T0185472

Lecture Notes in Computer Science   9206

Commenced Publication in 1973
Founding and Former Series Editors:
Gerhard Goos, Juris Hartmanis, and Jan van Leeuwen

More information about this series at http://www.springer.com/series/7407

Daniel Kroening · Corina S. Păsăreanu (Eds.)

Computer Aided Verification

27th International Conference, CAV 2015
San Francisco, CA, USA, July 18–24, 2015
Proceedings, Part I

 Springer

Editors
Daniel Kroening
University of Oxford
Oxford
UK

Corina S. Păsăreanu
Carnegie Mellon University
Moffett Field, CA
USA

ISSN 0302-9743   ISSN 1611-3349 (electronic)
Lecture Notes in Computer Science
ISBN 978-3-319-21689-8   ISBN 978-3-319-21690-4   (eBook)
DOI 10.1007/978-3-319-21690-4

Library of Congress Control Number: 2015943799

LNCS Sublibrary: SL1 – Theoretical Computer Science and General Issues

Springer Cham Heidelberg New York Dordrecht London

Printed on acid-free paper

Springer International Publishing AG Switzerland is part of Springer Science+Business Media
(www.springer.com)

Preface

It is our great pleasure to welcome you to CAV 2015, the 27th International Conference on Computer-Aided Verification, held in San Francisco, California, during July 18–24, 2015.

The CAV conference series is dedicated to the advancement of the theory and practice of computer-aided formal analysis methods for hardware and software systems. The conference covers the spectrum from theoretical results to concrete applications, with an emphasis on practical verification tools and the algorithms and techniques that are needed for their implementation. CAV considers it vital to continue spurring advances in hardware and software verification while expanding to new domains such as biological systems and computer security.

The CAV 2015 program included five keynotes, technical papers (58 long and 11 short papers accepted out of 252 submissions), 11 co-located events (VSTTE – Verified Software: Theories, Tools, and Experiments; SMT – Satisfiability Modulo Theories, EC2, IPRA – Interpolation: From Proofs to Applications; SYNT – Synthesis; VeriSure – Verification and Assurance; HCVS – Horn Clauses for Verification and Synthesis; VMW – Verification Mentoring Workshop, REORDER, SNR – Symbolic and Numerical Methods for Reachability Analysis; VEMDP – Verification of Engineered Molecular Devices and Programs), the Artifact Evaluation as well as briefings from the SMT and Synthesis competitions.

The invited keynote speakers were Philippa Gardner (Imperial College London), Leslie Lamport (Microsoft Research), Bob Kurshan (Cadence), William Hung (Synopsys), and Peter O'Hearn (University College London and Facebook).

Many people worked hard to make CAV 2015 a success. We thank the authors and the keynote speakers for providing the excellent technical material, the Program Committee for their thorough reviews and the time spent on evaluating all the submissions and discussing them during the on-line discussion period, and the Steering Committee for their guidance throughout the planning for CAV 2015.

We also thank Temesghen Kahsai, Local Chair, for his dedication and help with CAV 2015 planning and Hana Chockler, Sponsorship Chair, for helping to bring much needed financial support to the conference; Dirk Beyer, Workshop Chair, and all the organizers of the co-located events for bringing their events to the CAV week; Elizabeth Polgreen for the program and proceedings; Arie Gurfinkel, Temesghen Kahsai, Michael Tautschnig, and the Artifact Evaluation Committee for their work on evaluating the artifacts submitted.

We gratefully acknowledge NSF for providing financial support for student participants. We sincerely thank the CAV sponsors for their generous contributions:

- Google (Platinum sponsor)
- NASA, Fujitsu, SGT, Facebook, Microsoft (Gold sponsors)
- IBM, Cadence (Silver sponsors)
- Intel, Samsung (Bronze sponsors)

We also thank Carnegie Mellon University Silicon Valley and the University of Oxford for their support.

Finally, we hope you find the proceedings of CAV 2015 intellectually stimulating and practically valuable.

May 2015   Corina S. Păsăreanu
                                                                            Daniel Kroening

Organization

Program Committee

Aws Albarghouthi	University of Toronto, Canada
Jade Alglave	University College London, UK
Domagoj Babic	Google
Armin Biere	Johannes Kepler University, Austria
Roderick Bloem	Graz University of Technology, Austria
Ahmed Bouajjani	LIAFA, University of Paris Diderot, France
Marius Bozga	Verimag/CNRS, France
Aaron Bradley	Mentor Graphics
David Brumley	Carnegie Mellon University, USA
Tevfik Bultan	University of California at Santa Barbara, USA
Krishnendu Chatterjee	Institute of Science and Technology (IST)
Swarat Chaudhuri	Rice University, USA
Marsha Chechik	University of Toronto, Canada
Hana Chockler	King's College London, UK
Byron Cook	Microsoft Research
Isil Dillig	Stanford University, USA
Dino Distefano	Facebook
Alastair Donaldson	Imperial College London, UK
Azadeh Farzan	University of Toronto, Canada
Antonio Filieri	University of Stuttgart, Germany
Jasmin Fisher	Microsoft Research
Indradeep Ghosh	Fujitsu Labs of America
Patrice Godefroid	Microsoft Research
Aarti Gupta	Princeton University, USA
Arie Gurfinkel	Software Engineering Institute, CMU, USA
Gerard Holzmann	NASA/JPL, USA
Warren Hunt	University of Texas, USA
Ranjit Jhala	University of California San Diego, USA
Barbara Jobstmann	EPFL, Jasper DA, and CNRS-Verimag, Switzerland/France
Joost-Pieter Katoen	RWTH Aachen University, Germany
Daniel Kroening	University of Oxford, UK
Marta Kwiatkowska	University of Oxford, UK
Akash Lal	Microsoft Research, India
Darko Marinov	University of Illinois at Urbana-Champaign, USA
Ken McMillan	Microsoft Research
Kedar Namjoshi	Bell Labs

David Parker	University of Birmingham, UK
Corina Pasareanu	CMU/NASA Ames Research Center, USA
André Platzer	Carnegie Mellon University, USA
Zvonimir Rakamaric	University of Utah, USA
Grigore Rosu	University of Illinois at Urbana-Champaign, USA
Philipp Ruemmer	Uppsala University, Sweden
Mooly Sagiv	Tel Aviv University, Israel
Sriram Sankaranarayanan	University of Colorado, Boulder, USA
Koushik Sen	University of California, Berkeley, USA
Natarajan Shankar	SRI International
Natasha Sharygina	Università della Svizzera Italiana, Italy
Sharon Shoham	Technion, Israel
Nishant Sinha	IBM Research Labs
Fabio Somenzi	University of Colorado at Boulder, USA
Manu Sridharan	Samsung Research America
Ofer Strichman	Technion, Israel
Zhendong Su	UC Davis, USA
Cesare Tinelli	The University of Iowa, USA
Emina Torlak	U.C. Berkeley, USA
Tayssir Touili	LIAFA, CNRS and University Paris Diderot, France
Thomas Wahl	Northeastern University, USA
Georg Weissenbacher	Vienna University of Technology, Austria
Eran Yahav	Technion, Israel

Additional Reviewers

Abdelkader, Karam
Abdullah, Syed Md.
    Jakaria
Abraham, Erika
Aiswarya, C.
Akshay, S.
Alberti, Francesco
Alt, Leonardo
André, Etienne
Arechiga, Nikos
Asarin, Eugene
Astefanoaei, Lacramioara
Athanasiou, Konstantinos
Aydin, Abdulbaki
Backeman, Peter
Balakrishnan, Gogul
Bang, Lucas
Barbot, Benoit
Barrett, Clark

Bartocci, Ezio
Basset, Nicolas
Ben Sassi,
    Mohamed Amin
Ben-David, Shoham
Benes, Nikola
Berdine, Josh
Bertrand, Nathalie
Bhatt, Devesh
Blackshear, Sam
Bocic, Ivan
Bogomolov, Sergiy
Bornholt, James
Bortz, David
Brain, Martin
Brockschmidt, Marc
Brotherston, James
Bruns, Glenn
Bushnell, David

Calcagno, Cristiano
Ceska, Milan
Chakarov, Aleksandar
Chakravarthy, Venkat
Chan, May T.M.
Chapman, Martin
Chau, Cuong
Chen, Xin
Chen, Yuting
Cherini, Renato
Chiang, Wei-Fan
Chmelik, Martin
Choi, Wontae
Cimatti, Alessandro
Ciobaca, Stefan
Clancy, Kevin
Combaz, Jacques
Cox, Arlen
D'Antoni, Loris

D'Silva, Vijay
Dan, Andrei Marian
Dang, Thao
Darulova, Eva
David, Cristina
De Niz, Dionisio
Degorre, Aldric
Dehnert, Christian
Dhok, Monika
Diaz, Marcio
Dimjasevic, Marko
Dor, Nurit
Doyen, Laurent
Dragoi, Cezara
Dutertre, Bruno
Dutra, Rafael
Ebtekar, Aram
Ehlers, Rüdiger
Eide, Eric
Eisner, Cindy
Enea, Constantin
Fainekos, Georgios
Falcone, Ylies
Fedyukovich, Grigory
Feret, Jerome
Ferrere, Thomas
Fisman, Dana
Forejt, Vojtech
Fraer, Ranan
Frehse, Goran
Fu, Xiang
Fu, Zhoulai
Fuhs, Carsten
Fulton, Nathan
Gao, Sicun
Garg, Pranav
Garoche, Pierre-Loic
Gascon, Adria
Gerard, Leonard
Ghorbal, Khalil
Giacobbe, Mirco
Girard, Antoine
Gligoric, Milos
Goel, Shilpi
Gong, Liang
Gordon, Colin S.

Gotsman, Alexey
Gretz, Friedrich
Griesmayer, Andreas
Grinchtein, Olga
Grumberg, Orna
Gu, Yijia
Guck, Dennis
Gupta, Ashutosh
Gvero, Tihomir
Gyori, Alex
Günther, Henning
Haase, Christoph
Hadarean, Liana
Hahn, Ernst Moritz
Hall, Ben
Hall, Benjamin
Hallé, Sylvain
Hamza, Jad
He, Shaobo
Heizmann, Matthias
Henriques, David
Henry, Julien
Heule, Marijn
Hofferek, Georg
Horn, Alexander
Hyvärinen, Antti
Ivancic, Franjo
Ivrii, Alexander
Jain, Mitesh
Jansen, Nils
Jeannin, Jean-Baptiste
Ji, Ran
Jovanovic, Aleksandra
Jovanović, Dejan
Kafle, Bishoksan
Kahsai, Temesghen
Kahveci, Tuba
Kaminski, Benjamin
    Lucien
Kannan, Jayanthkumar
Kapinski, James
Karbyshev, Aleksandr
Karimi, Derrick
Keidar-Barner, Sharon
Keller, Chantal
Kennedy, Andrew

Khalimov, Ayrat
Khlaaf, Heidy
Kiefer, Stefan
Kim, Chang Hwan Peter
Kincaid, Zachary
King, Andy
King, Tim
Kini, Keshav
Koenighofer, Robert
Komuravelli, Anvesh
Konnov, Igor
Koskinen, Eric
Kretinsky, Jan
Kugler, Hillel
Kuncak, Viktor
Laarman, Alfons
Lahav, Ori
Lahiri, Shuvendu
Lampka, Kai
Lange, Martin
Lano, Kevin
Lawford, Mark
Le, Vu
Legay, Axel
Li, Goudong
Li, Guodong
Li, Peng
Li, Wenchao
Li, Yi
Liang, Tianyi
Lin, Yu
Liu, Peizun
Loos, Sarah
Luo, Qingzhou
Maler, Oded
Marescotti, Matteo
Martins, João G.
Martins, Ruben
Meel, Kuldeep
Mehne, Ben
Meller, Yael
Mereacre, Alexandru
Meshman, Yuri
Miné, Antoine
Misailovic, Sasa
Mitra, Sayan

Mitsch, Stefan
Moore, Brandon
Moses, Yoram
Mover, Sergio
Moy, Matthieu
Mukherjee, Rajdeep
Mukherjee, Suvam
Musuvathi, Madanlal
Müller, Andreas
Nadel, Alexander
Naiman, Lev
Natraj, Ashutosh
Navas, Jorge A.
Neider, Daniel
Nellen, Johanna
Nguyen, Huu Vu
Nickovic, Dejan
Nimal, Vincent
Nori, Aditya
Norman, Gethin
O'Hearn, Peter
Ober, Iulian
Oehlerking, Jens
Olivo, Oswaldo
Olmedo, Federico
Ong, Luke
Otop, Jan
Ouaknine, Joel
Owre, Sam
Padon, Oded
Palikareva, Hristina
Paoletti, Nicola
Papavasileiou, Vasilis
Park, Daejun
Partush, Nimrod
Pek, Edgar
Peleg, Hila
Piterman, Nir
Podelski, Andreas
Pommellet, Adrien
Pous, Damien
Prasad, Mukul
Prähofer, Herbert
Puggelli, Alberto

Qian, Xuehai
Qiu, Xiaokang
Quesel, Jan-David
Radoi, Cosmin
Ramachandran, Jaideep
Ratschan, Stefan
Ray, Sayak
Rinetzky, Noam
Rodríguez Carbonell,
    Enric
Roeck, Franz
Rungta, Neha
Ryvchin, Vadim
Safránek, David
Salay, Rick
Sawaya, Geof
Schewe, Sven
Schlaipfer, Matthias
Scholl, Christoph
Schrammel, Peter
Schäf, Martin
Schäfer, Andreas
See, Abigail
Seidl, Martina
Selfridge, Ben
Serbanuta, Traian Florin
Sethi, Divjyot
Sharma, Rahul
Sheinvald, Sarai
Shi, August
Shmulevich, Ilya
Sinz, Carsten
Slivovsky, Friedrich
Sogokon, Andrew
Solovyev, Alexey
Sousa Pinto, Joao
Srivathsan, B.
Stefanescu, Andrei
Stefanescu, Gheorghe
Sticksel, Christoph
Suda, Martin
Sun, Chengnian
Sun, Yutian
Szekeres, Laszlo

Taghdiri, Mana
Tautschnig, Michael
Thakur, Aditya
Tiwari, Ashish
Tonetta, Stefano
Topcu, Ufuk
Tracol, Mathieu
Tsiskaridze, Nestan
Tzoref-Brill, Rachel
Ulbrich, Mattias
Urban, Caterina
Urban, Christian
Vafeiadis, Viktor
Veitsman, Maor
Velner, Yaron
Vizel, Yakir
Voelzer, Hagen
Von Essen, Christian
Völp, Marcus
Wachter, Björn
Wang, Zilong
Wehrman, Ian
Wei, Ou
Wetzler, Nathan
Whalen, Mike
Wickerson, John
Wiltsche, Clemens
Wintersteiger, Christoph
Wolf, Karsten
Wolf, Verena
Wu, Zhilin
Yorav, Karen
Yorsh, Greta
Yoshida, Hiroaki
Younes, Håkan L.S.
Yu, Fang
Zawadzki, Erik
Zeljić, Aleksandar
Zhang, Qirun
Zhang, Yi
Zheng, Yunhui
Zutshi, Aditya

Abstracts of Invited Talks

A Trusted Mechanised Specification of JavaScript: One Year On

Philippa Gardner, Gareth Smith, Conrad Watt, and Thomas Wood

Imperial College London
{pg, gds, cw2312, tw1509}@ic.ac.uk
http://jscert.org

Abstract. The JSCert project provides a Coq mechanised specification of the core JavaScript language. A key part of the project was to develop a methodology for establishing trust, by designing JSCert in such a way as to provide a strong connection with the JavaScript standard, and by developing JSRef, a reference interpreter which was proved correct with respect to JSCert and tested using the standard Test262 test suite. In this paper, we assess the previous state of the project at POPL'14 and the current state of the project at CAV'15. We evaluate the work of POPL'14, providing an analysis of the methodology as a whole and a more detailed analysis of the tests. We also describe recent work on extending JSRef to include Google's V8 Array library, enabling us to cover more of the language and to pass more tests.

CAV: An Industrial Perspective

Robert Kurshan

The theory of computer-aided verification happily, in the past decade, has spawned a robust industrial utilization. This, after previous decades of wandering in a desert amply populated with disbelievers.

I recite some of the history of how this came about, review where it is today, together with some of the currently most pressing theoretical challenges that seem amenable to resolution, including memory systems, full systems and some significant tool enhancements left on the table, readily providable through current technology. (Inevitably), I speculate on where computer-aided verification may be headed.

Effective and Scalable Verification: Bridging Research and Industry

William N.N. Hung

Synopsys Inc., Mountain View CA 94043, USA
William.Hung@synopsys.com

Five decades ago, Moores law predicted the exponential growth of the semiconductor industry. Over the years, the increasing design complexity has called for effective and comprehensive verification of hardware and embedded systems. Functional verification has become a key concern in hardware and software system development. It is generally believed the majority of design effort is spent in functional verification, whose complexity explodes as the size of the design increases. The increasing adoption of high-level synthesis brings the consistency of C++ / System C / high-level model and register-transfer-level model into the picture. With the emergence of embedded system, functional verification of embedded software also becomes a key concern for the industry.

There are many approaches for functional verification: formal verification, dynamic verification, hardware emulation, hardware prototyping, etc. At present, constraint-based dynamic verification is still the mainstream approach in industry, especially for large complex designs. Dynamic verification is conducted by feeding input patterns to the design and simulating its behavior against a specification checker. The exponential nature of input patterns means, however, only a small subset of them can be sampled for dynamic verification. To quantify the extensiveness of dynamic verification, functional coverage is a criterion widely used. How to improve functional coverage is a key challenge to the industry.

In this talk, we will survey industrial standards, tools and methodologies to tackle the above verification problems, including the industry wide shift-left campaign, from software to hardware, formal, semi-formal, and constraint-based verification, accelerations, new ways of debugging and tackling complexity issues, ways to improve functional coverage, as well as new initiatives in software verification.

Contents – Part I

Software Analysis

Interpolation, IC3/PDR, and Invariants

Contents – Part II

Termination

Concurrency

Invited Paper

A Trusted Mechanised Specification of JavaScript: One Year On

Philippa Gardner, Gareth Smith, Conrad Watt, and Thomas Wood[(✉)]

Imperial College London, London, UK
{pg,gds,cw2312,tw1509}@ic.ac.uk
http://jscert.org

Abstract. The JSCert project provides a Coq mechanised specification of the core JavaScript language. A key part of the project was to develop a methodology for establishing trust, by designing JSCert in such a way as to provide a strong connection with the JavaScript standard, and by developing JSRef, a reference interpreter which was proved correct with respect to JSCert and tested using the standard Test262 test suite. In this paper, we assess the previous state of the project at POPL'14 and the current state of the project at CAV'15. We evaluate the work of POPL'14, providing an analysis of the methodology as a whole and a more detailed analysis of the tests. We also describe recent work on extending JSRef to include Google's V8 Array library, enabling us to cover more of the language and to pass more tests.

1 Introduction

JavaScript is the most widely used web language for client-side applications. However, JavaScript is complex and the associated ECMAScript standard (edition 5.1 in this paper, abbreviated ES5) is, by necessity, large and full of corner cases. In POPL'14, Gardner, Smith and others developed a Coq mechanised specification of the core JavaScript language, called JSCert ([1] and see acknowledgements). This work provides a foundation for future research projects based on, for example, program logics, type systems, sub-language analyses and abstract interpretation. It demonstrates that modern techniques of mechanised specification can handle the complexity of JavaScript.

An important part of the JSCert project was to develop a methodology for establishing trust: JSCert was designed so that each line of the core language of ES5 corresponds to one or two rules in JSCert; an executable reference interpreter, JSRef, was developed in parallel and proved to be correct with respect to JSCert; and JSRef was tested using Test262, the test suite that accompanies the ES5 standard. The methodology ensured that JSCert is a comparatively accurate formulation of the English standard, which will only improve with time.

In this paper, we describe the state of JSCert at POPL'14 and the current state of JSCert at CAV'15. With JSCert at POPL'14, we evaluate the methodology as a whole, report on the test results presented at the time, and assess our interpretation of the tests. We have found no errors in the Coq proof showing

© Springer International Publishing Switzerland 2015
D. Kroening and C.S. Păsăreanu (Eds.): CAV 2015, Part I, LNCS 9206, pp. 3–10, 2015.
DOI: 10.1007/978-3-319-21690-4_1

that JSRef is correct with respect to JSCert. We have identified a small number of cases where we have misinterpreted ES5, with these misinterpretations occurring consistently in both JSCert and JSRef. These misinterpretations have now been fixed; the close connection between ES5 and JSCert means that local misinterpretations of ES5 results in local fixes to JSCert and JSRef. We have found errors in the analysis of the tests, in particular by misattributing some test failures to the external parser instead of our parser interface code. Since POPL, we have greatly improved the test analysis and report on our results here.

For CAV'15, we give a snapshot of the current state of the JSCert project. The primary criticism of the POPL'14 work was that it only dealt with the core language, not with the associated libraries. In principle, we do not envisage difficulty in extending JSCert to the libraries[1], although covering all such libraries would be a mammoth task. Instead, we explore a different approach, to integrate an existing industrial-strength library implementation with JSRef. We focus on the Array library for illustration. We implement the Array library's low-level functionality using Coq and its high-level functionality using Google's V8 Array library implementation in core JavaScript. The V8 Array library is a good choice for us, as it provides a clear separation between the low-level and high-level functionality.

We can now run more code and pass more tests. We obtain trust in our extended JSRef in as far as we can trust the Google V8 Array library, trust our Coq implementation of the low-level functions, and trust the tests to identify errors in the industry code and our Coq code. However, this does not compete with the strong trust of the original JSCert project; for that, we need to extend JSCert to also specify the Array library.

2   JSCert at POPL'14

JSCert is an inductively-defined Coq semantics of the core part of ES5, suitable for carrying out formal proofs of, for example, safety properties of ES5 and security properties of sub-languages. It identifies the core language of ES5, comprising chapters 8–14 of ES5 and a small amount of Chap. 15. Chapters 1–7 are not directly relevant to JSCert[2]. Chapters 8–14 describe the bulk of the core language. The `for-in` command has not been specified, since it is notoriously difficult to understand and requires a global complication of the specification[3].

---

[1] Maksimović and Schmitt have begun to specify the core Array specification in JSCert and JSRef.

[2] Chapters 1–7 provide hints on how to read the later chapters, information about how the standard relates to the rest of the world and information that is only useful for parsing.

[3] During discussion on the `es-discuss` mailing list, even members of the ECMAScript committee had differing opinions of what the standard meant. The committee came to a consensus and we know how to specify the for-in command in JSCert. However, this specification would involve a global change, with the enumerable fields having to be explicitly recorded throughout the specification. The choice was to omit this

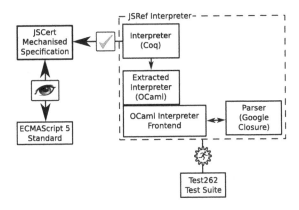

Fig. 1. The JSCert project at POPL'14.

The Array literal syntax has also not been specified, since the project did not specify the Array library.

Chapter 15 specifies objects and functions that should be present in the heap when the JavaScript interpreter is started. These functions provide both 'core' language functionality which must be directly implemented in the interpreter (such as special object constructors; eval; or control of property descriptors) and library or helper functionality which (such as URI decoding or array sorting). Unfortunately the split is not always clear, as all of these functions are defined in the ES5 specification in terms of the language's internal behaviour so it is not trivial to determine whether a function only makes use of state accessible to regular JavaScript programs. JSCert has specifications of the 'core' functions of Chap. 15, excluding the Array library.

JSCert is written using the pretty-big-step semantics of Charguéraud [2]. The original operational semantics of JavaScript, created by Maffeis, Mitchell and Taly [3] for ECMAScript 3, was written using a small-step semantics. By contrast, the prose of the standard has a big-step flavour. The aim was to design JSCert to be as close to the standard as possible. However, a traditional big-step operational semantics would lead to many duplicate rules since the JavaScript control flow is quite complex. The pretty-big-step semantics enables JSCert to be closer to the English prose. It was originally developed for a small ML-like language. The JSCert specification demonstrates that it scales to ES5, a real-world language which was not designed with formal methods in mind.

The main challenge was (and still is) to convince people (including ourselves) that JSCert can be trusted as an accurate formulation of the ES5 English standard. The design of the project is illustrated in Fig. 1. JSCert is 'eyeball close' to ES5, in the sense that we can place the English prose and the formal rules side-by-side and compare the two. This closeness is possible due to the

---

change, rather than complicate the specification, especially as the for-in command has essentially been replaced by the better behaved for-of command in the next standard.

pretty-big-step semantics. In most cases, each line of English corresponds to one or two Coq rules. The reason for the two rules is that, for simplicity, ES5 leaves much behaviour (such as state change and exception handling) implicit, whereas JSCert gives the behaviour explicitly to aid comparison and help with proofs. In some cases, the connection is not quite line by line. A typical example involves the while specification, where two lines of ES5 English specification correspond to two Coq rules: in ES5, the Boolean expression is evaluated to a reference then converted to a Boolean value; in Coq, this is done in one step.

JSCert is accompanied by the JSRef reference interpreter which comprises several parts. It comprises an interpreter written in Coq which is automatically extracted to an interpreter written in OCaml. This interpreter is then linked to a front-end which provides interfaces to the end-user and to a third-party JavaScript parser (for POPL'14, the Google Closure parser). The interpreter in Coq has been proved correct with respect to JSCert for Chaps. 8–14. More precisely, if the execution of a JavaScript program in JSRef returns a result, then there exists a reduction derivation in JSCert relating this program to this result. The creation of the interpreter in OCaml uses automatic Coq extraction techniques which are standard and well-used. Our trust that the extracted interpreter is an accurate reference interpreter for JSCert is based on the correctness proof for the interpreter in Coq, our trust in the Coq extraction process, the minimal amounts of unverified front-end code, and the testing using the ES5 conformance test suite, Test262.

The test results focused on Chaps. 8–14. Those reported in the POPL paper and talk are given in Table 1[4]. The paper stated that 'JSRef successfully executes all the tests *we expect to pass* given our coverage of ES5'. The original analysis reported that the failed and aborted tests were due to: for-in not implemented; Chap. 15 library functionality not implemented; and failures due to a non-conforming parser. This analysis was improved by the time of the POPL talk, hence the two rows in the table: the `for` command and associated tests (28 tests) had been omitted due to confusion with the `for-in` command; and some further tests (27 tests)[5] had been omitted.

Evaluation. An original aim of the project was to assess how much of ES5 it was possible to specify in Coq. JSCert covers the core language of ES5 (Chaps. 8–14 plus the some of Chap. 15), except for the for-in command and the Array literal syntax, as discussed. The fact that the specification was able to cope with all the corner cases was a surprise and a considerable achievement. The 'eyeball closeness' of JSCert with ES5 has been a success. In our experience, it is possible for a Coq expert reading JSCert and a JavaScript expert reading the ES5 standard to have a detailed discussion about the different formulations.

---

[4] We have separated the fails and the aborts. Most aborts are due to tests calling functions 'Not Yet Implemented', although a few aborts are real parser failures. Some fails are also due to tests calling functions 'Not Yet Implemented'. The other fails are more significant.

[5] Those associated with the Argument object and those calling the `hasOwnProperty` method.

Recall that JSRef comprises an interpreter in Coq which is extracted to an interpreter in OCaml. The correctness proof between JSCert and the interpreter in Coq has also stood the test of time. The proof was given for Chaps. 8–14. This gave a precise, clear description of what had been proved. In future, we would like extend the proof to the core language specified by JSCert. We have not found any mistakes in this proof. We have found some misinterpretations of the ES5 standard: for example, strict mode delete was not throwing an exception for unresolvable references. These misinterpretations are present in both JSCert and JSRef. JSCert and JSRef were developed separately, by different teams, but there was much interaction between the teams. When the ES5 standard was unclear, they reached consensus, both between themselves and with the help of `es-discuss`. So far, we have discovered that just a small amount of the ES5 core language was misinterpreted and this has been fixed.

The test analysis needs improvement. Many failed and aborted tests were due to for-in and Chap. 15 library functionality not being implemented, and this was correct. However, the failures of many strict-mode tests (at most 237 tests) were attributed solely to the parser, and this was incorrect: some failures were, indeed, due to the parser; other failures were due to the misinterpretation of ES5: for example, strict mode delete previously discussed; and most failures were due to mistakes in our parser interface code. These mistakes were not picked up by the tests because the test filtering at the time was ad-hoc and over-zealous for the strict-mode tests. The test filtering is now much better, the test failures and aborts are properly attributed, and the mistakes in our parser interface code are fixed.

Table 1. JSRef test results as at POPL'14 and CAV'15. The Array results for POPL'14 were not previously reported and are shown for comparison. Two rows of results are shown for CAV'15, the first without the Google V8 Array library loaded and the second with it loaded.

	Chs. 8–14			Ch. 15.4 – Array		
	Pass	Fail	Abort	Pass	Fail	Abort
POPL'14 paper results	1796	404	582	(139)	(873)	(1307)
POPL'14	1851	392	539	(149)	(864)	(1306)
CAV'15	2437	129	216	180	1204	935
CAV'15 (+V8 Array)	2440	126	216	1309	59	951

3 JSCert at CAV'15

We report on the current state of the JSCert project at CAV'15. JSCert remains largely the same. We have fixed the known inconsistencies with the ES5 standard as noted in the previous section. The JSRef interpreter has changed. From

POPL'14, many of the failed and aborted tests seemed to be due to library functions not yet implemented. In particular, there were many tests for the core language that called the Array library. We therefore extend the JSCert project with this library. One approach is to extend JSCert with a Coq specification of the Array library; Maksimović and Schmitt are beginning to do this. Another approach is to extend JSRef with an existing industrial-strength library implementation; we study this approach here.

Most of the Array functions (and, indeed, most of the Chap. 15 functions in general) do not directly access the language's internal state. They can, therefore, be implemented in the core JavaScript language and then loaded, parsed and interpreted to yield an initial heap state which declares these functions. The major JavaScript interpreters are using or moving towards this approach, which we explore here for the JSCert project. Rather than implementing this library ourselves, we use portions of Google's V8 Array library implementation as it has a clear separation of core functionality, which requires access to the language's internal state, and the higher-level functionality, which is implemented in the core JavaScript language.

The new structure of the JSCert project is given in Fig. 2. JSCert remains largely the same. The parser has been changed from Google's Closure to jQuery's Esprima for improved correctness, execution speed and web compliance. This change involved adding support for translation from the de facto SpiderMonkey AST to our internal AST representation, enabling us to use a wide range of third-party parsers for the front-end of JSRef. The JSRef interpreter has been extended to include the V8 Array library. To support the execution of this library, we extended the interpreter written in Coq with a number of low-level functions: some of these functions are defined in other sections of Chap. 15, such as those associated with `Object` or `Function`; and some provide access to a small amount of usually restricted internal state used, for example, to modify the prototype of an object or set the normally immutable `length` field of a function. In addition, V8 has some minor helper functions implemented in C++ to improve performance. We implement these helper functions in core JavaScript to minimise the size of the native/interpreted interface.

The test results are given in Table 1. We provide a more careful analysis of the tests for Chaps. 8–14. We also execute and analyse the tests for the Chap. 15.4. For the Chap. 8–14 tests, we believe that all the failed and aborted tests are doing so for valid reasons. These are mostly due to parts of the language that are not yet implemented: namely, the for-in statement (93 tests failing); array literal syntax (26 tests); 78 tests failing for missing Chap. 15 functionality; and 135 tests failing for other non-implemented features. In addition: 7 tests are failing because they use strictly invalid, but commonly used, syntax; 1 test is failing due to a parser bug (reported to the vendor); and 2 tests are failing due to the method of executing multiple programs in sequence by the unverified interpreter front-end.

We have run the tests for the Chap. 15.4, but currently have only a partial analysis of the tests. Since we use Google's V8 Array library, we can probably trust the implementation of the high-level functions and do not expect many

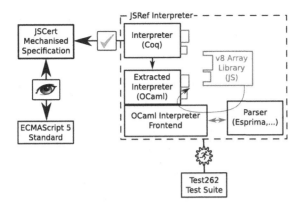

Fig. 2. The JSCert Project at CAV'15.

test failures associated with them. We do expect test failures in our Coq and JavaScript code which replaces the V8 C++ code, partially because it is code we have written and partially because the interface between the JavaScript and C++ code is not documented. The only way to establish trust in our code is through testing.

At the moment, 904 tests fail or abort due to Array literal syntax from Chaps. 8–14 not being implemented. This is potentially masking many bugs. For POPL'14, the Array literal syntax was not implemented because we were not calling the library. Now, the library is being called and the Array literal syntax needs to be specified in JSCert, interpreted in JSRef and the correctness proof extended. This is currently being done by Maksimović and Schmitt as part of their specification of the Array library. Many of the other tests fail due to parts of the language that are not yet implemented: namely, 30 tests because of the missing for-in statement; 53 because of missing Chap. 15 functionality; 19 tests because of other non-implemented features; and 1 test because of the use of invalid syntax. Additionally, 3 tests are failing due to an error in the ES5 specification[6]. This error was introduced as a typographic error between versions 3 and 5 of the ECMAScript specification. Test262 captures the intended semantics as per ES3, JSCert captured the incorrect semantics of ES5. The resulting discrepancy revealed itself as a set of test failures discovered during this test evaluation.

Evaluation. This paper assesses the current state of the JSCert project, reports on the improved analysis of the tests for chapters 8–14, and describes the extension of JSRef with Google's V8 Array library implementation.

JSCert provides a mechanised specification of the core JavaScript language, as described by the ES5 standard. It comprises Chaps. 8–14 and parts of Chap. 15, omitting the for-in command and the Array literal syntax. Following our work in POPL'14, the ES5 standard has also been specified in the K framework [4].

---

[6] https://bugs.ecmascript.org/show_bug.cgi?id=162.

In this work, the definition of the core language is that required to pass the core tests. In fact, it is not completely clear what the core language should be, since it is not precisely described by the ES5 standard. We should at some point compare the choices in the JSCert and the K specifications.

The proof that JSRef is correct with respect to JSCert has only been done for Chaps. 8–14, not the core language. The choice to focus on Chaps. 8–14 was made to present a clear boundary of what had been proved. However, in future, we would like to extend the proof to the core language. For now, the analysis of the tests focused on Chaps. 8–14 and the Chap. 15.4 Array library. The infrastructure for analysing the tests has been vastly improved: the test run takes considerably less time; the filtering is more accurate; and the test analysis can be more trusted. We believe the tests for Chaps. 8–14 are well done. The tests for Chap. 15.4 Array library are on-going. Many tests involve the Array literal syntax from chapters 8–14 which has not being implemented. These might be hiding many bugs, and we will investigate this once Maksimović and Schmitt have extended JSCert, JSRef and the proof to include the Array literal syntax. Otherwise, the other failed tests are understood.

We believe our experiment to extend JSRef with Google's V8 Array library has been a success. A next step is to extend this approach to the String, Boolean and Number libraries. Our overall aim is to pass as many tests as we can.

Acknowledgements. Two of the authors of this paper, Gardner and Smith, were part of the original team working on JSCert. We would like to thank the other co-authors for continuing invaluable discussions about this project: Martin Bodin, Arthur Charguéraud and Alan Schmitt from Inria; and Daniel Filaretti, Sergio Maffeis and Daiva Naudžiūnienė from Imperial. We also would like to thank Petar Maksimović and Alan Schmitt for interesting discussions and interaction about the Array library. They are beginning to specify the core Array library in Coq.

Gardner and Smith are supported by EPSRC Grant EP/K032089/1. Watt was supported by a GCHQ Undergraduate Internship Project award. Wood is supported by an EPSRC DTA award.

References

1. Bodin, M., Charguéraud, A., Filiaretti, D., Gardner, P., Maffeis, S., Naudžiūnienė, D., Schmitt, A., Smith, G.: A trusted mechanised javascript specification. In: Proceedings of the 41st Annual ACM SIGPLAN-SIGACT Symposium on Principles of Programming Languages. POPL 2014, ACM (2014)
2. Charguéraud, A.: Pretty-big-step semantics. In: Felleisen, M., Gardner, P. (eds.) ESOP 2013. LNCS, vol. 7792, pp. 41–60. Springer, Heidelberg (2013)
3. Maffeis, S., Mitchell, J.C., Taly, A.: An operational semantics for javascript. In: Ramalingam, G. (ed.) APLAS 2008. LNCS, vol. 5356, pp. 307–325. Springer, Heidelberg (2008)
4. Park, D., Ştefănescu, A., Roşu, G.: KJS: A complete formal semantics of javascript. In: Proceedings of the 36th ACM SIGPLAN Conference on Programming Language Design and Implementation. PLDI 2015, pp. 428–438. ACM (2015)

Model Checking and Refinements

On Automation of CTL* Verification
for Infinite-State Systems

Byron Cook[1], Heidy Khlaaf[1(✉)], and Nir Piterman[2]

[1] University College London, London, UK
h.khlaaf@ucl.ac.uk
[2] University of Leicester, Leicester, UK

Abstract. In this paper we introduce the first known fully automated tool for symbolically proving CTL* properties of (infinite-state) integer programs. The method uses an internal encoding which facilitates reasoning about the subtle interplay between the nesting of path and state temporal operators that occurs within CTL* proofs. A precondition synthesis strategy is then used over a program transformation which trades nondeterminism in the transition relation for nondeterminism explicit in variables predicting future outcomes when necessary. We show the viability of our approach in practice using examples drawn from device drivers and various industrial examples.

1 Introduction

In recent years, a number of systems have been proposed to automate the verification of either branching-time properties (e.g. expressed in CTL) or linear-time properties (e.g. LTL) of general integer manipulating programs [3,8,10–12]. Branching-time property verification requires reasoning about sets of *states* within a transition system that satisfy a particular temporal formula. Contrarily, linear-time property verification requires reasoning about sets of *paths* that satisfy a formula. However, these logics have significantly reduced expressiveness as they restrict or disallow the interplay between linear-time and branching-time operators. For example, a property involving the assertion "along *some* future an event occurs *infinitely often*" cannot be expressed in either LTL or CTL, yet is crucial when expressing the existence of fair paths spawning from every reachable state in an infinite-state system. Contrarily, CTL* is capable of expressing CTL, LTL, and properties necessitating their interplay, as demonstrated by examples further below.

Unfortunately, no fully automatic CTL* proving methods for infinite-state systems are known. Despite the existence of automated verification tools for branching-time and linear-time temporal logic, these tools do not allow for the verification of CTL*. A key problem is that CTL* formulae cannot merely be partitioned into isolated CTL and LTL sub-formulae, as such a partition fails to treat the intricate dependence between state-based and path-based reasoning. In this paper we introduce the first known automatic method capable of proving CTL*

D. Kroening and C.S. Păsăreanu (Eds.): CAV 2015, Part I, LNCS 9206, pp. 13–29, 2015.
DOI: 10.1007/978-3-319-21690-4_2

properties of infinite-state programs. Our contribution is a method that allows for the arbitrary nesting of state-based reasoning within path-based reasoning, and vice versa. Towards this purpose we recursively deconstruct a CTL* formula in a way that allows us to determine where the subtle interplay between the arbitrary nesting of path and state formulae occurs. To reason about the path subformulae, we find a sufficient set of branching nondeterministic decisions within a program's transition relation. We then devise a method of *temporarily* substituting said nondeterministic decisions with a *partially symbolic determinized* form. That is, nondeterministic decisions regarding which paths are taken are determined by variables that summarize the future of the program execution. When interchanging between path and state formulae, these determinized relations must then be collapsed to incorporate path quantifiers. Preconditions for the given CTL* property can then be acquired via existing CTL model checkers.

Based on our approach, we have developed a tool capable of automatically proving properties of programs that no tool could previously fully automate. The paper closes with a description of our experimental results using the developed tool on various programs drawn from industrial examples. Our tool is available under the MIT open-source license at https://github.com/hkhlaaf/T2/tree/T2Star.

Expressiveness of CTL*. CTL* allows us to express properties involving existential system stabilization, stating that an event can eventually become true and stay true from every reachable state. Additionally, it can express "possibility" properties, such as the viability of a system, stating that every reachable state can spawn a fair computation. Below are properties that can only be afforded by the extra expressive power of CTL*. These liveness properties are often imperative to verifying systems such as Windows kernel APIs that acquire resources and APIs that release resources, as later shown by our experiments.

For example, the property $EFG(\neg x \land (EGF\ x))$ conveys the divergence of paths. That is, there is a path in which a system stabilizes to $\neg x$, but every point on said path has a diverging path in which x holds infinitely often. This property is not expressible in CTL or in LTL, yet is crucial when expressing the existence of fair paths spawning from every reachable state in a system. In CTL, one can only examine sets of states, disallowing us to convey properties regarding paths. In LTL, one cannot approximate a solution by trying to *disprove* either $FG\ \neg x$ or $GF\ x$, as one cannot characterize these proofs within a path quantifier.

Another CTL* property $AG[(EG\ \neg x) \lor (EFG\ y)]$ dictates that from every state of a program, there exists either a computation in which x never holds or a computation in which y eventually always holds. The linear time property $G(Fx \rightarrow FG\ y)$ is significantly stricter as it requires that on every computation either the first disjunct or the second disjunct hold. Finally, the property $EFG[(x \lor (AF\ \neg y))]$ asserts that there exists a computation in which whenever x does not hold, all possible futures of a system lead to the falsification of y. This assertion is impossible to express in LTL.

Related Work. Proof systems for the verification of CTL*, first introduced by [14,21], have been well-studied. It is known that CTL* model checking for infinite-state systems generalizes termination and co-termination and is undecidable. A decision procedure exploring the structure of finite-state ω-automata was first introduced to determine the satisfaction of a CTL* formula over binary relations in [17], and later extended in [15]. A complete and sound axiomatization of propositional CTL* then followed in [26], which inspired the first sound and relatively complete deductive proof system for the verification of CTL* properties over possibly infinite-state reactive systems [20]. Proof rules for verifying CTL* properties of infinite-state systems were implemented in STeP [4]. However, the STeP system is only semi-automated, as it still requires users to construct auxiliary assertions and participate in the search for a proof.

Model checking CTL* [16] for finite-state programs and other decidable settings has been implemented in [18]. Their approach reduces a CTL* formula to μ-calculus using a system of fixed-point equations on relations with first-order quantifiers and equalities. They then invoke a μ-calculus model checker. Contrarily, we seek to verify the undecidable general class of infinite-state programs supporting both control-sensitive and integer properties. Given that μ-calculus model checking is polynomial-time equivalent to the solution of parity games [15], one can conceive that the approach in [2] could potentially solve CTL* model checking if the latter were reduced to solving parity games by combining [18] and [15]. However, we note that the resulting infinite-state game would integrate the (first-order μ-calculus) property within the program making it difficult to extract invariants pertaining to the program. For this reason, it is often the case that such a series of reductions inhibits tool performance. Furthermore, [2] requires a manual instantiation of the structure of assertions, characterizing subsets of the infinite-state game, that are to be found by their tool.

Existing automated tools for verification of infinite-state programs support *either* branching-time only *or* linear-time only reasoning, e.g., [3,5,8,10–12,27]. The important distinction however is that these tools do not allow for the interaction between linear-time and branching-time formulae.

Finally, we have adopted and repurposed a similar symbolic determinization technique introduced in [12] for the verification of LTL formulae in the infinite-state setting. Their symbolic determinization is based on the counterexample-guided refinement of generated tree counterexamples, or counterexamples with branching paths. That is, [8] produce a semantics-preserving transformation that encodes the structure of the nested CTL formulae within the state space, allowing for the generation of tree counterexamples. This causes precondition generation for syntactically partitioned formulae to be no longer possible, limiting the interplay between linear-time operators and path quantifiers allowed by our strategy.

Limitations. Our tool does not support programs with heap, nor do we support recursion or concurrency. The heap-based programs we consider during our experimental evaluation have been abstracted using an over-approximation technique introduced by [22]. Effective techniques for proving temporal properties of programs with heap remains an open research question. Our technique relies on the availability of CTL model checking and non-termination procedures. It is, in principle, applicable to every class of infinite-state systems for which such procedures are available (provided that integer variables are allowed). Additionally, our procedure is not complete as we use a series of techniques for safety [24], termination [9,25], nontermination [19], and CTL [3,11] that are not complete. Furthermore, our determinization procedure is not complete. We will further address this issue in later sections.

2 Preliminaries

Programs. As is standard [23], we treat programs as control-flow graphs, where edges are annotated by the updates they perform to variables. A program is a triple $P = (\mathcal{L}, E, \mathsf{Vars})$, where $\mathcal{L}$ is a set of locations, E is a set of edges/transitions, and Vars is a set of variables. Each edge $\tau = (\ell, \rho, \ell')$ in E, where $\ell, \ell' \in \mathcal{L}$ and ρ is a condition, specifies possible transitions in the program. The condition ρ is an assertion in terms of Vars and Vars', a primed copy of Vars, where constants range over Vals. That is, Vars refers to the values of variables before an update and Vars' refers to the values of variables after an update.

The set of locations includes the first location ℓ_I, which has no incoming transitions from other program locations. That is, for every $\tau = (\ell, \rho, \ell') \in E$ we have $\ell' \neq \ell_I$. Transitions exiting ℓ_I have their conditions expressed in terms of Vars'. Locations with incoming transitions from ℓ_I are *initial locations*. This allows us to encode more complex initial conditions. In figures, we omit ℓ_I and merely display the edges to locations with incoming transitions from ℓ_I.

A program gives rise to a transition system $T = (S, R)$, where S is the set of program states of the form $S = (\mathcal{L} - \{\ell_I\}) \times (\mathsf{Vars} \to \mathsf{Vals})$ and $R \subseteq S \times S$. That is, a program state is a pair (ℓ, f) where $\ell \neq \ell_I$ and f is a valuation, i.e., a function from program variables to values. A program can transition from (ℓ, f_1) to (ℓ', f_2) if there exists a transition $(\ell, \rho, \ell') \in E$ such that $(f_1, f_2) \models \rho$. The valuation (f_1, f_2) is a function from $\mathsf{Vars} \cup \mathsf{Vars}'$ to Vals such that for every $v \in \mathsf{Vars}$, $(f_1, f_2)(v) = f_1(v)$ and $(f_1, f_2)(v') = f_2(v)$. A state (ℓ, f) is considered initial if there is a transition (ℓ_I, ρ, ℓ) such that $(f_{-1}, f) \models \rho$, where f_{-1} is some arbitrary valuation. Notice that ρ is expressed in terms of Vars' and hence the valuation f_{-1} does not affect the satisfaction of ρ.

Given $V \subseteq \mathsf{Vars}$, the valuation obtained from f by restricting the valuation to variables in V is denoted by $f{\Downarrow}_V$. The restriction of states of the form (ℓ, f) and paths in the program is defined similarly, e.g., $\pi{\Downarrow}_V$.

Paths. A *path* or a *trace* π in P is an infinite sequence of states $(\ell_0, f_0), (\ell_1, f_1),$ ..., where for every $i \geq 0$, there exists some $(\ell_i, \rho_i, \ell_{i+1}) \in E$ where $(f_i, f_{i+1}) \models \rho_i$. We say that π is an (ℓ, f)-path if $\ell_0 = \ell$ and $f_0 = f$. Given a program P, a location ℓ, and a valuation f, we denote the set of (ℓ, f)-paths in P by $\mathsf{Path}(P, \ell, f)$. We say that π is a computation in P if (ℓ, f) is initial. Note that we restrict our attention to infinite paths and computations. In practice, we modify programs, transition systems, and temporal logic formulae to ensure that all paths are infinite, as is done, e.g., in [6].

CTL*. We are interested in verifying full computation tree logic (CTL*) [14,21]. The syntax of CTL* (written in negation normal form) includes state formulae φ, that are interpreted over states, and path formulae ψ, that are interpreted over paths. We assume that atomic propositions (ranged over by α) are expressed in some underlying theory over variables and constants (*e.g.* $\mathsf{x} < \mathsf{y}$). State formulas (φ) and path formulas (ψ) are co-defined:

$$\varphi ::= \alpha \mid \neg\alpha \mid \varphi \wedge \varphi \mid \varphi \vee \varphi \mid \mathsf{A}\psi \mid \mathsf{E}\psi$$
$$\psi ::= \varphi \mid \psi \wedge \psi \mid \psi \vee \psi \mid \mathsf{G}\psi \mid \mathsf{F}\psi \mid [\psi\mathsf{W}\psi] \mid [\psi\mathsf{U}\psi]$$

For a program P and a CTL^* state formula φ, we say that φ holds at a state s in P, denoted by $P, s \models \varphi$ if:

- If $\varphi = \alpha$, then $P, s \models \alpha$ iff $s \models \alpha$
- If $\varphi = \neg\alpha$, then $P, s \models \neg\alpha$ iff $s \not\models \alpha$
- If $\varphi = \varphi_1 \vee \varphi_2$, then $P, s \models \varphi_1 \vee \varphi_2$ iff $s \models \varphi_1$ or $s \models \varphi_2$
- If $\varphi = \varphi_1 \wedge \varphi_2$, then $P, s \models \varphi_1 \wedge \varphi_2$ iff $s \models \varphi_1$ and $s \models \varphi_2$
- If $\varphi = \mathsf{A}\psi$, then $P, s \models \mathsf{A}\psi$ iff $\forall \pi = (s, ...). \ P, \pi \models \psi$
- If $\varphi = \mathsf{E}\psi$, then $P, s \models \mathsf{E}\psi$ iff $\exists \pi = (s, ...). \ P, \pi \models \psi$

Path formulae are interpreted over paths. For a program P and a CTL^* path formula ψ, we say that ψ holds on a path $\pi = (s_0, s_1, ...)$ in P for location i, denoted by $P, \pi, i \models \psi$ if:

- If $\psi = \varphi$ is a state formula, then $P, \pi, i \models \varphi$ iff $P, s_i \models \varphi$.
- If $\psi = \psi_1 \vee \psi_2$, then $P, \pi, i \models \psi_1 \vee \psi_2$ iff $P, \pi, i \models \psi_1$ or $P, \pi, i \models \psi_2$
- If $\psi = \psi_1 \wedge \psi_2$, then $P, \pi, i \models \psi_1 \wedge \psi_2$ iff $P, \pi, i \models \psi_1$ and $P, \pi, i \models \psi_2$
- If $\psi = \mathsf{F}\psi_1$, then $P, \pi, i \models \mathsf{F}\psi_1$ iff $\exists j \geq i. \ P, \pi, j \models \psi_1$
- If $\psi = \mathsf{G}\psi_1$, then $P, \pi, i \models \mathsf{G}\psi_1$ iff $\forall j \geq i. \ P, \pi, j \models \psi_1$
- If $\psi = \psi_1\mathsf{W}\psi_2$, then $P, \pi, i \models \psi_1\mathsf{W}\psi_2$ iff either $\exists k \geq i. \ P, \pi, k \models \psi_2$ and $\forall i \leq j < k. \ P, \pi, j \models \psi_1$ or $\forall j \geq i. \ P, \pi, j \models \psi_1$
- If $\psi = \psi_1\mathsf{U}\psi_2$, then $P, \pi, i \models \psi_1\mathsf{U}\psi_2$ iff $\exists k \geq i. \ P, \pi, k \models \psi_2$ and $\forall i \leq j < k. \ P, \pi, j \models \psi_1$

A path formula ψ holds in a path π, denoted by $P, \pi \models \psi$, if $P, \pi, 0 \models \psi$. For a state formula φ, φ holds on P, denoted by $P \models \varphi$, if for every initial state s we have $P, s \models \varphi$. When the program P is is clear from the context, we may write $s \models \varphi$ for a state formula φ or $\pi, i \models \psi$ for a path formula ψ.

The branching-time logic CTL is a restricted subset of CTL^* in which temporal operators cannot be nested. That is, the only path formulas allowed are $\mathsf{G}\varphi_1$, $\mathsf{F}\varphi_1$, $\varphi_1\mathsf{U}\varphi_2$, and $\varphi_1\mathsf{W}\varphi_2$ for state formulas φ_1 and φ_2. The linear-time logic LTL is a fragment of CTL^* that only allows formulae of the form $\mathsf{A}\psi$, where A is the only occurrence of a path quantifier within ψ. When taking LTL as subset of CTL^*, LTL formulae are implicitly prefixed with the universal path quantifier A.

Strongly Connected Subgraphs. We provide some notation regarding strongly-connected subgraphs followed by the definition of *relation pairs* below. For a program P, we denote an ordered sequence of locations $\ell_0, ..., \ell_n$ as a cycle c if $\ell_n = \ell_0$ and for every $i \geq 0$ there exists some $(\ell_i, \rho_i, \ell_{i+1}) \in E$. Let C be the set of program locations such that $\ell \in \mathcal{L}$ appears in a cycle c. That is, $C = \{\ell \mid \exists c. \ \ell \in c\}$. For a program P and the set of locations C, we identify $\mathrm{SCS}(P, C)$ as some maximal set of non-trivial strongly-connected subgraphs (SCSs) of P such that every two subgraphs $G_1, G_2 \in \mathrm{SCS}(P, C)$ are either disjoint or one is contained in the other and for every $\ell \in C$, there exists at least one $G \in \mathrm{SCS}(P, C)$ such that $\ell \in G$. The details regarding the identification of C and $\mathrm{SCS}(P, C)$ are standard and thus omitted here (see, e.g., [13]). We denote the minimal SCS in $\mathrm{SCS}(P, C)$ that contains a location $\ell \in \mathcal{L}$ by $\mathrm{MINSCS}(P, C, \ell)$.

Identifying a program's strongly-connected subgraphs allows us to sufficiently find the set of *relation pairs* that characterize instances of branching nondeterministic decisions within a program's transition relation. A relation pair is thus (ρ_1, ρ_2) such that for some location ℓ we have (ℓ, ρ_1, ℓ_1) and (ℓ, ρ_2, ℓ_2) are transitions of P and $\ell_1 \in \mathrm{MINSCS}(P, C, \ell)$ and $\ell_2 \notin \mathrm{MINSCS}(P, C, \ell)$. That is, ρ_1 is the condition for remaining in the (minimal) SCS of ℓ and ρ_2 is the condition for leaving the (minimal) SCS of ℓ.

3   Overview

In this section, we present a quick overview of our CTL* verification procedure PROVECTL*, presented in Fig. 3 with an in-depth explanation provided later in Sect. 4. The procedure is designed to recurse over the structure of a given CTL* formula, and for each sub-formula θ we produce a precondition a that ensures its satisfaction. That is, a is an assertion over program variables and locations characterizing the states of the program that satisfy θ. We start by finding the precondition of the innermost sub-formula, followed by searching for the preconditions of the outer sub-formulae dependent on it.

A given CTL* formula is deconstructed to differentiate between state and path sub-formulae, as the crux of verifying CTL* formulae lies within identifying the interplay between the arbitrary nesting of path and state formulae. Preconditions for branching-time logic state formulae can be acquired via existing CTL model checking techniques which return an assertion characterizing the states in which a sub-formula holds. The essence of our algorithm is thus within how we acquire sufficient preconditions for path formulae that admit a sound interaction with state formulae. The algorithm is based on the procedures below, which are defined in later sections of the paper:

APPROXIMATE is a procedure that performs a syntactic conversion from a path formula to its corresponding over-approximated universal CTL formula (ACTL)[1]. The over-approximated formula can then be checked by an existing CTL model checker over a partially symbolic determinized form of the program to reduce path formula verification to state formula verification.

DETERMINIZE allows us to reason about path characterization through state characterization, as the satisfaction of an ACTL over-approximated formula

---

[1] ACTL is the universal subset of CTL where one can only address all possible paths with the universal quantifier A (e.g. AG or AF), but not the existence of some paths with E (e.g. EG or EF).

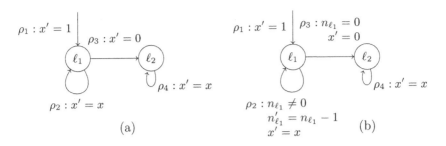

Fig. 1. (a) The control-flow graph of a program for which we wish to prove the CTL* property EFG $x = 1$. (b) The control-flow graph after calling DETERMINIZE, it includes the prophecy variable n_{ℓ_1} corresponding to the nondeterministic relation pair (ρ_2, ρ_3).

implies the satisfaction of the path formula. However, the inverse does not hold. The procedure thus constructs a form of a partially determinized program over the symbolic representations of all characterized instances of branching nondeterminism (i.e. *relation pairs*), stemming from the same program location ℓ. That is, nondeterministic decisions regarding which paths are taken would be determined by *prophecy variables*, which determine future outcomes of the program execution, and their values [1]. Recall that relation pairs are distinguished if they are not part of the same strongly connected subgraph.

QUANTELIM acquires the proper set of states that satisfy a formula which has been verified over a determinized program. This allows for the path quantification present within a CTL* formula, that is, whether all paths (or some paths) starting from a state satisfy a path formula. When a CTL* formula of the form $\theta ::= A\psi \mid E\psi$ is reached after acquiring a set of states satisfying ψ, θ is verified on the same determinized program used for ψ. We then must use quantifier elimination to acquire the proper set of states that satisfy θ, thus quantifying the assertions over the values of the prophecy variables. If the formula is of the form $A\psi$, we universally quantify the prophecy variables appearing in the set of states that satisfy $A\psi$. If the formula is of the form $E\psi$, we existentially quantify the prophecy variables.

Example. Consider the program in Fig. 1(a) and the property EFG $x = 1$ stating that there exists a possible future where $x = 1$ will eventually become true and stay true. This is a system stabilization property which can only be expressed in CTL*. We begin by identifying that G $x = 1$ is a path formula, and thus use APPROXIMATE to return the over-approximated state formula AG $x = 1$. We then initiate a CTL model checking task where we seek a set of states a_G such that EFa$_G$ holds, and for every state s such that $s \models a_G$ we have $s \models$ AG $x = 1$.

Our formula would now only be valid if we can find a set of states that are eventually reached in a possible future from the program's initial states such that AG $x = 1$ holds. However, no such set of states exists as the nondeterministic choice from ℓ_1 to ρ_2 and ρ_3 does not allow us to determine if we will eventually leave the loop or not. That is, there exists no set of states which can exemplify the infinite branching possibilities of leaving ρ_2 to possibly reaching ρ_3 or remaining in ρ_2 forever. In order to reason about the original sub-formula $G\ x = 1$, we must be observing sets of paths, not states. Given that we over-approximated our formula in a way that allows us to only reason about states, we thus symbolically determinize the program to simultaneously simulate all possible related paths through the control flow graph and try to separate them to originate from distinct states in the program.

Our procedure DETERMINIZE would then return a new partially symbolically determinized system in which a newly introduced prophecy variable, named n_{ℓ_1} in Fig. 1(b), is associated with the relation pair (ρ_2, ρ_3), and is used to make predictions about the occurrences of relations ρ_2 and ρ_3. Recall that relation pairs correspond to pairs of nondeterministic transitions, one remaining in a SCS and the other leaving the same SCS. In this case, ρ_3 is indeed disjoint from the strongly connected subgraph of ℓ_1.

Given that we initialize n_{ℓ_1} to a nondeterministic value, for every path in the program, a positive concrete number chosen at the nondeterministic assignment predicts the number of instances that transition ρ_2 is visited before transitioning to ρ_3. That is, we remain in ρ_2 until $n_{\ell_1} = 0$, with n_{ℓ_1} being decremented at each passage through the loop. Once we terminate the loop, the prophecy variable is nondeterministically reset (for the case that we return to the same loop again). A negative assignment to n_{ℓ_1} denotes remaining in ρ_2 forever, or non-termination.

We can now utilize an existing CTL model-checker to return an assertion characterizing the states in which $G\ x = 1$ holds by verifying the determinized program, denoted by P_D, using the over-approximated CTL formula $AG\ x = 1$. The assertion $a_G = (\ell_1 \wedge n_{\ell_1} < 0)$ is returned, and we proceed by replacing the sub-formula with its assertion in the original CTL* formula, resulting in EFa_G. To verify the outermost CTL* formula, EF, note that syntactically this is a readily acceptable CTL formula. However, we cannot simply use a CTL model checker as the path quantifier E exists within a larger relation context reasoning about paths given the inner formula FG. We thus must use the CTL model-checker to verify EFa_G over the same determinized program previously generated.

Our procedure returns with the same precondition $(\ell_1 \wedge n_{\ell_1} < 0)$. We then use quantifier elimination to existentially quantify out all introduced prophecy variables. The existential quantification corresponds to searching for some path (or paths) that satisfy the path formula. Thus, if there is a state s in the original program, and some value of the prophecy variables v such that *all* paths from the combined state $(s, n_{\ell_1} = v)$ in P_D satisfy the path formula then clearly, these paths give us a sufficient proof to conclude that $EFG\ x = 1$ holds from s in P.

4   Checking CTL* Formulae

In this section, we describe the details of our CTL* model checking procedure PROVECTL*. We first define the procedures utilized by PROVECTL*, namely DETERMINIZE and APPROXIMATE, followed by our model checking procedure and its utilization of QUANTELIM.

```
1 Let DETERMINIZE(P) : program =
2    P_D = P
3    SYNTH = [ ]
4    (L_D, E_D, Vars_D) = P_D
5    C = CYCLEPOINTS(P)
6    foreach (ℓ, ρ, ℓ') ∈ E_D do
7       G = MINSCS(P, C, ℓ) ∈ SCS(P, C)
8       if G ≠ ∅ ∧ MINSCS(P, C, ℓ') ≠ G then
9          SYNTH = ℓ :: SYNTH
10   done
11   foreach (ℓ, ρ, ℓ') ∈ E_D do
12      if ℓ ∈ SYNTH then
13         Vars_D = Vars_D ∪ n_ℓ ∈ ℤ
14         if ℓ' ∈ MINSCS(P, C, ℓ) then
15            ρ = ρ ∧ (n_ℓ ≠ 0) ∧ (n'_ℓ = n_ℓ − 1)
16         else
17            ρ = ρ ∧ (n_ℓ = 0)
18      done
19   return P_D
```

(a)

```
1 Let APPROXIMATE(ψ, a_{θ'_1}, a_{θ'_2}) :
2    φ = match (ψ) with
3    | Fθ'_1 → AFa_{θ'_1}
4    | Gθ'_1 → AGa_{θ'_1}
5    | Xθ'_1 → AXa_{θ'_1}
6    | θ'_1 W θ'_2 → Aa_{θ'_1} W a_{θ'_2}
7    | θ'_1 U θ'_2 → Aa_{θ'_1} U a_{θ'_2}
8    | θ'_1 ∧ θ'_2 → a_{θ'_1} ∧ a_{θ'_2}
9    | θ'_1 ∨ θ'_2 → a_{θ'_1} ∨ a_{θ'_2}
```

(b)

```
1 Let VERIFY(θ, P) : bool =
2    (L, E, Vars) = P
3    P_D = DETERMINIZE(P)
4    (a, _) = PROVECTL*(θ, P, P_D)
5    return ∀(ℓ_0, ρ, ℓ) ∈ E ∀s . (s, s) ⊨ ρ ⇒ a
```

(c)

```
1 Let QUANTELIM(a, φ) : AP =
2    a_EG = CTL(P_D, EG TRUE)
3    match (φ) with
4    | Aψ → ¬QE(∃n_ℓ∈L.a_EG ∧ ¬a)
5    | Eψ → QE(∃n_ℓ∈L.a_EG ∧ a)
```

(d)

Fig. 2. (a) DETERMINIZE identifies relation pairs and constructs a symbolically determinized program over them. (b) APPROXIMATE produces a syntactic conversion from a path formula to its corresponding over-approximation in ACTL. (c) VERIFY wraps PROVECTL* and then checks all initial states. (d) QUANTELIM applies quantifier elimination in order to convert path characterization to state characterization restricting attention to states from which an infinite path exists.

Determinize. The procedure DETERMINIZE constructs a form of partially symbolically determinized program over relation pairs that characterize instances of branching nondeterminism. We present our procedure in Fig. 2(a), where a program P is given and a partially determinized program P_D, contingent upon nondeterministic relation pairs, is returned. Ultimately, DETERMINIZE is designed to allow proof tools for branching-time logic state formulae to be used to reason about path formulae.

We begin by finding a sufficient set of relation pairs to symbolically determinize the program to one which has the same set of paths as the original. These relations are distinguished if there exist two nondeterministic relations stemming from the same location and yet are not part of the same strongly-connected subgraph. Our procedure thus begins by iterating over the set of a program's edges, $(ℓ, ρ, ℓ') ∈ E$ on line 6. We identify whether or not $ℓ ∈ C$ given that $G = $ MINSCS$(P, C, ℓ)$ and $G ≠ ∅$ on lines 7 and 8. If from some location $ℓ$, where $G = $ MINSCS$(P, C, ℓ)$, there is an edge to $ℓ'$ such that MINSCS$(P, C, ℓ')$

1 Let rec ProveCTL*$(\theta, P, P_D) : (formula, bool) =$	*17* $a_\theta = \text{QuantElim}(\text{CTL}(P_D, \varphi'), \varphi)$
2 $(\mathcal{L}, E, \text{Vars}) = P$	*18* Path $= \text{false}$
3 match (θ) with	*19* else
4 $\mid \varphi : state formula \rightarrow$	*20* $a_\theta = \text{CTL}(P, \varphi')$
5 match (φ) with	*21* Path $= \text{False}$
6 $\mid \alpha \rightarrow a_\theta = \alpha;$ Path $= \text{False}$	*22* $\mid \psi : path formula \rightarrow$
7 $\mid \theta_1' \wedge \theta_2' \mid \theta_1' \vee \theta_2' \mid E\theta_1' U\theta_2' \mid A\theta_1' W\theta_2'$	*23* match (ψ) with
8 $\mid E\theta_1' \wedge \theta_2' \mid E\theta_1' \vee \theta_2' \mid A\theta_1' \wedge \theta_2' \mid A\theta_1' \vee \theta_2' \rightarrow$	*24* $\mid \theta_1' \wedge \theta_2' \mid \theta_1' \vee \theta_2' \mid \theta_1' U\theta_2' \mid \theta_1' W\theta_2' \rightarrow$
9 $(a_{\theta_1'}, \text{Path}_1) = \text{ProveCTL}^*(\theta_1', P, P_D)$	*25* $(a_{\theta_1'}, \_) = \text{ProveCTL}^*(\theta_1', P, P_D)$
10 $(a_{\theta_2'}, \text{Path}_2) = \text{ProveCTL}^*(\theta_2', P, P_D)$	*26* $(a_{\theta_2'}, \_) = \text{ProveCTL}^*(\theta_2', P, P_D)$
11 $\mid AF\theta' \mid AG\theta' \mid AX\theta' \mid EF\theta' \mid EG\theta' \mid EX\theta' \rightarrow$	*27* $\mid F\theta' \mid G\theta' \mid X\theta' \rightarrow$
12 $(a_{\theta_1'}, \text{Path}_1) = \text{ProveCTL}^*(\theta', P, P_D)$	*28* $(a_{\theta_1'}, \_) = \text{ProveCTL}^*(\theta', P, P_D)$
13 Path$_2 = \text{False}$	*29* $\psi' = \text{Approximate}(\psi, a_{\theta_1'}, a_{\theta_2'})$
14 if $\varphi \neq \alpha$ then	*30* $a_\theta = \text{CTL}(P_D, \psi')$
15 $\varphi' = \text{Replace}(\psi, a_{\theta_1'}, a_{\theta_2'})$	*31* Path $= \text{true}$
16 if Path$_1 \vee$ Path$_2$ then	*32* (a_θ, Path)

Fig. 3. Our recursive CTL* verification procedure employs an existing CTL model checker and uses our procedures Approximate and QuantElim. It expects a CTL* property θ, a program P, and its determinized version P_D as parameters. An assertion characterizing the states in which θ holds is returned along with a boolean value indicating whether the formula checked was a path formula (and hence approximated).

is not equivalent to G, we can conclude that the transition from ℓ to ℓ' leaves the SCS of ℓ. We only desire that ℓ and ℓ' be elements of the most minimal SCS as such an edge eludes to the nondeterministic decision point where a transition diverted from remaining within an SCS. This nondeterministic point is key to the identification of where determinization must occur to facilitate the application of state-based reasoning to path-based reasoning for given a program P.

If the strongly connected subgraphs of ℓ and ℓ' do differ, we add ℓ to Synth, a list which tracks locations with nondeterministic points. For every such location, we identify a relation pair corresponding to the decision of either remaining in the same SCS, or leaving it. After finding all possible elements of Synth, on line 11 we iterate over the program edges, and for each relation pair encountered we introduce a new prophecy variable to predict the future outcome of the decision. Indeed, our motivation is to identify nondeterministic points so we can symbolically simulate all possible branching paths through a program, yet decisions regarding which paths are taken are determined by prophecy variables and their values. Information regarding different paths is now stored in the state of the modified program. This allows for a correspondence such that the verification path formulae can be reduced to the verification of ACTL formulae.

When an edge $(\ell, \rho, \ell') \in E$ is reached containing $\ell \in$ Synth, a prophecy variable $n_\ell \in \mathbb{Z}$ is added to the set of program variables Vars at line 13. If ℓ' is contained within MinSCS(P, C, ℓ), we constrain ρ by requiring that $n_\ell \neq 0$, and then decrement n_ℓ. If ℓ' is not contained within MinSCS(P, C, ℓ), we constrain ρ by $n_\ell = 0$, and n_ℓ' remains unconstrained, entailing a reset to a nondeterministic integer. The nondeterministic decision of the number of times a cycle is passed through is thus now determined by the prophecy variable n_ℓ. In the case that

$n_\ell < 0$, this rule corresponds to behaviors where every visit to ℓ is followed by a successor in the same SCS (i.e., the computation always remains in the SCS of ℓ). The nondeterminism within a transition relation is thus either determined at initialization by the initial choice of values for n_ℓ or else later in a path by choosing new nondeterministic values for n_ℓ.

We show that the determinization maintains the set of paths in the original program and the prophecy variables introduced merely trade nondeterminism in the transition relation for a larger, nondeterministic state space.

Theorem 1. *For every path π in P there is a path π' in P_D such that $\pi'\!\Downarrow_{\mathsf{Vars}} = \pi$. Furthermore, for every path π' in P_D it holds that $\pi'\!\Downarrow_{\mathsf{Vars}}$ is a path in P.*

Proof. *See TR [7], Appendix A.*

Approximate. In Fig. 2(b), we present a syntactic conversion from pure linear-time formulae in CTL*, that is LTL, to a corresponding over-approximation in ACTL. Our procedure is given a path formula ψ and two atomic preconditions, $a_{\theta_1'}$ and $a_{\theta_2'}$, corresponding to satisfaction of the nested CTL* formulae which appear within ψ. The precondition $a_{\theta_2'}$ is a conditional parameter utilized only when LTL formulae requiring two properties (e.g. W, U, $\wedge$, $\vee$) are given. Due to the recursive nature of PROVECTL*, presented in the next section, these preconditions would have already been priorly generated.

On lines 3–7, we instrument a universal path quantifier A preceding the appropriate temporal operators. Not only so, but the sub-formulae θ_1' and θ_2' are replaced with their corresponding preconditions $a_{\theta_1'}$ and $a_{\theta_2'}$, respectively. This aligns with how PROVECTL* will recursively iterate over each inner sub-formula followed by search for the preconditions of the outer sub-formulae dependent on it. Replacing a path formula by its CTL approximation indeed is sound in the sense that if the modified formula holds then the original holds as well.

Theorem 2. *For every program P, a state (ℓ, f), and a path formula ψ, if $P,(\ell, f) \models$ APPROXIMATE(ψ) then $P,(\ell, f) \models \mathsf{A}\psi$.*

Proof. *See TR [7], Appendix A.*

Theorem 2 does not consider existential path quantification. Recall that in order to conclude that the CTL* formula $P, s \models \mathsf{E}\psi$ for some path formula ψ, we require that there is some value v of the prophecy variables such that $P_D, (s, v) \models \mathsf{A}\psi$. This means that when restricting attention to a certain set of paths that start in a state s (those that match the valuation v for prophecy variables), *all* paths in the set satisfy the formula ψ. Clearly, this satisfies the requirement that there is some path that satisfies the formula.

4.1 ProveCTL*

In this section, we present our main CTL* verification procedure. Fig. 2(c) depicts VERIFY, which wraps the main procedure PROVECTL*, shown in Fig. 3. We then generate a determinized copy of the program, P_D, using the aforementioned procedure DETERMINIZE. This program is then passed into PROVECTL* along with the original program P and a CTL* property θ. PROVECTL* then returns an assertion a, characterizing the states in which θ holds. The second argument returned is disregarded, indicated by "_", as it is only used within the recursive calls of PROVECTL*. When PROVECTL* returns to VERIFY, it is only necessary to check if the precondition a is satisfied by the initial states of the program.

In order to synthesize a precondition for a CTL* property θ, we first recursively accumulate the preconditions generated when considering the sub-formulae of θ at lines 9, 10, 12, 25, 26, and 28. That is, for each sub-formula θ, we produce a precondition a_θ that ensures its satisfaction. We note that the precondition of an atomic proposition α is the proposition itself. A given CTL* formula is then deconstructed to differentiate between state and path sub-formulae, as the crux of verifying CTL* formulae lies within identifying the interplay between the arbitrary nesting of path and state formulae. On line 3, if θ can be identified as a state formula φ, we carry out the set of actions on lines 4 – 21. If θ is identified as a path formula ψ, we then we carry set of actions on lines 22 – 31.

Verifying Path Formulae. When a path formula ψ is reached, we begin by over-approximating the path formula by syntactically converting it to the universal subset of branching-time logic (ACTL) using the procedure APPROXIMATE. Recall that the preconditions generated when considering the sub-formula(e) of ψ at lines 25, 26, and 28 will be utilized by APPROXIMATE to replace θ'_1 and θ'_2 with their corresponding preconditions $a_{\theta'_1}$ and $a_{\theta'_2}$, respectively. On line 29, APPROXIMATE would then return a corresponding state formula ψ' where a universal path quantifier precedes every temporal operator within ψ.

A precondition for the newly attained ACTL formula ψ' can now be acquired via existing CTL model checkers which return an assertion characterizing the states in which ψ' holds. Existing tools which support this functionality include [3] and [11]. In our tool prototype, we build upon the latter. Recall that a precondition for a path formula requires more than a precondition for the corresponding state formula, as ψ' is merely an over-approximation. We thus must utilize the provided determinized program P_D when employing a CTL model checker rather than the original program P, as shown on line 30. The assertion a_θ is then returned characterizing the sets of states in which θ holds.

Recall that P_D leads to better correspondence between ψ and ψ'. That is, we find a sufficient set of relation pairs which determinize the program to one which has the same set of paths as the original, yet decisions regarding which paths are taken are determined by introduced prophecy variables and their values, allowing us to reduce path-based reasoning to state-based reasoning.

Finally, on line 31, we set the boolean flag PATH to true. This flag is the second argument to be returned by PROVECTL*. It indicates to the caller that the result a_θ returned by the recursive call is approximated. The value of PATH is used for deciding whether to use a_θ as is or modify it (in the case that the verified sub-formula is a state or a path formula, respectively), admitting a sound interaction between state and path formulae.

Verifying State Formulae. In the case that a state formula φ is reached, we partition the state sub-formulae by the syntax of CTL as shown on lines 6 – 8 and 11. This allows us to not only utilize existing CTL model checkers, but to also eliminate the redundant verification of a temporal operator, when it is already be preceded by a path quantifier. As a side effect of partitioning φ in such a way, a path formula ψ will always be in the form of a pure linear-time path formula, that is, LTL. This particular deconstruction of a CTL* formula is what allows us to identify the intricate interplay between path and state formulae.

We begin by recursively generating preconditions when considering the sub-formula(e) of φ at lines 9, 10, and 12. These preconditions will then be utilized by the procedure REPLACE on line 15. REPLACE substitutes θ_1' and θ_2' with their corresponding preconditions $a_{\theta_1'}$ and $a_{\theta_2'}$, respectively, and returns a new state formula φ'. Preconditions for branching-time logic state formulae can be acquired via existing CTL model checkers. However, in order to allow for the path quantification present within a CTL* formula to range over path formulae, we must consider whether all or some paths starting from a particular state satisfy a path formula. This is required in the case that the immediate inner sub-formula is a pure linear-time path formula, which is identified by the aforementioned boolean flag PATH given the partitioning of θ. The role of PATH is to track if a sub-formula of the current formula is a path formula. That is, PATH indicates that the path quantifier exists within the context of verifying a path formula, and not a branching-time state formula. Thus, it must be verified using P_D, yet the set of states of P_D that characterize it actually represents a set of paths. This set of paths must be collapsed later to a characterization of the set of states of P where the (state) formula holds. This is the key to allowing the interplay between state and path formulae.

The procedure QUANTELIM, presented in Fig. 2(d), which converts path characterization to state characterization, is thus executed at line 17. QUANTELIM takes in the assertion a returned from calling a CTL model checker on the determinized program P_D and the partitioned CTL formula φ', as well as the original formula φ. We then quantify the assertions over the values of the prophecy variables. If φ is a universal CTL formula, we universally quantify the prophecy variables appearing in the set of states that satisfy φ on line 4 in Fig. 2(d). If φ is an existential CTL formula, we existentially quantify the prophecy variables on line 5. Predictions of the prophecy variables may lead to finite paths to appear in the program, thus quantification must be restricted to states for which there does exist a prophecy value leading to infinite paths. Hence, on line 2 we acquire the precondition a_{EG} satisfying the CTL formula entailing nontermination, that is EG TRUE for P_D. The precondition a_{EG} is then conjuncted with a to ensure that the quantification of prophecy variables does not include finite paths generated due to invalid predictions of the prophecy variables. This is done according to the polarity of the quantification (universal or existential). The assertion a_θ is then returned by QUANTELIM characterizing the set of states in which θ holds.

In the case that PATH is false, the most immediate inner sub-formula would then be a state formula. This indicates that we can indeed use a CTL model checker using φ' and the original program P, as demonstrated on line 20. Upon the return of PROVECTL* to its caller VERIFY, a_θ will contain the precondition for the most outer temporal property of the original CTL* formula θ. Now it is only necessary to check if the precondition a_θ is satisfied by the initial states of the program to complete the verification of our CTL* formula. Finally, PATH is set to false, in order to carry out the above procedure again when necessary.

Theorem 3. *If* VERIFY(θ, P) *returns true then* $P \models \theta$.

Proof. *See TR [7], Appendix A.*

We note that the implication in Theorem 3 is only in one direction. That is, failing to prove that a property holds does not implicate that its negation holds (though this might be proved by negating the formula, converting it to negation normal form, and running our procedure on it). This incompleteness stems from the over-approximation of path formulae by a corresponding ACTL formulae, as although this over-approximation is checked over P_D, P_D does not determinize all paths. It is impossible to completely determinize a program as this requires uncountable branching (in the choice of prophecy variables). Countable nondeterminism is not a sufficient technique in the context of nondeterministic nested determinization of programs. For example, suppose that the prophecy variable value entails that an external loop does not terminate. Now consider all possible options for number of repetitions of the internal loop. In order to have a completely deterministic program, we must prophesize an infinite sequence of finite natural numbers. The number of such possible infinite sequences is uncountable.

5   Evaluation

In this section we discuss the results of our experiments with an implementation of the procedure from Fig. 2(c). Our implementation[2] is built as an extension to the open source project T2, which uses a safety prover similar to IMPACT [24] alongside previously published techniques for discovering ranking functions, etc. [9, 25] to prove both liveness and safety properties. The tool was executed on an Intel x64-based 2.8 GHz single-core processor. The format in which we interpret and parse a program's commands can be found in [11].

We have drawn out a set of CTL* problems from industrial code bases. Examples were taken from the I/O subsystems of the Windows OS kernel, the back-end infrastructure of the PostgreSQL database server, and the Apache web server. CTL* allows us to express "possibility" properties, such as the viability of a system, stating that any reachable state can spawn a fair computation. Additionally, we demonstrate that we can now verify properties involving existential system stabilization, stating that an event can eventually become true and stay true from any reachable state. For example, "OS frag. 1", "OS frag. 3", "PgSQL

---

[2] The source-code of our implementation and our benchmarks are available under the MIT open-source license at https://github.com/hkhlaaf/T2/tree/T2Star.

Program	LoC	Property	Time(s)	Res.
OS frag. 1	393	AG((EG(phi_io_compl $\leq$ 0)) $\vee$ (EFG(phi_nSUC_ret > 0))))	32.0	$\times$
OS frag. 1	393	EF((AF(phi_io_compl > 0)) $\wedge$ (AGF(phi_nSUC_ret $\leq$ 0))))	13.2	$\checkmark$
OS frag. 2	380	EFG((keA $\leq$ 0 $\wedge$ (AG keR = 0)))	28.3	$\checkmark$
OS frag. 2	380	EFG((keA $\leq$ 0 $\vee$ (EF keR = 1)))	16.5	$\checkmark$
OS frag. 3	50	EF(PPBlockInits > 0 $\wedge$ (((EFG IoCreateDevice = 0) $\vee$ (AGF status = 1)) $\wedge$ (EG PPBunlockInits $\leq$ 0)))	10.4	$\checkmark$
PgSQL arch 1	106	EFG(tt > 0 $\vee$ (AF wakend = 0))	1.5	$\times$
PgSQL arch 1	106	AGF(tt $\leq$ 0 $\wedge$ (EG wakend $\neq$ 0))	3.8	$\checkmark$
PgSQL arch 1	106	EFG(wakend = 1 $\wedge$ (EGF wakend = 0))	18.3	$\checkmark$
PgSQL arch 1	106	EGF(AG wakend = 1)	10.3	$\checkmark$
PgSQL arch 1	106	AFG(EF wakend = 0)	1.5	$\times$
PgSQL arch 2	100	AGF wakend = 1	1.4	$\checkmark$
PgSQL arch 2	100	EFG wakend = 0	0.5	$\times$
Bench 1	12	EFG(x = 1 $\wedge$ (EG y = 0))	1.0	$\checkmark$
Bench 2	12	EGF x > 0	0.1	$\checkmark$
Bench 3	12	AFG x = 1	0.1	$\checkmark$
Bench 4	10	AG((EFG y = 1) $\wedge$ (EF x $\geq$ t))	0.5	$\times$
Bench 5	10	AG(x = 0 U b = 0)	T/O	–
Bench 6	8	AG((EFG x = 0) $\wedge$ (EF x = 20))	0.1	$\checkmark$
Bench 7	6	(EFGx = 0) $\wedge$ (EFGy = 1)	0.5	$\times$
Bench 8	6	AG((AFG x = 0) $\vee$ (AFGx = 1))	0.5	$\checkmark$

Fig. 4. Experimental evaluations of infinite-state programs drawn from the Windows OS, PgSQL, and 8 toy examples. There are no competing tools available for comparison.

arch 1", and "Bench 2" are verified using said properties, described in detail in Sect. 1. We also include a few toy examples to further demonstrate further expressiveness of CTL* and its usefulness in verifying programs.

Given that our benchmarks tackle infinite-state programs, the only existing automated tool for verifying CTL* in the finite-state setting [18] is not applicable. In Fig. 4 we display the results of our benchmarks. For each program and its corresponding CTL* property to be verified, we display the number of lines of code (LoC), and report the time it took to verify a CTL* property (Time column) in seconds. We provide a **"Res."** column which indicates the results of our tool. A $\checkmark$ indicates that the tool was able to verify the property. Likewise, an $\times$ indicates that the tool failed to prove the property. The symbol "–" in the result column indicates that a result was not determined due to a timeout. A timeout or memory exception is indicated by T/O. A timeout is triggered if verification of an experiment exceeds 3000 seconds. Note that in various cases, we verify the same program using a CTL* property and its negation. Our tool thus allows us to prove each of the properties as well as disprove each of their negations.

Our experiments demonstrate the practical viability of our approach. Our runtimes show that our tool runs well within the range of performance previously exhibited by specialized tools such as as [3,8,10–12], which can only verify significantly less expressive properties over infinite-state programs. Our tool has successfully both verified and invalidated CTL* properties corresponding to their expected results for all but one of the benchmarks. This is due to the afore-mentioned limitation, that is, our countable nondeterministic determinization technique is not complete.

6 Concluding Remarks

We have introduced the first-known fully automatic method capable of proving CTL* of infinite-state (integer) programs. This allows us, for the first time ever, to automatically verify properties of programs that mix branching-time and linear-time temporal operators. We have developed an implementation capable of automatically proving properties of programs that no tool could previously prove. The method underlying our tool is one that uses a symbolic representation capable of facilitating reasoning about the interaction between sets of states and sets of paths.

References

1. Abadi, M., Lamport, L.: The existence of refinement mappings. Theoret. Comput. Sci. **82**, 253–284 (1991)
2. Beyene, T., Chaudhuri, S., Popeea, C., Rybalchenko, A.: A constraint-based app-roach to solving games on infinite graphs. In: POPL 2014, pp. 221–233. ACM (2014)
3. Beyene, T.A., Popeea, C., Rybalchenko, A.: Solving existentially quantified horn clauses. In: Sharygina, N., Veith, H. (eds.) CAV 2013. LNCS, vol. 8044, pp. 869–882. Springer, Heidelberg (2013)
4. Bjørner, N.S., Browne, A., Colón, M.A., Finkbeiner, B., Manna, Z., Sipma, H.B., Uribe, T.E.: Verifying temporal properties of reactive systems: a STeP tutorial. Form. Methods Syst. Des. **16**(3), 227–270 (2000)
5. Bodden, E.: A lightweight LTL runtime verification tool for Java. In: OOPSLA 2004, pp. 306–307. ACM (2004)
6. Cook, B., Khlaaf, H., Piterman, N.: Fairness for infinite-state systems. In: Baier, C., Tinelli, C. (eds.) TACAS 2015. LNCS, vol. 9035, pp. 384–398. Springer, Heidelberg (2015)
7. Cook, B., Khlaaf, H., Piterman, N.: On automation of CTL* verification for infinite-state systems. Technical report. University College London (2015). http://heidyk.com/publications/CAV15.pdf
8. Cook, B., Koskinen, E.: Reasoning about nondeterminism in programs. In: PLDI 2013, pp. 219–230. ACM (2013)
9. Cook, B., See, A., Zuleger, F.: Ramsey vs. lexicographic termination proving. In: Piterman, N., Smolka, S.A. (eds.) TACAS 2013 (ETAPS 2013). LNCS, vol. 7795, pp. 47–61. Springer, Heidelberg (2013)
10. Cook, B., Gotsman, A., Podelski, A., Rybalchenko, A., Vardi, M.Y.: Proving that programs eventually do something good. In: POPL 2007, pp. 265–276. ACM (2007)
11. Cook, B., Khlaaf, H., Piterman, N.: Faster temporal reasoning for infinite-state programs. In: FMCAD 2014, pp. 16:75–16:82. FMCAD Inc. (2014)
12. Cook, B., Koskinen, E.: Making prophecies with decision predicates. In: POPL 2011, pp. 399–410. ACM (2011)

13. Cormen, T.H., Stein, C., Rivest, R.L., Leiserson, C.E.: Introduction to Algorithms, 2nd edn. McGraw-Hill Higher Education, Boston (2001)
14. Emerson, E.A., Halpern, J.Y.: "Sometimes" and "Not Never"; revisited: on branching versus linear time temporal logic. J. ACM **33**(1), 151–178 (1986)
15. Emerson, E.A., Jutla, C.S.: The complexity of tree automata and logics of programs. SIAM J. Comput. **29**(1), 132–158 (1999)
16. Emerson, E.A., Lei, C.-L.: Modalities for model checking: branching time logic strikes back. Sci. Comput. Program. **8**(3), 275–306 (1987)
17. Emerson, E.A., Sistla, A.P.: Deciding branching time logic. In: STOC 1984, pp. 14–24. ACM (1984)
18. Griffault, A., Vincent, A.: The Mec 5 model-checker. In: Alur, R., Peled, D.A. (eds.) CAV 2004. LNCS, vol. 3114, pp. 488–491. Springer, Heidelberg (2004)
19. Gupta, A., Henzinger, T.A., Majumdar, R., Rybalchenko, A., Xu, R.-G.: Proving non-termination. SIGPLAN Not. **43**, 147–158 (2008)
20. Kesten, Y., Pnueli, A.: A compositional approach to CTL* verification. Theor. Comput. Sci. **331**(2–3), 397–428 (2005)
21. Lamport, L.: "Sometime" is sometimes "Not Never": on the temporal logic of programs. In: POPL 1980, pp. 174–185. ACM (1980)
22. Magill, S., Berdine, J., Clarke, E., Cook, B.: Arithmetic strengthening for shape analysis. In: Riis Nielson, H., Filé, G. (eds.) SAS 2007. LNCS, vol. 4634, pp. 419–436. Springer, Heidelberg (2007)
23. Manna, Z., Pnueli, A.: Temporal Verification of Reactive Systems: Safety, vol. 2. Springer, Heidelberg (1995)
24. McMillan, K.L.: Lazy abstraction with interpolants. In: Ball, T., Jones, R.B. (eds.) CAV 2006. LNCS, vol. 4144, pp. 123–136. Springer, Heidelberg (2006)
25. Podelski, A., Rybalchenko, A.: Transition invariants. In: LICS, pp. 32–41. IEEE, Turku, Finland (2004)
26. Reynolds, M.: An axiomatization of full computation tree logic. J. Symbolic Logic **66**(3), 1011–1057 (2001)
27. Song, F., Touili, T.: Pushdown model checking for malware detection. In: Flanagan, C., König, B. (eds.) TACAS 2012. LNCS, vol. 7214, pp. 110–125. Springer, Heidelberg (2012)

Algorithms for Model Checking HyperLTL and HyperCTL*

Bernd Finkbeiner[1], Markus N. Rabe[1 (✉)], and César Sánchez[2]

[1] Saarland University, Saarbrücken, Germany
{finkbeiner,rabe}@cs.uni-saarland.de
[2] IMDEA Software Institute, Madrid, Spain
cesar.sanchez@imdea.org

Abstract. We present an automata-based algorithm for checking finite state systems for hyperproperties specified in HyperLTL and HyperCTL*. For the alternation-free fragments of HyperLTL and HyperCTL* the automaton construction allows us to leverage existing model checking technology. Along several case studies, we demonstrate that the approach enables the verification of real hardware designs for properties that could not be checked before. We study information flow properties of an I2C bus master, the symmetric access to a shared resource in a mutual exclusion protocol, and the functional correctness of encoders and decoders for error resistant codes.

1 Introduction

HyperLTL and HyperCTL* are recent extensions to LTL and CTL* with the ability to express a wide range of hyperproperties [14]. Hyperproperties generalize trace properties and include properties from information-flow security such as noninterference [15]. Even though the complexity of model checking HyperLTL and HyperCTL* has been determined, no efficient algorithms are known so far. In this paper, we thus study the automatic verification of finite state systems for hyperproperties specified in HyperLTL and HyperCTL*.

HyperLTL and HyperCTL* allow us to specify relations over executions of the same system [14]. They introduce path quantifiers so computation paths can be referred to in the atomic propositions. For example, the following HyperLTL formula expresses noninterference [22] between input h and output o by requiring that all computation paths π and π' that only differ in h, have the same output o at all times:

$$\forall \pi. \forall \pi'. \ \Box \left(\bigwedge_{i \in I \setminus h} i_\pi = i_{\pi'} \right) \ \Rightarrow \ \Box \left(o_\pi = o_{\pi'} \right)$$

This work was partially supported by the Spanish Ministry of Economy under project "TIN2012-39391-C04-01 STRONGSOFT," the Madrid Regional Government under the project "S2013/ICE-2731 N-Greens Software-CM," the German Research Foundation (DFG) under the project SpAGAT in the Priority Program 1496 "Reliably Secure Software Systems - RS3," and the Graduate School of Computer Science at Saarland University.

D. Kroening and C.S. Păsăreanu (Eds.): CAV 2015, Part I, LNCS 9206, pp. 30–48, 2015.
DOI: 10.1007/978-3-319-21690-4_3

Quantifiers in CTL*, in contrast, are of the form $A\varphi$ and $E\varphi$ where the subformula φ can only (implicitly) refer to a single path—the path introduced by A and E respectively. Hence, CTL* cannot express noninterference [1,20].

Noninterference between i and o implies that o contains no information about i, and is therefore an important building block for properties in security [22]. By embedding noninterference in a temporal context, HyperLTL and HyperCTL* allow us to express a wide range of properties from information-flow security, including variants of declassification and quantitative information flow [3,5,16,41]. The use cases of HyperLTL and HyperCTL*, however, extend far beyond security, as we demonstrate in this paper.

The main result of this paper is an automata-theoretic algorithm for the model checking problem of HyperLTL and HyperCTL*. The automata approach to model checking LTL properties [46] reduces the verification problem to automata operations and decision problems, like automata product and check for emptiness. Typically, the LTL specification is translated into a Büchi word automaton that captures all violations of the specification. The product of the system with this automaton reveals the system's traces that violate the specification. We extend the approach based on Büchi word automata with the ability to quantify over new executions along the run, and thereby obtain an algorithm for HyperCTL* (Sect. 3). The construction for a quantifier $\exists\pi.\ \varphi$ corresponds to a product of the system and the automaton for the subformula φ. As in the classical approach, a final check of emptiness of the language of the automaton provides the answer to the model checking problem. The construction of the automaton involves the expensive nondeterminization of alternating automata [36] to handle quantifier alternations. For the rich class of alternation-free formulas, however, the algorithm is shown to be in NLOGSPACE in the size of the system. In Sect. 4 we use the alternating automaton construction to derive an approach to leverage existing model checking technology for model checking circuits for the alternation-free fragment of HyperCTL*.

We demonstrate the flexibility and the effectiveness of the proposed approach for the alternation-free fragment of HyperCTL* along three case studies (Sect. 5). The first case study concerns the information flow analysis of an I2C bus master. The second case study concerns the analysis of the symmetries in a mutual exclusion protocol. The typical fair-access properties against which mutual exclusion protocols are usually analyzed, such as accessibility and bounded overtaking [30], can be seen as abstractions of what is really expected from mutual exclusion protocols: *symmetric* access to the shared resource. HyperLTL enables a fine grained analysis of the symmetry between the processes, for example by expressing the property that switching the actions and roles between two components in a trace results in another legal trace, in which the access to the shared resource is switched accordingly. The third case study concerns the functional correctness of encoders and decoders of error resistant codes. The error resistance of a code is a property of its space of code words: all pairs of code words must have a certain minimum Hamming distance. We show that Hamming distance can be expressed in HyperLTL and demonstrate that this leads to an effective approach to the verification of encoders and decoders.

To summarize, our contributions are as follows:

- We develop the first direct automaton construction for model checking Hyper-LTL and HyperCTL* based on alternating automata.
- We present the first practical approach for model checking hardware systems for alternation-free HyperCTL* formulas.

Our evaluation shows that the approach enables the verification of industrial size hardware modules for hyperproperties. That is, we extend the state of the art in model checking hyperproperties from systems using only few (binary) variables [14,34] to systems with over 20.000 variables.

Related Work. In this paper, we present an automata-theoretic model checking algorithm for HyperLTL and HyperCTL*, together with a practical approach to the verification of hardware circuits against alternation-free formulas. Previous automata constructions for the problem [14] are based on *nondeterministic* Büchi automata, whereas we present an algorithm based on *alternating* Büchi automata, which allows us to leverage modern hardware verification techniques like IC3 [10]/PDR [18], interpolation [32], and SAT [8]. Our model checker can therefore be applied to significantly more complex systems than the proof-of-concept model checker for the one-alternation fragment of HyperLTL [14], which is limited to small explicitly given models.

HyperLTL and HyperCTL* are related to other logics for hyperproperties, such as variations of the μ-calculus, like the polyadic μ-calculus by Andersen [2], the higher-dimensional μ-calculus [38], and holistic hyperproperties [35]. The model checking problem for these logics can be reduced to the model checking problem of the modal μ-calculus [2,27] (or directly to parity games [34]) and involves, similar to our construction, an analysis of the product of several copies of the system. We are not aware, however, of any practical approaches that would allow the verification of complex hardware designs against specifications given in these logics. Another related class of logics are the epistemic temporal logics [19], which reason about the *knowledge of agents* and how it changes over time. While it has been shown that epistemic temporal logic can express certain information flow policies [4], most practical work with epistemic logics has focussed on applications from the area of multi-agent systems [21,28,29,33,39].

Lastly, in the area of information flow security, there are several verification techniques that focus on specific information flow properties—rather than on a general logic like HyperLTL and HyperCTL*—but use techniques that relate to our model checking algorithm. A construction based on the product of copies of a system, self-composition [6,7], has been tailored for various trace-based security definitions [17,23,44].

2 Temporal Logics for Hyperproperties

We now introduce the temporal logics for hyperproperties, their semantics, and their model checking problem.

A *Kripke structure* is a tuple $K = (S, s_0, \delta, \mathsf{AP}, L)$ consisting of a set of states S, an initial state s_0, a transition function $\delta : S \rightarrow 2^S$, a set of *atomic propositions* AP, and a *labeling function* $L : S \rightarrow 2^{\mathsf{AP}}$ decorating each state with a set of atomic propositions. We require that each state has a successor, that is $\delta(s) \neq \emptyset$, to ensure that every execution of a Kripke structure can always be extended to an infinite execution. A *path* of a Kripke structure is an infinite sequence of states $s_0 s_1 \ldots \in S^\omega$ such that s_0 is the initial state of K and $s_{i+1} \in \delta(s_i)$ for all $i \in \mathbb{N}$. We denote by $Paths(K, s)$ the set of all paths of K starting in state $s \in S$ and by $Paths^*(K, s)$ the set of their suffixes. Given a path p and a number $i \geq 0$, $p[i, \infty]$ denotes the suffix path where the first i elements are removed.

HyperLTL and HyperCTL* extend the standard temporal logics LTL and CTL* by *quantification over path variables*. Their formulas are generated by the following grammar, where $a \in \mathsf{AP}$ and π ranges over path variables:

$$\varphi ::= \mathsf{true} \mid a_\pi \mid \neg\varphi \mid \varphi \vee \varphi \mid \varphi \wedge \varphi$$
$$\mid \bigcirc\varphi \mid \varphi\, \mathcal{U}\, \varphi \mid \varphi\, \mathcal{R}\, \varphi \mid \exists\pi.\, \varphi \mid \forall\pi.\, \varphi$$

Additionally, we define the derived operators $\Diamond\varphi = \mathsf{true}\, \mathcal{U}\, \varphi$, $\Box\varphi = \neg\Diamond\neg\varphi$, and $\varphi_1\, \mathcal{W}\, \varphi_2 = \varphi_1\, \mathcal{U}\, \varphi_2 \vee \Box\varphi_1$.

For HyperLTL and HyperCTL* we require that temporal operators only occur inside the scope of path quantifiers. HyperLTL is the sublogic of formulas in *prenex normal form*. A formula is in prenex normal form, if it starts with a sequence of quantifiers, and is quantifier-free in the rest of the formula. The conceptual difference between HyperLTL and HyperCTL*, is that HyperLTL, like LTL, is a linear-time logic and that HyperCTL*, like CTL and CTL*, is a branching-time logic [20]. A formula φ is in *negation normal form* if the only occurrences of $\neg$ occur in front of propositions a_π.

Semantics. In the following we define the semantics for the operators a_π, $\neg\varphi$, $\varphi_1 \vee \varphi_2$, $\bigcirc\varphi$, $\varphi_1\, \mathcal{U}\, \varphi_2$, and $\exists\pi.\, \varphi$. The other operators are defined via the following equalities: $\forall\pi.\, \varphi = \neg\exists\pi.\, \neg\varphi$, $\varphi_1 \wedge \varphi_2 = \neg(\neg\varphi_1 \vee \neg\varphi_2)$, and $\varphi_1\mathcal{R}\varphi_2 = \neg(\neg\varphi_1\mathcal{U}\neg\varphi_1)$. These derived operators are kept in the syntax to guarantee the existence of equivalent formulas in negation normal form.

Let K be a Kripke structure and let s_0 be its initial state. The semantics of HyperLTL and HyperCTL* is given in terms of assignments $\Pi : N \rightarrow Paths^*(K, s_0)$ of a set of path variables N to suffixes of *paths*. We use $\Pi[i, \infty]$ for the map that assigns to each path variable π the suffix $\Pi(\pi)[i, \infty]$. We use the reserved path variable ε to denote the most recently quantified path and define the validity of a formula as follows:

$$\Pi \models_K a_\pi \qquad \text{whenever} \quad a \in L\big(\Pi(\pi)(0)\big)$$
$$\Pi \models_K \neg\varphi \qquad \text{whenever} \quad \Pi \not\models_K \varphi$$
$$\Pi \models_K \varphi_1 \vee \varphi_2 \qquad \text{whenever} \quad \Pi \models_K \varphi_1 \text{ or } \Pi \models \varphi_2$$
$$\Pi \models_K \bigcirc\varphi \qquad \text{whenever} \quad \Pi[1,\infty] \models_K \varphi$$
$$\Pi \models_K \varphi_1 \, \mathcal{U} \, \varphi_2 \qquad \text{whenever} \quad \text{for some } i \geq 0: \ \Pi[i,\infty] \models_K \varphi_2 \text{ and}$$
$$\text{for all } 0 \leq j < i: \ \Pi[j,\infty] \models_K \varphi_1$$
$$\Pi \models_K \exists\pi.\ \varphi \qquad \text{whenever} \quad \text{for some } p \in Paths(K, \Pi(\varepsilon)(0)):$$
$$\Pi[\pi \mapsto p, \ \varepsilon \mapsto p] \models_K \varphi$$

For the empty assignment $\Pi = \{\}$, we define $\Pi(\varepsilon)(0)$ to yield the initial state. Validity on states of a Kripke structure K, written $s \models_K \varphi$, is defined as $\{\} \models_K \varphi$. A Kripke structure $K = (S, s_0, \delta, \mathsf{AP}, L)$ satisfies formula φ, denoted with $K \models \varphi$ whenever $s_0 \models_K \varphi$.

3   Automata-Theoretic Model Checking of HyperCTL*

In this section, we present an automata-theoretic construction for the verification of HyperCTL* formulas. In Sect. 4 we will then use this construction to build a practical algorithm for the verification of circuits. We start with a brief review of alternating automata. Given a finite set Q, $\mathbb{B}(Q)$ denotes the set of Boolean formulas over Q and $\mathbb{B}^+(Q)$ the set of positive Boolean formulas, that is, formulas that do not contain negation. The satisfaction of a formula $\theta \in \mathbb{B}(Q)$ by a set $Q' \subseteq Q$ is denoted by $Q' \models \theta$.

Definition 1 (Alternating Büchi Automata). *An* alternating Büchi auto maton *(on words) is a tuple* $\mathcal{A} = (Q, q_0, \Sigma, \rho, F)$, *where* Q *is a finite set of states,* $q_0 \in Q$ *is the initial state,* Σ *is a finite alphabet,* $\rho : Q \times \Sigma \to \mathbb{B}^+(Q)$ *is a transition function that maps a state and a letter to a positive Boolean combination of states, and* $F \subseteq Q$ *are the accepting states.*

A run of an alternating automaton is a Q-labeled tree. A *tree* T is a subset of $\mathbb{N}_{>0}^*$ such that for every *node* $\tau \in \mathbb{N}_{>0}^*$ and every positive integer $n \in \mathbb{N}_{>0}$, (i) if $\tau \cdot n \in T$ then $\tau \in T$ (i.e., T is prefix-closed), and (ii) for every $0 < m < n$, $\tau \cdot m \in T$. The root of T is the empty sequence ε and for a node $\tau \in T$, $|\tau|$ is the length of the sequence τ, in other words, its distance from the root. A *run* of $\mathcal{A}$ on an infinite word $\pi \in \Sigma^\omega$ is a Q-labeled tree (T, r) such that $r(\varepsilon) = q_0$ and for every node τ in T with children $\tau_1, \ldots, \tau_k$ the following holds: $1 \leq k \leq |Q|$ and $\{r(\tau_1), \ldots, r(\tau_k)\} \models \rho(q, \pi[i])$, where $q = r(\tau)$ and $i = |\tau|$. A run r of $\mathcal{A}$ on $\pi \in \Sigma^\omega$ is *accepting* whenever for every infinite path $\tau_0 \tau_1 \ldots$ in T, there are infinitely many i with $r(\tau_i) \in F$. We say that π is accepted by $\mathcal{A}$ whenever there is an accepting run of $\mathcal{A}$ on π, and denote with $\mathcal{L}_\omega(\mathcal{A})$ the set of infinite words *accepted* by $\mathcal{A}$.

If the transition function of an alternating automaton does not contain any conjunctions, we call the automaton *nondeterministic*. The transition function ρ of a nondeterministic automaton thus identifies a disjunction over a set of successor states. Such a transition function can also be stated as a function $\rho : Q \times \Sigma \rightarrow 2^Q$ identifying the successors. Our model checking algorithm relies on the standard translation for alternation removal due to Miyano and Hayashi:

Theorem 1 ([36]). *Let $\mathcal{A}$ be an alternating Büchi automaton with n states. There is a nondeterministic Büchi automaton $\mathsf{MH}(\mathcal{A})$ with $2^{\mathcal{O}(n)}$ states that accepts the same language.*

3.1   The Alternation-Free Fragment

We present a model checking algorithm for the alternation-free fragment of HyperCTL*. This fragment is expressive enough to capture a broad range of other information-flow properties, like declassification mechanisms, quantitative noninterference, and information-flow requirements that change over time [14,16]. The case studies in Sect. 5 illustrate that this fragment also captures properties in application domains beyond information-flow security.

Definition 2 (Alternation-Free HyperCTL*). *A HyperCTL* formula φ in negation normal form is alternation-free, if φ contains only quantifiers of one type. Additionally, we require that no existential quantifier occurs in the left subformula of an until operator or in the right subformula of a release operator, and, symmetrically, that no universal quantifier occurs in the right subformula of an until operator or in the left subformula of a release operator.*

Similar to the automata-theoretic approach to LTL properties [37,45], we construct an alternating automaton bottom up from the formula, but handling multiple path quantifiers. For alternation-free HyperCTL*, the quantifiers may occur inside temporal operators (with the restrictions in Definition 2) as long as there is no quantifier alternation.

Let K be a Kripke structure $K = (S, s_0, \delta, \mathsf{AP}, L)$. To check the satisfaction of a HyperCTL* formula φ by K, we translate φ into a K-equivalent alternating automaton $\mathcal{A}_\varphi$. The construction of $\mathcal{A}_\varphi$ proceeds inductively following the structure of φ, as follows. Assume that φ is in negation normal form and starts with an existential quantifier, and consider a subformula ψ of φ. Let n be the number of path quantifiers occurring on the path from the root of the syntax tree of φ to ψ, and let these path quantifiers bind the variables $\pi_1, \ldots, \pi_n$. The alphabet Σ of $\mathcal{A}_\psi$ is S^n, the set of n-tuples of states of K. We say that a language $L \subseteq (S^n)^\omega$ is K-*equivalent* to ψ, if all sequences of state tuples $(s_0^0, \ldots, s_n^0)(s_0^1, \ldots, s_n^1) \ldots$ in L correspond to a path assignment Π satisfying ψ. That is, for all $(s_0^0, \ldots, s_n^0)(s_0^1, \ldots, s_n^1) \ldots \in L$ it holds $\Pi \models_K \psi$ for the path assignment $\Pi(\pi_i) = s_i^0 s_i^1 \ldots$ (for all $i \leq n$). An automaton is K-equivalent to ψ if its language is K-equivalent to ψ.

For atomic propositions, Boolean connectives, and temporal operators, our construction follows the standard translation from LTL to alternating automata [37,45]. Let $\mathcal{A}_{\psi_1} = (Q_1, q_{0,1}, \Sigma_1, \rho_1, F_1)$ and $\mathcal{A}_{\psi_2} = (Q_2, q_{0,2}, \Sigma_2, \rho_2, F_2)$ be the alternating automata for the subformulas ψ_1 and ψ_2:

$\psi = a_{\pi_k}$	$\mathcal{A}_\psi = (\{q_0\}, q_0, \Sigma, \rho, \emptyset)$, where $\rho(q_0, \boldsymbol{s}) = (a \in L(\boldsymbol{s}\mid_k))$
$\psi = \neg a_{\pi_k}$	$\mathcal{A}_\psi = (\{q_0\}, q_0, \Sigma, \rho, \emptyset)$, where $\rho(q_0, \boldsymbol{s}) = (a \notin L(\boldsymbol{s}\mid_k))$
$\psi = \psi_1 \vee \psi_2$	$\mathcal{A}_\psi = (Q_1 \cup Q_2 \cup \{q_0\}, q_0, \Sigma, \rho, F_1 \cup F_2)$
	where $\rho(q_0, \boldsymbol{s}) = \rho_1(q_{0,1}, \boldsymbol{s}) \vee \rho_2(q_{0,2}, \boldsymbol{s})$
	and $\rho(q, \boldsymbol{s}) = \rho_i(q, \boldsymbol{s})$ for $q \in Q_i, i \in \{1, 2\}$
$\psi = \psi_1 \wedge \psi_2$	$\mathcal{A}_\psi = (Q_1 \cup Q_2 \cup \{q_0\}, q_0, \Sigma, \rho, F_1 \cup F_2)$
	where $\rho(q_0, \boldsymbol{s}) = \rho_1(q_{0,1}, \boldsymbol{s}) \wedge \rho_2(q_{0,2}, \boldsymbol{s})$
	and $\rho(q, \boldsymbol{s}) = \rho_i(q, \boldsymbol{s})$ for $q \in Q_i, i \in \{1, 2\}$
$\psi = \bigcirc \psi_1$	$\mathcal{A}_\psi = (Q_1 \cup \{q_0\}, q_0, \Sigma, \rho, F_1)$
	where $\rho(q_0, \boldsymbol{s}) = q_{0,1}$
	and $\rho(q, \boldsymbol{s}) = \rho_1(q, \boldsymbol{s})$ for $q \in Q_1$
$\psi = \psi_1 \, \mathcal{U} \, \psi_2$	$\mathcal{A}_\psi = (Q_1 \cup Q_2 \cup \{q_0\}, q_0, \Sigma, \rho, F_1 \cup F_2)$
	where $\rho(q_0, \boldsymbol{s}) = \rho_2(q_{0,2}, \boldsymbol{s}) \vee (\rho_1(q_{0,1}, \boldsymbol{s}) \wedge q_0)$
	and $\rho(q, \boldsymbol{s}) = \rho_i(q, \boldsymbol{s})$ for $q \in Q_i, i \in \{1, 2\}$
$\psi = \psi_1 \, \mathcal{R} \, \psi_2$	$\mathcal{A}_\psi = (Q_1 \cup Q_2 \cup \{q_0\}, q_0, \Sigma, \rho, F_1 \cup F_2 \cup \{q_0\})$
	where $\rho(q_0, \boldsymbol{s}) = \rho_2(q_{0,2}, \boldsymbol{s}) \wedge (\rho_1(q_{0,1}, \boldsymbol{s}) \vee q_0)$
	and $\rho(q, \boldsymbol{s}) = \rho_i(q, \boldsymbol{s})$ for $q \in Q_i, i \in \{1, 2\}$

For a quantified subformula $\psi = \exists \pi.\psi_1$, we have to reduce the alphabet $\Sigma_{\psi_1} = S^{n+1}$ to $\Sigma = S^n$. The language for formula ψ contains exactly those sequences σ of state tuples, such that there is a path p through the Kripke structure K for which σ extended by p is in $\mathcal{L}(\mathcal{A}_{\psi_1})$. Let $\mathcal{N}'_{\psi_1} = (Q', q'_0, \Sigma, \rho', F')$ be the nondeterministic automaton $\mathcal{N}'_{\psi_1} = \mathsf{MH}(\mathcal{A}_{\psi_1})$ constructed from $\mathcal{A}_{\psi_1}$ by the construction in Theorem 1, and let $\mathcal{A}_\psi = (Q'', q''_0, \Sigma_\psi, \rho'', F'')$ be constructed from $\mathcal{N}'_{\psi_1}$ and the Kripke structure $K = (S, s_0, \delta, \mathsf{AP}, L)$ as follows:

$\psi = \exists \pi.\psi_1$	$\mathcal{A}_\psi = (Q' \times S \cup \{q''_0\}, q''_0, \Sigma_\psi, \rho'', F' \times S)$
	where $\rho''(q''_0, \boldsymbol{s}) = \{(q', s') \mid q' \in \rho'(q'_0, \boldsymbol{s} + \boldsymbol{s}\mid_n), s' \in \delta(\boldsymbol{s}\mid_n)\}$
	and $\rho''((q, s), \boldsymbol{s}) = \{(q', s') \mid q' \in \rho'(q, \boldsymbol{s} + s), s' \in \delta(s)\}$

For the case that $n = 0$ we define that $\boldsymbol{s}\mid_n$ is the initial state s_0 of K.

Since we consider the alternation-free fragment, there are no negated quantified subformulas and the construction is finished.

The correctness of the construction can be shown by structural induction.

Proposition 1. *Let φ be a HyperCTL* formula and $\mathcal{A}_\varphi$ the alternating automaton obtained by the previous construction. Then, φ and $\mathcal{A}_\varphi$ are K-equivalent.*

So far, we only considered alternation-free formulas that start with existential quantifiers. To decide $K \models \varphi$ for an arbitrary φ, we first transform φ in a Boolean combination over a set X of quantified subformulas. Each element ψ' of X is now in the form $\exists \pi.\varphi$ for which we apply the construction above. Since ψ' is of the form $\exists \pi.\psi_1$, $\mathcal{A}_{\psi'}$ is a nondeterministic Büchi automaton, for which we apply a standard nonemptiness test [47].

Theorem 2. *The model checking problem for the alternation-free fragment of HyperCTL* is PSPACE-complete in the size of the formula and NLOGSPACE-complete in the size of the Kripke structure.*

Proof. The alternating automaton $\mathcal{A}_{\psi_1}$ is a tree with self-loops, when we consider automata created for quantified subformulas as leafs of the tree. By structural induction, we show that the size of $\mathcal{A}_{\psi'}$ for an alternation-free formula ψ' is polynomial in $|\psi'|$ and in $|K|$ and that sub-automata for quantified subformulas are not reachable via actions that are self-loops with conjunctions.

Base Case: for atomic propositions and negated atomic propositions, the induction hypothesis is fulfilled.

Induction Step: Let $\psi = \exists \pi. \psi_1$. Only Until operators and Release operators in the formula lead to nodes that have two transitions, one with a self-loop and one without self-loops. By the restrictions in the definition of the alternation-free fragment, we guarantee that automata of quantified subformulas are not reachable via transitions with self-loops that contain conjunctions.

Conjunctive transitions that are not part of loops or self-loops only lead to a polynomial increase in size during nondeterminization. Emptiness of nondeterministic Büchi automata is in NLOGSPACE [47], so the upper bound of the theorem follows.

Since HyperCTL* subsumes LTL, the lower bound for LTL model checking [42] implies the lower bound for HyperCTL*.   □

3.2   The Full Logic

The construction from the previous subsection can be extended to full HyperCTL* by adding a construction for *negated* quantified subformulas. We compute an automaton for the complement language, based on the following theorem:

Theorem 3 ([25]). *For every alternating Büchi automaton $\mathcal{A} = (Q, q_0, \Sigma, \rho, F)$, there is an alternating Büchi automaton $\overline{\mathcal{A}}$ with $O(|Q|)^2$ states that accepts the complemented language: $\mathcal{L}_\omega(\overline{\mathcal{A}}) = \overline{\mathcal{L}_\omega(\mathcal{A})}$.*

We extend the previous construction with the following case:

$$\varphi = \neg \exists \pi. \psi_1 \,\Big|\, \overline{\mathcal{N}'_{\psi_1}}, \quad \text{where } \mathcal{N}'_{\psi_1} = \mathsf{MH}(\mathcal{A}_{\psi_1}) \text{ via Theorem 1}$$

We capture the complexity of the resulting model checking algorithm in terms of the alternation depth of the HyperCTL* formula. The formulas with alternation depth 0 are exactly the alternation-free formulas.

Definition 3 (Alternation Depth). *A HyperCTL* formula φ in negation normal form has alternation depth 0 plus the highest number of alternations from existential to universal and universal to existential quantifiers along any of* *the paths of the formula's syntax tree. Existential quantifiers in the left subformula of an until operator or in the right subformula of a release operator, and, symmetrically, universal quantifiers in the right subformula of an until operator or in the left subformula of a release operator count as additional alternation.*

For example, let ψ be a formula without additional quantifiers, then $\exists\pi.\ \psi$ has alternation depth 0, $\forall\pi_1.\exists\pi.\ \psi$ has alternation depth 1, $\exists\pi.\ \Diamond\exists\pi'.\ \psi$ has alternation depth 0, $\exists\pi.\ \Box\exists\pi'.\ \psi$ has alternation depth 1, and $(\forall\pi.\ \psi) \wedge (\exists\pi.\ \psi)$ has alternation depth 0.

Let $g_c(k,n)$ be a tower of exponentiations of height k, defined simply as $g_c(0,n) = n$ and $g_c(k,n) = c^{g_c(k-1,n)}$. We define NSPACE$(g(k,n))$ to be the languages that are accepted by a nondeterministic Turing machine that runs in SPACE $O(g_c(k,n))$ for some $c > 1$. For convenience, we define NSPACE$(g(-1,n))$ to be NLOGSPACE.

Proposition 2. *Let K be a Kripke structure and φ a HyperCTL* formula with alternation depth k. The alternating automaton $\mathcal{A}_\varphi$ resulting from the previous construction has $O(g(k+1,|\varphi|))$ and $O(g(k,|K|))$ states and can be constructed in NSPACE$(g(k,|\varphi|))$ and NSPACE$(g(k-1,|K|))$.*

Theorem 4. *Given a Kripke structure K and a HyperCTL* formula φ with alternation depth k, we can decide whether $K \models \varphi$ in NSPACE$(g(k,|\varphi|))$ and NSPACE$(g(k-1,|K|))$.*

The proof of Proposition 2 is an induction over the alternation depth. The proof of Theorem 4 uses that the nonemptiness problem for nondeterministic Büchi automata is in NLOGSPACE [47]. Theorem 4 subsumes the result for the alternation-free fragment:

Corollary 1. *For alternation depth 0, the model-checking problem $K \models \varphi$ is in PSPACE in $|\varphi|$ and in NLOGSPACE in $|K|$.*

4 Symbolic Model Checking of Circuits

In this section we translate the automaton-based construction from Sect. 3 for alternation-free formulas into a practical verification approach for circuits. Given a circuit C and an alternation-free formula φ the algorithm produces a new circuit C_φ that is linear in the size of C and also linear in the size of φ. The compactness of the encoding builds on the ability of circuits to describe systems of exponential size with a linear number of binary variables. The circuit C_φ is then checked for fair reachability to determine the validity of $C \models \varphi$. This check can be done with of-the-shelf model checkers leveraging modern hardware verification technology [8,11,12].

A $circuit^1$ $C = (X, init, I, O, T)$ consists of a set X of binary variables (latches with unit delay), a condition $init \in \mathbb{B}(X)$ characterizing a non-empty set of initial states of X, a set of input variables I, a set of output variables O, and a transition relation $T \in \mathbb{B}(X \times I \times O \times X)$. We require that T is input-enabled and input-deterministic, that is, for all $x \subseteq X$, $i \subseteq I$, there is exactly one $o \subseteq O$ and one $x' \subseteq X$ such that $T(x, i, o, x')$ holds. We denote a subset of X as a *state* of circuit C, indicating exactly those latches that are set to 1. The size of a circuit C, denoted $|C|$, is defined as the number of latches $|X|$.

A circuit C can be interpreted as a finite Kripke structure K_C of potentially exponential size. The state space of K_C is $S = s_0 \cup 2^X \times 2^I \times 2^O \times 2^X$, where s_0 is a fresh initial state. The transition relation distinguishes the initial step of the computation: $s' \in \delta(s_0)$ iff there is a circuit state $x \subseteq X$ with $init(x)$ and $x = s'|_X$ such that $T(x, s'|_I, s'|_O, s'|_X)$, where $s'|_I$, $s'|_O$, $s'|_X$, and $s'|_{X'}$ are the projections to variables I, O, the first copy of X, and the second copy of X respectively. For subsequent steps of computation we define $s' \in \delta(s)$ whenever $T(s|_X, s'|_I, s'|_O, s'|_{X'})$ and $s|_{X'} = s'|_X$. That is, the first copy X denotes the *previous* state, whereas X' denotes the *current* state. The labelling function of K_C maps each state s to the set $s|_I \cup s|_O \cup s|_X$. That is, the alphabet AP_{K_C} is $I \cup O \cup X$. The semantics of HyperCTL* on a circuit C is defined using the associated Kripke structure K_C. We write $C \models \varphi$ whenever $K_C \models \varphi'$, where φ' is obtained by replacing all atomic propositions a_π by $\bigcirc a_\pi$. This leads to a natural semantics on circuits: the atomic propositions always refer to the *current* value of the latches, the *next* input, and the *next* output.

Given a circuit C and an alternation-free HyperCTL* formula φ, we reduce the model checking problem $C \models \varphi$ to finding a computation path in a circuit C_φ that does not visit a bad state and satisfies a conjunction of strong fairness (or compassion) constraints $F = \{f_1, \ldots, f_k\}$. A strong fairness constraint f of a circuit consists of a tuple (a_1, a_2) of atomic propositions and a path p satisfies f, if a_1 holds only finitely often or a_2 holds infinitely often on p. We build C_φ bottom up following the formula structure. Without loss of generality, we assume that φ contains only existential quantifiers and is in negation normal form. Let ψ be a subformula of φ that occurs under n quantifiers. Let $C_{\psi_1} = (X_{\psi_1}, init_{\psi_1}, I_{\psi_1}, O_{\psi_1}, T_{\psi_1})$, $C_{\psi_2} = (X_{\psi_2}, init_{\psi_2}, I_{\psi_2}, O_{\psi_2}, T_{\psi_2})$ be the circuits, and let F_{ψ_1} and F_{ψ_2} be the fairness constraints for the subformulas ψ_1 and ψ_2. For LTL operators, the construction resembles the standard translation from LTL to circuits [13, 24]. We construct C_ψ and F_ψ as follows:

---

[1] Our definition of circuits can be considered as a model of and-inverter graphs in the Aiger standard [9], where the gate list is abstracted to a transition relation.

$\psi = a_{\pi_k}$	$C_\psi = (\emptyset, \text{true}, I_\psi, \{o_\psi\}, o_\psi \leftrightarrow a_{\pi_k}),$	$F_\psi = \emptyset$
$\psi = \neg a_{\pi_k}$	$C_\psi = (\emptyset, \text{true}, I_\psi, \{o_\psi\}, o_\psi \text{ xor } a_{\pi_k}),$	$F_\psi = \emptyset$
$\psi = \psi_1 \vee \psi_2$	$C_\psi = (X_{\psi_1} \uplus X_{\psi_2}, \; init_{\psi_1} \wedge init_{\psi_2},$ $\qquad I_{\psi_1} \cup I_{\psi_2} \uplus \{i_\psi\}, \; O_{\psi_1} \uplus O_{\psi_2} \uplus \{o_\psi\},$ $\qquad (o_\psi \leftrightarrow (i_\psi \Rightarrow o_{\psi_1}) \wedge (\neg i_\psi \Rightarrow o_{\psi_2})) \wedge T_{\psi_1} \wedge T_{\psi_2}),$ $F_\psi = F_{\psi_1} \cup F_{\psi_2}$	
$\psi = \bigcirc \psi_1$	$C_\psi = (X_{\psi_1} \uplus \{x_\psi\}, \; init_{\psi_1}, I_{\psi_1} \uplus \{i_\psi\}, \; O_{\psi_1} \uplus \{o_\psi, b_\psi\},$ $\qquad T_{\psi_1} \wedge (o_\psi \leftrightarrow i_\psi) \wedge (x'_\psi \leftrightarrow i_\psi) \wedge (\neg b_\psi \leftrightarrow (o_{\psi_1} \leftrightarrow x_\psi))),$ $F_\psi = F_{\psi_1}$	
$\psi = \psi_1 \, \mathcal{U} \, \psi_2$	$C_\psi = (X_{\psi_1} \uplus X_{\psi_2} \uplus \{x_\psi\}, \; init_{\psi_1} \wedge init_{\psi_2},$ $\qquad I_{\psi_1} \uplus I_{\psi_2} \uplus \{i_\psi, i'_\psi\}, \; O_{\psi_1} \uplus O_{\psi_2} \uplus \{o_\psi, b_\psi\},$ $\qquad T_{\psi_1} \wedge T_{\psi_2} \wedge (o_\psi \leftrightarrow x_\psi) \wedge (x'_\psi \leftrightarrow i_\psi) \wedge$ $\qquad (\neg b_\psi \leftrightarrow (((i'_\psi \Rightarrow o_{\psi_2}) \wedge (\neg i'_\psi \Rightarrow o_{\psi_1} \wedge x'_\psi)) \leftrightarrow x_\psi))),$ $F_\psi = F_{\psi_1} \cup F_{\psi_2} \cup \{(x_\psi, o_{\psi_2})\}$	
$\psi = \exists \pi. \; \psi_1$	$C_\psi = (X_{\psi_1} \uplus X_n, \; init_{\psi_1} \wedge (n = 1 \Rightarrow init(X_n)),$ $\qquad I_{\psi_1} \setminus X_n, \; (O_{\psi_1} \setminus O_n) \uplus \{o_\psi\},$ $\qquad T_{\psi_1} \wedge T(X_n) \wedge (\neg b_\psi \leftrightarrow (o_\psi \leftrightarrow o_{\psi_1} \wedge (X_n = X_{n-1})))),$ $F_\psi = F_{\psi_1}$	

Here $I_\psi = \bigcup_{i \le n} I_i \uplus O_i \uplus X_i$; $init(X_n)$ is the initial condition applied to copy X_n of the latches; and likewise $T(X_n)$ is the transition relation of C applied to the copy X_n. We use $X_n = X_{n-1}$ to denote the expression that all latches in X_n are equal to their counterparts in X_{n-1}. We omitted the construction for the conjunction and the Release operator due to the space limits. It is easy to verify that the transition relation is input-enabled and input-deterministic.

Proposition 3. *Given a circuit C and an alternation-free formula φ with k quantifiers, the size of the circuit C_φ is at most $|C| \cdot k + |\varphi|$.*

For each subformula ψ of φ, the output o_ψ in the circuit C_φ indicates that ψ must hold for the current computation path, and the latch x_ψ represent the requirements on the future of the computation that arise from the output o_ψ. The output b_ψ indicates that the requirements for subformula ψ are violated and a *bad state* is entered.

Proposition 4. *Let C be a circuit and let φ be an alternation-free HyperCTL* formula. $C \models \varphi$ holds iff the circuit C_φ admits a computation that shows output o_φ in the first step, that never outputs b_ψ for any of the subformulas ψ of φ, and that satisfies the fairness constraints.*

The proof of correctness proceeds again by structural induction on the structure of the formula. The search for paths of the form above can be performed by standard hardware model checkers.

5   Case Studies and Experimental Results

We have implemented the symbolic model checking approach from Sect. 4 as a transformation on Aiger circuits.[2] We rely on standard hardware synthesis tools to compile VHDL and Verilog files into a circuit to which we apply our tool to obtain a new circuit. As the backend engine, we use the ABC model checker [11], which provides many of the modern verification algorithms, including IC3 [10]/PDR [18], interpolation (INT) [32], and SAT-based bounded model checking (BMC) [8]. All experiments ran on an Intel Core i5 processor (4278U) with 2.6 GHz. Table 1 shows the verification times for the circuits and properties considered in our case studies. We used the default settings of ABC in all runs, except the entry marked with *. The symbol ✓ indicates that an invariant was found, and × that a (counter)example was found.

The experiments show that our approach enables the verification of hyper-properties for hardware modules with hundreds or even thousands of latches. For finding counterexamples, bounded model checking was most effective, and for cases where an invariant was needed, the relative performance of IC3/PDR vs. interpolation was inconclusive. In addition to benchmarking, our goal for these case studies has been to explore the versatility of alternation-free HyperCTL* model-checking and the potential of our prototype tool. In the following subsections, we report on the setup and results of the case studies, as well as on the verification workflow from a user perspective. Our case studies come from three different areas: information flow, symmetry, and error resistant codes.

5.1   Case Study 1: Information Flow Properties of I2C

Our first case study investigates the information flow properties of an I2C bus master. I2C is a widely used bus protocol that connects multiple components in a master-slave topology. Even though the I2C bus has no security features, it has been used in security-critical applications, such as the smart cards of the German public health insurance, which led to exploits [43]. We analyzed a I2C bus master implementation from the open source repository http://opencores. org. A typical setup consists of one *master*, one *controller*, and several *slaves*. The master communicates to the slaves via two physical wires, the clock line (SCL) and the data line (SDA). The interface of the master towards the *controller* consists of 8 bit wide words for input and output of data, a 3-bit wide address to encode slave numbers, a system clock input, and several reset and control signals. We checked the I2C bus master implementation against the information flow properties shown in Table 2.

From the Controller to the Bus. Property (NI1) states that there is no information flow with respect to the address to which the I2C master intends to send data, and (NI2) with respect to the data words themselves. Both information flows are intended, and our tool reports the violation. We tried to bound

---

[2] The tool and the experiments are available online [40].

Table 1. Experimental results for the case studies.

		Model	#Latches	#Gates	IC3	INT	BMC	
IF1	(NI1)				95.17	1.13	0.07	×
IF2	(NI2)				53.08	1.16	0.08	×
IF3	(NI3)				168.96	1.38	-	✓
IF4	(NI4)				438.41	1.01	0.09	×
IF5	(NI5)	I2C Master	254	1207	717.74	8.31	0.77	×
IF6	(NI6)				186.20	1.10	0.07	×
IF7	(NI7)				TO	6.82	0.55	×
IF8	(NI8)				1557.14	2.92	0.16	×
IF9	(NI2')	Ethernet	21093	70837	TO	155.77	6.27	×
Sym1	(S1)	Bakery	46	1829	6.34	0.88	0.08	×
Sym2	(S2)				168.59	464.52	7.00	×
Sym3		Bakery.a	47	1588	69.12	TO	71.92	×
Sym4	(S3)	Bakery.a.n	47	1618	26.31	4.75	0.39	×
Sym5		Bakery.a.n.s	47	1532	66.41	TO	-	✓
Sym6	(S4)				16.83	TO	-	✓
Sym7	(S5)	Bakery.a.n.s.5proc	90	3762	97.45	TO	-	✓
Sym8	(S6)				13.59	TO	-	✓
Sym9	(S7)	Bakery.a.n.s.7proc	136	6775	312.53*	TO	-	✓
Huff1	(HD1)	Huffman_enc	19	571	3.08	37.19	-	✓
Huff2	(HD2)				0.62	0.09	0.02	×
8b10b_1	(HD1)				0.32	0.09	0.02	×
8b10b_2	(HD1')	8b10b_enc	39	271	1.19	9.06	-	✓
8b10b_3	(HD2')				0.03	0.04	0.02	×
8b10b_4	(HD1'')	8b10b_dec	19	157	0.05	0.09	-	✓
Hamm1	(HD1$_1$)				0.02	0.04	0.02	×
Hamm2	(HD1$_2$)				0.02	0.03	0.02	×
Hamm3	(HD1$_3$)				0.03	0.04	0.02	×
Hamm3'	(HD1$_3'$)	Hamming_enc	27	47	7.34	0.18	-	✓
Hamm4	(HD1$_4$)				66.93	0.10	-	✓
Hamm5	(HD2$_1$)				11.83	1.31	-	✓
Hamm6	(HD2$_2$)				14.44	0.78	-	✓
Hamm7	(HD3)				12.23	1.25	-	✓

the information flow between the first valuation of the 3 bit wide address input and the bus data by encoding [14] the quantitative information-flow property. While the information flow of 3 bit could be determined (QNI1), checking the upper bound of $\log 9 \approx 3.17$ bit (QNI2) led to a timeout. Property (NI3) states that when the *write enable* bit is not set, no information should flow from the controller inputs to the bus. This property is satisfied by the implementation.

From the Bus to the Controller. Property (NI4) claims the absence of information flow from the slaves to the controller, which is again legitimately violated

Table 2. Information flow properties for the verification of the I2C bus master. In this list of properties, $P_\pi = P_{\pi'}$ is defined as $\bigwedge_{a \in P} a_\pi = a_{\pi'}$. $\overline{P_\pi} = \overline{P_{\pi'}}$ is defined as $(I \setminus P)_\pi = (I \setminus P)_{\pi'}$ where $P \subseteq \mathsf{AP}$ and $I \subseteq \mathsf{AP}$ are the inputs of the circuit.

(NI1)	$\forall \pi. \forall \pi'.\ \square(\overline{\mathrm{ADDR\_I}_\pi} = \overline{\mathrm{ADDR\_I}_{\pi'}}) \Rightarrow \square(\mathrm{SDA\_O}_\pi = \mathrm{SDA\_O}_{\pi'})$
(NI2)	$\forall \pi. \forall \pi'.\ \square \overline{\mathrm{DAT\_I}_\pi} = \overline{\mathrm{DAT\_I}_{\pi'}} \Rightarrow \square(\mathrm{SDA\_O}_\pi = \mathrm{SDA\_O}_{\pi'})$
(NI3)	$\forall \pi. \forall \pi'.\ \square(\neg \mathrm{WEn} \wedge \overline{\mathrm{DAT\_I}_\pi} = \overline{\mathrm{DAT\_I}_{\pi'}}) \Rightarrow \square(\mathrm{SDA\_O}_\pi = \mathrm{SDA\_O}_{\pi'})$
(NI4)	$\forall \pi. \forall \pi'.\ \square(\overline{\{\mathrm{SDA\_I,SCL\_I}\}}_\pi = \overline{\{\mathrm{SDA\_I,SCL\_I}\}}_{\pi'}) \Rightarrow \square(\mathrm{DAT\_O}_\pi = \mathrm{DAT\_O}_{\pi'})$
(NI5)	$\forall \pi.\ \square(\mathrm{SDA\_Enable} \Rightarrow \mathcal{H}_{\{\mathrm{SDA\_I,SCL\_I}\},\{\mathrm{DAT\_O}\}}\mathsf{false})$
(NI6)	$\forall \pi. \forall \pi'.\ \square(\overline{\mathrm{SDA\_I}_\pi} = \overline{\mathrm{SDA\_I}_{\pi'}}) \Rightarrow \square(\mathrm{SDA\_O}_\pi = \mathrm{SDA\_O}_{\pi'})$
(NI7)	$\forall \pi. \forall \pi'.\ \square(\overline{\mathrm{DAT\_I}_\pi} = \overline{\mathrm{DAT\_I}_{\pi'}}) \Rightarrow (\square(I_\pi = I_{\pi'}) \Rightarrow \Diamond\square(\mathrm{SDA\_O}_\pi = \mathrm{SDA\_O}_{\pi'}))$
(NI8)	$\forall \pi. \forall \pi'.\ \square(\overline{\{\mathrm{SDA\_I,SCL\_I}\}}_\pi = \overline{\{\mathrm{SDA\_I,SCL\_I}\}}_{\pi'}) \Rightarrow (\square(I_\pi = I_{\pi'}) \Rightarrow$ $\Diamond\square(\mathrm{DAT\_O}_\pi = \mathrm{DAT\_O}_{\pi'}))$

by the implementation. Property (NI5) refines (NI4) to determine whether the flow can still happen when we only consider information received on SDA *while* the master sends data too. The branching time operator $\mathcal{H}$ in (NI5), called the Hide operator $\mathcal{H}_{I,O}\varphi$, is borrowed from the logic SecLTL [16] and expresses that information from the inputs I do not interfere with the outputs O. The Hide operator is easily expressible in HyperCTL* [14]. Property (NI5) is violated by the implementation, because the concurrent transmission of data on the bus by multiple masters can bring I2C into arbitration mode and changes the interpretation of information sent over the bus later.

Long-term Information Flow: Properties (NI7) and (NI8) claim that the information flows from (NI1) and (NI4) cannot happen for an arbitrary delay. These properties are violated, which indicates that information may not be eventually forgotten by the I2C master.

All properties on the I2C Master were easily analyzed by the model checker. In order to determine if our approach scales to even larger designs, we checked an adapted version of property (NI2) on an Ethernet IP core with 21093 latches. The counterexample was still found within seconds.

5.2 Case Study 2: Symmetry in Mutual Exclusion Protocols

In our second case study, we investigate symmetry properties of mutual exclusion protocols. Mutual exclusion is a classical problem in distributed systems, for which several solutions have been proposed and analyzed. Violation of symmetry indicates that some clients have an unfair advantage over the other clients.

Our case study is based on a Verilog implementation of the Bakery protocol [26] from the VIS verification benchmark. The Bakery protocol works as follows. When a process wants to access the critical section it draws a "ticket", i.e., it obtains a number that is incremented every time a ticket is drawn. If there is more than one process who wishes to enter the critical section, the process with the smallest ticket number goes first. When two processes draw tickets concurrently, they may receive tickets with the same number, so ties among processes with the same ticket must be resolved by a different mechanism, for example by comparing process IDs. The Verilog implementation has an input *select* to indicate the process ID that runs in the next step, and an input *pause* to indicate whether the step is stuttering. Each process n has a program counter $pc(n)$. When process n is selected, the statement corresponding the program counter $pc(n)$ is executed. We are interested in the following HyperLTL property:

$$
\text{(S1)} \quad \forall \pi. \forall \pi'. \; \Box(sym(select_\pi, select_{\pi'}) \; \land \; pause_\pi = pause_{\pi'}) \Rightarrow \\
\Box(pc(0)_\pi = pc(1)_{\pi'} \; \land \; pc(1)_\pi = pc(0)_{\pi'})
$$

where $sym(select_\pi, select_{\pi'})$ means that process 0 is selected on path π when process 1 is selected on path π' and vice versa. Property (S1) states that, for every execution, there is another execution in which the *select* inputs corresponding to processes 0 and 1 are swapped and the outcome (i.e., the sequence of program counters of the processes) is also swapped. It is well known that it is impossible to accomplish mutual exclusion in an entirely symmetric fashion [31]. It is therefore not surprising that the implementation indeed violates Property (S1).

Inspecting the counterexample revealed, however, that the symmetry is broken even before the critical section is reached: if a non-existing process ID is selected by the variable *select*, process 0 proceeds instead. Property (S2) excludes paths on which a non-existing process ID is selected. The model-checker produced a counterexample in which processes 0 and 1 tried to access the critical section, but were treated differently.

$$
\text{(S2)} \quad \forall \pi. \forall \pi'. \; \Box(sym(select_\pi, select_{\pi'}) \; \land \; pause_\pi = pause_{\pi'} \; \land \\
select_\pi < 3 \land select_{\pi'} < 3) \Rightarrow \\
\Box(pc(0)_\pi = pc(1)_{\pi'} \; \land \; pc(1)_\pi = pc(0)_{\pi'})
$$

Next, we parameterized the necessary symmetry breaking in the system. We introduced additional inputs indicating which process may move, in case of a tie of the tickets and extended the property by the assumption that the symmetry is broken symmetrically.

$$
\text{(S3)} \quad \forall \pi. \forall \pi'. \; \Box(sym(select_\pi, select_{\pi'}) \; \land \; pause_\pi = pause_{\pi'} \; \land \\
select_\pi < 3 \land select_{\pi'} < 3 \; \land \; sym(sym\_break_\pi, sym\_break_{\pi'})) \Rightarrow \\
\Box(pc(0)_\pi = pc(1)_{\pi'} \; \land \; pc(1)_\pi = pc(0)_{\pi'})
$$

Property (S3) is still violated by the implementation: the order in which the processes were checked depends on the process IDs and causes delays in how the program counters evolve. After contracting the comparison of process IDs into a single step, property (S3) became satisfied.

In further experiments, we changed the structure of property from the form (S3) $\forall \pi. \forall \pi'. \Box\varphi \Rightarrow \Box\psi$ to (S7) $\forall \pi. \forall \pi'. \; \psi \, \mathcal{W} \, \neg\varphi$, which removes the liveness part of the property, while maintaining the semantics (for input-deterministic and input-enabled systems). This change significantly reduced the verification times and enabled the verification of the protocol for up to 7 participants.

5.3   Case Study 3: Error Resistant Codes

Error resistant codes enable the transmission of data over noisy channels. While the correct operation of encoder and decoders is crucial for communication systems, the formal verification of their functional correctness has received little attention. A typical model of errors bounds the number of flipped bits that may happen for a given code word length. Then, error correction coding schemes must guarantee that all code words have a minimal Hamming distance. Alternation-free HyperCTL* can specify that all code words produced by an encoder have a minimal Hamming distance of d:

$$(\text{HDd}) \quad \boxed{\forall \pi. \forall \pi'. \Diamond (\bigvee_{a \in I} a_\pi \neq a_{\pi'}) \Rightarrow \neg \text{Ham}_O(d-1, \pi, \pi')}$$

where I are the inputs denoting the data, O denote the code words, and the predicate $\text{Ham}_O(d, \pi, \pi')$ is defined as $\text{Ham}_O(-1, \pi, \pi') = \mathsf{false}$ and:

$$\text{Ham}_O(d, \pi, \pi') = \left(\bigwedge_{a \in O} a_\pi = a_{\pi'} \right) \mathcal{W} \left(\bigvee_{a \in O} a_\pi \neq a_{\pi'} \wedge \bigcirc \text{Ham}_O(d-1, \pi, \pi') \right).$$

We started with two simple encoders that are not intended to provide error resistance: a Huffman encoder from the VIS benchmarks, and an 8bit-10bit encoder from http://opencores.org that guarantees that the difference between the number of 1 s and the number of 0 s in the codeword is bounded by 2. As expected, encoders provide a Hamming distance of 1 (Huff1and 8b10b_2), but not more (Huff2and 8b10b_3). The experiments on these simple encoders were useful to determine the configuration of the command signals that enable the transmission of data. For example, checking the plain property as specified above for the 8bit-10bit encoder reveals that the reset signal must be set to false before sending data (8b10b_1). Similarly, for the 8bit-10bit *decoder*, we checked whether all codewords of Hamming distance 1 produce different outputs (8b10b_4).

Next, we considered an encoder for the 7-4-Hamming code, which encodes blocks of 4 bits into codewords of length 7, and guarantees a Hamming distance of 3. We started with finding out in which configuration the encoder actually sends encoded data (Hamm1to Hamm4). With Hamm3we discovered that the implementation deviates from the specification because the reset signal for the circuit is active high, instead of active low as specified. In Hamm3, we fixed the usage of the reset bit. We then scaled the specification to Hamming distances 2 and 3 (Hamm5to Hamm7).

6   Conclusions

We presented a novel automata-based automatic technique to model-check HyperLTL and HyperCTL* specifications, and an implementation integrated with a state-of-the-art hardware model checker. Our case studies show that the implementation scales to realistic hardware designs; in one case we successfully checked a design with more than 20.000 latches. The logics HyperLTL and HyperCTL* proved to be versatile tools for the analysis of various kinds of properties.

Acknowledgements. We thank Hans-Jörg Peter for valuable discussions and for synthesizing models for the case studies, Heinrich Ody for joint work on an early prototype of the tool, and Heidy Khlaaf for insightful comments on the paper.

References

1. Alur, R., Černý, P., Zdancewic, S.: Preserving secrecy under refinement. In: Bugliesi, M., Preneel, B., Sassone, V., Wegener, I. (eds.) ICALP 2006. LNCS, vol. 4052, pp. 107–118. Springer, Heidelberg (2006)
2. Andersen, H.R.: A polyadic modal μ-calculus. Technical report (1994)
3. Askarov, A., Myers, A.: A semantic framework for declassification and endorsement. In: Gordon, A.D. (ed.) ESOP 2010. LNCS, vol. 6012, pp. 64–84. Springer, Heidelberg (2010)
4. Balliu, M., Dam, M., Le Guernic, G.: Epistemic temporal logic for information flow security. In: Proceedings of PLAS, ACM (2011)
5. Banerjee, A., Naumann, D.A., Rosenberg, S.: Expressive declassification policies and modular static enforcement. In: Proceedings of S & P, pp. 339–353, IEEE CS Press (2008)
6. Barthe, G., Crespo, J.M., Kunz, C.: Beyond 2-safety: asymmetric product programs for relational program verification. In: Artemov, S., Nerode, A. (eds.) LFCS 2013. LNCS, vol. 7734, pp. 29–43. Springer, Heidelberg (2013)
7. Barthe, G., D'Argenio, P.R., Rezk, T.: Secure information flow by self-composition. In: Proceedings CSFW, pp. 100–114, June 2004
8. Biere, A., Clarke, E., Raimi, R., Zhu, Y.: Verifying safety properties of a PowerPC^{TM} microprocessor using symbolic model checking without BDDs. In: Halbwachs, N., Peled, D.A. (eds.) CAV 1999. LNCS, vol. 1633, pp. 60–71. Springer, Heidelberg (1999)
9. Biere, A., Heljanko, K., Wieringa, S.: AIGER 1.9 and beyond. http://fmv.jku.at/hwmcc11/beyond1.pdf (2011). Accessed Feb 6 2015. Via website: http://fmv.jku.at/aiger/
10. Bradley, A.R.: SAT-based model checking without unrolling. In: Jhala, R., Schmidt, D. (eds.) VMCAI 2011. LNCS, vol. 6538, pp. 70–87. Springer, Heidelberg (2011)
11. Brayton, R., Mishchenko, A.: ABC: an academic industrial-strength verification tool. In: Touili, T., Cook, B., Jackson, P. (eds.) CAV 2010. LNCS, vol. 6174, pp. 24–40. Springer, Heidelberg (2010)
12. Burch, J.R., Clarke, E.M., McMillan, K.L., Dill, D.L.: Sequential circuit verification using symbolic model checking. In: Proceedings of DAC 1990, pp. 46–51, IEEE CS Press (1990)
13. Claessen, K., Eén, N., Sterin, B.: A circuit approach to LTL model checking. In: Proceedings of FMCAD, pp. 53–60 (2013)

14. Clarkson, M.R., Finkbeiner, B., Koleini, M., Micinski, K.K., Rabe, M.N., Sánchez, C.: Temporal logics for hyperproperties. In: Abadi, M., Kremer, S. (eds.) POST 2014 (ETAPS 2014). LNCS, vol. 8414, pp. 265–284. Springer, Heidelberg (2014)
15. Clarkson, M.R., Schneider, F.B.: Hyperproperties.In: Proceedings IEEE Symposium on Computer Security Foundations, pp. 51–65, June 2008
16. Dimitrova, R., Finkbeiner, B., Kovács, M., Rabe, M.N., Seidl, H.: Model checking information flow in reactive systems. In: Kuncak, V., Rybalchenko, A. (eds.) VMCAI 2012. LNCS, vol. 7148, pp. 169–185. Springer, Heidelberg (2012)
17. D'Souza, D., Holla, R., Raghavendra, K.R., Sprick, B.: Model-checking trace-based information flow properties. J. Comput. Secur. **19**(1), 101–138 (2011)
18. Eén, N., Mishchenko, A., Brayton, R.K.: Efficient implementation of property directed reachability. In: Proceedings of FMCAD, pp. 125–134 (2011)
19. Fagin, R., Halpern, J.Y., Moses, Y., Vardi, M.Y.: Reasoning About Knowledge. MIT Press, Cambridge (1995)
20. Finkbeiner, B., Rabe, M.N.: The linear-hyper-branching spectrum of temporal logics. IT Inf. Technol. **56**, 273–279 (2014)
21. Gammie, P., van der Meyden, R.: MCK: model checking the logic of knowledge. In: Alur, R., Peled, D.A. (eds.) CAV 2004. LNCS, vol. 3114, pp. 479–483. Springer, Heidelberg (2004)
22. Goguen, J.A., Meseguer, J.: Security policies and security models. In: Proceedings IEEE Symposium on Security and Privacy, pp. 11–20, IEEE CS Press (1982)
23. Huisman, M., Worah, P., Sunesen, K.: A temporal logic characterisation of observational determinism. In: Proceedings of CSFW, IEEE CS Press (2006)
24. Kesten, Y., Pnueli, A., Raviv, L.: Algorithmic verification of linear temporal logic specifications. In: Larsen, K.G., Skyum, S., Winskel, G. (eds.) ICALP 1998. LNCS, vol. 1443, pp. 1–16. Springer, Heidelberg (1998)
25. Kupferman, O., Vardi, M.Y.: Weak alternating automata are not that weak. ACM TOCL **2**(3), 408–429 (2001)
26. Lamport, L.: A new solution of Dijkstra's concurrent programming problem. Commun. ACM **17**(8), 453–455 (1974)
27. Lange, M., Lozes, É.: Model-checking the higher-dimensional modal mu-calculus. In: Proceedings of FICS, EPTCS, vol. 77, pp. 39–46 (2012)
28. Lomuscio, A., Pecheur, C., Raimondi, F.: Automatic verification of knowledge and time with NuSMV. In: Proceedings of IJCAI, pp. 1384–1389 (2007)
29. Lomuscio, A., Qu, H., Raimondi, F.: MCMAS: a model checker for the verification of multi-agent systems. In: Bouajjani, A., Maler, O. (eds.) CAV 2009. LNCS, vol. 5643, pp. 682–688. Springer, Heidelberg (2009)
30. Manna, Z., Pnueli, A.: The Temporal Logic of Reactive and Concurrent Systems. Springer, New York (1992)
31. Manna, Z., Pnueli, A.: Temporal Verification of Reactive Systems: Safety. Springer, New York (1995)
32. McMillan, K.L.: Craig interpolation and reachability analysis. In: Cousot, R. (ed.) SAS 2003. LNCS, vol. 2694, p. 336. Springer, Heidelberg (2003)
33. Meski, A., Penczek, W., Szreter, M., Wozna-Szczesniak, B., Zbrzezny, A.: Bounded model checking for knowledge and linear time. In: Proceedings of AAMAS, pp. 1447–1448, IFAAMAS (2012)
34. Milushev, D.: Reasoning about hyperproperties. Ph.D thesis, Faculty of Engineering, Katholieke Universiteit Leuven, Celestijnenlaan 200A, box 2402, B3001 Heverlee, Belgium, 6 (2013)

35. Milushev, D., Clarke, D.: Towards incrementalization of holistic hyperproperties. In: Degano, P., Guttman, J.D. (eds.) Principles of Security and Trust. LNCS, vol. 7215, pp. 329–348. Springer, Heidelberg (2012)

36. Miyano, S., Hayashi, T.: Alternating finite automata on omega-words. Theor. Comput. Sci. **32**, 321–330 (1984)

37. Muller, D.E., Saoudi, A., Schupp, P.E.: Weak alternating automata give a simple explanation of why most temporal and dynamic logics are decidable in exponential time. In: Proceedings of LICS, pp. 422–427, IEEE CS Press (1988)

38. Otto, M.: Bisimulation-invariant PTIME and higher-dimensional μ-calculus. Theor. Comput. Sci. **224**, 237–265 (1998)

39. Pencze, W., Lomuscio, A.: Verifying epistemic properties of multi-agent systems via bounded model checking. In: Proceedings of AAMAS, pp. 209–216, IFAAMAS (2003)

40. Rabe, M.N.: MCHyper: a model checker for hyperproperties. http://www.react.uni-saarland.de/tools/mchyper/ (2015). Accessed Feb 6 2015

41. Sabelfeld, A., Myers, A.C.: A model for delimited information release. In: Futatsugi, K., Mizoguchi, F., Yonezaki, N. (eds.) ISSS 2003. LNCS, vol. 3233, pp. 174–191. Springer, Heidelberg (2004)

42. Sistla, P.A., Clarke, E.M.: The complexity of propositional linear temporal logics. J. ACM **32**(3), 733–749 (1985)

43. Thielke, W.: Code geknackt. Link to article in media archive: http://www.focus.de/finanzen/news/krankenkassen-code-geknackt_aid_148829.html (1994). Accessed Feb 6 2015

44. van der Meyden, R., Zhang, C.: Algorithmic verification of noninterference properties. Electr. Notes Theor. Comput. Sci. **168**, 61–75 (2007)

45. Vardi, M.Y.: Alternating automata and program verification. In: van Leeuwen, J. (ed.) Computer Science Today. LNCS, vol. 1000, pp. 471–485. Springer, Heidelberg (1995)

46. Vardi, M.Y., Wolper, P.: An automata-theoretic approach to automatic program verification. In: Proceedings of LICS 1986, pp. 332–344, IEEE CS Press (1986)

47. Vardi, M.Y., Wolper, P.: Reasoning about infinite computations. Inf. Comput. **115**(1), 1–37 (1994)

Fairness Modulo Theory: A New Approach to LTL Software Model Checking

Daniel Dietsch$^{(\boxtimes)}$, Matthias Heizmann,
Vincent Langenfeld, and Andreas Podelski

University of Freiburg, Freiburg im Breisgau, Germany
dietsch@informatik.uni-freiburg.de

Abstract. The construction of a proof for unsatisfiability is less costly than the construction of a ranking function. We present a new approach to LTL software model checking (i.e., to statically analyze a program and verify a temporal property from the full class of LTL including general liveness properties) which aims at exploiting this fact. The idea is to select finite prefixes of a path and check these for infeasibility before considering the full infinite path. We have implemented a tool which demonstrates the practical potential of the approach. In particular, the tool can verify several benchmark programs for a liveness property just with finite prefixes (and thus without the construction of a single ranking function).

1 Introduction

The long line of research on *software model checking*, i.e., on tools that statically analyze a given program in order to automatically verify a given temporal property, was initially restricted to safety properties [2,3,11,20,37,45,51]. It was later extended to termination [9,21,26,27,36,40,49,50,52]. The relative maturity of this research is reflected by the fact that software model checking tools successfully participate in the software verification competition SV-Comp [10], for safety [29,33,41,47] as well as for termination [33,55,56].

In a more recent trend, approaches to software model checking are emerging for the general class of LTL properties, and in particular general liveness properties [5,22–24]. In this paper, we introduce an approach to LTL software model checking which is based on *fairness modulo theory*, an extension of *reachability modulo theory* as introduced by Lal and Qadeer [42].

In the setting of [42], the existence of a program execution that violates a given safety property is proven via the reachability of an error location of the program along a *feasible* path. A path is feasible if the sequence of statements along the path is executable. This condition is checked by checking whether the corresponding logical formula is *satisfiable modulo theory* (i.e., satisfiable in the logical theory of integers, arrays, etc.). Today, quite efficient *SMT solvers* exist which can not only prove unsatisfiability but also compute *interpolants* [13,14, 17,19,46]. Interpolants can be used to generalize the proof of unsatisfiability in

D. Kroening and C.S. Păsăreanu (Eds.): CAV 2015, Part I, LNCS 9206, pp. 49–66, 2015.
DOI: 10.1007/978-3-319-21690-4_4

order to show the infeasibility of more and more paths and eventually prove the unreachability of an error location (which is the underlying idea in the approach to program verification of [35,36]).

We extend the setting of [42] to LTL by defining the construction of a new kind of program (a *Büchi program*) from the input program and the LTL property. The control flow graph of a Büchi program comes with a distinguished set of nodes which is used to define (infinite) *fair* paths (a path is fair if it visits the distinguished set of nodes infinitely often). Now, in our extension of the setting in [42], the existence of a program execution that violates a given LTL property is proven via the existence of a feasible *fair* path.

In general, to show that the infinite sequence of statements along a path is not executable, one needs to construct a *ranking function*. For example, for each of the two infinite sequences of statements below, one may construct the ranking function r defined by $r(x, y) = x - y$.

$$\tau_1 : \quad \boxed{\text{x--}} \ \boxed{\text{x>y}} \ \boxed{\text{x--}} \ \boxed{\text{x>y}} \ \boxed{\text{x--}} \ \boxed{\text{x>y}} \ \ldots$$
$$\tau_2 : \quad \boxed{\text{x:=y}} \ \boxed{\text{x>y}} \ \boxed{\text{x--}} \ \boxed{\text{x>y}} \ \boxed{\text{x--}} \ \boxed{\text{x>y}} \ \ldots$$

Every finite prefix of τ_1 is executable. In contrast, τ_2 has the prefix $\boxed{\text{x:=y}} \ \boxed{\text{x>y}}$ which already is not executable.

In the case where an infinite sequence of statements has a finite prefix such that already the prefix is not executable, it is not necessary to construct a ranking function. Instead, it is sufficient to consider the prefix and prove the unsatisfiability of the logical formula corresponding to the finite sequence of statements in the prefix.

Tools exist that, given an infinite sequence of statements like $(\boxed{\text{x>y}} \ \boxed{\text{x--}})^\omega$ or $\boxed{\text{x:=y}} \ \boxed{\text{x>y}} \ (\boxed{\text{x>y}} \ \boxed{\text{x--}})^\omega$, can construct a ranking function like r above automatically [7,12,48]. Recent efforts go into improving the scope and the scalability of such tools [8,25,34,43]. In comparison with proving unsatisfiability, the task of constructing a ranking function will always be more costly. Hence, substituting the construction of a ranking function by the construction of a proof of unsatisfiability carries an interesting potential for optimization. The goal of the work in this paper is to investigate whether this potential can be exploited practically. We develop a practical method and tool for LTL software model checking that shows that this is indeed the case.

In the remainder of the paper, after discussing an example, we introduce *Büchi programs* (as described above, we reduce the validity of an LTL property for a given program to the absence of a feasible fair path in a Büchi program). We present an algorithm that constructs such a Büchi program and checks whether it has a feasible fair path. The algorithm selects certain finite prefixes of a path for the check of feasibility before the full infinite path is considered. We then present the evaluation of a tool which implements the algorithm. Our evaluation shows the practical potential of our approach. In particular, the tool can verify several benchmark programs—for a liveness property—just with finite prefixes (and thus without the construction of a single ranking function).

2 Example

In this section we demonstrate how we apply our approach to the program $\mathcal{P}$ depicted in Fig. 1a and the LTL property $\varphi = \Box(x > 0 \rightarrow \Diamond(y = 0))$.

We represent the program $\mathcal{P}$ by the graph depicted in Fig. 1b. The edges of this graph are labeled with program statements. We use the Büchi automaton $\mathcal{A}_{\neg\varphi}$ depicted in Fig. 1c as representation of the negation of the LTL property φ.

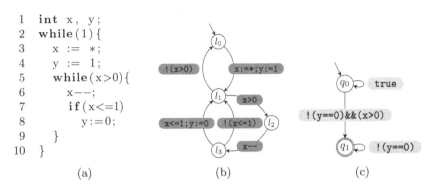

```
1    int x, y;
2    while (1) {
3        x := *;
4        y := 1;
5        while (x>0) {
6            x--;
7            if (x<=1)
8                y:=0;
9        }
10   }
```

(a)   (b)   (c)

Fig. 1. Program $\mathcal{P}$ is shown in (a) as pseudocode and in (b) as control flow graph. The Büchi automaton $\mathcal{A}_{\neg\varphi}$ that represents the negation of the LTL property $\varphi = \Box(x > 0 \rightarrow \Diamond(y = 0))$ is shown in (c).

As a first step we construct the *Büchi program* $\mathcal{B}$ depicted in Fig. 2. Afterwards we will show that this Büchi program $\mathcal{B}$ has no path that is fair and feasible, thus proving that $\mathcal{P}$ satisfies the LTL property φ.

A Büchi program is a program together with a fairness constraint: an execution is *fair* if a *fair location* is visited infinitely often. The fair locations of $\mathcal{B}$ are highlighted by double circles. The locations of the Büchi program $\mathcal{B}$ are pairs whose first element is a location of the program $\mathcal{P}$ and whose second element is a state of the Büchi automaton $\mathcal{A}_{\neg\varphi}$. The edges of the Büchi program $\mathcal{B}$ are labeled with sequential compositions of two statements where the first element is a statement of the program. The second element of the sequential composition is an assume statement that represents a letter of the Büchi automaton $\mathcal{A}_{\neg\varphi}$.

A key concept in our analysis is the notion of a *trace*. A trace is an infinite sequence of statements. We call a trace *fair* if it is the labeling of a path that visits some fair location infinitely often. A trace is *feasible* if it corresponds to some program execution. An example for a fair trace is $\tau_1 \tau_2^\omega$ where τ_1 and τ_2 are as follows.

τ_1 :   `x:=*;y:=1`   `!(y==0)&&(x>0)`   `!(x>0)`   `!(y==0)`

τ_2 :   `x:=*;y:=1`   `!(y==0)`   `!(x>0)`   `!(y==0)`

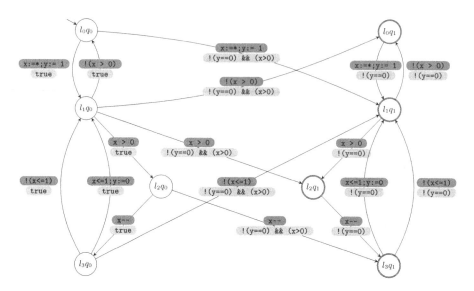

Fig. 2. The Büchi program $\mathcal{B}$ constructed from the program $\mathcal{P}$ (Fig. 1b) and the Büchi automaton representing $\neg\varphi$ (Fig. 1c). Each edge is labeled with the statements `s1` `s2` where `s1` comes from $\mathcal{P}$ and `s2` comes from $\neg\varphi$. The fair locations are l_0q_1, l_1q_1, l_2q_1 and l_3q_1, i.e., all locations that contain the Büchi automaton's accepting state q_1.

This trace is not feasible because the second statement `!(y==0)&&(x>0)` and the third statement `!(x>0)` are contradicting each other.

Our algorithm constructs Büchi programs such that each fair and feasible trace of the Büchi program corresponds to a feasible trace of the original program that violates the LTL property.

In order to show that $\mathcal{P}$ satisfies φ we show that no fair trace of the Büchi program $\mathcal{B}$ is feasible. Thus, our algorithm tries to find arguments for infeasibility of fair traces in $\mathcal{B}$:

Local Infeasibility. In the Büchi program $\mathcal{B}$ every trace that is the labeling of a path that contains the edge

$$l_3q_1 \quad \boxed{\text{x<=1; y:=0}} \quad \boxed{\text{!(y==0)}} \quad l_1q_1$$

is infeasible, because the statements `y:=0` and `!(y==0)` contradict each other. Another example for *local infeasibiliy* is the edge from l_1q_0 to l_0q_1 which is labeled with the two statements `!(x>0)` and `(x>0)` that contradict each other, too.

Infeasibility of a Finite Prefix. Every trace that is the labeling of a path that has the following finite prefix

$$
\begin{array}{llll}
l_0 q_0 & \text{x:=*;y:=1} & \text{true} & l_1 q_1 \\
l_1 q_1 & \text{x>0} & \text{!(y==0)\&\&(x>0)} & l_2 q_1 \\
l_2 q_1 & \text{x--} & \text{!(y==0)} & l_3 q_1 \\
l_1 q_1 & \text{!(x<=1)} & \text{!(y==0)} & l_1 q_1 \\
l_1 q_1 & \text{!(x>0)} & \text{!(y==0)} & l_0 q_1
\end{array}
$$

is infeasible because $\boxed{\text{!(x<=1)}}$ contradicts $\boxed{\text{!(x>0)}}$. Another example for infeasibiliy of a finite prefix is the trace $\tau_1 \tau_2^\omega$ that was discussed before.

ω-*Infeasibility.* Every trace that is the labeling of an infinite path that eventually loops along the following edges

$$
\begin{array}{llll}
l_1 q_1 & \text{x>0} & \text{!(y==0} & l_2 q_1 \\
l_2 q_1 & \text{x--} & \text{!(y==0)} & l_3 q_1 \\
l_3 q_1 & \text{!(x<=1)} & \text{!(y==0)} & l_1 q_1
\end{array}
$$

is infeasible because $\boxed{\text{x--}}$ infinitely often decreases x. Thus, the value of x will eventually contradict $\boxed{\text{!(x<=1)}}$. The formal termination argument is the ranking function $f(x) = x$.

Each fair trace of $\mathcal{B}$ is infeasible for one of the reasons mentioned above. Hence, we can conclude that program $\mathcal{P}$ indeed satisfies the LTL property φ.

All reasons for infeasibility that fall into the classes *Local infeasibility* or *infeasibility of a finite prefix* are comparatively cheap to detect. In this example we only needed to synthesize one ranking function, which is in general more expensive.

3   Preliminaries

Programs and Traces. In our formal exposition we consider a simple programming language whose statements are assignment, assume, and sequential composition. We use the syntax that is defined by the following grammar

$$
\text{s} := \text{assume bexpr} \mid \text{x := expr} \mid \text{s; s}
$$

where *Var* is a finite set of program variables, $\text{x} \in Var$, **expr** is an expression over *Var* and **bexpr** is a Boolean expression over *Var*. For brevity we use **bexpr** to denote the assume statement **assume bexpr**.

We represent a *program* over a given set of statements *Stmt* as a labeled graph $\mathcal{P} = (Loc, \delta, l_0)$ with a finite set of nodes *Loc* called locations, a set of edges labeled with statements, i.e., $\delta \subseteq Loc \times Stmt \times Loc$, and a distinguished node l_0 which we call the initial location.

In the following we consider only programs where each location has at least one outgoing edge, i.e. $\forall l \in Loc, \exists s \in Stmt, \exists l' \in Loc \bullet (l, s, l') \in \delta$. We note that each program can be transformed into this form by adding to each location without outgoing edges a selfloop that is labeled with **assume true**.

We call an infinite sequence of statements $\tau = s_0 s_1 s_2 \ldots$ a *trace of the program* $\mathcal{P}$ if τ is the edge labeling of an infinite path that starts at the initial location l_0. We define the set of all program traces formally as follows.

$$
T(\mathcal{P}) = \{s_0 s_1 \ldots \in Stmt^\omega \mid \exists l_1, l_2, \ldots \bullet (l_i, s_i, l_{i+1}) \in \delta, \text{ for } i = 0, 1, \ldots\}
$$

Let $\mathcal{D}$ be the set of values of the program's variables. We denote a program state σ as a function $\sigma : Var \rightarrow \mathcal{D}$ that maps program variables to values. We use S to denote the set of all program states. Each statement $\mathtt{s} \in Stmt$ defines a binary relation $\rho_{\mathtt{s}}$ over program states which we call the *successor relation*. Let $Expr$ be set of all expressions over the program variables Var. We assume a given interpretation function $\mathcal{I} : Expr \times (Var \rightarrow \mathcal{D}) \rightarrow \mathcal{D}$ and define the relation $\rho_{\mathtt{s}} \subseteq S \times S$ inductively as follows.

$$\rho_s = \begin{cases} \{(\sigma, \sigma') \mid \mathcal{I}(\mathtt{bexpr})(\sigma) = true \text{ and } \sigma = \sigma'\} & \text{if } s \equiv \mathtt{assume\ bexpr} \\ \{(\sigma, \sigma') \mid \sigma' = \sigma[\mathtt{x} \mapsto \mathcal{I}(\mathtt{expr})(\sigma)]\} & \text{if } s \equiv \mathtt{x:=expr} \\ \{(\sigma, \sigma') \mid \exists \sigma'' \bullet (\sigma, \sigma'') \in \rho_{\mathtt{s}_1} \text{ and } (\sigma'', \sigma') \in \rho_{\mathtt{s}_2}\} & \text{if } s \equiv \mathtt{s_1;s_2} \end{cases}$$

Given a trace $\tau = s_0 s_1 s_2 \ldots$, a sequence of program states $\pi = \sigma_0 \sigma_1 \sigma_2 \ldots$ is called a *program execution of the trace* τ if each successive pair of program states is contained in the successor relation of the corresponding statement of the trace, i.e., $(\sigma_i, \sigma_{i+1}) \in \rho_{s_i}$ for $i \in \{0, 1, \ldots\}$. We call a trace τ *infeasible* if it does not have any program execution, otherwise we call τ *feasible*. We use $\Pi(\tau)$ to denote the set of all program executions of τ. The set of all feasible trace of program $\mathcal{P}$ is denoted by $T_{feas}(\mathcal{P})$, and the set of all program executions of $\mathcal{P}$ is defined as follows.

$$\Pi(\mathcal{P}) = \bigcup_{\tau \in T_{feas}(\mathcal{P})} \Pi(\tau)$$

Büchi Automata and LTL Properties. We will not formally introduce linear temporal logic (LTL). Every LTL property can be expressed as a Büchi automaton [1]. In our formal presentation we use Büchi automata to represent LTL properties.

A *Büchi automaton* $\mathcal{A} = (\Sigma, Q, q_0, \longrightarrow, F)$ is a five tuple consisting of a finite alphabet Σ, a finite set of states Q, an initial state $q_0 \in Q$, a transition relation $\longrightarrow : Q \times \Sigma \times Q$, and a set of accepting states $F \subseteq Q$. A *word* over the alphabet Σ is an infinite sequence $w = a_0 a_1 a_2 \ldots$ such that $a_i \in \Sigma$ for all $i \geq 0$. A *run* r of a Büchi automaton $\mathcal{A}$ on w is an infinite sequence of states $q_0 q_1 \ldots$, starting in the initial state such that for all $a_i \in w$ there is a transition $(q_i, a_i, q_{i+1}) \in \longrightarrow$. A run r is called *accepting* if r contains infinitely many accepting states. A word w is *accepted* by $\mathcal{A}$ if there is an accepting run of $\mathcal{A}$ on w. The *language* $\mathcal{L}(\mathcal{A})$ of a Büchi automaton $\mathcal{A}$ is the set of all words that are accepted by $\mathcal{A}$.

An *atomic proposition* is a set of program states. An *LTL property* over a set of atomic propositions AP defines a set of words over the alphabet $\Sigma = 2^{AP}$. LTL properties are usually denoted by formulas, but several translations from formulas to equivalent Büchi automata are available [31, 32, 54]. We assume that we have given a Büchi automaton $\mathcal{A}_\varphi$ for each LTL property φ.

A program state σ *satisfies* a symbol a of the alphabet 2^{AP} if σ is an element of all atomic propositions in a. A sequence of program states $\sigma_0 \sigma_1 \ldots$ *satisfies* a word $a_0 a_1 a_2 \ldots \in (2^{AP})^\omega$, if σ_{i+1} satisfies a_i for each $i \geq 0$. A sequence of program states π *satisfies* the LTL property φ if π satisfies some word $w \in \mathcal{A}_\varphi$. A trace $\tau = s_0 s_1 \ldots$ *satisfies* φ if it has at least one program execution and all program executions of the trace satisfy φ. A program $\mathcal{P}$ *satisfies* φ if all program executions of $\mathcal{P}$ satisfy φ. We will use the $\models$ symbol to denote each of these "satisfies relations", e.g., we will write $\mathcal{P} \models \varphi$ if the program $\mathcal{P}$ satisfies the LTL property φ.

We note that these definitions do not put any restrictions on the initial state σ_0 of a sequence of program states. This accounts for the fact that our programs do not have to start in a given initial program state and allows programs that satisfy the LTL property $\Box(x = 0)$. For example, the program whose first statement sets the variable x to 0 and whose other statements do not modify x.

4   Büchi Program and Büchi Program Product

In this section we introduce the notion of a Büchi program, which is a program which is extended by a fairness constraint. We show that the problem whether a program satisfies an LTL property can be reduced to the problem whether a Büchi program has a fair program execution.

Definition 1 (Büchi Program). *A Büchi program* $\mathcal{B} = (Stmt, Loc, \delta, l_0, Loc_{fair})$ *is a program* $\mathcal{P} = (Loc, \delta, l_0)$ *whose set of statements is Stmt, with a distinguished subset of locations* $Loc_{fair} \subseteq Loc$. *We call the locations* Loc_{fair} *the* fair locations *of* $\mathcal{B}$.

An example for a Büchi program is the program depicted in Fig. 2 which was discussed in Sect. 2.

Definition 2 (Fair Trace). *A trace* $s_0 s_1 s_2 \ldots$ *of a Büchi program* $\mathcal{B}$ *is a* fair trace *if*

- *there exists a sequence of locations* $l_0, l_1, \ldots$ *such that* $l_0 \xrightarrow{s_0} l_1 \xrightarrow{s_1} l_2 \xrightarrow{s_2} \ldots$ *is a path in* $\mathcal{B}$, *i.e.,* $(l_i, s_i, l_{i+1}) \in \delta$ *for* $i = 0, 1, \ldots$, *and*
- *the sequence* $l_0, l_1, \ldots$ *contains infinitely many fair locations.*

We use $T_{fair}(\mathcal{B})$ *to denote the set of* fair traces *of* $\mathcal{B}$.

If we consider the Büchi program $\mathcal{B} = (Stmt, Loc, \delta, l_0, Loc_{fair})$ as a Büchi automaton where the alphabet is the set of program statements $Stmt$, the set of states is the set of program locations Loc, the transition relation is the labeled edge relation δ the initial state is the initial location l_0 and the set of accepting states is the set of fair locations Loc_{fair}, then the language of this Büchi automaton is exactly the set of fair traces of the Büchi program.

Definition 3 (Fair Program Execution). *A program execution* π *of a Büchi program* $\mathcal{B}$ *is a* fair program execution *of* $\mathcal{B}$ *if* π *is the program execution of some fair trace of* $\mathcal{B}$. *We use* $\Pi_{fair}(\mathcal{B})$ *to denote the set of all fair program execution of* $\mathcal{B}$.

We note that traces that are fair and feasible have at least one fair program execution.

Boolean expressions over the set of program variables Var, and atomic propositions both define sets of program states. For a letter $a \in 2^{AP}$, we will use assume a to denote the assume statement whose expression evaluates to *true* for each state σ that satisfies a. Hence assume a has the following successor relation.

$$\{(\sigma, \sigma') \mid \sigma \models p \text{ for each } p \in a\}$$

Definition 4 (Büchi Program Product). *Let $\mathcal{P} = (Loc, l_0, \delta_{\mathcal{P}})$ be a program over the set of statements Stmt, AP a set of atomic propositions over the program's variables Var, and let $\mathcal{A} = (\Sigma, Q, q_0, \rightarrow, F)$ be a Büchi automaton whose alphabet is $\Sigma = 2^{AP}$. The Büchi program product $\mathcal{P} \otimes \mathcal{A}$ is a Büchi program $\mathcal{B} = (Stmt_{\mathcal{B}}, Loc_{\mathcal{B}}, l_{0_{\mathcal{B}}}, \delta_{\mathcal{B}}, Loc_{F_{\mathcal{B}}})$ such that the set of statements consists of all sequential compositions of two statements where the first element is a statement of $\mathcal{P}$ and the second element is a statement that assumes that a subset of atomic propositions is satisfied, i.e.,*

$$Stmt_{\mathcal{B}} = \{s; \text{ assume } a \mid s \in Stmt, a \in 2^{AP}\},$$

the set of locations is the Cartesian product of program locations and Büchi automaton states, i.e.,

$$Loc_{\mathcal{B}} = \{(l, q) \mid l \in Loc \text{ and } q \in Q\},$$

the initial location is the pair consisting of the program's initial location and the Büchi automaton's initial state, i.e.,

$$l_{0_{\mathcal{B}}} = (l_0, q_0),$$

the labeled edge relation is a product of the program's edge relation and the transition relation of the Büchi automaton such that an edge is labeled by the statement that is a sequential composition of the program's edge label and an assume statement obtained from the transition's letter, formally defined as follows

$$\delta_{\mathcal{B}} = \{((l, q), \{s; \text{ assume } a, (l', q')) \mid (l, s, l') \in \delta_P \text{ and } (q, a, q') \in \rightarrow\},$$

the set of fair locations contains all pairs where the second component is an accepting state of the Büchi automaton, i.e.,

$$Loc_{F_{\mathcal{B}}} = \{(l, q) \mid l \in Loc \text{ and } q \in F\}.$$

The following theorem shows how we can use the Büchi program product to check if a program satisfies an LTL property.

Theorem 1. *The program $\mathcal{P}$ satisfies the LTL property φ if and only if the Büchi program product $\mathcal{B} = \mathcal{P} \otimes \mathcal{A}_{\neg\varphi}$ does not have a trace that is fair and feasible, i.e.,*

$$\mathcal{P} \models \varphi \qquad \textit{iff} \qquad T_{fair}(\mathcal{B}) \cap T_{feas}(\mathcal{B}) = \emptyset$$

Proof. For brevity, we give only a sketch of the proof. A more detailed proof is available in an extended version of this paper [30]. First, we use the definition of the Büchi program product to show the following connection between traces of $\mathcal{B}$, traces of $\mathcal{P}$ and words over 2^{AP}. $s_0;$ assume a_0 $s_1;$ assume $a_1 \ldots \in T_{fair}(\mathcal{B})$ if and only if $s_0 s_1 s_2 \ldots \in T(\mathcal{P})$ and $a_0 a_1 a_2 \ldots \in \mathcal{L}(\mathcal{A}_{\neg\varphi})$. Next, we use this equivalence to show that for a sequence of program states the following holds. $\pi \in \Pi_{fair}(\mathcal{B})$ if and only if $\pi \in \Pi(\mathcal{P})$ and $\pi \models \mathcal{A}_{\neg\varphi}$. A Büchi program has a fair program execution if and only if it has a fair and feasible trace. We conclude that the intersection $T_{fair}(\mathcal{B}) \cap T_{feas}(\mathcal{B})$ is empty if and only if each program execution of $\mathcal{P}$ satisfies the LTL property φ. □

5   LTL Software Model Checking

In this section we describe our LTL software model checking algorithm. The algorithm is based on counter example guided abstraction refinement (CEGAR) in the fashion of [35] extended by a check for termination of fair traces and a corresponding abstraction refinement.

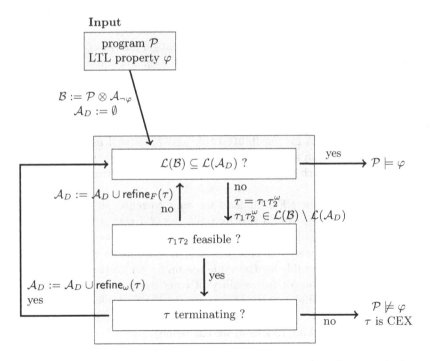

Fig. 3. The model checking algorithm. We use an automata-based approach that collects generalizations of infeasible traces in a Büchi automaton $\mathcal{A}_D$. The three inner boxes represent the three checks, which lead either to a refinement of $\mathcal{A}_D$, a result, or to a timeout (not shown).

Figure 3 shows an overview of the algorithm. The general idea is to create and continuously enlarge a Büchi automaton $\mathcal{A}_D$ whose language contains all fair traces of $\mathcal{B}$ that are already known to be infeasible. The algorithm starts by constructing a Büchi program $\mathcal{B}$ with the product construction from Sect. 4. Initially, $\mathcal{A}_D$ is a Büchi automaton that recognizes the empty language.

We use the similarities between Büchi programs and Büchi automata, i.e., that $\mathcal{L}(\mathcal{B}) = T_{feas}(\mathcal{B})$, throughout the whole algorithm. For example, in the first step of our CEGAR loop we check whether the set of fair traces represented by $\mathcal{A}_D$ is a superset of the fair traces of $\mathcal{B}$ (the first box in Fig. 3). This check for *trace inclusion* can be done with only Büchi automata operations.

If the set of fair traces of $\mathcal{A}_D$ is indeed a superset of the set of fair traces of $\mathcal{B}$, we know that there is no fair and feasible trace in $\mathcal{B}$ and our algorithm returns *safe*.

As the trace inclusion check is performed by computing $\mathcal{L}(\mathcal{B}) \setminus \mathcal{L}(\mathcal{A}_D)$, we will receive a fair trace τ of $\mathcal{B}$ that witnesses that the set of fair traces of $\mathcal{A}_D$ is no superset of the set of fair traces of $\mathcal{B}$. In this case, τ is always of the form $\tau_1 \tau_2^{\omega}$.

Next, our algorithm tries to decide whether τ is feasible or not. This is done by first checking various finite prefixes for feasibility. More precisely, the stem τ_1, the loop τ_2 and then the concatenation $\tau_1 \tau_2$ are checked for feasibility in that order. If none of those finite prefixes is infeasible, our algorithm tries to prove that the full infinite trace terminates. The termination analysis (inner lower box) tries to find a ranking function to prove that the loop will terminate eventually. When non-termination can be proven, we conclude that τ is feasible. Therefore, τ is a fair and feasible trace in $\mathcal{B}$ and thus a counterexample for the property φ. If instead termination can be shown, we know that τ is infeasible and the algorithm continues to the next step.

Note that the checks for feasibility of τ_1 and τ_2 as well as the termination analysis are based on – in general – undecidable methods. It is possible that they do not terminate. In such cases, our algorithm runs into a timeout and returns *unknown* as answer.

In the last step of the CEGAR loop we want to refine $\mathcal{A}_D$ by adding more fair and infeasible traces. We do this by replacing $\mathcal{A}_D$ with a Büchi automaton that is the union of the old Büchi automaton $\mathcal{A}_D$ and a new Büchi automaton which we create from trace τ. This new Büchi automaton recognizes all fair traces of $\mathcal{B}$ that are infeasible for the same reason for which trace τ is infeasible. Depending on the reason for infeasibility of trace τ, we use different methods for the construction of this new Büchi automaton: if τ was infeasible because we found an infeasible finite prefix, we use the method refine_F, if τ was infeasible because we found a ranking function, we use refine_ω.

The methods refine_F and refine_ω generalize a single trace to a set of traces. The input of these methods is the trace τ together with an infeasibility proof (resp. termination proof). The output is a Büchi automaton that accepts a set of traces whose infeasibility (resp. termination) can be shown by this infeasibility proof (resp. termination proof). refine_F and refine_ω guarantee that at least the single trace is contained in the language, but usually recognize a much larger set of traces. As the generalization performed by these methods is quite involved, it is not in the scope of this paper. We refer the interested reader to [35,36] for a detailed description.

6 Implementation and Evaluation

We implemented the algorithm from Sect. 5 as ULTIMATE LTLAUTOMIZER in the program analysis framework ULTIMATE [16]. This allowed us to use different, already available components for our implementation:

- a parser for ANSI C extended with specifications written in ACSL [6],
- various source-to-source transformations that optimize and simplify the input program,
- an implementation of the Trace Abstraction algorithm [35] to determine feasibility of finite trace prefixes,
- an implementation of a ranking function synthesis algorithm based on [34] to prove termination of fair traces in the Büchi program, and
- various automata operations like union, complementation and intersection of Büchi automata.

For the LTL property we use a custom annotation compatible to the ACSL format. After parsing, we transform the LTL property with LTL2BA [32] to a Büchi automaton, which is then together with an initial program the input for the product algorithm.

Our implementation of the product construction already contains some optimizations. For one, we already described that we remove locally infeasible traces by removing infeasible edges during the construction. We also convert the expression e of `assume e` statements to disjunctive normal form. If this results in edges labeled with more than one disjuncts, i.e. with `assume e1||e2||...||en`, we convert them to n edges labeled with `assume ei`. This improves the performance of the ranking function synthesis algorithm considerably.

Table 1 shows a comparison of our implementation against the benchmarks and the data provided by [23], in which the authors compare their novel LTL-checking approach based on decision predicates (DP) against a TERMINATOR-like procedure with an extension for fairness [21] (Term.). The set of benchmarks contains examples from "[...] the I/O subsystem of the windows kernel, the back-end infrastructure of the PostgreSQL database server, and the Apache web server", as well as "some toy examples". As the tools that were used in [23] are not publicly available, we could not re-run their implementations on our machine. Therefore, the results in the columns "Term." and "DP" are verbatim from the original publication.

We could solve most of the benchmarks in under five seconds. Notable exceptions are "Windows OS 5", where the other tools run into a timeout, and "Windows OS 8" where we performed much slower than DP. We are still unclear about the **OOM** result in "Apache `accept()`", but we suspect a bug in our tool.

Table 1. The results of the comparison with the benchmarks from [23]. "Program", "Lines", and "φ" contain the name of the benchmark, the lines of code of the program, and the checked property (atomic propositions have been abbreviated). "Result" states whether the tool proved the property (✔), produced a valid counterexample (✗), ran out of time (**T.O.**) or out of memory (**OOM**). **N.R.** shows the instance where we could not use the benchmark because the property was not specified explicitly and could not be guessed from the comments in the file. "Time" contains the runtime of the respective tool in seconds. For ULTIMATE LTLAUTOMIZER, there are additional statistics columns: "$|\mathbf{r}_F|$" states how many traces were refined using refine$_F$, and analogous "$|\mathbf{r}_\omega|$" for refine$_\omega$. "Inc." shows how much the product increased in size compared to the original CFG of the program. The timeout for "Term." and "DP" was four hours, our timeout was 20 min. Our memory limit was 8GB.

Program	Lines φ	Term. [21] Time (s)	Term. [21] Result	DP [23] Time (s)	DP [23] Result	ULTIMATE LTLAUTOMIZER Time (s)	Result	$|\mathbf{r}_F|$	$|\mathbf{r}_\omega|$	Inc. (%)
Ex. Sec. 2 of [23]	5 $\lozenge\square p$	2.32	✔	1.98	✔	0.51	✔	1	0	122
Ex. Fig. 8 of [21]	34 $\square(p \Rightarrow \lozenge q)$	209.64	✔	27.94	✔	0.72	✔	2	0	186
Toy acquire/release	14 $\square(p \Rightarrow \lozenge q)$	103.48	✔	14.18	✔	0.44	✔	1	1	129
Toy linear arith. 1	13 $p \Rightarrow \lozenge q$	126.86	(✔)	34.51	(✔)	1.10	✗	5	1	0.28
Toy linear arith. 2	13 $p \Rightarrow \lozenge q$	T.O.	T.O.	6.74	✔	0.82	✔	4	2	0.24
PostgreSQL strmsrv	259 $\square(p \Rightarrow \lozenge\square q)$	T.O.	T.O.	9.56	✔	1.04	✔	2	0	216
PostgreSQL strmsrv + bug	259 $\square(p \Rightarrow \lozenge\square q)$	87.31	(✗)	47.16	(✗)	0.66	✔	2	0	216
PostgreSQL pgarch	61 $\lozenge\square p$	31.50	(✔)	15.20	(✔)	0.33	✗	2	0	209
PostgreSQL dropbuf	152 $\square p$	T.O.	T.O.	1.14	(✔)	3.57	✗	1	1	148
PostgreSQL dropbuf	152 $\square(p \Rightarrow \lozenge q)$	53.99	✔	27.54	✔	1.37	✔	2	1	168
Apache accept()	314 $\square p \Rightarrow \square\lozenge q$	T.O.	T.O.	197.41	✔	502.15	OOM	-	-	209
Apache progress	314 $\square(p \Rightarrow (\lozenge q_1 \vee \lozenge q_2))$	685.34	✔	684.24	✔	2.01	✔	4	0	209
Windows OS 1	180 $\square(p \Rightarrow \lozenge q)$	901.81	✔	539.00	✔	43.59	✔	1	1	178
Windows OS 2	158 $\lozenge\square p$	16.47	✔	52.10	✔	0.11	✔	1	0	176
Windows OS 2 + bug	158 $\lozenge\square p$	26.15	✗	30.37	✗	0.22	✗	1	0	174
Windows OS 3	14 $\lozenge\square p$	4.21	✔	15.75	✔	0.08	✔	2	0	220
Windows OS 4	327 $\square(p \Rightarrow \lozenge q)$	T.O.	T.O.	1,114.18	✔	1.86	✔	1	3	207
Windows OS 4	327 $(\lozenge p) \vee (\lozenge q)$	1,223.96	✔	100.68	✔	-	N.R.	-	-	-
Windows OS 5	648 $\square(p \Rightarrow \lozenge q)$	T.O.	T.O.	T.O.	T.O.	20.76	✔	1	16	190
Windows OS 6	13 $\lozenge\square p$	149.41	✔	59.56	✔	T.O.	T.O.	6	8	158
Windows OS 6 + bug	13 $\lozenge\square p$	6.06	✗	22.12	✗	0.05	✗	0	0	61
Windows OS 7	13 $\square\lozenge p$	T.O.	T.O.	55.77	✔	0.91	✔	2	11	161
Windows OS 8	181 $\lozenge\square p$	T.O.	T.O.	5.24	✔	53.55	✔	4	55	168

In many instances with liveness properties we did not need to provide a ranking function, because the generalization from traces that are infeasible because of infeasible finite prefixes already excluded all fair traces of the Büchi program. For the remainder, the termination arguments were no challenge, except for "Windows OS 8": we had difficulties to generalize from many terminating traces, which also resulted in the slowdown compared to DP.

The expected increase in size of the Büchi program compared to the initial program's CFG (Inc.) was also manageable. Interestingly, in both instances of

"Toy linear arith." the product was even smaller than the original CFG, because we could remove many infeasible edges.

On four benchmarks ULTIMATE LTLAUTOMIZER results are different from the data in [23]: we contacted the authors and confirmed that our result for "Toy linear arith. 1" is indeed correct. We also could not run the benchmark "Windows OS 4", because the LTL property contained variables that were not defined in the source file. We did not yet receive a response regarding this issue as well as regarding the correctness of our results in the other three instances.

Table 2. Results of ULTIMATE LTLAUTOMIZER on other benchmark sets. "RERS" are the online problems from "The RERS Grey-Box Challenge 2012" [39] and "coolant" consists of toy examples modelled after real-world embedded systems with specifications based on the LTL patterns described in [53]. Each program set contains pairs of a file and a property. "Avg. Lines" states the average lines of code in the sample set, and |Set| the number of file-property pairs. In the next five columns we use the same symbols as in Table 1 except for ★, which represents abnormal termination of ULTIMATE LTLAUTOMIZER. The last four columns show the average runtime, the average number of refinements with refine$_F$ and refine$_\omega$, and how much the size of the optimized product increased on average compared to the original CFG. We used the same timeout and memory limits as in Table 1.

Program set	Avg. Lines	|Set|	✔	✗	T.O.	OOM	★ (N.R.)	Avg. Time (s)	Avg. |r$_F$|	Avg. |r$_\omega$|	Inc. (%)
RERS P14	514	50	19	21	2	0	8	107.21	21	< 1	329
RERS P15	1353	50	24	0	11	12	3	103.46	17	< 1	369
RERS P16	1304	50	15	1	16	14	4	297.34	32	< 1	362
RERS P17	2100	50	26	0	9	9	6	56.38	12	< 1	324
RERS P18	3306	50	21	0	17	10	2	262.03	24	< 1	297
RERS P19	8079	50	0	0	28	17	5	-	-	-	-
coolant	65	18	6	10	2	0	0	1.75	2	1	258
Benchmarks from Tab. 1	157	23	15	5	1	1	0 (1)	16.78	2	5	184

We also considered two other benchmark sets (see Table 2). First, we ran the on-site problems from the RERS Grey-Box Challenge 2012 [39] (RERS). RERS is about comparing program verification techniques on a domain of problems comparable to the ones seen in embedded systems engineering. For this, they generate control-flow-intensive programs that contain a so-called ECA-engine (event-condition-action): one non-terminating while loop which first reads an input symbol, then calls a function that based on the current state and the input calculates an output symbol, and finally writes this output symbol. We took all 6 problem classes from the on-site part of the challenge and tried to solve them with our tool. The classification (P14 to P19) encodes the size and assumed difficulty of the problem class: P14 and P15 are small, P16 and P17 are medium, and P18 and P19 are large problems. Inside a size bracket, the larger number means a higher difficulty.

We were able to verify roughly 43 % of the RERS benchmarks without any modifications. The RERS set also helped us finding a bug that one of our optimizations on the Büchi program product introduced and which is responsible for all but four of the ★ results. For the remaining four examples, ★ occurred because ULTIMATE LTLAUTOMIZER was unable to synthesize a ranking function. Interestingly, the RERS benchmarks did seldomly require generalizations with refine$_\omega$. In most cases, the refine$_F$ already excluded all fair traces from the Büchi program. This trend can also be observed in the number of refine$_\omega$ applications on the benchmarks that timed out (not shown in Table 2).

Second, we used a small toy example modeled after an embedded system, a coolant facility controller that encompasses two potentially non-terminating loops in succession. The first polls the user for the input of a sane temperature limit (except one example all versions of the coolant controller can loop infinitely in this step if the input is not suitable). The second loop polls the temperature, does some calculations, increments a counter and sets the "spoiled goods" flag if the temperature limit is exceeded. The LTL properties specify that the spoiled variable cannot be reset by the program (safety), that setup stages occur in the correct order (safety and liveness), and that the temperature controlling loop always progresses (safety and liveness). We then introduced various bugs in the original version of the program and checked against the property and its negation. Although the coolant examples are quite small, they contain complex inter-dependencies between traces which lead to timeouts in two cases.

An unexpected result of the evaluation was, that the initial size of the program does not seem to define the performance of the verification, both in time and success rate, as the larger programs from P17 and P18 had more results and were faster than their counterparts from P15 and P16. Also, the effective blow-up due to the product construction is no more than four times, which is still quite manageable.

The benchmark sets together with ULTIMATE LTLAUTOMIZER are available from [30].

7 Related Work

An earlier approach to LTL software model checking was done in [21]. There, the authors reduced the problem to fair termination checking. Our work can be seen as improvement upon this approach, as we also use fair termination checking, but only when it is necessary. We avoid a large number of (more costly) termination checks due to our previous check for infeasible finite prefixes and the resulting generalizing refinement.

In [23], the authors reduce the LTL model checking problem to the problem of checking ∀CTL by first approximating the LTL formula with a suitable CTL formula, and then refining counterexamples that represent multiple paths by introducing non-deterministic prophecy variables in their program representation. This non-determinism is then removed through a determinization procedure. By using this technique, they try to reduce their dependence on termination proofs, which they identified as the main reason for poor performance of automata-theoretic approaches. Our approach can be seen as another strategy to reduce the reliance on many termination proofs. By iteratively refining the Büchi program with different proof techniques, we often remove complex control structures from loops and thus reduce the strain on the termination proof engine.

There exist various publicly available finite-state model checking tools that support both LTL properties and programs, but are in contrast to ULTIMATE LTLAUTOMIZER limited to finite-state systems: SPIN [38] and Divine [4] are both based on the Vardi-Wolper product [57] for LTL model checking. Divine supports C/C++ via LLVM bytecode, SPIN can be used with different front-ends that translate programs to finite-state models, e.g. with Bandera [28] for Java. NuSMV [18] and Cadence SMV [44] reduce LTL model checking to CTL model checking. NuSMV can use different techniques like BDD symbolic model checking using symbolic fixed point, computation with BDDs, or bounded model checking using MiniSat. Cadence SMV uses Mu-calculus with additional fairness constraints [15].

8   Conclusion and Future Work

The encoding of the LTL program verification problem through the infeasibility of *fair* paths in a Büchi program has allowed us to define a sequence of semi-tests which can be scheduled before the full test of infeasibility of an infinite path. The occurrence of a successful semi-test (the proof of infeasibility for a finite prefix, by the construction of a proof of unsatisfiability) makes the full test redundant and avoids the relatively costly construction of a ranking function. Our experiments indicate that the corresponding approach leads to a practical tool for LTL software model checking.

We see several ways to improve performance. We may try to use alternatives to LTL2BA such as SPOT [31]; see [54]. The technique of large block encoding [11] adapted to Büchi programs, may help to reduce memory consumption.

References

1. Baier, C., Katoen, J.-P., et al.: Principles of Model Checking, vol. 26202649. MIT Press, Cambridge (2008)
2. Ball, T., Majumdar, R., Millstein, T.D., Rajamani, S.K.: Automatic predicate abstraction of C programs. In: PLDI, pp. 203–213 (2001)
3. Ball, T., Podelski, A., Rajamani, S.K.: Boolean and cartesian abstraction for model checking C programs. STTT 5(1), 49–58 (2003)
4. Barnat, J., Brim, L., Havel, V., Havlíček, J., Kriho, J., Lenčo, M., Ročkai, P., Štill, V., Weiser, J.: DiVinE 3.0 – an explicit-state model checker for multithreaded C & C++ programs. In: Sharygina, N., Veith, H. (eds.) CAV 2013. LNCS, vol. 8044, pp. 863–868. Springer, Heidelberg (2013)

5. Bauch, P., Havel, V., Barnat, J.: LTL model checking of LLVM bitcode with symbolic data. In: Hliněný, P., Dvořák, Z., Jaroš, J., Kofroň, J., Kořenek, J., Matula, P., Pala, K. (eds.) MEMICS 2014. LNCS, vol. 8934, pp. 47–59. Springer, Heidelberg (2014)

6. Baudin, P., Filliâtre, J.-C., Marché, C., Monate, B., Moy, Y., Prevosto, V., et al.: ACSL: ANSI/ISO C specification language, Feb 2015. http://frama-c.com/download.html

7. Ben-Amram, A.M.: Size-change termination, monotonicity constraints and ranking functions. In: Bouajjani, A., Maler, O. (eds.) CAV 2009. LNCS, vol. 5643, pp. 109–123. Springer, Heidelberg (2009)

8. Ben-Amram, A.M., Genaim, S.: On the linear ranking problem for integer linear-constraint loops. In: POPL, pp. 51–62 (2013)

9. Berdine, J., Cook, B., Distefano, D., O'Hearn, P.W.: Automatic termination proofs for programs with shape-shifting heaps. In: Ball, T., Jones, R.B. (eds.) CAV 2006. LNCS, vol. 4144, pp. 386–400. Springer, Heidelberg (2006)

10. Beyer, D.: Software verification and verifiable witnesses. In: Baier, C., Tinelli, C. (eds.) TACAS 2015. LNCS, vol. 9035, pp. 401–416. Springer, Heidelberg (2015)

11. Beyer, D., Cimatti, A., Griggio, A., Keremoglu, M.E., Sebastiani, R.: Software model checking via large-block encoding. In: FMCAD, pp. 25–32, IEEE (2009)

12. Bradley, A.R., Manna, Z., Sipma, H.B.: Linear ranking with reachability. In: Etessami, K., Rajamani, S.K. (eds.) CAV 2005. LNCS, vol. 3576, pp. 491–504. Springer, Heidelberg (2005)

13. Brillout, A., Kroening, D., Rümmer, P., Wahl, T.: An interpolating sequent calculus for quantifier-free presburger arithmetic. J. Autom. Reason. **47**(4), 341–367 (2011)

14. Bruttomesso, R., Pek, E., Sharygina, N., Tsitovich, A.: The openSMT solver. In: Esparza, J., Majumdar, R. (eds.) TACAS 2010. LNCS, vol. 6015, pp. 150–153. Springer, Heidelberg (2010)

15. Burch, J.R., Clarke, E.M., McMillan, K.L., Dill, D.L., Hwang, L.-J.: Symbolic model checking: 10^{20} states and beyond. In: LICS, pp. 428–439, IEEE (1990)

16. Christ, J., Dietsch, D., Ermis, E., Heizmann, M., Hoenicke, J., Langenfeld, V., Leike, J., Musa, B., Nutz, A., Schilling, C.: The program analysis framework ultimate, Feb 2015. http://ultimate.informatik.uni-freiburg.de

17. Christ, J., Hoenicke, J., Nutz, A.: SMTInterpol: an interpolating SMT solver. In: Donaldson, A., Parker, D. (eds.) SPIN 2012. LNCS, vol. 7385, pp. 248–254. Springer, Heidelberg (2012)

18. Cimatti, A., Clarke, E., Giunchiglia, E., Giunchiglia, F., Pistore, M., Roveri, M., Sebastiani, R., Tacchella, A.: NuSMV 2: an opensource tool for symbolic model checking. In: Brinksma, E., Larsen, K.G. (eds.) CAV 2002. LNCS, vol. 2404, pp. 359–364. Springer, Heidelberg (2002)

19. Cimatti, A., Griggio, A., Schaafsma, B.J., Sebastiani, R.: The MathSAT5 SMT solver. In: Piterman, N., Smolka, S.A. (eds.) TACAS 2013 (ETAPS 2013). LNCS, vol. 7795, pp. 93–107. Springer, Heidelberg (2013)

20. Clarke, E., Grumberg, O., Jha, S., Lu, Y., Veith, H.: Counterexample-guided abstraction refinement. In: Emerson, E.A., Sistla, A.P. (eds.) CAV 2000. LNCS, vol. 1855, pp. 154–169. Springer, Heidelberg (2000)

21. Cook, B., Gotsman, A., Podelski, A., Rybalchenko, A., Vardi, M.Y.: Proving that programs eventually do something good. ACM SIGPLAN Not. **42**, 265–276 (2007). ACM

22. Cook, B., Khlaaf, H., Piterman, N.: Fairness for infinite-state systems. In: Baier, C., Tinelli, C. (eds.) TACAS 2015. LNCS, vol. 9035, pp. 384–398. Springer, Heidelberg (2015)
23. Cook, B., Koskinen, E.: Making prophecies with decision predicates. ACM SIG-PLAN Not. 46, 399–410 (2011). ACM
24. Cook, B., Koskinen, E., Vardi, M.Y.: Temporal property verification as a program analysis task - extended version. FMSD 41(1), 66–82 (2012)
25. Cook, B., Kroening, D., Rümmer, P., Wintersteiger, C.M.: Ranking function synthesis for bit-vector relations. FMSD 43(1), 93–120 (2013)
26. Cook, B., Podelski, A., Rybalchenko, A.: Termination proofs for systems code. In: PLDI, pp. 415–426, ACM (2006)
27. Cook, B., Podelski, A., Rybalchenko, A.: Proving thread termination. In: PLDI, pp. 320–330 (2007)
28. Corbett, J.C., Dwyer, M.B., Hatcliff, J., Laubach, S., Pasareanu, C.S., Zheng, H., et al.: Bandera: extracting finite-state models from Java source code. In: ICSE, pp. 439–448, IEEE (2000)
29. Dangl, M., Löwe, S., Wendler, P.: Cpachecker with support for recursive programs and floating-point arithmetic - (competition contribution). In: Baier, C., Tinelli, C. (eds.) TACAS 2015. LNCS, vol. 9035, pp. 423–425. Springer, Heidelberg (2015)
30. Dietsch, D., Heizmann, M., Langenfeld, V.: Ultimate LTLAutomizer website, Feb 2015. http://ultimate.informatik.uni-freiburg.de/ltlautomizer
31. Duret-Lutz, A., Poitrenaud, D.: SPOT: an extensible model checking library using transition-based generalized Büchi automata. In: MASCOTS, pp. 76–83, IEEE (2004)
32. Gastin, P., Oddoux, D.: Fast LTL to Büchi automata translation. In: Berry, G., Comon, H., Finkel, A. (eds.) CAV 2001. LNCS, vol. 2102, pp. 53–65. Springer, Heidelberg (2001)
33. Heizmann, M., Dietsch, D., Leike, J., Musa, B., Podelski, A.: Ultimate automizer with array interpolation - (competition contribution). In: Baier, C., Tinelli, C. (eds.) TACAS 2015. LNCS, vol. 9035, pp. 455–457. Springer, Heidelberg (2015)
34. Heizmann, M., Hoenicke, J., Leike, J., Podelski, A.: Linear ranking for linear lasso programs. In: Van Hung, D., Ogawa, M. (eds.) ATVA 2013. LNCS, vol. 8172, pp. 365–380. Springer, Heidelberg (2013)
35. Heizmann, M., Hoenicke, J., Podelski, A.: Software model checking for people who love automata. In: Sharygina, N., Veith, H. (eds.) CAV 2013. LNCS, vol. 8044, pp. 36–52. Springer, Heidelberg (2013)
36. Heizmann, M., Hoenicke, J., Podelski, A.: Termination analysis by learning terminating programs. In: Biere, A., Bloem, R. (eds.) CAV 2014. LNCS, vol. 8559, pp. 797–813. Springer, Heidelberg (2014)
37. Henzinger, T.A., Jhala, R., Majumdar, R., Sutre, G.: Lazy abstraction. In: POPL, pp. 58–70, ACM (2002)
38. Holzmann, G.J.: The SPIN Model Checker Primer and Reference Manual, vol. 1003. Addison-Wesley, Reading (2004)
39. Howar, F., Isberner, M., Merten, M., Steffen, B., Beyer, D.: The RERS grey-box challenge 2012: analysis of event-condition-action systems. In: Margaria, T., Steffen, B. (eds.) ISoLA 2012, Part I. LNCS, vol. 7609, pp. 608–614. Springer, Heidelberg (2012)
40. Kroening, D., Sharygina, N., Tsitovich, A., Wintersteiger, C.M.: Termination analysis with compositional transition invariants. In: Touili, T., Cook, B., Jackson, P. (eds.) CAV 2010. LNCS, vol. 6174, pp. 89–103. Springer, Heidelberg (2010)

41. Kroening, D., Tautschnig, M.: CBMC – C bounded model checker. In: Ábrahám, E., Havelund, K. (eds.) TACAS 2014 (ETAPS). LNCS, vol. 8413, pp. 389–391. Springer, Heidelberg (2014)

42. Lal, A., Qadeer, S.: Reachability modulo theories. RP **2013**, 23–44 (2013)

43. Leike, J., Heizmann, M.: Ranking templates for linear loops. In: Ábrahám, E., Havelund, K. (eds.) TACAS 2014 (ETAPS). LNCS, vol. 8413, pp. 172–186. Springer, Heidelberg (2014)

44. McMillan, K.: Cadence SMV. Cadence Berkeley Labs, CA (2000). http://www.kenmcmil.com/smv.html

45. McMillan, K.L.: Lazy abstraction with interpolants. In: Ball, T., Jones, R.B. (eds.) CAV 2006. LNCS, vol. 4144, pp. 123–136. Springer, Heidelberg (2006)

46. McMillan, K.L.: Interpolants from Z3 proofs. In: FMCAD, pp. 19–27 (2011)

47. Ermis, E., Nutz, A., Dietsch, D., Hoenicke, J., Podelski, A.: Ultimate kojak. In: Ábrahám, E., Havelund, K. (eds.) TACAS 2014 (ETAPS). LNCS, vol. 8413, pp. 421–423. Springer, Heidelberg (2014)

48. Podelski, A., Rybalchenko, A.: A complete method for the synthesis of linear ranking functions. In: Steffen, B., Levi, G. (eds.) VMCAI 2004. LNCS, vol. 2937, pp. 239–251. Springer, Heidelberg (2004)

49. Podelski, A., Rybalchenko, A.: Transition invariants. In: LICS, pp. 32–41, IEEE Computer Society (2004)

50. Podelski, A., Rybalchenko, A.: Transition predicate abstraction and fair termination. In: POPL, pp. 132–144, ACM (2005)

51. Podelski, A., Rybalchenko, A.: ARMC: the logical choice for software model checking with abstraction refinement. In: Hanus, M. (ed.) PADL 2007. LNCS, vol. 4354, pp. 245–259. Springer, Heidelberg (2007)

52. Podelski, A., Rybalchenko, A., Wies, T.: Heap assumptions on demand. In: Gupta, A., Malik, S. (eds.) CAV 2008. LNCS, vol. 5123, pp. 314–327. Springer, Heidelberg (2008)

53. Post, A.C.: Effective Correctness Criteria for Real-time Requirements. Shaker, Aachen (2012)

54. Rozier, K.Y., Vardi, M.Y.: LTL satisfiability checking. In: Bošnački, D., Edelkamp, S. (eds.) SPIN 2007. LNCS, vol. 4595, pp. 149–167. Springer, Heidelberg (2007)

55. Ströder, T., Aschermann, C., Frohn, F., Hensel, J., Giesl, J.: Aprove: termination and memory safety of C programs - (competition contribution). In: Baier, C., Tinelli, C. (eds.) TACAS 2015. LNCS, vol. 9035, pp. 417–419. Springer, Heidelberg (2015)

56. Urban, C.: FuncTion: an abstract domain functor for termination. In: Baier, C., Tinelli, C. (eds.) TACAS 2015. LNCS, vol. 9035, pp. 464–466. Springer, Heidelberg (2015)

57. Vardi, M.Y., Wolper, P.: An automata-theoretic approach to automatic program verification. In: LICS, pp. 322–331, IEEE Computer Society (1986)

Model Checking Parameterized Asynchronous Shared-Memory Systems

Antoine Durand-Gasselin[1], Javier Esparza[1],
Pierre Ganty[2](✉), and Rupak Majumdar[3]

[1] TU Munich, Munich, Germany
[2] IMDEA Software Institute, Madrid, Spain
pierre.ganty@imdea.org
[3] MPI-SWS, Kaiserslautern, Germany

Abstract. We characterize the complexity of liveness verification for parameterized systems consisting of a leader process and arbitrarily many anonymous and identical contributor processes. Processes communicate through a shared, bounded-value register. While each operation on the register is atomic, there is no synchronization primitive to execute a sequence of operations atomically.

We analyze the case in which processes are modeled by finite-state machines or pushdown machines and the property is given by a Büchi automaton over the alphabet of read and write actions of the leader. We show that the problem is decidable, and has a surprisingly low complexity: it is NP-complete when all processes are finite-state machines, and is PSPACE-hard and in NEXPTIME when they are pushdown machines. This complexity is lower than for the non-parameterized case: liveness verification of finitely many finite-state machines is PSPACE-complete, and undecidable for two pushdown machines.

For finite-state machines, our proofs characterize infinite behaviors using existential abstraction and semilinear constraints. For pushdown machines, we show how contributor computations of high stack height can be simulated by computations of many contributors, each with low stack height. Together, our results characterize the complexity of verification for parameterized systems under the assumptions of anonymity and asynchrony.

1 Introduction

We study the verification problem for *parameterized asynchronous shared-memory systems* [9,12]. These systems consist of a *leader* process and arbitrarily many identical *contributors*, processes with no identity, running at arbitrary relative speeds. The shared-memory consists of a read/write register that all processes can access to perform either a read operation or a write operation. The register is bounded: the set of values that can be stored is finite. Read/write operations execute atomically but sequences of operations do not: no process can conduct an atomic sequence of reads and writes while excluding all other processes. In a previous paper [9], we have studied the complexity

D. Kroening and C.S. Păsăreanu (Eds.): CAV 2015, Part I, LNCS 9206, pp. 67–84, 2015.
DOI: 10.1007/978-3-319-21690-4_5

of safety verification, which asks to check if a safety property holds no matter how many contributors are present. In a nutshell, we showed that the problem is coNP-complete when both leader and contributors are finite-state automata and PSPACE-complete when they are pushdown automata.

In this paper we complete the study of this model by addressing the verification of liveness properties specified as ω-regular languages (which in particular encompasses LTL model-checking). Given a property like "every request is eventually granted" and a system with a fixed number of processes, one is often able to guess an upper bound on the maximal number of steps until the request is granted, and replace the property by the safety property "every request is granted after at most K steps." In parameterized systems this bound can depend on the (unbounded) number of processes, and so reducing liveness to safety, or to finitary reasoning, is not obvious. Indeed, for many parameterized models, liveness verification is undecidable even if safety is decidable [8,13].

Our results show that there is no large complexity gap between liveness and safety verification: liveness verification (existence of an infinite computation violating a property) is NP-complete in the finite-state case, and PSPACE-hard and in NEXPTIME in the pushdown case. In contrast, remember that liveness checking is already PSPACE-complete for a *finite* number of finite-state machines, and undecidable for a *fixed* number of pushdown systems. Thus, not only is liveness verification decidable in the parameterized setting but the complexity of the parameterized problem is *lower* than in the non-parameterized case, where all processes are part of the input. We interpret this as follows: in asynchronous shared-memory systems, the existence of arbitrarily many processes leads to a "noisy" environment, in which contributors may hinder progress by replying to past messages from the leader, long after the computation has moved forward to a new phase. It is known that imperfect communication can *reduce* the power of computation and the complexity of verification problems: the best known example are lossy channel systems, for which many verification problems are decidable, while they are undecidable for perfect channels (see e.g. [1,3]). Our results reveal another instance of the same phenomenon.

Technically, our proof methods are very different from those used for safety verification. Our previous results [9] relied on a fundamental Simulation Lemma, inspired by Hague's work [12], stating that the *finite* behaviors of an arbitrary number of contributors can be simulated by a finite number of *simulators*, one for each possible value of the register. Unfortunately, the Simulation Lemma does not extend to infinite behaviors, and so we have to develop new ideas. In the case in which both leader and contributors are finite-state machines, the NP-completeness result is obtained by means of a combination of an abstraction that overapproximates the set of possible infinite behaviors, and a semilinear constraint that allows us to regain precision. The case in which both leader and contributors are pushdown machines is very involved. In a nutshell, we show that pushdown runs in which a parameter called the *effective stack height* grows too much can be "distributed" into a number of runs with smaller effective stack height. We then prove that the behaviors of a pushdown machine with a bounded effective stack height can be simulated by an exponentially larger finite-state machine.

Related Work. Parameterized verification has been studied extensively, both theoretically and practically. While very simple variants of the problem are already undecidable [6], many non-trivial parameterized models retain decidability. There is no clear "rule of thumb" that allows one to predict what model checking problems are decidable, nor their complexities, other than "liveness is generally harder than safety." For example, coverability for Petri nets—in which finite-state, identityless processes communicate via rendezvous or global shared state— is EXPSPACE-complete, higher than the PSPACE-completeness of the non-parameterized version, and verification of liveness properties can be equivalent to Petri net reachability, for which we only know non-primitive recursive upper bounds, or even undecidable. Safety verification for extensions to Petri nets with reset or transfer, or broadcast protocols, where arbitrarily many finite-state processes communicate through broadcast messages, are non-primitive recursive; liveness verification is undecidable in all cases [2,8,13]. Thus, our results, which show simultaneously lower complexity than non-parameterized problems, as well as similar complexity for liveness and safety, are quite unexpected.

German and Sistla [10] and Aminof *et al.* [4] have studied a parameterized model with rendezvous as communication primitive, where processes are finite-state machines. Model checking the fully symmetrical case—only contributors, no leaders—runs in polynomial time (other topologies have also been considered [4]), while the asymmetric case with a leader is EXPSPACE-complete. In this paper we study the same problems, but for a shared memory communication primitive.

Population protocols [5] are another well-studied model of identityless asynchronous finite-state systems communicating via rendezvous. The semantics of population protocols is given over fair runs, in which every potential interaction that is infinitely often enabled is infinitely often taken. With this semantics, population protocols compute exactly the semilinear predicates [5]. In this paper we do not study what our model can compute (in particular, we are agnostic with respect to which fairness assumptions are reasonable), but what we can compute or decide about the model.

2   Formal Model: Non-atomic Networks

In this paper, we identify systems with languages. System actions are modeled as symbols in an alphabet, executions are modeled as infinite words, and the system itself is modeled as the language of its executions. Composition operations that combine systems into larger ones are modeled as operations on languages.

2.1   Systems as Languages

An *alphabet* Σ is a finite, non-empty set of *symbols*. A *word* over Σ is a finite sequence over Σ including the empty sequence denoted ε, and a *language* is a set of words. An ω-*word* over Σ is an infinite sequence of symbols of Σ, and an ω-*language* is a set of ω-words. We use Σ^* (resp. Σ^ω) to denote the language of all words (resp. ω-words) over Σ. When there is no ambiguity, we use "words" to refer to words or ω-words. We do similarly for languages. Let w be a sequence over some alphabet, define $\mathrm{dom}(w) = \{1, \ldots, n\}$ if $w = a_1 a_2 \ldots a_n$ is a word; else (w is an ω-word) $\mathrm{dom}(w)$ denote the set $\mathbb{N} \setminus \{0\}$. Elements of $\mathrm{dom}(w)$ are called *positions*. The *length* of a sequence w is defined to be $\sup \mathrm{dom}(w)$ and is denoted $|w|$. We denote by $(w)_i$ the symbol of w at position i if $i \in \mathrm{dom}(w)$, ε otherwise. Moreover, let $(w)_{i..j}$ with $i, j \in \mathbb{N}$ and $i < j$ denote $(w)_i (w)_{i+1} \ldots (w)_j$. Also $(w)_{i..\infty}$ denotes $(w)_i (w)_{i+1} \ldots$ For words $u, v \in (\Sigma^\omega \cup \Sigma^*)$, we say u is a *prefix* of v if either $u = v$ or $u \in \Sigma^*$ and there is a $w \in (\Sigma^\omega \cup \Sigma^*)$ such that $v = uw$.

Combining Systems: Shuffle. Intuitively, the shuffle of systems L_1 and L_2 is the system interleaving the executions of L_1 with those of L_2. Given two ω-languages $L_1 \subseteq \Sigma_1^\omega$ and $L_2 \subseteq \Sigma_2^\omega$, their *shuffle*, denoted by $L_1 \lozenge L_2$, is the ω-language over $(\Sigma_1 \cup \Sigma_2)$ defined as follows. Given two ω-words $x \in \Sigma_1^\omega, y \in \Sigma_2^\omega$, we say that $z \in (\Sigma_1 \cup \Sigma_2)^\omega$ is an *interleaving* of x and y if there exist (possibly empty) words $x_1, x_2, \ldots, x_i, \ldots \in \Sigma_1^*$ and $y_1, y_2, \ldots, y_i, \ldots \in \Sigma_2^*$ such that each $x_1 x_2 \cdots x_i$ is a prefix of x, and each $y_1 y_2 \cdots y_i$ is a prefix of y, and $z = x_1 y_1 x_2 y_2 \cdots x_i y_i \cdots \in \Sigma^\omega$ is an ω-word. Then $L_1 \lozenge L_2 = \bigcup_{x \in L_1, y \in L_2} x \lozenge y$, where $x \lozenge y$ denotes the set of all interleavings of x and y. For example, if $L_1 = ab^\omega$ and $L_2 = ab^\omega$, we get $L_1 \lozenge L_2 = (a + ab^*a)b^\omega$. Shuffle is associative and commutative, and so we can write $L_1 \lozenge \cdots \lozenge L_n$ or $\lozenge_{i=1}^n L_i$.

Combining Systems: Asynchronous product. The asynchronous product of $L_1 \subseteq \Sigma_1^\omega$ and $L_2 \subseteq \Sigma_2^\omega$ also interleaves the executions but, this time, the actions in the common alphabet must now be executed jointly. The ω-language of the resulting system, called the *asynchronous product* of L_1 and L_2, is denoted by $L_1 \parallel L_2$, and defined as follows. Let $Proj_\Sigma(w)$ be the word obtained by erasing from w all occurrences of symbols not in Σ. $L_1 \parallel L_2$ is the ω-language over the alphabet $\Sigma = \Sigma_1 \cup \Sigma_2$ such that $w \in L_1 \parallel L_2$ iff $Proj_{\Sigma_1}(w)$ and $Proj_{\Sigma_2}(w)$ are prefixes of words in L_1 and L_2, respectively. We abuse notation and write $w_1 \parallel L_2$ instead of $\{w_1\} \parallel L_2$ when $L_1 = \{w_1\}$. For example, let $\Sigma_1 = \{a, c\}$ and $\Sigma_2 = \{b, c\}$. For $L_1 = (ac)^\omega$ and $L_2 = (bc)^\omega$ we get $L_1 \parallel L_2 = ((ab + ba)c)^\omega$. Observe that the language $L_1 \parallel L_2$ depends on L_1, L_2 and also on Σ_1 and Σ_2. For example, if $\Sigma_1 = \{a\}$ and $\Sigma_2 = \{b\}$, then $\{a^\omega\} \parallel \{b^\omega\} = (a + b)^\omega$, but if $\Sigma_1 = \{a, b\} = \Sigma_2$, then $\{a^\omega\} \parallel \{b^\omega\} = \emptyset$. So we should more properly write $L_1 \parallel_{\Sigma_1, \Sigma_2} L_2$. However, since the alphabets Σ_1 and Σ_2 will be clear from the context, we will omit them. Like shuffle, asynchronous product is also associative and commutative, and so we write $L_1 \parallel \cdots \parallel L_n$. Notice finally that shuffle and asynchronous product coincide if $\Sigma_1 \cap \Sigma_2 = \emptyset$, but usually differ otherwise. For instance, if $L_1 = ab^\omega$ and $L_2 = ab^\omega$, we get $L_1 \parallel L_2 = ab^\omega$.

We describe systems as combinations of shuffles and asynchronous products, for instance we write $L_1 \parallel (L_2 \lozenge L_3)$. In these expressions we assume that $\lozenge$ binds tighter than $\parallel$, and so $L_1 \lozenge L_2 \parallel L_3$ is the language $(L_1 \lozenge L_2) \parallel L_3$, and not $L_1 \lozenge (L_2 \parallel L_3)$.

2.2 Non-atomic Networks

A non-atomic network is an infinite family of systems parameterized by a number k. The kth element of the family has $k+1$ components communicating through a global store by means of read and write actions. The store is modeled as an atomic register whose set of possible values is finite. One of the $k+1$ components is the leader, while the other k are the contributors. All contributors have exactly the same possible behaviors (they are copies of the same ω-language), while the leader may behave differently. The network is called non-atomic because components cannot atomically execute sequences of actions, only one single read or write.

Formally, we fix a finite set $\mathcal{G}$ of *global values*. A *read-write alphabet* is any set of the form $\mathcal{A} \times \mathcal{G}$, where $\mathcal{A}$ is a set of *read* and *write (actions)*. We denote a symbol $(a,g) \in \mathcal{A} \times \mathcal{G}$ by $a(g)$ and define $\mathcal{G}(a_1,\dots,a_n) = \{a_i(g) \mid 1 \le i \le n,\ g \in \mathcal{G}\}$.

We fix two languages $\mathcal{D} \subseteq \Sigma_{\mathcal{D}}^{\omega}$ and $\mathcal{C} \subseteq \Sigma_{\mathcal{C}}^{\omega}$, called the *leader* and the *contributor*, with alphabets $\Sigma_{\mathcal{D}} = \mathcal{G}(r_d, w_d)$ and $\Sigma_{\mathcal{C}} = \mathcal{G}(r_c, w_c)$, respectively, where r_d, r_c are called *reads* and w_c, w_d are called *writes*. We write $w_\star$ (respectively, $r_\star$) to stand for either w_c or w_d (respectively, r_c or r_d). We further assume that $Proj_{\{r_\star(g), w_\star(g)\}}(\mathcal{D} \cup \mathcal{C}) \ne \emptyset$ holds for every $g \in \mathcal{G}$, else the value g is never used and can be removed from $\mathcal{G}$.

Additionally, we fix an ω-language $\mathcal{S}$, called the *store*, over $\Sigma_{\mathcal{D}} \cup \Sigma_{\mathcal{C}}$. It models the sequences of read and write operations supported by an atomic register: a write $w_\star(g)$ writes g to the register, while a read $r_\star(g)$ succeeds when the register's current value is g. Initially the store is only willing to execute a write. Formally $\mathcal{S}$ is defined as $\left(\sum_{g \in \mathcal{G}} \left(w_\star(g)\,(r_\star(g))^* \right) \right)^{\omega} +$ $\left(\sum_{g \in \mathcal{G}} \left(w_\star(g)\,(r_\star(g))^* \right) \right)^* \sum_{g \in \mathcal{G}} \left(w_\star(g)\,(r_\star(g))^{\omega} \right)$ and any finite prefix thereof. Observe that $\mathcal{S}$ is completely determined by $\Sigma_{\mathcal{D}}$ and $\Sigma_{\mathcal{C}}$. Figure 1 depicts a store with $\{1,2,3\}$ as possible values as the language of a transition system.

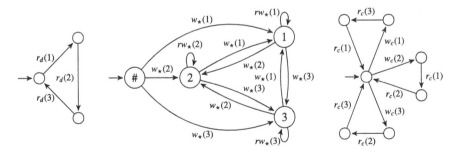

Fig. 1. Transition systems describing languages $\mathcal{D}$, $\mathcal{S}$, and $\mathcal{C}$. We write $rw_\star(g) = r_\star(g) \cup w_\star(g) = \{r_c(g), r_d(g)\} \cup \{w_c(g), w_d(g)\}$. The transition system for $\mathcal{S}$ is in state $i \in \{1,2,3\}$ when the current value of the store is i.

Definition 1. Let $\mathcal{D} \subseteq \Sigma_{\mathcal{D}}^\omega$ and $\mathcal{C} \subseteq \Sigma_{\mathcal{C}}^\omega$ be a leader and a contributor, and let $k \geq 1$. The *k-instance of the $(\mathcal{D}, \mathcal{C})$-network* is the ω-language $\mathcal{N}^{(k)} = (\mathcal{D} \parallel \mathcal{S} \parallel \lozenge_k \mathcal{C})$ where $\lozenge_k \mathcal{C}$ stands for $\lozenge_{i=1}^k \mathcal{C}$. The $(\mathcal{D}, \mathcal{C})$-network $\mathcal{N}$ is the ω-language $\mathcal{N} = \bigcup_{k=1}^\infty \mathcal{N}^{(k)}$. We omit the prefix $(\mathcal{D}, \mathcal{C})$ when it is clear from the context. It follows easily from the properties of shuffle and asynchronous product that $\mathcal{N} = (\mathcal{D} \parallel \mathcal{S} \parallel \lozenge_\infty \mathcal{C})$, where $\lozenge_\infty \mathcal{C}$ is an abbreviation of $\bigcup_{k=1}^\infty \lozenge_k \mathcal{C}$.

Next we introduce a notion of *compatibility* between a word of the leader and a multiset of words of the contributor (a multiset because several contributors may execute the same sequence of actions). Intuitively, compatibility means that all the words can be interleaved into a legal infinite sequence of reads and writes supported by an atomic register—that is, an infinite sequence belonging to $\mathcal{S}$. Formally:

Definition 2. Let $u \in \Sigma_{\mathcal{D}}^\omega$, and let $M = \{v_1, \ldots, v_k\}$ be a multiset of words over $\Sigma_{\mathcal{C}}^\omega$ (possibly containing multiple copies of a word). We say that u is *compatible* with M iff the ω-language $(u \parallel \mathcal{S} \parallel \lozenge_{i=1}^k v_i)$ is non-empty. When u and M are compatible, there exists a word $s \in \mathcal{S}$ such that $(u \parallel s \parallel \lozenge_{i=1}^k v_i) \neq \emptyset$. We call s a *witness* of compatibility.

Example 1. Consider the network with $\mathcal{G} = \{1, 2, 3\}$ where the leader, store, and contributor languages are given by the infinite paths of the transition systems from Fig. 1. The only ω-word of $\mathcal{D}$ is $(r_d(1)r_d(2)r_d(3))^\omega$ and the ω-language of $\mathcal{C}$ is $(w_c(1)r_c(3)r_c(1) + w_c(2)r_c(1)r_c(2) + w_c(3)r_c(2)r_c(3))^\omega$. For instance, $\mathcal{D} = (r_d(1)r_d(2)r_d(3))^\omega$ is compatible with the multiset M of 6 ω-words obtained by taking two copies of $(w(1)r(3)r(1))^\omega$, $(w(2)r(1)r(2))^\omega$ and $(w(3)r(2)r(3))^\omega$. The reader may be interested in finding another multiset compatible with $\mathcal{D}$ and containing only 4 ω-words.

Stuttering Property. Intuitively, the stuttering property states that if we take an ω-word of a network $\mathcal{N}$ and "stutter" reads and writes of the contributors, going e.g. from $w_d(1)r_c(1)w_c(2)r_d(2) \ldots$ to $w_d(1)r_c(1)r_c(1)w_c(2)w_c(2)w_c(2)r_d(2) \ldots$, the result is again an ω-word of the network.

Let $s \in \mathcal{S}$ be a witness of compatibility of $u \in \Sigma_{\mathcal{D}}^\omega$ and $M = \{v_1, \ldots, v_k\}$. Pick a set I of positions (viz. $I \subseteq \operatorname{dom}(s)$) such that $(s)_i \in \Sigma_{\mathcal{C}}$ for each $i \in I$, and pick a number $\ell_i \geq 0$ for every $i \in I$. Let s' be the result of simultaneously replacing each $(s)_i$ by $(s)_i^{\ell_i+1}$ in s. We have that $s' \in \mathcal{S}$. Now let $v_s = (s)_{i_1}^{\ell_{i_1}} \cdot (s)_{i_2}^{\ell_{i_2}} \cdots$, where $i_1 = \min(I)$, $i_2 = \min(I \setminus \{i_1\})$, ... It is easy to see that $(u \parallel s' \parallel \lozenge_{i=1}^k v_i) \neq \emptyset$, and so u is compatible with $M \oplus \{v_s\}$, the multiset consisting of M and v_s, and s' is a witness of compatibility.

An easy consequence of the stuttering property is the *copycat lemma* [9].

Lemma 1. (Copycat Lemma). *Let $u \in \Sigma_{\mathcal{D}}^\omega$ and let M be a multiset of words of $\Sigma_{\mathcal{C}}^\omega$. If u is compatible with M, then u is also compatible with $M \oplus \{v\}$ for every $v \in M$.*

2.3   The Model-Checking Problem for Linear-Time Properties

We consider the model checking problem for linear-time properties, that asks, given a network $\mathcal{N}$ and an ω-regular language L, decide whether $\mathcal{N} \parallel L$ is non-empty. We assume L is given as a Büchi automaton A over $\Sigma_{\mathcal{D}}$. Intuitively, A is a tester that observes the actions of the leader; we call this the *leader model checking problem*.

We study the complexity of leader model checking for networks in which the read-write ω-languages $\mathcal{D}$ and $\mathcal{C}$ of leader and contributor are generated by an abstract machine, like a finite-state machine (FSM) or a pushdown machine (PDM). (We give formal definitions later.) More precisely, given two classes of machines D, C, we study the model checking problem MC(D, C) defined as follows:

Given: machines $D \in$ D and $C \in$ C, and a Büchi automaton A
Decide: Is $\mathcal{N}_A = (L(A) \parallel L(D) \parallel \mathcal{S} \parallel \langle\!\langle_\infty L(C))$ non-empty?

In the next sections we prove that MC(FSM,FSM) and MC(PDM,FSM) are NP-complete, while MC(PDM,PDM) is in NEXPTIME and PSPACE-hard.

Example 2. Consider the instance of the model checking problem where $\mathcal{D}$ and $\mathcal{C}$ are as in Fig. 1, and A is a Büchi automaton recognizing all words over $\Sigma_{\mathcal{D}}$ containing infinitely many occurrences of $r_d(1)$. Since $\mathcal{D}$ is compatible with a multiset of words of the contributors, $\mathcal{N}_A$ is non-empty. In particular, $\mathcal{N}_A^{(4)} \neq \emptyset$.

Since $\Sigma_A = \Sigma_{\mathcal{D}}$, we can replace A and D by a machine $A \times D$ with a Büchi acceptance condition. The construction of $A \times D$ given A and D is standard. In what follows, we assume that D comes with a Büchi acceptance condition and forget about A.

There are two natural variants of the model checking problem, where $\Sigma_A = \Sigma_{\mathcal{C}}$, i.e., the alphabet of A contains the actions of all contributors, or $\Sigma_A = \Sigma_{\mathcal{D}} \cup \Sigma_{\mathcal{C}}$. In both these variants, the automaton A can be used to simulate atomic networks. Indeed, if the language of A consists of all sequences of the form $(w_d()r_c()w_c()r_d())^\omega$, and we design the contributors so that they alternate reads and writes, then the accepting executions are those in which the contributors read a value from the store and write a new value in an atomic step. So the complexity of the model-checking problem coincides with the complexity for atomic networks (undecidable for PDMs and EXPSPACE-complete for FSMs), and we do not study it further.

3   MC(FSM,FSM) is NP-Complete

We fix some notations. A finite-state machine (FSM) (Q, δ, q_0) over Σ consists of a finite set of states Q containing an initial state q_0 and a transition relation $\delta \subseteq Q \times \Sigma \times Q$. A word $v \in \Sigma^\omega$ is *accepted* by an FSM if there exists a sequence $q_1 q_2 \cdots$ of states such that $(q_i, (v)_{i+1}, q_{i+1}) \in \delta$ for all $i \geq 0$. We denote by $q_0 \xrightarrow{(v)_1} q_1 \xrightarrow{(v)_2} \cdots$ the *run* accepting v. A Büchi automaton (Q, δ, q_0, F) is an FSM (Q, δ, q_0) together with a set $F \subseteq Q$ of accepting states. An ω-word $v \in \Sigma^\omega$ is accepted by a Büchi automaton if there is a run $q_0 \xrightarrow{(v)_1} q_1 \xrightarrow{(v)_2} \cdots$ such that $q_j \in F$ for infinitely many positions j. The ω-language of a FSM or Büchi automaton A, denoted by $L(A)$, is the set of ω-words accepted by A.

In the rest of the section we show that MC(FSM,FSM) is NP-complete. Section 3.1 defines the infinite transition system associated to a (FSM,FSM)-network. Section 3.2 introduces an associated finite abstract transition system. Section 3.3 states and proves a lemma (Lemma 3) characterizing the cycles of the abstract transition system that, loosely speaking, can be concretized into infinite executions of the concrete transition system. Membership in NP is then proved using the lemma. NP-hardness follows from NP-hardness of reachability [9].

3.1   (FSM,FSM)-Networks: Populations and Transition System

We fix a Büchi automaton $D = (Q_D, \delta_D, q_{0D}, F)$ over $\Sigma_\mathcal{D}$ and an FSM $C = (Q_C, \delta_C, q_{0C})$ over $\Sigma_\mathcal{C}$. A *configuration* is a tuple $(q_D, g, \boldsymbol{p})$, where $q_D \in Q_D$, $g \in \mathcal{G} \cup \{\#\}$, and $\boldsymbol{p} \colon Q_C \to \mathbb{N}$ assigns to each state of C a natural number. Intuitively, q_D is the current state of D; g is a value or the special value $\#$, modelling that the store has not been initialized yet, and no process read before some process writes; finally, $\boldsymbol{p}(q)$ is the number of contributors currently at state $q \in Q_C$. We call $\boldsymbol{p}$ a *population* of Q_C, and write $|\boldsymbol{p}| = \sum_{q \in Q_C} \boldsymbol{p}(q)$ for the *size* of $\boldsymbol{p}$. Linear combinations of populations are defined componentwise: for every state $q \in Q_C$, we have $(k_1 \boldsymbol{p_1} + k_2 \boldsymbol{p_2})(q) := k_1 \boldsymbol{p_1}(q) + k_2 \boldsymbol{p_2}(q)$. Further, given $q \in Q_C$, we denote by $\boldsymbol{q}$ the population $\boldsymbol{q}(q') = 1$ if $q = q'$ and $\boldsymbol{q}(q') = 0$ otherwise, i.e., the population with one contributor in state q and no contributors elsewhere. A configuration is *accepting* if the state of D is accepting, that is whenever $q_D \in F$. Given a set of populations $\boldsymbol{P}$, we define $(q_D, g, \boldsymbol{P}) := \{(q_D, g, \boldsymbol{p}) \mid \boldsymbol{p} \in \boldsymbol{P}\}$.

The labelled transition system $TS = (X, T, X_0)$ associated to $\mathcal{N}_A$ is defined as follows:

- X is the set of all configurations, and $X_0 \subseteq X$ is the set of initial configurations, given by $(q_{0D}, \#, \boldsymbol{P_0})$, where $\boldsymbol{P_0} = \{k\boldsymbol{q_{0C}} \mid k \geq 1\}$;
- $T = T_D \cup T_C$, where
  - T_D is the set of triples $\big((q_D, g, \boldsymbol{p}), t, (q'_D, g', \boldsymbol{p}) \big)$ such that t is a transition of D, viz. $t \in \delta_D$, and one of the following conditions holds: (i) $t = (q_D, w_d(g'), q'_D)$; or (ii) $t = (q_D, r_d(g), q'_D)$, $g = g'$.
  - T_C is the set of triples $\big((q_D, g, \boldsymbol{p}), t, (q_D, g', \boldsymbol{p}') \big)$ such that $t \in \delta_C$, and one of the following conditions holds: (iii) $t = (q_C, w_c(g'), q'_C)$, $\boldsymbol{p} \geq \boldsymbol{q_C}$, and $\boldsymbol{p}' = \boldsymbol{p} - \boldsymbol{q_C} + \boldsymbol{q'_C}$; or (iv) $t = (q_C, r_c(g), q'_C)$, $\boldsymbol{p} \geq \boldsymbol{q_C}$, $g = g'$, and $\boldsymbol{p}' = \boldsymbol{p} - \boldsymbol{q_C} + \boldsymbol{q'_C}$.

Observe that $|\boldsymbol{p}| = |\boldsymbol{p}'|$, because the total number of contributors of a population remains constant. Given configurations c and c', we write $c \xrightarrow{t} c'$ if $(c, t, c') \in T$.

We introduce a notation important for Lemma 3 below. We define $\Delta(t) := \boldsymbol{p}' - \boldsymbol{p}$. Observe that $\Delta(t) = \boldsymbol{0}$ in cases (i) and (ii) above, and $\Delta(t) = -\boldsymbol{q_C} + \boldsymbol{q_C}'$ in cases (iii) and (iv). So $\Delta(t)$ depends only on the transition t, but not on $\boldsymbol{p}$.

3.2   The Abstract Transition System

We introduce an *abstraction function* α that assigns to a set $\boldsymbol{P}$ of populations the set of states of Q_C populated by $\boldsymbol{P}$. We also introduce a *concretization function* γ that assigns to a set $Q \subseteq Q_C$ the set of all populations $\boldsymbol{p}$ that only populate states of Q. Formally:

$$\alpha(\boldsymbol{P}) = \{q \in Q_C \mid \boldsymbol{p}(q) \geq 1 \text{ for some } \boldsymbol{p} \in \boldsymbol{P}\}$$
$$\gamma(Q) = \{\boldsymbol{p} \mid \boldsymbol{p}(q) = 0 \text{ for every } q \in Q_C \setminus Q\} \ .$$

It is easy to see that α and γ satisfy $\gamma(\alpha(\boldsymbol{P})) \supseteq \boldsymbol{P}$ and $\alpha(\gamma(Q)) = Q$, and so α and γ form a Galois connection (actually, a Galois insertion). An *abstract configuration* is a tuple (q_D, g, Q), where $q_D \in Q_D$, $g \in \mathcal{G} \cup \{\#\}$, and $Q \subseteq Q_C$. We extend α and γ to (abstract) configurations in the obvious way. An abstract configuration is *accepting* when the state of D is accepting, that is whenever $q_D \in F$.

Given $TS = (X, T, X_0)$, we define its *abstraction* $\alpha TS = (\alpha X, \alpha T, \alpha X_0)$ as follows:

- $\alpha X = Q_D \times (\mathcal{G} \cup \{\#\}) \times 2^{Q_C}$ is the set of all abstract configurations.
- $\alpha X_0 = (q_{0D}, \#, \alpha(\boldsymbol{P_0})) = (q_{0D}, \#, \{q_{0C}\})$ is the initial configuration.
- $(\ (q_D, g, Q),\ t,\ (q'_D, g', Q')\ ) \in \alpha T$ iff there is $\boldsymbol{p} \in \gamma(Q)$ and $\boldsymbol{p}'$ such that $(q_D, g, \boldsymbol{p}) \xrightarrow{t} (q'_D, g', \boldsymbol{p}')$ and $Q' = \alpha(\{\boldsymbol{p}' \mid \exists \boldsymbol{p} \in \gamma(Q) \colon (q_D, g, \boldsymbol{p}) \xrightarrow{t} (q'_D, g', \boldsymbol{p}')\})$.

Observe that the number of abstract configurations is bounded by $K = |Q_D| \cdot |\mathcal{G}| + 1 \cdot 2^{|Q_C|}$. Let us point out that our abstract transition system resembles but is different from that of Pnueli et al. [14]. We write $a \xrightarrow{t}_\alpha a'$ if $(a, t, a') \in \alpha T$. The abstraction satisfies the following properties:

(A) For each ω-path $c_0 \xrightarrow{t_1} c_1 \xrightarrow{t_2} c_2 \cdots$ of TS, there exists an ω-path $a_0 \xrightarrow{t_1}_\alpha a_1 \xrightarrow{t_2}_\alpha a_2 \cdots$ in αTS such that $c_i \in \gamma(a_i)$ for all $i \geq 0$.

(B) If $(q_D, g, Q) \xrightarrow{t}_\alpha (q'_D, g', Q')$, then $Q \subseteq Q'$.

To prove this claim, consider two cases:

- $t \in \delta_D$. Then $(q_D, g, \boldsymbol{p}) \xrightarrow{t} (q'_D, g', \boldsymbol{p})$ for every population $\boldsymbol{p}$ (because only the leader moves). So $(q_D, g, Q) \xrightarrow{t}_\alpha (q'_D, g', Q)$.
- $t \in \delta_C$. Consider the population $\boldsymbol{p} = 2 \sum_{q \in Q} \boldsymbol{q} \in \gamma(Q)$. Then $(q_D, g, \boldsymbol{p}) \xrightarrow{t} (q_D, g', \boldsymbol{p}')$, where $\boldsymbol{p}' = \boldsymbol{p} - \boldsymbol{q}_C + \boldsymbol{q}_C'$. But then $\boldsymbol{p}' \geq \sum_{q \in Q} \boldsymbol{q}$, and so $\alpha(\{\boldsymbol{p}'\}) \supseteq Q$, which implies $(q_D, g, Q) \xrightarrow{t}_\alpha (q_D, g', Q')$ for some $Q' \supseteq Q$.

So in every ω-path $a_0 \xrightarrow{t_1}_\alpha a_1 \xrightarrow{t_2}_\alpha a_2 \cdots$ of αTS, where $a_i = (q_{Di}, g_i, Q_i)$, there is an index i at which the Q_i stabilize, that is, $Q_i = Q_{i+k}$ holds for every $k \geq 0$. However, the converse of (A) does not hold: given a path $a_0 \xrightarrow{t_1}_\alpha a_1 \xrightarrow{t_2}_\alpha a_2 \cdots$ of αTS, there may be no path $c_0 \xrightarrow{t_1} c_1 \xrightarrow{t_2} c_2 \cdots$ in TS such that $c_i \in \gamma(a_i)$ for every $i \geq 0$. Consider a contributor machine C with two states q_0, q_1 and one single transition $t = (q_0, w_c(1), q_1)$. Then αTS contains the infinite path (omitting the state of the leader, which plays no role):

$$(\#, \{q_0\}) \xrightarrow{t}_\alpha (1, \{q_0, q_1\}) \xrightarrow{t}_\alpha (1, \{q_0, q_1\}) \xrightarrow{t}_\alpha (1, \{q_0, q_1\}) \cdots$$

However, the transitions of TS are of the form $(1, k_0 \boldsymbol{q_0} + k_1 \boldsymbol{q_1}) \xrightarrow{t} (1, (k_0 - 1)\boldsymbol{q_0} + (k_1 + 1)\boldsymbol{q_1})$, and so TS has no infinite paths.

3.3   Realizable Cycles of the Abstract Transition System

We show that the existence of an infinite accepting path in TS reduces to the existence of a certain lasso path in αTS. A lasso path consists of a stem and a cycle. Lemma 2 shows how every abstract finite path (like the stem) has a counterpart in TS. Lemma 3 characterizes precisely those cycles in αTS which have an infinite path counterpart in TS.

Lemma 2. *Let* (q_D, g, Q) *be an abstract configuration of* αTS *reachable from* $(q_{0D}, \#, \alpha(\boldsymbol{P_0}))$ *(*$= \alpha X_0$*). For every* $\boldsymbol{p} \in \gamma(Q)$, *there exists* $\hat{\boldsymbol{p}}$ *such that* $(q_D, g, \hat{\boldsymbol{p}})$ *is reachable from* $(q_{0D}, \#, \boldsymbol{P_0})$ *and* $\hat{\boldsymbol{p}} \geq \boldsymbol{p}$.

Lemma 2 does not hold for atomic networks. Indeed, consider a contributor with transitions $q_0 \xrightarrow{w_c(1)} q_1 \xrightarrow{r_c(1):w_c(2)} q_2 \xrightarrow{r_c(2):w_c(3)} q_3$, where $r_c(i) : w_c(j)$ denotes that the read and the write happen in one single atomic step. Then we have (omitting the state of the leader, which does not play any rôle here):

$$(\#, \{q_0\}) \xrightarrow{w_c(1)}_\alpha (1, \{q_0, q_1\}) \xrightarrow{r_c(1):w_c(2)}_\alpha (2, \{q_0, q_1, q_2\}) \xrightarrow{r_c(2):w_c(3)}_\alpha (3, \{q_0, \ldots, q_3\}) .$$

Let $\boldsymbol{p}$ be the population putting one contributor in each of $q_0, \ldots, q_3$. This population belongs to $\gamma(\{q_0, \ldots, q_3\})$ but no configuration $(3, \hat{\boldsymbol{p}})$ with $\hat{\boldsymbol{p}} > \boldsymbol{p}$ is reachable from any population that only puts contributors in q_0, no matter how many. Indeed, after the first contributor moves to q_2, no further contributor can follow, and so we cannot have contributors simultaneously in both q_2 and q_3. On the contrary, in non-atomic networks the Copycat Lemma states that what the move by one contributor can always be replicated by arbitrarily many.

   We proceed to characterized the cycles of the abstract transition system that can be "concretized". A *cycle* of αTS is a path $a_0 \xrightarrow{t_1}_\alpha a_1 \xrightarrow{t_2}_\alpha a_2 \cdots \xrightarrow{t_{n-1}}_\alpha a_n$ such that $a_n = a_0$. A cycle is *realizable* if there is an infinite path $c_0 \xrightarrow{t'_1} c_1 \xrightarrow{t'_2} c_2 \cdots$ of TS such that $c_k \in \gamma(a_{(k \bmod n)})$ and $t'_{k+1} = t_{(k+1 \bmod n)}$ for every $k \geq 0$.

Lemma 3. *A cycle* $a_0 \xrightarrow{t_1}_\alpha a_1 \xrightarrow{t_2}_\alpha a_2 \cdots \xrightarrow{t_n}_\alpha a_n$ *of* αTS *is realizable iff* $\sum_{i=1}^n \Delta(t_i) = \boldsymbol{0}$.

Theorem 1. *MC(FSM,FSM) is NP-complete.*

Proof. NP-hardness follows from the NP-hardness of reachability [9]. We show membership in NP with the following high-level nondeterministic algorithm whose correctness relies on Lemmas 2 and 3:

1. Guess a sequence $Q_1, \ldots, Q_\ell$ of subsets of Q_C such that $Q_i \subsetneq Q_{i+1}$ for all i, $0 < i < \ell$. Note that $\ell \leq |Q_C|$.
2. Compute the set $\mathcal{Q} = Q_D \times (\mathcal{G} \cup \{\#\}) \times \{\{q_{0C}\}, Q_1, \ldots, Q_\ell\}$ of abstract configurations and the set $\mathcal{T}$ of abstract transitions between configurations of $\mathcal{Q}$.
3. Guess an accepting abstract configuration $a \in \mathcal{Q}$, that is, an $a = (q_D, g, Q)$ such that q_D is accepting in D.
4. Check that a is reachable from the initial abstract configuration $(q_{0D}, \#, \{q_{0C}\})$ by means of abstract transitions of $\mathcal{T}$.
5. Check that the transition system with $\mathcal{Q}$ and $\mathcal{T}$ as states and transitions contains a cycle $a_0 \xrightarrow{t_1}_\alpha a_1 \cdots a_{n-1} \xrightarrow{t_n}_\alpha a_n$ such that $n \geq 1$, $a_0 = a_n = a$ and $\sum_{i=1}^{n} \Delta(t_i) = \mathbf{0}$.

We show that the algorithm runs in polynomial time. First, because the sequence guessed is no longer than $|Q_C|$, the guess can be done in polynomial time. Next, we give a polynomial algorithm for step (5):

– Compute an FSA[1] $A_a^\circlozenge$ over the alphabet $\delta_D \cup \delta_C$ with $\mathcal{Q}$ as set of states, $\mathcal{T}$ as set of transitions, a as initial state, and $\{a\}$ as set of final states.
– Use the polynomial construction of Seidl et al. [15] to compute an (existential) Presburger formula Ω for the Parikh image of $L(A_a^\circlozenge)$. The free variables of Ω are in one-to-one correspondence with the transitions of $\delta_D \cup \delta_C$. Denote by x_t the variable corresponding to transition $t \in \delta_D \cup \delta_C$.
– Compute the formula

$$\Omega' = \Omega \wedge \bigwedge_{q_c \in Q_c} \left(\sum_{tgt(t)=q_c} x_t = \sum_{src(t)=q_c} x_t \right) \wedge \sum_{t \in \delta_D \cup \delta_C} x_t > 0$$

where tgt and src returns the target and source states of the transition passed in argument. Ω' adds to Ω the realizability condition of Lemma 3.
– Check satisfiability of Ω'. This step requires nondterministic polynomial time because satisfiability of an existential Presburger formula is in NP [11].   □

4   MC(PDM,FSM) is NP-Complete

A pushdown system (PDM) $P = (Q, \Gamma, \delta, q_0)$ over Σ consists of a finite set Q of states including the initial state q_0, a *stack alphabet* Γ including the bottom stack symbol $\bot$, and a set of *rules* $\delta \subseteq Q \times \Sigma \times \Gamma \times Q \times (\Gamma \setminus \{\bot\} \cup \{\mathsf{pop}\})$ which either push or pop as explained below. A *PDM-configuration* qw consists of a state $q \in Q$ and a word $w \in \Gamma^*$ (denoting the stack content). For $q, q' \in Q$, $a \in \Sigma$, $\gamma, \gamma' \in \Gamma$, $w, w' \in \Gamma^*$, we say a PDM-configuration $q'w$ (resp. $q'\gamma'\gamma w$) a-follows $q\gamma w$ if $(q, a, \gamma, q', \mathsf{pop}) \in \delta$, (resp. $(q, a, \gamma, q', \gamma') \in \delta$); we write $qw \xrightarrow{a} q'w'$ if $q'w'$ a-follows qw, and call it a *transition*. A *run* $c_0 \xrightarrow{(v)_1} c_1 \xrightarrow{(v)_2} \cdots$ on a word $v \in \Sigma^\omega$ is a sequence of PDM-configurations such that $c_0 = q_0\bot$ and

---

[1] A finite-state automaton (FSA) is an FSM which decides languages of finite words. Therefore an FSA is an FSM with a set F of accepting states.

$c_i \xrightarrow{(v)_{i+1}} c_{i+1}$ for all $i \geq 0$. We write $c \xrightarrow{*} c'$ if there is a run from c to c'. The language $L(P)$ of P is the set of all words $v \in \Sigma^\omega$ such that P has a run on v.

A Büchi PDM is a PDM with a set $F \subseteq Q$ of accepting states. A word is accepted by a Büchi PDM if there is a run on the word for which some state in F occurs infinitely often along the PDM-configurations. The following lemma characterizes accepting runs.

Lemma 4. *[7] Let c be a configuration. There is an accepting run starting from c if there are states $q \in Q$, $q_f \in F$, a stack symbol $\gamma \in \Gamma$ such that $c \xrightarrow{*} q\gamma w$ for some $w \in \Gamma^*$ and $q\gamma \xrightarrow{*} q_f u \xrightarrow{*} q\gamma w'$ for some $u, w' \in \Gamma^*$.*

We now show MC(PDM, FSM) is decidable, generalizing the proof from Sect. 3. Fix a Büchi PDM $P = (Q_D, \Gamma_D, \delta_D, q_{0D}, F)$, and a FSM $C = (Q_C, \delta_C, q_{0C})$. A *configuration* is a tuple $(q_D, w, g, \boldsymbol{p})$, where $q_D \in Q_D$, $w \in \Gamma_D^*$ is the stack content, $g \in \mathcal{G} \cup \{\#\}$, and $\boldsymbol{p}$ is a population. Intuitively, $q_D w$ is the PDM-configuration of the leader. We extend the definitions from Sect. 3 like accepting configuration in the obvious way.

We define a labeled transition system $TS = (X, T, X_0)$, where X is the set of configurations including the set $X_0 = (q_{0D}, \bot, \#, \boldsymbol{P_0})$ of initial configurations, and the transition relation $T = T_D \cup T_C$, where T_C is as before and T_D is the set of triples $\left((q_D, w, g, \boldsymbol{p}), t, (q'_D, w', g', \boldsymbol{p})\right)$ such that t is a transition (not a rule) of D, and one of the following conditions holds: (i) $t = (q_D w \xrightarrow{w_d(g')} q'_D w')$; or (ii) $t = (q_D w \xrightarrow{r_d(g)} q'_D w')$ and $g = g'$. We define the abstraction αTS of TS as the obvious generalization of the abstraction in Sect. 3. An accepting path of the (abstract) transition system is an infinite path with infinitely many accepting (abstract) configurations. As for MC(FSM, FSM), not every accepting path of the abstract admits a concretization, but we find a realizability condition in terms of linear constraints. Here we use again the polynomial construction of Seidl *et al.* [15] mentioned in the proof of Theorem 1, this time to compute an (existential) Presburger formula for the Parikh image of a pushdown automaton.

Theorem 2. *MC(PDM,FSM) is NP-complete.*

5 MC(PDM,PDM) is in NEXPTIME

We show how to reduce MC(PDM,PDM) to MC(PDM,FSM). We first introduce the notion of *effective stack height* of a PDM-configuration in a run of a PDM, and define, given a PDM C, an FSM C_k that simulates all the runs of C of effective stack height k. Then we show that, for $k \in O(n^3)$, where n is the size of C, the language $(L(D) \parallel \mathcal{S} \parallel \lozenge_\infty L(C))$ is empty iff $(L(D) \parallel \mathcal{S} \parallel \lozenge_\infty L(C_k))$ is empty.

5.1 A FSM for Runs of Bounded Effective Stack Height

Consider a run of a PDM that repeatedly pushes symbol on the stack. The stack height of the configurations[2] is unbounded, but, intuitively, the PDM only uses

---

[2] For readability, we write "configuration" for "PDM-configuration.".

the topmost stack symbol during the run. To account for this we define the notion of effective stack height.

Definition 3. Let $\rho = c_0 \xrightarrow{(v)_1} c_1 \xrightarrow{(v)_2} \cdots$ be an infinite run of a PDM on ω-word v, where $c_i = q_i w_i$. The *dark suffix* of c_i in ρ, denoted by $ds(w_i)$, is the longest suffix of w_i that is also a proper suffix of w_{i+k} for every $k \geq 0$. The *active prefix* $ap(w_i)$ of w_i is the prefix satisfying $w_i = ap(w_i) \cdot ds(w_i)$. The *effective stack height* of c_i in ρ is $|ap(w_i)|$. We say that ρ is *effectively k-bounded* (or simply k-bounded for the sake of readability) if every configuration of ρ has an effective stack height of at most k. Further, we say that ρ is *bounded* if it is k-bounded for some $k \in \mathbb{N}$. Finally, an ω-word of the PDM is *k-bounded*, respectively bounded, if it is the word generated by some k-bounded, respectively bounded, run (other runs for the same word may not be bounded).

Intuitively, the effective stack height measures the actual memory required by the PDM to perform its run. For example, repeatedly pushing symbols on the stack produces a run with effective stack height 1. Given a position in the run, the elements of the stack that are never popped are those in the longest common suffix of all subsequent stacks. The first element of that suffix may be read, therefore only the longest *proper* suffix is effectively useless, so no configuration along an infinite run has effective stack height 0.

Proposition 1. *Every infinite run of a PDM contains infinitely many positions at which the effective stack height is 1.*

Proof. Let $p_0 w_0 \to p_1 w_1 \to p_2 w_2 \to \cdots$ be any infinite run. Notice that $|w_i| \geq 1$ for every $i \geq 0$, because otherwise the run would not be infinite. Let X be the set of positions of the run defined as: $i \in X$ iff $|w_i| \leq |w_j|$ for every $j > i$. Observe that X is infinite, because the first configuration of minimal stack height, say $p_k w_k$ belongs to it, and so does the first configuration of minimal stack height of the suffix $p_{k+1} w_{k+1} \to \cdots$, etc. By construction, the configuration at every position in X has effective stack height 1. $\qquad\square$

In a k-bounded run, whenever the stack height exceeds k, the $k + 1$-th stack symbol will never become the top symbol again, and so it becomes useless. So, we can construct a finite-state machine P_k recognizing the words of $L(P)$ accepted by k-bounded runs.

Definition 4. Given a PDM $P = (Q, \Gamma, \delta, q_0)$, the FSM $P_k = (Q_k, \delta_k, q_{0k})$, called the k-restriction of Ps, is defined as follows: (a) $Q_k = Q \times \bigcup_{i=1}^{k} \Gamma^i$ (a state of P_k consists of a state of P and a stack content no longer than k); (b) $q_{0k} = (q_0, \perp)$; (c) δ_k contains a transition $(q, (w)_{1..k}) \xrightarrow{a} (q', (w')_{1..k})$ iff $qw \xrightarrow{a} q'w'$ is a transition (not a rule) of P.

Theorem 3. *Given a PDM P, w admits a k-bounded run in P iff $w \in L(P_k)$.*

5.2   The Reduction Theorem

We fix a Büchi PDM D and a PDM C. By Theorem 3, in order to reduce MC(PDM,PDM) to MC(PDM,FSM) it suffices to prove the following Reduction Theorem:

Theorem 4. (Reduction Theorem). *Let* $N = 2|Q_C|^2|\Gamma_C| + 1$, *where* Q_C *and* Γ_C *are the states and stack alphabet of* C, *respectively. Let* C_N *be the* N-*restriction of* C. *We have:*

$$\big(L(D) \parallel S \parallel \lozenge_\infty L(C)\big) \neq \emptyset \quad \textit{iff} \quad \big(L(D) \parallel S \parallel \lozenge_\infty L(C_N)\big) \neq \emptyset . \qquad (\dagger)$$

There are PDMs D, C *for which* ($\dagger$) *holds only for* $N \in \Omega(|Q_C|^2|\Gamma_C|)$.

Theorems 4 and 2 provide an upper bound for MC(PDM,PDM). PSPACE-hardness of the reachability problem [9] gives a lower bound.

Theorem 5. *MC(PDM,PDM) is in NEXPTIME and PSPACE-hard. If the contributor is a one counter machine (with zero-test), it is NP-complete.*

The proof of Theorem 4 is very involved. Given a run of D compatible with a finite multiset of runs of C, we construct another run of D compatible with a finite multiset of N-bounded runs of C_N. (Here we extend compatibility to runs: runs are compatible if the words they accept are compatible.)

The proof starts with the Distributing lemma, which, loosely speaking, shows how to replace a run of C by a multiset of "smaller" runs of C without the leader "noticing". After this preliminary result, the first key proof element is the Boundedness Lemma. Let σ be an infinite run of D compatible with a finite multiset R of runs of C. The Boundedness Lemma states that, for any number Z, the first Z steps of σ are compatible with a (possibly larger) multiset R_Z of runs of C_N. Since the size of R_Z may grow with Z, this lemma does not yet prove Theorem 4: it only shows that σ is compatible with an *infinite* multiset of runs of C_N. This obstacle is overcome in the final step of the proof. We show that, for a sufficiently large Z, there are indices $i < j$ such that, not σ itself, but the run $(\sigma)_{1..i}\big((\sigma)_{i+1..j}\big)^\omega$ for adequate i and j is compatible with a *finite* multiset of runs of C_N. Loosely speaking, this requires to prove not only that the leader can repeat $(\sigma)_{i+1..j}$ infinitely often, but also that the runs executed by the instances of C_N while the leader executes $(\sigma)_{i+1..j}$ can be repeated infinitely often.

The Distributing Lemma. Let $\rho = c_0 \xrightarrow{a_1} c_1 \xrightarrow{a_2} c_2 \xrightarrow{a_3} \cdots$ be a (finite or infinite) run of C. Let r_i be the PDM-rule of C generating the transition $c_{i-1} \xrightarrow{a_i} c_i$. Then ρ is completely determined by c_0 and the sequence $r_1 r_2 r_3 \ldots$ Since c_0 is also fixed (for fixed C), in the rest of the paper we also sometimes write $\rho = r_1 r_2 r_3 \ldots$ This notation allows us to speak of $\mathrm{dom}(\rho)$, $(\rho)_k$, $(\rho)_{i..j}$ and $(\rho)_{i..\infty}$.

We say that ρ *distributes* to a multiset R of runs of C if there exists an *embedding function* ψ that assigns to each run $\rho' \in R$ and to each position $i \in \mathrm{dom}(\rho')$ a position $\psi(\rho', i) \in \mathrm{dom}(\rho)$, and satisfies the following properties:

- $(\rho')_i = (\rho)_{\psi(\rho',i)}$. (A rule occurrence in ρ' is matched to another occurrence of the same rule in ρ.)
- ψ is surjective. (For every position $k \in \text{dom}(\rho)$ there is at least one $\rho' \in R$ and a position $i \in \text{dom}(\rho')$ such that $\psi(\rho',i) = k$, or, informally, R "covers" ρ.)
- If $i < j$, then $\psi(\rho',i) < \psi(\rho',j)$. (So $\psi(\rho',1)\psi(\rho',2) \cdots$ is a scattered subword of ρ.)

Example 3. Let ρ be a run of a PDM P. Below are two distributions R and S of $\rho = r_a r_b r_b r_c r_c r_c$. On the left we have $R = \{\rho'_1, \rho'_2, \rho'_3\}$, and its embedding function ψ; on the right $S = \{\sigma'_1, \sigma'_2, \sigma'_3\}$, and its function ψ'.

ψ	1 2 3		1 2 3 4 5 6
ρ'_1	1 6	$\rho = r_a\ r_b\ r_b\ r_c\ r_c\ r_c$	
ρ'_2	1 2 5	$\rho'_1 = r_a$	$\qquad\quad r_c$
ρ'_3	1 3 4	$\rho'_2 = r_a\ r_b$	$\qquad r_c$
		$\rho'_3 = r_a$	$\quad r_b\ r_c$

ψ'	1 2 3 4		1 2 3 4 5 6
σ'_1	1 4	$\rho = r_a\ r_b\ r_b\ r_c\ r_c\ r_c$	
σ'_2	1 2 4 5	$\sigma'_1 = r_a$	$\qquad\quad r_c$
σ'_3	1 3 5 6	$\sigma'_2 = r_a\ r_b$	$\qquad r_c\ r_c$
		$\sigma'_3 = r_a$	$\quad r_b\qquad r_c\ r_c$

Lemma 5. (Distributing Lemma). *Let $u \in L(D)$, and let M be a multiset of words of $L(C)$ compatible with u. Let $v \in M$ and let ρ an accepting run of v in C that distributes to a multiset R of runs of C, and let M_R the corresponding multiset of words. Then $M \ominus \{v\} \oplus M_R$ is also compatible with u.*

The Boundedness Lemma. We are interested in distributing a multiset of runs of C into another multiset with, loosely speaking, "better" effective stack height.

Fix a run ρ of C and a distribution R of ρ with embedding function ψ. In Example 3, $(\rho)_{1..4}$ is distributed into $(\rho'_1)_{1..1}$, $(\rho'_2)_{1..2}$ and $(\rho'_3)_{1..3}$. Assume ρ is executed by one contributor. We can replace it by 3 contributors executing $\rho'_1, \rho'_2, \rho'_3$, without the rest of the network noticing any difference. Indeed, the three processes can execute r_a immediately after each other, which for the rest of the network is equivalent to the old contributor executing one r_a. Then we replace the execution of $(\rho)_{2..4}$ by $(\rho'_2)_2(\rho'_3)_{2..3}$.

We introduce some definitions allowing us to formally describe such facts. Given $k \in \text{dom}(\rho)$, we denote by $c(\rho, k)$ the configuration reached by ρ after k steps. We naturally extend this notation to define $c(\rho, 0)$ as the initial configuration. We denote by $last_\psi(\rho', i)$ the largest position $k \in \text{dom}(\rho')$ such that $\psi(\rho', k) \leq i$ (similarly if none exists, we fix $last_\psi(\rho', i) = 0$). Further, we denote by $c_\psi(\rho', k)$ the configuration reached by ρ' after k steps of ρ, that is, the configuration reached by ρ' after the execution of $last_\psi(\rho', k)$ transitions; formally, $c_\psi(\rho', k) = c(\rho', last_\psi(\rho', k))$.

Example 4. Let ρ, R, and ψ as in Example 3. Assuming that the PDM P has one single state p, stack symbols $\{\bot, \alpha\}$ such that the three rules r_a, r_b and r_c are given by $r_a \colon p\bot \to p\alpha\bot$, $r_b \colon p\alpha \to p\alpha\alpha$, and $r_c \colon p\alpha \to p$, then we have $c(\rho, 5) = p\alpha\bot$. Further, $last_\psi(\rho'_1, 5) = 1$, $last_\psi(\rho'_2, 5) = 3$, and $last_\psi(\rho'_3, 5) = 3$. Finally, $c_\psi(\rho'_1, 5) = p\alpha\bot$, $c_\psi(\rho'_2, 5) = p\alpha\bot$, and $c_\psi(\rho'_3, 5) = p\alpha\bot$.

Given $Z \in \text{dom}(\rho)$ and $K \in \mathbb{N}$, we say that a distribution R of ρ is (Z, K)-bounded if for every $\rho' \in R$ and for every $i \leq Z$, the effective stack height of

$c_\psi(\rho', i)$ is bounded by K. Further, we say that R is synchronized if for every configuration $c(\rho, i)$ with effective stack height 1 and for every $\rho' \in R$, $c_\psi(\rho', i) = c(\rho, i)$ (same control state and same stack content), and also has effective stack height 1.[3] The Boundedness Lemma states that there is a constant N, depending only on C, such that for every run ρ of C and for every $Z \in \mathrm{dom}(\rho)$ there is a (Z, N)-bounded and synchronized distribution R_Z of ρ. The key of the proof is the following lemma.

Lemma 6. *Let* $N = 2|Q_C|^2|\Gamma_C| + 1$. *Let* ρ *be a run of* C *and* $Z \in \mathrm{dom}(\rho)$ *be the first position of* ρ *such that* $c(\rho, Z)$ *is not* N-*bounded. Then there is a* (Z, N)-*bounded and synchronized distribution of* ρ.

Proof sketch. We construct a (Z, N)-bounded and synchronized distribution $\{\rho_a, \rho_b\}$ of ρ. Let $\alpha_{N+1}\alpha_N \cdots \alpha_1 w_0$ be the stack content of $c(\rho, Z)$. Define $\{\overrightarrow{p}_1, \overleftarrow{p}_1, \overrightarrow{p}_2, \overleftarrow{p}_2, \ldots, \overrightarrow{p}_N, \overleftarrow{p}_N\} \subseteq \mathrm{dom}(\rho)$ such that for each i, $1 \le i \le N$ we have $c(\rho, \overrightarrow{p}_i)$ and $c(\rho, \overleftarrow{p}_i)$ are the configurations immediately after the symbol α_i in $c(\rho, Z)$ is pushed, respectively popped and such that the stack content of each configuration between $\overrightarrow{p}_i$ (included) and $\overleftarrow{p}_i$ (excluded) equals $w_p \alpha_i \alpha_{i-1} \cdots \alpha_1 w_0$ for some $w_p \in \Gamma_C^*$. We get $c(\rho, \overrightarrow{p}_i) = q_i \alpha_i \alpha_{i-1} \ldots \alpha_0 w_0$ and $c(\rho, \overleftarrow{p}_i) = q_i' \alpha_{i-1} \ldots \alpha_0 w_0$ for some $q_i, q_i' \in Q_C$. Observe that the following holds: $\overrightarrow{p}_1 < \cdots < \overrightarrow{p}_{N-1} < \overrightarrow{p}_N < Z < \overleftarrow{p}_N < \overleftarrow{p}_{N-1} < \cdots < \overleftarrow{p}_1$.

Since $N = 2|Q_C|^2|\Gamma_C| + 1$, by the pigeonhole principle we find q, α, q' and three indices $1 \le j_1 < j_2 < j_3 \le N$ such that by letting $w_1 = \alpha_{j_1 - 1} \cdots \alpha_1$, $w_2 = \alpha_{j_2 - 1} \cdots \alpha_{j_1}$ and $w_3 = \alpha_{j_3 - 1} \cdots \alpha_{j_2}$, we have:

$$\rho = (\rho)_{1..\overrightarrow{p}_{j_1}} \ [q\alpha w_1] \ (\rho)_{\overrightarrow{p}_{j_1+1}..\overrightarrow{p}_{j_2}} \ [q\alpha w_2 w_1] \ (\rho)_{\overrightarrow{p}_{j_2+1}..\overrightarrow{p}_{j_3}} \ [q\alpha w_3 w_2 w_1]$$

$$(\rho)_{\overleftarrow{p}_{j_3+1}..\overleftarrow{p}_{j_3}} \ [q'w_3 w_2 w_1] \ (\rho)_{\overleftarrow{p}_{j_3+1}..\overleftarrow{p}_{j_2}} \ [q'w_2 w_1] \ (\rho)_{\overleftarrow{p}_{j_2+1}..\overleftarrow{p}_{j_1}} \ [q'w_1] \ (\rho)_{\overleftarrow{p}_{j_1+1}..\infty} \ .$$

Here, the notation indicates that we reach configuration $[q\alpha w_1]$ after $(\rho)_{1..\overrightarrow{p}_{j_1}}$, the configuration $[q\alpha w_2 w_1]$ after $(\rho_{1..\overrightarrow{p}_{j_2}}$, etc.

Now define ρ_a from ρ by simultaneously deleting $(\rho)_{\overrightarrow{p}_{j_1+1}..\overrightarrow{p}_{j_2}}$ and $(\rho)_{\overleftarrow{p}_{j_2+1}..\overleftarrow{p}_{j_1}}$. We similarly define ρ_b by deleting $(\rho)_{\overrightarrow{p}_{j_2+1}..\overrightarrow{p}_{j_3}}$ and $(\rho)_{\overleftarrow{p}_{j_3+1}..\overleftarrow{p}_{j_2}}$.

The following shows that ρ_a defines a legal run since it is given by

$$(\rho)_{1..\overrightarrow{p}_{j_1}} \ [q\alpha w_1] \ (\rho)_{\overrightarrow{p}_{j_2+1}..\overrightarrow{p}_{j_3}} \ [q\alpha w_3 w_1] (\rho)_{\overleftarrow{p}_{j_3+1}..\overleftarrow{p}_{j_3}} \ [q'w_3 w_1] \ (\rho)_{\overleftarrow{p}_{j_3+1}..\overleftarrow{p}_{j_2}} \ [q'w_1]$$

$$(\rho)_{\overleftarrow{p}_{j_1+1}..\infty} \ .$$

A similar reasoning holds for ρ_b. Finally, one can show that $\{\rho_a, \rho_b\}$ is a (Z, N)-bounded and synchronized distribution of ρ.

Lemma 7. (Boundedness Lemma). *Let* $N = 2|Q_C|^2|\Gamma_C| + 1$, *and let* ρ *be a run of* C. *For every* $Z \in \mathrm{dom}(\rho)$ *there is an* (Z, N)-*bounded and synchronized distribution* R_Z *of* ρ.

---

[3] Notice that the effective stack height of a configuration depends on the run it belongs to, and so $c(\rho, i) = c_\psi(\rho', i)$ does not necessarily imply that they have the same effective stack height.

The proof is by induction on Z. The distribution ψ_{Z+1}, R_{Z+1} is obtained from ψ_Z, R_Z by distributing each run ρ' of R_Z to a $(\psi_Z(\rho', Z) + 1, N)$-bounded run (applying Lemma 6).

Proof Sketch of Theorem 4. Given a run σ of D compatible with a finite multiset M of runs of C, we construct another run τ of D, and a multiset R of N-bounded runs of C_N such that τ and R are compatible as well. We consider only the special case in which M has one single element ρ (and one single copy of it). Since σ is compatible with ρ, we fix a witness $\pi \in S$ such that $\pi \in \sigma \between \rho$. We construct a "lasso run" out of π of the form $\lambda_1[\lambda_2]^\omega$. It suffices to find two positions in π where the content of the store is the same, the corresponding configurations of the leader are the same, and similarly for each contributor; the fragment between these two positions can be repeated (is "pumpable").

Given a position i of π, let i_ρ and i_σ denote the corresponding positions in ρ and σ.[4] Further, for every Z let R_Z be a (Z, N)-bounded and synchronized distribution of ρ with embedding function ψ (which exists by the Boundedness Lemma). Let $R_Z(i_\rho) = \{c_\psi(\eta, i_\rho) \mid \eta \in R_Z\}$ denote the multiset of configurations reached by the runs of R_Z after i steps of π. Using Proposition 1 and that (i)the store has a finite number of values, (ii) R_Z is (Z, N)-bounded, and (iii)there are only finitely many active prefixes of length at most N, we can apply the pigeonhole principle to find a sufficiently large number Z and three positions $i < j < k \le Z$ in π satisfying the following properties:

(1) The contents of the store at positions i and k of π coincide.
(2) The configurations $c(\sigma, i_\sigma)$ and $c(\sigma, k_\sigma)$ of the leader have effective stack height 1, same topmost stack symbol and same control state. Further, σ enters and leaves some accepting state between i_σ and k_σ.
(3) The configuration $c(\rho, j_\rho)$ has effective stack height 1.
(4) For every configuration of $R_Z(i_\rho)$ there is a configuration of $R_Z(k_\rho)$ with the same control state and active prefix, and vice versa.

Condition (4) means that, after removing the dark suffixes, $R_Z(i_\rho)$ and $R_Z(k_\rho)$ contain the same pruned configurations, although possibly a different number of times (same set, different multisets). If we obtain the same multiset, then the fragment of π between positions i and k is pumpable by (1) and (2), and we are done. Otherwise, we use (3) and the fact that R_Z is synchronized (which had not been used so far) to obtain a new distribution in which the multisets coincide. This is achieved by adding new runs to R_Z.

References

1. Abdulla, P.A., Bertrand, N., Rabinovich, A., Schnoebelen, P.: Verification of probabilistic systems with faulty communication. Inf. Comput. **202**(2), 105–228 (2005)
2. Abdulla, P.A., Cerans, K., Jonsson, B., Tsay, Y.K.: General decidability theorems for infinite-state systems. In: LICS'1996. pp. 313–321. IEEE Computer Society (1996)

---

[4] Position p in π defines position p_σ in σ such that $(\sigma)_{1..p_\sigma} = Proj_{\Sigma_D}((\pi)_{1..p})$, similarly p_ρ is defined as satisfying $(\rho)_{1..p_\rho} = Proj_{\Sigma_C}((\pi)_{1..p})$.

3. Abdulla, P.A., Jonsson, B.: Verifying programs with unreliable channels. Inf. Comput. **127**(2), 91–101 (1996)
4. Aminof, B., Kotek, T., Rubin, S., Spegni, F., Veith, H.: Parameterized model checking of rendezvous systems. In: Baldan, P., Gorla, D. (eds.) CONCUR 2014. LNCS, vol. 8704, pp. 109–124. Springer, Heidelberg (2014)
5. Angluin, D., Aspnes, J., Eisenstat, D., Ruppert, E.: The computational power of population protocols. Distrib. Comput. **20**(4), 279–304 (2007)
6. Apt, K.R., Kozen, D.C.: Limits for automatic verification of finite-state concurrent systems. Inf. Process. Lett. **22**(6), 307–309 (1986)
7. Bouajjani, A., Esparza, J., Maler, O.: Reachability analysis of pushdown automata: application to model-checking. In: CONCUR'1997: Proceedings of 8th International Conference on Concurrency Theory. LNCS, vol. 1243, pp. 135–150. Springer (1997)
8. Esparza, J., Finkel, A., Mayr, R.: On the verification of broadcast protocols. In: LICS'1999. pp. 352–359. IEEE Computer Society (1999)
9. Esparza, J., Ganty, P., Majumdar, R.: Parameterized verification of asynchronous shared-memory systems. In: Sharygina, N., Veith, H. (eds.) CAV 2013. LNCS, vol. 8044, pp. 124–140. Springer, Heidelberg (2013)
10. German, S.M., Sistla, A.P.: Reasoning about systems with many processes. J. ACM **39**(3), 675–735 (1992)
11. Grädel, E.: Subclasses of presburger arithmetic and the polynomial-time hierarchy. Theor. Comput. Sci. **56**, 289–301 (1988)
12. Hague, M.: Parameterised pushdown systems with non-atomic writes. In: Proceedings of FSTTCS'2011. LIPIcs, vol. 13, pp. 457–468. Schloss Dagstuhl (2011)
13. Meyer, R.: On boundedness in depth in the pi-calculus. In: Procedings of IFIP TCS 2008. IFIP, vol. 273, pp. 477–489. Springer (2008)
14. Pnueli, A., Xu, J., Zuck, L.D.: Liveness with $(0, 1, \infty)$-counter abstraction. In: Brinksma, E., Larsen, K.G. (eds.) CAV 2002. LNCS, vol. 2404, pp. 107–122. Springer, Heidelberg (2002)
15. Verma, K.N., Seidl, H., Schwentick, T.: On the complexity of equational horn clauses. In: Nieuwenhuis, R. (ed.) CADE 2005. LNCS (LNAI), vol. 3632, pp. 337–352. Springer, Heidelberg (2005)

SMT and POR Beat Counter Abstraction: Parameterized Model Checking of Threshold-Based Distributed Algorithms

Igor Konnov$^{(\boxtimes)}$, Helmut Veith, and Josef Widder

TU Wien (Vienna University of Technology), Vienna, Austria
konnov@forsyte.tuwien.ac.at

Abstract. Automatic verification of threshold-based fault-tolerant distributed algorithms (FTDA) is challenging: they have multiple parameters that are restricted by arithmetic conditions, the number of processes and faults is parameterized, and the algorithm code is parameterized due to conditions counting the number of received messages. Recently, we introduced a technique that first applies data and counter abstraction and then runs bounded model checking (BMC). Given an FTDA, our technique computes an upper bound on the diameter of the system. This makes BMC complete: it always finds a counterexample, if there is an actual error. To verify state-of-the-art FTDAs, further improvement is needed. In this paper, we encode bounded executions over integer counters in SMT. We introduce a new form of offline partial order reduction that exploits acceleration and the structure of the FTDAs. This aggressively prunes the execution space to be explored by the solver. In this way, we verified safety of seven FTDAs that were out of reach before.

1 Introduction

In recent work [28] we applied bounded model checking to verify reachability properties of threshold-based fault-tolerant distributed algorithms (FTDA), which are parameterized in the number of processes n and the fraction of faults t, e.g., $n > 3t$. Moreover, we showed how to make bounded model checking complete in the parameterized case. In particular, we considered counter systems where we record for each local state, how many processes are in this state. We have one counter per local state ℓ, denoted by $\kappa[\ell]$. A process step from local state ℓ to local state ℓ' is modeled by decrementing $\kappa[\ell]$ and incrementing $\kappa[\ell']$. When δ processes perform the same step one after the other, we allow the processes to do the *accelerated step* that instantaneously changes two counters by δ. The number δ is called *acceleration factor*, it can vary within a single run.

As we focus on FTDAs, we consider specific counter systems, namely those defined by *threshold automata*. Here, transitions are guarded by *threshold guards* that compare a shared integer variable to a linear combination of parameters, e.g., $x \geq n - t$ or $x < t$, where x is a shared variable and n and t are parameters.

Supported by the Austrian National Research Network S11403 and S11405 (RiSE), and project P27722 (PRAVDA) of the Austrian Science Fund (FWF).

© Springer International Publishing Switzerland 2015
D. Kroening and C.S. Păsăreanu (Eds.): CAV 2015, Part I, LNCS 9206, pp. 85–102, 2015.
DOI: 10.1007/978-3-319-21690-4_6

Completeness of the method [28] with respect to reachability is shown by proving a bound on the diameter of the accelerated system. Inspired by Lamport's view of distributed computation as partial order on events [30], our method is in essence an *offline* partial order reduction. Instead of pruning executions that are "similar" to ones explored before [22,38,43], we use the partial order to show (offline) that every run has a similar run of bounded length. Interestingly, the bound is independent of the parameters. In combination with the data abstraction of [25], we obtained the following automated method [28]:

1. Apply a parametric data abstraction to the process code to get a finite state process description, and construct the threshold automaton (TA) [25,27].
2. Compute the diameter bound, based on the control flow of the TA.
3. Construct a system with abstract counters, i.e., a counter abstraction [25,39].
4. Perform SAT-based bounded model checking [7,16] up to the diameter bound, to check whether bad states are reached in the counter abstraction.
5. If a counterexample is found, check its feasibility and refine, if needed [13,25].

While this allowed us to automatically verify several FTDAs not verified before, there remained two bottlenecks for scalability to larger and more complex protocols: First, due to abstraction there were spurious counterexamples. Second, counter abstraction works well in practice only for processes with a few dozens of local states, but it does not scale to hundreds of local states; partly because many different interleavings result in a large search space.

To address these bottlenecks, we make two crucial contributions in this paper: First, to eliminate one of the two sources of spurious counterexamples, namely, the non-determinism added by abstract counters, we do bounded model checking using SMT solvers with linear integer arithmetic on the accelerated system, instead of SAT-based bounded model checking on the counter abstraction.

Second, we reduce the search space dramatically: We introduce the notion of an *execution schema* that is defined as a sequence of local rules of the TA. By assigning to each rule of a schema an acceleration factor (possibly 0), one obtains a run of the counter system. Hence, each schema represents infinitely many runs. We show how to construct a set of schemas whose set of reachable states coincides with the set of reachable states of the accelerated counter system.

Our construction can be seen as an aggressive partial order reduction, where each run has a similar run generated by a schema from the set. To show this, we capture the guards that are locked and unlocked in a *locking context*. Our key insight is that a bounded number of transitions changes the context in each run. For example, of all transitions increasing a variable x, at most one makes $x \geq n - t$ true, and at most one makes $x < t$ false (the parameters n and t are fixed in a run). We fix those transitions that change the context, and apply the ideas of partial order reduction to the subexecutions between these transitions.

Our experiments show that SMT solvers and schemas outperform SAT solvers and counter abstraction in parameterized verification of threshold-based FTDAs. Indeed, we verified safety of complicated FTDAs [10,18,23,37,40,41] that have not been automatically verified before. In addition we achieved dramatic speedup and reduced memory footprint on previously verified FTDAs [9,12,42] (cf. [28]).

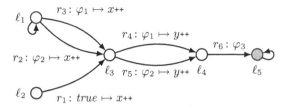

Fig. 1. An example threshold automaton.

2 A Motivating Example

Figure 1 is an example of a threshold automaton TA over two shared variables x and y and parameters n, t, and f. It is inspired by the distributed asynchronous broadcast protocol from [9], where $n - f$ correct processes concurrently execute TA, and f processes are Byzantine. As is typical for FTDAs, the parameters must satisfy a resilience condition, e.g., $n > 3t \wedge t \geq f \geq 0$ stating that less than a third of the processes is faulty. The circles depict the local states $\ell_1, \ldots, \ell_5$, two of them are the initial states ℓ_1, ℓ_2. The edges depict the rules $r_1, \ldots, r_6$ labeled with guarded commands $\varphi \mapsto$ act, where φ is one of the threshold guards "$\varphi_1 \colon x \geq \lceil (n + t)/2 \rceil - f$", "$\varphi_2 \colon y \geq (t + 1) - f$", and "$\varphi_3 \colon y \geq (2t + 1) - f$", and an action act increases the shared variables x or y by one, or zero (as in rule r_6).

Every local state ℓ_i has a non-negative counter $\kappa[\ell_i]$ that represents the number of processes in ℓ_i. Together with the values of x, y, n, t, and f, the values of the counters constitute a configuration of the system. In the initial configuration there are $n - f$ processes in initial states, i.e., $\kappa[\ell_1] + \kappa[\ell_2] = n - f$, and the other counters and the shared variables x and y are zero.

The rules define the transitions of the counter system. For instance, according to the rule r_2, if in the current configuration the guard $y \geq t + 1 - f$ holds true and $\kappa[\ell_1] \geq 5$, then five processes can instantaneously move out of the local state ℓ_1 to the local state ℓ_3, and increment x as prescribed by the action of r_2. This results in increase of x and the counter $\kappa[\ell_3]$ by five, and counter $\kappa[\ell_1]$ is decreased by five. When, as in this example, rule r_2 is conceptually executed by 5 processes, we denote this transition by r_2^5.

We now consider the runs more closely. As initially x and y are zero, threshold guards φ_1, φ_2, and φ_3 evaluate to false. As rules may only increase variables, these guards may eventually become true. (In this example we do not consider guards like $x < t$ that are initially true and become false, although we treat them later.) In fact, initially only r_1 is unlocked. Because r_1 increases x, it may unlock φ_1. Thus r_4 becomes unlocked. Rule r_4 increases y and thus repeated execution of r_4 (by different processes) first unlocks φ_2 and then φ_3. We call the set of conditions which evaluate to true in a configuration the *context*. For our example we observe that each run goes through the following sequence of contexts $\{\}$, $\{\varphi_1\}$, $\{\varphi_1, \varphi_2\}$, and $\{\varphi_1, \varphi_2, \varphi_3\}$. In fact, the sequence of contexts in an execution of a TA is always monotonic.

The conjunction of the guards in the context $\{\varphi_1, \varphi_2\}$ implies the guards of the rules r_1, r_2, r_3, r_4, r_5; we say they are unlocked in the context. A technical challenge addressed in this paper is to show that a fixed sequence of these rules can "capture" all schedules allowed in this context. To this end we analyze the control flow of the TA. Our example is acyclic up to self-loops, and thus the control flow establishes a partial order on the rules. We show in this paper that we can use any linear extension of this partial order as the required fixed sequence, e.g., $r_1 < r_2 < r_3 < r_4 < r_5$. (In this example we do not deal with loops, although we handle them in Sect. 4.1.) It remains to deal with transitions that actually change the context. In our example, only r_4 or r_5 can change the context from $\{\varphi_1, \varphi_2\}$ to $\{\varphi_1, \varphi_2, \varphi_3\}$. Therefore we append r_4, r_5 — that change the context — to the fixed sequence for the context. Thus, we obtain the following schema, where inside the curly brackets we give the contexts, and between two contexts the fixed sequences of rules. (We discuss the underlined rules below.)

$$S = \{\} \; \underline{r_1}, \underline{r_1} \; \{\varphi_1\} \; \underline{r_1}, \underline{r_3}, r_4, \underline{r_4} \; \{\varphi_1, \varphi_2\}$$
$$r_1, r_2, r_3, r_4, r_5, r_4, \underline{r_5} \; \{\varphi_1, \varphi_2, \varphi_3\} \; r_1, r_2, r_3, r_4, \underline{r_5}, \underline{r_6} \; \{\varphi_1, \varphi_2, \varphi_3\}$$

We now show how each schedule is captured by schema S. Consider, e.g., a schedule from the initial state σ_0 with $n = 5$, $t = f = 1$, $\kappa[\ell_1] = 1$, and $\kappa[\ell_2] = 3$. We are interested in whether there is a schedule that reaches a configuration, where all processes are in state ℓ_5. Consider the following schedule:

$$\tau = \underbrace{r_1^1, \; r_1^1,}_{\tau_1} \; \underbrace{r_3^1, r_1^1,}_{t_1 \quad \tau_2} \; \underbrace{r_4^1,}_{t_2 \quad \tau_3 \quad t_3} \; \underbrace{r_5^1, \; r_6^1, r_5^1, r_5^1, r_6^1, r_6^1, r_6^1}_{\tau_4}$$

Observe that after r_1^1, r_1^1, variable $x = 2$ and φ_1 is true. Hence transition t_1 changes the context from $\{\}$ to $\{\varphi_1\}$. Similarly t_2 and t_3 change the context. Context changing transitions are marked with curly brackets. Between them we have the subschedules $\tau_1, \dots, \tau_4$ (τ_3 is empty) marked with square brackets.

To show that this schedule is captured by the schema, we apply partial order arguments regarding distributed computations: As the guards φ_2 and φ_3 evaluate to true in τ_4, and r_5 precedes r_6 in the control flow of the TA, all transitions r_5^1 can be moved to the left in τ_4. Similarly, r_1^1 can be moved to the left in τ_2. The resulting schedule is applicable and leads to the same configuration as the original one. Further, we can accelerate the adjacent transitions with the same rule, e.g., the sequence r_5^1, r_5^1 can be transformed into r_5^2. Thus, we transform subschedules τ_i into τ_i', and arrive at the following schedule τ' that we call the representative schedule of τ. Importantly for reachability checking, if τ and τ' are applied to the same configuration, they end in the same configuration.

$$\tau' = \underbrace{r_1^1, \; r_1^1,}_{\tau_1'} \; \underbrace{r_1^1, r_3^1,}_{t_1 \quad \tau_2'} \; \underbrace{r_4^1,}_{t_2 \quad \tau_3' \quad t_3} \; \underbrace{r_5^1, \; r_5^2, r_6^4}_{\tau_4'}$$

Reconsidering schema S, we observe that the sequence of underlined rules in S matches the schedule τ'. In this paper we show that every schedule can be transformed into a representative schedule that matches one schema from a small set of schemas. Each schema in this set corresponds to one of the monotonic sequences of contexts, and is constructed following the ideas from above. Completeness regarding reachability follows from the fact that each schedule goes through a monotonic sequence of contexts. For each schema, reachability can be expressed by an SMT formula involving both state variables and parameters.

3 Parameterized Counter Systems

We extend the framework of [28]. A threshold automaton describes a process in a concurrent system, and is a tuple $\mathsf{TA} = (\mathcal{L}, \mathcal{I}, \Gamma, \Pi, \mathcal{R}, RC)$ defined below.

States. The finite set $\mathcal{L}$ contains the *local states*, and $\mathcal{I} \subseteq \mathcal{L}$ is the set of *initial states*. The finite set Γ contains the *shared variables* that range over $\mathbb{N}_0$. The finite set Π is a set of *parameter variables* that range over $\mathbb{N}_0$, and the *resilience condition RC* is a formula over parameter variables in linear integer arithmetic, e.g., $n > 3t$. The set of *admissible parameters* is $\mathbf{P}_{RC} = \{\mathbf{p} \in \mathbb{N}_0^{|\Pi|} : \mathbf{p} \models RC\}$.

Rules. A rule defines a conditional transition between local states that may update the shared variables. Formally, a *rule* is a tuple $(from, to, \varphi^{\leq}, \varphi^{>}, \mathbf{u})$: The local states *from* and *to* are from $\mathcal{L}$, and capture from which local state to which a process moves. A rule is only executed if the conditions $\varphi^{\leq}$ and $\varphi^{>}$ evaluate to true. Each condition is a conjunction of guards. Each guard is defined using some shared variable $x \in \Gamma$, coefficients $a_0, \ldots, a_{|\Pi|} \in \mathbb{Z}$, and parameter variables $p_1, \ldots, p_{|\Pi|} \in \Pi$ so that $a_0 + \sum_{i=1}^{|\Pi|} a_i \cdot p_i \leq x$ and $a_0 + \sum_{i=1}^{|\Pi|} a_i \cdot p_i > x$ are a *lower guard* and *upper guard*, respectively. Let Φ^U and Φ^L be the sets of lower and upper guards. The set $\mathsf{guard}(\varphi^{\leq}) \subseteq \Phi^U$ is the set of guards used in $\varphi^{\leq}$, while the set $\mathsf{guard}(\varphi^{>}) \subseteq \Phi^L$ is the set of guards used in $\varphi^{>}$.

Rules may increase shared variables using an update vector $\mathbf{u} \in \mathbb{N}_0^{|\Gamma|}$ that is added to the vector of shared variables. Finally, $\mathcal{R}$ is the finite set of rules.

Definition 1. *Given a threshold automaton $(\mathcal{L}, \mathcal{I}, \Gamma, \Pi, \mathcal{R}, RC)$, we define the precedence relation $\prec_P$: for a pair of rules $r_1, r_2 \in \mathcal{R}$, it holds that $r_1 \prec_P r_2$ if and only if $r_1.to = r_2.from$. We denote by $\prec_P^+$ the transitive closure of $\prec_P$. Further, we say that $r_1 \sim_P r_2$, if $r_1 \prec_P^+ r_2 \wedge r_2 \prec_P^+ r_1$, or $r_1 = r_2$.*

As in [28], we limit ourselves to threshold automata relevant for FTDAs, namely those where $r.\mathbf{u} = \mathbf{0}$ for all rules $r \in \mathcal{R}$ that satisfy $r \prec_P^+ r$.

Looplets. The relation $\sim_P$ defines equivalence classes of rules. An equivalence class corresponds to a loop or a single rule that is not part of a loop. Hence, we use the term looplet for one such equivalence class. For a given set of rules $\mathcal{R}$ let $\mathcal{R}/\sim$ be the set of equivalence classes defined by $\sim_P$. We denote by $[r]$ the equivalence class of rule r. For two classes c_1 and c_2 from $\mathcal{R}/\sim$ we write $c_1 \prec_c c_2$ iff there are two rules r_1 and r_2 in $\mathcal{R}$ satisfying $[r_1] = c_1$ and $[r_2] = c_2$ and $r_1 \prec_P^+ r_2$ and $r_1 \not\sim_P r_2$. As the relation $\prec_c$ is a strict partial order, there are linear extensions of $\prec_c$. Below, we fix an *arbitrary* of these linear extensions to sort transitions in a schedule: We denote by $\prec_c^{lin}$ a linear extension of $\prec_c$.

3.1   Counter Systems

Given a threshold automaton TA, a function $N : \mathbf{P}_{RC} \to \mathbb{N}_0$ that determines the number of processes to be modeled (typically, $N(n, t, f) = n - f$) and admissible parameter values $\mathbf{p} \in \mathbf{P}_{RC}$, we define a counter system as a transition system (Σ, I, R), that consists of the set of configurations Σ, which contain the counters and variables, the set of initial configurations I, and the transition relation R:

Configurations Σ and I. A configuration $\sigma = (\boldsymbol{\kappa}, \mathbf{g}, \mathbf{p})$ consists of a vector of *counter values* $\sigma.\boldsymbol{\kappa} \in \mathbb{N}_0^{|\mathcal{L}|}$ (for simplicity we use the convention that $\mathcal{L} = \{1, \ldots, |\mathcal{L}|\}$) a vector of *shared variable values* $\sigma.\mathbf{g} \in \mathbb{N}_0^{|\Gamma|}$, and a vector of *parameter values* $\sigma.\mathbf{p} = \mathbf{p}$. The set Σ is the set of all configurations. The set of initial configurations I contains the configurations that satisfy $\sigma.\mathbf{g} = \mathbf{0}$, $\sum_{i \in \mathcal{I}} \sigma.\boldsymbol{\kappa}[i] = N(\mathbf{p})$, and $\sum_{i \notin \mathcal{I}} \sigma.\boldsymbol{\kappa}[i] = 0$.

Transition Relation R. A *transition* is a pair $t = (rule, factor)$ of a rule of the TA and a non-negative integer called the *acceleration factor*, or just factor for short. For a transition $t = (rule, factor)$ we refer by $t.\mathbf{u}$ to $rule.\mathbf{u}$, by $t.\varphi^{>}$ to $rule.\varphi^{>}$, etc. We say a transition t is *unlocked* in configuration σ if $\forall k \in \{0, \ldots, t.factor - 1\}$. $(\sigma.\boldsymbol{\kappa}, \sigma.\mathbf{g} + k \cdot t.\mathbf{u}, \sigma.\mathbf{p}) \models t.\varphi^{\leq} \wedge t.\varphi^{>}$.

A transition t is *applicable (or enabled)* in configuration σ, if it is unlocked, and $\sigma.\boldsymbol{\kappa}[t.from] \geq t.factor$, or $t.factor = 0$. We say that σ' is the result of applying the enabled transition t to σ, and use the notation $\sigma' = t(\sigma)$, if

- $\sigma'.\mathbf{g} = \sigma.\mathbf{g} + t.factor \cdot t.\mathbf{u}$ and $\sigma'.\mathbf{p} = \sigma.\mathbf{p}$
- if $t.from \neq t.to$ then $\sigma'.\boldsymbol{\kappa}[t.from] = \sigma.\boldsymbol{\kappa}[t.from] - t.factor$ and $\sigma'.\boldsymbol{\kappa}[t.to] = \sigma.\boldsymbol{\kappa}[t.to] + t.factor$ and $\forall \ell \in \mathcal{L} \setminus \{t.from, t.to\}$. $\sigma'.\boldsymbol{\kappa}[\ell] = \sigma.\boldsymbol{\kappa}[\ell]$
- if $t.from = t.to$ then $\sigma'.\boldsymbol{\kappa} = \sigma.\boldsymbol{\kappa}$

The transition relation $R \subseteq \Sigma \times \Sigma$ of the counter system is defined as follows: $(\sigma, \sigma') \in R$ iff there is a $r \in \mathcal{R}$ and a $k \in \mathbb{N}_0$ such that $\sigma' = t(\sigma)$ for $t = (r, k)$. As updates to shared variables do not decrease their values, we obtain:

Proposition 1 ([28]). *For all configurations σ, all rules r, and all transitions t applicable to σ, the following holds:*

    1. If $\sigma \models r.\varphi^{\leq}$ then $t(\sigma) \models r.\varphi^{\leq}$ *3. If $\sigma \not\models r.\varphi^{>}$ then $t(\sigma) \not\models r.\varphi^{>}$*
    2. If $t(\sigma) \not\models r.\varphi^{\leq}$ then $\sigma \not\models r.\varphi^{\leq}$ *4. If $t(\sigma) \models r.\varphi^{>}$ then $\sigma \models r.\varphi^{>}$*

Schedules and Paths. A *schedule* is a sequence of transitions. For a schedule τ and an index $i : 1 \leq i \leq |\tau|$, by $t[i]$ we denote the ith transition of τ, and by τ^i we denote the prefix $t[1], \ldots, t[i]$ of τ. A schedule $\tau = t_1, \ldots, t_m$ is *applicable* to configuration σ_0, if there is a sequence of configurations $\sigma_1, \ldots, \sigma_m$ with $\sigma_i = t_i(\sigma_{i-1})$ for $1 \leq i \leq m$. If there is a $t_i.factor > 1$, then a schedule is *accelerated*.

By $\tau \cdot \tau'$ we denote the concatenation of two schedules τ and τ'. A sequence $\sigma_0, t_1, \sigma_1, \ldots, \sigma_{k-1}, t_k, \sigma_k$ of alternating configurations and transitions is called a (finite) *path*, if transition t_i is enabled in σ_i and $\sigma_i = t_i(\sigma_{i-1})$, for $1 \leq i \leq k$. For a configuration σ_0 and a schedule τ applicable to σ, by $\mathsf{path}(\sigma_0, \tau)$ we denote the path $\sigma_0, t_1, \ldots, t_{|\tau|}, \sigma_{|\tau|}$ with $t_i = \tau[i]$ and $\sigma_i = t_i(\sigma_{i-1})$, for $1 \leq i \leq |\tau|$.

3.2   Contexts and Slices

The evaluation of the guards in the sets Φ^U and Φ^L solely defines whether certain rules are unlocked. Due to Proposition 1, we infer that when the transitions of a schedule are applied, more and more guards from Φ^U become unlocked and more and more guards from Φ^L become locked. To capture this, we define:

Definition 2. *A* context *is a pair* (Ω^U, Ω^L) *of subsets* $\Omega^U \subseteq \Phi^U$ *and* $\Omega^L \subseteq \Phi^L$. *We denote by* Ω *the pair* (Ω^U, Ω^L), *and by* $|\Omega| = |\Omega^U| + |\Omega^L|$.

For two contexts (Ω_1^U, Ω_1^L) and (Ω_2^U, Ω_2^L), we define that $(\Omega_1^U, \Omega_1^L) \sqsubset (\Omega_2^U, \Omega_2^L)$ if and only if $\Omega_1^U \cup \Omega_1^L \subset \Omega_2^U \cup \Omega_2^L$. Then, a sequence of contexts $\Omega_1, \ldots, \Omega_m$ is *monotonically increasing*, if $\Omega_i \sqsubset \Omega_{i+1}$ for $1 \leq i < m$. Further, a monotonically increasing sequence of contexts $\Omega_1, \ldots, \Omega_m$ is *maximal*, if $\Omega_1 = (\emptyset, \emptyset)$ and $\Omega_m = (\Phi^U, \Phi^L)$ and $|\Omega_{i+1}| = |\Omega_i| + 1$, for $1 \leq i < m$. We obtain:

Proposition 2. *Every maximal monotonically increasing sequence of contexts is of length* $|\Phi^U| + |\Phi^L| + 1$. *There are at most* $(|\Phi^U| + |\Phi^L|)!$ *such sequences.*

Definition 3. *Given a threshold automaton, we define its* configuration context *as a function* $\omega : \Sigma \rightarrow 2^{\Phi^U} \times 2^{\Phi^L}$ *that for each configuration* $\sigma \in \Sigma$ *gives a context* (Ω^U, Ω^L) *with* $\Omega^U = \{\varphi \in \Phi^U : \sigma \models \varphi\}$ *and* $\Omega^L = \{\varphi \in \Phi^L : \sigma \not\models \varphi\}$.

Proposition 3. *If a transition* t *is enabled in a configuration* σ, *then either* $\omega(\sigma) \sqsubset \omega(t(\sigma))$, *or* $\omega(\sigma) = \omega(t(\sigma))$.

We say that a schedule τ is *steady* for a configuration σ, if for every prefix τ' of τ, the context does not change, i.e., $\omega(\tau'(\sigma)) = \omega(\sigma)$.

Proposition 4. *A schedule* τ *is steady for a configuration* σ *if and only if* $\omega(\sigma) = \omega(\tau(\sigma))$.

Given a configuration σ and a schedule τ applicable to σ, we say that $\mathsf{path}(\sigma, \tau)$ *is consistent with* a sequence of contexts $\Omega_1, \ldots, \Omega_m$, if the set of indices $\{0, \ldots, |\tau|\}$ can be partitioned into m (possibly empty) disjoint sets $I_1, \ldots, I_m$ such that $\omega(\tau^i(\sigma)) = \Omega_k$, for $1 \leq k \leq m$ and $i \in I_k$.

A context defines which rules of the TA are unlocked. As we consider steady schedules, we need to understand, which rules are unlocked in that schedule:

Definition 4. *Given a threshold automaton* $\mathsf{TA} = (\mathcal{L}, \mathcal{I}, \Gamma, \Pi, \mathcal{R}, RC)$ *and a context* Ω, *we define the* slice *of* TA *with context* Ω *as a threshold automaton* $\mathsf{TA}|_\Omega = (\mathcal{L}, \mathcal{I}, \Gamma, \Pi, \mathcal{R}|_\Omega, RC)$, *where a rule* $r \in \mathcal{R}$ *belongs to* $\mathcal{R}|_\Omega$ *if and only if* $\left(\bigwedge_{\varphi \in \Omega^U} \varphi \right) \rightarrow r.\varphi^{\leq}$ *and* $\left(\bigwedge_{\psi \in \Phi^L \setminus \Omega^L} \psi \right) \rightarrow r.\varphi^{>}$.

3.3   Parameterized Reachability

Given a threshold automaton TA, a *state property* B is a boolean combination of formulas that have the form $\bigwedge_{i \in Y} \kappa[i] = 0$, for some $Y \subseteq \mathcal{L}$. The *parameterized reachability* problem is to decide whether there are parameter values $\mathbf{p} \in \mathbf{P}_{RC}$, an initial configuration $\sigma_0 \in I$, with $\sigma_0.\mathbf{p} = \mathbf{p}$, and a schedule τ satisfying that τ is applicable to σ_0, and property B holds in the final state: $\tau(\sigma_0) \models B$.

4   Main Result: A Complete Set of Schemas

We introduce the notion of a schema that is an alternating sequence of contexts and sequences of rules. A schema serves as a pattern for an infinite set of paths, and can be used to efficiently encode parameterized reachability in SMT. We show how to construct a set of schemas $\mathcal{S}$ with the following property: for each schedule τ and each configuration σ, there is a representative schedule, i.e., a schedule that if applied to σ, ends in $\tau(\sigma)$, and is generated by a schema from $\mathcal{S}$.

Definition 5. *A* schema *is a sequence* $\Omega_0, \rho_1, \Omega_1, \ldots, \rho_m, \Omega_m$ *of alternating contexts and rule sequences. Often we write* $\{\Omega_0\}\rho_1\{\Omega_1\}\ldots\{\Omega_{m-1}\}\rho_m\{\Omega_m\}$ *for a schema. A schema with two contexts is called* simple.

Given two schemas $S_1 = \Omega_0, \rho_1, \ldots, \rho_k, \Omega_k$ and $S_2 = \Omega'_0, \rho'_1, \ldots, \rho'_m, \Omega'_m$ with $\Omega_k = \Omega'_0$, we define their *composition* $S_1 \circ S_2$ to be the schema that is obtained by concatenation of the two sequences: $\Omega_0, \rho_1, \ldots, \rho_k, \Omega'_0, \rho'_1, \ldots, \rho'_m, \Omega'_m$.

Definition 6. *Given a configuration σ and a schedule τ applicable to σ, we say that* $\mathsf{path}(\sigma, \tau)$ *is generated by a simple schema* $\{\Omega\}\,\rho\,\{\Omega'\}$*, if the following hold:*

- *For $\rho = r_1, \ldots, r_k$ there is a monotonically increasing sequence of indices $i(1), \ldots, i(m)$, i.e., $1 \leq i(1) < \cdots < i(m) \leq k$, and there are factors $f_1, \ldots, f_m > 0$, so that schedule $(r_{i(1)}, f_1), \ldots, (r_{i(m)}, f_m) = \tau$.*
- *The first and the last states match the contexts: $\omega(\sigma) = \Omega$ and $\omega(\tau(\sigma)) = \Omega'$.*

In general, we say that $\mathsf{path}(\sigma, \tau)$ is generated by a schema S, if $S = S_1 \circ \cdots \circ S_k$ for simple schemas $S_1, \ldots, S_k$ and $\tau = \tau_1 \cdots \tau_k$ such that each $\mathsf{path}(\pi_i(\sigma), \tau_i)$ is generated by the simple schema S_i, for $\pi_i = \tau_1 \cdots \tau_{i-1}$ and $1 \leq i \leq k$.

The *language of a schema* S—denoted with $\mathcal{L}(S)$—is the set of all paths generated by S. For a set of configurations $C \subseteq \Sigma$ and a set of schemas $\mathcal{S}$, we define the set $\mathsf{Reach}(C, \mathcal{S})$ to contain all configurations reachable from C via the paths generated by the schemas from $\mathcal{S}$, i.e., $\mathsf{Reach}(C, \mathcal{S}) = \{\tau(\sigma) \mid \sigma \in C, \exists S \in \mathcal{S}. \mathsf{path}(\sigma, \tau) \in \mathcal{L}(S)\}$. We say that a set $\mathcal{S}$ of schemas is *complete*, if: $\forall C \subseteq \Sigma. \{\tau(\sigma) \mid \sigma \in C, \tau$ is applicable to $\sigma\} = \mathsf{Reach}(C, \mathcal{S})$.

In [28, Thm. 1], we introduced a quantity $\mathcal{C}$ that depends on the number of conditions in a TA, and have shown that for every configuration σ and every schedule τ applicable to σ, there is a schedule τ' of length at most $d = |\mathcal{R}| \cdot (\mathcal{C} + 1) + \mathcal{C}$ that is also applicable to σ and results in $\tau(\sigma)$. Hence, by enumerating all sequences of rules of length up to d, one can construct a complete set of schemas:

Corollary 1. *For a threshold automaton, there is a complete schema set $\mathcal{S}_d$ of cardinality $|\mathcal{R}|^{|\mathcal{R}| \cdot (\mathcal{C}+1) + \mathcal{C}}$.*

Although the set $\mathcal{S}_d$ is finite, enumerating all its elements is impractical. We show that there is a complete set of schemas whose cardinality solely depends on the number of guards that syntactically occur in the TA. These numbers $|\Phi^U|$ and $|\Phi^L|$ are in practice much smaller than the number of rules $|\mathcal{R}|$:

Theorem 1. *For a threshold automaton, there is a complete schema set of cardinality at most $(|\Phi^U| + |\Phi^L|)!$, where the length of each schema does not exceed $(3 \cdot (|\Phi^U| + |\Phi^L|) + 2) \cdot |\mathcal{R}|$.*

Proof Idea. Construct the set Z of all maximal monotonically increasing sequences of contexts. From Proposition 2, there are at most $(|\Phi^U| + |\Phi^L|)!$ maximal monotonically increasing sequences of contexts. Therefore, $|Z| \leq (|\Phi^U| + |\Phi^L|)!$. Then, for each sequence $z \in Z$, we do the following:

1. Show that for each configuration σ and each schedule τ applicable to σ and consistent with the sequence z, there is a schedule $s(\tau)$ that has a specific structure, and is also applicable to σ. We call $s(\tau)$ the representative of τ.
2. Construct a schema and show that it generates all paths of all schedules $s(\tau)$ found in (1). The length of the schema is at most $(3 \cdot (|\Phi^U| + |\Phi^L|) + 2) \cdot |\mathcal{R}|$.

To prove Theorem 1, it remains to show existence of a representative schedule and of a schema as formulated in (1)–(2). We do this below in Proposition 9 and Theorem 2 respectively. Before that we consider special cases: when all rules of a schedule belong to the same looplet, and when a schedule is steady.

4.1   Special Case I: One Context and One Looplet

We show that for each schedule that uses only the rules from a fixed looplet and does not change its context, there exists a representative schedule of bounded length that reaches the same final state.

Proposition 5. *Fix a threshold automaton, a context Ω, and a looplet $c \in (\mathcal{R}|_\Omega)/_\sim$ in the slice $TA|_\Omega$. Let σ be a configuration and $\tau = t_1, \ldots, t_m$ a steady schedule applicable to σ, with $[t_i.rule] = c$ for $1 \leq i \leq |\tau|$. There exists a representative schedule $\mathsf{crep}_c^\Omega[\sigma, \tau]$ with the following properties:*

(a) schedule $\mathsf{crep}_c^\Omega[\sigma, \tau]$ is applicable to σ, and $\mathsf{crep}_c^\Omega[\sigma, \tau](\sigma) = \tau(\sigma)$,
(b) the rule of each transition t in $\mathsf{crep}_c^\Omega[\sigma, \tau]$ belongs to c, that is, $[t.rule] = c$,
(c) schedule $\mathsf{crep}_c^\Omega[\sigma, \tau]$ is not longer than $2 \cdot |c|$.

Proof Idea for Proposition 5. If $|c| = 1$, then we use a single accelerated transition or the empty schedule as representative. If $|c| > 1$, the rules of the slice $TA|_\Omega$ form a strongly connected component. Then, we can choose a node h, and construct two spanning trees: an *out-tree*, whose edges are pointing away from h, and an *in-tree*, whose edges are pointing to h. Using the trees, we construct two sequences of rules sorted in the topological order of the trees: the sequence $r_{\mathsf{in}}(1), \ldots, r_{\mathsf{in}}(k)$ moves processes to h, and the sequence $r_{\mathsf{out}}(1), \ldots, r_{\mathsf{out}}(m)$ distributes the processes from h to the locations. As a result, for each location ℓ in the graph, the processes are transferred from ℓ to the other locations, if $\sigma[\ell] > \tau(\sigma)[\ell]$, and additional processes arrive at ℓ, if $\sigma[\ell] < \tau(\sigma)[\ell]$.

Proposition 6. *Fix a threshold automaton, a context Ω, and a looplet $c \in (\mathcal{R}|_\Omega)/_\sim$ in the slice $TA|_\Omega$. There exists a schema $\mathsf{cschema}_c^\Omega$ with the following properties: For each configuration σ and each steady schedule $\tau = t_1, \ldots, t_m$ applicable to σ, if $[t_i.rule] = c$ for $1 \leq i \leq |\tau|$, then $path(\sigma, \tau')$ of the representative schedule $\tau' = \mathsf{crep}_c^\Omega[\sigma, \tau]$ from Proposition 5 is generated by $\mathsf{cschema}_c^\Omega$.*

Proof idea. We construct the schema using the same sequence of rules as in Proposition 5, i.e., $\mathsf{cschema}_c^\Omega = \{\Omega\}\, r_{\mathsf{in}}(1), \ldots, r_{\mathsf{in}}(k),\, r_{\mathsf{out}}(1), \ldots, r_{\mathsf{out}}(m)\, \{\Omega\}$. It follows that $\mathsf{cschema}_c^\Omega$ generates all paths of the representative schedules. $\square$

4.2 Special Case II: One Context and Multiple Looplets

In this section, we show that for each steady schedule, there exists a representative steady schedule of bounded length that reaches the same final state.

Proposition 7. *Fix a threshold automaton and a context Ω. For every configuration σ with $\omega(\sigma) = \Omega$ and every steady schedule τ applicable to σ, there exists a steady schedule $\mathsf{srep}_\Omega[\sigma, \tau]$ with the following properties:*

(a) $\mathsf{srep}_\Omega[\sigma, \tau]$ is applicable to σ, and $\mathsf{srep}_\Omega[\sigma, \tau](\sigma) = \tau(\sigma)$,
(b) $|\mathsf{srep}_\Omega[\sigma, \tau]| \leq 2 \cdot |(\mathcal{R}|_\Omega)/_\sim|$

To construct a representative schedule, we fix a context Ω of at TA, a configuration σ with $\omega(\sigma) = \Omega$, and a steady schedule τ applicable to σ. The key notion in our construction is a projection of a schedule on a set of looplets:

Definition 7. *Let $\tau = t_1, \ldots, t_k$ be a schedule and C be a set of looplets. Given an increasing sequence of indices $i(1), \ldots, i(m) \in \{1, \ldots, k\}$, i.e., $i(j) < i(j+1)$, for $1 \leq j < m$, a schedule $t_{i(1)} \ldots t_{i(m)}$ is a projection of τ on C, if each index $j \in \{1, \ldots, k\}$ belongs to $\{i(1), \ldots, i(m)\}$ if and only if $[t_j.rule] \in C$.*

In fact, each schedule τ has a unique projection on a set C. In the following, we write $\tau|_{c_1, \ldots, c_m}$ to denote the projection of τ on a set $\{c_1, \ldots, c_m\}$.

Provided that $c_1, \ldots, c_m$ are all looplets of the slice $(\mathcal{R}|_\Omega)/_\sim$ ordered with respect to $\prec_C^{lin}$, we construct the following sequences of projections on each looplet (note that π_0 is the empty schedule): $\pi_i = \tau|_{c_1} \cdot \ldots \cdot \tau|_{c_i}$ for $0 \leq i \leq m$.

Having defined $\{\pi_i\}_{0 \leq i \leq m}$, we construct the representative $\mathsf{srep}_\Omega[\sigma, \tau]$ simply as a concatenation of the representatives of each looplet:

$$\mathsf{srep}_\Omega[\sigma, \tau] = \mathsf{crep}_{c_1}^\Omega[\pi_0(\sigma), \tau|_{c_1}] \cdot \mathsf{crep}_{c_2}^\Omega[\pi_1(\sigma), \tau|_{c_2}] \cdots \mathsf{crep}_{c_m}^\Omega[\pi_{m-1}(\sigma), \tau|_{c_m}]$$

Lemma 1 (Looplet Sorting). *Given a threshold automaton, a context Ω, a configuration σ, a steady schedule τ applicable to σ, and a sequence $c_1, \ldots, c_m$ of all looplets in the slice $(\mathcal{R}|_\Omega)/_\sim$ with the property $c_i \prec_C^{lin} c_j$ for $1 \leq i < j \leq m$, the following holds:*

1. Schedule $\tau|_{c_1}$ is applicable to the configuration σ.
2. Schedule $\tau|_{c_2, \ldots, c_m}$ is applicable to the configuration $\tau|_{c_1}(\sigma)$.
3. Schedule $\tau|_{c_1} \cdot \tau|_{c_2, \ldots, c_m}$, when applied to σ, results in configuration $\tau(\sigma)$.

Proof (of Proposition 7). By iteratively applying Lemma 1, we prove by induction that schedule $\tau|_{c_1} \cdots \cdot \tau|_{c_m}$ is applicable to σ and results in $\tau(\sigma)$. From Proposition 5, we conclude that each schedule $\tau|_{c_i}$ can be replaced by its representative $\mathsf{crep}_{c_i}^{\Omega}[\pi_{i-1}(\sigma), \tau|_{c_i}]$. Thus, $\mathsf{srep}_{\Omega}[\sigma, \tau]$ is applicable to σ and results in $\tau(\sigma)$. By Proposition 4, schedule $\mathsf{srep}_{\Omega}[\sigma, \tau]$ is steady, since $\omega(\sigma) = \omega(\tau(\sigma))$. □

Finally, we show that for a given context, there is a schema that generates all paths of such representative schedules.

Proposition 8. *Fix a threshold automaton and a context Ω. Let $c_1, \ldots, c_m$ be the sorted sequence of all looplets of the slice $(\mathcal{R}|_{\Omega})/_{\sim}$, i.e., it holds that $c_1 \prec_C^{lin}$ $\ldots \prec_C^{lin} c_m$. Schema $\mathsf{sschema}_{\Omega} = \mathsf{cschema}_{c_1}^{\Omega} \circ \mathsf{cschema}_{c_2}^{\Omega} \circ \cdots \circ \mathsf{cschema}_{c_m}^{\Omega}$ satisfies: For each configuration σ with $\omega(\sigma) = \Omega$ and each steady schedule τ applicable to σ, $\mathsf{path}(\sigma, \tau')$ of the representative $\tau' = \mathsf{srep}_{\Omega}[\sigma, \tau]$ is generated by $\mathsf{sschema}_{\Omega}$.*

Proof. As for an arbitrary configuration σ with $\omega(\sigma) = \Omega$ and a steady schedule τ applicable to σ, we constructed $\mathsf{srep}_{\Omega}[\sigma, \tau]$ as a sorted sequence of representatives of the looplets, all paths of $\mathsf{srep}_{\Omega}[\sigma, \tau]$ are generated by $\mathsf{sschema}_{\Omega}$. □

4.3   The General Case

Using the results from Sects. 4.1 and 4.2, for each configuration and each schedule (without restrictions) we construct a representative schedule.

Proposition 9. *Given a threshold automaton, a configuration σ, and schedule τ applicable to σ, there exists a schedule $\mathsf{rep}[\sigma, \tau]$ with the following properties:*

(a) $\mathsf{rep}[\sigma, \tau]$ is applicable to σ, and $\mathsf{rep}[\sigma, \tau](\sigma) = \tau(\sigma)$,
(b) $|\mathsf{rep}[\sigma, \tau]| \leq 2 \cdot |\mathcal{R}| \cdot (|\Phi^U| + |\Phi^L| + 1) + |\Phi^U| + |\Phi^L|$.

Proof Idea. Consider the maximal monotonically increasing sequence $\Omega_0, \ldots, \Omega_m$ such that $\mathsf{path}(\sigma, \tau)$ is consistent with the sequence. Thus, τ contains at most m transitions that change their context, and schedules between these transitions are steady. By applying Proposition 7, we replace the steady schedules with their representatives and obtain $\mathsf{rep}[\sigma, \tau]$, which is applicable to σ and results in $\tau(\sigma)$. By Proposition 7, the representative of a steady schedule is not longer than $2 \cdot |\mathcal{R}|$, which together with m transitions gives us the bound $2 \cdot |\mathcal{R}| \cdot (m+1) + m$. By Proposition 2, the number m is $|\Phi^U| + |\Phi^L|$. This gives us the needed bound.

Further, given a maximal monotonically increasing sequence z of contexts, we construct a schema that generates all paths of the schedules consistent with z:

Theorem 2. *For a threshold automaton and a monotonically increasing sequence z of contexts, there exists a schema $\mathsf{schema}(z)$ that generates all paths of the representative schedules that are consistent with z, and the length of $\mathsf{schema}(z)$ does not exceed $(3 \cdot |\mathcal{R}| + 1) \cdot (|\Phi^U| + |\Phi^L|) + 2 \cdot |\mathcal{R}|$.*

Proof. Given a threshold automaton, let ρ_{all} be the sequence $r_1, \ldots, r_{|\mathcal{R}|}$ of all rules from $\mathcal{R}$, and $z = \Omega_0, \ldots, \Omega_m$ a monotonically increasing sequence of contexts. By the construction in Proposition 9, each representative schedule $\mathsf{rep}[\sigma, \tau]$ consists of the representatives of steady schedules terminated with transitions that change the context. Then, for each context Ω_i, for $0 \le i < m$, we compose $\mathsf{sschema}_\Omega$ with $\{\Omega_i\} \rho_{\mathsf{all}} \{\Omega_{i+1}\}$. This composition generates the representative of a steady schedule and the transition changing the context from Ω_i to Ω_{i+1}. Consequently, we construct the $\mathsf{schema}(z)$ as follows:

$$(\mathsf{sschema}_{\Omega_0} \circ \{\Omega_0\} \rho_{\mathsf{all}} \{\Omega_1\}) \circ \cdots \circ (\mathsf{sschema}_{\Omega_{m-1}} \circ \{\Omega_{m-1}\} \rho_{\mathsf{all}} \{\Omega_m\}) \circ \mathsf{sschema}_{\Omega_m}$$

By inductively applying Proposition 8, we prove that $\mathsf{schema}(z)$ generates all paths of schedules $\mathsf{rep}[\sigma, \tau]$ that are consistent with the sequence z. We get the needed bound on the length of $\mathsf{schema}(z)$ by using an argument similar to Proposition 9 and by noting that we add $|\mathcal{R}|$ extra rules per context.   □

Computing the Complete Set of Schemas. Our proofs show that the set of schemas is easily computed from the TA: The threshold guards are syntactic parts of the TA, and enable us to directly construct increasing sequences of contexts. To find a slice of the TA for a given context, we filter the rules with unlocked guards, i.e., check if the context contains the guard. To produce the simple schema of a looplet, we compute a spanning tree over the slice. To construct simple schemas, we do a topological sort over the looplets. For example, it takes just 30 s to compute the schemas in our longest experiment that runs for 4 h.

4.4   Optimization: Smaller Complete Sets of Schemas

Entailment Optimization. We say that a guard $\varphi_1 \in \Phi^U$ *entails* a guard $\varphi_2 \in \Phi^U$, if for all combinations of parameters $\mathbf{p} \in \mathbf{P}_{RC}$ and shared variables $\mathbf{g} \in \mathbb{N}_0^{|\Gamma|}$, it holds that $(\mathbf{g}, \mathbf{p}) \models \varphi_1 \rightarrow \varphi_2$. For instance, in our example, $\varphi_3 \colon y \ge (2t + 1) - f$ entails $\varphi_2 \colon y \ge (t + 1) - f$. If φ_1 entails φ_2, then we can omit all monotonically increasing sequences that contain a context (Ω^U, Ω^L) with $\varphi_1 \in \Omega^U$ and $\varphi_2 \notin \Omega^U$. If the number of schemas before applying this optimization is $m!$ and there are k entailments, then the number of schemas reduces from $m!$ to $(m - k)!$. A similar optimization is introduced for the guards from Φ^L.

Control Flow Optimization. Based on the proof of Lemma 1, we introduce the following optimization for TAs that are DAGs (possibly with self loops).

We say that a rule $r \in \mathcal{R}$ *may unlock* a lower guard $\varphi \in \Phi^U$, if there is a $\mathbf{p} \in \mathbf{P}_{RC}$ and $\mathbf{g} \in \mathbb{N}_0^{|\Gamma|}$ satisfying: $(\mathbf{g}, \mathbf{p}) \models r.\varphi^\le \wedge r.\varphi^>$ (the rule is unlocked); $(\mathbf{g}, \mathbf{p}) \not\models \varphi$ (the guard is locked); $(\mathbf{g} + r.\mathbf{u}, \mathbf{p}) \models \varphi$ (the guard is now unlocked).

In our example, the rule r_1 may unlock the guard φ_1.

Let $\varphi \in \Phi^U$ be a guard, $r_1', \ldots, r_m'$ be the rules that use φ, and $r_1, \ldots, r_k$ be the rules that may unlock φ. If $r_i \prec_c^{lin} r_j'$, for $1 \le i \le k$ and $1 \le j \le m$, then we exclude some sequences of contexts as follows (we call φ *forward-unlockable*). Let $\psi_1, \ldots, \psi_n \in \Phi^U$ be the guards of $r_1, \ldots, r_k$. Guard φ cannot be unlocked before

$\psi_1, \ldots, \psi_n$, and thus we can omit all sequences of contexts, where φ appears in the contexts before $\psi_1, \ldots, \psi_n$. Moreover, as $\psi_1, \ldots, \psi_n$ are the only guards of the rules unlocking φ, we omit the sequences with different combinations of contexts involving φ and the guards from $\Phi^U \setminus \{\varphi, \psi_1, \ldots, \psi_n\}$. Finally, as the rules $r'_1, \ldots, r'_m$ appear after the rules $r_1, \ldots, r_k$ in the order $\prec_C^{lin}$, the rules $r'_1, \ldots, r'_m$ appear after the rules $r_1, \ldots, r_k$ in a rule sequence of every schema. Thus, we omit the combinations of the contexts involving φ and $\psi_1, \ldots, \psi_n$.

Hence, we add all forward-unlockable guards to the initial context (we still check the guards of the rules in the SMT encoding in Sect. 5). If the number of schemas before applying this optimization is $m!$ and there are k forward-unlocking guards, then the number of schemas reduces from $m!$ to $(m - k)!$. A similar optimization is introduced for the guards from Φ^L.

5   Checking a Schema with SMT

The encoding for a schema is obtained by decomposing the schema into a sequence of simple schemas and encoding the simple schemas. Given a simple schema $S = \{\Omega_1\} \, r_1, \ldots, r_m \, \{\Omega_2\}$, we construct an SMT formula such that every model of the formula represents a path from $\mathcal{L}(S)$, and for every path in $\mathcal{L}(S)$ there is a corresponding model of the formula. Thus, we need to model a path of $m + 1$ configurations and m transitions (whose acceleration factors may be 0).

To represent a configuration σ_i, for $0 \le i \le m$, we introduce two vectors of SMT variables: a vector $\mathbf{k}^i = (k_1^i, \ldots, k_{|L|}^i)$ to represent the process counters, a vector $\mathbf{x}^i = (x_1^i, \ldots, x_{|\Gamma|}^i)$ to represent the shared variables. We call the pair $(\mathbf{k}^i, \mathbf{x}^i)$ the *layer i*, for $1 \le i \le m$.

A straightforward way to represent a bounded computation of length m is to encode the choice of a rule from $\mathcal{R}$ and to encode all the rules from $\mathcal{R}$ for each layer. In any case, we do not encode bounded computation but rather schemas, for which the sequence of rules $r_1, \ldots, r_m$ is fixed. We exploit this in two ways: First, instead of encoding the choice of a rule and encoding all rules, we encode for each layer i the constraints of rule r_i. Second, as this constraint may update only two counters — $r_i.from$ and $r_i.to$ — we do not need $|L|$ counter variables per layer, but only encode the two counters per layer that have actually changed. As is a common technique in bounded model checking, the counters that are not changed are "reused" from previous layers in our encoding. By doing so, we encode the schema rules with $|L| + |\Gamma| + m \cdot (2 + |\Gamma|)$ integer variables, $2m$ equations, and at most $m \cdot (|\Phi^U| + |\Phi^L|)$ inequalities over linear integer arithmetic.

6   Experiments

Implementation. We have implemented the technique in our tool ByMC (Byzantine Model Checker [2]), which integrates with an SMT solver via the interface provided by SMTLIB2. In our experiments, we used Z3 [17] as back-end solver.

Table 1. Summary of our experiments on AMD Opteron®6272, 32 cores, 192 GB. The symbols are: " ⊙ " for timeout of 24 h.; " 💣 " for memory overrun of 32 GB; " ⚠ " for BDD nodes overrun; " ↻ " for timeout in the refinement loop (24 h.); " ☹ " for spurious counterexamples due to counter abstraction. * In these cases, we used the control flow optimization from Sect. 4.4.

Input FTDA	Case (if more than one)	Threshold Automaton					Time, seconds				Memory, GB			
		$|\mathcal{L}|$	$|\mathcal{R}|$	$|\Phi^U|$	$|\Phi^L|$	$|\mathcal{S}|$	SMT	FAST	BMC	BDD	SMT	FAST	BMC	BDD
FRB	—	6	8	1	0	1	1	1	6	6	0.1	0.1	0.1	0.1
STRB	—	7	15	3	0	4	1	1	2	2	0.1	0.1	0.1	0.1
ABA	$\frac{n+t}{2} = 2t+1$	37	180	6	0	106	18	1103	12512	8	0.1	3.5	0.8	0.1
ABA	$\frac{n+t}{2} > 2t+1$	61	392	8	0	838	294	7782	⊙	18	0.4	12.3	⊙	0.1
CBC	$\lfloor \frac{n}{2} \rfloor < n-t \land f=0$	74	364	12*	0	1	21	⚠	12989	⊙	0.1	⚠	1.3	⊙
CBC	$\lfloor \frac{n}{2} \rfloor = n-t \land f=0$	40	137	12*	0	1	6	⚠	132	⊙	0.1	⚠	0.3	⊙
CBC	$\lfloor \frac{n}{2} \rfloor < n-t \land f>0$	115	896	17*	1	2	366	⚠	💣	💣	1.3	⚠	💣	💣
CBC	$\lfloor \frac{n}{2} \rfloor = n-t \land f>0$	71	408	17*	1	2	35	⚠	⊙	⊙	0.3	⚠	⊙	⊙
NBACC	—	109	1724	6	0	106	218	💣	💣	⊙	0.5	💣	💣	⊙
NBAC	—	77	1356	6	0	106	151	💣	↻	⊙	0.3	💣	↻	⊙
NBACG	—	24	44	4	0	14	2	⚠	275	⊙	0.1	⚠	0.2	⊙
CF1S	$f=0$	57	416	4	0	14	10	19089	12829	81	0.1	29.1	1.3	0.2
CF1S	$f=1$	57	416	4	1	60	22	💣	5583	309	0.1	💣	0.9	0.4
CF1S	$f>1$	98	1152	6	1	594	531	💣	⊙	49133	0.5	💣	⊙	6.0
C1CS	$f=0$	125	1992	8	0	838	1989	💣	💣	10591	1.4	💣	💣	2.0
C1CS	$f=1$	84	926	6	1	594	399	💣	💣	33033	0.4	💣	💣	1.0
C1CS	$f>1$	129	2128	8	1	5808	9876	💣	☹	⊙	8.2	💣	☹	⊙
BOSCO	$\lfloor \frac{n+3t}{2} \rfloor + 1 = n-t$	58	380	6	0	106	43	💣	☹	⊙	0.1	💣	☹	⊙
BOSCO	$\lfloor \frac{n+3t}{2} \rfloor + 1 > n-t$	88	740	8	0	838	598	💣	☹	⊙	0.5	💣	☹	⊙
BOSCO	$\lfloor \frac{n+3t}{2} \rfloor + 1 < n-t$	62	420	6	0	106	46	💣	☹	⊙	0.1	💣	☹	⊙
BOSCO	$n > 5t \land f=0$	134	1978	10	0	6802	13610	💣	💣	↻	9.9	💣	💣	↻
BOSCO	$n > 7t$	98	1080	8	0	838	797	💣	↻	↻	0.7	💣	↻	↻

Benchmarks. We revisited several asynchronous FTDAs that we evaluated in previous work [25,28]. In addition to these classic FTDAs, we considered asynchronous (Byzantine) consensus algorithms—namely, BOSCO [41], C1CS [10], and CF1S [18]—that are designed to work despite partial failure of the distributed system. All our benchmarks, their source code in our parametric extension of PROMELA, and the code of the threshold automata are freely available [1].

The challenge in the verification of FTDAs is the immense non-determinism caused by interleavings, asynchronous message passing, and faults. In our modeling, all these are reflected in non-deterministic choices in the PROMELA code. To obtain threshold automata, as required for our technique, our tool constructs a parametric interval data abstraction [25] that adds to non-determinism.

Evaluation. Table 1 summarizes our experiments conducted with nuXmv, FAST, and our new implementation. We evaluated four different tool configurations: our new implementation (SMT); our previous implementation that checks the counter abstraction with nuXmv [11], either using binary decision diagrams

(BDD), or SAT-based bounded model checking (BMC); and the acceleration-based tool FAST [4]. We compare our results with FAST, as TAs can be encoded with counter automata [3], which FAST receives at its input. For FAST, we give only the figures using the Mona plugin, which produced the best results in our experiments. For BMC, our tool first generates a SAT formula with nuXmv and then calls the solver Lingeling [6] to check satisfiability in non-incremental mode. This works better than the incremental mode with MiniSAT, built into nuXmv.

On large problems, our new technique works significantly better than BDD- and SAT-based model checking. BDDs work extremely well on smaller problems. Importantly, our new technique does not use abstraction refinement.

NBAC and NBACC are challenging as the model checker produces many spurious counterexamples, which are an artifact of counter abstraction losing or adding processes. When using SAT-based model checking, the individual calls to nuXmv are fast, but the abstraction-refinement loop times out, due to a large number of refinements (about 500). BDD-based model checking times out when looking for a counterexample. Our new technique, preserves the number of proceses, and thus, there are no spurious counterexamples of this kind.

In comparison to the general-purpose acceleration tool FAST, our tool uses less memory and is faster on the benchmarks where FAST is successful.

As predicted by the distributed algorithms literature, our tool finds counterexamples, when we relax the resilience condition. In contrast to counter abstraction, our new technique gives concrete values of the parameters and shows how many processes move at each step.

Our new method uses integer counters and thus does not introduce spurious behavior caused by counter abstraction, but still has spurious counterexamples from parameterized data abstraction for complex FTDAs such as BOSCO, C1CS, NBAC, and NBACC. In these cases, we manually refine the interval domain by adding new symbolic interval borders, see [25]. We believe that these interval borders can be derived directly from the TA, so that no refinement is necessary in the first place, and leave this question to future work.

7 Discussions

We introduced a method to efficiently check reachability properties of FTDAs in a parameterized way. If $n > 7t$ as for BOSCO, even the simplest interesting case with $t = 2$ leads to a system size that is out of range of explicit state model checking. Hence, FTDAs force us to develop parameterized verification methods.

The problem we consider is concerned with parameterized model checking, for which many interesting results exist [14,15,19–21,26]. However, the FTDAs considered by us run under the different assumptions. In [28], we discuss the relation between partial orders in accelerated counter systems of threshold automata and the following work: compact programs [35], counter abstraction [5,39], completeness thresholds [7,16,29], partial order reduction [8,22,38,43], and Lipton's movers [34]. We also discussed their relation to counter automata. Indeed, our result entails *flattability* [33] of every counter system of threshold automata: a complete set of schemas immediately gives us a flat counter automaton. Hence, the acceleration semi-algorithms [3,33] should terminate on the systems of TAs, though it rarely happens in our experiments. Further, our execution schemas are inspired by a general notion of *semi-linear path schemas* SLPS [32,33]. We construct a small complete set of schemas and thus a provably small SLPS. Besides, in our work we distinguish counter systems and counter abstraction: the former counts processes as integers, while the latter uses counters over a finite abstract domain, e.g., $\{0, 1, many\}$ [39].

Many distributed algorithms can be specified with I/O Automata [36] or TLA+ [31]. In these frameworks, correctness is typically shown with a proof assistant, while model checking is used as a debugger on small instances. Parameterized model checking is not a concern there, except one notable result [24].

Finally, to verify all properties of FTDAs, we have to check that they are not only safe, but also progress. Liveness properties is a subject to ongoing work.

References

1. https://github.com/konnov/fault-tolerant-benchmarks/tree/master/2015
2. ByMC: Byzantine model checker. http://forsyte.tuwien.ac.at/software/bymc/ (2013). Accessed Feb 2015
3. Bardin, S., Finkel, A., Leroux, J., Petrucci, L.: Fast: acceleration from theory to practice. STTT **10**(5), 401–424 (2008)
4. Bardin, S., Leroux, J., Point, G.: FAST extended release. In: Ball, T., Jones, R.B. (eds.) CAV 2006. LNCS, vol. 4144, pp. 63–66. Springer, Heidelberg (2006)
5. Basler, G., Mazzucchi, M., Wahl, T., Kroening, D.: Symbolic counter abstraction for concurrent software. In: Bouajjani, A., Maler, O. (eds.) CAV 2009. LNCS, vol. 5643, pp. 64–78. Springer, Heidelberg (2009)
6. Biere, A.: Lingeling, plingeling and treengeling entering the SAT competition 2013. In: Proceedings of SAT Competition 2013, Solver and p. 51 (2013)
7. Biere, A., Cimatti, A., Clarke, E., Zhu, Y.: Symbolic model checking without BDDs. In: Cleaveland, W.R. (ed.) TACAS 1999. LNCS, vol. 1579, pp. 193–207. Springer, Heidelberg (1999)
8. Bokor, P., Kinder, J., Serafini, M., Suri, N.: Efficient model checking of fault-tolerant distributed protocols. In: DSN, pp. 73–84 (2011)
9. Bracha, G., Toueg, S.: Asynchronous consensus and broadcast protocols. J. ACM **32**(4), 824–840 (1985)
10. Brasileiro, F., Greve, F.G.P., Mostéfaoui, A., Raynal, M.: Consensus in one communication step. In: Malyshkin, V.E. (ed.) PaCT 2001. LNCS, vol. 2127, pp. 42–50. Springer, Heidelberg (2001)
11. Cavada, R., Cimatti, A., Dorigatti, M., Griggio, A., Mariotti, A., Micheli, A., Mover, S., Roveri, M., Tonetta, S.: The nuXmv symbolic model checker. In: Biere, A., Bloem, R. (eds.) CAV 2014. LNCS, vol. 8559, pp. 334–342. Springer, Heidelberg (2014)
12. Chandra, T.D., Toueg, S.: Unreliable failure detectors for reliable distributed systems. JACM **43**(2), 225–267 (1996)
13. Clarke, E., Grumberg, O., Jha, S., Lu, Y., Veith, H.: Counterexample-guided abstraction refinement for symbolic model checking. J. ACM **50**(5), 752–794 (2003)

14. Clarke, E., Talupur, M., Veith, H.: Proving ptolemy right: the environment abstraction framework for model checking concurrent systems. In: Ramakrishnan, C.R., Rehof, J. (eds.) TACAS 2008. LNCS, vol. 4963, pp. 33–47. Springer, Heidelberg (2008)
15. Clarke, E., Talupur, M., Touili, T., Veith, H.: Verification by network decomposition. In: Gardner, P., Yoshida, N. (eds.) CONCUR 2004. LNCS, vol. 3170, pp. 276–291. Springer, Heidelberg (2004)
16. Clarke, E., Kroning, D., Ouaknine, J., Strichman, O.: Completeness and complexity of bounded model checking. In: Steffen, B., Levi, G. (eds.) VMCAI 2004. LNCS, vol. 2937, pp. 85–96. Springer, Heidelberg (2004)
17. De Moura, L., Bjørner, N.S.: Z3: an efficient SMT solver. In: Ramakrishnan, C.R., Rehof, J. (eds.) TACAS 2008. LNCS, vol. 4963, pp. 337–340. Springer, Heidelberg (2008)
18. Dobre, D., Suri, N.: One-step consensus with zero-degradation. In: DSN, pp. 137–146 (2006)
19. Emerson, E.A., Kahlon, V.: Model checking guarded protocols. In: LICS, pp. 361–370, IEEE (2003)
20. Emerson, E., Namjoshi, K.: Reasoning about rings. In: POPL, pp. 85–94 (1995)
21. Esparza, J., Ganty, P., Majumdar, R.: Parameterized verification of asynchronous shared-memory systems. In: Sharygina, N., Veith, H. (eds.) CAV 2013. LNCS, vol. 8044, pp. 124–140. Springer, Heidelberg (2013)
22. Godefroid, P.: Using partial orders to improve automatic verifcation methods. In: Clarke, E.M., Kurshan, R.P. (eds.) CAV. LNCS, vol. 531, pp. 176–185. Springer, Heidelberg (1990)
23. Guerraoui, R.: Non-blocking atomic commit in asynchronous distributed systems with failure detectors. Distrib. Comput. 15(1), 17–25 (2002)
24. Jensen, H.E., Lynch, N.A.: A proof of burns n-process mutual exclusion algorithm using abstraction. In: Steffen, B. (ed.) TACAS 1998. LNCS, vol. 1384, p. 409. Springer, Heidelberg (1998)
25. John, A., Konnov, I., Schmid, U., Veith, H., Widder, J.: Parameterized model checking of fault-tolerant distributed algorithms by abstraction. In: FMCAD, pp. 201–209 (2013)
26. Kaiser, A., Kroening, D., Wahl, T.: Efficient coverability analysis by proof minimization. In: Koutny, M., Ulidowski, I. (eds.) CONCUR 2012. LNCS, vol. 7454, pp. 500–515. Springer, Heidelberg (2012)
27. Kesten, Y., Pnueli, A.: Control and data abstraction: the cornerstones of practical formal verification. STTT 2, 328–342 (2000)
28. Konnov, I., Veith, H., Widder, J.: On the completeness of bounded model checking for threshold-based distributed algorithms: reachability. In: Baldan, P., Gorla, D. (eds.) CONCUR 2014. LNCS, vol. 8704, pp. 125–140. Springer, Heidelberg (2014)
29. Kroning, D., Strichman, O.: Efficient computation of recurrence diameters. In: Zuck, L.D., Attie, P.C., Cortesi, A., Mukhopadhyay, S. (eds.) VMCAI 2003. LNCS, vol. 2575, pp. 298–309. Springer, Heidelberg (2002)
30. Lamport, L.: Time, clocks, and the ordering of events in a distributed system. Commun. ACM 21(7), 558–565 (1978)
31. Lamport, L.: Specifying Systems: The TLA+ Language and Tools for Hardware and Software Engineers. Addison-Wesley Longman Publishing Co., Inc., Boston (2002)
32. Leroux, J., Sutre, G.: On flatness for 2-dimensional vector addition systems with states. In: Gardner, P., Yoshida, N. (eds.) CONCUR 2004. LNCS, vol. 3170, pp. 402–416. Springer, Heidelberg (2004)

33. Leroux, J., Sutre, G.: Flat counter automata almost everywhere!. In: Peled, D.A., Tsay, Y.-K. (eds.) ATVA 2005. LNCS, vol. 3707, pp. 489–503. Springer, Heidelberg (2005)

34. Lipton, R.J.: Reduction: a method of proving properties of parallel programs. Commun. ACM **18**(12), 717–721 (1975)

35. Lubachevsky, B.D.: An approach to automating the verification of compact parallel coordination programs. I. Acta Informatica **21**(2), 125–169 (1984)

36. Lynch, N.: Distributed Algorithms. Morgan Kaufman, San Francisco (1996)

37. Mostéfaoui, A., Mourgaya, E., Parvédy, P.R., Raynal, M.: Evaluating the condition-based approach to solve consensus. In: DSN, pp. 541–550 (2003)

38. Peled, D.: All from one, one for all: on model checking using representatives. CAV. LNCS **697**, 409–423 (1993)

39. Pnueli, A., Xu, J., Zuck, L.D.: Liveness with $(0, 1, \infty)$-counter abstraction. In: Brinksma, E., Larsen, K.G. (eds.) CAV 2002. LNCS, vol. 2404, pp. 93–111. Springer, Heidelberg (2002)

40. Raynal, M.: A case study of agreement problems in distributed systems: non-blocking atomic commitment. In: HASE, pp. 209–214 (1997)

41. Song, Y.J., Van Renesse, R.: Bosco: one-step byzantine asynchronous consensus. In: Taubenfeld, G. (ed.) DISC 2008. LNCS, vol. 5218, pp. 438–450. Springer, Heidelberg (2008)

42. Srikanth, T., Toueg, S.: Simulating authenticated broadcasts to derive simple fault-tolerant algorithms. Dist. Comp. **2**, 80–94 (1987)

43. Valmari, A.: Stubborn sets for reduced state space generation. In: Rozenberg, G. (ed.) Advances in Petri Nets 1990. LNCS, vol. 483, pp. 491–515. Springer, Heidelberg (1991)

Skipping Refinement

Mitesh Jain$^{(\boxtimes)}$ and Panagiotis Manolios

Northeastern University, Boston, USA
{jmitesh,pete}@ccs.neu.edu

Abstract. We introduce skipping refinement, a new notion of correctness for reasoning about optimized reactive systems. Reasoning about reactive systems using refinement involves defining an abstract, high-level *specification* system and a concrete, low-level *implementation* system. One then shows that every behavior allowed by the implementation is also allowed by the specification. Due to the difference in abstraction levels, it is often the case that the implementation requires many steps to match one step of the specification, hence, it is quite useful for refinement to directly account for *stuttering*. Some optimized implementations, however, can actually take multiple specification steps at once. For example, a memory controller can buffer the commands to the memory and at a later time simultaneously update multiple memory locations, thereby *skipping* several observable states of the abstract specification, which only updates one memory location at a time. We introduce skipping simulation refinement and provide a sound and complete characterization consisting of "local" proof rules that are amenable to mechanization and automated verification. We present case studies that highlight the applicability of skipping refinement: a JVM-inspired stack machine, a simple memory controller and a scalar to vector compiler transformation. Our experimental results demonstrate that current model-checking and automated theorem proving tools have difficulty automatically analyzing these systems using existing notions of correctness, but they can analyze the systems if we use skipping refinement.

1 Introduction

Refinement is a powerful method for reasoning about reactive systems. The idea is to prove that every execution of the concrete system being verified is allowed by the abstract system. The concrete system is defined at a lower level of abstraction, so it is usually the case that it requires several steps to match one high-level step of the abstract system. Thus, notions of refinement usually directly account for stuttering [5,10,13].

Engineering ingenuity and the drive to build ever more efficient systems has led to highly-optimized concrete systems capable of taking *single* steps that

This research was supported in part by DARPA under AFRL Cooperative Agreement No. FA8750-10-2-0233, by NSF grants CCF-1117184 and CCF-1319580, and by OSD under contract FA8750-14-C-0024.

© Springer International Publishing Switzerland 2015
D. Kroening and C.S. Păsăreanu (Eds.): CAV 2015, Part I, LNCS 9206, pp. 103–119, 2015.
DOI: 10.1007/978-3-319-21690-4_7

perform the work of *multiple* abstract steps. For example, in order to reduce memory latency and effectively utilize memory bandwidth, memory controllers often buffer requests to memory. The pending requests in the buffer are analyzed for address locality and then at some time in the future, multiple locations in the memory are read and updated simultaneously. Similarly, to improve instruction throughput, superscalar processors fetch multiple instructions in a single cycle. These instructions are analyzed for instruction-level parallelism (*e.g.*, the absence of data dependencies) and, where possible, are executed in parallel, leading to multiple instructions being retired in a single cycle. In both these examples, in addition to stuttering, a single step in the implementation may perform the work of multiple abstract steps, *e.g.*, by updating multiple locations in memory and retiring multiple instructions in a single cycle. Thus, notions of refinement that only account for stuttering are not appropriate for reasoning about such optimized systems. In Sect. 3, we introduce *skipping refinement*, a new notion of correctness for reasoning about reactive systems that "execute faster" and therefore can skip some steps of the specification. Skipping can be thought of as the dual of stuttering: stuttering allows us to "stretch" executions of the specification system and skipping allows us to "squeeze" them.

An appropriate notion of correctness is only part of the story. We also want to leverage the notion of correctness in order to mechanically verify systems. To this end, in Sect. 4, we introduce *Well-Founded Skipping*, a sound and complete characterization of skipping simulation that allows us to prove refinement theorems about the kind of systems we consider using only local reasoning. This characterization establishes that refinement maps always exist for skipping refinement. In Sect. 5, we illustrate the applicability of skipping refinement by mechanizing the proof of correctness of three systems: a stack machine with an instruction buffer, a simple memory controller, and a simple scalar-to-vector compiler transformation. We show experimentally that by using skipping refinement current model-checkers are able to verify systems that otherwise are beyond their capability to verify. We end with related work and conclusions in Sects. 6 and 7.

Our contributions include (1) the introduction of skipping refinement, which is the first notion of refinement to directly support reasoning about optimized systems that execute faster than their specifications (as far as we know) (2) a sound and complete characterization of skipping refinement that requires only local reasoning, thereby enabling automated verification and showing that refinement maps always exist (3) experimental evidence showing that the use of skipping refinement allows us to extend the complexity of systems that can be automatically verified using state-of-the-art model checking and interactive theorem proving technology.

2   Motivating Examples

To illustrate the notion of skipping simulation, we consider a running example of a discrete-time event simulation (DES) system. A state of the abstract, high-level specification system is a three-tuple $\langle t, E, A \rangle$ where t is a natural number corresponding to the current time, E is a set of pairs (e, t_e) where e is an event scheduled to be executed at time t_e (we require that $t_e \geq t$), and A is an assignment of values to a set of (global) state variables. The transition relation for the abstract DES system is defined as follows. If there is no event of the form $(e, t) \in E$, then there is nothing to do at time t and so t is incremented by 1. Otherwise, we (nondeterministically) choose and execute an event of the form $(e, t) \in E$. The execution of an event can modify the state variables and can also generate a finite number of new events, with the restriction that the time of any generated event is $> t$. Finally, execution involves removing (e, t) from E.

Now, consider an optimized, concrete implementation of the abstract DES system. As before, a state is a three-tuple $\langle t, E, A \rangle$. However, unlike the abstract system which just increments time by 1 when no events are scheduled for the current time, the optimized system uses a priority queue to find the next event to execute. The transition relation is defined as follows. An event (e, t_e) with the minimum time is selected, t is updated to t_e and the event e is executed, as above.

Notice that the optimized implementation of the discrete-time event simulation system can run faster than the abstract specification system by *skipping* over abstract states when no events are scheduled for execution at the current time. This is neither a stuttering step nor corresponds to a single step of the specification. Therefore, it is not possible to prove that the implementation refines the specification using notions of refinement that only allow stuttering [13,17], because that just is not true. But, intuitively, there is a sense in which the optimized DES system *does* refine the abstract DES system. Skipping refinement is our attempt at formally developing the theory required to rigorously reason about these kinds of systems.

Due to its simplicity, we will use the discrete-time event simulation example in later sections to illustrate various concepts. After the basic theory is developed, we provide an experimental evaluation based on three other motivating examples. The first is a JVM-inspired stack machine that can store instructions in a queue and then process these instructions in bulk at some later point in time. The second example is an optimized memory controller that buffers requests to memory to reduce memory latency and maximize memory bandwidth utilization. The pending requests in the buffer are analyzed for address locality and redundant writes and then at some time in the future, multiple locations in the memory are read and updated in a single step. The final example is a compiler transformation that analyzes programs for superword-level parallelism and, where possible, replaces multiple scalar instructions with a compact SIMD instruction that concurrently operates on multiple words of data. All of these examples require skipping refinement, because the optimized concrete systems can do more than inject stuttering steps in the executions specified by their specification systems; they can also collapse executions.

3   Skipping Simulation and Refinement

In this section, we introduce the notions of skipping simulation and refinement. We do this in the general setting of labeled transition systems where we allow state space sizes and branching factors of arbitrary infinite cardinalities.

We start with some notational conventions. Function application is some-times denoted by an infix dot "." and is left-associative. For a binary relation R, we often write xRy instead of $(x, y) \in R$. The composition of relation R with itself i times (for $0 < i \leq \omega$) is denoted R^i ($\omega = \mathbb{N}$ and is the first infinite ordinal). Given a relation R and $1 < k \leq \omega$, $R^{<k}$ denotes $\bigcup_{1 \leq i < k} R^i$ and $R^{\geq k}$ denotes $\bigcup_{\omega > i \geq k} R^i$. Instead of $R^{<\omega}$ we often write the more common R^+. $\uplus$ denotes the disjoint union operator. Quantified expressions are written as $\langle Qx \colon r \colon p \rangle$, where Q is the quantifier (e.g., $\exists, \forall$), x is the bound variable, r is an expression that denotes the range of x (*true* if omitted), and p is the body of the quantifier.

Definition 1. *A labeled transition system (TS) is a structure $\langle S, \rightarrow, L \rangle$, where S is a non-empty (possibly infinite) set of states, $\rightarrow \subseteq S \times S$ is a left-total transition relation (every state has a successor), and L is a labeling function: its domain is S and it tells us what is observable at a state.*

A path is a sequence of states such that for adjacent states s and u, $s \rightarrow u$. A path, σ, is a fullpath if it is infinite. fp.σ.s denotes that σ is a fullpath starting at s and for $i \in \omega$, $\sigma(i)$ denotes the ith element of path σ.

Our definition of skipping simulation is based on the notion of *matching*, which we define below. Informally, we say a fullpath σ matches a fullpath δ under relation B if the fullpaths can be partitioned into non-empty, finite segments such that all elements in a particular segment of σ are related to the first element in the corresponding segment of δ.

Definition 2 (Match). *Let INC be the set of strictly increasing sequences of natural numbers starting at 0. Given a fullpath σ, the ith segment of σ with respect to $\pi \in INC$, written $^\pi\sigma^i$, is given by the sequence $\langle \sigma(\pi.i), ..., \sigma(\pi.(i + 1) - 1) \rangle$. For $\pi, \xi \in INC$ and relation B, we define*

$$corr(B, \sigma, \pi, \delta, \xi) \equiv \langle \forall i \in \omega \colon\colon \langle \forall s \in {}^\pi\sigma^i \colon\colon sB\delta(\xi.i) \rangle \rangle \; and$$

$$match(B, \sigma, \delta) \equiv \langle \exists \pi, \xi \in INC \colon\colon corr(B, \sigma, \pi, \delta, \xi) \rangle.$$

In Fig. 1, we illustrate our notion of matching using our running example of a discrete-time event simulation system. Let the set of state variables be $\{v_1, v_2\}$ and let the set of events contain $\{(e_1, 0), (e_2, 2)\}$, where event e_i increments variable v_i by 1. In the figure, σ is a fullpath of the concrete system and δ is a fullpath of the abstract system. (We only show a prefix of the fullpaths.) The other parameter for *match* is B, which, for our example, is just the identity relation. In order to show that $match(B, \sigma, \delta)$ holds, we have to find π, ξ satisfying the definition. In the figure, we separate the partitions induced by our choice for π, ξ using $--$ and connect elements related by B with ⟿. Since all elements of a σ partition are related to the first element of the corresponding δ partition, $corr(B, \sigma, \pi, \delta, \xi)$ holds, therefore, $match(B, \sigma, \delta)$ holds.

Given a labeled transition system $\mathcal{M} = \langle S, \rightarrow, L \rangle$, a relation $B \subseteq S \times S$ is a *skipping simulation*, if for any $s, w \in S$ such that sBw, s and w are identically labeled and any fullpath starting at s can be matched by some fullpath starting at w.

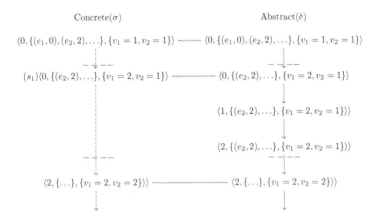

Fig. 1. Discrete-time Event simulation system

Definition 3 (Skipping Simulation). $B \subseteq S \times S$ *is a skipping simulation* (SKS) *on TS* $\mathcal{M} = \langle S, \rightarrow, L \rangle$ *iff for all* s, w *such that* sBw, *the following hold.*

(SKS1) $L.s = L.w$

(SKS2) $\langle \forall \sigma \colon fp.\sigma.s \colon \langle \exists \delta \colon fp.\delta.w \colon match(B, \sigma, \delta) \rangle \rangle$

It may seem counter-intuitive to define skipping refinement with respect to a single transition system, since our ultimate goal is to relate transition systems at different levels of abstraction. Our current approach has certain technical advantages and we will see how to deal with two transition systems shortly.

In our running example of a discrete-time event simulation system, neither the optimized concrete system nor the abstract system stutter, *i.e.*, they do not require multiple steps to complete the execution of an event. However, suppose that the abstract and concrete system are modified so that execution of an event takes multiple steps. For example, suppose that the execution of e_1 in the concrete system (the first partition of σ in Fig. 1) takes 5 steps and the execution of e_1 in the abstract system (the first partition of δ in Fig. 1) takes 3 steps. Now, our abstract system is capable of stuttering and the concrete system is capable of both stuttering and skipping. Skipping simulation allows this, *i.e.*, we can define π, ξ such that $corr B \sigma \pi \delta \xi$ still holds.

Note that skipping simulation differs from weak simulation [10]; the latter allows infinite stuttering. Since we want to distinguish deadlock from stuttering, it is important we distinguish between finite and infinite stuttering. Skipping simulation also differs from stuttering simulation, as the former allows an concrete system to skip steps of the abstract system and therefore run "faster" than the abstract system. In fact, skipping simulation is strictly weaker than stuttering simulation.

3.1   Skipping Refinement

We now show how the notion of skipping simulation, which is defined in terms of a *single* transition system, can be used to define the notion of skipping refinement, a notion that relates *two* transition systems: an *abstract* transition system and a *concrete* transition system. In order to define skipping refinement, we make use of *refinement maps*, functions that map states of the concrete system to states of the abstract system. Refinement maps are used to define what is observable at concrete states. If the concrete system is a skipping refinement of the abstract system, then its observable behaviors are also behaviors of the abstract system, modulo skipping (which includes stuttering). For example, in our running example, if the refinement map is the identity function then any behavior of the optimized system is a behavior of the abstract system modulo skipping.

Definition 4 (Skipping Refinement). *Let* $\mathcal{M}_A = \langle S_A, \overset{A}{\rightarrow}, L_A \rangle$ *and* $\mathcal{M}_C = \langle S_C, \overset{C}{\rightarrow}, L_C \rangle$ *be transition systems and let* $r : S_C \rightarrow S_A$ *be a* refinement map. *We say* $\mathcal{M}_C$ *is a skipping refinement of* $\mathcal{M}_A$ *with respect to* r, *written* $\mathcal{M}_C \lesssim_r \mathcal{M}_A$, *if there exists a relation* $B \subseteq S_C \times S_A$ *such that all of the following hold.*

1. $\langle \forall s \in S_C : : sBr.s \rangle$ *and*
2. B *is an SKS on* $\langle S_C \uplus S_A, \overset{C}{\rightarrow} \uplus \overset{A}{\rightarrow}, \mathcal{L} \rangle$ *where* $\mathcal{L}.s = L_A(s)$ *for* $s \in S_A$, *and* $\mathcal{L}.s = L_A(r.s)$ *for* $s \in S_C$.

Notice that we place no restrictions on refinement maps. When refinement is used in specific contexts it is often useful to place restrictions on what a refinement map can do, *e.g.*, we may require for every $s \in S_C$ that $L_A(r.s)$ is a projection of $L_C(s)$. Also, the choice of refinement map can have a big impact on verification times [18]. Our purpose is to define a general theory of skipping, hence, we prefer to be as permissive as possible.

4 Automated Reasoning

To prove that transition system $\mathcal{M}_C$ is a skipping refinement of transition system $\mathcal{M}_A$, we use Definitions 3 and 4, which require us to show that for any fullpath from $\mathcal{M}_C$ we can find a "matching" fullpath from $\mathcal{M}_A$. However, reasoning about the existence of infinite sequences can be problematic using automated tools. In order to avoid such reasoning, we introduce the notion of well-founded skipping simulation. This notion allows us to reason about skipping refinement by checking mostly local properties, *i.e.*, properties involving states and their successors. The intuition is, for any pair of states s, w, which are related and a state u such that $s \rightarrow u$, there are four cases to consider (Fig. 2): (a) either we can match the move from s to u right away, *i.e.*, there is a v such that $w \rightarrow v$ and u is related to v, or (b) there is stuttering on the left, or (c) there is stuttering on the right, or (d) there is skipping on the left.

Definition 5 (Well-founded Skipping). $B \subseteq S \times S$ *is a well-founded skipping relation on TS* $\mathcal{M} = \langle S, \rightarrow, L \rangle$ *iff :*

(WFSK1) $\langle \forall s, w \in S : sBw : L.s = L.w \rangle$

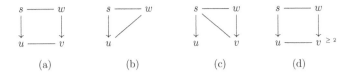

Fig. 2. Well-founded skipping simulation

(WFSK2) *There exist functions, rankt: $S \times S \to W$, rankl: $S \times S \times S \to \omega$, such that $\langle W, \prec \rangle$ is well-founded and*

$\langle \forall s, u, w \in S : s \to u \wedge sBw :$

(a) $\langle \exists v : w \to v : uBv \rangle$ ∨

(b) $(uBw \wedge rankt(u, w) \prec rankt(s, w))$ ∨

(c) $\langle \exists v : w \to v : sBv \wedge rankl(v, s, u) < rankl(w, s, u) \rangle$ ∨

(d) $\langle \exists v : w \to^{\geq 2} v : uBv \rangle \rangle$

In the above definition, notice that condition (2d) requires us to check that there exists a v such that v is *reachable* from w and uBv holds. Reasoning about reachability is not local in general. However, for the kinds of optimized systems we are interested in, we *can* reason about reachability using local methods because the number of abstract steps that a concrete step corresponds to is bounded by a constant. As an example, the maximum number of high-level steps that a concrete step of an optimized memory controller can correspond to is the size of the request buffer; this is a constant that is determined early in the design. Another option is to replace condition (2d) with a condition that requires only local reasoning. While this is possible, in light of the above comments, the increased complexity is not justified.

Next, we show that the notion of well-founded skipping simulation is equivalent to SKS and can be used as a sound and complete proof rule to check if a given relation is an SKS. This allows us to match infinite sequences by checking local properties and bounded reachability. To show this we first introduce an alternative definition for well-founded skipping simulation. The motivation for doing this is that the alternate definition is useful for proving the soundness and completeness theorems. It also allows us to highlight the idea behind the conditions in the definition of well-founded skipping simulation. The simplification is based on two observations. First, it turns out that (d) and (a) together subsume (c), so in the definition below, we do not include case (c). Second, if instead of $\to^{\geq 2}$ we use $\to^+$ in (d), then we subsume case (a) as well.

Definition 6. $B \subseteq S \times S$ *is a reduced well-founded skipping relation on TS* $\mathcal{M} = \langle S, \to, L \rangle$ *iff* :

(RWFSK1) $\langle \forall s, w \in S : sBw : L.s = L.w \rangle$

(RWFSK2) *There exists a function, rankt*: $S \times S \to W$, *such that* $\langle W, \prec \rangle$ *is well-founded and*

$\langle \forall s, u, w \in S : s \to u \wedge sBw :$

    (a) $(uBw \wedge rankt(u, w) \prec rankt(s, w)) \vee$

    (b) $\langle \exists v : w \to^+ v : uBv \rangle \rangle$

In the sequel, "WFSK" is an abbreviation for "well-founded skipping relation" and, similarly, "RWFSK" is an abbreviation for "reduced well-founded skipping relation."

We now show that WFSK and RWFSK are equivalent.

Theorem 1. *B is a WFSK on* $\mathcal{M} = \langle S, \to, L \rangle$ *iff B is an RWFSK on* $\mathcal{M}$.

Proof. ($\Leftarrow$ direction): This direction is easy.
($\Rightarrow$ direction): The key insight is that WFSK2c is redundant. Let $s, u, w \in S$, $s \to u$, and sBw. If WFSK2a or WFSK2d holds then RWFSK2b holds. If WFSK2b holds, then RWFSK2a holds. So, what remains is to assume that WFSK2c holds and neither of WFSK2a, WFSK2b, or WFSK2d hold. From this we will derive a contradiction.

Let δ be a path starting at w, such that only WFSK2c holds between $s, u, \delta.i$. There are non-empty paths that satisfy this condition, *e.g.*, let $\delta = \langle w \rangle$. In addition, any such path must be finite. If not, then for any adjacent pair of states in δ, say $\delta.k$ and $\delta(k + 1)$, $rankl(\delta(k + 1), s, u) < rankl(\delta.k, s, u)$, which contradicts the well-foundedness of *rankl*. We also have that for every $k > 0$, $u \not{B} \delta.k$; otherwise WFSK2a or WFSK2d holds. Now, let δ be a maximal path satisfying the above condition, *i.e.*, every extension of δ violates the condition. Let x be the last state in δ. We know that sBx and only WFSK2c holds between s, u, x, so let y be a witness for WFSK2c, which means that sBy and one of WFSK2a,b, or d holds between s, u, y. WSFK2b can't hold because then we would have uBy (which would mean WFSK2a holds between s, u, x). So, one of WFSK2a,d has to hold, but that gives us a path from x to some state v such that uBv. The contradiction is that v is also reachable from w, so WFSK2a or WFSK2d held between s, u, w. □

Let's now discuss why we included condition WFSK2c. The systems we are interested in verifying have a bound—determined early early in the design—on the number of skipping steps possible. The problem is that RWSFK2b forces us to deal with stuttering and skipping steps in the same way, while with WFSK any amount of stuttering is dealt with locally. Hence, WFSK should be used for automated proofs and RWFSK can be used for meta reasoning.

One more observation is that the proof of Theorem 1, by showing that WFSK2c is redundant, highlights why skipping refinement subsumes stuttering refinement. Therefore, skipping refinement is a weaker, but more generally applicable notion of refinement than stuttering refinement.

In what follows, we show that the notion of RWFSK (and by Theorem 1 WFSK) is equivalent to SKS and can be used as a sound and complete proof rule to check if a given relation is an SKS. This allows us to match infinite sequences by checking local properties and bounded reachability. We first prove soundness, *i.e.*, any RWFSK is an SKS. The proof proceeds by showing that given a RWFSK relation B, sBw, and any fullpath starting at s, we can recursively construct a fullpath δ starting at w, and increasing sequences π, ξ such that fullpath at s matches δ.

Theorem 2 (Soundness). *If B is an RWFSK on $\mathcal{M}$ then B is a SKS on $\mathcal{M}$.*

Proof. To show that B is an SKS on $\mathcal{M} = \langle S, \rightarrow, L \rangle$, we show that given B is a RWFSK on $\mathcal{M} = \langle S, \rightarrow, L \rangle$ and $x, y \in S$ such that xBy, SKS1 and SKS2 hold. SKS1 follows directly from condition 1 of RWSFK.

Next we show that SKS2 holds. We start by recursively defining δ. In the process, we also define partitions π and ξ. For the base case, we let $\pi.0 = 0$, $\xi.0 = 0$ and $\delta.0 = y$. By assumption $\sigma(\pi.0)B\delta(\xi.0)$. For the recursive case, assume that we have defined $\pi.0, \ldots, \pi.i$ as well as $\xi.0, \ldots, \xi.i$ and $\delta.0, \ldots, \delta(\xi.i)$. We also assume that $\sigma(\pi.i)B\delta(\xi.i)$. Let s be $\sigma(\pi.i)$; let u be $\sigma(\pi.i + 1)$; let w be $\delta(\xi.i)$. We consider two cases.

First, say that RWFSK2b holds. Then, there is a v such that $w \rightarrow^+ v$ and uBv. Let $\overrightarrow{v} = [v_0 = w, \ldots, v_m = v]$ be a finite path from w to v where $m \geq 1$. We define $\pi(i + 1) = \pi.i + 1, \xi(i + 1) = \xi.i + m, {}^{\xi}\delta^i = [v_0, \ldots, v_{m-1}]$ and $\delta(\xi(i + 1)) = v$.

If the first case does not hold, *i.e.*, RWFSK2b does not hold, and RWFSK2a does hold. We define J to be the subset of the positive integers such that for every $j \in J$, the following holds.

$$\langle \forall v : w \rightarrow^+ v : \neg(\sigma(\pi.i + j)Bv) \rangle \wedge \tag{1}$$
$$\sigma(\pi.i + j)Bw \wedge rankt(\sigma(\pi.i + j), w) \prec rankt(\sigma(\pi.i + j - 1), w)$$

The first thing to observe is that $1 \in J$ because $\sigma(\pi.i + 1) = u$, RWFSK2b does not hold (so the first conjunct is true) and RWFSK2a does (so the second conjunct is true). The next thing to observe is that there exists a positive integer $n > 1$ such that $n \notin J$. Suppose not, then for all $n \geq 1, n \in J$. Now, consider the (infinite) suffix of σ starting at $\pi.i$. For every adjacent pair of states in this suffix, say $\sigma(\pi.i + k)$ and $\sigma(\pi.i + k + 1)$ where $k \geq 0$, we have that $\sigma(\pi.i + k)Bw$ and that only RWFSK2a applies (*i.e.*, RWFSK2b does not apply). This gives us a contradiction because *rankt* is well-founded. We can now define n to be $min(\{l : l \notin J\})$. Notice that only RWFSK2a holds between $\sigma(\pi.i + n - 1)), \sigma(\pi.i + n)$ and w, hence $\sigma(\pi.i + n)Bw$ and $rankt(\sigma(\pi.i + n), w) \prec rankt(\sigma(\pi.i + n - 1), w)$. Since Formula 1 does not hold for n, there is a v such that $w \rightarrow^+ v \wedge \sigma(\pi.i + n)Bv$. Let $\overrightarrow{v} = [v_0 = w, \ldots, v_m = v]$ be a finite path from w to v where $m \geq 1$. We are now ready to extend our recursive definition as follows: $\pi(i + 1) = \pi.i + n$, $\xi(i + 1) = \xi.i + m$, and ${}^{\xi}\delta^i = [v_0, \ldots, v_{m-1}]$.

Now that we defined δ we can show that SKS2 holds. We start by unwinding definitions. The first step is to show that $fp.\delta.y$ holds, which is true by construction. Next, we show that $match(B, \sigma, \delta)$ by unwinding the definition of $match$. That involves showing that there exist π and ξ such that $corr(B, \sigma, \pi, \delta, \xi)$ holds. The π and ξ we used to define δ can be used here. Finally, we unwind the definition of $corr$, which gives us a universally quantified formula over the natural numbers. This is handled by induction on the segment index; the proof is based on the recursive definitions given above.   □

We next state completeness, $i.e.$, given a SKS relation B we provide as witness a well-founded structure $\langle W, \prec \rangle$, and a rank function $rankt$ such that the conditions in Definition 6 hold.

Theorem 3 (Completeness). *If B is an SKS on $\mathcal{M}$, then B is an RWFSK on $\mathcal{M}$.*

The proof requires us to introduce a few definitions and lemmas.

Definition 7. *Given TS $\mathcal{M} = \langle S, \rightarrow, L \rangle$, the computation tree rooted at a state $s \in S$, denoted $ctree(\mathcal{M}, s)$, is obtained by "unfolding" $\mathcal{M}$ from s. Nodes of $ctree(\mathcal{M}, s)$ are finite sequences over S and $ctree(\mathcal{M}, s)$ is the smallest tree satisfying the following.*

1. *The root is $\langle s \rangle$.*
2. *If $\langle s, \ldots, w \rangle$ is a node and $w \rightarrow v$, then $\langle s, \ldots, w, v \rangle$ is a node whose parent is $\langle s, \ldots, w \rangle$.*

Our next definition is used to construct the ranking function appearing in the definition of RWFSK.

Definition 8 *(ranktCt). Given an SKS B, if $\neg(sBw)$, then $ranktCt(\mathcal{M}, s, w)$ is the empty tree, otherwise $ranktCt(\mathcal{M}, s, w)$ is the largest subtree of $ctree(\mathcal{M}, s)$ such that for any non-root node $\langle s, \ldots, x \rangle$ of $ranktCt(\mathcal{M}, s, w)$, we have that xBw and $\langle \forall v : w \rightarrow^+ v : \neg(xBv) \rangle$.*

A basic property of our construction is the finiteness of paths.

Lemma 4. *Every path of $ranktCt(\mathcal{M}, s, w)$ is finite.*

Given Lemma 4, we define a function, $size$, that given a tree, t, all of whose paths are finite, assigns an ordinal to t and to all nodes in t. The ordinal assigned to node x in t is defined as follows: $size(t, x) = \bigcup_{c \in children.x} size(t, c) + 1$. We are using set theory, $e.g.$, an ordinal number is defined to be the set of ordinal numbers below it, which explains why it makes sense to take the union of ordinal numbers. The size of a tree is the size of its root, $i.e.$, $size(ranktCt(\mathcal{M}, s, w)) = size(ranktCt(\mathcal{M}, s, w), \langle s \rangle)$. We use $\preceq$ to compare ordinal and cardinal numbers.

Lemma 5. *If $|S| \preceq \kappa$, where $\omega \preceq \kappa$ then for all $s, w \in S$, $size(ranktCt(\mathcal{M}, s, w))$ is an ordinal of cardinality $\preceq \kappa$.*

Lemma 5 shows that we can use as the domain of our well-founded function in RWFSK2 the cardinal $max(|S|^+, \omega)$: either ω if the state space is finite, or $|S|^+$, the cardinal successor of the size of the state space otherwise.

Lemma 6. *If $sBw, s \to u, u \in ranktCt(\mathcal{M}, s, w)$ then $size(ranktCt(\mathcal{M}, u, w)) \prec size(ranktCt(\mathcal{M}, s, w))$.*

We are now ready to prove completeness.

Proof. (Completeness) We assume that B is an SKS on $\mathcal{M}$ and we show that this implies that B is also an RWFSK on $\mathcal{M}$. RWFSK1 follows directly. To show that RWFSK2 holds, let W be the successor cardinal of $max(|S|, \omega)$ and let $rankt(a, b)$ be $size(ranktCt(\mathcal{M}, a, b))$. Given $s, u, w \in S$ such that $s \to u$ and sBw, we show that either RWFSK2(a) or RWFSK2(b) holds.

There are two cases. First, suppose that $\langle \exists v : w \to^+ v : uBv \rangle$ holds, then RWFSK2(b) holds. If not, then $\langle \forall v : w \to^+ v : \neg(uBv) \rangle$, but B is an SKS so let σ be a fullpath starting at s, u. Then there is a fullpath δ such that $fp.\delta.w$ and $match(B, \sigma, \delta)$. Hence, there exists $\pi, \xi \in INC$ such that $corr(B, \sigma, \pi, \delta, \xi)$. By the definition of $corr$, we have that $uB\delta(\xi.i)$ for some i, but i cannot be greater than 0 because then uBx for some x reachable from w, violating the assumptions of the case we are considering. So, $i = 0$, *i.e.*, uBw. By lemma 6, $rankt(u, w) = size(ranktCt(\mathcal{M}, u, w)) \prec size(ranktCt(\mathcal{M}, s, w)) = rankt(s, w)$. □

Following Abadi and Lamport [13], one of the basic questions asked about new notions of refinement is: if a concrete system is an "implementation" of an abstract system, under what conditions do refinement maps (a local reasoning) exist that can be use to prove it? Abadi and Lamport required several rather complex conditions, but our completeness proof shows that for skipping refinement, refinement maps always exist. See Sect. 6 for more information.

Well-founded skipping gives us a simple proof rule to determine if a concrete transition system $\mathcal{M}_C$ is a skipping refinement of an abstract transition system $\mathcal{M}_A$ with respect to a refinement map r. Given a refinement map $r : S_C \to S_A$ and relation $B \subseteq S_C \times S_A$, we check the following two conditions: (a) for all $s \in S_C$, $sBr.s$ and (b) if B is a WFSK on disjoint union of $\mathcal{M}_C$ and $\mathcal{M}_A$. If (a) and (b) hold, from Theorem 2, $\mathcal{M}_C \lesssim_r \mathcal{M}_A$.

5   Experimental Evaluation

In this section, we experimentally evaluate the theory of skipping refinement using three case studies: a JVM-inspired stack machine, an optimized memory controller, and a vectorization compiler transformation. Our goals are to evaluate the specification costs and benefits of using skipping refinement as a notion of correctness and to determine the impact that the use of skipping refinement has on state-of-the-art verification tools in terms of capacity and verification times. We do that by comparing the cost of proving correctness using skipping refinement with the cost of using input-output equivalence: if the specification and the implementation systems start in equivalent initial states and get the same inputs, then if both systems terminate, the final states of the systems are also equivalent. We chose I/O equivalence since that is the most straightforward way of using existing tools to reason about our case studies. We cannot use existing notions of refinement because they do not allow skipping and, therefore, are not applicable. Since skipping simulation is a stronger notion of correctness than I/O equivalence, skipping proofs provide more information, *e.g.*, I/O equivalence holds even if the concrete system diverges, but skipping simulation does not hold and would therefore catch such divergence errors.

The first two case studies were developed and compiled to sequential AIGs using the BAT tool [20], and then analyzed using the TIP, IIMC, BLIMC, and SUPER_PROVE model-checkers [1]. SUPER_PROVE and IIMC are the top performing model-checkers in the single safety property track of the Hardware Model Checking Competition [1]. We chose TIP and BLIMC to cover tools based on temporal decomposition and bounded model-checking. The last case study involves systems whose state space is infinite. Since model checkers cannot be used to verify such systems, we used the ACL2s interactive theorem prover [8]. BAT files, corresponding AIGs, ACL2s models, and ACL2s proof scripts are publicly available [2], hence we only briefly describe the case studies.

Our results show that with I/O equivalence, model-checkers quickly start timing out as the complexity of the systems increases. In contrast, with skipping refinement much larger systems can be automatically verified. For the infinite state case study, interactive theorem proving was used and the manual effort required to prove skipping refinement theorems was significantly less than the effort required to prove I/O equivalence.

JVM-inspired Stack Machine. For this case study we defined BSTK, a simple hardware implementation of part of Java Virtual Machine (JVM) [11]. BSTK models an instruction memory, an instruction buffer and a stack. It supports a small subset of JVM instructions, including *push, pop, top, nop*. STK is the high-level specification with respect to which we verify the correctness of BSTK. The state of STK consists of an instruction memory (*imem*), a program counter (*pc*), and a stack (*stk*). STK fetches an instruction from the *imem*, executes it, increases the *pc* and possibly modifies the *stk*. The state of BSTK is similar to STK, except that it also includes an instruction buffer, whose capacity is a parameter. BSTK fetches an instruction from the *imem* and as long as the fetched instruction is not *top* and the instruction buffer (*ibuf*) is not full, it enqueues it to the end of the *ibuf* and increments the *pc*. If the fetched instruction is *top* or *ibuf* is full, the machine executes all buffered instructions in the order they were enqueued, thereby draining the *ibuf* and obtaining a new *stk*.

Memory Controller. We defined a memory controller, OptMEMC, which fetches a memory request from location *pt* in a queue of CPU requests, *reqs*. It enqueues the fetched request in the request buffer, *rbuf* and increments *pt* to point to the next CPU request in *reqs*. If the fetched request is a *read* or the request buffer is full (the capacity of *rbuf* is parameter), then before enqueuing the request into *rbuf*, OptMEMC first analyzes the request buffer for consecutive write requests to the same address in the memory (*mem*). If such a pair of writes exists in the buffer, it

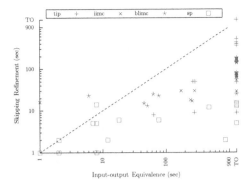

Fig. 3. Performance of model-checkers on case studies

marks the older write requests in the request buffer as redundant. Then it executes all the requests in the request buffer except the marked (redundant) ones. Requests in the buffer are executed in the order they were enqueued. We also defined MEMC, a specification system that processes each memory request atomically.

Results. To evaluate the computational benefits of skipping refinement, we created a benchmark suite including versions of the BSTK and STK machines—parameterized by the size of *imem*, *ibuf*, and *stk*—and OptMEMC and MEMC machines—parameterized by the size of *req*, *rbuf* and *mem*. These models had anywhere from 24 K gates and 500 latches to 2M gates and 23 K latches. We used a machine with an Intel Xeon X5677 with 16 cores running at 3.4GHz and 96GB main memory. The timeout limit for model-checker runs is set to 900 seconds. In Fig. 3, we plot the running times for the four model-checkers used. The x-axis represents the running time using I/O equivalence and y-axis represents the running time using skipping refinement. A point with $x =$ TO indicates that the model-checker timed out for I/O equivalence while $y =$ TO indicates that the model-checker timed out for skipping refinement. Our results show that model-checkers timeout for most of the configurations when using I/O equivalence while all model-checkers except TIP can solve all the configurations using skipping refinement. Furthermore, there is an improvement of several orders of magnitude in the running time when using skipping refinement. The performance benefits are partly due to the structure provided by the skipping refinement proof obligation. For example, we have a bound on the number of steps that the optimized systems can skip before a match occurs and we have rank functions for stuttering. This allows the model checkers to locally check correctness instead of having to prove correspondence at the input/output boundaries, as is the case for I/O equivalence.

Superword-level Parallelism with SIMD instructions. For this case study we verify the correctness of a compiler transformation from a source language containing only scalar instructions to a target language containing both scalar and vector instructions. We model the transformation as a function that given a program in the source language and generates a program in the target language. We use the translation validation approach to compiler correctness and prove that the target program implements the source program [4].

For presentation purposes, we make some simplifying assumptions: the state of the source and target programs (modeled as transition systems) is a tuple consisting of a sequence of instructions, a program counter and a store. We also assume that a SIMD instruction operates on two sets of data operands simultaneously and that the transformation identifies parallelism at the basic block level. Therefore, we do not consider control flow.

For this case study, we used deductive verification methodology to prove correctness. The scalar and vector machines are defined using the data-definition framework in ACL2s [6–8]. We formalized the operational semantics of the scalar and vector machines using standard methods. The sizes of the program and store are unbounded and thus the state space of the machines is infinite. Once the definitions were in place, proving skipping refinement with ACL2s was straightforward. Proving I/O equivalence requires significantly more theorem proving expertise and insight to come up with the right invariants, something we avoided with the skipping proof. The proof scripts are publicly available [2].

6   Related Work and Discussion

Notions of correctness. Notions of correctness for reasoning about reactive systems have been widely studied and we refer the reader to excellent surveys on this topic [10,15,22]. Lamport [12] argues that abstract and the concrete systems often only differ by stuttering steps; hence a notion of correctness should directly account stuttering. Weak simulation [10] and stuttering simulation [17] are examples of such notions. These notions are too strong to reason about optimized reactive systems, hence the need for skipping refinement, which allows both stuttering *and* skipping.

Refinement Maps. A basic question in a theory of refinement is whether refinement maps exist: if a concrete system implements an abstract system, does there exists a refinement map that can be use to prove it? Abadi and Lamport [13] showed that in the linear-time framework, a refinement map exists provided the systems satisfy a number of complex conditions. In [16], it was shown that for STS, a branching-time notion, the existence of refinement maps does not depend on any of the conditions found in the work of Abadi and Lamport and that this result can be extended to the linear-time case [17]. We show that like in the case of stuttering refinement, existence of refinement maps in skipping refinement does not depend on any conditions on the systems.

Hardware Verification. Several approaches to verification of superscalar processors appear in the literature and as new features are modeled new variants of correctness notions are proposed [3]. These variants can be broadly classified on the basis of whether (1) they support nondeterministic abstract systems or not (2) they support nondeterministic concrete systems or not (3) the kinds of refinement maps allowed. In contrast, the theory of skipping refinement provides a general framework that support nondeterministic abstract and concrete systems and arbitrary refinement maps. We believe that a uniform notion of correctness can significantly the verification effort.

Software Verification. Program refinement is widely used to verify the correctness of programs and program transformations. Several back-end compiler transformations are proven correct in CompCert [14] by showing that the source and the target language of a transformation are related by the notion of *forward simulation.* In [21], several compiler transformations, *e.g.,* dead-code elimination and control-flow graph compression, are analyzed stuttering refinement. Like CompCert, the semantics of the source and target languages are assumed to be deterministic and the only source of nondeterminism comes from initial states. In [9], *choice refinement* is introduced to account for compiler transformations that resolve internal nondeterministic choices in the semantics of the source language (*e.g.,* the left-to-right evaluation strategy). However, it is not possible to prove correctness of superword parallelism transformation(5) using these notions. Furthermore, skipping refinement does not place any restrictions on the kind of transition systems (deterministic or nondeterministic) and therefore provides a more general framework to analyze compiler transformations. In [19], it is shown how to prove the correctness of assembly programs running on a 7-stage pipelined processor. The proof proceeds by first proving the correctness of assembly code when running on a simple non-pipelined processor and, then proving that the pipelined processor is a stuttering refinement of the non-pipelined processor. Skipping refinement can similarly be used to combine hardware and software verification for optimized systems.

7   Conclusion and Future Work

In this paper, we introduced skipping refinement, a new notion of correctness for reasoning about optimized reactive systems where the concrete implementation can execute faster than its specification. This is the first notion of refinement that we know of that can directly deal with such optimized systems. We presented a sound and complete characterization of skipping that is local, *i.e.,* for the kinds of systems we consider, we can prove skipping refinement theorems by reasoning only about paths whose length is bounded by a constant. This characterization provides a convenient proof method and also enables mechanization and automated verification. We experimentally validated applicability of skipping refinement and our local characterization by performing three case studies. Our experimental results show that, for relatively simple configurations, proving correctness directly, without using skipping, is beyond the capabilities of current model-checking technology, but when using skipping refinement, current model-checkers are able to prove correctness. For future work, we plan to characterize the class of temporal properties preserved by skipping refinement, to develop and exploit compositional reasoning for skipping refinement, and to use skipping refinement for testing-based verification and validation.

References

1. Results of hardware model checking competition (2013). http://fmv.jku.at/hwmcc13/hwmcc13.pdf
2. Skipping simulation model. http://www.ccs.neu.edu/home/jmitesh/sks
3. Aagaard, M.D., Cook, B., Day, N.A., Jones, R.B.: A framework for microprocessor correctness statements. In: Margaria, T., Melham, T.F. (eds.) CHARME 2001. LNCS, vol. 2144, p. 433. Springer, Heidelberg (2001)
4. Barrett, C.W., Fang, Y., Goldberg, B., Hu, Y., Pnueli, A., Zuck, L.D.: TVOC: a translation validator for optimizing compilers. In: Etessami, K., Rajamani, S.K. (eds.) CAV 2005. LNCS, vol. 3576, pp. 291–295. Springer, Heidelberg (2005)
5. Browne, M.C., Clarke, E.M., Grümberg, O.: Characterizing finite kripke structures in propositional temporal logic. Theor. Comput. Sci. **59**, 115–131 (1988)
6. Chamarthi, H., Manolios, P.: ACL2s homepage (2015). http://acl2s.ccs.neu.edu/acl2s
7. Chamarthi, H.R., Dillinger, P.C., Manolios, P.: Data definitions in the ACL2 sedan. In: ACL2. ETPCS (2014)
8. Chamarthi, H.R., Dillinger, P., Manolios, P., Vroon, D.: The ACL2 sedan theorem proving system. In: Abdulla, P.A., Leino, K.R.M. (eds.) TACAS 2011. LNCS, vol. 6605, pp. 291–295. Springer, Heidelberg (2011)
9. Dockins, R.W.: Operational refinement for compiler correctness. Ph.D. thesis, Princeton University (2012)
10. van Glabbeek, R.J.: The linear time - branching time spectrum. In: Baeten, J.C.M., Klop, J.W. (eds.) CONCUR 1990. LNCS, vol. 458, pp. 278–297. Springer, Heidelberg (1990)
11. Hardin, D.S.: Real-time objects on the bare metal: an efficient hardware realization of the java tm virtual machine. In: ISORC (2001)
12. Lamport, L.: What good is temporal logic. In: Mason, R.E.A. (ed.) Information Processing. IFIP, North-Holland (1983)
13. Lamport, L., Abadi, M.: The existence of refinement mappings. Theor. Comput. Sci. **82**, 253–284 (1991)
14. Leroy, X.: A formally verified compiler back-end. J. Autom. Reason. **43**, 363–446 (2009)
15. Lynch, N., Vaandrager, F.: Forward and backward simulations:II. timing-based systems. Inf. Comput. **128**, 1–25 (1996)
16. Manolios, P.: Mechanical verification of reactive systems. Ph.D. thesis, University of Texas (2001)
17. Manolios, P.: A Compositional theory of refinement for branching time. In: Geist, D., Tronci, E. (eds.) CHARME 2003. LNCS, vol. 2860, pp. 304–318. Springer, Heidelberg (2003)
18. Manolios, P., Srinivasan, S.K.: A computationally efficient method based on commitment refinement maps for verifying pipelined machines. In: MEMOCODE (2005)
19. Manolios, P., Srinivasan, S.K.: A framework for verifying bit-level pipelined machines based on automated deduction and decision procedures. J. Autom. Reason. **37**, 93–116 (2006)
20. Manolios, P., Srinivasan, S.K., Vroon, D.: BAT: the bit-level analysis tool. In: Damm, W., Hermanns, H. (eds.) CAV 2007. LNCS, vol. 4590, pp. 303–306. Springer, Heidelberg (2007)

21. Namjoshi, K.S., Zuck, L.D.: Witnessing program transformations. In: Logozzo, F., Fähndrich, M. (eds.) Static Analysis. LNCS, vol. 7935, pp. 304–323. Springer, Heidelberg (2013)

22. Pnueli, A.: Linear and branching structures in the semantics and logics of reactive systems. In: Brauer, W. (ed.) Automata Languages and Programming. LNCS, vol. 194, pp. 15–32. Springer, Heidelberg (1985)

Quantitative Reasoning

Percentile Queries in Multi-dimensional Markov Decision Processes

Mickael Randour[1]($\boxtimes$), Jean-François Raskin[2], and Ocan Sankur[2]

[1] LSV, CNRS and ENS Cachan, Cachan, France
mickael.randour@gmail.com
[2] Département d'Informatique, Université Libre de Bruxelles (U.L.B.),
Brussels, Belgium

Abstract. Markov decision processes (MDPs) with multi-dimensional weights are useful to analyze systems with multiple objectives that may be conflicting and require the analysis of trade-offs. In this paper, we study the complexity of percentile queries in such MDPs and give algorithms to synthesize strategies that enforce such constraints. Given a multi-dimensional weighted MDP and a quantitative payoff function f, thresholds v_i (one per dimension), and probability thresholds α_i, we show how to compute a single strategy to enforce that for all dimensions i, the probability of outcomes ρ satisfying $f_i(\rho) \geq v_i$ is at least α_i. We consider classical quantitative payoffs from the literature (sup, inf, lim sup, lim inf, mean-payoff, truncated sum, discounted sum). Our work extends to the quantitative case the multi-objective model checking problem studied by Etessami et al. [16] in unweighted MDPs.

1 Introduction

Markov decision processes (MDPs) are central mathematical models for reasoning about (optimal) strategies in *uncertain environments*. For example, if rewards (given as numerical values) are assigned to actions in an MDP, we can search for a strategy (policy) that resolves the nondeterminism in a way that the *expected mean reward* of the actions taken by the strategy along time is maximized. See for example [23] for a solution to this problem. If we are risk-averse, we may want to search instead for strategies that ensure that the mean reward along time is larger than a given value with a high probability, i.e., a probability that exceeds a given threshold. See for example [17] for a solution.

Recent works are exploring several natural extensions of those problems. First, there is a series of works that investigate MDPs with multi-dimensional weights [6,12] rather than single-dimensional as it is traditionally the case. Multi-dimensional MDPs are useful to analyze systems with *multiple objectives* that are potentially conflicting and make necessary the analysis of trade-offs. For instance, we may want to build a control strategy that both ensures some good

Work partially supported by ERC starting grant inVEST (FP7-279499) and European project CASSTING (FP7-ICT-601148).

D. Kroening and C.S. Păsăreanu (Eds.): CAV 2015, Part I, LNCS 9206, pp. 123–139, 2015.
DOI: 10.1007/978-3-319-21690-4_8

quality of service and minimizes the energy consumption. Second, there are works that aim at synthesizing strategies enforcing *richer properties*. For example, we may want to construct a strategy that both ensures some minimal threshold with certainty (or probability one) and a good expectation [7]. An illustrative survey of such extensions can be found in [25].

Our paper participates in this general effort by providing algorithms and complexity results on the synthesis of strategies that enforce *multiple percentile constraints*. A *multi-percentile query* and the associated synthesis problem is as follows: given a multi-dimensionally weighted MDP M and an initial state s_{init}, synthesize a unique strategy σ such that it satisfies the conjunction of q constraints $\mathcal{Q} := \bigwedge_{i=1}^{q} \mathbb{P}^{\sigma}_{M,s_{\text{init}}}\left[f_{l_i} \geq v_i\right] \geq \alpha_i$, where each l_i refers to a dimension of the weight vectors, v_i is a value threshold, and α_i a probability threshold, and f a payoff function. Each constraint i expresses that the strategy ensures probability at least α_i to obtain payoff at least v_i in dimension l_i.

In this paper, we consider seven payoff functions: sup, inf, limsup, liminf, mean-payoff, truncated sum and discounted sum. This wide range covers most classical functions: our exhaustive study provides a *complete picture* for the new multi-percentile framework and we focus on establishing meta-theorems and connections whenever possible. Some of our results are obtained by reduction to the previous work of [16], but for mean-payoff, truncated sum and discounted sum, that are *non-regular payoffs*, we need to develop original techniques.

Consider some examples. In a stochastic shortest path problem, we may want a strategy ensuring that the probability to reach the target within d time units exceeds 50 percent: this is a single-constraint percentile query. With a *multi-constraint percentile query*, we can impose richer properties, for instance, enforcing that the duration is less than d_1 in 50 percent of the cases, and less than d_2 in 95 percent of the cases, with $d_1 < d_2$. We may also consider multi-dimensional systems. If in the model, we add information about fuel consumption, we may also enforce that we arrive within d time units in 95 percent of the cases, and that in half of the cases the fuel consumption is below some threshold c.

Contributions. We study percentile problems for a range of payoffs: we establish algorithms and prove complexity and memory bounds. Our algorithms solve multi-constraint multi-dimensional queries, but we also study interesting subclasses such as the single-dimensional case. We present an overview of our results in Table 1. For all payoff functions but the discounted sum, they only require *polynomial time in the size of the model* when the query size is fixed. In most applications, the query size is typically small while the model can be very large. So our algorithms have clear potential to be useful in practice.

(A) We show the PSPACE-hardness of the multiple reachability problem with exponential dependency on the query size (Theorem 2), and the PSPACE-completeness of the almost-sure case, refining the results of [16]. We also give a polynomial-time algorithm for *nested* target sets (Theorem 3).

(B) For inf, sup, lim inf and lim sup, we establish a polynomial-time algorithm for single-dimension (Theorem 5), and an algorithm that is only exponential in

Table 1. Some results for percentile queries. Here $\mathcal{F} = \{\inf, \sup, \lim\inf, \lim\sup\}$, $\overline{\text{MP}}$ (resp. $\underline{\text{MP}}$) stands for sup. (resp. inf.) mean-payoff, SP for shortest path, and DS for discounted sum. Parameters M and $\mathcal{Q}$ resp. represent model size and query size; $P(x)$, $E(x)$ and $P_{ps}(x)$ resp. denote polynomial, exponential and pseudo-polynomial time in parameter x. All results without reference are new.

	Single-constraint	Single-dim. Multi-constraint	Multi-dim. Multi-constraint
Reachability	P [23]	$P(M) \cdot E(\mathcal{Q})$ [16], PSPACE-h.	—
$f \in \mathcal{F}$	P [10]	P	$P(M) \cdot E(\mathcal{Q})$ PSPACE-h.
$\overline{\text{MP}}$	P [23]	P	P
$\underline{\text{MP}}$	P [23]	$P(M) \cdot E(\mathcal{Q})$	$P(M) \cdot E(\mathcal{Q})$
SP	$P(M) \cdot P_{ps}(\mathcal{Q})$ [21] PSPACE-h. [21]	$P(M) \cdot P_{ps}(\mathcal{Q})$ (one target) PSPACE-h. [21]	$P(M) \cdot E(\mathcal{Q})$ PSPACE-h. [21]
ε-gap DS	$P_{ps}(M, \mathcal{Q}, \varepsilon)$ NP-h.	$P_{ps}(M, \varepsilon) \cdot E(\mathcal{Q})$ NP-h.	$P_{ps}(M, \varepsilon) \cdot E(\mathcal{Q})$ PSPACE-h.

the query size for the general case (Theorem 6). We prove PSPACE-hardness for sup (Theorem 7), and give a polynomial time algorithm for lim sup (Theorem 8).

(C) In the mean-payoff case, we distinguish $\overline{\text{MP}}$ defined by the limsup of the average weights, and $\underline{\text{MP}}$ by their liminf. For the former, we give a polynomial-time algorithm for the general case (Theorem 10). For the latter, our algorithm is polynomial in the model size and exponential in the query size (Theorem 11).

(D) The truncated sum function computes the *sum* of weights until a target is reached. It models *shortest path* problems. We prove the multi-dimensional percentile problem to be undecidable when both negative and positive weights are allowed (Theorem 12). Therefore, we concentrate on the case of non-negative weights, and establish an algorithm that is polynomial in the model size and exponential in the query size (Theorem 13). We derive from recent results that even the single-constraint percentile problem is PSPACE-hard [21].

(E) Discounted sum turns out to be linked to a long-standing open problem, not known to be decidable (Lemma 8). Nevertheless, we give an algorithm for an approximation called ε-gap percentile problem. It guarantees correct answers up to an arbitrarily small zone of uncertainty (Theorem 14). We prove this problem is PSPACE-hard in general, and NP-hard for single-constraint queries. According to a very recent preprint by Haase and Kiefer [20], our reduction even proves PP-hardness of single-contraint queries, which suggests that the problem does not belong to NP at all otherwise the polynomial hierarchy would collapse.

We systematically study the memory requirement of strategies. We build our algorithms using different techniques. Here are a few of them. For inf and sup payoff functions, we reduce percentile queries to multiple reachability queries, and rely on the algorithm of [16]: those are the easiest cases. For lim inf, lim sup and $\overline{\mathsf{MP}}$, we additionally need to resort to maximal end-component decomposition of MDPs. For the following cases, there is no simple reduction to existing problems and we need non-trivial techniques to establish algorithms. For MP, we use linear programming techniques to characterize winning strategies, borrowing ideas from [6,16]. For shortest path and discounted sum, we consider unfoldings of the MDP, with particular care to bound their sizes, and for the latter, to analyze the cumulative error due to necessary roundings.

Related Work. There are works that study multi-dimensional MDPs: for discounted sum, see [12], and for mean-payoff, see [6,17]. In the latter papers, the following threshold problem is studied: given a threshold vector v and a probability threshold ν, does there exist a strategy σ such that $\mathbb{P}_s^\sigma [r \geq v] \geq \nu$, where r denotes the mean-payoff vector. The work [17] solves it for the single dimensional case, and the multi-dimensional for the *non-degenerate* case (w.r.t. solutions of a linear program). A general algorithm was given in [6]. This problem asks for a bound on the *joint probability* of the thresholds, i.e., the probability of satisfying *all* constraints simultaneously. In contrast, we bound the *marginal probabilities* separately, which may allow for more modeling flexibility. Maximizing the *expectation vector* was considered in [6]. An approach unifying the probability and expectation views for mean-payoff was recently presented in [11].

Multiple reachability objectives in MDPs were considered in [16]: given an MDP and multiple targets T_i, thresholds α_i, decide if there exists a strategy that forces each T_i with a probability larger than α_i. This work is the closest to our work and we show here that their problem is inter-reducible with our problem for the sup measure. In [16] the complexity results are given only for model size and not for query size: *we refine those results and answer questions left open.*

Several works consider percentile queries but only for *one* dimension and *one* constraint (while we consider multiple constraints and dimensions) and particular payoff functions. Single-constraint queries for lim sup and lim inf were studied in [10]. The threshold probability problem for truncated sum was studied for either all non-negative or all non-positive weights in [22,26]. *Quantile queries* in the single-constraint case were studied for the shortest path with non-negative weights in [29], and for energy-utility objectives in [1]. It has been recently extended to *cost problems* [21], in a direction orthogonal to ours. For fixed horizon, [32] studies maximization of the expected discounted sum subject to a single percentile constraint. Still for the discounted case, there are works studying *threshold problems* [30,31] and *value-at-risk problems* [5]. All can be related to single-constraint percentiles queries.

A long version of this paper with full details is available online [24].

2 Preliminaries

A finite *Markov decision process* (MDP) is a tuple $M = (S, A, \delta)$ where S is the finite set of *states*, A is the finite set of *actions* and $\delta \colon S \times A \to \mathcal{D}(S)$ is a partial function called the *probabilistic transition function*, where $\mathcal{D}(S)$ denotes the set of rational probability distributions over S. The set of actions that are available in a state $, \in S$ is denoted by $A(s)$. We use $\delta(s, a, s')$ as a shorthand for $\delta(s, a)(s')$. An *absorbing state* s is such that for all $a \in A(s)$, $\delta(s, a, s) = 1$. We assume w.l.o.g. that MDPs are *deadlock-free*: for all $s \in S$, $A(s) \neq \emptyset$ (if not the case, we simply replace the deadlock by an absorbing state with a unique action). An MDP where for all $s \in S$, $|A(s)| = 1$ is a fully-stochastic process called a *Markov chain*.

A *weighted* MDP is a tuple $M = (S, A, \delta, w)$, where w is a d-*dimension weight function* $w \colon A \to \mathbb{Z}^d$. For any $l \in \{1, \ldots, d\}$, we denote $w_l \colon A \to \mathbb{Z}$ the projection of w to the l-th dimension, i.e., the function mapping each action a to the l-th element of vector $w(a)$. A *run* of M is an infinite sequence $s_1 a_1 \ldots a_{n-1} s_n \ldots$ of states and actions such that $\delta(s_i, a_i, s_{i+1}) > 0$ for all $i \geq 1$. Finite prefixes of runs are called *histories*.

Fix an MDP $M = (S, A, \delta)$. An *end-component* (EC) of M is an MDP $C = (S', A', \delta')$ with $S' \subseteq S$, $\emptyset \neq A'(s) \subseteq A(s)$ for all $s \in S'$, and $\mathsf{Supp}(\delta(s, a)) \subseteq S'$ for all $s \in S', a \in A'(s)$ (here $\mathsf{Supp}(\cdot)$ denotes the support), $\delta' = \delta|_{S' \times A'}$ and such that C is *strongly connected*, i.e., there is a run between any pair of states in S'. The union of two ECs with non-empty intersection is an EC; one can thus define *maximal* ECs. We let $\mathsf{MEC}(M)$ denote the set of maximal ECs of M, computable in polynomial time [14].

A *strategy* σ is a function $(SA)^*S \to \mathcal{D}(A)$ such that for all $h \in (SA)^*S$ ending in s, we have $\mathsf{Supp}(\sigma(h)) \subseteq A(s)$. The set of all strategies is Σ. We consider *finite-* and *infinite-memory* strategies as strategies that can be encoded by Moore machines with finite or infinite states respectively. An MDP M, initial state s, and a strategy σ determines a Markov chain M_s^σ on which a unique probability measure is defined. Here, M_s^σ is defined on the state space that is product of M and that of the Moore machine encoding σ. Given an event $E \subseteq (SA)^\omega$, we denote by $\mathbb{P}_{M,s}^\sigma[E]$ the probability of runs of M_s^σ whose projection to M is in E. That is the probability of achieving event E when the MDP M is executed with initial state s and strategy σ.

Let $\mathsf{Inf}(\rho)$ denote the random variable representing the disjoint union of states and actions that occur infinitely often in the run ρ. By an abuse of notation, we see $\mathsf{Inf}(\rho)$ as a sub-MDP M' if it contains exactly the states and actions of M'. It was shown that for any MDP M, state s, strategy σ, $\mathbb{P}_{M,s}^\sigma[\mathsf{Inf}$ is an EC$] = 1$ [14].

Multiple Reachability. Given a subset T of states, let $\Diamond T$ be the *reachability objective* w.r.t. T, defined as the set of runs visiting a state of T at least once.

The *multiple reachability* problem consists, given MDP M, state s_{init}, target sets $T_1, \ldots, T_q$, and probabilities $\alpha_1, \ldots, \alpha_q \in [0, 1] \cap \mathbb{Q}$, in deciding whether there exists a strategy $\sigma \in \Sigma$ such that $\bigwedge_{i=1}^q \mathbb{P}_{M,s_{\mathsf{init}}}^\sigma[\Diamond T_i] \geq \alpha_i$. The *almost-sure multiple reachability* problem restricts to $\alpha_1 = \ldots = \alpha_q = 1$.

Percentile Problems. We consider *payoff functions* among inf, sup, lim inf, lim sup, mean-payoff, truncated sum (shortest path) and discounted sum. For any run $\rho = s_1 a_1 s_2 a_2 \ldots$, dimension $l \in \{1, \ldots, d\}$, and weight function w,

- $\mathsf{inf}_l(\rho) = \inf_{j \geq 1} w_l(a_j)$, $\mathsf{sup}_l(\rho) = \sup_{j \geq 1} w_l(a_j)$,

- $\liminf_l(\rho) = \liminf_{j\to\infty} w_l(a_j)$, $\limsup_l(\rho) = \limsup_{j\to\infty} w_l(a_j)$,
- $\mathsf{MP}_l(\rho) = \liminf_{n\to\infty} \frac{1}{n} \sum_{j=1}^{n} w_l(a_j)$, $\overline{\mathsf{MP}}_l(\rho) = \limsup_{n\to\infty} \frac{1}{n} \sum_{j=1}^{n} w_l(a_j)$,
- $\mathsf{DS}_l^{\lambda_l}(\rho) = \sum_{j=1}^{\infty} \lambda_l^j \cdot w_l(a_j)$, with $\lambda_l \in]0,1[\cap \mathbb{Q}$ a rational discount factor,
- $\mathsf{TS}_l^T(\rho) = \sum_{j=1}^{n-1} w_l(a_j)$ with s_n the first visit of a state in $T \subseteq S$. If T is never reached, then we assign $\mathsf{TS}_l^T(\rho) = \infty$.

For any payoff function f, $f_l \geq v$ defines the runs ρ that satisfy $f_l(\rho) \geq v$. A *percentile constraint* is of the form $\mathbb{P}_{M,s_{init}}^\sigma[f_l \geq v] \geq \alpha$, where σ is to be synthesized given threshold value v and probability α. We study *multi-constraint percentile queries* requiring to simultaneously satisfy q constraints each referring to a possibly different dimension. Formally, given a d-dimensional weighted MDP M, initial state $s_{init} \in S$, payoff function f, dimensions $l_1, \ldots, l_q \in \{1, \ldots, d\}$, value thresholds $v_1, \ldots, v_q \in \mathbb{Q}$ and probability thresholds $\alpha_1, \ldots, \alpha_q \in [0,1] \cap \mathbb{Q}$ the *multi-constraint percentile problem* asks if there exists a strategy $\sigma \in \Sigma$ such that query $\mathcal{Q} := \bigwedge_{i=1}^{q} \mathbb{P}_{M,s_{init}}^\sigma[f_{l_i} \geq v_i] \geq \alpha_i$ holds. We can actually solve queries $\exists? \sigma, \bigvee_{i=1}^{m} \bigwedge_{j=1}^{n_i} \mathbb{P}_{M,s_{init}}^\sigma[f_{l_{i,j}} \geq v_{i,j}] \geq \alpha_{i,j}$. We present our results for conjunctions of constraints only since the latter is equivalent to verifying the disjuncts independently: in other terms, to $\bigvee_{i=1}^{m} \exists\sigma \bigwedge_{j=1}^{n_i} \mathbb{P}_{M,s_{init}}^\sigma[f_{l_{i,j}} \geq v_{i,j}] \geq \alpha_{i,j}$.

We distinguish *single-dimensional percentile problems* ($d = 1$) from *multi-dimensional* ones ($d > 1$). We assume w.l.o.g. that $q \geq d$ otherwise one can simply neglect unused dimensions. sFor some cases, we will consider the *ε-relaxation* of the problem, which consists in ensuring each value $v_i - \varepsilon$ with probability α_i.

We assume binary encoding of constants, and define the *model size* $|M|$ as the size of the representation of M, and the *query size* $|\mathcal{Q}|$ that of the query. *Problem size* refers to the sum of the two. We study memory needs for strategies w.r.t. different classes of queries; but randomization is always necessary as shown in the next lemma.

Lemma 1. *Randomized strategies are necessary for multi-dimensional percentile queries for any payoff function.*

3   Multiple Reachability and Contraction of MECs

Multiple reachability. An algorithm to solve this problem was given in [16] based on a linear program (LP) of size polynomial in the model and exponential in the query; whereas restricting the target sets to absorbing states yields a polynomial-size LP. We will use this LP later in Fig. 1 in Sect. 5.

Theorem 1 [16]. *Memoryless strategies suffice for multiple reachability with absorbing target states, and can be computed in polynomial time. With arbitrary targets, exponential-memory strategies (in query size) can be computed in time polynomial in the model and exponential in the query.*

In this section, we improve over this result by showing that the case of almost-sure multiple reachability is PSPACE-complete, with a recursive algorithm and a reduction from QBF satisfiability. This also shows the PSPACE-hardness of the general problem. Moreover, we show that exponential memory is required for strategies, following a construction of [13].

Theorem 2. *The almost-sure multiple reachability problem is* PSPACE-*complete, and strategies need exponential memory in the query size.*

Despite the above lower bounds, it turns out that the polynomial time algorithm for the case of absorbing targets can be extended; we identify a subclass of the multiple reachability problem that admits a polynomial-time solution. In the *nested multiple reachability* problem, the target sets are nested, *i.e.* $T_1 \subseteq T_2 \subseteq \ldots \subseteq T_q$. The memory requirement for strategies is reduced as well to linear memory. Intuitively, we use $q + 1$ copies of the original MDP, one for each target set, plus one last copy. The idea is then to travel between those copies in a way that reflects the nesting of target sets whenever a target state is visited. The crux to obtain a polynomial-time algorithm is then to reduce the problem to a multiple reachability problem *with absorbing states* over the MDP composed of the $q + 1$ copies, and to benefit from the reduced complexity of this case.

Theorem 3. *The nested multiple reachability problem can be solved in polynomial time. Strategies have memory linear in the query size, which is optimal.*

Contraction of MECs. In order to solve percentile queries, we sometimes reduce our problems to multiple reachability by first contracting MECs of given MDPs, which is a known technique [14]. We define a transformation of MDP M to represent the events $\mathsf{Inf}(\rho) \subseteq C$ for $C \in \mathsf{MEC}(M)$ as fresh states. Intuitively, all states of a MEC will now lead to an absorbing state that will abstract the behavior of the MEC.

Consider M with $\mathsf{MEC}(M) = \{C_1, \ldots, C_m\}$. We define MDP M' from M as follows. For each C_i, we add state s_{C_i} and action a^* from each state $s \in C_i$ to s_{C_i}. All states s_{C_i} are absorbing, and $A(s_{C_i}) = \{a^*\}$. The probabilities of events $\mathsf{Inf}(\rho) \subseteq C_i$ in M are captured by the reachability of states s_{C_i} in M', as follows. We use the classical temporal logic symbols $\Diamond$ and $\Box$ to represent the *eventually* and *always* operators respectively.

Lemma 2. *Let M be an MDP and $\mathsf{MEC}(M) = \{C_1, \ldots, C_m\}$. For any strategy σ for M, there exists a strategy τ for M' such that for all $i \in \{1, \ldots, m\}$, $\mathbb{P}^\sigma_{M, s_{\mathsf{init}}}[\Diamond \Box C_i] = \mathbb{P}^\tau_{M', s_{\mathsf{init}}}[\Diamond s_{C_i}]$. Conversely, for any strategy τ for M' such that $\sum_{i=1}^m \mathbb{P}^\tau_{M', s_{\mathsf{init}}}[\Diamond s_{C_i}] = 1$, there exists σ such that for all i, $\mathbb{P}^\sigma_{M, s_{\mathsf{init}}}[\Diamond \Box C_i] = \mathbb{P}^\tau_{M', s}[\Diamond s_{C_i}]$.*

Under some hypotheses, solving multi-constraint percentile problems on ECs yield the result for all MDPs, by the transformation of Lemma 2. We prove a general theorem and then derive particular results as corollaries. Informally, for prefix-independent payoff functions, if for any EC, there is a strategy that is optimal in each dimension, and if optimal values are computable in polynomial time, then the percentile problem can be solved in polynomial time.

Theorem 4. *Consider all prefix-independent payoff functions f such that for all strongly connected MDPs M, and all $(l_i, v_i)_{1 \leq i \leq q} \in \{1, \ldots, d\} \times \mathbb{Q}$, there exists a strategy σ such that $\forall i \in \{1, \ldots, d\}, \mathbb{P}^\sigma_{M, s_{\text{init}}}[f_{l_i} \geq v_i] \geq \sup_\tau \mathbb{P}^\tau_{M, s_{\text{init}}}[f_{l_i} \geq v_i]$. If the value $\sup_\tau$ is computable in polynomial time for strongly connected MDPs, then the multi-constraint percentile problem for f is decidable in polynomial time. Moreover, if strategies achieving $\sup_\tau$ for strongly connected MDPs use $\mathcal{O}(g(M, q))$ memory, then the overall strategy use $\mathcal{O}(g(M, q))$ memory.*

The hypotheses are crucial. Essentially, we require payoff functions that are prefix-independent and for which strategies can be combined easily inside MECs (in the sense that if two constraints can be satisfied independently, they can be satisfied simultaneously). Prefix-independence also implies that we can forget about what happens before a MEC is reached. Hence, by using the MEC contraction, we can reduce the percentile problem to multiple reachability for absorbing target states.

4   Inf, Sup, LimInf, LimSup Payoff Functions

We give polynomial-time algorithms for the *single*-dimensional multi-constraint percentile problems. For inf, sup we reduce the problem to nested multiple reachability, while lim inf and lim sup are solved by applying Theorem 4.

Theorem 5. *The single-dimensional multi-constraint percentile problems can be solved in polynomial time in the problem size for inf, sup, lim inf, and lim sup functions. Computed strategies use memory linear in the query size for inf and sup, and constant memory for lim inf and lim sup.*

We are now interested in the multi-dimensional case. We show that all multi-dimensional cases can be solved in time polynomial in the model size and exponential in the query size by a reduction to multiple LTL objectives studied in [16]. Our algorithm actually solves a more general class of queries, where the payoff function can be different for each query.

Given an MDP M, for all $i \in \{1 \ldots q\}$ and value v_i, we denote $A_{l_i}^{\geq v_i}$ the set of actions of M whose rewards are at least v_i. We fix an MDP M. For any constraint $\phi_i \equiv f(w_{l_i}) \geq v_i$, we define an LTL formula denoted Φ_i as follows. For $f_{l_i} = \text{inf}$, $\Phi_i = \Box A_{l_i}^{\geq v_i}$, for $f_{l_i} = \text{sup}$, $\Phi_i = \Diamond A_{l_i}^{\geq v_i}$, for $f_{l_i} = \text{lim inf}$, $\Phi_i = \Diamond \Box A_{l_i}^{\geq v_i}$, and for $f_{l_i} = \text{lim sup}$, $\Phi_i = \Box \Diamond A_{l_i}^{\geq v_i}$. The percentile problem is then reduced to queries of the form $\wedge_{i=1}^q \mathbb{P}^\sigma_{M, s_{\text{init}}}[\Phi_i] \geq \alpha_i$, for which an algorithm was given in [16] that takes time polynomial in $|M|$ and doubly exponential in q. We improve this complexity since our formulae have bounded sizes.

Theorem 6. *The multi-dimensional percentile problems for sup, inf, lim sup and lim inf can be solved in time polynomial in the model size and exponential in the query size, yielding strategies with memory exponential in the query.*

The problem is **PSPACE**-hard for sup as shown in the following theorem.

Theorem 7. *The multi-dimensional percentile problem is* PSPACE-*hard for* sup.

Nevertheless, the complexity can be improved for lim sup functions, for which we give a polynomial-time algorithm by an application of Theorem 4.

Theorem 8. *The multi-dimensional percentile problem for* lim sup *is solvable in polynomial time. Computed strategies use constant-memory.*

The exact query complexity of the lim inf and inf cases are left open.

5 Mean-Payoff

We consider the multi-constraint percentile problem both for $\underline{\mathsf{MP}}$ and $\overline{\mathsf{MP}}$. We will see that strategies require infinite memory in both cases, in which case it is known that the two payoff functions differ. The *single-constraint* percentile problem was first solved in [17]. The case of multiple dimensions was mentioned as a challenging problem but left open. We solve this problem thus generalizing the previous work.

The Single-Dimensional Case. We start with a polynomial-time algorithm for the single-dimensional case obtained by an application of Theorem 4.

Theorem 9. *The single dimensional multi-constraint percentile problems for payoffs* $\underline{\mathsf{MP}}$ *and* $\overline{\mathsf{MP}}$ *are equivalent and solvable in polynomial time. Computed strategies use constant memory.*

Percentiles on Multi-dimensional $\overline{\mathsf{MP}}$. Let $\mathbb{E}^{\sigma}_{M,s_{\mathrm{init}}}[\overline{\mathsf{MP}}_i]$ be the *expectation* of $\overline{\mathsf{MP}}_i$ under strategy σ, and $\mathsf{Val}^*_{M,s_{\mathrm{init}}}(\overline{\mathsf{MP}}_i) = \sup_{\sigma} \mathbb{E}^{\sigma}_{M,s_{\mathrm{init}}}[\overline{\mathsf{MP}}_i]$, computable in polynomial time [23]. We solve the problem inside ECs, then apply Theorem 4. It is known that for strongly connected MDPs, for each i, some strategy σ satisfies $\mathbb{P}^{\sigma}_{M,s_{\mathrm{init}}}[\overline{\mathsf{MP}}_i = \mathsf{Val}^*_{M,s_{\mathrm{init}}}(\overline{\mathsf{MP}}_i)] = 1$, and that for all strategies τ, $\mathbb{P}^{\tau}_{M,s_{\mathrm{init}}}[\overline{\mathsf{MP}}_i > v] = 0$ for all $v > \mathsf{Val}^*_{M,s_{\mathrm{init}}}(\overline{\mathsf{MP}}_i)$. By switching between these optimal strategies for each dimension, with growing intervals, we prove that for strongly connected MDPs, a single strategy can simultaneously optimize $\overline{\mathsf{MP}}_i$ on *all* dimensions.

Lemma 3. *For any strongly connected MDP M, there is an infinite-memory strategy σ such that* $\forall i \in \{1,\dots,d\}$, $\mathbb{P}^{\sigma}_{M,s_{\mathrm{init}}}[\overline{\mathsf{MP}}_i \geq \mathsf{Val}^*_{M,s_{\mathrm{init}}}(\overline{\mathsf{MP}}_i)] = 1$.

Thanks to the above lemma, we fulfill the hypotheses of Theorem 4, and we obtain the following theorem.

Theorem 10. *The multi-dimensional percentile problem for* $\overline{\mathsf{MP}}$ *is solvable in polynomial time. Strategies use infinite-memory, which is necessary.*

Percentiles on Multi-dimensional $\underline{\mathsf{MP}}$. In contrast with the $\overline{\mathsf{MP}}$ case, our algorithm for $\underline{\mathsf{MP}}$ is more involved, and requires new techniques. In fact, the case of end-components is already non-trivial for $\underline{\mathsf{MP}}$, since there is no single strategy that satisfies all percentile constraints in general, and one cannot hope to apply Theorem 4 as we did in previous sections. We rather need to consider the set of strategies σ_I satisfying *maximal* subsets of percentile constraints; these are called *maximal strategies*. We then prove that any strategy satisfying all percentile queries can be written as a *linear combination* of maximal strategies, that is, there exists a strategy which chooses and executes each σ_I following a probability distribution.

For general MDPs, we first consider each MEC separately and write down the linear combination with unknown coefficients. We know that any strategy in a MDP eventually stays forever in a MEC. Thus, we adapt the linear program of [16] that encodes the reachability probabilities with multiple targets, which are the MECs here. We combine these reachability probabilities with the unknown linear combination coefficients, and obtain a linear program (Fig. 1), which we prove to be equivalent to our problem.

Single EC. Fix a strongly connected d-dimensional MDP M and pairs of thresholds $(v_i, \alpha_i)_{1 \leq i \leq q}$. We denote each event by $A_i \equiv \underline{\mathsf{MP}}_i \geq v_i$. In [6], the problem of maximizing the *joint* probability of the events A_i was solved in polynomial time. In particular, we have the following for strongly connected MDPs.

Lemma 4 [6]. *If M is strongly connected, then there exists σ such that $\mathbb{P}^\sigma_{M,s}[\wedge_{1 \leq i \leq q} A_i] > 0$ if, and only if there exists σ' such that $\mathbb{P}^{\sigma'}_{M,s}[\wedge_{1 \leq i \leq q} A_i] = 1$. Moreover, this can be decided in polynomial time, and for positive instances, for any $\varepsilon > 0$, a memoryless strategy τ can be computed in polynonomial time in M, $\log(v_i)$ and $\log(\frac{1}{\varepsilon})$, such that $\mathbb{P}^\tau_{M,s}[\wedge_{1 \leq i \leq q} \underline{\mathsf{MP}}_i \geq v_i - \varepsilon] = 1$.*

We give an overview of our algorithm. Using Lemma 4, we define strategy σ_I achieving $\mathbb{P}^{\sigma_I}_{M,s}[\wedge_{i \in I} A_i] = 1$ for any maximal subset $I \subseteq \{1, \ldots, q\}$ for which such a strategy exists. Then, to build a strategy for the multi-constraint problem, we look for a linear combination of these σ_I: given $\sigma_{I_1}, \ldots, \sigma_{I_m}$, we choose each $i_0 \in \{1, \ldots, m\}$ following a probability distribution to be computed, and we run $\sigma_{I_{i_0}}$.

We now formalize this idea. Let $\mathcal{I}$ be the set of maximal I (for set inclusion) such that some σ_I satisfies $\mathbb{P}^{\sigma_I}_{M,s}[\wedge_{i \in I} A_i] = 1$. Note that for all $I \in \mathcal{I}$, and $j \notin I$, $\mathbb{P}^{\sigma_I}_{M,s}[\wedge_{i \in I} A_i \wedge A_j] = 0$. Assuming otherwise would contradict the maximality of I, by Lemma 4. We consider the events $\mathcal{A}_I = \wedge_{i \in I} A_i \wedge_{i \notin I} \neg A_i$ for maximal I.

We are looking for a non-negative family $(\lambda_I)_{I \in \mathcal{I}}$ whose sum equals 1 with $\forall i \in \{1, \ldots, q\}, \sum_{I \in \mathcal{I} \text{ s.t. } i \in I} \lambda_I \geq \alpha_i$. This will ensure that if each σ_I is chosen with probability λ_I (among the set $\{\sigma_I\}_{I \in \mathcal{I}}$); with probability at least α_i, some strategy satisfying A_i with probability 1 is chosen. So each A_i is satisfied with probability at least α_i. This can be written in the matrix notation as

$$\mathcal{M}\boldsymbol{\lambda} \geq \boldsymbol{\alpha}, 0 \leq \boldsymbol{\lambda}, \mathbf{1} \cdot \boldsymbol{\lambda} = 1, \tag{1}$$

where $\mathcal{M}$ is a $q \times |\mathcal{I}|$ matrix with $\mathcal{M}_{i,I} = 1$ if $i \in I$, and 0 otherwise.

Lemma 5. *For any strongly connected MDP M, and an instance $(v_i, \alpha_i)_{1 \leq i \leq q}$ of the multi-constraint percentile problem for $\underline{\mathsf{MP}}$, (1) has a solution if, and only if there exists a strategy σ satisfying the multi-constraint percentile problem.*

$$\mathbf{1}_{s_{\text{init}}}(s) + \sum_{s' \in S, a \in A(s')} y_{s',a} \delta(s', a, s) = \sum_{a \in A'(s)} y_{s,a}, \qquad \forall s \in S, \tag{2}$$

$$\sum_{s \in S_{\text{MEC}}} y_{s,a^*} = 1, \tag{3}$$

$$\sum_{s \in C} y_{s,a^*} = \sum_{I \in \mathcal{I}^C} \lambda_I^C, \quad \forall C \in \mathsf{MEC}(M), \tag{4}$$

$$\lambda_I^C \geq 0, \quad \forall C \in \mathsf{MEC}(M), \forall I \in \mathcal{I}^C, \tag{5}$$

$$\sum_{C \in \mathsf{MEC}(M)} \sum_{I \in \mathcal{I}^C : i \in I} \lambda_I^C \geq \alpha_i, \qquad \forall i = 1 \dots d. \tag{6}$$

Fig. 1. Linear program (L) for the multi-constraint percentiles for MP.

Now (1) has size $O(q \cdot 2^q)$, and each subset I can be checked in time polynomial in the model size. The computation of $\mathcal{I}$, the set of maximal subsets, can be carried out in a top-down fashion; one might thus avoid enumerating all subsets in practice. We get the following result.

Lemma 6. *For strongly connected MDPs, the multi-dimensional percentile problem for* MP *can be solved in time polynomial in M and exponential in q. Strategies require infinite-memory in general. On positive instances, 2^q-memory randomized strategies can be computed for the ε-relaxation of the problem in time polynomial in $|M|, 2^q, \max_i \left(\log(v_i), \log(\alpha_i) \right), \log(\frac{1}{\varepsilon})$.*

General MDPs. Given MDP M, let us consider M' given by Lemma 2. We start by analyzing each maximal EC C of M as above, and compute the sets $\mathcal{I}^C$ of maximal subsets. We define a variable λ_I^C for each $I \in \mathcal{I}^C$, and also $y_{s,a}$ for each state s and action $a \in A'(s)$. Recall that $A'(s) = A(s) \cup \{a^*\}$ for states s that are inside a MEC, and $A'(s) = A(s)$ otherwise. Let S_{MEC} be the set of states of M that belong to a MEC. We consider the linear program (L) of Fig. 1.

The linear program follows the ideas of [6,16]. Note that the first two lines of (L) corresponds to the multiple reachability LP of [16] for absorbing target states. The equations encode strategies that work in two phases. Variables $y_{s,a}$ correspond to the expected number of visits of state-action s, a in the first phase. Variable y_{s,a^*} describes the probability of switching to the second phase at state s. The second phase consists in surely staying in the current MEC, so we require $\sum_{s \in S_{\text{MEC}}} y_{s,a^*} = 1$ (and we will have $y_{s,a^*} = 0$ if s does not belong to a MEC). In the second phase, we immediately switch to some strategy σ_I^C where C denotes the current MEC. Thus, variable λ_I^C corresponds to the probability with which we enter the second phase in C and switch to strategy σ_I^C (see (4)). Intuitively, given a solution $(\lambda_I)_I$ computed for one EC by (1), we have the correspondence $\lambda_I^C = \sum_{s \in C} y_{s,a^*} \cdot \lambda_I$. The interpretation of (6) is that each event A_i is satisfied with probability at least α_i.

Lemma 7. *The LP (L) has a solution if, and only if the multi-constraint percentiles problem for* $\underline{\mathsf{MP}}$ *has a solution. Moreover, the equation has size polynomial in M and exponential in q. From any solution of (L) randomized finite memory strategies can be computed for the ε-relaxation problem.*

Theorem 11. *The multi-dimensional percentile problem for* $\underline{\mathsf{MP}}$ *can be solved in time polynomial in the model, and exponential in the query. Infinite-memory strategies are necessary, but exponential-memory (in the query) suffices for the ε-relaxation and can be computed with the same complexity.*

6 Shortest Path

We study shortest path problems in MDPs, which generalize the classical graph problem. In MDPs, the problem consists in finding a strategy ensuring that a target set is reached with bounded truncated sum with high probability. This problem has been studied in the context of games and MDPs (e.g., [2,7,15]). We consider percentile queries of the form $\mathcal{Q} := \bigwedge_{i=1}^{q} \mathbb{P}_{M,s_{\mathsf{init}}}^{\sigma}\left[\mathsf{TS}_{l_i}^{T_i} \leq v_i\right] \geq \alpha_i$ (inner inequality $\leq$ is more natural but $\geq$ could be used by negating all weights). Each constraint i may relate to a different target set $T_i \subseteq S$.

Arbitrary Weights. We prove that without further restriction, the multi-dimensional percentile problem is undecidable, even for a fixed number of dimensions. Our proof is inspired by the approach of Chatterjee et al. for the undecidability of two-player multi-dimensional total-payoff games [8] but requires additional techniques to adapt to the stochastic case.

Theorem 12. *The multi-dimensional percentile problem is undecidable for the truncated sum payoff function, for MDPs with both negative and positive weights and four dimensions, even with a unique target set.*

Non-negative Weights. In the light of this result, we will restrict our setting to non-negative weights (we could equivalently consider non-positive weights with inequality $\geq$ inside percentile constraints). We first discuss recent related work.

Quantiles and Cost Problems. In [29], Ummels and Baier study *quantile queries* over non-negatively weighted MDPs. They are equivalent to minimizing $v \in \mathbb{N}$ in a single-constraint percentile query $\mathbb{P}_{M,s_{\mathsf{init}}}^{\sigma}\left[\mathsf{TS}^T \leq v\right] \geq \alpha$ such that there still exists a satisfying strategy, for some fixed α. Very recently, Haase and Kiefer extended quantile queries by introducing *cost problems* [21]. They can be seen as single-constraint percentile queries where inequality $\mathsf{TS}^T \leq v$ is replaced by an arbitrary Boolean combination of inequalities φ. Hence, it can be written as $\mathbb{P}_{M,s_{\mathsf{init}}}^{\sigma}\left[\mathsf{TS}^T \models \varphi\right] \geq \alpha$. Cost problems are studied on single-dimensional MDPs and all the inequalities relate to the same target T, in contrast to our setting which allows both for multiple dimensions and multiple target sets. The single probability threshold bounds the probability of the whole event φ.

Both settings are incomparable. Still, our queries share common subclasses with cost problems: atomic formulae φ exactly correspond to our single-constraint queries. Moreover, cost problems for such formulae are inter-reducible with quantile queries [21, Proposition 2]. Cost problems with atomic formulae are PSPACE-hard, so this also holds for *single-constraint* percentile queries. The best known algorithm in this case is in EXPTIME. In the following, we establish an algorithm that still only requires exponential time while allowing for *multi-constraint multi-dimensional multi-target* percentile queries.

Main Results. Our main contributions for the shortest path are as follows.

Theorem 13. *The percentile problem for the shortest path with non-negative weights can be solved in time polynomial in the model size and exponential in the query size (exponential in the number of constraints and pseudo-polynomial in the largest threshold). The problem is PSPACE-hard even for single-constraint queries. Exponential-memory strategies are sufficient and in general necessary.*

Sketch of Algorithm. Consider a d-dimensional MDP M and a q-query percentile problem, with potentially different targets for each query. Let $v_{\max}$ be the maximum of the thresholds v_i. Because weights are non-negative, extending a finite history never decreases the sum of its weights. Thus, any history ending with a sum exceeding $v_{\max}$ in all dimensions is surely losing under any strategy.

Based on this, we build an MDP M' by unfolding M and integrating the sum for each dimension in states of M'. We ensure its finiteness thanks to the above observation and we reduce its overall size to a *single*-exponential by defining a suitable equivalence relation between states of M': we only care about the current sum in each dimension, and we can forget about the actual path that led to it. Precisely, the states of M' are in $S \times \{0, \ldots, v_{\max} + 1\}^d$. Now, for each constraint, we compute a set of target states in M' that exactly captures all runs satisfying the inequality of the constraint. Thus, we are left with a multiple reachability problem on M': we look for a strategy σ' that ensures that each of these sets R_i is reached with probability α_i. This query can be answered in time polynomial in $|M'|$ but exponential in the number of sets R_i, i.e., in q (Theorem 1).

Remark 1. Percentile problems with unique target are solvable in time polynomial in the number of constraints but still exponential in the number of dimensions.

For single-dimensional queries with a unique target set (but still potentially multi-constraint), our algorithm remains pseudo-polynomial as it requires polynomial time in the thresholds values (i.e., exponential in their encoding).

Corollary 1. *The single-dimensional percentile problem with a unique target set can be solved in pseudo-polynomial time.*

Lower Bound. By equivalence with cost problems for atomic cost formulae, it follows from [21, Theorem 7] that no truly-polynomial-time algorithm exists for the single-constraint percentile problem unless P = PSPACE.

Memory. The upper bound is by reduction to multiple reachability over an exponential unfolding. The lower bound is via reduction from multiple reachability.

7 Discounted Sum

The *discounted sum* models that short-term rewards or costs are more important than long-term ones. It is well-studied in automata [3] and MDPs [9,12,23]. We consider queries of the form $\mathcal{Q} := \bigwedge_{i=1}^{q} \mathbb{P}^{\sigma}_{M,s_{\mathrm{init}}}[\mathsf{DS}_{l_i}^{\lambda_i} \geq v_i] \geq \alpha_i$, for discount factors $\lambda_i \in\ ]0,1[\cap \mathbb{Q}$ and the usual thresholds. That is, we study multi-dimensional MDPs and possibly distinct discount factors for each constraint.

Our setting encompasses a simpler question which is still not known to be decidable. Consider the *precise discounted sum problem*: given a rational t, and a rational discount factor $\lambda \in\ ]0,1[$, does there exist an infinite binary sequence $\tau = \tau_1 \tau_2 \tau_3 \ldots \in \{0,1\}^{\omega}$ such that $\sum_{j=1}^{\infty} \lambda^j \cdot \tau_j = t$? In [4], this problem is related to several long-standing open questions, such as decidability of the *universality problem for discounted-sum automata* [3]. A slight generalization to paths in graphs is also mentioned by Chatterjee et al. as a key open problem in [9].

Lemma 8. *The precise discounted sum problem can be reduced to an almost-sure percentile problem over a two-dimensional MDP with only one state.*

This suggests that answering percentile problems would require an important breakthrough. In the following, we establish a conservative algorithm that, in some sense, can approximate the answer.

The ε-gap Problem. Our algorithm takes as input a percentile query and an arbitrarily small *precision factor* $\varepsilon > 0$ and has three possible outputs: Yes, No and Unknown. If it answers Yes, then a satisfying strategy exists and can be synthesized. If it answers No, then no such strategy exists. Finally, the algorithm may output Unknown for a specified "zone" close to the threshold values involved in the problem and of width which depends on ε. It is possible to incrementally reduce the uncertainty zone, but it cannot be eliminated as the case $\varepsilon = 0$ would answer the precise discounted sum problem, which is not known to be decidable.

We actually solve an ε-*gap problem*, a particular case of *promise problems* [19], where the set of inputs is partitioned in three subsets: yes-inputs, no-inputs and the rest of them. The promise problem then asks to answer Yes for all yes-inputs and No for all no-inputs, while the answer may be arbitrary for the remaining inputs. In our setting, the set of inputs for which no guarantee is given can be taken arbitrarily small, parametrized by value $\varepsilon > 0$: this is an ε-gap problem. This notion is formalized in Theorem 15.

Related Work: Single-Constraint Case. There are papers considering models related to *single-constraint* percentile queries. Consider a single-dimensional MDP and a single-constraint query, with thresholds v and α. The *threshold problem* fixes v and maximizes α [30,31]. The *value-at-risk problem* fixes α and maximizes v [5]. This is similar to *quantiles* in the shortest path setting [29]. Paper [5] is the first to provide an exponential-time algorithm to approximate the optimal value v^* under a fixed α in the general setting. The authors also rely on approximation. While we do not consider optimization, we do extend the setting to *multi-constraint, multi-dimensional, multi-discount* problems, and we are able to remain in the same complexity class, namely EXPTIME.

Main Results. Our main contributions for the discounted sum are as follows.

Theorem 14. *The ε-gap percentile problem for the discounted sum can be solved in time pseudo-polynomial in the model size and the precision factor, and exponential in the query size: polynomial in the number of states, the weights, the discount factors and the precision factor, and exponential in the number of constraints. It is* PSPACE*-hard for two-dimensional MDPs and already* NP*-hard for single-constraint queries. Exponential-memory strategies are both sufficient and in general necessary to satisfy ε-gap percentile queries.*

Cornerstones of the Algorithm. Our approach is similar to the shortest path: we want to build an unfolding capturing the needed information w.r.t. the discounted sums, and then reduce the percentile problem to a multiple reachability problem over this unfolding. However, several challenges have to be overcome.

First, we need a *finite* unfolding. This was easy in the shortest path due to non-decreasing sums and corresponding upper bounds. Here, it is not the case as we put no restriction on weights. Nonetheless, thanks to the discount factor, weights contribute less and less to the sum along a run. In particular, cutting all runs after a pseudo-polynomial length changes the overall sum by at most $\varepsilon/2$.

Second, we reduce the overall size of the unfolding. For the shortest path we took advantage of integer labels to define equivalence. Here, the space of values taken by the discounted sums is too large for a straightforward equivalence. To reduce it, we introduce a *rounding* scheme of the numbers involved. This idea is inspired by [5]. We bound the error due to cumulated roundings by $\varepsilon/2$.

So, we control the amount of information lost to guarantee exact answers except inside an arbitrarily small ε-zone. Given a q-constraint query Q for thresholds v_i, α_i, dimensions l_i and discounts λ_i, we define the *x-shifted query* Q_x, for $x \in \mathbb{Q}$, as the exact same problem for thresholds $v_i + x$, α_i, dimensions l_i and discounts λ_i. Our algorithm satisfies the following theorem, which formalizes the ε-gap percentile problem mentioned in Theorem 14.

Theorem 15. *There is an algorithm that, given an MDP, a percentile query Q for the discounted sum and a precision factor $\varepsilon > 0$, solves the following ε-gap problem in exponential time. It answers*

- **Yes** *if there is a strategy satisfying the $(2 \cdot \varepsilon)$-shifted percentile query $Q_{2\cdot\varepsilon}$;*
- **No** *if there is no strategy satisfying the $(-2 \cdot \varepsilon)$-shifted percentile query $Q_{-2\cdot\varepsilon}$;*
- *and arbitrarily otherwise.*

Lower Bounds. The ε-gap percentile problem is PSPACE-hard by reduction from subset-sum games [28]. Two tricks are important. First, counterbalancing the discount effect via adequate weights. Second, simulating an equality constraint. This cannot be achieved directly because it requires to handle $\varepsilon = 0$. Still, by choosing weights carefully we restrict possible discounted sums to integer values only. Then we choose the thresholds and $\varepsilon > 0$ such that no run can take a value within the uncertainty zone. This circumvents the limitation due to uncertainty. For single-constraint ε-gap problems, we prove NP-hardness, even for Markov chains. Our proof is by reduction from the K-th largest subset problem [18], inspired by [7, Theorem 11]. A recent, not yet published, paper by Haase and Kiefer [20] claims that this K-th largest subset problem is actually PP-complete. If this claim holds, then it suggests that the single-constraint problem does not belong to NP at all, otherwise the polynomial hierarchy would collapse to P^{NP} by Toda's theorem [27].

Memory. For the precise discounted sum and generalizations, infinite memory is needed [9]. For ε-gap problems, the exponential upper bound follows from the algorithm while the lower bound is shown via a family of problems that emulate the ones used for multiple reachability (Theorem 2).

References

1. Baier, C., Daum, M., Dubslaff, C., Klein, J., Klüppelholz, S.: Energy-utility quantiles. In: Badger, J.M., Rozier, K.Y. (eds.) NFM 2014. LNCS, vol. 8430, pp. 285–299. Springer, Heidelberg (2014)
2. Bertsekas, D.P., Tsitsiklis, J.N.: An analysis of stochastic shortest path problems. Math. Oper. Res. **16**, 580–595 (1991)
3. Boker, U., Henzinger, T.A.: Exact and approximate determinization of discounted-sum automata. LMCS **10**(1), 1–33 (2014)
4. Boker, U., Henzinger, T.A., Otop, J.: The target discounted-sum problem. In: Proceedings of LICS. IEEE Computer Society (2015)
5. Brázdil, T., Chen, T., Forejt, V., Novotný, P., Simaitis, A.: Solvency Markov decision processes with interest. In: Proceedings of FSTTCS, LIPIcs, vol. 24, pp. 487–499. Schloss Dagstuhl - LZI (2013)
6. Brázdil, T., Brozek, V., Chatterjee, K., Forejt, V., Kucera, A.: Markov decision processes with multiple long-run average objectives. LMCS **10**(13), 1–29 (2014)
7. Bruyère, V., Filiot, E., Randour, M., Raskin, J.-F.: Meet your expectations with guarantees: beyond worst-case synthesis in quantitative games. In: Proceedings of STACS, LIPIcs, vol. 25, pp. 199–213. Schloss Dagstuhl - LZI (2014)
8. Chatterjee, K., Doyen, L., Randour, M., Raskin, J.-F.: Looking at mean-payoff and total-payoff through windows. In: Van Hung, D., Ogawa, M. (eds.) ATVA 2013. LNCS, vol. 8172, pp. 118–132. Springer, Heidelberg (2013)
9. Chatterjee, K., Forejt, V., Wojtczak, D.: Multi-objective discounted reward verification in graphs and MDPs. In: McMillan, K., Middeldorp, A., Voronkov, A. (eds.) LPAR-19 2013. LNCS, vol. 8312, pp. 228–242. Springer, Heidelberg (2013)
10. Chatterjee, K., Henzinger, T.A.: Probabilistic systems with limsup and liminf objectives. In: Archibald, M., Brattka, V., Goranko, V., Löwe, B. (eds.) ILC 2007. LNCS, vol. 5489, pp. 32–45. Springer, Heidelberg (2009)
11. Chatterjee, K., Komárková, Z., Kretínský, J.: Unifying two views on multiple mean-payoff objectives in Markov decision processes. In: Proceedings of LICS. IEEE Computer Society (2015)
12. Chatterjee, K., Majumdar, R., Henzinger, T.A.: Markov decision processes with multiple objectives. In: Durand, B., Thomas, W. (eds.) STACS 2006. LNCS, vol. 3884, pp. 325–336. Springer, Heidelberg (2006)
13. Chatterjee, K., Randour, M., Raskin, J.-F.: Strategy synthesis for multi-dimensional quantitative objectives. Acta Inform. **51**(3–4), 129–163 (2014)
14. de Alfaro, L.: Formal verification of probabilistic systems. Ph.D. thesis, Stanford University (1997)

15. de Alfaro, L.: Computing minimum and maximum reachability times in probabilistic systems. In: Baeten, J.C.M., Mauw, S. (eds.) CONCUR 1999. LNCS, vol. 1664, pp. 66–81. Springer, Heidelberg (1999)
16. Etessami, K., Kwiatkowska, M.Z., Vardi, M.Y., Yannakakis, M.: Multi-objective model checking of Markov decision processes. LMCS $4(4)$, 1–21 (2008)
17. Filar, J.A., Krass, D., Ross, K.W.: Percentile performance criteria for limiting average Markov decision processes. IEEE Trans. Aut. Control $40(1)$, 2–10 (1995)
18. Garey, Michael R., Johnson, David S.: Computers and Intractability: A Guide to the Theory of NP-Completeness. Freeman, New York (1979)
19. Goldreich, O.: On promise problems: a survey. In: Goldreich, O., Rosenberg, A.L., Selman, A.L. (eds.) Theoretical Computer Science. LNCS, vol. 3895, pp. 254–290. Springer, Heidelberg (2006)
20. Haase, C., Kiefer, S.: The complexity of the Kth largest subset problem and related problems. CoRR, abs/1501.06729 (2015)
21. Haase, C., Kiefer, S.: The odds of staying on budget. In: Halldórsson, M.M., Iwama, K., Kobayashi, N., Speckmann, B. (eds.) ICALP 2015. LNCS, vol. 9135, pp. 234–246. Springer, Heidelberg (2015)
22. Ohtsubo, Y.: Optimal threshold probability in undiscounted Markov decision processes with a target set. Appl. Math. Comput. $149(2)$, 519–532 (2004)
23. Puterman, M.L.: Markov Decision Processes: Discrete Stochastic Dynamic Programming, 1st edn. Wiley, New York (1994)
24. Randour, M., Raskin, J.-F., Sankur, O.: Percentile queries in multi-dimensional Markov decision processes. CoRR, abs/1410.4801 (2014)
25. Randour, M., Raskin, J.-F., Sankur, O.: Variations on the stochastic shortest path problem. In: D'Souza, D., Lal, A., Larsen, K.G. (eds.) VMCAI 2015. LNCS, vol. 8931, pp. 1–18. Springer, Heidelberg (2015)
26. Sakaguchi, M., Ohtsubo, Y.: Markov decision processes associated with two threshold probability criteria. J. Control Theor. Appl. $11(4)$, 548–557 (2013)
27. Toda, S.: PP is as hard as the polynomial-time hierarchy. SIAM J. Comput. $20(5)$, 865–877 (1991)
28. Travers, S.D.: The complexity of membership problems for circuits over sets of integers. Theor. Comput. Sci. $369(1–3)$, 211–229 (2006)
29. Ummels, M., Baier, C.: Computing quantiles in Markov reward models. In: Pfenning, F. (ed.) FOSSACS 2013 (ETAPS 2013). LNCS, vol. 7794, pp. 353–368. Springer, Heidelberg (2013)
30. White, D.J.: Minimizing a threshold probability in discounted Markov decision processes. J. Math. Anal. Appl. $173(2)$, 634–646 (1993)
31. Wu, C., Lin, Y.: Minimizing risk models in Markov decision processes with policies depending on target values. J. Math. Anal. Appl. $231(1)$, 47–67 (1999)
32. Xu, H., Mannor, S.: Probabilistic goal Markov decision processes. In: IJCAI, pp. 2046–2052 (2011)

Faster Algorithms for Quantitative Verification in Constant Treewidth Graphs

Krishnendu Chatterjee, Rasmus Ibsen-Jensen, and Andreas Pavlogiannis[(✉)]

IST Austria, Klostenneuburg, Austria
{kchatterjee,pavlogiannis}@ist.ac.at

Abstract. We consider the core algorithmic problems related to verification of systems with respect to three classical quantitative properties, namely, the mean-payoff property, the ratio property, and the minimum initial credit for energy property. The algorithmic problem given a graph and a quantitative property asks to compute the optimal value (the infimum value over all traces) from every node of the graph. We consider graphs with constant treewidth, and it is well-known that the control-flow graphs of most programs have constant treewidth. Let n denote the number of nodes of a graph, m the number of edges (for constant treewidth graphs $m = O(n)$) and W the largest absolute value of the weights. Our main theoretical results are as follows. First, for constant treewidth graphs we present an algorithm that approximates the mean-payoff value within a multiplicative factor of ϵ in time $O(n \cdot \log(n/\epsilon))$ and linear space, as compared to the classical algorithms that require quadratic time. Second, for the ratio property we present an algorithm that for constant treewidth graphs works in time $O(n \cdot \log(|a \cdot b|)) = O(n \cdot \log(n \cdot W))$, when the output is $\frac{a}{b}$, as compared to the previously best known algorithm with running time $O(n^2 \cdot \log(n \cdot W))$. Third, for the minimum initial credit problem we show that (i) for general graphs the problem can be solved in $O(n^2 \cdot m)$ time and the associated decision problem can be solved in $O(n \cdot m)$ time, improving the previous known $O(n^3 \cdot m \cdot \log(n \cdot W))$ and $O(n^2 \cdot m)$ bounds, respectively; and (ii) for constant treewidth graphs we present an algorithm that requires $O(n \cdot \log n)$ time, improving the previous known $O(n^4 \cdot \log(n \cdot W))$ bound. We have implemented some of our algorithms and show that they present a significant speedup on standard benchmarks.

1 Introduction

Boolean vs. Quantitative Verification. The traditional view of verification has been *qualitative (Boolean)* that classifies traces of a system as "correct" vs "incorrect". In the recent years, motivated by applications to analyze resource-constrained systems (such as embedded systems), there has been a huge interest

The research was partly supported by Austrian Science Fund (FWF) Grant No P23499- N23, FWF NFN Grant No S11407-N23 (RiSE/SHiNE), ERC Start grant (279307: Graph Games), and Microsoft faculty fellows award.

D. Kroening and C.S. Păsăreanu (Eds.): CAV 2015, Part I, LNCS 9206, pp. 140–157, 2015.
DOI: 10.1007/978-3-319-21690-4_9

to study *quantitative* properties of systems. A quantitative property assigns to each trace of a system a real-number that quantifies how good or bad the trace is, instead of classifying it as correct vs incorrect. For example, a Boolean property may require that every request is eventually granted, whereas a quantitative property for each trace can measure the average waiting time between requests and corresponding grants.

Variety of Results. Given the importance of quantitative verification, the traditional qualitative view of verification has been extended in several ways, such as, quantitative languages and quantitative automata for specification languages [15–17,21,27,28,44]; quantitative logics for specification languages [2,9,11]; quantitative synthesis for robust reactive systems [4,5,20]; a framework for quantitative abstraction refinement [13]; quantitative analysis of infinite-state systems [18,23]; and model measuring (that extends model checking) [33], to name a few. The core algorithmic question for many of the above studies is a graph algorithmic problem that requires to analyze a graph wrt a quantitative property.

Important Quantitative Properties. The three quantitative properties that have been studied for their relevance in analysis of reactive systems are as follows. First, the *mean-payoff* property consists of a weight function that assigns to every transition an integer-valued weight and assigns to each trace the long-run average of the weights of the transitions of the trace. Second, the *ratio* property consists of two weight functions (one of which is a positive weight function) and assigns to each trace the ratio of the two mean-payoff properties (the denominator is wrt the positive function). The *minimum initial credit for energy* property consists of a weight function (like in the mean-payoff property) and assigns to each trace the minimum number to be added such that the partial sum of the weights for every prefix of the trace is non-negative. For example, the mean-payoff property is used for average waiting time, worst-case execution time analysis [13,17,18]; the ratio property is used in robustness analysis of systems [5]; and the minimum initial credit for energy for measuring resource consumptions [10].

Algorithmic Problems. Given a graph and a quantitative property, the value of a node is the infimum value of all traces that start at the respective node. The algorithmic problem (namely, the *value* problem) for analysis of quantitative properties consists of a graph and a quantitative property, and asks to compute either the exact value or an approximation of the value for every node in the graph. The algorithmic problems are at the heart of many applications, such as automata emptiness, model measuring, quantitative abstraction refinement, etc.

Treewidth of Graphs. A very well-known concept in graph theory is the notion of *treewidth* of a graph, which is a measure of how similar a graph is to a tree (a graph has treewidth 1 precisely if it is a tree) [40]. The treewidth of a graph is defined based on a *tree decomposition* of the graph [31], see Sect. 2 for a formal definition. Beyond the mathematical elegance of the treewidth property for graphs, there are many classes of graphs which arise in practice and have constant treewidth. The most important example is that the control flow graphs of goto-free programs for many programming languages are of constant treewidth [42], and it was also shown in [30] that typically all Java programs have constant treewidth. For many other applications see the surveys [6,7]. The constant treewidth property of graphs has also played an important role in logic and verification; for example, MSO (Monadic Second Order logic) queries can be solved in polynomial time [24] (also in log-space [29]) for constant-treewidth graphs; parity games on graphs with constant treewidth can be solved in polynomial time [37]; and there exist faster algorithms for probabilistic models (like Markov decision processes) [14]. Moreover, recently it has been shown that the constant treewidth property is also useful for interprocedural analysis [18].

Previous Results and Our Contributions. In this work we consider general graphs and graphs with constant treewidth, and the algorithmic problems to compute the exact value or an approximation of the value for every node wrt to quantitative properties given as the mean-payoff, the ratio, or the minimum initial credit for energy. We first present the relevant previous results, and then our contributions.

Previous Results. We consider graphs with n nodes, m edges, and let W denote the largest absolute value of the weights. The running time of the algorithms is characterized by the number of arithmetic operations (i.e., each operation takes constant time); and the space is characterized by the maximum number of integers the algorithm stores. The classical algorithm for graphs with mean-payoff properties is the minimum mean-cycle problem of Karp [34], and the algorithm requires $O(n \cdot m)$ running time and $O(n^2)$ space. A different algorithm was proposed in [36] that requires $O(n \cdot m)$ running time and $O(n)$ space. Orlin and Ahuja [38] gave an algorithm running in time $O(\sqrt{n} \cdot m \cdot \log(n \cdot W))$. For some special cases there exist faster approximation algorithms [19]. There is a straightforward reduction of the ratio problem to the mean-payoff problem. For computing the exact minimum ratio, the fastest known strongly polynomial time algorithm is Burns' algorithm [12] running in time $O(n^2 \cdot m)$. Also, there is an algorithm by Lawler [35] that uses $O(n \cdot m \cdot \log(n \cdot W))$ time. Many pseudopolynomial algorithms are known for the problem, with polynomial dependency on the numbers appearing in the weight function, see [26]. For the minimum initial credit for energy problem, the decision problem (i.e., is the energy required for node v at most c?) can be solved in $O(n^2 \cdot m)$ time, leading to an $O(n^3 \cdot m \cdot \log(n \cdot W))$ time algorithm for the minimum initial credit for energy problem [10]. All the above algorithms are for general graphs (without the constant-treewidth restriction).

Our Contributions. Our main contributions are as follows.

1. *Finding the Mean-Payoff and Ratio Values in Constant-Treewidth Graphs.* We present two results for constant treewidth graphs. First, for the exact computation we present an algorithm that requires $O(n \cdot \log(|a \cdot b|))$ time and $O(n)$ space, where $\frac{a}{b} \neq 0$ is the (irreducible) ratio/mean-payoff of the output. If $\frac{a}{b} = 0$, the algorithm uses $O(n)$ time. Note that $\log(|a \cdot b|) \leq 2 \log(n \cdot W)$. We also present a space-efficient version of the algorithm that requires only $O(\log n)$ space. Second, we present an algorithm for finding an

ϵ-factor approximation of the mean-payoff value that requires $O(n \cdot \log(n/\epsilon))$ time, as compared to the $O(n^{1.5} \cdot \log(n \cdot W))$ time solution of Orlin & Ahuja, and the $O(n^2)$ time solution of Karp (see Table 1).

2. *Finding the Minimum Initial Credit in Graphs.* We present two results. First, we consider the exact computation for general graphs, and present (i) an $O(n \cdot m)$ time algorithm for the decision problem (improving the previously known $O(n^2 \cdot m)$ bound), and (ii) an $O(n^2 \cdot m)$ time algorithm to compute value of all nodes (improving the previously known $O(n^3 \cdot m \cdot \log(n \cdot W))$ bound). Finally, we consider the computation of the exact value for graphs with constant treewidth and present an algorithm that requires $O(n \cdot \log n)$ time (improving the previous known $O(n^4 \cdot \log(n \cdot W))$ bound) (see Table 2).

3. *Experimental Results.* We have implemented our algorithms for the minimum mean cycle and minimum initial credit problems and ran them on standard benchmarks (DaCapo suit [3] for the minimum mean cycle problem, and DIMACS challenges [1] for the minimum initial credit problem). For the minimum mean cycle problem, our results show that our algorithm has lower running time than all the classical polynomial-time algorithms. For the minimum initial credit problem, our algorithm provides a significant speedup over the existing method. Both improvements are demonstrated even on graphs of small/medium size. Note that our theoretical improvements (better asymptotic bounds) imply improvements for large graphs, and our improvements on medium sized graphs indicate that our algorithms have practical applicability with small constants.

Table 1. Time complexity of existing and our solutions for the minimum mean-cycle value and ratio-cycle value problem in constant treewidth weighted graphs with n nodes and largest absolute weight W, when the output is the (irreducible) fraction $\frac{a}{b} \neq 0$.

Minimum mean-cycle value			Minimum ratio-cycle value		
Orlin & Ahuja [38]	Karp [34]	Our result [Thm 4] (ε-approximate)	Burns [12]	Lawler [35]	Our result [Cor 2]
$O(n^{1.5} \cdot \log(n \cdot W))$	$O(n^2)$	$\mathbf{O(n \cdot \log(n/\epsilon))}$	$O(n^3)$	$O(n^2 \cdot \log(n \cdot W))$	$\mathbf{O(n \cdot \log(\vert a \cdot b \vert))}$

Table 2. Complexity of the existing and our solution for the minimum initial credit problem on weighted graphs of n nodes, m edges, and largest absolute weight W.

	Bouyer et al. [10]	Our result [Thm 5, Cor 3]	Our result [Thm 7] (constant treewidth)
Time (decision)	$O(n^2 \cdot m)$	$\mathbf{O(n \cdot m)}$	$\mathbf{O(n \cdot \log n)}$
Time	$O(n^3 \cdot m \cdot \log(n \cdot W))$	$\mathbf{O(n^2 \cdot m)}$	$\mathbf{O(n \cdot \log n)}$
Space	$O(n)$	$\mathbf{O(n)}$	$\mathbf{O(n)}$

Technical Contributions. The key technical contributions of our work are as follows:

1. *Mean-Payoff and Ratio Values in Constant-Treewidth Graphs.* Given a graph with constant treewidth, let c^* be the smallest weight of a simple cycle. First,

we present a linear-time algorithm that computes c^* exactly (if $c^* \geq 0$) or approximates c^* within a polynomial factor (if $c^* < 0$). Then, we show that if the minimum ratio value ν^* is the irreducible fraction $\frac{a}{b}$, then ν^* can be computed by evaluating $O(\log(|a \cdot b|))$ inequalities of the form $\nu^* \geq \nu$. Each such inequality is evaluated by computing the smallest weight of a simple cycle in a modified graph. Finally, for ϵ-approximating the value ν^*, we show that $O(\log(n/\epsilon))$ such inequalities suffice.

2. *Minimum Initial Credit Problem.* We show that for general graphs, the decision problem can be solved with two applications of Bellman-Ford-type algorithms, and the value problem reduces to finding non-positive cycles in the graph, followed by one instance of the single-source shortest path problem. We then show how the invariants of the algorithm for the value problem on general graphs can be maintained by a particular graph traversal of the tree-decomposition for constant-treewidth graphs.

2   Definitions

Weighted Graphs. We consider *finite weighted directed graphs* $G = (V, E, \mathsf{wt}, \mathsf{wt}')$ where V is the set of n *nodes*, $E \subseteq V \times V$ is the edge relation of m *edges*, $\mathsf{wt} : E \to \mathbb{Z}$ is a *weight function* that assigns an integer weight $\mathsf{wt}(e)$ to each edge $e \in E$, and $\mathsf{wt}' : E \to \mathbb{N}^+$ is a weight function that assigns strictly positive integer weights. For technical simplicity, we assume that there exists at least one outgoing edge from every node. In certain cases where the function wt' is irrelevant, we will consider weighted graphs $G = (V, E, \mathsf{wt})$, i.e., without the function wt'.

Finite and Infinite Paths. A *finite path* $P = (u_1, \ldots, u_j)$, is a sequence of nodes $u_i \in V$ such that for all $1 \leq i < j$ we have $(u_i, u_{i+1}) \in E$. The *length* of P is $|P| = j - 1$. A single-node path has length 0. The path P is *simple* if there is no node repeated in P, and it is a *cycle* if $j > 1$ and $u_1 = u_j$. The path P is a *simple cycle* if P is a cycle and the sequence $(u_2, \ldots u_j)$ is a simple path. The functions wt and wt' naturally extend to paths, so that the weight of a path P with $|P| > 0$ wrt the weight functions wt and wt' is $\mathsf{wt}(P) = \sum_{1 \leq i < j} \mathsf{wt}(u_i, u_{i+1})$ and $\mathsf{wt}'(P) = \sum_{1 \leq i < j} \mathsf{wt}'(u_i, u_{i+1})$. The *value* of P is defined to be $\overline{\mathsf{wt}}(P) = \frac{\mathsf{wt}(P)}{\mathsf{wt}'(P)}$. For the case where $|P| = 0$, we define $\mathsf{wt}(P) = 0$, and $\overline{\mathsf{wt}}(P)$ is undefined. An *infinite path* $\mathcal{P} = (u_1, u_2, \ldots)$ of G is an infinite sequence of nodes such that every finite prefix P of $\mathcal{P}$ is a finite path of G. The functions wt and wt' assign to $\mathcal{P}$ a value in $\mathbb{Z} \cup \{-\infty, \infty\}$: we have $\mathsf{wt}(\mathcal{P}) = \sum_i \mathsf{wt}(u_i, u_{i+1})$ and $\mathsf{wt}'(\mathcal{P}) = \infty$. For a (possibly infinite) path P, we use the notation $u \in P$ to denote that a node u appears in P, and $e \in P$ to denote that an edge e appears in P. Given a set $B \subseteq V$, we denote by $P \cap B$ the set of nodes of B that appear in P. Given a finite path P_1 and a possibly infinite path P_2, we denote by $P_1 \circ P_2$ the path resulting from the concatenation of P_1 and P_2.

Distances and Witness Paths. For nodes $u, v \in V$, we denote by $d(u, v) = \inf_{P : u \rightsquigarrow v} \mathsf{wt}(P)$ the *distance* from u to v. A finite path $P : u \rightsquigarrow v$ is a *witness* of the distance $d(u,v)$ if $\mathsf{wt}(P) = d(u,v)$. An infinite path $\mathcal{P}$ is a witness of the distance $d(u,v)$ if the following conditions hold:

1. $d(u,v) = \mathsf{wt}(\mathcal{P}) = -\infty$, and
2. $\mathcal{P}$ starts from u, and v is reachable from every node of $\mathcal{P}$.

Note that $d(u,v) = \infty$ is not witnessed by any path.

Tree Decompositions. A *tree-decomposition* $\mathrm{Tree}(G) = (V_T, E_T)$ of G is a tree such that the following conditions hold:

1. $V_T = \{B_0, \ldots, B_{n'-1} : \forall i\ B_i \subseteq V\}$ and $\bigcup_{B_i \in V_T} B_i = V$ (every node is covered).
2. For all $(u,v) \in E$ there exists $B_i \in V_T$ such that $u,v \in B_i$ (every edge is covered).
3. For all i,j,k such that there is a bag B_k that appears in the simple path $B_i \rightsquigarrow B_j$ in $\mathrm{Tree}(G)$, we have $B_i \cap B_j \subseteq B_k$ (every node appears in a contiguous subtree of $\mathrm{Tree}(G)$).

The sets B_i which are nodes in V_T are called *bags*. Conventionally, we call B_0 the root of $\mathrm{Tree}(G)$, and denote by $\mathsf{Lv}(B_i)$ the level of B_i in $\mathrm{Tree}(G)$, with $\mathsf{Lv}(B_0) = 0$. We say that $\mathrm{Tree}(G)$ is *balanced* if the maximum level is $\max_{B_i} \mathsf{Lv}(B_i) = O(\log n')$, and it is *binary* if every bag has at most two children bags. A bag B is called the *root bag* of a node u if B is the smallest-level bag that contains u, and we often use B_u to refer to the root bag of u. The *width* of a tree-decomposition $\mathrm{Tree}(G)$ is the size of the largest bag minus 1. The treewidth of G is the smallest width among the widths of all possible tree decompositions of G.

Theorem 1. *For every graph G with n nodes and constant treewidth, a balanced binary tree-decomposition $\mathrm{Tree}(G)$ of constant width and $O(n)$ bags can be constructed in (1) $O(n)$ time and space [8], (2) deterministic logspace (and hence polynomial time) [29].*

In the sequel we consider only balanced and binary tree-decompositions of constant width and $n' = O(n)$ bags (and hence of height $O(\log n)$). Additionally, we assume that every bag is the root bag of at most one node. Obtaining this last property is straightforward, simply by replacing each bag B which is the root of $k > 1$ nodes $x_1, \ldots x_k$ with a chain of bags $B_1, \ldots, B_k = B$, where each B_i is the parent of B_{i+1}, and $B_{i+1} = B_i \cup \{x_{i+1}\}$. Note that this keeps the tree binary and increases its height by at most a constant factor, hence the resulting tree is also balanced.

Throughout the paper, we follow the convention that the maximum and minimum of the empty set is $-\infty$ and ∞ respectively, i.e., $\max(\emptyset) = -\infty$ and $\min(\emptyset) = \infty$. Time complexity is measured in number of arithmetic and logical operations, and space complexity is measured in number of machine words. Given a graph G, we denote by $\mathcal{T}(G)$ and $\mathcal{S}(G)$ the time and space required for constructing a balanced, binary tree-decomposition $\mathrm{Tree}(G)$. We are interested in the following problems.

The Minimum Mean Cycle Problem [34]. Given a weighted directed graph $G = (V, E, \mathsf{wt})$, the minimum mean cycle problem asks to determine for each node u the *mean value* $\mu^*(u) = \min_{C \in \mathcal{C}_u} \frac{\mathsf{wt}(C)}{|C|}$, where $\mathcal{C}_u$ is the set of simple cycles reachable from u in G. A cycle C with $\frac{\mathsf{wt}(C)}{|C|} = \mu^*(u)$ is called a minimum mean cycle of u. For $0 < \epsilon < 1$, we say that a value μ is an ϵ-approximation of the mean value $\mu^*(u)$ if $|\mu - \mu^*(u)| \leq \epsilon \cdot |\mu^*(u)|$.

The Minimum Ratio Cycle Problem [32]. Given a weighted directed graph $G = (V, E, \mathsf{wt}, \mathsf{wt}')$, the minimum ratio cycle problem asks to determine for each node u the *ratio value* $\nu^*(u) = \min_{C \in \mathcal{C}_u} \overline{\mathsf{wt}}(C)$, where $\overline{\mathsf{wt}}(C) = \frac{\mathsf{wt}(C)}{\mathsf{wt}'(C)}$ and $\mathcal{C}_u$ is the set of simple cycles reachable from u in G. A cycle C with $\overline{\mathsf{wt}}(C) = \nu_u^*$ is called a minimum ratio cycle of u. The minimum mean cycle problem follows as a special case of the minimum ratio cycle problem for $\mathsf{wt}'(e) = 1$ for each edge $e \in E$.

The Minimum Initial Credit Problem [10]. Given a weighted directed graph $G = (V, E, \mathsf{wt})$, the minimum initial credit value problem asks to determine for each node u the smallest energy value $\mathsf{E}(u) \in \mathbb{N} \cup \{\infty\}$ with the following property: there exists an infinite path $\mathcal{P} = (u_1, u_2 \ldots)$ with $u = u_1$, such that for every finite prefix P of $\mathcal{P}$ we have $\mathsf{E}(u) + \mathsf{wt}(P) \geq 0$. Conventionally, we let $\mathsf{E}(u) = \infty$ if no finite value exists. The associated decision problem asks given a node u and an initial credit $c \in \mathbb{N}$ whether $\mathsf{E}(u) \leq c$.

3   Minimum Cycle

In this section we deal with a related graph problem, namely the detection of a minimum-weight simple cycle of a graph. In Sect. 4 we use our solution to this problem to obtain solutions for the minimum ratio and minimum mean cycle problems.

The Minimum Cycle Problem. Given a weighted graph $G = (V, E, \mathsf{wt})$, the minimum cycle problem asks to determine the weight c^* of a minimum-weight simple cycle in G, i.e., $c^* = \min_{C \in \mathcal{C}} \mathsf{wt}(C)$, where $\mathcal{C}$ is the set of simple cycles in G.

We describe the algorithm MinCycle that operates on a tree-decomposition Tree(G) of an input graph G, and has the following properties.

1. If G has no negative cycles, then MinCycle returns the weight c^* of a minimum-weight cycle in G.
2. If G has negative cycles, then MinCycle returns a value that is at most a polynomial (in n) factor smaller than c^*.

U-Shaped Paths. Following the recent work of [18], we define the important notion of U-shaped paths in a tree-decomposition Tree(G). Given a bag B and nodes $u, v \in B$, we say that a path $P : u \rightsquigarrow v$ is U-*shaped* in B, if one of the following conditions hold:

1. Either $|P| > 1$ and B is an ancestor of B_w for all intermediate nodes $w \in P$,
2. or $|P| \leq 1$ and B is B_u or B_v (i.e., B is the root bag of either u or v).

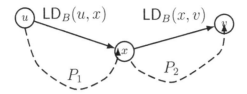

Fig. 1. Path shortening in MinCycle. When B_x is examined, $\mathsf{LD}_{B_x}(u,v)$ is updated with the weight of the U-shaped path $P = P_1 \circ P_2$. The paths P_1 and P_2 are U-shaped paths in the children bags B_1 and B_2 of B_x, and we have $\mathsf{LD}_{B_i}(u,x) = \mathsf{wt}(P_i)$.

Informally, given a bag B, a U-shaped path in B is a path that traverses intermediate nodes that exist only in the subtree of $\mathrm{Tree}(G)$ rooted in B. The following remark follows from the definition of tree-decompositions, and states that every simple cycle C can be seen as a U-shaped path P from the smallest-level node of C to itself. Consequently, we can determine the value c^* by only considering U-shaped paths in $\mathrm{Tree}(G)$.

Remark 1. Let $C = (u_1, \ldots, u_k)$ be a simple cycle in G, and $u_j = \arg\min_{u_i \in C} \mathsf{Lv}(u_i)$. Then $P = (u_j, u_{j+1}, \ldots u_k, u_1, \ldots, u_j)$ is a U-shaped path in B_{u_j}, and $\mathsf{wt}(P) = \mathsf{wt}(C)$.

Informal Description of MinCycle. Based on U-shaped paths, the work of [18] presented a method for computing algebraic path properties on tree-decompositions with constant width, where the weights of the edges come from a general semiring. Note that integer-valued weights are a special case of the tropical semiring. Our algorithm MinCycle is similar to the algorithm Preprocess from [18]. It consists of a depth-first traversal of $\mathrm{Tree}(G)$, and for each examined bag B computes a *local distance* map $\mathsf{LD}_B : B \times B \to \mathbb{Z} \cup \{\infty\}$ such that for each $u, v \in B$, we have (i) $\mathsf{LD}_B(u,v) = \mathsf{wt}(P)$ for some path $P : u \rightsquigarrow v$, and (ii) $\mathsf{LD}_B \le \min_P \mathsf{wt}(P)$, where P are taken to be simple $u \rightsquigarrow v$ paths (or simple cycles) that are U-shaped in B. This is achieved by traversing $\mathrm{Tree}(G)$ in post-order, and for each root bag B_x of a node x, we update $\mathsf{LD}_{B_x}(u,v)$ with $\mathsf{LD}_{B_x}(u,x) + \mathsf{LD}_{B_x}(x,v)$ (i.e., we do path-shortening from node u to node v, by considering paths that go through x). See Fig. 1 for an illustration. At the end, MinCycle returns the smallest $\mathsf{LD}_{B_x}(x,x)$ it has found.

The following lemma follows easily from [18, Lemma 2], and states that $\mathsf{LD}_B(u,v)$ is upper bounded by the smallest weight of a U-shaped simple $u \rightsquigarrow v$ path in B.

Lemma 1 ([18, Lemma 2]). *For every examined bag B and nodes $u, v \in B$, we have (1) $\mathsf{LD}_B(u,v) = \mathsf{wt}(P)$ for some path $P : u \rightsquigarrow v$ (and $\mathsf{LD}_B(u,v) = \infty$ if no such P exists), and (2) $\mathsf{LD}_B(u,v) \le \min_{P:u \rightsquigarrow v} \mathsf{wt}(P)$ where P ranges over U-shaped simple paths and simple cycles in B.*

Based on Lemma 1, we show that MinCycle returns $\min_x \mathsf{LD}_{B_x}(x,x)$, i.e., the weight of the smallest-weight U-shaped (not necessarily simple) cycle $C : x \rightsquigarrow x$

it has discovered. The cycle C has polynomial (in n) length, thus $|\mathsf{wt}(C)| = |c^*| \cdot n^{O(1)}$, and C is necessarily simple if there are no negative cycles in G, in which case $\mathsf{wt}(C) = c^*$. We refer to the full version for a detailed analysis [22]. This leads to the following theorem.

Theorem 2. *Let $G = (V, E, \mathsf{wt})$ be a weighted graph of n nodes with constant treewidth, and a balanced, binary tree-decomposition $\mathrm{Tree}(G)$ of G be given. Let c^*, be the smallest weight of a simple cycle in G. Algorithm $\mathsf{MinCycle}$ uses $O(n)$ time and $O(\log n)$ additional space, and returns a value c such that:*

1. *If G has no negative cycles, then $c = c^*$.*
2. *If G has a negative cycle, then $c \leq c^*$, and $|c| = |c^*| \cdot n^{O(1)}$.*

4   The Minimum Ratio and Mean Cycle Problems

In the current section we present algorithms for solving the minimum ratio and mean cycle problems for weighted graphs $G = (V, E, \mathsf{wt}, \mathsf{wt}')$ of constant treewidth.

Remark 2. If G is not strongly connected, we can compute its maximal strongly connected components (SCCs) in linear time [41], and use the algorithms of this section to compute the minimum cycle ratio ν_i^* in every component $\mathcal{G}_i$. Afterwards, we assign the ratio values $\nu^*(u)$ for all nodes u as follows. First, mark every SCC $\mathcal{G}_i$ with $M(\mathcal{G}_i) = \nu_i^*$. Then, for every bottom SCC $\mathcal{G}_i$, (i) for every u in $\mathcal{G}_i$ assign $\nu^*(u) = M(\mathcal{G}_i)$, (ii) for every neighbor SCC $\mathcal{G}_j$ of $\mathcal{G}_i$, mark $\mathcal{G}_j$ with $M(\mathcal{G}_j) = \min(M(\mathcal{G}_j), M(\mathcal{G}_i))$, (iii) remove $\mathcal{G}_i$ and repeat. Since these operations require linear time in total, they do not impact the time complexity. Therefore, we consider graphs G that are strongly connected, and we will speak about the minimum ratio ν^* and mean μ^* values of G.

Claim 1. Let ν^* be the ratio value of G. Then $\nu^* \geq \nu$ iff for every cycle C of G we have $\mathsf{wt}_\nu(C) \geq 0$, where $\mathsf{wt}_\nu(e) = \mathsf{wt}(e) - \mathsf{wt}'(e) \cdot \nu$ for each edge $e \in E$.

Hence, given a tree-decomposition $\mathrm{Tree}(G)$, and a guess ν of the ratio value ν^*, we can evaluate whether $\nu^* \geq \nu$ by executing algorithm $\mathsf{MinCycle}$ on input $G_\nu = (V, E, \mathsf{wt}_\nu)$. By Item 2a of Theorem 2 and Claim 1 we have that the returned value c of $\mathsf{MinCycle}$ is $c \geq 0$ iff $\mathsf{wt}_\nu(C) \geq 0$ for all cycles C, iff $\nu^* \geq \nu$ (and in fact $c = 0$ iff $\nu^* = \nu$).

4.1   Exact Solution

We now describe the method for determining the value ν^* of G exactly. This is done by making various guesses ν such that $\nu^* \geq \nu$ and testing for negative cycles in the graph $G_\nu = (V, E, \mathsf{wt}_\nu)$. We first determine whether $\nu^* = 0$, using Claim 1. In the remaining of this section we assume that $\nu^* \neq 0$.

Solution Overview. Consider that $\nu^* > 0$. First, we either find that $\nu^* \in (0, 1)$ (hence $\lfloor \nu^* \rfloor = 0$), or perform an *exponential search* of $O(\log \nu^*)$ iterations to determine $j \in \mathbb{N}^+$ such that $\nu^* \in [2^{j-1}, 2^j]$. In the latter case we perform a binary search of $O(\log \nu^*)$ iterations in the interval $[2^{j-1}, 2^j]$ to determine $\lfloor \nu^* \rfloor$. Then we can write $\nu^* = \lfloor \nu^* \rfloor + x$, where $x < 1$ is an irreducible fraction $\frac{a}{b}$. It has been shown [39] that such x can be determined by evaluating $O(\log b)$ inequalities of the form $x \geq \nu$. The case for $\nu^* < 0$ is handled similarly. We refer to the full version of the paper for a detailed description [22]. We thus obtain the following theorem, and by Theorem 1 the corollaries follow.

Theorem 3. *Let $G = (V, E, \mathsf{wt}, \mathsf{wt}')$ be a weighted graph of n nodes with constant treewidth, and $\lambda = \max_u |a_u \cdot b_u|$ such that $\nu^*(u)$ is the irreducible fraction $\frac{a_u}{b_u}$. Let $\mathcal{T}(G)$ and $\mathcal{S}(G)$ denote the required time and space for constructing a balanced binary tree-decomposition $\mathrm{Tree}(G)$ of G with constant width. The minimum ratio cycle problem for G can be computed in (1) $O(\mathcal{T}(G) + n \cdot \log \lambda)$ time and $O(\mathcal{S}(G) + n)$ space; and (2) $O(\mathcal{S}(G) + \log n)$ space.*

Corollary 1. *Let $G = (V, E, \mathsf{wt}, \mathsf{wt}')$ be a weighted graph of n nodes with constant treewidth, and $\lambda = \max_u |a_u \cdot b_u|$ such that $\nu^*(u)$ is the irreducible fraction $\frac{a_u}{b_u}$. The minimum ratio value problem for G can be computed in (1) $O(n \cdot \log \lambda)$ time and $O(n)$ space; and (2) $O(\log n)$ space.*

Corollary 2. *Let $G = (V, E, \mathsf{wt})$ be a weighted graph of n nodes with constant treewidth, and $\lambda = \max_u |\mu^*(u)|$. The minimum mean value problem for G can be computed in (1) $O(n \cdot \log \lambda)$ time and $O(n)$ space; and (2) $O(\log n)$ space.*

4.2 Approximating the Minimum Mean Cycle

We now focus on the minimum mean cycle problem, and present a method for ϵ-approximating the mean value μ^* of G for any $0 < \epsilon < 1$ in $O(n \cdot \log(n/\epsilon))$ time.

Approximate Solution in the Absence of Negative Cycles. We first consider graphs G that do not have negative cycles. Let C be a minimum weight simple cycle in G, and note that $\mu^* \in [0, \mathsf{wt}(C)]$. Additionally, we have $\mathsf{wt}(C) \leq n \cdot \mu^*$. Consider a binary search in the interval $[0, \mathsf{wt}(C)]$, which in step i approximates μ^* by the right endpoint μ_i of its current interval. The error is bounded by the length of the interval, hence $\mu_i - \mu^* \leq \mathsf{wt}(C) \cdot 2^{-i} \leq n \cdot \mu^* \cdot 2^{-i}$. To approximate within a factor ϵ it suffices to iterate for i steps, where $i \geq \log(n/\epsilon)$.

Approximate Solution in the Presence of Negative Cycles. We now turn our attention to ϵ-approximating μ^* in the presence of negative cycles in G. Let c be the value returned by $\mathsf{MinCycle}$ on input G. Item 2a of Theorem 2 guarantees that for the weight function $\mathsf{wt}_{-|c|}(e) = \mathsf{wt}(e) + |c|$, the graph $G_{-|c|} = (V, E, \mathsf{wt}_{-|c|})$ has no negative cycles (although it might still have negative edges). We show that μ^* can be ϵ-approximated by ϵ'-approximating the value μ'^* of $G_{-|c|}$, for some ϵ' polynomially (in n) smaller than ϵ (i.e., $\epsilon' = \epsilon/n^{O(1)}$). We refer to the full version for a detailed description [22].

Theorem 4. *Let $G = (V, E, \mathsf{wt})$ be a weighted graph of n nodes with constant treewidth. For any $0 < \epsilon < 1$, the minimum mean value problem can be ϵ-approximated in $O(n \cdot \log(n/\epsilon))$ time and $O(n)$ space.*

5   The Minimum Initial Credit Problem

In the current section we present algorithms for solving the minimum initial credit problem on weighted graphs $G = (V, E, \mathsf{wt})$. We first deal with arbitrary graphs, and provide an $O(n \cdot m)$ algorithm for the decision problem, and an $O(n^2 \cdot m)$ algorithm for the value problem, improving the previously best upper bounds. Afterwards we adapt our approach to graphs of constant treewidth to obtain an $O(n \cdot \log n)$ algorithm.

Non-positive Minimum Initial Credit. For technical convenience we focus on a variant of the minimum initial credit problem, where energies are non-positive, and the goal is to keep partial sums of path prefixes non-positive. Formally, given a weighted graph $G = (V, E, \mathsf{wt})$, the non-positive minimum initial credit value problem asks to determine for each node u the largest energy value $\mathsf{E}(u) \in \mathbb{Z}_{\leq 0} \cup \{-\infty\}$ with the following property: there exists an infinite path $\mathcal{P} = (u_1, u_2 \ldots)$ with $u = u_1$, such that for every finite prefix P of $\mathcal{P}$ we have $\mathsf{E}(u) + \mathsf{wt}(P) \leq 0$. We let $\mathsf{E}(u) = -\infty$ if no finite such value exists. Hence, minimality is wrt the absolute value of the energy. The associated decision problem asks given a node u and an initial credit $c \in \mathbb{Z}_{\leq 0}$ whether $\mathsf{E}(u) \geq c$.

   We start with some definitions and claims that will give the intuition for the algorithms to follow. First, we define the minimum initial credit of a pair of nodes u, v, which is the energy to reach v from u (i.e., the energy is wrt a finite path).

Finite Minimum Initial Credit. For nodes $u, v \in V$, we denote by $\mathsf{E}_v(u) \in \mathbb{Z}_{\leq 0} \cup \{-\infty\}$ the largest value with the following property: there exists a path $P : u \rightsquigarrow v$ such that for every prefix P' of P we have $\mathsf{E}_v(u) + \mathsf{wt}(P') \leq 0$. We let $\mathsf{E}_v(u) = -\infty$ if there is no path $u \rightsquigarrow v$. Note that for every pair of nodes $u, v \in V$, we have $\mathsf{E}(u) \geq \mathsf{E}_v(u) + \mathsf{E}(v)$.

Highest-Energy Nodes. Given a (possibly infinite) path P with $\mathsf{wt}(P) < \infty$, we say that a node $x \in P$ is a *highest-energy node* of P if there exists a *highest-energy prefix* P_1 of P ending in x such that for any prefix P_2 of P we have $\mathsf{wt}(P_1) \geq \mathsf{wt}(P_2)$. Note that since the weights are integers, for every pair of paths P_1', P_2', it is either $|\mathsf{wt}(P_1') - \mathsf{wt}(P_2')| = 0$ or $|\mathsf{wt}(P_1') - \mathsf{wt}(P_2')| \geq 1$. Therefore the set $\{\mathsf{wt}(P_i)\}_i$ of weights of prefixes of P has a maximum, and thus a highest-energy node always exists when $\mathsf{wt}(P) < \infty$. The following properties are easy to verify:

1. If x is a highest-energy node in a path $P : u \rightsquigarrow v$, then $\mathsf{E}_v(x) = 0$.
2. If x is a highest-energy node in an infinite path $\mathcal{P}$, then $\mathsf{E}(x) = 0$.

Using the above properties we establish Claim 2, which is central to our algorithms.

Claim 2. For every $u \in V$, we have $\mathsf{E}(u) = \max_{v:\mathsf{E}(v)=0} \mathsf{E}_v(u)$.

5.1   The Decision Problem for General Graphs

Recall the decision problem: given a node u and an initial credit $c \in \mathbb{Z}_{\leq 0}$, decide whether $\mathsf{E}(u) \geq c$. Our algorithm is based on Claim 3. The key idea is that

$E(u) \geq c$ iff there exists a witness path that reaches a non-positive cycle in less than n steps.

Claim 3. For every $u \in V$ and $c \in \mathbb{Z}_{\leq 0}$, we have that $E(u) \geq c$ iff there exists a simple cycle C such that (i) $\mathsf{wt}(C) \leq 0$ and (ii) for every $v \in C$ we have that $E_v(u) \geq c$, which is witnessed by a path $P_v : u \rightsquigarrow v$ with $|P_v| < n$.

Algorithm DecisionEnergy. Claim 3 suggests a way to decide whether $E(u) \geq c$. First, we start with energy c from u, and perform $n-1$ relaxation steps, similar to the Bellman-Ford algorithm, to discover the set V_u^c of nodes that can be reached from u with initial credit c by a path of length at most $n - 1$. Afterwards, we perform a Bellman-Ford computation on the subgraph $G \upharpoonright V_u^c$ induced by the set V_u^c. By Claim 3, we have that $E(u) \geq c$ iff $G \upharpoonright V_u^c$ contains a non-positive cycle. We refer to the full version for a detailed description [22]. We thus obtain the following theorem.

Theorem 5. Let $G = (V, E, \mathsf{wt})$ be a weighted graph of n nodes and m edges. Let $u \in V$ be an initial node, and $c \in \mathbb{Z}_{\leq 0}$ be an initial credit. The decision problem of whether $E(u) \geq c$ can be solved in $O(n \cdot m)$ time and $O(n)$ space.

5.2   The Value Problem for General Graphs

We now turn our attention to the value problem, where the task is to determine $E(u)$ for every node u. The following claim reduces the finite minimum initial credit problem to reach a node v to the shortest-path problem, when all energies to reach v are negative.

Claim 4. If for all $w \in V \setminus \{v\}$ we have $E_v(w) < 0$, then for each $u \in V \setminus \{v\}$ we have $E_v(u) = -d(u, v)$.

The rest of the section provides a $O(k \cdot n \cdot m)$ time solution, where $k = |X| + 1$ is the number of 0-energy nodes (plus one). This solution is faster in graphs where $k = o(n)$. This is achieved by algorithm ZeroEnergyNodes for obtaining the set X fast.

Determining the 0-Energy Nodes. To determine the set of 0-energy nodes, we construct the graph $G_2 = (V_2, E_2, \mathsf{wt}_2)$ with a fresh node $z \notin V$ as follows:

1. The node set is $V_2 = V \cup \{z\}$,
2. The edge set is $E_2 = E \cup (\{z\} \times V)$,
3. The weight function $\mathsf{wt}_2 : E_2 \to \mathbb{Z}$ is $\mathsf{wt}_2(u, v) = \begin{cases} 0 & \text{if } u = z \\ \mathsf{wt}(u, v) & \text{otherwise} \end{cases}$

Note that for every $u \in V$, the energy $E(u)$ is the same in G and G_2.

Algorithm ZeroEnergyNodes. Algorithm ZeroEnergyNodes is used for obtaining the set X of all 0-energy nodes in G_2. Informally, the algorithm performs a sequence of modifications on a graph $\mathcal{G}$, initially identical to G_2. In each step, the algorithm executes a Bellman-Ford computation on the current graph $\mathcal{G}$ with z as the source node, as long as a non-positive cycle C is discovered. For every

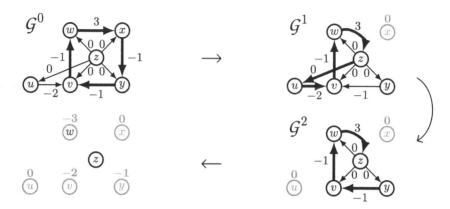

Fig. 2. Solving the value problem using operations on the graph $\mathcal{G}$. Initially we examine $\mathcal{G}^0$, and a non-positive cycle is found (boldface edges) with highest-energy node x. Thus $\mathsf{E}(x) = 0$, and we proceed with $\mathcal{G}^1$, to discover $\mathsf{E}(u) = 0$. In $\mathcal{G}^2$ all cycles are positive, and the energy of each remaining node is minus its distance to z.

such C, it determines a highest-energy node w of C, and modifies $\mathcal{G}$ by replacing every incoming edge (x, w) with an edge (x, z) of the same weight, and then removing w. See Fig. 2 for an illustration.

Determining the Negative-Energy Nodes. Given the set X of 0-energy nodes, it remains to determine the energy of every other node $u \in V \setminus X$. Let $\mathcal{G}^{|X|}$ be the modified graph $\mathcal{G}$ of algorithm ZeroEnergyNodes after the set X has been computed. To compute the energy $\mathsf{E}(u)$ of each node $u \in V \setminus X$, it suffices to compute its distance to z in $\mathcal{G}^{|X|}$. This reduces to a single-source shortest path instance from z on $\mathcal{G}^{|X|}$ with all edges reversed. Figure 2 illustrates the algorithms on an example. We refer to the full version of the paper for a detailed description [22]. We obtain the following theorem.

Theorem 6. *Let $G = (V, E, \mathsf{wt})$ be a weighted graph of n nodes and m edges, and $k = |\{v \in V : \mathsf{E}(v) = 0\}| + 1$. The minimum initial credit value problem for G can be solved in $O(k \cdot n \cdot m)$ time and $O(n)$ space.*

Corollary 3. *Let $G = (V, E, \mathsf{wt})$ be a weighted graph of n nodes and m edges. The minimum initial credit value problem for G can be solved in $O(n^2 \cdot m)$ time and $O(n)$ space.*

5.3   The Value Problem for Constant-Treewidth Graphs

We now turn our attention to the minimum initial credit value problem for constant-treewidth graphs $G = (V, E, \mathsf{wt})$. Note that in such graphs $m = O(n)$, thus Theorem 6 gives an $O(n^3)$ time solution as compared to the existing $O(n^4 \cdot \log(n \cdot W))$ time solution. This section shows that we can do significantly better, namely reduce the time complexity to $O(n \cdot \log n)$. This is mainly achieved by algorithm ZeroEnergyNodesTW for computing the set X of 0-energy nodes fast in constant-treewidth graphs.

Extended + and min Operators. Recall the graph $G_2 = (V_2, E_2, \text{wt}_2)$ from the last section. Given $\text{Tree}(G)$, a balanced and binary tree-decomposition $\text{Tree}(G_2)$ of G_2 with width increased by 1 can be easily constructed by (i) inserting z to every bag of $\text{Tree}(G)$, and (ii) adding a new root bag that contains only z. Let $\mathcal{I} = \mathbb{Z} \times V \times \mathbb{Z}$. For a map $f : V_2 \times V_2 \to \mathbb{Z}$, define the map $g_f : V_2 \times V_2 \to \mathcal{I}$ as

$$g_f(u,v) = \begin{cases} (f(u,v), u, 0) & \text{if } f(u,v) < 0 \text{ or } v = z \\ (f(u,v), v, f(u,v)) & \text{otherwise} \end{cases}$$

For triplets of elements $\alpha_1 = (a_1, b_1, c_1), \alpha_2 = (a_2, b_2, c_2) \in \mathcal{I}$, define the operations

1. $\min(\alpha_1, \alpha_2) = \alpha_i$ with $i = \arg\min_{j \in \{1,2\}} a_j$
2. $\alpha_1 + \alpha_2 = (a_1 + a_2, b, c)$, where $c = \max(c_1, a_1 + c_2)$ and $b = b_1$ if $c = c_1$ else $b = b_2$.

In words, if f is a weight function, then $g_f(u,v)$ selects the weight of the edge (u,v), its highest-energy node (i.e., u if $f(u,v) < 0$, and v otherwise, except when $v = z$), and the weight to reach that node from u. Recall that algorithm MinCycle from Sect. 3 traverses a tree-decomposition bottom-up, and for each encountered bag B stores a map LD_B such that $\text{LD}_B(u,v)$ is upper bounded by the weight of the shortest U-shaped simple path $u \rightsquigarrow v$ (or simple cycle, if $u = v$). Our algorithm ZeroEnergyNodesTW for determining all 0-energy nodes is similar, but now LD_B stores triplets (a, b, c) where a is the weight of a U-shaped path P, b is a highest-energy node of P, and c the weight of a highest-energy prefix of P. For triplets $\alpha_1 = (a_1, b_1, c_1), \alpha_2 = (a_2, b_2, c_2) \in \mathcal{I}$ corresponding to U-shaped paths P_1, P_2, $\min(\alpha_1, \alpha_2)$ selects the path with the smallest weight, and $\alpha_1 + \alpha_2$ determines the weight, a highest-energy node, and the weight of a highest-energy prefix of the path $P_1 \circ P_2$ (see Fig. 3).

Algorithm ZeroEnergyNodesTW. The algorithm ZeroEnergyNodesTW for computing the set of 0-energy nodes in constant-treewidth graphs follows the same principle as ZeroEnergyNodes for general graphs. It stores a map of edge weights

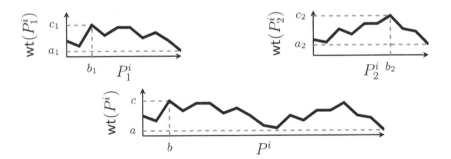

Fig. 3. Illustration of the $\alpha_1 + \alpha_2$ operation, corresponding to concatenating paths P_1 and P_2. The path P_j^i denotes the i-th prefix of P_j. We have $P = P_1 \circ P_2$, and the corresponding tripplet $\alpha = (a, b, c)$ denotes the weight a of P, its highest-energy node b, and the weight c of a highest-energy prefix.

$wt : E_2 \rightarrow \mathbb{Z} \cup \{\infty\}$, and initially $wt(u, v) = \mathsf{wt}_2(u, v)$ for each $(u, v) \in E_2$. The algorithm performs a bottom-up pass, and computes in each bag the local distance map $\mathsf{LD}_B : B \times B \rightarrow \mathcal{I}$ that captures U-shaped $u \leadsto v$ paths, together with their highest-energy nodes (similar to algorithm MinCycle from Sect. 3). When a non-positive cycle C is found, the algorithm modifies the edges of a highest-energy node w of C and its incoming neighbors (similar to algorithm ZeroEnergyNodes). These updates affect the distances between the remaining nodes, hence some local distance maps LD_B need to be corrected. We prove that each such edge modification only affects the local distance map of bags that appear in a path from a bag B' to some ancestor B'' of B'. Instead of restarting the computation as in ZeroEnergyNodes, the algorithm only updates those maps along the path $B' \leadsto B''$. We refer to the full version for a detailed description [22].

Theorem 7. *Let $G = (V, E, \mathsf{wt})$ be a weighted graph of n nodes with constant treewidth. The minimum initial credit value problem for G can be solved in $O(n \cdot \log n)$ time and $O(n)$ space.*

6   Experimental Results

Here we report on preliminary experimental evaluation of our algorithms, and compare them to existing methods. Our algorithm for the minimum mean cycle problem provides improvement for constant-treewidth graphs, and has thus been evaluated on constant-treewidth graphs obtained from the control-flow graphs of programs. For the minimum initial credit problem, we have implemented our algorithm for arbitrary graphs, thus the benchmarks in this case are general graphs (i.e., not constant-treewidth graphs).

Minimum Mean Cycle. We have implemented our approximation algorithm for the minimum mean cycle problem, and we let the algorithm run for as many iterations until a minimum mean cycle was discovered, instead of terminating after $O(\log(n/\epsilon))$ iterations required by Theorem 4. We have tested its performance in running time and space against six other minimum mean cycle algorithms from Table 3 in control-flow graphs of programs. The algorithms of Burns and Lawler solve the more general ratio cycle problem, and have been adapted to the mean cycle problem as in [26].

The algorithms were executed on control-flow graphs of methods of programs from the DaCapo benchmark suit [3], obtained using the Soot framework [43]. For each benchmark we focused on graphs of at least 500 nodes. This supplied a set of medium sized graphs (between 500 and 1300 nodes), in which integer weights were assigned uniformly at random in the range $\{-10^3, \ldots, 10^3\}$.

Table 3. Asymptotic complexity of compared minimum mean cycle algorithms.

	Madani [36]	Burns [12]	Lawler [35]	Dasdan-Gupta [25]	Hartmann-Orlin [32]	Karp [34]
Time	$O(n^2)$	$O(n^3)$	$O(n^2 \cdot \log(n \cdot W))$	$O(n^2)$	$O(n^2)$	$O(n^2)$

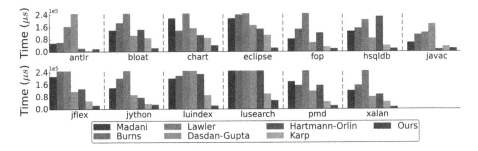

Fig. 4. Average performance of minimum mean cycle algorithms.

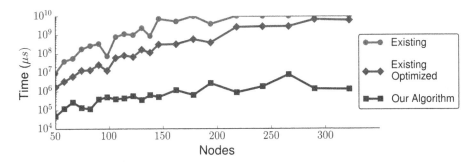

Fig. 5. Comparison of running times for the minimum initial credit value problem.

Figure 4 shows the average time performance of the examined algorithms (bars that exceeded the maximum value in the y-axis have been truncated). Our algorithm has much smaller running time than each other algorithm, in almost all cases.

Minimum Initial Credit. We have implemented our algorithm for the minimum initial credit problem on general graphs and evaluated its performance on a subset of benchmark weighted graphs from the DIMACS implementation challenges [1]. Our algorithm was tested against the existing method of [10], and an optimized version of that method. For each input graph we subtracted its minimum mean value μ^* from the weight of each edge to ensure that at least one non-positive cycle exists (thus the energies are finite). Figure 5 depicts the running time of the algorithm of [10] (with and without optimizations) vs our algorithm. A timeout was forced at $10^{10}\mu s$. Our algorithm is orders of magnitude faster, and scales better than the existing method.

References

1. DIMACS implementation challenges. http://dimacs.rutgers.edu/Challenges/
2. Almagor, S., Boker, U., Kupferman, O.: Formalizing and reasoning about quality. In: Fomin, F.V., Freivalds, R., Kwiatkowska, M., Peleg, D. (eds.) ICALP 2013, Part II. LNCS, vol. 7966, pp. 15–27. Springer, Heidelberg (2013)

3. Blackburn, S.M., Garner, R., Hoffmann, C., Khang, A.M., McKinley, K.S., Bentzur, R., Diwan, A., Feinberg, D., Frampton, D., Guyer, S.Z., Hirzel, M., Hosking, A., Jump, M., Lee, H., Moss, J.E.B., Phansalkar, A., Stefanović, D., VanDrunen, T., von Dincklage, D., Wiedermann, B.: The DaCapo benchmarks: Java benchmarking development and analysis. In: OOPSLA. ACM (2006)
4. Bloem, R., Chatterjee, K., Henzinger, T.A., Jobstmann, B.: Better quality in synthesis through quantitative objectives. In: Bouajjani, A., Maler, O. (eds.) CAV 2009. LNCS, vol. 5643, pp. 140–156. Springer, Heidelberg (2009)
5. Bloem, R., Greimel, K., Henzinger, T.A., Jobstmann, B.: Synthesizing robust systems. In: FMCAD (2009)
6. Bodlaender, H.L.: A tourist guide through treewidth. Acta Cybern. **11**, 1–22 (1993)
7. Bodlaender, H.L.: Discovering treewidth. In: Vojtáš, P., Bieliková, M., Charron-Bost, B., Sýkora, O. (eds.) SOFSEM 2005. LNCS, vol. 3381, pp. 1–16. Springer, Heidelberg (2005)
8. Bodlaender, H., Hagerup, T.: Parallel algorithms with optimal speedup for bounded treewidth. In: Fülöp, Z. (ed.) ICALP 1995. LNCS, vol. 944. Springer, Heidelberg (1995)
9. Boker, U., Chatterjee, K., Henzinger, T.A., Kupferman, O.: Temporal specifications with accumulative values. In: LICS (2011)
10. Bouyer, P., Fahrenberg, U., Larsen, K.G., Markey, N., Srba, J.: Infinite runs in weighted timed automata with energy constraints. In: Cassez, F., Jard, C. (eds.) FORMATS 2008. LNCS, vol. 5215, pp. 33–47. Springer, Heidelberg (2008)
11. Bouyer, P., Markey, N., Matteplackel, R.M.: Averaging in LTL. In: Baldan, P., Gorla, D. (eds.) CONCUR 2014. LNCS, vol. 8704, pp. 266–280. Springer, Heidelberg (2014)
12. Burns, S.M.: Performance analysis and optimization of asynchronous circuits. Technical report (1991)
13. Cerny, P., Henzinger, T.A., Radhakrishna, A.: Quantitative abstraction refinement. In: POPL. ACM (2013)
14. Chatterjee, K., Łącki, J.: Faster algorithms for markov decision processes with low treewidth. In: Sharygina, N., Veith, H. (eds.) CAV 2013. LNCS, vol. 8044, pp. 543–558. Springer, Heidelberg (2013)
15. Chatterjee, K., Doyen, L., Edelsbrunner, H., Henzinger, T.A., Rannou, P.: Mean-payoff automaton expressions. In: Gastin, P., Laroussinie, F. (eds.) CONCUR 2010. LNCS, vol. 6269, pp. 269–283. Springer, Heidelberg (2010)
16. Chatterjee, K., Doyen, L., Henzinger, T.A.: Expressiveness and closure properties for quantitative languages. LMCS (2010)
17. Chatterjee, K., Doyen, L., Henzinger, T.A.: Quantitative languages. Trans. Comput. Log. **11**, 1–38 (2010)
18. Chatterjee, K., Goyal, P., Ibsen-Jensen, R., Pavlogiannis, A.: Faster algorithms for algebraic path properties in recursive state machines with constant treewidth. In: POPL (2015)
19. Chatterjee, K., Henzinger, M., Krinninger, S., Loitzenbauer, V., Raskin, M.A.: Approximating the minimum cycle mean. Theor. Comput. Sci **547**, 104–116 (2014)
20. Chatterjee, K., Henzinger, T.A., Jobstmann, B., Singh, R.: Measuring and synthesizing systems in probabilistic environments. JACM **62**, 1–34 (2014)
21. Chatterjee, K., Henzinger, T.A., Otop, J.: Nested weighted automata. Technical report, IST Austria (2014)
22. Chatterjee, K., Ibsen-Jensen, R., Pavlogiannis, A.: Faster algorithms for quantitative verification in constant treewidth graphs. Technical report. http://arxiv.org/abs/1504.07384

23. Chatterjee, K., Velner, Y.: Mean-payoff pushdown games. In: LICS. IEEE Computer Society (2012)
24. Courcelle, B.: The monadic second-order logic of graphs. I. Recognizable sets of finite graphs. Inf. Comput. **85**, 12–75 (1990)
25. Dasdan, A., Gupta, R.: Faster maximum and minimum mean cycle algorithms for system-performance analysis. IEEE Trans. Comput.-Aided Des. Integr. Circ. Syst. **17**, 889–899 (1998)
26. Dasdan, A., Irani, S.S., Gupta, R.K.: An experimental study of minimum mean cycle algorithms. Technical report (1998)
27. Droste, M., Kuich, W., Vogler, H.: Handbook of Weighted Automata. Springer, Heidelberg (2009)
28. Droste, M., Meinecke, I.: Weighted automata and weighted MSO logics for average and long-time behaviors. Inf. Comput. **220**, 45–59 (2012)
29. Elberfeld, M., Jakoby, A., Tantau, T.: Logspace versions of the theorems of Bodlaender and Courcelle. In: FOCS. IEEE Computer Society (2010)
30. Gustedt, J., Mæhle, O.A., Telle, J.A.: The treewidth of java programs. In: Mount, D.M., Stein, C. (eds.) ALENEX 2002. LNCS, vol. 2409, pp. 86–97. Springer, Heidelberg (2002)
31. Halin, R.: S-functions for graphs. J. Geom. **8**, 171–186 (1976)
32. Hartmann, M., Orlin, J.B.: Finding minimum cost to time ratio cycles with small integral transit times. Networks **23**, 567–574 (1993)
33. Henzinger, T.A., Otop, J.: From model checking to model measuring. In: D'Argenio, P.R., Melgratti, H. (eds.) CONCUR 2013 – Concurrency Theory. LNCS, vol. 8052, pp. 273–287. Springer, Heidelberg (2013)
34. Karp, R.M.: A characterization of the minimum cycle mean in a digraph. Discrete Math. **23**, 309–311 (1978)
35. Lawler, E.: Combinatorial Optimization: Networks and Matroids. Saunders College Publishing, Fort Worth (1976)
36. Madani, O.: Polynomial value iteration algorithms for deterministic MDPs. In: UAI. Morgan Kaufmann Publishers (2002)
37. Obdržálek, J.: Fast Mu-calculus model checking when tree-width is bounded. In: Hunt Jr, W.A., Somenzi, F. (eds.) CAV 2003. LNCS, vol. 2725, pp. 80–92. Springer, Heidelberg (2003)
38. Orlin, J.B., Ahuja, R.K.: New scaling algorithms for the assignment and minimum mean cycle problems. Math. Program. **54**, 41–56 (1992)
39. Papadimitriou, C.H.: Efficient search for rationals. IPL **8**, 1–4 (1979)
40. Robertson, N., Seymour, P.: Graph minors. III. Planar tree-width. J. Comb. Theor. Ser. B **39**, 49–64 (1984)
41. Tarjan, R.: Depth-first search and linear graph algorithms. SIAM J. Comput. **1**, 146–160 (1972)
42. Thorup, M.: All structured programs have small tree width and good register allocation. Inf. Comput. **142**, 159–181 (1998)
43. Vallée-Rai, R. Co, P., Gagnon, E., Hendren, L., Lam, P., Sundaresan, V.: Soot - a java bytecode optimization framework. In: CASCON 1999. IBM Press (1999)
44. Velner, Y.: The complexity of mean-payoff automaton expression. In: Czumaj, A., Mehlhorn, K., Pitts, A., Wattenhofer, R. (eds.) ICALP 2012, Part II. LNCS, vol. 7392, pp. 390–402. Springer, Heidelberg (2012)

Counterexample Explanation by Learning Small Strategies in Markov Decision Processes

Tomáš Brázdil[1], Krishnendu Chatterjee[2], Martin Chmelík[2],
Andreas Fellner[2], and Jan Křetínský[2(✉)]

[1] Masaryk University, Brno, Czech Republic
[2] IST, Klosterneuburg, Austria
jan.kretinsky@ist.ac.at

Abstract. For deterministic systems, a counterexample to a property can simply be an error trace, whereas counterexamples in probabilistic systems are necessarily more complex. For instance, a set of erroneous traces with a sufficient cumulative probability mass can be used. Since these are too large objects to understand and manipulate, compact representations such as subchains have been considered. In the case of probabilistic systems with non-determinism, the situation is even more complex. While a subchain for a given strategy (or scheduler, resolving non-determinism) is a straightforward choice, we take a different approach. Instead, we focus on the strategy itself, and extract the most important decisions it makes, and present its succinct representation.

The key tools we employ to achieve this are (1) introducing a concept of importance of a state w.r.t. the strategy, and (2) learning using decision trees. There are three main consequent advantages of our approach. Firstly, it exploits the quantitative information on states, stressing the more important decisions. Secondly, it leads to a greater variability and degree of freedom in representing the strategies. Thirdly, the representation uses a self-explanatory data structure. In summary, our approach produces more succinct and more explainable strategies, as opposed to e.g. binary decision diagrams. Finally, our experimental results show that we can extract several rules describing the strategy even for very large systems that do not fit in memory, and based on the rules explain the erroneous behaviour.

1 Introduction

The standard models for dynamic stochastic systems with both probabilistic and nondeterministic behaviour are *Markov decision processes* (MDPs) [1–3]. They are widely used in verification of probabilistic systems [4,5] in several ways. Firstly, in concurrent probabilistic systems, such as communication protocols, the nondeterminism arises from scheduling [6,7]. Secondly, in probabilistic systems operating in open environments, such as various stochastic reactive systems, nondeterminism arises from environmental inputs [8,9]. Thirdly, for underspecified probabilistic systems, a controller is synthesized, resolving the nondeterminism in a way that optimizes some objective, such as energy consumption or time constraints in embedded systems [4,5].

© Springer International Publishing Switzerland 2015
D. Kroening and C.S. Păsăreanu (Eds.): CAV 2015, Part I, LNCS 9206, pp. 158–177, 2015.
DOI: 10.1007/978-3-319-21690-4_10

In analysis of MDPs, the behaviour under all possible strategies (schedulers, controllers, policies) is examined. For example, in the first two cases, the result of the verification process is either a guarantee that a given property holds under all strategies, or a counterexample strategy. In the third case, either a witness strategy guaranteeing a given property is synthesized, or its non-existence is stated. In all settings, it is desirable that the output *strategies should be "small and understandable"* apart from correct. Intuitively, it is a strategy with a representation small enough for the human debugger to read and understand where the bug is (in the verification setting), or for the programmer to implement in the device (in the synthesis setting). In this paper, we focus on the verification setting and illustrate our approach mainly on probabilistic protocols. Nonetheless, our results immediately carry over to the synthesis setting.

Obtaining a small and simple strategy may be impossible if the strategy is required to be optimal, i.e., in our setting reaching the error state with the highest possible probability. Therefore, there is a trade-off between simplicity and optimality of the strategies. However, in order to debug a system, a simple counterexample or a series thereof is more valuable than the most comprehensive, but incomprehensible counterexample. In practice, a simple strategy reaching the error with probability smaller by a factor of ε, e.g. one per cent, is a more valuable source of information than a huge description of an optimal strategy. Similarly, controllers in embedded devices should strive for optimality, but only as long as they are small enough to fit in the device. In summary, we are interested in finding small and simple close-to-optimal (ε-optimal) strategies.

How can one obtain a small and simple strategy? This seems to require some understanding of the particular system and the bug. How can we do something like that automatically? The approaches have so far been limited to BDD representations of the strategy, or generating subchains representing a subset of paths induced by the strategy. While BDDs provide a succinct representation, they are not well readable and understandable. Further, subchains do not focus on the decisions the strategy makes at all. In contrast, a huge effort has been spent on methods to obtain "understanding" from large sets of data, using *machine learning* methods. In this paper, we propose to extend their use in verification, namely of reachability properties in MDPs, in several ways. Our first aim of using these methods is to efficiently exploit the structure that is present in the models, written in e.g. PRISM language with variables and commands. This structure gets lost in the traditional numerical analysis of the MDPs generated from the PRISM language description. The second aim is to distil more information from the generated MDPs, namely the importance of each decision. Both lead to an improved understanding of the strategy's decisions.

Our Approach. We propose three steps to obtain the desired strategies. Each of them has a positive effect on the resulting size.

(1) Obtaining a (Possibly Partially Defined and Liberal) ε-optimal Strategy. The ε-optimal strategies produced by standard methods, such as value iteration of PRISM [10], may be too large to compute and overly specific. Firstly, as argued in [11], typically only a small fraction of the system needs to be explored in order to find an ε-optimal strategy, whereas most states are reached with only a very

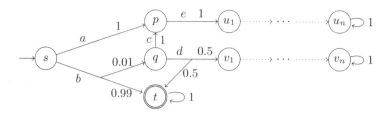

Fig. 1. An MDP M with reachability objective t

small probability. Without much loss, the strategy may not be defined there. For example, in the MDP M depicted in Fig. 1, the decision in q (and v_i's) is almost irrelevant for the overall probability of reaching t from s. Such a partially defined strategy can be obtained using learning methods [11].

Secondly, while the usual strategies prescribe which action to play, *liberal* strategies leave more choices open. There are several advantages of liberal strategies, and similar notions of strategies called permissive strategies have been studied in [12–14]. A liberal strategy, instead of choosing an action in each state, chooses a set of actions to be played uniformly at every state. First, each liberal strategy represents a set of strategies, and thus covers more behaviour. Second, in counter-example guided abstraction-refinement (CEGAR) analysis, since liberal strategies can represent sets of counter-examples, they accelerate the abstraction-refinement loop by ruling out several counter-examples at once. Finally, they also allow for more robust learning of smaller strategies in Step 3. We show that such strategies can be obtained from standard value iteration as well as [11]. Further processing of the strategies in Step 2 and 3 allows liberal strategies as input and preserves liberality in the small representation of the strategy.

(2) Identifying Important Parts of the Strategy. We define a concept of *importance* of a state w.r.t. a strategy, corresponding to the probability of visiting the state by the strategy. Observe that only a fraction of states can be reached while following the strategy, and thus have positive importance. On the unreachable states, with zero importance, the definition of the strategy is useless. For instance, in M, both states p and q must have been explored when constructing the strategy in order to find out whether it is better to take action a or b. However, if the resulting strategy is to use b and d, the information what to do in u_i's is useless. In addition, we consider v_i's to be of zero importance, too, since they are never reached on the way to target.

Furthermore, apart from ignoring states with zero importance, we want to partially ignore decisions that are unlikely to be made (in less important states such as q), and in contrast, stress more the decisions in important states likely to be visited (such as s). Note that this is difficult to achieve in data structures that remember all the stored data exactly, such as BDDs. Of course, we can store decisions in states with importance above a certain threshold. However, we obtain much smaller representations if we allow more variability and reflect the whole quantitative information, as shown in Step 3.

(3) Data Structures for Compact Representation of Strategies. The explicit representation of a strategy by a table of pairs (state, action to play) results in a huge amount of data since the systems often have millions of states. Therefore, a symbolic representation by binary decision diagrams (BDD) looks as a reasonable option. However, there are several drawbacks of using BDDs. Firstly, due to the bit-level representation of the state-action pairs, the resulting BDD is not very readable. Secondly, it is often still too large to be understood by human, for instance due to a bad ordering of the variables. Thirdly, it cannot quantitatively reflect the differences in the importance of states.

Therefore, we propose to use *decision trees* instead, e.g. [15], a structure similar to BDDs, but with nodes labelled by various predicates over the system's variables. They have several advantages. Firstly, they yield an explanation of the decision, as opposed to e.g. neural networks, and thus provide an explanation how the strategy works. Secondly, sophisticated algorithms for their construction, based on entropy, result in smaller representation than BDD, where a good ordering of variables is known to be notoriously difficult to find [4]. Thirdly, as suggested in Step 2, they allow for less probable remembering of less stressed data if this sufficiently simplifies the tree and decreases its size. Finally, the major drawback of decision trees in machine learning—frequent overfitting of the training data—is not an issue in our setting since the tree is not used for classification of test data, but only of the training data.

Summary of Our Contribution. In summary our contributions are as follows:

- We provide a method for obtaining succinct representation of ε-optimal strategies as decision trees. The method is based on a new concept of importance measure and on well-established machine learning techniques.
- Experimental data show that even for some systems larger than the available memory, our method yields trees with only several dozens of nodes.
- We illustrate the understandability of the representation on several examples from PRISM benchmarks [16], reading off respective bug explanations.

Related Work. In artificial intelligence, compact (factored) representations of MDP structure have been developed using dynamic Bayesian networks [17,18], probabilistic STRIPS [19], algebraic decision diagrams [20], and also decision trees [17]. Formalisms used to represent MDPs can, in principle, be used to represent values and policies as well. In particular, variants of decision trees are probably the most used [17,21,22]. For a detailed survey of compact representations see [23]. In the context of verification, MDPs are often represented using variants of (MT)BDDs [24–26], and strategies by BDDs [27].

Decision trees have been used in connection with real-time dynamic programming and reinforcement learning [28,29]. Learning a compact decision tree representation of a policy has been investigated in [30] for the case of body sensor networks, but the paper aims at a completely different application field (a simple model of sensor networks as opposed to generic PRISM models), uses different objectives (discounted rewards), and does not consider the importance of a state that, as we show, may substantially decrease sizes of resulting policies.

Our results are related to the problem of computing minimal/small counterexamples in probabilistic verification. Most papers concentrate on solving this problem for Markov chains and linear-time properties [31–34], branching-time properties [35–37], and in the context of simulation [38]. A couple of tools have been developed for probabilistic counterexample generation, namely DiPro [39] and COMICS [40]. For a detailed survey see [41]. While previous approaches focus on presenting diagnostic paths forming the counterexample, our approach focuses on decisions made by the respective strategy.

Concerning MDPs, [33] uses mixed integer linear programming to compute minimal critical sub-systems, i.e. whole sub-MDPs as opposed to a compact representation of "right" decisions computed by our methods. [42] uses a directed on-the-fly search to compute sets of most probable diagnostic paths (which somehow resembles our notion of importance), but the paths are encoded explicitly by AND/OR trees as opposed to our use of decision trees. Neither of these papers takes advantage of an internal structure of states and their methods substantially differ from ours. The notion of paths encoded as AND/OR trees has also been studied in [43] to represent probabilistic counter-examples visually as fault trees, and then derive causal (the cause and effect) relationship between events. [44] develops abstraction-based framework for model-checking MDPs based on games, which allows to trade compactness for precision, but does not give a procedure for constructing (a compact representation of) counterexample strategies. [45, 46] computes a smallest set of guarded commands (of a PRISM-like language) that induce a critical subsystem, but, unlike our methods, does not provide a compact representation of actual decisions needed to reach an erroneous state; moreover, there is not always a command based counterexample.

Counter-examples play a crucial role in CEGAR analysis of MDPs, and have been widely studied, such as, game-based abstraction refinement [47]; noncompositional CEGAR approach for reachability [48] and safe-pCTL [49]; compositional CEGAR approach for safe-pCTL and qualitative logics [38,50]; and abstraction-refinement for quantitative properties [51,52]. All of these works only consider a single strategy represented explicitly, whereas our approach considers a succinct representation of a set of strategies, and can accelerate the abstraction-refinement loop.

2   Preliminaries

We use $\mathbb{N}$, $\mathbb{Q}$, and $\mathbb{R}$ to denote the sets of positive integers, rational and real numbers, respectively. The set of all rational probability distributions over a finite set X is denoted by $Dist(X)$. Further, $d \in Dist(X)$ is Dirac if $d(x) = 1$ for some $x \in X$. Given a function $f : X \to \mathbb{R}$, we write $\arg\max_{x \in X} f(x) = \{x \in X \mid f(x) = \max_{x' \in X} f(x')\}$.

Markov Chains. A *Markov chain* is a tuple $M = (L, P, \mu)$ where L is a finite set of locations, $P : L \to Dist(L)$ is a probabilistic transition function, and $\mu \in Dist(L)$ is the initial probability distribution. We denote the respective unique probability measure for M by $\mathbb{P}$.

Markov Decision Processes. A *Markov decision process* (MDP) is a tuple $G = (S, A, Act, \delta, \hat{s})$ where S is a finite set of states, A is a finite set of actions, $Act : S \rightarrow 2^A \setminus \{\emptyset\}$ assigns to each state s the set $Act(s)$ of actions enabled in s, $\delta : S \times A \rightarrow Dist(S)$ is a probabilistic transition function that, given a state and an action, gives a probability distribution over the successor states, and $\hat{s}$ is the initial state. A *run* in G is an infinite alternating sequence of states and actions $\omega = s_1 a_1 s_2 a_2 \cdots$ such that for all $i \geq 1$, we have $a_i \in Act(s_i)$ and $\delta(s_i, a_i)(s_{i+1}) > 0$. A *path* of length k in G is a finite prefix $w = s_1 a_1 \cdots a_{k-1} s_k$ of a run in G.

Strategies and Plays. Intuitively, a strategy (or a policy) in an MDP G is a "recipe" to choose actions. Formally, a strategy is a function $\sigma : S \rightarrow Dist(A)$ that given the current state of a play gives a probability distribution over the enabled actions.[1] In general, a strategy may randomize, i.e. return non-Dirac distributions. A strategy is *deterministic* if it gives a Dirac distribution for every argument.

A *play* of G determined by a strategy σ and a state $\bar{s} \in S$ is a Markov chain $G_{\bar{s}}^{\sigma}$ where the set of locations is S, the initial distribution μ is Dirac with $\mu(\bar{s}) = 1$ and

$$P(s)(s') = \sum_{a \in A} \sigma(s)(a) \cdot \delta(s, a)(s').$$

The induced probability measure is denoted by $\mathbb{P}_{\bar{s}}^{\sigma}$ and "almost surely" or "almost all runs" refers to happening with probability 1 according to this measure. We usually write $\mathbb{P}^{\sigma}$ instead of $\mathbb{P}_{\hat{s}}^{\sigma}$ (here $\hat{s}$ is the initial state of G).

Liberal Strategies. A *liberal strategy* is a function $\varsigma : S \rightarrow 2^A$ such that for every $s \in S$ we have that $\emptyset \neq \varsigma(s) \subseteq Act(s)$. Given a liberal strategy ς and a state s, an action $a \in Act(s)$ is *good* (in s w.r.t. ς) if $a \in \varsigma(s)$, and *bad* otherwise. Abusing notation, we denote by ς the strategy that to every state s assigns the uniform distribution on $\varsigma(s)$ (which, in particular, allows us to use G_s^{ς}, $\mathbb{P}_s^{\varsigma}$ and apply the notion of ε-optimality to ς).

Reachability Objectives. Given a set $F \subseteq S$ of *target states*, we denote by $\Diamond F$ the set of all runs that visit a state of F. For a state $s \in S$, the *maximal reachability probability* (or simply *value*) in s, is $Val(s) := \max_{\sigma} \mathbb{P}_s^{\sigma}[\Diamond F]$. Given $\epsilon \geq 0$, we say that a strategy σ is ε-*optimal* if $\mathbb{P}^{\sigma}[\Diamond F] \geq Val(\hat{s}) - \varepsilon$, and we call a 0-optimal strategy *optimal*.[2] To avoid overly technical notation, we assume that states of F, subject to the reachability objective, are absorbing, i.e. for all $s \in F, a \in Act(s)$ we have $\delta(s, a)(s) = 1$.

End Components. A non-empty set $S' \subseteq S$ is an *end component* (EC) of G if there is $Act' : S' \rightarrow 2^A \setminus \{\emptyset\}$ such that (1) for all $s \in S'$ we have $Act'(s) \subseteq Act(s)$,

---

[1] In general, a strategy may be history dependent. However, for objectives considered in this paper, *memoryless* strategies (depending on the last state visited) are sufficient. Therefore, we only consider memoryless strategies in this paper.

[2] For every MDP, there is a memoryless deterministic optimal strategy, see e.g. [2].

(2) for all $s \in S'$, we have $a \in Act'(s)$ iff $\delta(s,a) \in Dist(S')$, and (3) for all $s,t \in S'$ there is a path $\omega = s_1 a_1 \cdots a_{k-1} s_k$ such that $s_1 = s$, $s_k = t$, and $s_i \in S', a_i \in Act'(s_i)$ for every i. An end component is a *maximal end component* (MEC) if it is maximal with respect to the subset ordering. Given an MDP, the set of MECs is denoted by MEC. Given a MEC, actions of $Act'(s)$ and $Act(s) \setminus Act'(s)$ are called *internal* and *external* (in state s), respectively.

3   Computing ε-Optimal Strategies

There are many algorithms for solving quantitative reachability in MDPs, such as the value iteration, the strategy improvement, linear programming based methods etc., see [2]. The main method implemented in PRISM is the value iteration, which successively (under)approximates the value $Val(s,a) = \sum_{s' \in A} \delta(s,a)(s') \cdot Val(s')$ of every state-action pair (s,a) by a value $V(s,a)$, and stops when the approximation is good enough. Denoting by $V(s) := \max_{a \in Act(s)} V(s,a)$, every step of the value iteration *improves* the approximation $V(s,a)$ by assigning $V(s,a) := \sum_{s' \in S} \delta(s,a)(s') \cdot V(s')$ (we start with V such that $V(s) = 1$ if $s \in F$, and $V(s) = 0$ otherwise).

The disadvantage of the standard value iteration (and also most of the above mentioned traditional methods) is that it works with the whole state space of the MDP (or at least with its reachable part). For instance, consider states u_i, v_i of Fig. 1. The paper [11] adapts methods of bounded real-time dynamic programming (BRTDP, see e.g. [53]) to speed up the computation of the value iteration by improving $V(s,a)^3$ only on "important" state-action pairs identified by simulations.

Even though RTDP methods may substantially reduce the size of an ε-optimal strategy, its explicit representation is usually large and difficult to understand. Thus we develop succinct representations of strategies, based on decision trees, that will reduce the size even further and also provide a human readable representation. Even though the above methods are capable of yielding *deterministic* ε-optimal strategies, that can be immediately fed into machine learning algorithms, we found it advantageous to give the learning algorithm more freedom in the sense that if there are more ε-optimal strategies, we let the algorithm choose (uniformly). This is especially useful within MECs where many actions have the same value. Therefore, we extract *liberal* ε-optimal strategies from the value approximation V, output either by the value iteration or BRTDP.

Computing Liberal ε-Optimal Strategies. Let us show how to obtain a liberal strategy ς from the value iteration, or BRTDP. For simplicity, we start with MDP without MECs.

MDP without End Components. We say that $V : S \times A \rightarrow [0,1]$ is a *valid ε-underapproximation* if the following conditions hold:

1. $V(s,a) \leq Val(s,a)$ for all $s \in S$ and $a \in A$
2. $Val(\hat{s}) - V(\hat{s}) \leq \varepsilon$
3. $V(s,a) \leq \sum_{s' \in S} \delta(s,a)(s') \cdot V(s')$ for all $s \in S$ and $a \in Acts$

---

[3] Here we use V for the lower approximation denoted by V_L in [11].

The outputs V of both the value iteration, and BRTDP are valid ε-underapproximations. We define a liberal strategy ς^V by $\varsigma^V(s) = \arg\max_{a \in Act(s)} V(s,a)$ for all $s \in S$.[4]

Lemma 1. *For every $\varepsilon > 0$ and a valid ε-underapproximation V, ς^V is ε-optimal.*[5]

General MDP. For MDPs with end components we have to extend the definition of the valid ε-underapproximation. Given a MEC $S' \subseteq S$, we say that $(s,a) \in S \times A$ is *maximal-external in* S' if $s \in S'$, $a \in Act(s)$ is external and $V(s,a) \geq V(s',a')$ for all $s' \in S'$ and $a' \in Act(s')$. A state $s' \in S'$ is an *exit* (of S') if (s,a) is maximal-external in S' for some $a \in Act(s)$. We add the following condition to the valid ε-underapproximation:

4. Each MEC $S' \subseteq S$ has at least one exit.

Now the definition of ς^V is also more complicated:

– For every $s \in S$ which is *not* in any MEC, we put $\varsigma^V(s) = \arg\max_{a \in Act(s)} V(s,a)$.
– For every $s \in S$ which *is* in a MEC S',
  • if s is an exit, then $\varsigma^V(s) = \{a \in Act(s) \mid (s,a) \text{ is maximal-external in } S'\}$
  • otherwise, $\varsigma^V(s) = \{a \in Act(s) \mid a \text{ is internal}\}$

Using these extended definitions, Lemma 1 remains valid. Further, note that $\varsigma^V(s)$ is defined even for states with trivial underapproximation $V(s) = 0$, for instance a state s that was never subject to any value iteration improvement. Then the values $\varsigma(s)$ may not be stored explicitly, but follow implicitly from *not* storing any $V(s)$, thus assuming $V(s,\cdot) = 0$.

4   Importance of Decisions

Note that once we have computed an ε-optimal liberal strategy ς, we may, in principle, compute a compact representation of ς (using e.g. BDDs), and obtain a strategy with possibly smaller representation than above.

   However, we go one step further as follows. Given a liberal strategy ς and a state $s \in S$, we define the *importance* of s by

$$Imp^\varsigma(s) := \mathbb{P}^\varsigma[\Diamond s \mid \Diamond F]$$

the probability of visiting s conditioned on reaching F (afterwards). Intuitively, the importance is high for states where a good decision can help to reach the target.[6]

---

[4] Furthermore, one could consider liberal strategies playing also ε-optimal actions. However, our experiments did not prove better performance.

[5] Intuitively this means that randomizing among good actions of ε-optimal strategies preserves ε-optimality in the reachability setting (in contrast to other settings, e.g. with parity objectives).

[6] Instead of the conditional probability of reaching s, we could consider the conditional expected number of visits of s. We discuss the differences and compare the efficiency together with the case of no conditioning on reaching the target in Sect. 6.

Example 1. For the MDP of Fig. 1 with the objective $\Diamond\{t\}$ and a strategy ς choosing b, we have $Imp^\varsigma(s) = 1$ and $Imp^\varsigma(q) = 5/995$. Trivially, $Imp^\varsigma(t) = 1$. For all other states, the importance is zero.

Obviously, decisions made in states of zero importance do not affect $\mathbb{P}^\varsigma[\Diamond F]$ since these states never occur on paths from $\hat{s}$ to F. However, note that many states of S may be reachable in G^ς with positive but negligibly small probability. Clearly, the value of $\mathbb{P}^\varsigma[\Diamond F]$ depends only marginally on choices made in these states. Formally, let ς_Δ be a strategy obtained from ς by changing each $\varsigma(s)$ with $Imp^\varsigma(s) \le \Delta$ to an arbitrary subset of $Act(s)$. We obtain the following obvious property:

Lemma 2. *For every liberal strategy ς, we have* $\lim\limits_{\Delta\to 0} \mathbb{P}^{\varsigma_\Delta}[\Diamond F] = \mathbb{P}^\varsigma[\Diamond F]$.

In fact, every $\Delta < \min(\{Imp^\varsigma(s) \mid s \in S\} \setminus \{0\})$ satisfies $\mathbb{P}^{\varsigma_\Delta}[\Diamond F] = \mathbb{P}^\varsigma[\Diamond F]$. But often even larger Δ may give $\mathbb{P}^{\varsigma_\Delta}[\Diamond F]$ sufficiently close to $\mathbb{P}^\varsigma[\Diamond F]$. Such Δ may be found using e.g. trial and error approach.[7]

Most importantly, we can use the importance of a state to affect the probability that decisions in this state are indeed remembered in the data structure. Data structures with such a feature are used in various learning algorithms. In the next section, we discuss decision trees. Due to this extra variability, which decisions to learn, the resulting decision trees are smaller than BDDs for strictly defined ς_Δ.

5   Efficient Representations

Let $G = (S, A, Act, \delta, \hat{s})$ be an MDP. In order to symbolically represent strategies in G, we need to assume that states and actions have some internal structure. Inspired by PRISM language [5], we consider a set $\mathcal{V} = \{v_1, \dots, v_n\}$ of *integer variables*, each v_i gets its values from a finite domain $Dom(v_i)$. We suppose that $S = \prod_{i=1}^n Dom(v_i) \subseteq \mathbb{Z}^n$, i.e. each state is a vector of integers. Further, we assume that the MDP arises as a product of m modules, each of which can separately perform non-synchronizing actions as well as synchronously with other modules perform a synchronizing action. Therefore, we suppose $A \subseteq \bar{A} \times \{0, \dots, m\}$, where $\bar{A} \subseteq \mathbb{N}$ is a finite set and the second component determines the module performing the action (0 stands for synchronizing actions).[8]

Since a liberal strategy is a function of the form $\varsigma : S \to 2^A$, assigning to each state its good actions, it can be *explicitly* represented as a list of state-action pairs, i.e., as a subset of

$$S \times A = \prod_{i=1}^n Dom(v_i) \times \bar{A} \times \{0, 1, \dots, m\} \qquad (1)$$

---

[7] One may give a theoretical bound on convergence of $\mathbb{P}^{\varsigma_\Delta}[\Diamond F]$ to $\mathbb{P}^\varsigma[\Diamond F]$ as $\Delta \to 0$, using e.g. Lemma 5.1 of [54]. However, for large MDPs the bound would be impractical.

[8] On the one hand, PRISM does not allow different modules to have local variables with the same name, hence we do not distinguish which module does a variable belong to. On the other hand, while PRISM declares no names for non-synchronizing actions, we want to exploit the connection between the corresponding actions of different copies of the same module.

In addition, standard optimization algorithms implemented in PRISM use an explicit "don't-care" value -2 for action in each unreachable state, meaning the strategy is not defined. However, one could simply not list these pairs at all. Thus a smaller list is obtained, with only the states where ς is defined. Recall that one may also omit states s satisfying $Imp^\varsigma(s) = 0$, thus ignoring reachable states with zero probability to reach the target. Further optimization may be achieved by omitting states s satisfying $Imp^\varsigma(s) < \Delta$ for a suitable $\Delta > 0$.

5.1 BDD Representation

The explicit set representation can be encoded as a binary decision diagram (BDD). This has been used in e.g. [27,55]. The principle of the BDD representation of a set is that (1) each element is encoded as a string of bits and (2) an automaton, in the form of a binary directed acyclic graph, is created so that (3) the accepted language is exactly the set of the given bit strings. Although BDDs are quite efficient, see Sect. 6, each of these three steps can be significantly improved:

1. Instead of a string of bits describing all variables, a string of integers (one per variable) can be used. Branching is then done not on the value of each bit, but according to an inequality comparing the variable to a constant. This significantly improves the readability.
2. Instead of building the automaton according to a chosen order of bits, we let a heuristic choose the order of the inequalities and the actual constants in the inequalities.
3. Instead of representing the language precisely, we allow the heuristic to choose which data to represent and which not. The likelihood that each datum is represented corresponds to its importance, which we provide as another input.

The latter two steps lead to significantly smaller graphs than BDDs. All this can be done in an efficient way using decision trees learning.

5.2 Representation Using Decision Trees

Decision Trees. A *decision tree* for a domain $\prod_{i=1}^{d} X_i \subseteq \mathbb{Z}^d$ is a tuple $\mathcal{T} = (T, \rho, \theta)$ where T is a finite rooted binary (ordered) tree with a set of inner nodes N and a set of leaves L, ρ assigns to every inner node a predicate of the form $[x_i \sim const]$ where $i \in \{1, \ldots, d\}$, $x_i \in X_i$, $const \in \mathbb{Z}$, $\sim \in \{\leq, <, \geq, >, =\}$, and θ assigns to every leaf a value *good*, or *bad*.[9]

Similarly to BDDs, the language $\mathcal{L}(\mathcal{T}) \subseteq \mathbb{N}^n$ of the tree is defined as follows. For a vector $\bar{x} = (\bar{x}_1, \ldots, \bar{x}_n) \in \mathbb{N}^n$, we find a path p from the root to a leaf such that for each inner node n on the path, the predicate $\rho(n)$ is satisfied by substitution $x_i = \bar{x}_i$ iff the first child of n is on p. Denote the leaf on this particular path by ℓ. Then $\bar{x}$ is in the language $\mathcal{L}(\mathcal{T})$ of $\mathcal{T}$ iff $\theta(\ell) = good$.

---

[9] There exist many variants of decision trees in the literature allowing arbitrary branching, arbitrary values in the leaves, etc., e.g. [15]. For simplicity, we define only a special suitable subclass.

Example 2. Consider dimension $d = 1$, domain $X_1 = \{1, \ldots, 7\}$. A tree representing a set $\{1, 2, 3, 7\}$ is depicted in Fig. 2. To depict the ordered tree clearly, we use unbroken lines for the first child, corresponding to the satisfied predicate, and dashed line for the second one, corresponding to the unsatisfied predicate.

In our setting, we use the domain $S \times A$ defined by Equation (1) which is of the form $\prod_{i=1}^{n+2} X_i$ where for each $1 \leq i \leq n$ we have $X_i = Dom(v_i)$, $X_{n+1} = \bar{A}$ and $X_{n+2} = \{0, 1, \ldots, m\}$. Here the coordinates $Dom(v_i)$ are considered "unbounded" and, consequently, the respective predicates use inequalities. In contrast, we know the possible values of $\bar{A} \times \{0, 1, \ldots, m\}$ in advance and they are not too many. Therefore, these coordinates are considered "discrete" and the respective predicates use

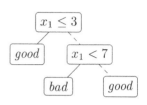

Fig. 2. A decision tree for $\{1, 2, 3, 7\} \subseteq \{1, \ldots, 7\}$

equality. Examples of such trees are given in Sect. 6 in Figs. 4 and 5. Now a decision tree $\mathcal{T}$ for this domain determines a liberal strategy $\varsigma : S \to 2^A$ by $a \in \varsigma(s)$ iff $(s, a) \in \mathcal{L}(\mathcal{T})$.

Learning. We describe the process of *learning a training set*, which can also be understood as storing the input data. Given a training sequence (repetitions allowed!) $x^1, \ldots, x^k$, with each $x^i = (x_1^i, \ldots, x_n^i) \in \mathbb{N}^d$, partitioned into the *positive* and *negative* subsequence, the process of learning according to the algorithm ID3 [15,56] proceeds as follows:

1. Start with a single node (root), and assign to it the whole training sequence.
2. Given a node n with a sequence τ,
   - if all training examples in τ are positive, set $\theta(n) = good$ and stop;
   - if all training examples in τ are negative, set $\theta(n) = bad$ and stop;
   - otherwise,
     - choose a predicate with the "highest gain" (with lowest entropy, see e.g. [15, Sects. 3.4.1, 3.7.2]),
     - split τ into sequences satisfying and not satisfying the predicate, assign them to the first and the second child, respectively,
     - go to step 2 for each child.

Intuitively, the predicate with the highest gain splits the sequence so that it maximizes the portion of positive data in the satisfying subsequence and the portion of negative data in the non-satisfying subsequence.

In addition, the final tree can be *pruned*. This means that some leaves are merged, resulting in a smaller tree at the cost of some imprecision of storing (the language of the tree changes). The pruning phase is quite sophisticated, hence for the sake of simplicity and brevity, we omit the details here. We use the standard C4.5 algorithm and refer to [15,57]. In Sect. 6, we comment on effects of parameters used in pruning.

Learning a Strategy. Assume that we already have a liberal strategy $\varsigma : S \rightarrow 2^A$. We show how we learn good and bad state-action pairs so that the language of the resulting tree is close to the set of good pairs. The training sequence will be composed of state-action pairs where good pairs are positive examples, and bad pairs are negative ones. Since our aim is to ensure that important states are learnt and not pruned away, we repeat pairs with more important states in the training sequence more frequently.

Formally, for every $s \in S$ and $a \in Act(s)$, we put the pair (s, a) to the training sequence $repeat(s)$-times, where

$$repeat(s) = c \cdot Imp^\varsigma(s)$$

for some constant $c \in \mathbb{N}$ (note that $Imp^\varsigma(s) \leq 1$). Since we want to avoid exact computation of $Imp^\varsigma(s)$, we estimate it using simulations. In practice, we thus run c simulation runs that reach the target and set $repeat(s)$ to be the number of runs where s was also reached.

6 Experiments

In this section, we present the experimental evaluation of the presented methods, which we have implemented within the probabilistic model checker PRISM [5]. All the results presented in this section were obtained on a single Intel(R) Xeon(R) CPU (3.50 GHz) with memory limited to 10 GB.

First, we discuss several alternative options to construct the training data and to learn them in a decision tree. Further, we compare decision trees to other data structures, namely sets and BDDs, with respect to the sizes necessary for storing a strategy. Finally, we illustrate how the decision trees can be used to gain insight into our benchmarks.

6.1 Decision Tree Learning

Generating Training Data. The strategies we work with come from two different sources. Firstly, we consider strategies constructed by PRISM, which can be generated using the explicit or sparse model checking engine. Secondly, we consider strategies constructed by the BRTDP algorithm [11], which are defined on a part of the state space only.

Recall that given a strategy, the training data for the decision trees is constructed from c simulation runs according to the strategy. In our experiments, we found that $c = 10000$ produces good results in all the examples we consider. Note that we stop each simulation as soon as the target or a state with no path to the target state is reached.

Decision Tree Learning in Weka. The decision trees are constructed using the Weka machine learning package [58]. The Weka suite offers various decision tree classifiers. We use the J48 classifier, which is an implementation of the C4.5 algorithm [57]. The J48 classifier offers two parameters to control the pruning that affect the size of the decision tree:

- The leaf size parameter $M \in \mathbb{N}$ determines that each leaf node with less than M instances in the training data is merged with its siblings. Therefore, only values smaller than the number of instances per classification class are reasonable, since higher numbers always result in the trivial tree of size 1.
- The confidence factor $C \in (0, 0.5)$ is used internally for determining the amount of pruning during decision tree construction. Smaller values incur more pruning and therefore smaller trees.

Detailed information and an empirical study of the parameters for J48 is available in [59].

Effects of the Parameters. We illustrate the effects of the parameters C and M on the resulting size of the decision tree on the mer benchmark. However, similar behaviour appears in all the examples. Figure 3a and b show the resulting size of the decision tree for several (random) executions. Each line in the plots corresponds to one decision tree, learned with 15 different values of the parameter. The C parameter scales linearly between 0.0001 and 0.5. The M parameter scales logarithmically between 1 and the minimum number of instances per class in the respective training set. The plots in Fig. 3 show that M is an effective parameter in calibrating the resulting tree size, whereas C plays less of a role. Hence, we use $C = 10^{-4}$. Furthermore, since the tree size is monotone in M, the parameter M can be used to retrieve a desired level of detail.

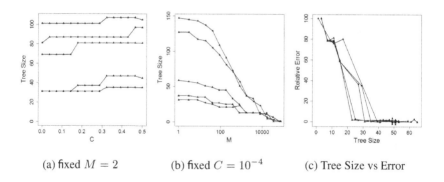

(a) fixed $M = 2$ (b) fixed $C = 10^{-4}$ (c) Tree Size vs Error

Fig. 3. Decision tree parameters

Figure 3c depicts the relation of the tree size to the relative error of the induced strategy. It shows that there is a threshold size under which the tree is not able to capture the strategy correctly anymore and the error rises quickly. Above the threshold size, the error is around 1 %, considered reasonable in order to extract reliable information. This threshold behaviour is observed in all our examples. Therefore, it is sensible to perform a binary search for the highest M ensuring the error at most 1 %.

Table 1. Comparison of representation sizes for strategies obtained from PRISM and from BRTDP computation. Sizes are presented as the number of states for explicit lists of values, the number of nodes for BDDs, and the number of nodes for decision trees (DT). For DT, we display the tree size obtained from the binary search described above. DT Error reports the relative error of the strategy determined by the decision tree (on the induced Markov chain) compared to the optimal value, obtained by model checking with PRISM.

			PRISM				BRTDP			
Example	$|S|$	Value	Explicit	BDD	DT	DT Error	Explicit	BDD	DT	DT Error
Firewire	481,136	1.000	479,834	4,233	1	0.000 %	766	4,763[1]	1	0.000 %
Investor	35,893	0.958	28,151	783	27	0.886 %	21,931	2,780	35	0.836 %
Mer_17M	1,773,664	0.200	Memory out				1,887	619	17	0.000 %
Mer_big[2]	Approx. 10^{13}	0.200	Memory out				1,894	646	19	0.692 %
Zeroconf	89,586	0.009	60,463	409	7	0.106 %	1,630	905	7	0.235 %

[1] Note that BDDs represent states in binary form. Therefore, one entry in the explicit state list corresponds to several nodes in the BDD.

[2] We did not measure the state size as the MDP does not fit in memory, but extrapolated it from the linear dependence of model size and one of its parameters, which we could increase to $2^{31} - 1$. The value is obtained from the BRTDP computation.

6.2 Results

First, we briefly introduce the four examples from the PRISM benchmark suite [16], which we tested our method on. Note that the majority of the states in the used benchmarks are non-deterministic, so the strategies are non-trivial in most states.

firewire models the Tree Identify Protocol of the IEEE 1394 High Performance Serial Bus, which is used to transport video and audio signals within a network of multimedia devices. The reachability objective is that one node gets the root and the other one the child role.

investor models a market investor and shares, which change their value probabilistically over time. The reachability objective is that the investor finishes a trade at a time, when his shares are more valuable than some threshold value.

Table 2. Effects of various learning variants on the tree size. Smallest trees computed from PRISM or BRTDP and the average time to compute one number are presented.

Example	I◊P	I∀P	I◊E	I∀E	O◊	O∀	Avg Time
firewire	1	1	1	1	1	1	45s
investor	27	25	31	35	37	37	135s
mer_17M	17	33	17	29	19	none	314s
mer_big	19	23	23	37	17	none	129s
zeroconf	7	7	7	7	7	17	141s

mer is a mutual exclusion protocol, that regulates the access of two users to two different resources. The protocol should prohibit that both resources are accessed simultaneously.

zeroconf is a network protocol which allows users to choose their IP addresses autonomously. The protocol should detected and prohibit IP address conflict.

For every example, Table 1 shows the size of the state space, the value of the optimal strategy, and the sizes of strategies obtained from explicit model checking by PRISM and by BRTDP, for each discussed data structure.

Learning Variants. In order to justify our choice of the importance function *Imp*, we compare it to several alternatives.

1. When constructing the training data, we can use the importance measure *Imp*, and add states as often as is indicated by its importance (I), or neglect it and simply add every visited state exactly once (O).
2. Further, states on the simulation are learned conditioned on the fact that the target state is reached (◊). Another option is to consider all simulations (∀).
3. Finally, instead of the probability to visit the state (ℙ), one can consider the expected number of visits (𝔼).

In Table 2, we report the sizes of the decision trees obtained for the all learning variants. We conclude that our choice (I◊ℙ) is the most useful one.

6.3   Understanding Decision Trees

We show how the constructed decision trees can help us to gain insight into the essential features of the systems.

zeroconf example. In Fig. 4 we present a decision tree that is a strategy for **zeroconf** and shows how an unresolved IP address conflict can occur in the protocol. First we present how to read the strategy represented in Fig. 4. Next we show how the strategy can explain the conflict in the protocol. Assume that we are classifying a state-action pair (s, a), where action a is enabled in state s.

1. No matter what the current state s is, the action **rec** is always classified as *bad* according to the root of the tree. Therefore, the action **rec** should be played with positive probability only if all other available actions in the current state are also classified as *bad*.
2. If action a is different from **rec**, the right son of the root node is reached. If action a is different from action `l>0&b=1&ip_mess=1 -> b'=0&z'=0&n1'=min (n1+1,8)&ip_mess'=0` (the whole PRISM command is a single action), then a is classified as *good* in state s. Otherwise, the left son is reached.
3. In node $z \leq 0$ the classification of action a (that is the action that labels the parent node) depends on the variable valuation of the current state. If the value of var. z is greater than 0, then a is classified as *good* in state s, otherwise it is classified as *bad*.

Action **rec** stands for a network host receiving a reply to a broadcast message, resulting in resolution of an IP address conflict if one is present, which clearly does not help in constructing an unresolved conflict. The action labelling the right son of the root represents the detection of an IP address conflict by an arbitrary network host. This action is only good, if variable z, which is a clock variable, in the current state is greater than 0. The combined meaning of the two nodes is that an unresolved IP address conflict can occur if the conflict is detected too late.

firewire example. For **firewire**, we obtain a trivial tree with a single node, labelled *good*. Therefore, playing all available actions in each state guarantees reaching the target almost surely. In contrast to other representations, we have

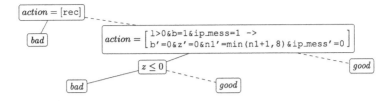

Fig. 4. A decision tree for zeroconf

automatically obtained the information that the network always reaches the target configuration, regardless of the individual behaviour of its components and their interleaving.

mer example. In the case of `mer`, there exists a strategy that violates the required property that the two resources are not accessed simultaneously. The decision tree for the `mer` strategy is depicted in Fig. 5. In order to understand how a state is reached, where both resources are accessed at the same time, it is necessary to determine which user accesses which resource in that state.

1. The two tree nodes labelled by 1 explain what resource *user 1* should access. The root node labelled by action `s1=0&r1=0 -> r1'=2` specifies that the request to access *resource 2* (variable `r1` is set to 2) is classified as *bad*. The only remaining action for *user 1* is to request access to *resource 1*. This action is classified as *good* by the right son of the root node.
2. Analogously, the tree nodes labelled by 2 specify that *user 2* actions should request access to *resource 2* (follows from `s2=0&r2=0 -> r2'=2`). Once *resource 2* is requested it should change its internal state `s2` to 1 (follows from `s2=0&r2=2 -> s2'=1`). It follows, that in the state violating the property, *user 1* has access to *resource 1* and *user 2* to *resource 2*.

The model is supposed to correctly handle such overlapping requests, but fails to do so in a specific case. In order to further debug the model, one has to find the action of the scheduler that causes this undesired behaviour. The lower part of the tree specifies that `u1_request_comm` is a candidate for such an action. Inspecting a snippet of the code of `u1_request_comm` from the PRISM source code (shown below) reveals that in the given situation, the scheduler reacts inappropriately with some probability p.

```
[u1_request_comm]   s=0 & commUser=0 & driveUser!=0 & k<n ->
            (1-p):(s'=1) & (r'=driveUser) & (k'=k+1) +
            p:(s'=-1) & (gc'=true) & (k'=k+1)
```

The remaining nodes of the tree that were not discussed are necessary to reset the situation if the non-faulty part (with probability $1-p$) of the `u1_request_comm` command was executed. It should be noted that executing the faulty `u1_request_comm` action does not lead to the undesired state right away. The action only grants *user 1* access rights in a situation, where he should not get these rights. Only a successive action leads to *user 1* accessing the resource and the undesired state

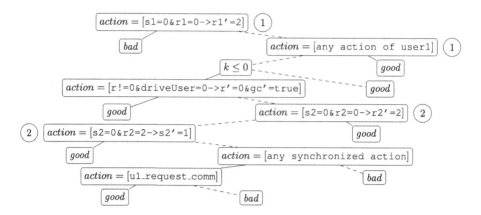

Fig. 5. A decision tree for `mer`

being reached. This is a common type of bug, where the command that triggered an error is not the cause of it.

7   Conclusion

In this work we presented a new approach to represent strategies in MDPs in a succinct and comprehensible way. We exploited machine learning methods to achieve our goals. Interesting directions of future works are to investigate whether other machine learning methods can be integrated with our approach, and to extend our approach from reachability objectives to other objectives (such as long-run average and discounted-sum).

Acknowledgements. This research was funded in part by Austrian Science Fund (FWF) Grant No P 23499-N23, FWF NFN Grant No S11407-N23 (RiSE) and Z211-N23 (Wittgenstein Award), European Research Council (ERC) Grant No 279307 (Graph Games), ERC Grant No 267989 (QUAREM), the Czech Science Foundation Grant No P202/12/G061, and People Programme (Marie Curie Actions) of the European Union's Seventh Framework Programme (FP7/2007–2013) REA Grant No 291734.

References

1. Howard, R.A.: Dynamic Programming and Markov Processes. The MIT press, New York, London, Cambridge (1960)
2. Puterman, M.L.: Markov Decision Processes. Wiley, New York (1994)
3. Filar, J., Vrieze, K.: Competitive Markov Decision Processes. Springer, New York (1997)
4. Baier, C., Katoen, J.-P.: Principles of Model Checking (Representation and Mind Series). The MIT Press, Cambridge (2008)
5. Kwiatkowska, M., Norman, G., Parker, D.: PRISM 4.0: verification of probabilistic real-time systems. In: Gopalakrishnan, G., Qadeer, S. (eds.) CAV 2011. LNCS, vol. 6806, pp. 585–591. Springer, Heidelberg (2011)

6. Courcoubetis, C., Yannakakis, M.: The complexity of probabilistic verification. J. ACM **42**(4), 857–907 (1995)
7. Vardi, M.: Automatic verification of probabilistic concurrent finite state programs. In: FOCS, pp. 327–338 (1985)
8. Segala, R.: Modeling and verification of randomized distributed real-time systems. Ph.D thesis, MIT Press (1995). Technical report MIT/LCS/TR-676
9. De Alfaro, L.: Formal verification of probabilistic systems. Ph.D thesis, Stanford University (1997)
10. Kwiatkowska, M., Parker, D.: Automated verification and strategy synthesis for probabilistic systems. In: Van Hung, D., Ogawa, M. (eds.) ATVA 2013. LNCS, vol. 8172, pp. 5–22. Springer, Heidelberg (2013)
11. Brázdil, T., Chatterjee, K., Chmelík, M., Forejt, V., Křetínský, J., Kwiatkowska, M., Parker, D., Ujma, M.: Verification of markov decision processes using learning algorithms. In: Cassez, F., Raskin, J.-F. (eds.) ATVA 2014. LNCS, vol. 8837, pp. 98–114. Springer, Heidelberg (2014)
12. Bernet, J., Janin, D., Walukiewicz, I.: Permissive strategies: from parity games to safety games. ITA **36**(3), 261–275 (2002)
13. Bouyer, P., Markey, N., Olschewski, J., Ummels, M.: Measuring permissiveness in parity games: mean-payoff parity games revisited. In: Bultan and Hsiung [60] pp. 135–149
14. Dräger, K., Forejt, V., Kwiatkowska, M., Parker, D., Ujma, M.: Permissive controller synthesis for probabilistic systems. In: Ábrahám, E., Havelund, K. (eds.) TACAS 2014 (ETAPS). LNCS, vol. 8413, pp. 531–546. Springer, Heidelberg (2014)
15. Mitchell, T.M.: Machine Learning, 1st edn. McGraw-Hill Inc., New York (1997)
16. Kwiatkowska, M., Norman, G., Parker, D.: The PRISM benchmark suite. In: QEST, pp. 203–204 (2012)
17. Boutilier, C., Dearden, R., Goldszmidt, M.: Exploiting structure in policy construction. In: IJCAI-95, pp. 1104–1111 (1995)
18. Kearns, M., Koller, D.: Efficient reinforcement learning in factored MDPs. In: IJCAI, pp. 740–747. Morgan Kaufmann Publishers Inc., San Francisco, CA, USA (1999)
19. Kushmerick, N., Hanks, S., Weld, D.: An algorithm for probabilistic least-commitment planning. In: Proceedings of AAAI-94, pp. 1073–1078 (1994)
20. Hoey, J., St-aubin, R., Hu, A., Boutilier, C.: Spudd: stochastic planning using decision diagrams. In: Proceedings of the Fifteenth Conference on Uncertainty in Artificial Intelligence, pp. 279–288. Morgan Kaufmann (1999)
21. Chapman, D., Kaelbling, L.P.: Input generalization in delayed reinforcement learning: an algorithm and performance comparisons. pp. 726–731. Morgan Kaufmann (1991)
22. Koller, D., Parr, R.: Computing factored value functions for policies in structured MDPs. In: Proceedings of the Sixteenth International Joint Conference on Artificial Intelligence, pp. 1332–1339. Morgan Kaufmann (1999)
23. Boutilier, C., Dean, T., Hanks, S.: Decision-theoretic planning: structural assumptions and computational leverage. JAIR **11**, 1–94 (1999)
24. De Alfaro, L., Kwiatkowska, M., Norman, G., Parker, D., Segala, R.: Symbolic model checking of probabilistic processes using MTBDDS and the kronecker representation. In: Graf, S. (ed.) TACAS 2000. LNCS, vol. 1785, pp. 395–410. Springer, Heidelberg (2000)
25. Hermanns, H., Kwiatkowska, M., Norman, G., Parker, D., Siegle, M.: On the use of MTBDDs for performability analysis and verification of stochastic systems. J. Log. Algebraic Program. Spec. Issue Probab. Tech. Des. Anal. Syst. **56**(1–2), 23–67 (2003)

26. Miner, A.S., Parker, D.: Symbolic representations and analysis of large probabilistic systems. In: Baier, C., Haverkort, B.R., Hermanns, H., Katoen, J.-P., Siegle, M. (eds.) Validation of Stochastic Systems. LNCS, vol. 2925, pp. 296–338. Springer, Heidelberg (2004)
27. Wimmer, R., Braitling, B., Becker, B., Hahn, E.M., Crouzen, P., Hermanns, H., Dhama, A., Theel, O.: Symblicit calculation of long-run averages for concurrent probabilistic systems. In: QEST, pp. 27–36, IEEE Computer Society, Washington, DC, USA (2010)
28. Boutilier, C., Dearden, R.: Approximating value trees in structured dynamic programming. In: Proceedings of the Thirteenth International Conference on Machine Learning, pp. 54–62 (1996)
29. Pyeatt, L.D.: Reinforcement learning with decision trees. In: The 21st IASTED International Multi-Conference on Applied Informatics (AI 2003), Innsbruck, Austria, pp. 26–31, 10–13 Feb 2003
30. Raghavendra, C.S., Liu, S., Panangadan, A., Talukder, A.: Compact representation of coordinated sampling policies for body sensor networks. In: Proceedings of Workshop on Advances in Communication and Networks (Smart Homes for Tele-Health), pp. 6–10, IEEE (2010)
31. Han, T., Katoen, J.-P., Damman, B.: Counterexample generation in probabilistic model checking. IEEE Trans. Softw. Eng. 35(2), 241–257 (2009)
32. Andrés, M.E., D'Argenio, P., Van Rossum, P.: Significant diagnostic counterexamples in probabilistic model checking. In: Chockler, H., Hu, A.J. (eds.) HVC 2008. LNCS, vol. 5394, pp. 129–148. Springer, Heidelberg (2009)
33. Wimmer, R., Jansen, N., Ábrahám, E., Katoen, J.-P., Becker, B.: Minimal counterexamples for linear-time probabilistic verification. TCS 549, 61–100 (2014)
34. Jansen, N., Ábrahám, E., Katelaan, J., Wimmer, R., Katoen, J.-P., Becker, B.: Hierarchical counterexamples for discrete-time markov chains. In: Bultan and Hsiung [60] pp. 443–452
35. Damman, B., Han, T., Katoen, J.-P.: Regular expressions for PCTL counterexamples. In: QEST, pp. 179–188, IEEE Computer Society (2008)
36. Fecher, H., Huth, M., Piterman, N., Wagner, D.: PCTL model checking of markov chains: truth and falsity as winning strategies in games. Perform. Eval. 67(9), 858–872 (2010)
37. Aljazzar, H., Leue, S.: Directed explicit state-space search in the generation of counterexamples for stochastic model checking. IEEE Trans. Softw. Eng. 36(1), 37–60 (2010)
38. Komuravelli, A., Păsăreanu, C.S., Clarke, E.M.: Assume-guarantee abstraction refinement for probabilistic systems. In: Madhusudan, P., Seshia, S.A. (eds.) CAV 2012. LNCS, vol. 7358, pp. 310–326. Springer, Heidelberg (2012)
39. Aljazzar, H., Leitner-Fischer, F., Leue, S., Simeonov, D.: DiPro - a tool for probabilistic counterexample generation. In: Groce, A., Musuvathi, M. (eds.) SPIN Workshops 2011. LNCS, vol. 6823, pp. 183–187. Springer, Heidelberg (2011)
40. Jansen, N., Ábrahám, E., Volk, M., Wimmer, R., Katoen, J.-P., Becker, B.: The COMICS tool - computing minimal counterexamples for DTMCs. In: Chakraborty, S., Mukund, M. (eds.) ATVA 2012. LNCS, vol. 7561, pp. 349–353. Springer, Heidelberg (2012)
41. Ábrahám, E., Becker, B., Dehnert, C., Jansen, N., Katoen, J.-P., Wimmer, R.: Counterexample generation for discrete-time markov models: an introductory survey. In: Bernardo, M., Damiani, F., Hähnle, R., Johnsen, E.B., Schaefer, I. (eds.) SFM 2014. LNCS, vol. 8483, pp. 65–121. Springer, Heidelberg (2014)
42. Aljazzar, H., Leue, S.: Generation of counterexamples for model checking of markov decision processes. In: QEST, pp. 197–206, IEEE Computer Society (2009)

43. Leitner-Fischer, F., Leue, S.: Probabilistic fault tree synthesis using causality computation. IJCCBS **4**(2), 119–143 (2013)
44. Kattenbelt, M., Huth, M.: Verification and refutation of probabilistic specifications via games. In: IARCS Annual Conference on Foundations of Software Technology and Theoretical Computer Science, FSTTCS 2009, IIT Kanpur, India, pp. 251–262, 15–17 Dec 2009
45. Wimmer, R., Jansen, N., Vorpahl, A., Ábrahám, E., Katoen, J.-P., Becker, B.: High-level counterexamples for probabilistic automata. In: Joshi, K., Siegle, M., Stoelinga, M., D'Argenio, P.R. (eds.) QEST 2013. LNCS, vol. 8054, pp. 39–54. Springer, Heidelberg (2013)
46. Dehnert, C., Jansen, N., Wimmer, R., Ábrahám, E., Katoen, J.-P.: Fast debugging of PRISM models. In: Cassez, F., Raskin, J.-F. (eds.) ATVA 2014. LNCS, vol. 8837, pp. 146–162. Springer, Heidelberg (2014)
47. Kwiatkowska, M.Z., Norman, G., Parker, D.: Game-based abstraction for Markov decision processes. In: QEST, pp. 157–166 (2006)
48. Hermanns, H., Wachter, B., Zhang, L.: Probabilistic CEGAR. In: Gupta, A., Malik, S. (eds.) CAV 2008. LNCS, vol. 5123, pp. 162–175. Springer, Heidelberg (2008)
49. Chadha, R., Viswanathan, M.: A counterexample-guided abstraction-refinement framework for Markov decision processes. ACM Trans. Comput. Log. **12**(1), 1 (2010)
50. Chatterjee, K., Chmelík, M., Daca, P.: CEGAR for qualitative analysis of probabilistic systems. In: Biere, A., Bloem, R. (eds.) CAV 2014. LNCS, vol. 8559, pp. 473–490. Springer, Heidelberg (2014)
51. D'Argenio, P.R., Jeannet, B., Jensen, H.E., Larsen, K.G.: Reachability analysis of probabilistic systems by successive refinements. In: De Luca, L., Gilmore, S. (eds.) PROBMIV 2001, PAPM-PROBMIV 2001, and PAPM 2001. LNCS, vol. 2165, pp. 39–56. Springer, Heidelberg (2001)
52. D'Argenio, P.R.: Reduction and refinement strategies for probabilistic analysis. In: Hermanns, H., Segala, R. (eds.) PROBMIV 2002, PAPM-PROBMIV 2002, and PAPM 2002. LNCS, vol. 2399, pp. 57–76. Springer, Heidelberg (2002)
53. McMahan, H.B., Likhachev, M., Gordon, G.J.: Bounded real-time dynamic programming: RTDP with monotone upper bounds and performance guarantees. In: ICML (2005)
54. Brázdil, T., Kiefer, S., Kučera, A.: Efficient analysis of probabilistic programs with an unbounded counter. J. ACM **61**(6), 41:1–41:35 (2014)
55. Von Essen, C., Jobstmann, B., Parker, D., Varshneya, R.: Semi-symbolic computation of efficient controllers in probabilistic environments. Technical report, Verimag (2012)
56. Quinlan, J.R.: Induction of decision trees. Mach. Learn. **1**(1), 81–106 (1986)
57. Quinlan, J.R.: C4.5: Programs for Machine Learning. Morgan Kaufmann, San Francisco (1993)
58. Hall, M., Frank, E., Holmes, G., Pfahringer, B., Reutemann, P., Witten, I.H.: The weka data mining software: an update. ACM SIGKDD Explor. Newsl. **11**(1), 10–18 (2009)
59. Drazin, S., Montag, M.: Decision tree analysis using weka. Machine Learning-Project II, University of Miami, pp. 1–3 (2012)
60. Bultan, T., Hsiung, P.-A. (eds.): Automated Technology for Verification and Analysis, ATVA 2011. 9th International Symposium, Taipei, Taiwan, October 11-14, 2011. Proceedings, vol. 6996, LNCS. Springer, Heidelberg (2011)

Symbolic Polytopes for Quantitative Interpolation and Verification

Klaus von Gleissenthall[1]([✉]), Boris Köpf[2], and Andrey Rybalchenko[3]

[1] Technische Universität München, Munich, Germany
gleissen@in.tum.de
[2] IMDEA Software Institute, Madrid, Spain
[3] Microsoft Research, Cambridge, UK

Abstract. Proving quantitative properties of programs, such as bounds on resource usage or information leakage, often leads to verification conditions that involve cardinalities of sets. Existing approaches for dealing with such verification conditions operate by checking cardinality bounds for given formulas. However, they cannot synthesize formulas that satisfy given cardinality constraints, which limits their applicability for inferring cardinality-based inductive arguments.

In this paper we present an algorithm for synthesizing formulas for given cardinality constraints, which relies on the theory of counting integer points in symbolic polytopes. We cast our algorithm in terms of a cardinality-constrained interpolation procedure, which we put to work in a solver for recursive Horn clauses with cardinality constraints based on abstraction refinement. We implement our technique and describe its evaluation on a number of representative examples.

1 Introduction

Proving quantitative properties of programs often leads to verification conditions that involve cardinalities of sets and relations over program states. For example, determining the memory requirements for memoization reduces to bounding the cardinality of the set of argument values passed to a function, and bounding information leaks of a program reduces to bounding the cardinality of the set of observations an attacker can make.

A number of recent advances for discharging verification conditions with cardinalities consider extensions of logical theories with cardinality constraints, such as set algebra and its generalizations [25,31,32], linear arithmetic [15,40], constraints over strings [27], as well as general SMT based settings [17]. At their core, these approaches operate by *checking* whether a cardinality bound holds for a given formula that describes a set of values. However, they cannot *synthesize* formulas that satisfy given cardinality constraints. As a consequence, the problem of automatically inferring cardinality-based inductive arguments that imply a specified assertion remains an open challenge.

In this paper, we present an approach for synthesizing linear arithmetic formulas that satisfy given cardinality constraints. Our approach relies on the theory of counting integer points in polytopes, however, instead of computing the

© Springer International Publishing Switzerland 2015
D. Kroening and C.S. Păsăreanu (Eds.): CAV 2015, Part I, LNCS 9206, pp. 178–194, 2015.
DOI: 10.1007/978-3-319-21690-4_11

cardinality of a given polytope (the typical use case of this theory) our approach synthesizes a polytope for a given cardinality constraint. Our synthesizer internally organizes the search space in terms of *symbolic polytopes*. Such polytopes are represented using symbolic vertices and hyperplanes, together with certain well-formedness constraints. We derive an expression for the number of points in the polytope in terms of this symbolic representation, which leads to a set of constraints that at the same time represent the shape *and* the cardinality of the polytope. For this, we restrict our attention to the class of *unimodular* polytopes. Unimodularity can be concisely described using constraints and provides an effective means for reducing the search space while being sufficiently expressive. We then resort to efficient SMT solvers specifically tuned to deal with the resulting kind of non-linear constraints, e.g., Z3 [16]. We cast our approach in terms of an algorithm #ITP$_{\text{LIA}}$ for cardinality constrained interpolation, that is, #ITP$_{\text{LIA}}$ generates formulas that satisfy cardinality constraints along with implication constraints.

We put cardinality-constrained interpolation to work within an automatic verification method #HORN for inferring cardinality-based inductive program properties, based on abstraction and its counterexample-guided refinement. Specifically, #HORN is a solver for recursive Horn clauses with cardinality constraints. We rely on Horn clauses as basis because they serve as a language for describing verification conditions for a wide range of programs, including those with procedures and multiple threads [8, 19, 34]. Adding recursion enables representing verification conditions that rely on inductive reasoning, such as loop invariants or procedure summaries. By offering support for cardinalities directly in the language in which we express verification conditions, our solver can effectively leverage the interplay between the qualitative and quantitative (cardinality) aspects of the constraints to be solved.

We implemented #ITP$_{\text{LIA}}$ and #HORN and applied them to analyze a collection of examples that show

- how a variety of cardinality-based properties (namely, bounds on information leaks, memory usage, and execution time) and different program classes (namely, while programs and programs with procedures) can be expressed and analyzed in a uniform manner.
- that our approach can establish resource bounds on examples from the recent literature at competitive performance and precision, and that it can handle examples whose precise analysis is out of scope of existing approaches.
- that our approach can be used for synthesizing a padding-based countermeasure against timing side channels, for a given bound on tolerable leakage.

In summary, our paper contributes and puts to work a synthesis method for polytopes that satisfy cardinality constraints, based on symbolic integer point counting algorithms.

2 Example

We consider a procedure mcm for *Matrix chain multiplication* [14] that recursively computes the cost of multiplying matrices $M_0, \ldots, M_n$ with optimal bracketing. mcm(i, j) returns the number of operations required for multiplying the subsequence $M_i, \ldots, M_j$, and c(k) returns the number of operations required for multiplying matrices M_k and M_{k+1}.

Even though the number of recursive function calls is exponential in n, mcm can be turned into an efficient algorithm by applying memoization. The amount of memory required to store results of recursive calls is bounded by $\frac{(n+1)\cdot(n+2)}{2}$, as mcm is only called with ordered pairs of arguments.

```
int mcm(int i, int j) {
  if (i == j) return 0;
  int minCost = infty;
  for (int k=i; k <= j-1; k++) {
    int v = mcm(i, k)+mcm(k+1, j)+c(k);
    if (v < minCost) minCost = v;
  }
  return minCost;
}
int main(n){
  mcm(0, n);
}
```

Proving such a bound requires reasoning about recursive procedure calls as well as tracking dependencies between variables i and j, i.e., estimating the range of each variable in isolation and combining the estimates is not precise enough.

When using #HORN, we first set up recursive Horn constraints on an assertion $args(i, j, n)$ that contains all triples (i, j, n) such that calling main(n) leads to a recursive call mcm(i, j), following [19]. Then, #HORN solves these constraints using a procedure based on counterexample-guided abstraction refinement. As an intermediate step, #HORN deals with an interpolation query that requires finding a polytope φ_{args} over i, j and n such that

$$n \geq 2 \wedge (i = 0 \wedge j = n \vee i = 1 \wedge j = 1) \rightarrow \varphi_{args} \quad (1)$$
$$n \geq 0 \rightarrow |\{(i, j) \mid \varphi_{args}\}| \leq \frac{(n+1)\cdot(n+2)}{2} . \quad (2)$$

Constraint (1) requires that φ_{args} contains triples obtained by symbolically executing mcm, a typical interpolation query, while (2) ensures that φ_{args} satisfies the bound by referring to the cardinality of φ_{args} through an application of cardinality operator $|\cdot|$.

Given (1) and (2), #ITP$_{\text{LIA}}$ computes the solution $\varphi_{args} = (0 \leq i \leq 1 \wedge i \leq j \leq n \wedge n \geq 2)$. The cardinality of $\{(i, j) \mid \varphi_{args}\}$ is $2n + 1$, hence φ_{args} satisfies the above bound. #HORN uses this solution to refine the abstraction function. In particular, it starts using the predicate $i \leq j$, which is crucial for tracking that mcm is only called on ordered pairs.

3 Counting Integer Points in Polytopes

In this section, we first revisit the theory of counting integer points in polytopes. We then discuss the derivation of expressions for the number of integer points in unimodular polytopes with symbolic vertices and hyperplanes.

Preliminaries. Let $g_1, \ldots, g_d \in \mathbb{R}^d$ be vectors in d-dimensional space. A *cone* with generators $g_1, \ldots, g_d$ is the set of all positive linear combinations of its generators. A cone is *unimodular* if the absolute value of the determinant of the matrix $(g_1 \cdots g_d)$ is equal to one. The *vertex cone* of a polytope P at vertex v is the smallest cone that originates from v and that includes P; we denote its generators by $g_{v1}, \ldots, g_{vd}$. Finally, a polytope P is unimodular if all its vertex cones are unimodular.[1]

Generating functions. The integer points contained in a set $S \subseteq \mathbb{R}^d$ in can be represented in terms of a *generating function* $f(S, x)$ which is a sum of monomials, one per integer point in S, defined as follows

$$f(S, x) = \sum_{m \in S \cap \mathbb{Z}^d} x^m, \tag{1}$$

where for $m = (m_1, \ldots, m_d)$ we define $x^m = x_1^{m_1} \cdot \ldots \cdot x_d^{m_d}$. This generating function is a Laurent series, i.e. its terms may have negative degree. Note that, for finite S, the value of $f(S, x)$ at $x = (1, \ldots, 1)$, corresponds to the number of integer points in S.

Rational function representation. Generating functions are a powerful tool for counting integer points in polytopes. This is due to two key results: First, Brion's theorem [9] allows to decompose the generating function of a polytope into the sum of the generating functions of its vertex cones. Second, the generating function of *unimodular* vertex cones can be represented through an equivalent yet short rational function. This rational function representation relies on a generalization of the equivalence $\frac{1}{1-x} = (1 + x + x^2 + x^3 + \ldots)$, which provides a concise representation of the set $\{0, 1, 2, 3, \ldots\}$.

This yields the following rational function representation for a unimodular polytope P with vertices $\mathcal{V}$:

$$r(P, x) = \sum_{v \in \mathcal{V}} \frac{x^v}{(1 - x^{g_{v1}}) \cdots (1 - x^{g_{vd}})} \tag{2}$$

Here, each summand represents the generating function of the vertex cone at v with generators $g_{v1}, \ldots, g_{vd}$. Rational function representations for arbitrary polytopes can be obtained through Barvinok's algorithm [3] that decomposes arbitrary vertex cones into unimodular cones.

Generating function evaluation. Since $x = (1, \ldots, 1)$ is a singularity of $r(P, x)$, computing the number of points in the polytope by direct evaluation leads to a division by zero. This can be avoided by performing a Laurent series expansion of $r(P, x)$ around $x = (1, \ldots, 1)$, however, the expansion requires a reduction of

---

[1] We provide additional examples and alternative definitions in the extended version of this article [37]. See e.g. [3,4,15] for more details.

$r(P, x)$ from a multivariate polynomial over $(x_1, \ldots, x_d)$ to a univariate polynomial over y, see [15]. The reduction is done by finding a vector $\mu = (\mu_1, \ldots, \mu_d)$ with

$$\mu \cdot g \neq 0, \qquad (3)$$

for all generators g of the polytope, and by replacing x_i with y^{μ_i}, for each $i \in 1 \ldots d$. Equation (3) ensures that no factor in the denominator of Eq. (2) becomes 0, and hence avoids introduction of singularities. Let $sub(r(P, x), y)$ denote the result of the above substitution. Then, the constant term of the Laurent expansion of $sub(r(P, x), y)$ around $y = 1$ yields the desired count. Computing Laurent series expansions is a standard procedure and implemented, e.g., in Wolfram Alpha [41].

Example 1. Consider the unimodular polytope $P = (x_1 \geq 0 \wedge x_2 \geq 0 \wedge x_1 + x_2 \leq 2)$ of dimension $d = 2$. P has vertices $v_1 = (0\ 0)$, $v_2 = (0\ 2)$, and $v_3 = (2\ 0)$ and contains 6 integer points, as shown by the circles below.

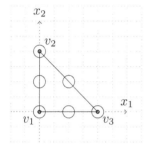

The generators of the vertex cones are given by

$$
\begin{aligned}
g_{v_1 1} &= (0\ 1) & g_{v_1 2} &= (1\ 0) \\
g_{v_2 1} &= (0\ -1) & g_{v_2 2} &= (1\ -1) \\
g_{v_3 1} &= (-1\ 0) & g_{v_3 2} &= (-1\ 1).
\end{aligned}
$$

Equation (2) yields the following rational generating function $r(P, x)$.

$$
\frac{x_1^0 x_2^0}{(1 - x_1^0 x_2^1)(1 - x_1^1 x_2^0)} + \frac{x_1^0 x_2^2}{(1 - x_1^0 x_2^{-1})(1 - x_1^1 x_2^{-1})} + \frac{x_1^2 x_2^0}{(1 - x_1^{-1} x_2^0)(1 - x_1^{-1} x_2^1)}
$$

Applying the substitution with $\mu = (-1\ 1)$ yields the expression $sub(r(P, x), y)$.

$$
\frac{1}{(1 - y)(1 - y^{-1})} + \frac{y^2}{(1 - y^{-1})(1 - y^{-2})} + \frac{y^{-2}}{(1 - y)(1 - y^2)}
$$

Computing the series expansion using the Wolfram Alpha command *series* $sub(r(P, x), y)$ at $y = 1$ produces $\cdots 5(y - 1)^3 + 5(y - 1)^2 + 6$, with the constant coefficient 6 yielding the expected count.   ∎

Symbolic cardinality expression. The rational function representation of the generating function of a unimodular polytope shown in Eq. 2 refers to the polytope's vertices and to the generators of its vertex cones. However, these generators and vertices do not have to be instantiated to concrete values in order for the evaluation of the generating function to be possible [40]. That is, the evaluation of the generating function can be carried out *symbolically* yielding a formula that expresses the cardinality of a polytope as a function of its generators, vertices, and a vector μ.

In our algorithm, we will use $\text{SYMCONECARD}(v, G, \mu)$ to refer to the result of the symbolic evaluation of the generating function for the cone of a symbolic vertex v with generators G. By summing up $\text{SYMCONECARD}(v, G, \mu)$ for all vertex cones we obtain a symbolic expression of the number of integer points in a symbolic polytope.[2]

Example 2. The cardinality of a two-dimensional polytope with symbolic vertices v_1, v_2, v_3 and generators $g_{v_i 1}$ and $g_{v_i 2}$, with $i \in 1..3$, is given by $\sum_{i=1}^{3} \text{SYMCONECARD}(v_i, \{g_{v_i 1}, g_{v_i 2}\}, \mu)$, where

$$\text{SYMCONECARD}(v_i, \{g_{v_i 1}, g_{v_i 2}\}, \mu)$$
$$= (\mu_1^2 + 3\mu_1(\mu_2 - 2\mu_v - 1) + \mu_2^2 - 3\mu_2(2\mu_v + 1) + 6\mu_v^2 + 6\mu_v + 1)(12\mu_1\mu_2)^{-1}$$
$$\text{with } \mu_1 = \mu \cdot g_{v_i 1}, \ \mu_2 = \mu \cdot g_{v_i 2} \text{ and } \mu_v = \mu \cdot v_i. \qquad\blacksquare$$

Note that in order for $\text{SYMCONECARD}(v, G, \mu)$ to yield a valid count, the vertices and generators must satisfy a number of conditions, e.g., the symbolic cones need to be unimodular and the employed vector μ needs to satisfy Eq. (3). We next present our interpolation procedure $\#\text{ITP}_{\text{LIA}}$ that creates constraints for ensuring these conditions.

4   Interpolation with Cardinality Constraints

In this section, we first define interpolation with cardinality constraints. Then we present the interpolation procedure $\#\text{ITP}_{\text{LIA}}$ that generates constraints on the cardinality of an interpolant and solves them using an SMT solver.

Cardinality Interpolation. Let k be a variable and let w be a tuple of variables. Let φ and ψ be constraints in a given first-order theory. Then, a *cardinality constraint* is an expression of the form

$$|\{w \mid \varphi\}| = k \wedge \psi$$

where $|\cdot|$ denotes the set cardinality operator. We call the free variables of φ that do not occur in w *parameters*. A cardinality constraint is *parametric* if it has at least one parameter and *non-parametric* otherwise. The expression ψ is used to constrain the cardinality.

Example 3. Consider the theory of linear integer arithmetic. The cardinality constraint $|\{x \mid 0 \le x \le 10\}| = k \wedge k \le 20$ is non-parametric, whereas the constraint $|\{x \mid 0 \le x \le n\}| = k \wedge k \le n+1$ is parametric in n. Both constraints are valid, since $|\{x \mid 0 \le x \le 10\}| = 11$ and $|\{x \mid 0 \le x \le n\}| = n+1$. $\blacksquare$

---

[2] This step relies on the fact that evaluating the generating function for each vertex cone separately and summing the results is equivalent to evaluating the sum of generating functions.

function $\#\mathrm{ITP_{LIA}}(w, \varphi^-, \varphi^+, \psi, \mathrm{TMPL})$

1   $\mathrm{CONS} := \mathit{true}$
2   $\mathrm{SYMCARD} := 0$
3   $d := $ length of w
4   $\mu := $ vector of d fresh variables
5   $\mathcal{H_V} := \bigcup\{\mathrm{TMPL}(v) \mid v \in \mathcal{V}\}$
6   **for** each $v \in \mathcal{V}$ **do**
7      $\mathcal{H} := \mathrm{TMPL}(v)$
8      $G := \emptyset$
9   **for** each $H \in \mathcal{H}$ **do**
10        $g_{vH} := $ vector of d fresh variables
11        $G := \{g_{vH}\} \cup G$
12     $\mathrm{CONS} := \mathrm{CONS} \wedge \mathrm{VERT}(v, \mathcal{H}, \mathcal{H_V}) \wedge \mathrm{GENR}(v, \mathcal{H}, G, \mu) \wedge \mathrm{UNIM}(v, G)$
13     $\mathrm{SYMCARD} := \mathrm{SYMCARD} + \mathrm{SYMCONECARD}(v, G, \mu)$
14 $\mathrm{CONS} := \mathrm{CONS} \wedge \mathrm{IMPL}(\varphi^-, \bigwedge \mathcal{H_V}) \wedge \mathrm{IMPL}(\bigwedge \mathcal{H_V}, \varphi^+)$
15 **return** $\mathrm{SMTSOLVE}(\mathrm{CONS} \wedge \mathrm{IMPL}(\mathrm{SYMCARD} = k, \psi(k)))$

Fig. 1. Function $\#\mathrm{ITP_{LIA}}$ computes cardinality constrained interpolants for template TMPL.

Assume constraints φ^- and φ^+ such that φ^- implies φ^+. A *cardinality-constrained interpolant* for φ^-, φ^+, and cardinality constraint $|\{w \mid \varphi\}| = k \wedge \psi$ is a constraint φ such that 1) φ^- implies φ, 2) φ implies φ^+, and 3) $|\{w \mid \varphi\}| = k \wedge \psi$ is valid. For a parametric cardinality constraint, we say that the interpolation problem is parametric, and call it non-parametric otherwise.

Example 4. Let $\varphi^- = (x = 0 \wedge n \geq 0)$ and $\varphi^+ = \mathit{true}$. Then $\varphi = (0 \leq x \leq n)$ is an interpolant that satisfies the cardinality constraint $|\{x \mid \varphi\}| = k \wedge k \leq n + 1$. For $\varphi^- = \mathit{false}$, $\varphi^+ = x \geq 0$ and cardinality constraint $|\{x \mid \varphi\}| = k \wedge 1 \leq k \leq 10$ the constraint $\varphi = (0 \leq x \leq 5)$ is a cardinality-constrained interpolant. ∎

Note that our definition of interpolation differs from the standard, cardinality-free definition given e.g. in [29] in that we do not require the free variables in φ to be common to both φ^- and φ^+. We exclude this requirement because it appears to be overly restrictive for the setting with cardinalities, as the cardinality constraint imposes a lower/upper bound in addition to φ^- and φ^+. In particular, the common variables condition rules out both interpolants in Example 4, as the set of common variables is empty in both cases.

In this paper, we focus on cardinality constraints with φ in linear arithmetic and ψ in (non-linear) arithmetic, which is an important combination for applications in software verification.

Interpolation Algorithm. We present an algorithm $\#\mathrm{ITP_{LIA}}$ for interpolation with cardinality constraints. For simplicity of exposition, we first consider the non-parametric case and discuss the parametric case in Sect. 5.

#ITP$_{LIA}$ finds an interpolant φ in a space of polytope candidates that is defined through a template. This template is given by a function TMPL that maps a symbolic vertex $v \in \mathcal{V}$ to a set of symbolic hyperplanes that are determined to intersect in v, where each hyperplane $H \in$ TMPL(v) is of the form $c_H \cdot w = \gamma_H$.

The algorithm #ITP$_{LIA}$ is described in Fig. 1. It collects a constraint CONS over the symbolic vertices and symbolic hyperplanes of φ, which ensures that any solution yields a unimodular polytope that satisfies conditions (1) – (3) of the definition of cardinality interpolation. In particular, #ITP$_{LIA}$ ensures that the cardinality of φ satisfies ψ by constructing a symbolic expression SYMCARD on the cardinality of φ in line 13, and requiring that this expression satisfies the cardinality constraint ψ in line 15. Line 12 produces well-formedness constraints VERT$(v, \mathcal{H}, \mathcal{H}_\mathcal{V})$ and GENR$(v, \mathcal{H}, G)$ that ensure a geometrically well-formed instantiation of the template TMPL. The final conjunct in line 12 poses constraints on the generators of the vertex cones in φ that ensure their unimodularity, as explained in Sect. 3. Finally, line 14 produces constraints that ensure the validity of the implications $\varphi^- \rightarrow \varphi$ and $\varphi \rightarrow \varphi^+$. The resulting constraint CONS is passed to an SMT solver that either returns a valuation of symbolic vertices and hyperplanes and hence determines φ, or fails.

Constraint generation. We will now describe the constraint generation of #ITP$_{LIA}$ in more detail. For each symbolic vertex v we make sure that it lies on the hyperplanes determined by TMPL(v) and in the appropriate half-space with respect to the remaning hyperplanes. This is achieved by the following constraint.

$$\text{VERT}(v, \mathcal{H}, \mathcal{H}_\mathcal{V}) = \bigwedge_{H \in \mathcal{H}} c_H \cdot v = \gamma_H \ \wedge \bigwedge_{H \in \mathcal{H}_\mathcal{V} \setminus \mathcal{H}} c_H \cdot v < \gamma_H$$

By making the inequalities strict, we ensure that the polytope does not collapse into a single point, since in this case Brion's theorem does not hold.

SYMCONECARD and UNIM refer to the generators of vertex cones determined by TMPL. Hence we produce a constraint that defines these generators in terms of symbolic hyperplanes. Let g_{vH} denote the generator of the cone at vertex v that lies in the half-space described by hyperplane H. Then we constrain the generators of the cone at v as follows.

$$\text{GENR}(v, \mathcal{H}, G, \mu) = \bigwedge_{H \in \mathcal{H}} (c_H \cdot g_{vH} \leq 0 \wedge \mu \cdot g_{vH} \neq 0$$
$$\wedge \bigwedge_{H' \in \mathcal{H} \setminus \{H\}} c_{H'} \cdot g_{vH} = 0)$$

Here we require each generator g_{vH} to lie on the facet formed by the intersection of all hyperplanes $H' \in \mathcal{H} \setminus \{H\}$, and to point in the appropriate half-space wrt. H. Additionally the generator is constrained according to Eq. 3. With the generators defined, we can ensure the unimodularity of vertex cones of the polytope by UNIM$(v, G) = (abs(det(g_{vH_1}, \ldots, g_{vH_d})) = 1)$, where $G = \{g_{vH_1}, \ldots, g_{vH_d}\}$. We then use SYMCONECARD(v, G, μ) to denote the counting expression of the symbolic cone of vertex v for our generators. We construct the counting expressions for the entire symbolic polytope φ by taking the sum over counting expressions for its vertex cones.

Finally, we generate constraints IMPL for the implication conditions $\varphi^- \to \varphi$ and $\varphi \to \varphi^+$ by applying Farkas' lemma [35], which is a standard tool for such tasks [13,33]. This lemma states that every linear consequence of a satisfiable set of linear inequalities can be obtained as a non-negative linear combination of these inequalities. Formally, if $Aw \leq b$ is satisfiable and $Aw \leq b$ implies $cw \leq \gamma$ then there exists $\lambda \geq 0$ such that $\lambda A = c$ and $\lambda b \leq \gamma$. When dealing with integers, Farkas' lemma is sound but not complete, see the discussion on completeness at the end of this section. Our implementation of IMPL handles non-conjunctive implication constraints by a standard method based on DNF conversion and Farkas' lemma.

Example 5. Consider $\varphi^- = (1 \leq x \wedge x - y \leq 1 \wedge x - y \geq -1 \wedge y \leq z \wedge z \leq 10)$, $\varphi^+ = \mathit{true}$, $w = (x, y)$, and $\psi = (k \leq 120)$. The solution φ is a polytope formed by three vertices $\mathcal{V} = \{v_1, v_2, v_3\}$. It is bounded by the supporting hyperplanes $\mathcal{H}_{\mathcal{V}} = \{H_1, H_2, H_3\}$ with normal vectors c_{H_1}, c_{H_2} and c_{H_3}, respectively. In our example, we use TMPL such that $v_1 \mapsto \{H_1, H_3\}$, $v_2 \mapsto \{H_1, H_2\}$, and $v_3 \mapsto \{H_2, H_3\}$, restricting φ to a triangular shape.

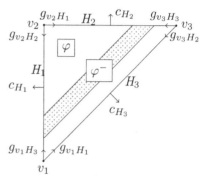

We obtain the following constraints:

$$\text{VERT}(v_1, \{H_1, H_3\}, \mathcal{H}_{\mathcal{V}}) = (c_{H_1} \cdot v_1 = \gamma_{H_1} \wedge c_{H_3} \cdot v_1 = \gamma_{H_3} \wedge c_{H_2} \cdot v_1 < \gamma_{H_2})$$
$$\text{VERT}(v_2, \{H_1, H_2\}, \mathcal{H}_{\mathcal{V}}) = (c_{H_1} \cdot v_2 = \gamma_{H_1} \wedge c_{H_2} \cdot v_2 = \gamma_{H_2} \wedge c_{H_3} \cdot v_2 < \gamma_{H_3})$$
$$\text{VERT}(v_3, \{H_2, H_3\}, \mathcal{H}_{\mathcal{V}}) = (c_{H_2} \cdot v_3 = \gamma_{H_2} \wedge c_{H_3} \cdot v_3 = \gamma_{H_3} \wedge c_{H_1} \cdot v_3 < \gamma_{H_1})$$

We get the following constraints on generators:

$$\text{GENR}(v_1, \{H_1, H_3\}, \{g_{v_1 H_1}, g_{v_1 H_3}\}, \mu) =$$
$$(c_{H_1} \cdot g_{v_1 H_1} \leq 0 \wedge c_{H_3} \cdot g_{v_1 H_1} = 0 \wedge c_{H_3} \cdot g_{v_1 H_3} \leq 0 \wedge c_{H_1} \cdot g_{v_1 H_3} = 0)$$
$$\text{GENR}(v_2, \{H_1, H_2\}, \{g_{v_2 H_1}, g_{v_2 H_2}\}, \mu) =$$
$$(c_{H_1} \cdot g_{v_2 H_1} \leq 0 \wedge c_{H_2} \cdot g_{v_2 H_1} = 0 \wedge c_{H_2} \cdot g_{v_2 H_2} \leq 0 \wedge c_{H_1} \cdot g_{v_2 H_2} = 0)$$
$$\text{GENR}(v_3, \{H_2, H_3\}, \{g_{v_3 H_2}, g_{v_3 H_3}\}, \mu) =$$
$$(c_{H_2} \cdot g_{v_3 H_2} \leq 0 \wedge c_{H_3} \cdot g_{v_3 H_2} = 0 \wedge c_{H_3} \cdot g_{v_3 H_3} \leq 0 \wedge c_{H_2} \cdot g_{v_3 H_3} = 0)$$

and unimodularity restrictions:

$$abs(det(g_{v_1 H_1}, g_{v_1 H_3})) = abs(det(g_{v_2 H_1}, g_{v_2 H_2})) = abs(det(g_{v_3 H_2}, g_{v_3 H_3})) = 1$$

The implication constraints in matrix notation are

$$
\overbrace{\begin{pmatrix} -1 & 0 \\ 1 & -1 \\ -1 & 1 \\ 0 & 1 \end{pmatrix}}^{A} \begin{pmatrix} x \\ y \end{pmatrix} \le \overbrace{\begin{pmatrix} -1 \\ 1 \\ 1 \\ 10 \end{pmatrix}}^{b} \quad \rightarrow \quad \overbrace{\begin{pmatrix} c_{11} & c_{12} \\ c_{21} & c_{22} \\ c_{31} & c_{32} \end{pmatrix}}^{C} \begin{pmatrix} x \\ y \end{pmatrix} \le \overbrace{\begin{pmatrix} \gamma_1 \\ \gamma_2 \\ \gamma_3 \end{pmatrix}}^{\gamma}
$$

where, for each $i \in \{1, 2, 3\}$, we obtain the following constraints for H_i by an application of Farkas' lemma: $\exists \lambda^i : \lambda^i \ge 0 \land \lambda^i A = C_i \land \lambda^i b \le \gamma_1$. We pass the constraints to an SMT solver and obtain the solution $\varphi = (1 \le x \land y \le 10 \land y \ge x - 3)$ with $|\{(x, y) \mid \varphi\}| = 91$. ∎

Theorem 1 (Soundness). *If* $\#\text{ITP}_{\text{LIA}}(w, \varphi^-, \varphi^+, \psi, \text{TMPL})$ *returns a solution* φ, *then* φ *is a cardinality-constrained interpolant for* φ^- *and* φ^+ *and cardinality constraint* $|\{w \mid \varphi\}| = k \land \psi$.

Proof. We show that φ satisfies conditions (1) to (3). Conditions (1) and (2) follow from the use of Farkas' lemma. Since the conditions posed by $\text{VERT}(v, \mathcal{H}, \mathcal{H}_{\mathcal{V}})$ ensure that each vertex is active (part of the polytope) and that vertices are distinct, Brion's theorem is applicable and hence the generating function of φ can be expressed as the sum of the generating functions of its vertex cones. Each of φ's vertex cones is unimodular by constraints $\text{UNIM}(v, G)$ and its generating function is hence given by the expression in Eq. 2. Summing over the evaluated rational generating functions of the vertex cones is equivalent to evaluating the sum of the rational generating functions by the fact that Laurent expansion distribute over sums. As a consequence, the expression SYMCARD corresponds to the cardinality of φ and, by the constraint in Line 15 in Fig. 1, satisfies the cardinality constraint ψ.   □

Completeness. For a given template, our method returns a solution whenever a solution expressed by the template exists, yet subject to the following two sources of incompleteness. First, solving non-linear integer arithmetic constraints is an undecidable problem and hence the call to SMTSOLVE may (soundly) fail. Second, Farkas' lemma is incomplete over the integers. Note that these sources of incompleteness did not strike on benchmarks from the literature, see Sect. 7.

5   Interpolation with Parametric Cardinalities

We now briefly discuss the parametric interpolation problem by contrasting it with the non-parametric case. Computing the number of integer points in a polytope in terms of a parameter uses the techniques described in Sect. 3. The key challenge we face when extending cardinality-constrained interpolation to the parametric case is a quantifier alternation. While in the non-parametric case the constraints CONS are quantified as $\exists \mathcal{H}_{\mathcal{V}} \exists \mathcal{V} : \text{CONS}$, introducing parameters changes the quantifier structure to $\exists \mathcal{H}_{\mathcal{V}} \forall p \exists \mathcal{V} : \text{CONS}$, where p is a tuple of parameters in the cardinality constraint. The alternation stems from the fact that the parameter valuation detemines the intesection points, that is, the vertices, for parametric polytopes. This alternation has two implication on the computation of interpolants: First, for different values of p the number of vertices of a polytope can vary due to changes in the relative position of the bounding hyperplanes. As a consequence, templates with fixed number of vertices are only valid for a specific parameter range, which is called a *chamber* [40]. We deal with this aspect by considering a predicate *cmb* that restricts the parameter range to the appropriate chamber and that satisfies the implication constraints. We then conjoin *cmb* to the inferred polytope.[3]

Second, solving the cardinality constraint requires quantifier elimination for non-linear arithmetic. For this task we devise a constraint-based method ensuring positivity of a polynomial on a given range by referring to its roots.

6   Verification of Programs with Cardinality Constraints

In this section, we sketch our algorithm #HORN for solving sets of Horn clauses with cardinality constraints. We choose Horn clauses as a basis for representing our verification conditions as they provide a uniform way to encode a variety of verification tasks [5–7,19]. The interpolation procedure #ITP$_{\text{LIA}}$ presented in Sect. 4 is a key ingredient for, but not restricted to, #HORN.

Horn Clauses with Cardinality Constraints. A *Horn clause* is a formula of the form $\varphi_0 \wedge q_1 \wedge \cdots \wedge q_k \rightarrow H$ where φ_0 is a linear arithmetic constraint, and $q_1, \ldots, q_k$ are uninterpreted predicates that we refer to as *queries*. We call the left-hand side of the implication *body* and the right-hand side *head* of the clause. H can either be a constraint φ, a query q, or a cardinality constraint of the form $|\{w \mid q\}| \leq \eta$, where η is a polynomial. By restricting cardinality constraints over queries to this shape, we ensure monotonicity, which is key for the soundness of over-approximation. For a clause $\varphi_0 \wedge q_1 \wedge \cdots \wedge q_k \rightarrow q$, we say that q *depends* on queries $q_1, \ldots, q_k$. We call a set of clauses *recursive* if the dependency relation contains a cycle, and *non-recursive* otherwise. For the semantics, we consider a *solution function* Σ that maps each query symbol q occurring in a given set of clauses into a constraint. The satisfaction relation $\Sigma \models cl$ holds for a clause $cl = (\varphi_0 \wedge q_1 \wedge \cdots \wedge q_k \rightarrow H)$ iff the body of cl entails the head, after replacing each q by $\Sigma(q)$. The lifting from clauses to sets of clauses is canonical.

Algorithm Description. #HORN takes as input a set C of recursive Horn clauses with cardinality constraints and produces as output either a solution to the clauses or a counterexample. Due the undecidability caused by recursion, #HORN may not terminate. The solver executes the following main steps: abstract inference, property checking, and refinement.

---

[3] Note that generators do not depend on the constant terms of thehyperplanes, which is why their constraints are not affected by variations in the parameters.

Abstract inference. We iteratively build a solution for the set of *inference clauses* $\mathcal{I} = \{cl \in C \mid cl = (\ldots \rightarrow q)\}$ by performing logical inference until a fixpoint is reached. This step uses abstraction to ensure that the inference terminates, where the abstraction is determined by a set of predicates *Preds*. This step is standard [19], as clauses $\mathcal{I}$ do not contain cardinality constraints.

Property checking. We check whether the constructed solution satisfies all *property clauses* in $\mathcal{P} = C \setminus \mathcal{I}$. The novelty in #HORN is the check for satisfaction of cardinality constraints $|\{w \mid \varphi\}| \leq \eta$, where φ is a linear arithmetic constraint. Here we rely on a parametric extension of Barvinok's algorithm [40], which on input φ returns a set of tuples $\mathscr{B}(\varphi, w) = \{(cmb_1, c_1), \ldots\}$ such that whenever the constraint cmb_i holds, the cardinality of $|\{w \mid \varphi\}|$ is given by the expression c_i, which may either be a polynomial c_i, or ω for the unbounded case. We hence reduce checking satisfaction of the cardinality constraint $|\{w \mid \varphi\}| \leq \eta$ to checking the following constraint.

$$\bigwedge_{(cmb,c) \in \mathscr{B}(\varphi,w)} (cmb \rightarrow c \leq \eta)$$

If the check succeeds, the algorithm returns the solution. Otherwise, the algorithm proceeds to a refinement phase to analyze the derivation that led to the violation of the property clause.

Refinement. We construct a counterexample, i.e., a set *CEX* of recursion-free Horn clauses with cardinality constraints that represents the derivation that led to the violation of the property clause. This counterexample may either be genuine or spurious due to abstraction. To determine which it is, we rely on a solver for *non-recursive* clauses with cardinality constraints that either produces a solution for the clauses or reports that no such solution exists. If no solution exists, the algorithm returns the counterexample that represents a genuine error derivation. Otherwise it uses #ITP$_{\text{LIA}}$ to eliminate the cardinality constraint from the clauses thus producing a set of *cardinality-free* Horn clauses. We solve these clauses using existing methods [22] and obtain a set of predicates that we use to refine the abstraction.

7 Experiments

We implemented our method in SICStus Prolog, and use its built-in constraint solver for the simplification and projection of linear constraints, HSF [19] for solving recursion- and cardinality-free Horn clauses, and Z3 [16] for non-linear/boolean constraint solving. We use BARVINOK [38] for checking whether a solution candidate satisfies a cardinality constraint. We use a 1.3 Ghz Intel Core i5 computer with 4 GB of RAM.

Benchmarks from the literature. We use #HORN to analyze a set of examples taken from the recent literature on resource bound computation (in particular:

Table 1. Application of #HORN on three classes of examples.

Program	Bound	Time
Dis1 [21]	$max(n - x_0, 0) + max(m - y_0, 0)$	0.19s
Dis2 [21]	$n - x_0 + m - z_0$	0.17s
SimpleSingle [21]	n	0.11s
SequentialSingle [21]	n	0.11s
NestedSingle [21]	$n + 1$	0.15s
SimpleSingle2 [21]	$max(n, m)$	0.13s
SimpleMultiple [21]	$n + m$	0.16s
NestedMultiple [21]	$max(n - x_0, 0) + max(m - y_0, 0)$	0.08s
SimpleMultipleDep [21]	$n \cdot (m + 1)$	0.15s
NestedMultipleDep [21]	$n \cdot (m + 1)$	0.09s
IsortList [23]	$n^2 \cdot m$	0.19s
LCS [23]	$n \cdot x$	0.15s
Example 1 [42]	n	0.15s
Sum [24]	$2n + 6$	0.15s
Flatten [24]	$8l + 8$	0.13s

(a) Examples of resource bound verification [21,23,24,42], with non-linear and disjunctive bounds on running time (the upper part of the tabe) and heap space usage (the lower part of the table), as well as imperative and functional programs. #HORN execution times are slightly faster than the literature. All bounds are precise.

Program	Bound	Time
mcm	$\frac{(n+1) \cdot (n+2)}{2}$	0.6s
band matrix	$3n + 1$	0.8s

(b) Examples tracking relational dependencies between variables.

Leakage bound, bits	Initialization	Time
$log(1)$	$j = i$	1s
$log(\frac{n}{2})$	$j = i + \frac{n}{2}$	0.7s
$log(\frac{n}{3})$	$j = \frac{2 \cdot i + n}{3}$	0.7s

(c) Synthesis of countermeasures.

time and heap space), with results given in Table 1a. We find that #HORN is able to prove all bounds in the literature while being slightly faster on average.

The time consumption of loops is bounded by synthesising a polytope containing all tuples of loop counter valuations. For example, for two loops with counters i and j bounded by parameters n and m, we synthesize a polytope of the form: $a \leq i \leq n + b \wedge c \leq j \leq m + d$, where a, b, c, d are inferred by our method. For heap consumption, we use the cost model of [24]. We encode max using disjunctions.

Dealing with relational dependencies. We use #HORN to analyze programs mcm for matrix chain multiplication of Sect. 2 and an array manipulating program *band matrix* for which code is provided in [37], with results in Table 1b. These examples require the tracking of relational dependencies between variables. The example mcm is particularly challenging as it requires reasoning about recursive function calls. We are not aware of any other method that can handle programs with both features. We use a template specifying that the sought polytope consists of three and four symbolic vertices, respectively. Choosing a template that is not expressive enough might only allow to prove coarser bounds, however, one can automate the problem of finding an appropriate template by iterating over templates with an increasing number of symbolic vertices.

Synthesis of countermeasures. By relying on recursive Horn clauses as input language, #HORN is readily applicable to a number of verification questions that go beyond reachability. We illustrate this using the example of procedure index(a, e), which returns the first position of an element e in an array a. Note that the execution time of index (modeled by the variable t) reveals the position of e. We apply #HORN for synthesizing a padding countermeasure against this timing side channel. Namely, we seek to instantiate the initialization of the variable

```
int index(a, e) {
  int r=-1; t=0;
  for(i=0; r<0 && i<n; i++){
    if (a[i]==e) r=i;
    t++;
  }
  /* Padding */
  for(j=?; j<n, j++) t++;
  return r;
}
/* assert: bound cardinality of
   set of final values of t. */
```

j such that it provides enough padding for a given bound on leakage. This is achieved by bounding the cardinality of the set of possible final values of t. We add an additional clause that constrains the cardinality of values for t upon termination, as the logarithm of this number corresponds to the amount of leaked information in bits, see e.g. [36]. Table 1c provides the timings and synthesized initialization of j for different bounds on leakage.

8   Related Work

Counting integer points in polytopes. The theory of counting integer points in polytopes has found wide-spread applications in program analysis. All applications we are aware of (including [2,17,28,40]) compute cardinalities for given polytopes, whereas our interpolation method computes polytopes for given cardinality constraints.

Verdoolaege et al. [40] also derive symbolic expressions for the number of integer points in parametric polytopes. In their approach, the parameter governs only the offset of the bounding hyperplanes (and hence the position of the vertices of the polytope) but not their tilt (and hence not the generators of the vertex cones). The advantage of fixing the vertex cones is that Barvinok's decomposition can be applied to handle arbitrary polytope shapes. In contrast, our interpolation procedure #ITP$_{\mathrm{LIA}}$ (see Sect. 4) leaves the vertices *and* the generators of the vertex cones symbolic, up to constraints that ensure their unimodularity. The benefit of this approach is the additional degree of freedom for the synthesis procedure. #HORN leverages both approaches: the one from [40] for checking cardinality constraints, and #ITP$_{\mathrm{LIA}}$ for refining the abstraction.

Recently, [17] presented a logic and decision procedure for satisfiability in the presence of cardinality constraints for the case of linear arithmetic. In contrast, we focus on synthesizing formulas that satisfy cardinality constraints, rather than checking their satisfiability.

Resource bounds. In [26] a static analysis estimates the worst case execution time of non-parametric loops using the box domain. To ensure precision, the widening operator intersects the current abstraction with polytopes derived from conditional statements. In contrast, our approach generates abstraction consisting of parametric unimodular polytopes (which include boxes as a special case). In [21], the authors compute parametric resource and time bounds by instrumenting the program with (multiple-) counters, using static analysis to compute a bound for the counters, and combining the results to yield a bound for the entire program. In contrast, we fit polytopes over each iteration domain of the program, thus avoiding the need to infer counter placement and enabling higher precision by tracking dependencies between variables. In [39] a pattern-matching based method extracts polytopes representing the iteration domain of for-loops from C source. In contrast our method operates on unstructured programs represented as Horn clauses. In [23,24], a type system for the amortized analysis for higher-order, polymorphic programs is developed. Their focus lies on recursive data-types while we mostly deal with recursion/loops over the integers. In [10], this line of work is extended to the verification of C programs. In [1,30] closed-form bounds on resource usage are established by solving recurrence relations.

Quantitative verification. Existing verification methods for other theories rely on cardinality extensions of SAT [18], or Boolean algebra of (uninterpreted) sets [25], multisets [31], and fractional collections [32]. These approaches focus on either computing the model size or checking satisfiability of a formula containing cardinality constraints. Cardinalities of uninterpreted sets are also used in [20] for establishing termination and memory usage bounds based on fixed abstractions. Finally, CEGAR approaches for weighted transition systems have been studied in [11,12]. These approaches considers abstractions for mean-payoff objectives such as limit-average or discounted sum.

9   Conclusion

We applied the theory of counting integer points in polytopes to devise an algorithm for a cardinality-constrained extension of Craig interpolation. This algorithm proceeds by posing constraints on a symbolic polytope that specify both its shape and cardinality and then solves the constraints via an SMT solver. We embedded our interpolation procedure into a solver for recursive Horn clauses with cardinality constraints and experimentally demonstrated its potential.

Acknowledgments. We thank Sven Verdoolaege for valuable feedback. Boris Köpf was partially funded by Spanish Project TIN2012-39391-C04-01 StrongSoft and Madrid Regional Project S2013/ICE-2731 N-GREENS. Klaus v. Gleissenthall was supported by a Microsoft Research scholarship.

References

1. Albert, E., Arenas, P., Genaim, S., Puebla, G., Zanardini, D.: Cost analysis of java bytecode. In: De Nicola, R. (ed.) ESOP 2007. LNCS, vol. 4421, pp. 157–172. Springer, Heidelberg (2007)
2. Backes, M., Köpf, B., Rybalchenko, A.: Automatic discovery and quantification of information leaks. In: IEEE S and P (2009)
3. Barvinok A.: A polynomial time algorithm for counting integral points in polyhedra when the dimension is fixed. In: FOCS (1993)
4. Barvinok, A.: A Course in Convexity. American Mathematical Society (2002)
5. Beyene, T.A., Chaudhuri, S., Popeea, C., Rybalchenko, A.: A constraint-based approach to solving games on infinite graphs. In POPL (2014)
6. Beyene, T.A., Popeea, C., Rybalchenko, A.: Solving existentially quantified Horn clauses. In: Sharygina, N., Veith, H. (eds.) CAV 2013. LNCS, vol. 8044, pp. 869–882. Springer, Heidelberg (2013)
7. Bjørner, N., McMillan, K., Rybalchenko, A.: On solving universally quantified Horn clauses. In: Logozzo, F., Fähndrich, M. (eds.) Static Analysis. LNCS, vol. 7935, pp. 105–125. Springer, Heidelberg (2013)
8. Bjørner, N., McMillan, K.L., Rybalchenko, A.: Program verification as satisfiability modulo theories. In: SMT@IJCAR (2012)
9. Brion, M.: Points entiers dans les polyedres convexes. Ann. Sci. Ecole Norm. Sup. **21**(4), 653–663 (1988)
10. Carbonneaux, Q., Hoffmann, J., Shao, Z.: Compositional certified resource bounds. In: PLDI (2015)
11. Cerny, P., Henzinger, T.A., Radhakrishna, A.: Quantitative abstraction refinement. In: POPL, ACM (2013)
12. Chatterjee, K., Pavlogiannis, A., Velner, Y.: Quantitative interprocedural analysis. In: POPL (2015)
13. Colón, M.A., Sankaranarayanan, S., Sipma, H.B.: Linear invariant generation using non-linear constraint solving. In: Hunt Jr., W.A., Somenzi, F. (eds.) CAV 2003. LNCS, vol. 2725, pp. 420–432. Springer, Heidelberg (2003)
14. Cormen, T.H., Stein, C., Rivest, R.L., Leiserson, C.E.: Introduction to Algorithms, 2nd edn. McGraw-Hill Higher Education, Boston (2001)
15. De Loera, J.A., Hemmecke, R., Tauzer, J., Yoshida, R.: Effective lattice point counting in rational convex polytopes. J. Symb. Comp. **38**(4), 1273–1302 (2004)
16. de Moura, L., Bjørner, N.S.: Z3: an efficient SMT solver. In: Ramakrishnan, C.R., Rehof, J. (eds.) TACAS 2008. LNCS, vol. 4963, pp. 337–340. Springer, Heidelberg (2008)
17. Fredrikson, M., Jha, S.: Satisfiability modulo counting: A new approach for analyzing privacy properties. In: LICS, IEEE (2014)
18. Gomes, C.P., Sabharwal, A., Selman, B.: Model counting. In: Biere, A., Heule, M., Maaren, H.V., Walsh, T. (eds.) Handbook of Satisfiability. IOS Press, Amsterdam (2009)
19. Grebenshchikov, S., Lopes, N.P., Popeea, C., Rybalchenko, A.: Synthesizing software verifiers from proof rules. In: PLDI (2012)
20. Gulwani, S., Lev-Ami, T., Sagiv, M.: A combination framework for tracking partition sizes. In: POPL. ACM (2009)
21. Gulwani, S., Mehra, K.K., Chilimbi, T.: Speed: precise and efficient static estimation of program computational complexity. In: POPL (2009)

22. Gupta, A., Popeea, C., Rybalchenko, A.: Predicate abstraction and refinement for verifying multi-threaded programs. In: POPL (2011)
23. Hoffmann, J., Aehlig, K., Hofmann, M.: Multivariate amortized resource analysis. In: POPL (2011)
24. Jost, S., Hammond, K., Loidl, H.-W., Hofmann, M.: Static determination of quantitative resource usage for higher-order programs. In: POPL (2010)
25. Kuncak, V., Nguyen, H.H., Rinard, M.: An algorithm for deciding BAPA: boolean algebra with presburger arithmetic. In: Nieuwenhuis, R. (ed.) CADE 2005. LNCS (LNAI), vol. 3632, pp. 260–277. Springer, Heidelberg (2005)
26. Lokuciejewski, P., Cordes, D., Falk, H., Marwedel, P.: A fast and precise static loop analysis based on abstract interpretation, program slicing and polytope models. In: CGO (2009)
27. Luu, L., Shinde, S., Saxena, P., Demsky, B.: A model counter for constraints over unbounded strings. In: PLDI. ACM (2014)
28. Mardziel, P., Magill, S., Hicks, M., Srivatsa, M.: Dynamic enforcement of knowledge-based security policies. In: CSF. IEEE (2011)
29. McMillan, K.L.: An interpolating theorem prover. TCS **345**(1), 101–121 (2005)
30. Navas, J.A., Méndez-Lojo, M., Hermenegildo, M.V.: User-definable resource usage bounds analysis for java bytecode. Electr. Notes Theor. Comput. Sci. **253**(5), 65–82 (2009)
31. Piskac, R., Kuncak, V.: Decision procedures for multisets with cardinality constraints. In: Logozzo, F., Peled, D.A., Zuck, L.D. (eds.) VMCAI 2008. LNCS, vol. 4905, pp. 218–232. Springer, Heidelberg (2008)
32. Piskac, R., Kuncak, V.: Fractional Collections with Cardinality Bounds, and Mixed Linear Arithmetic with Stars. In: Kaminski, M., Martini, S. (eds.) CSL 2008. LNCS, vol. 5213, pp. 124–138. Springer, Heidelberg (2008)
33. Podelski, A., Rybalchenko, A.: A complete method for the synthesis of linear ranking functions. In: Steffen, B., Levi, G. (eds.) VMCAI 2004. LNCS, vol. 2937, pp. 239–251. Springer, Heidelberg (2004)
34. Rümmer, P., Hojjat, H., Kuncak, V.: Disjunctive interpolants for Horn-clause verification. In: Sharygina, N., Veith, H. (eds.) CAV 2013. LNCS, vol. 8044, pp. 347–363. Springer, Heidelberg (2013)
35. Schrijver, A.: Theory of Linear and Integer Programming. Wiley, Chichester (1999)
36. Smith, G.: On the foundations of quantitative information flow. In: de Alfaro, L. (ed.) FOSSACS 2009. LNCS, vol. 5504, pp. 288–302. Springer, Heidelberg (2009)
37. von Gleissenthall, K., Köpf, B., Rybalchenko, A.: Symbolic polytopes for quantitative interpolation and verification - extended version (2015). https://www7.in.tum.de/~gleissen/papers/symb-polytopes.pdf
38. Verdoolaege, S.: Barvinok. http://freecode.com/projects/barvinok
39. Verdoolaege, S., Grosser, T.: Polyhedral extraction tool. In: IPACT (2012)
40. Verdoolaege, S., Seghir, R., Beyls, K., Loechner, V., Bruynooghe, M.: Counting integer points in parametric polytopes using Barvinok's rational functions. Algorithmica **48**(1), 37–66 (2007)
41. Wolfram, S.: Wolfram alpha, series expansion. http://www.wolframalpha.com/examples/SeriesExpansions.html
42. Zuleger, F., Gulwani, S., Sinn, M., Veith, H.: Bound analysis of imperative programs with the size-change abstraction. In: Yahav, E. (ed.) Static Analysis. LNCS, vol. 6887, pp. 280–297. Springer, Heidelberg (2011)

Adaptive Aggregation of Markov Chains: Quantitative Analysis of Chemical Reaction Networks

Alessandro Abate[1], Luboš Brim[2], Milan Češka[1,2(✉)], and Marta Kwiatkowska[1]

[1] Department of Computer Science, University of Oxford, Oxford, UK
milan.ceska@cs.ox.ac.uk
[2] Faculty of Informatics, Masaryk University, Brno, Czech Republic

Abstract. Quantitative analysis of Markov models typically proceeds through numerical methods or simulation-based evaluation. Since the state space of the models can often be large, exact or approximate state aggregation methods (such as lumping or bisimulation reduction) have been proposed to improve the scalability of the numerical schemes. However, none of the existing numerical techniques provides general, explicit bounds on the approximation error, a problem particularly relevant when the level of accuracy affects the soundness of verification results. We propose a novel numerical approach that combines the strengths of aggregation techniques (state-space reduction) with those of simulation-based approaches (automatic updates that adapt to the process dynamics). The key advantage of our scheme is that it provides rigorous precision guarantees under different measures. The new approach, which can be used in conjunction with time uniformisation techniques, is evaluated on two models of chemical reaction networks, a signalling pathway and a prokaryotic gene expression network: it demonstrates marked improvement in accuracy without performance degradation, particularly when compared to known state-space truncation techniques.

1 Introduction

Markov models are widely used in many areas of science and engineering in order to evaluate the probability of certain events of interest. Quantitative analysis of time-bounded properties of Markov models typically proceeds through numerical analysis, via solution of equations yielding the probability of the system residing in a given state at a given time, or via simulation-based exploration of its execution paths. For continuous-time Markov chains (CTMCs), a commonly employed method is uniformisation (also known as Jensen's method), which is

This work has been partially supported by the ERC Advanced Grant VERIWARE, the Czech Ministry of Education, Youth, and Sport project No. CZ.1.07/2.3.00/30.0009 (M. Češka), the Czech Grant Agency grant No. GA15-11089S (L. Brim), the John Fell Oxford University Press (OUP) Research Fund, and by the European Commission IAPP project AMBI 324432.

D. Kroening and C.S. Păsăreanu (Eds.): CAV 2015, Part I, LNCS 9206, pp. 195–213, 2015.
DOI: 10.1007/978-3-319-21690-4_12

based on the discretisation of the original CTMC and on the numerical computation of transient probabilities (that is, probability distributions over time). This can be combined with graph-theoretic techniques for probabilistic model checking against temporal logic properties [4].

There are many situations where highly accurate probability estimates are necessary, for example for reliability analysis in safety-critical systems or for predictive modelling in scientific experiments, but this is difficult to achieve in practice because of the state-space explosion problem. Imprecise values are known to lead to lack of robustness, in the sense that the satisfaction of temporal logic formulae can be affected by small changes to the formula bound or the probability distribution of the model. Simulation-based analysis does not suffer from this problem and additionally allows dynamic adaptation of the sampling procedure, as e.g. in importance sampling, to the current values of the transient probability distribution. However, this analysis provides only weak precision guarantees in the form of confidence intervals. In order to enable the handling of larger state spaces, two types of techniques have been introduced: state aggregation and state-space truncation. State aggregation techniques build a reduced state space using lumping [6] or bisimulation quotient [21], and have been proposed both in exact [21] and approximate form [10], with the latter deemed more robust than than the exact ones [11]. State-space truncation methods, e.g. fast adaptive uniformisation (FAU) [9,23], on the other hand, only consider the states whose probability mass is not negligible, while clustering states where the probability is less than a given threshold and computing the total probability lost. Unfortunately, though these methods allow the user to specify a desired precision, none provide explicit and general error bounds that can be used to quantify the accuracy of the numerical computation: more precisely, these truncation methods provide a lower bound on the probability distributions in time, and the total probability lost can be used to derive a (rather conservative) upper bound on the (point-wise) approximation error as the sum of the lower bound and of the total probability lost.

Key Contributions. We propose a novel adaptive aggregation method for Markov chains that allows us to control its approximation error based on explicitly derived error bounds. The method can be combined with numerical techniques such as uniformisation [9,23], typically employed in quantitative verification of Markov chains. The method works over a finite time interval by clustering the state space of a Markov chain sequentially in time, where the quality of the current aggregation is quantified by a number of metrics. These metrics, in conjunction with user-specified precision requirements, drive the process by automatically and adaptively reclustering its state space depending on the explicit error bounds. In contrast to related simulation-based approaches in the literature [13,31] that employ the current probability distribution of the aggregated model to selectively cluster the regions of the state space containing negligible probability mass, our novel use of the derived error bounds allows far greater accuracy and flexibility as it accounts also for the past history of the probability mass within specific clusters.

To the best of our knowledge, despite recent attempts [10, 11] the development and use of explicit bounds on the error associated with a clustering procedure is new for the simulation and analysis of Markov chains. The versatility of the method is further enhanced by employing a variety of different metrics to assess the approximation quality. More specifically, we use the following to control the error: (1) the probability distributions in time (namely, the point-wise difference between concrete and abstract distributions), (2) the time-wise likelihood of events (L_1 norm and total variation distance), as well as (3) the probability of satisfying a temporal logic specification.

We implement our method in conjunction with uniformisation for the computation of probability distributions of the process in time, as well as time-bounded probabilities (a key procedure for probabilistic model checking against temporal logic specifications), and evaluate it on two case studies of chemical reaction networks. Compared to fast adaptive uniformisation as implemented in PRISM [9], currently the best performing technique in this setting, we demonstrate that our method yields a marked improvement in numerical precision without degrading its performance.

Related Work. (Bio-)chemical reaction networks can be naturally analysed using discrete stochastic models. Since the discrete state space of these models can be large or even infinite, a number of numerical approaches have been proposed to alleviate the associated state-space explosion problem. For biochemical models with large populations of chemical components, fluid (mean-field) approximation techniques can be applied [5] and extended to approximate higher-order moments [12]: these deterministic approximations lead to a set of ordinary differential equations. In [16], a hybrid method is proposed that captures the dynamics using a discrete stochastic description in the case of small populations and a moment-based deterministic description for large populations. An alternative approach assumes that the transient probabilities can be compactly approximated based on quasi product forms [3]. All the mentioned methods do not provide explicit accuracy bounds of approximation.

A widely studied model reduction method for Markov models is state aggregation based on lumping [6] or (bi-)simulation equivalence [4], with the latter notion in its exact [21] or approximate [10] form. In particular, approximate notions of equivalence have led to new abstraction/refinement techniques for the numerical verification of Markov models over finite [11] as well as uncountably-infinite state spaces [1, 2, 26]. Related to these techniques, [27] presents an algorithm to approximate probability distributions of a Markov process forward in time, which serves as an inspiration for our adaptive scheme. From the perspective of simulations, adaptive aggregations are discussed in [13] but no precision error is given: our work differs by developing an adaptive aggregation scheme, where a formal error analysis steers the adaptation.

An alternative method to deal with large/infinite state spaces is truncation, where a lower bound on the transient probability distribution of the concrete model is computed, and the total probability mass that is lost due to this truncation is quantified. Such methods include finite state projections [24], sliding window abstractions [18], or fast adaptive uniformisation (FAU) [9,23]. Apart from truncating the state space by neglecting states with insignificant probability mass, FAU dynamically adapts the uniformisation rate, thus significantly reducing the number of uniformisation steps [30]. The efficiency of the truncation techniques depends on the distribution of the significant part of the probability mass over the states, and may result in poor accuracy if this mass is spread out over a large number of states, or whenever the selected window of states does not align with a property of interest.

Summarising, whilst a number of methods have been devised to study or to simulate complex biochemical models, in most cases a rigorous error analysis is missing [13,22,31], or the error analysis cannot be effectively used to obtain accurate bounds on the probability distribution or on the likelihood of events of interest [17].

Structure of this Article. Section 2 introduces the sequential aggregation approach to approximate the transient probability distribution (that is, the distribution over time) of discrete-time Markov chains, and quantifies bounds on the introduced error according to three different metrics. Section 3 applies the aggregation method for temporal logic verification of Markov chains. In Sect. 4, we implement adaptive aggregation for continuous-time Markov chain models of chemical reaction networks, in conjunction with known techniques such as uniformisation and threshold truncation. Finally, Sect. 5 discusses experimental results.

2   Computation of the Transient Probability Distribution

We first work with discrete-time labelled Markov chains (LMC), and in Sect. 4 we show how to apply the obtained results to (labelled) continuous-time Markov chains. Formally, an LMC is defined as a triple (S, P, L), where

- $S = \{s_1, \ldots, s_n\}$ is the finite state space of size n;
- $P : S \times S \to [0,1]$ is the transition probability matrix, which is such that $\forall j \in S : \sum_{i=1}^{n} P_{ji} = \sum_{i=1}^{n} P(j, i) = 1$;
- $L : S \to 2^{\Sigma}$ is a labelling function, where Σ is a finite alphabet built from a set of atomic propositions.

Whenever clear from the context, we refer to the model simply as (S, P). The model is initialised via distribution $\pi_0 : S \to [0,1], \sum_{s \in S} \pi_0(s) = 1$, and its transient probability distribution at time step $k \geq 0$ is

$$\pi_{k+1}(s) = \sum_{s' \in S} \pi_k(s')P(s', s), \qquad (1)$$

or more concisely as $\pi_{k+1} = \pi_k P$ (where the π_k's are row vectors). We are interested in providing a compact representation and an efficient computation of the vectors π_k.

Sequential Aggregations of the Markov Chain. Consider the finite time interval of interest $[0, 1, \ldots, N]$. Divide this interval into a given number (q) of sub-intervals, namely select $N_1, N_2, \ldots, N_q : \sum_{i=1}^{q} N_i = N$, and consider the evolution of the model within the corresponding l-th interval $[\sum_{i=0}^{l-1} N_i, \sum_{i=0}^{l} N_i]$, for $l = 1, \ldots q$, and where we have set $N_0 = 0$.

We assume that a specific state-space aggregation is given, for each of the q sub-intervals of time. Later, in Sect. 4, we show how such aggregations can be obtained adaptively, based on a number of measures (such as the current value of the aggregated transient probability distribution, or the accrued aggregation error in time). In particular, at the l-th step (where $l = 1, \ldots, q$), the state space is partitioned (clustered) as $S = \cup_{i=1}^{m_l} S_i^l$ (consider that the cardinality index m_l has been reasonably selected so that $m_l << n$), and denote the *abstract (aggregated) state space* simply as S^l and its elements (the *abstract states*) with $\phi_i, i = 1, \ldots, m_l$. Introduce abstraction and refinement maps as $\alpha^l : S \to S^l$ and $A^l : S^l \to 2^S$, respectively – the first takes concrete points into abstract ones, whereas the latter relates abstract states to concrete partitioning sets. For any pair of indices $i, j = 1, \ldots, m_l$, define the abstract transition matrix as

$$P^l(\phi_j, \phi_i) \doteq \frac{1}{\mid A^l(\phi_i) \mid} \sum_{s \in A^l(\phi_i)} \sum_{s' \in A^l(\phi_j)} P(s', s).$$

The intuition behind the aggregated matrix P^l is that it encompasses the average *incoming* probability from clusters S_j to S_i. The shape of this matrix is justified by the structure of the update equation in (1). Given the aggregated Markov chain, we shall work, for all $s \in S^l$, with the following recursions:

$$\pi_{k+1}^l(s) = \sum_{s' \in S^1} \pi_k^l(s') P^l(s', s).$$

The smaller, aggregated model (S^l, P^l) serves as basis for an approximate computation of the transient probability in time: we now calculate an explicit upper bound on the approximation error. In order to quantify this error, we define a function $\epsilon^l : [1, \ldots, m_l]^2 \to [0, 1]$, as follows:

$$\epsilon^l(j, i) \doteq \max_{s \in S_i^l} \left| \frac{\mid S_i^l \mid}{\mid S_j^l \mid} P(S_j, s) - P^l(\phi_j, \phi_i) \right|. \qquad (2)$$

Intuitively, this quantity accounts for the difference between the average incoming probability between a pair (j, i) of partitioning sets, and the worst-case (rescaled) point-wise incoming probability between those two sets. Introduce the terms $\epsilon^l(j) := \sum_{i=1}^{m_l} \epsilon^l(j, i)$.

Finally, define, for all $s \in S$, $\tilde{\pi}_k^l(s) = \pi_k^l(\alpha^l(s)) / \mid A^l(\alpha^l(s)) \mid$ as a (normalised) piecewise constant approximation of the abstract functions π_k^l. Functions $\tilde{\pi}_k^l$, being defined over the concrete state space S, will be employed for comparison with the original distribution functions π_k. Specifically, for the initial interval $[N_0, N_1]$ (with $l = 1$), approximate the initial distribution π_0 by π_0^1

as: $\forall s \in S^1, \pi_0^1(s) = \sum_{s' \in A^1(s)} \pi_0(s')$. Similarly, we have that $\forall s \in S, \tilde{\pi}_0^1(s) = \pi_0^1(\alpha^1(s)) / \mid A^1(\alpha^1(s)) \mid$.

Remark 1. Exact and approximate probabilistic bisimulations [10,21] build a quotient or a cover of the state space of the original model based on matching or approximating the "outgoing probability" from concrete states – for example, exact probabilistic bisimulation compares, for state pairs (s_1, s_2) within a partition, the "outgoing" probabilities $P(s_1, B)$ and $P(s_2, B)$ over partitions B. On the other hand, in (2) we approximate the "incoming probability", as motivated by the approximation of the recursions in (1). □

Explicit Error Bounds for the Quality of the Sequential Aggregations. Let us consider the aggregated model (S^1, P^1) (for $l = 1$) and, given the aggregated vector π_0^1, the time-wise updates $\pi_{k+1}^1 = \pi_k^1 P^1, k = N_0, \ldots, N_1 - 1$. Introduce the interpolated vectors $\tilde{\pi}_{k+1}^1(s), s \in S$, defined as $\tilde{\pi}_{k+1}^1(s) = \pi_{k+1}^1(\alpha^1(s)) / \mid A^1(\alpha^1(s)) \mid$. We are interested in a bound on the point-wise error defined over the concrete state space, namely $\forall s \in S, k = N_0, \ldots, N_1$, $|\pi_k(s) - \tilde{\pi}_k^1(s)|$, or equivalently a bound for $\left| \pi_k(s) - \frac{\pi_k^1(\alpha^1(s))}{|A^1(\alpha^1(s))|} \right|$. Such a point-wise bound directly allows for expressing a global error for the infinity norm of the difference between the two distribution vectors, namely

$$\left\| \pi_k - \tilde{\pi}_k^1 \right\|_\infty = \max_{s \in S} \left| \pi_k(s) - \tilde{\pi}_k^1(s) \right|.$$

Beyond the first aggregation $(l = 1)$, the next statement explicitly characterises such a bound over the entire sequence of q re-aggregations and the time interval $[0, 1, \ldots, N]$.

Proposition 1. *Consider a sequential q-step aggregation strategy, characterised by times $N_l : \sum_{l=1}^q N_l = N$, partitions $S = \cup_{i=1}^{m_l} S_i^l$, and matrices P^l. We obtain*

$$\left| \pi_N(s) - \tilde{\pi}_N^q(s) \right| \leq c(s)^N \left| \pi_0(s) - \tilde{\pi}_0^1(s) \right|$$

$$+ \sum_{l=1}^q c(s)^{N - \sum_{i=0}^l N_i} \left\{ \frac{1}{\mid A^l(\alpha^l(s)) \mid} \sum_{j=1}^{m_l} \epsilon^l(j, \alpha^l(s)) \sum_{k=0}^{N_l - 1} \pi_{\sum_{i=0}^{l-1} N_i + k}^l(j) + \gamma_{l-1}^l(s) \right\},$$

where we have set $c(s) = P(S, s)$, and $\gamma_{l-1}^l(s) = \left| \tilde{\pi}_{\sum_{i=0}^{l-1} N_i}^{l-1}(s) - \tilde{\pi}_{\sum_{i=0}^{l-1} N_i}^l(s) \right|$ for $l = 1, \ldots, q$, with $\gamma_0^1(s) = 0, \forall s \in S$.

Remark 2. A few comments on the structure of the error bounds are in order. The overall error is composed of two main contributions, one depending on the error accrued within single aggregation steps, and the other $(\gamma_{l-1}^l(s))$ depending on the q re-aggregations (that is, an update from the current partition to the next).

The first term of the first contribution further depends on the point-wise error in the distributions initialised at each aggregation, namely, $\left| \pi_{\sum_{i=0}^{l} N_i}(s) - \tilde{\pi}^l_{\sum_{i=0}^{l} N_i}(s) \right|$: this quantity, discounted by the N_l-th power of the factor $c(s)$ (accounting for contractive or expansive dynamics), builds up recursively to yield the global (over the q aggregation steps) quantity $c(s)^N \left| \pi_0(s) - \tilde{\pi}^1_0(s) \right|$. The second term of the first contribution, on the other hand, accounts for the error due to the approximation of the transition probability matrix (terms ϵ^l), averaged over the accrued running distribution functions (factors π^l).

The intuition on factor $c(s)$ is the following: if the model is "contractive" (in a certain probabilistic sense) towards a point s, the factor $c(s)$ is likely to be greater than one; on the other hand, if the distribution in time is "dispersed," then it is likely that $c(s) < 1$ over a large subset of the state space. The quantity $c(s) = P(S, s)$ might be decreased if we work on a subset of S: this might happen with a discrete-time chain obtained from a corresponding continuous-time model via FAU [9, 23], or through the interaction of the factor $c(s), s \in S$, with atomic propositions defined specifically over subsets of the state space S.   □

Corollary 1. *Consider the same setup as in Proposition 1. A bound for the quantity $\| \pi_N - \tilde{\pi}^q_N \|_\infty$ can be obtained from that in Proposition 1 by straightforward adaptation and setting $c = \max_{s \in S} c(s)$, and $\gamma^l_{l-1} = \max_{s \in S} \gamma^l_{l-1}(s), l = 1, \ldots, q$.*

In addition to point-wise errors, we seek a bound for the following global error,

$$\left\| \pi_k - \tilde{\pi}^1_k \right\|_1 = \sum_{s \in S} \left| \pi_k(s) - \tilde{\pi}^1_k(s) \right|, \quad \forall k = 0, \ldots, N_1,$$

and its further extension to successive aggregations and time steps $k = N_1 + 1, \ldots, N$. This L_1-norm measure is related to the "total variation distance" over events in the σ-algebra 2^S at each time step k. This measure is commonly used in related literature [8, 29], and refers to differences in probability of events defined over sets in S at a specific point in time k. The corresponding error bound is explicitly quantified as follows.

Proposition 2. *Consider a q-step sequential aggregation strategy characterised by the times $N_l : \sum_{l=1}^q N_l = N$, partitions $S = \cup_{i=1}^{m_l} S^l_i$, and matrices P^l. We obtain*

$$\left\| \pi_N - \tilde{\pi}^q_N \right\|_1 \le \left\| \pi_0 - \tilde{\pi}^1_0 \right\|_1 + \sum_{l=1}^q \left\{ \sum_{j=1}^{m_l} \epsilon^l(j) \sum_{k=0}^{N_l-1} \pi^l_{\sum_{i=0}^{l-1} N_i + k}(j) + \Gamma^l_{l-1} \right\},$$

where for $l = 1, \ldots, q$, $\Gamma^l_{l-1} = \left\| \tilde{\pi}^{l-1}_{\sum_{i=0}^{l-1} N_i} - \tilde{\pi}^l_{\sum_{i=0}^{l-1} N_i} \right\|_1$, and where we have set $\Gamma^1_0 = 0$.

3 Aggregations for Model Checking of Time-Bounded Specifications

In Sect. 2, we have introduced a sequential aggregation procedure to approximate the computation of the transient probability distribution of a Markov chain. The derived bounds allow for a comparison of aggregated and concrete models either point-wise, or according to a global measure of the differences in the probability of events over the state space, at a specific point in time. We now show how to employ the aggregation method for quantitative verification against probabilistic temporal logics such as PCTL. We focus on a bounded variant of the probabilistic safety (invariance) property, which corresponds to time-bounded invariance for continuous-time Markov chains.

Consider the LMP (S, P, L). We focus on properties expressed over the atomic propositions AP, namely the set of finite strings over the labels 2^{AP}, and on how to approximately compute the likelihood associated to such strings. In particular, consider a step-bounded safety formula [4], namely $\mathbb{P}_{=?}(G^{\leq N}\Phi)$, where $N \in \mathbb{N}$, and $\Phi \in 2^{\Sigma}$, $\mathrm{Sat}(\Phi) \subseteq S^{1}$. This specification expresses the likelihood that a trajectory, initialised according to a distribution (say, π_0) over the state space S, resides within set Φ over the time interval $[0, 1, \dots, N]$. The specification of interest can be characterised as follows: for any $s \in S, k = 0, 1, \dots, N-1$,

$$V_0(s) = 1_{\Phi}(s)\pi_0(s), \qquad V_{k+1}(s) = 1_{\Phi}(s)\sum_{s' \in S} V_k(s')P(s', s),$$

so that $\mathbb{P}_{=?}(G^{\leq N}\Phi) = \sum_{s \in S} V_N(s)$. It is well known that the computed quantity depends on the choice of the initial distribution π_0 (which can in particular be a point mass for a distinguished initial state). As should be clear from the recursion above (use of indicator functions 1_{Φ}), it is sufficient to restrict the recursive updates to within the set of points labelled by Φ.

As before, consider the global finite interval $[0, 1, \dots, N]$, and divide it via intervals of duration $N_1, N_2, \dots, N_q : \sum_{i=1}^{q} N_i = N$. Specifically, for the initial interval $[N_0, N_1]$ (corresponding to index $q = 1$), partition set Φ as $\Phi = \cup_{i=1}^{m_1}\Phi_i^1$ – notice that the partition does not cross the boundaries of the set Φ. Thus $S^1 = \Phi^1 \cup \{a_1\} = \{1, \dots, m_1, a_1\}$, where a_1 is associated with the complement set $S\backslash\Phi$. Introduce abstraction and refinement maps as $\alpha^1 : S \to S^1$ and $A^1 : S^1 \to 2^S$, the abstract transition matrix P^1, and function $\epsilon^1 : [1, \dots, m_1]^2 \to [0, 1]$ as

$$\epsilon^1(j, i) \doteq \max_{s \in \Phi_i^1} \left| \frac{|\Phi_i^1|}{|\Phi_j^1|}P(\Phi_j^1, s) - P^1(\phi_j, \phi_i) \right|.$$

Further, approximate π_0 as: $\forall s \in S^1, \pi_0^1(s) = \sum_{s' \in A^1(s)} \pi_0(s')$. Introduce, $\forall s \in S^1$, cost functions V_i via the following recursions:

$$V_0^1(s) = 1_{\Phi^1}(s)\pi_0^1(s), \qquad V_{k+1}^1(s) = 1_{\Phi^1}(s)\sum_{s' \in S^1} V_k^1(s')P^1(s', s),$$

---

[1] For the sake of simplicity, we shall often loosely identify the set $\mathrm{Sat}(\Phi)$ with label Φ.

and, $\forall s \in S$, $\tilde{V}_k^1(s) = V_k^1(\alpha^1(s))/|A^1(\alpha^1(s))|$, as a (normalised) piecewise constant approximation of the abstract functions V_k^1, and in particular initialised as $\tilde{\pi}_0^1(s) = \pi_0^1(\alpha^1(s))/|A^1(\alpha^1(s))|$. We shall derive explicit bounds on the computation of the error:

$$\left| \sum_{s \in \Phi} V_{N_1}(s) - \sum_{s \in \Phi} \tilde{V}_{N_1}^1(s) \right| = \left| \sum_{i=1}^{m_1} \sum_{s \in \Phi_i} \left(V_{N_1}(s) - \tilde{V}_{N_1}^1(s) \right) \right|,$$

and extend them over successive aggregation and time steps $k = N_1 + 1, \ldots, N$. Notice that, in this instance, we are comparing two scalars, comprising the likelihoods associated with the specification of interest computed over the concrete and abstract models, respectively. More precisely, in general we have:

$$\left| \sum_{s \in \Phi_i} V_{N_1}(s) - \sum_{s \in \Phi_i} \tilde{V}_{N_1}^1(s) \right| = \left| \sum_{s \in \Phi_i} V_{N_1}(s) - \sum_{s \in \Phi_i} \frac{V_{N_1}^1(\alpha^1(s))}{|A^1(\alpha^1(s))|} \right| = \left| \sum_{s \in \Phi_i} V_{N_1}(s) - V_{N_1}^1(i) \right|.$$

Proposition 3. *Consider a q-step sequential aggregation strategy characterised by corresponding times $N_l : \sum_{l=1}^{q} N_l = N$, partitions $\Phi = \cup_{i=1}^{m_l} \Phi_i^l$, and matrices P^l. We obtain:*

$$\left| \sum_{s \in \Phi} V_N(s) - \sum_{s \in \Phi} \tilde{V}_N^q(s) \right| \le \sum_{l=1}^{q} \sum_{i=1}^{m_l} \epsilon^l(i) \sum_{k=0}^{N_l-1} V_{\sum_{i=0}^{l-1} N_i + k}^l(i).$$

Remark 3. We give some intuition regarding the structure of the bounds. The quantity depends on a summation over q aggregation steps. It expresses the accrual of the error incurred over the outgoing probability from the i-th partition (term $\epsilon^l(i)$), averaged over the history of the cost function over that partition. Note the symmetry between the shape of the bound and the recursive definition of the quantities of interest. □

4 Quantitative Analysis of Chemical Reaction Networks

A chemical reaction network describes a biochemical system containing M chemical species participating in a number of chemical reactions. The state of a model of the system at time $t \in \mathbb{R}^+$ is the vector $\mathbf{X}(t) = (X_1(t), X_2(t), \ldots, X_M(t))$, where X_i denotes the number of molecules of the i-th species [15]. Whenever a single reaction occurs the state changes based on the stoichiometry of the corresponding reaction. We use S to denote the set of (discrete) states. Further, for $s \in S$, $\pi_t(s)$ denotes the probability $\mathbb{P}(\mathbf{X}(t) = s)$. Assuming finite volume and temperature, the model can be interpreted as a continuous-time Markov chain (CTMC) $C = (S, R)$, where the rate matrix $R(s, s')$ gives the rate of a transition from states s to s', and π_0 specifies the initial distribution over S. The time evolution of the model is governed by the Chemical Master Equation (CME) [15], namely $\frac{d}{dt}\pi_t = \pi_t \cdot Q$, where Q is the infinitesimal generator matrix, defined as $Q(s, s') = R(s, s')$ if $s \neq s'$, and as $1 - \sum_{s'' \neq s} R(s, s'')$ otherwise. The exact solution of the CME is in general intractable, which has led to a number of possible numerical approximations [25]. We employ uniformisation [30], which in many cases outperforms other methods and also provides an arbitrary, user-defined approximation precision.

Uniformisation is based on a time-discretisation of the CTMC. The distribution π_t is obtained as a sum (over index i) of terms giving the probability that i discrete reaction steps occur up to time t: this is a Poisson random variable $\gamma_{i, \lambda \cdot t} = e^{-\lambda \cdot t} \cdot \frac{(\lambda \cdot t)^i}{i!}$, where the time delay is exponentially distributed with rate λ. More formally, $\pi_t = \sum_{i=0}^{\infty} \gamma_{i, \lambda \cdot t} \cdot \pi_0 \cdot \tilde{Q}^i \approx \sum_{i=0}^{N} \gamma_{i, \lambda \cdot t} \cdot \pi_0 \cdot \tilde{Q}^i$, where $\tilde{Q}$ is the uniformised infinitesimal generator matrix defined using terms $\frac{R(s, s')}{\lambda}$, and where the uniformisation constant λ is equal to the maximal exit rate $\sum_{s'' \neq s} R(s, s'')$. Although the sum is in general infinite, for a given precision an upper bound N can be estimated using techniques in [14], which also allow for efficient computation of the Poisson probabilities $\gamma_{i, \lambda \cdot t}$.

For complex models with very large or possibly infinite state spaces, the above numerical approximations are computationally infeasible, and are typically combined with (dynamical) state-space truncation methods, such as finite state projection [24], sliding window abstraction [18], or fast adaptive uniformisation [9,23] (FAU). The key idea of these truncation methods is to restrict the analysis of the model to a subset of states containing significant probability mass. One can easily compute the probability lost at each uniformisation step and thus obtain the total probability lost by truncation. As such, these truncation methods provide a lower bound on the quantities π_t, and the quantified probability lost can be used to derive a (rather conservative) upper bound on the approximation error: the sum of the lower bound and the probability lost gives an upper bound for the point-wise error. Moreover, a (pessimistic) bound on the L_1-norm over a general subset of the state space is obtained by multiplying the probability lost by the number of states in the concrete subset.

Adaptive Aggregation for CTMC Models of Chemical Reaction Networks. The aggregation methods in the previous sections can be directly applied to uniformised CTMCs, such as those arising from chemical reaction networks. We now discuss how the aggregation unfolds sequentially in time and how the derived error bounds can be used for the aggregation method in this setting.

Recall from Eq. (2) that the derivation of the error bounds for the aggregation procedure requires a finite state space: for *infinite-state* CTMCs, the aggregation method can be combined with state-space truncation (alongside time uniformisation), in order to accelerate computations in cases where the set of significant states is still too large. On the other hand, for *finite-state* CTMC models, adaptive aggregations can be regarded as an orthogonal strategy to truncation, and can be directly applied in conjunction with time uniformisation. In order to compare the precision and reduction capability of our method to that of FAU,

---

Algorithm 1. Adaptive aggregation for computation of transient probability

---

Require: Finite CTMC $C = (S, R)$, initial distribution π_0, time t, and bound θ on L_1-norm error
Ensure: $globalError \leq \theta$
1: $(P, N) \leftarrow$ uniformise (C, t); $l \leftarrow 1$
2: $(S^l, P^l, \pi_k^l, \epsilon^l) \leftarrow$ initAggregation (S, P, π_0)
3: **for** $(k \leftarrow 0; k \leq N, k \leftarrow k + 1)$ **do**   ▷ perform N uniformisation steps
4:     $(globalError, AccumErrors) \leftarrow$ computeErrors $\left(\pi_k^l, \epsilon^l, k\right)$
5:     $\pi_{k+1}^l(s) = \sum_{s' \in S^1} \pi_k^1(s') P^l(s', s)$ ▷ update the probability distribution
6:     **if** checkAggregation $\left(\epsilon^l, \pi_{k+1}^l, AccumErrors, \theta\right)$ = false **then**
7:         $(S^{l+1}, P^{l+1}, \pi_{k+1}^{l+1}, \epsilon^{l+1}) \leftarrow$ Recluster $\left(S^l, P^l, \pi_{k+1}^l, \epsilon^l, AccumErrors\right)$
8:         $AccumErrors \leftarrow 0$; $l \leftarrow l + 1$

---

we thus assume that the population of each species is bounded, which ensures fairness of experimental evaluation.

The key ingredient of the proposed aggregation method is a partitioning strategy that controls and adapts the clustering of the state space over the given finite time interval. Algorithm 1 summarises the scheme for transient probability calculation (the adaptive aggregation for an invariant property as in Sect. 3 unfolds similarly). The procedure starts with a given partition S^1 of the state space S (obtained by the procedure initAggregation on line 2). It dynamically (and automatically) updates the current partition when needed, thus providing new abstract state spaces S^l over the l-th time interval $[\sum_{i=0}^{l-1} N_i, \sum_{i=0}^{l} N_i]$, where $l = 2, \ldots, q$ and $q \ll N$. The update of the current l-th clustering is performed after N_l steps, that is, whenever the error accrual exceeds a threshold ensuring the user-defined precision θ (function checkAggregation on line 6). At the same time, the aggregation strategy aims to minimise the average size of the abstract state space, defined as $avg = \sum_{l=0}^{q} N_l \cdot |S^l|/N$. We consider two adaptive strategies, one time-*local* and the other *history*-dependent, both of which are driven by the shape of the derived error bounds – in particular, the history-dependent strategy exactly employs the calculated error bounds. Both strategies are parametrised by thresholds, which ensure the required overall precision θ and account for the size of the concrete state space as well as the number of uniformisation steps N.

The *history*-dependent strategy is based on the available history contributing to the shape of the derived errors: for the l-th aggregation step and the given i-th cluster of the current partition, it tracks the sum of the errors accumulated in the interval $[\sum_{i=0}^{l-1} N_i, \sum_{i=0}^{l-1} N_i + k]$ for $k = 1, \ldots, N_l$, according to the explicit bounds derived in Sect. 2 (line 4 of Algorithm 1). At each step k, the obtained value (averaged over k steps) reflects the (averaged) error accrual for each cluster (array $AccumErrors$) and is used to drive the partitioning procedure.

The function checkAggregation determines (using $AccumErrors$) if the current clustering meets the desired threshold, or if a refinement is desirable: during re-clustering, a locally coarser abstraction may as well be suggested by merging clusters. The function Recluster provides the new clustering based on the error bounds, which are functions of $AccumErrors$, of the local contributions ϵ^l, and of the (history of the) distribution π_k^l (or of the cost V_k^l in the case of safety verification). In contrast to the adaptive method presented in [13] and based exclusively on local heuristics, our strategy closely reflects the shape of the derived, history-dependent error bounds. Note that the aggregation strategy applied to chemical reaction networks aligns well with the known structure of the underlying CTMCs. In particular, the state-space clustering employs the spatial locality of the distribution of transitions in the M-dimensional space [13,31] (M is the number of chemical species), usually leading to relatively uniform probability mass over adjacent states and thus to strategies that cluster neighbouring states.

A simpler re-clustering strategy (denoted in the experiments as *local*) employs at each uniformisation step k only the product of the local error ϵ^l with the probability distribution π_k^l (or with the cost function V_k^l). In other words, a local re-clustering is performed if the local error depending on $\epsilon^l \pi_k^l$ (respectively, on $\epsilon^l V_k^l$) is above a given threshold. This intuitive scheme is similar to the local heuristic employed in [13].

We will show that the history-based strategy is more flexible with respect to the required precision and aggregation size. Our experiments confirm that, while based on error bounds that over-estimate the actual empirical error incurred in the aggregation, the history-based strategy tends to outperform the more intuitive and easier local strategy, with respect to key performance metrics affecting the practical use of the adaptive aggregation. This shows that the computed errors not only serve as a means to certify the accuracy of approximation, but can also be used to effectively drive the aggregation procedure. In particular, the metrics we are interested in are: (1) the value of avg representing the state-space reduction; (2) the accuracy of the empirical results of the abstract model; (3) the total number of re-clusterings; and (4) the actual value of the error bounds (compared to the empirical errors).

The number of re-clusterings (denoted by q) is crucial for the performance of the overall scheme, since each re-clustering requires $\mathcal{O}(|S| + |P|)$ steps, which is similar to performing a few uniformisation steps for the concrete model. As such, the number of re-clusterings should be significantly smaller than the total number of uniformisation steps. Therefore, in our experiments we use thresholds that favour fewer re-clusterings over coarser abstractions. Finally, note that the adaptive aggregation scheme can be combined with the adaptive uniformisation step as well as with dynamic state-space truncation [9,23,30], which updates the uniformisation constant λ for different time intervals, thus decreasing the number of overall uniformisation steps N.

Illustrative Example. We resort to a two-dimensional discrete Lotka-Volterra "predator-prey" model [15] to illustrate the history-dependent aggregation strategy. The maximal population of each species is bounded by 2000, thus the concrete model has 4M states. The initial population is set to 200 predators and 400 preys.

Figure 1 displays the outcome of the adaptive procedure (top row) at three distinct time steps and (bottom row) the current probability distribution of the concrete model. For ease of visualisation, the top plots display for each point of the concrete model the size of its corresponding cluster, where we have limited the maximal size to 100 states. Note the close correspondence between the error bounds and the computed empirical errors, and the limited number of re-clusterings needed (one in about 200 uniformisation steps). Observe that the single-state clusters (red colour in the plots) tend to collect where the current probability distribution peaks. The figure also illustrates a memory effect due to the history-dependent error bounds employed by the aggregation.

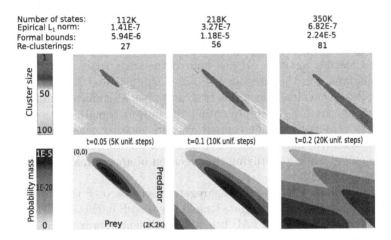

Fig. 1. Transient analysis of the Lotka-Volterra model using history-based adaptive aggregation.

5 Experimental Evaluation on Two Case Studies

We have developed a prototype implementation of the adaptive aggregation for the quantitative analysis of chemical reaction networks modelled in PRISM [20]. We have evaluated the scheme on two case studies in comparison with FAU [9] as implemented in the explicit engine of PRISM. In order to ensure comparability between the two schemes, which employ different data structures, rather than measuring execution time we have focused on assessing performance based on measures that are independent of implementation, and specifically focused on the metrics (1)–(4) introduced in Sect. 4 (model reduction, empirical accuracy, number of re-clusterings, and formal error bounds). For the same reason, we have not incorporated heuristics such as varying the maximal cluster size, optimally selecting error thresholds, or use of advanced clustering methods, which can be employed to further optimise the adaptive scheme.

We run all experiments on a MackBook Air^{TM} with 1.8GHz Intel Core i5 and 4 GB 1600 MHz RAM. As expected, for comparable state space reductions (value *avg*), FAU can be faster but in the same order of magnitude as our prototype, due to the overhead of clustering and adaptive uniformisation not being fully integrated in our implementation.

Recall that FAU eliminates states with incoming probability lower than a defined threshold, and as such leads to an under-approximation of the concrete probability distribution with no tailored error bounds: all we can say is that, point-wise, the concrete transient probability distribution resides between this under-approximation and a value obtained by adding the total probability lost, and similarly for the invariance likelihood.

Two-Component Signalling Pathway. [7] has analysed the robustness of the output signal of an input-output signal response mechanisms introduced in [28]. It is a two-component signalling pathway including the histidine kinase H, the response regulator R, and their phosphorylated forms (Hp and Rp). In order to ensure a feasible analysis, [7] has limited the state space by bounding the total populations over the intervals $25 \leq H + Hp \leq 35$ and $25 \leq R + Rp \leq 35$ (dimensionless quantities). Since this truncation has a significant impact on the distribution of variable Rp (representing the output signal), in this work we consider less conservative (but computationally more expensive) bounds and employ the adaptive aggregation scheme, which allows for a reduction in the size of the model while quantifying the precision of approximation by means of the derived error bounds.

We first evaluate the adaptive aggregation scheme over the verification of an invariant property with associated small likelihood: in this scenario dynamic truncation techniques such as FAU provide insufficient approximation precision. We compute the probability that the population of Rp stays below the level 15 for $t = 5\,\mathrm{s}$ (a relevant time window due to the fast-scale phosphorylation). The results for the new, less restrictive population bounds [5,55] are reported in Fig. 2. We present empirical satisfaction probabilities ("Empirical") and their formal bounds ("Bound") computed using Proposition 3 for the adaptive aggregation scheme, and lower bounds and probability lost for the FAU algorithm. For both schemes we report the obtained state-space size *avg*. We can observe a clear

Adaptive aggregation					Fast adaptive uniformisation			
Strategy	avg	Empirical	Bound	Re-clust.	Threshold	avg	Lower	Prob. lost
Local 1	62K	9.55E-12	2.34E-8	65	1E-10	15K	0.0	2.68E-5
Local 2	93K	6.32E-13	4.43E-10	81	1E-12	25K	0.0	1.98E-6
Local 3	115K	4.54E-14	2.39E-11	97	1E-15	44K	0.0	1.20E-6
History 1	54K	5.08E-16	4.68E-11	37	1E-20	91K	0.0	1.00E-6
History 2	66K	4.71E-16	4.60E-12	19	1E-25	160K	2.12E-17	1.80E-6
History 3	90K	2.20E-16	4.26E-14	20	1E-30	242K	2.15E-17	1.94E-6

Fig. 2. Statistics for the invariant property. Population bounds [5,55]: 1.2M states (less than those in Fig. 3 due to the property of interest), 16489 steps. The satisfaction probability of the property for the concrete model is equal to 2.15E-17.

relationship between the state-space reduction and the precision of the analysis. For adaptive aggregations, the parametrisation of each strategy is denoted by an index (1, 2, 3) representing the thresholds affecting the precision. Note that the parameterization for the history-based aggregation, in contrast to the local strategy, allows us to obtain the user-defined precision (e.g. in this experiment for the history-dependent strategy index 1 denotes a restriction of the bounds to 5E-11, whereas 2 to 5E-12, and 3 to 5E-14), since the aggregation employs exactly the errors. The results also demonstrate that the history-based strategy significantly outperforms the local strategy in all four key performance metrics.

Since the invariant property is associated with a small probability, we require accurate error bounds. The data in Fig. 2 shows that, for upper bounds of the adaptive scheme that are at least 5 orders of magnitude better compared to those from FAU, the adaptive aggregation method provides more than a twenty-fold reduction with respect to the size of the concrete model, and about a three-fold improvement with respect to the compression obtained via FAU. The results also demonstrate that different parameterisations of the aggregation strategy allow us to control the bounds, and via the bounds also to improve the empirical results (which confirms the usefulness of the derived bounds). However, decreasing the truncation threshold of FAU only improves the lower bounds (from 0.0 to 2.15E-17), but the probability lost is not considerably improved (it is even slightly worse for the very small thresholds, probably due to rounding errors). Notice that, whilst the global errors are still much more conservative, FAU provides better state-space reduction when a lower bound around 2.15E-17 (which is very close to the true probability) is required for the adaptive scheme.

Population	Adaptive aggregation					Fast adaptive uniformisation		
	Strategy	avg	Empirical	Bound	Re-clust.	Threshold	avg	Prob. lost
[25, 35]	History 1	70K	1.83E-4	2.56E-2	16	1E-10	72K	1.26E-3
	History 2	88K	2.69E-6	2.95E-4	17	1E-14	105K	1.98E-6
[5, 55]	History 1	453K	2.54E-4	4.73E-2	16	1E-10	132K	1.65E-3
	History 2	515K	4.16E-6	5.31E-4	24	1E-18	493K	1.96E-6

Fig. 3. Statistics for the L_1 norm of the error. Population bounds [25,35]: 116K states, 6924 uniformisation steps. Population bounds [5,55]: 2.5M states, 16489 uniformisation steps.

Next, we employ this example to compare the computation of the L_1 norm of the probability distribution at time $t = 5$ s. The table in Fig. 3 depicts the results for the L_1 norm over the whole state space, whereas the table in Fig. 4 depicts the results for the L_1 norm over a certain subset of interest. The formal bounds for the adaptive scheme (column "Empirical" in Fig. 3) have been computed using Proposition 2, whilst the corresponding bounds for Fig. 4 (middle part) have been obtained as the sum of the point-wise errors, defined in Proposition 1, over the subset of interest. The upper part of the tables corresponds to the

Pop.	Adaptive aggregation					Fast adaptive uniformisation			
	Strategy	avg	Empirical	Bound	Re-clust.		Threshold	avg	Empirical	Bound
[25, 35]	Hist. 1	71K	2.92E-8	4.89E-4	18		1E-12	93K	1.77E-9	2.18E-1
	Hist. 2	86K	5.80E-10	3.83E-6	8		1E-14	105K	2.04E-11	2.77E-2
[5, 55]	Hist. 1	354K	2.79E-6	1.75E-3	13		1E-16	388K	7.12E-13	6.02E-1
	Hist. 2	430K	1.10E-8	1.67E-5	19		1E-20	597K	2.68E-14	5.71E-1

Fig. 4. Statistics for the L_1 norm of the error computed over a set, characterised by the population of at least one species that is equal to 0. Population bounds [25,35]: 116K states, 6924 uniformisation steps - the set has 14 K states and the probability distribution within the set at time $t = 5$ is equal to 1.31E-8. Population bounds [5,55]: 2.5M states, 16489 uniformisation steps - the set has 307 K states and the probability distribution within the set at time $t = 5$ is equal to 1.36E-8.

population bounds [25, 35] (as in [7]), whereas the lower part to the less restrictive bounds [5,55]. Compared to the local strategy, the history-based aggregation again provides better performance, namely it requires significantly (up to ten-times) smaller numbers of re-clusterings ("Re-clust."): we thus present the results only for the history-dependent strategy. We ensure the comparability of the two outcomes by empirically selecting the threshold for FAU to obtain a truncated model of size (*avg*) similar to that resulting from our technique. Note that, in the case of the L_1 norm over the state space, the probability lost reported by FAU provides the safe bound on the L_1 norm and is equal to the empirical error between the concrete and truncated probability distributions. However, in the case of the L_1 norm over a general subset of the state space the probability lost has to be multiplied by the cardinality of the subset to obtain the correct formal bounds. Such bounds are reported in Fig. 4 (right part) as "Bound," whereas the empirical error between the distribution over the subset is depicted as "Empirical".

Summarising Figs. 3 and 4, when requiring a tight bound for the smaller state space (population [25, 35]), either approach does not lead to more than a two-fold reduction in the size of the space. This suggests a limit on the possible state-space reduction resulting from the model dynamics. However, for the larger model (population [5, 55]), up to a seven-fold reduction can be obtained using adaptive aggregation. We can see that FAU outperforms the adaptive aggregation scheme in the case of the L_1 norm error over the whole state space (where it leads to a nineteen-fold reduction) but, in contrast to our approach, is not able to provide useful bounds for a general L_1 norm (especially for the larger model).

Prokaryotic Gene Expression. The second case study deals with a more complex model for prokaryotic gene expression. The chemical reaction model has been introduced in [19] and includes 12 species and 11 reactions. We bound the maximal population of particular species (left column in Fig. 5) to obtain a finite and tractable state space. We focus our experiments exclusively on the history-dependent aggregation scheme.

Max pop.	Adaptive aggregation				Fast adaptive uniformisation			
	Strategy	avg	Empirical	Bound	Re-clust.	Threshold	avg	Empirical	Bound
10	Hist. 1	127K	6.36E-7	1.77E-4	35	1E-12	141K	2.55E-7	1.00E+0
10	Hist. 2	207K	2.94E-9	3.77E-7	37	1E-20	386K	7.24E-9	8.05E-1
20	Hist. 1	287K	7.38E-6	2.83E-4	56	1E-12	176K	1.49E-6	1.00E+0
20	Hist. 2	428K	2.56E-8	4.26E-7	59	1E-20	628K	3.35E-8	1.00E+0

Fig. 5. Statistics for the L_1 norm of the error restricted to a set of interest, a strict subset of the state space. Maximal population 10: 1.2M states, 33162 uniformisation steps - the set has 516 K states and the probability distribution within the set at time $t = 1000$ is equal to 5.84E-3. Maximal population 20: 4.4M states, 53988 uniformisation steps - the set has 1.8M states and the probability distribution within the set at time $t = 1000$ is equal to 2.21E-2.

In contrast with the previous case study that focused on events with very small likelihood, we now discuss results for events with non-negligible likelihood. Figure 5 reports basic statistics on the computation of the L_1 norm over a certain subset of the state space at time $t = 1000$ s. Providing useful error bounds on the L_1 norm (computed from the point-wise errors in Proposition 1), the adaptive aggregation leads to almost a ten-fold state space reduction for the smaller model (1.2M vs 127K) and a fifteen-fold reduction for the larger model (4.4M vs 287K). Due to the large cardinality of the subset of interest, FAU fails to provide any informative formal bounds. Note that in this case study the adaptive aggregation scheme also provides better empirical bounds than FAU.

Finally, we have evaluated both approaches on an invariant property (the population of a species stays below the level 10, for 1000 s) with a significant satisfaction probability (more than 15 % and 20 % on the small and large model, respectively). We observe that this choice is favourable to FAU, since for invariant properties with high likelihood the state space truncated via FAU is aligned with the property of interest, and thus the lost probability mass is slightly smaller than the error introduced by the state-space aggregations. In this scenario FAU yields better reductions than the adaptive aggregation scheme (especially for the larger model), while providing similar error bounds, since it is able to successfully identify the relevant part of the state space. This scenario advantageous to FAU is in contrast to that discussed in Fig. 2, as well as to the general case where for an arbitrary model it is not known how the probability mass is distributed in relation to the states satisfying the property of interest.

6 Conclusions

We have proposed a novel adaptive aggregation algorithm for approximating the probability of an event in a Markov chain with rigorous precision guarantees. Our approach provides error bounds that are in general orders of magnitude more accurate compared to those from fast adaptive uniformisation, and significantly decreases the size of models without performance degradation. This has allowed us to efficiently analyse larger and more complex models. Future work will include effective combinations of the adaptive aggregation with robustness analysis and parameter synthesis. We also plan to apply our approach to the verification and performance analysis of complex safety-critical computer systems, where precision guarantees play a key role.

References

1. Abate, A., Katoen, J.-P., Lygeros, J., Prandini, M.: Approximate model checking of stochastic hybrid systems. Eur. J. Control **16**, 624–641 (2010)
2. Abate, A., Kwiatkowska, M., Norman, G., Parker, D.: Probabilistic model checking of labelled Markov processes via finite approximate bisimulations. In: van Breugel, F., Kashefi, E., Palamidessi, C., Rutten, J. (eds.) Horizons of the Mind. LNCS, vol. 8464, pp. 40–58. Springer, Heidelberg (2014)
3. Angius, A., Horváth, A., Wolf, V.: Quasi Product form approximation for markov models of reaction networks. In: Priami, C., Petre, I., de Vink, E. (eds.) Transactions on Computational Systems Biology XIV. LNCS, vol. 7625, pp. 26–52. Springer, Heidelberg (2012)
4. Baier, C., Katoen, J.-P.: Principles of Model Checking. The MIT Press, Cambridge (2008)
5. Bortolussi, L., Hillston, J.: Fluid model checking. In: Koutny, M., Ulidowski, I. (eds.) CONCUR 2012. LNCS, vol. 7454, pp. 333–347. Springer, Heidelberg (2012)
6. Buchholz, P.: Exact performance equivalence: an equivalence relation for stochastic automata. Theor. Comput. Sci. **215**(1–2), 263–287 (1999)
7. Česka, M., Šafránek, D., Dražan, S., Brim, L.: Robustness analysis of stochastic biochemical systems. PloS One **9**(4), e94553 (2014)
8. Chen, T., Kiefer, S.: On the total variation distance of labelled Markov chains. In: Computer Science Logic (CSL) and Logic in Computer Science (LICS) (2014)
9. Dannenberg, F., Hahn, E.M., Kwiatkowska, M.: Computing cumulative rewards using fast adaptive uniformisation. ACM Trans. Model. Comput. Simul. Spec. Issue Comput. Methods Syst. Biol. (CMSB) **25**, 9 (2015)
10. Desharnais, J., Laviolette, F., Tracol, M.: Approximate analysis of probabilistic processes: logic, simulation and games. In: Quantitative Evaluation of SysTems (QEST), pp. 264–273 (2008)
11. D'Innocenzo, A., Abate, A., Katoen, J.-P.: Robust PCTL model checking. In: Hybrid Systems: Computation and Control (HSCC), pp. 275–285. ACM (2012)
12. Engblom, S.: Computing the moments of high dimensional solutions of the master equation. Appl. Math. Comput. **180**(2), 498–515 (2006)
13. Ferm, L., Lötstedt, P.: Adaptive solution of the master equation in low dimensions. Appl. Numer. Math. **59**(1), 187–204 (2009)
14. Fox, B.L., Glynn, P.W.: Computing poisson probabilities. Commun. ACM **31**(4), 440–445 (1988)
15. Gillespie, D.T.: Exact stochastic simulation of coupled chemical reactions. J. Phys. Chem. **81**(25), 2340–2381 (1977)
16. Hasenauer, J., Wolf, V., Kazeroonian, A., Theis, F.: Method of conditional moments (MCM) for the chemical master equation. J. Math. Biol. **69**(3), 687–735 (2014)
17. Hegland, M., Burden, C., Santoso, L., MacNamara, S., Booth, H.: A solver for the stochastic master equation applied to gene regulatory networks. J. Comput. Appl. Math. **205**(2), 708–724 (2007)

18. Henzinger, T.A., Mateescu, M., Wolf, V.: Sliding window abstraction for infinite Markov chains. In: Bouajjani, A., Maler, O. (eds.) CAV 2009. LNCS, vol. 5643, pp. 337–352. Springer, Heidelberg (2009)

19. Kierzek, A.M., Zaim, J., Zielenkiewicz, P.: The effect of transcription and translation initiation frequencies on the stochastic fluctuations in prokaryotic gene expression. J. Biol. Chem. **276**(11), 8165–8172 (2001)

20. Kwiatkowska, M., Norman, G., Parker, D.: PRISM 4.0: verification of probabilistic real-time systems. In: Gopalakrishnan, G., Qadeer, S. (eds.) CAV 2011. LNCS, vol. 6806, pp. 585–591. Springer, Heidelberg (2011)

21. Larsen, K.G., Skou, A.: Bisimulation through probabilistic testing. Inf. Comput. **94**(1), 1–28 (1991)

22. Madsen, C., Myers, C., Roehner, N., Winstead, C., Zhang, Z.: Utilizing stochastic model checking to analyze genetic circuits. In: Computational Intelligence in Bioinformatics and Computational Biology (CIBCB), pp. 379–386. IEEE Computer Society (2012)

23. Mateescu, M., Wolf, V., Didier, F., Henzinger, T.A.: Fast adaptive uniformization of the chemical master equation. IET Syst. Biol. **4**(6), 441–452 (2010)

24. Munsky, B., Khammash, M.: The finite state projection algorithm for the solution of the chemical master equation. J. Chem. Phys. **124**, 044104 (2006)

25. Sidje, R., Stewart, W.: A numerical study of large sparse matrix exponentials arising in Markov chains. Comput. Stat. Data Anal. **29**(3), 345–368 (1999)

26. Soudjani, S.E.Z., Abate, A.: Adaptive and sequential gridding procedures for the abstraction and verification of stochastic processes. SIAM J. Appl. Dyn. Syst. **12**(2), 921–956 (2013)

27. Esmaeil Zadeh Soudjani, S., Abate, A.: Precise approximations of the probability distribution of a markov process in time: an application to probabilistic invariance. In: Ábrahám, E., Havelund, K. (eds.) TACAS 2014 (ETAPS). LNCS, vol. 8413, pp. 547–561. Springer, Heidelberg (2014)

28. Steuer, R., Waldherr, S., Sourjik, V., Kollmann, M.: Robust signal processing in living cells. PLoS Comput. Biol. **7**(11), e1002218 (2011)

29. Tkachev, I., Abate, A.: On approximation metrics for linear temporal model-checking of stochastic systems. In: Hybrid Systems: Computation and Control (HSCC), pp. 193–202. ACM (2014)

30. van Moorsel, A.P., Sanders, W.H.: Adaptive uniformization. Stoch. Models **10**(3), 619–647 (1994)

31. Zhang, J., Watson, L.T., Cao, Y.: Adaptive aggregation method for the chemical master equation. Int. J. Comput. Biol. Drug Des. **2**(2), 134–148 (2009)

PROPhESY: A PRObabilistic ParamEter SYnthesis Tool

Christian Dehnert$^{(\boxtimes)}$, Sebastian Junges, Nils Jansen, Florian Corzilius,
Matthias Volk, Harold Bruintjes, Joost-Pieter Katoen, and Erika Ábrahám

RWTH Aachen University, Aachen, Germany
dehnert@cs.rwth-aachen.de

Abstract. We present PROPhESY, a tool for analyzing parametric Markov chains (MCs). It can compute a rational function (i.e., a fraction of two polynomials in the model parameters) for reachability and expected reward objectives. Our tool outperforms state-of-the-art tools and supports the novel feature of conditional probabilities. PROPhESY supports incremental automatic parameter synthesis (using SMT techniques) to determine "safe" and "unsafe" regions of the parameter space. All values in these regions give rise to instantiated MCs satisfying or violating the (conditional) probability or expected reward objective. PROPhESY features a web front-end supporting visualization and user-guided parameter synthesis. Experimental results show that PROPhESY scales to MCs with millions of states and several parameters.

1 Introduction

The mainstream model-checking methods so far focus on safety (is a "bad" state reachable?) and liveness (is some progress made?) properties. For applications in which randomization and uncertainty play an important role, probabilistic properties are of prime importance. These applications include randomized distributed algorithms (where randomization breaks the symmetry between processes), security (e.g., key generation at encryption), systems biology (where species randomly react depending on their concentration), embedded systems (interacting with unknown and varying environments), and so forth. For instance, the *crowds* protocol [1] employs random routing to ensure anonymity. Nodes randomly choose to deliver a packet or to route it to another randomly picked node. In the presence of "bad" nodes that eavesdrop, we could be interested in analyzing probabilistic safety properties such as "the probability of a bad node identifying the sender's identity is less than 5 %".

This has led to the development of different automata- and tableau-based *probabilistic model-checking* techniques to prove model properties specified by, e.g., probabilistic ω-regular languages or probabilistic branching-time logics such as pCTL and pCTL*. Probabilistic model checking is applicable to a

---

This work was supported by the Excellence Initiative of the German federal and state government and the EU FP7 projects SENSATION and CARP.

D. Kroening and C.S. Păsăreanu (Eds.): CAV 2015, Part I, LNCS 9206, pp. 214–231, 2015.
DOI: 10.1007/978-3-319-21690-4_13

plethora of probabilistic models, ranging from discrete-time Markov chains to continuous-time Markov decision processes and probabilistic timed automata, possibly extended with notions of resource consumption (such as memory footprint and energy usage) using rewards (or prices). PRISM [2], MRMC [3], CADP [4] and iscasMc [5] are mature probabilistic model checkers and have been applied successfully to a wide range of benchmarks. Recently, Alur *et al.* [6] identified probabilistic model checking as a promising new direction as it establishes correctness *and* evaluates performance aspects; see also [7].

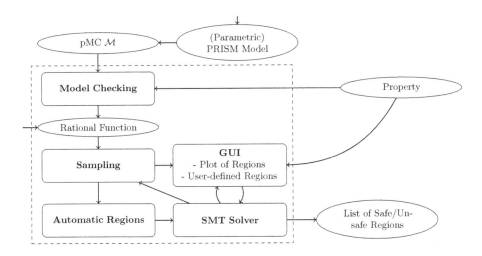

Fig. 1. The verification process of PROPhESY.

A major practical obstacle is that probabilistic model-checking techniques and tools work under the assumption that all probabilities in models are a priori known. However, at early development stages, certain system quantities such as faultiness, reliability, reaction rates, packet loss ratios, etc. are often not—or at the best partially—known. In such cases, *parametric* probabilistic models can be used for specification, where transition probabilities are specified as arithmetic expressions using real-valued parameters. In addition to checking instantiated models for fixed parameter values, the important problem of *parameter synthesis* arises, posing the question which parameter values lead to the satisfaction of certain properties of interest. For the crowds protocol it is of interest to establish for which routing probabilities the sender's identity can be revealed in at most 5 % of all protocol runs. Similar questions arise in systems biology when determining the concentration of species such that, e.g., catalytic reactions diminish other species within a given time frame with high likelihood. Parametric models are also quite natural in adaptive software where "continuous" verification frequently amends system models during deployment [8] as well as in model repair [9], where probabilities are tuned so as to satisfy a desired property. There is little work done on model checking of parametric probabilistic models, with the notable exception of the PARAM tool [10] and recently also PRISM [2].

This paper presents the tool PROPhESY for the analysis of *parametric (discrete-time) Markov chains (pMCs)*. Inputs are a pMC (specified in the input language of PRISM) together with a requirement imposing an upper bound on the measure-of-interest, see Fig. 1 depicting the workflow of the tool. Transitions in pMCs are labelled with rational functions, i.e., fractions of polynomials over a set of parameters. These measures are (conditional) reachability probabilities or expected costs to reach target states. Once the state space of a pMC is generated, the focus is on determining parameter valuations meeting the requirement, e.g., values for which (a) bad states can be reached in at most 1 % of all runs, (b) the expected resource consumption to reach a successful state is within a given budget, or (c) the conditional probability to reach a good state given that eventually a terminating state is reached is above 99 %. To do so, PROPhESY supports a palette of advanced techniques relying on computing and efficient manipulation of rational functions and incremental synthesis techniques (á la CEGAR).

In the next section, we will elaborate on PROPhESY's features and summarize the contributions. Section 3 lays the formal background needed for the algorithms and techniques presented in Sect. 4. In Sect. 5 we explain details on implementation issues and give a thorough experimental evaluation. Finally, in Sects. 6 and 7 we discuss the related work and conclude.

2   Features and Contributions

In this overview on PROPhESY's workflow and contributions we emphasize all steps as depicted in Fig. 1.

The Core Engine. The core *model-checking* engine of the tool determines and returns a *rational function* in terms of the parameters of the (conditional) reachability probability or expected cost. Daws [11] showed that these rational functions can be obtained using state elimination in the pMC, a technique similar to reducing finite-state automata to regular expressions. This was implemented in PARAM [10] and PRISM [2]. Note that finding the minimal-sized regular expression for an automaton is NP-complete; the efficiency of the construction strongly depends on the order in which states are eliminated [12]. We employ several dedicated heuristics in our algorithms. New techniques exploit SCC decomposition for state elimination together with advanced gcd-computations on rational functions [13].

Apart from the these techniques, the PROPhESY tool supports new algorithms dedicated to determine conditional probabilities, which are introduced in this paper. Conditional probabilities are central in—amongst others—the field of Bayesian programming.

Parameter Synthesis. In general, to determine whether the given requirement is met, one has to consider all possible parameter valuations. For a feasible and usable approach, we aim for an (approximate) partitioning of the parameter space into *safe* and *unsafe regions*. Each parameter instantiation within a safe region satisfies the requirement under consideration. These *parameter synthesis* problems are challenging and substantially more complex than verifying standard MCs—just checking whether a pMC is realizable (having a parameter evaluation inducing a well-defined MC) is exponential in the number of parameters [14].

Incremental Parameter Synthesis. Our approach to parameter synthesis can be summarized as follows. After the model checking engine has computed a rational function for the property at hand, the first step is to *sample* the rational function up to a user-adjustable degree. This amounts to instantiating parameter values (determined by dedicated heuristics) over the entire parameter space. This yields a coarse approximation of parts of the solution space that are safe or unsafe and can be viewed as an abstraction of the true partitioning into safe or unsafe parts. The goal is now to divide the parameter space into regions which are *certified* to be safe or unsafe. This is done in an iterative CEGAR-like fashion [15]. First, a region candidate assumed to be safe or unsafe is automatically generated. An *SMT solver* is then used to verify the assumption. In case it was wrong, a *counterexample* in the form of a contradicting sample point is provided along which the abstraction/sampling is *refined*, giving a finer abstraction of the solution space. Using this, new region candidates are generated.

Sensitivity Analysis. In addition to determining whether a property is satisfied, the robustness of selected parameters which are subject to perturbation is of utter importance, see [16]. That is, for a region of the parameter space, one wants to certify that changing parameter values within certain "robust" bounds has limited impact on the investigated property. A *sensitivity analysis* for parameters leads to obtaining such bounds. As an initial approach, we benefit from computing the rational function for the measure-of-interest where we simply compute the derivative of this function.

Visualization. The PROPhESY tool includes a *web front-end* as part of a service-oriented architecture for *visualization* as well as steering and guiding the verification process. Concretely, the sampling result and the final or intermediate regions can be visualized in the GUI. The user has the possibility to change the properties dynamically such that the sample points are updated. This offers a direct help to find good parameter evaluations, akin to fitting [17]. Regions in the form of convex polygons can be manually specified and again be verified by an SMT solver. At all times, intermediate results can be used by the automatic CEGAR-like synthesis procedure.

Contributions. The main contribution of this paper is a tool offering a palette of analysis techniques for parametric Markov chains. It significantly extends the efficiency, functionality, and analysis techniques of the currently available tools that can handle parameters, PRISM [2] and PARAM [10]:

- An efficient core engine based on a dedicated library for the costly arithmetic operations yielding a substantial speed up and improved scalability;
- The first algorithmic approach for computing conditional probabilities over parametric MCs. Its instantiation to ordinary (i.e., non-parametric) MCs is orders of magnitudes faster than reported in [18];
- Incremental parameter synthesis (á la CEGAR) exploiting advanced SMT techniques. For many benchmarks, over 90 % of the solution space can be split into safe and unsafe regions within a minute.
- Initial support for sensitivity and perturbation analysis;
- A user-friendly GUI based on an integrated web-server for guiding the synthesis process.

3   Formal Foundations

In order for this paper to be self-contained, we briefly introduce the formal models and properties we consider. Let in the following V be a finite set of variables over the domain $\mathbb{R}$. A *valuation* for V is a function $u\colon V \to \mathbb{R}$. Following [19], we use rational functions $f = g_1/g_2$ over V to describe parameterized probabilities, where g_1 and g_2 are (multivariate) polynomials over V with rational coefficients. Let $\mathbb{Q}_V$ be the set of all rational functions over V. The evaluation $g(u)$ of a polynomial g under u replaces each $x \in V$ by $u(x)$. For $f = g_1/g_2 \in \mathbb{Q}_V$ and evaluation u with $g_2(u) \neq 0$ we define $f(u) = \frac{g_1(u)}{g_2(u)} \in \mathbb{R}$.

Definition 1 (pMC). *A* parametric discrete-time Markov chain (pMC) *is a tuple* $\mathcal{M} = (S, V, s_I, P)$ *with a finite set of states* S, *a finite set of parameters* $V = \{x_1, \ldots, x_n\}$ *with domain* $\mathbb{R}$, *an initial state* $s_I \in S$, *and a parametric transition probability matrix* $P\colon S \times S \to \mathbb{Q}_V$. $\mathcal{M}$ *is called a* discrete-time Markov chain (MC) *if* $P\colon S \times S \to \mathbb{R}$. *Together with a (state) reward function* rew$\colon S \to \mathbb{R}_{\geq 0}$, *a pMC is called a* parametric Markov reward model.

For a pMC $\mathcal{M} = (S, V, s_I, P)$, the *underlying graph* of $\mathcal{M}$ is $\mathcal{G}_\mathcal{M} = (S, E)$ with $E = \{(s, s') \in S \times S \mid P(s, s') \not\equiv 0\}$. *Successor or predecessor states of* $s \in S$ are succ$(s) = \{s' \in S \mid (s, s') \in E\}$ and pred$(s) = \{s' \in S \mid (s', s) \in E\}$. We define $P(s, S') = \sum_{s' \in S'} P(s, s')$ and $\overline{S'} = S \setminus S'$. State s is *absorbing* iff succ$(s) = \{s\}$.

A *path* of $\mathcal{M}$ is a non-empty sequence $\pi = s_0 s_1 \ldots$ of states $s_i \in S$ such that $P(s_i, s_{i+1}) > 0$ for $i > 0$. A state $s' \in S$ is *reachable* from $s \in S$, written $s \rightsquigarrow s'$, iff there is a path leading from s to s'. The property $\Diamond T$ is overloaded to describe the set of paths finally reaching a set of target states $T \subseteq S$ starting from s_I.

For a pMC $\mathcal{M} = (S, V, s_I, P)$ and a valuation $u\colon V \to \mathbb{R}$ of V, the *instantiated pMC under* u is given by the tuple $\mathcal{M}_u = (S, s_I, P_u)$ with $P_u(s, s') = P(s, s')(u)$ for all $s, s' \in S$. A valuation u is *well-defined* for the pMC $\mathcal{M}$ iff $P_u(s, s') \in [0, 1]$ with $\sum_{s'' \in S} P_u(s, s'') = 1$ for all $s, s' \in S$ and $\mathcal{G}_\mathcal{M} = \mathcal{G}_{\mathcal{M}_u}$. $\mathcal{M}$ is called *realizable* iff there is a well-defined valuation for $\mathcal{M}$. We assume all pMCs to be realizable. The instantiated pMC $\mathcal{M}_u$ induced by a well-defined valuation u is an MC, enabling to use all definitions and concepts for mere MCs also for pMCs.

Example 1. Consider the pMC $\mathcal{M}$ with parameters $V = \{p, q\}$ depicted in Fig. 2a on Page 8. The valuation $u(p) = u(q) = 0.25$ is well-defined, while $u(p) = u(q) = 0.5$ would induce probabilities larger than 1.

A unique probability measure $\mathrm{Pr}^{\mathcal{M}}$ on sets of paths is defined via the usual *cylinder set construction*, see [20]. For instance, $\mathrm{Pr}^{\mathcal{M}}(\Diamond T)$ describes the probability of reaching $T \subseteq S$ states from s_I in $\mathcal{M}$. For a set of *stochastically independent* paths, the individual probabilities of these paths can be summed.

The *conditional probability* for two reachability objectives is given by

$$\mathrm{Pr}^{\mathcal{M}}(\Diamond T \mid \Diamond C) = \frac{\mathrm{Pr}^{\mathcal{M}}(\Diamond T \cap \Diamond C)}{\mathrm{Pr}^{\mathcal{M}}(\Diamond C)}$$

for $\mathrm{Pr}^{\mathcal{M}}(\Diamond C) > 0$. Considering a (parametric) Markov reward model, the *reward* $\mathrm{rew}(s)$ is earned upon leaving s. The *expected reward* $\mathrm{ExpRew}^{\mathcal{M}}(\Diamond T)$ is the expected amount of reward that has been accumulated until a set of target states $T \subseteq S$ is reached when starting in the initial state s_I. We often omit the superscript $\mathcal{M}$ if it is clear from the context. For more details on probability measures and the considered properties we refer to [20].

Finally, we give a formal definition the model checking problems for pMCs.

Definition 2 (Parametric Probabilistic Model Checking). *For a pMC $\mathcal{M} = (S, V, s_I, P)$ the parametric probabilistic model checking problem is to find either*

- *$f^r \in \mathbb{Q}_V$ for $\mathrm{Pr}^{\mathcal{M}}(\Diamond T)$ with $T \subseteq S$,*
- *$f^c \in \mathbb{Q}_V$ for $\mathrm{Pr}^{\mathcal{M}}(\Diamond T \mid \Diamond C)$ with $T, C \subseteq S$,*
- *or $f^e \in \mathbb{Q}_V$ for $\mathrm{ExpRew}^{\mathcal{M}}(\Diamond T)$ with $T \subseteq S$*

such that for all well-defined valuations u, the instantiated rational function f^r, f^c, or f^e, and the instantiated pMC $\mathcal{M}_u$ it holds that:

$$f^r_u = \mathrm{Pr}^{\mathcal{M}_u}(\Diamond T), \qquad f^c_u = \mathrm{Pr}^{\mathcal{M}_u}(\Diamond T \mid \Diamond C), \qquad f^e_u = \mathrm{ExpRew}^{\mathcal{M}_u}(\Diamond T).$$

4 Supported Techniques

In this section we briefly recall incorporated methods introduced in former works and explain new methods and concepts in detail.

4.1 Model Checking

We start by briefly explaining how model checking for a pMC $\mathcal{M} = (S, V, s_I, P)$ and the different properties as in Definition 2 is performed.

Reachability Probabilities and Expected Rewards. Let $T \subseteq S$ be a set of target states and assume w.l.o.g. that all states in T are absorbing and that $s_I \notin T$. Let us briefly recall the concept of the *state elimination* [11,19] used to compute a rational function describing reachability probabilities (**eliminate_state** in Algorithm 1). The basic idea is to "bypass" a state s by removing it from the model and increasing the probabilities $P(s_1, s_2)$ of the transitions from each predecessors s_1 to each successors s_2 by the probability of moving from s_1 to s_2 via s, possibly including a self-loop on s. Note that it is well possible to eliminate a single transition (s_1, s_2) by only calling the function **eliminate_transition**(P, s_1, s_2).

The state elimination approach can also be adapted to compute *expected rewards* [19] for Markov reward models. When eliminating a state s, in addition to adjusting the probabilities of the transitions from all predecessors s_1 of s to all successors s_2 of s, it is also necessary to "summarize" the reward that would have been gained from s_1 to s_2 via s.

Algorithm 1. State elimination for pMCs

---

eliminate_state$(P, s \in S$ not absorbing$)$
    for each $s_1 \in \mathit{pred}(s), s_1 \neq s$ **do**
        eliminate_transition(P, s_1, s)

eliminate_transition$(P, s_1 \in \mathit{pred}(s), s \in S$ not absorbing$)$
    if $s_1 \neq s$ **then**
        for each $s_2 \in \mathit{succ}(s), s \neq s_2$ **do**
            $P(s_1, s_2) := P(s_1, s_2) + \frac{P(s_1, s) \cdot P(s, s_2)}{1 - P(s, s)}$
        $P(s_1, s) := 0$
    else
        for each $s_2 \in \mathit{succ}(s), s \neq s_2$ **do**
            $P(s, s_2) := \frac{P(s, s_2)}{1 - P(s, s)}$
        $P(s, s) := 0$

Example 2. Consider again the pMC from Example 1. Assume, state s_3 is to be eliminated. The states that are relevant for this procedure are the only predecessor s_0 and the successors s_0 and s_5. Applying the function **eliminate_state**(P, s_3) of Algorithm 1 yields the model in Fig. 2(b).

Conditional Probabilities. The probability $\mathrm{Pr}^{\mathcal{M}}(\Diamond T \mid \Diamond C)$ measures the reachability of $T \subseteq S$ given that C is reached. We assume $s_I \notin T \cup C$, because otherwise the result is the constant one function or coincides with the probability of reaching T, respectively. We assume w.l.o.g. all states in $T \cap C$ to be absorbing.

We will now show how to compute this function using the elimination framework. Let $S_{\mathrm{rest}} = (\overline{T} \cap \overline{C}) \setminus \{s_I\}$. Consider the path fragment in $\mathcal{M}$ as illustrated

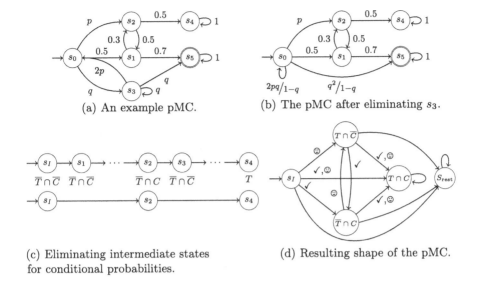

(a) An example pMC.

(b) The pMC after eliminating s_3.

(c) Eliminating intermediate states for conditional probabilities.

(d) Resulting shape of the pMC.

Fig. 2. pMC model checking.

the upper part of Fig. 2(c). It finally reaches T (s_4) after visiting C (s_2) and intermediately visits only S_{rest}. By eliminating the transitions to and from the *intermediate states* in S_{rest}, we essentially summarize the probability of moving from s_I to $\overline{T} \cap C$ and from there on to T; see the second path fragment in Fig. 2(c). Therefore, the conditional probability from s_I remains the same.

We use this key insight to convert the shape of $\mathcal{M}$ to the one depicted in Fig. 2(d). First, we bypass all non-absorbing intermediate states via state elimination and keep only the states that are relevant for the conditional probability and the absorbing states in S_{rest}. Then, we eliminate *backward transitions* from all states s targeting the initial state s_I by applying **eliminate_transition** from Algorithm 1. It remains to eliminate transitions between states in $T \cap \overline{C}$ as well as transitions between states in $\overline{T} \cap C$. After this final step, the shape of the resulting system is the one depicted in Fig. 2(d). Note that the abstract states and transitions in this pMC correspond to sets of states and sets of transitions, respectively. We are interested in computing the fraction

$$\frac{\Pr^{\mathcal{M}}(\lozenge T \cap \lozenge C)}{\Pr^{\mathcal{M}}(\lozenge C)} =: \frac{f_1}{f_2} \qquad f_1, f_2 \in \mathbb{Q}_V$$

For the sake of clarity, we label an (abstract) transition $s \to s'$ with ☺ if $s' \in T$, and with ✓ if $s' \in C$. To this end, we notice that it suffices to consider path fragments of length two, since we have either seen both ☺ and ✓ along such a fragment (and it therefore contributes to f_1 and f_2), or we are in S_{rest}. In the latter case, we saw only ✓ (contributing to f_2), only ☺, or none of them and there is no way of reaching any one of them in the future.

The functions are computed as follows. f_2 corresponds to the probability mass of all paths along which $\checkmark$ is seen. That is, we either (i) start with a $\odot$ and then see a $\checkmark$, (ii) directly see both a $\checkmark$ and a $\odot$, or (iii) encounter only a $\checkmark$ along the first step. f_1 corresponds to the probability mass of all paths along which both $\checkmark$ and $\odot$ are seen. Such paths either (i) start with $\checkmark$, and require a subsequent $\odot$ (corresponding to the path from Fig. 2(c)), (ii) start with both $\odot$ and $\checkmark$, or (iii) start with $\odot$, and require a subsequent $\checkmark$. This directly leads to the following equation, where the three cases for f_1 and f_2 correspond to the three summands in the numerator and denominator in the order from left to right.

$$\frac{\Pr^{\mathcal{M}}(\lozenge T \cap \lozenge C)}{\Pr^{\mathcal{M}}(\lozenge C)} = \frac{\sum\limits_{t \in T \cap \overline{C}} P(s_I, t) \cdot P(t, C) + \sum\limits_{t \in T \cap C} P(s_I, t) + \sum\limits_{t \in \overline{T} \cap C} P(s_I, t) \cdot P(t, T)}{\sum\limits_{t \in T \cap \overline{C}} P(s_I, t) \cdot P(t, C) + \sum\limits_{t \in T \cap C} P(s_I, t) + \sum\limits_{t \in \overline{T} \cap C} P(s_I, t)}$$

The pseudo code of the elimination algorithm is given in Algorithm 2.

Algorithm 2. Computing conditional probabilities for pMCs

---

conditional(pMC $\mathcal{M} = (S, V, s_I, P)$, $T \subseteq S$, $C \subseteq S$)
    while $\exists s \in (\overline{T} \cap \overline{C}) \setminus \{s_I\}$, s not absorbing **do**
        eliminate_state(P, s)
    for each s_1 with $P(s_1, s_I) > 0$ **do**
        eliminate_transition(P, s_1, s_I)
    while $\exists s_1, s_2 \in (T \cap \overline{C})$ or $\exists s_1, s_2 \in (\overline{T} \cap C)$ with $P(s_1, s_2) > 0$ **do**
        eliminate_transition(P, s_1, s_2)
    $g_1 := \sum_{t \in T \cap \overline{C}} P(s_I, t) \cdot P(t, C)$ $g_2 := \sum_{t \in T \cap C} P(s_I, t)$
    $g_3 := \sum_{t \in \overline{T} \cap C} P(s_I, t) \cdot P(t, T)$ $g_4 := \sum\limits_{t \in \overline{T} \cap C} P(s_I, t)$
    return $\frac{g_1 + g_2 + g_3}{g_1 + g_2 + g_4}$

Theorem 1 (Correctness). *For a given pMC $\mathcal{M} = (S, V, s_I, P)$ and sets of states $T \subseteq S$ and $C \subseteq S$, the procedure $\mathbf{conditional}(\mathcal{M}, T, C)$ computes the rational function describing the conditional probability $\Pr^{\mathcal{M}}(\lozenge T \mid \lozenge C)$.*

The proof relies on the fact that state elimination preserves reachability probabilities [19]. As we obtain a structure as in Fig. 2, the summation over all path fragments of length (at most) two that contribute to the conditioned probability yields the same result as in the original system.

4.2 Parameter Synthesis

Instantiating the rational functions yields model checking probabilities for the corresponding instantiated MCs. However, this only gives a very rough impression of the behavior of the pMC for different parameter values, which is unsatisfactory if one aims to certify expected behavior over a non-singular parameter space. Instead we determine which parts of the parameter space give rise to a safe system. As explained in Sect. 2, we do this in a CEGAR-like manner; consider again Fig. 1. The underlying concepts are presented in the following.

We assume upper bounds[1] $\lambda \in [0, 1]$ for (conditional) reachability probabilities and $\kappa \in \mathbb{R}_{\geq 0}$ for expected rewards. For all parameter valuations inside a region the bound shall either be violated or met in the corresponding instantiated MC. Typically, the parameter space consists of both safe and unsafe regions.

Formally, let a *half-space* for parameters $V = \{p_1, \ldots, p_n\}$ be given by the linear inequality $a_1 p_1 + \ldots + a_n p_n \leq b$ with $a_1, \ldots, a_n, b \in \mathbb{Q}$. A *region* is a *convex polytope* defined by m half-spaces, i.e., a system of linear inequalities $A\mathbf{p} \leq b$ with $A \in \mathbb{Q}^{m \times n}$, $\mathbf{p} = (p_1 \ldots p_n)^T \in V^{n \times 1}$ and $b \in \mathbb{Q}^{m \times 1}$. Assume a rational function $f^r \in \mathbb{Q}_V$, $f^c \in \mathbb{Q}_V$, or $f^e \in \mathbb{Q}_V$ according to Definition 2 to be computed for a pMC $\mathcal{M}$ as explained in the previous section.

Definition 3 (Safe/Unsafe Region). *A region is safe iff there is no valuation u such that $A\mathbf{u} \leq b$ with $f^r_u > \lambda$, $f^c_u > \lambda$, or $f^e_u > \kappa$ with $\lambda \in [0, 1]$ and $\kappa \in \mathbb{R}_{\geq 0}$ where $\mathbf{u} = (u(p_1) \ldots u(p_n))^T$. A region is unsafe iff there is no valuation such that $f^r_u \leq \lambda$, $f^c_u \leq \lambda$, or $f^e_u \leq \kappa$. Otherwise, the region is called undetermined.*

By safe, unsafe, or undetermined we also refer to the *type* of a region. Given a region and a rational function together with a threshold, certifying the assumed type boils down to checking satisfiability of a conjunction of

– linear inequalities encoding the candidate region,
– nonlinear inequalities ensuring well-definedness of valuations, and
– a nonlinear inequality stating that the bound is violated or satisfied,

using an SMT solver such as Z3 [21]. The solver can then determine whether there exists a valuation inside the candidate region whose corresponding instantiated MC exceeds the threshold on the probability or the expected reward. If so, we obtain such a valuation from the solver and can conclude that the region is not safe. The obtained valuation serves as a *counterexample* to this region candidate.

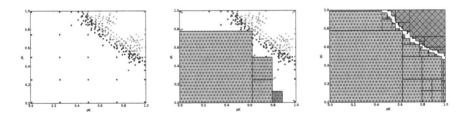

Fig. 3. Sampling and region analysis.

Sampling. As a guide for determining candidates for safe or unsafe regions, we apply sampling w.r.t. the property. An initially coarse sampling is iteratively refined by adding points based on the linear interpolation between samples from a safe and an unsafe region. Sampling can either be performed by instantiating a rational function describing these reachability probabilities or by instantiating the pMC and performing (non-parametric) probabilistic model checking, e. g., via PRISM. The latter is faster for a moderate number of sample points because of the costly computation of the rational function. However, the rational function is needed for verifying the safety of a region as described above.

Figure 3(left) shows an example sampling of the *Bounded Retransmission Protocol* (BRP) benchmark [22]. Red crosses indicate that λ is exceeded (i.e. the instantiated pMC is unsafe) while green dots indicate a safe instantiation.

Finding Region Candidates. For the construction of region candidates based on sample points, three methods are available. It is possible to generate *half-spaces* separating safe from unsafe points, successively enlarge rectangles containing only safe or only unsafe points, a technique that is commonly referred to as *growing rectangles*, or recursively separate the search space in *quadrants* that only contain either safe or unsafe points. In each iteration, the intermediate regions are checked for either safety or unsafety, based on the information from the sampling. The middle and right images in Fig. 3 show an example of region generation in the BRP benchmark, based on the initial sampling in the first figure. After 5 iterations, a large part of the solution space is already determined to be (un)safe. After 80 iterations, over 97 % of the area was covered by certified safe and unsafe regions, respectively. The remaining white space indicates that not the whole parameter space could yet be categorized into safe or unsafe points, but the approximation can be further refined in subsequent iterations. Currently, only pMCs with at most two parameters are supported, but all existing benchmark models satisfy this criterion. We plan to alleviate this restriction by supporting multi-dimensional convex regions, which is a straightforward extension for the rectangle and quadrant approaches, but challenging for the hyperplane approach.

Sensitivity Analysis. Besides analyzing in which regions the system behaves correctly w. r. t. the specification, it is often desirable to perform a sensitivity analysis [16], i. e., to determine in which regions of the parameter space a small perturbation of the system leads to a relatively large change in the considered measure. In our setting, such an analysis can be conducted with little additional effort. Given a rational function for a measure of interest, its derivations w. r. t. all parameters can be easily computed. Passing the derivations with user-specified thresholds to the SMT solver then allows for finding parameter regions in which the system behaves robustly. Adding the safety constraints described earlier, the SMT solver can find regions that are both safe *and* robust.

5   Implementation and Experiments

The complete tool chain is available online[2]. We implemented the model checking algorithms as described in Sect. 4 in the framework of a probabilistic model checker that is a redevelopment of MRMC [3] in C++. As for PARAM and PRISM, models are specified in a parametric version of PRISM's input language. From the model description, we construct the explicit transition matrix, which can then be reduced w.r.t. both *strong* [23] and *weak bisimulation* [24] in order to speed up the computation. As the state elimination process frequently deletes old transitions and creates new ones, we chose not to represent the transition matrix in the compressed row storage format [25], but rather implemented a hybrid between a sparse and a dense representation that only stores non-zero entries but does not store all rows consecutively in memory. Furthermore, for the representation of rational functions, we employ the newly developed modular arithmetic library CArL [26]. Since the simplification involves the costly computation of the greatest common divisor of polynomials, CArL tries to speed this up by caching and refining a partial factorization of rational functions, optimizing the ideas of [13].

The tool chain—integrating the model checking backend with the sampling algorithms, region generation and the web service—is implemented in Python using the SciPy packages [27] and the Shapely package. Currently supported SMT-solvers are Z3 [21] and SMT-RAT [28]. They are interfaced via the standard SMT-LIB format [29], in principle enabling to use all SMT solvers supporting non-linear real arithmetic. Due to numerical instabilities when sampling the rational function, we use exact arithmetics. As the performance of SciPy proved to be insufficient in this regard, we use CArL as sampling backend.

Experimental Evaluation. We evaluated the performance of our model checking backend on well-known benchmark models available on PRISM's [30] and param's [31] website, respectively. We compared the running times of our tool with those of PRISM and PARAM on reachability properties and expected reward properties. We ran the experiments on an HP BL685C G7 machine with 48 cores clocked with 2.0GHz each and possessing 192GB of RAM. However, we restricted the available RAM to 12GB for all experiments. We briefly explain the benchmark models, but refer to our website [32] for further details and a full list of benchmark results.

The first case study is the probabilistic *Bounded Retransmission Protocol* [22] that tries to send a file via an unreliable network. This model has two parameters: the reliability of each lossy channel. The *Crowds Protocol* [1] aims at anonymizing the sender of a message by routing it probabilistically through a larger crowd of communication parties. The parameters govern the probability that a message is once more forwarded in the crowd as well as the probability that a member of the crowd is not trustworthy. The *Zeroconf Protocol* [33] governs how hosts joining a network are being assigned a network address by probabilistically choosing

---

[2] http://moves.rwth-aachen.de/prophesy/.

one and then checking for possible collisions. This model is parametric in the probability that a collision happens and the probability that this is successfully detected. *Probabilistic Contract Signing* [34] tries to establish the commitment of two parties to a contract where no one trusts each other. It does so by revealing secrets bit by bit with a certain probability that is the single parameter of this model. Finally, *NAND Multiplexing* [35] describes fault-tolerant hardware using unreliable hardware by having copies of a NAND unit all doing the same job. Parameters are the probabilities of faultiness of the units and of erroneous inputs.

Table 1 shows the runtimes (in seconds) of PRISM, PARAM and PROPhESY on the selected benchmarks for different objectives where we chose the best-performing settings for each tool and benchmark instance. These concrete settings are given on our webpage to enable the reproducibility of our results. Note that to the best of our knowledge, no symbolic representation of pMCs is available.

Table 1. Runtimes of model checking on different benchmark models.

		instance	#states	#trans	PRISM verif.	PRISM total	PARAM verif.	PARAM total	PROPhESY verif.	PROPhESY total
reachability	brp	(128, 5)	10376	13827	215	218	5	7	2	**3**
		(256, 5)	20744	27651	1237	1242	32	33	8	**10**
	crowds	(15, 5)	592060	1754860	TO	TO	18*	48*	1	**46**
		(20, 5)	2061951	7374951	TO	TO	75*	194*	4	**165**
	nand	(20, 2)	154942	239832	886	901	44	48	16	**22**
		(20, 5)	384772	594792	TO	TO	319	328	89	**104**
exp. reward	egl	(5, 4)	74750	75773	5	11	–	–	< 1	**5**
		(8, 4)	7536638	7602173	543	910	–	–	7	**607**
	nand	(20, 2)	154942	239832	TO	TO	264	2033	5	**12**
		(20, 5)	384772	594792	TO	TO	TO	TO	47	**64**
	zconf	(10000)	10004	20005	TO	TO	TO*	TO*	4	**4**
		(100000)	100004	200005	TO	TO	TO*	TO*	255	**263**
conditional	brp	(256, 2)	10757	13827	–	–	–	–	< 1	1
		(256, 5)	20744	27651	–	–	–	–	1	3
	crowds	(15, 5)	592060	1754860	–	–	–	–	5	50
		(20, 5)	2061951	7374951	–	–	–	–	14	174

		instance	#states	#trans	PRISM verif.	PRISM total	Baier *et al.*[18] verif.	Baier *et al.*[18] total	PROPhESY verif.	PROPhESY total
conditional	brp	(256, 2)	10757	13827	6	10	13	16	< 1	**< 1**
		(256, 5)	20744	27651	10	14	65	69	< 1	**< 1**
		(256, 10)	37389	50691	16	20	325	328	< 1	**1**
	crowds	(10, 5)	111294	261444	95	99	11	16	< 1	**1**
		(15, 5)	592060	1754860	699	702	69	84	< 1	**6**
		(20, 5)	2061951	7374951	TO	TO	184	242	1	**19**

Besides the total time taken by the respective tool (columns "total"), we list the verification time (columns "verif."), i.e. the time needed to reduce the model and compute the rational function. The total time also includes the time needed to build the model. Each row of the table corresponds to one benchmark instance. As we observed that PARAM produced wrong results on some case studies when using specific settings, we list the times of the best setup that returned the correct result and marked the entries with a little star. All experiments marked with "TO" exceeded the time limit of one hour and the best total time is **boldfaced**.

When computing the rational function representing the reachability probability, PROPhESY is faster than PARAM, whereas PRISM is significantly slower than both its competitors. E.g. both PARAM and PROPhESY solve the larger crowds instances within less than four minutes, while PRISM is unable to compute a result within the time limit. Note that for the crowds case study, the raw verification times of PROPhESY are always strictly better than those of PARAM, even though the total time is not (always), because PARAM employs an efficient model building procedure that PROPhESY does not implement. Even without this technical advantage, PROPhESY beats PARAM on almost all instances. For the expected reward benchmarks, we did not list the times for PARAM for the egl case study, because the tool produced an incorrect rational function for the smaller instance for all settings and was unable to build the model for the larger instance. Overall, we observe that PROPhESY outperforms the other tools on all benchmark models.

The runtimes of PROPhESY on the case studies of the first "conditional" section of the table illustrate that our elimination-based algorithm to compute parametric conditional probabilities on pMCs is able to solve instances with millions of states and transitions. For instance, it takes only a few seconds longer to compute the conditional probability rather than the reachability probability on the largest crowds instance despite the more complicated objective.

Thanks to the authors of [18], we could compare the performance of our algorithm for computing conditional probabilities on *non-parametric* models with both (i) the "naive" quotient method available in PRISM and (ii) the prototypical implementation used in [18]. The second section "conditional" of Table 1 shows that we are able to compute the result at least one order of magnitude faster than both PRISM and the prototypical tool of [18] for all benchmarks.

Figure 4 shows a scatter plot of all mere verification times except for parametric conditional probability. The data shows how PROPhESY performs in comparison to the best competitor on any given instance. All points above the main diagonal indicate that our tool could solve the instance faster than the competitor, which is the case for all larger benchmarks; above the dashed diagonal, PROPhESY is more than ten times faster.

Finally, recall Fig. 3 showing how growing rectangles cover the parameter space starting from a sampling. For a practical evaluation, see Fig. 5 illustrating that large parts of the solution space are covered quickly by the

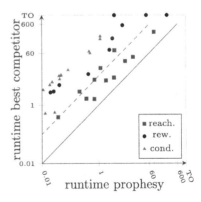

Fig. 4. The summarized results.

growing rectangles or using quadrants, but covering more area is increasingly

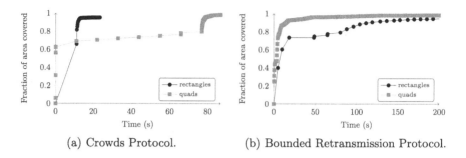

(a) Crowds Protocol.   (b) Bounded Retransmission Protocol.

Fig. 5. Area of solution space covered.

costly. Moreover, it depends strongly on the benchmark which of the technique performs best.

6   Related Work

Parameter synthesis for probabilistic models is a relatively new and challenging field. Daws [11] proposed to represent reachability probabilities by means of rational functions, which are obtained by state elimination (as for obtaining a regular expression from automata). This technique has been improved by Hahn *et al.* [19] by directly computing and simplifying intermediate functions, as a major drawback of these techniques is the rapid growth of functions. The simplification involves the addition of functions where the costly operation of computing the greatest common divisor (gcd) needs to be performed. Jansen *et al.* [13] further improved the state elimination technique by combining it with SCC decomposition, and a dedicated gcd-computation operating on partial factorizations of polynomials. State elimination is the core of the tool PARAM [10] and has recently been adopted in PRISM [2]. These are—to the best of our knowledge—the only available tools for computing reachability probabilities and expected rewards of pMCs. Note that all these tools just output the rational function—sometimes accompanied by constraints ensuring well-definedness—while none of them directly addresses the synthesis problem.

Other works include parameter synthesis of timed reachability in parametric CTMCs [36–38], synthesis for interval MCs and ω-regular properties [39].

Seshia *et al.* [40] investigate probabilities which are modeled as convex functions over independent parameters. In model repair [9,41], models refuting a given property are amended so as to satisfy this property. In this setting, parametric MCs are used as underlying model. The verification of MCs against parametric LTL formulas has been considered in [42]. Improved methods for single-parameter pMCs and nested reachability properties were presented in [43]. Finally, [16] presents several complexity results for perturbation analysis of pMCs.

Computing *conditional probabilities* for MCs has been considered in [18,44]. Usually, conditional probabilities are computed by the so-called quotient method involving verifying ω-regular properties. Baier *et al.* [18] presented an elegant algorithm reducing the problem to compute reachability probabilities in the MC and a copy of it and experimentally showed the superiority of this approach.

7 Conclusion and Future Work

We presented the new tool PROPhESY dedicated to parameter synthesis for pMCs. Beyond the superior model checking times over existing tools, it offers automated and user-guided methods for partitioning the parameter space into safe and unsafe parts. The service oriented architecture and modularity allow for a high usability. Future work will consider the extension to parametric Markov decision processes as well as continuous-time MCs. A further important extension will be parameter synthesis for a higher number of parameters.

Acknowledgements. We want to thank Ernst Moritz Hahn for valuable discussions on computing conditional probabilities for parametric MCs.

References

1. Reiter, M.K., Rubin, A.D.: Crowds: anonymity for web transactions. ACM Trans. Inf. Syst. Secur. **1**(1), 66–92 (1998)
2. Kwiatkowska, M., Norman, G., Parker, D.: PRISM 4.0: verification of probabilistic real-time systems. In: Gopalakrishnan, G., Qadeer, S. (eds.) CAV 2011. LNCS, vol. 6806, pp. 585–591. Springer, Heidelberg (2011)
3. Katoen, J.P., Zapreev, I.S., Hahn, E.M., Hermanns, H., Jansen, D.N.: The ins and outs of the probabilistic model checker MRMC. Perform. Eval. **68**(2), 90–104 (2011)
4. Garavel, H., Lang, F., Mateescu, R., Serwe, W.: CADP 2011: a toolbox for the construction and analysis of distributed processes. Softw. Tools Technol. Transf. **15**(2), 89–107 (2013)
5. Hahn, E.M., Li, Y., Schewe, S., Turrini, A., Zhang, L.: iscasMc: a web-based probabilistic model checker. In: Jones, C., Pihlajasaari, P., Sun, J. (eds.) FM 2014. LNCS, vol. 8442, pp. 312–317. Springer, Heidelberg (2014)
6. Alur, R., Henzinger, T.A., Vardi, M.: Theory in practice for system design and verification. ACM SIGLOG News **2**(1), 46–51 (2015)
7. Baier, C., Haverkort, B.R., Hermanns, H., Katoen, J.P.: Performance evaluation and model checking join forces. Commun. ACM **53**(9), 76–85 (2010)
8. Calinescu, R., Ghezzi, C., Kwiatkowska, M.Z., Mirandola, R.: Self-adaptive software needs quantitative verification at runtime. Commun. ACM **55**(9), 69–77 (2012)
9. Bartocci, E., Grosu, R., Katsaros, P., Ramakrishnan, C.R., Smolka, S.A.: Model repair for probabilistic systems. In: Abdulla, P.A., Leino, K.R.M. (eds.) TACAS 2011. LNCS, vol. 6605, pp. 326–340. Springer, Heidelberg (2011)
10. Hahn, E.M., Hermanns, H., Wachter, B., Zhang, L.: PARAM: a model checker for parametric markov models. In: Touili, T., Cook, B., Jackson, P. (eds.) CAV 2010. LNCS, vol. 6174, pp. 660–664. Springer, Heidelberg (2010)
11. Daws, C.: Symbolic and parametric model checking of discrete-time markov chains. In: Liu, Z., Araki, K. (eds.) ICTAC 2004. LNCS, vol. 3407, pp. 280–294. Springer, Heidelberg (2005)

12. Gruber, H., Johannsen, J.: Optimal lower bounds on regular expression size using communication complexity. In: Amadio, R.M. (ed.) FOSSACS 2008. LNCS, vol. 4962, pp. 273–286. Springer, Heidelberg (2008)

13. Jansen, N., Corzilius, F., Volk, M., Wimmer, R., Ábrahám, E., Katoen, J.-P., Becker, B.: Accelerating parametric probabilistic verification. In: Norman, G., Sanders, W. (eds.) QEST 2014. LNCS, vol. 8657, pp. 404–420. Springer, Heidelberg (2014)

14. Lanotte, R., Maggiolo-Schettini, A., Troina, A.: Parametric probabilistic transition systems for system design and analysis. Form. Asp. Comput. **19**(1), 93–109 (2007)

15. Clarke, E.M., Grumberg, O., Jha, S., Lu, Y., Veith, H.: Counterexample-guided abstraction refinement. In: Emerson, E.A., Sistla, A.P. (eds.) CAV 2000. LNCS, vol. 1855, pp. 154–169. Springer, Heidelberg (2000)

16. Chen, T., Feng, Y., Rosenblum, D.S., Su, G.: Perturbation analysis in verification of discrete-time markov chains. In: Baldan, P., Gorla, D. (eds.) CONCUR 2014. LNCS, vol. 8704, pp. 218–233. Springer, Heidelberg (2014)

17. Su, G., Rosenblum, D.S.: Asymptotic bounds for quantitative verification of perturbed probabilistic systems. In: Groves, L., Sun, J. (eds.) ICFEM 2013. LNCS, vol. 8144, pp. 297–312. Springer, Heidelberg (2013)

18. Baier, C., Klein, J., Klüppelholz, S., Märcker, S.: Computing conditional probabilities in markovian models efficiently. In: Ábrahám, E., Havelund, K. (eds.) TACAS 2014 (ETAPS). LNCS, vol. 8413, pp. 515–530. Springer, Heidelberg (2014)

19. Hahn, E.M., Hermanns, H., Zhang, L.: Probabilistic reachability for parametric Markov models. Softw. Tools Technol. Transf. **13**(1), 3–19 (2010)

20. Baier, C., Katoen, J.P.: Principles of Model Checking. The MIT Press, Cambridge (2008)

21. Jovanović, D., de Moura, L.: Solving non-linear arithmetic. In: Gramlich, B., Miller, D., Sattler, U. (eds.) IJCAR 2012. LNCS, vol. 7364, pp. 339–354. Springer, Heidelberg (2012)

22. Helmink, L., Sellink, M., Vaandrager, F.: Proof-checking a data link protocol. In: Barendregt, H., Nipkow, T. (eds.) TYPES 1993. LNCS, vol. 806, pp. 127–165. Springer, Heidelberg (1994)

23. Jonsson, B., Larsen, K.G.: Specification and refinement of probabilistic processes. In: Proceedings of LICS, pp. 266–277, IEEE CS (1991)

24. Baier, C., Hermanns, H.: Weak bisimulation for fully probabilistic processes. In: Grumberg, O. (ed.) CAV 1997. LNCS, vol. 1254, pp. 119–130. Springer, Heidelberg (1997)

25. Barrett, R., Berry, M., Chan, T.F., Demmel, J., Donato, J., Dongarra, J., Eijkhout, V., Pozo, R., Romine, C., Der Vorst, H.V.: Templates for the Solution of Linear Systems: Building Blocks for Iterative Methods, 2nd edn. SIAM, Philadelphia (1994)

26. CArL Website (2015). http://goo.gl/8QsVxv

27. Jones, E., Oliphant, T., Peterson, P., et al.: SciPy: open source scientific tools for python (2001)

28. Corzilius, F., Loup, U., Junges, S., Ábrahám, E.: SMT-RAT: an SMT-compliant nonlinear real arithmetic toolbox. In: Cimatti, A., Sebastiani, R. (eds.) SAT 2012. LNCS, vol. 7317, pp. 442–448. Springer, Heidelberg (2012)

29. Barrett, C., Stump, A., Tinelli, C.: The satisfiability modulo theories library (SMT-LIB) (2010). www.SMT-LIB.org

30. PRISM website (2015). http://prismmodelchecker.org

31. PARAM website (2015). http://depend.cs.uni-sb.de/tools/param/

32. Prophesy website (2015). http://moves.rwth-aachen.de/prophesy/
33. Bohnenkamp, H., Stok, P.V.D., Hermanns, H., Vaandrager, F.: Cost-optimization of the IPv4 zeroconf protocol. In: Proceedings of DSN, pp. 531–540, IEEE CS (2003)
34. Even, S., Goldreich, O., Lempel, A.: A randomized protocol for signing contracts. Commun. ACM **28**(6), 637–647 (1985)
35. Han, J., Jonker, P.: A system architecture solution for unreliable nanoelectronic devices. IEEE Trans. Nanotechnol. **1**, 201–208 (2002)
36. Han, T., Katoen, J.P., Mereacre, A.: Approximate parameter synthesis for probabilistic time-bounded reachability. In: Proceedings of RTSS, pp. 173–182, IEEE CS (2008)
37. Brim, L., Češka, M., Dražan, S., Šafránek, D.: Exploring parameter space of stochastic biochemical systems using quantitative model checking. In: Sharygina, N., Veith, H. (eds.) CAV 2013. LNCS, vol. 8044, pp. 107–123. Springer, Heidelberg (2013)
38. Češka, M., Dannenberg, F., Kwiatkowska, M., Paoletti, N.: Precise parameter synthesis for stochastic biochemical systems. In: Mendes, P., Dada, J.O., Smallbone, K. (eds.) CMSB 2014. LNCS, vol. 8859, pp. 86–98. Springer, Heidelberg (2014)
39. Benedikt, M., Lenhardt, R., Worrell, J.: LTL model checking of interval markov chains. In: Piterman, N., Smolka, S.A. (eds.) TACAS 2013 (ETAPS 2013). LNCS, vol. 7795, pp. 32–46. Springer, Heidelberg (2013)
40. Puggelli, A., Li, W., Sangiovanni-Vincentelli, A.L., Seshia, S.A.: Polynomial-time verification of PCTL properties of MDPs with convex uncertainties. In: Sharygina, N., Veith, H. (eds.) CAV 2013. LNCS, vol. 8044, pp. 527–542. Springer, Heidelberg (2013)
41. Chen, T., Hahn, E.M., Han, T., Kwiatkowska, M., Qu, H., Zhang, L.: Model repair for Markov decision processes. In: Proceedings of TASE, pp. 85–92, IEEE CS (2013)
42. Chakraborty, S., Katoen, J.-P.: Parametric LTL on markov chains. In: Diaz, J., Lanese, I., Sangiorgi, D. (eds.) TCS 2014. LNCS, vol. 8705, pp. 207–221. Springer, Heidelberg (2014)
43. Su, G., Rosenblum, D.S.: Nested reachability approximation for discrete-time markov chains with univariate parameters. In: Cassez, F., Raskin, J.-F. (eds.) ATVA 2014. LNCS, vol. 8837, pp. 364–379. Springer, Heidelberg (2014)
44. Andrés, M.E., van Rossum, P.: Conditional probabilities over probabilistic and nondeterministic systems. In: Ramakrishnan, C.R., Rehof, J. (eds.) TACAS 2008. LNCS, vol. 4963, pp. 157–172. Springer, Heidelberg (2008)

Software Analysis

Effective Search-Space Pruning for Solvers of String Equations, Regular Expressions and Length Constraints

Yunhui Zheng[1]($\boxtimes$), Vijay Ganesh[2], Sanu Subramanian[2], Omer Tripp[1], Julian Dolby[1], and Xiangyu Zhang[3]

[1] IBM T.J. Watson Research Center, Yorktown Heights, USA
zhengyu@us.ibm.com
[2] University of Waterloo, Waterloo, Canada
[3] Purdue University, West Lafayette, USA

Abstract. In recent years, string solvers have become an essential component in many formal-verification, security-analysis and bug-finding tools. Such solvers typically support a theory of string equations, the length function as well as the regular-expression membership predicate. These enable considerable expressive power, which comes at the cost of slow solving time, and in some cases even nontermination. We present two techniques, designed for word-based SMT string solvers, to mitigate these problems: (i) sound and complete detection of overlapping variables, which is essential to avoiding common cases of nontermination; and (ii) pruning of the search space via bi-directional integration between the string and integer theories, enabling new cross-domain heuristics. We have implemented both techniques atop the Z3-str solver, resulting in a significantly more robust and efficient solver, dubbed Z3str2, for the quantifier-free theory of string equations, the regular-expression membership predicate and linear arithmetic over the length function. We report on a series of experiments over four sets of challenging real-world benchmarks, where we compared Z3str2 with five different string solvers: S3, CVC4, Kaluza, PISA and Stranger. Each of these tools utilizes a different solving strategy and/or string representation (based e.g. on words, bit vectors or automata). The results point to the efficacy of our proposed techniques, which yield dramatic performance improvement. We argue that the techniques presented here are of broad applicability, and can be integrated into other SMT-backed string solvers to improve their performance.

1 Introduction

Reasoning over strings is gaining increasing importance due to the security threats imposed by improper handling of untrusted string values [7,19,27]. In response, different powerful string solvers have been developed, including, e.g., HAMPI [19], Kaluza [28], PISA [30], Stranger [32], CVC4 [22], S3 [31], Norn [6] and Z3-str [35]. These tools primarily solve the satisfiability problem over string

© Springer International Publishing Switzerland 2015
D. Kroening and C.S. Păsăreanu (Eds.): CAV 2015, Part I, LNCS 9206, pp. 235–254, 2015.
DOI: 10.1007/978-3-319-21690-4_14

(aka word) equations, with some of them also providing support for regular-expression (RE) membership predicates and linear arithmetic over the length function. While these tools have improved dramatically in recent years, the demand for even more efficient solvers continues to grow unabated.

Motivated by this need for efficient string solvers, we present two new techniques to solve combined string, regular-expression and integer constraints. These techniques are applicable primarily to SMT solvers that treat strings without abstractions or representation conversions, which we refer to collectively as *word-based string solvers*. Examples of such solvers include the Z3-str, CVC4 and S3 string solvers.

For the sake of completeness, we compare and contrast our techniques against solvers that use automata (e.g., PISA and Stranger) and bit-vector (e.g., Kaluza) string representations. Word-based string solvers have several important advantages: First, unlike bit-vector-based solvers, they can precisely model unbounded strings and string equalities without over-approximation, a feature that is crucial to string analysis of web applications. Second, by modeling strings and length in native domains, word-based string solvers can leverage the state of the art in integer constraint solving, and further enable hybrid techniques via powerful SMT engines. Finally, such solvers can take advantage of well-developed application-specific rewrite rules.

At the same time, a fundamental problem of word-based string solvers (unlike those based on bit vectors, which impose a finite domain) is that it is unclear, at present, whether the satisfiability problem for the quantifier-free theory of word equations, regular-expression membership predicate and length function is decidable [24]. All current practical string solvers suffer from incompleteness and nontermination. Addressing these problems is of primary importance, calling for new techniques to effectively explore the solution space. In light of this motivation, we have developed two techniques that address the respective problems of nontermination and search-space explosion.

First, a well-known reason for nontermination is overlapping variables [6,11,35], as we illustrate with the equation $a \cdot X = X \cdot b$, where a, b are constant strings and X is a string variable. Stated intuitively, the solution for X has to be in the form of $a \cdot X_1 \cdot b$, where X_1 is a string variable. The reduction step results in $a \cdot X_1 = X_1 \cdot b$, which is in the same form as the original equation, and thus leads to nontermination. However, this equation is obviously unsatisfiable. We revisit this example in Sect. 3, which highlights the need for a robust procedure to detect overlapping variables.

The second technique, given the tight interplay between string and integer values (in index-sensitive string operations), is bi-directional solver-level integration between the string and integer theories. This can be leveraged to drastically reduce the search space for typical constraints obtained from practical applications.

We have implemented both of these techniques atop the Z3-str solver as the Z3str2 solver for the satisfiability problem over a quantifier-free theory of word equations, regular-expression membership predicate as well as the length function. We report on a comprehensive set of experiments that validate the efficacy of our proposed techniques by comparing Z3str2 with Kaluza, PISA, Stranger, S3 and CVC4 over four sets of benchmarks derived from the real world.[1] We emphasize that our techniques are applicable also to other word-based string solvers such as S3 and CVC4.

Contributions. To summarize, this paper makes the following principal contributions:

1. Guided Search: We present two techniques designed for string solvers that treat strings as primitive types. The first is a sound and complete method to detect overlapping variables, which optimizes performance and avoids exploration of certain paths that may lead to nontermination. The second technique is a two-way integration between the string and integer theories, which enables effective pruning based on cross-domain heuristics.

2. Z3-str Integration: We have integrated both of the aforementioned techniques into the core solving algorithm of Z3-str. We describe the architecture of the resulting tool, Z3str2, and prove its soundness.

3. Experimental Study: To validate the efficacy of our techniques, we have conducted a comprehensive set of experiments where we compare Z3str2 against five solvers — namely, S3, CVC4, Kaluza, PISA and Stranger — on four benchmark suites. The results show that Z3str2 is significantly faster than competing solvers (often by orders of magnitude) in all but few cases.

1.1 Related Work

The theory considered in this paper – namely the quantifier-free (QF) theory T_{wlr} over word equations, membership predicate over REs, and length function – is a multi-sorted theory with string (str) and numeric (num) sorts. Makanin was the first to show, in 1977, that the QF theory of word equations is decidable [23]. Since, many have improved upon this seminal result [15,16,25,26,29]. In particular, Plandowski proved that this problem is in PSPACE [26]. Despite decades of effort, the satisfiability problem for T_{wlr} remains open [11,15,23,26]. Still, many practical solvers have been proposed.

Automata-Based Solvers. Regular languages (or automata), as well as context-free grammars (CFGs), can be used to represent strings and handling regex-related operations. JSA [8] computes CFGs for string variables in Java programs. Hooimeijer et al. [13] suggest an optimization whereby automata are built lazily. A primary challenge faced by automata-based approaches, which we do not suffer from, is to capture the connections between strings and other domains, e.g., integers. To overcome this limitation, refinements have been proposed. JST [12] extends JSA. It asserts length constraints in each automaton, and handles numeric constraints after conversion. PISA [30] encodes Java programs into M2L formulas that it discharges to the MONA solver to obtain

---

[1] The Z3str2 code, as well as the data pertaining to our experiments, are all available at [1].

path- and index-sensitive string approximations. PASS [20,21] combines automata and parametrized arrays for efficient treatment of unsat cases. Stranger is a powerful extension of string automata with arithmetic automata [32,33].

Bit-Vector Based Solvers. Another group of solvers converts string constraints to constraints into other domains such as integers or bit-vectors. HAMPI [19] is an efficient solver that represents strings as bit-vectors, though it requires the user to provide an upper bound on string lengths. Early versions of Kaluza [28] extended both STP [10] and HAMPI to support mixed string and numeric constraints represented as bit-vector. A similar approach powers Pex [7], though strings are reduced to integer abstractions.

Word-Based String Solvers. CVC4 [22] handles constraints over the theory of unbounded strings with length and RE membership. Solving is based on multi-theory reasoning backed by the DPLL(T) architecture combined with existing SMT theories. The Kleene star operator in RE formulas is dealt with via unrolling as in Z3str2. S3 [31] is another word-based solver, and it can be viewed as an extension of an early version of Z3-str. Roughly speaking, CVC4, S3 and Z3str2 embody similar approaches, and hence CVC4 and S3 can also benefit from the techniques proposed in this paper.

1.2   Formal Preliminaries

Syntax of Word Equations, RE Membership, and Length. We fix a disjoint two-sorted set of variables $var = var_{str} \cup var_{int}$; var_{str} consists of string variables, denoted $X, Y, S, \ldots$ and var_{int} consists of integer variables, denoted $m, n, \ldots$. We also fix a two-sorted set of constants $Con = Con_{str} \cup Con_{int}$. Moreover, $Con_{str} \subset \Sigma^*$ for some finite alphabet, Σ, whose elements are denoted $f, g, \ldots$. Elements of Con_{str} will be referred to as *string constants* or *strings*. Elements of Con_{int} are nonnegative integers. The empty string is represented by ϵ, and length 0. Terms may be string terms or integer terms. A string term is either an element of var_{str}, an element of Con_{str}, or a concatenation of string terms (denoted by the function *concat* or interchangeably by $\cdot$). An integer term is an element of var_{int}, an element of Con_{int}, the length function applied to a string term, a constant integer multiple of a integer term, or a sum of integer terms. The theory contains three types of atomic formulas, namely, word equations, length constraints, and RE membership predicates. REs are defined inductively, where constants and the empty string form the base case, and the operations of concatenation, alternation, and Kleene star are used to build up more complicated expressions (see details in [14]). REs may not contain variables. Z3str2 supports a list of common string-related operators such as charAt, containts, startswith, endswith, indexof, lastindexof, substring and etc. They are desugared to word equations with length functions. Formulas are defined inductively over atomic formulas and are quantifier-free.

Semantics of Word Equations, RE Membership, and Length. For a word, w, $len(w)$ denotes the length of w. The universe of discourse for the str sort is the set of strings Σ^*, and for the int sort is the set of natural numbers. For a word equation $t_1 = t_2$, we refer to t_1 as the left hand side (LHS), and t_2 as the right hand side (RHS). We fix a string alphabet, Σ. Given a formula θ, an *assignment* for θ (with respect to Σ) is a map from the set of variables in θ to $\Sigma^* \cup \mathbb{N}$ (where string variables are mapped to strings and integer variables are mapped to numbers). Given such an assignment, θ can be interpreted as an assertion about Σ^* and $\mathbb{N}$. If this assertion is true, then θ is *satisfiable* or SAT. A formula with no satisfying assignment is *unsatisfiable* or UNSAT. Two formulas θ, ϕ are *equisatisfiable* if θ is SAT iff ϕ is SAT. The *satisfiability problem* for a set S of formulas is to decide whether any given formula in S is SAT or not. The satisfiability problem for a set of formulas is decidable if there exists an algorithm (or *satisfiability procedure*) that solves its satisfiability problem. Satisfiability procedures must have three properties: soundness, completeness, and termination. Soundness and completeness guarantee that the procedure returns SAT if and only if the input formula is indeed SAT. More precisely, the procedure is sound if the procedure says UNSAT then the input is indeed unsatisfiable. Completeness is the converse of soundness.

2   Overview of the Design Z3str2 String Solver

The Z3str2 solver is essentially a string plug-in built into the Z3 SMT Solver [9], with an efficient integration between the string plug-in and Z3's integer solver. As can be seen from the architectural schematic of the Z3str2 string solver given in Fig. 1 (and an algorithmic description is given in Algorithm 1), the first step is to purify the input into two, namely, string constraints (word equations and RE membership) on the one hand, and integer linear arithmetic constraints over the length function on the other. Next, the word equations and RE constraints are input to the string plug-in. The plug-in may consult the Z3 core to detect equivalent terms. The word equations are solved using an algorithm described in detail in the Sect. 3 below. The RE constraints are solved by unrolling as described also in Sect. 3. The length constraints are converted into a system of pure integer linear arithmetic inequations and solved using Z3's integer solver. During the solving process, the string plug-in may generate length constraints that are incrementally added on demand to Z3's integer solver, that are regularly checked for consistency with both the input length constraints and previously added ones.

On any well-formed input as described in Sect. 1.2, Z3str2 may return SAT, UNSAT or UNKNOWN. Note that while Z3str2 can handle a boolean combination of atomic formulas, we refer only to conjunction of literals in the rest of paper without loss of generality. If either Z3's integer solver or our string plug-in determines that their respective purified inputs are UNSAT, Z3str2 reports UNSAT. If the string plug-in detects that the input equations have complicated overlaps that its heuristics cannot handle, it reports UNKNOWN. This is a source of incompleteness in Z3str2's implementation. Note that Z3str2, like other competing solvers such as CVC4, is sound but not complete.

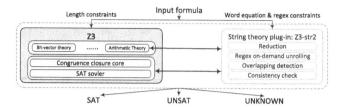

Fig. 1. Architecture of Z3str2.

The third and only remaining possibility is that both Z3's integer solver and the string plug-in determine that their respective purified inputs are SAT. However, this does not necessarily mean that the input is SAT. It could be that the solution produced by the integer solver is inconsistent with the solution produced by the string solver, or vice-versa. For example, the integer solver may say that a particular string variable, say X, has length equal to 1, while the string plug-in might produce a specific assignment for X that is of length equal to 2. One way to overcome this problem is to iterate through all possible solutions until a consistent one is found, assuming one exists. However, given that the domain of strings and natural numbers is infinite, it is possible that such an iterative procedure may loop forever in the event there are no consistent solutions to be found. In other words, if the input is indeed SAT, the procedure discussed here will correctly establish consistency and determine that the input is SAT. Unfortunately, it is possible that, when the input is in fact UNSAT, both the integer solver and string plug-in may determine that their respective purified inputs are SAT and may then loop forever searching for a combined consistent solution. They are obviously not going to find a combined consistent solution in such cases given that the input is in fact UNSAT, and hence the iterative procedure may not terminate.

The above-described problem of non-termination due to the interaction between the integer and string parts of the theory is not specific to Z3str2. In fact, the problem of deciding the satisfiability problem for the quantifier-free theory of word equations and length function remains open after decades of research and is a major open problem in mathematical logic [24]. In conclusion, if Z3str2 reports that the input is UNSAT, then indeed the input is UNSAT (soundness). However, the converse is not necessarily true, i.e., just like all other competing practical solvers, Z3str2 is not complete.

3   Word Equation Sub-solver in Z3str2

In this section, we focus on the word equation solving component of Z3str2. Starting with the work of Makanin [23], many decision procedures [15,26,29] have been proposed. While most procedures are not accompanied by practical implementations, they are a rich source of ideas for all the solvers that have recently been implemented. For example, the Z3str2 solver follows ideas, namely, *boundary labels, generalized word equations and arrangements* (discussed in greater

Algorithm 1. A high-level description of Z3str2's Algorithm

Input: Word equations $\mathcal{Q}_w$, and the corresponding integer linear arithmetic constraints $\mathcal{Q}_l$ over the length function
Output: SAT / UNSAT / UNKNOWN
1: **procedure** SOLVESTRINGCONSTRAINT($\mathcal{Q}_w$, $\mathcal{Q}_l$)
2:    **if** equations in $\mathcal{Q}_w$ are all in solved form and $\mathcal{Q}_w$ is UNSAT **or** $\mathcal{Q}_l$ is UNSAT **then**
3:      **return** UNSAT
4:    **if** equations in $\mathcal{Q}_w$ are all in solved form **and** $\mathcal{Q}_w$ and $\mathcal{Q}_l$ can be consistently determined as SAT together **then**
5:      **return** SAT
6:    Convert $\mathcal{Q}_w$ equisatisfiably in disjunctive normal form (DNF) formula $\mathcal{Q}_a$
7:    **for each** disjunct D in $\mathcal{Q}_a$ **do**
8:      Convert each equation in D to an arrangement consistent with the length constraints from the integer theory
9:      **for each** string variable x **do**
10:        Merge per-equation arrangements to a set of possible global arrangements, denoted as $G(x)$
11:        Detect arrangements with overlaps in $G(x)$
12:        **if** there is any overlap **then**
13:          Prune the global arrangements with the overlap from $G(x)$
14:      **for each** global arrangement combination selected from $G(x)$, $G(y)$..., for all variables x, y,... **do**
15:        Split each variable to sub-variables according to the selected global arrangement
16:        Convert $\mathcal{Q}_w$ equisatisfiably to a system $\mathcal{Q}'_w$ of simpler equation based on the new variables
17:        $\mathcal{Q}'_l$ is the corresponding new set of length constraints
18:        $r = $ **solveStringConstraint**($\mathcal{Q}'_w$, $\mathcal{Q}'_l$)
19:        **if** $r \equiv$ SAT **then**
20:          **return** SAT
21:    **if** overlapping variables have ever been detected **then**
22:      **return** UNKNOWN
23:    **else**
24:      **return** UNSAT

detail in Subsect. 4.1), that have their roots in the very first decision procedure for word equations by Makanin.

The key technique used by Z3str2 to solve a word equation W is to recursively convert W equisatisfiably into disjunction of conjunctions of simpler equations we call arrangements. These arrangements are computed by aligning the concatenation function on the LHS and RHS of a given equation such that an occurrence of concatenation function in the LHS (resp. RHS) may "split" or "cut" variables on the RHS (resp. LHS).

As an illustration, consider the following formula composed of three equations: $Z = X \cdot Y \ \wedge \ Z = W \cdot c \ \wedge \ c \cdot Y = c \cdot b \cdot c$, where X, Y, Z and W are string variables, and b and c are characters. A simple rewriting is the following:

$$Z = X \cdot Y \implies Z_1 = X \ \wedge \ Z_2 = Y \ ^{[1.1]}$$

$$Z = W \cdot \ c \implies Z_1 = W \ \wedge \ Z_2 = c \ ^{[1.2]}$$

$$c \cdot Y = c \cdot b \cdot c \implies Y = b \cdot c \ ^{[1.3]}$$

Observe that Z is split into Z_1 and Z_2, which are constrained differently. However, this rewriting is not satisfiable because $Y = c$ from equations [1.1] and [1.2], and $Y = b \cdot c$ from equation [1.3]. Now observe that the alignment described above is not the only one we can consider. Below is a different alignment that leads to a new splitting and in fact yields a satisfying assignment:

$$Z = W \cdot c \Longrightarrow Z_1 = W_1{}^{[1.4]} \wedge Z_2 = W_2 \cdot c^{[1.5]}$$

The difference now is that W is also split (into W_1 and W_2), and hence this splitting yields a satisfying assignment. In particular, from $[1.1], [1.3]$ and $[1.5]$, we have $W_2 = b$. Also note that X, Z_1 and W_1 become free variables as they are all equivalent but not constrained by any other variable.

What the above example highlights is that there are many different alignments of variable boundaries in the LHS (resp. RHS) that can split variables in the RHS (resp. LHS). We call every such alignment an *arrangement*. Here is the crucial fact about word equations: every equation can be equisatisfiably rewritten into a finite set of arrangements, where each arrangement is a finite set of word equations obtained from the splitting procedure described above. The Z3str2 solver exploits this fact, and solves word equations by converting them into finite sets of arrangements and inspecting each one individually to see if they are satisfiable. The input word equation is SAT if and only if at least one arrangement is SAT. This in a nutshell is how the word equations are solved by the Z3str2 solver, i.e., by recursively converting equations into a disjunction of arrangements (where each arrangement is a simpler set of equations) until a set of arrangements is derived where the satisfiability can determined purely via inspection.

Supporting Regular Expression Membership Predicates: A RE membership predicate $X \in \mathcal{R}$ is reduced to word equations by a transformation function $\rho(X, \mathcal{R})$, where X is a string variable and $\mathcal{R}$ is a regular expression. The function is defined as follows:

$$
\begin{aligned}
\rho(X, s) &::= && X = s, \text{ where } s \text{ is a constant string} \\
\rho(X, \mathcal{R}_1 | \mathcal{R}_2) &::= && \rho(X, \mathcal{R}_1) \vee \rho(X, \mathcal{R}_2) \\
\rho(X, \mathcal{R}_1 \cdot \mathcal{R}_2) &::= && X = T_1 \cdot T_2 \wedge \rho(T_1, \mathcal{R}_1) \wedge \rho(T_2, \mathcal{R}_2) \\
\rho(X, \mathcal{R}^*) &::= && X = unroll(\mathcal{R}, n) \wedge n \geq 0
\end{aligned}
$$

where n is a fresh integer variable for each Kleene star operation; T_1 and T_2 are fresh string variables; $unroll(\mathcal{R}, n)$ represents the expression obtained by unrolling $\mathcal{R}$ n times. After the RE membership predicates are replaced by word equations, the string solver proceeds as usual. When the solver explores various arrangements, the $unroll()$ functions are further simplified by the following rules.

$$
\begin{aligned}
X = unroll(\mathcal{R}, n_1) \quad &::= \text{ if } (n_1 = 0) \text{ then } \{X = \epsilon\} \text{ else } \{X = T_3 \cdot unroll(\mathcal{R}, n_1 - 1) \wedge \rho(T_3, \mathcal{R})\} \\
X \cdot Y = unroll(\mathcal{R}, n_1) &::= \text{ if } (n_1 = 0) \text{ then } \{X = \epsilon \wedge Y = \epsilon\} \text{ else } \{X = unroll(\mathcal{R}, n_2) \cdot T_3 \\
&\qquad \wedge Y = T_4 \cdot unroll(\mathcal{R}, n_3) \wedge n_1 = n_2 + n_3 + 1 \wedge \rho(T_3 \cdot T_4, \mathcal{R})\}
\end{aligned}
$$

Note that $\mathcal{R}$ is essentially unrolled once in the else branch of both rules. Just like in other existing solvers that support RE, the unrolling process may not terminate, especially when there are no length constraints associated with the involved variables. We hence rely on a timeout mechanism.

While simple, elegant and efficient for typical equations obtained from program analysis, the word equation solver described here may fall into infinite loops under certain circumstances. This problem and our approach are described at length below. In fact, the problem of "overlapping" variables described below is recognized by logicians as the crucial source of complexity in solving word equations.

Fig. 2. Graphical representation of an arrangement of $a \cdot X = X \cdot b$, where the two occurrences of X overlap represented by X_1.

A Word Equation that Highlights the Crucial Overlap Detection Problem: To illustrate the problem, consider the example: $a \cdot X = X \cdot b$, where X is a string variable. X appears both as the LHS suffix and as the RHS prefix. This equation is not satisfiable. However, if we solve it analogously, then the solving procedure will not terminate. In particular, the equation has three arrangements: The first arrangement is where $X = \epsilon$, resulting in the equation $a = b$ which is unsatisfiable. The second arrangement is where the concatenation function in the LHS and RHS align exactly such that we get $X = a \wedge X = b$. The third arrangement is where the LHS occurrence of X cuts the RHS occurrence in the RHS illustrated in Fig. 2.

Note that the suffix of X in the RHS (bottom part of Fig. 2) of the equation overlaps with the prefix of X in the LHS (top part of Fig. 2). We represent this overlapping part with a new variable X_1. By applying some simple rewrites we derive the following:

$$a \cdot X = X \cdot b \implies X = a \cdot X_1{}^{[2.1]} \wedge X = X_1 \cdot b \ ^{[2.2]}$$

From [2.1] and [2.2], we can infer $a \cdot X_1 = X_1 \cdot b$. Note this derived equation has the same form as the input formula. As a result, the above-mentioned decision procedure will not terminate, unless some steps are taken to detect such "overlaps" and determine their satisfiability without computing arrangements ad infinitum.

One could imagine heuristics to detect and handle relatively simple overlaps described above. However, in general, when many equations are involved with variables overlapping indirectly, the problem is not easy to detect or decide. In fact, overlapping variables get to the crux of the difficulty of solving word equations, for otherwise simple rewrites can solve such equations. Hence, any solution to detecting overlaps is of universal value, and can be used as subroutine by many different types of string solvers.

4 New Techniques for Improving Efficiency of String Solvers

In this section, we present two search space pruning techniques to improve performance of word-based string solvers.

4.1 Subroutine for Detecting Overlapping Variables in Word Equations

Here we provide details about detecting overlapping variables in word equations.

Definition 1 (Boundary Labels, Generalized Word Equations, Label Sets). *We define boundary labels (aka labels) using special symbols $\triangleright_n^\star$ (left) and $\triangleleft_n^\star$ (right), where $\star$ is either a character c or a variable X, and n denotes its n-th occurrence in the equation. A left/right pair of labels on either side of a variable or character uniquely identifies the boundaries of that occurrence of that character or variable. A set of labels is simply called a label set. A word equation E annotated with label sets, where these sets replace every (implicit) occurrence of the concatenation function in the words of E, is called a generalized word equation.*

Below is an example of the word equation $a \cdot X = X \cdot b$ annotated with boundary labels. Note that the right label of the character "a" and the left label of the variable X are grouped into the set $\{\triangleleft_1^a, \triangleright_1^X\}$:

$$\{\triangleright_1^a\} a \{\triangleleft_1^a, \triangleright_1^X\} X \{\triangleleft_1^X\} \; = \; \{\triangleright_2^X\} X \{\triangleleft_2^X, \triangleright_1^b\} b \{\triangleleft_1^b\}$$

Definition 2 (Label Arrangements and Merging of Label Sets). *Given a word equation E, a label arrangement or simply arrangement A of E is an ordered sequence of label sets, where each label set in A is obtained by taking the union (aka "merging") of sequences of label sets from the LHS and RHS of E. We define the merge of two sequences $S_1 \equiv \{l_1, \cdots, l_k\}$ and $S_2 \equiv \{r_1, \cdots, r_k\}$ as some sequence S_3 whose elements are either simply elements of S_1 or S_2 or the union of some elements of S_1 and S_2.*

The intuition behind the construction of an arrangement A of given equation $l = r$ is very straightforward, namely, that we align the natural boundaries of the LHS l and RHS r by appropriately merging the label sets of the LHS and the RHS of E to obtain arrangements. The reason we construct arrangement is that it allows us to recursively derive simpler equations from a given equation E, until they are so simple that their satisfiability can be trivially determined.

By construction, a word equation can be equisatisfiably reduced to a finite disjunction of arrangements (The satisfiability of an arrangement is defined in terms of the word equations it implies). To better understand how arrangements are derived from an equation (or more precisely a generalized word equation) consider the following:

$$\{\triangleright_1^a\} a \{\triangleleft_1^a, \triangleright_1^Y\} Y \{\triangleleft_1^Y\} \; = \; \{\triangleright_1^X\} X \{\triangleleft_1^X, \triangleright_1^b\} b \{\triangleleft_1^b\}$$

A possible arrangement of its two words is the following:

$$\{\triangleright_1^a, \triangleright_1^X\} \; \cdot \; \{\triangleleft_1^a, \triangleleft_1^X, \triangleright_1^Y, \triangleright_1^b\} \cdot \{\triangleleft_1^Y, \triangleleft_1^b\}$$

From this arrangement, we can easily derive two smaller equations, $X = a$ and $Y = b$, which directly yield a solution. In our tech report (TR) [34] we describe, in much greater detail, several operations for label set manipulation and of "merging" label sets to obtain arrangements, and merging arrangements from multiple word equations. These operations are key for detecting complex overlapping variables that occur over multiple equations, and are not immediately obvious as is the case in $a \cdot X = X \cdot b$.

Detecting Overlapping Variables by Merging Arrangements: Just as we can construct arrangements by merging the ordered sequence of labels over words from a single equation, we can merge the arrangements obtained from multiple word equations, when these equations contain occurrences of the same variable. Intuitively, the arrangements from multiple equations may imply a variable being cut/split differently (e.g., X is cut by the boundary of Y in one equation and by the boundary of Z in another). Our algorithm explores all the possible orders of the cuts from different arrangements, denoted as label sets, for the same variable. Each order yields a *global arrangement* for the variable. As such, each variable is divided into a set of sub-variables guided by the global arrangement; the previous system of equations is hence reduced to a new system of equations with shorter and simpler words. More details can be found in our TR.

Detection of overlapping variable can be done by checking the following condition in any global arrangement: in the ordered sequence of label sets of a global arrangement, there exists a left label of an occurrence of a variable X that occurs in a label set in between two label sets where the first contains the left label and the second contains the right label of another occurrence of X. We say that X is an overlapping variable in the given system of word equations. As an example, consider the arrangement in Fig. 2 that has overlapping variables. This arrangement written per the formal definition as a sequence of label sets we have:

$$\{\triangleright_1^a, \triangleright_2^X\} \cdot \{\triangleleft_1^a, \triangleright_1^X\} \cdot \{\triangleleft_2^X, \triangleright_1^b\} \cdot \{\triangleleft_1^X, \triangleleft_1^b\}$$

Theorem 1. *The subroutine for detecting overlapping variables is sound, complete and terminating, i.e., it correctly detects all overlapping variables and terminates.*

4.2   String and Integer Theory Integration

Basic Length Rules. For strings X and Y, we assert the following: (1) $|X| \geq 0$ (2) $|X| = 0 \leftrightarrow X = \epsilon$ (3) $X = Y \rightarrow |X| = |Y|$ (4) $|X \cdot ... \cdot Y| = |X| + ... + |Y|$.

String and Integer Theory Integration: As discussed in Sect. 2, finding a consistent solution for both strings and numbers can be expensive due to the infinite search space. The goal of string and integer theory integration is to achieve synergy from the two such that the procedure can converge faster. In particular, one theory will generate new assertions in the domain of the other theory, and vice versa. Inside the string theory, the set of arrangements that is explored is constrained by the assertions on string lengths, which are provided by the integer theory. On the other hand, the string theory will derive new length assertions when it makes progress in exploring new arrangements. These assertions are provided to the integer theory so that the search space is pruned.

Consider $X \cdot Y = M \cdot N$, where X, Y, M and N are nonempty string variables. It has three possible arrangements: $[a1]$ $X = M \cdot T_1 \wedge N = T_1 \cdot Y$; $[a2]$ $X = M \wedge N = Y$; $[a3]$ $M = X \cdot T_2 \wedge Y = T_2 \cdot N$. Assume the integer theory infers that $|X| > |M|$ or $|Y| < |N|$. Thus, only $[a1]$ is consistent with the length conditions.

The string solver only needs to explore one arrangement instead of three. On the other hand, assume the string solver is exploring arrangement $[a1]$. It generates a new assertion $[a1] \rightarrow |X| = |M \cdot T_1| \wedge |N| = |T_1 \cdot Y| \wedge |X| > |M| \wedge |N| > |Y|$, which in turn triggers the Z3 core to add an integer assertion.

Note that different string solvers implement string and integer integrations in vastly different ways [7,22,31,33]. [7] focuses on integration in a staged manner. [33] focuses on integration via automata manipulations. [22,31] and Z3str2 are integrations within the DPLL(T) architecture, where the algorithm only solves parts of the formula on demand and learns new constraints as it solves such that these implied constraints often cut the search dramatically. Compared to [22,31], our integration is tighter, powered by the bi-directional heuristics.

5   Soundness of the Z3str2 Algorithm

In this section we sketch the soundness proof of Z3str2's algorithm given in Algorithm 1. For a detailed formal analysis we refer the reader to the associated tech-report. The soundness property of any decision procedure in an SMT solving context can be stated as "If the procedure returns UNSAT, then input formula is indeed UNSAT".

Theorem 2. *Algorithm 1 is sound, i.e., when Algorithm 1 reports UNSAT, the input constraint is indeed UNSAT.*

Proof. To see that Z3str2 is sound, we show that the UNSAT returned at line 3 and line 24 are both sound. First observe that line 3 returns an UNSAT if either string or integer constraints are determined to be UNSAT. For string constraints, we use the algorithms described in [11] to decide the satisfiability of word (dis)equations in the solved form. The soundness of line 3 relies on the soundness of the procedure [11] and the integer solver (here Z3).

For the UNSAT returned at line 24, we show transformations impacting it are all satisfiability-preserving. If a transformation is satisfiability-preserving, it means its output formula is satisfiable if and only if its input formula is satisfiable. In particular, transformations at (i) line 6 (ii) line 8 (iii) line 10 and (iv) lines 15–16 are satisfiability-preserving: (i) The disjunctive normal form conversion at line 6 is obviously satisfiability-preserving. (ii) The conversion in line 8 is probably the most involved in terms of establishing soundness. This step is a variant of the idea of sound transformation of word equations to arrangements mentioned in Makanin's paper [23]. We can show that arrangement generation is satisfiability-preserving because each arrangement is a finite set of equations implied by the input system of equations. In addition, we extract length constraints from arrangements and they may conflict with the existing integer constraints. If so, we drop inconsistent arrangements based on the UNSAT results determined by the integer theory. Similarly, since we assume the integer theory is sound, this step is also satisfiability-preserving. (iii) At line 10, we systematically enumerate all feasible orders among boundary labels according to the Definition 2. This step is satisfiability-preserving. (iv) In lines 15 and 16, this step derives simpler equations by a satisfiability-preserving rewriting. Please see the technical report for proof details. Note the REs are reduced to word equations so that they can be handled by this same procedure. In addition, although we prune arrangements at line 13, the answer can only be SAT or UNKNOWN once this happens. The algorithm is still sound. Therefore, we return UNSAT exactly when we can prove this to be the case.

6 Experimental Results

In this section, we describe the implementation of Z3str2, as well as experiments to validate the efficacy of the new techniques proposed in this paper, namely, overlapping-variable detection and deeper string/integer theory integration. Both techniques improve solver efficiency in isolation, as well as when switched on simultaneously. However, in the interest of space we only report their combined contributions.

1. Detection of Overlapping Variables. During solving, Z3str2 prunes away arrangements with overlapping variables, leading to a smaller search space. Thus, if the technique is effective, we would be able to observe that other solvers time out on the cases reported as UNKNOWN by Z3str2. In Z3str2, an UNKNOWN result is returned when no SAT can be established in all arrangements with non-overlapping variables.

2. Evaluating String and Integer Theory Integration. The contribution of the string and integer integration will be illustrated by the improvement on the performance in resolving both the SAT and UNSAT cases, in comparison with other solvers.

We compare Z3str2 against five state-of-the-art string solvers, namely, CVC4 [22], S3 [31], Kaluza [28], PISA [30], and Stranger [32] across four different suites of benchmarks obtained from Kudzu/Kaluza [28], PISA [30], AppScan Source [2]

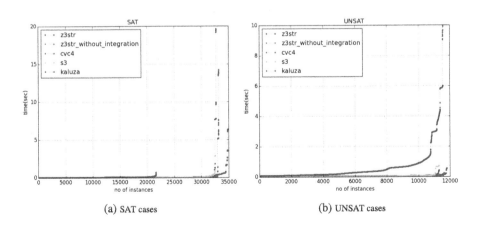

(a) SAT cases   (b) UNSAT cases

Fig. 3. Cactus plots for the Kaluza benchmark suite (incorrect results excluded)

and Kausler's [18] projects. Given the rich and diversified landscape of string problems, we chose to validate our approach using benchmarks from real-world applications with different characteristics. Additionally, the total number of tests on which we compared Z3str2 with other solvers is approximately 69,000.

Kaluza Benchmark Suite. The Kaluza constraints were generated by a JavaScript symbolic execution engine [28], where length, concatenation and (finite) RE membership queries occur frequently. Both CVC4 and S3 were originally evaluated only on this suite, which consists of approximately 50 K problems in the Kaluza format. The CVC4 team selected 47, 284 of them, and translated them into the CVC4 format. The S3 team did the translation to S3 format. We wrote translators from CVC4 to Z3str2, and from Z3str2 to CVC4. The timeout threshold for comparison over this suite was set at 20 seconds per problem, which was the threshold used in CVC4 [22].

PISA Benchmark Suite. While the Kaluza suite is large and diverse, and includes string problems of varying sizes, it only contains a small subset of string operations. To make the comparison more comprehensive, we included constraints from real-world Java sanitizer methods that were used in the evaluation of the PISA system [30]. Sanitizers cleanse user input to remove the threat of an injection attack. They are usually complex and utilize various primitive string operations. We generated two groups of constraints: First, as in the PISA paper, we encode the semantics of the sanitizers and check the return value(s) against predefined attack patterns (such as cross-site scripting (XSS)). In the second group, we also encode input constraints per the application defining the sanitizer. For the PISA suite, we set a timeout value of 200 seconds due to its higher complexity.

AppScan Benchmark Suite. The third suite of benchmarks is derived from security warnings output by IBM Security AppScan Source Edition [2], an application sold commercially by IBM. These reflect potentially vulnerable information flows, represented as traces of program statements, which yield more representative real-world constraints than focusing on sanitizers only. We ran AppScan on popular websites to obtain traces. Similar to the PISA benchmarks, the AppScan constraints also utilize a rich set of string operators. As with PISA, timeout here too was set at 200 seconds per benchmark.

Kausler Benchmark Suite. The final suite is extracted from 8 Java programs by Scott Kausler [18]. They represent path conditions obtained from dynamic symbolic execution, and are pure string constraints [17]. Unlike other benchmarks, Kausler's suite does not dump string constraints to file but instead calls the solvers via an API. The suite contains 174 path condition encoding files, and the resulting constraints are input to the solvers in-memory via their APIs. The comparison [18] was originally done using a driver interface [3]. However, we observed bugs ranging from JNI issues for Stranger to generating invalid constraints for Z3str2. We made our best attempt to compare Z3str2 with Stranger using modified interfaces [1] patched by both the Stranger team and us.

Table 1. Results on Kaluza suite [28].

	Z3str2		Z3str2 w/o integration		CVC4		S3		Kaluza	
	$\checkmark$	$\times$	$\checkmark$	$\times$	$\checkmark$	$\times$	$\checkmark$	$\times$	$\checkmark$	$\times$
sat	34859	0	32752	0	33190	0	32503	488	21651	n/a
unsat	11799	0	11313	0	11625	0	11351	412	12099	10909
unknown	626†		395†		0		0		0	
timeout	0		2824		2469		989		340	
tool reports error	0		0		0		2		2285	
crash	0		0		0		1539		0	
Total time (sec)	4288.8**(1x)**		61232.8**(14.3x)**		52478.8 **(12.2x)**		22543.4 **(5.3x)**		46753.9 **(10.9x)**	

† 'unknown' indicates Z3str2 detected and avoided overlapping arrangements.

6.1 Performance Results

The results we obtained are summarized in Tables 1–3 and Fig. 3 with appropriate references to the various benchmark suites[2].

Kaluza Suite. In Table 1, "tool reports error" counts the number of inputs on which the solver reports an error. "crash", instead, refers to runtime errors such as segfaults. For "sat" and "unsat", $\times$ denotes the number of provably incorrect results (either an "unsat" response where the problem has a verified solution or a "sat" response with an infeasible solution, as defined in [22]), and $\checkmark$ the rest. The comparison involves Z3str2 without bi-directional integration, CVC4 and S3, but not PISA, as PISA cannot model string lengths or symbolic arithmetic operations that are intensive in the suite.

According to Table 1, neither Z3str2 nor CVC4 report any provably incorrect result, though Z3str2 is more effective and can solve more cases (46658 compared to 44815) without timeouts. Though Z3str2 additionally has 626 unknown cases, CVC4 times out on all these cases. Z3str2 without bi-directional integration solves 2593 fewer cases and timeouts more often. S3 has errors in both directions, as well as an overall of 989 timeouts, while Kaluza suffers less from timeouts (340) but has many sat-as-unsat errors (10909). Kaluza therefore is unsound. Since Kaluza only provides assignments for variables matching the query, sat answers are not verifiable. Both S3 and Kaluza also have tool errors (2 and 2285, respectively). In addition, S3 crashes on 1539 cases. To compare performance on the sat and unsat Kaluza cases across the different solvers, we created the cactus plots in Figs. 3a (sat) and 3b (unsat). Incorrect results are excluded. In both categories, Z3str2 and CVC4 have comparable performance, while Z3str2 solves more cases and is faster on complex cases. S3 and Z3str2 without string-integer integration are slower. Kaluza has the worst performance.

---

[2] All experiments were performed on a workstation running Ubuntu 12.04 with an i7-3770 CPU and 8GB of RAM memory. For reproducibility, we have made the Z3str2 source code publicly available [1]. We used V1.5-prerelease of CVC4; the version of S3 from the original paper [31]; the Kaluza version from the CVC4 paper with "var" as the query string; and Stranger from [4].

PISA Suite. Table 2 presents the results on the PISA benchmarks. The "string operators stats" column lists the involved operations and their number of occurrences. In addition, we also count the number of variables and predicates for each format. In this comparison, we included CVC4 and PISA, but not S3 and Kaluza, as we were not able to model popular string operations such as indexof using their language. Besides, for PISA, while one group of constraints is equivalent to the MONA program generated by PISA, enabling proper comparison, the other group requires changes to the PISA translation algorithm (to fix the input constraints as well as the negative output constraints), and thus the respective comparisons were not possible. From Table 2, we have the following observations. First, Z3str2 reports 8 sat cases compared to 6 by CVC4 and 2 timeouts. For the 6 sats in common, Z3str2 solves them in $1.069s$ while CVC4 requires $51.394s$. Second, MONA and Z3str2 are in agreement. MONA runs faster on the sat cases, though it cannot generate satisfying string assignments, and has comparable performance to Z3str2 on the unsat cases.

AppScan Suite. The results of the third comparison over the AppScan suite appear in Table 3. Z3str2 reports sat on 8 cases while CVC4 agrees on 4 and times out on the rest. The performance gap between the solvers on sat cases in agreement is significant: Z3str2 completes in $0.707s$, whereas the CVC4 solving time is $154.852s$.

Kausler Suite. We were able to run the Stranger tool on 5 sets in this suite — namely, *beasties, jerichoHTMLParser, mathParser, mathQuizGame* and *natural-CLI* — without crashing or hanging. Across these 5 sets, we found that the average solving time per constraint instance for Z3str2 are $6.4ms$, $10.7ms$, $39.9ms$, $7.1ms$ and $23.4ms$ respectively, and for Stranger are $51.8ms$, $5.9ms$, $1.4ms$, $9.4ms$ and $3.0ms$. Z3str2 is faster than Stranger on two of these sets, Stranger is faster than Z3str2 on the remaining three.

However, these findings should be qualified. First, Stranger crashes or hangs on 98 files. Z3str2 neither crashes nor hangs nor times out on any of the gen-

Table 2. Results on constraints generated from sanitizers detected by PISA [30].

input	string operators stats (omitting eq and dis-eq)	Z3str2				CVC4				PISA-MONA			
		var	pred	result	time (s)	var	pred	result	time (s)	var	pred	result	time (s)
pisa-000.smt2	contains (3), indexof (1), substring (1)	4	12	sat (√)	0.164	4	12	sat (√)	0.264	9	301	sat (?[+])	0.029
pisa-001.smt2	contains (1), indexof (1), substring (1)	4	9	sat (√)	0.114	4	9	sat (√)	0.032	—[+]	—[+]	—[+]	—[+]
pisa-002.smt2	contains (4)	2	10	sat (√)	0.114	2	10	sat (√)	50.871	—	—	—	—
pisa-003.smt2	contains (3), concat (1)	3	11	unsat (√)	0.064	3	11	timeout	200.00	—	—	—	—
pisa-004.smt2	contains (2), indexof (1), length (1), lastIndexof[†] (1), substring (2)	7	22	unsat (√)	0.038	10	32	timeout	200.00	9	331	unsat (√)	0.041
pisa-005.smt2	indexof (1), lastIndexof[†] (1), length (1), substring (2),	7	23	sat (√)	0.115	10	33	sat (√)	0.165	—	—	—	—
pisa-006.smt2	indexof (1), lastIndexof[†] (1), length (1), substring (2), contains (1)	7	24	unsat (√)	0.039	11	36	timeout	200.00	9	331	unsat (√)	0.038
pisa-007.smt2	indexof (2), lastIndexof[†] (1), length (1), substring (2), contains (1)	8	26	unsat (√)	0.042	11	36	timeout	200.00	9	324	unsat (√)	0.039
pisa-008.smt2	replace[*] (5), contains (2)	6	13	sat (√)	0.214	6	13	timeout	200.00	9	283	sat (?[+])	0.031
pisa-009.smt2	replace (2), concat (1), contains (2)	3	8	sat (√)	0.447	3	8	sat (√)	0.046	9	292	sat (?[+])	0.054
pisa-010.smt2	replace (2), concat (1)	3	6	sat (√)	0.165	3	6	timeout	200.00	—	—	—	—
pisa-011.smt2	replace (1), concat (2)	3	6	sat (√)	0.115	3	6	sat (√)	0.016	—	—	—	—

+ We could not generate constraints without changing PISA. No string solutions are generated so it's not verifiable.

† CVC4 doesn't provide operator 'lastIndexof'. We encode it with operators "concat", "length" and "contains".

* replace applies to the first occurrence of the argument string for both Z3str2 and CVC4.

Table 3. Results on constraints derived from AppScan traces [2].

input	string operators stats (omitting eq and dis-eq)	Z3str2				CVC4			
		var	pred	result	time (s)	var	pred	result	time (s)
t01.smt2	indexof (4), substring (3)	7	37	sat ($\checkmark$)	0.265	7	37	timeout	200.00
t02.smt2	concat (3), membership (1), regexConcat (2), regexUnion (14), str2Regex (17), length (1)	5	47	sat ($\checkmark$)	0.215	5	33	sat ($\checkmark$)	0.026
t03.smt2	concat (3), membership (1), regexConcat (2), regexUnion(14), str2Regex (17), length(1)	5	46	sat ($\checkmark$)	2.519	5	32	timeout	200.00
t04.smt2	concat (5), membership (1), regexConcat (2), regexUnion (14), str2Regex (17), length(1)	6	50	sat ($\checkmark$)	4.574	6	35	timeout	200.00
t05.smt2	concat (3), membership (1), regexConcat (2), indexof (1) regexUnion (14), str2Regex (17), length (2), substring (1)	8	56	sat ($\checkmark$)	2.770	8	42	timeout	200.00
t06.smt2	concat (1), indexof (3), endsWith (5)	5	33	sat ($\checkmark$)	0.214	5	33	sat ($\checkmark$)	3.021
t07.smt2	concat (6), regexStar (2), str2Regex (4), endsWith (2) regexUnion (2), membership (2), startsWith (2)	8	32	sat ($\checkmark$)	0.114	8	29	sat ($\checkmark$)	0.115
t08.smt2	concat (2), regexStar (2), str2Regex (4), endsWith (2) regexUnion (2), membership (2), startsWith (2)	5	23	sat ($\checkmark$)	0.164	5	22	sat ($\checkmark$)	151.663

erated instances. We have omitted these 98 files from our comparison. Additionally, Stranger over-approximates disequalities ($\neq$ operator) among variables that can represent multiple strings [5]. We observe that such cases commonly exist in all sets (the percentages of instances with $\neq$ operators in each set are 83.4 %, 61.7 %, 79.0 %, 96.0 % and 95.0 % respectively, and many fall into this category of disequalities among variables that represent multiple strings). This implies that Stranger produces unsound results. We believe that some of these constraints are easy for Stranger thanks to this over-approximation. By contrast Z3str2 correctly implements all operators and predicates in its input language. Finally, Stranger requires that integers occurring as indices and length bounds be constant, whereas Z3str2 and most other competing solvers support integers symbolically thus providing expressive power that is essential in practice.

6.2 Interpretation of Results

The general trend, across all benchmark suites, is that CVC4 has comparable performance to Z3str2 although CVC4 times out far more often than Z3str2, whereas S3 is significantly slower. These results establish the efficacy of both techniques presented in this paper.

Detection of Overlapping Variables. Z3str2 can decide either sat or unsat on 98.7 %, 100 % and 100 % of the instances in the Kaluza, PISA and AppScan suites, respectively. CVC4, in comparison, achieves 94.8 %, 50 % and 50 %. For unknowns reported by Z3str2 on the Kaluza instances, which occur in merely 1.3 % of the cases, CVC4 times out on all of them. This lends support to our design choice of purposely pruning away parts of the solution space (those with overlapping arrangements) to avoid nontermination.

String and Integer Theory Integration. As the comparisons between Z3str2 versions with and without the integration clearly demonstrate, there is significant gain thanks to tightening the integer and string theory integration, which enables generation of implied constraints in both domains for more aggressive elimination of assignments unsatisfying for combined string-integer constraints.

7   Conclusion

We have described two techniques that dramatically improve the efficiency of word-based string solvers: (i) a sound and complete procedure to detect overlapping variables, thereby automatically identifying and avoiding sources of nontermination; and (ii) tight bi-directional integer/string theory integration, thereby pruning a vast array of inconsistent search candidates. We have implemented both of these techniques on top of Z3-str as Z3str2. We show the efficacy of these techniques through an extensive set of experiments, comparing Z3str2 with the CVC4, S3, Kaluza, PISA and Stranger solvers over four benchmark suites derived from real-world applications.

References

1. Z3str2 String constraint solver. https://sites.google.com/site/z3strsolver/
2. IBM security AppScan source. http://www-03.ibm.com/software/products/en/appscan-source
3. Kausler suite. https://github.com/BoiseState/string-constraint-solvers
4. LibStranger. https://github.com/vlab-cs-ucsb/LibStranger
5. Personal communications with the stranger team (2015)
6. Abdulla, P.A., Atig, M.F., Chen, Y.-F., Holík, L., Rezine, A., Rümmer, P., Stenman, J.: String constraints for verification. In: Biere, A., Bloem, R. (eds.) CAV 2014. LNCS, vol. 8559, pp. 150–166. Springer, Heidelberg (2014)
7. Bjørner, N., Tillmann, N., Voronkov, A.: Path feasibility analysis for string-manipulating programs. In: Kowalewski, S., Philippou, A. (eds.) TACAS 2009. LNCS, vol. 5505, pp. 307–321. Springer, Heidelberg (2009)
8. Christensen, A.S., Møller, A., Schwartzbach, M.I.: Precise analysis of string expressions. In: Cousot, R. (ed.) SAS 2003. LNCS, vol. 2694, pp. 1–18. Springer, Heidelberg (2003)
9. De Moura, L., Bjørner, N.S.: Z3: an efficient SMT solver. In: Ramakrishnan, C.R., Rehof, J. (eds.) TACAS 2008. LNCS, vol. 4963, pp. 337–340. Springer, Heidelberg (2008)
10. Ganesh, V., Dill, D.L.: A decision procedure for bit-vectors and arrays. In: Damm, W., Hermanns, H. (eds.) CAV 2007. LNCS, vol. 4590, pp. 519–531. Springer, Heidelberg (2007)
11. Ganesh, V., Minnes, M., Solar-Lezama, A., Rinard, M.: Word equations with length constraints: what's decidable? In: Biere, A., Nahir, A., Vos, T. (eds.) HVC. LNCS, vol. 7857, pp. 209–226. Springer, Heidelberg (2013)
12. Ghosh, I., Shafiei, N., Li, G., Chiang, W.-F.: JST: an automatic test generation tool for industrial java applications with strings. In: Proceedings of the 2013 International Conference on Software Engineering, ICSE 2013, pp. 992–1001 (2013)
13. Hooimeijer, P., Weimer, W.: Solving string constraints lazily. In: Proceedings of the IEEE/ACM International Conference on Automated Software Engineering, ASE 2010, pp. 377–386 (2010)

14. Hopcroft, J.E., Motwani, R., Ullman, J.D.: Introduction to Automata Theory, Languages, and Computation. Pearson/Addison Wesley, Upper Saddle River (2007)
15. Jeż, A.: Recompression: word equations and beyond. In: Béal, M.-P., Carton, O. (eds.) DLT 2013. LNCS, vol. 7907, pp. 12–26. Springer, Heidelberg (2013)
16. Karhumäki, J., Mignosi, F., Plandowski, W.: The expressibility of languages and relations by word equations. J. ACM **47**(3), 483–505 (2000)
17. Kausler, S.: Evaluation of string constraint solvers using dynamic symbolic execution. Master's thesis, Boise State University (2014)
18. Kausler, S., Sherman, E.: Evaluation of string constraint solvers in the context of symbolic execution. In: Proceedings of the 29th ACM/IEEE International Conference on Automated Software Engineering, ASE 2014, pp. 259–270. ACM, New York, NY, USA (2014)
19. Kiezun, A., Ganesh, V., Guo, P.J., Hooimeijer, P., Ernst, M.D.: Hampi: a solver for string constraints. In: Proceedings of the Eighteenth International Symposium on Software Testing and Analysis, ISSTA 2009, pp. 105–116 (2009)
20. Li, G., Andreasen, E., Ghosh, I.: SymJS: automatic symbolic testing of javascript web applications. In: Proceedings of the 22nd ACM SIGSOFT International Symposium on Foundations of Software Engineering, FSE 2014, pp. 449–459 (2014)
21. Li, G., Ghosh, I.: PASS: string solving with parameterized array and interval automaton. In: Bertacco, V., Legay, A. (eds.) HVC 2013. LNCS, vol. 8244, pp. 15–31. Springer, Heidelberg (2013)
22. Liang, T., Reynolds, A., Tinelli, C., Barrett, C., Deters, M.: A DPLL(T) theory solver for a theory of strings and regular expressions. In: Biere, A., Bloem, R. (eds.) CAV 2014. LNCS, vol. 8559, pp. 646–662. Springer, Heidelberg (2014)
23. Makanin, G.S.: The problem of solvability of equations in a free semigroup. Math. Sbornik **103**, 147–236 (1977). English transl. in Math USSR Sbornik 32 (1977)
24. Matiyasevich, Y.: Word equations, fibonacci numbers, and hilbert's tenth problem. In: Workshop on Fibonacci Words (2007)
25. Plandowski, W.: Satisfiability of word equations with constants is in pspace. J. ACM **51**(3), 483–496 (2004)
26. Plandowski, W.: An efficient algorithm for solving word equations. In: Proceedings of the 38th Annual ACM Symposium on Theory of Computing, STOC 2006, pp. 467–476 (2006)
27. Redelinghuys, G., Visser, W., Geldenhuys, J.: Symbolic execution of programs with strings. In: Proceedings of the South African Institute for Computer Scientists and Information Technologists Conference, SAICSIT 2012, pp. 139–148 (2012)
28. Saxena, P., Akhawe, D., Hanna, S., Mao, F., McCamant, S., Song, D.: A symbolic execution framework for javascript. In: Proceedings of the 2010 IEEE Symposium on Security and Privacy, SP 2010, pp. 513–528 (2010)
29. Schulz, K.: Makanin's algorithm for word equations-two improvements and a generalization. In: Schulz, K. (ed.) Word Equations and Related Topics. LNCS, vol. 572, pp. 85–150. Springer, Heidelberg (1992)
30. Tateishi, T., Pistoia, M., Tripp, O.: Path- and index-sensitive string analysis based on monadic second-order logic. ACM Trans. Softw. Eng. Methodol. **22**(4), 33:1–33:33 (2013)
31. Trinh, M.-T., Chu, D.-H., Jaffar, J.: S3: A symbolic string solver for vulnerability detection in web applications. In: Proceedings of the 2014 ACM SIGSAC Conference on Computer and Communications Security, CCS 2014, pp. 1232–1243 (2014)
32. Yu, F., Alkhalaf, M., Bultan, T.: STRANGER: an automata-based string analysis tool for PHP. In: Esparza, J., Majumdar, R. (eds.) TACAS 2010. LNCS, vol. 6015, pp. 154–157. Springer, Heidelberg (2010)

33. Yu, F., Bultan, T., Ibarra, O.H.: Symbolic string verification: combining string analysis and size analysis. In: Kowalewski, S., Philippou, A. (eds.) TACAS 2009. LNCS, vol. 5505, pp. 322–336. Springer, Heidelberg (2009)
34. Zheng, Y., Ganesh, V., Subramanian, S., Tripp, O., Dolby, J., Zhang, X.: Effective search-space pruning for solvers of string equations, regular expressions and length constraints. Technical report (2015). https://sites.google.com/site/z3strsolver/publications
35. Zheng, Y., Zhang, X., Ganesh, V.: Z3-str: a z3-based string solver for web application analysis. In: Proceedings of the 2013 9th Joint Meeting on Foundations of Software Engineering, ESEC/FSE 2013, pp. 114–124 (2013)

Automata-Based Model Counting
for String Constraints

Abdulbaki Aydin$^{(\boxtimes)}$, Lucas Bang, and Tevfik Bultan

University of California, Santa Barbara, USA
{baki,bang,bultan}@cs.ucsb.edu

Abstract. Most common vulnerabilities in Web applications are due
to string manipulation errors in input validation and sanitization code.
String constraint solvers are essential components of program analysis techniques for detecting and repairing vulnerabilities that are due
to string manipulation errors. For quantitative and probabilistic program analyses, checking the satisfiability of a constraint is not sufficient,
and it is necessary to count the number of solutions. In this paper, we
present a constraint solver that, given a string constraint, (1) constructs
an automaton that accepts all solutions that satisfy the constraint, (2)
generates a function that, given a length bound, gives the total number
of solutions within that bound. Our approach relies on the observation
that, using an automata-based constraint representation, model counting reduces to path counting, which can be solved precisely. We demonstrate the effectiveness of our approach on a large set of string constraints
extracted from real-world web applications.

1 Introduction

Since many computer security vulnerabilities are due to errors in string manipulating code, string analysis has become an active research area in the last
decade [3,9,12,17,31,36,38,39]. Symbolic execution is a well-known automated
bug detection technique which has been applied to vulnerability detection [28].
In order to apply symbolic execution to analysis of string manipulating programs, it is necessary to check satisfiability of string constraints [6]. Several
string constraint solvers have been proposed in recent years to address this problem [1,18,19,21,23,24,32,40].

This material is based on research sponsored by NSF under grant CCF-1423623 and
by DARPA under agreement number FA8750-15-2-0087. The U.S. Government is
authorized to reproduce and distribute reprints for Governmental purposes notwith-
standing any copyright notation thereon. The views and conclusions contained herein
are those of the authors and should not be interpreted as necessarily representing
the official policies or endorsements, either expressed or implied, of DARPA or the
U.S. Government. Part of this research was conducted while Tevfik Bultan was visiting Koç University in İstanbul, Turkey, supported by a research fellowship from
TÜBİTAK under the BİDEB 2221 program.

© Springer International Publishing Switzerland 2015
D. Kroening and C.S. Păsăreanu (Eds.): CAV 2015, Part I, LNCS 9206, pp. 255–272, 2015.
DOI: 10.1007/978-3-319-21690-4_15

There are two recent research directions that aim to extend symbolic execution beyond assertion checking. One of them is quantitative information flow, where the goal is to determine how much secret information is leaked from a given program [10,26,27,29], and another one is probabilistic symbolic execution where the goal is to compute probability of the success and failure paths in order to establish reliability of the given program [7,13]. Interestingly, both of these approaches require the same basic extension to constraint solving: They require a model-counting constraint solver that not only determines if a constraint is satisfiable, but it also computes the number of satisfying instances.

In this paper, we present an automata-based model-counting technique for string constraints that consists of two main steps: (1) Given a string constraint and a variable, we construct an automaton that accepts all the string values for that variable for which the string constraint is satisfiable. (2) Given an automaton we generate a function that takes a length bound as input and returns the total number of strings that are accepted by the automaton that have a length that is less than or equal to the given bound.

Our constraint language can handle regular language membership queries, word equations that involve concatenation and replacement, and arithmetic constraints on string lengths. For a class of constraints that we call *pseudo-relational*, our approach gives the precise model-count. For constraints that are not in this class our approach computes an upper bound. We implemented a tool called Automata-Based model Counter for string constraints (ABC) using the approach we present in this paper. Our experiments demonstrate that ABC is effective and efficient when applied to thousands of string constraints extracted from real-world web applications.

Related Work: Our inspiration for this work was the recently proposed model-counting string constraint solver SMC [25]. Similar to SMC, we also utilize generating functions in model-counting. However, due to some significant differences in how we utilize generating functions, our approach is strictly more precise than the approach used in SMC. For example, SMC cannot determine the precise model count for a regular expression constraint such as $x \in (a|b)^*|ab$, whereas our approach is precise for all regular expressions. More importantly, SMC cannot propagate string values across logical connectives which reduces its precision. For example, for a simple constraint such as $(x \in a|b) \lor (x \in a|b|c|d)$ SMC will generate a model-count range which consists of an upper bound of 6 and a lower bound of 2, whereas our approach will generate the exact count which is 4. Moreover, SMC always generates a lower bound of 0 for conjunctions that involve the same variable. So, the range generated for $(x \in a|b) \land (x \in a|b|c|d)$ would be 0 to 2, whereas our approach generates the exact count which is 2. The set of constraints we handle is also larger than the constraints that SMC can handle. In particular, we can handle constraints with replace operations which is common in server-side input sanitization code.

There has been significant amount of work on string constraint solving in recent years [1,15,18,19,21,23,24,28,32,40]. Some of these constraints solvers bound the string length [21,23,28] whereas our approach handles strings of arbitrary length. None of these string constraint solvers provide model-counting functionality. Our modal-counting constraint solver, ABC, builds on the automata-based string analysis tool Stranger [36,38,39], which was determined to be the best in terms of precision and efficiency in a recent empirical study for evaluating string constraint solvers for symbolic execution of Java programs [20]. In addition to checking satisfiability, ABC also generates an automaton that accepts all possible solutions and provides model-counting capability. To the best of our knowledge, ABC is the only tool that supports all of these. In addition to enabling quantitative and probabilistic analysis by model counting, our constraint solver also enables automated program repair synthesis by generating a characterization of all solutions [2,37].

2   Automata Construction for String Constraints

In this section, we discuss how to construct automata for string constraints. Given a constraint and a variable, our goal is to construct an automaton that accepts all strings, which, when assigned as the value of the variable in the given constraint, results in a satisfiable constraint.

2.1   String Constraint Language

We define the set of string constraints using the following abstract grammar:

$$F \rightarrow C \mid \neg F \mid F \wedge F \mid F \vee F \tag{1}$$
$$C \rightarrow S \in R \tag{2}$$
$$\mid \ S = S \tag{3}$$
$$\mid \ S = S \, . \, S \tag{4}$$
$$\mid \ \text{LEN}(S) \ O \ n \tag{5}$$
$$\mid \ \text{LEN}(S) \ O \ \text{LEN}(S) \tag{6}$$
$$\mid \ \text{CONTAINS}(S, s) \tag{7}$$
$$\mid \ \text{BEGINS}(S, s) \tag{8}$$
$$\mid \ \text{ENDS}(S, s) \tag{9}$$
$$\mid \ n = \text{INDEXOF}(S, s) \tag{10}$$
$$\mid \ S = \text{REPLACE}(S, s, s) \tag{11}$$
$$S \rightarrow v \mid s \tag{12}$$
$$R \rightarrow s \mid \varepsilon \mid R \, R \mid R \mid R \mid R^* \tag{13}$$
$$O \rightarrow \ < \ \mid \ = \ \mid \ > \tag{14}$$

where C denotes the basic constraints, n denotes integer values, $s \in \Sigma^*$ denotes string values, ε is the empty string, v denotes string variables, . is the string concatenation operator, $\text{LEN}(v)$ denotes the length of the string value that is assigned to variable v, and the string functions are defined as follows:

- CONTAINS$(v, s) \Leftrightarrow \exists s_1, s_2 \in \Sigma^* : v = s_1 s s_2$
- BEGINS$(v, s) \Leftrightarrow \exists s_1 \in \Sigma^* : v = s s_1$
- ENDS$(v, s) \Leftrightarrow \exists s_1 \in \Sigma^* : v = s_1 s$
- $n = $ INDEXOF$(v, s) \Leftrightarrow ($CONTAINS$(v, s) \wedge (\exists s_1, s_2 \in \Sigma^* : LEN(s_1) = n \wedge v = s_1 s s_2) \wedge$ $(\forall i < n : \neg(\exists s_1, s_2 \in \Sigma^* : LEN(s_1) = i \wedge v = s_1 s s_2))) \vee (\neg$CONTAINS$(v, s) \wedge n = -1)$
- $v = $ REPLACE$(v', s_1, s_2) \Leftrightarrow (\exists s_3, s_4, s_5 \in \Sigma^* : v' = s_3 s_1 s_4 \wedge v = s_3 s_2 s_5 \wedge s_5 = $ REPLACE$(s_4, s_1, s_2) \wedge (\forall s_6, s_7 \in \Sigma^* : v' = s_6 s_1 s_7 \Rightarrow LEN(s_6) \geq LEN(s_3))) \vee$ $(\neg$CONTAINS$(v', s_1) \wedge v = v')$

and the definitions of these functions when the string variable v is replaced with a string constant are similar.

Given a constraint F, let V_F denote the set of variables that appear in F. Let $F[s/v]$ denote the constraint that is obtained from F by replacing all appearances of $v \in V_F$ with the string constant s. We define the truth set of the formula F for variable v as $[\![F, v]\!] = \{s \mid F[s/v] \text{ is satisfiable}\}$.

We identify three classes of constraints: (1) *Single-variable constraints* are constructed using at most one string variable (i.e., $V_F = \{v\}$ or $V_F = \emptyset$), they do not contain constraints of type (4), (6), and (11), and have a single variable on the left hand side of constraints of type (3). (2) *Pseudo-relational constraints:* are a set of constraints that we define in the next section, for which the truth sets are regular (i.e., each $[\![F, v]\!]$ is a regular set). (3) *Relational constraints* are the constraints that are not pseudo-relational constraints (truth sets of relational constraints can be non-regular).

2.2 Mapping Constraints to Automata

A Deterministic Finite Automaton (DFA) A is a 5-tuple $(Q, \Sigma, \delta, q_0, F)$, where $Q = \{1, 2, \ldots, n\}$ is the set of n states, Σ is the input alphabet, $\delta \subseteq Q \times Q \times \Sigma$ is the state transition relation set, $q_0 \in Q$ is the initial state, and $F \subseteq Q$ is the set of final, or accepting, states.

Given an automaton A, let $\mathcal{L}(A)$ denote the set of strings accepted by A. Given a constraint F and a variable v, our goal is to construct an automaton A, such that $\mathcal{L}(A) = [\![F, v]\!]$.

Automata Construction for Single-Variable Constraints: Let us define an automata constructor function $\mathcal{A}$ such that, given a formula F and a variable v, $\mathcal{A}(F, v)$ is an automaton where $\mathcal{L}(\mathcal{A}(F, v)) = [\![F, v]\!]$. In this section we discuss how to implement the automata constructor function $\mathcal{A}$.

Consider the following string constraint $F \equiv \neg(x \in (01)^*) \wedge $ LEN$(x) \geq 1$ over the alphabet $\Sigma = \{0, 1\}$. Let us name the sub-constraints of F as $C_1 \equiv x \in (01)^*$, $C_2 \equiv $ LEN$(x) \geq 1$, $F_1 \equiv \neg C_1$, where $F \equiv F_1 \wedge C_2$. The automata construction algorithm starts from the basic constraints at the leaves of the syntax tree (C_1 and C_2), and constructs the automata for them. Then it traverses the syntax tree towards the root by constructing an automaton for each node using the automata constructed for its children (where the automaton for F_1 is constructed using the automaton for C_1 and the automaton for F is constructed using the automata

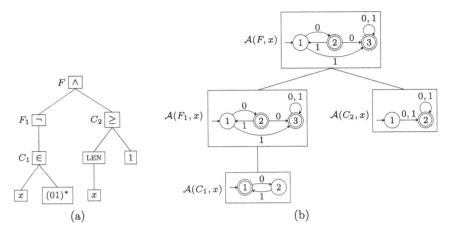

Fig. 1. (a) The syntax tree for the string constraint $\neg(x \in (01)^*) \wedge \text{LEN}(x) \geq 1$ and (b) the automata construction that traverses the syntax tree from the leaves towards the root.

for F_1 and C_2). Figure 1 demonstrates the automata construction algorithm on our running example.

Let $\mathcal{A}(\Sigma^*), \mathcal{A}(\Sigma^n), \mathcal{A}(s)$, and $\mathcal{A}(\emptyset)$ denote automata that accept the languages Σ^*, Σ^n, $\{s\}$, and $\emptyset$, respectively. We construct the automaton $\mathcal{A}(F, v)$ recursively on the structure of the single-variable constraint F as follows:

- case $V_F = \emptyset$ (i.e., there are no variables in F): Evaluate the constraint F. If $F \equiv \mathbf{true}$ then $\mathcal{A}(F, v) = \mathcal{A}(\Sigma^*)$, otherwise $\mathcal{A}(F, v) = \mathcal{A}(\emptyset)$.
- case $F \equiv \neg F_1$: $\mathcal{A}(F, v)$ is constructed using $\mathcal{A}(F_1, v)$ and it is an automaton that accepts the complement language $\Sigma^* - \mathcal{L}(\mathcal{A}(F_1, v))$.
- case $F \equiv F_1 \wedge F_2$ or $F \equiv F_1 \vee F_2$: $\mathcal{A}(F, v)$ is constructed using $\mathcal{A}(F_1, v)$ and $\mathcal{A}(F_2, v)$ using automata product, and it accepts the language $\mathcal{A}(F_1, v) \cap \mathcal{A}(F_2, v)$ or $\mathcal{A}(F_1, v) \cup \mathcal{A}(F_2, v)$, respectively.
- case $F \equiv v \in R$: $\mathcal{A}(F, v)$ is constructed using regular expression to automata conversion algorithm and accepts all strings that match the regular expression R.
- case $F \equiv v = s$: $\mathcal{A}(F, v) = \mathcal{A}(s)$.
- case $F \equiv \text{LEN}(v) = n$: $\mathcal{A}(F, v) = \mathcal{A}(\Sigma^n)$.
- case $F \equiv \text{LEN}(v) < n$: $\mathcal{A}(F, v)$ is an automaton that accepts the language $\{\varepsilon\} \cup \Sigma^1 \cup \Sigma^2 \cup \ldots \cup \Sigma^{n-1}$.
- case $F \equiv \text{LEN}(v) > n$: $\mathcal{A}(F, v)$ is constructed using $\mathcal{A}(\Sigma^{n+1})$ and $\mathcal{A}(\Sigma^*)$ and then constructing an automaton that accepts the concatenation of those languages, i.e., $\Sigma^{n+1}\Sigma^*$.
- case $F \equiv \text{CONTAINS}(v, s)$: $\mathcal{A}(F, v)$ is an automaton that is constructed using $\mathcal{A}(\Sigma^*)$ and $\mathcal{A}(s)$ and it accepts the language $\Sigma^* s \Sigma^*$.
- case $F \equiv \text{BEGINS}(v, s)$: $\mathcal{A}(F, v)$ is constructed using $\mathcal{A}(\Sigma^*)$ and $\mathcal{A}(s)$, and it accepts the language $s\Sigma^*$.
- case $F \equiv \text{ENDS}(v, s)$: $\mathcal{A}(F, v)$ is constructed using $\mathcal{A}(\Sigma^*)$ and $\mathcal{A}(s)$, and it accepts the language $\Sigma^* s$.
- case $F \equiv n = \text{INDEXOF}(v, s)$: Let L_i denote the language $\Sigma^i s \Sigma^*$. Automata that accept the languages L_i can be constructed using $\mathcal{A}(\Sigma^i)$, $\mathcal{A}(s)$, and $\mathcal{A}(\Sigma^*)$.

Then $\mathcal{A}(F, v)$ is the automaton that accepts the language $\Sigma^n s \Sigma^* - (\{\varepsilon\} \cup L_1 \cup L_2 \cup \ldots \cup L_{n-1})$ which can be constructed using $\mathcal{A}(\Sigma^n)$, $\mathcal{A}(s)$, $\mathcal{A}(\Sigma^*)$, and the automata that accept L_i.

Pseudo-Relational Constraints: Pseudo-relational constraints are multi-variable constraints. Note that, using multiple variables, one can specify constraints with non-regular truth sets. For example, given the constraint $F \equiv x = y \cdot y$, $[\![F, x]\!]$ is not a regular set, so we cannot construct an automaton precisely recognizing its truth set. Below, we define a class of constraints called pseudo-relational constraints for which $[\![F, v]\!]$ is regular.

We assume that constraint F is converted to DNF form where $F \equiv \vee_{i=1}^{n} F_i$, $F_i \equiv \wedge_{j=1}^{m} C_{ij}$, and each C_{ij} is either a basic constraint or negation of a basic constraint. The constraint F is pseudo-relational if each F_i is pseudo-relational.

Given $F \equiv C_1 \wedge C_2 \wedge \ldots \wedge C_n$, where each C_i is either a basic constraint or negation of a basic constraint, for each C_i, let V_{C_i} denote the set of variables that appear in C_i. We call F pseudo-relational if the following conditions hold:

1. Each variable $v \in V_F$ appears in each C_i at most once.
2. There is only one variable, $v \in V_F$, that appears in more than one constraint C_i where $v \in V_{C_i} \wedge |V_{C_i}| > 1$, and in each C_i that v appears in, v is on the left hand side of the constraint. We call v the *projection variable*.
3. For all variables $v' \in V_F$ other than the projection variable, there is a single constraint C_i where $v' \in V_{C_i} \wedge |V_{C_i}| > 1$ and the projection variable v appears in C_i, i.e., $v \in V_{C_i}$.
4. For all constraints C_i where $|V_{C_i}| > 1$, C_i is not negated in the formula F.

Many string constraints extracted from programs via symbolic execution are pseudo-relational constraints, or can be converted to pseudo-relational constraints. The projection variable represents either the variable that holds the value of the user's input to the program (for example, user input to a web application that needs to be validated), or the value of the string expression at a program sink. A program sink is a program point (such as a security sensitive function) for which it is necessary to compute the set of values that reach to that program point in order to check for vulnerabilities.

For example, following constraint is a pseudo-relational constraint extracted from a web application (regular expressions are simplified):

$$(x = y \cdot z) \wedge (\text{LEN}(y) = 0) \wedge \neg(z \in (0|1)) \wedge (x = t) \wedge \neg(t \in 0^*)$$

Automata Construction for Pseudo-Relational Constraints: Given a pseudo-relational constraint F and the projection variable v, we now discuss how to construct the automaton $\mathcal{A}(F, v)$ that accepts $[\![F, v]\!]$. As above, we assume that F is converted to DNF form where $F \equiv \vee_{i=1}^{n} F_i$, $F_i \equiv \wedge_{j=1}^{m} C_{ij}$, and each C_{ij} is either a basic constraint or negation of a basic constraint.

In order to construct the automaton $\mathcal{A}(F, v)$ we first construct the automata $\mathcal{A}(F_i, v)$ for each F_i where $\mathcal{A}(F_i, v)$ accepts the language $[\![F_i, v]\!]$. Then we combine the $\mathcal{A}(F_i, v)$ automata using automata product such that $\mathcal{A}(F, v)$ accepts the language $[\![F_1, v]\!] \cup [\![F_2, v]\!] \cup \ldots \cup [\![F_m, v]\!]$.

Since we discussed how to handle disjunction, from now on we focus on constraints of the form $F \equiv C_1 \wedge C_2 \wedge \ldots \wedge C_n$ where each C_i is either a basic constraint or negation of a basic constraint. For each C_i, let V_{C_i} denote the set of variables that appear in C_i. If V_{C_i} is a singleton set, then we refer to the variable in it as v_{C_i}.

First, for each single-variable constraint C_i that is not negated, we construct an automaton that accepts the truth set of the constraint C_i, $[\![C_i, v_{C_i}]\!]$, using the techniques we discussed above for single-variable constraints. If C_i is negated, then we construct the automaton that accepts the complement language $\Sigma^* - [\![C_i, v_{C_i}]\!]$ (note that, only single-variable constraints can be negated in pseudo-relational constraints). Let us call these automata $\mathcal{A}(C_i, v_{C_i})$ (some of which may correspond to negated constraints).

Then, for any variable $v' \in V_F$ that is not the projection variable, we construct an automaton $\mathcal{A}(F, v')$ which accepts the intersection of the languages $\mathcal{A}(C_i, v')$ for all single-variable constraints that v' appears in, i.e., $\mathcal{L}(\mathcal{A}(F, v')) = \bigcap_{V_{C_i}=\{v'\}} \mathcal{L}(\mathcal{A}(C_i, v'))$.

Next, for each multi-variable constraint C_i we construct an automaton that accepts the language $[\![C_i, v]\!]$ where v is the projection variable as follows:

- case $C_i \equiv v = v'$: $\mathcal{A}(C_i, v) = \mathcal{A}(F, v')$.
- case $C_i \equiv v = v_1 \cdot v_2$: $\mathcal{A}(C_i, v)$ is constructed using the automata $\mathcal{A}(F, v_1)$ and $\mathcal{A}(F, v_2)$ and it accepts the concatenation of the languages $\mathcal{L}(\mathcal{A}(F, v_1))$ and $\mathcal{L}(\mathcal{A}(F, v_2))$.
- case $C_i \equiv \text{LEN}(v) = \text{LEN}(v')$: Given the automaton $\mathcal{A}(F, v')$, we construct an automaton $A_{\text{LEN}(F,v')}$ such that $s \in \mathcal{L}(A_{\text{LEN}(F,v')}) \Leftrightarrow \exists s' : \text{LEN}(s) = \text{LEN}(s') \wedge s' \in \mathcal{L}(\mathcal{A}(F, v'))$. Then, $\mathcal{A}(C_i, v) = A_{\text{LEN}(F,v')}$.
- case $C_i \equiv \text{LEN}(v) < \text{LEN}(v')$: Given the automaton $\mathcal{A}(F, v')$ we find the length of the maximum word accepted by $\mathcal{A}(F, v')$, which is infinite if $\mathcal{A}(F, v')$ has a loop that can reach an accepting state. If it is infinite then $\mathcal{A}(C_i, v) = A(\Sigma^*)$. If not, then given the maximum length m, $\mathcal{A}(C_i, v)$ is the automaton that accepts the language $\{\varepsilon\} \cup \Sigma^1 \cup \Sigma^2 \cup \ldots \cup \Sigma^{m-1}$. Note that if $m = 0$ then $\mathcal{A}(C_i, v) = A(\emptyset)$.
- case $C_i \equiv \text{LEN}(v) > \text{LEN}(v')$: Given the automaton $\mathcal{A}(F, v')$ we find the length of the minimum word accepted by $\mathcal{A}(F, v')$. Given the minimum length m, $\mathcal{A}(C_i, v)$ is the automaton that accepts the concatenation of the languages accepted by $\mathcal{A}(\Sigma^{m+1})$ and $\mathcal{A}(\Sigma^*)$, i.e., $\Sigma^{m+1}\Sigma^*$.
- case $C_i \equiv v = \text{REPLACE}(v', s, s)$: Given the automaton $\mathcal{A}(F, v')$ we use the construction presented in [38,39] for language based replacement to construct the automaton $\mathcal{A}(C_i, v)$.

The final step of the construction is to construct $\mathcal{A}(F, v)$ using the automata $\mathcal{A}(C_i, v)$ where $\mathcal{L}(\mathcal{A}(F, v)) = \bigcap_{v \in V_{C_i}} \mathcal{L}(\mathcal{A}(C_i, v))$.

For pseudo-relational constraints, the automaton $\mathcal{A}(F, v))$ constructed based on the above construction accepts the truth set of the formula F for the projected variable, i.e., $\mathcal{L}(\mathcal{A}(F, v)) = [\![F, v]\!]$. However, the replace function has different variations in different programming languages (such as first-match versus longest-match replace) and the match pattern can be given as a regular expression. The language-based replace automata construction we use [38,39] over-approximates the replace operation in some cases, which would then result in over-approximation of the truth set: $\mathcal{L}(\mathcal{A}(F, v)) \supseteq [\![F, v]\!]$.

Automata Construction for Relational Constraints: For constraints that are not pseudo-relational, we extend the above algorithm to compute an over approximation of $[\![F, v]\!]$. In relational constraints, more than one variable can be involved in multi-variable constraints which creates a cycle in constraint evaluation.

Given a relational constraint in the form $F \equiv C_1 \wedge C_2 \wedge \ldots \wedge C_n$, we start with initializing each $\mathcal{A}(F, v)$ to $\mathcal{A}(\Sigma^*)$, i.e., initially variables are unconstrained. Then, we process each constraint as we described above to compute new automata for the variables in that constraint using the automata that are already available for each variable. We can stop this process at any time, and, for each variable v, we would get an over-approximation of the truth-set $\mathcal{A}(F, v) \supseteq [\![F, v]\!]$. We can state this algorithm as follows:

Algorithm 1. AUTOMATA FOR CONSTRAINT($F \equiv C_1 \wedge C_2 \wedge \ldots \wedge C_n$)

1: **for** $v \in V_F$ **do**
2:    $\mathcal{A}(F, v) = \mathcal{A}(\Sigma^*)$;
3: **end for**
4: $count = 0$; $done = $ **false**;
5: **while** $count < bound \wedge \neg done$ **do**
6:    **for each** $C \in F$ and $v \in V_C$ **do**
7:       construct A' where $\mathcal{L}(A') = \mathcal{L}(\mathcal{A}(F, v)) \cap \mathcal{L}(\mathcal{A}(C, v))$;
8:       $\mathcal{L}(\mathcal{A}(F, v)) = A'$;
9:    **end for**
10:    **if** none of the $\mathcal{L}(\mathcal{A}(F, v))$ changed during the current iteration of the while loop **then**
11:       $done = $ **true**;
12:    **end if**
13:    $count = count + 1$;
14: **end while**

In order to improve the efficiency of the above algorithm, we first build a constraint dependency graph where, 1) a multi-variable constraint C_i depends on a single variable constraint C_j if $V_{C_j} \subseteq V_{C_i}$, and 2) a multi-variable constraint C_i depends on a multi-variable constraint C_j if $V_{C_j} \cap V_{C_i} \neq \emptyset$. We traverse the constraints based on their ordering in the dependency graph and iteratively refine the automata in case of cyclic dependencies. Note that, in the constructions we described above we only constructed automaton for the variable on the left-hand-side of a relational constraint using the automata for the variables on the right-hand-side of the constraint. In the general case we need to construct automata for variables on the right-hand-side of the relational constraints too. We do this using techniques similar to the ones we described above. Constructing automata for the right-hand-side variables is equivalent to the pre-image computations used during backward symbolic analysis as discussed in [35] and we use the constructions given there. Finally, unlike pseudo-relational constraints, a relational constraint can contain negation of a basic constraint C_i where $|V_{C_i}| > 1$. In such cases, in constructing the truth set of $\neg C_i$ we can use the complement language $\Sigma^* - [\![C_i, v]\!]$ only if $[\![C_i, v]\!]$ is a singleton set. Otherwise, we construct an over approximation of the truth set of $\neg C_i$.

3 Automata-Based Model Counting

Once we have translated a set of constraints into an automaton we employ algebraic graph theory [5] and analytic combinatorics [14] to perform model counting. In our method, model counting corresponds exactly to counting the accepting paths of the constraint DFA up to a given length bound k. This problem can be solved using dynamic programming techniques in $O(k \cdot |\delta|)$ time where δ is the DFA transition relation [11,16]. However, for each different bound, the dynamic programming technique requires another traversal of the DFA graph.

A preferable solution is to derive a symbolic function that given a length bound k outputs the number of solutions within bound k. To achieve this, we use the *transfer matrix method* [14,30] to produce an ordinary generating function which in turn yields a linear recurrence relation that is used to count constraint solutions. We will briefly review the necessary background and then describe the model counting algorithm.

Given a DFA A, consider its corresponding language $\mathcal{L}$. Let $\mathcal{L}_i = \{w \in \mathcal{L} : |w| = i\}$, the language of strings in $\mathcal{L}$ with length i. Then $\mathcal{L} = \bigcup_{i \geq 0} \mathcal{L}_i$. Define $|\mathcal{L}_i|$ to be the cardinality of $\mathcal{L}_i$. The cardinality of $\mathcal{L}$ can be computed by the sum of a series $a_0, a_1, \ldots, a_i, \ldots$ where each a_i is the cardinality of the corresponding language $\mathcal{L}_i$, i.e., $a_i = |\mathcal{L}_i|$.

For example, recall the automaton in Fig. 1. Let $\mathcal{L}^x$ be the language over $\Sigma = \{0,1\}$ that satisfies the formula $(x \notin (01)^* \wedge \mathrm{LEN}(x) \geq 1)$. Then $\mathcal{L}^x$ is described by the expression $\Sigma^* - (01)^*$. In the language $\mathcal{L}^x$, we have zero strings of length 0 ($\varepsilon \notin \mathcal{L}^x$), two strings of length 1 ($\{0,1\}$), three strings of length 3 ($\{00, 10, 11\}$), and so on. The sequence is then $a_0 = 0, a_1 = 2, a_2 = 3, a_3 = 8, a_4 = 15$, etc. For any length i, $|\mathcal{L}_i^x|$, is given by a 3rd order linear recurrence relation:

$$a_0 = 0, a_1 = 2, a_2 = 3 \atop a_i = 2a_{i-1} + a_{i-2} - 2a_{i-3} \text{ for } i \geq 3 \tag{15}$$

In fact, using standard techniques for solving linear homogeneous recurrences, we can derive a closed form solution to determine that

$$|\mathcal{L}_i^x| = (1/2)(2^{i+1} + (-1)^{i+1} - 1). \tag{16}$$

In the following discussion we give a general method based on generating functions for deriving a recurrence relation and closed form solution that we can use for model counting.

Generating Functions: Given the representation of the size of a language $\mathcal{L}$ as a sequence $\{a_i\}$ we can encode each $|\mathcal{L}_i|$ as the coefficients of a polynomial, an ordinary generating function (GF). The *ordinary generating function* of the sequence $a_0, a_1, \ldots, a_i, \ldots$ is the infinite polynomial [14,30]

$$g(z) = \sum_{i \geq 0} a_i z^i \tag{17}$$

Although $g(z)$ is an infinite polynomial, $g(z)$ can be interpreted as the Taylor series of a finite rational expression. I.e., we can also write $g(z) = p(z)/q(z)$, where $p(z)$ and $q(z)$ are finite degree polynomials. If $g(z)$ is given as a finite rational expression, each a_i can be computed from the Taylor expansion of $g(z)$:

$$a_i = \frac{g^{(i)}(0)}{i!} \qquad (18)$$

where $g^{(i)}(z)$ is the ith derivative of $g(z)$. We write $[z^i]g(z)$ for the ith Taylor series coefficient of $g(z)$. Returning to our example, we can write the generating function for $|\mathcal{L}_i^x|$ both as a rational function and as an infinite Taylor series polynomial. The reader can verify the following equivalence by computing the right hand side coefficients via Eq. (18).

$$g(z) = \frac{2z - z^2}{1 - 2z - z^2 + 2z^3} = 0z^0 + 2z^1 + 3z^2 + 8z^3 + 15z^4 + \dots \qquad (19)$$

Generating Function for a DFA: Given a DFA A and length k we can compute the generating function $g_A(z)$ such that the kth Taylor series coefficient of $g_A(z)$ is equal to $|\mathcal{L}_k(A)|$ using the transfer-matrix method [14, 30].

We first apply a transformation and add an extra state, s_{n+1}. The resulting automaton is a DFA A' with λ-transitions from each of the accepting states of A to s_{n+1} where λ is a new padding symbol that is not in the alphabet of A. Thus, $\mathcal{L}(A') = \mathcal{L}(A) \cdot \lambda$ and furthermore $|\mathcal{L}_i(A)| = |\mathcal{L}_{i+1}(A')|$. That is, the augmented DFA A' preserves both the language and count information of A. Recalling the automaton from Fig. 1, the corresponding augmented DFA is shown in Fig. 2(b). (Ignore the dashed λ transition for the time being.)

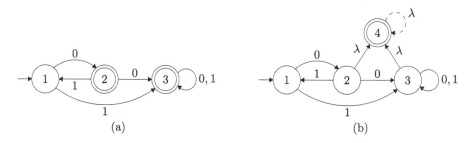

Fig. 2. (a) The original DFA A, and (b) the augmented DFA A' used for model counting (sink state omitted).

From A' we construct the $(n+1) \times (n+1)$ transfer matrix T. A' has $n+1$ states $s_1, s_2, \dots s_{n+1}$. The matrix entry $T_{i,j}$ is the number of transitions from state s_i to state s_j. Then the generating function for A is

$$g_A(z) = (-1)^n \frac{\det(I - zT : n+1, 1)}{z \det(I - zT)}, \qquad (20)$$

where $(M : i, j)$ denotes the matrix obtained by removing the ith row and j^{th} column from M, I is the identity matrix, $\det M$ is the matrix determinant, and

n is the number of states in the original DFA A. The number of accepting paths of A with length exactly k, i.e. $|\mathcal{L}_k(A)|$, is then given by $[z^k]g_A(z)$ which can be computed through symbolic differentiation via Eq. 18.

For our running example, we show the transition matrix T and the terms $(I - zT)$ and $(I - zT : n, 1)$. Here, $T_{1,2}$ is 1 because there is a single transition from state 1 to state 2, $T_{3,3}$ is 2 because there are two transitions from state 3 to itself, $T_{2,4}$ is 1 because there is a single (λ) transition from state 2 to state 4, and so on for the remaining entries.

$$T = \begin{bmatrix} 0 & 1 & 1 & 0 \\ 1 & 0 & 1 & 1 \\ 0 & 0 & 2 & 1 \\ 0 & 0 & 0 & 1 \end{bmatrix}, I - zT = \begin{bmatrix} 1 & -z & -z & 0 \\ -z & 1 & -z & -z \\ 0 & 0 & 1 - 2z & -z \\ 0 & 0 & 0 & 1 \end{bmatrix}, (I - zT : n, 1) = \begin{bmatrix} -z & -z & 0 \\ 1 & -z & -z \\ 0 & 1 - 2z & -z \end{bmatrix}$$

Applying Eq. (20) results in the same GF that counts $\mathcal{L}_i(A)$ given in (19).

$$g_{A'}(z) = -\frac{\det(I - zT : n, 1)}{z \det(I - zT)} = \frac{2z - z^2}{1 - 2z - z^2 + 2z^3}. \tag{21}$$

Suppose we now want to know the number of solutions of length six. We compute the sixth Taylor series coefficient to find that $|\mathcal{L}_6^x(A)| = [z^6]g(z) = 63$.

Deriving a Recurrence Relation: We would like a way to compute $[z^i]g(z)$ that is more direct than symbolic differentiation. We describe how a linear recurrence for $[z^i]g(z)$ can be extracted from the GF. Before we describe how to accomplish this in general, we demonstrate the procedure for our example. Combining Eqs. (17) and (21) and multiplying by the denominator, we have

$$2z - z^2 = (1 - 2z - z^2 + 2z^3) \sum_{i \geq 0} a_i z^i.$$

Expanding the sum for $0 \leq i < 3$ and collecting terms,

$$2z - z^2 = a_0 + (a_1 - 2a_0)z + (a_2 - 2a_1 - a_0)z^2 + \sum_{i \geq 3}(a_i - 2a_{i-1} - a_{i-2} + 2a_{i-3})z^i.$$

Comparing each coefficient of z^i on the left side to the coefficient of z^i on the right side, we have the set of equations

$$a_0 = 0$$
$$a_1 - 2a_0 = 2$$
$$a_2 - 2a_1 - a_0 = -1$$
$$a_i - 2a_{i-1} - a_{i-2} + 2a_{i-3} = 0, \text{ for } i \geq 3$$

One can see that this results in the same solution given in Eq. (15).

This idea is easily generalized. Recall that $g(z) = p(z)/q(z)$ for finite degree polynomials p and q. Suppose that the maximum degree of p and q is m. Then

$$g(z) = \frac{b_m z^m + \ldots + b_1 z + b_0}{c_m z^m + \ldots + c_1 z + c_0} = \sum_{i \geq 0} a_i z^i.$$

Multiplying by the denominator, expanding the sum up to m terms, and comparing coefficients we have the resulting system of equations which can be solved for $\{a_i : 0 \le i \le m\}$ using standard linear algebra:

$$\sum_{j=0}^{i} c_j a_{i-j} = \begin{cases} b_i, & \text{for } 0 \le i \le m \\ 0, & \text{for } i > m \end{cases}$$

For any DFA A, since each coefficient a_i is associated with $|\mathcal{L}_k(A)|$, the recurrence gives us an $O(kn)$ method to compute $|\mathcal{L}_k(A)|$ for any string length bound k. In addition, standard techniques for solving linear homogeneous recurrence relations can be used to derive a closed form solution for $|\mathcal{L}_i(A)|$ [22].

Counting All Solutions within a Given Bound: The above described method gives a generating function that encodes each $|\mathcal{L}_i(A)|$ *separately*. Instead, we seek a generating function that encodes the number of *all solutions within a bound*. To this end we define the automata model counting function

$$\mathcal{MC}_A(k) = \sum_{i \ge 0}^{k} |\mathcal{L}_i(A)|. \tag{22}$$

In order to compute $\mathcal{MC}_A(k)$ we make a simple adjustment. All that is needed is to add a single λ-cycle (the dashed transition in Fig. 2(b)) to the accepting state of the augmenting DFA A'. Then $\mathcal{L}_{k+1}(A') = \bigcup_{i=0}^{k} \mathcal{L}_i(A) \cdot \lambda^{k-i}$ and the accepting paths of strings in $\mathcal{L}_{k+1}(A')$ are in one-to-one correspondence with the accepting paths of strings in $\bigcup_{i=0}^{k} \mathcal{L}_i(A)$. Consequently, $|\mathcal{L}_{k+1}(A')| = \sum_{i=0}^{k} |\mathcal{L}_i(A)|$ and so $\mathcal{MC}_A(k) = |\mathcal{L}_{k+1}(A')|$. Hence, we can compute $\mathcal{MC}_A$ using the recurrence for $|\mathcal{L}_i(A')|$ with the additional λ-cycle.

4   Implementation

We implemented Automata-Based model Counter for string constraints (ABC) using the symbolic string analysis library provided by the Stranger tool [36,38, 39]. We used the symbolic DFA representation of the MONA DFA library [8] to implement the constructions described in Sect. 2. In MONA's DFA library, the transition relation of the DFA is represented as a Multi-terminal Binary Decision Diagram (MBDD) which results in a compact representation of the transition relation. ABC supports more operations (such as TRIM, SUBSTRING) than the ones listed in Sect. 2 using constructions similar to the ones given in that section.

ABC supports the SMT-LIB 2 language syntax. We specifically added support for CVC4 string operations [24]. In string constraint benchmarks provided by CVC4, boolean variables are used to assert the results of subformulas. In our automata-based constraint solver, we check the satisfiability of a formula by checking if its truth set is empty or not. We eliminated the boolean variables that are only used to check the results of string operations (such as string equivalence, string membership) and instead substituted the corresponding expressions directly. We converted if-then-else structures into disjunctions. We also searched for several patterns between length equations and word equations to infer the values of the string variables whenever possible (for example when we see the constraint LEN(x) = 0 we can infer that the string variable x must be equal to the empty string). These transformations allow us to convert some constraints to pseudo-relational constraints that we can precisely solve. If these transformations do not resolve all the cyclic dependencies in a constraint then the resulting DFA may recognize an over-approximation of all possible solutions.

We implemented the automata-based model counting algorithm of Sect. 3 by passing the automaton transfer matrix to Mathematica for computing the generating function, corresponding recurrence relation, and the model count for a specific bound. Because the DFAs we encountered in our experiments typically have sparse transition graphs, we make use of Mathematica's powerful and efficient implementations of symbolic sparse matrix determinant functions [33].

5   Experiments

To evaluate ABC we experimented with a set of Java application benchmarks, SMT-LIB 2 translation of Kaluza JavaScript benchmarks, and several examples from the SMC distribution. In our experiments we compared ABC to SMC [25] and CVC4 [24]. We ran all the experiments on an Intel I5 machine with 2.5GHz X 4 processors and 32 GB of memory running Ubuntu 14.04[1].

Table 1. Constraint characteristics

| Benchmarks | # Constraints | Frequency of Operations Per 1000 Formulas | | | | | | | | | |
		∈	.	=	LEN	REPLACE	INDEXOF	CONTAINS	BEGINS	ENDS	SUBSTRING
ASE	116164	0.42	386.10	129.39	382.54	639.28	4.11	7.52	16.91	7.51	41.17
Kaluza Small	368433	30.29	93.89	224.87	46.84	0	0	0	0	0	0
Kaluza Big	5138323	38.12	129.53	164.64	60.46	0	0	0	0	0	0

Table 1 shows the frequency of string operations from our string constraint grammar that are contained in the ASE, Kaluza Small, and Kaluza Big benchmark sets. ASE benchmarks are from Java programs and represent server-side code [20]. The Kaluza benchmarks are taken from JavaScript programs and represent client-side code [28]. All three benchmarks have regular expression membership (∈), concatenation (.), string equality (=), and length constraints. However, the ASE benchmark contains additional string operations that are typically used for input sanitization, like REPLACE and SUBSTRING.

Java Benchmarks. String constraints in these benchmarks are extracted from 7 real-world Java applications: Jericho HTML Parser, jxml2xql (an xml-to-sql converter), MathParser, MathQuizGame, Natural CLI (a natural language command line tool), Beasties (a command line game), HtmlCleaner, and iText (a PDF library) [20]. These benchmarks represent server-side code and employ many input-sanitizing string operators such as REPLACE and SUBSTRING as seen

---

[1] Results of our experiments are available at http://www.cs.ucsb.edu/~vlab/ABC/.

in Table 1. These string constraints were generated by extracting program path constraints through dynamic symbolic execution [20].

In [20], an empirical evaluation of several string constraint solvers is presented. As a part of this empirical evaluation, the authors use the symbolic string analysis library of Stranger [36, 38, 39] to construct automata for path constraints on strings. In order to evaluate the model counting component of ABC, we ran their tool on the 7 benchmark sets and output the resulting automata whenever the constraint is satisfiable. Out of 116,164 string path constraints, 66,236 were found to be satisfiable and we performed model counting on those cases. The constraints in Java benchmarks are all single-variable or pseudo-relational constraints. The resulting automata do not have any over-approximation caused by relational constraints. As a measure of the size of the resulting automata, we give the number of BDD nodes used in the symbolic transition relation representation of MONA. The average number of BDD nodes for the satisfiable path constraints is 69.51 and the size of the each BDD node is 16 bytes. For these benchmarks our model-counter is efficient; the average running time of model counting per path constraint is 0.0015 seconds and the resulting model-counting recurrence is precise, i.e., gives the exact count for any given bound.

SMC and CVC4 are not able to handle the constraints in this data set since they do not support sanitization operations such as REPLACE.

SMC Examples. For a comparative evaluation of our tool with SMC, we used the examples that are listed on SMC's web page. We translated the 6 example constraints listed in Table 2 into SMT-LIB2 language format that we support. We inspected the examples to confirm that they are pseudo-relational, i.e., our analysis generates a precise model-counting function for these constraints. We compare our results with the results reported in SMC's web page. The first column of the Table 2 shows the file names of these example constraints. The second column shows the bounds used for obtaining the model counts. The next two columns show the log-scale SMC lower and upper bound values for the model counts. The last column shows the log-scale model count produced by ABC. We omit the decimal places of the numbers to fit them on the page. For all the cases ABC generates a precise count given the bound. ABC's count is exactly equal to SMC's upper bound for four of the examples and is exactly equal to SMC's lower bound for one example. For the last example ABC reports a count that is between the lower and upper bound produced by SMC. Note that these are log scaled values and actual differences between a lower and an upper-bound values are huge. Although SMC is unable to produce an exact answer for any of these examples, ABC produces an exact count for each of them.

JavaScript Benchmarks. We also experimented with Kaluza benchmarks which were extracted from JavaScript code via dynamic symbolic execution [28]. These benchmarks are divided to a small and large set based on the sizes of the constraints. These benchmarks have been used by both SMC and CVC4 tools. ABC handles 19,731 benchmark constraints in the satisfiable small set with an average of 0.32 seconds per constraint for model counting, whereas SMC handles 17,559 constraints with an average of 0.26 seconds per constraint. ABC handles

Table 2. Log scaled comparison between SMC and ABC

	bound	SMC lower bound	SMC upper bound	ABC count
nullhttpd	500	3752	3760	3760
ghttpd	620	4880	4896	4896
csplit	629	4852	4921	4921
grep	629	4676	4763	4763
wc	629	4281	4284	4281
obscure	6	0	3	2

1,587 benchmark constraints in satisfiable big set with an average of 0.34 seconds per constraint for model counting, whereas SMC handles 1,342 constraints with an average of 5.29 seconds per constraint. We were not able to do a one-to-one timing and precision comparison between ABC and SMC for each constraint due to an error in the SMC data file (the mapping between file names and results is incorrect).

Table 3. Constraint-solver comparison

	ABC	CVC4	ABC	CVC4	ABC	CVC4	ABC	CVC4	ABC	CVC4
	sat - sat		unsat-unsat		sat-unsat		unsat-sat		sat-timeout	
sat/small	19728		3		0		0		0	
sat/big	1587		0		0		0		0	
unsat/small	8139		3013		74		0		0	
unsat/big	3419		5904		2385		0		2359	

Satisfiability Checking Evaluation. We ran ABC on SMT-LIB 2 translation of the full set of JavaScript benchmarks. We put a 20-second CPU timeout limit on ABC for each benchmark constraint. Table 3 shows the comparison between ABC and the CVC4 [24] constraint solver based on the CVC4 results that are available online. The first column shows the initial satisfiability classification of the data set by the creators of the benchmarks [28]. The next two columns show the number of results that ABC and CVC4 agree. The last three columns show the cases where ABC and CVC4 differ. Note that, since ABC over-approximates the solution set, if the given constraint is not single-valued or pseudo-relational, it is possible for ABC to classify a constraint as satisfiable even if it is unsatisfiable. However, it is not possible for ABC to classify a constraint unsatisfiable if it is satisfiable. Out of 47,284 benchmark constraints ABC and CVC4 agree on 41,793 of them. As expected ABC never classifies a constraint as unsatisfiable if CVC4 classifies it as satisfiable. However, due to over-approximation of relational constraints, ABC classifies 2,459 constraints as satisfiable although CVC4 classifies them as unsatisfiable. A practical approach would be to use ABC together with a satisfiability solver like CVC4, and, given a constraint, first use the satisfiability solver to determine the satisfiability of the formula, and then use ABC to generate its truth set and the model counting function.

The average automata construction time for big benchmark constraints is 0.44 seconds and for small benchmark constraints it is 0.01 seconds. CVC4 average running times are 0.18 seconds and 0.015 seconds respectively (excluding timeouts). CVC4 times out for 2359 constraints, whereas ABC never times out. For those 2359 constraints, ABC reports satisfiable. ABC is unable to handle 672 constraints; the automata package we use (MONA) is unable to handle the resulting automata and we believe that these cases can be solved by modifying MONA. For these 672 constraints; CVC4 times out for 29 of them, reports unsat for 246 of them, and reports sat for 397 of them. There are also a few thousand constraints from the Kaluza benchmarks that CVC4 is unable to handle.

6 Conclusions and Future Work

We presented a model-counting string constraint solver that, given a constraint, generates: (1) An automaton that accepts all solutions to the given string constraint; (2) A model-counting function that, given a length bound, returns the number of solutions within that bound. Our experiments on thousands of constraints extracted from real-world web applications demonstrates the effectiveness and efficiency of the proposed approach. Our string constraint solver can be used in quantitative information flow, probabilistic analysis and automated repair synthesis. We plan to extend our automata-based model-counting approach to Presburger arithmetic constraints using an automata-based representation for Presburger arithmetic constraints [4,34].

References

1. Abdulla, P.A., Atig, M.F., Chen, Y.-F., Holík, L., Rezine, A., Rümmer, P., Stenman, J.: String constraints for verification. In: Biere, A., Bloem, R. (eds.) CAV 2014. LNCS, vol. 8559, pp. 150–166. Springer, Heidelberg (2014)
2. Alkhalaf, M., Aydin, A., Bultan, T.: Semantic differential repair for input validation and sanitization. In: Proceedings of the International Symposium on Software Testing and Analysis (ISSTA), pp. 225–236 (2014)
3. Alkhalaf, M., Bultan, T., Gallegos, J.L.: Verifying client-side input validation functions using string analysis. In: Proceedings of the 34th International Conference on Software Engineering (ICSE), pp. 947–957 (2012)
4. Bartzis, C., Bultan, T.: Efficient symbolic representations for arithmetic constraints in verification. Int. J. Found. Comput. Sci. **14**(4), 605–624 (2003)
5. Biggs, N.: Algebraic Graph Theory. Cambridge University Press, Cambridge Mathematical Library, Cambridge (1993)
6. Bjørner, N., Tillmann, N., Voronkov, A.: Path feasibility analysis for string-manipulating programs. In: Kowalewski, S., Philippou, A. (eds.) TACAS 2009. LNCS, vol. 5505, pp. 307–321. Springer, Heidelberg (2009)

7. Borges, M., Filieri, A., d'Amorim, M., Pasareanu, C.S., Visser, W.: Compositional solution space quantification for probabilistic software analysis. In: Proceedigns of the ACM SIGPLAN Conference on Programming Language Design and Implementation (PLDI) (2014)
8. BRICS. The MONA project. http://www.brics.dk/mona/
9. Christensen, A.S., Møller, A., Schwartzbach, M.I.: Precise analysis of string expressions. In: Proceedings of the 10th International Static Analysis Symposium (SAS), pp. 1–18 (2003)
10. Clark, D., Hunt, S., Malacaria, P.: A static analysis for quantifying information flow in a simple imperative language. J. Comput. Secur. **15**(3), 321–371 (2007)
11. Cormen, T.H., Stein, C., Rivest, R.L., Leiserson, C.E.: Introduction to Algorithms, 2nd edn. McGraw-Hill Higher Education, Boston (2001)
12. D'Antoni, L., Veanes, M.: Static analysis of string encoders and decoders. In: Giacobazzi, R., Berdine, J., Mastroeni, I. (eds.) VMCAI 2013. LNCS, vol. 7737, pp. 209–228. Springer, Heidelberg (2013)
13. Filieri, A., Pasareanu, C.S., Visser, W.: Reliability analysis in symbolic pathfinder. In: Proceedings of the 35th International Conference on Software Engineering (ICSE), pp. 622–631 (2013)
14. Flajolet, P., Sedgewick, R.: Analytic Combinatorics, 1st edn. Cambridge University Press, New York (2009)
15. Ganesh, V., Minnes, M., Solar-Lezama, A., Rinard, M.: Word equations with length constraints: what's decidable? In: Biere, A., Nahir, A., Vos, T. (eds.) HVC. LNCS, vol. 7857, pp. 209–226. Springer, Heidelberg (2013)
16. Gross, J.L., Yellen, J., Zhang, P.: Handbook of Graph Theory, 2nd edn. Chapman and Hall/CRC, Boca Raton (2013)
17. Hooimeijer, P., Livshits, B., Molnar, D., Saxena, P., Veanes, M.: Fast and precise sanitizer analysis with bek. In: Proceedings of the 20th USENIX Conference on Security (2011)
18. Hooimeijer, P., Weimer, W.: A decision procedure for subset constraints over regular languages. In: Proceedings of the ACM SIGPLAN Conference on Programming Language Design and Implementation (PLDI), pp. 188–198 (2009)
19. Hooimeijer, P., Weimer, W.: Solving string constraints lazily. In: Proceedings of the 25th IEEE/ACM International Conference on Automated Software Engineering (ASE), pp. 377–386 (2010)
20. Kausler, S., Sherman, E.: Evaluation of string constraint solvers in the context of symbolic execution. In: Proceedings of the 29th ACM/IEEE International Conference on Automated Software Engineering (ASE), pp. 259–270 (2014)
21. Kiezun, A., Ganesh, V., Guo, P.J., Hooimeijer, P., Ernst, M.D.: Hampi: a solver for string constraints. In: Proceedings of the 18th International Symposium on Software Testing and Analysis (ISSTA), pp. 105–116 (2009)
22. Knuth, D.E.: The Art of Computer Programming, Volume 1: Fundamental Algorithms. Addison-Wesley, Reading (1968)
23. Li, G., Ghosh, I.: PASS: string solving with parameterized array and interval automaton. In: Bertacco, V., Legay, A. (eds.) HVC 2013. LNCS, vol. 8244, pp. 15–31. Springer, Heidelberg (2013)
24. Liang, T., Reynolds, A., Tinelli, C., Barrett, C., Deters, M.: A DPLL(T) Theory solver for a theory of strings and regular expressions. In: Biere, A., Bloem, R. (eds.) CAV 2014. LNCS, vol. 8559, pp. 646–662. Springer, Heidelberg (2014)
25. Luu, L., Shinde, S., Saxena, P., Demsky, B.: A model counter for constraints over unbounded strings. In: Proceedings of the ACM SIGPLAN Conference on Programming Language Design and Implementation (PLDI), p. 57 (2014)

26. McCamant, S., Ernst, M.D.: Quantitative information flow as network flow capacity. In: Proceedings of the ACM SIGPLAN Conference on Programming Language Design and Implementation (PLDI), pp. 193–205 (2008)
27. Phan, Q.-S., Malacaria, P., Tkachuk, O., Păsăreanu, C.S.: Symbolic quantitative information flow. SIGSOFT Softw. Eng. Notes **37**(6), 1–5 (2012)
28. Saxena, P., Akhawe, D., Hanna, S., Mao, F., McCamant, S., Song, D.: A symbolic execution framework for javascript. In: Proceedings of the 31st IEEE Symposium on Security and Privacy (2010)
29. Smith, G.: On the foundations of quantitative information flow. In: de Alfaro, L. (ed.) FOSSACS 2009. LNCS, vol. 5504, pp. 288–302. Springer, Heidelberg (2009)
30. Stanley, R.P.: Enumerative Combinatorics: vol. 1, 2nd edn. Cambridge University Press, New York (2011)
31. Tateishi, T., Pistoia, M., Tripp, O.: Path- and index-sensitive string analysis based on monadic second-order logic. In: Proceedings of the International Symposium on Software Testing and Analysis (ISSTA), pp. 166–176 (2011)
32. Trinh, M.-T., Chu, D.-H., Jaffar, J.: S3: a symbolic string solver for vulnerability detection in web applications. In: Proceedings of the ACM SIGSAC Conference on Computer and Communications Security (CCS), pp. 1232–1243 (2014)
33. Wolfram Research Inc., Mathematica (2014). http://www.wolfram.com/mathematica/
34. Wolper, P., Boigelot, B.: On the construction of automata from linear arithmetic constraints. In: Graf, S. (ed.) TACAS 2000. LNCS, vol. 1785, pp. 1–19. Springer, Heidelberg (2000)
35. Yu, F.: Automatic verification of string manipulating programs. Ph.D. thesis. University of California, Santa Barbara (2010)
36. Yu, F., Alkhalaf, M., Bultan, T.: STRANGER: an automata-based string analysis tool for PHP. In: Esparza, J., Majumdar, R. (eds.) TACAS 2010. LNCS, vol. 6015, pp. 154–157. Springer, Heidelberg (2010)
37. Yu, F., Alkhalaf, M., Bultan, T.: Patching vulnerabilities with sanitization synthesis. In: Proceedings of the 33rd International Conference on Software Engineering (ICSE), pp. 131–134 (2011)
38. Fang, Y., Alkhalaf, M., Bultan, T., Ibarra, O.H.: Automata-based symbolic string analysis for vulnerability detection. Formal Methods Syst. Des. **44**(1), 44–70 (2014)
39. Yu, F., Bultan, T., Cova, M., Ibarra, O.H.: Symbolic string verification: an automata-based approach. In: Havelund, K., Majumdar, R. (eds.) SPIN 2008. LNCS, vol. 5156, pp. 306–324. Springer, Heidelberg (2008)
40. Zheng, Y., Zhang, X., Ganesh, V.: Z3-str: a z3-based string solver for web application analysis. In: Proceedings of the 9th Joint Meeting on Foundations of Software Engineering (ESEC/FSE), pp. 114–124 (2013)

OpenJDK's Java.utils.Collection.sort() Is Broken: The Good, the Bad and the Worst Case

Stijn de Gouw[1,2]([✉]), Jurriaan Rot[1,3], Frank S. de Boer[1,3], Richard Bubel[4], and Reiner Hähnle[4]

[1] CWI, Amsterdam, The Netherlands
cdegouw@gmail.com
[2] SDL, Amsterdam, The Netherlands
[3] Leiden University, Leiden, The Netherlands
[4] Technische Universität Darmstadt, Darmstadt, Germany

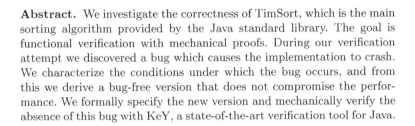

Abstract. We investigate the correctness of TimSort, which is the main sorting algorithm provided by the Java standard library. The goal is functional verification with mechanical proofs. During our verification attempt we discovered a bug which causes the implementation to crash. We characterize the conditions under which the bug occurs, and from this we derive a bug-free version that does not compromise the performance. We formally specify the new version and mechanically verify the absence of this bug with KeY, a state-of-the-art verification tool for Java.

1 Introduction

Some of the arguments often invoked against the usage of formal software verification include the following: it is expensive, it is not worthwhile (compared to its cost), it is less effective than bug finding (e.g., by testing, static analysis, or model checking), it does not work for "real" software. In this article we evaluate these arguments in terms of a case study in formal verification.

The goal of this paper is functional verification of sorting algorithms written in Java with mechanical proofs. Because of the complexity of the code under verification, it is essential to break down the problem into subtasks of manageable size. This is achieved with *contract-based deductive verification* [3], where the functionality and the side effects of each method are precisely specified with expressive first-order contracts. In addition, each class is equipped with an invariant that has to be re-established by each method upon termination. These formal specifications are expressed in the Java Modeling Language (JML) [11].

We use the state-of-art Java verification tool KeY [4], a semi-automatic, interactive theorem prover, which covers nearly full sequential Java. KeY typically finds more than 99 % of the proof steps automatically (see Sect. 6), while the

Partly funded by the EU project FP7-610582 ENVISAGE and the NWO project 612.063.920 CoRE.

remaining ones are interactively done by a human expert. This is facilitated by the use in KeY of symbolic execution plus invariant reasoning as its proof paradigm. That results in a close correspondence between proof nodes and symbolic program states which brings the experience of program verification somewhat close to that of debugging.

The work presented here was motivated by our recent success to verify executable Java versions of counting sort and radix sort in KeY with manageable effort [6]. As a further challenge we planned to verify a complicated sorting algorithm taken from the widely used OpenJDK core library. It turns out that *the default implementation* of Java's `java.util.Arrays.sort()` and `java.util.Collection.sort()` method is an ideal candidate: it is based on a complex combination of merge sort and insertion sort [12,15]. It had a bug history[1], but was reported as fixed as of Java version 8. We decided to verify the implementation, stripped of generics, but otherwise completely unchanged and fully executable. The implementation is described in Sect. 2.

During our verification attempt we discovered that the fix to the bug mentioned above is in fact not working. We succeeded to characterize the conditions under which the bug occurs and results in a crash (Sect. 4) and from this we could derive a bug-free version (Sect. 5) that does not compromise the performance.

We provide a detailed experience report (Sect. 6) on the formal specification and mechanical verification of correctness and termination of the fixed version with KeY (Sects. 5, 6). Summarizing, our real-life case study shows that formal specification and verification, at least of library code, pays off, but also shows the limitations of current verification technology. In Sect. 7 we draw conclusions.

Related Work. Several industrial case studies have already been carried out in KeY [1,13,14]. The implementation considered here and its proof is the most complex and one of the largest so far. The first correctness proof of a sorting algorithm is due to Foley and Hoare, who formally verified Quicksort by hand [9]. Since then, the development and application of (semi)-automated theorem provers has become standard in verification. The major sorting algorithms Insertion sort, Heapsort and Quicksort were proven correct by Filliâtre and Magaud [8] using Coq, and Sternagel [16] formalized a proof of Mergesort within the interactive theorem prover Isabelle/HOL.

2   Implementation of TimSort

The default implementation of `java.util.Arrays.sort` for non-primitive types is TimSort, a hybrid sorting algorithm based on mergesort and insertion sort. The algorithm reorders a specified segment of the input array incrementally from left to right by finding consecutive (disjoint) sorted segments. If these segments are not large enough, they are extended using insertion sort. The starting positions and the lengths of the generated segments are stored on a stack. During execution some of these segments are merged according to a condition on the

---

[1] http://bugs.java.com/view_bug.do?bug_id=8011944.

top elements of the stack, ensuring that the lengths of the generated segments are decreasing and the length of each generated segment is greater than the sum of the next two. In the end, all segments are merged, yielding a sorted array.

We explain the algorithm in detail based on the important parts of the Java implementation. The stack of runs (a sorted segment is called here a "run") is encapsulated by the object variable ts. The stack of starting positions and run lengths is represented by the arrays of integers runBase and runLen, respectively. The length of this stack is denoted by the instance variable stackSize. The main loop is as follows (with original comments):

Listing 1. Main loop of TimSort

```
1   do {
2     // Identify next run
3     int runLen = countRunAndMakeAscending(a, lo, hi, c);
4     // If run is short, extend to min(minRun, nRemaining)
5     if (runLen < minRun) {
6       int force = nRemaining <= minRun ? nRemaining : minRun;
7       binarySort(a, lo, lo + force, lo + runLen, c);
8       runLen = force;
9     }
10    // Push run onto pending−run stack, and maybe merge
11    ts.pushRun(lo, runLen);
12    ts.mergeCollapse();
13    // Advance to find next run
14    lo += runLen;
15    nRemaining −= runLen;
16  } while (nRemaining != 0);
17  // Merge all remaining runs to complete sort
18  assert lo == hi;
19  ts.mergeForceCollapse();
20  assert ts.stackSize == 1;
```

In each iteration of the above loop, the next run is constructed. First, a maximal ordered segment from the current position lo is constructed (the parameter hi denotes the upper bound of the entire segment of the array a to be sorted). This construction consists in constructing a maximal descending or ascending segment and reversing the order in case of a descending one. If the constructed run is too short (that is, less than minRun) then it is extended to a run of length minRun using binary insertion sort (nRemaining is the number of elements yet to be processed). Next, the starting position and the length of the run is pushed onto the stack of the object variable ts by the method pushRun below.

Listing 2. pushRun

```
1   private void pushRun(int runBase, int runLen) {
2     this.runBase[stackSize] = runBase;
3     this.runLen[stackSize] = runLen;
4     stackSize++; }
```

The method mergeCollapse subsequently checks whether the invariant (lines 4—5 of Listing 3) on the stack of runs still holds, and merges runs until the invariant is restored (explained in detail below). When the main loop terminates, the method mergeForceCollapse completes sorting by merging all stacked runs.

Listing 3. mergeCollapse

```
1  /**
2   * Examines the stack of runs waiting to be merged and merges
3   * adjacent runs until the stack invariants are reestablished:
4   *    1. runLen[i - 3] > runLen[i - 2] + runLen[i - 1]
5   *    2. runLen[i - 2] > runLen[i - 1]
6   * This method is called each time a new run is pushed onto the stack,
7   * so the invariants are guaranteed to hold for i < stackSize upon
8   * entry to the method.
9   */
10 private void mergeCollapse() {
11   while (stackSize > 1) {
12     int n = stackSize - 2;
13     if (n > 0 && runLen[n-1] <= runLen[n] + runLen[n+1]) {
14       if (runLen[n - 1] < runLen[n + 1])
15         n--;
16       mergeAt(n);
17     } else if (runLen[n] <= runLen[n + 1]) {
18       mergeAt(n);
19     } else {
20       break; // Invariant is established
21     }
22   }
23 }
```

The method `mergeCollapse` ensures that the top three elements of the stack satisfy the invariant given in the comments above. In more detail, let `runLen[n-1]` = C, `runlen[n]` = D, and `runLen[n+1]` = E be the top three elements. Operationally, the loop is based on the following cases: 1. If $C \leq D + E$ and $C < E$ then the runs at `n-1` and `n` are merged. 2. If $C \leq D + E$ and $C \geq E$ then the runs at `n` and `n+1` are merged. 3. If $C > D + E$ and $D \leq E$ then the runs at `n` and `n+1` are merged. 4. If $C > D + E$ and $D > E$ then the loop exits.

3 Breaking the Invariant

We next show that the method `mergeCollapse` does not preserve the invariant in the entire run stack, contrary to what is suggested in the comments. To see this, consider as an example the situation where `runLen` consists of 120, 80, 25, 20, 30 on entry of `mergeCollapse`, directly after 30 has been added by `pushRun`. In the first iteration of the `mergeCollapse` loop there will be a merge at 25, since $25 \leq 20 + 30$ and $25 < 30$, resulting in (Listing 3, lines 15 and 16): $120^{\times}$, 80, 45, 30. In the second iteration, it is checked that the invariant is satisfied at 80 and 45 (lines 13 and 17), which is the case since $80 > 45 + 30$ and $45 > 30$, and `mergeCollapse` terminates. But notice that the invariant does not hold at 120, since $120 \leq 80 + 45$. Thus, `mergeCollapse` has not fully restored the invariant.

More generally, an error (violation of the invariant) can only be introduced by merging the second-to-last element and requires precisely four elements after the position of the error, i.e., at `runLen[stackSize-5]`. Indeed, suppose `runLen` consists of four elements A, B, C, D satisfying the invariant (so $A > B + C$, $B > C + D$ and $C > D$). We add a fifth element E to `runLen` using `pushRun`, after which `mergeCollapse` is called. The only possible situation in which an error can be introduced, is when $C \leq D + E$ and $C < E$. In this case, C and D will be merged, yielding the stack $A, B, C + D, E$. Then `mergeCollapse` checks whether the invariant is satisfied by the new three top elements. But A is not among those, so it is not checked whether $A > B + C + D$. As shown by the above example, this latter inequality does not hold in general.

3.1   The Length of runLen

The invariant affects the maximal size of the stack of run lengths during exection; recall that this stack is implemented by `runLen` and `stackSize`. The length of `runLen` is declared in the constructor of TimSort, based on the length of the input array `a` and, as shown below, on the assumption that the invariant holds. For performance reasons it is crucial to choose `runLen.length` as small as possible (but so that `stackSize` does not exceed it). The original Java implementation is as follows[2] (in a recent update the number 19 was changed to 24, see Sect. 4):

Listing 4. Bound of runLen based on length of the input array

```
1   int len = a.length;
2   int stackLen = (len <      120  ? 5 :
3                   len <     1542  ? 10 :
4                   len <   119151  ? 19 : 40);
```

We next explain these numbers, assuming the invariant to hold. Consider the sequence $(b_i)_{i \geq 0}$, defined inductively by $b_0 = 0$, $b_1 = 16$ and $b_{i+2} = b_{i+1} + b_i + 1$. The number 16 is a general lower bound on the run lengths. Now $b_0, \ldots, b_n$ are lower bounds on the run lengths in an array `runLen` of length n that satisfy the invariant; more precisely, $b_{i-1} \leq$ `runLen[n-i]` for all i with $0 < i \leq n$.

Let `runLen` be a run length array arising during execution, assume it satisfies the invariant, and let $n =$ `stackSize`. We claim that for any number B such that $1 + \sum_{i=0}^{B} b_i >$ `a.length` we have $n \leq B$ throughout execution. This means that B is a safe bound, since the number of stack entries never exceeds B.

The crucial property of the sequence (b_i) is that throughout execution we have $\sum_{i=0}^{n-1} b_i < \sum_{i=0}^{n-1}$ `runLen[i]` using that $b_0 = 0 <$ `runLen[n-1]` and $b_{i-1} \leq$ `runLen[n-i]`. Moreover, we have $\sum_{i=0}^{n-1}$ `runLen[i]` $\leq$ `a.length` since the runs in `runLen` are disjoint segments of `a`. Now for any B chosen as above, we have $\sum_{i=0}^{n-1} b_i < \sum_{i=0}^{n-1}$ `runLen[i]` $\leq$ `a.length` $< 1 + \sum_{i=0}^{B} b_i$ and thus $n \leq B$. Hence, we can safely take `runLen.length` to be the least B such that $1 + \sum_{i=0}^{B} b_i >$ `a.length`. If `a.length` < 120 we thus have 4 as the minimal choice of the bound, for `a.length` < 1542 it is 9, etc. This shows that the bounds used in OpenJDK (Listing 4) are slightly suboptimal (off by 1). The default value 40 (39 is safe) is based on the maximum $2^{31} - 1$ of integers in Java.

4   Worst Case Stack Size

In Sect. 3 we showed that the declared length of `runLen` is based on the invariant, but that the invariant is not fully preserved. However, this does not necessarily

---

[2] TimSort can also be used to sort only a segment of the input array; in this case, `len` should be based on the length of this segment. In the current implementation this is not the case, which negatively affects performance.

result in an actual error at runtime. The goal is to find a bad case, i.e., an input array for TimSort of a given length k, so that `stackSize` becomes larger than `runLen.length`, causing an ArrayIndexOutOfBoundsException in `pushRun`. In this section we show how to achieve the *worst case*: the maximal size of a stack of run lengths which does not satisfy the invariant. For certain choices of k this *does* result in an exception during execution of TimSort, as we show in Sect. 4.1. Not only does this expose the bug, our analysis also provides a safe choice for `runLen.length` that avoids the out-of-bounds exception.

The general idea is to construct a list of run lengths that leads to the worst case. This list is then turned into a concrete input array for TimSort by generating actual runs with those lengths. For instance, a list $(2,3,4)$ of run lengths is turned into the input array $(0,1,0,0,1,0,0,0,1)$ of length $k = 9$.

The sum of all runs should eventually sum to k. Hence, to maximize the stack size, the runs in the worst case are short. A run that breaks the invariant is too short, so the worst case occurs with a maximal number of runs that break the invariant. However, the invariant holds for at least half of the entries:

Lemma 1. *Throughout execution of TimSort, the invariant cannot be violated at two consecutive runs in* `runLen`.

Proof. Suppose, to the contrary, that two consecutive entries A and B of the run length stack violate the invariant. Consider the moment that the error at B is introduced, so A is already incorrect. The analysis of Sect. 3 reveals that there must be exactly four more entries after B on the stack (labelled $C \dots F$) satisfying $D \leq E + F$ and $D < F$ to trigger the merge below:

$$
\begin{array}{cccccc}
A^{\times} & B & C & D & E & F \\
A^{\times} & B^{\times} & C & D+E & F &
\end{array}
$$

Merging stops here (otherwise $B^{\times}$ would be corrected), and we have 1. $D < F$ and 2. $C > D + E + F$. Next, consider the moment that C was generated. Since $A^{\times}$ is incorrect, C must be the result of merging some C_1 and C_2:

$$
\begin{array}{ccccc}
A & B & C_1 & C_2 & D'
\end{array}
$$

This gives: 3. $C_1 + C_2 = C$, 4. $C_1 > C_2$, 5. $C_1 < D'$, 6. $D' \leq D$. Finally, all run lengths must be positive, thus: 7. $E > 0$. It is easy to check that constraints 1.–7. yield a contradiction. □

The above lemma implies that in the worst case, `runLen` has the form:

$$
Y_n, X_n^{\times}, Y_{n-1}, X_{n-1}^{\times}, \dots, Y_1, X_1 \tag{1}
$$

where each X_i invalidates the invariant, i.e., $X_i \leq Y_{i-1} + X_{i-1}$, and each Y_i satisfies it, i.e., $Y_i > X_i + Y_{i-1}$ (except when $i \leq 2$, since at least 5 elements are required to break the invariant). In the remainder of this section we show how to compute an input (in terms of run lengths) on which execution of TimSort results in a run length stack of the form (1).

Observe that the above sequence (1) can not be reached by simply choosing an input with these run lengths: each X_i would be merged away when X_{i-1} is pushed. Instead, we choose the input run lengths in such a way that each X_i arises as a sum of elements $x_1^i, \ldots, x_{n_i}^i$ and each Y_i occurs literally in the input.

In order to calculate the X_i's, suppose the top three elements of the stack are X_i, Y_{i-1}, x_1^{i-1}. Since X_i must not be merged away, we have $X_i > Y_{i-1} + x_1^{i-1}$. Thus, the minimal choice of X_i's and Y_i's is:

$$X_i = Y_{i-1} + x_1^{i-1} + 1 \qquad Y_i = X_i + Y_{i-1} + 1 \qquad (2)$$

The base cases are $X_1 = m$ (with $x_1^1 = m$) and $Y_1 = m + 4$, where $m = 16$ is the minimal run length. From (2) we then derive that $X_2 = 20 + 16 + 1 = 37$. The next step is to show how the elements x_j^i are computed from X_i, $i \geq 2$. To minimize the X_i's and Y_i's, each x_1^i should be as small as possible. Moreover, the merging pattern that arises while adding x_j^i's needs to preserve the previous X_{i+1} and Y_{i+1}, thus the top three elements of the stack before pushing x_j should be (omitting the index i from the x's for readability):

$$X_{i+1}, Y_i, x_1 + \ldots + x_{j-2}, x_{j-1}$$

Pushing x_j should then result in the merge:

$$X_{i+1}, Y_i, x_1 + \ldots + x_{j-2} + x_{j-1}, x_j \, .$$

and merging should stop, so $x_1 + \ldots + x_{j-1} > x_j$. The above merge only occurs when $x_1 + \ldots + x_{j-2} < x_j$. Thus, we obtain the desired merging behaviour by choosing the sequences $x_1, \ldots, x_{n_i}$ such that $X_i = x_1 + \ldots + x_{n_i}$ and

$$\text{for all } j \leq n_i : \quad x_j \geq m \text{ and } x_1 + \ldots + x_{j-2} < x_j < x_1 + \ldots + x_{j-1} \qquad (3)$$

Further, x_1 should be chosen as small as possible to minimize X_{i+1} (2).

To compute such a sequence $x_1, \ldots, x_n$ from a number X, we distinguish between the case that X lies within certain intervals for which we have a fixed choice (with optimal x_1), and other ranges, for which we apply a default computation. The default computation starts with $x_n = X - (\lfloor \frac{X}{2} \rfloor + 1)$ and proceeds to compute $x_1, \ldots, x_{n-1}$ from $\lfloor \frac{X}{2} \rfloor + 1$. By repeatedly applying this computation, we always end up in one of the intervals for which we have a fixed choice. Because of space limitations, we treat only the fixed choices for the intervals $[m, 2m]$, $[2m+1, 3m+2]$ and $[3m+3, 4m+1]$. In the first case the only possible choice is $x_1 = X$. In the second case we take $x_1 = \lfloor \frac{X}{2} \rfloor + 1$ and $x_2 = X - x_1$. Finally, in the last case we take $x_1 = m + 1$, $x_2 = m$ and $x_3 = X - (x_2 + x_1)$.

Proposition 1. *For any X, the above strategy yields a sequence that satisfies (3) with a minimal value of x_1.*

Proof. We have fixed choices for any X in $[0, 2m]$, $[2m+1, 3m+2]$, $[3m+3, 4m+1]$, $[5m+5, 6m+5]$, $[8m+9, 10m+9]$, $[13m+15, 16m+17]$. An X in the first interval results in a sequence of length 1, in the second a sequence of length 2, etc. Except for the first two intervals $x_1 = m + 1$ is always chosen. The requirements (3) imply $x_1 > x_2 \geq m$, thus for any $X > m$, $x_1 = m + 1$ is the best we can hope for. Next, observe that if $x_1 = m + 1$ is produced for $X \in [l, r]$ then $x_1 = m + 1$, for any $X \in [2l - 1, 2r - 1]$ as well (since then $(\lfloor \frac{X}{2} \rfloor + 1) \in [l, r]$). Applying this to the interval $[3m + 3, 4m + 1]$ gives $[6m + 5, 8m + 1]$, which combined with $[5m + 5, 6m + 5]$ gives $[5m + 5, 8m + 1]$. We thus also get $[10m + 9, 16m + 1]$, and combining this with $[8m + 9, 10m + 9]$ yields $[8m + 9, 16m + 1]$. Combining the latter with $[13m + 15, 16m + 17]$ we obtain $[8m + 9, 16m + 17]$. Since this interval gives the optimal $x_1 = m + 1$, so do $[16m + 17, 32m + 33]$, $[32m + 33, 64m + 65]$, etc. Hence, we have the minimal $x_1 = m + 1$, for any $X \geq 8m + 9$.

For $X \leq 8m + 9$ a (tedious) case analysis shows minimality of x_1.   □

All in all, we have shown how to construct an input that generates the worst case which is of the form (1) and where each of the sequences of x_j^i's is constructed using the above strategy, yielding a minimal x_1^i by Proposition 1.

Theorem 1. *An input corresponding to the sequence of run lengths as constructed above produces the largest possible stack of run lengths for a given input length, which does not satisfy the invariant.*

4.1 Breaking TimSort

We implemented the above construction of the worst case [7]. Executing TimSort on the generated input yields the following stack sizes (given array sizes):

array size	64	128	160	65536	131072	67108864	1073741824
required stack size	3	4	5	21	23	41	49
`runLen.length`	5	10	10	19 (24)	40	40	40

The table above lists the required stack size for the worst case of a given length. The third row shows the declared bounds in the TimSort implementation (see Listing 4). The number 19 was recently updated to 24 after a bug report[1].

This means that, for instance, the worst case of length 160 requires a stack size of 5, and thus the declared `runLen.length` $= 10$ suffices. Further observe that 19 does not suffice for arrays of length at least 65536, whereas 24 does. For the worst case of length 67108864, the declared bound 40 does not suffice, and running TimSort yields an unpleasant result:

Listing 5. Exception during exection of TimSort

```
Exception in thread"main" java.lang.ArrayIndexOutOfBoundsException: 40
    at java.util.TimSort.pushRun(TimSort.java:386)
    at java.util.TimSort.sort(TimSort.java:213)
    at java.util.Arrays.sort(Arrays.java:659)
    at TestTimSort.main(TestTimSort.java:18)
```

5   Verification of a Fixed Version

In Sect. 3 we showed that `mergeCollapse` does not fully re-establish the invariant, which led to an ArrayIndexOutOfBoundsException in `pushRun`. The previous section provides a possible workaround: adjust `runLen.length` using a worst-case analysis. That section also made clear that this analysis is based on an intricate argument that seems infeasible for a mechanized correctness proof.

Therefore, we provide a more principled solution. We fix `mergeCollapse` so that the class invariant *is* re-established, formally specify the new implementation in JML and provide a formal correctness proof, focussing on the most important specifications and proof obligations. This formal proof has been fully mechanized in the theorem prover KeY [4] (see Sect. 6 for an experience report).

Listing 6. Fixed version of mergeCollapse

```
 1   private void mergeCollapse() {
 2       while (stackSize > 1) {
 3           int n = stackSize - 2;
 4           if ( n >= 1 && runLen[n-1] <= runLen[n] + runLen[n+1]
 5               || n >= 2 && runLen[n-2] <= runLen[n] + runLen[n-1]) {
 6               if (runLen[n-1] < runLen[n+1])
 7                   n--;
 8           } else if (runLen[n] > runLen[n+1]) {
 9               break; // Invariant is established
10           }
11           mergeAt(n);
12       }
13   }
```

Listing 6 shows the new version of `mergeCollapse`. The basic idea is to check validity of the invariant on the top 4 elements of `runLen` (lines 4, 5 and 8), instead of only the top 3, as in the original implementation. Merging continues until the top 4 elements satisfy the invariant, at which point we break out of the merging loop (line 9). We prove below that this ensures that *all* runs obey the invariant.

To obtain a human readable specification and a feasible (mechanized) proof, we introduce suitable abstractions using the following auxiliary predicates:

Name	Definition
elemBiggerThanNext2(arr, idx)	$(0 \leq idx \land idx + 2 < arr.length) \rightarrow$ $arr[idx] > arr[idx + 1] + arr[idx + 2]$
elemBiggerThanNext(arr, idx)	$0 \leq idx \land idx + 1 < arr.length \rightarrow$ $arr[idx] > arr[idx + 1]$
elemLargerThanBound(arr, idx, v)	$0 \leq idx < arr.length \rightarrow arr[idx] \geq v$
elemInv(arr, idx, v)	elemBiggerThanNext2$(arr, idx)\land$ elemBiggerThanNext$(arr, idx)\land$ elemLargerThanBound(arr, idx, v)

Intuitively, the formula elemInv($runLen, i, 16$) is that `runLen[i]` satisfies the invariant as given in lines 4—5 of Listing 3, and has length at least 16 (recall that this is a lower bound on the minimal run length). Aided by these predicates we are ready to express the formal specification, beginning with the class invariant.

Class Invariant. A class invariant is a property that all instances of a class should satisfy. In a design by contract setting, each method is proven in isolation (assuming the contracts of methods that it calls), and the class invariant can be assumed in the precondition and must be established in the postcondition, as well as at all call-sites to other methods. The latter ensures that it is safe to assume the class invariant in a method precondition. A precondition in JML is given by a **requires** clause, and a postcondition is given by **ensures**. To avoid manually adding the class invariant at all these points, JML offers an **invariant** keyword which *implicitly* conjoins the class invariant to all pre- and postconditions. A seemingly natural candidate for the class invariant states that all runs on the stack satisfy the invariant and have a length of at least 16. However, **pushRun** does not preserve this invariant. Further, inside the loop of **mergeCollapse** (Listing 6) the **mergeAt** method is called, so the class invariant must hold. But at that point the invariant can be temporarily broken by the last 4 runs in **runLen** due to ongoing merging. Finally, the last run pushed on the stack in the main sorting loop (Listing 1) can be shorter than 16 if fewer items remain. The class invariant given below addresses all this:

Listing 7. Class invariant of TimSort

```
 1  /*@ invariant
 2  @        runBase.length == runLen.length
 3  @ && (a.length < 120 ==> runLen.length==4)
 4  @ && (a.length >= 120 && a.length < 1542 ==> runLen.length==9)
 5  @ && (a.length>=1542 && a.length<119151 ==> runLen.length==18)
 6  @ && (a.length >= 119151 ==> runLen.length==39)
 7  @ && (runBase[0] + (\sum int i; 0<=i && i<stackSize; (\bigint)runLen[i]) <= a.length)
 8  @ && (0 <= stackSize && stackSize <= runLen.length)
 9  @ && (\forall int i; 0<=i && i<stackSize-4; elemInv(runLen, i, 16))
10  @ && elemBiggerThanNext(runLen, stackSize-4)
11  @ && elemLargerThanBound(runLen, stackSize-3, 16)
12  @ && elemLargerThanBound(runLen, stackSize-2, 16)
13  @ && elemLargerThanBound(runLen, stackSize-1, 1)
14  @ && elemLargerThanBound(runBase, 0, 0)
15  @ && (\forall int i; 0<=i && i<stackSize-1;
16  @          (\bigint)runBase[i] + runLen[i] == runBase[i+1]);
17  @*/
```

Lines 3–6 specify the length of **runLen** in terms of the length of the input array **a**. Line 7–8 formalizes the property that the length of all runs together (i.e., the sum of all run lengths) does not exceed **a.length**. Line 9 contains bounds for **stackSize**. Line 10 expresses that all but the last 4 elements satisfy the invariant. The properties satisfied by the last 4 elements are specified on lines 11–14. Lines 15–17 formalize that run i starts at **runBase[i]** and extends for **runLen[i]** elements. As JML by default uses Java integer types, which can overflow, we need to make sure this does not happen by casting those expressions that potentially can overflow to \bigint.

The pushRun method. This method adds a new run of length **runLen** to the stack, starting at index **runBase**[3]. Lines 4–5 of Listing 8 express that the starting index of the new run (**runBase**) directly follows after the end index of the last run (at index **stackSize-1** in **this.runLen** and **this.runBase**). The assignable clause indicates which locations can be modified; intuitively the assignable clause below says that previous runs on the stack are unchanged.

Listing 8. Contract of pushRun

```
1   /*@ normal_behavior
2   @ requires
3   @       runLen > 0 && runLen <= a.length && runBase >= 0
4   @ && (stackSize > 0  ==> runBase ==
5   @   (\bigint)this.runBase[stackSize−1]+this.runLen[stackSize−1])
6   @ && ((\bigint)runLen + runBase <= a.length)
7   @ && (\forall int i; 0<=i && i<ts.stackSize−2; elemInv(ts.runLen,i,16))
8   @ && elemBiggerThanNext(ts.runLen, ts.stackSize−2)
9   @ && elemLargerThanBound(ts.runLen, ts.stackSize−1, 16)
10  @ ensures
11  @    this.runBase[\old(stackSize)] == runBase
12  @ && this.runLen[\old(stackSize)] == runLen
13  @ && stackSize == \old(stackSize)+1;
14  @ assignable
15  @    this.runBase[stackSize], this.runLen[stackSize], this.stackSize;
16  @*/
17  private void pushRun(int runBase, int runLen)
```

The mergeCollapse method. The new implementation of **mergeCollapse** restores the invariant at all elements in **runLen**; this is stated in lines 6–7 of Listing 9. As **mergeCollapse** just merges existing runs, the sum of all run lengths should be preserved (lines 8–9). Line 10 expresses that the length of the last run on the stack after merging never decreases (merging increases it). This is needed to ensure that all runs, except possibly the very last one, have length ≥ 16.

Listing 9. Contract of mergeCollapse

```
1   /*@ normal_behavior
2   @ requires
3   @       stackSize > 0  && elemInv(runLen, stackSize−4, 16)
4   @   && elemBiggerThanNext(runLen, stackSize−3);
5   @ ensures
6   @    (\forall int i; 0<=i && i<stackSize−2; elemInv(runLen, i, 16))
7   @ && elemBiggerThanNext(runLen, stackSize−2)
8   @ && ((\sum int i; 0<=i && i<stackSize; (\bigint)runLen[i])
9   @    == \old((\sum int i; 0<=i && i<stackSize; (\bigint)runLen[i])))
10  @ && (runLen[stackSize−1] >= \old(runLen[stackSize−1]))
11  @ && (0 < stackSize && stackSize <= \old(stackSize));
12  @*/
13  private void mergeCollapse()
```

The loop invariant of **mergeCollapse** is given in Listing 10. As discussed above, merging preserves the sum of all run lengths (lines 2–3). Line 4 expresses that all but the last four runs satisfy the invariant: a merge at index **stackSize-3** (*before* merging) can break the invariant of the run at index **stackSize-4** *after* merging (beware: **stackSize** was decreased). Lines 5–8 state the conditions satisfied by the

---

[3] These parameters shadow the instance variables with the same name; to refer to the instance variables in specifications one prefixes **this**, just like in Java.

last 4 runs. Lines 9–10 specify consistency between `runLen` and `runBase`. The last line states that `stackSize` can only decrease through merging.

Listing 10. Loop Invariant of mergeCollapse

```
1   /*@ loop_invariant
2   @        ((\sum int i; 0<=i && i<stackSize; runLen[i])
3   @           == \old((\sum int i; 0<=i && i<stackSize; runLen[i])))
4   @ && (\forall int i; 0<=i && i<stackSize-4; elemInv(runLen, i, 16))
5   @ && elemBiggerThanNext(runLen, stackSize-4)
6   @ && elemLargerThanBound(runLen, stackSize-3, 16)
7   @ && elemLargerThanBound(runLen, stackSize-2, 16)
8   @ && elemLargerThanBound(runLen, stackSize-1, 1)
9   @ && (\forall int i; 0<=i && i<stackSize-1;
10  @        (\bigint)runBase[i] + runLen[i] == runBase[i+1])
11  @ && (runLen[stackSize-1] >= \old(runLen[stackSize-1]))
12  @ && (0 < stackSize && stackSize <= \old(stackSize));
13  @*/
```

To prove the contracts, several verification conditions must be established. We discuss the two most important ones. The first states that on entry of `pushRun`, the `stackSize` must be smaller than the stack length. The ArrayIndexOutOf-BoundsException of Listing 5 was caused by the violation of that property:

`requires(pushRun) &&` cl. invariant `==> stackSize < this.runLen.length`

Proof. Line 9 of the class invariant implies `stackSize ≤ this.runLen.length`. We derive a contradiction from `stackSize = this.runLen.length` by considering four cases: `a.length < 120`, or `a.length ≥ 120 && a.length < 1542`, or `a.length ≥ 1542 && a.length < 119151`, or `a.length ≥ 119151`. We detail the case `a.length < 120`, the other cases are analogous. Since `a.length < 120`, line 3 of the class invariant implies `stackSize = this.runLen.length = 4`.

Let `SUM = this.runLen[0] + ... + this.runLen[3]`. Suitable instances of lines 16–17 of the class invariant imply `this.runBase[3] + this.runLen[3] = this.runBase[0] + SUM`. Together with line 15 of the class invariant and lines 4–6 of the `pushRun` contract we get `runLen + SUM < 120`. But the `\requires` clause of `pushRun` implies `runLen > 0`, so `SUM < 119`. The `\requires` clause also implies `runLen[3] ≥ 16` (line 9), `runLen[2] ≥ 17` (line 8), `runLen[1] ≥ 34` and `runLen[0] ≥ 52` (line 7). So `SUM ≥ 16 + 17 + 34 + 52 = 119`, a contradiction.   □

The second verification condition arises from the break statement in the `mergeCollapse` loop (Listing 6, line 9). At that point the guards on line 4 and 5 are false, the one on line 8 is true, and the `\ensures` clause of `mergeCollapse` (which implies that the invariant holds for all runs in `runLen`) must be proven:

$$
\begin{pmatrix}
\text{loop invariant of } \texttt{mergeCollapse} \; \&\& \; \texttt{n = stackSize-2} \\
\&\& \; \texttt{n > 0 ==> runLen[n-1] > runLen[n] + runLen[n+1]} \\
\&\& \; \texttt{n > 1 ==> runLen[n-2] > runLen[n-1] + runLen[n]} \\
\&\& \; \texttt{n >= 0 ==> runLen[n] > runLen[n+1]}
\end{pmatrix}
$$

$$==> \texttt{\textbackslash ensures (mergeCollapse)}$$

Proof. Preservation of sums (lines 8–9 of `\ensures`) follows directly from lines 2–3 of the loop invariant. Lines 10–11 of `\ensures` are implied by lines 11–12 of the loop invariant. The property `elemBiggerThanNext(runLen,stackSize-2)` follows directly from `n >= 0 ==> runLen[n] > runLen[n+1]`. We show by cases that `\forall int i; 0<=i && i<stackSize-2; elemInv(runLen, i, 16)`.

- `i < stackSize − 4`: from line 4 of the loop invariant.
- `i = stackSize − 4`: from line 3 of the premise. The original `mergeCollapse` implementation (Listing 3) did not cover this case, which was the root cause that the invariant `elemInv(runLen, i, 16)` could be false for some i.
- `i = stackSize − 3`: from the second line of the premise.   □

Of course, these proof obligations (plus all others) were formally shown in KeY.

5.1 Experimental Evaluation

The new version of `mergeCollapse` passes all relevant OpenJDK unit tests[4]. However, it introduces a potential extra check in the loop, which might affect performance. We compared the new version with the OpenJDK implementation using the benchmark created by the original author of the Java port of TimSort. This benchmark is part of OpenJDK[5]. It generates input of several different types, of varying sizes and repetitions. We executed the benchmark on three different setups: (Sys. 1): MacBookPro, Intel Core i7 @ 2.6 GHz, 8 GB, 4 core; (Sys. 2): Intel Core i7 @ 2.8 GHz, 6 GB, 2 core; (Sys. 3): Intel(R) Core(TM) i7 @ 3.4 GHz, 16 GB, 4 core. The table below summarizes the average speedup over 25 runs on each setup (see [7] for full results). The speedup is computed by dividing the benchmark result of the new version by the result of the original version. Thus, a value larger than 1 means that the new version wins.

	Sys. 1	Sys. 2	Sys. 3	Average
ALL_EQUAL_INT	0.9796	1.0094	1.0058	0.9983
ASCENDING_10_RND_AT_END_INT	0.9982	0.9997	0.9942	0.9974
ASCENDING_3_RND_EXCH_INT	1.0084	1.0130	1.0021	1.0079
ASCENDING_INT	0.9810	1.0082	1.0039	0.9977
DESCENDING_INT	0.9740	0.9897	0.9868	0.9835
DUPS_GALORE_INT	0.9910	0.9980	0.9981	0.9957
PSEUDO_ASCENDING_STRING	0.9652	0.9926	0.9929	0.9836
RANDOM_BIGINT	1.0064	1.0057	1.0047	1.0056
RANDOM_INT	0.9912	0.9989	0.9993	0.9965
RANDOM_WITH_DUPS_INT	0.9956	0.9971	0.9999	0.9975
WORST_CASE	1.0062	1.0075	1.0127	1.0088
All together (average)	0.9906	1.0018	1.0000	0.9975

---

[4] http://hg.openjdk.java.net/jdk7u/jdk7u/jdk/file/70e3553d9d6e/test/java/util/Arrays/Sorting.java.

[5] http://hg.openjdk.java.net/jdk7u/jdk7u/jdk/file/70e3553d9d6e/test/java/util/TimSort.

The first column contains the type of input. We added WORST_CASE, which generates the worst case as presented in Sect. 4. This case is important because it discriminates the two versions as much as possible. The other types of input are defined in `ArrayBuilder.java` which is part of the OpenJDK benchmark. We conclude that the new version does not negatively affect the performance.

6   Experience with KeY

We constructed a mechanized proof in KeY, showing correctness of the class invariant, the absence of exceptions and termination for all methods that affect the bug. Due to the complexity of Timsort, this requires interactivity as well as powerful automated search strategies.

However, two methods (`mergeLo` and `mergeHi`) we did not manage despite a considerable effort. Each has over 100 lines of code and exhibits a complex control flow with many nested loops, six breaks, and several `if`-statements. This leads to a memory overflow while proving due to an explosion in the number of symbolic execution paths. These methods obviously do not invalidate the class invariant as they do not access `runLen` and `runBase`. All other 15 methods were fully verified, which required specifications of all methods. In total, there are 460 lines of specifications, compared to 928 lines of code (including whitespace).

Our analysis resulted in one of the largest case studies carried out so far in KeY with over 2 million proof steps in total. The KeY proof targets the actual implementation in the OpenJDK standard library, rather than an idealized model of it. That implementation uses low-level bitwise operations, abrupt termination of loops and arithmetic overflows. This motivated several improvements to KeY, such as new support for reasoning about operations on bit-vectors.

	Rule Apps	Interact	Call	Loop	Q-inst	Spec	LoC
binarySort	536.774	470	3	2	16	27	35
sort(a,lo,hi,c)	235.632	695	14	1	54	38	52
mergeCollapse	415.133	1529	7	1	225	48	13
mergeAt	279.155	690	4	0	1064	32	39
pushRun	26.248	94	0	0	69	18	5
mergeForceColl	53.814	294	1	1	113	39	10
Other (sum)	664.507	1257	135	20	195	132	179
Total	2.211.263	5029	164	25	1736	334	333

One reason for the large number of proof steps is their fine granularity. However, notice that only a relatively small number was applied manually ("Interact"). Most of the manual interactions are applications of elementary weakening rules (hiding large irrelevant formulas) for guiding the automated proof search. Approximately 5–10 % required ingenuity, such as introducing crucial lemmas and finding suitable quantifier instantiations ("Q-inst"). The columns ("Call") and ("Loop") show the number of rule applications concerning calls and loops encountered in symbolic execution paths. Since multiple paths can lead to the same call, this is higher than the number of calls in the source code. The last two columns show the number of lines of specification and code (without comments).

The specification was constructed incrementally, by repeated attempts to complete the proof and, when failing, enhancing the (partial) specifications based on the feedback given by KeY. In particular, KeY can provide a symbolic counter example. For instance, KeY produces the following uncloseable goal when verifying the original **mergeCollapse** implementation:

```
runLen[stackSize−3] > runLen[stackSize−2] + runLen[stackSize−1],
\forall int i; 0<=i && i<stackSize−4; runLen[i] > runLen[i+1]+runLen[i+2]
==> runLen[stackSize−4] > runLen[stackSize−3] + runLen[stackSize−2]
```

The quantified formula says: the invariant holds except for the last five runs. The first formula establishes it for the last three runs. Nevertheless, it is broken by the fourth-last run, as the right hand side states. This information shows precisely where the invariant breaks (Sect. 3) and suggests how to fix the algorithm (Sect. 5): add a test for index **stackSize**-4 "somewhere". Due to symbolic execution, KeY produces proof trees that correspond closely to the structure of the program. This allows identifying *where* to add the extra check in the code.

While specifications were written incrementally, small changes to the class invariant required reproving instance methods almost from scratch. Indeed, a major challenge for properly supporting this incremental process is: how to avoid proof duplication? This could be partially addressed by introducing user-defined predicates to abstract from certain concrete parts of the specification. KeY already supports ad hoc introduction of user-defined predicates (Sect. 5). A systematic treatment is given in [5, 10]; its integration in KeY is ongoing work.

To reduce the number of symbolic paths, we heavily used block contracts around if-statements as a form of state merging. Current work focusses on more general techniques for merging different symbolic execution branches.

7   Conclusion and Future Work

Beyond the correctness result obtained in this paper, our case study allows to draw a number of more general conclusions:

1. State-of-art formal verification systems allow to prove functional correctness of actual implementations of complex algorithms that satisfy a minimum degree of structure and modularity.
2. Even core library methods of mainstream programming languages contain subtle bugs that can go undetected for years. Extensive testing was not able to exhibit the bug. Sections 3 and 4 explain why: the smallest counterexample is an array of 67+ million elements (with non-primitive type) and a very

complex structure. It is interesting to note that the affected sorting implementation was ported to Java from the Python library.[6] It turns out that the bug is present in Python as well, ever since the method was introduced.[7] It can be fixed in the same manner as described above. Though the bug is unlikely to occur by accident, it can be used in denial-of-service attacks[8].

3. Software verification is often considered too expensive. However, precise formal specification allowed us to discover that the invariant is not preserved, in an afternoon. Section 6 shows that this fact also inevitably arises during verification with KeY. The combination of interactivity with powerful automated strategies was essential to formally verify the fixed version.

4. Static analysis and model checking are not precise, expressive and modular enough to fully capture the functionality of the involved methods. Expressive contracts are crucial to break down the problem into feasible chunks.

We conclude that functional deductive verification of core libraries of mainstream programming languages with expressive, semi-automated verification tools is feasible. To reach beyond the current limits, improvements based on program transformations, refinement, and proof reuse are mandatory. Further, it is clearly worthwhile: the OpenJDK implementation of sort() is used daily in billions of program runs, often in safety- or security-critical scenarios. The infamous Intel Pentium bug cost a lot of revenue and reputation, even though the actual occurrence of a defect was not more likely than in the case of TimSort. Since then, formal verification of microprocessors is standard (e.g., [2]). Isn't it time that we begin to apply the same care to core software components?

Acknowledgment. We thank Peter Wong for suggesting to verify TimSort.

References

1. Ahrendt, W., Mostowski, W., Paganelli, G.: Real-time Java API specifications for high coverage test generation. In: Proceedings of the 10th International Workshop on Java Technologies for Real-time and Embedded Systems, JTRES 2012, pp. 145–154. ACM, New York (2012)
2. Akbarpour, B., Abdel-Hamid, A.T., Tahar, S., Harrison, J.: Verifying a synthesized implementation of IEEE-754 floating-point exponential function using HOL. Comput. J. **53**(4), 465–488 (2010)
3. Beckert, B., Hähnle, R.: Reasoning and verification. IEEE Intell. Syst. **29**(1), 20–29 (2014)
4. Beckert, B., Hähnle, R., Schmitt, P.H. (eds.): Verification of Object-Oriented Software: The KeY Approach. LNCS, vol. 4334. Springer, Heidelberg (2007)
5. Pelevina, M., Bubel, R., Hähnle, R.: Fully abstract operation contracts. In: Margaria, T., Steffen, B. (eds.) ISoLA 2014, Part II. LNCS, vol. 8803, pp. 120–134. Springer, Heidelberg (2014)

---

[6] http://svn.python.org/projects/python/trunk/Objects/listsort.txt.
[7] As the Python version works with 64bit integer types and uses larger bounds for runLen, it is even more unlikely to occur, however.
[8] http://bugs.java.com/view_bug.do?bug_id=6804124.

6. de Gouw, S., de Boer, F.S., Rot, J.: Proof pearl: the key to correct and stable sorting. J. Autom. Reasoning **53**(2), 129–139 (2014)
7. de Gouw, S., et al: Web appendix of this paper. http://envisage-project.eu/?page_id=1412 (2015)
8. Filliâtre, J.-C., Magaud, N.: Certification of sorting algorithms in the system Coq. In: Theorem Proving in Higher Order Logics: Emerging Trends. Nice (1999)
9. Foley, M., Hoare, C.A.R.: Proof of a recursive program: quicksort. Comput. J. **14**(4), 391–395 (1971)
10. Hähnle, R., Schaefer, I., Bubel, R.: Reuse in software verification by abstract method calls. In: Bonacina, M.P. (ed.) CADE 2013. LNCS, vol. 7898, pp. 300–314. Springer, Heidelberg (2013)
11. Leavens, G.T., Poll, E., Clifton, C., Cheon, Y., Ruby, C., Cok, D., Müller, P., Kiniry, J., Chalin, P., Zimmerman, D.M., Dietl, W.:. JML Reference Manual, Draft revision 2344 (2013)
12. McIlroy, P.M.: Optimistic sorting and information theoretic complexity. In: Ramachandran, V. (ed.) Proceedings of the Fourth Annual ACM/SIGACT-SIAM Symposium on Discrete Algorithms, pp. 467–474. ACM/SIAM, Austin (1993)
13. Mostowski, W.: Formalisation and verification of Java Card security properties in dynamic logic. In: Cerioli, M. (ed.) FASE 2005. LNCS, vol. 3442, pp. 357–371. Springer, Heidelberg (2005)
14. Mostowski, W.: Fully verified Java card API reference implementation. In: Beckert, B. (ed.) Proceedings of the 4th International Verification Workshop in Connection with CADE-21, CEUR Workshop Proceedings, Vol. 259, CEUR-WS.org, Bremen (2007)
15. Peters, T.: Timsort description. http://svn.python.org/projects/python/trunk/Objects/listsort.txt. Accessed Feb 2015
16. Sternagel, C.: Proof pearl - a mechanized proof of ghc's mergesort. J. Autom. Reasoning **51**(4), 357–370 (2013)

Tree Buffers

Radu Grigore$^{(\boxtimes)}$ and Stefan Kiefer

University of Oxford, Oxford, UK
radugrigore@gmail.com

Abstract. In *runtime verification*, the central problem is to decide if a given program execution violates a given property. In *online* runtime verification, a monitor observes a program's execution as it happens. If the program being observed has hard real-time constraints, then the monitor inherits them. In the presence of hard real-time constraints it becomes a challenge to maintain enough information to produce *error traces*, should a property violation be observed. In this paper we introduce a data structure, called *tree buffer*, that solves this problem in the context of automata-based monitors: If the monitor itself respects hard real-time constraints, then enriching it by tree buffers makes it possible to provide error traces, which are essential for diagnosing defects. We show that tree buffers are also useful in other application domains. For example, they can be used to implement functionality of *capturing groups* in regular expressions. We prove optimal asymptotic bounds for our data structure, and validate them using empirical data from two sources: regular expression searching through Wikipedia, and runtime verification of execution traces obtained from the DaCapo test suite.

1 Introduction

In runtime verification, a program is instrumented to emit events at certain times, such as method calls and returns. A monitor runs in parallel, observes the stream of events, and identifies bad patterns. Often, the monitor is specified by an automaton (for example, see [1,2,8,13,23]). When the accepting state of the automaton is reached, the last event of the program corresponds to a bug. At this point, developers want to know how was the bug reached. For example, the bug could be that an invalid iterator is used to access its underlying collection. An iterator becomes invalid when its underlying collection is modified, for instance by calling the REMOVE method of another iterator for the same collection. In order to diagnose the root cause of the bug, developers will want to determine how exactly the iterator became invalid. Of particular interest will be an *error trace*: the last few relevant events that led to a bug. In the context of static verification, error traces have proved to be invaluable in diagnosing the root cause of bugs [19]. However, runtime verification tools (such as [5,14,21]) shy away from providing error traces, perhaps because adding this functionality would impact efficiency. The goal of this paper is to provide the algorithmic foundations of efficient monitors that can provide error traces for a very general class of specifications.

© Springer International Publishing Switzerland 2015
D. Kroening and C.S. Păsăreanu (Eds.): CAV 2015, Part I, LNCS 9206, pp. 290–306, 2015.
DOI: 10.1007/978-3-319-21690-4_17

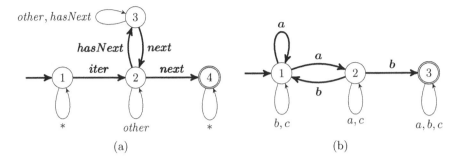

Fig. 1. Two automata with relevant transitions in boldface.

Nondeterministic automata provide a convenient specification formalism for monitors. They define both bugs and relevant events. Figure 1a shows an example automaton that specifies incorrect usage of an iterator: it is a bug if an iterator is created (event *iter*), and afterwards its NEXT() method is called without a preceding call to HASNEXT(). Throughout the paper we assume that the user specifies which transitions are *relevant*. In most applications, there is a natural way to choose the relevant transitions. For example, in Fig. 1a and in many other runtime verification properties, the natural choice are the non-loop transitions. Since the choice is natural, it can be automated; since the choice is dependent on application details, we do not focus on it.

We have to consider nondeterministic automata in general. Nondeterministic finite automata allow exponentially more succinct specifications than deterministic finite automata. In addition, in the runtime verification context we must use an automaton model that handles possibly infinite alphabets. For most models of automata over infinite alphabets, the nondeterministic variant is strictly more expressive than the deterministic variant [3,16,26]. Thus, we must consider nondeterminism not only to allow concise specifications, but also because some specifications cannot be defined otherwise.

Let us consider a concrete example: the automaton in Fig. 1b, consuming the stream of letters *cabbcab*. (We say *stream* when we wish to emphasize that the elements of the sequence must be processed one by one, in an online fashion.) One of the automaton computations labeled by *cabbcab* is $1 \xrightarrow{c} 1 \xrightarrow{a} 1 \xrightarrow{b} 1 \xrightarrow{b} 1 \xrightarrow{c} 1 \xrightarrow{a} 2 \xrightarrow{b} 3$, where relevant transitions are bold. We say that the subsequence formed by the relevant transitions is an *error trace*; here, $1 \xrightarrow{a} 1 \xrightarrow{a} 2 \xrightarrow{b} 3$.

The main contribution of this paper is the design of a data structure that allows the monitor to do the following while reading a stream:

1. The monitor keeps track of the states that the nondeterministic automaton could currently be in. Whenever the automaton could be in an accepting state, the monitor reports (i) the occurrence of a bug, and (ii) the last h relevant transitions of a run that drove the automaton into an accepting state. Here, h is a positive integer constant that the user fixes upon initializing the monitor.

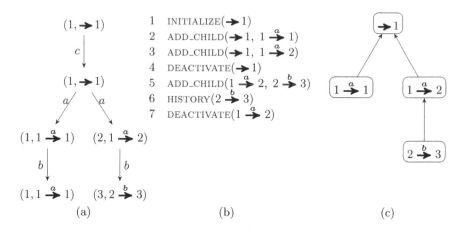

Fig. 2. Illustration of a monitor run of the automaton from Fig. 1b on the stream *cab*. Part (a) shows the monitor's traversal of the automaton with some instrumentation. Part (b) shows the sequence of tree buffer operations that the monitor invokes. Part (c) shows the tree-buffer data structure that the monitor builds.

Due to the nondeterminism, a bug may have multiple such error traces, but the monitor needs to report only one of them.

2. The monitor processes each event in a constant amount of *time*, thus paving the way for implementing real-time runtime verifiers that track error traces. (There is a need for real-time verifiers [22].) Not only the time is constant, but also not much *space* is wasted. Wasted space occurs if the monitor keeps transitions that are not among the h most recent relevant transitions.

Due to the nondeterminism of the automaton, those constraints force the monitor to keep track of a *tree* of computation histories. For properties that can be monitored with *slicing* [23] the tree of computation histories has a very particular shape. That shape allows for a relatively straightforward technique for providing error traces, using linear buffers. However, it has been shown that some interesting program properties, including *taint* properties, cannot be expressed by slicing [1,9].

In this paper we provide a monitor for *general* nondeterministic automata, at the same time satisfying the properties 1 and 2 mentioned above. The single most crucial step is the design of an efficient data structure, which we call *tree buffer*. A tree buffer operates on general trees and may be of independent interest.

Tree Buffers for Monitoring. A tree buffer is a data structure that stores parts of a tree. Its two main operations are ADD_CHILD(x, y), which adds to the tree a new node y as a child of node x, and HISTORY(x), which requests the h ancestors of x, where h is a constant positive integer. For memory efficiency the tree buffer distinguishes between *active* and *inactive* nodes. When ADD_CHILD(x, y) or HISTORY(x) is called, node x must be active. In the case of ADD_CHILD(x, y), the new node y becomes active. There is also a

DEACTIVATE(x) operation with the obvious semantics. One of the main contributions of this paper is the design of efficient algorithms that provide the functionality of tree buffers with asymptotically optimal time and space complexity. More precisely, the ADD_CHILD and DEACTIVATE operations take constant time, and the space wasted by nodes that are no longer accessible via HISTORY calls is bounded by a constant times the space occupied by nodes that *are* accessible via HISTORY calls.

In the following, we give an example of how an efficient monitor operates, assuming that an efficient tree buffer is available. Consider the automaton from Fig. 1b and the stream cab. The monitor keeps pairs of (1) a current automaton state q, and of (2) a *tree buffer node* with the most recent relevant transition of a run that led to q. Initially, this pair is $(1, \rightarrow 1)$, as 1 is the initial state of the automaton (see Fig. 2).

Upon reading c, the automaton takes the transition $1 \overset{c}{\rightarrow} 1$, and the monitor simulates the automaton by evolving from $(1, \rightarrow 1)$ to a new pair $(1, \rightarrow 1)$: the first component remains unchanged because $1 \overset{c}{\rightarrow} 1$ is a loop; the second component remains unchanged because $1 \overset{c}{\rightarrow} 1$ is irrelevant.

Next, a is read. The automaton takes transitions $1 \overset{a}{\rightarrow} 1$ and $1 \overset{a}{\rightarrow} 2$, both relevant. Corresponding to the automaton transition $1 \overset{a}{\rightarrow} 1$, the monitor evolves $(1, \rightarrow 1)$ into a new pair $(1, 1 \overset{a}{\rightarrow} 1)$: the first component remains unchanged because $1 \overset{a}{\rightarrow} 1$ is a loop; the second component *changes* because $1 \overset{a}{\rightarrow} 1$ is *relevant*. Corresponding to the automaton transition $1 \overset{a}{\rightarrow} 2$, the monitor *also* evolves $(1, \rightarrow 1)$ into a new pair $(2, 1 \overset{a}{\rightarrow} 2)$. Now that two relevant transitions were taken, they are added to the tree buffer: both $1 \overset{a}{\rightarrow} 1$ and $1 \overset{a}{\rightarrow} 2$ are children of $\rightarrow 1$. Moreover, because $\rightarrow 1$ is not anymore in any pair kept by the monitor, it is deactivated in the tree buffer.

Next, b is read. The automaton takes transitions $1 \overset{b}{\rightarrow} 1$, $2 \overset{b}{\rightarrow} 1$, and $2 \overset{b}{\rightarrow} 3$. Out of the two transitions with the same target the monitor will pick only one to simulate, using an application specific heuristic. In Fig. 2, the monitor chose to ignore $2 \overset{b}{\rightarrow} 1$. Moreover, because $1 \overset{a}{\rightarrow} 2$ used to be in the monitor's pairs before b was read but is not anymore, its corresponding tree buffer node is deactivated. Finally, since state 3 is accepting, the monitor will ask the tree buffer for an error trace, by calling $(2 \overset{b}{\rightarrow} 3)$.

In Fig. 7 we provide pseudocode formalizing the sketched algorithm.

The full version of the paper [10] includes missing proofs and further details.

2   Tree Buffers

Consider a procedure that handles a stream of events. At any point in time the procedure should be able to output the previous h events in the stream, where h is a fixed constant. Such *linear buffers* are ubiquitous in computer science, with applications, for example, in instruction pipelines [25], voice-over-network protocols [12], and distributed operating systems [15]. Linear buffers can be easily implemented using *circular buffers*, using $\Theta(h)$ memory and constant update time, which is clearly optimal.

INITIALIZE(x)
1   $parent(x) :=$ nil
2   $children(x) := 0$
3   $Nodes := \{x\}$
4   $Active := \{x\}$
5   $mem := 1$
6   $memOld := 1$

ADD_CHILD(x, y)
1   **assert** that $x \in Active$ and $y \notin Nodes$
2   $parent(y) := x$
3   $children(x) := children(x) + 1$
4   $Nodes := Nodes \cup \{y\}$
5   $Active := Active \cup \{y\}$

DEACTIVATE(x)
1   $Active := Active - \{x\}$

HISTORY(x)
1   **assert** that $x \in Active$
2   $xs := []$
3   **repeat** h times, or until $x =$ nil
4       $xs := x \cdot xs$
5       $x := parent(x)$
6   **return** xs

EXPAND$(x, \{y_1, \ldots, y_n\})$
1   **for** $i \in \{1, \ldots, n\}$
2   ADD_CHILD(x, y_i)
3   DEACTIVATE(x)

Fig. 3. The naive algorithm.

While this buffering approach is simple and efficient, it is less appropriate if the streamed data is organized *hierarchically*. Consider a stream of events, each of which contains a link to one of the previous events. We already saw an example of how such streams arise in runtime verification (Fig. 2). But, there are many other situations where such streams could arise; for example, when trees such as XML data are transmitted over a network, or when recording the spawned processes of a parallel computation, or when recording Internet browsing history.

A natural requirement for a buffer is to store the most recent data. For a tree this could mean, for example, the leaves of the tree, or the h ancestors of each leaf, where h is a constant. Observe that a linear buffer does not satisfy such requirements, because an old leaf or the parent of a new leaf may have been streamed much earlier, so that they have been removed from the buffer already.

A *tree buffer* is a tree-like data structure that satisfies such requirements. It supports the following operations:

- INITIALIZE(x) initializes the tree with the single node x and makes x active
- ADD_CHILD(x, y) adds node y as a child of the active node x and makes y active
- DEACTIVATE(x) makes x inactive
- EXPAND$(x, \{y_1, \ldots, y_n\})$ adds nodes $y_1, \ldots, y_n$ as children of the active node x, makes x inactive, and makes $y_1, \ldots, y_n$ active
- HISTORY(x) requests the h ancestors of the active node x, where h is a constant positive integer

A simple use case of a tree buffer consists of an INITIALIZE operation, followed by EXPAND operations with $n > 0$. In this case the active nodes are always exactly the leaves.

The functionality of tree buffers is defined by the naive algorithm shown in Fig. 3. The notation $f(x)$ stands for the field f of the node x, while the notation

F(x) stands for a call to function F with argument x. The field *children* and the variables *mem* and *memOld* do not affect the behavior of the naive algorithm: they are used later. The assertions at the beginning of ADD_CHILD and HISTORY detect sequences of operations that are invalid. For example, any sequence that does not start with a call to INITIALIZE is invalid. For such invalid sequences, tree buffer implementations are not required to behave like the naive algorithm. For valid sequences we require implementations to be functionally equivalent, albeit performance is allowed to be different.

The naive algorithm is time optimal: INITIALIZE, ADD_CHILD, and DEACTIVATE all take constant time; and HISTORY takes $O(h)$ time. However, it is not space efficient, as it does not take advantage of DEACTIVATE operations: it does not delete nodes that are out of reach of HISTORY. The challenge in designing tree buffers lies in preserving both time and space efficiency. On the one hand, it is not space efficient to store the whole tree. On the other hand, it is not time efficient to exactly identify the nodes that must be stored.

3   Space Efficient Algorithms

The naive algorithm is time efficient but not space efficient. This section presents several other algorithms. First, if each DEACTIVATE is followed by garbage collection, then the implementation becomes space efficient but not time efficient. Second, if DEACTIVATE is followed by garbage collection only at certain times, then the implementation becomes both space and time efficient, but only in an amortized sense. Third, we present an algorithm that is both space and time efficient in a strict sense. The last algorithm is somewhat sophisticated, and its correctness requires a non-obvious proof. The implementation of all four algorithms, which fully specifies all the details, is available online [11].

3.1   The Garbage Collecting Algorithm

A space optimal implementation uses no more memory than needed to answer HISTORY queries. To make this precise, let us define the *height* of a node x to be the shortest distance from x to an active node in the subtree of x, were we to use the naive algorithm. Active nodes have height 0. A node with no active node in its subtree has height ∞. Let H_i be the set of nodes with height i, and let $H_{<i}$ be the set of nodes with height less than i.

The memory needed to answer HISTORY queries is $\Omega(|H_{<h}|)$, and the gc algorithm of Fig. 4 achieves this bound. On line 5 of GC, the list *Level* represents H_{i-1}, and *Seen* represents $H_{<i}$. Thus, on line 13, the list *Level* represents H_{h-1}, and *Seen* represents $H_{<h}$. The procedure DELETE_PARENT implements a reference counting scheme.

Let us consider a sequence of ADD_CHILD and DEACTIVATE operations, coming after INITIALIZE. We call ADD_CHILD and DEACTIVATE *modifying operations*. Let $H_i^{(k)}$ be the H_i corresponding to the tree obtained after k modifying operations, and let $s_{gc}^{(k)}$ be the space used by the gc algorithm after k modifying operations.

```
GC()
1  Seen := COPY_OF(Active)
2  Level := CONVERT_TO_LIST(Active)
3  i := 1
4  while i < h and Level is nonempty
5      NextLevel := []
6      for y ∈ Level
7          x := parent(y)
8          if x ∉ Seen
9              Seen := {x} ∪ Seen
10             NextLevel := x · NextLevel
11     Level := NextLevel
12     i := i + 1
13 for y ∈ Level
14     DELETE_PARENT(y)

DEACTIVATE(x)
1  Active := Active − {x}
2  GC()
```

```
DELETE_PARENT(y)
1  x := parent(y)
2  if x ≠ nil
3      children(x) := children(x) − 1
4      if children(x) = 0
5          DELETE_PARENT(x)
6          delete x
7          mem := mem − 1
8      parent(y) := nil

ADD_CHILD(x, y)
1  assert that x ∈ Active
2  parent(y) := x
3  children(x) := children(x) + 1
4  Active := Active ∪ {y}
5  mem := mem + 1
```

Fig. 4. The gc algorithm. The tree buffer operations INITIALIZE, EXPAND, and HISTORY are those defined in Fig. 3.

Proposition 1. *Consider the* gc *algorithm from Fig. 4. The memory used after* k *modifying operations is optimal:* $s_{gc}^{(k)} \in \Theta(|H_{<h}^{(k)}|)$. *The runtime used to process* k *modifying operations is* $\Theta(k^2)$.

The space bound is obvious. For the time bound, the following sequence exhibits the quadratic behavior: INITIALIZE(0), ADD_CHILD(0, 1), ADD_CHILD(0, 2), DEACTIVATE(2), ADD_CHILD(0, 3), ADD_CHILD(0, 4), DEACTIVATE(4), . . .

3.2 The Amortized Algorithm

Our aim is to mitigate or even solve the time problem of the gc algorithm, but to retain space optimality up to a constant. One idea is to invoke the garbage collector rarely, so that the time spent in garbage collection is amortized. To this end, we call GC when the number of nodes in memory has doubled since the end of the last garbage collection. We obtain the amortized algorithm from Fig. 5. It is here that the counters mem and memOld are finally used.

```
ADD_CHILD(x, y)
1  assert that x ∈ Active
2  parent(y) := x
3  children(x) := children(x) + 1
4  Active := Active ∪ {y}
5  mem := mem + 1
6  if mem = 2 · memOld
7      GC()
8      memOld := mem
```

Fig. 5. The amortized algorithm. The tree buffer operations INITIALIZE, DEACTIVATE, EXPAND, HISTORY are those defined in Fig. 3. The subroutine GC is that defined in Fig. 4.

The following theorem states that the amortized algorithm is space efficient, by comparing it with the gc algorithm, which is space optimal. As before, let us consider a sequence of modifying operations. We write $s_{\text{amo}}^{(k)}$ for the space used by the amortized implementation after the first k operations. Call a sequence of operations *extensive* if every DEACTIVATE(x) is immediately preceded by an ADD_CHILD(x, y) for some y. For example, a sequence is extensive if it consists of an INITIALIZE operation followed by EXPAND operations with $n > 0$.

Theorem 2. *Consider the* amortized *algorithm in Fig. 5. A sequence of ℓ modifying operations takes $O(\ell)$ time. We have $s_{\text{amo}}^{(k)} \in O\big(\max_{j \leq k} s_{\text{gc}}^{(j)}\big)$ for all $k \leq \ell$. If the sequence is extensive then $s_{\text{amo}}^{(k)} \in O\big(s_{\text{gc}}^{(k)}\big)$ for all $k \leq \ell$.*

Loosely speaking, the theorem says that the space wasted in-between two garbage collections is bounded by the space that would be needed by the space optimal implementation at some earlier time, up to a constant. It also says that the time used is optimal *for a sequence* of operations.

3.3   The Real-Time Algorithm

In general, interactive applications should not have amortized implementations. Interactive applications include graphical user interfaces, but also real-time systems and runtime verification monitors for real-time systems. More generally speaking, the environment, be it human or machine, does not accumulate patience as the time goes by. Thus, time bounds that apply to each operation are preferable to bounds that apply to the sequence of operations performed so far.

The difficulty of designing a real-time algorithm stems from the fact that whether a node is needed depends on its height, but the heights cannot be maintained efficiently. This is because one DEACTIVATE operation may change the heights of many nodes, possibly far away.

The key idea is to under-approximate the set of unneeded nodes; that is, to find a property that is easily computable, and only unneeded nodes have it. To do so, we maintain three other quantities instead of heights. The *depth* of a node is its distance to the root via *parent* pointers, were we to use the naive algorithm. The *representative* of a node is its closest ancestor whose depth is a multiple of h. The *active count* of a node is the number of active nodes that have it as a representative. Unlike height, these three quantities — depth, representative, active count — are easy to maintain explicitly in the data structure. The depth only needs to be computed when the node is added to the tree. The representative of a node is either itself or the same as the representative of its parent, depending on whether the depth is a multiple of h. Finally, when a node is deactivated (added to the tree, respectively), only one active count changes: the active count of the node's representative is decreased (increased, respectively) by one.

The active count of a representative becomes 0 only if its height is at least h, which means it is unneeded to answer subsequent HISTORY queries. Thus, the set of nodes that are representatives and have an active count of 0 constitutes

INITIALIZE(x)

1   $Active := \{x\}$
2   $parent(x) := \mathsf{nil}$
3   $children(x) := 0$
4   $depth(x) := 0$
5   $rep(x) := x$
6   $cnt(x) := 1$

PROCESS_QUEUE$()$

1   **if** $queue$ is nonempty
2       $x := \text{DEQUE}()$
3   CUT_PARENT(x)
4   **delete** x

DEACTIVATE(x)

1   $Active := Active - \{x\}$
2   $cnt(rep(x)) := cnt(rep(x)) - 1$
3   **if** $children(x) = 0$
4   ENQUE(x)
5   **if** $cnt(rep(x)) = 0$
6   CUT_PARENT$(rep(x))$
7   PROCESS_QUEUE$()$

ADD_CHILD(x, y)

1   **assert** that $x \in Active$
2   **assert** that $cnt(y) = children(y) = 0$
3   $Active := Active \cup \{y\}$
4   $parent(y) := x$
5   $children(x) := children(x) + 1$
6   $depth(y) := depth(x) + 1$
7   **if** $depth(y) \equiv 0 \pmod{h}$
8       $rep(y) := y$
9   **else**
10      $rep(y) := rep(x)$
11 $cnt(rep(y)) := cnt(rep(y)) + 1$
12 PROCESS_QUEUE$()$

CUT_PARENT(y)

1   $x := parent(y)$
2   **if** $x \neq \mathsf{nil}$
3       $children(x) := children(x) - 1$
4   **if** $children(x) = 0$ **and** $x \notin Active$
5   ENQUE(x)
6   $parent(y) := \mathsf{nil}$

Fig. 6. The real-time algorithm. The tree buffer operations EXPAND and HISTORY are those defined in Fig. 3. The ENQUE and DEQUE operations are the standard operations of a queue data structure.

an under-approximation of the set of unneeded nodes. The resulting real-time algorithm appears in Fig. 6.

As DELETE_PARENT did in the gc algorithm, the function DEACTIVATE implements a reference counting scheme, using *children* as the counter. Unlike the gc algorithm, the node is not deleted immediately, but *scheduled for deletion*, by being placed in a queue. This queue is processed whenever the user calls ADD_CHILD or DEACTIVATE. When the queue is processed, by PROCESS_QUEUE, one node is deleted from memory, and perhaps its parent is scheduled for deletion.

The proof of the following theorem [10] is subtle. Similarly as before, we write $s_{\mathsf{rt}}^{(k)}$ for the space that the real-time algorithm has allocated and not deleted after k operations.

Theorem 3. *Consider the real-time algorithm from Fig. 6, and a sequence of ℓ modifying operations. Every operation takes $O(1)$ time. We have $s_{\mathsf{rt}}^{(k)} \in O\big(\max_{j \leq k} s_{\mathsf{gc}}^{(j)}\big)$ for all $k \leq \ell$. If the sequence is extensive then $s_{\mathsf{rt}}^{(k)} \in O\big(s_{\mathsf{gc}}^{(k)}\big)$ for all $k \leq \ell$.*

4   Monitoring

Consider a nondeterministic automaton $\mathcal{A} = (Q, E, q_0, F, \delta_i, \delta_r)$, where Q is a set of states, E is the alphabet of events, $q_0 \in Q$ is the initial state, $F \subseteq Q$ contains the accepting states, and $\delta_i, \delta_r \subseteq Q \times E \times Q$ are, respectively, the irrelevant and the relevant transitions. We aim to construct a monitor that reads a stream of events and reports an error trace when an accepting state has been reached. Since $\mathcal{A}$ is in general nondeterministic and there are both irrelevant and relevant transitions, building an efficient monitor for $\mathcal{A}$ is not straightforward. We have sketched in the introduction how to use a tree buffer for such a monitor. The algorithm in Fig. 7 makes this precise.

The main invariants (line 4) are the following:

- If the pair $(q, node)$ is in the list now, then HISTORY$(node)$ would return the last $\leq h$ relevant transitions of some computation $q_0 \xrightarrow{w}^* q$ of $\mathcal{A}$, where w is the stream read so far.
- If there is a computation $q_0 \xrightarrow{w}^* q$ of $\mathcal{A}$, then, after reading w, a pair $(q, node)$ is in the list now, for some $node$.

A node x is created and added to the tree buffer when a relevant transition is taken (lines 10–11). The node x is deactivated (line 19) when and only when it is about to be removed from the list now (line 20), since neither ADD_CHILD$(x, \cdot)$ nor HISTORY(x) can be invoked later.

In the following subsections we give two applications for this monitor. The $location$, which accompanies events (lines 5 and 10), is application dependent. For regular expression searching, the $location$ is an index in a string; for runtime verification, the $location$ is a position in the program text.

4.1   Regular-Expression Searching

We show that regular-expression searching with *capturing groups* can be implemented by constructing an automaton with irrelevant and relevant transitions, and then running the monitor from Fig. 7. Suppose we want to search Wikipedia for famous people with reduplicated names, like 'Ford Madox Ford'. One approach is to use the following (Python) regular expression:

$$\text{Ford}(\_[A-Z][a-z]*)\{m,n\}\_\text{Ford} \tag{1}$$

This expression matches names starting and ending with 'Ford', and with at least m and at most n middle names in-between. The parentheses indicate so-called *capturing groups*: The regular-expression engine is asked to remember (and possibly later output) the position in the text where the group was matched. We can implement this as follows. First, we compile the regular expression with capturing groups into an automaton with relevant and irrelevant transitions. Which transitions are relevant could be determined automatically using the capturing groups, or the user could specify it using a special-purpose extension of the syntax of regular expressions. Whenever the automaton takes a relevant transition, the position in the text should be remembered. Then we run the monitor from Fig. 7 on this automaton. In this way we can output the last h matches of capturing groups. In contrast, standard regular-expression engines would report only the last occurrence of each match. In the example expression (1), they

MONITOR()

```
1    root_node := MAKE_NODE(➤ q_0, nil)
2    INITIALIZE(root_node)
3    now, nxt := [(q_0, root_node)], []
4    forever
5        a, location := GET_NEXT_EVENT_AND_LOCATION()
6        for each (q, parent) in the list now
7            for each a-labeled transition t = (q →ᵃ q') ∈ δ_i ⊎ δ_r
8                if ¬in_nxt(q')
9                    if t ∈ δ_r
10                       child := MAKE_NODE(t, location)
11                       ADD_CHILD(parent, child)
12                   if t ∈ δ_i
13                       child := parent
14                   append (q', child) to nxt
15                   in_nxt(q'), in_nxt(child) := true, true
16                   if q' ∈ F
17                       REPORT_ERROR(HISTORY(child))
18       for each (q, node) in the list now
19           if ¬in_nxt(node) then DEACTIVATE(node)
20       now, nxt := nxt, []
21       for each (q, node) in the list now
22           in_nxt(q), in_nxt(node) := false, false
```

Fig. 7. A monitor for the automaton $\mathcal{A} = (Q, E, q_0, F, \delta_i, \delta_r)$. The monitor reports error traces by using a tree buffer.

would report only the last of Ford's middle names. One would have to unroll the expression n times in order to make a standard engine report them all.

For the regular expression (1), we remark that any equivalent *deterministic* automaton has $\Omega(2^m)$ states, so nondeterminism is essential for feasibility[1].

4.2 Runtime Verification

For runtime verification we use the monitor from Fig. 7 as well, in the way we sketched in the introduction. Clearly, for real-time runtime verification the real-time tree buffer algorithm needs to be used.

We have not yet emphasized one feature of our monitor, which is essential for runtime verification: The automaton $\mathcal{A} = (Q, E, q_0, F, \delta_i, \delta_r)$ may have an infinite set Q of states, and it may deal with infinite event alphabets E. Note that we did

---

[1] We use a large value for m when we want to find people with reduplicated names that are long. By searching Wikipedia with large values for m we found, for example, 'José María del Carmen Francisco Manuel Joaquín *Pedro* Juan Andrés Avelino Cayetano Venancio Francisco de Paula Gonzaga Javier Ramón Blas Tadeo Vicente Sebastián Rafael Melchior Gaspar Baltasar Luis *Pedro* de Alcántara Buenaventura Diego Andrés Apostol Isidro' (a Spanish don).

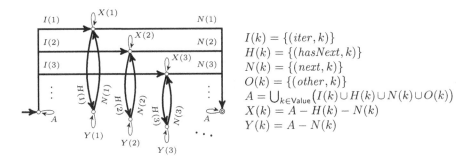

$$I(k) = \{(iter, k)\}$$
$$H(k) = \{(hasNext, k)\}$$
$$N(k) = \{(next, k)\}$$
$$O(k) = \{(other, k)\}$$
$$A = \bigcup_{k \in \mathsf{Value}} \big(I(k) \cup H(k) \cup N(k) \cup O(k)\big)$$
$$X(k) = A - H(k) - N(k)$$
$$Y(k) = A - N(k)$$

Fig. 8. The configuration graph of Fig. 1a. The arcs are labeled by *sets* of events, meaning that there is one transition for each event in the set. The picture shows only three values from $\mathsf{Value} = \{1, 2, 3, \dots\}$

not require any finiteness of the automaton for our monitor. We can implement the monitor from Fig. 7, as long as we have a finite *description* of $\mathcal{A}$, which allows us to loop over transitions (line 7) and to store individual states and events. One can view this as constructing the (infinite) automaton on the fly. For instance, the event alphabet could be $E = \Sigma \times \mathsf{Value}$, where $\Sigma = \{iter, hasNext, next, other\}$ and Value is the set of all program values, which includes integers, booleans, object references, and so on. There are various works on automata over infinite alphabets and with infinitely many states. In those works, infinite (-state or -alphabet) automata are usually called *configuration graphs*, whereas the word *automaton* refers to a finite description of a configuration graph. In contrast to the rest of the paper, we use that terminology in the rest of this paragraph. Often there exists an explicitly defined translation of an automaton to a configuration graph (for example, for register automata [16], class memory automata [3], and history register automata [26]). Even when the semantics are not given in terms of a configuration graph, it is often easy to devise a natural translation. For example, the configuration graph in Fig. 8 is obtained from the automaton of Fig. 1a using an obvious translation that would also apply in the case of data automata [6] and in the case of slicing [23].

5   Experiments

This section complements the asymptotic results of Sect. 3 with experimental results from three data sets.

5.1   Datasets

1. The first dataset is a sequence of $n = 10^7$ operations that simulate a sequence of linear buffer operations. That is, we called the tree buffer as follows: INITIALIZE(0); EXPAND(0, {1}); … ; EXPAND($n - 1$, {n}).
2. We produced (manually) the automaton in Fig. 9 from the regular expression '.*a(⌴*[^]){8}⌴*a', and ran the monitor from Sect. 4 on the text of Wikipedia. This dataset contains $7 \cdot 10^8$ tree buffer operations.

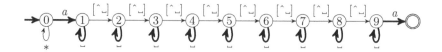

Fig. 9. A nondeterministic automaton without a small, deterministic equivalent: It finds substrings that contain 10 non-space characters, the first and last of which are 'a'. The structure of the automaton is similar to the one corresponding to the regular expression from Sect. 4.1.

3. We ran the monitor from Sect. 4 on infinite automata alongside the DaCapo test suite. The property we monitored was specified using a TOPL automaton [9], and it was essentially the one in Fig. 1a: it is an error if there is a NEXT without a preceding HASNEXT that returned true. We used the projects avrora (simulator of a grid of microcontrollers), eclipse (development environment), fop (XSL to PDF converter), h2 (in memory database), luindex (text indexer), lusearch (text search engine), pmd (simple code analyzer), sunflow (ray tracer), tomcat (servlet server), and xalan (XML to HTML converter) from version 9.12 of the DaCapo test suite [4]. This dataset contains $8 \cdot 10^7$ tree buffer operations.

5.2   Empirical Results

We measure space and time in a way that is machine independent. For space, there is a natural measure: the number of nodes in memory. For time, it is less clear what the best measure is: We follow Knuth [18], and count memory references.

Runtime Versus History. Figure 10 gives the *average* number of memory references per operation. We observe that this number does not depend on h, except for very small values of h, thus validating the asymptotic results about time from Sect. 3.

Runtime Variability. Figure 11 shows that for the amortized and gc algorithms there exist operations that take a long time. In contrast, the plots for the naive and the real-time algorithms are almost invisible because they are completely concentrated on the left side of Fig. 11.

Memory Versus History. In Fig. 12, we notice that the memory usage of the amortized and the real-time algorithms is within a factor of 2 of the memory usage of the gc algorithm, thus validating the asymptotic results about space from Sect. 3. The naive algorithm is excluded from Fig. 12 because its memory usage is much bigger than that of the other algorithms.

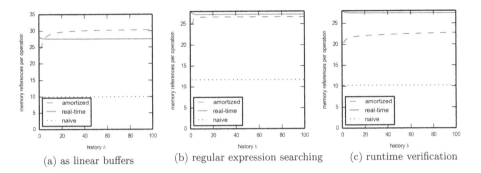

Fig. 10. The average number of memory references per tree buffer operation.

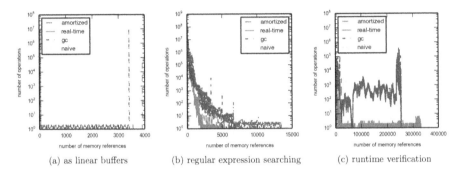

Fig. 11. Histogram for the number of memory references per operation, for $h = 100$.

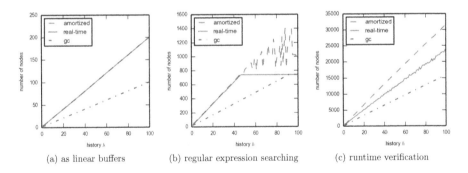

Fig. 12. How much space is necessary.

6   Conclusions, Related Work, and Future Work

We have designed *tree buffers*, a data structure that generalizes linear buffers. A tree buffer consumes a stream of events each of which declares its parent to be one of the preceding events. Tree buffers can answer queries that ask for the h ancestors of a given event. Implementing tree buffers with good performance is not easy. We have explored the design space by developing four possible algorithms (naive, gc, amortized, real-time). Two of those are straightforward: naive is time optimal, and gc is space optimal. The other two algorithms are time and space optimal at the same time: amortized is simpler but not suitable for real-time use, and real-time is more involved but suitable for real-time use. Proving the amortized and the real-time algorithms correct requires some care. We have validated our algorithms on data sets from three different application areas.

Algorithms that process their input in a gradual manner have been studied under the names of online algorithms, dynamic data structures, and, more recently, streaming algorithms. These algorithms address different problems than tree buffers. For example, streaming algorithms [7,20] fall into two classes: those that process numeric streams, and those that process graph streams. Graph streaming algorithms are concerned with problems such as: 'Are vertices u and v connected in the graph described so far?' One of the basic tools used for answering such questions are link-cut trees [24]. Yet, like all the existing graph streaming algorithms, link-cut trees do not give more weight to the recent parts of the tree, in the way tree buffers do. Such a preference for recent data has been studied only in the context of numeric streams. For example, the following problem has been studied: 'Which movie is most popular *currently*?' [20, Sect. 4.7]

The closest relatives of tree buffers remain the simple and ubiquitous linear buffers. Since tree buffers extend linear buffers naturally, it is easy to imagine a wide array of applications. We have discussed an engine for regular expression searching as one example. The main motivation of our research is to enhance *runtime verification monitors* with the ability to provide error traces, fulfilling real-time constraints if needed, and covering general nondeterministic automata specifications. We have described this application in detail.

Several automata models that are used in runtime verification, including the TOPL automata used in our implementation, are nondeterministic [9,13,23], which led us to a tree data structure that can track such automata. Some automata models are even more general, such as quantified event automata [1] and alternating automata [8]. The construction of error-trace providing monitors for such automata is an intriguing challenge that seems to raise further fundamental algorithmic questions.

Acknowledgements. Grigore is supported by EPSRC Programme Grant Resource Reasoning (EP/H008373/2). Kiefer is supported by a Royal Society University Research Fellowship. We thank the reviewers for their comments. We thank Rasmus Lerchedahl Petersen for his contribution to the implementation of an early version of the amortized algorithm in the runtime verifier TOPL.

References

1. Barringer, H., Falcone, Y., Havelund, K., Reger, G., Rydeheard, D.: Quantified event automata: towards expressive and efficient runtime monitors. In: Giannakopoulou, D., Méry, D. (eds.) FM 2012. LNCS, vol. 7436, pp. 68–84. Springer, Heidelberg (2012)

2. Bauer, A., Küster, J.-C., Vegliach, G.: From propositional to first-order monitoring. In: Legay, A., Bensalem, S. (eds.) RV 2013. LNCS, vol. 8174, pp. 59–75. Springer, Heidelberg (2013)

3. Björklund, H., Schwentick, T.: On notions of regularity for data languages. Theor. Comput. Sci. **411**(4–5), 702–715 (2010)

4. Blackburn, S.M., Garner, R., Hoffmann, C., Khan, A.M., McKinley, K.S., Bentzur, R., Diwan, A., Feinberg, D., Frampton, D., Guyer, S.Z., Hirzel, M., Hosking, A.L., Jump, M., Lee, H.B., Moss, J.E.B., Phansalkar, A., Stefanovic, D., VanDrunen, T., von Dincklage, D., Wiedermann, B.: The DaCapo benchmarks: Java benchmarking development and analysis. In: Tarr, P.L., Cook, W.R. (eds.) Proceedings of the 21th Annual ACM SIGPLAN Conference on Object-Oriented Programming, Systems, Languages, and Applications, OOPSLA 2006, 22–26 Oct 2006, Portland, Oregon, USA, pp. 169–190. ACM (2006)

5. Bodden, E.: MOPBox: A library approach to runtime verification – (tool demonstration). In: Khurshid and Sen [17], pp. 365–369

6. Bojanczyk, M., Muscholl, A., Schwentick, T., Segoufin, L., David, C.: Two-variable logic on words with data. In: Proceedings of the 21th IEEE Symposium on Logic in Computer Science (LICS 2006), 12–15 Aug 2006, Seattle, WA, USA, pp. 7–16. IEEE Computer Society (2006)

7. Amit, C.: CS49: Data Stream Algorithms. Lecture Notes. Dartmouth College, New Hampshire (2014)

8. Finkbeiner, B., Sipma, H.: Checking finite traces using alternating automata. Form. Methods Syst. Des. **24**(2), 101–127 (2004)

9. Grigore, R., Distefano, D., Petersen, R.L., Tzevelekos, N.: Runtime verification based on register automata. In: Piterman, N., Smolka, S.A. (eds.) TACAS 2013 (ETAPS 2013). LNCS, vol. 7795, pp. 260–276. Springer, Heidelberg (2013)

10. Grigore, R., Kiefer, S.: Tree buffers. http://arxiv.org/abs/1504.04757. Full version, with proofs

11. Grigore, R., Kiefer, S.: Tree buffers. http://github.com/rgrig/treebuffers/. Implementation

12. Gündüzhan, E., Momtahan, K.: Linear prediction based packet loss concealment algorithm for PCM coded speech. IEEE Trans. Speech Audio Process. **9**(8), 778–785 (2001)

13. Havelund, K.: Monitoring with data automata. In: Margaria, T., Steffen, B. (eds.) ISoLA 2014, Part II. LNCS, vol. 8803, pp. 254–273. Springer, Heidelberg (2014)

14. Jin, D., Meredith, P.O., Lee, C., Rosu, G.: JavaMOP: Efficient parametric runtime monitoring framework. In: Glinz, M., Murphy, G.C., Pezzè, M. (eds.) 34th International Conference on Software Engineering, ICSE 2012, 2–9 June 2012, Zurich, Switzerland, pp. 1427–1430. IEEE (2012)

15. Kaashoek, M.F., Tanenbaum, A.S.: Group communication in the Amoeba distributed operating system. In: Distributed, Computing Systems, pp. 222–230 (1991)

16. Kaminski, M., Francez, N.: Finite-memory automata (extended abstract). In: FOCS, pp. 683–688. IEEE Computer Society (1990)

17. Stoller, S.D., Bartocci, E., Seyster, J., Grosu, R., Havelund, K., Smolka, S.A., Zadok, E.: Runtime verification with state estimation. In: Khurshid, S., Sen, K. (eds.) RV 2011. LNCS, vol. 7186, pp. 193–207. Springer, Heidelberg (2012)

18. Knuth, D.E.: The stanford graphBase – a platform for combinatorial computing. ACM (1993)

19. Rustan, K., Leino, M., Millstein, T.D.: Generating error traces from verification-condition counterexamples. Sci. Comput. Program. **55**(1–3), 209–226 (2005)

20. Leskovec, J., Rajaraman, A., Ullman, J.D.: Mining Massive Datasets. http://mmds.org/ (2014)
21. Luo, Q., Zhang, Y., Lee, C., Jin, D., Meredith, P.O.N., Şerbănuţă, T.F., Roşu, G.: RV-Monitor: efficient parametric runtime verification with simultaneous properties. In: Bonakdarpour, B., Smolka, S.A. (eds.) RV 2014. LNCS, vol. 8734, pp. 285–300. Springer, Heidelberg (2014)
22. Pike, L., Niller, S., Wegmann, N.: Runtime verification for ultra-critical systems. In: Khurshid, S., Sen, K. (eds.) RV 2011. LNCS, vol. 7186, pp. 310–324. Springer, Heidelberg (2012)
23. Rosu, G., Chen, F.: Semantics and algorithms for parametric monitoring. Log. Methods Comput. Sci. $8(1)$, 1–47 (2012)
24. Sleator, D.D., Tarjan, R.E.: A data structure for dynamic trees. In: Proceedings of the 13th Annual ACM Symposium on Theory of Computing, 11–13 May 1981, Milwaukee, Wisconsin, USA, pp. 114–122. ACM (1981)
25. Smith, J.E., Pleszkun, A.R.: Implementing precise interrupts in pipelined processors. IEEE Trans. Comput. $37(5)$, 562–573 (1988)
26. Tzevelekos, N., Grigore, R.: History-register automata. In: Pfenning, F. (ed.) FOSSACS 2013 (ETAPS 2013). LNCS, vol. 7794, pp. 17–33. Springer, Heidelberg (2013)

Learning Commutativity Specifications

Timon Gehr, Dimitar Dimitrov$^{(\boxtimes)}$, and Martin Vechev

Department of Computer Science, ETH Zürich,
Zürich, Switzerland
dimitar.dimitrov@inf.ethz.ch

Abstract. In this work we present a new sampling-based "black box" inference approach for learning the behaviors of a library component. As an application, we focus on the problem of automatically learning *commutativity specifications* of data structures. This is a very challenging problem, yet important, as commutativity specifications are fundamental to program analysis, concurrency control and even lower bounds.

Our approach is enabled by three core insights: (i) *type-aware sampling* which drastically improves the quality of obtained examples, (ii) *relevant predicate discovery* critical for reducing the formula search space, and (iii) an *efficient search* based on weighted-set cover for finding formulas ranging over the predicates and capturing the examples.

More generally, our work learns formulas belonging to fragments consisting of quantifier-free formulas over a finite number of relation symbols. Such fragments are expressive enough to capture useful specifications (e.g., commutativity) yet are amenable to automated inference.

We implemented a tool based on our approach and have shown that it can quickly learn non-trivial and important commutativity specifications of fundamental data types such as hash maps, sets, array lists, union find and others. We also showed experimentally that learning these specifications is beyond the capabilities of existing techniques.

1 Introduction

In this work we present a new and scalable "black box" technique for learning complex library specifications. Our technique is based on sampling of library behaviors, is fully automatic, and quickly learns succinct and precise specifications of complex interactions beyond the reach of current techniques. Concretely, our approach learns specifications in fragments of the quantifier-free formulas over a finite number of relation symbols. Such fragments are expressive enough to capture useful specifications yet are amenable to automated inference. Note that even though the fragment is quantifier-free, the relations in the fragment can be defined using quantifiers and hence the learned formulas may include quantifiers.

We have instantiated our approach to learning *commutativity specifications* of data structures, a hard yet practically important problem as these specifications are fundamental to concurrency (e.g., program analysis [4], concurrency control [9,13,14,23], and lower bounds [1]). This is the first automatic approach that

© Springer International Publishing Switzerland 2015
D. Kroening and C.S. Păsăreanu (Eds.): CAV 2015, Part I, LNCS 9206, pp. 307–323, 2015.
DOI: 10.1007/978-3-319-21690-4_18

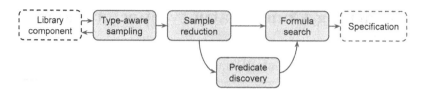

Fig. 1. Our approach to specification inference.

can precisely and quickly infer commutativity specifications for useful data types such as hash map, union find, array list and others[1].

The flow and ingredients of our approach are shown in Fig. 1. Given a library component (e.g., a data structure), instead of blindly sampling its behaviors and obtaining redundant examples, a key insight is to introduce the notion of *type-aware sampling* which allows us to obtain a diverse set of quality examples (informally, two examples have the same type if they are indistinguishable by a formula in the logical fragment). However, even with advanced sampling, the sheer number of examples can overwhelm the search. That is why we reduce the size of this set by filtering out examples indistinguishable by the logical fragment. Once the final set of examples is obtained, a critical step is to reduce the search space of candidate formulas by *discovering relevant predicates* (a fundamental step in many static analysis approaches [15]). The key insight of this step is to filter out a predicate if it cannot be distinguished from its negation by any positive-negative example pair. Finally, we search for formulas over the relevant predicates that cover our set of examples. We show that a greedy algorithm based on weighted set-cover is quite effective in finding non-trivial and optimal specifications quickly – it infers complex commutativity conditions in seconds.

Main contributions. The main contributions of this work are:

- A new sampling-based "black box" approach for learning specifications in fragments consisting of quantifier-free formulas over a finite number of relation symbols. The key insights of our technique are: type-aware sampling, sample reduction, relevant predicate discovery and efficient formula search.
- An instantiation of the approach for learning commutativity specifications including a specialized sampling procedure.
- An experimental evaluation illustrating that our approach quickly learns practical commutativity specifications of fundamental data types such as hash map, set, array list, union find and others. We further show that learning these specifications is beyond the reach of current approaches.

2   Overview

We next illustrate our approach on an example: inferring the conditions for when two insertions in a `Map` data type commute. The aim of this section is to provide an intuitive understanding of the general framework presented later.

---

[1] Specifications and source code available at http://www.srl.inf.ethz.ch/core.

Commutativity. Consider a standard `Map` data type, supporting the methods $get(k)/r$ and $put(k,v)/r$, where `put` returns the old value r under the key k. We seek to infer the commutativity specification for the method pair `put`/`put`. Two method invocations *commute* if they can always be reordered without any observable effect. In our case, $put(k_1, v_1)/r_1$ and $put(k_2, v_2)/r_2$ commute if and only if they access different keys or both leave the map unmodified, captured as:

$$\varphi(k_1, v_1, r_1, k_2, v_2, r_2) := k_1 \neq k_2 \vee v_1 = r_1 \wedge v_2 = r_2. \tag{1}$$

When inferring logical specifications, we assume a fixed logical fragment that defines our search space. Let us set this fragment to consist of arbitrary boolean combinations of constraints over the numeric relations $<$ and $=$.

Type-Aware Sampling. We treat the data type as a black box, sampling it at random in order to obtain examples of commuting/non-commuting behaviors. We first prepare a random data type state, then choose random arguments for the methods, and finally invoke them in both orders. This way we obtain tuples of arguments and return values which are classified as positive (commuting) or negative (non-commuting). Figure 2 shows a sample of several examples for `put`/`put`. As a pure random sample may contain many redundant examples, we use a sampling method that tries to rule out a large number of candidate specifications.

#	k_1	v_1	r_1	k_2	v_2	r_2	+/-
1.	3	2	2	4	2	1	+
2.	1	0	0	2	0	-1	+
3.	2	0	0	1	0	-1	+
4.	2	0	-2	1	0	-1	+
5.	1	2	2	1	1	2	-
6.	1	-1	-1	1	1	-1	-

Fig. 2. Commutativity and non-commutativity examples of `put`/`put`.

We say that examples have the same *logical type* if they cannot be distinguished by any formula in the fragment. For instance, examples 1 and 2 in Fig. 2 have the same logical type, as all basic predicates of the form $x = y$ and $x < y$ have the same truth value on both 1 and 2 (where $x, y \in \{k_i, v_i, r_i\}$). To rule out as many candidates as possible, we need to diversify the logical types observed in a sample. Thus, we first choose a formula representing the logical type of the method arguments (e.g., $v_1 = v_2 < k_1 < k_2$ for examples 1 and 2), and then select concrete values that satisfy that formula. We finally test for commutativity with these arguments.

Sample Size Reduction. We would ideally like to diversify the logical type of the complete example, and not only the arguments. However, we cannot control what the return values are, as we obtain these *after* executing the commutativity test. This can lead to redundancy in the sample as some examples will have the same logical type. We filter out such uninformative examples and obtain a significantly smaller sample which covers exactly the same variety of logical types. Inference over this reduced sample is much faster than over the larger one.

Discovery of Relevant Predicates. Logical specifications in our fragment consist of disjunctions and conjunctions of literals. For example, when inferring a specification for `put`/`put` we search for a formula built from all possible literals over the relations $<$, $=$, and the variables k_i, v_i, r_i, namely, $k_1 = k_2$, $k_1 \neq k_2$, $k_1 < k_2$, $k_1 \geq k_2$, $v_1 = r_1$, $v_2 = r_2$, etc. As we can see, literals such as $k_1 < k_2$ and $k_1 \geq k_2$ do not occur in the target specification (1), and are therefore irrelevant for the search. Thus, to reduce the formula search space, we introduce a procedure that identifies irrelevant literals from the information provided by the sample. Informally, the idea is to look at a contradicting pair of literals such as $k_1 < k_2$ and $k_1 \geq k_2$. We then consider those pairs of commutativity examples that can be distinguished only by the two contradicting literals. Examples 2 and 3 in Fig. 2 form such a pair and can be distinguished only by $k_1 < k_2$ and $k_1 \geq k_2$. If the two examples are either both positive or both negative, then the pair of literals is irrelevant for distinguishing these examples. We rule out the pair if it is irrelevant for all pairs of examples (later we describe a more elaborate technique that is able to rule out more literals). In our example, we obtain a reduced set of literals: $k_1 \neq k_2$, $v_1 = r_1$, $v_2 = r_2$, ...

Formula Search. Finally, given a data sample (as in Fig. 2) and a set of literals, we search for a formula which is consistent with the sample. We aim to infer *sound* specifications. In the case of commutativity, this means that the specification should always imply that two invocations do commute. Therefore, we search for a formula which does not evaluate to *true* on negative examples yet evaluates to *true* in as many positive examples as possible. To prevent overfitting, we search for the smallest such formula. This is the reason why our approach requires both positive and negative examples, for otherwise the formulas *true* and *false* would be trivial solutions. To infer a formula meeting or objective, we developed a procedure that interleaves exhaustive and greedy search.

Determining Sample Size. For the inference to be self-contained, we need an automatic way to determine the sample size. We employ an intuitive approach: new examples are drawn until the result of the formula search stabilizes. To confirm the stabilization, we draw examples in blocks, each block being twice as large as the previous one. For every new block we run the formula search, and if it produces the same outcome twice in a row, we declare the formula as stable. The exponential increase of the block size ensures that we restart the search at most a logarithmic number of times, and that we draw at most linearly more examples than required.

In what follows, we first describe a general framework for learning specifications belonging to fragments consisting of quantifier-free formulas over a finite number of relation symbols. Then, we show how to instantiate our approach for learning practical commutativity specifications (belonging to a restriction of the general fragment), and finally we discuss an experimental evaluation on a number of real world data structures.

3   Background

In this section we introduce several key notions from logic that are essential for addressing the problem of specification inference. In particular, the two concepts that we will rely upon later sections are *definable relations* and *logical types*. The family of definable relations forms the hypothesis class that an inference algorithm considers to explain the observed data, and the complexity of that class governs the difficulty of inference. A logical type abstracts all data points carrying the same information with respect to the hypothesis class. Among other uses, types are crucial when estimating the quality of a data sample.

Definition 1. *A structure $\mathfrak{X}$ consists of a carrier set, a set of relations and functions over the carrier, and relation and function symbols naming them.*

We think of a structure $\mathfrak{X}$ as providing the context for interpreting logical formulas. The first-order *language* of $\mathfrak{X}$ consists of all first-order formulas built using equality and the symbols mentioned by the structure. For a formula $\varphi(\boldsymbol{u})$ from the language and a tuple $\boldsymbol{u}$ of elements from the carrier, we shall use the standard notation $\mathfrak{X} \models \varphi(\boldsymbol{u}/\boldsymbol{x})$ to state that $\varphi(\boldsymbol{x})$ holds true for $\boldsymbol{u}$.

In general, not all relations over the carrier can be expressed by formulas over a structure's language. In the present work, we consider relations expressible in a boolean closed fragment $\mathcal{L}$ of the full language of $\mathfrak{X}$:

Definition 2. *A relation h over $\mathfrak{X}$ is $\mathcal{L}$-definable if there exists a formula $\varphi(\boldsymbol{x}) \in \mathcal{L}$ such that for any tuple $\boldsymbol{u} \in h$ we have that $\boldsymbol{u} \in h \iff \mathfrak{X} \models \varphi(\boldsymbol{u}/\boldsymbol{x})$.*

Looking for a specification in the fragment $\mathcal{L}$ implies that we need to approximate an unknown relation c with an $\mathcal{L}$-definable relation h, given a finite sample of c. Thus, the family $\mathcal{H}$ of all $\mathcal{L}$-definable relations forms our hypothesis class.

We will make heavy use of a natural abstraction that a logic induces over tuples of elements. Two tuples $\boldsymbol{u}$ and $\boldsymbol{v}$ have the same *logical type*[2,3] if they satisfy the same $\mathcal{L}$-formulas:

Definition 3. *The $\mathcal{L}$-type $tp_{\mathcal{L}}(\boldsymbol{u})$ of a any tuple $\boldsymbol{u}$ over the carrier of $\mathfrak{X}$ is the set of formulas $\Phi(\boldsymbol{x}) = \{\varphi(\boldsymbol{x}) \in \mathcal{L} \mid \mathfrak{X} \models \varphi(\boldsymbol{u}/\boldsymbol{x})\}$ that it satisfies.*

In other words, tuples having the same $\mathcal{L}$-type are indistinguishable by formulas in the fragment $\mathcal{L}$. In turn, this determines the structure of the $\mathcal{L}$-definable relations. Let us call the set $\{\boldsymbol{u} \in X^n \mid tp_{\mathcal{L}}(\boldsymbol{u}) = \Phi(\boldsymbol{x})\}$ the *preimage* of $\Phi(\boldsymbol{x})$. The collection of all such preimages partitions the set of tuples, and moreover.

Observation 1. *Every $\mathcal{L}$-definable relation is an unique disjoint union of preimages of $\mathcal{L}$-types.*

Therefore, a relation is $\mathcal{L}$-definable if and only if it does not separate any type preimage into two parts. Later, we will make extensive use of this fact.

In our work, we often need a tangible way to manipulate logical types: we would like to replace a type (a potentially infinite collection of formulas) with a finite description (i.e., just a single formula).

Definition 4. *A type $\Phi(\boldsymbol{x})$ is called* isolated *when some formula $\varphi(\boldsymbol{x}) \in \Phi(\boldsymbol{x})$ generates it, that is for all $\psi(\boldsymbol{x}) \in \Phi(\boldsymbol{x})$ we have that $\mathfrak{X} \models \forall \boldsymbol{x}. \varphi(\boldsymbol{x}) \to \psi(\boldsymbol{x})$.*

---

[2] Logical types should not be confused with the concept of types in type theory.

[3] To find more about logical types the reader can consult [2,17], or the classic [3,10].

However, we would like an even stronger property to hold true, namely that the preimage of the type $\Phi(\boldsymbol{x})$ be $\mathcal{L}$-definable. This is important for obtaining data samples with a chosen type. Fortunately, the boolean closedness of the fragment ensures that a preimage is $\mathcal{L}$-definable if and only if the type is isolated:

$$tp_{\mathcal{L}}(\boldsymbol{u}) = \Phi(\boldsymbol{x}) \iff \mathfrak{X} \models \Phi(\boldsymbol{u}/\boldsymbol{x}) \iff \mathfrak{X} \models \varphi(\boldsymbol{u}/\boldsymbol{x}) \tag{2}$$

In order to guarantee that we work with isolated types we will impose certain restrictions on the family of definable relations. Let $\mathcal{L}(\boldsymbol{x})$ denote the subfragment of $\mathcal{L}$ consisting of all the formulas $\varphi(\boldsymbol{x}) \in \mathcal{L}$ having free variables among $\boldsymbol{x}$, where as usual $\boldsymbol{x}$ is a finite list of distinct variables.

Observation 2. *If the family of $\mathcal{L}(\boldsymbol{x})$-definable relations is finite, then there are finitely many $\mathcal{L}(\boldsymbol{x})$-types, and all of them are isolated.*

We shall focus on the setting where: (i) the structure $\mathfrak{X}$ is relational, i.e., it mentions no function symbols (including constants); (ii) the relation symbols are finitely many; and (iii) $\mathcal{L}(\boldsymbol{x})$ is the quantifier-free fragment of $\mathfrak{X}$. Combined, these conditions guarantee that there are finitely many $\mathcal{L}(\boldsymbol{x})$-definable relations in the structure $\mathfrak{X}$, and therefore we can leverage Observation 2. We will further assume that formulas are in *negation normal form*, i.e., that all negations are pushed in front of atomic subformulas.

4   Learning Formulas

We next describe our approach to learning logical formulas from examples over a structure $\mathfrak{X}$. We first state our learning objective, i.e., which formula to select given a sample. Then, we discuss how we search for such a formula. Finally, we present a way to reduce the formula search space by discarding irrelevant literals.

4.1   Learning Objective

Given a sample (s_+, s_-) of positive and negative examples from an unknown relation c over the carrier of $\mathfrak{X}$, we would like to infer a definition of c in the logical fragment $\mathcal{L}(\boldsymbol{x})$. It is important to note that such a definition need not exist in general. That is why, our goal will be to find a formula that defines a relation $h \in \mathcal{H}$ that best approximates c in our *hypothesis class* $\mathcal{H}$ of $\mathcal{L}(\boldsymbol{x})$-definable relations. Two natural approximation criteria are: best under-approximation, i.e., the maximal $h \subseteq c$, and best over-approximation, i.e., the minimal $h \supseteq c$. We shall work with under-approximations but all the machinery can be used directly for over-approximations directly as the two notions are dual. Recalling Observation 1 and 2 we establish the existence of best approximations:

Theorem 1. *The best under-approximation $h \in \mathcal{H}$ to any relation c over $\mathfrak{X}$ equals the disjoint union $\bigcup\{t \subseteq c \mid t \text{ is a preimage of some type}\}$.*

However, we can search for this h only indirectly, for we merely have an access to the finite sample (s_+, s_-) instead of the complete relation c. Our learning objective will be to find a hypothesis h that includes a maximum number of positive examples, while excluding all negative ones. In other words, we have the following optimization problem over the hypothesis class $\mathcal{H}$:

$$\text{maximize } |h \cap s_+|, \quad \text{subject to } h \cap s_- = \varnothing \tag{3}$$

In general, an optimal solution to this objective is not unique. Moreover, for a learning procedure we need an effective criterion telling us when a candidate hypothesis satisfies (3).

Definition 5 (Observed Status). *Call the* observed status *of a type $\Phi(x)$ with a preimage t:* positive *if $s_+ \cap t \neq \varnothing$ and $s_- \cap t = \varnothing$;* negative *if $s_+ \cap t = \varnothing$ and $s_- \cap t \neq \varnothing$;* ambiguous *if $s_+ \cap t \neq \varnothing$ and $s_- \cap t \neq \varnothing$. Otherwise, call it* missing.

Theorem 2. *A hypothesis $h \in \mathcal{H}$ is optimal with respect to (3) for a given sample (s_+, s_-) if and only if for every tuple $\boldsymbol{u}$ from $\mathfrak{X}$ with non-missing type*

$$\boldsymbol{u} \in h \iff tp_{\mathcal{L}(x)}(\boldsymbol{u}) \text{ is positive}$$
$$\boldsymbol{u} \notin h \iff tp_{\mathcal{L}(x)}(\boldsymbol{u}) \text{ is negative or ambiguous}$$

The theorem follows from Observation 1. Note that even if a tuple belongs to s_+, its type might still be ambiguous as another tuple of the same type might belong to s_-. Optimal hypotheses cannot be further distinguished by the sample (s_+, s_-), and so we need an additional principle to select one of them such that we avoid overfitting. We shall rely on the minimum description length principle [18,19,22], which suggests to search for a solution of (3) defined by a formula of minimal size. This is also important for human-readability.

4.2   Formula Search

To find a solution to (3) we combine an exhaustive search interleaved with a greedy algorithm. In accordance with Observation 2 we consider the subset $s'_+ \subseteq s_+$ of positive examples having a type with a positive observed status. We search until we find a formula that evaluates to true on all of s'_+, and evaluates to false on all of s_-. By Theorem 2, the discovered formula satisfies (3). By Theorem 1, at least one optimal hypothesis exists, and therefore the search always terminates. During the search, we try to minimize the size measure given by:

$$\|true\| = \|false\| = 0; \quad \|\text{literal}\| = 1; \quad \|\varphi \wedge \psi\| = \|\varphi \vee \psi\| = 1 + \|\varphi\| + \|\psi\| \tag{4}$$

We enumerate the formulas of $\mathcal{L}(x)$ in increasing size, via a simple dynamic programming approach that alone guarantees finding a formula of minimum size. We employ the standard heuristic to consider two formulas equivalent if they produce the same results on the sample $s_+ \cup s_-$. Exhaustive enumeration, however, is feasible for inferring small formulas only. This is why we interleave it with a greedy algorithm, which does not guarantee minimality, but is much faster in practice. For each formula size i, we consider the set G of conjunctions which have size smaller than i, and also evaluate to false on all of s_-. From those, we try to build a disjunction $\bigvee F$ which covers all of s'_+, where $F \subseteq G$. To find a disjunction of small size, we phrase the problem as an instance of weighted set cover, and use a greedy approximation. We weight each conjunction $\varphi \in G$ with $\|\varphi\|$ and seek a cover $F \subseteq G$ of s'_+ with small total weight. We run a standard greedy algorithm to produce a cover F. If the cover has less than $2i$ formulas, we terminate the search; else, we move on to size $i + 1$.

4.3 Predicate Discovery

We now describe how to reduce the formula search space $\mathcal{L}(\boldsymbol{x})$ by restricting the set of literals considered during formula enumeration. We prune formulas that contain literals irrelevant for explaining the sample (s_+, s_-). The approach has to be instantiated for the specific structure $\mathfrak{X}$ under consideration, and we first illustrate it for the two-valued boolean algebra $\{0, 1\}$, or equivalently for the case of learning propositional formulas.

Two-Valued Case. Here, free variables range over 0–1, and our fragment $\mathcal{L}(\boldsymbol{x})$ has a relation T interpreted as $T(x) \iff x = 1$. The logical type of every tuple $\boldsymbol{u}$ is characterized by a single conjunction $\bigwedge Q_i$, where $Q_i = T(x_i) \iff u_i = 1$ and $Q_i = \neg T(x_i) \iff u_i = 0$. Therefore, in the two-valued case no distinct tuples can have the same logical type, and we can identify the type of a tuple with the tuple itself, i.e., a 0–1 valued vector.

Definition 6. *A sample (s_+, s_-) of n-tuples is* monotone *in the i-th coordinate, if for all tuples $\boldsymbol{u}$ and $\boldsymbol{v}$ with $|\boldsymbol{u}| = i-1$, $|\boldsymbol{u}|+|\boldsymbol{v}| = n-1$ we have that $(\boldsymbol{u}, 0, \boldsymbol{v}) \in s_+$ implies $(\boldsymbol{u}, 1, \boldsymbol{v}) \notin s_-$. Similarly, the sample is* antitone *in the i-th coordinate if we instead require that $(\boldsymbol{u}, 1, \boldsymbol{v}) \in s_+$ implies $(\boldsymbol{u}, 0, \boldsymbol{v}) \notin s_-$.*

If a sample (s_+, s_-) is monotone in i, then we can extend it to an optimal hypothesis h with the similar property of $(\boldsymbol{u}, 0, \boldsymbol{v}) \in h$ implying $(\boldsymbol{u}, 1, \boldsymbol{v}) \in h$. A folk theorem states that any formula defining a relation with this property can be converted to an equivalent formula not containing the literal $\neg T(x_i)$. Therefore, in our search for an optimal hypothesis we can prune formulas containing this literal. Analogously, we can prune $T(x_i)$ when (s_+, s_-) is antitone in i.

Generalization. To handle more general logical fragments, we shall abstract the notion of monotonicity from the two-valued case. There, the concept of a tuple and its type essentially coincided; we had a condition over pairs tuples $(\boldsymbol{u}, 0, \boldsymbol{v})$, $(\boldsymbol{u}, 1, \boldsymbol{v})$ that increase (or decrease) in their i-th coordinate. In the more general case, we shall use a condition over logical types and not tuples. As a type assigns a truth value to every literal and (in our fragment) formulas are combinations of literals, the role of coordinates will be played by the literals themselves. For each literal λ we assume a *neighbor relation* $\mathcal{N}_\lambda$ that relates pairs of types for which the truth value of λ increases from *false* to *true*, i.e., $(\Phi, \Psi) \in \mathcal{N}_\lambda$ must imply $\neg\lambda \in \Phi$ and $\lambda \in \Psi$ (the converse need not hold).

Definition 7. *Given a literal λ and a neighbor relation $\mathcal{N}_\lambda$, we say that a sample (s_+, s_-) is $\mathcal{N}_\lambda$-unate when for all pairs of types $(\Phi, \Psi) \in \mathcal{N}_\lambda$, if Φ has a positive observed status, then Ψ has a positive or a missing observed status.*

In the two-valued case, we implicitly used the relation: $(\Phi, \Psi) \in \mathcal{N}_\lambda$ if and only if the Ψ is obtained from Φ by switching the truth value of λ, but of no other literals. This is too restrictive in general, as switching the truth value of one literal may require a switch in another. For example, consider logical types in the order structure $(\mathbb{Z}, <)$ of the integers. There, switching $x \neq y$ from *false* to *true* also requires switching either $x < y$ or $y < x$ from *false* to *true*.

We now define when a neighbor relation $\mathcal{N}_\lambda$ is admissible. In general such relations have to be derived for the specific structure under consideration. To gain more flexibility, we shall allow $\mathcal{N}_\lambda$ to depend on the sample (s_+, s_-) for which we are doing predicate discovery, i.e., $\mathcal{N}_\lambda = \mathcal{N}_\lambda(s_+, s_-)$.

Definition 8. *A family of neighbor relations $\mathcal{N}_\lambda(s_+, s_-)$ is admissible if for every sample (s_+, s_-) with no missing types the best hypothesis is definable without any literals $\neg\lambda$ for which (s_+, s_-) is $\mathcal{N}_\lambda(s_+, s_-)$-unate.*

Neighbors for linear orders. We now give a suitable neighbor relation $\mathcal{N}_\lambda$ for the order structure $(\mathbb{Z}, <)$ of the integers (used in Sect. 6.1). Here, every logical type is equivalent to an ordered partition of the variables $\boldsymbol{x}$: equal variables form a class, and classes are ordered linearly. For example, the type generated by the formula $x_1 < x_2 = x_3 < x_4$ is equivalent to the ordered partition $\{x_1\} < \{x_2, x_3\} < \{x_4\}$. We shall manipulate types via two operations on *adjacent* classes: we can *swap* their position, or we can *merge* them into a single class. Given a sample (s_+, s_-), we say that two types *conflict* if one is positive, while the other is either negative or ambiguous. We are now ready to define $\mathcal{N}_\lambda$ ($[x]$ denotes the class of x):

1. $(\Phi, \Psi) \in \mathcal{N}_{x<y} \iff y < x \in \Phi$, $x < y \in \Psi$; swapping $[x]$ and $[y]$ in Ψ gives Φ; merging $[x]$ and $[y]$ in Ψ gives a type in conflict with Ψ.
2. $(\Phi, \Psi) \in \mathcal{N}_{x \neq y} \iff x = y \in \Phi$, $x \neq y \in \Psi$; merging $[x]$ and $[y]$ in Ψ gives Φ; swapping $[x]$ and $[y]$ in Ψ gives a type not in conflict with Ψ.
3. $(\Phi, \Psi) \in \mathcal{N}_{x \leq y} \iff (\Psi, \Phi) \in \mathcal{N}_{y<x}$ and $(\Phi, \Psi) \in \mathcal{N}_{x=y} \iff (\Psi, \Phi) \in \mathcal{N}_{y \neq x}$.

From an admissible family $\mathcal{N}_\lambda$ we obtain the resulting predicates by pruning literals $\neg\lambda$ for which the sample (s_+, s_-) is $\mathcal{N}_\lambda$-unate. We then search for a formula as described in Sect. 4.2. Because of missing types, the above method may prune literals which are required for finding the optimal hypothesis. Thus, our pruning approach is a heuristic that relies on good samples.

5   Sampling

When inferring specifications from data, it is important to ensure the data is of sufficient quality. In this section we present a sampling strategy based on a heuristic measure of the informativeness of a sample. Then, we give a simple algorithm for removing redundant observations from a sample. Finally, we describe a method to adaptively determine the sample size.

5.1 Type-Aware Sampling

Recall that our learning objective is to identify a hypothesis h that best approximates an unknown relation c. We have access to c only as a black-box: we can basically choose a tuple u and test whether it belongs to c or not, thus obtaining a sample of positive s_+ and negative s_- examples. We want to draw tuples such that the obtained sample (s_+, s_-) gives us most information about c. We shall consider one sample more informative than another if it rules out more candidate hypotheses from our class $\mathcal{H}$ of $\mathcal{L}(x)$-definable relations.

Measure. We can roughly quantify this notion of informativeness via logical types. Observation 2 tells us that if the observed status of a type is not missing, we know how to classify all other tuples having that type. This suggests that we should increase the number of types observed in the sample. However, we also need to account for the case where c is not definable in our fragment. It might be that the observed status of some type is positive, but there exists some example that when added to our sample will switch this status to ambiguous, forcing us to reclassify all tuples having this type as negative. Let us call the *true status* of a type $\Phi(x)$ its status with respect to the "sample" $c_+ = \{u \mid u \in c\}$, $c_- = \{u \mid u \notin s_-\}$, i.e., when we add all possible tuples. Then our goal is to maximize the measure given by the number of types that have their true status (i.e., w.r.t. (c_+, c_-)) equal to their observed status (i.e., w.r.t. (s_+, s_-)).

Strategy. Of course, we cannot calculate this measure directly, as all we know is the observed status of a type. Thus, in the process of sampling we need to balance two conflicting factors: diversity and confidence. On one hand, we would like the sample to be as diverse as possible and to contain examples from many types. On the other hand, we would like to have high confidence that the observed status of every type matches its true status. To control this trade-off we assume two parameters: the total number m of examples to draw (discussed further in Sect. 5.3) controls the diversity, and the number k of examples to draw from a single type controls the confidence. Note that once the observed status of a type becomes ambiguous, we can stop drawing more examples from that type, as it will remain ambiguous. The strategy is summarized in Fig. 3.

Sample Size Reduction. Once we have a sample we can optimize its size without reducing its informativeness by removing examples as long as we preserve the observed status of every type. We need to keep a single example of any type with a positive or a negative observed status, and two examples, one positive and one negative, from any type with an ambiguous observed status. This size reduction plays a role when we decide how many examples to draw (Sect. 5.3).

Guarantees. If we obtain a sample of maximal informativeness, i.e., in which every type has its observed status equal to its true status, then we are guaranteed to infer (the best) sound approximation. Such a sample always exists (as there are finitely many logical types) but obtaining it is often infeasible in practice. Thus, we can combine our black-box approach with white-box verification, e.g., [12].

SAMPLE($\mathfrak{X}, \mathcal{L}, c, m, k$)

$\quad s_+, s_- \leftarrow \varnothing, \varnothing$

$\quad$**while** $|s_+| + |s_-| < m$

$\quad\quad$choose an unambiguous $\mathcal{L}$-type $\Phi(x)$ at random

$\quad\quad$**while** $\Phi(x)$ is unambiguous and $\#\{u \in s_+ \cup s_- \mid \mathfrak{X} \models \Phi(u/x)\} < k$

$\quad\quad\quad$choose $u : \mathfrak{X} \models \Phi(u/x)$ at random

$\quad\quad\quad s_+ \leftarrow s_+ \cup \{u\}$ **if** $u \in c$

$\quad\quad\quad s_- \leftarrow s_- \cup \{u\}$ **if** $u \notin c$

$\quad$**return** (s_+, s_-)

Fig. 3. Type-aware sampling from a relation c. The algorithm draws m examples in total, with at most k of them having the same logical type.

5.2 Black-Box Interface

In our sampling algorithm we assumed that we sample the unknown relation c by generating tuples u and feeding them to a black-box which classifies them as positive or negative. However, this is not always the case in general (e.g., for commutativity, Sect. 6.2). We might be able to feed the black-box only a part v of u, and only then obtain the rest w (i.e., $u = (v, w)$). In this case, we cannot control the type of the whole u but only of v. This requires only a local change to the type-aware sampling algorithm: we choose a random type $\Phi(y), y \subseteq x$ to generate v, and then feed v to the black-box to obtain the complete example u. From there on, we continue as before, considering the type of u and not v.

5.3 Hypothesis Stabilization

We now discuss how to reliably determine the sample size m. Instead of fixing the number m a priori, we draw new examples until the result of the formula search stabilizes. We realize this strategy by interleaving a sampling step with a formula search step. If the search gives the same result two consecutive times, then we return the discovered formula. The sampling begins with an initial number of m_0 examples and, at each subsequent step $i + 1$ draws twice as many new examples as the previous step, i.e., $m_{i+1} = 2m_i$. After each sampling step, we run the search from scratch on all examples collected so far. As the search might take too long due to insufficient data, we run each search no longer than the time t_i taken for sampling at the same step. The total running time is not much longer compared to a single run over m examples: we restart the search $\Theta(\log m)$ times. The following theorem guarantees that we terminate:

Theorem 3. *If sample size reduction is applied, the required search time t_i' grows sublinearly with the time limit t_i, i.e., $t_i' = o(t_i)$.*

The theorem holds because t_i' grows with the reduced sample size which in turn is bounded by the number of types in the logical fragment. On the other hand, without sample size reduction we are unlikely to terminate, as then the number of examples for which we perform a search is proportional to m_i, and therefore we have that $t_i' = \Omega(t_i)$ (provided the sampling time t_i is linear in m_i).

6   Inferring Commutativity Specifications

In this section, we apply the approach discussed so far to the problem of learning commutativity specifications. Given a data structure (described via an abstract specification or a concrete implementation), our goal is to infer a commutativity specification for every pair of its methods.

6.1   Commutativity Specifications

A commutativity specification states when two method invocations commute. Consider two executions that start in the same initial state σ:

$$m_1(u_1)/v_1 \; ; \; m_2(u_2)/v_2 \quad m_2(u_2)/w_2 \; ; \; m_2(u_1)/w_1 \tag{5}$$

If both executions end in the same state, $v_1 = w_1$, and $v_2 = w_2$, we say that the two invocations $m_1(u_1)/v_2$ and $m_2(u_1)/v_2$ commute in σ. A commutativity specification for m_1, m_2 is a formula $\varphi(\sigma, x, y)$, which given a concrete initial state σ, arguments $x = u_1 u_2$, and return values $y = v_1 v_2$ describes if $m_1(u_1)/v_2$ and $m_2(u_1)/v_2$ commute. Sound specifications always imply that invocations commute (cf. the objective from Sect. 4.1). State independent ones do not mention the state σ, i.e., they have the form $\varphi(x, y)$. Our work is able to learn optimal state independent approximations of state dependent specifications.

The logical fragment we will use consists of quantifier-free formulas built from integer and boolean variables, the predicates $=$ and $<$, and the standard boolean operations. Formulas in this fragment have an arbitrary boolean structure and are expressive enough to capture a large number of commutativity specifications.

6.2   Sampling for Commutativity

We now describe an instantiation of the sampling approach from Sect. 5.1. Here, an example $u_1 u_2 v_1 v_2$ consists of the combined arguments and return values of a pair of commuting or non-commuting method invocations. To produce an example, we generate random arguments $u_1 u_2$ and an initial state σ, and then execute the methods in both orders. The outcome is two states σ_1 and σ_2, and two pairs of return values $v_1 v_2$ and $w_1 w_2$. If the states and the return values match, we have a positive example of commutativity. Otherwise, we have two negative examples. To compare states we assume that an abstract equality check, $\text{EQUAL}(\sigma_1, \sigma_2)$, is provided (naturally, we reason at the abstract level as opposed to the bit for bit concrete level).

7   Evaluation

We implemented our approach, and experimented with inferring commutativity specifications for method pairs of 21 data types. Some of these (e.g., accumulator, set, map, array list, 1-d tree, union-find) are well-known in the context of commutativity [1,4,9,12–14,23] while others are variants of multiset, partial map, bit list, 6 variations of union-find, etc. We also selected classic data structures such as stack, queue and heap. For all data structures, we aimed to discover a state independent specification in the fragment of Sect. 6. We used the strategy from Sect. 5.3, obviating the need for setting the sample size in advance. We have set the initial sample size to 5000 by experimenting with Set and Map. We have used this value for all other structures. Our tool inferred the best approximation in all cases. For example, we inferred the following specification for the method pair $\mathtt{unite}(a_1, b_1)/r_1$, $\mathtt{unite}(a_2, b_2)/r_2$ of UnionFind 6, where $\mathtt{unite}(a, b)/r$ unites the classes of a and b under the representative of the class of a, and also returns whether a modification was actually performed:

$$\left[(a_1 = a_2 \vee a_1 = b_2 \vee a_2 = b_1) \wedge r_1 \wedge r_2\right] \vee a_1 = b_1 \vee a_2 = b_2 \vee (\neg r_1 \wedge \neg r_2) \quad (6)$$

Data structure	Pairs	Size	Disj.	#Samples	#Types	Sampl.	Search	P.d.
Set	10	5	3	15 001	11/12	120	0.4	16.0x
Map	3	5	3	15 000	2492/4683	1.4s	600	33.3x
MaxRegister	3	3	3	15 000	20/75	80	3.2	10.9x
1DTree	6	9	3	15 000	31/75	240	2.6	11.9x
IntProximityQuery	10	5	3	15 000	19/75	130	1.4	18.6x
RangeUpdate	3	11	1	15 000	208/300	330	54	3.7x
Accumulator	3	1	1	15 000	3/3	35	0.06	3.3x
Queue	10	7	3	15 001	6/6	96	0.6	4.7x
Stack	10	7	3	15 001	6/6	83	0.3	3.3x
MinHeap	10	7	3	15 001	6/6	85	0.8	4.0x
MultiSet	10	9	3	15 000	51/75	170	3.3	2.3x
PartialMap	15	5	3	22 500	1987/4683	1.4s	440	43.2x
UnionFind 1	6	3	3	17 500	75/75	140	9.7	8.0x
UnionFind 2	6	5	3	32 500	75/75	290	31	2.7x
UnionFind 3	6	5	1	45 000	75/75	380	59	2.5x
UnionFind 4	6	3	3	30 001	247/300	520	110	2.5x
UnionFind 5	6	11	3	105 001	247/300	2.3s	470	1.6x
UnionFind 6	6	17	9	75 000	247/300	1.6s	550	36.4x
BitTextEditor	36	7	3	15 001	4/4	42	0.3	4.3x
ArrayList	28	7	3	145 001	1403/4683	2.4s	710	23.9x
BitList	120	19	9	75 000	150/150	920	210	19.5x

Fig. 4. Experimental results averaged over 8 runs. Times are in ms (unless indicated).

Figure 4 summarizes our experimental results over 8 runs. For every data structure we show the averaged maximum over all method pairs. These numbers are: inferred formula size (**Size**), largest disjunct size (**Disj.**), number of drawn examples (**#Sample**), number of observed logical types vs. their upper bound (**#Types**), sampling time (**Sampl.**), formula search time (**Search**), and the search speedup achieved via predicate discovery (**P.d.**). The reduced sample size is proportional to the number of observed types.

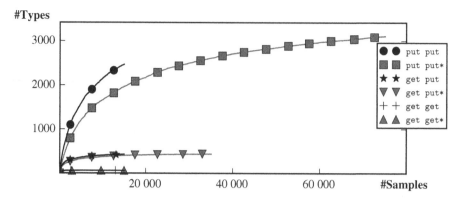

Fig. 5. Type-aware vs. random sampling (*) for 6 method pairs of Map. The method pairs produce tuples with 6 (put/put), 5 (get/put), and 4 (get/get) components.

Our results indicate that the approach is effective for learning non-trivial specifications. Further, stabilizing the inferred formula is a reliable way to determine a good sample size. By filtering examples of the same logical type, we significantly reduced the input sample size for the later formula search, and combining exhaustive and greedy search was fully sufficient for inferring all of the specifications. The results also show that predicate discovery dramatically reduces search time for more complex specifications. Finally, type-aware sampling successfully provided all observations necessary for inference.

We also compared type-aware with pure random sampling. Figure 5 shows the number of examples vs. observed types of typical inference runs for Map. The curve of each run ends when formula stabilization was confirmed. We observe that: (i) type-aware sampling explored new types more quickly than pure random sampling, but only when sampling larger tuples (about 6 components in this particular case); and (ii) type-aware sampling stabilized the inferred formula much earlier (15 000 vs. 75 000 examples). In fact, in our experiments, we observed large variance in stabilization time when sampling purely at random.

8   Related Work

There has been substantial interest in learning program invariants from concrete executions [5–8, 16, 20, 21]. We evaluated several of these approaches, including [5, 16, 20, 21]. Unfortunately, none of them could infer the necessary specifications and match our results.

Daikon [5] infers conjunctions of predefined templates that stay invariant during program execution. DIG [16] infers polynomial invariants over various algebras, e.g., min-plus and max-plus. Even though both tools support some form of disjunctive invariants, in our case they could only infer rather crude approximations to the target specification. A reason for this is that disjunctions abound in the context of commutativity [12]. That is why, in contrast to

Daikon and DIG, our approach aims at learning free-form boolean expressions. That said, our approach is not strictly better. Daikon scales well when the number of relations in the fragment increases, and DIG specializes in polynomial invariants.

Similarly to us, the approaches outlined in [6,20,21] also focus on fragments with rich support for disjunctions. However, their goal is to support program verification, and so they learn invariant properties that separate all positive from all negative examples in a given sample. This is not suitable for learning specifications, due to the fact that: (i) learning fails if a sample cannot be separated by a classifier, even though a good approximation exists (cf. (3) in Sect. 4.1); (ii) even if the sample can be separated, the inferred classifier can be too approximative to be useful, compared to the best approximation.

These points are especially true for the method in [21] which is tied to an expressive fragment (arbitrary boolean combinations of half-planes) and prone to overfitting, as we observed in our experiments with it. In [20] formula search is performed stochastically. This has the flexibility of supporting a variety of fragments, but can be highly sensitive to randomness, and can also have issues with convergence. We could not observe the approach terminating when inferring commutativity specifications over five or more variables.

Program synthesis methods are also applicable to our problem, i.e., we can simply ask for a program encoding the target specification. The technique in [11] synthesizes a program by querying a black-box input-output oracle. However, it also relies on a verification oracle, and in our setting this requirement can be too strong: the oracle needs to reason about the data type implementation, which in turn can be quite complex. The approach in [7] replaces the verification oracle with "universal examples" which distinguish every possible candidate specification. However, in the case of commutativity, we cannot directly query whether such an example is positive or negative, as a part of the example (the method return values) is actually generated by the query itself. Interestingly, our type-aware sampling can be seen as generalization of the "universal examples".

9   Conclusion

We presented a new "black-box" approach for learning specifications in the fragment of quantifier-free formulas over a finite number of relation symbols. The key insight is to treat uniformly the examples of the same logical type, i.e., examples that are indistinguishable by the logical fragment. Our approach introduces new techniques for obtaining small and informative samples, discovering relevant predicates, fast search procedure, and a way to adaptively determine sample size.

For our evaluation, we focused on automatically learning commutativity specifications. These are fundamental to various areas of computer science, yet are tricky to write manually. Our results indicate that the approach is practically effective – our tool quickly inferred non-trivial, useful commutativity specifications, beyond the reach of any existing work.

References

1. Attiya, H., Guerraoui, R., Hendler, D., Kuznetsov, P., Michael, M.M., Vechev, M.T.: Laws of order: expensive synchronization in concurrent algorithms cannot be eliminated. In: Proceedings of the 38th ACM SIGPLAN-SIGACT Symposium on Principles of Programming Languages, POPL 2011, Austin, TX, USA, 26–28 Jan 2011 (2011)
2. Cameron, P.J.: Oligomorphic Permutation Groups. Cambridge University Press, Cambridge (1990)
3. Chang, C.C., Keisler, H.J.: Model Theory. Studies in Logic and the Foundations of Mathematics. Elsevier Science, North-Holland (1990)
4. Dimitrov, D., Raychev, V., Vechev, M.T., Koskinen, E.: Commutativity race detection. In: ACM SIGPLAN Conference on Programming Language Design and Implementation, PLDI2014, Edinburgh, UK - 09–11 June 2014 (2014)
5. Ernst, M.D., Perkins, J.H., Guo, P.J., McCamant, S., Pacheco, C., Tschantz, M.S., Xiao, C.: The Daikon system for dynamic detection of likely invariants. Sci. Comput. Program. **69**(1–3), 35–45 (2007)
6. Garg, P., Löding, C., Madhusudan, P., Neider, D.: ICE: A robust framework for learning invariants. In: Biere, A., Bloem, R. (eds.) CAV 2014. LNCS, vol. 8559, pp. 69–87. Springer, Heidelberg (2014)
7. Godefroid, P., Taly, A.: Automated synthesis of symbolic instruction encodings from i/o samples. In: PLDI2012, pp. 441–452, New York, ACM (2012)
8. Gupta, A., Majumdar, R., Rybalchenko, A.: From tests to proofs. In: Kowalewski, S., Philippou, A. (eds.) TACAS 2009. LNCS, vol. 5505, pp. 262–276. Springer, Heidelberg (2009)
9. Herlihy, M., Koskinen, E.: Transactional boosting: a methodology for highly-concurrent transactional objects. In: Proceedings of the 13th ACM SIGPLAN Symposium on Principles and Practice of Parallel Programming, PPOPP 2008, Salt Lake City, UT, USA, 20–23 Feb 2008 (2008)
10. Hodges, W.: Model Theory: Encyclopedia of Mathematics and its Applications. Cambridge University Press, Cambridge (2008)
11. Jha, S., Gulwani, S., Seshia, S.A., Tiwari, A.: Oracle-guided component-based program synthesis. In: Proceedings of the 32Nd ACM/IEEE International Conference on Software Engineering - Volume 1, ICSE'2010, pp. 215–224, New York, NY, USA, ACM (2010)
12. Kim, D., Rinard, M.C.: Verification of semantic commutativity conditions and inverse operations on linked data structures. In: PLDI'2011, pp. 528–541, New York, NY, USA, ACM (2011)
13. Kulkarni, M., Nguyen, D., Prountzos, D., Sui, X., Pingali, K.: Exploiting the commutativity lattice. SIGPLAN Not. **46**(6), 542–555 (2011)
14. Kulkarni, M., Pingali, K., Walter, B., Ramanarayanan, G., Bala, K., Chew, L.P.: Optimistic parallelism requires abstractions. In: Proceedings of the ACM SIGPLAN 2007 Conference on Programming Language Design and Implementation, San Diego, California, USA, 10–13 June 2007 (2007)
15. McMillan, K.L.: Relevance heuristics for program analysis. In: Proceedings of the 35th ACM SIGPLAN-SIGACT Symposium on Principles of Programming Languages, POPL 2008, San Francisco, California, USA, 7–12 Jan 2008 (2008)
16. Nguyen, T., Kapur, D., Weimer, W., Forrest, S.: Using dynamic analysis to generate disjunctive invariants. In: ICSE 2014, pp. 608–619. ACM (2014)

17. Poizat, B.: A Course in Model Theory: An Introduction to Contemporary Mathematical Logic Universitext. Springer, New York (2000)
18. Rissanen, J.: Modeling by shortest data description. Automatica **14**(5), 465–471 (1978)
19. Rissanen, J.: Information and Complexity in Statistical Modeling. Springer, New York (2010)
20. Sharma, R., Aiken, A.: From invariant checking to invariant inference using randomized search. In: Biere, A., Bloem, R. (eds.) CAV 2014. LNCS, vol. 8559, pp. 88–105. Springer, Heidelberg (2014)
21. Sharma, R., Gupta, S., Hariharan, B., Aiken, A., Nori, A.V.: Verification as learning geometric concepts. In: Logozzo, F., Fähndrich, M. (eds.) Static Analysis. LNCS, vol. 7935, pp. 388–411. Springer, Heidelberg (2013)
22. Vapnik, V.N.: Statistical Learning Theory. Adaptive and Learning Systems for Signal Processing, Communications, and Control. Wiley, New York (1998)
23. Weihl, W.E.: Commutativity-based concurrency control for abstract data types. IEEE Trans. Comput. **37**(12), 1488–1505 (1988)

Angelic Verification: Precise Verification Modulo Unknowns

Ankush Das[1], Shuvendu K. Lahiri[1]([✉]), Akash Lal[1], and Yi Li[2]

[1] Microsoft Research, Bangalore, India
{t-ankdas,shuvendu,akashl}@microsoft.com
[2] University of Toronto, Toronto, Canada
liyi@cs.toronto.edu

Abstract. Verification of open programs can be challenging in the presence of an unconstrained environment. Verifying properties that depend on the environment yields a large class of uninteresting false alarms. Using a verifier on a program thus requires extensive initial investment in modeling the environment of the program. We propose a technique called *angelic verification* for verification of open programs, where we constrain a verifier to report warnings only when no acceptable environment specification exists to prove the assertion. Our framework is parametric in a vocabulary and a set of angelic assertions that allows a user to configure the tool. We describe a few instantiations of the framework and an evaluation on a set of real-world benchmarks to show that our technique is competitive with industrial-strength tools even without models of the environment.

1 Introduction

Scalable software verifiers offer the potential to find defects early in the development cycle. The user of such a tool can specify a property (e.g. correct usage of kernel/security Apis) using some specification language and the tool validates that the property holds on all feasible executions of the program. There has been a significant progress in the area of software verification, leveraging ideas from model checking [13], theorem proving [34] and invariant inference algorithms [16,22,33]. Tools based on these principles (e.g. SDV [3], F-Soft [24]) have found numerous bugs in production software.

However, a fundamental problem still limits the adoption of powerful software verifiers in the hands of end users. Most (interprocedural) program verifiers aim to verify that a program does not fail assertions under all possible feasible executions of the program. This is a good match when the input program is "closed", i.e., its execution starts from a well-defined initial state, and external library methods are included or accurately modeled. Scalability concerns preclude performing monolithic verification that includes all transitive callers and library source code. In practice, a significant portion of verification tool development requires closing a program by (i) either providing a *harness* (a client program) or a *module invariant* [30] to constrain the inputs and (ii) *stubs* for external library

© Springer International Publishing Switzerland 2015
D. Kroening and C.S. Păsăreanu (Eds.): CAV 2015, Part I, LNCS 9206, pp. 324–342, 2015.
DOI: 10.1007/978-3-319-21690-4_19

```
 1 // inconsistency                            20 // globals
 2 procedure Bar(x:int) {                      21 var gs:int, m:[int]int;
 3     if (x != NULL) { gs := 1; }             22
 4     else { gs := 2; }                       23 // external call
 5     // possible BUG or dead code            24 procedure FooBar() {
 6     assert x != NULL;                       25     var x, w, z:int;
 7     m[x] := 5;                              26     call z := Lib1();
 8 }                                           27     assert z != NULL;
 9 // internal bug                             28     m[z] := NULL;
10 procedure Baz(y:int) {                      29     call x := Lib2();
11     assert y != NULL; //DEFINITE BUG        30     assert x != NULL;
12     m[y] := 4;                              31     w := m[x];
13 }                                           32     assert w != NULL;
14 // entry point                              33     m[w] := 4;
15 procedure Foo(z:int) {                      34 }
16     call Bar(z);        // block + relax    35 // library
17     call Baz(NULL); // internal bug         36 procedure Lib1() returns (r:int);
18     call FooBar();      // external calls   37 procedure Lib2() returns (r:int);
19 }
```

Fig. 1. Running example.

procedures [3]. The effect of modeling is to *constrain* the set of *unknowns* in the program to rule out infeasible executions. Absence of such modeling results in numerous uninteresting alarms and deters a user from further interacting with the tool. *"A stupid false positive implies the tool is stupid"* [6]. The significant initial modeling overhead often undermines the value provided by verifiers. Even "bounded" versions of verifiers (such as CBMC [14]) suffer from this problem because these unknowns are present even in bounded executions.

Example 1. Consider the example program (written in the Boogie language [4]) in Fig. 1. The program has four procedures Foo, Bar, Baz, FooBar and two external *library* procedures Lib1, Lib2. The variables in the programs can be scalars (of type int) or *arrays* (e.g. m) that map int to int. The Boogie program is an encoding of a C program [15]: pointers and values are uniformly modeled as integers (e.g. parameter x of Bar, or the return value of Lib1), and memory dereference is modeled as array lookup (e.g. m[x]). The procedures have assertions marked using assert statements. The entry procedure for this program is Foo.

There are several sources of *unknowns* or unconstrained values in the program: the parameter z to Foo, the global variable m representing the heap, and the return values of library procedures Lib1 and Lib2. Even a precise verifier is bound to return assertion failures for *each* of the assertions in the program. This is due to the fact that all the assertions, except the one in Baz (the only *definite bug* in the program) are assertions over unknowns in the program and (sound) verifiers tend to be conservative (over-approximate) in the face of unknowns. Such *demonic* nature of verifiers will result in several false alarms.

Overview. Our goal is to push back on the demonic nature of the verifier by prioritizing alarms with higher evidence. In addition to the warning in Baz, the assertion in Bar is suspicious as the only way to avoid the bug is to make the "else" branch unreachable in Bar. For the remaining assertions, relatively *simple* constraints on the unknown values suffice to explain the correctness of these assertions. For example, it is *reasonable* to assume that calls to library methods do not return NULL, their dereferences (m[x]) store non-null values and calls to two different library methods do not return aliased pointers. We tone down the demonic nature of verifiers by posing a more *angelic* decision problem for the verifier (also termed as *abductive inference* [10,20]):

> For a given assertion, does there exists an *acceptable* specification over the unknowns such that the assertion holds?

This forces the verifier to work harder to exhaust the space of *acceptable* specifications before showing a warning for a given assertion. Of course, this makes the verification problem less defined as it is parameterized by what constitutes "acceptable" to the end user of the tool. At the same time, it allows a user to be able to configure the demonic nature of the tool by specifying a vocabulary of acceptable specifications.

In this paper, we provide a user a few dimensions to specify a vocabulary *Vocab* that constitutes a specification (details can be found in Sect. 4). The vocabulary can indicate a template for the atomic formulas, or the Boolean and quantifier structure. Given a vocabulary *Vocab*, we characterize an acceptable specification by how (a) *concise* and (b) *permissive* the specification is. Conciseness is important for the resulting specifications to be understandable by the user. Permissiveness ensures that the specification is not overly strong, thus masking out true bugs. The failure in Bar is an example, where a specification x ≠ NULL is not permissive as it gives rise to dead code in the "else" branch before the assertion. To specify desired permissiveness, we allow the users to augment the program with a set of *angelic assertions* $\hat{A}$. The assertions in $\hat{A}$ should *not* be provable in the presence of any inferred specification over the unknowns. An angelic assertion assert $e \in \hat{A}$ at a program location l indicates that the user expects at least one state to reach l and satisfy $\neg e$. For Bar one can add two assertions assert false inside each of the branches. The precondition x ≠ NULL would be able to prove that assert false in the "else" branch is unreachable (and thus provable), which prevents it from being permissive. We describe a few such useful instances of angelic assertions in Sect. 3.1.

We have implemented the angelic verification framework in a tool called *AngelicVerifier* for Boogie programs. Given a Boogie program with a set S of entrypoints, *AngelicVerifier* invokes each of the procedures in S with unknown input states. In the absence of any user-provided information, we assume that S is the set of all procedures in the program. Further, the library procedures are assigned a body that assigns a non-deterministic value to the return variables and adds an assume statement with a predicate unknown_i (Fig. 2). This predicate will be used to constrain the return values of a procedure for *all possible call sites* (Sect. 4) within an entrypoint.

AngelicVerifier invokes a given (demonic) verifier on this program with all entrypoints in S. If the verifier returns a trace that ends in an assertion failure, *AngelicVerifier* tries to infer an acceptable specification over the unknowns. If it succeeds, it installs the specification as a precondition of the entry point and

```
function unknown_0(a: int ): bool;
function unknown_1(a: int ): bool;

procedure Lib1() returns (r: int) {
    assume unknown_0(r);
    return;
}

procedure Lib2() returns (r: int) {
    assume unknown_1(r);
    return;
}
```

```
// Trace: Bar → assert on line 6
SPEC :: x ≠ NULL, Spec not permissive
ANGELIC_WARNING: Assertion x != NULL fails in proc Bar
// Trace: Baz → assert on line 11
SPEC :: y ≠ NULL
// Trace: FooBar → assert on line 27
SPEC :: (∀ x_1: unknown_0(x_1) ⇒ x_1 ≠ NULL)
// Trace: FooBar → assert on line 30
SPEC :: (∀ x_2: unknown_1(x_2) ⇒ x_2 ≠ NULL)
// Trace: FooBar → assert on line 32
SPEC :: (∀ x_2, x_1: unknown_1(x_2) ∧
        unknown_0(x_1)⇒ (x_2 ≠ x_1 ∧ m[x_2] ≠ NULL))
// Trace: Foo → Baz → assert on line 11
ANGELIC_WARNING: Assertion y != NULL fails in proc Baz
```

Fig. 2. Modeling of external procedures by *AngelicVerifier*. All variables are non-deterministically initialized.

Fig. 3. Output of *AngelicVerifier* on the program shown in Fig. 1. A line with "SPEC" denotes an inferred specification to suppress a trace.

iterates. If it is unable to infer an acceptable specification, the trace is reported as a defect to the user.

Figure 3 shows the output of *AngelicVerifier* applied to our example:

- For a trace that starts at Bar and fails the assert on line 6, we conjecture a specification x ≠ NULL but discover that it is not permissive. The line with "ANGELIC_WARNING" is a warning shown to the user.
- For the trace that starts at Baz and fails the assert on line 11, we block the assertion failure by installing the constraint y ≠ NULL. The code of Bar does not have any indication that it expects to see NULL as input.
- For the three traces that start at FooBar and fail an assertion inside it, we block them using constraints on the return values of library calls. Notice that the return values are not in scope at the entry to FooBar; they get constrained indirectly using the unknown_i predicates. The most interesting block is for the final assertion which involves assuming that (a) the returns from the two library calls are never aliased, and (b) the value of the array m at the value returned by Lib2 is non-null. (See Sect. 4)
- The trace starting at Foo that calls Baz and fails on line 11 cannot be blocked (other than by using the non-permissive specification *false*), and is reported to the user.

Contributions. In summary, the paper makes the following contributions: (a) We provide a framework for performing angelic verification with the goal of highlighting highest confidence bugs. (b) We provide a parametric framework based on *Vocab* and $\hat{A}$ to control the level of angelism in the tool that a user can configure. (c) We describe a scalable algorithm for searching specifications using *Explain-Error* (Sect. 4). We show an effective way to deal with internal non-determinism resulting from calls to library procedures. (d) We have implemented the ideas in a prototype tool *AngelicVerifier* and evaluated it on real-world benchmarks. We show that *AngelicVerifier* is competitive with industrial-strength tools even without access to the environment models.

2   Programming Language

Syntax. We formalize the ideas in the paper in the context of a simple subset of the Boogie programming language [4]. A program consists of a set of *basic blocks Block*; each block consists of a *label BlockId*, a body $s \in Stmt$ and a (possibly empty) set of *successor* blocks. A program has a designated first block *Start* $\in$ *Block*. Most statements are standard; the havoc x statement assigns a non-deterministic value to the variable x. An expression (*Expr*) can be a variable identifier or an application of function $f \in$ *Functions*. A formula (*Formula*) includes Boolean constants, application of a predicate $p \in$ *Predicates*, and closed under Boolean connectives and quantifiers. The constructs are expressive enough to model features of most programming languages such as C [15] or Java [1]. Conditional statements are modeled using assume and goto statements; heap is modeled using *interpreted* array functions $\{read, write\} \subseteq$ *Functions* [35] (Fig. 4).

$$
\begin{aligned}
P &\in Program ::= Block^+ \\
BL &\in Block \quad ::= BlockId : s; \text{ goto } BlockId^* \\
s, t &\in Stmt \quad ::= \text{skip} \mid \text{assert } \phi \mid \text{assume } \phi \mid x := e \mid \text{havoc } x \mid s; s \\
x, y &\in Vars \\
e &\in Expr \quad ::= x \mid f(e, \ldots, e) \\
\phi, \psi &\in Formula ::= \text{true} \mid \text{false} \mid p(e, \ldots, e) \mid \phi \wedge \phi \mid \forall x : \phi \mid \neg \phi
\end{aligned}
$$

Fig. 4. A simple programming language.

Semantics. A *program state* , is a type-consistent valuation of variables in scope in the program. The set of all states is denoted by $\Sigma \cup \{Err\}$, where *Err* is a special state to indicate an *assertion failure*. For a given state $\in \Sigma$ and an expression (or formula) e, e denotes the evaluation of e in the state. For a formula $\phi \in Formula$, $\models \phi$ holds if ϕ evaluates to true. The semantics of a program is a set of *execution traces*, where a trace corresponds to a sequence of program states. We refer the readers to earlier works for details of the semantics [4]. Intuitively, an execution trace for a block *BL* corresponds to the sequence of states obtained by executing the body, and extending the *terminating* sequences with the traces of the successor blocks (if any). A sequence of states for a block does not terminate if it either executes an assume ϕ or an assert ϕ statement in a state $\in \Sigma$ such that $\not\models \phi$. In the latter case, the successor state is *Err*. The traces of a program is the set of traces for the start block *Start*. Let $\mathcal{T}(P)$ be the set of all traces of a program P. A program P is *correct* (denoted as $\models P$) if $\mathcal{T}(P)$ does not contain a trace that ends in the state *Err*. For a program P that is not correct, we define a *failure trace* as a trace τ that starts at *Start* and ends in the state *Err*.

3 Angelic Verification

In this section, we make the problem of *angelic verification* more concrete. We are given a program P that cannot be proved *correct* in the presence of unknowns from the environment (e.g. parameters, globals and outputs of library procedures). If one takes a conservative approach, we can only conclude that the program P has a *possible* assertion failure. In this setting, verification failures offer no information to a user of the tool. Instead, one can take a more pragmatic approach. If the user can characterize a class of *acceptable* missing specifications Φ that precludes verification (based on experience), one can instead ask a weaker verification question: *does there exist a specification $\phi \in \Phi$ such $\phi \models P$?*. One can characterize the acceptability of a specification ϕ along two axes: (i) *Conciseness* — the specification should have a concise representation in some vocabulary that the user expects and can inspect. This usually precludes specifications with several levels of Boolean connectives, quantifiers, or complex atomic expressions. (ii) *Permissive* — the specification ϕ should not be too strong to preclude feasible states of P that are known to exist. We allow two mechanisms for an expert user to control the set of acceptable specifications:

- The user can provide a *vocabulary Vocab* of acceptable specifications, along with a checker that can test membership of a formula ϕ in *Vocab*. We show instances of *Vocab* in Sect. 4.
- The user can augment P with a set of *angelic* assertions $\hat{\mathcal{A}}$ at specific locations, with the expectation that any specification should not prove an assertion assert $e \in \hat{\mathcal{A}}$.

We term the resulting verification problem *angelic* as the verifier co-operates with the user (as opposed to playing an adversary) to find specifications that can prove the program. This can be seen as a particular mechanism to allow an expert user to customize the *abductive inference* problem tailored to their needs [20]. If no such specification can found, it indicates that the verification failure of P cannot be categorized into previously known buckets of false alarms.

We make these ideas more precise in the next few sections. In Sect. 3, we describe the notion of *angelic correctness* given P, *Vocab* and $\hat{\mathcal{A}}$. In Sect. 3.2, we describe an algorithm to prove *angelic correctness* using existing program verifiers.

3.1 Problem Formulation

Let $\phi \in$ *Formula* be a well-scoped formula at the block *Start* of a program P. We say that a program P is *correct under ϕ* (denoted as $\phi \models P$), if the augmented program $Start_0$: assume ϕ ; goto *Start* with "Start" block as $Start_0$ is correct. In other words, the program P is correct with a *precondition* ϕ.

Let $\mathcal{A}$ be the set of assertions in program P. Additionally, let the user specify an additional set $\hat{\mathcal{A}}$ of angelic assertions at various blocks in P. We denote the program P_{A_1, A_2} as the instrumented version of P that has two sets of assertions enabled:

- *Normal* assertions $A_1 \subseteq \mathcal{A}$ that constitute a (possibly empty) subset of the original assertions present in P, and
- *Angelic* assertions $A_2 \subseteq \hat{\mathcal{A}}$ that constitute a (possibly empty) subset of set of additional user supplied assertions.

Definition 1 (Permissive Precondition). *For a program* $P_{\mathcal{A},\hat{\mathcal{A}}}$ *and formula* ϕ, *Permissive*$(P_{\mathcal{A},\hat{\mathcal{A}}}, \phi)$ *holds if for every assertion* $s \in \hat{\mathcal{A}}$, *if* $\phi \models P_{\emptyset,\{s\}}$, *then* true $\models P_{\emptyset,\{s\}}$.

In other words, a specification ϕ is not allowed to prove any assertion $s \in \hat{\mathcal{A}}$ that was not provable under the unconstrained specification true.

Definition 2 (Angelic Correctness). *Given (i) a program* P *with a set of normal assertions* $\mathcal{A}$, *(ii) an angelic set of assertions* $\hat{\mathcal{A}}$, *and (iii) a vocabulary Vocab constraining a set of formulas at Start,* P *is* angelically correct under $(Vocab, \hat{\mathcal{A}})$ *if there exists a formula* $\phi \in Vocab$ *such that: (i)* $\phi \models P_{\mathcal{A},\emptyset}$, *and (ii) Permissive*$(P_{\emptyset,\hat{\mathcal{A}}}, \phi)$ *holds.*

If no such specification ϕ exists, then we say that P has an *angelic* bug with respect to $(Vocab, \hat{\mathcal{A}})$. In this case, we try to ensure the angelic correctness of P with respect to a subset of the assertions in P; the rest of the assertions are flagged as angelic warnings.

Examples of Angelic Assertions $\hat{\mathcal{A}}$. If one provides assert false at *Start* to be part of $\hat{\mathcal{A}}$, it disallows preconditions that are inconsistent with other preconditions of the program [20]. If we add assert false at the end of every basic block, it prevents us from creating preconditions that create dead code in the program. This has the effect of detecting *semantic inconsistency* or *doomed* bugs [19,21,23,36]. Further, we can allow checking such assertions interprocedurally and at only a subset of locations (e.g. exclude defensive checks in callees). Finally, one can encode other domain knowledge using such assertions. For example, consider checking the correct lock usage for if(∗){L1 : assert ¬locked(l1); lock(l1); } else {L2 : assert locked(l2); unlock(l2); }. If the user expects an execution where l1 = l2 at L2, the angelic assertion assert l1 ≠ l2 ∈ $\hat{\mathcal{A}}$ precludes the precondition ¬locked(l1) ∧ locked(l2), and reveals a warning for at least one of the two locations. As another example, if the user has observed a runtime value v for variable x at a program location l, she can add an assertion assert x ≠ v ∈ $\hat{\mathcal{A}}$ at l to ensure that a specification does not preclude a known feasible behavior; further, the idea can be extended from feasible values to feasible intraprocedural path conditions.

3.2 Finding Angelic Bugs

Algorithm 1 describes a (semi) algorithm for proving angelic correctness of a program. In addition to the program, it takes as inputs the set of angelic assertions $\hat{\mathcal{A}}$, and a vocabulary *Vocab*. On termination, the procedure returns a specification E and a subset $\mathcal{A}_1 \subseteq \mathcal{A}$ for which the resultant program is angelically correct under E. Lines 1 and 2 initialize the variables E and $\mathcal{A}_1$, respectively. The loop from line 3 — 16 performs the main act of blocking failure traces in P. First, we verify the assertions $\mathcal{A}_1$ over P. The routine tries to establish $E \models P$ using a sound and complete program verifier; the program verifier itself may never terminate. We return in line 6 if verification succeeds and P contains no failure traces (NO_TRACE). In the event a failure trace τ is present, we query a procedure $ExplainError$ (see Sect. 4) to find a specification ϕ that can prove that none of the executions along τ fail an assertion. Line 10 checks if the addition of the new constraint ϕ still ensures that the resulting specification E_1 is permissive. If not, then it suppresses the assertion a that failed in τ (by removing it from $\mathcal{A}_1$) and outputs the trace τ to the user. Otherwise, it adds ϕ to the set of constraints collected so far. The loop repeats forever until verification succeeds in Line 4. The procedure may fail to terminate if either the call to $Verify$ does not terminate, or the loop in Line 3 does not terminate due to an unbounded number of failure traces.

Theorem 1. *On termination, Algorithm 1 returns a pair of precondition E and a subset $\mathcal{A}_1 \subseteq \mathcal{A}$ such that (i) $E \models P$ when only assertions in $\mathcal{A}_1$ are enabled, and (ii) $Permissive(P_{\mathcal{A},\hat{\mathcal{A}}}, E)$.*

The proof follows directly from the check in line 4 that establishes (i), and line 10 that ensures permissiveness.

Input: Program P with assertions $\mathcal{A}$,
Input: Angelic Assertions $\hat{\mathcal{A}}$,
Input: Vocabulary $Vocab$,
Output: A permissive specification E,
Output: A set of assertions $\mathcal{A}_1 \subseteq \mathcal{A}$ for
      which $E \models P_{\mathcal{A}_1, \emptyset}$
1: $E \leftarrow \emptyset$
2: $\mathcal{A}_1 \leftarrow \mathcal{A}$
3: **loop**
4:    $\tau \leftarrow Verify(P_{\mathcal{A}_1, \emptyset}, E)$ /* $E \models P$ */
5:    **if** $\tau = $ NO_TRACE **then**
6:       **return** $(E, \mathcal{A}_1)$
7:    **end if**
8:    $\phi \leftarrow ExplainError(P, \tau, Vocab)$
9:    $E_1 \leftarrow E \cup \{\phi\}$
10:   **if** $\neg Permissive(P_{\emptyset, \mathcal{A}}, E_1)$ **then**
11:      Let a be the failing assert in τ
12:      $\mathcal{A}_1 \leftarrow \mathcal{A}_1 \setminus \{a\}$ /* Report a */
13:   **else**
14:      $E \leftarrow E_1$
15:   **end if**
16: **end loop**
Algorithm 1: *AngelicVerifier*

Input: Program P, failure trace τ, vocabulary
      $Vocab$
Output: A formula that blocks τ
1: $\tau_1 \leftarrow ControlSlice(P, \tau)$
2: $\phi_1 \leftarrow wlp(\tau_1, \text{true})$
3: $\phi_2 \leftarrow EliminateMapUpdates(\phi_1)$
4: $atoms_1 \leftarrow FilterAtoms(GetAtoms(\phi_2), Vocab.Atoms)$
5: **if** $Vocab.Bool = $ MONOMIAL **then**
6:    $S \leftarrow \{a \mid a \in atoms_1, \text{ and } a \models \phi_2\}$
7:    **return** $S = \emptyset$? false : $(\bigvee_{a \in S} a)$
8: **else**
9:    **return** $ProjectAtoms(\phi_2, atoms_1)$
10: **end if**
Algorithm 2: *ExplainError*

4 ExplainError

Problem. Given a program P that is not correct, let τ be a failure trace of P. Since a trace can be represented as a valid program (*Program*) in our language (with a single block containing the sequence of statements ending in an assert statement), we will treat τ as a program with a single control flow path.

Informally, the goal of ExplainError is to return a precondition ϕ from a given vocabulary *Vocab* such that $\phi \models \tau$, or false if no such precondition exists. ExplainError takes as input the following: (a) a program P, (b) a failure trace τ in P represented as a program and (c) a *vocabulary Vocab* that specifies syntactic restrictions on formulas to search over. It returns a formula ϕ such that $\phi \models \tau$ and $\phi \in Vocab \cup \{\mathsf{false}\}$. It returns false either when (a) the vocabulary does not contain any formula ϕ for which $\phi \models \tau$, or (b) the search does not terminate (say due to a timeout).

Note that the *weakest liberal precondition* (*wlp*) of the trace [18] is guaranteed to be the weakest possible blocking constraint; however, it is usually very specific to the trace and may require enumerating all the concrete failing traces inside Algorithm 1. Moreover, the resulting formula for long traces are often not suitable for human consumption. When ExplainError returns a formula other than false, one may expect ϕ to be the *weakest* (most permissive) constraint in *Vocab* that blocks the failure path. However, this is not possible for several reasons (a) efficiency concerns preclude searching for the weakest, (b) *Vocab* may not be closed under disjunction and therefore the weakest constraint may not be defined. Thus the primary goals of ExplainError are to be (a) scalable (so that it can be invoked in the main loop in Algorithm 1), and (b) the resulting constraints are concise even if not the weakest over *Vocab*.

Algorithm. Algorithm 2 provides the high-level flow of ExplainError. Currently, the algorithm is parameterized by *Vocab* that consists of two components:

- *Vocab.Atoms*: a template for the set of atomic formulas that can appear in a blocking constraint. This can range over equalities ($e_1 = e_2$), difference constraints ($e_1 \leq e_2 + c$), or some other syntactic pattern.
- *Vocab.Bool*: the complexity of Boolean structure of the blocking constraint. One may choose to have a *clausal* formula ($\bigvee_i e_i$), *cube* formulas ($\bigwedge_i e_i$), or an arbitrary *conjunctive normal form* (CNF) ($\bigvee_j (\bigwedge_i e_i)$) over atomic formulas e_i.

Initially, we assume that we do not have internal non-determinism in the form of havoc or calls to external libraries in the trace τ – we will describe this extension later in this section.

Let $wlp(s, \phi)$ be the weakest liberal precondition transformer for a $s \in Stmt$ and $\phi \in Formula$ [18]. $wlp(s, \phi)$ is the weakest formula representing states from which executing s does not lead to assertion failure and on termination satisfies ϕ. It is defined as follows on the structure of statements: $wlp(\mathsf{skip}, \phi) = \phi$, $wlp(\mathsf{x} := e, \phi) = \phi[e/\mathsf{x}]$ (where $\phi[e/\mathsf{x}]$ denotes substituting e for all free occurrences of x), $wlp(\mathsf{assume}\ \psi, \phi) = \psi \Rightarrow \phi$, $wlp(\mathsf{assert}\ \psi, \phi) = \psi \wedge \phi$, and

$wlp(s; t, \phi) = wlp(s, wlp(t, \phi))$. Thus $wlp(\tau, \mathsf{true})$ will ensure that no assertion fails along τ. Our current algorithm (Algorithm 2) provides various options to create *predicate (under) covers* of $wlp(\tau, \mathsf{true})$ [22], formulas that imply $wlp(\tau, \mathsf{true})$. Such formulas are guaranteed to block the trace τ from failing.

The first step *ControlSlice* performs an optimization to prune conditionals from τ that do not control dominate the failing assertion, by performing a variant of the *path slicing* approach [25]. Line 2 performs the *wlp* computation on the resulting trace τ_1. At this point, ϕ_1 is a Boolean combination of literals from arithmetic, equalities and array theories in *satisfiability modulo theories* (SMT) [34]. *EliminateMapUpdates* (in line 3) eliminates any occurrence of *write* from the formula using rewrite rules such as $read(write(e_1, e_2, e_3), e_4) \rightarrow e_2 = e_4 ? e_3 : read(e_1, e_4)$. This rule introduces new equality (aliasing) constraints in the resulting formula that are not present directly in τ. Line 4 chooses a set of atomic formulas from ϕ_2 that match the vocabulary. Finally, the conditional in Line 5 determines the Boolean structure in the resulting expression.

The MONOMIAL option specifies that the block expression is a disjunction of atoms from $atoms_1$. Line 7 collects the set of atoms in $atoms_1$ that imply ϕ_2, which in turn implies $wlp(\tau, \mathsf{true})$. We return the clause representing the disjunction of such atoms, which in turn implies $wlp(\tau, \mathsf{true})$. The more expensive *ProjectAtoms*$(\phi_2, atoms_1)$ returns a formula ϕ_3 that is a CNF expression over $atoms_1$, such that $\phi_3 \Rightarrow \phi_2$, by performing Boolean quantifier elimination of the atoms not present in $atoms_1$. We first transform the formula ϕ_2 into a *conjunctive normal form* (CNF) by repeatedly applying rewrite rules such as $\phi_1 \vee (\phi_2 \wedge \phi_3) \rightarrow (\phi_1 \vee \phi_2) \wedge (\phi_1 \vee \phi_3)$. We employ a theorem prover at each step to try simplify intermediate expressions to true or false. Finally, for each clause c in the CNF form, we remove any literal in c that is not present in the set of atoms $atoms_1$.

Example. Consider the example FooBar in Fig. 1, and the trace τ that corresponds to violation of assert $w \neq \mathsf{NULL}$. The trace is a sequential composition of the following statements: $z := x\_1$, $m[z] := \mathsf{NULL}$, $x := x\_2$, $w := m[x]$, assert $w \neq \mathsf{NULL}$, where we have replaced calls to Lib1 and Lib2 with x_1 and x_2 respectively. $wlp(\tau, \mathsf{true})$ is $read(write(m, x\_1, \mathsf{NULL}), x\_2) \neq \mathsf{NULL}$, which after applying *EliminateMapUpdates* would result in the expression $(x\_1 \neq x\_2 \wedge m[x\_2] \neq \mathsf{NULL})$. Notice that this is nearly identical to the blocking clause (except the quantifiers and triggers) returned while analyzing FooBar in Fig. 3. Let us allow any disequality $e_1 \neq e_2$ atoms in *Vocab*. If we only allow MONOMIAL Boolean structure, there does not exist any clause over these atoms (weaker than false) that suppresses the trace.

Internal Non-determinism. In the presence of only *input* non-determinism (parameters and globals), the $wlp(\tau, \mathsf{true})$ is a well-scoped expression at entry in terms of parameters and globals. In the presence of *internal* non-determinism (due to havoc statements either present explicitly or implicitly for non-deterministic initialization of local variables), the target of a havoc is universally quantified away ($wlp(\mathsf{havoc}\ x, \phi) = \forall u : \phi[u/x]$). However, this is unsatisfactory for several reasons: (a) one has to introduce a fresh quantified variable for different call sites of a function (say Lib1 in Fig. 1). (b) Moreover, the quantified formula does not have good *trigger* [17] to instantiate the universally quantified variables u. For a quantified formula, a trigger is a set of sub-expressions containing all the bound variables. To address both these issues, we introduce a distinct predicate unknown_i after the i-th syntactic call to havoc and introduce an assume statement after the havoc (Fig. 2): assume unknown_i(x), The *wlp* rules for assume and havoc ensure that the quantifiers are more well-behaved as the resultant formulas have unknown_i(x) as a trigger (see Fig. 3).

5   Evaluation

We have implemented the ideas described in this paper (Algorithms 1 and 2) in a tool called *AngelicVerifier*, available with sources.[1] *AngelicVerifier* uses the *Corral* verifier [31] as a black box to implement the check *Verify* used in Algorithm 1. *Corral* performs interprocedural analysis of programs written in the Boogie language; the Boogie program can be generated from either C [15], .NET [5] or Java programs [1]. As an optimization, while running ExplainError, *AngelicVerifier* first tries the MONOMIAL option and falls back to *ProjectAtoms* when the former returns false.

We empirically evaluate *AngelicVerifier* against two industrial tools: the *Static Driver Verifier* (SDV) [3] and *PREfix* [9]. Each of these tools come packaged with models of the environment (both harness and stubs) of the programs they target. These models have been designed over several years of testing and tuning by a product team. We ran *AngelicVerifier* with none of these models and compared the number of code defects found as well as the benefit of treating the missing environment as *angelic* over treating it as *demonic*.

5.1   Comparison with SDV

Benchmarks	Procedures	KLOC	CPU(Ks)
Correct (5)	71-235	2.0-19.1	1.1
Buggy (13)	23-139	1.5-6.7	1.7

Fig. 5. SDV Benchmarks

SDV is a tool offered by Microsoft to third-party driver developers. It checks for typestate properties (e.g., locks are acquired and released in strict alternation) on Windows device drivers. SDV checks these properties by introducing monitors in the program in the form of global variables, and instrumenting the property as assertions in the program. We chose a subset of benchmarks and properties from SDV's verification suite that correspond to drivers distributed in the Windows Driver Kit (WDK); their characteristics are mentioned in Fig. 5. We picked a total of 18 driver-property pairs, in which SDV reports a defect on 13 of them. Figure 5 shows the range for the number of procedures, lines of code (contained in C files) and the total time taken by SDV (in 1000s of seconds) on all of the buggy or correct instances.

---

[1] At http://corral.codeplex.com, project AddOns\AngelicVerifierNull.

We ran various instantiations of *Angelic Verifier* on the SDV benchmarks:

- DEFAULT: The vocabulary includes aliasing constraints $(e_1 \neq e_2)$ as well as arbitrary expressions over monitor variables.
- NOTS: The vocabulary only includes aliasing constraints.
- NOALIAS: The vocabulary only includes expressions over the monitor variables.
- NOEE: The vocabulary is empty. In this case, all traces returned by Corral are treated as bugs without running ExplainError. This option simulates a demonic environment.
- DEFAULT+HARNESS: This is the same as DEFAULT, but the input program includes a stripped version of the harness used by SDV. This harness initializes the monitor variables and calls specific procedures in the driver. (The actual harness used by SDV is several times bigger and includes initializations of various data structures and flags as well.)

Example: Fig. 6 contains code snippets inspired from real code in our benchmarks. We use it to highlight the differences between the various configurations of *Angelic Verifier* described above.

- The assertion in Fig. 6(a) will be reported as a bug by NOTS but not DEFAULT because LockDepth > 1 is not a valid atom for NOTS.
- The assertion in Fig. 6(c) will be reported as a bug by NOALIAS but not DEFAULT because it requires a specification that constrains aliasing in the environment. For instance, DEFAULT constrains the environment by imposing $(x \neq \text{irp} \land y \neq \text{irp}) \lor (z \neq \text{irp} \land y \neq \text{irp})$, where x is devobj $\rightarrow$ DeviceExtension $\rightarrow$ FlushIrp, y is devobj $\rightarrow$ DeviceExtension $\rightarrow$ LockIrp and z is devobj $\rightarrow$ DeviceExtension $\rightarrow$ BlockIrp.
- The procedures called Harness in Fig. 6 are only available under the setting DEFAULT+HARNESS. The assertion in Fig. 6(a) will not be reported by DEFAULT as it is always possible (irrespective of the number of calls to KeAcquireSpinLock and KeReleaseSpinLock) to construct an initial value of LockDepth that suppresses the assertion. When the (stripped) harness is present, this assertion will be reported. Note that the assertion failure in Fig. 6(b) will be caught by both DEFAULT and DEFAULT+HARNESS.

The results on SDV benchmarks are summarized in Table 1. For each *Angelic Verifier* configuration, we report the cumulative running time in thousands of seconds (**CPU**), the numbers of bugs reported (**B**), and the number of false positives (**FP**) and false negatives (**FN**). The experiments were run (sequentially, single-threaded) on a server class machine with two Intel(R) Xeon(R) processors (16 logical cores) executing at 2.4 GHz with 32 GB RAM.

NOEE reports a large number of false positives, confirming that a demonic environment leads to spurious warnings. The DEFAULT configuration, on the other hand, reports no false positives! It is overly-optimistic in some cases resulting in missed defects. It is clear that the out-of-the-box experience, i.e., before environment models have been written, of *Angelic Verifier* (low false positives,

```
// monitor variable
int LockDepth;

// This procedure is only
// available under the option
// default +harness
void Harness() {
  LockDepth = 0;
  IoCancelSpinLock();
}

void IoCancelSpinLock() {
  KeReleaseSpinLock();

  ...
  KeReleaseSpinLock();

  ...
  KeAcquireSpinLock();

  ...
  KeCheckSpinLock();
}

void KeAcquireSpinLock()
{ LockDepth ++; }

void KeReleaseSpinLock()
{ LockDepth − −; }

void KeCheckSpinLock()
{ assert LockDepth > 0; }

        (a)
```

```
const int PASSIVE = 0;
const int DISPATCH = 2;
//monitor variable
int irqlVal ;

// This procedure is only
// available under the option
// default +harness
void Harness() {
  irqlVal = PASSIVE;
  KeRaiseIrql ();
}

void KeRaiseIrql () {
  ...
  irqlVal = DISPATCH;
  ...
  KeReleaseIrql ();
}

void KeReleaseIrql () {
  assert irqlVal == PASSIVE;
  irqlVal = DISPATCH;
}

        (b)
```

```
int completed;
IRP * global_irp ;

void DispatchRoutine(DO *devobj,
          IRP *irp) {
  completed = 0;
  global_irp  = irp ;
  DE *de = devobj→DeviceExtension;
  ...
  IoCompleteRequest(de→FlushIrp);
  ...
  IoCompleteRequest(de→BlockIrp);
  ...
  IoCompleteRequest(de→LockIrp);
}

void IoCompleteRequest(IRP *p) {
  if (p == global_irp ) {
    assert completed != 1;
    completed = 1;
  }
}

        (c)
```

Fig. 6. Code snippets, in C, illustrating the various settings of *Angelic Verifier*

Table 1. Results on SDV benchmarks

Bench	DEFAULT				DEFAULT+HARNESS				NoEE				NoTS				NoAlias			
	CPU (Ks)	B	FP	FN	CPU (Ks)	B	FP	FN	CPU (Ks)	B	FP	FN	CPU (Ks)	B	FP	FN	CPU (Ks)	B	FP	FN
Correct	9.97	0	0	0	16.8	0	0	0	0.28	12	12	0	4.20	2	2	0	15.1	0	0	0
Buggy	3.19	9	0	4	3.52	13	0	0	0.47	21	13	5	2.58	14	3	2	1.42	10	3	6

few false negatives) is far superior to a demonic verifier (very high false positives, few false negatives).

The DEFAULT+HARNESS configuration shows that once the tool could use the (stripped) harness, it found all bugs reported by SDV. The configurations NoTS and NoAlias show that the individual components of the vocabulary were necessary for inferring the right environment specification in the DEFAULT configuration. We also note that the running time of our tool is several times higher than that of SDV; instead of the tedious manual environment modeling effort, the cost shifts to higher running time of the automated verifier.

5.2   Comparison Against PREfix

PREfix is a production tool used internally within Microsoft. It checks for several kinds of programming errors, including checking for null-pointer dereferences,

Table 2. Comparison against PREfix on checking for null-pointer dereferences

Bench	stats		PREfix	DEFAULT							DEFAULT-AA	
	Procs	KLOC	B	CPU(Ks)	B	PM	FP	FN	PRE-FP	PRE-FN	CPU(Ks)	B
Mod 1	453	37.2	14	2.7	26	14	4	0	0	1	1.8	26
Mod 2	64	6.5	3	0.2	0	0	0	3	0	0	0.2	0
Mod 3	479	56.6	5	5.8	11	3	4	2	0	1	1.7	6
Mod 4	382	37.8	4	1.8	3	0	0	0	4	3	1.1	2
Mod 5	284	30.9	6	0.8	12	6	1	0	0	0	0.4	11
Mod 6	37	8.4	7	0.1	10	7	0	0	0	0	0.1	10
Mod 7	184	20.9	10	0.6	11	10	0	0	0	1	0.4	11
Mod 8	400	43.8	5	2.9	15	5	1	0	0	1	1.0	15
Mod 9	40	3.2	7	0.1	8	7	0	0	0	0	0.1	8
Mod 10	998	76.5	7	24.9	8	3	1	4	0	4	16.0	4
total	–	321	68	39.9	104	54	11	9	4	11	22.8	93

on the Windows code base. We targeted *AngelicVerifier* to find null-pointer exceptions and compared against PREfix on 10 modules selected randomly, such that PREfix reported at least one defect in the module. Table 2 reports the sizes of these modules. (The names are hidden for proprietary reasons.)

We used two *AngelicVerifier* configurations: DEFAULT-AA uses a vocabulary of only aliasing constraints. DEFAULT uses the same vocabulary along with angelic assertions: an assert false is injected after any statement of the form assume e == null. This enforces that if the programmer anticipated an expression being *null* at some point in the program, then *AngelicVerifier* should not impose an environment specification that makes this check redundant.

Scalability. This set of benchmarks were several times harder than the SDV benchmarks for our tool chain. This is because of the larger codebase, but also because checking *null*-ness requires tracking of pointers in the heap, whereas SDV's type-state properties are mostly control-flow based and require minimal tracking of pointers. To address the scale, we use two standard tricks. First, we use a cheap alias analysis to prove many of the dereferences safe and only focus *AngelicVerifier* on the rest. Second, *AngelicVerifier* explores different entrypoints of the program in parallel. We used the same machine as for the previous experiment, and limited parallelism to 16 threads (one per available core). Further, we optimized ExplainError to avoid looking at assume statements along the trace, i.e., it can only block the failing assertion. This can result in ExplainError returning a stronger-than-necessary condition but improves the convergence time of *AngelicVerifier*. This is a limitation that we are planning to address in future work.

Table 2 shows the comparison between PREfix and *AngelicVerifier*. In each case, the number of bug reports is indicated as **B** and the running time as **CPU** (in thousands of seconds). We found *AngelicVerifier* to be more verbose than PREfix, producing a higher number of reports (104 to 68). However, this was mostly because *AngelicVerifier* reported multiple failures with the same cause. For instance, x = null; if(...){*x = ...}else{*x = ...} would be flagged as two buggy traces by *Angelic Verifier* but only one by PREfix. Thus, there is potential for post-processing *Angelic Verifier*'s output, but this is orthogonal to the goals of this paper.

We report the number of PREfix traces matched by some trace of *Angelic Verifier* as **PM**. To save effort, we consider all such traces as true positives. We manually examined the rest of the traces. We classified traces reported by *Angelic Verifier* but not by PREfix as either false positives of *Angelic Verifier* (**FP**) or as false negatives of PREfix (**PRE-FN**). The columns **FN** and **PRE-FP** are the duals, for traces reported by PREfix but not by *Angelic Verifier*.

PREfix is not a desktop application; one can only invoke it as a background service that runs on a dedicated cluster. Consequently, we do not have the running times of PREfix. *Angelic Verifier* takes 11 hours to consume all benchmarks, totaling 321 KLOC, which is very reasonable (for, say, overnight testing on a single machine).

Most importantly, *Angelic Verifier* is able to find most (80 %) of the bugs caught by PREfix, without any environment modeling! We verified that under a demonic environment, the Corral verifier reports 396 traces, most of which are false positives.

Angelic Verifier has 11 false positives; 5 of these are due to missing stubs (e.g., a call to the KeBugCheck routine does not return, but *Angelic Verifier*, in the absence of its implementation, does not consider this to be a valid specification). All of these 5 were suppressed when we added a model of the missing stubs. The other 6 reports turn out to be a bug in our compiler front-end, where it produced the wrong IR for certain features of C. (Thus, they are not issues with *Angelic Verifier*.) *Angelic Verifier* has 9 false negatives. Out of these, 1 is due to a missing stub (where it was valid for it to return a *null* pointer), 4 due to Corral timing out, and 5 due to our front-end issues.

Interestingly, PREfix misses 11 valid defects that *Angelic Verifier* reports. Out of these, 6 are reported by *Angelic Verifier* because it finds an inconsistency with an angelic assertion; we believe PREfix does not look for inconsistencies. We are unsure of the reason why PREfix misses the other 5. We have reported these new defects to the product teams and are awaiting a reply. We also found 4 false positives in PREfix's results (due to infeasible path conditions).

A comparison between DEFAULT and DEFAULT-AA reveals that 11 traces were found because of an inconsistency with an angelic assertion. We have already mentioned that 6 of these are valid defects. The other 5 are again due to front-end issues.

In summary, *Angelic Verifier* matched 80 % of PREfix's reports, found new defects, and reported very few false positives.

6   Related Work

Our work is closely related to previous work on abductive reasoning [7,10,11,20] in program verification. Dillig et al. [20] perform abductive reasoning based on quantifier elimination of variables in wlp that do not appear in the minimum satisfying assignment of $\neg wlp$. The method requires quantifier elimination that is difficult in the presence of richer theories such as quantifiers and uninterpreted functions. Our method *ProjectAtoms* can be seen as a (lightweight) method for performing Boolean quantifier elimination (without interpreting the theory predicates) that we have found to be effective in practice. It can be shown that the specifications obtained by the two methods can be incomparable, even for arithmetic programs. Calcagno et al. use bi-abductive reasoning to perform bottom-up shape analysis [10] of programs, but performed only in the context of intraprocedural reasoning. In comparison of this work, we provide configurability by being able to control parts of vocabulary and the check for permissiveness using $\hat{\mathcal{A}}$. The work on *almost-correct specifications* [7] provides a method for *minimally* weakening the wlp over a set of predicates to construct specifications that disallow dead code. However, the method is expensive and can be only applied intraprocedurally.

Several program verification techniques have been proposed to detect semantic inconsistency bugs [21] in recent years [19,23,36]. Our work can be instantiated to detect this class of bugs (even interprocedurally); however, it may not be the most scalable approach to perform the checks. The work on *angelic non-determinism* [8] allows for checking if the non-deterministic operations can be replaced with deterministic code to succeed the assertions. Although similar in principle, our end goal is bug finding with high confidence, as opposed to program synthesis. The work on *angelic debugging* [12] and BugAssist [26] similarly look for relevant expressions to relax to fix a failing test case. The difference is that the focus is more on debugging failing test cases and repairing a program.

The work on ranking static analysis warnings using statistical measures is orthogonal and perhaps complementary to our technique [28]. Since these techniques do not exploit program semantics, such techniques can only be used as a post-processing step (thus offering little control to users of a tool). Finally, work on *differential static analysis* [2] can be leveraged to suppress a class of warnings with respect to another program that can serve as a specification [29,32]. Our work does not require any additional program as a specification and therefore can be more readily applied to standard verification tasks. The work on CBUGS [27] leverages sequential interleavings as a specification while checking concurrent programs.

7 Conclusions

We presented the angelic verification framework that constrains a verifier to search for warnings that cannot be precluded with acceptable specifications over unknowns from the environment. Our framework is parameterized to allow a user to choose different instantiations to fit the precision-recall tradeoff. Preliminary experiments indicate that such a tool can indeed be competitive with industrial tools, even without any modeling effort. With subsequent modeling (e.g. adding a harness), the same tool can find more interesting warnings.

References

1. Arlt, S., Schäf, M.: Joogie: infeasible code detection for java. In: Madhusudan, P., Seshia, S.A. (eds.) CAV 2012. LNCS, vol. 7358, pp. 767–773. Springer, Heidelberg (2012)
2. Lahiri, S.K., Vaswani, K., Hoare, C.A.R.: Differential static analysis: opportunities, applications, and challenges. In: Proceedings of the Workshop on Future of Software Engineering Research, FoSER 2010, at the 18th ACM SIGSOFT, International Symposium on Foundations of Software Engineering, November 7-11, 2010, pp. 201–2014, Santa Fe, NM, USA (2010)
3. Ball, T., Levin, V., Rajamani, S.K.: A decade of software model checking with SLAM. Commun. ACM **54**(7), 68–76 (2011)
4. Barnett, M., Leino, K.R.M.: Weakest-precondition of unstructured programs. In: Program Analysis For Software Tools and Engineering (PASTE 2005), pp. 82–87 (2005)
5. Barnett, M., Qadeer, S.: BCT: a translator from MSIL to Boogie. In: Seventh Workshop on Bytecode Semantics, Verification, Analysis and Transformation (2012)
6. Bessey, A., Block, K., Chelf, B., Chou, A., Fulton, B., Hallem, S., Henri-Gros, C., Kamsky, A., McPeak, S., Engler, D.: A few billion lines of code later: using static analysis to find bugs in the real world. Commun. ACM **53**(2), 66–75 (2010)
7. Blackshear, S., Lahiri, S.K.: Almost-correct specifications: a modular semantic framework for assigning confidence to warnings. In: ACM SIGPLAN Conference on Programming Language Design and Implementation, PLDI 2013, pp. 209–218, Seattle, WA, USA, 16–19 Jun 2013
8. Bodík, R., Chandra, S., Galenson, J., Kimelman, D., Tung, N., Barman, S., Rodarmor, C.: Programming with angelic nondeterminism. In: Principles of Programming Languages (POPL 2010), pp. 339–352 (2010)
9. Bush, W.R., Pincus, J.D., Sielaff, D.J.: A static analyzer for finding dynamic programming errors. Softw. Pract. Exper. **30**(7), 775–802 (2000)
10. Calcagno, C., Distefano, D., O'Hearn, P.W., Yang, H.: Compositional shape analysis by means of bi-abduction. In: Proceedings of the 36th ACM SIGPLAN-SIGACT Symposium on Principles of Programming Languages, POPL 2009, pp. 289–300, Savannah, GA, USA, 21–23 Jan 2009
11. Chandra, S., Fink, S.J., Sridharan, M.: Snugglebug: a powerful approach to weakest preconditions. In: Programming Language Design and Implementation (PLDI 2009), pp. 363–374 (2009)
12. Chandra, S., Torlak, E., Barman, S., Bodik, R.: Angelic debugging. In: Proceedings of the 33rd International Conference on Software Engineering, ICSE 2011, pp. 121–130. ACM, New York, NY, USA (2011)
13. Clarke, E.M., Grumberg, O., Peled, D.A.: Model Checking. MIT Press, Cambridge (2000)
14. Clarke, E.M., Kroening, D., Yorav, K.: Behavioral consistency of C and verilog programs using bounded model checking. In: Proceedings of the 40th Design Automation Conference, DAC 2003, pp. 368–371, Anaheim, CA, USA, 2–6 Jun 2003
15. Condit, J., Hackett, B., Lahiri, S.K., Qadeer, S.: Unifying type checking and property checking for low-level code. In: Principles of Programming Languages (POPL 2009), pp. 302–314 (2009)
16. Cousot, P., Cousot, R.: Abstract interpretation : a unified lattice model for the static analysis of programs by construction or approximation of fixpoints. In: Symposium on Principles of Programming Languages (POPL 1977), ACM Press (1977)

17. Detlefs, D., Nelson, G., Saxe, J.B.: Simplify: a theorem prover for program checking. J. ACM **52**(3), 365–473 (2005)
18. Dijkstra, E.W.: Guarded commands, nondeterminacy and formal derivation of programs. Commun. ACM **18**(8), 453–457 (1975)
19. Dillig, I., Dillig, T., Aiken, A.: Static error detection using semantic inconsistency inference. In: Programming Language Design and Implementation (PLDI 2007), pp. 435–445 (2007)
20. Dillig, I., Dillig, T., Aiken, A.: Automated error diagnosis using abductive inference. In: Proceedings of the 33rd ACM SIGPLAN Conference on Programming Language Design and Implementation, PLDI 2012, pp. 181–192. ACM, New York, NY, USA, (2012)
21. Engler, D.R., Chen, D.Y., Chou, A.: Bugs as inconsistent behavior: a general approach to inferring errors in systems code. In: Symposium on Operating Systems Principles (SOSP 2001), pp. 57–72 (2001)
22. Graf, S., Saïdi, H.: Construction of abstract state graphs with PVS. In: Grumberg, O. (ed.) CAV 1997. LNCS, vol. 1254, pp. 72–83. Springer, Heidelberg (1997)
23. Hoenicke, J., Leino, K.R.M., Podelski, A., Schäf, M., Wies, T.: Doomed program points. Form. Meth. Syst. Des. **37**(2–3), 171–199 (2010)
24. Ivančić, F., Yang, Z., Ganai, M.K., Gupta, A., Shlyakhter, I., Ashar, P.: F-SOFT: software verification platform. In: Etessami, K., Rajamani, S.K. (eds.) CAV 2005. LNCS, vol. 3576, pp. 301–306. Springer, Heidelberg (2005)
25. Jhala, R., Majumdar, R.: Path slicing. In: Proceedings of the ACM SIGPLAN 2005 Conference on Programming Language Design and Implementation, pp. 38–47, Chicago, IL, USA, 12–15 Jun 2005
26. Jose, M., Majumdar, R.: Cause clue clauses: error localization using maximum satisfiability. In: Proceedings of the 32nd ACM SIGPLAN Conference on Programming Language Design and Implementation, PLDI 2011, pp. 437–446, San Jose, CA, USA, 4–8 Jun 2011
27. Joshi, S., Lahiri, S.K., Lal, A.: Underspecified harnesses and interleaved bugs. In: Principles of Programming Languages (POPL 2012), pp. 19–30, ACM (2012)
28. Kremenek, T., Engler, D.R.: Z-ranking: using statistical analysis to counter the impact of static analysis approximations. In: Cousot, R. (ed.) SAS 2003. LNCS, vol. 2694, pp. 295–315. Springer, Heidelberg (2003)
29. Lahiri, S.K., McMillan, K.L., Sharma, R., Hawblitzel, C.: Differential assertion checking. In: Joint Meeting of the European Software Engineering Conference and the ACM SIGSOFT Symposium on the Foundations of Software Engineering, ESEC/FSE 2013, pp. 345–355, Saint Petersburg, Russian Federation, 18–26 Aug 2013
30. Lahiri, S.K., Qadeer, S., Galeotti, J.P., Voung, J.W., Wies, T.: Intra-module inference. In: Bouajjani, A., Maler, O. (eds.) CAV 2009. LNCS, vol. 5643, pp. 493–508. Springer, Heidelberg (2009)
31. Lal, A., Qadeer, S., Lahiri, S.K.: A solver for reachability modulo theories. In: Madhusudan, P., Seshia, S.A. (eds.) CAV 2012. LNCS, vol. 7358, pp. 427–443. Springer, Heidelberg (2012)
32. Logozzo, F., Lahiri, S.K., Fähndrich, M., Blackshear, S.: Verification modulo versions: towards usable verification. In: ACM SIGPLAN Conference on Programming Language Design and Implementation, PLDI 2014, p. 32, Edinburgh, United Kingdom, 09–11 Jun 2014
33. McMillan, K.L.: An interpolating theorem prover. In: Jensen, K., Podelski, A. (eds.) TACAS 2004. LNCS, vol. 2988, pp. 16–30. Springer, Heidelberg (2004)

34. Satisfiability modulo theories library (SMT-LIB). http://goedel.cs.uiowa.edu/smtlib/
35. Stump, A., Barrett, C.W., Dill, D.L., Levitt, J.R.: A decision procedure for an extensional theory of arrays. In: IEEE Symposium of Logic in Computer Science (LICS 2001) (2001)
36. Tomb, A., Flanagan, C.: Detecting inconsistencies via universal reachability analysis. In: International Symposium on Software Testing and Analysis (ISSTA 2012) (2012)

The SeaHorn Verification Framework

Arie Gurfinkel[1]([✉]), Temesghen Kahsai[2], Anvesh Komuravelli[3],
and Jorge A. Navas[4]

[1] Software Engineering Institute, Carnegie Mellon University, Pittsburgh, USA
arie@sei.cmu.edu
[2] NASA Ames, Carnegie Mellon University, Pittsburgh, USA
temesghen.kahsaiazene@nasa.gov
[3] Computer Science Department, Carnegie Mellon University, Pittsburgh, USA
anvesh@cs.cmu.edu
[4] NASA Ames, SGT, Pittsburgh, USA
jorge.a.navaslaserna@nasa.gov

Abstract. In this paper, we present SEAHORN, a software verification framework. The key distinguishing feature of SEAHORN is its modular design that separates the concerns of the syntax of the programming language, its operational semantics, and the verification semantics. SEAHORN encompasses several novelties: it (a) encodes verification conditions using an efficient yet precise inter-procedural technique, (b) provides flexibility in the verification semantics to allow different levels of precision, (c) leverages the state-of-the-art in software model checking and abstract interpretation for verification, and (d) uses Horn-clauses as an intermediate language to represent verification conditions which simplifies interfacing with multiple verification tools based on Horn-clauses. SEAHORN provides users with a powerful verification tool and researchers with an extensible and customizable framework for experimenting with new software verification techniques. The effectiveness and scalability of SEAHORN are demonstrated by an extensive experimental evaluation using benchmarks from SV-COMP 2015 and real avionics code.

1 Introduction

In this paper, we present SEAHORN, an LLVM-based [38] framework for verification of safety properties of programs. SEAHORN is a fully automated verifier that verifies user-supplied assertions as well as a number of built-in safety properties. For example, SEAHORN provides built-in checks for buffer and signed integer

This material is based upon work funded and supported by NASA Contract No. NNX14AI09G, NSF Award No. 1422705 and by the Department of Defense under Contract No. FA8721-05-C-0003 with Carnegie Mellon University for the operation of the Software Engineering Institute, a federally funded research and development center. Any opinions, findings and conclusions or recommendations expressed in this material are those of the author(s) and do not necessarily reflect the views of the United States Department of Defense, NASA or NSF. This material has been approved for public release and unlimited distribution. DM-0002153.

© Springer International Publishing Switzerland 2015
D. Kroening and C.S. Păsăreanu (Eds.): CAV 2015, Part I, LNCS 9206, pp. 343–361, 2015.
DOI: 10.1007/978-3-319-21690-4_20

overflows. More generally, SEAHORN is a framework that simplifies development and integration of new verification techniques. Its main features are:

1. *It decouples a programming language syntax and semantics from the underlying verification technique.* Different programming languages include a diverse assortments of features, many of which are purely syntactic. Handling them fully is a major effort for new tool developers. We tackle this problem in SEAHORN by separating the language syntax, its operational semantics, and the underlying verification semantics – the semantics used by the verification engine. Specifically, we use the LLVM front-end(s) to deal with the idiosyncrasies of the syntax. We use LLVM intermediate representation (IR), called the *bitcode*, to deal with the operational semantics, and apply a variety of transformations to simplify it further. In principle, since the bitcode has been formalized [54], this provides us with a well-defined formal semantics. Finally, we use Constrained Horn Clauses (CHC) to logically represent the verification condition (VC).

2. *It provides an efficient and precise analysis of programs with procedure using new inter-procedural verification techniques.* SEAHORN summarizes the input-output behavior of procedures efficiently without inlining. The expressiveness of the summaries is not limited to linear arithmetic (as in our earlier tools) but extends to richer logics, including, for instance, arrays. Moreover, it includes a program transformation that lifts deep assertions closer to the main procedure. This increases context-sensitivity of intra-procedural analyses (used both in verification and compiler optimization), and has a significant impact on our inter-procedural verification algorithms.

3. *It allows developers to customize the verification semantics and offers users with verification semantics of various degrees of precision.* SEAHORN is fully parametric in the (small-step operational) semantics used for the generation of VCs. The level of abstraction in the built-in semantics varies from considering only LLVM numeric registers to considering the whole heap (modeled as a collection of non-overlapping arrays). In addition to generating VCs based on small-step semantics [48], it can also automatically lift small-step semantics to large-step [7,28] (a.k.a. Large Block Encoding, or LBE).

4. *It uses Constrained Horn Clauses (CHC) as its intermediate verification language.* CHC provide a convenient and elegant way to formally represent many encoding styles of verification conditions. The recent popularity of CHC as an intermediate language for verification engines makes it possible to interface SEAHORN with a variety of new and emerging tools.

5. *It builds on the state-of-the-art in Software Model Checking (SMC) and Abstract Interpretation (AI).* SMC and AI have independently led over the years to the production of analysis tools that have a substantial impact on the development of real world software. Interestingly, the two exhibit complementary strengths and weaknesses (see e.g., [1,10,24,27]). While SMC so far has been proved stronger on software that is mostly control driven, AI is quite effective on data-dependent programs. SEAHORN combines SMT-based model checking techniques with program invariants supplied by an abstract interpretation-based tool.

6. Finally, *it is implemented on top of the open-source LLVM compiler infrastructure*. The latter is a well-maintained, well-documented, and continuously improving framework. It allows SEAHORN users to easily integrate program analyses, transformations, and other tools that targets LLVM. Moreover, since SEAHORN analyses LLVM IR, this allows to exploit a rapidly-growing frontier of LLVM front-ends, encompassing a diverse set of languages. SEAHORN itself is released as open-source as well (source code can be downloaded from http://seahorn.github.io).

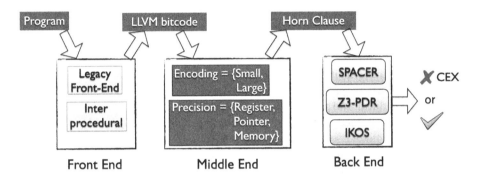

Fig. 1. Overview of SEAHORN architecture.

The design of SEAHORN provides users, developers, and researchers with an extensible and customizable environment for experimenting with and implementing new software verification techniques. SEAHORN is implemented in C++ in the LLVM compiler infrastructure [38]. The overall approach is illustrated in Fig. 1. SEAHORN has been developed in a modular fashion; its architecture is layered in three parts:

Front-End: Takes an LLVM based program (e.g., C) input program and generates LLVM IR bitcode. Specifically, it performs the pre-processing and optimization of the bitcode for verification purposes. More details are reported in Sect. 2.

Middle-End: Takes as input the optimized LLVM bitcode and emits verification condition as Constrained Horn Clauses (CHC). The middle-end is in charge of selecting the encoding of the VCs and the degree of precision. More details are reported in Sect. 3.

Back-End: Takes CHC as input and outputs the result of the analysis. In principle, any verification engine that digests CHC clauses could be used to discharge the VCs. Currently, SEAHORN employs several SMT-based model checking engines based on PDR/IC3 [13], including SPACER [35,36] and GPDR [33]. Complementary, SEAHORN uses the abstract interpretation-based analyzer IKOS (Inference Kernel for Open Static Analyzers) [14] for providing numerical invariants[1]. More details are reported in Sect. 4.

---

[1] While conceptually, IKOS should run on CHC, currently it uses its own custom IR.

The effectiveness and scalability of SEAHORN are demonstrated by our extensive experimental evaluation in Sect. 5 and the results of SV-COMP 2015.

Related Work. Automated analysis of software is an active area of research. There is a large number of tools with different capabilities and trade-offs [6,8,9,15–18,20,42]. Our approach on separating the program semantics from the verification engine has been previously proposed in numerous tools. From those, the tool SMACK [49] is the closest to SEAHORN. Like SEAHORN, SMACK targets programs at the LLVM-IR level. However, SMACK targets Boogie intermediate verification language [22] and Boogie-based verifiers to construct and discharge the proof obligations. SEAHORN differs from SMACK in several ways: (i) SEAHORN uses CHC as its intermediate verification language, which allows to target different solvers and verification techniques (ii) it tightly integrates and combines both state-of-the-art software model checking techniques and abstract interpretation and (iii) it provides an automatic inter-procedural analysis to reason modularly about programs with procedures.

Inter-procedural and modular analysis is critical for scaling verification tools and has been addressed by many researchers (e.g., [2,33,35,37,40,51]). Our approach of using mixed-semantics [30] as a source-to-source transformation has been also explored in [37]. While in [37], the mixed-semantics is done at the verification semantics (Boogie in this case), in SEAHORN it is done in the front-end level allowing mixed-semantics to interact with compiler optimizations.

Constrained Horn clauses have been recently proposed [11] as an intermediate (or exchange) format for representing verification conditions. However, they have long been used in the context of static analysis of imperative and object-oriented languages (e.g., [41,48]) and more recently adopted by an increasing number of solvers (e.g., [12,23,33,36,40]) as well as other verifiers such as UFO [4], HSF [26], VeriMAP [21], Eldarica [50], and TRACER [34].

2 Pre-Processing for Verification

In our experience, performance of even the most advanced verification algorithms is significantly impacted by the front-end transformations. In SEAHORN, the front-end plays a very significant role in the overall architecture. SEAHORN provides two front-ends: a *legacy* front-end and an *inter-procedural* front-end.

The Legacy Front-End. This front-end has been used by SEAHORN for the SV-COMP 2015 competition [29] (for C programs). It was originally developed for UFO [3]. First, the input C program is pre-processed with CIL [46] to insert line markings for printing user-friendly counterexamples, define missing functions that are implicitly defined (e.g., malloc-like functions), and initialize all local variables. Moreover, it creates stubs for functions whose addresses can be taken and replaces function pointers to those functions with function pointers to the stubs. Second, the result is translated into LLVM-IR bitcode, using `llvm-gcc`. After that, it performs compiler optimizations and preprocessing to simplify the verification task. As a preprocessing step, we further initialize any uninitialized registers using non-deterministic functions. This is used to bridge the gap between the verification semantics (which assumes a non-deterministic assignment) and the compiler semantics, which tries to take advantage of the undefined behavior of uninitialized variables to perform code optimizations. We perform a number of program transformations such as function inlining, conversion to static single assignment (SSA) form, dead code elimination, peephole optimizations, CFG simplifications, etc. We also internalize all functions to enable global optimizations such as replacement of global aggregates with scalars.

The legacy front-end has been very effective for solving SV-COMP (2013, 2014, and 2015) problems. However, it has its own limitations: its design is not modular and it relies on multiple unsupported legacy tools (such as `llvm-gcc` and LLVM versions 2.6 and 2.9). Thus, it is difficult to maintain and extend.

The Inter-Procedural Front-End. In this new front-end, SEAHORN can take any input program that can be translated into LLVM bitcode. For example, SEAHORN uses `clang` and `gcc` via `DragonEgg` [2]. Our goal is to make SEAHORN not to be limited to C programs, but applicable (with various degrees of success) to a broader set of languages based on LLVM (e.g., C++, Objective C, and Swift).

Once we have obtained LLVM bitcode, the front-end is split into two main sub-components. The first one is a pre-processor that performs optimizations and transformations similar to the ones performed by the legacy front-end. Such pre-processing is optional as its only mission is to optimize the LLVM bitcode to make the verification task 'easier'. The second part is focused on a reduced set of transformations mostly required to produce correct results even if the pre-processor is disabled. It also performs SSA transformation and internalizes functions, but in addition, lowers `switch` instructions into `if-then-else`s, ensures only one exit block per function, inlines global initializers into the main procedure, and identifies `assert`-like functions.

Although this front-end can optionally inline functions similarly to the legacy front-end, its major feature is a transformation that can significantly help the verification engine to produce procedure summaries.

One typical problem in proving safety of large programs is that assertions can be nested very deep inside the call graph. As a result, counterexamples are longer and it is harder to decide for the verification engine what is relevant for the property of interest. To mitigate this problem, the front-end provides a transformation based on the concept of *mixed semantics*[3] [30,37]. It relies on the simple observation that any call to a procedure P either fails inside the call and therefore P does not return, or returns successfully from the call. Based on this, any call to P can be instrumented as follows:

---

[2] `DragonEgg` (http://dragonegg.llvm.org/) is a GCC plugin that replaces GCC's optimizers and code generators with those from LLVM. As result, the output can be LLVM bitcode.

[3] The term *mixed* semantics refers to a combination of small- with big-step operational semantics.

– if P may fail, then make a copy of P's body (in main) and jump to the copy.
– if P may succeed, then make the call to P as usual. Since P is known not to fail each assertion in P can be safely replaced with an *assume*.

Upon completion, only the main function has assertions and each procedure is inlined at most once. The explanation for the latter is that a function call is inlined only if it fails and hence, its call stack can be ignored. A key property of this transformation is that it preserves reachability and non-termination properties (see [30] for details). Since this transformation is not very common in other verifiers, we illustrate its working on an example.

main ()	*main$_{new}$* ()	$p1_{entry}$:	$p1_{new}$ ()
$\quad$ p1 (); p1 ();	$\quad$ if (*) goto $p1_{entry}$;	$\quad$ if (*) goto $p2_{entry}$;	$\quad$ $p2_{new}$ ();
$\quad$ assert (c1);	$\quad$ else $p1_{new}$ ();	$\quad$ else $p2_{new}$ ();	$\quad$ assume (c2);
p1 ()	$\quad$ if (*) goto $p1_{entry}$;	$\quad$ if ($\neg$c2) goto *error*;	$p2_{new}$ ()
$\quad$ p2 ();	$\quad$ else $p1_{new}$ ();	$p2_{entry}$:	$\quad$ assume (c3);
$\quad$ assert (c2);	$\quad$ if ($\neg$c1) goto *error*;	$\quad$ if ($\neg$c3) goto *error*;	
p2 ()	$\quad$ assume (false);	$\quad$ assume (false);	
$\quad$ assert (c3);		*error* : assert (false);	

Fig. 2. A program before and after mixed-semantics transformation.

Example 1 (Mixed-semantics transformation). On the left in Fig. 2 we show a small program consisting of a main procedure calling two other procedures $p1$ and $p2$ with three assertions $c1$, $c2$, and $c3$. On the right, we show the new program after the mixed-semantics transformation. First, when main calls $p1$ it is transformed into a non-deterministic choice between (a) jumping into the entry block of $p1$ or (b) calling $p1$. The case (a) represents the situation when $p1$ fails and it is done by inlining the body of $p1$ (labeled by $p1_{entry}$) into *main* and adding a goto statement to $p1_{entry}$. The case (b) considers the case when $p1$ succeeds and hence it simply duplicates the function $p1$ but replacing all the assertions with assumptions since no failure is possible. Note that while $p1$ is called twice, it is inlined only once. Furthermore, each inlined function ends up with an "assume (false)" indicating that execution dies. Hence, any complete execution of a transformed program corresponds to a bad execution of the original one. Finally, an interesting side-effect of mixed-semantics is that it can provide some context-sensitivity to context-insensitive intra-procedural analyses.

3   Flexible Semantics for Developers

SEAHORN provides out-of-the-box verification semantics with different degrees of precision. Furthermore, to accommodate a variety of applications, SEAHORN is designed to be easily extended with a custom semantics as well. In this section, we illustrate the various dimensions of semantic flexibility present in SEAHORN.

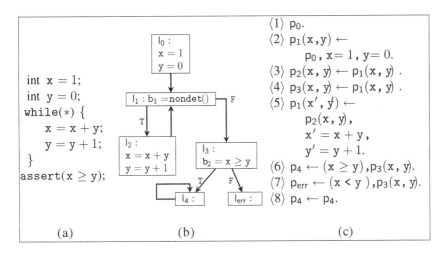

Fig. 3. (a) Program, (b) Control-Flow Graph, and (c) Verification Conditions.

Encoding Verification Conditions. SEAHORN is parametric in the semantics used for VC encoding. It provides two different semantics encodings: (a) a small-step encoding (exemplified below in Fig. 3) and (b) a large-block encoding (LBE) [7]. A user can choose the encoding depending on the particular application. In practice, LBE is often more efficient but small-step might be more useful if a fine-grained proof or counterexample is needed. For example, SEAHORN used the LBE encoding in SV-COMP [29].

Regardless of the encoding, SEAHORN uses CHC to encode the VCs. Given the sets $\mathcal{F}$ of function symbols, $\mathcal{P}$ of predicate symbols, and $\mathcal{V}$ of variables, a *Constrained Horn Clause (CHC)* is a formula

$$\forall \mathcal{V} \cdot (\phi \wedge p_1[X_1] \wedge \cdots \wedge p_k[X_k] \rightarrow h[X]), \text{ for } k \geq 0$$

where: ϕ is a constraint over $\mathcal{F}$ and $\mathcal{V}$ with respect to some background theory; $X_i, X \subseteq \mathcal{V}$ are (possibly empty) vectors of variables; $p_i[X_i]$ is an application $p(t_1, \ldots, t_n)$ of an n-ary predicate symbol $p \in \mathcal{P}$ for first-order terms t_i constructed from $\mathcal{F}$ and X_i; and $h[X]$ is either defined analogously to p_i or is $\mathcal{P}$-free (i.e., no $\mathcal{P}$ symbols occur in h). Here, h is called the *head* of the clause and $\phi \wedge p_1[X_1] \wedge \ldots \wedge p_k[X_k]$ is called the *body*. A clause is called a *query* if its head is $\mathcal{P}$-free, and otherwise, it is called a *rule*. A rule with body true is called a *fact*. We say a clause is *linear* if its body contains at most one predicate symbol, otherwise, it is called *non-linear*. In this paper, we follow the Constraint Logic Programming (CLP) convention of representing Horn clauses as $h[X] \leftarrow \phi, p_1[X_1], \ldots, p_k[X_k]$.

A set of CHCs is satisfiable if there exists an interpretation $\mathcal{I}$ of the predicate symbols $\mathcal{P}$ such that each constraint ϕ is true under $\mathcal{I}$. Without loss of generality, to check if a program $\mathcal{A}$ satisfies a safety property α_{safe} amounts to establishing the (un)satifiability of CHCs encoding the VCs of $\mathcal{A}$, as described next.

Example 2 (Small-step encoding of VCs using Horn clauses). Fig. 3(a) shows a program which increments two variables x and y within a non-deterministic loop. After the loop is executed we would like to prove that x cannot be less than y. Ignoring wraparound situations, it is easy to see that the program is safe since x and y are initially non-negative numbers and x is greater than y. Since the loop increases x by a greater amount than y, at its exit x cannot be smaller than y. Figure 3(b) depicts, its corresponding Control Flow Graph (CFG) and Fig. 3(c) shows its VCs encoded as a set of CHCs.

The set of CHCs in Fig. 3(c) essentially represents the *small-step* operational semantics of the CFG. Each basic block is encoded as a Horn clause. A basic block label l_i in the CFG is translated into $\mathsf{p}_i(X_1, \ldots, X_n)$ such that $\mathsf{p}_i \in \mathcal{P}$ and $\{X_1, \ldots, X_n\} \subseteq \mathcal{V}$ is the set of live variables at the entry of block l_i. A Horn clause can model both the control flow and data of each block in a very succinct way. For instance, the fact $\langle 1 \rangle$ represents that the entry block l_0 is reachable. Clause $\langle 2 \rangle$ describes that if l_0 is reachable then l_1 should be reachable too. Moreover, its body contains the constraints $x = 1 \wedge y = 0$ representing the initial state of the program. Clause $\langle 5 \rangle$ models the loop body by stating that the control flow moves to l_2 from l_1 after transforming the state of the program variables through the constraints $x' = x + y$ and $y' = y + 1$, where the primed versions represent the values of the variables after the execution of the arithmetic operations. Based on this encoding, the program in Fig. 3(a) is safe if and only if the set of recursive clauses in Fig. 3(c) augmented with the query $\mathsf{p}_{\mathsf{err}}$ is unsatisfiable. Note that since we are only concerned about proving unsatisfiability any safe final state can be represented by an infinite loop (e.g., clause (8)).

SEAHORN middle-end offers a very simple interface for developers to implement an encoding of the verification semantics that fits their needs. At the core of the SEAHORN middle-end lies the concept of a symbolic store. A *symbolic store* simply maps program variables to symbolic values. The other fundamental concept is how different parts of a program are *symbolically executed*. The small-step verification semantics is provided by implementing a symbolic execution interface that symbolically executes LLVM instructions relative to the symbolic store. This interface is automatically lifted to large-step semantics as necessary.

Modeling Statements with Different Degrees of Abstraction. The SEAHORN middle-end includes verification semantics with different levels of abstraction. Those are, from the coarsest to the finest:

Registers only: only models LLVM numeric registers. In this case, the constraints part of CHC is over the theory of Linear Integer Arithmetic (LIA).

Registers + Pointers (without memory content): models numeric and pointer registers. This is sufficient to capture pointer arithmetic and determine whether a pointer is NULL. Memory addresses are also encoded as integers. Hence, the constraints remain over LIA.

Registers + Pointers + Memory: models numeric and pointer registers and the heap. The heap is modeled by a collection of non-overlapping arrays. The constraints are over the combined theories of arrays and LIA.

To model heap, SEAHORN uses a heap analysis called *Data Structure Analysis (DSA)* [39]. In general, DSA is a context-sensitive, field-sensitive heap analysis that builds an explicit model of the heap. However, in SEAHORN, we use a simpler context-insensitive variant that is similar to Steensgaard's pointer analysis [52].

In DSA, the memory is partitioned into a heap, a stack, and global objects. The analysis builds for each function a *DS graph* where each node represents a potentially infinite set of memory objects and distinct *DSA nodes* express disjoint sets of objects. Edges in the graph represents *points-to* relationships between DS nodes. Each node is typed and determines the number of fields and outgoing edges in a node. A node can have one outgoing edge per field but each field can have at most one outgoing edge. This restriction is key for scalability and it is preserved by *merging* nodes whenever it is violated. A DS graph contains also *call nodes* representing the effect of function calls.

Given a DS graph we can map each DS node to an array. Then each memory load (read) and store (write) in the LLVM bitcode can be associated with a particular DS node (i.e., array). For memory writes, SEAHORN creates a new array variable representing the new state of the array after the write operation.

Inter-Procedural Proofs. For most real programs verifying a function separately from each possible caller (i.e., *context-sensitivity*) is necessary for scalability. The version of SEAHORN for SV-COMP 2015 [29] achieved full context-sensitivity by inlining all program functions. Although in-lining is often an effective solution for small and medium-size programs it is well known that suffers from an exponential blow up in the size of the original program. Even more importantly inlining cannot produce inter-procedural proofs nor counterexamples which are often highly desired.

We tackle this problem in SEAHORN, by providing an encoding that allows inter-procedural proofs. We illustrate this procedure via the example in Fig. 4. The upper box shows a program with three procedures: *main*, *foo*, and *bar*. The program swaps two numbers x and y. The procedure *foo* adds two numbers and *bar* subtracts them. At the exit of *main* we want to prove that the program indeed swaps the two inputs. To show all relevant aspects of the inter-procedural encoding we add a trivial assertion in *bar* that checks that whenever x and y are non-negative the input x is greater or equal than the return value.

The lower box of Fig. 4 illustrates the corresponding verification conditions encoded as CHCs. The new encoding follows a small-step style as the intra-procedural encoding shown in Fig. 3 but with two major distinctions. First, notice that the CHCs are not linear anymore (e.g., the rule denoted by m_{assrt}). Each function call has been replaced with a *summary rule* (f and b) representing the effect of calling to the functions foo and bar, respectively. The second difference is how assertions are encoded. In the intra-procedural case, a program is

$main()$	
$x = \mathsf{nondet}();$	$foo(x, y)$
$y = \mathsf{nondet}();$	$res = x + y;$
$x_{old} = x;$	return $res;$
$y_{old} = y;$	$bar(x, y)$
$x = foo(x, y);$	$res = x - y;$
$y = bar(x, y);$	assert $(\neg\,(x \geq 0 \wedge y \geq 0 \wedge x < res));$
$x = bar(x, y);$	return $res;$
assert $(x = y_{old} \wedge y = x_{old});$	

$\mathsf{m_{entry}}.$	$\mathsf{f_{entry}}(x, y).$
$\mathsf{m_{assrt}}(x_{old}, y_{old}, x, y, e_{out}) \leftarrow$	$\mathsf{f_{exit}}(x, y, res) \leftarrow$
$\quad \mathsf{m_{entry}},$	$\quad \mathsf{f_{entry}}(x, y),$
$\quad x_{old} = x, y_{old} = y,$	$\quad res = x + y.$
$\quad \mathsf{f}(x, y, x_1),$	$\mathsf{f}(x, y, res) \leftarrow \mathsf{f_{exit}}(x, y, res).$
$\quad \mathsf{b}(x_1, y, y_1, \mathsf{false}, e),$	$\mathsf{b_{entry}}(x, y).$
$\quad \mathsf{b}(x_1, y_1, x_2, e, e_{out}).$	$\mathsf{b_{exit}}(x, y, res, e_{out}) \leftarrow$
$\mathsf{m_{err}}(e_{out}) \leftarrow$	$\quad \mathsf{b_{entry}}(x, y),$
$\quad \mathsf{m_{assrt}}(x_{old}, y_{old}, x, y, e), \neg\, e,$	$\quad res = x - y,$
$\quad e_{out} = \neg\,(x = y_{old}, y = x_{old}).$	$\quad e_{out} = (x \geq 0 \wedge y \geq 0 \wedge x < res).$
$\mathsf{m_{err}}(e_{out}) \leftarrow$	$\mathsf{b}(x, y, z, \mathsf{true}, \mathsf{true}).$
$\quad \mathsf{m_{assrt}}(x_{old}, y_{old}, x, y, e_{out}), e_{out}.$	$\mathsf{b}(x, y, z, \mathsf{false}, e_{out}) \leftarrow \mathsf{b_{exit}}(x, y, z, e_{out})$

Fig. 4. A program with procedures (upper) and its verification condition (lower).

unsafe if the query $\mathsf{p_{err}}$ is satisfiable, where $\mathsf{p_{err}}$ is the head of a CHC associated with a special basic block to which all can-fail blocks are redirected. However, with the presence of procedures assertions can be located deeply in the call graph of the program, and therefore, we need to modify the CHCs to propagate error to the main procedure.

In our example, since a call to bar can fail we add two arguments e_{in} and e_{out} to the predicate b where e_{in} indicates if there is an error before the function is called and e_{out} indicates whether the execution of bar produces an error. By doing this, we are able to propagate the error in clause $\mathsf{m_{assrt}}$ across the two calls to bar. We indicate that no error is possible at $main$ before any function is called by unifying false with e_{in} in the first occurrence of b. Within a can-fail procedure we skip the body and set e_{out} to true as soon as an assertion can be violated. Furthermore, if a function is called and e_{in} is already true we can skip its body (e.g., first clause of b). Functions that cannot fail (e.g., foo) are unchanged. The above program is safe if and only if the query $\mathsf{m_{err}}(\mathsf{true})$ is unsatisfiable.

Finally, it is worth mentioning that this propagation of error can be, in theory, avoided if the mixed-semantics transformation described in Sect. 2 is applied. However, this transformation assumes that all functions can be inlined in order to raise all assertions to the main procedure. However, recursive functions and functions that contain LLVM indirect branches (i.e., branches that can jump to a label within the current function specified by an address) are not currently inlined in SEAHORN. For these reasons, our inter-procedural encoding must always consider the propagation of error across Horn clauses.

4   Verification Engines

In principle, SEAHORN can be used with any Horn clause-based verification tool. In the following, we describe two such tools developed recently by ourselves. Notably, the tools discussed below are based on the contrasting techniques of SMT-based model checking and Abstract Interpretation, showcasing the wide applicability of SEAHORN.

4.1   SMT-Based Model Checking with Spacer

SPACER is based on an efficient SMT-based algorithm for model checking procedural programs [35]. Compared to existing SMT-based algorithms (e.g., [2, 26, 31, 40]), the key distinguishing characteristic of SPACER is its compositionality. That is, to check safety of an input program, the algorithm iteratively creates and checks *local* reachability queries for individual procedures (or the unknown predicates of the Horn-clauses). This is crucial to avoid the exponential growth in the size of SMT formulas present in approaches based on monolithic Bounded Model Checking (BMC). To avoid redundancy and enable reuse, we maintain two kinds of summaries for each procedure: *may* and *must*. A may (must) summary of a procedure is a formula over its input-output parameters that over-approximates (under-approximates) the set of all feasible pairs of pre- and post-states.

However, the creation of new reachability queries and summaries involves existentially quantifying auxiliary variables (e.g., local variables of a procedure). To avoid dependencies on such auxiliary variables, we use a technique called *Model Based Projection* (MBP) for lazily and efficiently eliminating existential quantifiers for the theories of Linear Real Arithmetic and Linear Integer Arithmetic. At a high level, given an existentially quantified formula $\exists \overline{x} \cdot \varphi(\overline{x}, \overline{y})$, where φ is quantifier-free, it is expensive to obtain an equivalent quantifier-free formula $\psi(\overline{y})$. Instead, MBP obtains a quantifier-free under-approximation $\eta(\overline{y})$ of $\exists \overline{x} \cdot \varphi(\overline{x}, \overline{y})$. To ensure that η is a useful under-approximation, MBP uses a model-based approach such that given a model $M \models \varphi(\overline{x}, \overline{y})$, it ensures that $M \models \eta(\overline{y})$.

As mentioned in Sect. 3, SEAHORN models memory operations using the extensional theory of arrays (ARR). To handle the resulting Horn clauses, we have recently developed an MBP procedure for ARR. First of all, given a quantified formula $\exists a \cdot \varphi(a, \overline{y})$ where a is an array variable with index sort I and value sort V and φ is quantifier-free, one can obtain an equivalent formula $\exists \overline{i}, \overline{v} \cdot \varphi(\overline{i}, \overline{v}, \overline{y})$ where $\overline{i}$ and $\overline{v}$ are fresh variables of sort I and V, respectively. This can be achieved by a simple modification of the decision procedure for ARR by Stump et al. [53] and we skip the details in the interest of space.[4] We illustrate our MBP procedure below using an example, which is based on the above approach for eliminating existentially quantified array variables.

---

[4] The authors thank Nikolaj Bjørner and Kenneth L. McMillan for helpful discussions.

Let φ denote $(b = a[i_1 \leftarrow v_1]) \vee (a[i_2 \leftarrow v_2][i_3] > 5 \wedge a[i_4] > 0)$, where a and b are array variables whose index and value sorts are both Int, the sort of integers, and all other variables have sort Int. Here, for an array a, we use $a[i \leftarrow v]$ to denote a *store* of v into a at index i and use $a[i]$ to denote the value of a at index i. Suppose that we want to existentially quantify the array variable a. Let $M \models \varphi$. We will consider two possibilities for M:

1. Let $M \models b = a[i_1 \leftarrow v_1]$, i.e., M satisfies the array equality containing a. In this case, our MBP procedure substitutes the term $b[i_1 \leftarrow x]$ for a in φ, where x is a fresh variable of sort Int. That is, the result of MBP is $\exists x \cdot \varphi[b[i_1 \leftarrow x]/a]$.
2. Let $M \models b \neq a[i_1 \leftarrow v_1]$. We use the second disjunct of φ for MBP. Furthermore, let $M \models i_2 \neq i_3$. We then reduce the term $a[i_2 \leftarrow v_2][i_3]$ to $a[i_3]$ to obtain $a[i_3] > 5 \wedge a[i_4] > 0$, using the relevant disjunct of the select-after-store axiom of ARR. We then introduce fresh variables x_3 and x_4 to denote the two select terms on a, obtaining $x_3 > 5 \wedge x_4 > 0$. Finally, we add $i_3 = i_4 \wedge x_3 = x_4$ if $M \models i_3 = i_4$ and add $i_3 \neq i_4$ otherwise, choosing the relevant case of Ackermann reduction, and existentially quantify x_3 and x_4.

The MBP procedure outlined above for ARR is implemented in SPACER. Additionally, the version of SPACER used in SEAHORN contains numerous enhancements compared to [35].

4.2 Abstract Interpretation with Ikos

IKOS [14] is an open-source library of abstract domains with a state-of-the-art fixed-point algorithm [5]. Available abstract domains include: intervals [19], reduced product of intervals with congruences [25], DBMs [43], and octagons [44].

SEAHORN users can choose IKOS as the only back-end engine to discharge proof obligations. However, even if the abstract domain can express precisely the program semantics, due to the join and widening operations, we might lose some precision during the verification. As a consequence, IKOS alone might not be sufficient as a back-end engine. Instead, a more suitable job for IKOS is to supply program invariants to the other engines (e.g. SPACER).

To exemplify this, let us come back to the example of Fig. 3. SPACER alone can discover $x \geq y$ but it misses the vital invariant $y \geq 0$. Thus, it does not terminate. On the contrary, IKOS alone with the abstract domain of DBMs can prove safety immediately. Interestingly, SPACER populated with invariants supplied by IKOS using intervals proves safety even faster.

Although we envision IKOS to be part of the back-end it is currently part of the middle-end translating bitcode to its own custom IR. Note that there is no technical impediment to move IKOS to the back-end. Abstract interpretation tools over Horn clauses have been previously explored successfully, e.g., [32].

5   Experimental Evaluation

In this section, we describe the results of our evaluation on various C program benchmarks. First, we give an overview of SEAHORN performance at SV-COMP 2015 that used the legacy non-inter-procedural front-end. Second, we showcase the new inter-procedural verification flow on the hardest (for SEA-HORN) instances from the competition. Finally, we illustrate a case study of the use of SEAHORN built-in buffer overflow checks on autopilot control software.

Results of SV-COMP 2015. For the competition, we used the legacy front-end described in Sect. 2. The middle-end was configured with the large step semantics and the most precise level of small-step verification semantics (i.e., registers, pointers, and heap). Note, however, that for most benchmarks the heap is almost completely eliminated by the front-end. IKOS with interval abstract domain and Z3-PDR were used on the back-end. Detailed results can be found at http://tinyurl.com/svcomp15.

Overall, SEAHORN won one gold medal in the *Simple* category – benchmarks that depend mostly on control-flow structure and integer variables – two silver medals in the categories *Device Drivers* and *Control Flow*. The former is a set of benchmarks derived from the Linux device drivers and includes a variety of C features including pointers. The latter is a set of benchmarks dependent mostly on the control-flow structure and integer variables. In the device drivers category, SEAHORN was beaten only by BLAST [8] – a tool tuned to analyzing Linux device drivers. Specifically, BLAST got 88 % of the maximum score while SEA-HORN got 85 %. The *Control Flow* category, was won by CPAChecker [9] getting 74 % of the maximum score, while SEAHORN got 69 %. However, SEAHORN is significantly more efficient than most other tools solving most benchmarks much faster.

Results on Hard Benchmarks. SEAHORN participated in SV-COMP 2015 with the *legacy* front-end and using Z3-PDR as the verification back-end. To test the efficiency of the new verification framework in SEAHORN, we ran several experiments on the 215 benchmarks that we either could not verify or took more than a minute to verify in SV-COMP. All experiments have been carried out on an Ubuntu machine with a 2.2 GHz AMD Opteron(TM) Processor 6174 and 516GB RAM with resource limits of 30 min and 15GB for each verification task. In the scatter plots that follow, a diamond indicates a *time-out*, a star indicates a *mem-out*, and a box indicates an anomaly in the back-end tool.

For our first experiment, we used inlining in the front-end and Fig. 5a shows a scatter plot comparing Z3-PDR and SPACER in the back-end. The plot clearly shows the advantages of the various techniques we developed in SPACER, and in particular, of Model Based Projection for efficiently and lazily eliminating existential quantifiers for integers and arrays.

Figure 5b compares the two back-end tools when SEAHORN is using inter-procedural encoding. As the plot shows, Z3-PDR runs out of time on most of the benchmarks whereas SPACER is able to verify many of them.

As mentioned in Sect. 2, inter-procedural encoding is advantageous from a usability point of view. It turns out that it also makes verification easier over-all. To see the advantage of inter-procedural encoding, we used the same tool SPACER in the back-end and compared the running times with and without inlining in

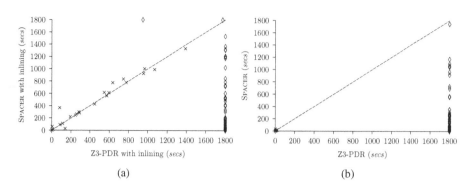

Fig. 5. SPACER vs. Z3-PDR on hard benchmarks (a) with and (b) without inlining

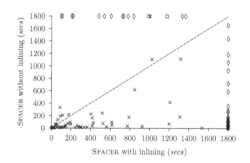

Fig. 6. Advantage of inter-procedural encoding using SPACER.

the front-end. Figure 6 shows a scatter plot of the running times and we see that SPACER takes less time on many benchmarks when inlining is disabled.

SPACER also has a compositional BMC mode (see Sect. 4.1 for details), where no additional computation is performed towards invariant generation after checking safety for a given value of the bound. This helps SPACER show the failure of safety in two additional hard benchmarks, as shown in Table 1. The figure also shows the number of benchmarks verified by Z3-PDR, the back-end tool used in SV-COMP, for comparison.

Table 1. Number of hard benchmarks that are verified as safe/unsafe by SPACER in its normal and BMC mode, and Z3-PDR, with inlining disabled.

	SPACER	SPACER BMC	Z3-PDR	Total verified
SAFE	21	–	3	21
UNSAFE	74	76	7	81

Case Study: Checking Buffer Overflow in Avionics Software. We have evaluated the SEAHORN built-in buffer overflow checks on two autopilot control

Table 2. A comparison between SEAHORN and ANALYZER on autopilot software.

Program	#C	ANALYZER		SEAHORN					
		%W	T	T_F	T_M	T_{SPACER}	T_{FMS}	$T_{\text{SPACER}} + T_{\text{IKOS}}$	T_{FMSI}
mnav.inlined	607	4.7 %	36	2	18	744	764	116 + 52	187
mnav.mixed	815	8.2 %	10	1	8	278	287	139 + 5	153
paparazzi.inlined	343	0 %	85	2	1	–	3	–	3
paparazzi.mixed	684	43 %	15	1	2	3	6	2 + 1	6

software. To prove absence of buffer overflows, we only need to add in the front-end a new LLVM transformation pass that inserts the corresponding checks in the bitcode. The middle-end and back-end are unchanged. If SEAHORN proves the program is safe then it guarantees that the program is free of buffer overflows.

Table 2 shows the results of our evaluation comparing SEAHORN with an abstract interpretation-based static analyzer using IKOS (labelled ANALYZER) developed at NASA Ames [14]. We have used two open-source autopilot control software mnav [45] (160K LOC) and paparazzi [47] (20K LOC). Both are versatile autopilot control software for a fixed-wing aircrafts and multi-copters. For each benchmark, we created two versions: one inlining all functions (inlined) and the other applying the mixed-semantics transformation (mixed). SEAHORN front-end instruments the programs with the buffer overflow and underflow checks. In the middle-end, we use large-step encoding and the inter-procedural encoding (for mixed). For mnav, we had to model the heap, while for paparazzi, modeling registers and pointers only was sufficient. For ANALYZER, we neither inline nor add the checks explicitly as these are handled internally. Both SEAHORN and ANALYZER used intervals as the abstract domain.

In Table 2, #C denotes the number of overflow and underflow checks. For ANALYZER, we show the warning rate %W and the total time of the analysis T. For SEAHORN, we show the time spent by the front-end (T_F) and the middle-end (T_M). All times are in seconds. For the back-end, we record the time spent when SPACER alone is used (T_{SPACER}), and the time spent when both SPACER and IKOS are used ($T_{\text{SPACER}} + T_{\text{IKOS}}$). The column T_{FMS} and T_{FMSI} denote the total time, from front-end to the back-end, when SPACER alone and SPACER together with IKOS are used, respectively. SEAHORN proves absence of buffer overflows for both benchmarks, while ANALYZER can only do it for paparazzi; although, for mnav the number of warnings was low (4 %). To the best of our knowledge, this is the first time that absence of buffer overflows has been proven for mnav. For the inlined paparazzi benchmark, SEAHORN was able to discharge the proof obligations using front-end only (probably because all global array accesses were lowered to scalars and all loops are bound). The performance of SEAHORN on mnav reveals that the inter-procedural encoding significantly better than the inlined version. Furthermore, IKOS has a significant impact on the results. Specially, SEAHORN with IKOS dramatically helps when the benchmark is inlined. The best configuration is the inter-procedural encoding with IKOS.

6 Conclusion

We have presented SEAHORN, a new software verification framework with a modular design that separates the concerns of the syntax of the language, its operational semantics, and the verification semantics. Building a verifier from scratch is a very tedious and time-consuming task. We believe that SEAHORN is a versatile and highly customizable framework that can help significantly the process of building new tools by allowing researchers experimenting only on their particular techniques of interest. To demonstrate the practicality of this framework, we shown that SEAHORN is a very competitive verifier for proving safety properties both for academic benchmarks (SV-COMP) and large industrial software (autopilot code).

References

1. Albarghouthi, A., Gurfinkel, A., Chechik, M.: Craig interpretation. In: Miné, A., Schmidt, D. (eds.) SAS 2012. LNCS, vol. 7460, pp. 300–316. Springer, Heidelberg (2012)
2. Albarghouthi, A., Gurfinkel, A., Chechik, M.: WHALE: an interpolation-based algorithm for inter-procedural verification. In: Kuncak, V., Rybalchenko, A. (eds.) VMCAI 2012. LNCS, vol. 7148, pp. 39–55. Springer, Heidelberg (2012)
3. Albarghouthi, A., Gurfinkel, A., Li, Y., Chaki, S., Chechik, M.: UFO: verification with interpolants and abstract interpretation. In: Piterman, N., Smolka, S.A. (eds.) TACAS 2013 (ETAPS 2013). LNCS, vol. 7795, pp. 637–640. Springer, Heidelberg (2013)
4. Albarghouthi, A., Li, Y., Gurfinkel, A., Chechik, M.: UFO: a framework for abstraction- and interpolation-based software verification. In: Madhusudan, P., Seshia, S.A. (eds.) CAV 2012. LNCS, vol. 7358, pp. 672–678. Springer, Heidelberg (2012)
5. Amato, G., Scozzari, F.: Localizing widening and narrowing. In: Logozzo, F., Fähndrich, M. (eds.) Static Analysis. LNCS, vol. 7935, pp. 25–42. Springer, Heidelberg (2013)
6. Arlt, S., Rubio-González, C., Rümmer, P., Schäf, M., Shankar, N.: The gradual verifier. In: Badger, J.M., Rozier, K.Y. (eds.) NFM 2014. LNCS, vol. 8430, pp. 313–327. Springer, Heidelberg (2014)
7. Beyer, D., Cimatti, A., Griggio, A., Keremoglu, M.E., Sebastiani, R.: Software model checking via large-block encoding. In: FMCAD, pp. 25–32 (2009)
8. Beyer, D., Henzinger, T.A., Jhala, R., Majumdar, R.: The software model checker blast. STTT 9(5–6), 505–525 (2007)
9. Beyer, D., Keremoglu, M.E.: CPACHECKER: a tool for configurable software verification. In: Gopalakrishnan, G., Qadeer, S. (eds.) CAV 2011. LNCS, vol. 6806, pp. 184–190. Springer, Heidelberg (2011)
10. Bjørner, N., Gurfinkel, A.: Property directed polyhedral abstraction. In: D'Souza, D., Lal, A., Larsen, K.G. (eds.) VMCAI 2015. LNCS, vol. 8931, pp. 263–281. Springer, Heidelberg (2015)
11. Bjørner, N., McMillan, K.L., Rybalchenko, A.: Program verification as satisfiability modulo theories. In: SMT, pp. 3–11 (2012)

12. Bjørner, N., McMillan, K., Rybalchenko, A.: On solving universally quantified horn clauses. In: Logozzo, F., Fähndrich, M. (eds.) Static Analysis. LNCS, vol. 7935, pp. 105–125. Springer, Heidelberg (2013)
13. Bradley, A.R.: IC3 and beyond: incremental, inductive verification. In: Madhusudan, P., Seshia, S.A. (eds.) CAV 2012. LNCS, vol. 7358, pp. 4–4. Springer, Heidelberg (2012)
14. Brat, G., Navas, J.A., Shi, N., Venet, A.: IKOS: a framework for static analysis based on abstract interpretation. In: Giannakopoulou, D., Salaün, G. (eds.) SEFM 2014. LNCS, vol. 8702, pp. 271–277. Springer, Heidelberg (2014)
15. Chatterjee, S., Lahiri, S.K., Qadeer, S., Rakamarić, Z.: A reachability predicate for analyzing low-level software. In: Grumberg, O., Huth, M. (eds.) TACAS 2007. LNCS, vol. 4424, pp. 19–33. Springer, Heidelberg (2007)
16. Clarke, E., Kroning, D., Lerda, F.: A tool for checking ANSI-C programs. In: Jensen, K., Podelski, A. (eds.) TACAS 2004. LNCS, vol. 2988, pp. 168–176. Springer, Heidelberg (2004)
17. Cohen, E., Dahlweid, M., Hillebrand, M.A., Leinenbach, D., Moskal, M., Santen, T., Schulte, W., Tobies, S.: Vcc: A practical system for verifying concurrent c. In: TPHOL. pp. 23–42 (2009)
18. Cordeiro, L., Fischer, B., Marques-Silva, J.: Smt-based bounded model checking for embedded ANSI-C software. IEEE Trans. Softw. Eng. 38(4), 957–974 (2012)
19. Cousot, P., Cousot, R.: Static determination of dynamic properties of programs. In: Proceedings of the second international symposium on Programming, Paris, France. pp. 106–130 (1976)
20. Cuoq, P., Kirchner, F., Kosmatov, N., Prevosto, V., Signoles, J., Yakobowski, B.: Frama-C. In: Eleftherakis, G., Hinchey, M., Holcombe, M. (eds.) SEFM 2012. LNCS, vol. 7504, pp. 233–247. Springer, Heidelberg (2012)
21. De Angelis, E., Fioravanti, F., Pettorossi, A., Proietti, M.: VeriMAP: a tool for verifying programs through transformations. In: Ábrahám, E., Havelund, K. (eds.) TACAS 2014 (ETAPS). LNCS, vol. 8413, pp. 568–574. Springer, Heidelberg (2014)
22. DeLine, R., Leino, K.R.M.: BoogiePL: A typed procedural language for checking object-oriented programs. Technical report MSR-TR-2005-70, Microsoft Research (2005)
23. Gange, G., Navas, J.A., Schachte, P., Søndergaard, H., Stuckey, P.J.: Failure tabled constraint logic programming by interpolation. TPLP 13(4—5), 593–607 (2013)
24. Garoche, P.-L., Kahsai, T., Tinelli, C.: Incremental invariant generation using logic-based automatic abstract transformers. In: Brat, G., Rungta, N., Venet, A. (eds.) NFM 2013. LNCS, vol. 7871, pp. 139–154. Springer, Heidelberg (2013)
25. Granger, P.: Static analysis of arithmetical congruences. Int. J. Comput. Math. 30, 165–190 (1989)
26. Grebenshchikov, S., Lopes, N.P., Popeea, C., Rybalchenko, A.: Synthesizing software verifiers from proof rules. In: PLDI, pp. 405–416 (2012)
27. Gurfinkel, A., Chaki, S.: Combining predicate and numeric abstraction for software model checking. STTT 12(6), 409–427 (2010)
28. Gurfinkel, A., Chaki, S., Sapra, S.: Efficient predicate abstraction of program summaries. In: Bobaru, M., Havelund, K., Holzmann, G.J., Joshi, R. (eds.) NFM 2011. LNCS, vol. 6617, pp. 131–145. Springer, Heidelberg (2011)
29. Gurfinkel, A., Kahsai, T., Navas, J.A.: SeaHorn: a framework for verifying C programs (Competition Contribution). In: Baier, C., Tinelli, C. (eds.) TACAS 2015. LNCS, vol. 9035, pp. 447–450. Springer, Heidelberg (2015)

30. Gurfinkel, A., Wei, O., Chechik, M.: Model checking recursive programs with exact predicate abstraction. In: Cha, S.S., Choi, J.-Y., Kim, M., Lee, I., Viswanathan, M. (eds.) ATVA 2008. LNCS, vol. 5311, pp. 95–110. Springer, Heidelberg (2008)
31. Heizmann, M., Christ, J., Dietsch, D., Ermis, E., Hoenicke, J., Lindenmann, M., Nutz, A., Schilling, C., Podelski, A.: Ultimate automizer with SMTInterpol. In: Piterman, N., Smolka, S.A. (eds.) TACAS 2013 (ETAPS 2013). LNCS, vol. 7795, pp. 641–643. Springer, Heidelberg (2013)
32. Hermenegildo, M.V., Puebla, G., Bueno, F., López-García, P.: Program development using abstract interpretation (and the ciao system preprocessor). In: SAS, pp. 127–152 (2003)
33. Hoder, K., Bjørner, N.: Generalized property directed reachability. In: Cimatti, A., Sebastiani, R. (eds.) SAT 2012. LNCS, vol. 7317, pp. 157–171. Springer, Heidelberg (2012)
34. Jaffar, J., Murali, V., Navas, J.A., Santosa, A.E.: TRACER: a symbolic execution tool for verification. In: Madhusudan, P., Seshia, S.A. (eds.) CAV 2012. LNCS, vol. 7358, pp. 758–766. Springer, Heidelberg (2012)
35. Komuravelli, A., Gurfinkel, A., Chaki, S.: SMT-based model checking for recursive programs. In: Biere, A., Bloem, R. (eds.) CAV 2014. LNCS, vol. 8559, pp. 17–34. Springer, Heidelberg (2014)
36. Komuravelli, A., Gurfinkel, A., Chaki, S., Clarke, E.M.: Automatic abstraction in SMT-based unbounded software model checking. In: Sharygina, N., Veith, H. (eds.) CAV 2013. LNCS, vol. 8044, pp. 846–862. Springer, Heidelberg (2013)
37. Lal, A., Qadeer, S.: A program transformation for faster goal-directed search. In: FMCAD, pp. 147–154 (2014)
38. Lattner, C., Adve, V.S.: LLVM: a compilation framework for lifelong program analysis & transformation. In: CGO, pp. 75–88 (2004)
39. Lattner, C., Adve, V.S.: Automatic pool allocation: improving performance by controlling data structure layout in the heap. In: PLDI, pp. 129–142 (2005)
40. McMillan, K., Rybalchenko, A.: Solving constrained horn clauses using interpolation. Technical report MSR-TR-2013-6 (2013)
41. Méndez-Lojo, M., Navas, J., Hermenegildo, M.V.: A flexible, (C)LP-based approach to the analysis of object-oriented programs. In: King, A. (ed.) LOPSTR 2007. LNCS, vol. 4915, pp. 154–168. Springer, Heidelberg (2008)
42. Merz, F., Falke, S., Sinz, C.: LLBMC: bounded model checking of C and C++programs using a compiler IR. In: VSTTE. pp. 146–161 (2012)
43. Miné, A.: A few graph-based relational numerical abstract domains. In: Hermenegildo, M.V., Puebla, G. (eds.) SAS 2002. LNCS, vol. 2477, pp. 117–132. Springer, Heidelberg (2002)
44. Miné, A.: The octagon abstract domain. High. Order Symb. Comput. 19(1), 31–100 (2006)
45. Micro NAV autopilot software. Available http://sourceforge.net/projects/micronav/
46. Necula, G.C., McPeak, S., Rahul, S.P., Weimer, W.: CIL: intermediate language and tools for analysis and transformation of C programs. In: CC, pp. 213–228 (2002)
47. Paparazzi autopilot software. Available http://wiki.paparazziuav.org/wiki/Main_Page
48. Peralta, J.C., Gallagher, J.P., Saglam, H.: Analysis of imperative programs through analysis of constraint logic programs. In: Levi, G. (ed.) SAS 1998. LNCS, vol. 1503, pp. 246–261. Springer, Heidelberg (1998)

49. Rakamarić, Z., Emmi, M.: SMACK: decoupling source language details from verifier implementations. In: Biere, A., Bloem, R. (eds.) CAV 2014. LNCS, vol. 8559, pp. 106–113. Springer, Heidelberg (2014)

50. Rümmer, P., Hojjat, H., Kuncak, V.: Disjunctive interpolants for horn-clause verification. In: Sharygina, N., Veith, H. (eds.) CAV 2013. LNCS, vol. 8044, pp. 347–363. Springer, Heidelberg (2013)

51. Sinha, N., Singhania, N., Chandra, S., Sridharan, M.: Alternate and learn: finding witnesses without looking all over. In: Madhusudan, P., Seshia, S.A. (eds.) CAV 2012. LNCS, vol. 7358, pp. 599–615. Springer, Heidelberg (2012)

52. Steensgaard, B.: Points-to analysis in almost linear time. In: POPL, pp. 32–41 (1996)

53. Stump, A., Barrett, C.W., Dill, D.L., Levitt, J.R.: A decision procedure for an extensional theory of arrays. In: LICS, pp. 29–37 (2001)

54. Zhao, J., Nagarakatte, S., Martin, M.M.K., Zdancewic, S.: Formalizing the LLVM intermediate representation for verified program transformations. In: POPL, pp. 427–440 (2012)

Automatic Rootcausing for Program Equivalence Failures in Binaries

Shuvendu K. Lahiri[1(✉)], Rohit Sinha[2], and Chris Hawblitzel[1]

[1] Microsoft Research, Redmond, WA, USA
{shuvendu,chrishaw}@microsoft.com
[2] University of California, Berkeley, CA, USA
rsinha@berkeley.edu

Abstract. Equivalence checking of imperative programs has several applications including compiler validation and cross-version verification. Debugging equivalence failures can be tedious for large examples, especially for low-level binary programs. In this paper, we formalize a simple yet precise notion of *verifiable rootcause* for equivalence failures that leverages semantic similarity between two programs. Unlike existing works on program repair, our definition of rootcause avoids the need for a template of fixes or the need for a complete repair to ensure equivalence. We show progressively weaker checks for detecting rootcauses that can be applicable even when multiple fixes are required to make the two programs equivalent. We provide optimizations based on Maximum Satisfiability (MAXSAT) and binary search to prune the search space of such rootcauses. We have implemented the techniques in SymDiff and provide an evaluation on a set of real-world compiler validation binary benchmarks.

1 Introduction

Equivalence checking between two imperative programs has several applications in software validation. It has been used widely in the translation validation of compilers [10,14,19], regression verification [6], cross-version verification [7,11] and checking independent implementations [17,21]. Applications such as compiler validation [7], or automatic comparison of student attempts to reference implementations [21], can result in thousands of equivalence checking failures. Automated debugging and identification of the rootcause of a verification failure is crucial for the usability of these verification tools.

The problem of rootcausing is more involved while analyzing assembly or binary programs. Such problems come up naturally in various compiler validation tasks, such as comparing (a) intermediate representations with binaries, (b) binaries with different optimizations, (c) binaries generated for two different platforms (e.g. x86 vs. ARM), or even (iv) binaries from different versions of a compiler [7]. Comparing binaries (instead of source code or intermediate representations) allows discovering low-level bugs that are introduced during compilation and linking. However, debugging verification failures is tedious due

© Springer International Publishing Switzerland 2015
D. Kroening and C.S. Păsăreanu (Eds.): CAV 2015, Part I, LNCS 9206, pp. 362–379, 2015.
DOI: 10.1007/978-3-319-21690-4_21

to the lack of (type-based) non-aliasing; most instructions read or modify the registers, flags or the heap.

In a prior work on such binary comparisons, the number of failures even with a modest 2 % failure rate, ran into thousands [7]. Equivalence failures resulted from diverse sources such as modeling imprecision, missing environmental specifications, and presence of true defects. Moreover, for many such applications the syntax of the two programs (e.g. x86 vs. ARM) differ too much to benefit from syntactic difference based tools. To cope with such large-scale applications of equivalence checking for binaries, there is a growing need for automated techniques for understanding and bucketing failures.

In this paper, we provide a simple yet precise notion of a *verifiable rootcause* for equivalence failures of two similar programs. Our work is inspired by work on program repair [9,15,18], however our technique attempts to leverage semantic similarity of the two programs. In a nutshell, we attempt to "fix" an equivalence failure by changing an assignment r in one program with a value computed by an assignment l in the other program. The pair of assignments (l, r) from the two programs constitute a rootcause (whenever it exists) by pointing to the two assignments where the two programs diverge. The simple formulation has several advantages when applicable: (a) it provides correspondence points in two programs that is useful in the setting of comparing two programs, (b) it is completely automatic as it does not require any template of fix that is customary in program repair (e.g., [9,15]), and (c) the rootcause can be found without the need to repair the program, which we find too stringent in the presence of multiple repairs.

On the other hand, the notion of such a singleton fix as a rootcause may appear overly restrictive and less applicable in practice. Therefore, we propose several mechanisms that exploit similarity between programs to improve the applicability of this approach. First, we formulate two progressively weaker checks (with progressively weaker guarantees) that work by looking for singleton fixes for weaker equivalence problems. Second, we show examples of additional domain-specific weakening through preprocessing to increase the applicability of such rootcauses.

Although it is easy to symbolically encode the search for such a rootcause in existing program synthesis tools [9,15,22], our initial attempt did not scale for the binary benchmarks studied in this paper. We therefore provide a more enumerative solution to search for a rootcause. We provide optimizations based on Maximum Satisfiability (MAXSAT) and binary search to prune the space of candidate fixes. We have implemented the techniques [23] and provide preliminary evaluation on a set of real-world compiler validation benchmarks [7]; our technique finds verified rootcauses for 74 % and 80 % respectively of the cases on two sets of benchmarks.

1.1 Overview

We illustrate the concepts informally with the aid of two simplified models of assembly programs generated from a common C# procedure using different

```
1  procedure p1(M:[int]int, x:int)          1  procedure p2(M:[int]int, x:int)
2  returns (r1:int, M1:[int]int)            2  returns (r2:int, M2:[int]int)
3  {                                         3  {
4    M1 := M;                                4    M2 := M;
5    r5 := M1[x];        //ld r5, [x]        5    r6 := M2[x];        //ld r6, [x]
6    assume(r5@5 = r5);                      6    M2, r2 := f(M2,r6); //call f
7    M1, r1 := f(M1,r5); //call f            7    r2 := M2[x];        //ld r2, [x]
8    r1 := r5;           //mov r1, r5        8    r2 := r5@5;
9    M1, r1 := g(M1,r1); //call g            9    M2, r2 := g(M2,r2); //call g
10   return;                                 10   return;
11 }                                         11 }
```

Fig. 1. Optimizing loads. The rootcause pair is highlighted and underlined lines are part of program instrumentation.

compiler versions [7]. For most of these examples, the heap is modeled as an array variable M and the effect of a procedure call is modeled by applying uninterpreted functions such as f (line 7 in Fig. 1) to the arguments. We refer the reader to earlier works for further details of translating assembly instructions into the language (§ 2) used in this paper [7].

Single Fix. Figure 1 describes two procedures p_1 and p_2 that differ in an extra load from memory M in p_2. The underlined lines are additional instrumentation inserted by our tool, and not part of the original programs. Procedure p_2 has two loads (lines 5 and 7) from x; the two loads can yield different results if the procedure call f can modify M at the location x. The compiler for p_1 optimizes the second load in p_1 based on the knowledge that the call to f does not modify M at the location x. Such internal assumptions from the compiler are often not readily available to the equivalence checker, thereby resulting in equivalence failure.

For this example, our tool first inserts the underlined lines in the two procedures. The assume in line 6 in p_1 uses a symbolic constant r5@5 to capture the symbolic value computed in r5 after the load in line 5. The assignment in line 8 in p_2 overwrites the assignment in line 7 with the value in r5@5, thereby making the two procedures equivalent. We highlight the rootcause as the pair of original instructions (5, 7) that participate in the fix. Note that we do not actually "repair" the program p_2, since it contains values (e.g. r5@5) that are only computed by p_1.

Weaker Fixes. Figure 2 illustrates a case where our technique can identify a fix even though multiple fixes are required to make the two procedures equivalent. The source of difference between the two procedures is that fields of a class are laid out at different offsets by the two compilers. The field accesses are reflected in the accesses to the heap M using different offsets from a base location x (e.g. lines 7, 11, 14 in p_1). Note that the fields in p_2 have an additional offset of 4 compared to fields in p_1. This example is challenging since at least 3 fixes are required to make the two procedures equivalent. Searching for multiple fixes is significantly more expensive and a complete repair may be elusive when two programs have several differences. However, for the purpose of rootcausing, we have observed that it suffices to highlight the *earliest* instruction pair where the two programs diverge. By exploiting the semantic similarity, we can often pose

```
1  procedure p1(M:[int]int, x:int)      1  procedure p2(M:[int]int, x:int)
2  returns (r1:int, M1:[int]int)        2  returns (r2:int, M2:[int]int)
3  {                                     3  {
4    M1 := M;                            4    M2 := M;
5    assume(M1[x] = 42); //Fix path      5    if (M2[x] != 42) {
6    if (M1[x] = 42) {                   6      r2 := M2[x+20];
                                         7      M2 := g(M2,r2);
7      r1 := M1[x + 4]; assume(r1@7 = r1);  8    }
8      M1 := f(M1,r1); assume(M1@8 = M1);   9    else {
9    }                                   10     r2 := M2[x + 8];
10   else {                             11     r2 := r1@7;
11     r1 := M1[x+16];                  12     M2 := f(M2,r2);
12     M1 := g(M1,r1);                  13     assume (M1@8 != M2); //Early assume
13   }                                  14    }
14   r1 := M1[x+32];                    15    r2 := M2[x+36];
15   ...                                16    ...
16 }                                    17 }
```

Fig. 2. Partial fix. The rootcause pair is highlighted and underlined lines are part of program instrumentation.

weaker equivalence checks (with weaker guarantees) that may still be verified with a single fix.

Let us assume that the equivalence failure provides a counterexample cex that takes the "then" branch of the conditional in p_1 and the "else" branch in p_2. (Notice that the branches are rearranged to mimic common compiler transformations.) We present two separate ideas to create a weaker equivalence problem. (i) First, we constrain p_1 to take only that path that was taken by the counterexample; this is achieved by instrumenting assumptions denoting branch conditions satisfied in the counterexample (e.g. line 5 in p_1). (ii) Second, we exploit the fact that semantically similar programs often have intermediate program points where the two programs are expected to *synchronize* — i.e. certain part of the states are expected to be equal. In the presence of such synchronization points, we can look for fixing the violations of such intermediate equalities in addition to the final equivalence. For compiler validation, it is often assumed that the two procedures synchronize on procedure calls — the sequence of procedure calls and the values returned from them are equal on both sides on a common input [7,10,11,14]. One reason for this assumption is that the heap is passed as a map in and out of procedure calls in these settings (we discuss exceptions in Fig. 4). Let us assume that the counterexample cex assigns different outputs for M1 and M2 at lines 8 and 12 respectively. We add the underlined assume after the update in line 12 in p_2 to make the two maps disequal, assuming procedures synchronize on calls to f. Intuitively, the assumption weakens the final equivalence assertion with an equality over intermediate state of the two programs. The singleton fix $(7, 10)$ does not satisfy this assumption and therefore blocks execution of the instrumented program after line 13 in p_2, which leads to the equivalence check to succeed.

Contributions. The contributions of the paper include (a) the first precise formulation of rootcause for the problem of equivalence failure that does not require a template of fixes or the need to repair a program, (b) mechanisms to improve the applicability of the rootcause by postulating weaker checks by leveraging similarity of the two programs, and (c) an implementation and evaluation on a set of challenging real-world binary equivalence failures.

Organization. We describe a simple programming language used to model binary programs in Sect. 2. We formalize our notion of rootcause for equivalence failures in Sect. 3 along with the weaker checks. We describe an algorithm to search for rootcauses in Sect. 4 along with various optimizations. We present our evaluation in Sect. 5, and discuss related work in Sect. 6.

2 Background

Programs. Figure 3 describes the syntax of programs. *Vars* denotes the set of variables and includes parameters and locals; we assume that the programs contain no globals for simplicity. We distinguish scalar variables (denoted by x) from array or map variables (denoted by X). *Consts* denotes a set of symbolic constants. *Rels* and *Funcs* denote the set of relations and functions, and can either be uninterpreted or be interpreted by an underlying theory (e.g. $\{\leq, \geq\}$ $\in$ *Rels* and $\{+, -, *\} \in$ *Funcs*). Map operations x := X[y] and X[y] := x are modeled as x := sel(X, y) and X := upd(X, y, x) respectively, where sel and upd are functions in *Funcs* interpreted by the theory of arrays [20]. Maps can also be updated at an *unbounded* number of locations by functions returning map values (e.g. X := f(X, ...)).

Statements in *Stmt* include assignments, conditionals, assertions, assumptions, and sequential composition ($s; s$). Parallel assignments (e.g. line 7 in Fig. 1) are desugared as assignments using additional temporary variables.

A procedure p consists of a list of parameters and return variables, and a body ($s_g \in$ *Stmt*). Procedures are side-effect free, and all the modifications are reflected explicitly by the return vari-

$$
\begin{aligned}
&x, X \in Vars \\
&\theta \quad \in Consts \\
&q \quad \in Rels \\
&f, g \in Funcs \\
&e \quad \in Expr \quad ::= x \mid X \mid \theta \mid f(e, \ldots, e) \\
&\phi \quad \in Formula ::= \text{true} \mid \text{false} \mid e = e \mid \\
&\qquad\qquad\qquad q(e, \ldots, e) \mid \phi \wedge \phi \mid \neg\phi \\
&s \quad \in Stmt \quad ::= x := e \mid s; s \mid \text{if } (\phi) \{s\} \text{ else } \{s\} \\
&\qquad\qquad\qquad \text{assert } \phi \mid \text{assume } \phi \\
&p \quad \in Proc \quad ::= g(x_g, \ldots) : (r_g, \ldots) \{ s_g \}
\end{aligned}
$$

Fig. 3. Syntax of programs.

ables. As is standard in most prior works on compiler equivalence checking [6,10,11,14], a procedure call is either inlined or is modeled by assigning the return variables an uninterpreted function over the parameters (e.g. line 7 in Fig. 1). The treatment in this paper ignores loops; we assume they are either unrolled to a bounded depth or modeled as tail-recursive procedures [12].

Semantics. A state σ of a program at a given program location is a valuation of the variables in scope. Let Σ be the set of all program states. We omit the definition of an execution as it is quite standard for the statements [1]. We recall that the semantics of $\texttt{assume}\ \phi$ is to block execution when executed in a state σ that does not satisfy ϕ. For a procedure p, an *input state* is a valuation of the parameters at entry and an *output state* is a valuation of the returns at exit. The semantics of a procedure p is given by a relation $\mathcal{R}(p) \subseteq \Sigma \times \Sigma$ over pairs of input and output states, where $(\sigma, \sigma') \in \mathcal{R}(p)$ if and only if there is an execution of p starting at σ and ending in σ'.

Equivalence Checking. Given two procedures p_1 and p_2 and a one-one mapping of the parameters $\overrightarrow{x}$ and returns $\overrightarrow{r}$, we define p_1 and p_2 to be *partially equivalent* if for every $(\sigma, \sigma') \in \mathcal{R}(p_1)$ and $(\sigma, \sigma'') \in \mathcal{R}(p_2)$, $\sigma' = \sigma''$. In other words, if both p_1 and p_2 terminate on an input σ, then the outputs are equivalent. We drop the term partial henceforth when referring to partial equivalence. We check equivalence of two such procedures p_1 and p_2 by creating the composed procedure p_{12} (where p_1 and p_2 are inlined) and checking the final assertion:

$$p_{12}(\overrightarrow{x})\{\overrightarrow{r_1} := p_1(\overrightarrow{x}); \overrightarrow{r_2} := p_2(\overrightarrow{x}); \texttt{assert}\ \overrightarrow{r_1} = \overrightarrow{r_2}; \}$$

Since we assume p_1 and p_2 are loop-free, p_{12} is a bounded program. Several well-known techniques [1] exist to transform a loop-free and call-free procedure with assertions into a compact logical formula in the Satisfiability Modulo Theories (SMT) format by a process called verification-condition (VC) generation. For our purpose, we define $VC(p)$ to be a logical formula that is *valid* if and only if p does not fail any assertion. If $VC(p_{12})$ is valid then p_1 and p_2 are equivalent; otherwise we obtain a counterexample *cex* along paths in p_1 and p_2 for which at least one of the return variables differ.

3 Problem Formulation

When p_1 and p_2 are not equivalent, the counterexample *cex* allows the user to debug the equivalence failure. However, such counterexamples can often be hundreds of lines long and finding the relevant instructions that lead to the failure can be cumbersome. Understanding counterexamples of equivalence failures is often laborious due to several factors: (a) most statements in a program are relevant to an equivalence assertion, and (b) one has to proceed simultaneously along both p_1 and p_2. In our prior experience of debugging equivalence failures from compiler validation, summarizing the "core reason" (or rootcause) for equivalence failure was the main ask for the adoption of equivalence checking tools in a production setting [7].

In this section, we formulate a natural notion of rootcause for equivalence failure that exploits the structure of both programs. We pose the rootcause problem as the problem of finding a pair of scalar assignments $l : x_1 := e_1$ (from p_1) and $r : x_2 := e_2$ (from p_2) at labels l and r respectively, such that replacing e_2 in p_2 with the value of e_1 computed in p_1 makes the two procedures equivalent.

Observe that the proposal is different from replacing the expression e_2 with e_1 in p_2; such a change may not even yield a well-typed program as the expression e_1 may contain local variables not in scope in p_2. Thus, the rootcause does not really repair the program p_2, but rather yields (when the pair exists) a pair of program points where the two procedures should have been equivalent. We term such a pair (l, r) as a *fix*.

A reader may be concerned about *trivial fixes* in the form of setting the outputs of p_2 to the outputs of p_1. In our experience this seldom happens due to the following reasons: (a) Binary programs contain arrays to model the heap. Most equivalence failures result in the output maps being different at a large (even unbounded) number of locations. Since we do not consider updates to entire maps for potential fixes, a trivial fix does not work in such cases. (b) A similar argument holds when a procedure has multiple outputs that differ. In addition, for cases when multiple such fixes exist, we always pick the fix that appears earliest in the lexicographic ordering of the pair of labels.

Another concern would be the adequacy of the space of our fixes. This concern is indeed justified due to either (i) several paths may require a fix, or (ii) a long counterexample requires several fixes to align the outputs. We leverage the semantic similarity between the two programs to formulate two progressively weaker checks (with progressively weaker guarantees) that work by looking for singleton fixes for weaker equivalence problems. Let us refer to the first (original) check that checks to fix p_{12} with the pair (l, r) as *AllFix* check. The second check (*LeftPathFix*) attempts to only fix the subset of inputs along a single counterexample path, thereby avoiding the need to make the program equivalent on all inputs. The third check (*LeftPathEarliestFix*) leverages the presence of intermediate synchronization points such as procedure calls to look for fixing the earliest synchronization point where the two programs diverge.

In the next few sections, we formalize the different notions of rootcauses with the aid of a program instrumentation.

3.1 Instrumentation

For a pair of procedures p_1 and p_2, let L and R be the sequence of labels in the left (respectively p_1) and right (respectively p_2) procedures. Each label l corresponds to a scalar assignment $\mathsf{x}_l := \mathsf{e}_l$. We sometimes treat L and R as sets instead of a sequence. We define an instrumentation that transforms a statement to another statement:

- For each scalar assignment instruction $l : \mathsf{x} := \mathsf{e}$ with a label $l \in L$, we transform it to:

$$l : \mathsf{x} := \mathsf{e}; \mathsf{assume}(\theta@l = \mathsf{x})$$

  where $\theta@l$ is a *fresh* constant for storing the value of x after the assignment at label l.
- For each assignment instruction $r : \mathsf{x} := \mathsf{e}$ with a label $r \in R$, we transform it to:

$$r : \mathsf{x} := \mathsf{e};\ \mathsf{x} := \gamma_r?\ \theta@r :\ \mathsf{x};\ \mathsf{assume} \bigwedge_{l \in L} (\beta_r^l \Rightarrow \mathsf{x} = \theta@l)$$

Here $\theta@r$ and γ_r are fresh constants for label r. Setting γ_r to true replaces the current assignment at r with a completely unconstrained value $\theta@r$ in p_2. For each $l \in L$, we also create a Boolean constant β_r^l to denote a candidate fix (l, r). The constant β_r^l constrains x to be equal to the value assigned at label $l \in L$. It is easy to see that setting γ_r to true and exactly one of β_r^l to true (and other candidates $\beta_r^{l'}$ to false) is equivalent to an assignment x := $\theta@l$, which is the intended fix.

For all further discussions, we refer p_{12} to mean the instrumented version of p_{12}. We next describe the meaning of two operations *ConstrainFix* and *AssignFix*, that weaken the formula being checked by the SMT solver:

– *ConstrainFix*(p_{12}, L', R') takes two sets of labels $L' \subseteq L$ and $R' \subseteq R$ and constrains all the candidates in $L' \times R'$ to true. It generates the following logical formula:

$$\left(\bigwedge_{r \in R} \neg\gamma_r \wedge \bigwedge_{(l,r)\in L'\times R'} \beta_r^l \wedge \bigwedge_{(l,r)\in(L\times R)\backslash(L'\times R')} \neg\beta_r^l \right) \Rightarrow VC(p_{12})$$

– *AssignFix*$(p_{12}, (l', r'))$ takes a fix (l', r') and overwrites the assignment at r' with value computed at l'. It generates the following logical formula:

$$\left(\gamma_{r'} \wedge \beta_{r'}^{l'} \wedge \bigwedge_{r \in R\backslash\{r'\}} \neg\gamma_r \wedge \bigwedge_{(l,r)\in L\times R\backslash\{(l',r')\}} \neg\beta_r^l \right) \Rightarrow VC(p_{12})$$

The encodings give rise to a few simple facts.

Lemma 1. *For $L_1 \subseteq L_2 \subseteq L$ and $R_1 \subseteq R_2 \subseteq R$, if ConstrainFix$(p_{12}, L_1, R_1)$ is valid, then ConstrainFix(p_{12}, L_2, R_2) is valid.*

Lemma 1 follows from the fact that setting more β_r^l constants to true adds more assumes to p_{12}, thus making the specification weaker.

Lemma 2. *For $l \in L$ and $r \in R$, if the formula AssignFix$(p_{12}, (l, r))$ is valid, then the formula ConstrainFix$(p_{12}, \{l\}, \{r\})$ is valid.*

Lemma 2 follows from the observation that replacing an unconstrained constant $\theta@r$ with a more constrained expression e in the assignment $r : x := e$ can never change a valid formula into an invalid formula.

Theorem 1. *For $L_1 \subseteq L$ and $R_1 \subseteq R$, if ConstrainFix(p_{12}, L_1, R_1) is not valid, then AssignFix$(p_{12}, (l, r))$ is not valid for any $(l, r) \in L_1 \times R_1$.*

The theorem follows immediately from the two lemmas. The utility of the theorem is in providing a sufficient condition to prune a subset of candidate fixes, without explicitly trying each of them. We use this for optimizations in Sect. 4.

3.2   Different Checks

We now formalize the different checks starting with the strongest check.

Definition 1 (*AllFix*). *AllFix*(p_1, p_2) is true if there exists a fix $(l, r) \in L \times R$ such that $AssignFix(p_{12}, (l, r))$ is valid.

For the example in Fig. 1, both $(5, 7)$ and $(8, 7)$ constitute a fix according to the *AllFix* check. We highlight the pair $(5, 7)$ since it is lexicographically smaller than $(8, 7)$.

If *AllFix* does not hold, then we can try a weaker check. Given a counterexample path *cex*, we define $HoldLeftPath(p_{12}, cex)$ as constraining p_1 to only take the path taken in *cex*. Figure 2 shows an example (line 5 in p_1) where the branch condition of the taken branch is assumed before the conditional statement.

Definition 2 (*LeftPathFix*). *LeftPathFix*(p_1, p_2, cex) is true if there exists a fix $(l, r) \in L \times R$ such that $AssignFix(HoldLeftPath(p_{12}, cex), (l, r))$ is valid.

Observe that the check *LeftPathFix* does not yield a fix for the example in Fig. 2. This is because even this single path requires at least two fixes to constants in lines 10 and 15. Note that we do not constrain both the left and the right paths together while looking for a fix, because (a) the fix may require changing the control flow in p_2 and (b) a vacuous fix may be found that avoids this combined path.

We can further weaken the final assertion by exploiting statically defined intermediate synchronization points for the two procedures, where certain variables are expected to match up on the two sides. For example, for compiler translation validation, it is common to assume that the sequence of procedure calls and the values returned from them are equal on both programs on a common input. In the presence of such synchronization points, we can look for fixing the violations of such intermediate equalities in *cex* in addition to the final equivalence.

For a counterexample *cex*, let $l_1, \ldots, l_m$ and $r_1, \ldots, r_n$ be the sequence of assignment labels from p_1 and p_2 respectively. Further, let a subset of instruction pairs $(l^1, r^1), \ldots, (l^j, r^j)$ (ordered by *cex*) are expected to be the synchronization points. We find the *earliest* pair where the synchronization is violated in the traces. Let (l^k, r^k) be the earliest violation of synchronization (it may not always exist) and let x be the variable assigned in r^k. We insert the following assume statement after the assignment at r^k:

$$r^k : \mathsf{x} := e; \ \mathtt{assume}(\mathsf{x} \neq \theta @ l^k)$$

Intuitively, the assume weakens the final equivalence check by pruning behaviors that satisfy the synchronization at (l^k, r^k). In turn, this expects less from a fix: a fix does not need to check the final equivalence if it can synchronize (l^k, r^k). For compiler validation, it is often assumed that p_1 and p_2 synchronize on procedure calls, for which x would represent the heap that is passed out of the procedure calls. We define the instrumentation $AddEarlyDiseqAssumes(p_{12}, cex)$ to insert such assumes into p_{12}. Figure 2 shows an instance of such assume in line 13 in p_2 for map variable M.

These assumptions are most useful when the counterexample path is constrained to cex. Otherwise, the verifier can find an alternate path and avoid the inserted assume statement. Hence we use this in conjunction with $HoldLeftPath(p_{12}, cex)$.

Definition 3 (*LeftPathEarliestFix*). *LeftPathEarliestFix*(p_1, p_2, cex) is true if there exists a fix $(l, r) \in L \times R$ such that the logical formula represented by $AssignFix(HoldLeftPath(AddEarlyDiseqAssumes(p_{12}, cex), cex), (l, r))$ is valid.

The example in Fig. 2 satisfies this weaker check and yields the rootcause pair highlighted in the figure.

It is worth pointing the difference with an alternate option of inserting an assertion $\mathtt{assert}(\mathsf{x} = \theta@l^k)$ at r^k and removing the final assertion. Such a check can be verified with spurious fixes that avoid the path leading to the assertion, and we have found it to be true in practice. Finally, the following theorem formalizes the relationship between the three checks:

Theorem 2. *Given procedures p_1 and p_2, and a counterexample cex to $VC(p_{12})$, $AllFix(p_1, p_2, cex)$ $\Rightarrow$ $LeftPathFix(p_1, p_2, cex)$ $\Rightarrow$ $LeftPathEarliestFix(p_1, p_2, cex)$.*

In summary, there are several advantages to our natural formulation of rootcause: (a) We can exploit the semantic similarity of the two closely related programs by moving "values" computed in p_1 into p_2 for the fix. Our notion of rootcause is verifiable, but does not require a complete repair to the program. (b) The formulation does not require separate templates for repairing a program [15,21]. This is useful when the repair templates may not be obvious (e.g. the repair of p_2 in Fig. 1 requires strengthening the environment assumptions of callees). (c) When such a fix exists, it points to correspondence points in the two programs that differ under cex but are *necessary* for equivalence. We have found this to be much more informative than fixing one statement in p_2, as would be done by existing rootcause methods [21]. (d) The semantic similarity between the two programs (as opposed to a specification versus a program) can be exploited to formulate weaker checks that can yield a rootcause with weaker guarantees.

4   Searching for a Fix

Our first attempt was to leverage *counterexample-guided inductive synthesis* (CEGIS) to symbolically encode the search for a fix [15,22]. The algorithm searches for an assignment to boolean constants $\beta \cup \gamma$ (at most one fix for each $r \in R$) such that p_1 and p_2 are equivalent. Promisingly, CEGIS can find multiple fixes; in the case of Fig. 2, it finds all 3 fixes needed to make p_1 and p_2 equivalent. However, we did not succeed in scaling the CEGIS-based algorithm to the compiler validation benchmarks due to timeouts in the theorem prover. There are several reasons why CEGIS does not scale for our benchmarks:

Algorithm 1. $FindRootCause(p_{12}, cex)$

Input: Combined procedure p_{12}, a counterexample cex to equivalence failure of p_{12}
Output: $\{NOROOTCAUSE, ROOTCAUSE(l, r)\}$
 1: $(L, R) \leftarrow$ Sequences of scalar assignment labels as they appear in cex
 2: $PruneCandidatesStatic(cex, L, R)$
 3: **if** $CheckSAT(ConstrainFix(p_{12}, L, R)) \neq UNSAT$ **then**
 4:     **return** $NOROOTCAUSE$ /* No fix exists */
 5: **end if**
 6: /* Binary search based pruning */
 7: $(low, up) \leftarrow (0, |R|)$
 8: **while** $(up - low > 1)$ **do**
 9:     $curr \leftarrow low + (up - low)/2$
10:     **if** $CheckSAT(ConstrainFix(p_{12}, L, [1, curr])) \neq UNSAT$ **then**
11:         $low \leftarrow curr$
12:     **else**
13:         $up \leftarrow curr$
14:     **end if**
15: **end while**
16: /* MAXSAT based pruning */
17: **for** $r \in [low + 1, |R|]$ **do**
18:     $L' \leftarrow L \setminus CheckMAXSAT(ConstrainFix(p_{12}, L, \{r\}), \{\beta_r^l \mid l \in L\})$
19:     **for** $l \in L'$ in program order **do**
20:         **if** $CheckSAT(AssignFix(p_{12}, (l, r))) = UNSAT$ **then**
21:             **return** $ROOTCAUSE(l, r)$
22:         **end if**
23:     **end for**
24: **end for**
25: **return** $NOROOTCAUSE$

(a) the benchmarks contain several hundred lines along with heavy use of quantifiers to model semantics of binary programs, and (b) the size of the instrumented program fed to CEGIS is quadratic in the size of the two input programs. The combination of these two factors make the problem of generating a model or satisfiable input more difficult for SMT solvers.

We now present an alternate algorithm for searching for a fix in Algorithm 1. We assume that p_{12} has already been instrumented with one of the three checks $\{AllFix, LeftPathFix, LeftPathEarliestFix\}$. It returns $NOROOTCAUSE$ to denote that no singleton rootcause exists, and returns $ROOTCAUSE(l, r)$ for a pair (l, r) that fixes p_{12}. A naïve solution will enumerate every pair of assignments (l, r) over p_1 and p_2 and check for $AssignFix(p_{12}, (l, r))$. This can lead to a best case quadratic (in the size of p_{12}) number of theorem prover checks when no such fix exists. In section, we describe a few techniques to prune the space of candidate fixes where a fix cannot be found.

The search for a singleton fix enables a few simple optimizations. Given a counterexample cex, the first step is to collect into (L, R) only the scalar assignments that appear along cex (line 1). The method $PruneCandidatesStatic$ prunes pairs (l, r) such that $cex(l) = cex(r)$, i.e. the assignments that produce equal value in cex. For any such pair (l, r), applying that fix will not prevent the counter-example cex. Therefore, $PruneCandidatesStatic$ fixes the β_r^l constants to false permanently.

For the remaining pairs, we perform pruning based on calls to an automated theorem prover. The operation $CheckSAT(\phi)$ checks if $\neg\phi$ is satisfiable (SAT) or unsatisfiable $(UNSAT)$; these cases correspond to ϕ being invalid and valid respectively. Line 3 checks if constraining p_{12} with all the remaining assumes guarded by β_r^l (except those disabled in line 2 earlier) can verify p_{12}. If the result is SAT, there can be no fix with (L, R) (Theorem 1). The check for a fix is done in line 20; if the formula is valid, then we return the rootcause pair (l, r). Lines 6–15 use *binary search* to prune a subset of candidates. Lines 16–24 use Maximum Satisfiability (MAXSAT) to prune a subset of candidates. We describe these optimizations below.

Binary Search Based Pruning. We are interested in pruning the sub-range of R where no fix can lie. We observe that for any fix (l, r) (such that $AssignFix(p_{12}, (l, r))$ is valid), the following condition follows from Theorem 1: $r > r'$ for any $r' \in R$ for which $ConstrainFix(p_{12}, L, [1, r'])$ is not valid. We use binary search over $[1, |R|]$ to find the largest r (returned in the variable low) such that $ConstrainFix(p_{12}, L, [1, r])$ is invalid. We use two markers low and up with the following loop invariants: (i) $ConstrainFix(p_{12}, L, [1, low])$ is invalid, and (ii) $ConstrainFix(p_{12}, L, [1, up])$ is valid, and (iii) $low \leq up$. The binary search converges in at most $\log(|R|)$ steps since the distance between low and up is halved at each step.

MAXSAT Based Pruning. For a fixed $r \in R$, we are also interested in pruning a subset of L where no fixes can lie. We use Maximum Satisfiability (MAXSAT) to perform this. For a given $r \in R$ if $ConstrainFix(p_{12}, L, \{r\})$ is valid, then we find the largest subset $L'' \subseteq L$ such that $ConstrainFix(p_{12}, L'', \{r\})$ is invalid. From Theorem 1 we know that a fix (l, r) cannot be found for any $l \in L''$. Computing the largest (invalid) subset L'' can be performed by the call to $CheckMAXSAT(ConstrainFix(p_{12}, L, \{r\}), \{\beta_r^l \mid l \in L\})$, where the first argument is a formula ϕ and the second argument is a set S of Boolean constants that are "soft". $CheckMAXSAT(\phi, S)$ returns the largest subset $S' \subseteq S$ such that $\neg\phi \wedge \bigwedge_{s\in S'} s$ is satisfiable. For our purpose, the set of soft constants consists of the set of all candidate fixes from L for a given $r \in R$.

As an example, consider this optimization in the context of Fig. 1. Consider the MAXSAT query when considering the statement r2 := M2[x]. The potential set of candidates from p_1 are (ignoring updates to maps):

$$L \doteq \{5 : \text{r5} := \text{M1}[\text{x}], 7 : \text{r1} := \text{f}(\text{M1}, \text{r5}), 8 : \text{r1} := \text{r5}, 9 : \text{r1} := \text{g}(\text{M1}, \text{r1})\}$$

The instrumentation of $7 : \text{r2} := \text{M2}[\text{x}]$ is as follows:

$$7 : \text{r2} := \text{M2}[\text{x}]; \ \text{r2} := \gamma_7? \ \theta@7 : \ \text{r2}; \ \text{assume} \bigwedge_{l\in[5,7,8,9]} (\beta_7^l \Rightarrow \text{r2} = \theta@l)$$

For this program, both $(5, 7)$ and $(8, 7)$ are valid (singleton) fixes and make the two program equivalent.

Consider the case when γ_7 is false and the subset $\{\beta_7^7, \beta_7^9\}$ are true. The two programs are not equivalent under this constraint. In other words, the verification condition $VC(p_{12})$ is SAT even with these constraints. The call to $CheckMAXSAT$ with $\{\beta_7^l \mid l \in \{5,7,8,9\}\}$ as the soft clauses will return the largest set $\{\beta_7^7, \beta_7^9\}$ that is satisfiable, thereby pruning the set of candidates that have to be explicitly tested by 2.

5   Evaluation

In this section, we describe an implementation of the techniques and an evaluation on a set of binary benchmarks from compiler validation. Our implementation is part of SYMDIFF sources [23], and takes as input a Boogie program p_{12} generated by the equivalence checker tool SYMDIFF [11]. The inputs to SYMDIFF are Boogie programs p_1 and p_2 and a mapping between the two procedures. These Boogie programs can be generated from various languages such as C [4], or from various compiler back-end formats [7,25]. For this section, we only focus on Boogie programs generated from compiler validation benchmarks [7].

The main goal of our experiment is to determine how often our notion of rootcause can be found in real benchmarks. The evaluation consists of two parts. In Sect. 5.1, we evaluate the implementation on 15 *smallest* benchmarks of equivalence failures resulting from comparing the output of the .NET CLR compiler across two different optimization levels. In Sect. 5.2, we evaluate the implementation on 46 benchmarks comparing the output of the .NET CLR compiler in Just In Time (JIT) mode to the compiler in mostly-ahead-of-time mode (based on the MDIL [16] machine-dependent intermediate language). We restrict to the smallest 15 for the former category to be able to manually establish the ground truth (the true reason for failure) of these failures, which can be quite tedious. For the latter benchmarks, previous syntactic heuristics provided good starting points for establishing the ground truth. Thus we report more quantitative evaluation for the latter category.

5.1   Different Optimization Levels

We successfully find a total of 12 rootcauses (80 % of the cases) out of the 15 benchmarks in this category. These benchmarks have 68 lines of assembly code on average, and the generated Boogie programs have 510 Boogie statements on average. In most cases, we found a fix with either the *LeftPathFix* and *LeftPathEarliestFix* checks. However, some of the examples do not satisfy the assumption that the two programs have equal set of callees. We illustrate the problem and an additional *preprocessing* step that alleviates the problem without any changes to the algorithm.

Figure 4 illustrates a case where our technique fails to identify a fix when a procedure call in p_1 is replaced by access to the object's field in p_2. This is an instance of a common compiler optimization of inlining simple methods (such as side-effect free "getter" methods) with their implementations. Our tool

```
1  procedure p1(M:[int]int, x:int)      1  procedure p2(M:[int]int, x:int)
2  returns (r1:int, M1:[int]int)        2  returns (r2:int, M2:[int]int)
3  {                                    3  {
4    M1 := M; r1 := M1[x];              4    M2 := M; r2 := M2[x];
5    assume(M1@5 = M1);                 5    r2 := M2[r2 + 8];
6    M1,r1 := getLength(M1,r1);         6    r2 := r1@6;
7    assume(M1 = M1@5) //preprocessing  7    if (r2 > 0) {
8    assume(r1@6 = r1);                 8      M2, r2 := writeToFile(M2,r2);
9    if (r1 > 0) {                      9    }
10     M1, r1 := writeToFile(M1,r1);    10   ...
11   }                                  11 }
12   ...
13 }
```

Fig. 4. Example for side-effect free preprocessing heuristic.

fails to find a rootcause because (i) procedure call to getLength can modify the heap M1 arbitrarily and cause it to differ from M2, and (ii) return value r1 of getLength is allowed to differ from the field access M2[r1 + 8]. To account for (i), we exploit the fact if a procedure call only appears in one program, then it is likely to not modify the heap M. In a preprocessing step, we modify p_1 to insert an assume in line 5 and restore M1 in line 7. Then, our rootcause analysis identifies the singleton fix $(6, 5)$. Similarly, we find examples that make several calls to the same procedure in p_1 that are optimized to only one call in p_2 because the compiler is able to prove idempotence. We perform a similar instrumentation as Fig. 4 to handle such cases. Conceptually, these preprocessing provide a weaker guarantee on the rootcause by constraining the summaries of callees (e.g. side-effect free, idempotent); this is analogous to how *LeftPathFix* provides a rootcause by constraining the entry state of the procedures.

5.2 JIT Versus Compiled Binaries

Benchmarks. These benchmarks have 165 lines of assembly code on average, with the largest benchmark having 574 lines. The generated Boogie programs have 1242 Boogie statements on average, with the largest benchmark having 4323 statements. The considerable sizes make it difficult to apply program synthesis to find the rootcauses. In fact, we needed a few domain-specific heuristics to prune the search space to be able to find the rootcauses within 800 seconds. Note that the heuristics only sacrifice the *completeness* of our technique — we may fail to find a rootcause even though it may exist.

Heuristics for pruning candidates. We define the following three domain-specific syntactic heuristics for finding rootcauses of binary programs. The *callee* heuristic only considers assignments to the callee register before an indirect call. The heuristic *load* only considers loads from a memory address, and the heuristic *imm* only considers assignments with arithmetic constants or operations. In addition, we also use a heuristic that exploits the synchronization of p_1 and p_2 across procedure calls. Let $f_1, \ldots, f_m$ and $g_1, \ldots, g_n$ be the sequence of procedure calls along cex in p_1 and p_2 respectively. We define a pair of calls (f_i, g_i) as the *earliest mismatched calls* if the calls $(f_1, g_1), \ldots, (f_{i-1}, g_{i-1})$ return matching outputs and (f_i, g_i) mismatch. We define a heuristic $callWind_k$ that only

Heuristic	Candidate s	AllFix R/NR	time(sec)	LeftPathFix R/NR	time(sec)	LeftPathEarliestFix R/NR	time(sec)
$callee$	125	12/27	85.4	14/25	77.8	24/15	85.0
$load$	128	2/37	113.1	3/36	98.6	6/32	129.1
imm	128	7/5	193.8	7/4	191.0	16/0	181.0
$callWind_1$	107	13/9	142.1	14/9	154.7	23/0	212.7
$callWind_2$	272	6/8	264.7	7/8	251.7	14/0	289.8
Total	140	15/24	134.1	18/22	128.4	34/5	154.4

Fig. 5. Summary on benchmarks returning either $ROOTCAUSE$ or $NOROOTCAUSE$.

considers fixes in the region between $f_{i-k}, \ldots, f_i$ and $g_{i-k}, \ldots, g_i$ in p_1 and p_2 respectively.

Experimental setup. Each benchmark consists of two procedures p_1 and p_2 being compared, and a syntactic filter $\in \{callee, load, imm, callWind_1, callWind_2\}$. With each of the 5 syntactic filters, we experiment with 46 pairs of procedures, giving us 230 benchmarks in total. Each benchmark is run with all optimizations from Sect. 4 enabled. We instantiate *LeftPathEarliestFix* by synchronizing at procedure call boundaries. A run can fail with *UNKNOWN* due to timeouts or out-of-memory exceptions in Boogie/Z3.

Results. Figure 5 presents the results. The table presents the following metrics (for non *UNKNOWN* cases): (1) average number of candidates generated for each benchmark, (2) benchmarks for which a rootcause is found (R) or not found (NR), and (3) average runtime (in seconds). These results indicate that progressively weakening the check to *LeftPathFix* and *LeftPathEarliestFix* identifies rootcause in more benchmarks. The "Total" row describes the total number of distinct rootcauses found across the different heuristics. We find a total of 34 out of 46 rootcauses (74 % of the cases), which we find quite encouraging. For the remaining examples, the most common reasons for *NOROOTCAUSE* include: (i) the need for multiple fixes even for the weakest check *LeftPathEarliestFix*, (ii) insufficient semantic similarity between p_1 and p_2, whereby p_1 is devoid of a value that fixes p_2, and (iii) several missing assumptions about the read and write sets of callees and aliasing assumptions.

We also measured the impact of an optimization $\in \{$Binary Search, MAXSAT$\}$ with respect to (a) the number of candidates pruned, and (b) the reduction in runtime. For each optimization, we study the effect of the optimization by disabling it. Both optimizations perform a substantial reduction in candidates, more pronounced for larger instances, with MAXSAT (resp., Binary Search) giving us a significant 49 % (resp., 12 %) reduction in runtime and 691 % (resp., 34 %) reduction in candidates[1]. The average runtime improvement is lower than the average improvement in candidates; there are few cases in Binary Search and MAXSAT where the optimization results in a slowdown due to the overhead of the prover.

---

[1] Detailed plots in Appendix of extended technical report [13].

6   Related Work

Automated debugging and repair are certainly not new problems. Our work is inspired in part by program repair techniques [2,15,21,24], and in part by error localization techniques [3,8]. The novelty of our work is in providing a sweet spot — formal guarantees for the rootcause (unlike localization approaches) without requiring a complete repair the program. Unlike our work, none of these approaches deal with the complexities of analyzing binary programs.

Error Localization. BugAssist by Jose et al. [8] analyzes a specific failing input to compute a minimal set of program statements that can be potentially changed to prevent the failing execution. Ermis et al. [5] propose a concept of error invariants to slice error traces using interpolants. In our context, we observe that most instructions in the program are relevant for equivalence failure. Consequently, both techniques end up retaining most of the instructions along the counterexample path. However, there is no guarantee that these rootcauses (program expressions) can be changed to repair the program.

Repair. On the other hand, there is active research in using synthesis for repairing programs. Nguyen et al. [15] assume a single-fix assumption to synthesize a repair such that the program passes all its test cases. Recent repair approaches perform template-based repair using a counterexample guided inductive synthesis (CEGIS) loop [9]. Singh et al. [21] use constraint-based synthesis to automatically provide feedback to students in an introductory programming course. They use the instructor's solution only as a specification for synthesizing a set of fixes to the student's solution i.e. their approach extends to the multiple-fix model. The sizes of examples from compiler validation are at least an order bigger than the benchmark sizes for student attempts; Furthermore, the space of all repairs is quite large in our setting (all x86 instructions with all possible operands). Our work differs from all three of [15,21], and [9] by (i) exploiting similarity in the two programs and therefore not requiring repair templates, and (ii) alleviating scalability issues by not insisting on a complete fix. However, our approach may fail to identify a rootcause when the program requires multiple fixes, or when p_1 does not possess a value that can fix p_2. In other related work, Samanta et al. [18] repair boolean programs with the single-fix assumption using QBF solving. In our setting, we do not abstract assembly language programs as boolean programs.

7   Conclusion

We have proposed a new formulation of rootcause for equivalence failures of similar programs. We have implemented our technique and evaluated it on several real-world binary equivalence failures and report the potential to be useful. We believe the idea is general and can be applied to other equivalence checking domains (e.g. grading assignments). We are currently extending the formulation to handle multiple fixes and combining with synthesis methods.

References

1. Barnett, M., Leino, K.R.M.: Weakest-precondition of unstructured programs. In: PASTE'2005, pp. 82–87 (2005)
2. Chandra, S., Torlak, E., Barman, S., Bodik, R.: Angelic debugging. In: Proceedings of the 33rd International Conference on Software Engineering, ICSE'2011, pp. 121–130, New York, NY, USA. ACM (2011)
3. Cleve, H., Zeller, A.: Locating causes of program failures. In: Proceedings of the 27th International Conference on Software Engineering, ICSE'2005, pp. 342–351, New York, NY, USA. ACM (2005)
4. Condit, J., Hackett, B., Lahiri, S.K., Qadeer, S.: Unifying type checking and property checking for low-level code. In: POPL, pp. 302–314 (2009)
5. Ermis, E., Schäf, M., Wies, T.: Error invariants. In: Giannakopoulou, D., Méry, D. (eds.) FM 2012. LNCS, vol. 7436, pp. 187–201. Springer, Heidelberg (2012)
6. Godlin, B., Strichman, O.: Regression verification. In: DAC, pp. 466–471 (2009)
7. Hawblitzel, C., Lahiri, S.K., Pawar, K., Hashmi, H., Gokbulut, S., Fernando, L., Detlefs, D., Wadsworth, S.: Will you still compile me tomorrow? static cross-version compiler validation. In: Proceedings of the 2013 9th Joint Meeting on Foundations of Software Engineering, ESEC/FSE 2013, pp. 191–201, New York, NY, USA. ACM (2013)
8. Jose, M., Majumdar, R.: Cause clue clauses: error localization using maximum satisfiability. In: Proceedings of the 32Nd ACM SIGPLAN Conference on Programming Language Design and Implementation, PLDI'2011, pp. 437–446, New York, NY, USA. ACM (2011)
9. Konighofer, R., Bloem, R.: Automated error localization and correction for imperative programs. Formal Methods Comput. Aided Des. **2011**, 91–100 (2011)
10. Kundu, S., Tatlock, Z., Lerner, S.: Proving optimizations correct using parameterized program equivalence. In: Programming Language Design and Implementation (PLDI'2009), pp. 327–337. ACM (2009)
11. Lahiri, S.K., Hawblitzel, C., Kawaguchi, M., Rebêlo, H.: SYMDIFF: a language-agnostic semantic diff tool for imperative programs. In: Madhusudan, P., Seshia, S.A. (eds.) CAV 2012. LNCS, vol. 7358, pp. 712–717. Springer, Heidelberg (2012)
12. Lahiri, S.K., McMillan, K.L., Sharma, R., Hawblitzel, C.: Differential assertion checking. In: Proceedings of the 2013 9th Joint Meeting on Foundations of Software Engineering, ESEC/FSE 2013, pp. 345–355, New York, NY, USA. ACM (2013)
13. Lahiri, S.K., Sinha, R., Hawblitzel, C.: Automatic rootcausing for program equivalence failures in binaries. Technical Report MSR-TR-2014-11, Microsoft Research (2014)
14. Necula, G.C.: Translation validation for an optimizing compiler. In: ACM SIGPLAN Conference on Programming Language Design and Implementation (PLDI'2000), pp. 83–94 (2000)
15. Nguyen, H.D.T., Qi, D., Roychoudhury, A., Chandra, S.: Semfix: Program repair via semantic analysis. In: Proceedings of the 2013 International Conference on Software Engineering, ICSE'2013, pp. 772–781., Piscataway, NJ, USA, IEEE Press (2013)
16. Ramaswamy, S.: Deep dive into the kernel of .NET on Windows Phone 8. In: Build Conference (2012)
17. Ramos, D.A., Engler, D.R.: Practical, low-effort equivalence verification of real code. In: Gopalakrishnan, G., Qadeer, S. (eds.) CAV 2011. LNCS, vol. 6806, pp. 669–685. Springer, Heidelberg (2011)

18. Samanta, R., Deshmukh, J.V., Emerson, E.A.: Automatic generation of local repairs for boolean programs. In: Proceedings of the 2008 International Conference on Formal Methods in Computer-Aided Design, FMCAD'2008, pp. 27:1–27:10, Piscataway, NJ, USA. IEEE Press (2008)
19. Samet, H.: Compiler testing via symbolic interpretation. In: In Proceedings of the ACM 29th Annual Conference, pp. 492–497 (1976)
20. Satisfiability Modulo Theories Library (SMT-LIB). Available http://goedel.cs.uiowa.edu/smtlib/
21. Singh, R., Gulwani, S., Solar-Lezama, A.: Automated feedback generation for introductory programming assignments. In: Proceedings of the 34th ACM SIGPLAN Conference on Programming Language Design and Implementation, PLDI'2013, pp. 15–26, New York, NY, USA. ACM (2013)
22. Solar-Lezama, A., Arnold, G., Tancau, L., Bodik, R., Saraswat, V., Seshia, S.: Sketching stencils. SIGPLAN Not. **42**(6), 167–178 (2007)
23. SymDiff source code. Available http://symdiff.codeplex.com
24. Weimer, W.: Patches as better bug reports. In: Generative Programming and Component Engineering, 5th International Conference, GPCE 2006, pp. 181–190. ACM (2006)
25. Yang, J., Hawblitzel, C.: Safe to the last instruction: automated verification of a type-safe operating system. In: Proceedings of the 2010 ACM SIGPLAN Conference on Programming Language Design and Implementation (PLDI), pp. 99–110 (2010)

Fine-Grained Caching of Verification Results

K. Rustan M. Leino[1]([✉]) and Valentin Wüstholz[2]([✉])

[1] Microsoft Research, Redmond, WA, USA
leino@microsoft.com
[2] Department of Computer Science, ETH Zurich, Zurich, Switzerland
valentin.wuestholz@inf.ethz.ch

Abstract. Developing provably correct programs is an incremental process that often involves a series of interactions with a program verifier. To increase the responsiveness of the program verifier during such interactions, we designed a system for fine-grained caching of verification results. The caching system uses the program's call graph and control-flow graph to focus the verification effort on just the parts of the program that were affected by the user's most recent modifications. The novelty lies in how the original program is instrumented with cached information to avoid unnecessary work for the verifier. The system has been implemented in the Boogie verification engine, which allows it to be used by different verification front ends that target the intermediate verification language Boogie; we present one such application in the integrated development environment for the Dafny programming language. The paper describes the architecture and algorithms of the caching system and reports on how much it improves the performance of the verifier in practice.

1 Introduction

Making formal program verification useful in practice requires not only automated logical theories and formal programming-language semantics, but also—inescapably—a human understanding of why the program under verification might actually be correct. This understanding is often gained by trial and error, debugging verification attempts to discover and correct errors in programs and specifications and to figure out crucial inductive invariants. To support this important trial and error process, it is essential that the integrated development environment (IDE) provides rapid feedback to the user.

In this paper, we enhance the IDE for the specification-aware programming language Dafny [20] by adding fine-grained caching of results from earlier runs of the verifier. The effect of this caching is to reduce the time from user keystrokes in the editor to the reporting of verification errors that are gathered in the background. In some cases, this lag time can now be around a second for examples where it previously may have taken tens of seconds for the verifier to repeat the checking of proof obligations that were not affected by the change.

© Springer International Publishing Switzerland 2015
D. Kroening and C.S. Păsăreanu (Eds.): CAV 2015, Part I, LNCS 9206, pp. 380–397, 2015.
DOI: 10.1007/978-3-319-21690-4_22

These improvements rely on a basic caching technique that tracks dependencies using the program's call graph to avoid re-verification of methods that were not affected by the most recent change to the program. Our fine-grained caching takes this a step futher. It is motivated by the fact that when a proof obligation is not automatically verified, a user tends to spend human focus and editing in one small area of the program. Often, this area can be in one branch of a method, so if the tool can rapidly re-verify just what has changed, the user can make progress more quickly. Our fine-grained caching thus makes use of the program's control-flow graph.

Like other verifiers, the Dafny verifier generates proof obligations by translating Dafny to an intermediate verification language (IVL), namely Boogie [2,21]. We designed our fine-grained caching to operate at the level of the IVL, which makes it possible for other Boogie front ends to make use of the new functionality. Our novel caching approach compares the current *snapshot* of a Boogie program with a previously verified snapshot. It then instruments the current snapshot to adjust the proof obligations accordingly. Finally, it passes the instrumented Boogie program to the underlying satisfiability-modulo-theories (SMT) solver in the usual way. Our implementation is available as part of the Boogie and Dafny open source projects.

In Sect. 2, we explain a motivating example in more detail. Sect. 3 gives background on the architecture of the Dafny verifier and describes the basic, coarse-grained caching based on the program's call graph. We describe our fine-grained caching in Sect. 4 and evaluate how both techniques improve the performance of the verifier in Sect. 5.

2   Motivating Example

Let us consider some typical steps in the interactive process of developing a verifiably correct program, indicating where our caching improvements play a role. Figure 1 shows an incomplete attempt at specifying and implementing the Dutch Flag algorithm, which sorts an array of colors.

The program gives rise to several proof obligations, following the rules of Hoare logic. The loop invariants are checked when control flow first reaches the loop. The loop body with its three branches is checked to decrease a termination metric (here provided by the tool: the absolute difference between w and b) and to maintain the loop invariants. The postcondition of the method is checked to follow from the loop invariants and the negation of the guard (without further inspection of the loop body). For every call to method `Sort` in the rest of the program, the method's precondition is checked and its postcondition is assumed.

In addition, all statements and expressions, including those in specifications, are verified to be well-formed. For example, for the assignment that swaps two array elements in the loop body (line 18), the well-formedness checks ensure that the array is not `null`, that the indices are within bounds of the array, that the method is allowed to modify the heap at these locations, and that the parallel assignment does not attempt to assign different values to the same heap location.

```
0    datatype Color = Red | White | Blue
1
2    predicate Ordered(c: Color, d: Color) { c = Red ∨ d = Blue }
3
4    method Sort(a: array<Color>)
5      requires a ≠ null
6      modifies a
7      ensures forall i,j • 0 ≤ i < j < a.Length ⟹ Ordered(a[i], a[j])
8    {
9      var r, w, b := 0, 0, a.Length;
10     while w ≠ b
11       invariant 0 ≤ r ≤ w ≤ b ≤ a.Length
12       invariant forall i • 0 ≤ i < r ⟹ a[i] = Red
13       invariant forall i • r ≤ i < w ⟹ a[i] = White
14       invariant forall i • b ≤ i < a.Length ⟹ a[i] = Blue
15     {
16       match a[w]
17         case Red ⟹
18           a[r], a[w] := a[w], a[r]; r := r + 1;
19         case White ⟹
20           w := w + 1;
21         case Blue ⟹
22           b := b - 1;
23     }
24   }
```

Fig. 1. Incomplete attempt at implementing the Dutch Flag algorithm. As written, the program contains a specification omission, a specification error, and two coding errors. As the program is edited, our fine-grained caching of verification results enables a more responsive user experience by avoiding re-verification of unaffected proof obligations.

To provide *design-time* feedback to the user, the Dafny IDE automatically runs the verifier in the background as the program is being edited. This allows the verifier to assist the user in ways that more closely resemble those of a background spell checker. Given the program in Fig. 1, the Dafny verifier will report three errors.

The first error message points out that the method body may not establish the postcondition. Selecting this error in the Dafny IDE brings up the verification debugger [18], which readily points out the possibility that the array contains two White values. To fix the error, we add a disjunct c = d to the definition of predicate Ordered. Instead of expecting the user to re-run the verifier manually, the Dafny IDE will do so automatically. To speed up this process, the basic caching technique will already avoid some unnecessary work by using the call graph: only methods that depend on the predicate Ordered will be re-verified, which includes the body of Sort and, since the postcondition of Sort mentions the predicate, all callers of Sort. Caller dependencies get lower scheduling priority, since they are likely to be further away from the user's current focus of attention. However, we can hope for something even better: the maintenance of the loop invariant in `Sort` need not be re-verified, but only the fact that the loop invariant and the negation of the guard establish the postcondition. Our fine-grained caching technique makes this possible.

The second error message points out that the loop may fail to terminate. Selecting the error shows a trace through the `Red` branch of the `match` statement, and we realize that this branch also needs to increment `w`. As we make that change, the tool re-verifies only the loop body, whereas it would have re-verified the entire method with just the basic caching technique.

The third error message points out that the last loop invariant is not maintained by the `Blue` branch. It is fixed by swapping `a[w]` and `a[b]` after the update to `b`. After doing so, the re-verification proceeds as for the second error.

Finally, it may become necessary to strengthen `Sort`'s postcondition while verifying some caller—it omits the fact that the final array's elements are a permutation of the initial array's. If only the basic caching was used, the addition of such a postcondition would cause both `Sort` and all of its callers to be re-verified. By using the fine-grained caching, the body of `Sort` is re-verified to check only the new postcondition (which in this case will require adding the postcondition also as a loop invariant). For callers, the situation is even better: since the change of `Sort`'s specification only strengthens the postcondition, proof obligations in callers that succeeded before the change are not re-verified.

The performance improvements that we just gave a taste of have the effect of focusing the verifier's attention on those parts of the program that the user is currently, perhaps by trial and error, editing. The result is a user experience with significantly improved response times. In our simple example program, the time to re-verify the entire program is about 0.25 seconds, so caching is not crucial. However, when programs have more methods, contain more control paths, and involve more complicated predicates, verification times can easily reach tens of seconds. In such cases, our fine-grained caching can let the user gain insight from the verification tool instead of just becoming increasingly frustrated and eventually giving up all hopes of ever applying formal verification techniques.

3 Verification Architecture and Basic Caching

In this section, we describe the role of the intermediate verification language Boogie and the basic caching technique that the fine-grained caching builds on. We have presented an informal overview of the basic caching technique in a workshop paper describing different novel features of the Dafny IDE [22].

3.1 Architecture

Like many other verifiers, such as Spec# [3] and VCC [8], Dafny uses the Boogie [2] intermediate verification language to express proof obligations to be discharged by the Boogie verification engine using an SMT solver, such as Z3 [10]. The language constructs of the source language are translated into more primitive constructs of

Boogie, including variables, axioms, and procedures. For example, a Dafny *method* is translated to several Boogie constructs: (1) a *procedure (declaration)* that captures the specification of the method, (2) a *procedure implementation* that captures the method body and checks that it adheres to the method specification, and (3) a second procedure implementation that captures the well-formedness conditions for the method specification [19]. As another example, a Dafny *function* is translated to a corresponding Boogie *function* and a procedure implementation that captures the function's well-formedness conditions. Boogie functions are given meaning by *axioms*, but to simplify our presentation, we omit some details of the translation of Dafny functions.

Boogie supports a modular verification approach by verifying procedure implementations individually. More precisely, calls in procedure implementations are reasoned about only in terms of their specification (i.e., the corresponding procedure declaration). Consequently, a change to a program often does not invalidate verification results obtained for independent program entities. In particular, a change in a given procedure implementation does not invalidate verification results of other procedure implementations, and a change in a procedure's specification may invalidate verification results only of its callees and of the corresponding procedure implementation.

3.2   Basic Caching

While the Boogie pipeline accepts a single program, obtains verification results, and then reports them, the basic caching mechanism turns Boogie into more of a verification service: it accepts a stream of programs, each of which we refer to as a *snapshot*.

The basic caching approach exploits the modular structure of Boogie programs by determining which program entities have been changed *directly* in the latest program snapshot and which other program entities are *indirectly* affected by those changes. To determine direct changes, Boogie relies on the client front end (Dafny in our case) to provide an *entity checksum* for each function, procedure, and procedure implementation. For example, the Boogie program in Fig. 2 shows entity checksums provided by a front end to Boogie via the : checksum custom attribute. In our implementation, Dafny computes them as a hash of those parts of the Dafny abstract syntax tree that are used to generate the corresponding Boogie program entities. This makes checksums insensitive to certain textual changes, such as ones that concern comments or whitespace.

To determine indirect changes, Boogie computes *dependency checksums* for all functions, procedures, and procedure implementations based on their own entity checksum and the dependency checksums of entities they depend on directly (e.g., callees). These checksums allow the basic caching to reuse verification results for an entity if its dependency checksum is unchanged in the latest snapshot.

For example, when computing dependency checksums from entity checksums in Fig. 2, Boogie takes into account that both implementations depend on the

```
0  procedure {:checksum "727"} abs(a: int) returns (r: int)
1    ensures 0 ≤ r;
2
3  implementation {:checksum "733"} abs(a: int) returns (r: int)
4  { r := 0; }
5
6  implementation {:checksum "739"} main()
7  { var x: int; call x := abs(-585); assert x = 585; }
```

Fig. 2. Boogie program that shows how a front end uses custom attributes on declarations to assign entity checksums, which can be computed in front-end specific ways.

procedure declaration of `abs` (implementation `abs` needs to adhere to its procedure declaration and `main` contains a call to `abs`). Consequently, a change that only affects the entity checksum of *procedure* `abs` (e.g., to strengthen the postcondition) will prevent Boogie from returning cached verification results for both implementations. However, a change that only affects the entity checksum of *implementation* `abs` (e.g., to return the *actual* absolute value) will allow Boogie to return cached verification results for implementation `main`.

Figure 3 gives an architectural overview of the caching system. In terms of it, the basic caching works as follows. First, Boogie computes dependency checksums for all entities in a given program snapshot. Then, for each procedure implementation P, the cache is consulted. If the cache contains the dependency checksum for P, branch (0) is taken and the cached verification results are reported immediately. Otherwise, branch (1) is taken and the procedure implementation is verified as usual by the Boogie pipeline. Our fine-grained caching may also choose branch (2), as we explain in Sect. 4.

3.3   Prioritizing Procedure Implementations Using Checksums

Besides using them for determining which procedure implementations do not need to be re-verified, we use the checksums for determining the order in which the others should be verified. Ideally, procedure implementations that are more directly related to the user's latest changes are given higher priority, since these most likely correspond to the ones the user cares about most and wants feedback on most quickly. The checksums provide a metric for achieving this by defining four priority levels for procedure implementations:

- low (unlike the entity checksum, the dependency checksum in the cache is different from the current one): Only dependencies of the implementation changed.
- medium (entity checksum in the cache is different from the current one): The implementation itself changed.
- high (no cache entry was found): The implementation was added recently.
- highest (both the entity and the dependency checksum is the same as the one in the cache): The implementation was not affected by the change and a cache lookup is sufficient for reporting verification results to the user *immediately*, instead of waiting for other implementations to be verified.

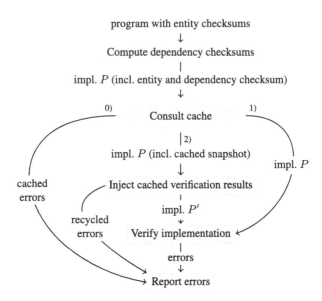

Fig. 3. Overview of the verification process for procedure implementations. Boxes correspond to components and arrows illustrate data flow. The caching component produces three possible outputs: 0) cached errors in case the entity and dependency checksums are unchanged, 1) the implementation P in case it is not contained in the cache, or 2) the implementation P and the cached snapshot in case either the entity or the dependency checksum have changed. Cached snapshots are used to inject verification results into the implementation and to identify errors that can be recycled.

4 Fine-Grained Caching

Basic caching can determine which procedure implementations in a new snapshot do not need to be re-verified at all, but it does not track enough information to allow us to reuse verification results for parts of an implementation. In this section, we present an extension of the basic caching that reuses verification results in fine-grained ways. In particular, our extension avoids re-verification of checks that were not affected by the most recent change and it recycles errors that are still present in the current snapshot.

Before giving our full algorithm, we sketch how it works in two common scenarios we want to address: when an isolated part of a procedure implementation (e.g., one of two branches or a loop body) has been changed, and when the specification of a procedure has been changed. We proceed by example, starting from the program in Fig. 4. Running Boogie on this program results in two errors: a failure to establish the postcondition on line 2 and an assertion violation on line 7. To fix the postcondition error in the program in Fig. 4, the user might add an explicit else branch on line 10 and insert statement r := x. This is an instance of the common change-in-isolated-part scenario. In particular,

```
0   procedure gcd(x, y: int) returns (r: int)
1     requires 0 < x ∧ 0 < y;
2     ensures 0 ≤ r;
3
4   implementation gcd(x, y: int) returns (r: int) {
5     if (x < y) {
6       call r := gcd(x, y - x);
7       assert 1 ≤ r;
8     } else if (y < x) {
9       call r := gcd(x - y, y);
10    }
11    assert 0 < x + y;
12  }
```

Fig. 4. Incomplete attempt at implementing a Boogie procedure for computing the greatest common denominator. Boogie reports a postcondition violation for the implementation and an assertion violation on line 7.

the change has no effect on the assertion on line 7, and thus we would hope to be able to cache and recycle the error.

4.1 Fine-Grained Dependency Tracking Using Statement Checksums

To cache and reuse verification results at this fine granularity, we need to know what each statement depends on. To determine this, we compute a *statement checksum* for every statement from a hash of its pretty-printed representation and—to keep the overhead small—the statement checksums of *all* statements that precede it in the control flow (as opposed to ones that actually affect it). If a statement contains a function call in some subexpression, then the statement depends on the callee's definition and we include the callee's dependency checksum when computing the statement checksum.

The computation of statement checksums occurs after the Boogie program has undergone some simplifying transformations. For example, loops have been transformed using loop invariants and back-edges of loops have been cut [4]; thus, the computation of statement checksums does not involve any fixpoint computation. As another example, the checks for postconditions have been made explicit as **assert** statements at the end of the implementation body and the preconditions of procedure implementations have been transformed into **assume** statements at the beginning of the implementation body; thus, these statements are taken into account for computing the statement checksums. In contrast to an **assert** statement, which instructs the verifier to check if a condition holds at the given program point, an **assume** statement instructs the verifier to blindly assume a condition to hold at the given program point.

After the simplifications from above, there are only two kinds of statements that lead to checks: assertions and calls (precondition of callee). We will refer to them as *checked statements*. We introduce a cache that associates statement checksums of such statements in a given implementation with verification results. Before verifying a new snapshot, we compute statement checksums for the new snapshot and then instrument the snapshot by consulting this cache.

Let us describe this in more detail using our example. We will refer to the program in Fig. 4 as Snapshot 0 and the program resulting from adding the else branch and assignment on line 10 as Snapshot 1. After verifying Snapshot 0, the cache will have entries for the statement checksums of the following checked statements: the failing assertion on line 7, the succeeding precondition checks for the calls on lines 6 and 9, the succeeding assertion on line 11, and the failing check of the postcondition from line 2. The statement checksums for the first three checked statements (on lines 6, 7, and 9) in Snapshot 1 are the same as in Snapshot 0. Since the cache tells us the verification results for these, we report the cached error immediately and we add `assume` statements for the checked condition before these checked statements in Snapshot 1. The statement checksums of the fourth and fifth checked statement are different in Snapshot 1, since they are affected by the modification of line 10. Since the new checksums are not found in the cache, the statements are not rewritten. As a result, Boogie needs to only verify those checks. Indeed, Boogie is now able to prove both and it updates the cache accordingly. With reference to Fig. 3, what we have just described takes place along branch (2) after the basic cache has been consulted.

4.2   Injecting Explicit Assumptions and Partially Verified Checks

To fix the failing assertion on line 7 in Fig. 4, the user might now decide to strengthen the postcondition of the procedure by changing it to 1 ≤ r. This is an instance of the common change-in-specification scenario. In particular, since the change involves a strengthened postcondition, we would hope to avoid re-verifying any previously succeeding checks downstream of call sites.

We will refer to the program resulting from the user's change as Snapshot 2. After Boogie computes the statement checksums, only the statement checksum for the assertion of the postcondition will be different from the ones in the cached snapshot. However, since the dependency checksums of the callee changed for both calls, we introduce an *explicit assumption* [7] after each call to capture the condition assumed at this point in the cached snapshot. We do so by introducing an *assumption variable* for each such call that is initialized to `true` and is only assigned to once (here, after the corresponding call) using a statement of the form `a := a ∧ P`, where `a` is the assumption variable and P is a boolean condition. The variable allows us to later refer to an assumption that was made at a specific program point; e.g., to mark a check that was not failing in the corresponding cached snapshot as *partially verified* under a conjunction of assumption variables.

To illustrate, consider the rewrite of Snapshot 2 in Fig. 5. At this stage, the precondition is assumed explicitly on line 2 and the postcondition is asserted explicitly on line 15 as described earlier. On line 0, we introduce one assumption variable for each call to a procedure with a different dependency checksum, and these are initialized to `true` on line 1. The call on line 5 gets to assume the new postcondition of `gcd`. If that call happens to return in a state that was allowed by the previous postcondition ($0 \leq \mathtt{r}$), then assumption variable a0 will remain true after the update on line 6. But if the call returns in a state that does not satisfy the previously assumed postcondition, then a0 will be set to `false`. In our example, since the postcondition of the callee is strengthened, the explicit assumption $0 \leq \mathtt{r}$ will always evaluate to true. Indeed, this works particularly well when postconditions are not weakened, but, depending on the calling context, it may also simplify the verification otherwise. For instance, it would work for a call where the state is constrained such that for this particular call site the previous postcondition holds after the call, even though the new postcondition is indeed weaker.

Next, we inject assumptions into the program about checked statements that are found to be non-failing in the cached snapshot based on their statement checksum. More precisely, for each statement with checked condition P whose statement checksum is in the cache and that was non-failing in the cached snapshot, we inject an assumption $A \implies P$, where A is the conjunction of all assumption variables. Intuitively, this tells the verifier to skip this check if all assumption variables are true. Otherwise, the verifier will perform the check since a state was reached for which it has not already been verified in the cached snapshot. We say that the check has been marked as *partially verified*. As an optimization, we include in A only those assumption variables whose update statement definition can reach this use; we refer to these as *relevant* assumption variables. Figure 5 shows the assumptions being introduced on lines 4, 9, and 13, preceding the precondition checks and the assert statement, thus marking these checks as partially verified. Note that the assertion on line 7 is not marked as partially verified, since it is a failing assertion in Snapshot 1. Since the assumption variables remain true, the partially verified checks in effect become fully verified in this example. Note that the verifier may discover that only some partially verified checks are in effect fully verified depending on the state at those checks. For instance, this may happen if the state after some call was not always allowed by the callee's previous postcondition, but some partially verified checks after that call are in a conditional branch where the branching condition constrains the state such that all states are allowed by the previous postcondition *there*.

4.3   Algorithm for Injecting Cached Verification Results

In this subsection, we present our algorithm for injecting cached verification results in procedure implementations of medium or low priority, for which no limit on the number of reported errors was hit when verifying the cached implementation. At this point, most existing Boogie transformations have been applied to the implementation as described earlier (e.g., eliminating loops using loop invariants and adding explicit assertions for procedure postconditions).

As a first step, we compute statement checksums for all statements in an implementation as defined earlier. As a second step, we insert explicit assumptions for calls if the dependency checksum of the callee has changed in the current snapshot. More precisely, for each call, we distinguish between three different cases, in order:

```
0   var {:assumption} a0, a1: bool;
1   a0, a1 := true, true;
2   assume 0 < x ∧ 0 < y;   // precondition
3   if (x < y) {
4       assume (true) ⟹ (0 < x ∧ 0 < y - x);
5       call r := gcd(x, y - x);
6       a0 := a0 ∧ (0 ≤ r);
7       assert 1 ≤ r;
8   } else if (y < x) {
9       assume (true) ⟹ (0 < x - y ∧ 0 < y);
10      call r := gcd(x - y, y);
11      a1 := a1 ∧ (0 ≤ r);
12  } else { r := x; }
13  assume (a0 ∧ a1) ⟹ (0 < x + y);
14  assert 0 < x + y;
15  assert 0 ≤ r;   // postcondition
```

Fig. 5. Body of the procedure implementation for Snapshot 2 after injecting cached verification results (underlined). The instrumented program contains two explicit assumptions [7] on lines 6 and 11 derived from the postcondition of the cached callee procedure. Also, all checks that did not result in errors in the cached snapshot have been marked as partially verified by introducing **assume** statements on lines 7, 9, and 13.

1. Dependency checksum of callee is the same as in the cached snapshot: We do not need to do anything since the asserted precondition and the assumed postcondition are the same as in the cached snapshot.
2. All functions that the callee transitively depended on in the cached snapshot are still defined and unchanged in the current snapshot: Before the call, we add the statement assume ? ⟹ P, where ? is a placeholder that will be filled in during the final step of the algorithm and P is the precondition of the callee in the cached snapshot. This may allow us to reuse the fact that the precondition of a call has been verified in the cached snapshot. To simplify the presentation, we will only later determine if the precondition has indeed been verified and under which condition. Since the dependency checksum of the callee is different from the one in the cached snapshot, we additionally introduce an explicit assumption to capture the condition that was assumed after the call in the cached snapshot. This condition depends on the callee's *modifies clause* (which lists the global variables that the callee is allowed to modify) and its postcondition. To capture the former, let V be the set of global variables that were added to the callee's modifies clause since the cached snapshot. We now add ov := v for each global variable v in this set V before the call, where ov is a fresh, local variable. This allows us to express the explicit assumption by adding the statement a := a ∧ (Q ∧ M) after the call, where a is a fresh assumption variable, Q is the postcondition of the callee in the cached snapshot and M contains a conjunct ov == v for each global variable v in the set V. Note that M does not depend on global variables that

were removed from the callee's modifies clause since the cached snapshot; the statements after the call have already been verified for all possible values of such variables.

3. Otherwise: Since we cannot easily express the pre- and postcondition of the callee in the cached snapshot, we need to be conservative. We therefore do not add any assumption about the precondition and we add the statement a := a ∧ false after the call, where a is a fresh assumption variable.

As a third step, we transform each checked statements with the checked condition P to express cached verification results. We distinguish four cases, in order:

1. Some relevant assumption variable is definitely false when performing constant propagation: We do not do anything, since we cannot determine under which condition the check may have been verified.
2. There was an error for this check in the cached implementation and there are no relevant assumption variables: Since it has previously resulted in an error under identical conditions, we add the statement assume P before and report the error immediately to avoid unnecessary work.
3. There was no error for this check in the cached implementation: Since it has been verified previously, we add the statement assume $A \implies P$ before, where A is the conjunction of all relevant assumption variables. If there are any such assumption variables, we say that the check has been marked as *partially* verified; otherwise, we say that it has been marked as *fully* verified.
4. Otherwise: We do not do anything. For instance, this may happen if we cannot determine that we have seen the same check in the cached snapshot.

As a last step, we replace the placeholder ? in each statement assume ? $\implies$ P with the conjunction of all relevant assumption variables, if none of the relevant assumption variables are definitely false and there was no error for the corresponding call in the cached implementation. Otherwise, we drop the statement.

Optimization for Explicit Assumptions Within Loops. By default, loop bodies are verified modularly in Boogie. That is, on entry to a loop body, all variables that are modified within the body are "havocked" by assigning a nondeterministic value and the invariant is assumed. After the loop body, only the invariant remains to be checked. For this reason, an assumption (e.g., as a result of a procedure call) that was made in the loop body when verifying the cached snapshot was neither used for verifying statements after the loop (provided there is no break statement in the loop) nor for verifying statements within the loop that precede the assignment to the corresponding assumption variable. To reproduce this behavior for the current snapshot, it is safe not to havoc assumption variables that would usually be havocked in this case. By doing so, such assumption variables usually remain true at that point unless the corresponding loop has previously been unrolled a number of times.

5   Evaluation

To evaluate the effectiveness of our caching techniques *in practice*, we recorded eight verification sessions during expert use of the Dafny IDE for regular development tasks. Those sessions were not scripted and therefore cover real workloads that such a tool faces when it is being used by a user to develop provably correct software. The sessions span a wide range of activities (including extension, maintenance, and refactoring) that are encountered when developing programs of several hundred lines. Sessions consist of up to 255 individual program snapshots (see Fig. 6) since the Dafny IDE automatically verifies the program as the user is editing it. To make this a pleasant experience for the user, the responsiveness of the tool is of paramount importance.

Figure 6 clearly shows that this user experience could not be achieved without caching. The basic caching alone decreases the running times of the verifier tremendously (more than an order of magnitude for many sessions) and complementing it with fine-grained caching decreases them even more. This confirms the positive feedback that we received from users of the Dafny IDE, including members of the Ironclad project at Microsoft Research, whose codebase includes more than 30'000 lines of Dafny code [15]. Interestingly, caching turned out to have a more significant effect on the responsiveness of the tool than parallelization of verification tasks in Boogie using multiple SMT solver instances.

Figure 7 sheds more light on why the basic caching is so effective by showing the priorities of the procedure implementations that are sent to the verifier for each snapshot in session 5: most of the procedure implementations do not need to be re-verified at all and only two implementations (originating from a single Dafny method) need to be verified for most snapshots. This data looks very similar for the other sessions and demonstrates that the basic caching benefits significantly from the modular verification approach in Dafny. Besides this, we can see that there are occasional spikes with procedure implementations of low priority. For example, snapshot 2 consists of a change to a function that may affect all callers. In fact, due to the way that functions are handled, all *transitive* callers are affected, which is not the case for procedures. While in this case the basic caching needs to re-verify 11 procedure implementations from scratch, the fine-grained caching is able to mark 400 out of 971 checked statements in Boogie as fully verified. This reduces the running time from 28 s to 14 s and at the same time avoids a timeout (by default, 10 s per procedure implementation) for one of those procedure implementations.

Overall, Fig. 6 shows that the fine-grained caching performs even better than the basic caching for all sessions (42 % faster for session 3 and on average 17 % faster compared to the basic caching). For session 7, there is no significant speedup even though the fine-grained caching is able to mark a large number of checks as verified. It seems that, in this case, most of the time is spent on verifying a single check (e.g., the postcondition of the edited method) that could not be marked as verified. Such cases can come up occasionally since the times that are needed for verifying different checks are usually not distributed uniformly.

SESSION	SNAPSHOTS	TIME (IN SECONDS)			NUMBER OF TIMEOUTS		
		NC	BC	FGC	NC	BC	FGC
0	70	4'395.3	315.3	277.5	58	3	1
1	13	758.5	88.2	74.8	11	4	2
2	59	3'648.0	220.2	206.1	83	5	4
3	254	13'977.6	1'734.7	1'008.7	2	1	0
4	255	6'698.6	533.8	499.8	16	6	5
5	27	1'956.0	785.7	519.7	0	0	0
6	29	106.9	33.3	27.3	0	0	0
7	7	765.5	20.5	20.0	0	0	0

Fig. 6. Comparison of three configurations for verifying eight recorded IDE sessions: no caching (**NC**), basic caching (**BC**) and fine-grained caching (**FGC**). The second column shows the number of program snapshots per session. The next three columns show the running times for each configuration and the rightmost three columns show the number of timed-out procedure implementations for each configuration.

Besides increasing responsiveness, caching helps in reducing the number of procedure implementations that fail to verify due to timeouts (see Fig. 6). Again, the basic caching avoids the majority of timeouts and the fine-grained caching avoids even more of them (between 17 % and 100 % less), which is not obvious given our program transformations. This additional reduction over the basic caching is due to the fact that Boogie is able to focus on fewer unverified or partially verified checks.

To provide a better indication of how much the fine-grained caching is able to reduce the verification effort, Fig. 8 shows the number of checked statements for each snapshot in session 5 that were transformed when injecting cached verification results. This demonstrates that for many snapshots, more than half of the checks can be marked as fully verified or errors from the cached snapshot can be recycled (two errors each for snapshots 5 and 6 and one error each for snapshots 7 and 8). At an early development stage, fewer checks were marked as verified since statement checksums changed more often. It turned out that small changes in a Dafny program could result in significant changes to the

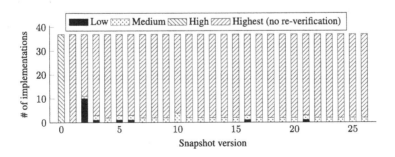

Fig. 7. Priorities of procedure implementations for session 5. The bars show the number of procedure implementations of a given priority for each snapshot version. Most implementations are assigned the highest priority and do not need to be re-verified.

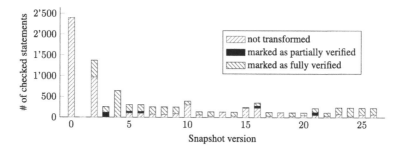

Fig. 8. Transformed checked statements in session 5. The bars show the number of checked statements for each snapshot version that are marked as fully verified, partially verified, or not transformed at all. Additionally, a number of errors are recycled: two errors each for snapshots 5 and 6 and one error each for snapshots 7 and 8.

corresponding Boogie program due to the way in which names (e.g., of auxiliary variables) were generated. After taking this into account during the translation of Dafny into Boogie, performance improved significantly.

6   Related Work

Caching is a widely used technique for reusing information that was computed in the past. More specifically, there are several existing approaches for reusing results from previous runs of static analyzers, model checkers, program verifiers, and automatic test-case generation tools. Clousot [12], a static analyzer for .NET, uses caching to retrieve the results of previous runs of its cloud-based analysis service [1]. Unlike our fine-grained caching, it only reuses such results if a method itself did not change *and* if the specifications of all its callees did not change. Clousot also supports "verification modulo versions" [23], which uses conditions inferred for a previous version of a program to only report new errors for the current version. The Why3 verification platform uses checksums to maintain program proofs in the form of *proof sessions* as the platform evolves (e.g., by generating different proof obligations). In particular, it matches goals from the existing proof with new goals using both checksums and *goal shapes*, a heuristic similarity measure. Maintenance of proofs is particularly important for interactive proof assistants since proofs are largely constructed by users and, ideally, do not need to be changed once they are completed. Such work has been done for the KIV [24] and KeY [17] tools. Grigore and Moskal [14] have worked on such techniques for proofs that were generated by SMT solvers to verify programs using ESC/Java2.

There are several approaches for reusing information that was computed when running a non-modular tool on an earlier revision of a program. In the area of model checking, such information can consist of summaries computed using Craig interpolation [25], *derivation graphs* that record analysis progress [9], or parts of the reachable, abstract state space [16]; even the precision of the analysis that was sufficient for analyzing an earlier program revision may be used later [5]. Work on incremental compositional dynamic test generation [13] presents techniques for determining if function summaries that were obtained for an earlier version of a program can be safely reused when performing symbolic execution on the current version of the program.

Regression verification [26] is another area that developed techniques for reusing information that was collected during runs of a tool on earlier versions of a program. Unlike in our approach, the goal is to check if the behavior of the latest version of a program is equivalent to the one of an earlier version, much like in regression testing.

In spirit, our caching scheme is an instance of a truth maintenance system [11]. However, the mechanisms used are quite different. For example, a truth maintenance system records justifications for each fact, whereas our caching scheme tracks snapshots of the programs that give rise to proof obligations, not the proofs of the proof obligations themselves.

7 Conclusions and Future Work

We have presented two effective techniques for using cached verification results to improve the responsiveness and performance of the Dafny IDE. Both techniques are crucial for providing *design-time feedback* at every keystroke to users of the IDE, much like background spell checkers. The key novelties of our technique are its use of checksums for determining which parts of a program are affected by a change and how a program is instrumented with cached information to focus the verification effort. In particular, we use explicit assumptions to express the conditions under which we can reuse cached verification results. We have designed our technique to work on the level of an intermediate verification language. This makes it immediately usable for other verifiers that use the Boogie verification engine (e.g., VCC [8] or AutoProof [27]) and should make possible to adopt by other intermediate verification languages, such as Why3 [6].

As future work, we would like to make the existing caching more fine-grained in cases where assumptions in the program (e.g., resulting from user-provided assume statements, preconditions, and user-provided or inferred loop invariants) are affected by a change. We believe that—much like for procedure calls—we can use explicit assumptions to capture assumptions that were made in the cached snapshot, and thereby mark more checks as partially verified. We would also like to look into techniques, such as slicing, for determining if certain partially verified checks could be marked as fully verified by identifying the explicit assumptions they depend on more precisely.

Acknowledgments. We are grateful to the users of the Dafny IDE—notably, Nada Amin, Maria Christakis, Arjun Narayan, and Bryan Parno—for providing feedback on its caching system. We thank Maria for comments on a draft of this paper and the reviewers for their constructive comments.

References

1. Barnett, M., Bouaziz, M., Fähndrich, M., Logozzo, F.:. A case for static analyzers in the cloud. In: Workshop on Bytecode Semantics, Verification, Analysis, and Transformation (Bytecode 2013) (2013)
2. Barnett, M., Chang, B.-Y.E., DeLine, R., Jacobs, B., Leino, K.R.M.: Boogie: a modular reusable verifier for object-oriented programs. In: de Boer, F.S., Bonsangue, M.M., Graf, S., de Roever, W.-P. (eds.) FMCO 2005. LNCS, vol. 4111, pp. 364–387. Springer, Heidelberg (2006)
3. Barnett, M., Fähndrich, M., Leino, K.R.M., Müller, P., Schulte, W., Venter, H.: Specification and verification: the Spec# experience. Commun. ACM **54**(6), 81–91 (2011)
4. Barnett, M., Leino, K.R.M.: Weakest-precondition of unstructured programs. In: Workshop on Program Analysis for Software Tools and Engineering (PASTE), pp. 82–87. ACM (2005)
5. Beyer, D., Löwe, S., Novikov, E., Stahlbauer, A., Wendler, P.: Precision reuse for efficient regression verification. In: ESEC/FSE, pp. 389–399. ACM (2013)
6. Bobot, F., Filliâtre, J.-C., Marché, C., Paskevich, A.: Why3: shepherd your herd of provers. In: Boogie 2011: First International Workshop on Intermediate Verification Languages, pp. 53–64 (2011)
7. Christakis, M., Müller, P., Wüstholz, V.: Collaborative verification and testing with explicit assumptions. In: Giannakopoulou, D., Méry, D. (eds.) FM 2012. LNCS, vol. 7436, pp. 132–146. Springer, Heidelberg (2012)
8. Cohen, E., Dahlweid, M., Hillebrand, M., Leinenbach, D., Moskal, M., Santen, T., Schulte, W., Tobies, S.: VCC: a practical system for verifying concurrent C. In: Berghofer, S., Nipkow, T., Urban, C., Wenzel, M. (eds.) TPHOLs 2009. LNCS, vol. 5674, pp. 23–42. Springer, Heidelberg (2009)
9. Conway, C.L., Namjoshi, K.S., Dams, D.R., Edwards, S.A.: Incremental algorithms for inter-procedural analysis of safety properties. In: Etessami, K., Rajamani, S.K. (eds.) CAV 2005. LNCS, vol. 3576, pp. 449–461. Springer, Heidelberg (2005)
10. de Moura, L., Bjørner, N.S.: Z3: an efficient SMT solver. In: Ramakrishnan, C.R., Rehof, J. (eds.) TACAS 2008. LNCS, vol. 4963, pp. 337–340. Springer, Heidelberg (2008)
11. Doyle, J.: A truth maintenance system. Artif. Intell. **12**(3), 231–272 (1979)
12. Fähndrich, M., Logozzo, F.: Static contract checking with abstract interpretation. In: Beckert, B., Marché, C. (eds.) FoVeOOS 2010. LNCS, vol. 6528, pp. 10–30. Springer, Heidelberg (2011)
13. Godefroid, P., Lahiri, S.K., Rubio-González, C.: Statically validating must summaries for incremental compositional dynamic test generation. In: Yahav, E. (ed.) SAS 2011. LNCS, vol. 6887, pp. 112–128. Springer, Heidelberg (2011)
14. Grigore, R., Moskal, M.: Edit and verify. In: Workshop on First-Order Theorem Proving (FTP) (2007)
15. Hawblitzel, C., Howell, J., Lorch, J.R., Narayan, A., Parno, B., Zhang, D., Zill, B.: Ironclad apps: End-to-end security via automated full-system verification. In: OSDI, USENIX Association, pp. 165–181 (2014)
16. Henzinger, T.A., Jhala, R., Majumdar, R., Sanvido, M.A.A.: Extreme model checking. In: Dershowitz, N. (ed.) Verification: Theory and Practice. LNCS, vol. 2772, pp. 332–358. Springer, Heidelberg (2004)
17. Klebanov, V.: Extending the reach and power of deductive program verification. Ph.D. thesis. Department of Computer Science, Universität Koblenz-Landau (2009)

18. Le Goues, C., Leino, K.R.M., Moskal, M.: The Boogie verification debugger (tool paper). In: Barthe, G., Pardo, A., Schneider, G. (eds.) SEFM 2011. LNCS, vol. 7041, pp. 407–414. Springer, Heidelberg (2011)

19. Leino, K.R.M.: Specification and verification of object-oriented software. In: Engineering Methods and Tools for Software Safety and Security, Volume 22 of NATO Science for Peace and Security Series D: Information and Communication Security, Summer School Marktoberdorf 2008 Lecture Notes, pp. 231–266. IOS Press (2009)

20. Leino, K.R.M.: Dafny: an automatic program verifier for functional correctness. In: Clarke, E.M., Voronkov, A. (eds.) LPAR-16 2010. LNCS, vol. 6355, pp. 348–370. Springer, Heidelberg (2010)

21. Leino, K.R.M., Rümmer, P.: A polymorphic intermediate verification language: design and logical encoding. In: Esparza, J., Majumdar, R. (eds.) TACAS 2010. LNCS, vol. 6015, pp. 312–327. Springer, Heidelberg (2010)

22. Leino, K.R.M., Wüstholz, V.: The Dafny integrated development environment. In: Workshop on Formal Integrated Development Environment (F-IDE), Electronic Notes in Theoretical Computer Science, vol. 149, pp. 3–15 (2014)

23. Logozzo, F., Lahiri, S.K., Fähndrich, M., Blackshear, S.: Verification modulo versions: towards usable verification. In: PLDI, pp. 294–304. ACM (2014)

24. Reif, W., Stenzel, K.: Reuse of proofs in software verification. In: Shyamasundar, R.K. (ed.) FSTTCS 1993. LNCS, vol. 761, pp. 284–293. Springer, Heidelberg (1993)

25. Sery, O., Fedyukovich, G., Sharygina, N.: Incremental upgrade checking by means of interpolation-based function summaries. In: FMCAD, pp. 114–121. IEEE (2012)

26. Strichman, O., Godlin, B.: Regression verification - a practical way to verify programs. In: Meyer, B., Woodcock, J. (eds.) VSTTE 2005. LNCS, vol. 4171, pp. 496–501. Springer, Heidelberg (2008)

27. Tschannen, J., Furia, C.A., Nordio, M., Polikarpova, N.: AutoProof: auto-active functional verification of object-oriented programs. In: Baier, C., Tinelli, C. (eds.) TACAS 2015. LNCS, vol. 9035, pp. 566–580. Springer, Heidelberg (2015)

Predicting a Correct Program in Programming by Example

Rishabh Singh$^{(\boxtimes)}$ and Sumit Gulwani

Microsoft Research, Redmond, USA
risin@microsoft.om

We study the problem of efficiently predicting a correct program from a large set of programs induced from few input-output examples in Programming-by-Example (PBE) systems. This is an important problem for making PBE systems usable so that users do not need to provide too many examples to learn the desired program. We first formalize the two classes of sharing that occurs in version-space algebra (VSA) based PBE systems, namely set-based sharing and path-based sharing. We then present a supervised machine learning approach for learning a hierarchical ranking function to efficiently predict a correct program. The key observation of our learning approach is that ranking any correct program higher than all incorrect programs is sufficient for generating the correct output on new inputs, which leads to a novel loss function in the gradient descent based learning algorithm. We evaluate our ranking technique for the FlashFill PBE system on over 175 benchmarks obtained from the Excel product team and help forums. Our ranking technique works in real-time, reduces the average number of examples required for learning the desired transformation from 4.17 to 1.48, and learns the transformation from just one input-output example for 74 % of the benchmarks. The ranking scheme played a pivotal role in making FlashFill usable for millions of Excel users.

1 Introduction

Millions of computer end users need to perform repetitive tasks, but unfortunately lack the programming expertise required to do such tasks automatically. Example-based program synthesis techniques have the potential to enhance the productivity of such end users by enabling them to create small scripts using examples [8,9]. These techniques have been developed for a wide variety of domains including repetitive text-editing [14], syntactic string transformations [7], semantic string transformations [23], table transformations [11], and number transformations [24]. FlashFill [1,7] is a recent system in Excel 2013 that learns syntactic string transformation programs from examples.

Many recent Programming-By-Example (PBE) techniques use version-space algebra (VSA) [14] based methodology of computing the set of *all* programs in an underlying domain-specific language (DSL) that are consistent with a given set of input-output examples. The number of such programs is huge; but they are all succinctly represented using appropriate data-structures that share common program fragments. Given a representative set of input-output examples

© Springer International Publishing Switzerland 2015
D. Kroening and C.S. Păsăreanu (Eds.): CAV 2015, Part I, LNCS 9206, pp. 398–414, 2015.
DOI: 10.1007/978-3-319-21690-4_23

for a task, all synthesized programs would be *correct*, i.e. the programs would correspond to the intended task. However, if only a few input-output examples are given (i.e. the task is under-specified), the set of synthesized programs will include both correct and incorrect programs. The user would then need to refine the specification by providing additional input-output examples to avoid learning an incorrect program. The number of representative input-output examples required to learn a desired task is a function of the underlying DSL and has also been referred to as the *learning dimension* [6] of the DSL. A more expressive DSL makes the synthesizer more useful (since it can assist users with a larger variety of tasks), but it also makes the synthesizer less usable (since users now need to provide more examples).

We study the problem of predicting a correct program from a huge set of programs in an expressive DSL that have been induced by a *small* number of examples. We propose a machine learning based ranking technique to rank the induced programs by assigning them a likelihood score based on their features. While machine learning has been used in the past to improve the efficiency of heuristic-based enumerative search in program synthesis [17], we leverage machine learning in a different manner: the VSA based programming-by-example techniques set up the space of programs (that are consistent with the user-provided examples) over which machine-learning based ranking is performed to predict a correct program. There are two key challenges that our technique addresses, namely that of automatically learning the ranking function, and that of efficiently identifying the highest ranked program from a large set of induced programs in a VSA representation.

We formalize the problem of learning a ranking function as a machine learning problem and present a novel solution to it. Traditional learning-to-rank approaches [2–4,12] either aim to rank all relevant documents over all non-relevant documents or rank the most relevant document at the top. We, instead, study the problem of ranking *some* correct program over *all* incorrect programs as any correct program would be sufficient to generate the desired outputs on new inputs. Our solution involves two key ideas: (a) we present a gradient descent based approach to learn the coefficients (weights) of a linear ranking function with the goal of ranking some correct program over all incorrect programs. (b) we also provide an automated method to obtain the labeled training data for our learning algorithm from training benchmark tasks.

A key challenge in using any ranking methodology for VSA based PBE systems is that of efficiency. The naïve approach of explicitly computing the rank for each induced program does not scale because the number of induced programs is often huge (more than 10^{20} [23]). These programs are represented using succinct data structures that allow sharing of expressions across different levels. We formalize two general classes of sharing that occurs in these data-structures [7,11,23,24], namely *set-based sharing* and *path-based sharing*. We learn a separate ranking function for each level of sharing—this enables us to apply the ranking methodology efficiently in practice.

We instantiate our ranking technique for the FlashFill synthesis algorithm [7]. The VSA based data-structure in FlashFill involves two levels of sharing.

We learn a separate ranking function for each level over corresponding efficient features (Sect. 5). We present the evaluation of our ranking technique on over 175 string manipulation tasks obtained from Excel product team and help-forums. The ranking scheme works in real-time and reduces the average number of examples required per benchmark to 1.48 as compared to 4.17 examples needed by a manually defined ranking scheme based on Occam's razor [7]. Our machine-learning based ranking scheme played a pivotal role in making FlashFill successful and usable for millions of Excel users.

This paper makes the following contributions.

- We formalize the two different classes of sharing used in VSA based representations, namely set-based sharing and path-based sharing(Sect. 3).
- We describe a machine-learning based technique to rank *some* correct program over all incorrect programs for most benchmarks in the training set (Sect. 4.3).
- We demonstrate the efficacy of our ranking technique for FlashFill on over 175 real-world benchmarks (Sect. 5.2).

2 Motivating Examples

In this section, we present a few motivating examples from FlashFill that show three observations: (i) there are multiple correct programs in the set of programs induced from an input-output example, (ii) simple features such as size are not sufficient for preferring a correct program over incorrect programs, and (iii) there are huge number of programs induced from a given input-output example.

Example 1. An Excel user had a series of names in a column and wanted to add the title Mr. before each name. She gave the input-output example as shown in the table to express her intent. The intended program concatenates the constant string "Mr." with the input string in column v_1.

	Input v_1	Output
1	Roger	Mr. Roger
2	Simon	
3	Benjamin	
4	John	

The challenge for FlashFill to learn the desired transformation in this case is to decide which substrings in the output string "Mr. Roger" are constant strings and which are substrings of the input string "Roger". We use the notation $s[i..j]$ to refer to a substring of s of length $j - i + 1$ starting at index i and ending at index j. FlashFill infers that the substring $out_1[0..0] \equiv$ "M" has to be a constant string since "M" is not present in the input string. On the other hand, the substring $out_1[1..1] \equiv$ "r" can come from two different substrings in the input string ($in_1[0..0] \equiv$ "R" and $in_1[4..4] \equiv$ "r"). FlashFill learns more than 10^3 regular expressions to compute the substring "r" in the output string from the input string, some of which include: 1st capital letter, 1st character, 5th character from end, 1st character followed by a lower case string etc. Similarly, FlashFill learns more than 10^4 expressions to extract the substring "Roger" from the input string, thereby learning more than 10^7 programs from just one input-output example. All programs in the set of learnt programs that include an expression for extracting "r" from the input string are incorrect, whereas programs that treat "r" as a constant string are correct. Some hints than can help FlashFill rank constant expressions for "r" higher are:

- Length of substring: Since the length of substring "r" is 1, it is less likely to be an input substring.
- Relative length of substring: The relative length of substring "r" as compared to the output string is small $\frac{1}{9}$.
- Constant neighboring characters: The neighboring characters "M" and "." of "r" are both constant expressions.

Example 2. An Excel user had a list of names consisting of first and last names, and wanted to format the names such that the first name is abbreviated to its first initial and is followed by the last name as shown in the table.

	Input v_1	Output
1	Mark Sipser	M.Sipser
2	Louis Johnson	
3	Edward Davis	
4	Robert Mills	

This example requires the output substring $out_1[0..0] \equiv$ "M" to come from the input string instead of it being the constant string "M". The desired behavior in this example of preferring the substring "M" to be a non-constant string is in conflict with the desired behavior of preferring smaller substrings as constant strings in Example 1. Some hints that can help FlashFill prefer the substring expression for "M" over the constant string expression are:

- Output Token: The substring "M" of the output string is a Capital token.
- String case change: The case of the substring does not change from input.
- Regular expression Frequency: The regular expression to extract 1st capital letter occurs frequently in practice.

Example 3. An Excel user had a series of addresses in a column and wanted to extract the city names from them. The user gave the input-output example shown in the table.

	Input v_1	Output
1	243 Flyer Dr,Cambridge, MA 02145	Cambridge
2	512 Wir Ave,Los Angeles, CA 78911	
3	64 128th St,Seattle, WA 98102	
4	560 Heal St,San Mateo, CA 94129	

FlashFill learns more than 10^6 different substring expressions to extract the substring "Cambridge" from the input string "243 Flyer Drive,Cambridge, MA 02145", some of which are listed below.

- p_1: Extract the 3rd alphabet token string.
- p_2: Extract the 4th alphanumeric token string.
- p_3: Extract substring between 1st and 2nd comma tokens.
- p_4: Extract substring between 3rd capital and the 1st comma.
- p_5: Extract substring between 1st and last comma tokens.

The problem with learning the substring expression p_1 is that on the input string "512 Wright Ave, Los Angeles, CA 78911", it produces the output string "Los" that is not the desired output. On the other hand, the expression p_3 (or p_5) generates the desired output string "Los Angeles". Some features that can help FlashFill rank the expression p_3 higher are:

- Same left and right position logics: The regular expression tokens for left and right position logics for p_3 are similar (comma).
- Match Id: The match count of substring between two comma tokens is 1 as compared to 3 for the alphabet token of p_1.

3   Domain-Specific Languages (DSLs) for PBE in VSA

There have been many recent proposals for DSLs for PBE systems in the domains of string [1,7], table [23], numbers [24], and layout manipulations [11]. The key idea in designing these DSLs is to make them expressive enough to capture majority of the desired tasks, but concise enough for amenable learning from examples. Since the specification mechanism of input-output examples is inherently incomplete and ambiguous, there are typically a huge number of expressions in these expressive languages that conform to the provided examples. These large number of consistent expressions are represented succinctly using VSA based data structures that allow for sharing expressions. In this section, we describe an abstract language $\mathcal{L}_a$ that captures two major kinds of expressions that allow for such sharing, namely *fixed arity* expressions and *associative* expressions. We then present the syntax and semantics of the VSA based data structure and the algorithm to efficiently compute the highest ranked expression.

$$
\begin{aligned}
&\text{Expr } e := v \mid c \\
&\qquad\quad\; \mid e_f \mid e_h \\
&\text{Fixed Arity Expr } e_f := f(e_1, \cdots, e_n) \\
&\text{Associative Expr } e_h := h(e_1, \cdots, e_k) \\
&\qquad\qquad\qquad\qquad (a)
\end{aligned}
\qquad
\begin{aligned}
&\text{Union Expr } \tilde{e} := \{c_i, v_j, \cdots, \tilde{e}_f, \tilde{e}_h\} \\
&\text{Join Expr } \tilde{e}_f := f(\tilde{e}_1, \cdots, \tilde{e}_n) \\
&\text{DAG Expr } \tilde{e}_h := \mathcal{D}(\tilde{\eta}, \eta^s, \eta^t, W), \text{where} \\
&\qquad W : (\eta_1, \eta_2) \to \tilde{e}, |\tilde{\eta}| = k+1 \\
&\qquad\qquad\qquad\qquad (b)
\end{aligned}
$$

Fig. 1. (a) Syntax for a general abstract language $\mathcal{L}_a$ for a VSA based PBE system, and (b) a data structure for succinctly representing a set of $\mathcal{L}_a$ expressions.

3.1   An Abstract Language $\mathcal{L}_a$ for PBE Systems

An abstract language $\mathcal{L}_a$ that captures the major kinds of expression sharing in DSLs of several VSA based PBE systems is shown in Fig. 1(a). The top-level expression e in $\mathcal{L}_a$ can either be a constant string c, a variable v, a fixed arity expression e_f, or an associative expression e_h.

Definition 1 (Fixed Arity Expression). *Let f be any constructor for n independent expressions ($n \geq 1$). We use the notation $f(e_1, \ldots, e_n)$ to denote a fixed arity expression with n arguments.*

Example 4. The position pair expression in the FlashFill language $\mathtt{SubStr}(v_i, p_1, p_2)$ is a fixed arity expression that represents the left and right position logic expressions p_1 and p_2 independently. The Boolean expression predicate $(C_1 = e_t \wedge \cdots \wedge C_k = e_t)$ for a candidate key of size k in the lookup transformation language [23], and the decimal and exponential number formatting expressions $\mathtt{Dec}(u, \eta_1, f)$ and $\mathtt{Exp}(u, \eta_1, f, \eta_2)$ in the number transformation language [24] are also examples of fixed arity expressions with independent arguments.

Definition 2 (Associative Expression). *Let h be a binary associative constructor for independent expressions. We use the simplified notation $h(e_1, \ldots, e_k)$ to denote the associative expression $h(e_1, h(e_2, h(e_3, \ldots, h(e_{k-1}, e_k) \ldots)))$ for any $k \geq 1$ (where $h(e)$ simply denotes e).*

Example 5. The $\mathtt{Concatenate}(f_1, .., f_n)$ expression in FlashFill is an an associative expression with $\mathtt{Concatenate}$ as the associative constructor. The top-level select expression $e_t := \mathtt{Select}(C, T, C_i = e_t)$ in the lookup transformation language [23] and the associative program $\mathtt{Assoc}(F, s_0, s_1)$ in the table layout transformation language [11] are also examples of associative expressions.

Associative expressions involve applying an associative operator with input and output type T to an unbounded sequence of expressions of type T. They differ from the fixed arity expressions in two ways: (i) they have unbounded arity, and (ii) their input and output types are restricted to be the same.

$$[\![c]\!]_\sigma := c$$
$$[\![v]\!]_\sigma := \sigma(v)$$
$$[\![\tilde{e}]\!]_\sigma := \{e_j \mid e_j \in [\![e_i]\!]_\sigma, e_i \in \tilde{e}\}$$
$$[\![\tilde{e}_f]\!]_\sigma := \{f(e_1, \cdots e_n) \mid e_i \in [\![\tilde{e}_i]\!]_\sigma\}$$
$$[\![\tilde{e}_h]\!]_\sigma := \{h(e_1, \cdots, e_k) \mid (\eta_0, \cdots, \eta_k) \in \tilde{\eta},$$
$$\eta_0 = \eta^s, \eta_k = \eta^t,$$
$$e_i \in [\![W(\eta_{i-1}, \eta_i)]\!]_\sigma\}$$

(a)

$$\mathcal{R}(\{\tilde{e}_1, \cdots, \tilde{e}_n\}, \sigma) := r_u(e_1, \cdots, e_n, \sigma)$$
$$e_i = \mathcal{R}(\tilde{e}_i, \sigma)$$
$$\mathcal{R}(f(\{\tilde{e}_{11}, \cdots, \tilde{e}_{1n}\}, := r_f(e_{11}, \cdots, e_{2m}, \sigma)$$
$$\{\tilde{e}_{21}, \cdots, \tilde{e}_{2m}\}), \sigma) \quad e_{ij} = \mathcal{R}(\tilde{e}_{ij}, \sigma)$$
$$\mathcal{R}(\mathcal{D}(\tilde{\eta}, \eta^s, \eta^t, W), \sigma) := r_g(e_{12}, \cdots, e_{ij}, \cdots, \sigma)$$
$$e_{ij} = \mathcal{R}(W(\eta_i, \eta_j), \sigma)$$

(b)

Fig. 2. (a) Semantics of the VSA based data structure for $\mathcal{L}_a$ expressions, and (b) Ranking functions for efficiently identifying the top-ranked expressions.

3.2   Data Structure for Representing a Set of $\mathcal{L}_a$ Expressions

The data structure to succinctly represent a huge number of $\mathcal{L}_a$ expressions is shown in Fig. 1(b). The Union Expression $\tilde{e}$ represents a set of top-level expressions as an explicit set without any sharing. The Join Expression $\tilde{e}_f$ represents a set of fixed arity expressions by maintaining independent sets for its arguments $e_1, \cdots, e_n$. The DAG expression $\tilde{e}_h$ represents a set of associative expressions using a DAG $\mathcal{D}$, where the edges correspond to a set of expressions $\tilde{e}$ and each path from the start node η^s to the end node η^t represents an associative expression. The semantics of the data structure is shown in Fig. 2(a).

Join Expressions (Set-based Sharing): There can often be a huge number of fixed-arity expressions that are consistent with a given example(s). Consider the input-output example pair (u, v). Suppose v_1, v_2, v_3 are values such that $v = f(v_1, v_2, v_3)$. Suppose E_1, E_2, and E_3 are sets of expressions that are respectively consistent with the input-output pairs (u, v_1), (u, v_2), and (u, v_3). Then, $f(e_1, e_2, e_3)$ is consistent with (u, v) for any $e_1 \in E_1$, $e_2 \in E_2$, and $e_3 \in E_3$. The number of such expressions is $|E_1| \times |E_2| \times |E_3|$. However, these can be succinctly represented using the data-structure $f(E_1, E_2, E_3)$, which denotes the set of expressions $\{f(e_1, e_2, e_3) \mid e_1 \in E_1, e_2 \in E_2, e_3 \in E_3\}$, using space that is proportional to $|E_1| + |E_2| + |E_3|$.

Example 6. The position pair expressions $\mathtt{SubStr}(v_i, \{\tilde{p}_j\}_j, \{\tilde{p}_k\}_k)$ in FlashFill represents the set of left and right position logic expressions $\{\tilde{p}_j\}_j$ and $\{\tilde{p}_j\}_j$ independently. The generalized Boolean conditions in the select expression $\mathtt{Select(C,T,B)}$ of the lookup transformation language [23] also exhibit set-based sharing. The data structure for representing a set of decimal and exponential number formatting expressions in the number transformation language $\mathtt{Dec}(u, \tilde{\eta}_1, \tilde{f})$ and $\mathtt{Exp}(u, \tilde{\eta}_1, \tilde{f}, \tilde{\eta}_2)$ represents integer formats ($\tilde{\eta}_1$), fractional formats ($\tilde{f}$), and exponent formats ($\tilde{\eta}_2$) as independent sets.

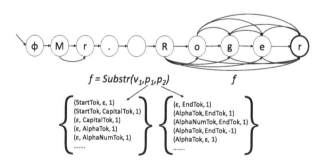

Fig. 3. The DAG data structure for representing the induced programs in Example 1.

DAG Expressions (Path-based Sharing): There can often be a huge number of associative expressions that can be consistent with a given example(s). Consider the input-output example pair (u, v). Suppose $v_1, \ldots, v_n$ are n values such that $v = h(v_1, \ldots, v_n)$ and let $e_{i,j}$ be an expression that evaluates to the value $v_{i,j} \equiv h(v_i, \ldots, v_j)$ on input u ($1 \leq i < j \leq n$). Let $\sigma = [\sigma_0, \ldots, \sigma_m]$ be a subsequence of $[0, \ldots, n]$ such that $\sigma_0 = 0$ and $\sigma_m = n$ and e_σ be the expression

$h(e'_1, \ldots, e'_m)$, where $e'_i = e_{\sigma_{i-1}, \sigma_i}$. Note that the number of such subsequences σ is exponential in n, and for any such subsequence σ, e_σ evaluates to $v_{1,n}$. Such an exponential sized set of associative expressions can be represented succinctly as a DAG whose nodes correspond to $0, \ldots, n$ and an edge between two nodes i and j corresponds to the value $v_{i,j}$ and is labeled with $e_{i,j}$. A path in the DAG from source node 0 to sink node n is some subsequence $[\sigma_1, \ldots, \sigma_m]$ of $[0, \ldots, n]$ where $\sigma_1 = 0$ and $\sigma_m = n$, and it represents the expression $F(e'_1, \ldots, e'_m) = v$, where $e'_i = e_{\sigma_{i-1}, \sigma_i}$. An example DAG data structure representing all programs consistent with the input-output example in Example 1 is shown in Fig. 3. The graph data structure for generalized expression nodes for representing select expressions [23] also uses such path-based sharing for succinctly representing exponential number of expressions.

3.3   Ranking the Set of $\mathcal{L}_a$ Expressions

Given an input-output example, the PBE system learns a huge number of conforming expressions and represents them succinctly using the data structure shown in Fig. 1(b). Some of these learnt expressions are correct (desired) and others are incorrect (undesired). A user typically needs to provide more input-output examples to refine their intent until the set of expressions learnt by the system consists of only correct expressions. Our goal is to learn the desired expression from minimal number of examples (preferably 1). We formulate this problem as learning a ranking function that can rank the correct expression as the highest ranked expression.

We need to define the ranking function such that it can identify the top-ranked expression without explicitly enumerating the constituent sets. The ranking function $\mathcal{R}$ (shown in Fig. 2(b)) takes a set of $\mathcal{L}_a$ expressions and the set of input-output examples , as input, and returns the highest ranked expression. For maintaining the version-space algebra based sharing, the ranking function is defined hierarchically in terms of individual ranking functions at different levels, namely r_u, r_f, and r_h. The ranking function r_u computes the highest ranked expression from a Union Expression. It first recursively computes the top-ranked expression e_i for each of its constituent expression $\tilde{e}_i$, and then computes the highest ranked expression amongst them.

The ranking function r_f computes the highest-ranked expression from a Join expression $f(E_1, .., E_n)$. Since we assume the ranking function to be a linear weighted function of features, if all features depended on only one column (say E_i), we can easily enumerate the expressions individually for each column ($e \in E_i$) and compute the highest ranked expression $f(e_1, .., e_n)$ by selecting the highest ranked expression e_i for each individual column E_i. But often times the features depend on multiple columns, which leads to challenges in efficiently identifying the highest ranked expression. A key observation we use for computing such features is that these features typically do not depend on all concrete values of other columns, but only on a few abstract values (defined as the *abstract dimension* of the feature). For a given set of features, the columns can be extended to a set whose size is bounded by the product of abstract dimensions of features such that a feature now depends on only one column.

The ranking function r_h efficiently computes the highest ranked expression from a DAG Expression by exploiting the notion of *associative* features. A feature g over associative expressions is said to be *associative* if there exists an associative monotonically increasing binary operator $\circ$ and a numerical feature h over expressions e_i such that $g(F(e_1, \ldots, e_n)) = g(F(e_1, \ldots, e_{n-1})) \circ h(e_n)$. The ranking function uses a dynamic programming algorithm similar to the Dijkstra's shortest path algorithm for computing the highest-ranked expression, where each DAG node maintains the highest-ranked path from the start node to itself, together with the corresponding edge feature values.

The key challenge now is to learn these ranking functions automatically at different levels. We present a supervised learning-to-rank approach for learning the ranking functions.

4   Learning the Ranking Function

Most previous approaches for *learning to rank* [2–4,12] aim at ranking all relevant documents above all non-relevant documents or ranking the most relevant document as highest. However, in our case, we want to learn a ranking function that ranks any correct program higher than all incorrect programs. We use a supervised learning approach to learn such a function, but it requires us to solve two main challenges. First, we need some labeled training data for the supervised learning. We present a technique to automatically generate labeled training data from a set of input-output examples and the corresponding set of induced programs. Second, we need to learn a ranking function based on this training data. We use a gradient descent based method to optimize a novel loss function that aims to rank *any* correct program higher than *all* incorrect programs.

4.1   Preliminaries

The training phase consists of a set of tasks $T = \{t_1, \cdots, t_n\}$. Each task t_i consists of a set of input-output examples $E^i = \{e_1^i, \cdots, e_{n(t_i)}^i\}$, where example $e_j^i = (\mathtt{in}_j^i, \mathtt{out}_j^i)$ denotes a pair of input ($\mathtt{in}_i$) and output ($\mathtt{out}_i$). We assume that for each training task t_i, sufficiently large number of input-output examples E^i are provided such that only correct programs are consistent with the examples. The task labels i on examples e_j^i are used only for assigning the training labels, and we will drop the labels to refer the examples simply as e_j for notational convenience. The complete set of input-output examples for all tasks is obtained by taking the union of the set of examples for each task $E = \{e_1, \cdots, e_{n(e)}\} = \cup_t E^t$. Let p_i denote the set of synthesized programs that are consistent with example e_i such that $p_i = \{p_i^1, \cdots, p_i^{n(i)}\}$, where $n(i)$ denotes the number of programs in the set p_i. We define positive and negative programs induced from an input-output example as follows.

Definition 3 (Positive and Negative Programs). *A program $p \in p_j$ is said to be a positive (or correct) program if it belongs to the set intersection of the set of programs for all examples of task t_i, i.e. $p \in p_1 \cap p_2 \cap \cdots \cap p_{n(t_i)}$. Otherwise, the program $p \in p_j$ is said to be a negative (or incorrect) program i.e. $p \notin p_1 \cap p_2 \cap \cdots \cap p_{n(t_i)}$.*

4.2 Automated Training Data Generation

We now present a technique to automatically generate labeled training data from the training tasks specified using input-output examples. Consider a training task t_i consisting of the input-output examples $E^i = \{(e_1, \cdots, e_{n(t_i)}\}$ and let p_j be the set of programs synthesized by the synthesis algorithm that are consistent with the input-output example e_j. For a task t_i, we construct the set of all positive programs by computing the set $p_1 \cap p_2 \cap \cdots \cap p_{n(t_i)}$. We compute the set of all negative programs by computing the set $\{p_k \setminus (p_1 \cap p_2 \cap \cdots \cap p_{n(t_i)}) \mid 1 \leq k \leq n(t_i)\}$. The version-space algebra based representation allows us to construct these sets efficiently by performing intersection and difference operations over corresponding shared expressions.

We associate a set of programs $p_i = \{p_i^1, \cdots, p_i^{n(i)}\}$ for an example e_i with a corresponding set of labels $y_i = \{y_i^1, \cdots, y_i^{n(i)}\}$, where label y_i^j denotes the label for program p_i^j. The labels y_i^j take binary values such that the value $y_i^j = 1$ denotes that the program p_i^j is a positive program for the task, whereas the label value 0 denotes that program p_i^j is a negative program for the task.

4.3 Gradient Descent Based Learning Algorithm

From the training data generation phase, we obtain a set of programs p_i associated with labels y_i for each input-output example e_i of a task. Our goal now is to learn a ranking function that can rank a positive program higher than all negative programs for each example of the task. We present a brief overview of our gradient descent based method to learn the ranking function for predicting a correct program by optimizing a novel loss function.

We compute a feature vector $x_i^j = \phi(e_i, p_i^j)$ for each example-program pair $(e_i, p_i^j), e_i \in E, p_i^j \in p_i$. For each example e_i, a training instance (x_i, y_i) is added to the training set, where $x_i = \{x_i^1, \cdots, x_i^{n(i)}\}$ denotes the list of feature vectors and $y_i = \{y_i^1, \cdots, y_i^{n(i)}\}$ denotes their corresponding labels. The goal now is to learn a ranking function f that computes the ranking score $z_i = (f(x_i^1), \cdots, f(x_i^{n(i)}))$ for each example such that a positive program is ranked as highest.

This problem formulation is similar to the problem formulation of listwise approaches for learning-to-rank [2,25]. The main difference comes from the fact that while previous listwise approaches aim to rank most documents in accordance with their training scores or rank the most relevant document as highest, our approach aims to rank any one positive program higher than all negative

$$L(E) = \sum_{i=1}^{n(e)} L(y_i, z_i) = \sum_{i=1}^{n(e)} \mathtt{sign}(\mathtt{Max}(\{f(x_i^j) \mid y_i^j = 0\}) - \mathtt{Max}(\{f(x_i^k) \mid y_i^k = 1\}))$$

$$(1)$$

$$L(y_i, z_i) = \mathtt{tanh}(c_1 \times (\frac{1}{c_2} \times \log(\sum_{y_i^j = 0} e^{c_2 \times f(x_i^j)}) - \frac{1}{c_2} \times \log(\sum_{y_i^k = 1} e^{c_2 \times f(x_i^k)})))$$

$$(2)$$

programs. Therefore, our loss function counts the number of examples where a negative program is ranked higher than all positive programs, as shown in Eq. 1. For each example, the loss function compares the maximum rank of a negative program ($\mathtt{Max}(\{f(x_i^j) \mid y_i^j = 0\})$) with the maximum rank of a positive program ($\mathtt{Max}(\{f(x_i^k) \mid y_i^k = 1\})$), and adds 1 to the loss function if a negative program is ranked highest (and subtracts 1 otherwise).

The presence of $\mathtt{sign}$ and $\mathtt{Max}$ functions in the loss function in Eq. 1 makes the function non-continuous. The non-continuity of the loss function makes it u nsuitable for gradient descent based optimization as the gradient of the function can not be computed. We, therefore, perform smooth approximations of the $\mathtt{sign}$ and $\mathtt{Max}$ functions using the hyperbolic $\mathtt{tanh}$ function and softmax function respectively (with scaling constants c_1 and c_2) to obtain a continuous and differentiable loss function in Eq. 2.

We assume the desired ranking function $f(x_i^j) = \boldsymbol{w} \cdot x_i^j$ to be a linear function over the features. Let there be m features in the feature vector $x_i^j = \{g_1, \cdots, g_m\}$ such that $f(x_i^j) = w_0 + w_1 g_1 + \cdots + w_m g_m$. We use the gradient descent algorithm to the learn the weights w_i of the ranking function that minimizes the loss function from Eq. 2. Although our loss function is differentiable, it is not convex, and therefore the algorithm only achieves a local minima. We need to restart the gradient descent algorithm from multiple random initializations to avoid getting stuck in non-desirable local minimas.

5 Case Study: FlashFill

We instantiate our ranking method for the FlashFill synthesis algorithm [7]. We chose FlashFill because of the availability of several real-world benchmarks. FlashFill uses a version-space algebra based data-structure shown to succinctly represent a huge set of programs. The expressions in FlashFill are shared at three different levels: (i) set-based sharing of position pair expressions at the lowest level, (ii) union expressions for atomic expressions on the DAG edges, and (iii) path-based sharing of concatenate expressions at the top level. We describe efficient features for expressions at each of the levels.

5.1 Efficient Expression Features

Position Pair Expression Features: The binary position pair expressions take two position logic expressions as arguments. The features used for ranking the position pair expressions are shown in Fig. 4(a) together with their low abstract-dimensions. These features include frequency-based features denoting frequencies of: token sequences of left and right position logic expression arguments ($g_1, g_2,$ g_7, g_8), occurrence Id and the position logics (g_3,g_4, g_9, g_{10}),and length of token sequences of position logics (g_5,g_6, g_{11}, g_{12}). In addition to frequency-based features, there are also Boolean features that include whether the right token sequence of left position logic is equal to the left token sequence of the right position logic (g_{13}), the right token sequence (resp. left) of left position logic and left token sequence (resp. right) of right position logic are empty (g_{14}, g_{15}).

Fixed Arity Feature	Abs. Dim.
$g_1 : \nu(r_1^l), g_2 : \nu(r_2^l)$	1
$g_3 : \nu(c^l), g_4 : \nu((r_1^l, r_2^l))$	1
$g_5 : \nu(|r_1^l|), g_6 : \nu(|r_2^l|)$	1
$g_7 : \nu(r_1^r), g_8 : \nu(r_2^r)$	1
$g_9 : \nu(c^r), g_{10} : \nu((r_1^r, r_2^r))$	1
$g_{11} : \nu(|r_1^r|), g_{12} : \nu(|r_2^r|)$	1
$g_{13} : r_2^l = r_1^r$	$|\tilde{p}_k|$
$g_{14} : r_2^l = \epsilon \wedge r_1^r = \epsilon$	2
$g_{15} : r_1^l = \epsilon \wedge r_2^r = \epsilon$	2

(a)

Associative Feature	Binary Operator o	Numerical Feature h
$g_1 :$ NumArgs	+	$c(1)$
$g_2 :$ SumWeights	+	weight
$g_3 :$ ProdWeights	×	weight
$g_4 :$ MaxWeight	Max	weight
$g_5 :$ MinWeight	Min	weight

(b)

Fig. 4. (a) The set of features for ranking position pair expression SubStr($v_i, \{\tilde{p}_j\}_j, \{\tilde{p}_k\}_k$), where $\tilde{p}_j = $ Pos(r_1^l, r_2^l, c^l), $\tilde{p}_k = $ Pos(r_1^r, r_2^r, c^r). (b) The set of associative features for ranking a set of Concatenate($f_1, .., f_n$) expressions.

Atomic Expression Features: An atomic expression corresponds to a substring of the output string, which can come from several positions in the input string in addition to being a constant string. This leads to multiple atomic expression edges between any two nodes of the DAG, which are represented explicitly using a Union expression. The features for ranking these expressions are: whether the left and right positions of output (input resp.) substring matches a token (g_1, g_2, g_3, g_4), expression is a constant string or a position pair (g_5, g_6), there is a case change (g_7), absolute and relative lengths of the substring as compared to input and output strings (g_8, g_9, g_{10}),the left and right expressions of the output substring are constant expressions or not (g_{11}, g_{12}), and the rank of position pair expression obtained from the previous level (g_{13}).

Concatenate Expression Features: At the top-level of DAG, we use associative features to compute the ranking of paths. The set of associative features together with their corresponding binary operator and numerical feature are shown in Fig. 4(b). These features include number of arguments in the Concatenate expression (g_1), the sum of weights of edges on the path (g_2), the product of weights of edges on the path (g_3), and the maximum (g_4) and minimum (g_5) weights of an edge on the path.

5.2 Experimental Evaluation

We now present the evaluation of our ranking scheme for FlashFill on a set of 175 benchmark tasks obtained from Excel product team and help forums. We evaluate our algorithm on three different train-test partition strategies, namely 20–80, 30–70 and 40–60. For each partition strategy, we randomly assign the corresponding number of benchmarks to the training and test set. For each benchmark problem, we provide 5 input-output examples. The experiments were performed on an Intel Core i7 3.20 GHz CPU with 32 GB RAM.

Training Phase: We run the gradient descent algorithm 1000 times with different random values for initialization of weights, while also varying the value of the learning rate α from 10^{-5} to 10^5 (in increments of multiples of 10). We learn the weights for the ranking functions for the initialization and α values for which best ranking performance is achieved on the training set.

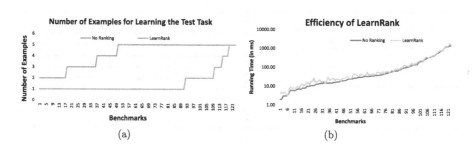

(a)   (b)

Fig. 5. Comparison of LearnRank with the Baseline scheme for a random 30–70 partition on (a) number of examples required for learning and (b) running time.

Test Phase: We compare the following two ranking schemes on the basis of number of input-output examples required to learn the desired task.

- **Baseline:** The manual ranking algorithm that chooses smallest and simplest program [7]. The algorithm prefers lesser number of arguments for the concatenate expressions, prefers simpler token expressions (such as Alphabets over AlphaNumeric), and ranks regular expression based position expression higher than constant position expressions.

- **LearnRank**: Our ranking scheme that uses the gradient descent algorithm to learn the ranking functions for position pair, atomic, and concatenate expressions in DAG.

Comparison with Baseline: The average number of input-output examples required to learn a test task for 10 runs of different train-test partitions is shown in the table. The LearnRank scheme performs much better than Baseline in terms of average number of examples required to learn the desired task (1.49 vs 4.17). For

Train-Test	Average Examples	
Partition	Baseline	LearnRank
20–80	4.19	**1.52** $\pm$ 0.07
30–70	4.17	**1.49** $\pm$ 0.06
40–60	4.18	**1.44** $\pm$ 0.07

a random 30–70 partition run, the number of input-output examples required to learn the 123 test benchmark tasks under the two ranking schemes is shown in Fig. 5(a). The LearnRank scheme learns the desired task from just 1 example for 91 tasks (74 %) as compared to 0 for Baseline, and from at most 2 examples for 110 tasks (89 %), as compared to only 18 tasks (14 %) for Baseline. Moreover, Baseline is not able to learn any program for 72 benchmarks (needing all 5 examples) as compared to 4 such benchmarks for LearnRank.

Efficiency of LearnRank: For evaluating the overhead of LearnRank scheme, we compare the running times of FlashFill with the Baseline ranking and Flash-Fill augmented with the LearnRank scheme over the same number of input-output examples for each test task. The running times of the two FlashFill versions is shown in Fig. 5(b). We observe that the overhead of LearnRank is small. The average overhead of LearnRank over Baseline is about 20 milliseconds (ms) per benchmark task whereas the median overhead is about 8 ms. This translates to an average overhead of about 29 % and a median overhead of 25 % in running times as compared to Baseline.

6 Related Work

In this section, we describe several work related to our technique which can be broadly divided into two areas: ranking techniques for program synthesis and machine learning for program synthesis.

Ranking in Program Synthesis: There have been several related work on using a manual ranking function for ranking of synthesized programs (or expressions). Gvero et al. [10] use weights to rank the expressions for efficient synthesis of likely program expressions of a given type at a given program point. These weights depend on the lexical nesting structure of declarations and also on the statistical information about the usage of declarations in a code corpus. PROSPECTOR [16] synthesizes jungloid code fragments (chain of objects and method calls from type τ_{in} to type τ_{out}) by ranking jungloids using the primary criterion of length, and secondary criteria of number of crossed package boundaries and generality of output type. Perelman et al. [20] synthesize hole values in partial expressions for code completion by ranking potential completed expressions based on features such as class hierarchy of method parameters, depth of sub-expressions, in-scope static methods, and similar names. PRIME [18] uses relaxed inclusion matching to search for API-usage from a large collection of code corpuses, and ranks the results using the frequency of similar snippets. The SEMFIX tool [19] uses a manual characterization of components in different complexity levels for synthesizing simpler expression repairs. Our ranking scheme also uses some of these features, but we learn the ranking function automatically using machine learning unlike these techniques which need manual definition and parameter tuning for the ranking function.

SLANG [22] uses the regularities found in sequences of method invocations from large code repositories to synthesize likely method invocation sequences for code completion. It uses alias and history analysis to extract precise sequences of method invocations during the training phase, and then trains a statistical language model on the extracted data. CodeHint [5] is an interactive and dynamic code synthesis system that also employs a probabilistic model learnt over ten million lines of code to guide and prune the search space. The main difference in our technique is that it is based on a VSA based representation where it is possible to compute all conforming programs.

Machine Learning for Programming by Example: A recent work by Menon et al. [17] uses machine learning to bias the search for finding a composition of a given set of typed operators based on clues obtained from the examples. Raychev et al. [21] use A^* search based on a heuristic function of length of current refactoring sequence and estimated distance from target tree for efficient learning of software refactorings from few user edits. On the other hand, we use machine learning to identify an intended program from a given set of programs that are consistent with a given set of examples. Our technique is applicable to domains where it is possible to compute the set of all programs that are consistent with a given set of examples [8,9]. SMARTedit [14] is a PBD (Programming By Demonstration) text-editing system where a user presents demonstration(s) of the text-editing task and the system tries to generalize the demonstration(s) to a macro by extending the notion of version-spaces to model plausible macro hypotheses. The macro language of SMARTedit is not as expressive as FlashFill's, and furthermore the task demonstrations in SMARTedit reduce a lot of ambiguity in the hypothesis space. Liang et al. [15] introduce hierarchical Bayesian prior in a multi-task setting that allows sharing of statistical strength across tasks. Our underlying language and representation of string manipulation programs is different from the combinatory logic based representation used by Liang et al., which requires us to use a different learning approach.

7 Conclusion

Learning programs from few examples is an important problem to make PBE systems usable. In this paper, we presented a general approach for efficiently predicting a correct program from a large number of programs induced by few examples. Our solution of using gradient descent based algorithm for learning the ranking function for VSA representations is at the intersection of machine learning and formal methods. We show the efficacy of our ranking technique for the FlashFill system. This machine-learning based ranking technique played a pivotal role in making FlashFill successful and usable for millions of Excel users.

References

1. Flash Fill (Microsoft Excel 2013 feature). http://research.microsoft.com/users/sumitg/flashfill.html
2. Cao, Z., Qin, T., Liu, T.-Y., Tsai, M.-F., Li, H.: Learning to rank: from pairwise approach to listwise approach. In: ICML (2007)
3. Cossock, D., Zhang, T.: Subset ranking using regression. In: Lugosi, G., Simon, H.U. (eds.) COLT 2006. LNCS (LNAI), vol. 4005, pp. 605–619. Springer, Heidelberg (2006)
4. Freund, Y., Iyer, R., Schapire, R.E., Singer, Y.: An efficient boosting algorithm for combining preferences. J. Mach. Learn. Res. **4**, 933–969 (2003)
5. Galenson, J., Reames, P., Bodík, R., Hartmann, B., Sen, K.: Codehint: dynamic and interactive synthesis of code snippets. In: ICSE, pp. 653–663 (2014)
6. Goldman, S.A., Kearns, M.J.: On the complexity of teaching. J. Comput. Syst. Sci. **50**, 303–314 (1992)
7. Gulwani, S.: Automating string processing in spreadsheets using input-output examples. In: POPL (2011)
8. Gulwani, S.: Synthesis from examples: interaction models and algorithms. In: 14th International Symposium on Symbolic and Numeric Algorithms for Scientific Computing (2012)
9. Gulwani, S., Harris, W., Singh, R.: Spreadsheet data manipulation using examples. Commun. ACM **55**(8), 97–105 (2012)
10. Gvero, T., Kuncak, V., Kuraj, I., Piskac, R.: Complete completion using types and weights. In: PLDI, pp. 27–38 (2013)
11. Harris, W.R., Gulwani, S.: Spreadsheet table transformations from examples. In: PLDI (2011)
12. Herbrich, R., Graepel, T., Obermayer, K.: Large margin rank boundaries for ordinal regression. In: Smola, A. J., Bartlett, P. L., Scholkopf, B., Schuur-mans, D. (eds.) Advances in Neural Information Processing Systems, pp. 115–132 (1999)
13. Jha, S., Gulwani, S., Seshia, S., Tiwari, A.: Oracle-guided component-based program synthesis. In: ICSE (2010)
14. Lau, T., Wolfman, S., Domingos, P., Weld, D.: Programming by demonstration using version space algebra. Mach. Learn. **53**(1–2), 111–156 (2003)
15. Liang, P., Jordan, M.I., Klein, D.: Learning programs: a hierarchical bayesian approach. In: ICML (2010)
16. Mandelin, D., Xu, L., Bodík, R., Kimelman, D.: Jungloid mining: helping to navigate the api jungle. In: PLDI, pp. 48–61 (2005)
17. Menon, A., Tamuz, O., Gulwani, S., Lampson, B., Kalai, A.: A machine learning framework for programming by example. In: ICML (2013)
18. Mishne, A., Shoham, S., Yahav, E.: Typestate-based semantic code search over partial programs. In: OOPSLA, pp. 997–1016 (2012)
19. Nguyen, H.D.T., Qi, D., Roychoudhury, A., Chandra, S.: Semfix: program repair via semantic analysis. In: ICSE (2013)

20. Perelman, D., Gulwani, S., Ball, T., Grossman, D.: Type-directed completion of partial expressions. In: PLDI, pp. 275–286 (2012)
21. Raychev, V., Schäfer, M., Sridharan, M., Vechev, M.T.: Refactoring with synthesis. In: OOPSLA, pp. 339–354 (2013)
22. Raychev, V., Vechev, M.T., Yahav, E.: Code completion with statistical language models. In: PLDI (2014)
23. Singh, R., Gulwani, S.: Learning semantic string transformations from examples. PVLDB 5(8), 740–751 (2012)
24. Singh, R., Gulwani, S.: Synthesizing number transformations from input-output examples. In: Madhusudan, P., Seshia, S.A. (eds.) CAV 2012. LNCS, vol. 7358, pp. 634–651. Springer, Heidelberg (2012)
25. Xia, F., Liu, T.-Y., Wang, J., Zhang, W., Li, H.: Listwise approach to learning to rank: theory and algorithm. In: ICML (2008)

Abstract Interpretation with Higher-Dimensional Ellipsoids and Conic Extrapolation

Mendes Oulamara[1]([✉]) and Arnaud J. Venet[2]

[1] École Normale Supérieure, 45 Rue D'Ulm, 75005 Paris, France
mendes.oulamara@ens.fr
[2] NASA Ames Research Center, Carnegie Mellon University, Moffett Field,
Mountain View, CA 94035, USA
arnaud.venet@west.cmu.edu

Abstract. The inference and the verification of numerical relationships among variables of a program is one of the main goals of static analysis. In this paper, we propose an Abstract Interpretation framework based on higher-dimensional ellipsoids to automatically discover symbolic quadratic invariants within loops, using loop counters as implicit parameters. In order to obtain non-trivial invariants, the diameter of the set of values taken by the numerical variables of the program has to evolve (sub-)linearly during loop iterations. These invariants are called ellipsoidal cones and can be seen as an extension of constructs used in the static analysis of digital filters. Semidefinite programming is used to both compute the numerical results of the domain operations and provide proofs (witnesses) of their correctness.

Keywords: Static analysis · Semidefinite programming · Ellipsoids · Conic extrapolation

1 Introduction

Ellipsoids have been widely used to overapproximate convex sets. For instance, in Control Theory they naturally arise as sublevel sets of quadratic Lyapunov functions. They are chosen to minimize some criterion, such as the volume. In Abstract Interpretation [8], they have been used to compute bounds on the output of linear digital filters [3,4]. Roux *et al.* [5,6] further extended that approach by borrowing techniques from Semidefinite Programming (SDP). However, all those works try to recover an ellipsoid that is known to exist as the Lyapunov invariant of some control system from the numerical algorithm implementing that system. The analysis algorithms are tailored for the particular type of numerical code considered. Ellipsoids are interesting in and of themselves

M. Oulamara—This material is based upon work supported by the National Science Foundation under Grant No. 1136008.

D. Kroening and C.S. Păsăreanu (Eds.): CAV 2015, Part I, LNCS 9206, pp. 415–430, 2015.
DOI: 10.1007/978-3-319-21690-4_24

because they provide a space-efficient yet expressive representation of convex sets in higher dimensions (quadratic compared to exponential for polyhedra). In this paper, we devise an Abstract Interpretation framework [9] to automatically compute an overapproximation of the values of the numerical variables in a program by an ellipsoid.

We focus our attention on the case when the program variables grow linearly with respect to the enclosing loop counters. We call this approximation an 'ellipsoidal cone'. Our work also relates to the gauge domain [7], which discovers simple linear relations between loop counters and the numerical variables of a program. Even though the definitions of the abstract operations are general, this model arises more naturally when the analyzed system naturally tends to exhibit quadratic invariants, for instance in the analysis of switched linear systems. Section 2 defines the basic ellipsoidal operations and their verification, and Sect. 4 extends this to the conic extrapolation. The soundness of our analysis relies on the verification of Linear Matrix Inequalities (LMI), which we describe in Sect. 3 before delving into the description of ellipsoidal cones. Finally Sect. 5 presents experiments and discusses applications to switched linear systems.

2   Ellipsoidal Operations

Ellipsoids are the building blocks of our conic extrapolation. We define how to compute the result of basic operations (union, affine transformation...). Since there is generally no minimal ellipsoid in the sense of inclusion, we choose the heuristic of minimizing the volume. Other choices, such as minimizing the so called 'condition number' or preserving the shape, are compared in [5].

We mainly rely on SDP optimization methods [2,10,11] both to find a covering ellipsoid and test the soundness of our result. However, we do not rely on the correctness of the SDP solver. For each operation whose arguments and results are expressed in function of matrices $(A_i)_{1 \leq i \leq r}$, we define a linear matrix inequality (LMI) of the form $\sum_{i=0}^{r} \alpha_i A_i \succeq 0$, where $A \succeq 0$ means "A is semidefinite positive", such that proving the soundness of the result is equivalent to showing that the LMI is satisfied for some reals (α_i). We find (α_i) candidates using an SDP solver and then verify the inequality with a sound procedure described in Sect. 3.

Definition 1 (Ellipsoid). $\mathrm{Ell}(Q, c) = \{x \in \mathbb{R}^n | (x - c)^T Q(x - c) \leq 1\}$ *is the definition of an ellipsoid where* $c \in \mathbb{R}^n$ *and* Q *is a definite positive* $n \times n$ *matrix. For practical use, we also define the function* $F : (Q, c) \mapsto \begin{pmatrix} Q & -Qc \\ -c^T Q & c^T Qc - 1 \end{pmatrix}$.

2.1   A Test of Inclusion

Let $\mathrm{Ell}(Q, c)$ and $\mathrm{Ell}(Q^*, c^*)$ be two ellipsoids, using the function F of Definition 1 we have the following duality result (proven in [1]):

Theorem 1

$$\max_{x \in \text{Ell}(Q,c)} \left((x - c^*)^T Q^* (x - c^*) - 1 \right) =$$

$$\min_{\lambda, \beta \in \mathbb{R}} \{ \beta \ s.t. \ \lambda \geq 0 \ and \ \beta E_{n+1} + \lambda F(Q,c) \succeq F(Q^*, c^*) \}$$

Where E_{n+1} is an $(n+1) \times (n+1)$ matrix, with $(E_{n+1})_{i,j} = 1$ if $i = j = n+1$, else $(E_{n+1})_{i,j} = 0$. Hence $\text{Ell}(Q,c) \subset \text{Ell}(Q^*, c^*)$ if and only if the minimizing value β^* is nonpositive.

For given $\text{Ell}(Q,c)$, $\text{Ell}(Q^*, c^*)$ and candidates λ and β computed by the SDP solver, the right hand term provides the LMI to check.

2.2   Computation of the Union

Let $(\text{Ell}(Q_i, c_i))_{1 \leq i \leq p}$ be p ellipsoids, we want to find an ellipsoid $\text{Ell}(Q^*, c^*)$ which is of nearly minimal volume containing them. To do so, we can solve the following SDP problem. It is decomposed into a first part ensuring the inclusion, proven in [1], and a second part describing the volume minimization criterion, proven in [2, example 18d].

The unknowns of the SDP problem are X an $n \times n$ symmetric matrix, $z \in \mathbb{R}^n$ a vector, Δ a lower triangular matrix and real numbers t, $(\tau_i)_{1 \leq i \leq p}$ $(u_i)_{1 \leq i \leq 2^{l+1} - 2}$ where $n \leq 2^l < 2n$:

maximize; t such that

Inclusion conditions, see [1]:

$\forall i, 1 \leq i \leq p, \ \exists \tau_i \geq 0$ s.t.

$$\tau_i \begin{pmatrix} Q_i & -Q_i c_i & 0 \\ -c_i^T Q_i & c_i^T Q_i c_i - 1 & 0 \\ 0 & 0 & 0 \end{pmatrix} \succeq \begin{pmatrix} X & -z & 0 \\ -z^T & -1 & z^T \\ 0 & z & -X \end{pmatrix}$$

Volume minimization, see [3, example 18d]:

$$\begin{pmatrix} X & \Delta \\ \Delta^T & D(\Delta) \end{pmatrix} \succeq 0$$

where $D(\Delta)$ is the diagonal matrix with the diagonal of Δ.

$$\begin{pmatrix} u_1 & t \\ t & u_2 \end{pmatrix} \succeq 0 \ \text{and} \ \forall i, 1 \leq i \leq 2^l - 2, \begin{pmatrix} u_{2i+1} & u_i \\ u_i & u_{2i+2} \end{pmatrix} \succeq 0$$

$\forall i, 2^l - 1 \leq i < 2^l - 1 + n, u_i = \delta_{i-2^l+2}$

where $(\delta_1, \ldots, \delta_n)$ are the diagonal coefficients of Δ.

$$\forall i, 2^l - 1 + n \leq i \leq 2^{l+1} - 2, u_i = 1 \tag{1}$$

We then define $Q^* = X$ and $c^* = Q^{*-1} z$ (in floating-point numbers, then we possibly increase the ratio of Q to ensure the inclusion condition). We can check that the resulting ellipsoid really contains the others with Theorem 1.

2.3   Affine Assignments

In this section, we are interested in computing the sound counterpart of an assignment $x \leftarrow Ax + b$, where x is the vector of variables, A is a matrix and b a vector.

Computation. We want to find a minimal volume ellipsoid such that the inclusion $\mathrm{Ell}(Q^*, c^*) \supset \{Ax + b | (x - c)^T Q(x - c) \leq 1\}$ is verified.

By a symmetry argument, we can set $c^* = Ac + b$. By expanding the inclusion equation, we find $\{Ax + b | x \in \mathrm{Ell}(Q, c)\} \subset \mathrm{Ell}(Q^*, Ac + b) \iff Q \succeq A^T Q^* A$.

Hence Q^* is a solution of the following SDP problem with unknowns X an $n \times n$ symmetric matrix, $z \in \mathbb{R}^n$ a vector, Δ a lower triangular matrix and real numbers t, $(\tau_i)_{1 \leq i \leq p}$ $(u_i)_{1 \leq i \leq 2^{l+1}-2}$ where $n \leq 2^l < 2n$:

Volume Minimization:

The same constraints and objective as in (1).

Inclusion Conditions:

$$Q \succeq A^T X A \text{ and } \frac{1}{\epsilon} \mathrm{Id} \succeq X \text{ where Id is the } n \times n \text{ identity matrix and } \epsilon > 0 \tag{2}$$

We then set $Q^* = X$ and $c^* = Ac + b$.

The second inclusion condition is here to ensure the numerical convergence of the SDP solving algorithm: if A is singular, the image by A of an ellipsoid is a flat ellipsoid. With this condition, we ensure that $\mathrm{Ell}(Q^*, c^*)$ contains a ball of radius ϵ.

To add an input defined by the convex hull of a finite set of vectors (for instance a hypercube), we can just compute the sum for every one of these vectors and compute the union [5].

Verification. The previous procedure gives us inequalities whose correctness ensures that the ellipsoid $\mathrm{Ell}(Q^*, Ac + b)$ contains the image of $\mathrm{Ell}(Q, c)$ by $x \mapsto Ax + b$. However, $c^* = Ac + b$ is computed in floating-point arithmetic, hence the soundness does not extend to our actual result $\mathrm{Ell}(Q^*, c^*)$. Therefore, we have to devise a test of inclusion for an arbitrary c^*. Let us compute the resulting center in two steps: we first assume that $b = 0$. We have from [1]:

$$(\forall x, x \in \mathrm{Ell}(Q, c) \Rightarrow Ax \in \mathrm{Ell}(Q^*, c^*))$$

$$\iff \max_{x \in \mathrm{Ell}(Q,c)} (x^T A^T Q^* A x - 2x^T A^T Q^* c^* + c^{*T} Q^* c^*) \leq 1$$

$$\iff \min_{\lambda, \beta \in \mathbb{R}} \{\beta | \lambda \geq 0 \text{ and } \lambda F(Q, c) + \beta E_{n+1} \succeq G\} \leq 0 \tag{3}$$

$$\text{where } G = \begin{pmatrix} A^T Q^* A & -A^T Q^* c^* \\ (-A^T Q^* c^*)^T & c^{*T} Q^* c^* - 1 \end{pmatrix}$$

We can hence verify the inclusion by finding suitable parameters and verifying the resulting LMI.

We finally have to perform the sound computation of the center translation $(c + b)$. Again, this is computed in floating-point arithmetic and we may have to increase the ratio of Q to ensure the verification of the inclusion condition in interval arithmetics: in the test of Theorem 1, we first compute $(c + b)$ and $F(Q, c+b)$ in floating-point arithmetic (and possibly increase the ratio), and with the LMI we check that it "contains" $F(Q, c + b)$ directly computed in interval arithmetic.

2.4   Variable Packing

It can be useful to analyze groups of variables independently, and merge the results. Given a set of variables $\{x_1, \ldots, x_p, x_{p+1}, \ldots, x_{p+q}\}$ and an ellipsoidal constraint over these variables (Q, c), we can find an ellipsoidal constraint linking $x_1, \ldots, x_p$ by computing the assignment defined by the matrix $\begin{pmatrix} I_p & 0 \\ 0 & 0 \end{pmatrix}$.

Given two sets of variables $\{x_1, \ldots, x_p\}$ and $\{x_{p+1}, \ldots, x_{p+q}\}$ linked respectively by (Q_1, c_1) and (Q_2, c_2), their product is tightly overapproximated by:
$$\text{Ell}\left(\begin{pmatrix} \frac{Q_1}{2} & 0 \\ 0 & \frac{Q_2}{2} \end{pmatrix}, \begin{pmatrix} c_1 \\ c_2 \end{pmatrix} \right).$$

3   Verifying Linear Matrix Inequalities

We now describe how we check the LMI's that determine the soundness of our analysis. We use interval arithmetic: the coefficients are intervals of floating-point numbers. Each atomic operation (addition, multiplication...) is overapproximated in the interval domain.

3.1   Cholesky Decomposition

Recall that the SDP solver gives us an inequality of the form $\sum_{i=0}^{r} \alpha_i A_i \succeq 0$, and candidate coefficients (α_i).

We translate each matrix and coefficient into the interval domain, and sum them up in interval arithmetic so that the soundness of the result does not depend on the floating-point computation of the linear expression.

Then, we compute the Cholesky decomposition of the resulting matrix in interval arithmetic. That is, we decompose [15] the matrix A into $A = LDL^T$ where D is an interval diagonal matrix and L a (non interval) lower triangular matrix with ones on the diagonal. Checking that D has only positive coefficients implies that A is definite positive.

3.2   Practical Aspects of the Ellipsoidal Operations

The Precision Issue. The limitation in the precision of the computations makes us unable to actually test whether a matrix is semidefinite positive: we can only decide when a matrix is definite positive "enough". For instance, standard libraries[1] fail at deciding that the null matrix 0 is semidefinite positive.

It means that for all the operations and verifications, we have to perform additional overapproximations in addition to those made by the SDP solver, such as multiplying the ratio of the ellipsoid by a number $(1 + \epsilon)$. Moreover, in the verification of LMI's, it can prove useful to explore the neighborhood $\alpha_i \pm \epsilon > 0$ of the parameters (α_i). As Roux and Garoche write in [6]: "Finding a good way to pad equations to get correct results, while still preserving the best accuracy, however remains some kind of black magic."

Complexity Results. From the complexity results of Porkolab and Khachiyan, the resolution of an LMI with m terms in dimension n has a complexity of $O(mn^4) + n^{O(\min(m,n^2))}$ [12]. Hence the complexity of the abstract operations is polynomial as a function of the dimension n (i.e., the number of variables), with a degree almost always smaller than 4 (for most operations, $m \leq 4$). The complexity of the Cholesky decomposition can be directly computed and is $O(n^3)$.

4   Conic Extrapolation

Now that the ellipsoidal operations are well defined, we can describe the construction of the conic extrapolation. The goal is to analyze variable transformations when the ellipsoidal radius evolves (sub-)linearly in the value of the loop counters.

Let us have numerical variables $x = (x_1, \ldots, x_n)$ and loop counters $y = (y_1, \ldots, y_k)$, we want to control the evolution of x depending on the counters y, which are expected to be monotonically increasing.

Inspired by the ellipsoidal constraints, we can use intersections of linear inequalities and a quadratic constraint of the form:

Definition 2 (Conic extrapolation). *Let q be a definite positive quadratic form (that is, there is a matrix $Q \succ 0$ such that $\forall x \in \mathbb{R}^n$, $q(x) = x^T Q x$), $c \in \mathbb{R}^n$, and for $i \in [\![1, k]\!]$, $\beta_i > 0$, $\delta_i \in \mathbb{R}^n$, $\lambda_i \in \mathbb{R}$, and b_i a boolean value. We define the ellipsoidal cone:*

$$\mathrm{Con}((q,c),(\beta_i, \delta_i, \lambda_i, b_i)_{1 \leq i \leq k}) =$$
$$\{(x,y) \in \mathbb{R}^n \times \mathbb{R}^k | \forall i \in [\![1, k]\!], y_i \geq \lambda_i \ \wedge$$
$$\forall i \in [\![1, k]\!], (b_i \vee (y_i = \lambda_i)) \ \wedge$$
$$q(x - c - \sum_{i=1}^{k}(y_i - \lambda_i)\delta_i) \leq (\sum_{i=1}^{k}\beta_i(y_i - \lambda_i) + 1)^2\}$$

---

[1] E.g mpmath [15].

Let Q be the matrix associated with q, $\text{Ell}(Q, c)$ is the ellipsoidal base of the cone. The $\lambda_i \in \mathbb{R}$ are the base levels of the cone, that is the minimum values of the loop counters (usually zero). The $\delta_i \in \mathbb{R}^n$ are the directions toward which the cone is "leaning" (for instance, with a single loop iterating $x \leftarrow x + 1$, we would want δ to be equal to 1). The $\beta_i \in \mathbb{R}$ determine the slope of the cone in each dimension. The b_i are boolean values stating, for each dimension, whether an extrapolation has been made in this dimension. That is, do we consider only the (x, y) with $y_i = \lambda_i$ (case $b_i = \text{False}$) or all those with $y_i \geq \lambda_i$ and verifying the other conditions (case $b_i = \text{True}$).

4.1   Conditions of Inclusion

We need to be able to test the inclusion of two cones. The following theorem shows that this inclusion can be reframed as conditions that can be verified with an SDP solver.

Theorem 2. *If we consider two cones $C = \text{Con}((q, c), (\beta_i, \delta_i, \lambda_i, b_i)_{1 \leq i \leq k})$ and $C' = \text{Con}((q', c'), (\beta_i', \delta_i', \lambda_i', b_i')_{1 \leq i \leq k})$, then $C \subset C'$ if and only if*

$$
\begin{cases}
(i) & \forall i \in [\![1, k]\!], \lambda_i' \leq \lambda_i \text{ and } \lambda_i > \lambda_i' \Rightarrow b_i' \\[2ex]
(ii) & \text{Ell}(q, c) \subset \text{Ell}\left(\dfrac{q'}{(1 + \sum\limits_{i=1}^{k} \beta_i'(\lambda_i - \lambda_i'))^2}, c' + \sum\limits_{i=1}^{k}(\lambda_i - \lambda_i')\delta_i' \right) \\[3ex]
(iii) & \forall i \in [\![1, k]\!], b_i \Rightarrow \left(b_i' \text{ and } \beta_i'^2 \geq \max\limits_{u \in \mathbb{R}^n, q(u) \leq 1} q'(\beta_i u + \delta_i - \delta_i') \right)
\end{cases}
$$

To prove this theorem, we first consider the case when the two cones have the same base levels. That is, we reduce it to the case when all the λ_i's are equal to 0.

Lemma 1. *If we consider two cones $C = \text{Con}((q, c), (\beta_i, \delta_i, 0, b_i)_{1 \leq i \leq k})$ and $C' = \text{Con}((q', c'), (\beta_i', \delta_i', 0, b_i')_{1 \leq i \leq k})$, then $C \subset C'$ if and only if*

$$
\begin{cases}
(i) & \text{Ell}(q, c) \subset \text{Ell}(q', c') \\[2ex]
(ii) & \forall i \in [\![1, k]\!], b_i \Rightarrow \left(b_i' \text{ and } \beta_i'^2 \geq \max\limits_{u \in \mathbb{R}^n, q(u) \leq 1} q'(\beta_i u + \delta_i - \delta_i') \right)
\end{cases}
$$

The proof of these two results is postponed to the end of the section.

4.2   Test of Inclusion

Theorem 2 enables us to build a sound test of inclusion between two cones C and C'. Condition (i) can be directly tested. We can use the procedure of the previous section to test the ellipsoidal inclusion of condition (ii).

Note that in practice, the test of inclusion will be used (during widening iterations) on cones with the same ellipsoidal base. In these cases, we do not want the overapproximations of the SDP solver to reject the inclusion. Therefore we should directly test whether the bases (Q, c) and the λ_i's are equal (as numerical values) and answer True for the test of base inclusion in this case.

To perform a sound test on the subcondition of (iii):

$$\beta_i'^2 \geq \max_{u \in \mathbb{R}^n, q(u) \leq 1} q'(\beta_i u + \delta_i - \delta_i')$$

we can compute an overapproximation of $M = \max_{u \in \mathbb{R}^n, q(u) \leq 1} q'(\beta_i u + \delta_i - \delta_i')$
From Theorem 1, we know that

$$M = 1 + \min_{s,t \in \mathbb{R}} \left\{ t \mid s \geq 0 \text{ and } sF(\frac{Q}{\beta_i^2}, 0) + tE_{n+1} \succeq F(Q', \delta_i' - \delta_i) \right\}$$

So for any feasible solution (s, t) of this SDP problem, $1 + t$ is a sound overapproximation of M.

4.3   Affine Operations on Cones

Counter Increment. The abstract counterpart of a statement $y_i \leftarrow y_i + v$ for some value v, is the operation $\lambda_i \leftarrow \lambda_i + v$: after the statement, the constraint is verified for $y_i - v$, and making this change in Definition 2 leads to the new value of λ_i. To have a sound result, we can compute the sum in interval arithmetic, and take the lower bound. Note that, in general, the loop counters are integer valued. In that case, the value can be computed exactly.

Affine Transformations. We want to have a sound counterpart for the affine assignment $x \leftarrow Ax + b$ where A is a matrix and b a vector. Let us fix the values of $(y_i)_{1 \leq i \leq k}$ and note $R = (1 + \sum_{i=1}^{k} \beta_i(y_i - \lambda_i))$ and $\hat{c} = c + \sum_{i=1}^{k} (y_i - \lambda_i)\delta_i$. Let Q be the matrix of q. We first want to find (Q', c') such that we have the inclusion $\{Ax+b|x \in \text{Ell}(\frac{Q}{R^2}, \hat{c})\} \subset \text{Ell}(\frac{Q'}{R^2}, c')$. By symmetry, we can set $c' = A\hat{c}+b$. Thus, by doing the same calculations as in Sect. 2.3, we have

$$\{Ax + b|x \in \text{Ell}(\frac{Q}{R^2}, \hat{c})\} \subset \text{Ell}(\frac{Q'}{R^2}, c') \iff Q \succeq A^T Q' A$$

The last condition does not depend on the y_i's, so for any quadratic form q' whose matrix Q' verifies $Q \succeq A^T Q' A$ (which is an SDP equation, we can add the conditions of volume minimization of (1), and $Q' \preceq \frac{1}{\epsilon} I_n$ with ϵ small enough, to ensure numerical convergence), we have

$$\{(Ax, y)|(x, y) \in \text{Con}((q, c), (\beta_i, \delta_i, \lambda_i, b_i)_{1 \leq i \leq k})\} \subset$$
$$\text{Con}((q', Ac), (\beta_i, A\delta_i, \lambda_i, b_i)_{1 \leq i \leq k})$$

As in the case of ellipsoidal assignments, $Ac + b$ and $A\delta_i$ are computed in floating-point arithmetic. Hence once they are computed, we have to ensure that the resulting numerical cone contains the formally defined cone, i.e. we need to verify the inclusion of ellipsoidal bases with (3) and the procedure described in Sect. 2.3. We also need to verify the conic inclusion, i.e. the fact that $\beta_i' \geq \beta_i + \sqrt{q'(A\delta_i - \delta_i')}$, where β_i' and δ_i' are the parameters of the resulting cone. So we may have to update the parameters and verify the inequalities in a sound manner.

4.4   Addition and Removal of Counters

When the analyzer enters a new loop, it needs to take into account the previous constraint and add a dependency on the current loop counter y_i. Moreover, when it exits a loop, it needs to build a new constraint overapproximating the previous one that does not involve the counter y_i.

Ellipsoidal constraints can be seen as conic constraints with $k = 0$. Hence we study the problem of adding and removing counters to a conic constraint $\mathrm{Con}((q,c), (\beta_i, \delta_i, \lambda_i, b_i)_{1 \leq i \leq k})$.

Adding a Counter. Let y_{k+1} be the counter we want to add. Let λ_{k+1} be the minimal value of the counter inferred at this point. We set $\beta_{k+1} = 0$, $\delta_{k+1} = 0$ and $b_{k+1} = $ True if the value of y_{k+1} at this point of the analysis is not known precisely, else if we know that $y_{k+1} = \lambda_{k+1}$, then $b_{k+1} = $ False.

That gives us the constraint $\mathrm{Con}((q,c), (\beta_i, \delta_i, \lambda_i, b_i)_{1 \leq i \leq k+1})$.

Proof. It is immediate from Definition 2 and the distinction made on what we know about y_i, that this constraint overapproximates the set of reachable (x, y) at this point. □

Removing a Counter. We now want to remove the counter y_k from the conic constraint, provided that we know that $y_k \in [\lambda_k, M]$ with $M < +\infty$ (note that if it happens that $b_k = $ False, then $M = \lambda_k$).

Theorem 3. *Let $C = \mathrm{Con}((q,c), (\beta_i, \delta_i, \lambda_i, b_i)_{1 \leq i \leq k+1})$. Then C is convex and we have*

$$C_{|y_k \in [a,b]} = C \cap \{(x,y) | y_k \in [a,b]\} = \mathrm{Conv}(C \cap \{(x,y) | y_k = a \vee y_k = b\}).$$

where we suppose $a \geq \lambda_k$ and where $\mathrm{Conv}(X)$ is the convex hull of X.

Proof. Up to translation, we can assume that $\forall i \in [\![1, k]\!], \lambda_i = 0$. If $a = b$, it is immediate. We suppose $a < b$. Then, if Q is the matrix of q, let S be the inverse of its square root $(S^{-2} = Q)$. We have

$$(x, y) \in C \iff q(x - c - \sum_{i=1}^{k} y_i \delta_i) \leq (1 + \sum_{i=1}^{k} \beta_i y_i)^2$$

$$\iff \exists u \in \mathbb{R}^p, ||u||_2 \leq 1, x - c - \sum_{i=1}^{k} y_i \delta_i = (1 + \sum_{i=1}^{k} \beta_i y_i) Su$$

$$\iff \exists u \in \mathbb{R}^p, ||u||_2 \leq 1, x = \frac{y_k - a}{b - a} x_b + (1 - \frac{y_k - a}{b - a}) x_a$$

$$\text{where } x_b = (c + \sum_{i=1}^{k-1} y_i \delta_i + (1 + \sum_{i=1}^{k-1} \beta_i y_i) Su + b(\delta_k + \beta_k Su))$$

$$x_a = (c + \sum_{i=1}^{k-1} y_i \delta_i + (1 + \sum_{i=1}^{k-1} \beta_i y_i) Su + a(\delta_k + \beta_k Su))$$

From the previous equivalences, we have $z_a = (x_a, y_1, \ldots, y_{k-1}, a) \in C$ and $z_b = (x_b, y_1, \ldots, y_{k-1}, b) \in C$. Moreover $(x, y) = \frac{y_k - a}{b-a} z_b + (1 - \frac{y_k - a}{b-a}) z_a$. □

Let π_{y_k} be the projection along y_k. Since convexity and barycenters are preserved up to projections, $\pi_{y_k}(C_{|y_k \in [a,b]}) = \text{Conv}(\pi_{y_k}(C_{|y_k = a}) \cup \pi_{y_k}(C_{|y_k = b}))$. So, by a direct calculation

$$\pi_{y_k}(C_{|y_k=a}) = \text{Con}((\frac{q}{(1 + \beta_k(a - \lambda_k))^2}, c + (a - \lambda_k)\delta_k),$$

$$(\frac{\beta_i}{1 + (a - \lambda_k)\beta_k}, \delta_i, \lambda_i, b_i)_{1 \leq i \leq k-1})$$

We have a similar equality for $\pi_{y_k}(C_{|y_k=b})$, hence we just have to compute the join $(\pi_{y_k}(C_{|y_k=a}) \bigsqcup_{\text{Con}} \pi_{y_k}(C_{|y_k=b}))$, which is an overapproximation of the convex hull of the union.

However, we have to implement this operation such that it is sound when computed in floating-point arithmetic. Via affine transformation, we can soundly compute an ellipsoidal base $\text{Ell}(q^*, c^*)$ such that

$$\begin{cases} q(x - (c + (a - \lambda_k)\delta_k)) \leq (1 + \beta_k(a - \lambda_k))^2 \\ q(x - (c + (b - \lambda_k)\delta_k)) \leq (1 + \beta_k(b - \lambda_k))^2 \end{cases} \Rightarrow q^*(x - c^*) \leq 1$$

Then, for any $i \in [\![1, k - 1]\!]$ such that $b_i = \text{True}$, if we note β_i^* and δ_i^* the parameters of the resulting cone, in order to have an inclusion of $C_{|y_k=a}$ and $C_{|y_k=b}$ in C^*, we need to establish by Theorem 2 that:

$$\begin{cases} \beta_i^{*2} \geq \max_{\frac{q(u)}{(1+\beta_k(a-\lambda_k))^2} \leq 1} q^*(\frac{\beta_i}{1 + (a - \lambda_k)\beta_k} u + \delta_i - \delta_i^*) \\ \beta_i^{*2} \geq \max_{\frac{q(u)}{(1+\beta_k(b-\lambda_k))^2} \leq 1} q^*(\frac{\beta_i}{1 + (b - \lambda_k)\beta_k} u + \delta_i - \delta_i^*) \end{cases}$$

And since from our hypothesis on $\mathrm{Ell}(q^*, c^*)$ we know that $q \succeq q^*$, we can just set $\delta_i^* = \delta_i$ and the condition becomes $\beta_i^* \geq \beta_i$. So we can just define $\beta_i^* = \beta_i$, hence the resulting cone after the removing of the kth counter is

$$\mathrm{Con}((q^*, c^*), (\beta_i, \delta_i, \lambda_i, b_i)_{1 \leq i \leq k-1})$$

4.5   A Widening Operator

Let $C = \mathrm{Con}((q, c), (\beta_i, \delta_i, \lambda_i, b_i)_{1 \leq i \leq k})$ and $C' = \mathrm{Con}((q', c'), (\beta_i', \delta_i', \lambda_i', b_i')_{1 \leq i \leq k})$. We suppose that $\forall i \in [\![1, k]\!], \lambda_i \leq \lambda_i'$ and $\exists i \in [\![1, k]\!], \lambda_i < \lambda_i'$.

We want to define a widening operator $\bigtriangledown$ over cones. The intuitive idea is that if C "starts strictly below" C' (cf. the conditions on the λ_i's), then $C^* = C \bigtriangledown C'$ has the same ellipsoidal base as C, but its opening has been "widened" to contain C'. The decision of only changing the opening and the orientation of the cone (i.e., to change only the β_i's and δ_i's) relies on the hypothesis that the relative shift of C' from C has good chances to be reproduced again. Hence the name of "conic extrapolation".

Definition of $\bigtriangledown_p$. More formally, we first study the special case in which we know that $\mathrm{Ell}(q', c') \subset C$ and we define a partial widening operator $\bigtriangledown_p$.

Let $C^* = C \bigtriangledown_p C' = \mathrm{Con}((q, c), (\beta_i^*, \delta_i^*, \lambda_i, b_i^*)_{1 \leq i \leq k})$. We note $(i), (ii), (iii)$ (resp. $(i'), (ii'), (iii')$) the conditions of Theorem 2 relative to the inclusion $C \subset C^*$ (resp. $C' \subset C^*$). By construction of C^*, we already have (ii) and with our hypothesis $\mathrm{Ell}(q', c') \subset C'$, we just need to verify $C \subset C^*$ to have (ii'). We can define $\forall i \in [\![1, k]\!], b_i^* = (b_i \vee b_i' \vee \lambda_i < \lambda_i')$, which gives us (i) and (i').

Finally to verify (iii) and (iii'), we only need to define the β_i^*'s and δ_i^*'s such that

$$\forall i \in [\![1, k]\!], \begin{cases} b_i \Rightarrow \beta_i^{*2} \geq \max_{q(u) \leq 1} q(\beta_i u + \delta_i - \delta_i^*) \\ b_i' \Rightarrow \beta_i^{*2} \geq \max_{q'(u) \leq 1} q(\beta_i' u + \delta_i' - \delta_i^*) \end{cases}$$

which we overapproximate by a triangle inequality for the norm defined by q:

$$\forall i \in [\![1, k]\!], \begin{cases} b_i \Rightarrow \beta_i^* \geq \beta_i + \sqrt{q(\delta_i - \delta_i^*)} \\ b_i' \Rightarrow \beta_i^* \geq \beta_i' r + \sqrt{q(\delta_i' - \delta_i^*)} \\ \text{where } r \geq \min\{\rho > 0 | \frac{q'}{\rho^2} \preceq q\} \end{cases}$$

With the SDP methods of the first section, we can compute an overapproximating r. For each i, if none of b_i or b_i' is True, then from our hypothesis $\mathrm{Ell}(q', c') \subset C'$, $b_i^* = \mathrm{False}$ and we do not have to give values to either β_i or δ_i. If only b_i (resp. b_i') is True, then we define $\delta_i^* = \delta_i$ and $\beta_i^* = \beta_i$ (resp. $\delta_i^* = \delta_i'$ and $\beta_i^* \geq r\beta_i'$).

If $b_i = b_i' = \mathrm{True}$, we want to minimize $\max(\beta_i + \sqrt{q(\delta_i - \delta_i^*)}, \beta_i' r + \sqrt{q(\delta_i' - \delta_i^*)})$. If we fix the q-distance $\sqrt{q(\delta_i - \delta_i^*)}$, we want to minimize the

q-distance $\sqrt{q(\delta'_i - \delta^*_i)}$. With this geometrical point of view, we see that the optimal δ^*_i is a barycenter of δ_i and δ'_i.

So we define $\delta^*_i = \mu\delta_i + (1-\mu)\delta'_i$ where we want to find $\mu \in [0,1]$ minimizing

$$\max(\beta_i + \sqrt{q(\delta_i - \mu\delta_i - (1-\mu)\delta'_i)}, \beta'_i r + \sqrt{q(\delta'_i - \mu\delta_i - (1-\mu)\delta'_i)}) =$$

$$\max(\beta_i + (1-\mu)\sqrt{q(\delta_i - \delta'_i)}, \beta'_i r + \mu\sqrt{q(\delta_i - \delta'_i)}).$$

Hence, we can exactly (up to floating-point approximations) compute μ, define δ^*_i and then β^*_i. This construction of $(\beta^*_i, \delta^*_i, b^*_i)_{1 \le i \le k}$ ensures that $C, C' \subset C^*$ and defines ∇_p.

Definition of ∇. We now study the general case in which the only assumption made is that $\forall i \in [\![1,k]\!], \lambda_i \le \lambda'_i$ and $\exists i \in [\![1,k]\!], \lambda_i < \lambda'_i$.

We define a cone $C^+ = \mathrm{Con}((q,c),(\beta^+_i, \delta^+_i, \lambda_i, b^+_i)_{1 \le i \le k})$, which contains the ellipsoidal base of the two cones. The definition (with q, c and the λ_i) ensures the inclusion of the ellipsoidal base of C. Let $R = 1 + \sum_{i=1}^{k} \beta^+_i(\lambda'_i - \lambda_i)$ and

$$\Delta = \sum_{i=1}^{k} \delta^+_i(\lambda'_i - \lambda_i).$$

We define $\forall i \in [\![1,k]\!], b^+_i = (\lambda_i < \lambda'_i)$. Let $r = \min\{\rho > 0 | \frac{q}{\rho^2} \preceq q'\}$, if we have $\mathrm{Ell}(\frac{q}{r^2}, c') \subset \mathrm{Ell}(\frac{q}{R^2}, c + \Delta)$ then $\mathrm{Ell}(q', c') \subset \mathrm{Ell}(\frac{q}{R^2}, c + \Delta)$ and from the definitions of the b^+_i's and Definition 2, we would have $\mathrm{Ell}(q', c') \times \{(\lambda'_1, \ldots, \lambda'_k)\} \subset C^+$. To get this result, we need:

$$\mathrm{Ell}(\frac{q}{r^2}, c') \subset \mathrm{Ell}(\frac{q}{R^2}, c + \Delta) \iff \{q(c' - c - \Delta) \le (R - r)^2\} \wedge \{R \ge r\}$$

If the transformations applied to the cone are affine, the shift can be seen as the difference between centers. So we choose to define $\Delta = c' - c$. Then we choose the minimal possible value of R to have a cone as tight as possible: once the δ_i's corresponding to Δ are computed in floating-point arithmetic, we can define an upper bound on $\sqrt{q(c' - c - \Delta)} + r$ and define R accordingly, so that the above inequality is verified.

These definitions of Δ and R must be implemented in terms of β^+_i and δ^+_i. Since we ensured that there is at least one i such that $(\lambda'_i - \lambda_i) \ne 0$, there is always a solution. If only one i fits this criterion the solution is unique, otherwise a choice must be made on how to weight the different variable.

This uncertainty can be easily explained: recall that in real programs, only one loop counter is increased at a time, so we know what causes the change in our constraint. This is not the case if many loop counters are increased at the same time.

Finally, this definition of C^+ allows us to define the widening operator ∇ by: $C \nabla C' = (C \nabla_p C^+) \nabla_p C'$. Note that the assumptions of ∇_p are verified since C and C^+ have the same ellipsoidal base, and C^+, hence $C \nabla_p C^+$, contains the base of C'.

To ensure the convergence of the widening sequence in the cases described in Sect. 5, we can use a real widening operator on the β_i's that sets them to $+\infty$ after a certain number of steps, for instance.

4.6   Proof of the Characterization of Conic Inclusion

Proof (Proof of Lemma 1)
- We first prove that $(i) \wedge (ii) \Rightarrow C \subset C'$. From (i), we know that $\forall u \in \mathbb{R}^p, q(u) \leq 1 \Rightarrow q'(u+c-c') \leq 1$. Thus, for $(x, y) \in \mathbb{R}^p \times \mathbb{R}_+^k$ such that $q(x -$

$$c - \sum_{i=1}^{k} y_i \delta_i) \leq (1 + \sum_{i=1}^{k} \beta_i y_i)^2, \text{ we define } \nu = (1 + \sum_{i=1}^{k} \beta_i y_i) \geq \sqrt{q(x - c - \sum_{i=1}^{k} y_i \delta_i)}$$

and $u = \frac{1}{\nu}(x - c - \sum_{i=1}^{k} y_i \delta_i)$. We have $q(u) \leq 1$.

$$
q'(x - c' - \sum_{i=1}^{k} y_i \delta_i') = q'\left(u + (c - c') + (\nu - 1)u + \sum_{i=1}^{k} y_i (\delta_i - \delta_i') \right)
$$
$$
\leq \left(\sqrt{q'(u + c - c')} + \sum_{i=1}^{k} y_i \sqrt{q'(\beta_i u + \delta_i - \delta_i')} \right)^2
\tag{4}
$$

So if b_i = False then $y_i = 0$, hence $y_i \sqrt{q'(\beta_i u + \delta_i - \delta_i')} \leq y_i \beta_i'$, and from (ii), if b_i = True, then we have the same inequality since $q(u) \leq 1$. So this inequality is true for all $i \in [\![1, k]\!]$.

Thus, we have $q'(x - c' - \sum_{i=1}^{k} y_i \delta_i') \leq (1 + \sum_{i=1}^{k} \beta_i' y_i)^2$ and $\forall i \in [\![1, k]\!]$ we have $y_i \geq 0$ and from (ii), $y_i > 0 \Rightarrow b_i \Rightarrow b_i'$. So $(x, y) \in C'$. So $C \subset C'$.
- Now we prove that $C \subset C' \Rightarrow (i) \wedge (ii)$. It is obvious that $C \subset C' \Rightarrow (i)$ by taking the intersections of the cones with the set $\{(x, 0) \in \mathbb{R}^{p+k}\}$.

If $\exists i \in [\![1, k]\!]$ s.t. b_i' = False and b_i = True, then there exist a point (x, y) of C with $y_i > 0$, so $(x, y) \notin C'$ and $C \not\subset C'$.

If $\exists i \in [\![1, k]\!]$ s.t. b_i = True and $\beta_i' < \max_{q(u) \leq 1} \sqrt{q'(\beta_i u + \delta_i - \delta_i')}$, then let us take $u \in \mathbb{R}^p$ such that $q(u) \leq 1$ and $\beta_i' < \sqrt{q'(\beta_i u + \delta_i - \delta_i')}$. We define $x(t) = (1 + \beta_i t)u + t\delta_i + c$.

For any $t \geq 0$, $q'(x(t) - c' - t\delta_i') \geq \left(\sqrt{q'(u + c - c')} - t\sqrt{q'(\beta_i u + \delta_i - \delta_i')} \right)^2$

Since $\beta_i' < \sqrt{q'(\beta_i u + \delta_i - \delta_i')}$, and from the previous inequality, we have for t big enough, $q'(x(t) - t\delta_i' - c') > (1 + \beta_i')^2$. By a direct computation $q(x(t) - t\delta_i - c) \leq (1 + \beta_i t)^2$. And since b_i = True, we have for $y(t)$ such that $y(t)_i = t$ and $y(t)_{j \neq i} = 0$, $(x(t), y(t)) \in C$, $(x(t), y(t)) \notin C'$ so $C \not\subset C'$.

We have proven $\neg(i) \vee \neg(ii) \Rightarrow C \not\subset C'$, so we finally have $(i) \wedge (ii) \Longleftrightarrow C \subset C'$. □

Proof (Proof of Theorem 2). Since $(c, (\lambda_i)_{1 \leq i \leq k}) \in C$, it is clear that (i) is a necessary condition. Moreover, $C \subset \{(x, y) \in \mathbb{R}^{p+k} | \forall i \in [\![1, k]\!], y_i \geq \lambda_i\} =:$ Orth$_\lambda$, therefore $C \subset C' \iff C \subset C' \cap \text{Orth}_\lambda \iff C \subset C' \cap \text{Orth}_\lambda \wedge (i)$.

Directly from Definition 2, we have for $R = (1 + \sum\limits_{i=1}^{k} \beta'_i(\lambda_i - \lambda'_i))$ the implication

$(i) \Rightarrow C' \cap \mathrm{Orth}_\lambda = \mathrm{Con}((\frac{q'}{R^2}, c' + \sum\limits_{i=1}^{k}(\lambda_i - \lambda'_i)\delta'_i), (\frac{\beta'_i}{R}, \delta'_i, \lambda_i, b'_i)_{1 \le i \le k})$. So up to translation, we can reduce this case to $\lambda_i = \lambda'_i = 0$ and apply Lemma 1.

$$C \subset C' \iff C \subset C' \cap \mathrm{Orth}_\lambda \wedge (i)$$

$$\iff (i) \wedge \mathrm{Ell}(q, c) \subset \mathrm{Ell}(\frac{q'}{R^2}, c' + \sum\limits_{i=1}^{k}(\lambda_i - \lambda'_i)\delta'_i)$$

$$\wedge \forall i \in [\![1, k]\!], b_i \Rightarrow \left(b'_i \text{ and } \frac{\beta'^2_i}{R^2} \ge \max_{q(u) \le 1} \frac{q'}{R^2}(\beta_i u + \delta_i - \delta'_i) \right)$$

$$\iff (i) \wedge (ii) \wedge (iii)$$

$\square$

5   Application and Convergence

In the definition of the conic extrapolation, we did not describe how to choose the ellipsoidal base. For instance, it is possible to get an ellipsoidal shape by computing some iterates of the loop. This seems to work well in the case of programs composed of loops and nondeterministic counter increments: the iterations capture in which direction the counters globally increase (Fig. 1). Since the diameter of the set containing the numerical variables grows linearly, any cone will be overapproximating for β big enough.

```
1: x ← 0 ∈ ℝⁿ
2: for y from 0 to ∞ do
3:     pick i ∈ [1, n]
4:     pick ε ∈ {−1, 1}
5:     xᵢ ← xᵢ + ε
```

n	2	4	6	8	10	12	14	16
Ell. cones	3s	7s	19s	49s	1m56s	4m16s	8m	12m
Polyhedra	<0.1s	<0.1s	0.3s	2.5s	54s	47m	>1h	>1h

Fig. 1. Example of a program and its average analysis time on a 2GHz CPU. Ellipsoidal cones have been prototyped in Python using NumPy [16], CVXOPT [14], mpmath [15]. The Apron [17] C library has been used for polyhedra. The prototype Python code and details about benchmarks are available on http://www.eleves.ens.fr/home/oulamara/ellcones.html.

5.1   Switched Linear Systems

However, the picture is not as nice if we add linear transformation. This is the case, for instance, for switched linear systems in control theory (Fig. 2): if the quadratic form associated with the ellipsoid is not a Lyapunov function of the

```
1: x ← 0 ∈ ℝⁿ
2: (Aᵢ, bᵢ)₁≤ᵢ≤ₖ
3:     where bᵢ ∈ ℝⁿ, Aᵢ ∈ Mₙ(ℝ)
4: for y from 0 to ∞ do
5:     i ← rand(1, n)
6:     x ← Aᵢx + bᵢ
```

Benchmark	1	2	3	4	5	6	7
Ell. Cones	1s	2s	2s	2s	1.8s	1.2s	1.3s
Polyhedra	3.2s	16.6s	18s	24s	>1h	>1h	2m35s

Fig. 2. The structure of a Switched Linear System and some benchmarks. Experimental conditions are the same as in Fig. 1. Except for Benchmarks 1 and 2, the resulting polyhedron is trivial.

linear part of the system (of the matrices A_i in Fig. 2), then the growth of its radius is exponential in the loop counters, and cannot be captured by our conic extrapolation. So if Q is the matrix of the ellipsoidal base of the cone, the Lyapunov conditions should be verified simultaneously : $\forall i, Q - A_i^T Q A_i \succeq 0$. This is not always possible, but one can use the SDP solver to try to find a suitable Q. Note that the identity matrix is not stable in the sense of control theory and should not be included in the search of Q. When Q verifies the Lyapunov conditions, it is easy to show that for β_i large enough, the cone will be invariant during loops iterations.

6 Concluding Remarks and Perspectives

We proposed an abstract interpretation framework based on ellipsoidal cones to study systems with (sub-)linear growth in loop counters. The aim of this work is twofold: to build an extension of the formal verification of linear systems, and to devise a framework that can be used outside the context of digital filters. Indeed, only the choice of the ellipsoidal base of the cone has to deal with control theory considerations.

The next step is obviously to go beyond the prototype and have a robust implementation to test this framework on actual systems. This will involve a research on how to accurately tune and use the SDP solver, how to deal with precision issues.

The main tools are the SDP solver and the SDP duality to check the soundness of the results of operations via LMI's. However, we are not bound to use SDP solvers to compute these results, and exploring other options might speed up the analysis.

It would also be interesting to generalize this framework to switched linear systems that are more complex than those studied above. An example is the analysis in [13].

Acknowledgments. We want to thank Pierre-Loïc Garoche and Léonard Blier for the fruitful conversations we had with each of them during this work, as well as the anonymous referees for the time and efforts taken to review this work.

References

1. Yildirim, E.: Alper. On the minimum volume covering ellipsoid of ellipsoids. SIAM J. Optim. **17**(3), 621–641 (2006)
2. Ben-Tal, A., Nemirovski, A.: Lectures on Modern Convex Optimization: Analysis, Algorithms, and Engineering Applications, vol. 2. SIAM, Philadelphia (2001)
3. Feret, J.: Static analysis of digital filters. In: Schmidt, D. (ed.) ESOP 2004. LNCS, vol. 2986, pp. 33–48. Springer, Heidelberg (2004)
4. Feret, J.: Numerical abstract domains for digital filters. In: International Workshop on Numerical and Symbolic Abstract Domains (NSAD 2005) (2005)
5. Roux, P., Jobredeaux, R., Garoche, P. L., Féron, É.: A generic ellipsoid abstract domain for linear time invariant systems. In: Proceedings of the 15th ACM International Conference on Hybrid Systems: Computation and Control, pp. 105–114. ACM (2012)
6. Roux, P., Garoche, P.-L.: Computing quadratic invariants with min- and max-policy iterations: a practical comparison. In: Jones, C., Pihlajasaari, P., Sun, J. (eds.) FM 2014. LNCS, vol. 8442, pp. 563–578. Springer, Heidelberg (2014)
7. Venet, A.J.: The gauge domain: scalable analysis of linear inequality invariants. In: Madhusudan, P., Seshia, S.A. (eds.) CAV 2012. LNCS, vol. 7358, pp. 139–154. Springer, Heidelberg (2012)
8. Cousot, P., Cousot, R.: Abstract interpretation: a unified lattice model for static analysis of programs by construction or approximation of fixpoints. In: Proceedings of the 4th ACM SIGACT-SIGPLAN Symposium on Principles of Programming Languages. ACM (1977)
9. Cousot, P., Cousot, R.: Abstract interpretation frameworks. J. Logic Comput. **2**(4), 511–547 (1992)
10. Blekherman, G., Parrilo, P.A., Thomas, R.R.: Semidefinite Optimization and Convex Algebraic Geometry, vol. 13. SIAM, Philadelphia (2013)
11. Vandenberghe, L., Boyd, S.: Semidefinite programming. SIAM Rev. **38**, 49–95 (1996)
12. Porkolab, L., Khachiyan, L.: On the complexity of semidefinite programs. J. Global Optim. **10**(4), 351–365 (1997)
13. Daafouz, J., Riedinger, P., Iung, C.: Stability analysis and control synthesis for switched systems: a switched lyapunov function approach. IEEE Trans. Autom. Control **47**(11), 1883–1887 (2002)
14. Andersen, M.S., Dahl, J., Vandenberghe, L.: CVXOPT: A Python package for convex optimization, version 1.1.6. (2013). http://www.cvxopt.org
15. Johansson, F., et al.: mpmath: a Python library for arbitrary-precision floating-point arithmetic, version 0.18, December 2013
16. van der Walt, S., Colbert, S.C., Varoquaux, G.: The NumPy array: a structure for efficient numerical computation. Comput. Sci. Eng. **13**, 22–30 (2011)
17. Jeannet, B., Miné, A.: APRON: A library of numerical abstract domains for static analysis. In: Bouajjani, A., Maler, O. (eds.) CAV 2009. LNCS, vol. 5643, pp. 661–667. Springer, Heidelberg (2009)

Lightning Talks

ADAM: Causality-Based Synthesis of Distributed Systems

Bernd Finkbeiner[1], Manuel Gieseking[2]([⊠]), and Ernst-Rüdiger Olderog[2]

[1] Universität des Saarlandes, Saarbrücken, Germany
[2] Carl von Ossietzky Universität Oldenburg,
Oldenburg, Germany
finkbeiner@cs.uni-saarland.de,
manuel.gieseking@informatik.uni-oldenburg.de,
olderog@informatik.uni-oldenburg.de

Abstract. We present ADAM, a tool for the automatic synthesis of distributed systems with multiple concurrent processes. For each process, an individual controller is synthesized that acts on locally available information obtained through synchronization with the environment and with other system processes. ADAM is based on Petri games, an extension of Petri nets where each token is a player in a multiplayer game. ADAM implements the first symbolic game solving algorithm for Petri games. We report on experience from several case studies with up to 38 system processes.

1 Introduction

Research on the *reactive synthesis* problem, i.e., the challenge of constructing a reactive system automatically from a formal specification, dates back to the early years of computer science [5,6,16]. Over the past decade, this research has led to tools like Acacia+ [4], Ratsy [3], and Unbeast [7], which translate a formal specification automatically into an implementation that is correct in the sense that the system reacts to every possible input from the system's environment in a way that ensures that the specification is satisfied. The tools have been used in nontrivial applications, such as the synthesis of bus arbiter circuits [2] and robotic control [12]. The key limitation of the current state of the art is that the underlying system model consists of a single process. If the system under construction consists of several distributed parts, such as several robots, then the implementation is always based on a central controller with whom the entire system must constantly synchronize. This is unfortunate, because in practice, it is specifically the design of the *distributed* implementation with multiple concurrent processes that is most error-prone and would, therefore, benefit most from a synthesis tool.

In this paper, we present ADAM, a synthesis tool designed for distributed systems with multiple concurrent processes. Unlike previous tools based on

This research was partially supported by the German Research Council (DFG) in the Transregional Collaborative Research Center SFB/TR 14 AVACS.

D. Kroening and C.S. Păsăreanu (Eds.): CAV 2015, Part I, LNCS 9206, pp. 433–439, 2015.
DOI: 10.1007/978-3-319-21690-4_25

automata, ADAM uses concurrent processes in the form of Petri nets as its underlying system model. (ADAM is named in honor of Carl *Adam* Petri.) Our aim is to automate the construction of complex distributed systems, such as production plants with multiple independent robots. Rather than creating a central controller, with whom all robots must constantly synchronize, ADAM creates an individual controller for each robot, which acts on locally available information such as the information obtained through observations and through synchronization with nearby robots.

The most well-studied model for the synthesis of distributed systems is due to Pnueli and Rosner [14]. This model captures the *partial information* available to the processes by specifying for each process the subset of events that are visible to the process. The decisions of the process are based only on the history of its observations, not on the full state history. Unfortunately, the Pnueli/Rosner model has never been translated into practical tools; the synthesis problem under the Pnueli/Rosner

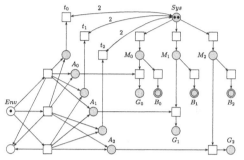

Fig. 1. Example Petri game from the synthesis of two independent robots in a manufacturing situation with k orders on n machines (here: $k = 2, n = 3$), where one machine is chosen by the environment to be defective.

model is undecidable in general, and very expensive (nonelementary) in the special cases where it can be decided [10,15].

ADAM is based on the more recently developed model of *Petri games* [9]. The synthesis problem is modeled as a game between a team of system players, representing the processes, and an environment (player), representing the user (and other external influences) of the system. Both the system players and the environment are represented as tokens of a Petri net. As Petri nets, the games capture the complex *causal dependencies* (and independence) between the processes (cf. [17]). Figure 1 shows a typical application scenario, taken here from the synthesis of robot controllers in a production plant, addressing concurrency, usage constraints, and uncertain availability of machines. The robots are expected to process k orders on n machines (here: $k = 2, n = 3$), despite the actions of a hostile environment, which is allowed to declare one machine to be defective. The environment, initially at place Env, chooses which machine is defective and activates the remaining machines by putting tokens on two of the places A_i, $i \in \{0, 1, 2\}$. The two system players in place Sys represent the two robots. Different robots can take their orders concurrently to different machines. If a robot chooses a machine M_i right away, it does not know whether M_i is defective, i.e., without a token on A_i. Then from M_i only the bad place B_i is reachable. If a robot chooses an active machine M_i (with a token on A_i) then from M_i the good place G_i is reachable by consuming the token from A_i. If a robot chooses M_i again, the token on A_i is missing, and only the bad place B_i

is reachable. A winning strategy for the robots must avoid any transitions to a bad place. To this end, the robots first inform themselves, via the synchronizing transitions t_0, t_1 and t_2, which machines are broken (this is done simultaneously by the two robots due to the arc multiplicity 2) and then use two different active machines.

In recent work [9], we showed that solving Petri games with safety objectives, a single environment player and an arbitrary (but fixed) number of system players is EXPTIME-complete, and thus dramatically cheaper than comparable synthesis problems in the Pnueli/Rosner setting. ADAM represents the first practical implementation of this theoretical result.

2 The Synthesis Game

We model the synthesis problem as a game between a team of system players on one side and a hostile environment player on the other side. The system players have a joint objective, to defeat the environment, but are independent of each other in the sense that they have no information of each other's state unless they explicitly communicate. A *Petri game* [9] is a refinement of a Petri net. The players are the tokens in the underlying Petri net. They are organized into two teams, the system players and the environment players, where the system players wish to avoid a certain "bad" place (i.e., they follow a safety objective), while the environment players wish to reach just such a marking. To partition the tokens into the teams, we distinguish each place p as belonging to either the system ($p \in \mathcal{P}_S$) or the environment ($p \in \mathcal{P}_E$). A token belongs to one of these teams whenever it is on a place that belongs to that team. Formally, a Petri game is a structure $\mathcal{G} = (\mathcal{P}_S, \mathcal{P}_E, \mathcal{T}, \mathcal{F}, In, \mathcal{B})$, where the underlying Petri net of $\mathcal{G}$ is $\mathcal{N} = (\mathcal{P}, \mathcal{T}, \mathcal{F}, In)$ with set of places $\mathcal{P} = \mathcal{P}_S \cup \mathcal{P}_E$, set of transitions $\mathcal{T}$, flow relation $\mathcal{F}$, initial marking In, and set of bad places $\mathcal{B}$. We depict places of $\mathcal{P}_S$ in gray and of $\mathcal{P}_E$ in white. In the following, we assume that there is a single environment player and an arbitrary (but bounded) number of system players. We further assume that the Petri net is safe, i.e., every place is, at all times, occupied by at most one token. Petri games that are bounded, but not necessarily safe, like the example from the introduction, can be translated into an equivalent game with a safe net using the standard transformation.

A player (token) is always informed about its causal past. As long as different players move in concurrent places of the net, they do not know of each other. Only when they communicate, i.e., synchronize at a joint transition, they exchange their knowledge about the past. Formally, this is modelled by the net unfolding.

A *strategy* σ for the system players will eliminate at each place of the net unfolding some of the available branches. A strategy is *winning* for the system players if all branches that lead to a bad place are eliminated. For each player we can obtain a *local controller* by isolating the part of σ that is relevant for this player. These local controllers can proceed independently unless they have to synchronize at a joint transition with other local controllers as described by σ. Since the winning condition of a game is a *safety objective*, the system players can satisfy it by doing nothing. To avoid such trivial solutions, we look for

0	1	2	3	4	5	6	7	8
	p_i (binary-coded)		type	$\top$	t_1		$\cdots$	$t_{|\mathcal{T}|}$

Fig. 2. Bitvector representation of a cut. The subvector encodes the ith system token.

strategies that are *deadlock-avoiding* in the sense that in every reachable marking, whenever there is a transition enabled in the unfolding then there is some transition enabled in the strategy. A marking where there is no enabled transition in the unfolding either is not a deadlock. Then we say that the game has *terminated*. A *play* π (conforming to a strategy σ) is obtained from σ by eliminating all remaining choices such that at each place there is only one transition left (determinism). The system players win the play π if it does not contain a bad place. Otherwise, the environment wins.

3   Solving Petri Games

Petri games can be solved via a reduction to two-player games over finite graphs. In this section, we give an informal sketch of the reduction, focusing on the symbolic representation and the fixed point iteration of the game solving algorithm. For a more formal presentation of the reduction from Petri games to two-player games over finite graphs, the reader is referred to [9].

The two-player game simulates the Petri game through a sequence of *cuts*, i.e., maximal sets of concurrent places. We annotate the system places in a cut with a *decision set*, i.e., a set of transitions currently selected by the player represented by the token on the system place. In each cut, we designate a subset of the system places as *type-2*, which means that its strategy will no longer synchronize (directly or indirectly through other system tokens) with the environment. Additionally, we designate a subset of the system places as *type-1*. These are places that still require a synchronization with the environment but are, in the current cut, not able to move (following their decision sets) before the environment makes its next move.

Cuts where all system places are either type-1 or type-2 are called *mcuts*. Mcuts correspond to situations in which the system players have progressed maximally in the sense that all non-type-2 places are blocked until the environment moves. The key idea of the reduction is to delay all environment decisions until an mcut is reached. This ensures that all system decisions that should be made independently of the environment choice have actually been made *before* the environment decision is made, and are, hence, guaranteed to be independent of this decision. A winning strategy for the system players must thus legally move from mcut to mcut, in response to the environment decisions at the mcuts, without encountering bad situations (such as bad places), either until the Petri net terminates or forever, if the play never terminates.

The symbolic representation of cuts. Our representation of a cut is organized by the tokens, rather than places: this is motivated by the fact that the number of tokens in a Petri net is usually much smaller than the number of places; it is therefore cheaper to assign to each token the currently occupied place instead of simply representing an (arbitrary) subset of the places. A cut is represented as a bitvector, which is composed of several subvectors, one for each token. Figure 2 depicts such a subvector for a system token i. The first part of the bitvector encodes the place p_i and its type (type-1 vs. type-2). The second part encodes the decision of the strategy. The bit t_j is set iff the player represented by token i chooses to allow the jth transition of the Petri net. The T-bit is set right after a transition is executed. It indicates that the player is allowed to choose a new set of transitions. For the special case of the environment token, we only need to encode the place, without the type, T-, and transition flags. We use BDDs to represent sets of cuts and relations on cuts.

The game solving algorithm. The game solving algorithm consists of three phases. *Phase 1* is a preprocessing step that identifies the type-2 places in the cuts. The strategy from type-2 places must guarantee that the tokens on the type-2 places have no further interaction with the environment. The set of all cuts with correct type-2 annotation is computed as a largest fixed point. *Phase 2* identifies the winning mcuts, i.e., mcuts where the strategy from type-1 places guarantees that the game continues with an infinite sequence of mcuts or reaches an mcut with only type-2 tokens. The set of mcuts is computed as a largest fixed point. Nested inside the largest fixed point computation is a least fixed point iteration that finds the predecessor mcuts, by first identifying all cuts from which the system players can force the game without further interaction with the environment into some mcut of the current approximation of the largest fixed point. Phase 2 also computes, as a least fixed point, the set of all cuts from which the system players can enforce a visit of such an mcut. The game is won by the system players iff the initial cut is in this set. *Phase 3* constructs a winning strategy if the game is won by the system players. The strategy first enforces the visit of a winning mcut according to the computation in Phase 2. From there, the strategy from type-1 places forces the game into new winning mcuts, and the strategy from type-2 places ensures, according to the computation in Phase 1, the safe continuation without any further interaction with the environment.

4 Experience with ADAM

ADAM is a Java-based implementation of the fixed point construction described in Sect. 3. For the BDD operations, ADAM uses BuDDy [13], a BDD library written in C. The size of the BDDs is reduced with various optimizations, including a compact representation of the place encodings, based on net invariants (which reduce the set of potential places for each token). We use the DOT [1] format as output for Graphviz for the visualization of the Petri games and the strategy graph of the 2-player game, as well as the Petri game strategies.

We have applied ADAM in several case studies from robotic control, workflow management, and other distributed applications. Table 1 shows representative results from several synthesis problems. The tool, more examples and their benchmarks are available online [8].

For each benchmark, the table shows the number $\#Tok$ of tokens, the number $\#Var$ of BDD variables used, and the numbers $\#P$ and $\#T$ of places and transitions, respectively, of the Petri game. We give the elapsed CPU *time* in s, and the used *memory* in GB for solving the problem. For the resulting solution, $\#P_s$ and $\#T_s$ are the number of places and transitions of the strategy, respectively. *Par* states the parameter size(s) of the example. The time and memory values are an average of 10 runs. The results were obtained on an Intel i7-2700K CPU with 3.50GHz and 32 GB RAM. The experiments refer to the following scalable benchmarks:

• CM: *Concurrent Machines* (see Fig. 1). The environment decides which of n machines is functioning. On these machines, k orders should be processed, each order by one machine. Different orders can be processed concurrently on different machines. No machine should be used twice for processing orders. *Parameters*: n machines/k orders

Table 1. Experimental results.

Ben.	Par.	#Tok	#Var	#P	#T	time	memory	#Ps	#Ts
CM	2/1	6	66	13	10	1.4	0.31	14	8
	2/2	7	96	18	16	1.3	0.29	-	-
	...								
	2/6	11	216	38	40	206.5	5.43	-	-
	3/1	8	92	18	15	1.3	0.29	26	12
	3/2	9	132	25	24	2.1	0.3	36	18
	3/3	10	172	32	33	3.3	0.38	-	-
	3/4	11	212	39	42	11.6	0.8	-	-
	3/5	12	252	46	51	180.9	5.43	-	-
	4/1	10	120	23	20	1.6	0.29	42	16
	4/2	11	172	32	32	3.9	0.38	55	24
	4/3	12	224	41	44	14.4	0.8	68	32
	4/4	13	276	50	56	155.3	4.27	-	-
	5/1	12	146	28	25	4.0	0.38	62	20
	5/2	13	208	39	40	24.3	0.8	78	30
	5/3	14	270	50	55	468.3	3.5	94	40
	6/1	14	172	33	30	19.6	0.8	86	24
	6/2	15	244	46	48	1042.2	2.51	105	36
SR	2/1	5	86	18	17	1.3	0.29	32	16
	2/2	6	116	24	26	1.6	0.29	-	-
	2/3	7	144	30	35	4.4	0.39	-	-
	2/4	8	174	36	44	42.7	0.8	-	-
	3/1	6	204	34	49	1155.6	10.05	79.7	45
JP	2	3	46	12	13	1.1	0.31	16	13
	3	4	76	18	23	1.8	0.31	34	28
	...								
	10	11	612	88	149	146.9	5.43	552	385
	11	12	762	102	175	434.8	16.62	706	484
DW	1	3	46	12	10	0.9	0.25	10	6
	2	4	72	19	16	1.8	0.30	22	15
	...								
	19	21	492	138	118	1411.8	15.93	1144	780
	20	22	516	145	124	1734.7	15.85	1264	861
DWs	1	3	36	11	6	0.8	0.31	8	3
	2	5	70	21	12	1.6	0.31	23	10
	...								
	18	37	588	181	108	1027.3	11.94	1351	666
	19	39	620	191	114	1451.9	15.99	1502	741

'-' means no winning strategy exists.

machine. Different orders can be processed concurrently on different machines. No machine should be used twice for processing orders. *Parameters*: n machines/k orders

• SR: *Self-reconfiguring Robots* [11]. Each piece of material needs to be processed by n different tools. There are n robots having all n tools to their disposal, of which only one tool is currently used. The environment may (repeatedly) destroy a tool on a robot R. Then the robots reconfigure themselves so that R uses another tool and the other robots adapt their usage of tools accordingly. *Parameters*: n robots with n tools/k tools will be successively destroyed

• JP: *Job Processing*. The environment chooses a subset of n different processors and a job that requires handling by each processor in this subset in ascending order. *Parameter*: n processors

• DW: *Document Workflow*. The environment hands over a document to one of n clerks. The document then circulates among the clerks. Each clerk should endorse it or not, but wants to make the decision dependent on who has endorsed it already. Altogether they should reach a unanimous decision. In a simpler variant DWs, all clerks should endorse it. *Parameter*: n clerks

The benchmarks represent essential building blocks for modeling various manufacturing and workflow scenarios that can be analyzed automatically by synthesizing winning strategies with ADAM.

References

1. AT&T, Bell-Labs: DOT file format for Graphviz - Graph visualization software. http://www.graphviz.org/
2. Bloem, R., Galler, S., Jobstmann, B., Piterman, N., Pnueli, A., Weiglhofer, M.: Automatic hardware synthesis from specifications: a case study. In: Proceedings of the Conference on Design, Automation and Test in Europe (DATE), pp. 1188–1193 (2007)
3. Bloem, R.P., Gamauf, H.J., Hofferek, G., Könighofer, B., Könighofer, R.: Synthesizing robust systems with RATSY. In: Association, O.P. (ed.). Electronic Proceedings in Theoretical Computer Science SYNT 2012, vol. 84, pp. 47–53 (2012)
4. Bohy, A., Bruyère, V., Filiot, E., Jin, N., Raskin, J.-F.: Acacia+, a tool for LTL synthesis. In: Madhusudan, P., Seshia, S.A. (eds.) CAV 2012. LNCS, vol. 7358, pp. 652–657. Springer, Heidelberg (2012)
5. Büchi, J.R., Landweber, L.H.: Solving sequential conditions by finite-state strategies. Trans. Am. Math. Soc. 138, 295–311 (1969)
6. Church, A.: Logic, arithmetic and automata. In: Proceedings of the International Congress of Mathematicians 1962, pp. 23–25. Uppsala (1963)
7. Ehlers, R.: Unbeast: symbolic bounded synthesis. In: Abdulla, P.A., Leino, K.R.M. (eds.) TACAS 2011. LNCS, vol. 6605, pp. 272–275. Springer, Heidelberg (2011)
8. Finkbeiner, B., Gieseking, M., Olderog, E.: ADAM - Analyzer of distributed asynchronous models. University of Oldenburg and Saarland University. http://www.uni-oldenburg.de/csd/adam (2014)
9. Finkbeiner, B., Olderog, E.: Petri games: Synthesis of distributed systems with causal memory. In: Peron, A., Piazza, C. (eds.) Proceedings of Fifth International Symposium on Games, Automata, Logics and Formal Verification (GandALF). EPTCS, vol. 161, pp. 217–230 (2014). http://dx.doi.org/10.4204/EPTCS.161.19
10. Finkbeiner, B., Schewe, S.: Coordination logic. In: Dawar, A., Veith, H. (eds.) CSL 2010. LNCS, vol. 6247, pp. 305–319. Springer, Heidelberg (2010)
11. Güdemann, M., Ortmeier, F., Reif, W.: Formal modeling and verification of systems with self-x properties. In: Yang, L.T., Jin, H., Ma, J., Ungerer, T. (eds.) ATC 2006. LNCS, vol. 4158, pp. 38–47. Springer, Heidelberg (2006)
12. Kress-Gazit, H., Fainekos, G., Pappas, G.: Temporal-logic-based reactive mission and motion planning. Robot. IEEE Trans. 25(6), 1370–1381 (2009)
13. Lind-Nielsen, J.: BuDDy - Binary decision diagram package. IT-University of Copenhagen. http://sourceforge.net/projects/buddy/
14. Pnueli, A., Rosner, R.: On the synthesis of a reactive module. In: Proc. POPL'1989. pp. 179–190. ACM Press, New York (1989)
15. Pnueli, A., Rosner, R.: Distributed reactive systems are hard to synthesize. In: Proceedings of the FOCS'1990, pp. 746–757 (1990)
16. Rabin, M.O.: Automata on Infinite Objects and Church's Problem, Regional Conference Series in Mathematics, vol. 13. American Mathematical Society, Rhode Island (1972)
17. Reisig, W.: Elements of Distributed Algorithms - Modeling and Analysis with Petri Nets. Springer, New York (1998)

Alchemist: Learning Guarded Affine Functions

Shambwaditya Saha[✉], Pranav Garg[✉], and P. Madhusudan[✉]

University of Illinois, Urbana-Champaign, USA
{ssaha6,garg11,madhu}@illinois.edu

Abstract. We present a technique and an accompanying tool that learns guarded affine functions. In our setting, a teacher starts with a guarded affine function and the learner learns this function using equivalence queries only. In each round, the teacher examines the current hypothesis of the learner and gives a counter-example in terms of an input-output pair where the hypothesis differs from the target function. The learner uses these input-output pairs to learn the guarded affine expression. This problem is relevant in synthesis domains where we are trying to synthesize guarded affine functions that have particular properties, provided we can build a teacher who can answer using such counter-examples. We implement our approach and show that our learner is effective in learning guarded affine expressions, and more effective than general-purpose synthesis techniques.

1 Introduction

We consider the problem of learning guarded affine functions, where the function is expressed using linear inequality guards that delineate regions, and where in each region, the function is expressed using an affine function. More precisely, guarded affine functions are those expressible as guarded linear expressions, which are given by the following grammar:

$$gle := ite(lp, gle, gle) \mid le$$
$$lp := le < le \mid le \leq le \mid le = le$$
$$le := c \mid cx \mid le + le$$

where x ranges over a fixed finite set of variables V with domain D (which can be reals, rationals, integers or natural numbers), and where c ranges over rationals.

We are interested in the problem of learning guarded affine functions using only a sample of its behavior on a finite set of points. More precisely, consider the learning setting where we have a teacher that has a target guarded affine function $f : \mathbb{R}^d \longrightarrow \mathbb{R}$. We start with the behavior on a finite set of samples $S \subseteq \mathbb{R}^d$, and the teacher gives the value of the function on these points. The learner then must respond with a guarded linear expression hypothesis H that is consistent with these points. The teacher then examines H and checks if the learner has learned the target function (i.e., checks whether $H \equiv f$). If yes, we

© Springer International Publishing Switzerland 2015
D. Kroening and C.S. Păsăreanu (Eds.): CAV 2015, Part I, LNCS 9206, pp. 440–446, 2015.
DOI: 10.1007/978-3-319-21690-4_26

are done; otherwise, the teacher *adds* a new sample $s \in \mathbb{R}^d$ where they differ (i.e., $H(s) \neq f(s)$), and we iterate the learning process with the learner coming up with a new hypothesis. The goal of the learner is to learn the target guarded affine function f.

The above model can be seen as a learning model with *equivalence queries* only, or an *online learning model* [3]. This learning model is motivated by synthesis problems, where the idea is to synthesize functions that satisfy certain properties. For instance, in an effort to help a programmer identify a guarded affine function within a program, we can consider the program with this *hole*, capture the correctness requirement (perhaps expressed using input-output examples to the program) and then build a teacher who can check correctness of hypothesized expressions [10]. Combined with the learner that we build, we will then obtain synthesis algorithms for this problem.

We do emphasize, however, that the problem and solution we consider here works only if there is an effective teacher who knows the target concept. In some synthesis contexts, where the specification admits *many* acceptable guarded affine functions as solutions, we would have to use heuristics to use our approach (for example, the teacher may decide how the function behaves on some inputs, from the class of possible outputs, to instruct the learner). However, as a learning problem, our problem formulation is simple and clean.

The black-box learning approach to synthesis is in fact very common in synthesis solvers. For instance, the CEGIS (counter-example guided inductive synthesis) approach [11] is similar to learning in the sense that it too synthesizes from samples, and solvers in the SyGuS format for synthesis, including the enumerative solver, the stochastic solver, the symbolic solver, and Sketch [10], are based on synthesizing using concrete valuations of variables in the specification [1].

There has also been previous work on the construction of piece-wise affine models of hybrid dynamical systems from input-output examples [2,4,5,12] (also see [7] for an extensive survey of the existing techniques). The problem setting, in these works, attacks a different problem, where the goal is to learn guarded linear functions that *approximate* the sample. Consequently, the work in [2] uses techniques such as regression, while we use accurate algorithms. Also, in our setting, we have an active learning setup where the learner keeps learning using counterexamples till the process converges to the target function.

Contribution: In this paper, we build a learning algorithm for guarded affine functions, that learns from a sample of points and how the target function evaluates on that sample: $\{(\boldsymbol{x}_i, f(\boldsymbol{x}_i))\}_{i=1,\ldots,n}$. Our goal is to learn a *simple* guarded linear expression that is consistent with this sample (the learning bias is towards simpler expressions). A guarded linear expression can be thought of as a nested if-then-else expression with linear guards, and linear expressions at its leaves. Our algorithm is composed of two distinct phases:

- Phase 1: [Geometry] First, we synthesize the set of linear expressions that will occur at the leaves of our guarded linear expression. This problem is to essentially find a small set of planes that include all the given points in the

$(d + 1)$-dimensional space (viewing the space describing the inputs and the output of the function being synthesized), and we use a greedy algorithm that uses computational geometry techniques for achieving this. At the end of this phase, we have *labeled* every point in the sample with a plane that correctly gives the output for that point.

– Phase 2: [Classifier] Given the linear expressions from the first phase, we then synthesize the guards. This is done using a classification algorithm, which decides how to assign all points in $\mathbb{R}^d$ to planes such that all the samples get mapped to the correct planes. We use a decision tree classifier [6,8] for this, which is a fast and scalable machine-learning algorithm that can discover such a classification based on Boolean guards.

Neither phase is meant to return the best solution. The geometry phase tries to find k planes that cover all points, and uses a greedy algorithm that need not necessarily work; in this case, we may increase k, and hence our algorithm might find more planes than necessary. The second phase for finding guards also does not necessarily find the minimal tree. Needless to say, the optimal versions of these problems are intractable. However, the algorithms we employ are extremely efficient; there are no NP oracles (SAT/SMT solvers) used. The learning of decision trees is based on information theory to choose the best guards at each point, and work well in practice in producing small trees [6].

We implement our learning algorithm and also build a teacher who has particular target functions, and instructs the learner using counter-examples obtained with the help of an SMT solver. We show that for many functions with reasonable guards and linear expressions, our technique performs extremely well. Furthermore, we can express the problem of learning guarded affine functions in the SyGuS framework [1], and hence use the black-box synthesis algorithms that are implemented for SyGuS. We show that our tool performs much better than these general-purpose synthesis techniques for this class of problems.

2   A Learning Algorithm Based on Geometry and Decision Trees

The learner learns from a set of sample points $S = \{(\boldsymbol{x}_i, v_i), i = 1, \ldots n\}$. A guarded linear expression e satisfies such a set of samples S if the function f defined by the expression e maps each $\boldsymbol{x}_i$ to v_i.

As we mentioned earlier, the learner works in two phases. The first phase finds the leaf expressions using geometry and the second phase finds a guarded expression that maps points to these planes. We now describe these two phases.

2.1   Finding Leaf Planes Using Geometric Techniques

The first phase, based on geometry, finds a small set of (unguarded) linear expressions P such that for every sample point, there is at least one linear expression in P that will produce the right output for that point. This phase hence discovers the set of leaf expressions in the guarded linear expression. Let $|S| = n$ where n is large, and let us assume that we want to find k planes that cover all the points, where k is small. Let the function being synthesized be of arity d. Each sample point in S can be viewed as an input-output pair, $p = (\boldsymbol{x}, y)$ such that $f(\boldsymbol{x}) = y$. We view them as points in a $(d + 1)$-dimensional space, and try to find, using a greedy strategy, a small number of planes such that every point falls on at least one plane. We start with a small budget for k and increase k when it doesn't suffice.

Assuming that there are k planes that cover all the points, there must be at least $\lceil n/k \rceil$ points that are covered by a single plane. Hence, our strategy is to find a plane in a greedy manner that covers at least these many points. Once we find such a plane, we can remove all the points that are covered by that plane, and recurse, decrementing k.

Note that in a $(d + 1)$-dimensional space, one can always a construct a plane that passes through any $(d + 1)$ points. Hence, our strategy is to choose sets of $(d + 2)$ points and check if they are coplanar (and then check if they cover enough points in the sample). Since we are synthesizing a guarded linear expression, it is likely that the leaf planes are defined over a local region, and hence we would like to choose the $d + 2$ points such that they are *close* to each other. Our algorithm Construct-Plane, depicted below, searches for a plane by (a) choosing a random point p and taking the closest $2d$ points next to p, by computing the distance of all points to p, sorting them, and picking the closest $2d$ points and (b) choosing *every* combination of $(d + 2)$ points from this set and checking it for coplanarity.

CONSTRUCT-PLANE(S)
1   Select a random point $p = (\boldsymbol{x}, y) \in S$
2   C = set of $2d$ points closest to p
3   Y = collection of all subsets of $(d + 1)$ points in C
4   **repeat** for all Z in Y
5   **if** the set of points in $(Z \cup p)$ are coplanar
6            $pln = find\_plane\,(Z \cup p)$
7   Sel = set of points in S that lie on plane pln
8   **if** $|Sel| > \lceil |S|/k \rceil$
9   label the points in Sel as pln
10   **return** Sel, pln

$$
\begin{vmatrix}
x_1^1 & x_1^2 & \dots & x_1^{d+1} & 1 \\
x_2^1 & x_2^2 & \dots & x_2^{d+1} & 1 \\
\vdots & \vdots & & \vdots & \vdots \\
x_{d+2}^1 & x_{d+2}^2 & \dots & x_{d+2}^{d+1} & 1
\end{vmatrix} = 0
$$

Fig. 1. (a) Algorithm for constructing planes that cover the input points (b) Co-planarity check for a set of points.

Coplanarity can be verified by checking the value of determinant as above (Fig. 1b), and the plane defined by these $(d + 2)$ points can be constructed by solving for the co-efficients c_i in the set of equations $\Sigma_{i=1}^{n} c_i x_i = c_{n+1}$, where we substitute the x_i's with the points we have chosen. The above two require numerical solvers and can be achieved using software like MatLab or Octave.

If the above process discovers k planes that cover all points in the sample, then we are done. If not, we are either left with too few points ($< d + 2$) or too many points and have run out of the budget of planes. In the former case, we ignore these points, compute a guarded linear expression for the points that we have already covered using the second phase, and then add these points back as special points on which the answers are fixed using the appropriate constants in the sample. In the latter case, we increase our budget k, and continue.

There are several parameters that can be tuned for performance, including (a) how many points the teacher returns in each round, (b) the number of points in the window from which we select points to find planes, (c) the threshold of coverage for selecting a plane, etc. These parameters can be tweaked for better performance on the application at hand.

2.2 Finding Conditionals Using Decision Tree Learning

The first phase identifies a set of planes and labels each input in the sample with a plane from this set that correctly maps it to its output. In the second phase, we use state-of-the-art decision tree classification algorithm [6,8] to synthesize the conditional guards that classify all inputs such that the inputs in the sample are mapped to the correct planes. Decision trees can classify points according to a finite set of *numerical attributes*. We choose numerical attributes that are linear combinations of the variables with bounded integer coefficients (since we expect the coefficients in the guards to be small, the learner considers attributes of the form $\Sigma a_i x_i$ where $\Sigma a_i < K$ for a small K, where K increases in an outer loop). The decision-tree learner then constructs a classifier that uses Boolean combinations of formulas of the form $a \leq t$, where a is a numerical attribute and t is a threshold (constant) which it synthesizes. Note that the linear coefficients for the guards are enumerated by our tool— the decision tree learner just picks appropriate numerical attribute and synthesizes the thresholds.

The decision tree learner that we use is a standard state-of-the-art decision tree algorithm, called C5.0 [8,9], and is extremely scalable and has an inductive bias to learn smaller trees. It constructs trees using an algorithm that does no back-tracking, but chooses the best attributes heuristically using *information gain*, calculated using Shannon's entropy measure. We disable some features in the C5.0 algorithm such as *pruning*, which is traditionally performed to reduce overfitting, since we want a classifier that works precisely on the given sample and cannot tolerate errors. During the construction of the tree, if there are several attributes with the highest information gain, we choose the attribute that has the smallest absolute value. This heuristic biases the learner towards synthesizing guards that have smaller threshold values.

3   Evaluation

We implemented the two phases of the learner as follows: The geometric phase is implemented using a numerical solver, Octave, and the classifier phase is implemented using decision tree classification algorithm C5.0. The output of both these two phases is then combined to construct a hypothesis that is conjectured as the target guarded linear expression.

Table 1. Experimental results. The timeout is set to $600s$.

Target Guarded Affine Function	Enumerative solver	Stochastic solver	Symbolic solver	Alchemist
$x + y$	$0.0s$	$0.3s$	$5.4s$	$0.7s$
$3x + 3y + 3$	$2m12.4s$	$16.1s$	timeout	$0.7s$
$5x + 5y + 5$	timeout	$4m1.1s$	timeout	$0.7s$
$max2 : ite(x < y,\ y,\ x)$	$0.0s$	$0.2s$	$2.6s$	$0.6s$
$max3 : ite(x < y, ite(y < z,\ z,\ y)), ite(x < z,\ z,\ x))$	timeout	$5.4s$	timeout	$1.1s$
$max4(x, y, z, u)$	timeout	$6m21.6s$	timeout	$20.5s$
$max5(x, y, z, u, v)$	timeout	timeout	timeout	$1m30.0s$
$ite(x + y \leq 1, x + y, x - y)$	$1.2s$	$2.5s$	timeout	$0.9s$
$ite(x + y + z \leq 1, x + y, x - y)$	$12.8s$	$6.5s$	timeout	$0.8s$
$ite(2x + y + z \leq 1, x + y, x - y)$	$6m42.7s$	$8.1s$	timeout	$1.4s$
$ite(2x + 2y + z \leq 1, x + y, x - y)$	timeout	$7.9s$	timeout	$1.4s$
$ite(x + y \geq 1, ite(x + z \geq 1, x + 1, y + 1), z + 1)$	timeout	$20.7s$	timeout	$1.8s$
$ite(x + y \geq 1, ite(x + z \geq 1, x + 1, y + 1),$ $ite(y + z \geq 1, y + 1, z + 1))$	timeout	$4m37.2s$	timeout	$2.9s$
$ite(x \geq 5, 5x + 3y + 17, 3x + 1)$	timeout	timeout	timeout	$0.9s$
$ite(x \leq y + 4, min(x, y, z), max(x, y, z))$	timeout	timeout	timeout	$1.8s$
$if\ x + y <= 1\ then\ 10x + 10y + 10$ $elseif\ x + y <= 2\ then\ 20x + 20y - 20$ $elseif\ x + y <= 3\ then\ 30x + 30y + 30$ $elseif\ x + y <= 4\ then\ 40x + 40y - 40$ $elseif\ x + y <= 5\ then\ 50x + 50y + 50$ $else\ \ \ 60x + 60y - 60$	timeout	timeout	timeout	$27.9s$

In order to evaluate our tool, we also implemented a teacher which knows a target guarded affine function f and provides counter-examples to the learner using a constraint solver. Given a hypothesis H the teacher checks if there is some valuation for variables x such that $H(x) \neq f(x)$. If such a valuation exists, the teacher returns $(x, f(x))$ as a counterexample to the learner.

All experiments were performed on a system with an Intel Core i7 2.2 GHz processor and 4GB RAM running 64-bit Ubuntu 14.04 OS, with a timeout of $600s$. In Table 1 we tabulate our experimental results comparing our learner[1] with the enumerative, the stochastic, and the symbolic SyGus solver [1] for learning various target guarded affine functions of increasing complexity, both in terms of the Boolean structure and in terms of the coefficients. We also evaluate on relevant SyGuS benchmarks. For the stochastic solver, we report the time averaged over ten runs. From the results, it seems the SyGus solvers are very general and do not exploit the geometry of this domain well. Also, the machine learning algorithms seem better at sifting through candidate guards and picking a small subset that work.

Apart from the above mentioned solvers, we also tried the SyGus solver based on Sketch [10] but it failed to execute for most of the problems. We could not try [2] as being a passive algorithm which approximates the solution makes it very hard to compare the tools empirically.

---

[1] Our tool can be accessed at http://web.engr.illinois.edu/~ssaha6/Alchemist/.

4 Conclusions

The learning based synthesis of guarded affine functions we have proposed seems very promising and a good alternative to existing synthesis techniques. An earlier version of this solver was submitted as a solver to the SyGuS synthesis competition; however, note that in a more general setting, building a teacher is not easy as the teacher does not know precisely the function to be synthesized. We hence built a teacher who would identify at least certain inputs on which the function was determined and feed these to the learner. A more general approach that extends our work to solving general synthesis problems involving guarded affine functions is an interesting direction for future work.

Acknowledgments. We thank Sariel Har-Peled for discussions on geometric techniques for synthesizing leaf expressions. This work was partially supported by NSF Expeditions in Computing ExCAPE Award #1138994.

References

1. Alur, R., Bodík, R., Juniwal, G., Martin, M.M.K., Raghothaman, M., Seshia, S.A., Singh, R., Solar-Lezama, A., Torlak, E., Udupa, A.: Syntax-guided synthesis. In: Formal Methods in Computer-Aided Design, FMCAD 2013, Portland, OR, USA, 20–23 October 2013, pp. 1–17 (2013)
2. Alur, R., Singhania, N.: Precise piecewise affine models from input-output data. In: Proceedings of the 14th International Conference on Embedded Software, EMSOFT 2014, pp. 3:1–3:10. ACM, New York, NY, USA (2014)
3. Angluin, D.: Queries and concept learning. Mach. Learn. **2**(4), 319–342 (1988)
4. Bemporad, A., Garulli, A., Paoletti, S., Vicino, A.: A bounded-error approach to piecewise affine system identification. IEEE Trans. Automat. Contr. **50**(10), 1567–1580 (2005)
5. Ferrari-Trecate, G., Muselli, M., Liberati, D., Morari, M.: A clustering technique for the identification of piecewise affine systems. Automatica **39**(2), 205–217 (2003)
6. Mitchell, T.M.: Machine Learning. McGraw Hill Series in Computer Science, New York (1997)
7. Paoletti, S., Juloski, A.L., Ferrari-Trecate, G., Vidal, R.: Identification of hybrid systems: a tutorial. Eur. J. Control **13**(2–3), 242–260 (2007)
8. Quinlan, J.R.: Induction of decision trees. Mach. Learn. **1**(1), 81–106 (1986)
9. Quinlan, J.R.: C4.5: Programs for Machine Learning. Morgan Kaufmann, San Francisco (1993)
10. Solar-Lezama, A.: Program sketching. STTT **15**(5–6), 475–495 (2013)
11. Solar-Lezama, A., Tancau, L., Bodík, R., Seshia, S.A., Saraswat, V.A.: Combinatorial sketching for finite programs. In: Proceedings of the 12th International Conference on Architectural Support for Programming Languages and Operating Systems, ASPLOS 2006, San Jose, CA, USA, 21–25 October 2006, pp. 404–415 (2006)
12. Vidal, R., Soatto, S., Sastry, S.: An algebraic geometric approach to the identification of a class of linear hybrid systems. In: Proceedings of the IEEE Conference on Decision and Control, vol. 1, pp. 167–172, December 2003

OptiMathSAT: A Tool for Optimization Modulo Theories

Roberto Sebastiani and Patrick Trentin[(✉)]

DISI, University of Trento, Trento, Italy
patrick.trentin@unitn.it

Abstract. Many SMT problems of interest may require the capability of finding models that are *optimal* wrt. some objective functions. These problems are grouped under the umbrella term of *Optimization Modulo Theories – OMT*. In this paper we present OPTIMATHSAT, an OMT tool extending the MATHSAT5 SMT solver. OPTIMATHSAT allows for solving a list of optimization problems on SMT formulas with linear objective functions –on the Boolean, the rational and the integer domains, and on their combination thereof– including MaxSMT. Multiple objective functions can be combined together and handled either independently, or lexicographically, or in a min-max/max-min fashion.

OPTIMATHSAT ships with an extended SMT-LIBV2 input syntax and C API bindings, and it preserves the incremental attitude of its underlying SMT solver.

1 Introduction

SMT solvers are currently used as backend engines in many formal verification (FV) tools for Hardware, Software and Hybrid Systems. Many SMT problems of interest for FV or for other disciplines, however, require the capability of finding models that are *optimal* wrt. some objective functions [6,8,9,11,13–16,18–20]. These problems are grouped under the umbrella term of *Optimization Modulo Theories – OMT*.

For instance, in SMT-based model checking with timed or hybrid systems, you may want to find executions which optimize the value of some parameter while fulfilling/violating some property –e.g., to find the minimum opening time interval for a railcrossing causing a safety violation. (See e.g. [19] for some examples.) Also, a recent application of OMT is the SMT-based computation of the worst-case execution time (WCET) of loop-free programs [12], which finds tighter over-approximations of the WCET than other state-of-the-art approaches. A longer list of OMT applications in formal verification and in other disciplines can be found in [8,11,14–16,19].

This work is supported by Semiconductor Research Corporation (SRC) under GRC Research Project 2012-TJ-2266 WOLF. We thank Alberto Griggio for support with MATHSAT5 code.

© Springer International Publishing Switzerland 2015
D. Kroening and C.S. Păsăreanu (Eds.): CAV 2015, Part I, LNCS 9206, pp. 447–454, 2015.
DOI: 10.1007/978-3-319-21690-4_27

In this paper we present OPTIMATHSAT, an OMT tool extending the MATHSAT5 SMT solver [3,10], implementing the OMT procedures described in [18–20]. OPTIMATHSAT allows for solving a list of optimization problems on SMT formulas with linear objective functions –on the Boolean, the rational and the integer domains, and on their combination thereof– including MAXSMT. Multiple objective functions can be combined together and handled either independently, or lexicographically, or in a MIN-MAX/MAX-MIN fashion. Like MATH-SAT5, it is freely available for research and evaluation purposes [4], and it is currently used in some innovative projects (see Sect. 5).

Related Tools. Currently few other OMT tools exist. Closest to OPTIMATHSAT are SYMBA [14] and the very-recent νZ [6,7], which are both built on top of Z3. [14] considered the problem of optimizing multiple rational cost functions at the same time. SYMBA uses the underlying SMT solver as black-box, and it features additional ad hoc techniques for detecting unbounded costs and optimization. νZ supports both single-objective linear optimization –over a real, integer or bit-vector term – and multi-objective optimization in either boxed, lexicographic or Pareto-optimization mode. It ships with several specialized engines for MaxSMT and with pre-processing techniques that re-encode the 0-1 integer variables of the input formula into Pseudo-Boolean or MaxSMT constraints. We refer the reader to the related work section of [19] for a more-detailed analysis of other OMT-related approaches and tools.

Content. This paper is structured as follows. Section 2 provides a brief outline of OPTIMATHSAT architecture, followed by a description of its optimization functionalities and interfaces in Sect. 3. Section 4 presents a short example, and Sect. 5 reviews some recent interesting applications of OPTIMATHSAT. Section 6 concludes the paper with hints of some future developments. An extended version of this paper, containing a performance evaluation and some more details, is available from OPTIMATHSAT web page [4].

2   Architecture

OPTIMATHSAT is written in $C++$ and it is built as an extension of MATH-SAT5, which implements the standard lazy SMT paradigm (see [5]). Unlike the OMT algorithms in [6,14], which are based on an *offline* architecture –in which the SMT Solver is incrementally called multiple times as a black-box– OPTIMATHSAT is based on an *inline architecture* –in which the SMT solver is run only once and its internal SAT solver is modified to handle the search for the optima [18–20]. Although harder to implement, the *inline* architecture has showed better performance for OPTIMATHSAT than the *offline* one [18,19]. (We refer the reader to [19] for a comparison of the two architectures.)

The optimization algorithm can explore the search space in *linear-search* mode, by pruning one intermediate solution at a time, or in *binary-search* mode, by introducing cuts bisecting the search space, or in *adaptive-search* mode, which uses adaptive heuristics to choose among the linear- and binary-search modes at each search step.

Some functionalities, such as the control loop for *lexicographic* optimization and the assertion of soft clauses, are handled at a higher level of abstraction by means of a combination of MATHSAT5 and OPTIMATHSAT API calls.

3 Optimization Functionalities

OPTIMATHSAT is mainly a tool for (single- and multiple-objective) OMT with linear objective functions OMT($\mathcal{LA} \cup \mathcal{T}$) s.t. "$\mathcal{LA}$" denotes linear arithmetic over either the rationals ($\mathcal{LRA}$), or the integers ($\mathcal{LIA}$) or their combination $\mathcal{LRIA}$, and $\mathcal{T}$ denotes any other Nelson-Oppen theory supported by MATHSAT5. For each objective it is possible to specify both global and local bounds, if known.[1] OPTIMATHSAT can use this information to explore the search space in binary or in adaptive search mode, which might improve the overall performance of the solver. We support objective functions over the rational, integer and Boolean domains[2], or their combinations.

Here we provide a brief list of OPTIMATHSAT optimization functionalities, omitting the functionalities inherited from MATHSAT5 [10]. A detailed description of the implemented algorithms is presented in [18–20].

3.1 Single-Objective Optimization

We discuss first the case in which we have only one objective function, namely *obj*.

Linear Arithmetic Optimization over $\mathcal{LRA}$, $\mathcal{LIA}$ and $\mathcal{LRIA}$. Given some term *obj* on $\mathcal{LA}$, OPTIMATHSAT finds a solution (if any) which makes the term *obj* minimum/maximum. This is based on a combination of SMT and linear [integer] programming techniques.

Partial Weighted MaxSMT and SMT with Pseudo-Boolean Objectives (PB-SMT). Given an input formula $\varphi_h \wedge \varphi_s$, where φ_h contains hard constraints and φ_s contains soft constraints with positive weights, the goal of *partial weighted* MAXSMT [9,16] is to find a model M s.t. $M \models \varphi_h \wedge \varphi_s^M$ and φ_s^M is a subset of φ_s in which the soft-constraints have the largest cumulative weight possible. Similarly, OPTIMATHSAT allows also for defining Pseudo-Boolean objective functions in the form $\sum_i w_i \psi_i$, where w_i are numerical constants and ψ_i are sub-formulas.

Unlike with the procedures in [6,8,9,16], which use specialized algorithms for MAXSMT/PB-SMT, OPTIMATHSAT works by encoding the problem into the optimization of an $\mathcal{LRA}$ term, as described in [19]. This allows for combining the MaxSMT terms with other objectives, as we describe in Sect. 3.2.

---

[1] Local bounds have a special use in boxed multi-objective optimization (see Sect. 3.2). In single-objective and lexicographic optimization, they coincide with global bounds.
[2] i.e. MaxSMT and SMT with Pseudo-Boolean objective functions.

Notice that it is possible to interrupt the search of OPTIMATHSAT (e.g., by setting a timeout) and to still have access to the current sub-optimal solutions and its model.

3.2 Multi-objective Combination

The interface of OPTIMATHSAT allows for combining multiple objective functions obj_1, ..., obj_N in various ways.

Multiple Independent Objectives [14]. (Aka Boxed Optimization [6].) OPTI-MATHSAT can solve simultaneously N independent optimization problems $\langle \varphi, obj_1 \rangle$, ..., $\langle \varphi, obj_N \rangle$, optionally building the corresponding optimum models M_0, ..., M_N.[3] (In the empirical evaluation presented in [20], we showed that using this optimization strategy can be considerably more efficient than solving N single-objective optimization problems.) This option is the default configuration.

Lexicographic Optimization. OPTIMATHSAT optimizes lexicographically the objectives obj_1, ..., obj_N by decreasing level of priority. If any objective obj_i is unsatisfiable or unbounded, the search returns.

Min-max and Max-min. The goal of a MIN-MAX problem is to find the maximum value of an obj s.t. $\bigwedge_{i=0}^{N} (obj \leq obj_i) \wedge \bigvee_{i=0}^{N} (obj_i = obj)$, obj being a fresh variable.[4] Max-min is dual. OPTIMATHSAT provides syntactic-sugar extensions to SMT-LIBv2 that allow for encoding this type of objectives.

Linear Combination. Obviously, one can also create objectives that are a linear combination of other objectives obj_1, ..., obj_N, i.e., $obj = \sum_{i=1}^{N} w_i \cdot obj_i$.

We remark that all the above combinations hold for obj_i cost functions over every domain, including Boolean. For instance, you can combine together MaxSMT with OMT optimization over Integer or Real objectives.

3.3 Interfaces

Input Language. OPTIMATHSAT functions are accessible through a list of commands, extending the SMT-LIBv2 syntax, which is shown in a concise description in Fig. 1. Notice that, differently from νZ [7], in case of a MAXSMT problem we require the user to build *explicitly* a minimization objective using the ID associated with the asserted soft clauses, i.e., by writing "(minimize ID)". The advantage of this requirement is that we allow for arbitrary composition of the MAXSMT objective with other linear arithmetic functions, which can be useful in particular contexts (for instance, to build obj functions on mixed Boolean/numeric domains, as with Linear Generalized Disjunctive Programming (LGDP) problems [17]).

---

[3] Since the N input problems are independent to one another, the local bounds of each objective obj_i do not have any side effect on the feasible solutions of all other objectives obj_j, as if the N problems were solved separately.

[4] Notice that in the actual encoding we drop the "$\bigvee$" part of the formula, since it is unnecessary and may cause extra Boolean search.

```
; assert soft clauses for MaxSMT (weight/dweight
;    defaults to 1, id defaults to 'I')
(assert-soft <term> [:weight <numeral>] [:id <string>])
(assert-soft <term> [:dweight <decimal>] [:id <string>])
; push new objectives on the stack
(minimize|maximize <term> [:local-lb <decimal>]
                          [:local-ub <decimal>])
(minmax|maxmin <term>...<term> [:local-lb <decimal>]
                          [:local-ub <decimal>])
; set multi-objective optimization mode
(set-option :opt.priority box|lex)
; optimize objective(s) in the stack
(check-sat)
; load model of objective with stack index <numeral>
(set-model <numeral>)
; retrieve model values
(get-model)
(get-value <VAR>)
```

Fig. 1. SMT-LIBv2 Optimization Extensions, square brackets corresponds to optional parameters, whereas "|" stands for alternative choices.

```
; set goods quantity
(assert (= 250 (+ q1 q2 q3 q4)))
; set goods offered by each supplier
(assert (and (or (= q1 0) (and (<=  50 q1) (<= q1 250)))
             (or (= q2 0) (and (<= 100 q2) (<= q2 150)))
             (or (= q3 0) (and (<= 100 q3) (<= q3 100)))
             (or (= q4 0) (and (<=  50 q4) (<= q4 100)))))
; a supplier is 'used' if sends more than zero items
(assert (and (=> s1 (not (= q1 0))) (=> s2 (not (= q2 0)))
             (=> s3 (not (= q3 0))) (=> s4 (not (= q4 0)))))
; supply from the largest number of suppliers
(assert-soft s1 :id ignored_suppliers)
(assert-soft s2 :id ignored_suppliers)
(assert-soft s3 :id ignored_suppliers)
(assert-soft s4 :id ignored_suppliers)
; set goal (A)
(minimize (+ (* q1 23) (* q2 21) (* q3 20) (* q4 10)))
; set goal (B)
(minimize ignored_suppliers)
; optimize lexicographically
(set-option :opt.priority lex)
(check-sat)
; print model
(set-model 1)
(get-model)
```

Fig. 2. SMT-LIBv2 encoding of the problem.

C API. The optimization functions of OPTIMATHSAT are also available through its C API, which extends that of MATHSAT5 [3]. A detailed documentation of the *C API*, the SMT-LIBv2 language extensions and some usage examples are accessible on OPTIMATHSAT website [4].

Incremental Interface. Like MATHSAT5, OPTIMATHSAT provides a PUSH/POP interface for adding and removing objectives and pieces of formulas from the formula stack, which allows for reusing information from one optimization search to another to improve the global performance of the search [20].

4 Example

In Fig. 2 we present a toy example that illustrates how to encode a problem into the extended SMT-LIBv2 language of OPTIMATHSAT. A small company urgently needs 250 units of some goods. Suppliers s_1, s_2, s_3, s_4 offer to supply up to $250, 150, 100, 100$ units of goods starting from the minimum quantity of $50, 100, 100, 50$ units respectively. Their prices are 23\$, 21\$, 20\$, 10\$ per unit respectively. Our goal is (A) to minimize the overall purchase cost and, at cost tie, (B) to maximize the number of suppliers.

A simple OMT encoding of the problem is shown in Fig. 2. In this example there are two combinations of suppliers $-s_2, s_4$ and s_1, s_3, s_4- from which we can purchase the goods at the minimum cost of 4150\$. Therefore, the tie is broken by our secondary goal (B), which imposes our preference on the second solution. The optimum model of a lexicographic optimization is always associated with the top-most objective on the internal stack. Since in this example there are only two objectives, this objective can be selected by passing 1 to the `set-model` command. As mentioned in Sect. 3.3, notice that we explicitly ask for `ignored_suppliers`, the label of the MAXSMT constraints, to be minimized. OPTIMATHSAT solved the problem in 10ms.

5 Applications

We briefly mention two examples of recent applications –which are very innovative in their respective domains– that have been technologically enabled by OMT and use OPTIMATHSAT as backend automated-reasoning engine.

Structured Learning Modulo Theories. In Machine Learning applications, performing inference and learning in hybrid domains –characterized by both continuous and Boolean/discrete variables– is a particularly daunting task. *Structured Learning Modulo Theories (SLMT)* [21] addresses the problem by combining (Structured-Output) Support Vector Machines (SVNs) with OMT, so that the latter plays the role of inference and separation oracle for the former. The tool LMT implementing the SLMT method [2] uses OPTIMATHSAT as backend OMT engine.

Automated Reasoning on Constrained Goal Models. Goal Models (GM) are used in Requirements Engineering to represent software requirements, objectives, and design qualities [22]. *Constrained Goal Models (CGM)* are a novel, formal version of GM which are enriched with constraints so that to handle preferences, numerical attributes and resources (e.g., scores, financial cost, workforce, etc.). OPTIMATHSAT is used as a backend reasoning engine of CGM-TOOL [1], a tool for building and reasoning on *CGM*s, allowing for automatically verifying the realizability of a CGM and for finding optimal realizations according to some specified criterion.

6 Future Developments

We plan to extend OPTIMATHSAT capabilities along several directions. For instance, we are interested into generalizing our implementation to support objective functions extended on other theories, i.e. bit-vector. We are also considering to add the possibility of combining multiple objectives for Pareto-optimization. Finally, we plan to parallelize OMT so that to exploit the multi-core architectures of modern CPUs.

References

1. CGM-Tool. www.cgm-tool.eu
2. LMT. http://disi.unitn.it/teso/lmt/lmt.tgz
3. MathSAT 5. http://mathsat.fbk.eu/
4. OptiMathSAT. http://optimathsat.disi.unitn.it/
5. Barrett, C.W., Sebastiani, R., Seshia, S.A., Tinelli, C.: Satisfiability modulo theories. In: Handbook of Satisfiability, chap. 26, pp. 825–885. IOS Press (2009)
6. Bjorner, N., Phan, A.-D.: νZ - Maximal satisfaction with Z3. In: Proceedings of SCSS. Invited presentation., Gammart, Tunisia, December 2014. EasyChair Proceedings in Computing (EPiC). http://www.easychair.org/publications/?page=862275542
7. Bjørner, N., Phan, A.-D., Fleckenstein, L.: νZ - An optimizing SMT solver. In: Baier, C., Tinelli, C. (eds.) TACAS 2015. LNCS, vol. 9035, pp. 194–199. Springer, Heidelberg (2015, to appear)
8. Cimatti, A., Franzén, A., Griggio, A., Sebastiani, R., Stenico, C.: Satisfiability modulo the theory of costs: foundations and applications. In: Esparza, J., Majumdar, R. (eds.) TACAS 2010. LNCS, vol. 6015, pp. 99–113. Springer, Heidelberg (2010)
9. Cimatti, A., Griggio, A., Schaafsma, B.J., Sebastiani, R.: A modular approach to maxSAT modulo theories. In: Järvisalo, M., Van Gelder, A. (eds.) SAT 2013. LNCS, vol. 7962, pp. 150–165. Springer, Heidelberg (2013)
10. Cimatti, A., Griggio, A., Schaafsma, B.J., Sebastiani, R.: The mathSAT5 SMT solver. In: Piterman, N., Smolka, S.A. (eds.) TACAS 2013 (ETAPS 2013). LNCS, vol. 7795, pp. 93–107. Springer, Heidelberg (2013)
11. Dillig, I., Dillig, T., McMillan, K.L., Aiken, A.: Minimum satisfying assignments for SMT. In: Madhusudan, P., Seshia, S.A. (eds.) CAV 2012. LNCS, vol. 7358, pp. 394–409. Springer, Heidelberg (2012)

12. Henry, J., Asavoae, M., Monniaux, D., Maïza, C.: How to compute worst-case execution time by optimization modulo theory and a clever encoding of program semantics. SIGPLAN Not. **49**(5), 43–52 (2014)
13. Larraz, D., Oliveras, A., Rodríguez-Carbonell, E., Rubio, A.: Minimal-model-guided approaches to solving polynomial constraints and extensions. In: Sinz, C., Egly, U. (eds.) SAT 2014. LNCS, vol. 8561, pp. 333–350. Springer, Heidelberg (2014)
14. Li, Y., Albarghouthi, A., Kincad, Z., Gurfinkel, A., Chechik, M.: Symbolic optimization with SMT solvers. In: POPL. ACM Press (2014)
15. Manolios, P., Papavasileiou, V.: ILP modulo theories. In: Sharygina, N., Veith, H. (eds.) CAV 2013. LNCS, vol. 8044, pp. 662–677. Springer, Heidelberg (2013)
16. Nieuwenhuis, R., Oliveras, A.: On SAT modulo theories and optimization problems. In: Biere, A., Gomes, C.P. (eds.) SAT 2006. LNCS, vol. 4121, pp. 156–169. Springer, Heidelberg (2006)
17. Raman, R., Grossmann, I.: Modelling and computational techniques for logic based integer programming. Comput. Chem. Eng. **18**(7), 563–578 (1994)
18. Sebastiani, R., Tomasi, S.: Optimization in SMT with $\mathcal{LA}\mathbb{Q}$ Cost Functions. In: Gramlich, B., Miller, D., Sattler, U. (eds.) IJCAR 2012. LNCS, vol. 7364, pp. 484–498. Springer, Heidelberg (2012)
19. Sebastiani, R., Tomasi, S.: Optimization modulo theories with linear rational costs. ACM Trans. Comput. Logics 16(2) (2015). doi:10.1145/2699915
20. Sebastiani, R., Trentin, P.: Pushing the envelope of optimization modulo theories with linear-arithmetic cost functions. In: Baier, C., Tinelli, C. (eds.) TACAS 2015. LNCS, vol. 9035, pp. 335–349. Springer, Heidelberg (2015)
21. Teso, S., Sebastiani, R., Passerini, A.: Structured learning modulo theories. Artificial Intelligence (2015). http://disi.unitn.it/rseba/publist.html
22. Van Lamsweerde, A.: Goal-oriented requirements engineering: a guided tour. In: Proceedings of the Fifth IEEE International Conference on Requirements Engineering, RE 2001, pp. 249–262. IEEE Computer Society (2001)

Systematic Asynchrony Bug Exploration for Android Apps

Burcu Kulahcioglu Ozkan[1]([✉]), Michael Emmi[2], and Serdar Tasiran[1]

[1] Koç University, Istanbul, Turkey
{bkulahcioglu,stasiran}@ku.edu.tr
[2] IMDEA Software Institute, Madrid, Spain
michael.emmi@imdea.org

Abstract. Smartphone and tablet "apps" are particularly susceptible to asynchrony bugs. In order to maintain responsive user interfaces, events are handled asynchronously. Unexpected schedules of event handlers can result in apparently-random bugs which are notoriously difficult to reproduce, even given the user-event sequences that trigger them.
  We develop the AsyncDroid tool for the systematic discovery and reproduction of asynchrony bugs in Android apps. Given an app and a user-event sequence, AsyncDroid systematically executes alternate schedules of the same asynchronous event handlers, according to a programmable schedule enumerator. The input user-event sequence is given either by user interaction, or can be generated by automated UI "monkeys". By exposing and controlling the factors which influence the scheduling order of asynchronous handlers, our programmable enumerators can explicate reproducible schedules harboring bugs. By enumerating all schedules within a limited threshold of reordering, we maximize the likelihood of encountering asynchrony bugs, according to prevailing hypotheses in the literature, and discover several bugs in Android apps found in the wild.

1 Introduction

Android apps execute asynchronously: typically a number of background threads exist to prevent long-running tasks from tying up the main UI thread. Threads execute asynchronously-called procedures concurrently with other threads. Programmers tend to imagine atomically-handled events, without taking all possible thread interleavings into consideration. However, event handlers often call other asynchronous methods, and so the execution of multiple events can interleave and result in hard-to-reproduce bugs.

  In this work we present AsyncDroid[1], the first concurrency testing tool for Android apps. AsyncDroid takes a sequence of user events given by user interaction or automated UI "monkeys" and explores different thread interleavings to

---

This work is supported in part by the Scientific and Technological Research Council of Turkey (TUBITAK).
[1] http://github.com/imdea-software/async-droid.

detect thrown exceptions and assertion violations. Focusing on the systematic exploration of alternate schedules of asynchronously-executing methods, and prioritizing those schedules derived from few re-orderings, our technique uncovers many violations quickly, and uncovers all violations given enough time.

Our prototype implementation explores all deviations from a base schedule within a user-specified bound. In addition to providing a default thread scheduler from which the base schedule can be generated, we also provide an interface allowing users to implement their own scheduler to guide the exploration process along their own insights. Besides control over the thread schedules, our implementation can also record a given sequence of user events, and then replay the same sequence events along alternate thread schedules. We implement both scheduler control and event recording/replaying via program instrumentation, without modifying Android runtime libraries.

Related Work. Existing approaches to bug detection in Android apps fall into two basic categories. The first category focuses on UI input testing [1,2,4,9]. Orthogonally to these techniques, which test a single execution of any given UI-event sequence, our goal is to explore the alternate schedules of execution for a given UI-event sequence, thus uncovering elusive concurrency-related bugs. The second category of techniques investigates race detection [3,7,8,10]. Our work is complementary to these techniques and it is novel in two respects: it is a dynamic analysis rather than static, and it does not report false positives.

While prioritized systematic exploration of concurrent program executions has been studied before [5,11], the adaptation to event driven programs poses some specific difficulties. A tool must explore different possible concurrent behaviors for a given, fixed user interaction with the program. This requires the recording and replay of user input events while exploring alternate schedules. Moreover, it is nontrivial to design effective thread schedulers for the typical Android "looper" threads, which do nothing but execute the handlers of received messages.

2   Design and Implementation

The basic functionality of AsyncDroid is to repeat a sequence of UI events over a systematic enumeration of thread schedules. We achieve this functionality via a program instrumentation which provides explicit control over thread scheduling, and recording/replaying of UI events for given thread schedules.

2.1   Recording and Repeating User Events

To record the user events, we instrument each visible UI component with an additional event handler. When run in record mode, the instrumented handler records each event and forwards it to the original handler. This allows us to capture both direct user interaction, and simulated "monkey" interaction.

In replay mode, we use an input repeater which reads and replays the recorded events for every thread schedule to be tested. The input repeater runs in its own thread and feeds the user events to the application concurrently to the execution of the other threads. AsyncDroid schedules this thread as well as the other application threads, controlling the interleaving between sending an event and the execution in the other threads.

In approaches in the literature, the user events are recorded by saving the coordinates of an input event and replayed by giving the same input on the same coordinates [6]. However, the timing of the inputs differ in each schedule and a UI component might not be visible at a time we want to replay it. Repeating an event using only the coordinates might result in the invocation of a wrong event, since a different view might exist on the original event's input coordinates at the time of replay. To overcome this, we use an abstraction of an input event close to the application semantics. Our event abstraction keeps the path to UI component of the user event. While replaying an event, we make sure that the recorded path to an event fully matches to the view on the currently visible UI.

2.2 Thread Scheduling

AsyncDroid controls the scheduling of the input repeater, UI, and background threads. To explore different execution schedules, AsyncDroid treats the beginnings and ends of asynchronous methods as scheduling points, only preempting threads at these points to determine a complete schedule.

AsyncDroid's default scheduler runs threads until becoming blocked in a round-robin fashion. The input repeater thread is enabled if it has more events to replay and the next event's UI component is visible. Similarly, the UI thread and other threads are enabled if they have some tasks to execute. In Android, it is likely that the UI thread have repetitive runtime tasks (for interprocess communication, UI update, etc.) in its queue and never becomes disabled during an execution. In this case, the standard preemption bounding approach would spend a preemption to switch from the UI thread. Our tool blocks a thread and switches to another thread when the message queue of a current thread is empty or it has only recurring Android-runtime messages.

Though the default scheduler runs the threads in round-robin fashion, we use delay bounding [5] to prioritize our search of alternate executions. For a given bound k, we systematically explore all executions which correspond to thread schedules which are k-delay deviations from the default schedule.

AsyncDroid also allows the programmer to specify his own default scheduler by implementing certain scheduling hooks. To this end, we provide an interface which exposes the current list of application threads, whether each thread is blocked, the list of pending events in the input-repeater thread, and the lists of pending tasks in the UI and background threads. The programmer and access these lists in deciding which thread to dispatch at any given scheduling point.

3 Case Studies

As an instructive case study, we investigate an asynchrony bug in the Vlille Checker app used with the public bicycle-sharing program in the city of Lille,

France.[2] The app displays a list of bicycle stations together with their status and information. The user can (un)mark a station as a favorite, and limit their view to favorite stations. While the list is being viewed, station information is updated asynchronously in a background thread to keep the UI thread responsive.

The following scenario triggers our bug, depending on the execution order of asynchronous methods. Figure 1 shows the relevant application code with distinguished statements labeled L1, L2, and L3.

– The user clicks to view their favorites list.

L1 To initiate the status update of the favorite stations which are currently visible on the screen, the application creates a sublist of visible favorite stations. Crucially for the bug in question, this sublist is not represented by a new data structure, but is instead backed by the same data structure as the full list of favorite stations.

– The user clicks to remove a station from the favorites list.

L2 An asynchronous task executing on the UI thread removes the station from the favorites list.

L3 An asynchronous task executing on a background thread iterates over the visible favorites list in order to update their statuses.

Since L2 and L3 are executed asynchronously on separate threads, they can execute in any order, depending on hard-to-determine system scheduling factors. In the case that L2 is executed before L3, the ArrayList constructor throws a *ConcurrentModificationException* as the favorites list backing the visible favorites sublist has been modified.

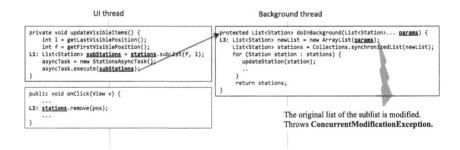

Fig. 1. An exception thrown only in executions of the Vlille Checker app in which the list removal at Statement L2 is executed between the sublist creation at L1 and its use in the constructor at L3 of the asynchronously-called doInBackground method.

To produce the bug, we record the following event sequence and systematically explore possible schedules of asynchronous methods:[3]

---

[2] The bug report: https://github.com/ojacquemart/vlilleChecker/issues/60.

[3] The test which produces this bug is available on AsyncDroid's Github repository.

1. click on a menu item to display all stations,
2. click on a station to add it into the favorites,
3. click on a menu item to display the favorite stations, and
4. click on the favorite station to remove it from the favorites.

Note that many schedules of asynchronous methods for this event sequence do not expose the bug. For instance, without incurring delays, AsyncDroid's default scheduler runs each thread until it is no longer enabled before moving on to the next thread in a round-robin fashion. The input repeater thread becomes blocked after Event 3 is actuated, since Event 4 is not enabled until the favorite stations list becomes visible. Next, the scheduler executes the pending UI-thread tasks, causing the asynchronous *doInBackground* method to become pending on the background thread. Once the UI thread becomes idle, the scheduler executes the background task to completion before returning to the input repeater thread where Event 4 is enabled, the favorite stations list having been updated and made visible. In this way, our default scheduler, without delaying, executes Statement L3 before L2, and does not expose the bug.

However, by enumerating all 1-delay executions, AsyncDroid does discover an execution in which the *ConcurrentModificationException* is thrown, by delaying the background thread before executing Statement L3. This delay causes our default scheduler to return to the input repeater thread where Event 4 is enabled, due to the UI thread having made the favorite stations list visible. After actuating Event 4, we return to the UI thread to process its *onClick* handler before returning to the background thread. This 1 delay execution thus executes Statement L2 before L1, and throws the exception.

We also applied our tool to the ACV comics and image viewer app[4], the Jamendo online music player app[5], and a hand-crafted microbenchmark with an injected asynchrony bug. We test the ACV app by providing tap inputs to browse, view, and rotate images. Since tap inputs are always enabled in this app, independently of the app state, our replay is not guaranteed to be faithful to the original event sequence, e.g., in the case that certain taps are ignored in certain states. This limitation could be overcome by more precise tracking of UI state.

The Jamendo music player app is tested by browsing, selecting and playing a radio channel. While playing music, recurring messages are sent to the UI thread to display track progress. As AsyncDroid repetitively runs all schedules without restarting the app, these recurring tasks remain in the message queue after the execution of a schedule completes. This causes the next schedule to start with some leftover tasks. AsyncDroid overcomes this problem by calling an optional finalizer method implemented by the programmer in his app itself to clean up the tasks in the message queues. We tested the Jamendo app by adding a finalizer method into its source code.

Our hand-crafted microbenchmark inserts into and deletes from a list of items, in response to user events. When the user wants to insert an item, it

---

[4] https://github.com/robotmedia/droid-comic-viewer.
[5] https://github.com/telecapoland/jamendo-android.

B.K. Ozkan et al.

Table 1. Quantitative results of our case studies.

	# of events	# of switch	# of sch. dec	0 delay		1 delay	
				# of conf.	Bug?	# of conf.	Bug?
Vlille checker	5	9	29	30	No	59	Yes
	7	8	33	34	No	69	Yes
ACV comic viewer	6	9	19	14	No	31	No
	8	9	23	19	No	40	No
Jamendo music player	3	23	100	69	No	87	No
	5	21	37	24	No	61	No
Microbenchmark	3	5	7	8	No	10	Yes
	5	5	11	12	No	19	Yes

increases the items count and performs the insertion in a background thread. If the removal of the item in the last index is processed before the background thread, the app throws an *IndexOutOfBoundsException*.

Table 1 lists the quantitative results of our case studies. As a rough measure of behavioral coverage, we measure the number of "abstract" program configurations encountered in each exploration, which distinguish only the number of asynchronous tasks pending on each thread. For each run, the table depicts the length of a fixed input event sequence, the number of context switches and the number of scheduling decision points encountered in the zero-delay execution, and the number of abstract configurations encountered. AsyncDroid quickly reproduces the known, yet previously nondeterministically-occurring, bugs in the Vlille Checker and our microbenchmark in a matter of minutes using a single delay. While we do not know whether the ACV and Jamendo apps contain a bug, AsyncDroid does not discover one within a single delay.

4 Limitations and Future Work

Applying systematic concurrency exploration to event driven programs faces the fundamental obstacle that some schedules may become infeasible due to the unavailability of a given UI component at a given time. When the component corresponding to a scheduled-for-replay event is not visible on the screen, we delay its activation, disrupting the intended schedule. This limitation raises research questions about how to integrate the treatment of UI events in concert with systematic concurrency exploration.

Controlling all scheduling decisions is a key implementation challenge. In our current prototype, we focus on the systematic analysis of interleavings between the asynchronous methods created by the given app, and leave the scheduling of other asynchronous methods (e.g., periodic system events) uncontrolled.

AsyncDroid currently only supports recording and replaying of certain types of UI events: we handle simple clicks, but not text inputs nor gestures. Capturing a wider set of UI events will allow us to test a larger set of applications. Our future work also involves developing coverage metrics to evaluate how various scheduling strategies compare with respect to coverage of program behaviors.

References

1. Anand, S., Naik, M., Harrold, M.J., Yang, H.: Automated concolic testing of smart-phone apps. In: Proceedings of the ACM SIGSOFT 20th International Symposium on the Foundations of Software Engineering. pp. 59:1–59:11. FSE 2012, ACM, New York, NY, USA (2012). http://doi.acm.org/10.1145/2393596.2393666
2. Azim, T., Neamtiu, I.: Targeted and depth-first exploration for systematic testing of android apps. In: Proceedings of the 2013 ACM SIGPLAN International Conference on Object Oriented Programming Systems Languages & Applications. pp. 641–660. OOPSLA 2013, ACM, New York, NY, USA (2013). http://doi.acm.org/10.1145/2509136.2509549
3. Bielik, P.: Effective Race Detection for Android. Master's thesis, ETH Zurich, Switzerland (2014)
4. Choi, W., Necula, G., Sen, K.: Guided GUI testing of Android apps with minimal restart and approximate learning. In: Proceedings of the 2013 ACM SIGPLAN International Conference on Object Oriented Programming Systems Languages and Applications. pp. 623–640. OOPSLA 2013, ACM, New York, NY, USA (2013). http://doi.acm.org/10.1145/2509136.2509552
5. Emmi, M., Qadeer, S., Rakamarić, Z.: Delay-bounded scheduling. In: Proceedings of the 38th Annual ACM SIGPLAN-SIGACT Symposium on Principles of Programming Languages. pp. 411–422. POPL 2011, ACM, New York, NY, USA (2011). http://doi.acm.org/10.1145/1926385.1926432
6. Gomez, L., Neamtiu, I., Azim, T., Millstein, T.: Reran: Timing- and touch-sensitive record and replay for Android. In: Proceedings of the 2013 International Conference on Software Engineering. pp. 72–81. ICSE 2013, IEEE Press, Piscataway, NJ, USA (2013). http://dl.acm.org/citation.cfm?id=2486788.2486799
7. Hsiao, C.H., Yu, J., Narayanasamy, S., Kong, Z., Pereira, C.L., Pokam, G.A., Chen, P.M., Flinn, J.: Race detection for event-driven mobile applications. In: Proceedings of the 35th ACM SIGPLAN Conference on Programming Language Design and Implementation. pp. 326–336. PLDI 2014, ACM, New York, NY, USA (2014). http://doi.acm.org/10.1145/2594291.2594330
8. Lin, Y., Radoi, C., Dig, D.: Retrofitting concurrency for Android applications through refactoring. In: Proceedings of the 22nd ACM SIGSOFT International Symposium on Foundations of Software Engineering. pp. 341–352. FSE 2014, ACM, New York, NY, USA (2014). http://doi.acm.org/10.1145/2635868.2635903
9. Machiry, A., Tahiliani, R., Naik, M.: Dynodroid: An input generation system for Android apps. In: Proceedings of the 2013 9th Joint Meeting on Foundations of Software Engineering. pp. 224–234. ESEC/FSE 2013, ACM, New York, NY, USA (2013). http://doi.acm.org/10.1145/2491411.2491450
10. Maiya, P., Kanade, A., Majumdar, R.: Race detection for Android applications. In: Proceedings of the 35th ACM SIGPLAN Conference on Programming Language Design and Implementation. pp. 316–325. PLDI 2014, ACM, New York, NY, USA (2014). http://doi.acm.org/10.1145/2594291.2594311
11. Musuvathi, M., Qadeer, S.: Iterative context bounding for systematic testing of multithreaded programs. In: Proceedings of the 2007 ACM SIGPLAN Conference on Programming Language Design and Implementation. pp. 446–455. PLDI 2007, ACM, New York, NY, USA (2007). http://doi.acm.org/10.1145/1250734.1250785

Norn: An SMT Solver for String Constraints

Parosh Aziz Abdulla[1], Mohamed Faouzi Atig[1], Yu-Fang Chen[2], Lukáš Holík[3],
Ahmed Rezine[4], Philipp Rümmer[1], and Jari Stenman[1 (✉)]

[1] Department of Information Technology, Uppsala University, Uppsala, Sweden
jari.stenman@it.uu.se
[2] Institute of Information Science, Academia Sinica, Taipei, Taiwan
[3] Faculty of Information Technology, Brno University of Technology,
Brno, Czech Republic
[4] Department of Computer and Information Science,
Linköping University, Linköping, Sweden

Abstract. We present version 1.0 of the Norn SMT solver for string constraints. Norn is a solver for an expressive constraint language, including word equations, length constraints, and regular membership queries. As a feature distinguishing Norn from other SMT solvers, Norn is a decision procedure under the assumption of a set of acyclicity conditions on word equations, without any restrictions on the use of regular membership.

1 Introduction

We introduce version 1.0 of the Norn SMT solver. Norn targets an expressive constraint language that includes word equations, length constraints, and regular membership queries. Norn is based on the calculus introduced in [1]. This version adopts several improvements on the original version, which allow it to efficiently establish or refute the satisfiability of benchmarks that are out of the reach of existing state of the art solvers.

Norn aims to establish satisfiability of constraints written as Boolean combinations of: (i) word equations such as equalities ($a \cdot u = v \cdot b$) or disequalities ($a \cdot u \neq v \cdot b$), where a, b are letters and u, v are string variables denoting words of arbitrary lengths, (ii) length constraints such as ($|u| = |v| + 1$), where $|u|$ refers to the length of the word denoted by string variable u, and (iii) predicates representing membership in regular expressions, e.g., $u \in c \cdot (a + b)^*$. The analysis is not trivial as it needs to capture subtle interactions between different types of predicates. The general decidability problem is still open. We guarantee termination of our procedure in case the considered initial constraints are *acyclic*. Acyclicity is a syntactic condition and it ensures that no variable appears more than once in word (dis)equalities during the analysis. This defines a fragment that is rich enough to capture all the practical examples we have encountered.

This work was supported by the Czech Science Foundation project 202/13/37876P, the Ministry of Science and Technology of Taiwan (103- 2221-E-001 -019 -MY3 and 103-2221-E-001 -020 -MY3), Uppsala Programming for Multicore Architectures Research Center (UPMARC), and the Linköping CENIIT Center (12.04).

D. Kroening and C.S. Păsăreanu (Eds.): CAV 2015, Part I, LNCS 9206, pp. 462–469, 2015.
DOI: 10.1007/978-3-319-21690-4_29

This version of the Norn solver follows a DPLL(T) architecture in order to turn the calculus introduced in [1] into an effective proof procedure, and introduces optimizations that are key to its current efficiency: an improved approach to handling disequalities, and a better strategy for splitting equalities compared to [1]. Norn accepts SMT-LIB scripts as input, both in the format proposed in [2] and in the CVC4 dialect [6], and can handle the combination of string constraints and linear integer arithmetic. In addition, Norn contains a fixed-point engine for processing recursive programs in the form of Horn constraints, which are expressed as SMT-LIB scripts with uninterpreted predicates; the algorithm for solving such Horn constraints was introduced in [1, 9].

Related work. Over the last years, several SMT solvers for strings and related logics have been introduced. A number of tools handled strings by means of a translation to bit-vectors [5, 10, 11], thus assuming a fixed upper bound on the length of the possible words. More recently, DPLL(T)-based string solvers lift the restriction to strings of bounded length; this generation of solvers includes Z3-str [14], CVC4 [6], and S3 [12], which are all compared to Norn in Sect. 4. Most of those solvers are more restrictive than Norn in their support for language constraints. In our experience, such restrictions are particularly problematic for software model checking, where regular membership constraints offer an elegant and powerful way of expressing and synthesising program invariants. Another related technique are automata-based solvers for analyzing string-manipulated programs [13]. According to [4], automata-based solvers are faster than the SMT-based ones on checking single execution trace. On the other hand, Norns ability to derive loop invariants and to verify entire programs can allow it to conclude even in the presence of an infinite number of possible single executions. Automata-based solvers would need to provide widening operators to handle such cases.

2 Logic and Calculus

Our constraint language includes word equations, membership queries in regular languages and length and arithmetic inequalities. We assume a finite alphabet Σ and write Σ^* to mean the set of finite words over Σ. We assume w.l.o.g. that each letter in our alphabet is represented by its unique Unicode character. We work with a set U of string variables denoting words in Σ^* and write $\mathbb{Z}$ for the set of integer numbers.

Assume variables $u, v \in U$, integers $k \in \mathbb{Z}$, letters $c \in \Sigma$, and words $w \in \Sigma^*$. We further write $|t|$ for length of word t. The syntax of the constraints is then given by:

$$
\begin{array}{llll}
\phi & ::= & \phi \wedge \phi \mid \neg \phi \mid \varphi & \text{constraints} \\
\varphi & ::= & t = t \mid e \leq e \mid t \in \mathcal{R} & \text{atomic predicates} \\
t & ::= & \varepsilon \mid c \mid u \mid t \cdot t & \text{terms} \\
\mathcal{R} & ::= & \emptyset \mid \varepsilon \mid c \mid w \mid \mathcal{R} \cdot \mathcal{R} \mid \mathcal{R} + \mathcal{R} \mid \mathcal{R} \cap \mathcal{R} \mid \mathcal{R}^C \mid \mathcal{R}^* & \text{regular expressions} \\
e & ::= & k \mid |t| \mid k * e \mid e + e & \text{integer expressions}
\end{array}
$$

A constraint is *linear* if no variable appears more than once in any of its (dis)equalities. We write w_t to mean a word denoted by a term t. Semantics of the constraints are in [1].

Given a constraint ϕ in our logic, we build a proof tree rooted at ϕ by repeatedly applying inference rules. We assume here, without loss of generality, that ϕ is given in Disjunctive Normal Form. An inference rule is of the form:

$$\frac{B_1 \ B_2 \ ... \ B_n}{A} \ \text{N}\text{AME}_{cond}$$

NAME is the name of the rule, *cond* is a side condition on A for the application of the rule, $B_1 \ B_2 \ ... \ B_n$ are the premises, and A is the conclusion. Premises and conclusions are constraints. Each application consumes a conclusion and produces premises. In our calculus, if one of the produced premises turns out to be satisfiable, then ϕ is also satisfiable. If none of the produced premises is satisfiable, then ϕ is unsatisfiable. The inference rules are introduced in [1]. The repeated application of the rules starting from a constraint ϕ is guaranteed to terminate (i.e., giving a decision procedure) in case ϕ is *acyclic*. Intuitively, *acyclicity* is a syntactic condition on the occurences of variables. This condition ensures all (dis)equalities are linear, whether in ϕ or after the application of some inference rule. We describe one rule. Other rules are introduced in [1].

Rule EQ-VAR eliminates variable u from the equality $u \cdot t_1 = t_2 \wedge \phi$. The equality is satisfied if a word w_u coincides with the prefix of a word w_{t_2}. We assume $u \cdot t_1 = t_2 \wedge \phi$ is linear (see [1] for the general case). There are two sets of premises. The first set corresponds to all the cases where w_u coincides with a word w_{t_3} where t_2 is the concatenation $t_3 \cdot t_4$. The second set represents all situations where w_{t_3} is a prefix of w_u which is a prefix of $w_{t_3 \cdot v}$ with t_2 being written as the concatenation $t_3 \cdot v \cdot t_4$.

$$\frac{\{t_1 = t_4 \wedge \phi[u/t_3] \mid t_2 = t_3 \cdot t_4\} \ \cup}{\{t_1 = v_2 \cdot t_4 \wedge \phi[u/t_3 \cdot v_1][v/v_1 \cdot v_2] \mid t_2 = t_3 \cdot v \cdot t_4\}}{u \cdot t_1 = t_2 \wedge \phi} \ \text{E}\text{Q-V}\text{AR}_{(u \cdot t_1 = t_2 \text{ is linear})}$$

3 A DPLL(T)-Style Proof Procedure for Strings

We follow the classical DPLL(T)-architecture [8] to turn the calculus from Sect. 2 into an effective proof procedure. For a given (quantifier-free) formula in our logic, first a Boolean skeleton is computed, abstracting every atom to a Boolean variable. A SAT-solver is then used to check satisfiability of the Boolean skeleton, producing (in the positive case) an implicant of the skeleton; the implicant is subsequently translated back to a conjunction of string literals, and checked for satisfiability in the string logic.

Our theory solver for checking conjunctions of string literals implements the rules of Sect. 2 and Sect. 3.1, and handles all necessary splitting internally, i.e., without involving the SAT-solver. In our experience (which is consistent with observations in other domains, e.g., [3]), this approach makes it easier to integrate splitting heuristics, and often shows better performance in practice. In particular, our approach to split equalities is model-based and exploits information extracted from arithmetic constraints in order to prune the search space; the method is explained in Sect. 3.2.

Starting from a conjunction $\phi = (\phi_= \wedge \phi_{\neq} \wedge \phi_\in \wedge \phi_a)$ of literals (which is here split into equalities $\phi_=$, disequalities $\phi_{\neq}$, membership constraints $\phi_\in$, and arithmetic constraints ϕ_a) the theory solver performs depth-first exploration until either a proof branch is found that cannot be closed (and constitutes a model), or all branches have been closed and discharged. In the latter case, information about the string literals involved in showing unsatisfiability is propagated back to the SAT-solver as a blocking clause.

Rules are applied to $\phi = (\phi_= \wedge \phi_{\neq} \wedge \phi_\in \wedge \phi_a)$ in the following order: (i) Satisfiability of ϕ_a (in Presburger arithmetic) is checked, (ii) Compound disequalities in $\phi_{\neq}$ are eliminated (Sect. 3.1), (iii) Equalities in $\phi_=$ with complex left-hand side are split (Sect. 3.2), (iv) Membership constraints in $\phi_\in$ with complex term are split, and (v) Satisfiability of all remaining membership literals and arithmetic constraints is checked.

3.1 Efficient Handling of Disequalities

To handle disequalities, we proceed differently than the method presented in [1]. For each disequality of the form $t \neq t'$, the rule DISEQ-SPLIT produces only two premises. The first premise corresponds to the case where the words w_t and $w_{t'}$ have different length. The second case is when w_t and $w_{t'}$ have the same length but contain different letters $c \neq c'$ after a common prefix. Rather than constructing a premise for each pair of different letters (as it is done in [1]), we introduce two special variables μ and μ' (called *witness variables*) such that the letters c and c' correspond to the words denoted by μ and μ'. Therefore, the length of these witness variables is one and this fact is added to the arithmetic constraints. Furthermore, we add a disequality $\mu \neq \mu'$ in order to denote that c is different from c'. Assuming fresh variables u, v and v', we rewrite $t \neq t'$ as two equalities $t = u \cdot \mu \cdot v$ and $t' = u \cdot \mu' \cdot v'$. Finally, w.l.o.g. we restrict the inference rules such that witness variables can only be substituted by other witness variables.

$$\frac{\{|t| \neq |t'| \wedge \phi\} \cup}{\{|v| = |v'| \wedge t = u \cdot \mu \cdot v \wedge t' = u \cdot \mu' \cdot v' \wedge |\mu| = 1 \wedge |\mu'| = 1 \wedge \mu \neq \mu' \wedge \phi\}}{t \neq t' \wedge \phi} \; \text{DISEQ-SPLIT}$$

The new Rule REG-WITNESS can only be applied to a witness variable μ in a certain case. For a formula ϕ, we define the condition $\Theta(\phi, \mu)$ to denote that μ appears in ϕ only in disequalities. The Rule REG-WITNESS replaces all membership predicates $\{\mu \in R_i\}_{i=1}^n$ with an arithmetic constraint Unicode$(R_1, R_2, \ldots, R_n, \mu)$. This constraint uses a fresh variable μ_{uni} s.t. the set of possible lengths of the word denoted by μ_{uni} represents the set of Unicode characters belonging to the intersection of all regular expressions $\{R_i\}_{i=1}^n$. In order to do so, we construct a finite state automaton A accepting the intersection of $\{R_i\}_{i=1}^n$. Furthermore, we restrict A to accept only words of size exactly one (since μ is a witness variable). The obtained automaton is then determined. Notice that the determined automaton B has only transitions from the initial state to the final one. Each transition of B is labelled by a Unicode character interval as specified by the automata library [7] we are using. Then, for each transition labeled by an interval of the form $\{min, \ldots, max\}$, we associate the arithmetic constraint $min \leq |\mu_{uni}| \leq max$. Finally, our arithmetic constraint $\mathsf{Unicode}(R_1, R_2, \ldots, R_n, \mu)$ will be the disjunction of all associated arithmetic constraints to all the transitions of B. In the case that the intersection is empty, we set $\mathsf{Unicode}(R_1, R_2, \ldots, R_n, \mu)$ to $\mathtt{false}$.

$$\frac{\mathsf{Unicode}(\mathcal{R}_1 \cap \ldots \cap \mathcal{R}_m, u) \wedge \phi}{\mu \in \mathcal{R}_1 \wedge \ldots \wedge u \in \mathcal{R}_m \wedge \phi} \ \ \text{REG-WITNESS}(\Theta(\phi, \mu))$$

Finally, the Rule DISEQ-WITNESS replaces a disequality of the form $\mu \neq \mu'$ by the arithmetic constraint $|\mu_{uni}| \neq |\mu'_{uni}|$.

$$\frac{|\mu_{uni}| \neq |\mu'_{uni}| \wedge \phi}{\mu \neq \mu' \wedge \phi} \ \ \text{DISEQ-WITNESS}(\Theta(\phi, \mu))$$

3.2 Length-Guided Splitting of Equalities

The original calculus rule for handling complex equalities is EQ-VAR, which systematically enumerates the different ways of matching up left-hand and right-hand side terms. For a practical proof procedure, naive use of this rule is suboptimal in two respects: the number of cases to be considered grows quickly (in the worst case, exponentially in the number of equalities); and the rule does not provide any guidance on the order in which the cases should be considered, which can have dramatic impact on the performance for satisfiable problems. We found that both aspects can be improved by eagerly taking arithmetic constraints on the length of strings into account.

To present the approach, we assume that conjunctions $\phi = (\phi_= \wedge \phi_{\neq} \wedge \phi_\in \wedge \phi_a)$ are continuously saturated by propagating length information from $\phi_=$ to ϕ_a: for every equality $s = t$, a corresponding length equality $|s| = |t|$ is added, compound expressions $|s \cdot t|$ are rewritten to $|s| + |t|$, and the length $|w|$ of concrete words $w \in \Sigma^*$ is evaluated. In addition, for every variable v an inequality $|v| \geq 0$ is generated. Similar propagation is possible for membership constraints in $\phi_\in$.

Prior to splitting equalities from $\phi_=$, it is then possible to check the satisfiability of arithmetic constraints ϕ_a (using any solver for Presburger arithmetic), and compute a satisfying assignment β. This assignment defines the length $val_\beta(|v|)$ of all string variables v, and thus uniquely determines how the right-hand side of an equality $u \cdot t_1 = t_2$ should be split into a prefix corresponding to u, and a suffix corresponding to t_1. We obtain the following modified splitting rule, which has the side condition that $u \cdot t_1 = t_2 \cdot v \cdot t_3$ is linear, and that a satisfying assignment β of ϕ_a exists such that $val_\beta(|t_2|) \le val_\beta(|u|) \le val_\beta(|t_2 \cdot v|)$:

$$\frac{\begin{array}{l}((t_1 = v_2 \cdot t_3 \wedge \phi_a \wedge \phi)[u/t_2 \cdot v_1])[v/v_1 \cdot v_2] \\ u \cdot t_1 = t_2 \cdot v \cdot t_3 \wedge (|u| < |t_2| \wedge \phi_a) \wedge \phi \\ u \cdot t_1 = t_2 \cdot v \cdot t_3 \wedge (|t_1| < |t_3| \wedge \phi_a) \wedge \phi \end{array}}{u \cdot t_1 = t_2 \cdot v \cdot t_3 \wedge \phi_a \wedge \phi} \text{ Len-Eq-Split}$$

A similar rule is introduced to cover the situation that the right-hand side has to be split between two concrete letters, i.e., in case we have $val_\beta(|u|) = val_\beta(|t_2|)$ and $val_\beta(|t_1|) = val_\beta(|t_3|)$ for an equation $u \cdot t_1 = t_2 \cdot t_3$.

4   Implementation and Experiments

We compare the new version of Norn[1] to other solvers on two sets of benchmarks. First, we use the well-known set of Kaluza benchmarks, which were translated to SMT-LIB by the authors of CVC4 [6]. These benchmarks contain constraints generated by a Javascript analysis tool, and are mainly equational, with relatively little use of regular expressions. Results are given in Table 1, and show that currently Z3-str [14] performs best for this kind of benchmarks; however, Norn can solve 27 benchmarks that no other tool can handle (Table 2). S3 [12] produced internal errors on a larger number of the Kaluza benchmarks, and sometimes results that were contradictory with the other solvers: for 95 problems, S3 claimed unsat, whereas Z3-str and CVC4 reported sat. For 27 of those, also Norn gave the answer sat. No contradictions were observed between CVC4, Z3-str, and Norn. A direct comparison with Norn 0.3 [1] was not possible due to lacking support for SMT-LIB input. Instead, we internally modified Norn and reverted back to the old version of the calculus. The results indicate that our new rules significantly improve the performance specially on large benchmarks.

As a second set of benchmarks, we considered queries generated during CEGAR-based verification of string-processing programs [1]; those queries are quite small, but make heavy use of regular expressions and operators like the Kleene star. Norn could solve all of the benchmarks. We did not observe any major difference between the two versions of the calculus (runtimes are typically very small). Comparison with Z3-str was not possible, since the solver does not support regular expressions.[2] CVC4 and S3 showed timeouts, ran out of memory, or crashed on a large number of the benchmarks. S3 and Norn gave contradicting answers in altogether 413 cases, with manual inspection indicating that the answers by Norn were correct. This was confirmed by the S3 authors, and will be fixed in the near future; a corrected version was not available by the deadline.

---

[1] Tool and benchmarks are available on http://user.it.uu.se/%7Ejarst116/norn/.

[2] The recently released Z3-str2 supports regular expressions, but in a format different from all other compared tools, so that experiments could not be carried out by the deadline.

Table 1. Experimental results. All experiments were done on an AMD Opteron 2220 SE machine, running 64-bit Linux and Java 1.8. Runtime was limited to 240 s (wall clock time), and heap space to 1.5 GB. CEGAR were benchmarks downsized from UTF16 when necessary.

		Norn 1.0	Norn 0.3	CVC4 1.5pre	Z3-str 1.0.0	S3
Kaluza	(Sat)	33 072	31 018	33 772	34 770	30 925
	(Unsat)	11 595	11 256	11 625	11 799	11 408
	(Unknown)	2 617	5 010	1 887	715	3 081
	(Crash)	0	0	0	0	1 870
CEGAR	(sat)	712	712	292	–	307
	(Unsat)	315	315	98	–	530
	(Unknown)	0	0	637	–	158
	(Crash/OOM)	0	0	0	–	32

Table 2. Complementarity of the results: number of problems for which one tool can show sat/unsat, whereas another tool times out or crashes. For instance, Norn can prove satisfiability of 435 Kaluza benchmarks on which CVC4 times out.

		Norn 1.0		CVC4		Z3-str		S3	
		Sat	Unsat	Sat	Unsat	Sat	Unsat	Sat	Unsat
Norn	(Kaluza)	–	–	+1 135	+57	+1 698	+231	+64	+125
	(CEGAR)	–	–	0	0	–	–	0	0
CVC4	(Kaluza)	+435	+27	–	–	+998	+174	0	0
	(CEGAR)	+420	+217	–	–	–	–	+124	+398
Z3-str	(Kaluza)	0	+27	0	0	–	–	0	0
	(CEGAR)	–	–	–	–	–	–	–	–
S3	(Kaluza)	+2 184	+339	+2 752	+312	+3 750	+486	–	–
	(CEGAR)	+134	+56	+57	+18	–	–	–	–

References

1. Abdulla, P.A., Atig, M.F., Chen, Y.-F., Holík, L., Rezine, A., Rümmer, P., Stenman, J.: String Constraints for Verification. In: Biere, A., Bloem, R. (eds.) CAV 2014. LNCS, vol. 8559, pp. 150–166. Springer, Heidelberg (2014)
2. Bjorner, N., Ganesh, V., Michel, R., Veanes, M.: Smt-lib sequences and regular expressions. In: Fontaine, P., Goel, A. (eds.) SMT 2012. EPiC Series, vol. 20, pp. 77–87. EasyChair (2013)
3. Griggio, A.: A practical approach to satisfiability modulo linear integer arithmetic. JSAT 8(1/2), 1–27 (2012)

4. Kausler, S., Sherman, E.: Evaluation of string constraint solvers in the context of symbolic execution. In: Crnkovic, I., Chechik, M., Grünbacher, P. (eds.) ACM/IEEE International Conference on Automated Software Engineering, ASE'2014, Vasteras, Sweden - 15–19 Sept 2014. pp. 259–270. ACM (2014). http://doi.acm.org/10.1145/2642937.2643003

5. Kiezun, A., Ganesh, V., Guo, P.J., Hooimeijer, P., Ernst, M.D.: HAMPI: A Solver for String Constraints. In: ISTA. pp. 105–116. ACM (2009)

6. Liang, T., Reynolds, A., Tinelli, C., Barrett, C., Deters, M.: A DPLL(T) theory solver for a theory of strings and regular expressions. In: Biere, A., Bloem, R. (eds.) CAV 2014. LNCS, vol. 8559, pp. 646–662. Springer, Heidelberg (2014)

7. Møller, A.: dk.brics.automaton - finite-state automata and regular expressions for Java (2010). http://www.brics.dk/automaton/

8. Nieuwenhuis, R., Oliveras, A., Tinelli, C.: Solving SAT and SAT modulo theories: from an abstract Davis-Putnam-Logemann-Loveland procedure to DPLL(T). J. ACM **53**(6), 937–977 (2006)

9. Rümmer, P., Hojjat, H., Kuncak, V.: Disjunctive interpolants for horn-clause verification. In: Sharygina, N., Veith, H. (eds.) CAV 2013. LNCS, vol. 8044, pp. 347–363. Springer, Heidelberg (2013)

10. Saxena, P., Akhawe, D., Hanna, S., Mao, F., McCamant, S., Song, D.: A symbolic execution framework for JavaScript. In: IEEE Symposium on Security and Privacy. pp. 513–528. IEEE Computer Society (2010)

11. Saxena, P., Hanna, S., Poosankam, P., Song, D.: FLAX: Systematic discovery of client-side validation vulnerabilities in rich web applications. In: NDSS. The Internet Society (2010)

12. Trinh, M.T., Chu, D.H., Jaffar, J.: S3: A symbolic string solver for vulnerability detection in web applications. In: Ahn, G., Yung, M., Li, N. (eds.) CCS. pp. 1232–1243. ACM (2014)

13. Yu, F., Alkhalaf, M., Bultan, T.: STRANGER: an automata-based string analysis tool for PHP. In: Esparza, J., Majumdar, R. (eds.) TACAS 2010. LNCS, vol. 6015, pp. 154–157. Springer, Heidelberg (2010)

14. Zheng, Y., Zhang, X., Ganesh, V.: Z3-str: A Z3-based string solver for web application analysis. In: Meyer, B., Baresi, L., Mezini, M. (eds.) ESEC/FSE. pp. 114–124. ACM (2013)

Pvsio-web 2.0: Joining PVS to HCI

Paolo Masci[1]([✉]), Patrick Oladimeji[3], Yi Zhang[2], Paul Jones[2],
Paul Curzon[1], and Harold Thimbleby[3]

[1] Queen Mary University of London, London, UK
{p.m.masci,p.curzon}@qmul.ac.uk
[2] U.S. Food and Drug Administration, Silver Spring, MD, USA
{yi.zhang2,paul.jones}@fda.hhs.gov
[3] Swansea University, Swansea, UK
{p.oladimeji,h.thimbleby}@swansea.ac.uk

Abstract. PVSio-web is a graphical environment for facilitating the
design and evaluation of interactive (human-computer) systems. Using
PVSio-web, one can generate and evaluate realistic interactive prototypes
from formal models. PVSio-web has been successfully used over the last
two years for analyzing commercial, safety-critical medical devices. It has
been used to create training material for device developers and device
users. It has also been used for medical device design, by both formal
methods experts and non-technical end users.
This paper presents the latest release of PVSio-web 2.0, which will be
part of the next PVS distribution. The new tool architecture is discussed,
and the rationale behind its design choices are presented.

PVSio-web Tool: http://www.pvsioweb.org

Keywords: Prototyping · User interface analysis · Practical formal
tools

1 Introduction

Inadequate user interface design is repeatedly reported as a root cause of many
incidents in healthcare [1,2], avionics [3], and other safety-critical domains [4].
Design and analysis of user interfaces often requires a multidisciplinary team
of human factors specialists, engineers, and end users to validate requirements,
specifications, and implementation details. Rigorous formal methods tools can
enable early identification of potential design issues. State-of-the-art verification
tools like PVS [5], however, generally have minimal front-ends that create barriers when formal methods experts need to work in a multidisciplinary team
and engage with non-experts of formal methods technologies — e.g., to validate
hypotheses included in the formal models, or to discuss formal analysis results.

US Government (outside the US) 2015. The rights of this work are transferred to
the extent transferrable according to title 17 U.S.C. 105.

© Springer International Publishing Switzerland 2015
D. Kroening and C.S. Păsăreanu (Eds.): CAV 2015, Part I, LNCS 9206, pp. 470–478, 2015.
DOI: 10.1007/978-3-319-21690-4_30

The tool presented in this paper, PVSio-web, significantly reduces these barriers. PVSio-web is a web-based environment for modeling and prototyping interactive (human-computer) systems in PVS, and is particularly suitable for: *validating hypotheses* included in formal models and formal properties before starting the verification process; *demonstrating formal analysis results* to engineers and domain specialists in a way that is easy to comprehend; and *enabling lightweight formal analysis* of user interfaces based on user-centred design methods, such as user testing and expert walkthroughs of prototypes. PVSio-web can be freely downloaded with the latest version of PVS [6] or from our repository [7].

Related Work. SCR [8] is a toolset for the analysis of system requirements and specifications. Using SCR, one can formally specify the behavior of a system, use visual front-ends for demonstrating the system behavior based on the specifications, and use a group of formal methods tools (including PVS) for the analysis of system properties. In contrast to our tool, SCR lacks specialized functionalities needed for the analysis of user interfaces, such as rapid generation of user interface prototypes, deployment of prototypes on mobile devices, and logging of user interactions. Simulink [9] is a de-facto standard environment for model-based design and analysis of dynamic systems. It provides a graphical model editor based on Statecharts, and functions for rapid generation of realistic prototypes. Unlike our tool, Simulink offers very limited functions for prototyping user interface designs. More importantly, its architecture is not open, preventing it from being used with PVS or other formal analysis tools. In [10], an approach to develop realistic device prototypes using graph models and interactive pictures is presented, but the approach is not supported by a development environment, and the prototypes are manually crafted. PetShop [11], IVY [12] and similar verification tools for formal analysis of user interfaces lack functions for rapid generation of realistic prototypes. Other verification tools like Bandera [13] and PVSioChecker [14] are not specialized for user interface analysis, and features such as rapid prototyping are out of their intended functionalities.

2   PVSio-web: System Overview and Applications

PVSio-web provides a formal methods based, sophisticated graphical front-end for modeling and prototyping interactive (human-computer) systems. It transforms the animation capabilities of PVS, and enables the user to rapidly generate realistic prototypes in two steps: first, a picture of the user interface is loaded into the tool; second, programmable areas are created over the picture and linked to the formal model specifying the human-system interaction. Programmable areas for input widgets (e.g., buttons) over the user interface picture define how user actions are translated into PVS expressions that can be animated within PVSio [15], the native animation environment of PVS. Programmable areas for output widgets (e.g., displays), on the other hand, define how results returned by PVSio are rendered into visual elements of the prototype, so the visual appearance of the prototype can closely resemble the appearance of the real system in the corresponding state.

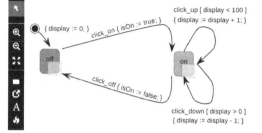

(a) Prototype Builder.   (b) Emucharts Editor and example diagram.

```
Compile    Import Files   Set As Main File   Save Selected File                    ←  →  Q Find text

1 ▾ emucharts th: THEORY BEGIN IMPORTING utils_th                                         ∨ ▦ defaultProject
2                                                                                          ▪ emucharts.pvs
3   MachineState: TYPE = { off, on }
4   State: TYPE = [# current_state : MachineState, previous_state: MachineState, display: real, isOn: bool #]  ▪ MDNumberpad.pvs
5
6   per_click_up(st: State): bool = ((current_state(st) = on) AND (display(st) < 100))    ▪ ivpump1.jpg
7 ▾ click_up(st: (per_click_up)): State =
8 ▾   COND (current_state(st) = on) AND (display(st) < 100)                                ▪ widgetDefinition.json
9 ▾   -> LET new_st = leave_state(on)(st),
10        new_st = new_st WITH [ display := display(st) + 1 ]
11      IN enter_into(on)(new_st) ENDCOND
```

(c) Model Editor and a model snippet generated from the diagram in Figure 1(b).

Fig. 1. Screenshots of the main tools provided by the PVSio-web environment.

Figure 1(a) is a screenshot of PVSio-web generating a prototype, where framed boxes are programmable overlay areas: thus, our tool embeds a script in the area over button "0" that translates click actions over the button into a PVS expression click_0(st), and evaluates this expression in PVSio. The function click_0 is defined in the PVS model of the system, st being the current model state. Our tool automatically keeps track of model states during interaction with the prototype, and seamlessly replaces st with the current model state. The overlay over the display region renders the value of PVS expressions returned by PVSio (here, as numbers).

Applications. PVSio-web has been applied successfully in the analysis of commercial medical devices. Using PVSio-web, we have:

- demonstrated previously undetected design issues in medical devices [16,17],
- validated requirements for medical devices [18–21], and
- created training material [22] for device developers and users.

For example, the prototype shown in Fig. 1(a) is one of many that have been used to analyze real medical devices, here a drug infusion pump. Our analysis focused on the data entry defining how the infusion pump responds when the user enters configuration parameters, such as therapy data or patient data. The PVS model of the infusion pump's user interface was obtained by translating the source-code implementation of its user interface software into a PVS theory. Using PVSio-web, we generated a realistic prototype based on the formal model, and used it to perform quick exploratory analyses of the model to understand how to

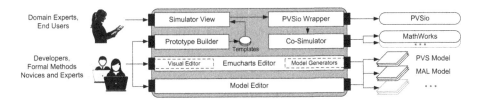

Fig. 2. PVSio-web architecture. Rectangular boxes represent the main modules of the tool; arrows between boxes represent use relationships between modules.

best formalize human factors principles as PVS theorems. An example human factors principle is **consistency**, asserting that the same user actions should produce the same results in logically equivalent situations. We formalized this principle as a PVS theorem that checks whether the data entry interaction of the device consistently registered button clicks in all states. This theorem allowed us to discover previously undetected issues with the decimal point (full details of the analysis are in [16]). The same prototype was also used to demonstrate the identified design issues to regulators and real device users (nurses, doctors, medical device trainers), resulting in the recognition of the safety implications of these issues. This and other prototypes generated using PVSio-web are currently used in training material for hospitals [23], device manufacturers, and regulators to raise awareness about general user interface software issues [22].

3   The PVSio-web Architecture

The architecture of the latest release of PVSio-web is shown in Fig. 2. It follows the Model-View-Controller design pattern [24], creating a clear separation between modules responsible for the behavior of the prototype and those for its visual appearance. In particular, the behavior of a prototype is entirely specified using PVS executable models animated within PVSio. PVSio is used *as is*, without any modification that might compromise its correctness or sound integration with PVS.

PVSio-web provides multiple facets; that is, it combines different development environments specifically designed for different target users. One facet, Simulator View, is designed for domain specialists and end users: it includes only elements and functionalities for exploring the behavior of prototypes generated with PVSio-web. The other facets are designed for developers and formal methods specialists. They provide tools for creating the visual appearance of the prototype (Prototype Builder), and for editing the PVS model. Advanced PVS users can use the Model Editor for editing and type-checking PVS models; developers who are novice PVS users can use a visual model editor (Emucharts Editor) for developing formal models using a graphical notation based on Statecharts [25]. The facets work well together, allowing people with different background and expertise to work together with the same underlying formal models.

▶ The **Simulator View** handles the execution of prototypes developed within PVSio-web, and logs user interactions with the prototype. This module renders the visual elements of the prototype, and implements functions for detecting and logging user actions over input widgets. It also translates user actions performed on the input widgets into PVS expressions; triggers the evaluation of PVS expressions in PVSio; and renders PVS expressions returned by PVSio into visual elements of the prototype. Translation of user actions into PVS expressions, and rendering of PVS expressions into visual elements are performed in real time using template scripts created with Prototype Builder. Example prototypes executed within Simulator View are illustrated in [17, 22].

▶ The **Prototype Builder** automates the generation of a prototype, providing a graphical environment with functions for defining the visual aspect of the prototype (typically, a picture) and for creating programmable overlay areas that enable interaction with the prototype. Overlay areas corresponding to input widgets define which user actions are recognized (e.g., press, release, click) and how these actions are translated into PVS expressions. The translation is performed using templates that map user actions to PVS functions on the basis of naming conventions. An example template is `click_<btn>(<st>)`, which translates clicks performed by the user over a button `<btn>` into a PVS function that takes one parameter `<st>`, representing the current model state. Areas corresponding to output widgets use string filters to extract the actual value of the widget from PVS expressions returned by PVSio.

▶ The **EmuCharts Editor** implements a visual editor and code generators for creating executable formal models. With this module, developers can: *define states* by drawing labelled boxes; *define transitions* by drawing labelled arrows; *define variables* representing relevant characteristics of the system; and *generate executable models* from the visual diagram. Model generators employ constructs from languages supported by popular analysis tools and programming languages: state labels are translated into enumerated type constants; state variables are translated into fields of a record type defining the system state; state transitions are translated into transition functions over system states. Language constructs for checking well-formedness of the model are automatically embedded in the generated models. For example, the PVS model generator introduces subtyping [26] relations so that consistency and coverage of conditions can be checked with the PVS type-checker (e.g., see the PVS model snippet in Fig. 1(c)).

▶ The **Model Editor** is a text editor for editing formal models, providing the typical functionalities of modern IDEs (syntax highlighting, autocomplete, search, etc.) as well as a file browser to perform operations on the file system.

▶ The **PVSio Wrapper** spawns PVSio processes needed for model animation, and hides the native read-eval-print loop of PVSio behind an API implementing a standard observer pattern [27], with functions for sending commands to PVSio, and for receiving call-backs when PVSio returns a result. This module implements mechanisms to disable inappropriate configurations of our tool, e.g., it disallows spawning multiple concurrent instances of PVSio for demonstrating concurrent systems (the demonstration of such systems must be based on a PVS model that explicitly defines the concurrent behavior).

▶ The **Co-Simulator** creates a communication infrastructure that enables exchange of simulation events and data between PVS models animated within PVSio and models animated within other simulation environments. This module is particularly useful for the development and evaluation of complex systems. In particular, a development team can employ different modeling and analysis tools for different parts of a complex system, while using the Co-Simulator to verify system properties in a coordinated simulation environment. Example prototypes using this module to perform co-simulation of PVS models and Simulink models are described in [28, 29].

4   Implementation

The core modules of PVSio-web are entirely implemented in JavaScript, which eases the deployment of PVSio-web to mobile devices (tablets, smartphones, etc.) allowing demonstrations to be given conveniently to domain experts. A client-server architecture is used, in which the server builds on NodeJS [30] and the client relies on the JavaScript engine of web browsers. Jison [31] is employed to automatically generate language parsers from production rules. Model generators use Handlebars [32] for generating formal specifications from model templates. PVSio-web 2.0 includes model generators for PVS, MAL [12], PIM [33], and VDM-SL [34]. PVSio-web text editors build on CodeMirror [35]. PVSio-web visual editors build on D3.js [36].

PVSio-web was first released in early 2013 [37]. The tool has been continuously extended with new features, and re-engineered to improve modularity and the overall code quality. JSLint [38] and Jasmine [39] are routinely used to ensure that our implementation is compliant with established coding standards and that the code is well-formed. The latest version of PVSio-web consists of 18,000 lines of JavaScript code.

5   Conclusions and Future Directions

PVSio-web shows it is possible and productive to make realistic user interfaces, with all the benefits of web access (mobility, platform independence), connected closely to formal methods tools. PVSio-web makes professional formal methods accessible to end users and others, as is required in best practice for user interface design. We believe that our tool has the potential to improve the development of safe and dependable device user interfaces, as it facilitates using formal methods practices in an area of product design that has typically not made use of this technology. The tool is gaining popularity: it was downloaded over 1,600 times in 2014 [40]; research groups are exploring applications of the tool to the analysis of commercial products in other application domains (e.g., Honeywell is using it to analyze flight decks [41]). PVSio-web has been successfully used in tutorials [42, 43] to explain the structure of PVS models, and the meaning of PVS theorems to researchers and students that were not familiar with formal methods. Other universities [44–47] are also using our tool as a basis for projects and student theses. Current and future development directions include improved support for advanced formal verification techniques. For example, we are developing a new visual front-end, Proof Explorer [48], to ease the demonstration of formal proofs, the generation of test cases from verification results, and the development of proof strategies specialized for the analysis of user interface software (example strategies are informally described in [21]). We are additionally developing model generators and co-simulators to link our tool with other popular formal methods tools, including SAL [49], KeYmaera [50], and Uppaal [51]. We are also regularly adding new case studies in medical and other domains, e.g., for avionics and aerospace.

Acknowledgements. This work is part of CHI+MED (EPSRC grant [EP/G059 063/1]). The authors would like to thank SRI International, in particular John Rushby, Sam Owre and Natarajan Shankar for supporting the development of our tool.

Disclaimer. The mention of commercial products, their sources, or their use in connection with material reported herein is not to be construed as either an actual or implied endorsement of such products by the U.S. Department of Health and Human Services.

References

1. Simone, L.: Software-related recalls: an analysis of records. Biomed. Instrum. Technol. **47**(6), 514–522 (2013)
2. US Food and Drug Administration (FDA), Manufacturer and User Facility Device Experience Database (MAUDE). http://www.fda.gov/MedicalDevices/Device RegulationandGuidance/PostmarketRequirements/ReportingAdverseEvents/ ucm127891.htm
3. Gelman, G., Feigh, K., Rushby, J.: Example of a complementary use of model checking and human-performance simulation. IEEE Trans. Hum. Mach. Syst. **44**(5), 576–590 (2014)
4. Millett, L., Thomas, M., Jackson, D., et al.: Software for Dependable Systems: Sufficient Evidence?. National Academies Press, Washington, DC (2007)
5. Owre, S., Rushby, J., Shankar, N.: PVS: a prototype verification system. In: Kapur, D. (ed.) CADE 1992. LNCS, vol. 607, pp. 748–752. Springer, Heidelberg (1992)
6. PVS Specification and Verification System – GitHub repository. https://github. com/samowre/PVS
7. PVSio-web - Interactive human-computer systems modelling and prototyping tool. http://www.pvsioweb.org
8. Heitmeyer, C., Kirby, J., Labaw, B., Bharadwaj, R.: SCR: a toolset for specifying and analyzing software requirements. In: Vardi, M.Y., Hu, A.J. (eds.) CAV 1998. LNCS, vol. 1427, pp. 526–531. Springer, Heidelberg (1998)
9. Mathworks Simulink. http://www.mathworks.com/products/simulink
10. Thimbleby, H., Gow, J.: Applying graph theory to interaction design. In: Gulliksen, J., Harning, M.B., van der Veer, G.C., Wesson, J. (eds.) EIS 2007. LNCS, vol. 4940, pp. 501–519. Springer, Heidelberg (2008)
11. Palanque, P., Ladry, J.-F., Navarre, D., Barboni, E.: High-Fidelity Prototyping of Interactive Systems Can Be Formal Too. In: Jacko, J.A. (ed.) HCI International 2009, Part I. LNCS, vol. 5610, pp. 667–676. Springer, Heidelberg (2009)

12. Campos, J., Harrison, M.: Interaction engineering using the IVY tool. In: Proceedings of the ACM SIGCHI Symposium on Engineering Interactive Computing Systems (EICS09), pp. 35–44. ACM (2009)
13. Hatcliff, J., Dwyer, M.B., Păsăreanu, C.S.: Foundations of the Bandera abstraction tools. In: Mogensen, T.Æ., Schmidt, D.A., Sudborough, I.H. (eds.) The Essence of Computation. LNCS, vol. 2566, pp. 172–203. Springer, Heidelberg (2002)
14. Dutle, A.M., Muñoz, C.A., Narkawicz, A.J., Butler, R.W.: Software validation via model animation. In: Blanchette, J.C., Kosmatov, N. (eds.) TAP 2015. LNCS, vol. 9154, pp. 92–108. Springer, Heidelberg (2015)
15. Muñoz, C.: Rapid prototyping in PVS, Technical report NIA Report No. 2003–03, NASA/CR-2003-212418. National Institute of Aerospace (2003)
16. Masci, P., Zhang, Y., Jones, P., Curzon, P., Thimbleby, H.: Formal verification of medical device user interfaces using PVS. In: Gnesi, S., Rensink, A. (eds.) FASE 2014 (ETAPS). LNCS, vol. 8411, pp. 200–214. Springer, Heidelberg (2014)
17. Masci, P., Oladimeji, P., Curzon, P., Thimbleby, H.: Tool demo: Using PVSio-web to demonstrate software issues in medical user interfaces. In: 4th International Symposium on Foundations of Healthcare Information Engineering and Systems (FHIES 2014) (2014)
18. Masci, P., Ayoub, A., Curzon, P., Harrison, M., Lee, I., Thimbleby, H.: Verification of interactive software for medical devices: PCA infusion pumps and FDA regulation as an example. In: EICS2013, 5th ACM SIGCHI Symposium on Engineering Interactive Computing Systems. ACM Digital Library (2013)
19. Masci, P., Ayoub, A., Curzon, P., Lee, I., Sokolsky, O., Thimbleby, H.: Model-based development of the generic PCA infusion pump user interface prototype in PVS. In: Bitsch, F., Guiochet, J., Kaâniche, M. (eds.) SAFECOMP. LNCS, vol. 8153, pp. 228–240. Springer, Heidelberg (2013)
20. Masci, P., Rukšėnas, R., Oladimeji, P., Cauchi, P., Gimblett, A., Li, Y., Curzon, P., Thimbleby, H.: The benefits of formalising design guidelines: a case study on the predictability of drug infusion pumps. Innovations Syst. Softw. Eng. 11(2), 73–93 (2013)
21. Harrison, M., Masci, P., Campos, J., Curzon, P.: Demonstrating that medical devices satisfy user related safety requirements. In: 4th International Symposium on Foundations of Healthcare Information Engineering and Systems (FHIES 2014) (2014)
22. Masci, P.: Design issues in medical user interfaces. https://www.youtube.com/watch?v=T0QmUe0bwL8
23. Masci, P.: Data entry issues in medical devices. Seminar given within the Washington Adventist Hospital's Continuing Medical Education (CME) Program (2014)
24. Krasner, G., Pope, S.: A description of the model-view-controller user interface paradigm in the Smalltalk-80 system. J. Object Oriented Program. 1(3), 26–49 (1988)
25. Harel, D.: Statecharts: a visual formalism for complex systems. Sci. Comput. Program. 8, 231–274 (1987)
26. Shankar, N., Owre, S.: Principles and pragmatics of Subtyping in PVS. In: Bert, D., Choppy, C., Mosses, P.D. (eds.) WADT 1999. LNCS, vol. 1827, pp. 37–52. Springer, Heidelberg (2000)
27. Gamma, E., Helm, R., Johnson, R., Vlissides, J.: Design Patterns: Elements of Reusable Object-oriented Software. Pearson Education, Upper Saddle River (1994)
28. Masci, P., Zhang, Y., Jones, P., Oladimeji, P., D'Urso, E., Bernardeschi, C., Curzon, P., Thimbleby, H.: Combining PVSio with Stateflow. In: Badger, J.M., Rozier, K.Y. (eds.) NFM 2014. LNCS, vol. 8430, pp. 209–214. Springer, Heidelberg (2014)

29. Bernardeschi, C., Domenici, A., Masci, P.: Integrated simulation of implantable cardiac pacemaker software and heart models. In: 2nd International Conference on Cardiovascular Technologies (CARDIOTECHNIX 2014). ScitePress Digital Library (2014). http://www.scitepress.org
30. Node.js. http://nodejs.org
31. Jison - JavaScript Parser Generator. http://jison.org
32. Handlebars Semantic Templates. http://handlebarsjs.com
33. Bowen, J., Reeves, S.: Modelling safety properties of interactive medical systems. In: Proceedings of the 5th ACM SIGCHI Symposium on Engineering Interactive Computing Systems, EICS 2013, pp. 91–100. ACM (2013)
34. Masci, P., Couto, L., Larsen, P., Curzon, P.: Integrating the PVSio-web modelling and prototyping environment with Overture. In: 13th Overture Workshop, Satellite Event of FM 2015 (2015)
35. CodeMirror text editor for web browsers. http://codemirror.net
36. D3.js JavaScript library for dynamic creation and control of graphical elements. http://d3js.org
37. Oladimeji, P., Masci, P., Curzon, P., Thimbleby, H.: PVSio-web: a tool for rapid prototyping device user interfaces in PVS. In: 5th International Workshop on Formal Methods for Interactive Systems (FMIS 2013) (2013). http://www.pvsioweb.org
38. JSLint - JavaScript Code Quality Tool. http://www.jslint.com
39. Jasmine - JavaScript Testing Tool. http://jasmine.github.io
40. Download statistics for package pvsio-web. http://npm-stat.com/charts.html?package=pvsio-web
41. Hall, B., Bhatt, D.: Formal Specification and Verification of Human Interactive Interfaces Incorporating Voice Control. Project Proposal, Honeywell (2013)
42. Medical devices and HCI. Full day tutorial at NordiCHI (2014). http://cs.swan.ac.uk/~cspo/2014/nordichi/
43. Masci, P.: Design and analysis of software for interactive medical devices. Ph.D. module at University of Pisa (2014). http://phd.dii.unipi.it/formazione/item/85-dr-paolo-masci
44. Robb, N.: Exploring Aspects of Automated Test Generation on Models. Waikato University, New Zealand, Honour Project (2015)
45. Pascoe, I.: Usability study of a system that models interactive systems. Waikato University, New Zealand, Honour Project (2015)
46. D'Urso, E.: Emulink: a graphical modelling environment for PVS, Master's thesis. University of Pisa, Italy (2014)
47. Faria, C.: Web-base user interface prototyping and simulation, Master's thesis. University of Minho, Portugal (2014)
48. Proof Explorer. https://github.com/thehogfather/ProofExplorer
49. de Moura, L., Owre, S., Rueß, H., Rushby, J., Shankar, N., Sorea, M., Tiwari, A.: SAL 2. In: Alur, R., Peled, D.A. (eds.) CAV 2004. LNCS, vol. 3114, pp. 496–500. Springer, Heidelberg (2004)
50. Platzer, A., Quesel, J.-D.: KeYmaera: a hybrid theorem prover for hybrid systems (system description). In: Armando, A., Baumgartner, P., Dowek, G. (eds.) IJCAR 2008. LNCS (LNAI), vol. 5195, pp. 171–178. Springer, Heidelberg (2008)
51. Behrmann, G., David, A., Larsen, K., Hakansson, J., Petterson, P., Yi, W., Hendriks, M.: Uppaal 4.0. In: Third International Conference on Quantitative Evaluation of Systems. QEST 2006, pp. 125–126. IEEE (2006)

The Hanoi Omega-Automata Format

Tomáš Babiak[1], František Blahoudek[1], Alexandre Duret-Lutz[2],
Joachim Klein[3]([✉]), Jan Křetínský[5], David Müller[3], David Parker[4],
and Jan Strejček[1]

[1] Faculty of Informatics, Masaryk University, Brno, Czech Republic
[2] LRDE, EPITA, Le Kremlin-Bicêtre, France
[3] Technische Universität Dresden, Dresden, Germany
klein@tcs.inf.tu-dresden.de
[4] University of Birmingham, Birmingham, UK
[5] IST Austria, Klosterneuburg, Austria

Abstract. We propose a flexible exchange format for ω-automata, as typically used in formal verification, and implement support for it in a range of established tools. Our aim is to simplify the interaction of tools, helping the research community to build upon other people's work. A key feature of the format is the use of very generic acceptance conditions, specified by Boolean combinations of acceptance primitives, rather than being limited to common cases such as Büchi, Streett, or Rabin. Such flexibility in the choice of acceptance conditions can be exploited in applications, for example in probabilistic model checking, and furthermore encourages the development of acceptance-agnostic tools for automata manipulations. The format allows acceptance conditions that are either state-based or transition-based, and also supports alternating automata.

1 Introduction

Finite automata over infinite words, ω-automata, play a crucial role in formal verification. For instance, they are a key component in the automata-theoretic approach to LTL model checking [21], where the property in question is encoded as an ω-automaton. There is a long history of research and ongoing tool development, trying to produce more compact automata in theory and in practice.

T. Babiak, F. Blahoudek, and J. Strejček have been supported by The Czech Science Foundation, grant GBP202/12/G061. J. Klein and D. Müller have been supported by the DFG through the collaborative research centre HAEC (SFB 912), the Excellence Initiative by the German Federal and State Governments (cluster of excellence cfAED and Institutional Strategy), the Graduiertenkolleg QuantLA (1763), and the DFG/NWO-project ROCKS, and the EU-FP-7 grant MEALS (295261). J. Křetínský has been supported in part by the European Research Council (ERC) under grant 267989 (QUAREM), by the Austrian Science Fund (FWF) under grants S11402-N23 (RiSE) and Z211-N23 (Wittgenstein Award), and by the People Programme (Marie Curie Actions) of the European Union's Seventh Framework Programme (FP7/2007–2013) under REA grant agreement No 291734.

© Springer International Publishing Switzerland 2015
D. Kroening and C.S. Păsăreanu (Eds.): CAV 2015, Part I, LNCS 9206, pp. 479–486, 2015.
DOI: 10.1007/978-3-319-21690-4_31

Formats to represent ω-automata have mostly been defined in an ad-hoc manner, tailored to their particular tools, setting and scope, and tend to be restricted to a few specific acceptance conditions. For classical Büchi automata, tools often use Spin's never claims [8] (see Fig. 1(c)), or LBT's format [17] (see Fig. 1(b)), which can also represent generalized Büchi automata and which was extended with transition-based acceptance by LBTT [19]. For Rabin and Streett automata, the format of ltl2dstar [10] can be used, provided those automata are complete, deterministic, and use state-based acceptance.

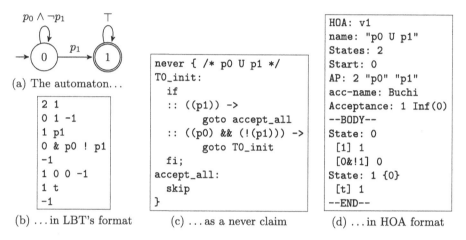

(a) The automaton...

(b) ...in LBT's format   (c) ...as a never claim   (d) ...in HOA format

Fig. 1. A Büchi automaton for the LTL formula $p_0 U p_1$ encoded in three formats.

The one format that covers most common acceptance conditions (Büchi, generalized Büchi, co-Büchi, Rabin, Streett, etc.) and automata structures (deterministic, non-deterministic, and alternating) is the XML-based Goal File Format (GFF) used internally by the Goal tool [20]. It uses specific encodings for the different acceptance conditions. For instance, there is a special notation to define the sets in each acceptance pair of Rabin conditions. This necessitates changes to the format and its parsers when introducing new acceptance conditions and makes acceptance-agnostic manipulations difficult.

Based on our experience as implementers of tools producing, consuming, and manipulating ω-automata, we have set out to define a common, flexible, and extensible format for representing ω-automata in a uniform way. The result is the *Hanoi Omega-Automata (HOA)* format.[1] A crucial feature is the introduction of a *generic* way to specify the acceptance condition as an arbitrary Boolean formula over the acceptance primitives "infinitely often" and "finitely often", covering the common acceptance conditions discussed so far and more.

Firstly, this approach facilitates the exchange and usage of new acceptance conditions, which can provide important gains in efficiency. For instance, the generalized Rabin condition [13] has led to an orders-of-magnitude speed-up of probabilistic LTL model checking [3,12]. Secondly, it offers flexibility in the

---

[1] The discussion about this format started during ATVA'13 in Hanoi, hence the name.

choice of acceptance conditions, which can again be quite beneficial in practice, such as for deterministic Streett and Rabin automata [9], where there is an exponential worst-case size difference in both directions [16].

Thirdly, arbitrary Boolean combinations of acceptance conditions can be exploited. For example, building a deterministic automaton for an LTL formula using a product of the automata constructed for its subformulas can be beneficial in practice [9]. But this normally only works when the structure of the formula and acceptance condition are aligned, e.g., conjunctive formulas and a conjunctive acceptance condition such as Streett. With generic acceptance, it becomes possible to compositionally construct automata using disjunction, conjunction, and negation of deterministic automata with unrelated acceptance conditions. For some verification problems, such as probabilistic model checking of LTL in Markov chains, this generic acceptance condition can be used directly for verification.

The HOA format offers flexibility in other respects too. It supports various structural variants of ω-automata such as labels on states or transitions and state-based or transition-based acceptance, and can describe deterministic, non-deterministic, and alternating automata. Despite its generality, the format also contains features that allow a concise and readable representation in special circumstances, such as when dealing with deterministic complete automata, where the number of transitions per state is constant.

We have implemented support for the HOA format in various established tools, as detailed in Sect. 3, and are already seeing several of the intended benefits. Interaction between existing tools has become significantly easier: they are no longer restricted by the particular format of automata used, but only by the algorithms implemented to work with them. This shortens development time and can bring performance gains, as described above. It also facilitates research into new types of automata; for instance the intermediate co-Büchi alternating automata built by ltl3ba can now be exported to an easily-readable format. More generally, we hope to stimulate the development of acceptance-agnostic tools for the automata construction pipeline, e.g., for doing structural transformations such as switching between state- and transition-based acceptance or for reduction algorithms that do not rely on a particular acceptance condition.

2   Main Features of the HOA Format

The HOA format currently supports the following:

- deterministic, non-deterministic, and alternating ω-automata,
- both state-labelled and transition-labelled ω-automata,
- generic acceptance conditions, specified in a uniform and extensible way,
- both state-based and transition-based acceptance.

The format was also designed to:

- be succinct and human-readable,
- be extensible, by allowing additional information to be stored in the headers,
- support streaming, for processing automata in batches.

The full specification of the format and some examples can be found at http://adl.github.io/hoaf/. Below, we discuss a few of the most important features.

As seen in Fig. 1(d), an automaton is defined in two parts: a header that specifies the characteristics of the automaton, and a body that gives the transition structure, the labels of states or transitions (in square brackets), and the acceptance sets (in curly brackets). Numbers in the body outside any brackets always refer to states. Labels (in square brackets) are Boolean formulas over integers that index the atomic propositions listed in the AP: header. Using indices instead of atomic propositions makes it easy to rename an atomic proposition, and allows using arbitrarily long names without bloating the resulting file.

Header lines that start with a capital letter are supposed to affect the semantics of the automaton, while header lines that start with a lower-case letter are only informative. The HOA specification reserves a few header names, but additional headers can be added as needed. This gives an easy and robust way for automata producers to extend the format and emit additional information about the automaton: Consumers that encounter a capitalized header they do not understand should report an error, but can safely ignore a lower-case one.

The Acceptance line specifies the acceptance condition formally. This line has the form "Acceptance: n acc", where n gives the number of acceptance sets used, subsequently named $0, \ldots, n - 1$, and acc is a formula built according to the following grammar.

$$acc ::= \text{f} \mid \text{t} \mid \text{Inf}(s) \mid \text{Inf}(!s) \mid \text{Fin}(s) \mid \text{Fin}(!s) \mid acc\&acc \mid acc\,|\,acc \mid (acc)$$

Above, s denotes one of the acceptance sets. Membership in these sets for states and transitions is defined in the body of the automaton. A run satisfies an acceptance primitive $\text{Inf}(s)$ or $\text{Fin}(s)$ iff it visits the acceptance set s infinitely often or at most finitely often, respectively. The same notations with $!s$ refer to the complement of the set s.[2] A run is accepting if it satisfies the acceptance condition acc. We do not need a negation operator, as negation can be pushed into the acceptance primitives, e.g., $\neg\text{Inf}(s)$ is equivalent to $\text{Fin}(s)$.

In the case of Fig. 1(d), there is only one acceptance set, and accepting runs should visit this acceptance set infinitely often. In the body of the automaton, state 1 is marked with $\{0\}$, meaning that it belongs to the set 0.

Rabin acceptance with 3 pairs of acceptance sets could be defined as follows:

```
Acceptance: 6 (Fin(0)&Inf(1))|(Fin(2)&Inf(3))|(Fin(4)&Inf(5))
```

Here, a run is accepting if it visits set 0 finitely and set 1 infinitely often, or set 2 finitely and set 3 infinitely often, or analogously for sets 4 and 5.

---

[2] Readers familiar with LTL can interpret $\text{Inf}(s)$, $\text{Fin}(s)$, $\text{Inf}(!s)$, $\text{Fin}(!s)$ as meaning $\text{GF}p_s$, $\text{FG}\neg p_s$, $\text{GF}\neg p_s$, $\text{FG}p_s$, where p_s is the property "belongs to set s".

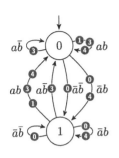

```
HOA: v1                          State: 0
name: "G(Fa && XFb)"             [ 0 & !1] 0 {3}
States: 2                        [ 0 &  1] 0 {1 3 4}
Start: 0                         [!0 & !1] 1 {0}
acc-name:                        [!0 &  1] 1 {0 4}
  generalized-Rabin 2 1 2        State: 1
Acceptance:                      [ 0 & !1] 0 {3}
  5 (Fin(0)&Inf(1))              [ 0 &  1] 0 {1 3 4}
   | (Fin(2)&Inf(3)&Inf(4))      [!0 & !1] 1 {0}
AP: 2 "a" "b"                    [!0 &  1] 1 {0 4}
--BODY--                         --END--
```

(a) The automaton...   (b) ... and its HOA representation.

Fig. 2. A (non-simplified) transition-based generalized deterministic Rabin automaton for the LTL formula G(Fa ∧ XFb).

Figure 2 shows an example of a transition-based generalized deterministic Rabin automaton (such as produced internally by ltl3dra before optimizations). Here, acceptance sets are expressed in terms of transitions. As a final example, Fig. 3 shows an alternating transition-based co-Büchi automaton, such as those studied in [18]. Alternation is supported by allowing a transition to have multiple destinations. Runs over alternating automata are trees, and in this example a run is accepting iff the only transition in the acceptance set 0 is visited finitely often in all the branches, as specified by the Acceptance: line. This example also demonstrates that states may be named.

In general, most of the tools that are the ultimate consumers of HOA automata, such as model checkers, will employ algorithms restricted to particular acceptance conditions. There are often multiple ways to syntactically structure the acceptance condition. For example, the Rabin acceptance can be expressed with the sets in the pairs swapped or complemented, as in [14]. Therefore, we specify canonical expression and acceptance set indices for the common acceptance conditions, and an optional acc-name: header line which helps tools to detect acceptance conditions they support. However, as discussed in the introduction, some verification procedures can make direct use of generic acceptance conditions.

3   Application Support

We have implemented support for HOA in a range of tools, with the current status available at http://adl.github.io/hoaf/support.html, including links to releases of each tool and a Live CD ISO for easy investigation of them all.

HOA Generation. Generating automata in the HOA format is now supported by several tools: ltl2dstar [10], which translates LTL to deterministic Rabin or Street automata; ltl3ba [1], which generates Büchi automata,

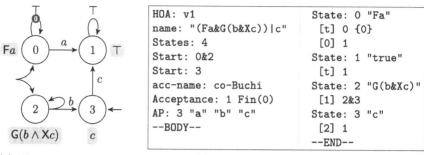

(a) The automaton...   (b) ...and its HOA representation.

Fig. 3. Alternating transition-based co-Büchi automaton for $(Fa \wedge G(b \wedge Xc)) \vee c$.

transition-based generalized Büchi automata, and very weak alternating co-Büchi automata; ltl3dra [2], which converts a fragment of LTL to deterministic Rabin automata, transition-based generalized deterministic Rabin automata, and very weak alternating co-Büchi automata; and Rabinizer3 [12], which translates LTL into state- and transition-based variants of deterministic Rabin automata and generalized deterministic Rabin automata.

Furthermore, Spot [6] offers many tools for generating automata in the HOA format: ltl2tgba [5] can translate LTL/PSL into Büchi automata, transition-based generalized Büchi automata or monitors; randaut generates random Büchi automata, transition-based generalized Büchi automata or monitors; and finally dstar2tgba converts deterministic automata in the dstar format into Büchi automata, transition-based generalized Büchi automata or monitors. The Spot tool autfilt filters, transforms, and converts formats for Büchi automata, generalized Büchi automata, and monitors and supports reading and writing HOA, with ltldo wrapping other LTL/PSL-to-automata translators to convert their input and output. This command and the previous one can be used to produce HOA output from existing tools that only output never claims or the LBT format.

HOA Parsing. There are two parsers for the HOA format. The first, in C++, is included in Spot and is able to read a stream of automata whose format can be either HOA, LBT or never claim. This parser powers the tools autfilt and ltldo (presented above), and also ltlcross [4] (a verifier for LTL translators). At the time of writing, Spot does not yet support alternation.

The second is the jhoafparser library [11], which provides a Java-based parser. This provides a convenient interface for applications to consume the different elements of the HOA format, taking care of basic sanity checks. The library is accompanied by a command-line tool that checks the well-formedness of an automaton in the HOA format and performs basic manipulations.

HOA Import. We have extended the probabilistic model checker PRISM [15] to interface with external tools for the conversion from LTL to deterministic automata. This is done using the HOA format and jhoafparser. In parallel, we have expanded PRISM's ω-automata verification procedures: Markov chains can now be model checked against generic acceptance conditions, giving producers of deterministic automata full flexibility in terms of acceptance conditions. Markov decision processes can be checked against both generalized or standard Rabin acceptance conditions. As a result, we have successfully interfaced PRISM with Rabinizer3, ltl2dstar, and ltl3dra.

4 Conclusion

We have presented a new format for ω-automata that supports generic acceptance conditions, and implemented it in several tools. Besides smoothing the interaction between tools, this representation of acceptance conditions allows a significant flexibility and performance increase, which has already been harnessed in PRISM, and encourages tool developers to expand the range of supported acceptance conditions. The HOA format has been developed openly on GitHub, and an issue tracker keeps a public archive of our discussion and decisions. We encourage other tool authors to report issues and suggest improvements.

References

1. Babiak, T., Křetínský, M., Řehák, V., Strejček, J.: LTL to Büchi automata translation: fast and more deterministic. In: Flanagan, C., König, B. (eds.) TACAS 2012. LNCS, vol. 7214, pp. 95–109. Springer, Heidelberg (2012)
2. Babiak, T., Blahoudek, F., Křetínský, M., Strejček, J.: Effective translation of LTL to deterministic Rabin automata: beyond the (F,G)-fragment. In: Van Hung, D., Ogawa, M. (eds.) ATVA 2013. LNCS, vol. 8172, pp. 24–39. Springer, Heidelberg (2013)
3. Chatterjee, K., Gaiser, A., Křetínský, J.: Automata with generalized Rabin pairs for probabilistic model checking and LTL synthesis. In: Sharygina, N., Veith, H. (eds.) CAV 2013. LNCS, vol. 8044, pp. 559–575. Springer, Heidelberg (2013)
4. Duret-Lutz, A.: Manipulating LTL formulas using Spot 1.0. In: Van Hung, D., Ogawa, M. (eds.) ATVA 2013. LNCS, vol. 8172, pp. 442–445. Springer, Heidelberg (2013)
5. Duret-Lutz, A.: LTL translation improvements in Spot 1.0. Int. J. Crit. Comput. Based Syst. 5(1/2), 31–54 (2014)
6. Duret-Lutz, A., Poitrenaud, D.: SPOT: an extensible model checking library using transition-based generalized Büchi automata. In: MASCOTS 2004, pp. 76–83. IEEE Computer Society Press (2004)
7. Gerth, R., Peled, D., Vardi, M.Y., Wolper, P.: Simple on-the-fly automatic verification of linear temporal logic. In: PSTV 1995, pp. 3–18. Chapman and Hall (1996)
8. Holzmann, G.J.: The Spin Model Checker: Primer and Reference Manual. Addison-Wesley, Reading (2003)
9. Klein, J., Baier, C.: Experiments with deterministic ω-automata for formulas of linear temporal logic. Theor. Comput. Sci. 363(2), 182–195 (2006)
10. Klein, J., Baier, C.: On-the-fly stuttering in the construction of deterministic ω-automata. In: Holub, J., Žďárek, J. (eds.) CIAA 2007. LNCS, vol. 4783, pp. 51–61. Springer, Heidelberg (2007)

11. Klein, J., Müller, D.: The jhoafparser library (2015). http://automata.tools/hoa/jhoafparser/
12. Komárková, Z., Křetínský, J.: Rabinizer 3: Safraless translation of LTL to small deterministic automata. In: Cassez, F., Raskin, J.-F. (eds.) ATVA 2014. LNCS, vol. 8837, pp. 235–241. Springer, Heidelberg (2014)
13. Křetínský, J., Esparza, J.: Deterministic automata for the (F,G)-fragment of LTL. In: Madhusudan, P., Seshia, S.A. (eds.) CAV 2012. LNCS, vol. 7358, pp. 7–22. Springer, Heidelberg (2012)
14. Krishnan, S.C., Puri, A., Brayton, R.K.: Deterministic ω-automata vis-a-vis deterministic Büchi automata. In: Du, D.-Z., Zhang, X.-S. (eds.) ISAAC 1994. LNCS, vol. 834, pp. 378–386. Springer, Heidelberg (1994)
15. Kwiatkowska, M., Norman, G., Parker, D.: PRISM 4.0: verification of probabilistic real-time systems. In: Gopalakrishnan, G., Qadeer, S. (eds.) CAV 2011. LNCS, vol. 6806, pp. 585–591. Springer, Heidelberg (2011)
16. Löding, C.: Optimal bounds for transformations of ω-automata. In: Pandu Rangan, C., Raman, V., Sarukkai, S. (eds.) FST TCS 1999. LNCS, vol. 1738, pp. 97–109. Springer, Heidelberg (1999)
17. Rönkkö, M.: LBT: LTL to Büchi conversion. http://www.tcs.hut.fi/Software/maria/tools/lbt/ (1999). Implements [7]
18. Tauriainen, H.: Automata and linear temporal logic: translation with transition-based acceptance. Ph.D thesis, Helsinki University of Technology, Espoo, Finland, Sept 2006
19. Tauriainen, H., Heljanko, K.: Testing LTL formula translation into Büchi automata. Int. J. Softw. Tools Technol. Transf. 4(1), 57–70 (2002)
20. Tsai, M.-H., Tsay, Y.-K., Hwang, Y.-S.: GOAL for games, omega-automata, and logics. In: Sharygina, N., Veith, H. (eds.) CAV 2013. LNCS, vol. 8044, pp. 883–889. Springer, Heidelberg (2013)
21. Vardi, M.Y.: Automata-theoretic model checking revisited. In: Cook, B., Podelski, A. (eds.) VMCAI 2007. LNCS, vol. 4349, pp. 137–150. Springer, Heidelberg (2007)

The Open-Source LearnLib
A Framework for Active Automata Learning

Malte Isberner[1][(✉)], Falk Howar[2], and Bernhard Steffen[1]

[1] TU Dortmund University, 44221 Dortmund, Germany
{malte.isberner,steffen}@cs.tu-dortmund.de
[2] IPSSE/TU Clausthal, 38678
Clausthal-Zellerfeld, Germany
falk.howar@tu-clausthal.de

Abstract. In this paper, we present *LearnLib*, a library for active automata learning. The current, open-source version of *LearnLib* was completely rewritten from scratch, incorporating the lessons learned from the decade-spanning development process of the previous versions of *LearnLib*. Like its immediate predecessor, the open-source *LearnLib* is written in Java to enable a high degree of flexibility and extensibility, while at the same time providing a performance that allows for large-scale applications. Additionally, *LearnLib* provides facilities for visualizing the progress of learning algorithms in detail, thus complementing its applicability in research and industrial contexts with an educational aspect.

1 Introduction

Active automata learning, from its early beginnings almost thirty years ago [6], inspired a number of applications in quite a number of fields (see [19] for a survey). However, it took almost a decade for the software verification and testing community to recognize its value of being able to provide models of black-box systems for the plethora of model-based tools and techniques. More precisely, it was not until the seminal works of Peled *et al.* [36], employing automata learning to model check black-box systems, and Steffen *et al.* [18], who used it to automatically generate test cases for legacy computer-telephony integrated systems, that this use case of automata learning was discovered.

Since then, however, active automata learning has enjoyed quite a success story, having been used as a valuable tool in areas as diverse as automated GUI testing [13], fighting bot-nets [12], or typestate analysis [5,41]. Most of these works, however, used their custom, one-off implementation of the well-known L* learning algorithm [6], and hence invested relatively little effort for optimizations, or using a more sophisticated (but harder to implement and lesser-known) algorithm altogether.[1]

---

[1] An elaborate discussion on the theoretical aspects of active automata learning, as well as on the challenges that arise in practice, are outside the scope of this paper. We refer the interested reader to [39] for an introduction focusing on these matters.

© Springer International Publishing Switzerland 2015
D. Kroening and C.S. Păsăreanu (Eds.): CAV 2015, Part I, LNCS 9206, pp. 487–495, 2015.
DOI: 10.1007/978-3-319-21690-4_32

488   M. Isberner et al.

We started developing the *LearnLib*[2] library to provide researchers and prac-
titioners with a reusable set of components to facilitate and promote the use of
active automata learning, and to enable access to cutting-edge automata learning technology. From the beginnings of the development of *LearnLib*, started in
2003, until now, more than a decade has passed. In these years, many lessons
were learned on what makes for a usable, efficient and practically feasible product
that fulfills this goal (cf. [25,35,37]).

These lessons form the basis of the new *LearnLib* presented in this paper.
The new *LearnLib* is not just an overhaul of the prior version, but completely
re-written from scratch. It provides a higher level of abstraction and increased
flexibility, while simultaneously being the fastest version of *LearnLib* to date
(cf. Sect. 4). As a service to the community and to encourage contributions by
and collaborations with other research groups, we decided to make *LearnLib*
available under an open-source license (the *Apache License, version 2.0*[3]). In the
remainder of this paper we highlight two aspects that we address with *LearnLib*.

Advanced Features. This is what we consider the strongest case for preferring
a comprehensive automata learning framework such as *LearnLib* over a custom
implementation. While implementing the original version of L* is not a challenging task, the situation is different for more refined active learning algorithms,
such as Rivest & Schapire's [38], Kearns & Vazirani's [30] or even the very recent
TTT algorithm [28]. While we found these algorithms to consistently outperform L*, the latter remains the most widely used. Also, several other advanced
optimizations such as query parallelization or efficient query caches are typically neglected. Through *LearnLib*'s modular design, changing filters, algorithm
parameters or even the whole algorithm is a matter of a few lines of code, yielding valuable insights on how different algorithms perform on certain input data.
Many of these features rely on *AutomataLib*, the standalone finite-state machine
library that was developed for *LearnLib*, which provides a rich toolbox of data
structures and algorithms for finite-state machines. The design of *AutomataLib*
is presented in Sect. 2, while Sect. 3 provides a more comprehensive overview of
LearnLib's feature set.

Performance. The implementation of a learning algorithm comes with many
performance pitfalls. Even though in most cases the time taken by the actual
learning algorithm is an uncritical aspect (compared to the time spent in executing queries, which may involve, e.g., network communication), it should be kept
as low as reasonably possible. Besides, an efficient management of data structures is necessary to enable learning of large-scale systems without running into
out-of-memory conditions or experiencing huge performance slumps. In *Learn-
Lib*, considerable effort was spent on efficient implementations while providing
a conveniently high level of abstraction. This will be detailed in Sect. 4.

Finally, we conclude the paper by briefly discussing envisioned future work
in Sect. 5.

---

[2] http://www.learnlib.de.
[3] https://www.apache.org/licenses/LICENSE-2.0.

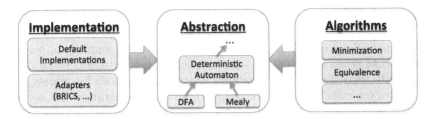

Fig. 1. Architecture of *AutomataLib*

2 AutomataLib

One of the main architectural changes of the open-source *LearnLib* is that it uses a dedicated, stand-alone library for representing and manipulating automata, called *AutomataLib*.[4] While *AutomataLib* is formally independent of *LearnLib*, its development process is closely intertwined with the one of *LearnLib*. For this reason, *AutomataLib* mainly focuses on deterministic automata, even though selected classes of non-deterministic automata are supported as well (e.g., NFAs).

AutomataLib is divided into an *abstraction layer*, automata *implementations*, and *algorithms* (cf. Fig. 1). The abstraction layer comprises a set of *Java* interfaces to represent various types of automata and graphs, organized in a complex, fine-grained type hierarchy. Furthermore, these interfaces were designed in a generic fashion, to integrate existing, third-party automata implementations into *AutomataLib*'s interface landscape with as little effort and run-time overhead as possible. For instance, a proof-of-concept adapter for the BRICS automaton library[5] could be realized in as little as 20 lines of *Java* code.

Adapters like for the BRICS library form one part of the implementation layer. The other part are generic automaton implementations, e.g., for DFAs or Mealy machines, that provide good defaults for general setups, and are also used by most algorithms in *LearnLib* to store hypotheses.

Sample algorithms shipped with *AutomataLib* include minimization, equivalence testing, or visualization (via *GraphVIZ*'s[6] dot tool). The set of functionalities will be continuously extended, with a strong focus on functionality either directly required in *LearnLib*, or desirable in a typical automata learning application context.

An important aspect is that the algorithms operate solely on the abstraction layer, meaning that they are implementation agnostic: they can be used with a (wrapped) BRICS automaton as well as with other automaton implementations. Furthermore, the generic design enables a high degree of code reuse: the minimization (or equivalence checking) algorithm can be used for both DFA and Mealy machines, as it is designed to only require a *deterministic automaton*, instead of a concrete machine type (or even implementation).

---

[4] http://www.automatalib.net/.
[5] http://www.brics.dk/automaton/.
[6] http://www.graphviz.org/.

3   LearnLib

LearnLib provides a set of components to apply automata learning in practical settings, or to develop or analyze automata learning algorithms. These can be grouped into three main classes: learning algorithms, methods for finding counterexamples (so-called *Equivalence Queries*), and infrastructure components.

Learning Algorithms. *LearnLib* features a rich set of learning algorithms, covering the majority of algorithms which have been published (and many beyond that). Care was taken to develop the algorithms in a modular and parameterizable fashion, which allows us to use a single "base" algorithm to realize several algorithms described in the literature, e.g., by merely exchanging the involved counterexample analysis strategy. Perhaps the best example for this is the L^* algorithm [6], which can be configured to pose as **Maler & Pnueli's** [31], **Rivest & Schapire's** [38], or **Shahbaz's** [26] algorithm, **Suffix1by1** [26], or variants thereof. Other base algorithms available in *LearnLib* are the **Observation Pack** [21] algorithm, **Kearns & Vazirani's** [30] algorithm, the **DHC** [34] algorithm, and the **TTT** [28] algorithm. These, too, can be adapted in the way they handle counterexamples, e.g., by linear search, binary search (à la Rivest & Schapire), or exponential search [29]. With the exception of **DHC**, all these algorithms are available in both DFA and Mealy versions. Furthermore, *LearnLib* features the NL^* algorithm for learning NFAs [8].

Equivalence Tests and Finding Counterexamples. Once a learning algorithm converges to a stable hypothesis, a *counterexample* is needed to ensure further progress. In the context of active learning, the process of searching for a counterexample is also referred to as an *equivalence query.* "Perfect" equivalence queries are possible only when a model of the target system is available. In this case, *LearnLib* uses Hopcroft and Karp's near-linear equivalence checking algorithm [4,20] available through *AutomataLib.* In black-box scenarios, equivalence queries can be approximated using conformance tests. *AutomataLib* provides implementations of the W-method [14] and the Wp-method [16], two of the few conformance tests that can find missing states. Often, the cheapest and fastest way of approximating equivalence queries is searching for counterexamples directly: *LearnLib* implements a random walk (only for Mealy machines), randomized generation of tests, and exhaustive generation of test inputs (up to a certain depth).

Infrastructure. The third class of components that come with *LearnLib* provide useful infrastructure functionality such as a logging facility, an import/export mechanism to store and load hypotheses, or utilities for gathering statistics. An important component for many practical applications are (optimizing) *filters,* which pre-process the queries posed by the learning algorithm. A universally useful example of such a filter is a *cache filter* [32], eliminating duplicate queries that most algorithms pose. Other examples include a parallelization component that distributes queries across multiple workers [22], a mechanism for reusing system states to reduce the number of resets [7], and for prefix-closed systems [32].

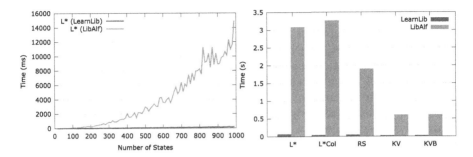

Fig. 2. Performance comparison between the new *LearnLib* and *libalf*. Left: run-time of the classic L* algorithm on a series of randomly generated automata with state counts between 10 and 1000. Right: run-time of five comparable algorithms from *LearnLib* and *libalf* on a DFA with 500 states.

For a learning algorithm to work in practice, some interface to the system under learning (SUL) needs to be available. While this is generally specific to the SUL itself, *LearnLib* provides *SUL adapters* for typical cases, e.g., *Java* classes, web-services, or processes that are interfaced with via standard I/O.

4   Evaluation

We are aware of two other open-source automata learning libraries that provide implementations of textbook algorithms, complemented by own developments:

libalf[7]. The *Automata Learning Framework* [9], was developed primarily at the RWTH Aachen. It is available under LGPLv3 and written in C++. Its active development seems to have ceased; the last version was released in April 2011.

AIDE[8]. The *Automata-Identification Engine*, under active development, is available under the open-source license LGPLv2.1 and written in C#.

The ambitions behind *LearnLib* go further: It is specifically designed to easily compose new custom learning algorithms on the basis of components for counterexample analysis, approximations of equivalence queries, as well as connectors to real life systems. Moreover, *LearnLib* provides a variety of underlying data structures, and various means for visualizing the algorithm and its statistics. This does not only facilitate the construction of highly performant custom solutions, but also provides a deeper understanding of the algorithms' characteristics. The latter has been essential, e.g., for designing the TTT algorithm [28], which almost uniformly outperforms all the previous algorithms.

Performance. As we have mentioned earlier, the open-source *LearnLib* is the fastest version of *LearnLib* to date, and moreover the fastest automata learning

---

[7] http://libalf.informatik.rwth-aachen.de/.
[8] http://aide.codeplex.com/.

implementation that we are aware of. We have conducted a preliminary performance evaluation, comparing the new *LearnLib* to *libalf* and the old, closed-source version of *LearnLib* (which we will refer to as *JLearn* in order to avoid confusion). A visualization of some of the results comparing *LearnLib* and *libalf* is shown in Fig. 2. It can be clearly seen that in the considered setting, *Learn-Lib* is more than an order of magnitude faster than *libalf* (even though the former is implemented in Java while the latter is implemented in C++). More importantly, the gap grows with the size of the system to be learned. In our experiments, the open-source *LearnLib* also outperformed *JLearn* on a similar scale. More detailed performance data can be found on the *LearnLib* website.[9]

Applications. The performance data demonstrates that *LearnLib* provides a robust basis for fast and scalable active automata learning solutions. Consequently, in its ten years of continued development, *LearnLib* has been used in a number of research and industry projects, of which we briefly present some of the more recent ones. A more complete list can be found on the *LearnLib* homepage. *LearnLib* has been used to infer models of smart card readers [11] and of bank cards [3]. The models were used to verify security properties of these systems. In [2,15], models of communication protocols are inferred using *LearnLib*. The models are used to verify the conformance of protocol implementations to the corresponding specifications. At TU Dortmund, *LearnLib* has been used in an industry project [40] to generate models of a web application. The models were used to test regressions in the user interface and in the business processes of this application. The authors of [33] propose a method for generating checking circuits for functions implemented in FPGAs. The method uses models of the functions that are inferred with *LearnLib*. *LearnLib* is also used in other tools: PSYCO [17,23] is a tool for generating precise interfaces of software components developed at CMU and NASA Ames. The tool combines concolic execution and active automata learning (i.e., *LearnLib*). Tomte, developed at the Radboud University of Nijmegen [1] leverages regular inference algorithms provided by *LearnLib* to infer richer classes of models by simultaneously inferring sophisticated abstractions (or "mappers").

5   Conclusion

In this paper we have presented *LearnLib*, a versatile open-source library of active automata learning algorithms. *LearnLib* is unique in its modular design, which has furthered the development of new learning algorithms (e.g., the TTT algorithm [28]) and tools (e.g., Tomte [1] and PSYCO [17,23]).

While in many aspects the open-source *LearnLib* by far surpasses the capabilities of the previous version, there are two major features which have yet to be ported. The first is *LearnLib Studio* (cf. [35]), a graphical user interface for *LearnLib*, and the second is an extension for learning *Register Automata*. An extension for learning Register Automata with the theory of equality only was

---

[9] http://learnlib.de/features/performance.

available upon request for the old *LearnLib* in binary form [24,27]. We are currently working on a generalized approach [10], which will be included in the open-source release.

References

1. Aarts, F., Heidarian, F., Kuppens, H., Olsen, P., Vaandrager, F.: Automata learning through counterexample guided abstraction refinement. In: Giannakopoulou, D., Méry, D. (eds.) FM 2012. LNCS, vol. 7436, pp. 10–27. Springer, Heidelberg (2012)
2. Aarts, F., Jonsson, B., Uijen, J., Vaandrager, F.W.: Generating models of infinite-state communication protocols using regular inference with abstraction. Form. Meth. Syst. Des. **46**(1), 1–41 (2015)
3. Aarts, F., De Ruiter, J., Poll, E.: Formal models of bank cards for free. In: 2013 IEEE Sixth International Conference on Software Testing, Verification and Validation, Workshops Proceedings, pp. 461–468, Luxembourg, 18–22 Mar 2013
4. Almeida, M., Moreira, N., Reis, R.: Testing the equivalence of regular languages. In: Proceedings Eleventh International Workshop on Descriptional Complexity of Formal Systems, DCFS 2009, pp. 47–57, Magdeburg, Germany, 6–9 Jul 2009. http://dx.doi.org/10.4204/EPTCS.3.4
5. Alur, R., Cerný, P., Madhusudan, P., Nam, W.: Synthesis of interface specifications for java classes. In: Palsberg, J., Abadi, M. (eds.) Proceedings of the 32nd ACM SIGPLAN-SIGACT Symposium on Principles of Programming Languages, POPL 2005, pp. 98–109. ACM, Long Beach, California, USA, 12–14 Jan 2005. http://doi.acm.org/10.1145/1040305.1040314
6. Angluin, D.: Learning regular sets from queries and counterexamples. Inf. Comput. **75**(2), 87–106 (1987)
7. Bauer, O., Neubauer, J., Steffen, B., Howar, F.: Reusing system states by active learning algorithms. In: Moschitti, A., Scandariato, R. (eds.) EternalS 2011. CCIS, vol. 255, pp. 61–78. Springer, Heidelberg (2012)
8. Bollig, B., Habermehl, P., Kern, C., Leucker, M.: Angluin-style learning of NFA. In: Proceedings IJCAI 2009, pp. 1004–1009. IJCAI 2009, San Francisco, CA, USA (2009)
9. Bollig, B., Katoen, J.-P., Kern, C., Leucker, M., Neider, D., Piegdon, D.R.: libalf: The automata learning framework. In: Touili, T., Cook, B., Jackson, P. (eds.) CAV 2010. LNCS, vol. 6174, pp. 360–364. Springer, Heidelberg (2010)
10. Cassel, S., Howar, F., Jonsson, B., Steffen, B.: Learning extended finite state machines. In: Giannakopoulou, D., Salaün, G. (eds.) SEFM 2014. LNCS, vol. 8702, pp. 250–264. Springer, Heidelberg (2014)
11. Chalupar, G., Peherstorfer, S., Poll, E., De Ruiter, J.: Automated reverse engineering using lego. In: 8th USENIX Workshop on Offensive Technologies, WOOT 2014, San Diego, CA, USA, 19 Aug 2014
12. Cho, C.Y., Babić, D., Shin, R., Song, D.: Inference and analysis of formal models of botnet command and control protocols. In: Proceedings CCS 2010, pp. 426–440, ACM, Chicago, Illinois, USA (2010)
13. Choi, W., Necula, G., Sen, K.: Guided gui testing of android apps with minimal restart and approximate learning. In: Proceedings of the 2013 ACM SIGPLAN International Conference on Object Oriented Programming Systems Languages & Applications, pp. 623–640. OOPSLA 2013, ACM, New York, NY, USA (2013). http://doi.acm.org/10.1145/2509136.2509552

14. Chow, T.S.: Testing software design modeled by finite-state machines. IEEE Trans. Softw. Eng. **4**(3), 178–187 (1978)
15. Fiterău-Broştean, P., Janssen, R., Vaandrager, F.: Learning fragments of the TCP network protocol. In: Lang, F., Flammini, F. (eds.) FMICS 2014. LNCS, vol. 8718, pp. 78–93. Springer, Heidelberg (2014)
16. Fujiwara, S., Von Bochmann, G., Khendek, F., Amalou, M., Ghedamsi, A.: Test selection based on finite state models. IEEE Trans. Softw. Eng. **17**(6), 591–603 (1991)
17. Giannakopoulou, D., Rakamarić, Z., Raman, V.: Symbolic learning of component interfaces. In: Miné, A., Schmidt, D. (eds.) SAS 2012. LNCS, vol. 7460, pp. 248–264. Springer, Heidelberg (2012)
18. Hagerer, A., Hungar, H.: Model generation by moderated regular extrapolation. In: Kutsche, R.-D., Weber, H. (eds.) FASE 2002. LNCS, vol. 2306, p. 80. Springer, Heidelberg (2002)
19. De la Higuera, C.: A bibliographical study of grammatical inference. Pattern Recogn. **38**(9), 1332–1348 (2005). http://dx.doi.org/10.1016/j.patcog.2005.01.003
20. Hopcroft, J., Karp, R.: A linear algorithm for testing equivalence of finite automata. Technical report 0, Deptartment of Computer Science, Cornell U, Dec 1971
21. Howar, F.: Active learning of interface programs. Ph.D. thesis, TU Dortmund University (2012). http://dx.doi.org/2003/29486
22. Howar, F., Bauer, O., Merten, M., Steffen, B., Margaria, T.: The teachers' crowd: the impact of distributed oracles on active automata learning. In: Hähnle, R., Knoop, J., Margaria, T., Schreiner, D., Steffen, B. (eds.) ISoLA 2011 Workshops 2011. CCIS, vol. 336, pp. 232–247. Springer, Heidelberg (2012)
23. Howar, F., Giannakopoulou, D., Rakamarić, Z.: Hybrid learning: interface generation through static, dynamic, and symbolic analysis. In: Proceedings of the International Symposium on Software Testing and Analysis (ISSTA), pp. 268–279, ACM (2013)
24. Howar, F., Steffen, B., Jonsson, B., Cassel, S.: Inferring canonical register automata. In: Kuncak, V., Rybalchenko, A. (eds.) VMCAI 2012. LNCS, vol. 7148, pp. 251–266. Springer, Heidelberg (2012)
25. Hungar, H., Niese, O., Steffen, B.: Domain-specific optimization in automata learning. In: Hunt Jr, W.A., Somenzi, F. (eds.) CAV 2003. LNCS, vol. 2725, pp. 315–327. Springer, Heidelberg (2003)
26. Irfan, M.N., Oriat, C., Groz, R.: Angluin style finite state machine inference with non-optimal counterexamples. In: 1st International Workshop on Model Inference In Testing (2010)
27. Isberner, M., Howar, F., Steffen, B.: Learning register automata: from languages to program structures. Mach. Learn. **96**(1–2), 65–98 (2014). http://dx.doi.org/10.1007/s10994-013-5419-7
28. Isberner, M., Howar, F., Steffen, B.: The TTT algorithm: a redundancy-free approach to active automata learning. In: Bonakdarpour, B., Smolka, S.A. (eds.) RV 2014. LNCS, vol. 8734, pp. 307–322. Springer, Heidelberg (2014)
29. Isberner, M., Steffen, B.: An abstract framework for counterexample analysis in active automata learning. In: Clark, A., Kanazawa, M., Yoshinaka, R. (eds.) Proceedings of the 12th International Conference on Grammatical Inference, ICGI 2014, Kyoto, Japan, 17–19 Sep 2014. JMLR Proceedings, vol. 34, pp. 79–93, http://JMLR.org (2014). http://jmlr.org/proceedings/papers/v34/isberner14a.html
30. Kearns, M.J., Vazirani, U.V.: An Introduction to Computational Learning Theory. MIT Press, Cambridge (1994)

31. Maler, O., Pnueli, A.: On the learnability of infinitary regular sets. Inf. Comput. **118**(2), 316–326 (1995)

32. Margaria, T., Raffelt, H., Steffen, B.: Knowledge-based relevance filtering for efficient system-level test-based model generation. Innov. Syst. Softw. Eng. **1**(2), 147–156 (2005)

33. Matuova, L., Kastil, J., Kotásek, Z.: Automatic construction of on-line checking circuits based on finite automata. In: 17th Euromicro Conference on Digital System Design, DSD 2014, pp. 326–332, Verona, Italy, 27–29 Aug 2014

34. Merten, M., Howar, F., Steffen, B., Margaria, T.: Automata learning with on-the-fly direct hypothesis construction. In: Hähnle, R., Knoop, J., Margaria, T., Schreiner, D., Steffen, B. (eds.) ISoLA 2011 Workshops 2011. CCIS, vol. 336, pp. 248–260. Springer, Heidelberg (2012)

35. Merten, M., Steffen, B., Howar, F., Margaria, T.: Next generation LearnLib. In: Abdulla, P.A., Leino, K.R.M. (eds.) TACAS 2011. LNCS, vol. 6605, pp. 220–223. Springer, Heidelberg (2011)

36. Peled, D., Vardi, M.Y., Yannakakis, M.: Black box checking. In: Wu, J., Chanson, S.T., Gao, Q. (eds.) Proceedings FORTE 1999, pp. 225–240, Kluwer Academic (1999)

37. Raffelt, H., Steffen, B., Berg, T., Margaria, T.: LearnLib: a framework for extrapolating behavioral models. Int. J. Softw. Tools Technol. Transf. **11**(5), 393–407 (2009)

38. Rivest, R.L., Schapire, R.E.: Inference of finite futomata using homing sequences. Inf. Comput. **103**(2), 299–347 (1993)

39. Steffen, B., Howar, F., Merten, M.: Introduction to active automata learning from a practical perspective. In: Bernardo, M., Issarny, V. (eds.) SFM 2011. LNCS, vol. 6659, pp. 256–296. Springer, Heidelberg (2011)

40. Windmüller, S., Neubauer, J., Steffen, B., Howar, F., Bauer, O.: Active continuous quality control. In: CBSE, pp. 111–120 (2013)

41. Xiao, H., Sun, J., Liu, Y., Lin, S., Sun, C.: Tzuyu: learning stateful typestates. In: Denney, E., Bultan, T., Zeller, A. (eds.) 2013 28th IEEE/ACM International Conference on Automated Software Engineering, ASE 2013, pp. 432–442, IEEE, Silicon Valley, CA, USA, 11–15 Nov 2013. http://dx.doi.org/10.1109/ASE.2013. 6693101

Bbs: A Phase-Bounded Model Checker for Asynchronous Programs

Rupak Majumdar and Zilong Wang$^{(\boxtimes)}$

MPI-SWS, Kaiserslautern, Germany
{rupak,zilong}@mpi-sws.org

Abstract. A popular model of asynchronous programming consists of a single-threaded worker process interacting with a task queue. In each step of such a program, the worker takes a task from the queue and executes its code atomically to completion. Executing a task can call "normal" functions as well as post additional asynchronous tasks to the queue. Additionally, tasks can be posted to the queue by the environment.

Bouajjani and Emmi introduced *phase-bounding* analysis on asynchronous programs with unbounded FIFO task queues, which is a systematic exploration of all program behaviors up to a fixed *task phase*. They showed that phase-bounded exploration can be sequentialized: given a set of recursive tasks, a task queue, and a phase bound $L > 0$, one can construct a sequential recursive program whose behaviors capture all states of the original asynchronous program reachable by an execution where only tasks up to phase L are executed. However, there was no empirical evaluation of the method.

We describe our tool Bbs that implements phase-bounding to analyze embedded C programs generated from TinyOS applications, which are widely used in wireless sensor networks. Our empirical results indicate that a variety of subtle safety-violation bugs are manifested within a small phase bound (3 in most of the cases). While our evaluation focuses on TinyOS, our tool is generic, and can be ported to other platforms that employ a similar programming model.

1 Introduction

In many asynchronous applications, a single-threaded worker process interacts with a task queue. In each scheduling step of these programs, the worker takes a task from the queue and executes its code atomically to completion. Executing a task can call "normal" functions as well as post additional asynchronous tasks to the queue. Additionally, tasks can be posted to the queue by the environment. This basic concurrency model has been used in many different settings: in low-level server and networking code, in embedded code and sensor networks [6], in smartphone programming environments such as Android or iOS, and in Javascript. While the concurrency model enables the development of responsive applications, interactions between tasks and the environment can give rise to subtle bugs.

© Springer International Publishing Switzerland 2015
D. Kroening and C.S. Păsăreanu (Eds.): CAV 2015, Part I, LNCS 9206, pp. 496–503, 2015.
DOI: 10.1007/978-3-319-21690-4_33

Bouajjani and Emmi introduced *phase-bounding* [1]: a bounded systematic search for asynchronous programs that explores all program behaviors up to a certain phase of asynchronous tasks. Intuitively, the *phase* of a task is defined as its depth in the task tree: the main task has phase 1, and each task posted asynchronously by a task at phase i has phase $i + 1$. Their main result is a sequentialization procedure for asynchronous programs for a given fixed bound L on the task phase.

In this paper, we describe our tool BBS[1] that implements phase-bounding to analyze C programs generated from TinyOS applications, which are widely used in wireless sensor networks. Our empirical results indicate that a variety of subtle memory-violation bugs are manifested within a small phase bound (3 in most of the cases). From our evaluation, we conclude that phase-bounding is an effective approach in bug finding for asynchronous programs.

While our evaluation focuses on TinyOS, our tool is generic, and can be ported to other platforms that employ a similar programming model. We leave certain extensions, such as handling multiple worker threads, and the experimental evaluation of this technique to other domains, such as smartphone applications or Javascript programs, for future work.

2   Sequentialization Overview

We now give an informal overview of Bouajjani and Emmi's sequentialization procedure. Given an asynchronous program, we first perform the following simple transformation to reduce assertion checking to checking if a global bit is set: (1) we add a global Boolean variable gError whose initial value is *false*; (2) we replace each assertion **assert**(e) by gError = !e; **if**(gError) **return**; and (3) we add **if**(gError) **return**; at the beginning of each task's body and after each procedure call. The translation ensures that an assertion fails iff gError is *true* at the end of **main**.

Intuitively, the sequentialization replaces asynchronous posts with "normal" function calls. These function calls carry an additional parameter that specifies the phase of the call: the phase of a call corresponding to an asynchronous post is one more than the phase of the caller. The sequentialization maintains several versions of the global state, one for each phase, and calls the task on the copy of the global state at its phase. The task can immediately execute on that global state, without messing up the global state at the posting task's phase. Since tasks are executed in FIFO order, notice that when two tasks t_1 and t_2 are posted sequentially (at phase i, say), the global state after running t_1 is exactly the global state at which t_2 starts executing. Thus, the copy of the global state at phase i correctly threads the global state for all tasks executing at phase i.

The remaining complication is connecting the various copies of the global state. For example, the global state when phase i starts is the same as the global state at the *end* of executing phase $i - 1$, but we do not know what that state is

---

[1] BBS stands for *Buffer phase-Bounded Sequentializer* and can be downloaded at https://github.com/zilongwang/bbs.

(without executing phase $i-1$ first). Here, we use non-determinism. We guess the initial values of the global state for each phase at the beginning of the execution. At the end of the execution, we check that our guess was correct, using the then available values of the global states at each phase. If the guess was correct, we check if some copy of gError is set to true: this would imply a semantically consistent run that had an assertion failure.

We now make the translation a bit more precise. Given a phase bound $L \in \mathbb{N}$, i.e., the maximal number of phases to explore, the sequentialization consists of four steps:

1. Track the phase of tasks at which they run in an execution. Intuitively, the phase of main, the initial task, is 1, and if a task at phase i executes post $p(e)$, then the new task p is at phase $i + 1$. As an example, consider an error trace in Fig. 1, task t_0 is at phase 1, and tasks t_1, t_2 are at phase 2. This tracking can be done by augmenting each procedure's parameter list with an integer k that tracks the phase of the procedure. Consequently, we also replace each normal synchronous procedure call $p(e)$ by $p(e, k)$, and each asynchronous call post $p(e)$ by post $p(e, k + 1)$.
2. Replace each post $p(e, k + 1)$ by if$(k < L)$ $p(e, k + 1)$;, meaning that if some task at phase k posts the task p and $k + 1$ does not exceed the phase bound L, the task p is immediately called and runs at phase $k + 1$ instead of putting it into the task queue.
3. For each global variable g, create L copies of it, denoted by $g[1], \ldots, g[L]$. Set the initial value of the first copy $g[1]$ to the initial value of g, and nondeterministically guess the initial values of the other copies. For each statement of a program, if g appears, then replace it by $g[k]$. Intuitively, the i-th copy of global variables is used to record the evolution of global valuations along an execution at phase i.
4. Run the initial task t_0 at phase 1. When t_0 returns, for each phase $i \in [2, L]$, enforce that the guessed initial values of the i-th copy are indeed equal to the final values of the $(i - 1)$-th copy. Finally, a bug is found if some copy of gError equals *true*.

Step 4 is better explained through an example. We present how a sequentialized execution in Fig. 2 is related to an error trace of Fig. 1. Suppose that the phase bound $L = 2$ and the above first three steps have been done correctly.

Consider segment (a) in Fig. 2 and segment (1) in Fig. 1. When task t_0 starts, notice that the global state x in segment (1) and its first copy $x[1]$ in segment (a) are always the same because both are initialized to v_0, and in each step of their executions, the way that segment (1) modifies x is the same as the way that segment (a) modifies $x[1]$. In this case, we say that segment (a) uses the first copy of the global state to "mimic" the evolution of the global state in segment (1).

Since the last statement of segment (a) is if$(k < L)$ $p(e, k + 1)$; and the current phase $k = 1$, segment (b) starts. Notice that segment (b) runs at phase 2 and only modifies the second copy of the global state $x[2]$. Additionally, if

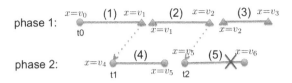

Fig. 1. An error trace before sequentialization. Circles denote the starting or end-ing points of tasks. Solid lines denote the execution of tasks. Triangles with dashed arrows indicate a post statement that posts a task to the queue; triangles without dashed arrows are statements right after post statements. The cross represents where the assertion fails. This error trace is read as follows: task t_0 runs, posts tasks t_1 and t_2 to the task queue, and completes. Then t_1 and t_2 runs one after another. We divided the error trace into execution segments (1)–(5), ordered by their execution order. Val-ues of the global state x at each segment are shown. E.g., when segment (1) starts and ends, $x = v_0$ and $x = v_1$, respectively. When segment (4) starts and ends, $x = v_4$ and $x = v_5$, respectively. Note that due to the FIFO order, $v_3 = v_4$.

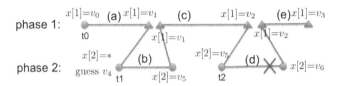

Fig. 2. The sequentialized error trace after sequentialization. Values of each copy of the global state x at each segment are shown. E.g., when segment (a) starts and ends, the first copy $x[1] = v_0$ and $x[1] = v_1$, respectively. When segment (b) starts, the second copy $x[2]$ is guessed to v_4. When segment (b) ends, $x[2] = v_5$.

we assume that the initial value of $x[2]$ are guessed correctly, i.e., v_4, shown in Fig. 2, then segment (b) uses the second copy of the global state to "mimic" the evolution of the global state in segment (4).

After segment (b) completes, the control goes back to phase 1 and segment (c) starts. Note that segment (b) does not modify the first copy x[1], and hence when segment (c) starts, the value of $x[1]$ is still v_1. As a result, segment (c) uses the first copy of the global state to "mimic" the evolution of the global state in segment (2).

After segment (c) completes, segment (d) starts. Note that since segment (c) does not modify the second copy $x[2]$, the value of $x[2]$ is still v_5 at the beginning of segment (d), which is the same as the value of x at the beginning of segment (5). Hence segment (d) uses $x[2]$ to mimic x in segment (5). When segment (d) completes, segment (e) starts to use the first copy $x[1]$ to mimic segment (3).

Finally, When segment (e) completes, by using assume statements, we enforce that the initial value for the second copy $x[2]$ is indeed guessed to v_4 in order to satisfy the FIFO order imposed by the task queue. After the enforcement, the sequential execution in Fig. 2 and the error trace in Fig. 1 reach exactly the same set of global states. Hence we conclude that a bug is found.

3   Experimental Evaluation

We first provide a brief introduction to TinyOS applications. We then present the design of Bbs and elaborate on our experimental results.

3.1   TinyOS Execution Model

TinyOS [7] is a popular operating system designed for wireless sensor networks. It uses nesC [6] as the programming language and provides a toolchain that translates nesC programs into embedded C code and then compiles the C code into executables which are deployed on sensor motes to perform operations such as data collection.

TinyOS provides a programming language (nesC) and an execution model tailored towards asynchronous programming. A nesC program consists of tasks and interrupt handlers. When the program runs, TinyOS associates a scheduler, a stack, and a task queue with it, and starts to run the "main" task on the stack. Tasks run to completion and can post additional tasks into the task queue. When a task completes, the scheduler dequeues the first task from the task queue, and runs it on the stack.

Hardware interrupts may arrive at any time (when the corresponding interrupt is enabled). For instance, a timer interrupt may occur periodically so that sensors can read meters, or a receive interrupt may occur to notice sensors that packets arrived from outside. When an (enabled) interrupt occurs, TinyOS preempts the running task and executes the corresponding interrupt handler defined in the nesC program. An interrupt handler can also post tasks to the task queue, which is used as a mechanism to achieve deferred computation and hide the latency of time-consuming operations such as I/O. Once the interrupt handler completes, the interrupted task resumes.

3.2   Bbs Overview

We implemented Bbs to perform phase-bounded analysis for TinyOS applications. Bbs checks user-defined assertions as well as two common memory violations in C programs: out-of-bound array accesses (OOB) and null-pointer dereference.

The workflow of Bbs is shown in Fig. 3. First, given a TinyOS application consisting of nesC files, the nesC compiler nescc combines them together and generates a self-contained embedded C file. nescc supports many mote platforms and generates different embedded C code based on platforms. In our work, we let nescc generate embedded C code for MSP430 platforms.

Bbs takes as inputs the MSP430 embedded C file containing assertions and a phase bound, and executes three modules.

The first module performs preprocessing and static analysis on the C program to instrument interrupts and assertions. Interrupt handlers are obtained from nescc-generated attributes in the code. A naive way to instrument interrupts is to insert them before each statement of the C program. However, if a

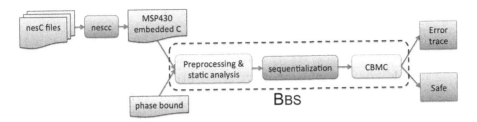

Fig. 3. The workflow of Bbs

statement does not have potentially raced variables[2], we do not need to instrument interrupts before it, because the execution of such statements commutes with the interrupt handler: either order of execution leads to the same final state. Thus Bbs performs static analysis to compute potentially raced variables and instruments interrupts accordingly.

The second module implements the sequentialization algorithm. The resulting sequential C program is fed into the bounded model checker CBMC [3,4], which outputs either an error trace or "program safe" up to the phase bound and the bound imposed by CBMC.

3.3 Experimental Experience with BBS

We used Bbs to analyze eight TinyOS applications in the **apps** directory from TinyOS's source tree. These benchmarks cover most of the basic functionalities provided by a sensor mote such as timers, radio communication, and serial transmission.

In Table 1, we summarize the size and complexity of these benchmarks in terms of (1) lines of code in the cleanly reformatted ANSI C program after the preprocessing stage, (2) the number of types of tasks that can be posted, (3) the number of types of hardware interrupts that are expected, (4) the number of global variables as well as the number of potentially raced variables (found by the static analysis).

In each of the first three benchmarks, we manually injected a realistic memory violation bug that programmers often make. The rest five benchmarks were previously known to be buggy [2,5,8,9]. The TestSerial benchmark contains two bugs and each of the rest has one bug. We ran Bbs on these benchmarks to see whether it could find these bugs efficiently within small phase bounds.

Experimental Results. All experiments were performed on a 2 core Intel Xeon X5650 CPU machine with 64GB memory and 64bit Linux (Debian/Lenny). Table 2 lists the analysis results, showing that Bbs successfully uncovered all bugs that are injected in the first three benchmarks, as well as all previously known bugs in the rest five benchmarks. We report the type of bugs, the minimal

---

[2] A potentially raced variable is accessed by both tasks and interrupt handlers, and at least one access from both is a write.

Table 1. TinyOS benchmarks

Benchmark	LOC	Tasks	Interrupt types	Global variables	Potentially raced global variables
TestAdc	6738	9	2	100	19
TestEui	7467	13	3	138	17
TestAM	11259	13	5	154	27
BlinkFail	3153	3	1	64	5
TestSerial	6590	10	3	127	17
TestPrintf	6882	13	3	136	18
TestDissemination	13004	17	5	166	37
TestDip	17091	25	7	243	49

Table 2. Experimental results

Benchmark	Bug type	Min phase	Time Seq. (s)	Time CBMC (s)	Error trace (in steps)
TestAdc	NullPtr	2	3.92	15.92	2014
TestEui	OOB	2	3.97	12.78	9425
TestAM	NullPtr	3	5.88	342.99	12925
BlinkFail	OOB	3	2.55	2.69	3773
TestSerial	OOB	4	3.75	23.92	13531
	User-defined	4		39.01	14161
TestPrintf	OOB	3	3.78	30.32	14154
TestDissemination	NullPtr	3	5.95	843.68	17307
TestDip	NullPtr	3	7.69	681.81	20274

phases that are required to uncover the bugs, the time used in both sequentialization and CBMC, and the lengths of error traces. Notice that all bugs were found within small phase bounds, that is, at most 4 phases. This result indicates that the phase-bounded approach effectively uncovers interesting bugs within small phase bounds for realistic C programs.

References

1. Bouajjani, A., Emmi, M.: Bounded phase analysis of message-passing programs. STTT **16**(2), 127–146 (2014)
2. Bucur, D., Kwiatkowska, M.Z.: Software verification for TinyOS. In: Proceedings of the 9th ACM/IEEE International Conference on Information Processing in Sensor Networks, IPSN 2010, pp. 400–401, ACM (2010)
3. Clarke, E., Kroning, D., Lerda, F.: A tool for checking ANSI-C programs. In: Jensen, K., Podelski, A. (eds.) TACAS 2004. LNCS, vol. 2988, pp. 168–176. Springer, Heidelberg (2004)

4. Clarke, E., Kroening, D., Yorav, K.: Behavioral consistency of C and Verilog programs using bounded model checking. In: Proceedings of the 40th Annual Design Automation Conference, DAC 2003, pp. 368–371. ACM, New York, NY, USA (2003)
5. Cooprider, N., Archer, W., Eide, E., Gay, D., Regehr, J.: Efficient memory safety for TinyOS. In: Proceedings of the 5th International Conference on Embedded Networked Sensor Systems, SenSys 2007, pp. 205–218. ACM, New York, NY, USA (2007)
6. Gay, D., Levis, P., von Behren, R., Welsh, M., Brewer, E., Culler, D.: The nesC language: a holistic approach to networked embedded systems. In: Proceedings of the ACM SIGPLAN 2003 Conference on Programming Language Design and Implementation, PLDI 2003, pp. 1–11. ACM, New York, NY, USA (2003)
7. Hill, J., Szewczyk, R., Woo, A., Hollar, S., Culler, D., Pister, K.: System architecture directions for networked sensors. In: Proceedings of the Ninth International Conference on Architectural Support for Programming Languages and Operating Systems, ASPLOS IX, pp. 93–104. ACM, New York, NY, USA (2000)
8. Li, P., Regehr, J.: T-check: bug finding for sensor networks. In: Proceedings of the 9th ACM/IEEE International Conference on Information Processing in Sensor Networks, IPSN 2010, pp. 174–185. ACM, New York, NY, USA (2010)
9. Safe TinyOS. http://docs.tinyos.net/index.php/Safe_TinyOS

Time-Aware Abstractions in HybridSal

Ashish Tiwari[✉]

SRI International, Menlo Park, CA, USA
ashish.tiwari@sri.com

Abstract. HybridSal is a tool for enabling verification of hybrid systems using infinite bounded model checking and k-induction. The core component of the tool is an abstraction engine that automatically creates a discrete, but infinite, state transition system abstraction of the continuous dynamics in the system. In this paper, we describe Hybrid-Sal's new capability to create time-aware relational abstractions, which gives users control over the precision of the abstraction. We also describe a novel approach for abstracting nonlinear expressions that allows us to create time-aware relational abstractions that are more precise than those described previously. We show that the new approach enables automatic verification of systems that could not be verified previously.

1 Introduction

Hybrid automata is a modeling formalism in which discrete transitions and continuous evolution can be intermixed to describe fairly complex cyber-physical systems. HybridSal [15] is a tool for performing verification of hybrid automata models [2,3,5,6,8,9,11,14,16]. It is a tool built over the SAL tool [7] that can be used to model and verify discrete (finite or infinite) state transition systems. The core component of HybridSal is an *abstraction* engine that takes a hybrid model and outputs a discrete (SAL) model that is a sound abstraction of the hybrid model [13]. The abstract SAL model can be analyzed using the usual SAL model checking tools (such as the infinite bounded model checker or the k-induction prover).

In this paper, we revisit the relational abstraction technique [13] and its improvement to time-aware relational abstraction [10], which are both available in the current version of HybridSal [15]. We identify a class of problems for which these techniques yield very coarse abstractions, and present an approach to fix this shortcoming. The approach is based on creating sound approximations of nonlinear functions using sound approximations of the natural logarithm (ln) function. We present examples that can be verified using the new approach that could not be verified previously by HybridSal.

This work was supported, in part, by the National Science Foundation under grant CNS-1423298, and the Defense Advanced Research Projects Agency (DARPA) and Air Force Research Laboratory (AFRL), under contract FA8750-12-C-0284. The views, opinions, and/or findings contained in this report are those of the authors and should not be interpreted as representing the official views or policies, either expressed or implied, of the funding agencies.

© Springer International Publishing Switzerland 2015
D. Kroening and C.S. Păsăreanu (Eds.): CAV 2015, Part I, LNCS 9206, pp. 504–510, 2015.
DOI: 10.1007/978-3-319-21690-4_34

2   Relational Abstraction

The HybridSal abstraction engine constructs a so-called *relational abstraction* of the system. A relational abstraction does not abstract the state space of the system, but only over-approximates the transition relation [13]. Concretely, the relational abstraction of a transition system $(S, \rightarrow)$ (with state space S and transition relation $\rightarrow$) is another transition system $(S, \rightarrow^a)$ such that $\rightarrow \subseteq \rightarrow^a$.

The semantics of a hybrid system is given as a state transition system $(S, \rightarrow_d \cup \rightarrow_c)$, where $\rightarrow_d$ are transitions that capture the "discrete" behavior of the system, and $\rightarrow_c$ are transitions that capture the "continuous" behavior. The HybridSal tool constructs relational abstraction of hybrid systems by abstracting only the relation $\rightarrow_c$; that is, the abstract system is $(S, \rightarrow_d \cup \rightarrow_c^a)$. We next briefly describe the relations $\rightarrow_c$ and $\rightarrow_c^a$.

The continuous behavior of a hybrid system is typically specified using ordinary differential equations. Consider a system of differential equations, $dx/dt = f(x)$, whose dynamics are constrained to remain within invariant Inv. The concrete semantics of this continuous behavior is defined by the relation $\rightarrow_c$:

$$x_1 \rightarrow_c x_2 \text{if } \exists F : \exists (t \geq 0) : x_1 = F(0), x_2 = F(t), dF/dt = f(F(t)),$$
$$\forall (0 \leq t' \leq t) : F(t') \in \text{Inv} \qquad (1)$$

Here, the function F is a solution of the differential equations [1].

It is extremely difficult to reason with the relation in Eq. 1. Relational abstraction overcomes this problem by constructing an over-approximation of this relation that is much easier to analyze. Henceforth, let us assume that continuous dynamics are specified using *linear* ordinary differential equations; for simplicity, say $dx/dt = Ax$, where A is an $n \times n$ matrix.

2.1   Time-Oblivious Relational Abstraction

A relational abstraction that does not mention the *time* variable, t, explicitly is called a *time-oblivious relational abstraction*. By default, HybridSal constructs time-oblivious abstractions [15]. If c^T is a left-eigenvector of A corresponding to eigenvalue λ, then it is easily proved that if $x \rightarrow_c x'$, then

$$c^T x' = c^T x e^{\lambda(t'-t)} \qquad (2)$$

When $\lambda > 0$, we can over-approximate the relationship between x and x' in the form of the following time-oblivious abstraction:

$$(c^T x' = c^T x = 0) \vee (c^T x' \geq c^T x > 0) \vee (c^T x' \leq c^T x < 0) \qquad (3)$$

Note there is no mention of the time elapsed $(t' - t)$ in the above expression. Furthermore, all expressions above are *linear*. Each left eigenvector of A corresponding to a real eigenvalue will generate one constraint of the form in Eq. 3. If the eigenvalue λ has a nonzero imaginary part, we can still get a *piecewise linear time-oblivious relational abstraction* on the real and imaginary parts of the corresponding eigenvector [15].

There are two shortcomings in the time-oblivious abstraction computed above. First, it is too coarse. It loses all time-related information. For example, if we have a 2-d system $dx/dt = -x, dy/dt = -y$, the time-oblivious abstraction forgets that the (exponential) decay rates of x and y are the same. Second, if matrix A is *defective*, that is, it has fewer eigenvectors corresponding to eigenvalue λ than the algebraic multiplicity of λ, then we do not even know how to construct a reasonably good time-oblivious abstraction.

As an example, consider the 2-d system $dx/dt = x + y, dy/dt = y$. The corresponding matrix $A = [1, 1; 0, 1]$ is defective – it has eigenvalue 1 with multiplicity 2, but there is only one associated left eigenvector $[0,1]$. The solution of the ODE is given by the equations:

$$y(t) = y(0)e^t, \quad x(t) = x(0)e^t + y(0)te^t \tag{4}$$

The default time-oblivious relational abstraction constructed by HybridSal would just have inequalities (as in Eq. 3) for $y(t)$, but $x(t)$ would be unconstrained. This is because HybridSal lacked a general technique for handling defective A matrices.

2.2 Time-Aware Relational Abstraction

The first shortcoming of the time-oblivious abstraction computed by Hybrid-Sal was recently recognized and it resulted in the introduction of *time-aware relational abstractions* [10].

A *time-aware* relational abstraction relates the change in the value of an expression to the time elapsed. It can be more precise than a time-oblivious abstraction. Consider the exponentially increasing/decaying expression in Eq. 2 constructed from the left eigenvector c^T corresponding to a real eigenvalue λ. Taking the natural logarithm on both sides of Eq. 2, we get

$$\ln(c^T x') = \ln(c^T x) + \lambda(t' - t) \tag{5}$$

The expressions $c^T x'$, $c^T x$, and $\lambda(t' - t)$ (for a fixed value of λ) are *linear* in the state variables x and the time variable t (and their *next* values). So, we just need a *piecewise-affine* (lower and upper) approximation of the natural logarithm function $\ln$ to construct a *time-aware* relational abstraction. Such an approximation exists and is shown in Fig. 1: intuitively, the upper bound $\ln_{ub}$ is defined by first-order Taylor approximations of $\ln$ at points $e^{i+1} - e^i$ [4].

Using the piecewise-linear approximation functions $\ln_{lb}$ and $\ln_{ub}$ defined in Fig. 1, we abstract Eq. 5 using the following linear arithmetic formula:

$$\ln_{lb}(c^T x') \leq \ln_{ub}(c^T x) + \lambda(t' - t) \;\wedge\; \ln_{ub}(c^T x') \geq \ln_{lb}(c^T x) + \lambda(t' - t) \tag{6}$$

Since the number of intervals that define the piecewise linear approximation of the $\ln$ function is unbounded (Fig. 1), HybridSal creates an approximation that uses only *finitely* many intervals: $(-\infty, e^{-n}], [e^m, +\infty)$, and $[e^i, e^{i+1}]$,

$i = -n, \ldots, -1, 0, 1, \ldots, m - 1$. When creating time-aware relational abstractions in HybridSal, the *precision parameters* n, m are chosen by the user (via a commandline argument): picking a higher value increases precision.

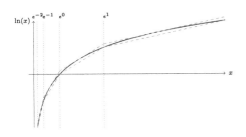

Fig. 1. Piecewise-linear lower and upper approximation for natural logarithm function.

The $\ln(x)$ function in Fig. 1 is approximated by dividing the x axis into the (infinitely many) intervals $[e^i, e^{i+1}]$, $i \in \mathbb{Z}$. In the interval $[e^i, e^{i+1}]$, a lower-bound, $\ln_{\mathrm{lb}}(x)$, for $\ln(x)$ is given by the line joining the two end-points; that is, $\ln_{\mathrm{lb}}(x) := \frac{(x-e^i)}{(e^{i+1}-e^i)} + i$; whereas an upper-bound is given by $\ln_{\mathrm{ub}}(x) := \ln_{\mathrm{lb}}(x) + 0.12$. The tangents at the end-points also provide an upper-bound; hence, a better upper-bound, $\ln_{\mathrm{ub}}^{(2)}(x)$, is $\min(\ln_{\mathrm{ub}}(x), \frac{(x-e^i)}{e^i}+i, \frac{(x-e^{i+1})}{e^{i+1}}+i+1)$.

Using $\ln_{\mathrm{lb}}$ and $\ln_{\mathrm{ub}}$, we know how to create time-aware abstractions for exponentially changing expressions (Eq. 2), as well as, periodically changing expressions ($x(t) = \frac{x(0)}{\cos(\theta_0)} e^{\lambda t} \cos(\omega t + \theta_0)$); see [10].

2.3 Defective Matrices

If the dynamics are specified by an A matrix that is not defective, then, for an n-dimensional system, we can always find n linearly independent vectors, such that for each vector c, the value of the linear expression $c^T x$ is either exponentially changing or periodically changing. Hence, for such systems, we can get relatively good linear, time-aware relational abstractions.

If A is defective, then we can still find n linearly independent vectors, but now their dynamics can *additionally* contain terms that are "products" of exponential/trigonometric function and t^k, where t is the time variable and k is some natural number. See the dynamics of $x(t)$ in Eq. 4 for an example.

The main observation we make in this paper is that we can abstract a product of two terms by using the approximations for ln function described above. In particular, the equation $z = xye^u$ can be abstracted by the expression:

$$(z = 0 \leftrightarrow (x = 0 \lor y = 0)) \land (z > 0 \leftrightarrow ((x > 0 \land y > 0) \lor (x < 0 \land y < 0))) \; \land$$
$$\ln_{\mathrm{lb}}(|x|) + \ln_{\mathrm{lb}}(|y|) + u \le \ln_{\mathrm{ub}}(|z|) \land \ln_{\mathrm{ub}}(|x|) + \ln_{\mathrm{ub}}(|y|) + u \ge \ln_{\mathrm{lb}}(|z|) \qquad (7)$$

Let $\phi(u, x, y, z)$ denote the above formula. The formula ϕ contains only *linear* expressions, and hence we can use a linear theory solver to reason about it.

We can now use the abstraction ϕ to construct abstractions of linear systems whose dynamics are specified by defective matrices. Concretely, we construct a relational abstraction of the dynamics for $x(t)$ given in Eq. 4, namely $x' = xe^{t'-t} + y(t'-t)e^{t'-t}$, as follows:

$$x' = z_1 + z_2 \land \phi(t'-t, x, 1, z_1) \land \phi(t'-t, y, t'-t, z_2) \qquad (8)$$

where z_1, z_2 are new variables. For an arbitrary A matrix, defective or not, we can now compute time-aware relational abstractions by first transforming A into Jordan normal form J; say $A = U^{-1}JU$. The value of each expression $c^T x$, where c^T is a row of U, is a linear combination of terms of the form $t^k e^{\lambda t}$ (or $t^k \cos(bt) e^{at}$ or $t^k \sin(bt) e^{at}$). Thus, using ϕ, we can get piecewise linear abstractions for each expression by straight-forwardly extending the ideas used to construct the abstraction in Eq. 8 (and combine the ideas with [10] for periodic dynamics).

3   Experiments

Dynamics where the A matrix is defective are quite common. Some of the simplest examples turn out to have defective matrices. For example, a linear motion with constant velocity is described by $[\dot{x}; \dot{v}] = A[x; v] + \boldsymbol{b}$, where $A = [0, 1; 0, 0]$ is defective. Similarly, linear motion with constant acceleration also gives rise to defective A matrices. Even real-world examples appear to more often have defective A matrices than not. So, it was important for us to improve the quality of abstraction HybridSal generates on these dynamics.

One good verification challenge benchmark is the adaptive cruise controller from [12]. The controller sets the acceleration of the *following* car, a_f, as $\dot{a}_f = -3a_f - 3(v_f - v_l) + gap - (v_f + 10)$, where v_l, a_l denote the velocity and acceleration of the *leading* car, v_f, a_f are those of the *following* car, and gap is the distance between the cars. We assume that the controller is engaged whenever $gap \geq 5, 0 \leq v_l, v_f \leq 30$ and $gap - 0.1(v_f^2 - v_l^2) - 10 - (v_f - v_i) \geq 0$. We assume that a_l is an input and is constrained to be within $-5m/s^2$ and $2m/s^2$, and the velocities v_l, v_f are always non-negative. The goal is to prove that after it is engaged, the controller guarantees that $gap \geq 0$ always.

The currently released version of HybridSal, which includes an option to create time-aware relational abstraction, fails to verify the above example since it fails to use the equation $v'_l - v_l = a_l(t' - t)$ (because the A matrix is defective). However, if we add a constraint that abstracts this equation (using the ϕ formula), then HybridSal can prove safety. Even though a_l can vary arbitrarily, this equation still holds (for some a_l due to mean value theorem). Note that the quadratic term in the initial set had to be approximated by linear terms in the HybridSal model.

To further evaluate the precision of the proposed abstraction function, we also created several simple examples of linear systems whose A matrices were defective, but whose explicit solutions could be worked out by hand. For the safety property, we had an upper-bound on the value of the variable whose solution expression had the highest degree in the time variable t. Using knowledge of the explicit solution, we created initial sets and unsafe regions. We report the results in Table 1. The current version of HybridSal, of course, fails on all these examples. The new approach presented in this paper allowed us to prove conservative bounds in each case. In Table 1, Column `truebnd.` contains the true bound (computed by hand using the analytical solution), Column `proved/CE` is

Table 1. Experimental results: All six examples have 1 jordan block in the A matrix. For each example, Column #vars denotes the number of state variables, λ is the eigenvalue(s), `alg.mult.` is the (sum of) algebraic multiplicity of the eigenvalue(s), #evecs is the number of eigenvectors, `truebnd.` is the true upper bound (analytically calculated) for the "top" variable, `proved/CE` is the bound proved by the tool followed by the bound that generated a (spurious) counter-example, and `time` is the time (in seconds) taken by Yices to prove/generate a counter-example. The last two columns report the same results, but using a refined upper bound for ln function.

name	#vars	λ	alg. mult.	#evecs	true bnd.	New Approach (default and refined)			
						proved/CE	time	proved/CE	time
real_j2	2	-1	2	1	2.2	2.8/2.7	0.5/0.5	2.6/2.5	1.7/2.3
real_j3	3	-1	3	1	1.6	2.0/1.9	0.8/1.2	1.9/1.8	5.3/9.1
real_j4	4	-1	4	1	3.8	4.6/4.5	2.1/4.5	4.3/4.2	41/50
real_j5	5	-1	5	1	1.4	2.1/2.0	3.1/7.0	1.8/1.7	4.4/7.3
comp_j4	4	$-1\pm i$	4	2	1.8	2.8/2.7	1.8/2.8	2.7/2.6	2.3/7.6
comp_j6	6	$-1\pm i$	6	2	2.1	3.6/3.5	27/37	3.0/2.9	52/92

the bound that our approach was able to prove, followed by a bound that yielded a (spurious) counter-example. Column `time` reports the time it took the SMT solver (Yices) to prove the bound in Column `proved/CE`, followed by the time it took Yices to find a counter-example for the second bound in Column `proved/CE`.

To further validate the claim that the sound approximations for ln are the key, we used a slightly better (refined) upper-bound, $\ln_{ub}^{(2)}$ defined in Fig. 1, for ln function and re-ran the experiments, and in each case, the tool proved a tighter safety property than before (last two columns in Table 1). As expected, using the refined approximation caused Yices to take more time. The tool and examples are all available from the HybridSal webpage [15].

We note that on examples that contain only non-defective matrices, there is no overhead added by our new extension: the piecewise-linear approximation of product terms is not triggered and the new approach becomes identical to the old [10]. We also note that for matrices that have large eigenvalues, we may need to create a more precise abstraction by choosing large values for the precision parameters. Consequently, the cost of analysis (model checking) increases for such examples. In future work, we plan to address this issue.

4 Conclusion

We presented an approach for improving the time-aware relational abstraction that is currently computed by the HybridSal tool. In particular, we improved the precision of the abstraction for linear systems whose A matrices are defective. We showed that the new approach enables HybridSal to prove correctness of systems that could not be proved correct using an approach that performed coarse abstraction for defective A matrices. This extension is significant since defective matrices occur frequently in models of real systems.

References

1. Alur, R., Courcoubetis, C., Halbwachs, N., Henzinger, T.A., Ho, P.-H., Nicollin, X., Olivero, A., Sifakis, J., Yovine, S.: The algorithmic analysis of hybrid systems. Theor. Comput. Sci. **138**(3), 3–34 (1995)
2. Alur, R., Dang, T., Ivančić, F.: Counter-example guided predicate abstraction of hybrid systems. In: Garavel, H., Hatcliff, J. (eds.) TACAS 2003. LNCS, vol. 2619, pp. 208–223. Springer, Heidelberg (2003)
3. Alur, R., Henzinger, T., Lafferriere, G., Pappas, G.: Discrete abstractions for hybrid systems. Proc. IEEE **88**(2), 971–984 (2000)
4. Chen, X., Ábrahám, E., Sankaranarayanan, S.: Taylor model flowpipe construction for non-linear hybrid systems. In: Proceedings of 33rd IEEE Real-Time Systems Symposium, RTSS, pp. 183–192. IEEE Computer Society (2012)
5. Chen, X., Ábrahám, E., Sankaranarayanan, S.: Flow: an analyzer for non-linear hybrid systems. In: Sharygina, N., Veith, H. (eds.) CAV 2013. LNCS, vol. 8044, pp. 258–263. Springer, Heidelberg (2013)
6. Clarke, E., Fehnker, A., Han, Z., Krogh, B.H., Stursberg, O., Theobald, M.: Verification of hybrid systems based on counterexample-guided abstraction refinement. In: Garavel, H., Hatcliff, J. (eds.) TACAS 2003. LNCS, vol. 2619, pp. 192–207. Springer, Heidelberg (2003)
7. de Moura, L., Owre, S., Rueß, H., Rushby, J., Shankar, N., Sorea, M., Tiwari, A.: SAL 2. In: Alur, R., Peled, D.A. (eds.) CAV 2004. LNCS, vol. 3114, pp. 496–500. Springer, Heidelberg (2004)
8. Frehse, G., Le Guernic, C., Donzé, A., Cotton, S., Ray, R., Lebeltel, O., Ripado, R., Girard, A., Dang, T., Maler, O.: SpaceEx: scalable verification of hybrid systems. In: Gopalakrishnan, G., Qadeer, S. (eds.) CAV 2011. LNCS, vol. 6806, pp. 379–395. Springer, Heidelberg (2011)
9. Henzinger, T.A., Ho, P.-H., Wong-Toi, H.: HyTech: a model checker for hybrid systems. Softw. Tools Technol. Transf. **1**, 110–122 (1997). http://www-cad.eecs.berkeley.edu/~tah/HyTech/
10. Mover, S., Cimatti, A., Tiwari, A., Tonetta, S.: Time-aware relational abstraction for hybrid systems. In: EMSOFT (2013)
11. Pham, M.-D., Boncz, P., Erling, O.: S3G2: A scalable structure-correlated social graph generator. In: Nambiar, R., Poess, M. (eds.) TPCTC 2012. LNCS, vol. 7755, pp. 156–172. Springer, Heidelberg (2013)
12. Puri, A., Varaiya, P.: Driving safely in smart cars. In: Proceedings of the 1995 American Control Conference (1995)
13. Sankaranarayanan, S., Tiwari, A.: Relational abstractions for continuous and hybrid systems. In: Gopalakrishnan, G., Qadeer, S. (eds.) CAV 2011. LNCS, vol. 6806, pp. 686–702. Springer, Heidelberg (2011)
14. Silva, B.I., Krogh, B.H.: Formal verification of hybrid system using CheckMate: a case study. In: American Control Conference (2000)
15. Tiwari, A.: HybridSAL relational abstracter. In: Madhusudan, P., Seshia, S.A. (eds.) CAV 2012. LNCS, vol. 7358, pp. 725–731. Springer, Heidelberg (2012)
16. Wongpiromsarn, T., Mitra, S., Murray, R.M., Lamperski, A.: Verification of periodically controlled hybrid systems application to an autonomous vehicle. ACM Tans. Embed. Comput. Syst. (ACM TECS). **11**, 53 (2012)

A Type-Directed Approach to Program Repair

Alex Reinking and Ruzica Piskac[✉]

Yale University, New Haven, USA
{ruzica.piskac,alexander.reinking}@yale.edu

Abstract. Developing enterprise software often requires composing several libraries together with a large body of in-house code. Large APIs introduce a steep learning curve for new developers as a result of their complex object-oriented underpinnings. While the written code in general reflects a programmer's intent, due to evolutions in an API, code can often become ill-typed, yet still syntactically-correct. Such code fragments will no longer compile, and will need to be updated. We describe an algorithm that automatically repairs such errors, and discuss its application to common problems in software engineering.

1 Introduction

While coding, a developer often knows the approximate structure of the expression she is working on, but may yet write code that does not compile because some fragments are not well-typed. Such mistakes occur mainly because modern libraries often evolve into complex application programming interfaces (APIs) that provide a large number of declarations. It is difficult, if not impossible, to learn the specifics of every declaration and its utilization.

In this paper we propose an approach that takes ill-typed expressions and automatically suggests several well-typed corrections. The suggested code snippets follow the structure outlined in the original expression as closely as possible, and are ranked based on their similarity to the original code. This approach can also be seen as code synthesis. In fact, our proposed method extends the synthesis functionality described in [3,6,10]. In light of program repair, plain expression synthesis can be seen as a repair of the empty expression.

We have implemented an early prototype of our algorithm, and empirically tested it on synthesis and repair benchmarks. The initial evaluation strongly supports the idea of a graph-based type-directed approach to code repair and snippet synthesis. Compared to the results reported in [3], our approach outperforms on similar benchmarks, sometimes by several orders of magnitude, while still producing high-quality results.

2 Related Work

Our work is largely inspired by two synthesis tools: Prospector [6] and InSynth [3,4]. Prospector is a tool for synthesizing code snippets containing only unary

© Springer International Publishing Switzerland 2015
D. Kroening and C.S. Păsăreanu (Eds.): CAV 2015, Part I, LNCS 9206, pp. 511–517, 2015.
DOI: 10.1007/978-3-319-21690-4_35

API methods. The basic synthesis algorithm used in [6] encodes method signatures using a graph. Although we also encode function information in a graph structure, our synthesis graph is more general. As explained in Sect. 4.1, we distinguish nodes into types and functions, as opposed to just types. In a way, the connections to each function node models its succinct type as described in [3]. While our approach acts as a generalization of both these tools, we significantly extend their capability. Our algorithm can repair ill-typed expressions, as well.

Debugging and locating errors in code [1,8] play an important role in the process of increasing software reliability. While our approach suggests repairs based only on a given ill-typed expression and its environment, other tools that tackle this problem [2,5,7,9] additionally require test cases, code contracts and/or symbolic execution.

3 Motivating Example: Correcting Multiple Errors

In this section, we show how our algorithm efficiently repairs ill-typed expressions. Sometimes, such expressions might poorly reflect the structure of the desired expression, while still retaining other useful information. This is the case when the correct structure is obscured by passing too many or too few arguments to a function, or by passing them in the wrong order.

The following code fragment attempts to read a compressed file though a buffered stream while using an extensive number of calls to the standard Java API. The developer attempts to instantiate an `InputStream` object:

```
int buffSize = 1024, compLevel = Deflater.BEST_SPEED;
String fileName = "compressed.txt";

InputStream input =
    new BufferedInputStream(buffSize, new DeflaterInputStream(
        new FileInputStream(), compLevel, true)); // error
```

In this example, the single variable assignment contains three errors. First, the constructor for the `FileInputStream` requires at least one argument, yet has received none; second, the `DeflaterInputStream` constructor has been passed too many arguments; and finally, the `BufferedInputStream` has been passed valid arguments, but in the wrong order.

To repair this expression, our algorithm proceeds from the bottom, viewed as a parse tree, up to the top-level. Thus, it begins by correcting the innermost sub-expression: `new FileInputStream()`. From the entire available code, our repair algorithm returns `new FileInputStream(fileName)` as the closest match. To repair code, we consider the visible user-defined values along with the standard libraries, favoring the values that appear closest to the point in the program where the repair was initiated.

After substituting the new expression, the repair proceeds to correct the `DeflaterInputStream` call. Since all of its arguments are well-typed, the repair will attempt to re-use them while synthesizing a replacement. After searching through the space of possible repairs, the algorithm finds the following snippet:

```
new DeflaterInputStream(new FileInputStream(fileName), new
   Deflater(compLevel, true))
```

Here, the repair wraps the extra arguments in a call to the `Deflater` constructor from the Java API. Notice that even though `Deflater` was not previously present in the expression, our repair algorithm was able to discover it by examining the valid constructor calls for a `DeflaterInputStream`.

Finally, the algorithm rebuilds the overall expression by interchanging the arguments in the top-level expression to arrive at the final, correct result:

```
new BufferedInputStream(new DeflaterInputStream(
   new FileInputStream(fileName),new Deflater(compLevel, true)),
   buffSize);
```

As we discuss in Sect. 5, the whole search and repair takes under a second to complete.

4 The Algorithm

4.1 Synthesis Graph Construction

Our algorithm operates by searching through a data structure we call the *synthesis graph*. Each node of the synthesis graph corresponds to either a value-producing language entity, such as a function, variable, constant, or literal, or to a type in the language. We therefore divide nodes into two sets V_t (type nodes) and V_f (function nodes). Since variables, constants, and literals can be considered functions taking the empty set to their value, they belong to V_f. To every function node, there is an incoming edge from the type it produces, and for each distinct type that the function takes as an argument, there is an outgoing edge from the function node to the type node. Importantly, this means that a function on three input parameters of the same type will have out-degree exactly one.

In addition, we assign to every edge a cost, which is a subjective measure that guides the search towards desirable traits. Such traits could include smaller expressions or lower memory usage, similar to [4]. The cost of an expression is defined to be an accumulation of the costs of the edges it includes.

4.2 Synthesis Procedure

We now outline the synthesis portion of our algorithm, Algorithm 1. The algorithm takes as input the synthesis graph $G = (V_t \cup V_f, E)$, the type of expression to synthesize τ, and two numbers $C_{\max}$ and N. N is the number of expressions to synthesize, and $C_{\max}$ is an upper bound on the cost of an expression. The synthesis algorithm returns a list of expressions of type τ. The first two steps can be done using Dijkstra's algorithm. The types in V_t' are explored in reverse order to avoid performing expensive recomputations. The loop finds N expressions of type σ with the shortest cost-distance to τ in G' and stores them in snips. This way, GetExpressions is able to reuse these computations without reducing the search space.

Algorithm 1. Synthesis Algorithm

---

input : $G = (V_t \cup V_f, E)$, $\tau \in V_t$, $C_{\max}$, N
output : exprs, the list of expressions

1 $G' = (V_t' \cup V_f', E') \longleftarrow$ subgraph of G reachable within $C_{\max}$ from τ ;
2 Sort V_t' in descending distance away from τ ;
3 snips $\longleftarrow$ Hash table mapping types to snippets ;
4 **foreach** $\sigma \in V_t'$ **do**
5 $\quad \lfloor$ snips $[\sigma] \longleftarrow$ getExpressions(G', snips, σ, $C_{\max}-$ Dist(σ), N) ;
6 exprs $\longleftarrow$ snips $[\tau]$;

Procedure. GetExpressions $(G' = (V_t' \cup V_f', E')$, snips, $\tau, C_{now}, N)$

---

1 **if** $\tau \in$ Keys(snips) **then return** snips $[\tau]$
2 results $\leftarrow \emptyset$;
3 **foreach** $g \in V_f'$ *of the form* $g : (\tau_1 \times \cdots \times \tau_k) \to \tau$ **do**
4 $\quad$ **if** Cost$(g) > C_{now}$ **then continue**
5 $\quad$ For all i, let $s_i \leftarrow$ GetExpressions(G', snips, $\tau_i, C_{now}-$ Cost$(g), N)$;
6 $\quad$ **foreach** $args \in s_1 \times \cdots \times s_k$ **do**
7 $\quad\quad$ **if** Cost$(g(args)) \leq C_{now}$ **then**
8 $\quad\quad\quad \lfloor$ Add g(args) to results ;
9 $\quad\quad$ **while** $\mid$ results $\mid > N$ **do**
10 $\quad\quad\quad \lfloor$ Remove the most costly entry from results ;

11 **return** results

Next we describe the GetExpressions procedure, whose task is to find the N best snippets of type τ in G' within a prescribed cost bound C_{now}. The procedure operates recursively, and it checks the snips table to see whether it can reuse the existing computations. To compute candidates for $\tau \in V_t$, the procedure looks at its outgoing neighbors, which are all functions whose output is of type τ. For each function that does not immediately break the cost constraint, GetExpressions attempts to synthesize subexpressions for each of its arguments recursively. This only needs to be done once for each type. Then, for every possible set of arguments to the function, it adds the allowable expressions to the results. Furthermore, it pushes out the worst few results if the size of the set would exceed N.

4.3 Repair Algorithm

Finally, we describe the repair algorithm, Algorithm 2. The key step in our approach is biasing the previously-described synthesis procedures towards the correctly-typed subexpressions of the broken expression. The intuition for this is that the search should be directed to favor those components that the programmer intended to use. To do this, we adjust the Cost function used by GetExpressions to assign the lowest possible cost to the well-typed subexpressions.

Informally, we call these zero-cost subexpressions "reinforced". This lowers the weights of results that contain these expressions, thus improving their ranking among the returned results.

This scheme has a few advantages: first, it will very strongly prefer those expressions that occurred as part of the given incorrect expression; second, in cases where more than one of the same type is required, it will favor using multiple, distinct subexpressions; and finally, if no expressions are given, then Cost actually remains unchanged.

With this modification in place, the repair algorithm proceeds from the bottom up. For each broken sub-expression in the input, we first reinforce each of its well-typed subexpressions and then initiate a synthesis for the desired type of the current subexpression. If any of its children are ill-typed, we recurse and repair them first.

Notice that this means the repaired subexpressions will also be reinforced. This behavior is desirable because it favors reusing the subexpressions generated once the repair synthesizes a higher level. Additionally, the recursion guarantees that reinforcing a subexpression will not interfere with a synthesis that occurs at the same level as that subexpression. Although this algorithm, as described, returns up to N possible repairs, in our preliminary implementation, the first returned result was mostly the correct one, so we speculate that setting N really low might be acceptable in a practical setting.

Algorithm 2. Repair Algorithm

---

    input   : $G = (V_t \cup V_f, E)$, the synthesis graph; expr, the broken expression; $C_{\max}$, the maximum allowable cost; N, the number of repairs to synthesize

    output: repairs, a list

1 **if** expr *is well-typed* **then return** *[expr]*
2 Write expr as expr $(x_1, \ldots, x_k)$ where x_i are its subexpressions of type τ_i ;
3 **foreach** $x \in \{x_1, \ldots, x_k\}$ **do**
4     $x \longleftarrow$ Repair $(G, x, C_{\max}, N)$;   `// Replace x with a list of either`
        `itself or its possible corrections`
5 **foreach** subs $\in x_1 \times \ldots \times x_k$ **do**
6   Reinforce all expressions in subs ;
7   Add all results of Synthesize $(G, \tau, C_{\max}, N)$ to repairs ;
8   Clear reinforcements ;
9 repairs $\longleftarrow$ Best N results in repairs

---

5   Preliminary Evaluation

We empirically evaluated our approach on benchmarks based on those found in [4]. Table 1 shows the summary of the results. The runtimes were measured on a standard university-supplied computer. For each benchmark, the best of 50

Table 1. Typical-use runtimes in various benchmarks. "Nodes" and "Edges" refer to the size of the searched subgraph, and "Rank" indicates the correct expression's position among the results. The "size" refers to the number of subexpressions in the output expression. Each test case was initialized with a small environment consisting of five variables, and produced ten results.

Benchmark	Type	Size	Time (ms)	Nodes	Edges	Rank
SequenceInputStream	Synthesis	3	< 1	141	149	1
SequenceInputStream	Repair	5	4	–	–	1
BufferedReader	Synthesis	3	16	3119	4225	2
BufferedReader	Repair	3	18	–	–	1
AudioClip (applet)	Synthesis	3	27	6808	9291	2
InputStreamReader	Synthesis	2	29	7064	9673	1
FileInputStream	Synthesis	2	38	7832	10516	1
Matcher (regex)	Synthesis	4	93	14505	24740	1
InputStream (from byte array)	Synthesis	2	116	13163	20581	2
DeflaterInputStream	Repair	8	380	–	–	1

consecutive trials was recorded to account for variance in process scheduling, cache behavior, and JVM warmup. It was not uncommon to see four-to-five-fold speed increases between the best and the worst runtimes of the algorithm. This is due to the delay in program optimization afforded by Oracle's JIT compiler.

It is important to note that these numbers represent a worst-case scenario for our algorithm. Since the full set of Java libraries are rarely imported, the algorithm should run even faster in practice as it will have smaller graphs to search. We imported the whole Java standard library which resulted in a graph of 45,557 nodes and 102,377 edges.

These benchmarks show that repair is fast and accurate even in the face of multiple, difficult errors. The compressed stream example in Sect. 3 had several distinct errors: a missing parameter, two parameters transposed, and additional parameters passed to a function that did not accept them. Still, in three calls to the synthesis routine, our algorithm automatically corrected *all three* errors in around a third of a second.

Although it is impossible to test the full range of possible type errors everywhere they might appear in the Java standard library, if these speeds are indeed representative of the whole space of possible errors, then our repair algorithm is sufficiently fast to operate in an interactive setting.

6   Conclusions and Future Directions

We have seen that our algorithm efficiently subsumes the work done in [3,6,10] and extends it to the problem of program repair. Using our novel graph-theoretic approach, we efficiently solve instances of this problem to synthesize a correct expression from the salvageable parts of a broken one. We believe that the algorithm in its current state has two compelling uses. First, it can assist programmers in writing complex expressions. Second, it could be integrated into a compiler to provide enhanced error messages that not only point to errors, but offer ways to correct them. We believe that our algorithm will perform useful and effective repairs that are well-aligned with the developer's intentions, even when the given ill-typed expression requires several steps to repair.

Acknowledgments. We thank Tihomir Gvero and Ivan Kuraj for early discussions about program repair.

References

1. Chandra, S., Torlak, E., Barman, S., Bodik, R.: Angelic debugging. In: Proceedings of the 33rd International Conference on Software Engineering, ICSE 2011, pp. 121–130. ACM, New York, NY, USA (2011)
2. Goues, C.L., Nguyen, T., Forrest, S., Weimer, W.: GenProg: a generic method for automatic software repair. IEEE Trans. Software Eng. **38**(1), 54–72 (2012)
3. Gvero, T., Kuncak, V., Kuraj, I., Piskac, R.: Complete completion using types and weights. In: PLDI, pp. 27–38 (2013)
4. Gvero, T., Kuncak, V., Piskac, R.: Interactive synthesis of code snippets. In: Gopalakrishnan, G., Qadeer, S. (eds.) CAV 2011. LNCS, vol. 6806, pp. 418–423. Springer, Heidelberg (2011)
5. Kaleeswaran, S., Tulsian, V., Kanade, A., Orso, A.: Minthint: automated synthesis of repair hints. In: Proceedings of the 36th International Conference on Software Engineering, ICSE 2014, pp. 266–276. ACM, New York, NY, USA (2014)
6. Mandelin, D., Xu, L., Bodík, R., Kimelman, D.: Jungloid mining: helping to navigate the api jungle. In: PLDI (2005)
7. Nguyen, H.D.T., Qi, D., Roychoudhury, A., Chandra, S.: Semfix: program repair via semantic analysis. In: Notkin, D., Cheng, B.H.C., Pohl, K. (eds.) 35th International Conference on Software Engineering, ICSE 2013, San Francisco, CA, USA, 18–26 May 2013, pp. 772–781. IEEE/ACM (2013)
8. Pavlinovic, Z., King, T., Wies, T.: Finding minimum type error sources. In: Proceedings of the 2014 ACM International Conference on Object Oriented Programming Systems Languages & Applications, OOPSLA 2014, pp. 525–542. ACM, New York, NY, USA (2014)
9. Pei, Y., Wei, Y., Furia, C.A., Nordio, M., Meyer, B.: Code-based automated program fixing. In: Alexander, P., Pasareanu, C.S., Hosking, J.G. (eds.) 26th IEEE/ACM International Conference on Automated Software Engineering, ASE 2011, Lawrence, KS, USA, 6–10 November 2011, pp. 392–395. IEEE (2011)
10. Perelman, D., Gulwani, S., Ball, T., Grossman, D.: Type-directed completion of partial expressions. In: PLDI, pp. 275–286 (2012)

Formal Design and Safety Analysis of AIR6110 Wheel Brake System

M. Bozzano[1], A. Cimatti[1], A. Fernandes Pires[1(✉)], D. Jones[2], G. Kimberly[2], T. Petri[2], R. Robinson[2(✉)], and S. Tonetta[1]

[1] Fondazione Bruno Kessler, Trento, Italy
{bozzano,cimatti,anthony,tonettas}@fbk.eu
[2] The Boeing Company, P.O. Box 3707, Seattle, WA 98124, USA
{david.h.jones,greg.kimberly,tyler.j.petri,
richard.v.robinson}@boeing.com

Abstract. SAE Aerospace Information Report 6110, "Contiguous Aircraft/System Development Process Example," follows the development of a complex wheel brake system (WBS) using processes in the industry standards ARP4754A, "Guidelines for Development of Civil Aircraft and Systems," and ARP4761, "Guidelines and Methods for Conducting the Safety Assessment Process on Civil Airborne Systems and Equipment."

AIR6110 employs informal methods to examine several WBS architectures which meet the same requirements with different degrees of reliability.

In this case study, we analyze the AIR6110 with formal methods. First, WBS architectures in AIR6110 formerly using informal steps are recreated in a formal manner. Second, methods to automatically analyze and compare the behaviors of various architectures with additional, complementary information not included in the AIR6110 are presented. Third, we provide an assessment of distinct formal methods ranging from contract-based design, to model checking, to model based safety analysis.

Keywords: Aerospace recommended practices · Case study · Model checking · Safety analysis · Fault tree · Contract-based design

1 Introduction

General Context. As aerospace systems become more complex and integrated, it becomes increasingly important that the development of these systems proceeds in a way that minimizes development errors. Advisory Circular (AC) 20-174 [13] from the FAA specifies the Society for Automotive Engineering (SAE) guidance, Aerospace Recommended Practice (ARP) ARP4754A [24], "Guidelines for Development of Civil Aircraft and Systems," as a method (but not the only method) for developing complex systems. ARP4754A along with its companion ARP4761 [23], "Guidelines and Methods for Conducting the Safety Assessment Process on Civil Airborne Systems and Equipment," provide the guidance that

© Springer International Publishing Switzerland 2015
D. Kroening and C.S. Păsăreanu (Eds.): CAV 2015, Part I, LNCS 9206, pp. 518–535, 2015.
DOI: 10.1007/978-3-319-21690-4_36

original equipment manufacturers (OEMs) such as Boeing and Airbus may utilize to demonstrate that adequate development and safety practices were followed, and that final products meet performance and safety requirements while minimizing development errors.

System safety assessment is a development process compatible with ARP4761 which ensures that system architectures meet functional and safety requirements. Architecture decisions take system functions and safety into account through the use of countermeasures to faults such as redundancy schemas, fault reporting, maintenance, and dynamic system reconfiguration based on fault detection, isolation, and recovery (FDIR). The role of safety assessment is to evaluate whether a selected design is sufficiently robust with respect to the criticality of the function and the probability of fault occurrence. For example, functions with catastrophic hazards must not have any single failure that can result in that hazard. Also, each level of hazard category (catastrophic, hazardous, major, minor) has an associated maximum probability that must be ensured by the design. For all functions, the system architecture and design must support availability and integrity requirements commensurate with the functional hazards. Among the various analyses, the construction of fault trees [26] is an important practice to compare different architectural solutions and ensure a compliant design.

The AIR6110 *Document.* Aerospace Information Report (AIR) AIR6110 [25] is an informational document issued by the SAE that provides an example of the application of the ARP4754A and ARP4761 processes to a specific aircraft function and implementing systems. The non-proprietary example of a wheel brake system (WBS) in this AIR demonstrates the applicability of design and safety techniques to a specific architecture. The WBS in this example comprises a complex hydraulic plant controlled by a redundant computer system with different operation modes and two landing gears each with four wheels. The WBS provides symmetrical and asymmetrical braking and anti-skid capabilities. AIR6110 steps the reader through a manual process leading to the creation of several architectural variants satisfying both functional and safety requirements, and cost constraints.

Contribution. In this paper, the informal process employed in AIR6110 is examined and enhanced using a thorough, formal methodology. We show how formal methods can be applied to model and analyze the case study presented in AIR6110. This formal method supports multiple phases of the process, explores the different architectural solutions, and compares them based on automatically produced artifacts.

The formal modeling and analysis are based on the integration of several techniques, supported by a contract-based design tool (OCRA [7]), a model checker (NUXMV [6]), and a platform for model-based safety analysis (XSAP [1]). Using these techniques and tools, we create models for the various architectures described in AIR6110, demonstrate their functional correctness, and analyze a number of requirements from the safety standpoint, automatically producing fault trees with a large number of fault configurations, and probabilistic reliability measures.

Distinguishing Features. The work described in this paper is important for several reasons. First, it describes a fully-automated analysis of a complex case study, covering not only functional verification but also safety assessments. Second, we propose the integration of different formal techniques (e.g., architectural decomposition, contract-based design, model checking, model-based safety analysis, and contract-based safety analysis) within an automated, unifying flow, which we analyze in terms of scalability and accuracy. Finally, we report interesting results from the standpoint of the AIR6110. Specifically, we provide qualitative and quantitative analyses of the WBS, through an examination of the respective merits of the various architectures. We also show that a flaw affects more architectures than reported in AIR6110.

Related Work. The WBS described in ARP4761 has been used in the past as a case study for techniques on formal verification, contract-based design and/or safety analyses (see, e.g., [9,11,20,21]). With respect to these works, this case study is much more comprehensive, describes a more elaborate design, and is the only one to automatically produce fault trees. In [3], contract-based fault-tree generation is applied to the ARP4761 WBS, but on a much smaller architecture than those considered in this paper. Moreover, the current work is unique in the literature, in that it takes into account the process described in AIR6110 and analyzes the differences between the various architectures.

There are many applications of formal methods in the industrial avionics process. The ESACS [12], ISAAC [19], and MISSA [22] projects pioneered the ideas of model extension and model-based safety assessment, and proposed automatic generation of fault trees. However, we are not aware of other significant case studies combining contract-based design, formal verification, and model-based safety analysis (with automated fault tree generation) as in the methodology described in this paper.

Plan of the Paper. In Sect. 2 we present the informal AIR6110 application and process. In Sect. 3 we give an overview of our formal process. In Sect. 4 we discuss the formal models of the WBS. In Sect. 5 we present the results of the formal analyses. In Sect. 6 we discuss the lessons learned, and outline future work.

2 AIR 6110

2.1 Overview of the Standards

ARP4754A [24] and ARP4761 [23] define Recommended Practices for development and safety assessment processes for the avionics field. The practices prescribed by these documents are recognized by the Federal Aviation Administration (FAA) as acceptable means for showing compliance with federal regulations [13,14], and have been used by the industry of the field for years.

The Aerospace Information Report 6110 (AIR6110) document was released by SAE in 2011. It describes the development of sub-systems for a hypothetical aircraft following the principles defined in ARP4754A, and shows the relationships with the ARP4761. AIR6110 focuses on the Wheel Brake System (WBS) of a passenger aircraft designated model S18. The hypothetical S18 aircraft is capable of transporting between 300 and 350 passengers, and has an average flight duration of 5 h.

2.2 Overview of the Wheel Brake System

The WBS of the S18 is a hydraulic brake system implementing the aircraft function *"provide primary stopping force"*. In particular, it provides braking of the left and right main landing gears, each with four wheels. In addition to coupled braking, each landing gear can be individually controlled by the pilot through a dedicated (left/right) brake pedal.

WBS Architecture and Behavior. An overview of the WBS architecture is shown in Fig. 1. For the sake of clarity, the control system is not decomposed and sensors for the pedal position and the wheels' angular speed are not represented.

The WBS is composed of a physical system and a control system. The physical system includes hydraulic circuits running from hydraulic pumps to wheel brakes and thus providing braking force to each of the 8 wheels. The physical system can be electrically controlled by the Braking System Control Unit (BSCU) of the control system, or mechanically controlled directly through the pedals' mechanical position, depending on the operation mode of the WBS.

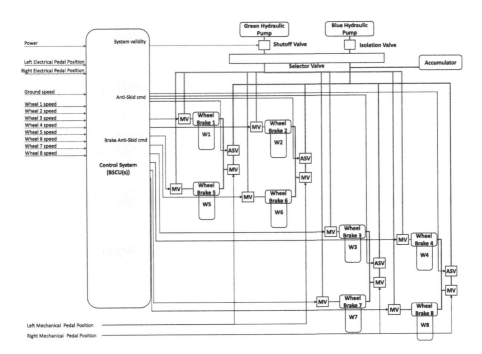

Fig. 1. WBS architecture overview (MV=Meter Valve; ASV=AntiskidShutoff Valve; W=Wheel)

522   M. Bozzano et al.

There are 3 different operation modes. In *normal mode*, braking is effected by the primary hydraulic circuit, referred to as the green circuit. The green circuit is composed of a hydraulic pump and 8 meter valves, one valve for each wheel. Each valve is individually controlled by electrical commands provided by the BSCU. The BSCU signals a combined brake and antiskid command, which may be different for each wheel. The brake command depends on the electrical signal received from the pilot pedal. The antiskid command is computed based using sensor inputs that indicate ground speed, wheel speed and brake command.

In *alternate mode*, braking is effected by a second hydraulic circuit, called the blue circuit. The 8 wheels are mechanically braked in pair, 2 pairs per landing gear. The blue circuit is composed of a hydraulic pump, 4 meter valves and 4 anti-skid shutoff valves. Each meter valve is mechanically commanded by its associated pilot pedal. The switch between green and blue circuits is mechanically controlled via a selector valve. When the selector valve detects a lack of pressure in the green circuit, it automatically switches to the blue circuit. When the green circuit becomes available again, it switches from the blue circuit back to the green circuit. A lack of pressure in the green circuit can occur if the hydraulic pump of the circuit fails or if the pressure is cut by a shutoff valve. The shutoff valve is closed if the BSCU becomes invalid.

Emergency mode is supported by the blue circuit, operating only in case the hydraulic pump fails. In this case, an accumulator backs up the circuit with hydraulic pressure, supplying sufficient pressure to mechanically brake the aircraft. An isolation valve placed before the pump prevents pressure from flowing back to the pump.

WBS Requirements. The AIR6110 document contains several requirements for the WBS. These can be grouped in two main categories: Requirements corresponding to safety, e.g., *the loss of all wheel braking shall be extremely remote*, and others, e.g., *the WBS shall have at least two hydraulic pressure sources*.

Our case study focuses on five safety requirements, that are well representative of safety requirements that should be handled during safety assessment:

S18-WBS-R-0321. *Loss of all wheel braking (unannunciated or annunciated) during landing or RTO shall be extremely remote*

S18-WBS-R-0322. *Asymmetrical loss of wheel braking coupled with loss of rudder or nose wheel steering during landing or RTO shall be extremely remote*

S18-WBS-0323. *Inadvertent wheel braking with all wheels locked during takeoff roll before V1 shall be extremely remote*

S18-WBS-R-0324. *Inadvertent wheel braking of all wheels during takeoff roll after V1 shall be extremely improbable*

S18-WBS-R-0325. *Undetected inadvertent wheel braking on one wheel w/o locking during takeoff shall be extremely improbable*

Intuitively, a safety requirement associates the description of an undesirable behaviour or condition (e.g. "inadvertent wheel braking") with a lower bound on its likelihood, according to terminology (e.g. "extremely improbable") defined in [15].

2.3   The Informal Development Process

The AIR6110 document describes the development process shown in Fig. 2 as applied to the WBS. It details the development of the WBS system architecture in four versions, each obtained after design choices of different types.

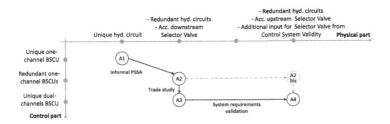

Fig. 2. Five architectures

ARCH1 is the high-level architecture of the WBS. It represents the first step in the architecture definition by defining the main functional elements of the WBS. It incorporates only one hydraulic circuit and one Control Unit.

ARCH2 is the first concrete architecture which meets basic safety requirements. The development of ARCH2 is motivated by performing a Preliminary System Safety Assessment (PSSA) on ARCH1, which results in the introduction of redundancy in the hydraulic circuits and in command computation with two BSCUs in the control system.

ARCH3 is motivated by trade studies on ARCH2. The purpose of the trade study is to assess other architectures answering to the same safety requirements as ARCH2 and which are less expensive and easier to maintain. Only the control system architecture is modified by going from two BSCUs to one dual-channeled BSCU.

ARCH4 is driven by validation of safety requirements on ARCH3. Specifically, a safety requirement addressing mutual exclusion of the operating modes of the WBS is shown to be unmet. ARCH3 is modified to meet the requirement. Only the physical system is modified, by adding an input to the selector valve corresponding to the validity of the control system and moving the accumulator in front of the selector valve.

For our case study, we added an architecture variant called ARCH2BIS which is based on the control system architecture of ARCH2 and the physical system architecture of ARCH4. The purpose is to show that it is possible to detect the issue that motivated the change to ARCH4 earlier in the design process at ARCH2.

3   Formal Approach

The formal approach to modeling and analyzing the case study follows the process depicted in Fig. 3. The main steps are: component-based modeling of the

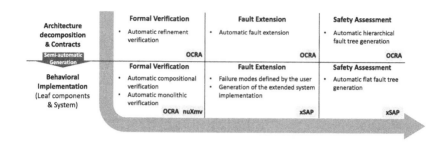

Fig. 3. Overview of the process and the related tool support.

system architecture and contract-based specification of the architectural decomposition; definition of the behavioral implementation of components at the leaves of the architecture, generation of the full system implementation and formal verification of the properties; extension of the model with failures to include faulty behaviors of components; production of a safety analysis based on fault-tree analysis.

The formal approach is supported by a set of tools developed by the Fondazione Bruno Kessler, namely OCRA [7,9,10,17] for contract-based specification, verification, and safety analysis of the architecture decomposition; nuXmv [6,16] for formal verification of the behavioral implementation; and xSAP [1,4,18] for model-based safety analysis of the behavioral implementation.

Formal Verification of the Architectural Decomposition. The architecture decomposition is expressed in the OCRA language and the component contracts are expressed in linear temporal logic (LTL). The system architecture is hierarchically decomposed into constituent components, until leaf components of the system are reached. Each component has an interface defining the boundary between the component implementation and its environment. An interface consists of a set of input and output ports through which the component implementation interacts with its environment. A composite component is refined into a synchronous composition of sub-components. The decomposition also defines interconnections among the ports of the subcomponents and the composite component. The implementation of a composite component is given by the composition of the implementations of the subcomponents. Similarly, the environment of a subcomponent is given by the composition of the other subcomponents.

The properties in component contracts are formalized into LTL formulas following the Contract-Based Design supported by OCRA. Each component is enriched with contracts that define the correct refinement of the architecture. A contract is composed of an assume clause, which represents the property that the environment of the component must ensure, and a guarantee clause which describes the property that the component must ensure. Contracts of refined components are refined by the contracts of their sub-components. This refinement can be automatically checked by OCRA by generating and discharging a set of proof obligations that are validity problems for LTL.

Formal Verification of the Behavioral Implementation. OCRA can also generate implementation templates for leaf components of the architecture. Implementation templates are generated in the SMV language [6]. The user needs to provide only the implementations of leaf components in the template. Once done, OCRA can take into account these implementations to automatically generate a full system implementation in the SMV language. During this generation, the component contracts are automatically translated as LTL properties in the system implementation. Each leaf component implementation can be checked according to the component contracts defined in the architecture decomposition using OCRA. The full system implementation can also be monolithically checked using the symbolic model checker NUXMV.

Model-Based Safety Analysis (MBSA). xSAP is used to support extending a nominal model with failure modes provided by the user. A failure mode represents the behavior of a component in the context of a given failure. Failure modes can be defined from the xSAP fault library using a dedicated language for fault-extension. Once failure modes are defined for each component, xSAP can proceed to the fault extension of the nominal model and generate a new SMV implementation taking into account failure behaviors.

This extended model is used to conduct Model-Based Safety Analysis on the system using xSAP. More precisely, xSAP can generate flat fault trees based on this extended model. Such fault tree is a set of Minimal Cut Sets (MCS), which are the minimal configurations of faults leading to a Top Level Event (TLE). Here, the TLEs of the fault trees are the violations of the LTL properties resulting from the contracts provided in the architecture decomposition. Notice that a probability can be attached to each failure mode by the user, which will allow xSAP to compute the probability for the TLE to happen.

Contract-Based Safety Analysis (CBSA). An alternative way to perform safety analysis is provided by OCRA given the contract-based specification of the architecture [3]. The architecture decomposition is automatically extended with failure modes based on the contracts to generate a hierarchical fault tree. The TLEs of these fault trees are violations of the system contracts of the architecture. The intermediate events are violations of the subcomponents' contracts.

4 Formal Models

4.1 Modeling Nominal Aspect

Key Features. The WBS architectures presented in AIR6110 are modeled following the formal approach described in Sect. 3. In order to formalize the case study, we applied some simplifying abstractions to the concrete system. First, we consider the hydraulic circuits as a unidirectional circuit, thus avoiding relational modeling of the circuit. As a consequence, the isolation valve present in Fig. 1 is not relevant for the modeling and is removed from our models.

Another abstraction concerns the representation of hydraulic pressure in the hydraulic components, for example at the valve interfaces. All ports representing hydraulic pressure are expressed as bounded integers between 0 and 10 (represented as enumeration), as are ports representing braking force. A similar abstraction is applied to commands sent by the BSCU. All commands are represented as boolean values. The angular speed of each wheel is treated similarly. The angular speed of a wheel is represented by a wheel status, stopped or rolling. Under this representation, the wheel is considered to be skidding if the aircraft is moving and the wheel is stopped. These choices were made to limit complexity of the models while keeping a sufficient level of detail to obtain relevant results from the analysis.

We consider two behaviors for pressure supplied to hydraulic circuits. First, a hydraulic pump supplies hydraulic pressure only if the pump is supplied by electrical power and hydraulic fluid. This allows emphasizing the different mode changes defined in the WBS, depending on the pressure supply of each circuit. Second, the accumulator is considered to have an infinite reserve of pressure. This choice is justified by the fact that the model does not incorporate a concept of measuring "sufficient" pressure necessary to brake the aircraft.

Finally, all models are defined using discrete time and all component behaviors are instantaneous, i.e., all inputs are computed at the same time step where inputs are provided. There is only one exception that concerns the wheel component: Braking force applied on the wheel determines the status of the wheel at the next step.

Architecture Decomposition. The decomposition of the WBS architectures is accomplished according to information provided in the AIR6110, extended by clarifications from brake system subject matter experts. Each architecture is decomposed into numerous sub-components. For example, the BSCU is decomposed into sub-modules that monitor the system and that create commands. The wheel brake is decomposed into a hydraulic fuse[1], a hydraulic piston and a brake actuator. Metrics for the different architectures are given in Table 1.

Behavior Implementation. The implementation of the leaf components is provided by the user, based on the implementation templates generated by OCRA. The architecture decomposition allows a wide reuse of the leaf component implementations through the architecture variants. For example, the leaf component implementations of ARCH2 and ARCH3 are identical. The only differences are due to the architecture decomposition at upper-levels, as introduced in Sect. 2. Similarly, ARCH2BIS and ARCH4 have the same leaf components; they differ from ARCH2 and ARCH3 in the implementation of the selector valve that is not only commanded by the pressure in inputs, but also by the control system validity. The largest delta between architectures is the change from ARCH1 to the rest. Due to the lack of redundancy, some of the leaf component implementations are different from ARCH2, ARCH2BIS, ARCH3 and ARCH4, or even not present at all, e.g., the selector valve.

---

[1] We consider that the hydraulic fuse is a simple pipe in the nominal model.

Table 1. Formal modeling metrics

		ARCH1	ARCH2	ARCH2BIS	ARCH3	ARCH4
Architecture decomposition	Total components types	22	29	29	30	30
	Leaf components types	15	20	20	20	20
	Total components instances	100	168	168	169	169
	Leaf components instances	79	143	143	143	143
	Max depth	5	5	5	6	6
	Nb. contracts	121	129	129	142	142
System implementation	Nb. properties	199	291	291	304	304
	State variables Bool.	31	79	79	79	79
	Enum	55	88	88	88	88
Extended System implementation	Failure modes	28	33	33	33	33
	Fault variables	170	261	261	261	261
	State variables Bool.	74	156	156	156	156
	Enum	184	311	311	311	311

The full system implementation is automatically generated by OCRA, using the architecture decomposition and the leaf component implementations. The translation from the OCRA architecture to the SMV file preserves the structure, leveraging the use of modules. The contracts present in the OCRA file are translated as LTL properties in the system implementation. Metrics about the system implementation are given in Table 1, where we report the number of state variables and the number of property instances available for the system implementation, based on the properties generated from the contracts for each component type.

Requirements Formalization and Decomposition. The five safety requirements expressed in Sect. 2.2 are translated as contracts at the system level. They are modeled as follows: First, we remove flight phase and speed value from the requirements, as we do not have sufficiently details about them in the models. The treatment of the required likelihood is ignored in the modeling, and is delayed to the phase of safety analysis. The undesirable condition is instead stated never to occur. For example, the requirements S18-WBS-0323 becomes "never inadvertent wheel braking with all wheels locked".

```
COMPONENT MeterValve
 INTERFACE
  INPUT PORT elec_cmd: boolean;
  INPUT PORT mech_cmd: boolean;
  INPUT PORT hyd_pressure_in: 0..10;
  OUTPUT PORT hyd_pressure_out: 0..10;

  CONTRACT apply_command
  assume: true;
  guarantee: always(((elec_cmd or mech_cmd) and hyd_pressure_in>0)
                 iff (hyd_pressure_out>0));
```

Listing 1.1. Architectural specification in OCRA for the Meter Valve

In addition, the requirements S18-WBS-R-0322 is split into two different contracts, one for the left side and one for the right side. The requirement S18-WBS-R-0325 is also split in eight contracts, one for each wheel.

In the subsequent phase of contract decomposition, these five safety requirements are in turn broken down into contracts for sub-components, describing the properties they must ensure, based on the description provided in AIR6110 and clarifications provided by subject matter experts. Additional contracts are also added to ensure the expected behavior of each component (e.g., braking force is applied when commanded). The number of contracts defined on each architecture is given in Table 1.

These contracts are then automatically translated into LTL properties in the system implementation, as described in Sect. 3.

```
MODULE MeterValve(elec_cmd, mech_cmd, hyd_pressure_in)
VAR
  hyd_pressure_out : {0, 1, 2, 3, 4, 5, 6, 7, 8, 9, 10};
LTLSPEC NAME apply_command_norm_guarantee :=
  (TRUE -> G(((elec_cmd | mech_cmd) & hyd_pressure_in>0) <-> hyd_pressure_out>0));
ASSIGN
  hyd_pressure_out := ((mech_cmd | elec_cmd) ? hyd_pressure_in : 0) ;
```

Listing 1.2. Example of SMV implementation for the Meter Valve

Example of the Meter Valve. A meter valve is a valve that will open if it receives a command. There are two possible commands: electrical or mechanical, both described as boolean in our model. The specification of the Meter Valve in the architecture decomposition is given Listing 1.1. Its behavioral implementation is given Listing 1.2.

In this implementation, the only part added by the user is the ASSIGN part. All the rest is automatically generated by OCRA based on the architecture decomposition.

4.2   Modeling Safety Aspects

Failure Modes and Extended Model. A set of failure modes for the WBS has been defined for each component, based on expert clarifications: hydraulic pumps can fail to supply pressure to the hydraulic circuit; valves can fail open or closed (meter valves and antiskid shutoff valves can also be stuck at the last commanded position or at a random position); the accumulator can fail open or closed; hydraulic fuses can close the circuit; brake pistons and brake actuators can be stuck on, or off, or at the last position; wheels can fail with no rotation; sensors or BSCU components can send erroneous signals: the selector valve (occurring in ARCH2, ARCH2BIS, ARCH3, ARCH4) can fail only to its last position; switch gates (occurring in the control system of ARCH2, ARCH2BIS, ARCH3, ARCH4) can fail at the last position or in an intermediate position.

All failure modes described above can be encoded using predefined failure modes in the XSAP fault library. The user specifies possible failure modes for each component (a single component may be associated to more than one failure mode) using XSAP fault extension language. Then, the generation of the extended model is automatically carried out by XSAP. The extended model is typically two to three times larger than the model before extension.

An example of failure mode for the meter valve is given Listing 1.3. It describes a failure "failed closed" based on the predefined failure mode *StuckAt-ByValue* available in the XSAP fault library. For more details about the fault extension language, see [18].

```
EXTENSION OF MODULE MeterValve
    SLICE MeterValve_faults AFFECTS hyd_pressure_out WITH
    MODE MeterValve_FailedClosed {3.25e-6} : Permanent StuckAtByValue_I(
        data term << 0,
        data input << hyd_pressure_out,
        data varout >> hyd_pressure_out,
        event failure);
```

Listing 1.3. Example of failure mode "failed closed" for the Meter Valve

Availability of the fault extension affords a number of advantages. First, it guarantees the alignment of the nominal and extended models, avoiding a typical problem in safety analysis practice. Second, it saves a substantial amount of tedious modeling of faults, and thus improves productivity. Third, as for the implementation of the leaf components, the definition of failure modes for each component allows a similar rate of reuse for each architecture. Metrics about the failure modes and the extended model of each architecture are given in Table 1. To conduct a safety analysis on the extended models, the violation of the safety requirements described above are used as TLE.

Contract Based Safety Analysis (CBSA). The fault extension for the CBSA is automatically managed by the tool on the architecture decomposition. In comparison with the fault extension provided by the user in the MBSA, the CBSA approach takes into account all possible failure modes that will disprove the contract of a component.

5   Automated Analyses

For the models described in the previous section, we carried out an experimental evaluation along the following dimensions: formal verification, construction of Fault Trees, and comparison of architectures.

Formal Verification. The monolithic models, in form of SMV files, were analyzed with respect to properties resulting from the contracts in the architecture. We used NUXMV, running different verification engines: BDD-based model checking and IC3 [5]. The same results were also obtained via the contract-based approach of OCRA. The contract based verification process is based on the following steps: the top level properties are stated as contracts in the form of temporal logic formulae at the system level; each component is associated with contracts; the correctness of each contract refinement is proved by means of temporal entailment checks; the SMV module associated with each leaf component is proved to correctly implement the corresponding contracts.

Table 2. Results of the formal verification (time in seconds)

Arch	Monolithic approach		Compositional approach			
	BDD	IC3	Ref.	Impl.	Tot.	VPar
ARCH1	38.32	56.62	1422.24	6.07	1428.31	439.62
ARCH2	2700.64	153.28	102.04	1.26	103.30	24.12
ARCH2BIS	3069.82	153.19	32.38	1.26	33.64	1.39
ARCH3	2935.88	159.01	72.87	1.29	74.16	10.74
ARCH4	3429.59	158.51	29.74	1.29	31.03	1.78

All experiments have been performed on a cluster of 64-bit Linux machines with 2.7 Ghz Intel Xeon X5650 CPU, using one core with a memory limit set to 10Gb. The results are reported in Table 2 (with Ref. and Impl. representing time taken for the contract refinement and leaf implementation checks).

The results show that the compositional approach is often faster than the monolithic analysis. Consider also that contract refinement and implementation checks are fully independent and localized, and can in principle be executed in parallel. The VPar column in Table 2 reports maximum computation time across various individual checks, corresponding to the limit case where each check is run on a dedicated machine.

Aside from performance considerations, the most important result of the formal verification is that the analysis of some sanity checks pinpointed a problem with ARCH2 that is not reported in AIR6110. The problem is caused by the fact that the accumulator is positioned downstream of the selector valve, so that a fault in the accumulator can cause inadvertent braking. The problem is only reported for ARCH3; ARCH2BIS was included in the analysis to correct the problem.

Fault-Tree Analysis. We now consider the construction of Fault Trees for each of the architectures and requirements, from the models obtained with the model extension functionality of xSAP, as described in Sect. 3. Each TLE is the violation of a system requirement. In order to cope with scalability issues, we limited the space of the problem in two ways: restricting the set of faults, and limiting the cardinality of the cut sets. This follows a standard practice in traditional safety analysis: given the manual effort required, priority is given to cut sets of lower cardinality or greater likelyhood.

The analyses have been run on the five architectures, for all safety properties and two additional properties. For each property, cardinality goes from 1 to 5, and also with no restriction. In addition to the complete set of faults, six different restricted sets of faults have been defined and observed. In total, 3150 fault tree constructions have been launched. Overall the activity resulted in 3089 computed fault trees and 61 computations timed out. The fault trees have minimal cut sets ranging from 0 to tens of thousands. All fault tree constructions have been performed using IC3 engine on a cluster of 64-bit Linux machines with CPU going from 2.4 Ghz to 2.7 Ghz Intel Xeon, with a memory limit set to 30Gb and a time limit of 10 h.

Table 3. Fault trees results for ARCH4 (- represents a timed out computation)

Arch/Prop		Prob.	$|mcs| = 1$	$|mcs| = 2$	$|mcs| = 3$	$|mcs| = 4$	$|mcs| = 5$	Full
Arch4	S18-WBS-R-0321	4.51e-10	0	6	627	629	-	N
	S18-WBS-R-0322-left	1.00e-05	2	2	203	46287	-	N
	S18-WBS-R-0322-right	1.00e-05	2	2	203	46287	-	N
	S18-WBS-0323	0	0	0	0	0	0	N
	S18-WBS-R-0324	2.50e-11	0	1	0	2	8729	N
	S18-WBS-R-0325-wheel1	1.20e-04	9	12	2596	0	0	Y
	S18-WBS-R-0325-wheel2	1.20e-04	9	12	2596	0	0	Y
	S18-WBS-R-0325-wheel3	1.20e-04	9	12	2596	0	0	Y
	S18-WBS-R-0325-wheel4	1.20e-04	9	12	2596	0	0	Y
	S18-WBS-R-0325-wheel5	1.20e-04	9	12	2596	0	0	Y
	S18-WBS-R-0325-wheel6	1.20e-04	9	12	2596	0	0	Y
	S18-WBS-R-0325-wheel7	1.20e-04	9	12	2596	0	0	Y
	S18-WBS-R-0325-wheel8	1.20e-04	9	12	2596	0	0	Y
	cmd implies braking w1	1.13e-04	13	30	7428	3815	1768	Y
	braking implies cmd w1	1.25e-04	10	24	2647	4530	59	Y

For lack of space, we report only a sample of the results obtained for ARCH4. A detailed account of the results for all architectures, as well as the formal models and artifacts produced by the analyses, are available at [2]. Table 3 reports the number of minimal cut sets for the 15 chosen properties, for the full set of faults, with cardinality going from 1 to 5. The last column indicates whether the computation has been completed without cardinality bound (Y) or if it timed out (N). We also report the probability (Prob.) for each of the top-level events, for an association of the basic faults with a probability (in the N cases, the reported value is a lower bound). The execution time required to generate results ranges from seconds (for fault tree with dozens of minimal cut sets) to minutes or hours (for fault tree with thousands of minimal cut sets).

The problem was also tackled by means of contract-based safety analysis [3]. Given the inherent scalability of the contract based approach, we were able to produce hierarchical fault trees (HFT). The fault trees have been produced in a few minutes for all top level contracts for the full configurations. As discussed in [3], the compositional approach produces hierarchical fault trees whose corresponding set of minimal cut sets is an over-approximation of the one obtained with the monolithic approach. This was confirmed in the experiments. We also notice that over-approximation is a common practice in safety analysis. The two approaches can be considered complementary.

Architectures Comparison. We carried out a global comparison of the architectures, based on the results obtained for each of them. Basically, the findings confirmed the weaknesses of ARCH1: its number of "single points of failure", i.e. minimal cut sets of cardinality 1, is always greater, or equal, than in the other architectures. The probabilities associated to the TLEs concerning the loss of wheel braking (S18-WBS-R-0321, S18-WBS-R-0322-left/right) are also greater than in the other architectures. The probability associated to the inadvertent braking of one wheel without locking (S18-WBS-R-0325-wheelX) is better in

ARCH1 than in the other architectures. This is due to the fact that even if there is the same number of minimal cut sets at lower cardinality, the components at fault are not the same and neither is reliability.

The fault trees for the pair ARCH2 and ARCH3 are the same, which suggests that the modification of the control system (i.e. the difference between the two architectures) has no impact on the safety; same observations hold for the pair ARCH2BIS and ARCH4. This is to be expected, since the change is triggered by a trade study aiming at reducing costs and easing maintenance, but the two control systems are designed according to the same redundancy principles, i.e. double Control Unit. The difference is that in one case the two CU's can be physically positioned in different places, while in the other they are part of a unique subsystem (which can, in very rare situations, break the assumption of independence of the two CU's). Common Cause Analysis, in particular Zonal Safety Analysis (ZSA), could confirm this point, and will be part of future activity.

The superiority of ARCH2BIS on ARCH2 (and similarly of ARCH4 on ARCH3) is demonstrated by a lower number of minimal cut sets with cardinality greater than 1. For the TLEs concerning the loss of wheel braking (S18-WBS-R-0321, S18-WBS-R-0322-left/right), the lower number of minimal cut sets appears at cardinality 3. For the TLE concerning the inadvertent braking of all wheels with locking (S18-WBS-0323), there is no difference up to cardinality 5. Concerning the inadvertent braking of all wheels (S18-WBS-R-0324), the lower number of minimal cut sets appears at cardinality 4. For the TLEs concerning the inadvertent braking of one wheel without locking (S18-WBS-R-0325-wheelX) the lower number of minimal cut sets appears at cardinality 2.

6 Conclusions, Lessons Learned and Further Work

We presented a complete formal analysis of the AIR6110 [25], a document describing the informal design of a Wheel Brake System. We covered all the phases of the process, and modeled the case study by means of a combination of formal methods including contract-based design, model checking and safety analysis. We were able to produce modular descriptions of five architectures, and to analyze their characteristics in terms of a set of safety requirements, automatically producing over 3000 fault trees, as well as quantitative reliability measures. We remark that one of the analyzed architectures (ARCH2BIS) was the result of detecting an unexpected dependency in the phases of the AIR6110. Specifically, the trade study on the control system (leading from ARCH2 to ARCH3) was carried out on an architecture suffering from a misplaced position of the accumulator (fixed in ARCH4). In the following, we discuss some lessons learned, and outline directions for future activities.

Lessons Learned. The value in going from an informal description to a formal model was clearly recognized: the AIR6110 omits important information that is assumed to be background knowledge. The ability to produce the artifacts of the traditional design flow (e.g., architectural diagrams for visual inspection, fault trees) supported the interaction with subject matter experts, who were able to provide fundamental information to increase the accuracy of the models.

MBSA is a fundamental factor for this kind of application. First, it provides for automated construction of models encompassing faults from models containing only nominal behaviours. Second, traditional verification techniques, that allow to prove or disprove properties, are not sufficient: the automated synthesis of the set of minimal cut sets (i.e. the configurations causing property violations) is required to support the informal process and to provide a suitable granularity for the comparison of various architectural solutions. This approach also provides strong support for trade studies.

A key factor is the availability of automated and efficient engines. IC3 and its extensions to the computation of minimal cut sets allowed for the analysis of architectures that were completely out of reach for BDD-based safety assessment algorithms.

The use of an architectural modeling language, as proposed in the Contract Based approach supported by OCRA (and its integration with NUXMV), allows to reuse both models and contracts. For example, the similar architectures (e.g., ARCH3 and ARCH4) share a very large part of their models. This also makes it possible to analyze architectural variants with moderate effort.

There is a fundamental role for contract-based design. Its key advantages are the ability to mimic the informal process, thus ensuring traceability, and to support proof reuse. Contract-based design also supports the construction of Hierarchical Fault Trees, which are a fundamental artifact compared to the flat presentation of the set of minimal cut sets. The CBSA approach outlined in [3] enables for hierarchical fault tree generation, which are much easier to compute, and exhibit more structure when compared to a flat presentation of minimal cut sets. The open problem is how to evaluate the amount of approximation associated with the method.

Future Work. We will continue this work along the following directions, also driven by the findings in the case study. We will explore the use of alternative and more expressive modeling formalisms that may be more adequate to describe systems at a higher level of detail. For example, we will consider the use of SMT and more expressive logics, both on discrete and hybrid traces [8].

Contract-based design poses important challenges in terms of debugging. In particular, there is a need for suitable diagnostic information to support contract formulation (e.g., to understand why a certain contract refinement does not hold).

Another direction concerns increasing scalability for safety analysis. Realistic cases require the analysis of tens of thousands of minimal cut sets. We will investigate techniques to gain efficiency by introducing approximations (e.g., limiting cardinality and likelihood of cut sets); an important requirement will be the ability to calculate the degree of approximation of the result.

References

1. Bittner, B., Bozzano, M., Cavada, R., Cimatti, A., Gario, M., Griggio, A., Mattarei, C., Micheli, A., Zampedri, G.: The xSAP Safety Analysis Platform. ArXiv e-prints (2015)
2. Bozzano, M., Cimatti, A., Fernandes Pires, A., Jones, D., Kimberly, G., Petri, T., Robinson, R., Tonetta, S.: AIR6110 Wheel Brake System case study. https://es.fbk.eu/projects/air6110
3. Bozzano, M., Cimatti, A., Mattarei, C., Tonetta, S.: Formal safety assessment via contract-based design. In: Cassez, F., Raskin, J.-F. (eds.) ATVA 2014. LNCS, vol. 8837, pp. 81–97. Springer, Heidelberg (2014)
4. Bozzano, M., Villafiorita, A.: Design and Safety Assessment of Critical Systems. CRC Press (Taylor and Francis), Boca Raton (2010). An Auerbach Book
5. Bradley, A.R.: SAT-based model checking without unrolling. In: Jhala, R., Schmidt, D. (eds.) VMCAI 2011. LNCS, vol. 6538, pp. 70–87. Springer, Heidelberg (2011)
6. Cavada, R., Cimatti, A., Dorigatti, M., Griggio, A., Mariotti, A., Micheli, A., Mover, S., Roveri, M., Tonetta, S.: The nuXmv symbolic model checker. In: Biere, A., Bloem, R. (eds.) CAV 2014. LNCS, vol. 8559, pp. 334–342. Springer, Heidelberg (2014)
7. Cimatti, A., Dorigatti, M., Tonetta, S.: OCRA: a tool for checking the refinement of temporal contracts. In: 28th IEEE/ACM International Conference on Automated Software Engineering (ASE), pp. 702–705 (2013)
8. Cimatti, A., Roveri, M., Tonetta, S.: Requirements validation for hybrid systems. In: Bouajjani, A., Maler, O. (eds.) CAV 2009. LNCS, vol. 5643, pp. 188–203. Springer, Heidelberg (2009)
9. Cimatti, A., Tonetta, S.: A property-based proof system for contract-based design. In: 38th Euromicro Conference on Software Engineering and Advanced Applications (SEAA), pp. 21–28 (2012)
10. Cimatti, A., Tonetta, S.: Contracts-refinement proof system for component-based embedded systems. Sci. Comput. Program. **97**, 333–348 (2014)
11. Damm, W., Hungar, H., Josko, B., Peikenkamp, T., Stierand, I.: Using contract-based component specifications for virtual integration testing and architecture design. In: Design, Automation and Test in Europe (DATE), pp. 1023–1028 (2011)
12. ESACS: The ESACS Project. www.transport-research.info/web/projects/project_details.cfm?ID=2658. Accessed 20 May 2015
13. FAA: F.A.A.: Advisory Circular (AC) 20–174. http://www.faa.gov/documentLibrary/media/Advisory_Circular/AC%2020-174.pdf
14. FAA: F.A.A.: Advisory Circular (AC) 23–1309-1E. http://www.faa.gov/documentLibrary/media/Advisory_Circular/AC%2023.1309-1E.pdf
15. FAA: F.A.A.: Advisory Circular (AC) 25.1309-1A. http://rgl.faa.gov/Regulatory_and_Guidance_Library/rgAdvisoryCircular.nsf/list/AC%2025.1309-1A/$FILE/AC25.1309-1A.pdf (1988)
16. FBK: nuXmv: a new eXtended model verifier. https://nuxmv.fbk.eu
17. FBK: OCRA: A tool for Contract-Based Analysis. https://ocra.fbk.eu
18. FBK: xSAP: eXtended Safety Analysis Platform. https://xsap.fbk.eu
19. ISAAC: The ISAAC Project. http://ec.europa.eu/research/transport/projects/items/isaac_en.htm. Accessed 20 May 2015
20. Joshi, A., Heimdahl, M.P.E.: Model-based safety analysis of simulink models using SCADE design verifier. In: Winther, R., Gran, B.A., Dahll, G. (eds.) SAFECOMP 2005. LNCS, vol. 3688, pp. 122–135. Springer, Heidelberg (2005)

21. Joshi, A., Whalen, M., Heimdahl, M.: Model-based safety analysis final report. Technical Report, NASA/CR-2006-213953, NASA (2006)
22. MISSA: The MISSA Project. www.missa-fp7.eu. Accessed 20 May 2015
23. SAE: ARP4761: Guidelines and Methods for Conducting the Safety Assessment Process on Civil Airborne Systems and Equipment (1996)
24. SAE: ARP4754A: Guidelines for Development of Civil Aircraft and Systems (2010)
25. SAE: AIR6110: Contiguous Aircraft/System Development Process Example (2011)
26. Vesely, W., Stamatelatos, M., Dugan, J., Fragola, J., Minarick III, J., Railsback, J.: Fault tree handbook with aerospace applications. Technical report, NASA (2002)

Meeting a Powertrain Verification Challenge

Parasara Sridhar Duggirala$^{(\boxtimes)}$, Chuchu Fan, Sayan Mitra,
and Mahesh Viswanathan

University of Illinois, Urbana-champaign, USA
{duggira3,cfan10,mitras,vmahesh}@illinois.edu

Abstract. We present the verification of a benchmark powertrain control system using the hybrid system verification tool C2E2. This model comes from a suite of benchmarks that were posed as a challenge problem for the hybrid systems community, and to our knowledge, we are reporting its first verification. For this work, we implemented the algorithm reported in [10] in C2E2, to automatically compute local discrepancy (rate of convergence or divergence of trajectories) of the model. We verify the key requirements of the model, specified in signal temporal logic (STL), for a set of driver behaviors.

1 A Challenge Problem

As the targets for fuel efficiency, emissions, and drivability become more demanding, automakers are becoming interested in pushing the design automation and verification technologies for automotive control systems. The benchmark suite of powertrain control systems were published in [11,12] as challenge problems that capture some of the difficulties that arise in verification of realistic systems. It consists of a sequence of Simulink^{TM}/Stateflow^{TM} models of the engine with increasing levels of sophistication and fidelity. At a high-level, the models take inputs from a driver (throttle angle) and the environment (sensor failures), and define the dynamics of the engine. The key controlled quantity is the air to fuel ratio which in turn influences the emissions, the fuel efficiency, and torque generated. The requirements for the system are stated in signal temporal logic (STL). A typical property, for example, $\Diamond_t(x \in [x_{eq} - \epsilon, x_{eq} + \epsilon])$, states that after t units of time, the continuous variable x is within the range $x_{eq} \pm \epsilon$. Breach [4] and STaliro [2] have been used for finding counterexamples (or falsifying) models in [5,12–14]. These techniques can show the presence of executions that violate a requirement, but not their absence. The technique used in this paper proves that all the executions from a given set of initial states and a set of switching signals satisfies (or violates) the requirement. To the best of our knowledge, this is the first time a model in the powertrain control benchmark is verified.

The model we consider in this paper is polynomial hybrid automata model (Model 3, Sect. 3.3) of [12]. Although this model is given as a Simulink^{TM} diagram with switch blocks, it can be transformed to a hybrid automaton with 4 locations and 5 continuous variables. The dynamics of the system is given by highly nonlinear polynomial differential equations. The mode transitions are

© Springer International Publishing Switzerland 2015
D. Kroening and C.S. Păsăreanu (Eds.): CAV 2015, Part I, LNCS 9206, pp. 536–543, 2015.
DOI: 10.1007/978-3-319-21690-4_37

brought about by the input signal from the driver and there are uncertainties in the initial set owing to measurement inaccuracies. Using an improved version of the C2E2 tool [6,7] we are able to perform reachability analysis of this model and we verify the requirements with respect to a set of relevant driver behaviors. In principle, Flow* [3] is designed to handle polynomial hybrid automata models, however, it was unable to verify the models considered in this paper, owing to the complexity of nonlinear dynamics.

C2E2 is a verification tool for a general class of nonlinear hybrid systems. The previous version of C2E2 [6,7] required the user to provide a special type of annotation for the model, called *discrepancy function*, which essentially captures the rate of convergence (or divergence) of neighboring trajectories. Finding discrepancy functions for nonlinear models can be challenging. One of the main developments that enabled this verification, is the implementation of a new algorithm in C2E2 (presented in detail in [10]) for automatic computation of local discrepancy along trajectories of the system. Using this improved C2E2, we were not only able to find counterexamples, but also verify the key STL requirements of the powertrain benchmark in the order of minutes.

2 Nonlinear Hybrid Powertrain Model

Simulink^{TM} model for the powertrain control system is shown in Fig. 1(a). The system has four continuous variables p, λ, p_e, i (see Fig. 1(b)), and four modes of operation: *startup*, *normal*, *power*, and *sensor_fail*. The mode switches (also called *transitions*) are brought about by changes in the input *throttle angle* θ_{in} or *failure* events.

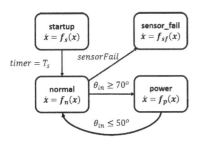

Variable	Description
p	Intake manifold pressure
p_e	Intake manifold pressure estimate
λ	Air-fuel ratio
i	Integrator state, control variable
θ_{in}	Throttle angle

(a) Hybrid automata model of powertrain control system.

(b) Table with state variables and their description.

Fig. 1. Figure showing the model in (a) and the model variables in (b).

The rest of the Simulink^{TM} diagram defines polynomial differential equations that govern the evolution of the continuous variables in the four different modes. As an example, we reproduce the differential equation for normal mode of operation.

$$\dot{p} = c_1(2\theta_{in}(c_{20}p^2 + c_{21}p + c_{22}) - c_{12}(c_2 + c_3\omega p + c_4\omega p^2 + c_5\omega^2 p))$$
$$\dot{\lambda} = c_{26}(c_{15} + c_{16}c_{25}F_c + c_{17}c_{25}^2 F_c^2 + c_{18}\dot{m}_c + c_{19}\dot{m}_c c_{25}F_c - \lambda)$$
$$\dot{p}_e = c_1(2c_{23}\theta_{in}(c_{20}p^2 + c_{21}p + c_{22}) - (c_2 + c_3\omega p_e + c_4\omega p_e^2 + c_5\omega^2 p_e))$$
$$\dot{i} = c_{14}(c_{24}\lambda - c_1 1).$$

Here $F_c = \frac{1}{c_{11}}(1 + i + c_{13}(c_{24}\lambda - c_{11}))(c_2 + c_3\omega p_e + c_4\omega p_e^2 + c_5\omega^2 p_e)$, $\dot{m}_c = c_{12}(c_2 + c_3\omega p + c_4\omega p^2 + c_5\omega^2 p)$, and all the c_i's are constant parameters of the model.

This model is translated to a hybrid automaton form that is accepted by C2E2. The operating modes correspond to the locations of the automaton, the variables correspond to the above continuous variables, the differential equations define the trajectories, and the discrete transitions among the locations is defined by a piecewise constant input signal θ_{in} from the driver behavior. C2E2 currently handles only closed automaton models. Therefore, for every driver behavior of interest, we explicitly construct a family of switching signals that determine the timing of the mode switches. The initial set of the automaton is a ball in the state space which corresponds to the measurement uncertainty in state components.

The goal of the powertrain control system is to maintain the air-fuel ratio at a desired value for optimal functioning of internal combustion engine under different driving behaviors and conditions. These control objectives or requirements are stated in [12] using STL formulas. An example requirement for the *normal* mode of operation is the following:

$$rise \Rightarrow \Box_{(\eta,\zeta)}(0.98\lambda_{ref} \leq \lambda \leq 1.02\lambda_{ref}), \tag{1}$$

which can be read as "If the throttle angle θ_{in} changes from 0 to 60, denoted by the event *rise*, then the air-fuel ratio λ should be in the range $[0.98\lambda_{ref}, 1.02\lambda_{ref}]$ after η time units and stay in that region until ζ time units". Here λ_{ref} is the reference (desired) air-fuel ratio and η and ζ are parameters of the property. We note that this type of requirements can also be expressed as bounded time invariants— the class of properties currently handled by C2E2. We simply need to introduce a *timer* variable that keeps track of time elapsed since the last occurrence of the relevant events like *rise* in the above example.

3   Verification Using C2E2 with Local Discrepancy

C2E2 implements a generic, simulation-based, algorithm for bounded time verification of invariant and temporal precedence properties of nonlinear hybrid models (see [6–8] for details). The algorithm iteratively computes more precise over-approximations of the reachable states of the system until it either proves the property (the requirement) or finds a counter-example. These over-approximations are computed for each location and for the duration that the system is in that location. The set of reachable states at the end of that interval serves as the starting set for the next location and so on. Thus, the key step in the algorithm is to compute and refine reach set over-approximations for ODEs for a given location. This step uses validated simulations and discrepancy functions [6].

A *validated simulation* of an ordinary differential equation (ODE) $\dot{x} = f(x)$ from an initial state x_0 with error bound ϵ is a sequence of time-stamped regions $\psi = (R_0, t_0), \ldots, (R_k, t_k)$ such that for each time interval $[t_{i-1}, t_i]$ the solution $\xi(x_0, .)$ resides in the region R_i and $dia(R_i) \leq \epsilon$. A uniformly continuous function $\beta : \mathbb{R}^n \times \mathbb{R}^n \times \mathbb{R}_{\geq 0} \to \mathbb{R}_{\geq 0}$ is a *discrepancy function* of the above ODE if (a) for any pair of states $x, x' \in \mathbb{R}^n$, and any time $t > 0$, $\|\xi(x, t) - \xi(x', t)\| \leq \beta(x, x', t)$, and (b) for any t, as $x \to x'$, $\beta(., ., t) \to 0$. Thus, β gives an upper bound on the rate of divergence of two neighboring trajectories and this bound vanishes as their initial states approach each other.

In order to check whether the system satisfies an invariant I over a time horizon T, the C2E2 algorithm starts with a δ-cover of the initial set and proceeds as follows: from each point x_0 in the cover C a validated simulation is generated and then bloated by a factor given by the discrepancy function. This bloated set is an over-approximation of the reachset from the δ-neighborhood $(B_\delta(x_0))$ of x_0. If this set is disjoint from (or contained in) I^c then the algorithm infers that the initial set $B_\delta(x_0)$ satisfies (or violates, respectively) I. Otherwise, a finer cover of $B_\delta(x_0)$ is created and added to C for computing a more precise over-approximation of the reach set from $B_\delta(x_0)$. The first property of the discrepancy function gives the soundness of this algorithm, and the second property gives relative completeness (see, Theorem 13 from [6]).

This approach requires the user to provide discrepancy functions which can be burdensome. Although Lipschitz constants, contraction metrics [15], and incremental Lyapunov functions [1] can be used to get discrepancy for certain classes of models, none of these approaches give an algorithm for computing β for general nonlinear ODEs. In this paper, we use the algorithm presented in [10] for computing local discrepancy functions on-the-fly along validated simulations. This algorithm uses the Jacobian J_f and a Lipschitz constant L_f of the ODE. First it computes a coarse over-approximation $S(x_i)$ of the reach set from a simulation point for a short duration. Then it computes an exponential (possibly negative) bound on the divergence rate of trajectories over $S(x_0)$ by finding a bound on the maximum eigenvalue of the symmetric part of the Jacobian J_f over the region $S(x_0)$. We refer the reader to the technical report [10] for the details of this algorithm.

3.1   Tool Implementation and Engineering

Implementation. For verifying the powertrain system, we implemented the local discrepancy algorithm in C2E2[1]. This modified implementation only requires

---

[1] The modified tool and related files are available from http://publish.illinois.edu/c2e2-tool/powertrain-challenge/.

the user to supply the Jacobian matrix of the system. The eigenvalues of the symmetric parts of the Jacobian are computed using Eigen library [9]. For maximizing the norm of error matrices our implementation uses interval arithmetic.

Coordinate Transformation. An important technical detail that makes the implementation scale is the coordinate transformation proposed in [10]. For Jacobian matrices with complex eigenvalues the local discrepancy computed directly using the above algorithm can be a positive exponential even though the actual trajectories are not diverging. This problem can be avoided by first computing a local coordinate transformation and then applying the algorithm. Coordinate transformation provides better convergence, but comes with a multiplicative cost in the error term. This trade-off between the exponential divergence rate and the multiplicative error has be tuned by choosing the time horizon over which the coordinate transformation is computed.

Model Reduction. In *start up* and *power* mode of the system, the differential equation does not update the value of the integrator variable i, i.e., $\dot{i} = 0$. Moreover, i does not appear in the right hand side of the differential equations for variables p, λ, p_e. We take advantage of these observations, and consider only the dynamics of the variables p, λ, and p_e for computing local discrepancy.

4   Experimental Results on Powertrain Challenge

We have implemented the algorithm described in Sect. 3 as a prototype extension of the tool C2E2. Verification of key properties of powertrain systems is typically performed on a standard set of driver behaviors as the number of switching signals corresponding to driver behaviors are infinite. In this paper, we pick two sets of driver behaviors provided in [12] that visit all the modes of the system. Further, to enable verification with C2E2, the STL properties were encoded as bounded time safety properties. Hence, the properties in [12] which involved integrals over paths, could not be verified. Table 1 provides the results of verifying different STL properties.

The first six properties provided in Table 1 are invariant properties. These invariant properties can be global (i.e. correspond to all modes) or could be restricted to a certain mode of operation provided in the *Mode* column. The invariants assert that the air-fuel ratio should not go out of the specified bounds. Observe that C2E2 could not only prove that the given specification is satisfied, but also that a stricter version of invariants for *startup* and *power* modes is violated. The next four properties are about the settling time requirements. These requirements enforce that in a given mode, whenever an action is triggered, the fuel air ratio should be in the given range provided after η (or η^{pwr} for power mode) time units. Similar to the invariant properties, C2E2 could also find counterexample for a stricter version of the settling time requirement (η^s settling time instead of η) in *power* mode. When C2E2 finds an overapproximation that violates a given property, it immediately terminates and hence C2E2 takes less time when it finds counterexamples. The parameters used for verification are $\eta = \eta^{pwr} = 1$, $\eta^s = 0.5$, $T_s = 9$, $T = 20$, $\lambda_{ref} = 14.7$, $\lambda_{ref}^{pwr} = 12.5$, and

Table 1. Table showing the result and the time taken for verifying STL specification of the powertrain control system. Sat: Satisfied, Sim: Number of simulations performed. All the experiments are performed on Intel Quad-Core i7 processor, with 8 GB ram, on Ubuntu 11.10.

Property	Mode	Sat	Sim	Time
$\Box_{T_s,T}\lambda \in [0.8\lambda_{ref}, 1.2\lambda_{ref}]$	*all modes*	yes	53	11 m 58 s
$\Box_{[0,T_s]}\lambda \in [0.8\lambda_{ref}, 1.2\lambda_{ref}]$	*startup*	yes	50	10 m 21 s
$\Box_{[T_s,T]}\lambda \in [0.95\lambda_{ref}, 1.05\lambda_{ref}]$	*normal*	yes	50	10 m 28 s
$\Box_{[T_s,T]}\lambda \in [0.8\lambda_{ref}^{pwr}, 1.2\lambda_{ref}^{pwr}]$	*power*	yes	53	11 m 12 s
$\Box_{[0,T_s]}\lambda \in [0.98\lambda_{ref}, 1.02\lambda_{ref}]$	*startup*	no	2	0 m 24 s
$\Box_{[T_s,T]}\lambda \in [0.9\lambda_{ref}^{pwr}, 1.1\lambda_{ref}^{pwr}]$	*power*	no	4	0 m 43 s
$rise \Rightarrow \Box_{(\eta,\zeta)}\lambda \in [0.9\lambda_{ref}, 1.1\lambda_{ref}]$	*startup*	yes	50	10 m 40 s
$rise \Rightarrow \Box_{(\eta,\zeta)}\lambda \in [0.98\lambda_{ref}, 1.02\lambda_{ref}]$	*normal*	yes	50	10 m 15 s
$(\ell = power) \Rightarrow \Box_{(\eta^{pwr},\zeta)}\lambda \in [0.95\lambda_{ref}^{pwr}, 1.05\lambda_{ref}^{pwr}]$	*power*	yes	53	11 m 35 s
$(\ell = power) \Rightarrow \Box_{(\eta^s,\zeta)}\lambda \in [0.95\lambda_{ref}^{pwr}, 1.05\lambda_{ref}^{pwr}]$	*power*	no	4	0 m 45 s

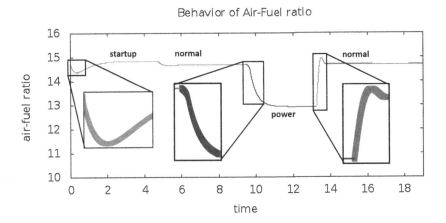

Fig. 2. Figure showing the reachable set of the powertrain control system for a given user behavior that visits different modes.

$\zeta = 4$. Set of reachable states of the powertrain control system for a given driver behavior is provided in Fig. 2.

5 Conclusions and Future Work

In this paper, we have successfully applied the simulation based verification technique with local discrepancy functions to find counterexamples and verify the polynomial hybrid automata model of powertrain benchmark challenge. This case study suggests that verification using on-the-fly discrepancy function along with the coordinate transformation can handle complex nonlinear dynamics. In future, we wish to extend these techniques to handle higher fidelity models in the powertrain verification challenge. These models contain delay differential equations, actuation delays, and look up tables, which C2E2 cannot currently handle.

Acknowledgment. We thank Jim Kapinski, Jyo Desmukh, and Xiaoqing Jin of Toyota for several useful discussions on the powertrain models. This research is funded by research grants from the National Science Foundation (grant: CAR 1054247 and NSF CSR 1016791) and the Air Force Office of Scientific Research (AFOSR YIP FA9550-12-1-0336).

References

1. Angeli, D.: A lyapunov approach to incremental stability properties. IEEE Trans. Autom. Control **47**(3), 410–421 (2000)
2. Annpureddy, Y., Liu, C., Fainekos, G., Sankaranarayanan, S.: S-TaLiRo: a tool for temporal logic falsification for hybrid systems. In: Abdulla, P.A., Leino, K.R.M. (eds.) TACAS 2011. LNCS, vol. 6605, pp. 254–257. Springer, Heidelberg (2011)
3. Chen, X., Ábrahám, E., Sankaranarayanan, S.: Flow*: an analyzer for non-linear hybrid systems. In: Sharygina, N., Veith, H. (eds.) CAV 2013. LNCS, vol. 8044, pp. 258–263. Springer, Heidelberg (2013)
4. Donzé, A.: Breach, a toolbox for verification and parameter synthesis of hybrid systems. In: Touili, T., Cook, B., Jackson, P. (eds.) CAV 2010. LNCS, vol. 6174, pp. 167–170. Springer, Heidelberg (2010)
5. Dreossi, T., Dang, T., Donzé, A., Kapinski, J., Jin, X., Deshmukh, J.V.: Efficient guiding strategies for testing of temporal properties of hybrid systems. In: Havelund, K., Holzmann, G., Joshi, R. (eds.) NFM 2015. LNCS, vol. 9058, pp. 127–142. Springer, Heidelberg (2015)
6. Duggirala, P.S., Mitra, S., Viswanathan, M.: Verification of annotated models from executions. In: Proceedings of the International Conference on Embedded Software, EMSOFT 2013, pp. 1–10. IEEE (2013)
7. Duggirala, P.S., Mitra, S., Viswanathan, M., Potok, M.: C2E2: a verification tool for stateflow models. In: Baier, C., Tinelli, C. (eds.) TACAS 2015. LNCS, vol. 9035, pp. 68–82. Springer, Heidelberg (2015)
8. Duggirala, P.S., Wang, L., Mitra, S., Viswanathan, M., Muñoz, C.: Temporal precedence checking for switched models and its application to a parallel landing protocol. In: Jones, C., Pihlajasaari, P., Sun, J. (eds.) FM 2014. LNCS, vol. 8442, pp. 215–229. Springer, Heidelberg (2014)
9. Eigen, a C++ template library for linear algebra. http://eigen.tuxfamily.org Accessed Feb 2015
10. Fan, C., Mitra, S.: Bounded verification using on-the-fly discrepancy computation. Technical report UILU-ENG-15-2201, Coordinated Science Laboratory. University of Illinois at Urbana-Champaign (2015)
11. Jin, X., Deshmukh, J.V., Kapinski, J., Ueda, K., Butts, K.: Benchmarks for model transformations and conformance checking. In: 1st International Workshop on Applied Verification for Continuous and Hybrid Systems (ARCH) (2014)

12. Jin, X., Deshmukh, J.V., Kapinski, J., Ueda, K., Butts, K.: Powertrain control verification benchmark. In: Proceedings of the 17th international conference on Hybrid systems: computation and control, pp. 253–262. ACM (2014)

13. Jin, X., Donzé, A., Deshmukh, J.V., Seshia, S.A.: Mining requirements from closed-loop control models. In: Proceedings of the 16th international conference on Hybrid systems: computation and control, pp. 43–52. ACM (2013)

14. Jin, X., Donzé, A., Deshmukh, J.V., Seshia, S.A.: Mining requirements from closed-loop control models. In: EEE Transactions on Computer-Aided Design of Integrated Circuits and Systems (2016, to appear)

15. Lohmiller, W., Slotine, J.J.E.: On contraction analysis for non-linear systems. Automatica **36**(4), 683–696 (1998)

Synthesising Executable Gene Regulatory Networks from Single-Cell Gene Expression Data

Jasmin Fisher[1,2], Ali Sinan Köksal[3], Nir Piterman[4],
and Steven Woodhouse[1](✉)

[1] University of Cambridge, Cambridge, UK
[2] Microsoft Research Cambridge, Cambridge, UK
[3] University of California, Berkeley, USA
[4] University of Leicester, Leicester, UK
sjw229@cam.ac.uk

Abstract. Recent experimental advances in biology allow researchers to obtain gene expression profiles at single-cell resolution over hundreds, or even thousands of cells at once. These single-cell measurements provide snapshots of the states of the cells that make up a tissue, instead of the population-level averages provided by conventional high-throughput experiments. This new data therefore provides an exciting opportunity for computational modelling. In this paper we introduce the idea of viewing single-cell gene expression profiles as states of an asynchronous Boolean network, and frame model inference as the problem of reconstructing a Boolean network from its state space. We then give a scalable algorithm to solve this synthesis problem. We apply our technique to both simulated and real data. We first apply our technique to data simulated from a well established model of common myeloid progenitor differentiation. We show that our technique is able to recover the original Boolean network rules. We then apply our technique to a large dataset taken during embryonic development containing thousands of cell measurements. Our technique synthesises matching Boolean networks, and analysis of these models yields new predictions about blood development which our experimental collaborators were able to verify.

1 Introduction

As biological data becomes more accurate and becomes available in larger volumes, researchers are increasingly adopting concepts from computer science to the modelling and analysis of living systems. Formal methods have been successfully applied to gain insights into biological processes and to direct the design of new experiments [3–5,12]. New single-cell resolution gene expression measurement technology provides an exciting opportunity for modelling biological systems at the cellular level. Single-cell gene expression profiles provide a snapshot of the true states that cells can reach in the real experimental system, a level of detail which has not been available before [15,18]. A major challenge for

© Springer International Publishing Switzerland 2015
D. Kroening and C.S. Păsăreanu (Eds.): CAV 2015, Part I, LNCS 9206, pp. 544–560, 2015.
DOI: 10.1007/978-3-319-21690-4_38

researchers is to move beyond established methods for the analysis of population data, to new techniques that take advantage of single-cell resolution data [14]. Uncovering and understanding the gene regulatory networks (GRNs) which underlie the behaviour of stem and progenitor cells is a central issue in molecular cell biology. These GRNs control the self-renewal and differentiation capabilities of the stem cells that maintain adult tissues, and become perturbed in diseases such as cancer. They also specify the complex developmental processes that lead to the initial formation of tissues in the embryo. Understanding how to effectively control GRNs can lead to important insights for the programmed generation of clinically-relevant cell types important for regenerative medicine, as well as into the design of molecular therapies to target cancerous cells.

Biological systems can be modelled at different levels of abstraction. At a molecular level, the biochemical events which occur inside a cell can be captured by stochastic processes, given by chemical master equations [24]. These chemical events are fundamentally stochastic, driven by random fluctuations of molecules present at low concentrations and by Brownian motion. Asynchronous Boolean networks abstract away details of transcription, translation and molecular binding reactions and represent the status of each modelled substance as either active (on) or inactive (off), while using non-determinism to capture different options that arise from stochastic behaviour [7,13,27]. In the cell, gene activity is controlled by combinatorial logic in which proteins called transcription factors cooperate to physically bind to a regulatory DNA region of a gene and trigger (or inhibit) its transcription. Target genes may in turn code for transcription factors, forming a complex GRN. Asynchronous Boolean networks are particularly well suited to modelling GRNs because the combinatorial logic regulating gene activity can be expressed as a Boolean function. For example, gene X may be activated by either the presence of gene A or by the presence of both genes B and C. The presence of a repressor D may prevent X from becoming triggered by the presence of these activating genes. When modelling the differentiation of a cell using an asynchronous Boolean network, dynamics proceed by a series of single–gene changes. Mature, differentiated cell types correspond to stable attractor states of the model.

Predictions about the modes of interaction between genes resulting from computational analysis can be tested experimentally through a range of assays. For example, if analysis of a model predicts that gene X is activated by gene A, a ChIP (Chromatin ImmunoPrecipitation) assay can be used to assess whether the protein coded for by A binds to a regulatory region of X. Then, perturbations which prevent the binding of A to this region can be introduced, and the effect that this has on the expression of X can be examined.

State–space analyses of hand–built asynchronous Boolean network models based on literature–derived gene regulatory interactions have been successfully applied to model cell fate decisions, and to reproduce known experimental results (e.g., [2,11,13]). Here we address the problem of automatically constructing such models directly from data. If we think of single-cell gene expression profiles as the state space of an asynchronous Boolean network, can we identify the underlying gene regulatory logic that could have generated this data?

We encode the matching of an asynchronous Boolean network to a state space as a synthesis problem and use constraint (satisfiability) solving techniques for answering the synthesis problem. The synthesised network has to match the data in two aspects. First, the resulting network should try to minimise transitions to expression points that are not part of the sampled data. Second, the resulting network should allow for a progression through the state space in a way that matches the flow of time through the different experiments that produced the data. A direct encoding of this problem into a satisfiability problem does not scale well. We suggest a modular search that handles parts of the state space and the network and does not need to reason about the entire network at once. We consider two test cases. First, we try to reconstruct an existing asynchronous Boolean network from its state space. We are able to reconstruct Boolean rules from the original network. Second, we apply our technique to experimental data derived from blood cell development. The network that is produced by our technique matches known dependencies and suggests interesting novel predictions. Some of these predictions were validated by our collaborators.

This paper describes the algorithm that we used to obtain the results in a recently published biological paper on a single-cell resolution study of embryonic blood development [16]. The biological paper includes full details of the experiment that generated the data, and the biological validation of our resulting synthesised model. Here, we cover the algorithmic aspects of our method.

2   Biological Motivation

Single-cell gene expression experiments produce gene expression profiles for individually measured cells. Each of these gene expression profiles is a vector where each element gives the level of expression of one gene in that cell. Figure 1 plots the level of the genes *Etv2* and *Runx1* over 3934 cells.

Our experimental collaborators performed such gene expression profiling on five batches of cells taken from four sequential developmental time points of a mouse embryo. For each time point, the experiment aimed to capture every cell with the potential to develop into a blood cell, providing a comprehensive

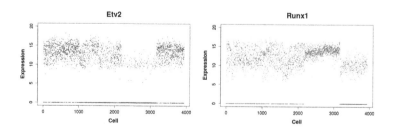

Fig. 1. Single–cell gene expression measurements for two genes, in 3934 cells.

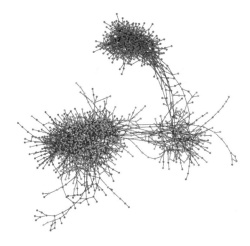

Fig. 2. State graph. Node colours correspond to the time point at which a state was measured. States from the earliest of the time points are coloured blue, and states from the last time point are coloured red (Color figure online).

single–cell resolution picture of the developmental timecourse of blood development. This resulted in a data set of 3934 cell measurements. Full details of this experiment and our analysis can be found in [16]. This data set is the first of its kind, attempting to capture an entire tissue's worth of progenitor cells across a developmental time course. This level of coverage of the potential cell state space is required for our approach to accurately recover gene regulatory networks, and requires the measurement of thousands of cell profiles. Later we will introduce a synthetic data set of a few hundred cell states in order to illustrate how our approach works, but we would like to stress that to be usable on real experimental data our algorithm needs to be able to scale thousands of cell states.

For each of 3934 cells, the level of expression of 33 transcription factor genes was measured. Expression levels are non-negative real numbers, where the value 0 indicates that the given gene is unexpressed in the cell (see Fig. 1).

The key idea introduced in this paper is to view this gene-expression data as a sample from the state-space of an asynchronous Boolean network. In the past, manually curated Boolean networks have been successfully used to recapitulate experimental results [2,11,13]. Such Boolean networks were hand–constructed from biological knowledge that has accumulated in the literature over many years. Here, we aim to produce such Boolean networks automatically, directly from gene expression data, by employing synthesis techniques. We aim to produce a Boolean network that can explain the data and can be used to inform biological experiments for uncovering the nature of gene regulatory networks in real biological systems.

In order to convert the data into a format that can be viewed as a Boolean network state space, we first discretise expression values to binary, assigning the value 1 to all non-zero gene expression measurements. A value of zero corresponds to the discovery threshold of the equipment used to produce the data. Discretising the

3934 expression profiles in this way yields 3070 unique binary states, where every state is a vector of 33 Boolean values corresponding to the activation/inactivation level of each of 33 genes in a given cell. In an asynchronous Boolean network, transitions correspond to the change of value of a single variable. Hence, we next look for pairs of states that differ by only one gene (that is, the Hamming distance between the two vectors is 1). An analysis of the strongly-connected components of this graph shows that one strongly connected component contains 44 % of the states. We note that in a random sample of 3934 elements from a space of 2^{33}, the chance of seeing repeats or neighbours with Hamming–distance 1 is negligible.

A plot of the graph of the largest strongly connected component is given in Fig. 2. We add an edge for every Hamming–distance 1 pair and cluster together highly connected nodes. The colours of nodes correspond to the developmental time the measurements was taken. Note that there is a clear separation between the earliest developmental time point and the latest one. This representation already suggests a clear change of states over the development of the embryo, with separate clusters identifiable and obvious fate transitions between clusters.

We wish to find an asynchronous Boolean network that matches this graph. For that we impose several restrictions on the Boolean network. Connections between states correspond to a change in the value of one gene, however, we do not know the direction of the change. Thus, we search simultaneously for directions and update functions of the different genes that satisfy the following two conditions: states from the earliest developmental time point should be able to evolve, through a series of single–gene transitions, to the states from the latest developmental time point. Secondly, the update functions must minimise the number of transitions that lead to additional, unobserved states, that were not measured in the experiment.

3   Example: Reconstructing an ABN from its State Space

We first illustrate our synthesis method using an example. We take an existing Boolean network, construct its associated state space, and then use this state space as input to our synthesis method in order to try to reconstruct the Boolean network that we started with.

Krumsiek *et al.* introduce a Boolean network model of the core regulatory network active in common myeloid progenitor cells [13]. Their network is based upon a comprehensive literature survey. It includes a set of 11 Boolean variables (corresponding to genes) and a Boolean update function for each variable (Fig. 3).[1] The model is given

Gene	Update function
Gata2	$Gata2 \land \neg(Pu.1 \lor (Gata1 \land Fog1))$
Gata1	$(Gata1 \lor Gata2 \lor Fli1) \land \neg Pu.1$
Fog1	$Gata1$
EKLF	$Gata1 \land \neg Fli1$
Fli1	$Gata1 \land \neg EKLF$
Scl	$Gata1 \land \neg Pu.1$
Cebpa	$Cebpa \land \neg(Scl \lor (Fog1 \land Gata1))$
Pu.1	$(Cebpa \lor Pu.1) \land \neg(Gata1 \lor Gata2)$
cJun	$Pu.1 \land \neg Gfi1$
EgrNab	$(Pu.1 \land cJun) \land \neg Gfi1$
Gfi1	$Cebpa \land \neg EgrNab$

Fig. 3. Boolean update functions for a manually curated network.

---

[1] The function of *Cebpa* is modified from that in [13] to match the format we assume.

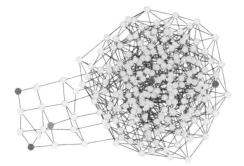

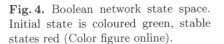

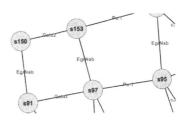

Fig. 4. Boolean network state space. Initial state is coloured green, stable states red (Color figure online).

Fig. 5. Close–up of Boolean network state space.

a well-defined initial starting state, representing the expression profile of the common myeloid progenitor, and computational analysis reveals an acyclic, hierarchical state space of 214 states with four stable state attractors (Fig. 4).

These stable attractors are in agreement with experimental expression profiles of megakaryocytes, erythrocytes, granulocytes and monocytes; four of the mature myeloid cell types that develop from common myeloid progenitors.

We treat the state space of this Boolean network as we would treat experimental data, forgetting all directionality information, and connecting all states which differ in the expression of only one gene by an undirected edge (Figs. 4 and 5, where each edge is labelled with the single gene that changes in value between the states it connects). We would now like to reconstruct the Boolean network given in Fig. 3 from this undirected state space.

For each gene, we would like to assign a direction to each of its labelled edges (or decide that it does not exist), in a way that is compatible with a Boolean update function. For example, in Fig. 5, we may orient the $Pu.1$-labelled edge between states 97 and 95 in the direction $s_{97} \to s_{95}$, in the direction $s_{95} \to s_{97}$, or decide that this is not a possible update. We also allow the edge to be directed in both directions. If $s_{97} \to s_{95}$, we want a Boolean update function $u_{Pu.1}$ that takes state s_{97} to state s_{95}. Since there is no $Pu.1$-labelled edge leaving state s_{150}, we can also add the constraint that $u_{Pu.1}$ takes s_{150} to s_{150}.

We also add reachability constraints that restrict which edges are included and their orientation. Since the state space was constructed starting from a well-defined initial state, we would like to enforce the constraint that each non-initial state ought to be reachable by some directed path from the initial state. Since cell development proceeds hierarchically and unidirectionally, we favour short paths over long paths. This eliminates routes that seem biologically implausible, for example routes that cross a fate transition and then return to where they began. It also reduces the space of paths we have to search through. By increasing the lengths of allowed paths, we can increase the number of considered solutions.

Gene	Synthesised update functions	Comments
Gata2	$Gata2 \wedge \neg(Fog1 \vee Pu.1)$ $Gata2 \wedge \neg(Fog1 \vee (Pu.1 \wedge Cebpa))$ $Gata2 \wedge \neg(Fog1 \vee (Pu.1 \wedge Gata2))$ $Gata2 \wedge \neg(Gata2 \wedge (Pu.1 \vee Fog1)$ $\mathbf{Gata2 \wedge \neg(Pu.1 \vee (Gata1 \wedge Fog1))}$ $Gata2 \wedge \neg(Pu.1 \vee (Gata2 \wedge Fog1))$	
Gata1	$(Gata1 \vee Cebpa) \wedge \neg Pu.1$ $(Gata2 \vee Fog1) \wedge \neg Pu.1$ $(Gata1 \vee Gata2) \wedge \neg Pu.1$ $\mathbf{(Gata1 \vee Gata2 \vee Fli1) \wedge \neg Pu.1}$ Other functions of the form $(X \vee Y \vee Z) \wedge \neg Pu.1$	
Fog1	$\mathbf{Gata1}$	Unique
EKLF	$\mathbf{Gata1 \wedge \neg Fli1}$	Unique
Fli1	$\mathbf{Gata1 \wedge \neg EKLF}$	Unique
Scl	$Gata1$ $\mathbf{Gata1 \wedge \neg Pu.1}$	
Cebpa	$Cebpa \wedge \neg(Fog1 \vee Scl)$ $Cebpa \wedge \neg(Cebpa \wedge (Scl \vee Fog1))$ $Cebpa \wedge \neg(Fog1 \wedge (Scl \vee Cebpa))$ $Cebpa \wedge \neg(Fog1 \vee (Scl \wedge Gata1))$ $Cebpa \wedge \neg(Fog1 \vee (Scl \wedge Gata2))$ $Cebpa \wedge \neg(Gata1 \wedge (Fog1 \vee Scl)$ $Cebpa \wedge \neg(Scl \vee (Fog1 \wedge Cebpa)$ $\mathbf{Cebpa \wedge \neg(Scl \vee (Fog1 \wedge Gata1))}$	
Pu.1	$Pu.1 \wedge \neg Gata2$ $(Pu.1 \wedge Cebpa) \wedge \neg Gata2$ $Pu.1 \wedge \neg(Gata1 \vee Gata2)$ Other functions of the form $Pu.1 \wedge \neg(Gata2 \vee X)$ $Pu.1 \wedge \neg(Gata2 \wedge Cepba)$ $Pu.1 \wedge \neg(Gata2 \wedge Pu.1)$ $Cebpa \wedge \neg(Gata1 \vee Gata2)$ $Cebpa \wedge \neg(Gata2 \vee Fog1)$ $\mathbf{(Cebpa \vee Pu.1) \wedge \neg(Gata1 \vee Gata2)}$ $(Cebpa \wedge Pu.1) \wedge \neg(Gata1 \vee Gata2)$ Other functions of the form $(Cebpa \vee X) \wedge \neg(Gata2 \vee Y)$ Other functions of the form $(Pu.1 \vee X) \wedge \neg(Gata2 \vee Y)$ Other functions of the form $(Cebpa \wedge Pu.1) \wedge \neg(Gata2 \vee X)$	
cJun	$\mathbf{Pu.1 \wedge \neg Gfi1}$	Unique
EgrNab	$\mathbf{(cJun \vee Gata1) \wedge \neg Gfi1}$	Incorrect with shortest paths
Gfi1	$\mathbf{Cebpa \wedge \neg EgrNab}$	Unique

Fig. 6. Synthesised update functions.

The results of applying our technique are shown in Figure 6. The method reconstructs the Boolean update functions for all but one gene (*EgrNab*), in some cases uniquely identifying the original function. We note that when multiple solutions are found for an update function, these solutions, while not exact, all provide useful regulatory information that could be verified experimentally. For example, both solutions for *Scl* successfully predict *Scl*'s activation by *Gata1*, although one of the two solutions omits its repression by *Pu.1*.

4   Background to Asynchronous Boolean Networks

An *asynchronous Boolean network* (ABN) is $B(V, U)$, where $V = \{v_1, v_2, \ldots, v_n\}$ is a set of *variables*, and $U = \{u_1, u_2, \ldots, u_n\}$ is a set of Boolean *update functions*. For every $u_i \in U$ we have $u_i : \{0,1\}^n \rightarrow \{0,1\}$ associated with variable v_i. A *state* of the system is a map $s : V \rightarrow \{0,1\}$. We say that an update function

u_i is *enabled* at state s if $u_i(s) \neq s(v_i)$, i.e. applying the update function u_i to state s changes the value of variable v_i.

State $s' = (d'_1, d'_2, \ldots, d'_n)$ is a *successor* of state $s = (d_1, d_2, \ldots, d_i, \ldots, d_n)$ if for some i we have u_i is enabled, $d'_i = u_i(s)$, and for all $j \neq i$ we have $d'_j = d_j$. That is, we get to the next state s', by non-deterministically selecting an enabled update function u_i and updating the value of the associated variable: $s' = (d_1, d_2, \ldots, u_i(d_i), \ldots, d_n)$. If no update function is enabled, the system remains in its current, stable, state, where it will remain: $s' = s$.

An ABN induces a labelled transition system $T = (N, R)$, where N is the set of 2^n states of the ABN, and $R \subseteq N \times V \times N$ is the successor relation. Each transition (s_1, v_i, s_2) is labelled with the variable v_i such that $s_1(v_i) \neq s_2(v_i)$.

The *undirected state space* of an ABN is an undirected graph $S = (N, E)$, where each vertex $n \in N$ is uniquely labelled with a state s of the Boolean network, and there is an edge $\{s_1, s_2\} \in E$ iff s_1 and s_2 differ in the value of exactly one variable, v. The edge $\{s_1, s_2\}$ is labelled with v. In general, an undirected state space does not have to include all 2^n states induced by a Boolean network.

An ABN $B(V, U)$ *induces* a *directed state space* on an undirected state space $S = (N, E)$. Consider the transition system $T = (2^V, R)$ of $B(U, V)$. Then, the induced directed state space is $S' = (N, A)$, where $(s_1, s_2) \in A$ implies that there is a variable v_i such that $(s_1, v_i, s_2) \in R$. We say that (s_1, s_2) is *compatible* with u_i, if $s_2(v_i) = u_s(s_1)$, and for every $j \neq i$ we have $s_2(v_j) = s_1(v_j)$.

5   Formal Definition of the Problem

Our synthesis problem can be stated as follows: we are given an undirected state space S over a given set of variables V. We would like to extract a set of Boolean update functions that induce a directed state space from S such that each of the states in S are reachable from a given set of initial states. We also want to ensure that no additional, undesired states not in S are reachable, by ruling out transitions which 'exit' the state space.

More formally, we are given a set of variables $V = \{v_1, v_2, \ldots, v_n\}$, an undirected state space $S = (N, E)$ over V, and a set $I \subseteq N$ of *initial* vertices.

We would like to find an update function $u_i : \{0,1\}^n \to \{0,1\}$ for each variable $v_i \in V$, such that the following conditions hold. Let $U = \{u_i \mid v_i \in V\}$ be the set of update functions.

1. Every non-initial vertex $s \in N - I$ is reachable from some initial vertex $s_i \in I$ by a directed path in the directed state space induced by $B(V, U)$ on S.
2. For every variable $v_i \in V$, let N_i be the set of states without an outgoing v_i-labelled arc. For every i we require that for each $s \in N_i$, $u_i(s) = s(v_i)$.

5.1   Generalising the Definition to Partial Data

Since we intend to apply our method in an experimental setting, where we only have an incomplete sample from the possible states of the system, we relax this definition to extend it to partial data. Instead of requiring that *every* state is reachable from those initial states that we have measured, we only require that a set of *final* states are reachable. Instead of requiring that every undesired transition is ruled out, we seek to maximise the number of such transitions which are eliminated. This is formally stated next.

As before, we are given a set of variables $V = \{v_1, v_2, \ldots, v_n\}$, an undirected state space $S = (N, E)$ over V, and a designated set $I \subseteq N$ of *initial* vertices. In addition, we are given a designated set $F \subseteq N$ of *final* vertices, along with a *threshold* t_i for each variable $v_i \in V$. The threshold t_i specifies how many undesired transitions must be ruled out.

We would like to find an update function $u_i : \{0,1\}^n \to \{0,1\}$ for each variable $v_i \in V$, such that the following conditions hold. Let $U = \{u_i \mid v_i \in V\}$ be the set of update functions.

1. Every final vertex $s_f \in F$ is reachable from some initial vertex $s_i \in I$ by a directed path in the directed state space induced by $B(V, U)$ on S.
2. For every variable $v_i \in V$, let N_i be the set of states without an outgoing v_i-labelled arc. For every i the number of states $s \in N_i$ such that $u_i(s) = s(v_i)$ is greater or equal to t_i.

In the remainder of the text, we refer to condition 1 as the *reachability condition* and condition 2 as the *threshold condition*.

We restrict the search to update functions of the form $f_1 \wedge \neg f_2$, where f_i is a monotone Boolean formula. The inputs to f_1 are the activating inputs to the gene and the inputs to f_2 are the the the repressing inputs. This restriction was chosen after discussion with biologist colleagues and consultation of the literature (e.g., [2,13]).

6   A Direct Encoding

We start with a direct encoding of the search for a matching Boolean network. The search is parameterised by the shape of update functions (how many activators and how many repressors each variable has), the length of paths from initial states to final states, and the thresholds for each variable. By increasing the first two parameters and decreasing the last we can explore all possible Boolean networks.

6.1   Possible Update Functions

In order to represent the Boolean update function for gene v_i, $u_i = f_1 \wedge \neg f_2$, we use a bitvector encoding. We represent the Boolean formula f_j by a set of bitvectors, $\{a_1, a_2, \ldots a_n\}$, $a_j \in V \cup \{\vee, \wedge\}$, where each bitvector a_i represents a variable or a Boolean operator, and solutions take the form of a binary tree. For example, the formula $v_1 \wedge (v_2 \vee v_3)$ is represented by the solution $a_1 = \wedge, a_2 = \vee, a_3 = v_1, a_4 = v_2, a_5 = v_3$. We restrict the syntactic form of possible update functions so that each variable appears only once, and each possible function has one canonical representation. For example, the function $(v_1 \wedge (v_2 \vee v_3))$ is included in our search space while $(v_1 \wedge v_2) \vee (v_1 \wedge v_3)$ is not. We search for functions up to a maximum number of activators, A_i, and a maximum number of repressors, R_i.

To encode the application of function u_i to a state s, $u_i(s)$, we add implications which unwrap the bitvector encoding of u_i to the constituent variables and logical operators; substituting values, $s(v_j)$, for variables, v_j, and directly mapping operations to logical constraints in the Boolean satisfiability formula. For example, the application of the function $(v_1 \vee v_2) \wedge \neg v_3$ to the state s_1 is mapped to $(s_1(v_1) \vee s_1(v_2)) \wedge \neg s_1(v_3)$.

6.2   Ensuring Reachability

To enforce the global reachability condition we consider all of the underlying directed edges in the undirected state space $S = (N, E)$, and their associated single–gene transitions.

Recall that we require every final vertex to be reachable from some initial vertex by a directed path in the directed state space induced on S by the Boolean network. That is, we require that every final vertex is reachable by a directed path, and that every v_j-labelled edge along this path is compatible with its associated update function, u_j.

To enforce this we add constraints that track the compatibility of edges with update functions and define reachability recursively. We consider reachability by paths up to a maximum length: recall that we consider shorter paths to be more biologically likely. By iteratively increasing the length of the paths considered, we can obtain all satisfying models.

We introduce a pair of Boolean variables e_{ij}, e_{ji} for each v_i-labelled undirected edge $\{s_i, s_j\} \in E$, which track the value of the application of u_i to s_i and to s_j (and the compatibility of the underlying directed edges (s_i, s_j) and (s_j, s_i) with u_i). e_{ij} is true iff $u_i(s_i) = s_j(v)$.

We introduce an integer given by a bitvector encoding, r_n, for each node $n \in N$. Bitvector r_n encodes the fact that node n is reachable from an initial node in r_n steps, up to some maximum encodable value $2^{|r_n|} - 1$. Bitvector r_n is given a value of -1 to indicate that n is not reachable in this maximum number of steps.

Reachability is then defined inductively:

1. Initial nodes are reachable in zero steps: for every $i \in I$, $r_i = 0$.
2. A non–initial node s_i is reachable in M steps if there is a compatible incoming edge (s_j, s_i) from another node s_j, and s_j is itself reachable in fewer than M steps. That is, for every $n = s_j \in N - I$ and $m = s_i \in N$ such that $\{s_i, s_j\} \in E$ we have $e_{ij} \to r_m < r_n$. We also have that non–initial nodes cannot be reached in zero steps: For every $n \in N - I$, $r_n = -1 \vee r_n > 0$.

Finally, we add a constraint that every final node $n \in F$ is reachable from some initial node: $r_n \neq -1$.

6.3   Enforcing the Threshold Condition

We enforce the threshold condition for each update function as follows.

Consider an update function $u_i : V \rightarrow \{0, 1\}$. We say that a node $s \in N_i$ is *negatively matched* by u_i if $u_i(s) = s(v_i)$. That is, by using u_i as the update function of variable v_i, u_i does not change the value of v_i from node s. We are searching for an update function such that a maximum number of nodes from N_i are negatively matched.

We add a variable, m_{is} for each node $s \in N_i$ to record whether u_i negatively matches s. We then add a constraint demanding that the number of negatively matched nodes is greater than or equal to the threshold: $\sum_{s \in N_i} m_{is} \geq t_i$.

We search for satisfying assignments to the constraint variables encoding the representation of the Boolean update functions u_i for all v_i in V. The resulting synthesised Boolean network is the combination of these update functions.

Unfortunately, in practice the direct encoding of the search does not scale to handle our experimental data. In the next section we suggest a compositional way to solve the problem.

7   A Compositional Algorithm

We now introduce our compositional algorithm, which scales better than the direct encoding given above. The problem of synthesising a Boolean network from the data is partitioned to three stages. Crucially, we avoid searching for a complete Boolean network and consider parts of the network that can be constructed independently.

7.1   Pruning the Set of Possible Edges

We start by building a directed graph from the given undirected state space $S = (N, E)$, by considering which of the underlying directed edges in E are compatible with some Boolean update function, and pruning those that are not. We consider each underlying directed edge (s_1, s_2) and (s_2, s_1) of each of the v_i-labelled undirected edges $\{s_1, s_2\}$ in E independently.

We pose a decision problem for each directed edge (s_1, s_2): whether there exists some Boolean update function u_i satisfying the threshold condition (condition 2, Sect. 5.1) such that $u_i(s_1) = s_2(v_i)$. This is encoded as a Boolean satisfiability problem, adding constraints to represent the encoding of the update function, the threshold condition, and the evaluation of the function at the specific edge under consideration. We say that a satisfying function, u_i, is *compatible* with (s_1, s_2). Once a compatible function has been found, it can quickly be evaluated outside the solver at other edges to try reduce the number of SAT queries we have to make.

After making a query for each edge, we are left with a directed graph, which is the existential projection of all compatible update functions for each of the variables $v \in V$. We have eliminated edges which have no compatible update function, and cannot participate in the reachability condition. On the example data set from Sect. 3, this step removes 18 % of the possible edges.

7.2 Ensuring Reachability

We now come to the only part of the algorithm that considers the edges of all variables together, in order to enforce the global reachability condition (condition 1, Sect. 5.1). This phase does not require the solving of a Boolean satisfiability problem, and as a result is very efficient.

We construct, for each pair of initial nodes $i \in I$ and final nodes $f \in F$, the shortest path p_{if} from i to f in the directed graph that was built in the previous phase of the algorithm. These paths can be computed via a breadth–first search.

Due to the edge pruning of the previous phase of the algorithm, if there is no path to a final node f, this implies that there are no satisfying models (at the given threshold and function size parameters). Otherwise, our reachability condition will be enforced by fixing a set of directed edges P_i for each variable $v_i \in V$ corresponding to these shortest paths. We will then require that the update function we search for, u_i, is compatible with each of the edges in P_i.

We choose, for each final node f, one path $p_f = p_{if}$ from one of the initial nodes i. By fixing this path, we ensure that f is reachable from an initial node. We define $p_f|_i$ as the set of v_i-labelled edges in the path p_f. We define P_i, the v_i-labelled edges which must be fixed to ensure reachability via the chosen paths, as the the set of v_i-labelled edges in p_f for each final node f:

$$P_i = \bigcup_{f \in F} \{(s_1, s_2) \mid (s_1, s_2) \in p_f|_i\} \qquad (1)$$

By considering only the edges in P_i, we can search for an update function for v_i independently of all other variables, while ensuring the global reachability condition holds.

7.3 Final Update Functions

We can now search for the update function of variable v_i, u_i, independently of all other variables. We fix the v_i-labelled edges computed in the previous phase and encode the search for u_i as a Boolean satisfiability problem.

As before we add constraints to encode the representation of u_i, and to enforce the threshold condition. We fix each of the v_i-labelled edges $(s_1, s_2) \in P_i$ to establish reachability, by adding a conjunction requiring that u_i is compatible with each of them: $u_i(s_1) = s_2(v_i)$.

We search for satisfying assignments of the constraint variables encoding u_i, using an ALLSAT procedure to extract all possible update functions for variable v_i. This gives rise to a set of update functions per variable and a set of Boolean networks from the product of the set of update functions per variable.

We note that this final phase of the algorithm can fail to find update functions for a variable v_i, because there are no possible update functions compatible with all of the path edges P_i that were computed in the previous phase. That is, while each edge in P_i is individually compatible with some update function, there may be no update function that is compatible with every edge in P_i. In order to cope with this limitation, we can extract the minimal unsatisfiable core of the

Data set	Genes	States	Direct (seconds)	Compositional (seconds)
CMP (synthetic)	11	214	25	77
Blood stem cells	21	753	OUT OF MEMORY	5114
Embryonic (66% of states)	33	956	OUT OF MEMORY	3364
Embryonic (full)	33	1448	OUT OF MEMORY	8709

Fig. 7. Performance of direct encoding and compositional algorithm on example data sets.

Boolean formula, and search for replacement paths that exclude incompatible combinations of edges. This step can be iterated until satisfying solutions are found for all variables, or until no path can be found, implying that there are no valid models.

By extending our search from the shortest paths between initial and final node pairs in the directed graph to the k-shortest paths between pairs and incrementally increasing k [26], we can increase the number of possible update functions that we consider. In the limit, we will obtain all satisfying models.

An implementation of our algorithm, which is written in F# and uses Z3 as the satisfiability solver, is available at https://github.com/swoodhouse/SCNS-Toolkit. In Fig. 7 we present experimental results from running our implementation of the direct encoding from Sect. 6 and compositional algorithm on four data sets: the small synthetic data set from Sect. 3, the large embryonic experimental data set from Sect. 2, and a second experimental data set covering blood stem cells. We also show results from rerunning on the embryonic data set with a third of states removed. All experiments were performed on an Intel Core i5 @ 1.70GHz with 8GB of RAM, using a single thread.

While the direct encoding synthesised a matching Boolean network on the small synthetic data set faster than our compositional algorithm, it cannot scale to the real experimental data sets, quickly running out of memory. The compositional algorithm, on the other hand, can scale to handle real data sets of the sort produced by our experimental collaborators. All experiments terminated within a few hours, when running on a single thread. The compositional algorithm can easily be parallelised over variables, which would further increase its efficiency.

8   Application to the Experimental Dataset

We now return to the experimental data set introduced in Sect. 2.

Recall that cell measurements were taken from four sequential developmental time points, and that the state graph resulting from discretisation of the data (Fig. 2) exhibited a clear separation between the earliest developmental time point (states coloured blue) and the latest (states coloured red). We applied our synthesis technique to this data, taking the initial states to be the states from the first time point, and the final states to be the states from the latest time point. For complete details, we direct the reader to [16].

The result of the synthesis was a set of possible Boolean update functions for each of the 33 genes, with several genes having a uniquely identified update function. By applying standard techniques for the analysis of Boolean networks, we found the stable state attractors and performed computational perturbations. The synthesised network, along with the subsequent computational analysis led to a set of predictions which were then tested experimentally. We found that our results were robust when performing bootstrapping, removing a third of the data at random and rerunning the synthesis algorithm.

Our experimental collaborators were able to validate key predictions made by our analysis. The update function for one of the genes at the core of this network, *Erg*, which directly activates many other genes, was tested experimentally by a range of assays. Evidence was found that the activators specified in the gene's synthesised update function (*Hoxb4* and *Sox17*) do indeed activate expression of the gene, and furthermore in a fashion consistent with the Boolean "OR" logic of the synthesised update function. This could be regarded as a "local" validation of our model, testing two of the directed edges in the network.

Computational perturbations to another gene at the core of the network, *Sox7*, indicated that when *Sox7* was forced to always be expressed, stable states corresponding to cells from the final developmental time point (blood progenitors) no longer exist. Cell differentiation assays confirmed this prediction experimentally, finding that when this gene was forced to be expressed, the number of cells which normally emerge at this final time point is significantly reduced. This can be thought of as a "global" validation of our model, as it is a prediction about the behaviour of the whole network under a certain perturbation.

9   Related Work

Previous analyses of single-cell gene expression data have mostly been based on statistical properties of the data viewed as a whole, such as the correlation in the level of expression of pairs of genes [8,15]. Such analysis cannot recover mechanistic Boolean logic, does not infer the direction of interactions and cannot easily distinguish direct from indirect influence.

Boolean networks were introduced by Kauffman in order to study random models of genetic regulatory networks [10]. They have since been applied in a range of contexts, from modelling blood stem and progenitor differentiation [2,13], to the yeast apoptosis network [11], to the network regulating pluripotency in embryonic stem cells [9]. BDD-based algorithms for state-space exploration and finding attractors of Boolean networks have been introduced [7,27].

Synthesis is the problem of producing programs or designs from their specifications. In recent years much progress has been made on the usage of SAT and SMT solvers for synthesis. Essentially, the existence of a program that solves a certain problem is posed as a satisfiability query. Then, a solver tries to search for a solution to the query, which corresponds to a program. For example, Srivastava *et al.* [22,23] show that the capabilities of SMT solvers to solve quantified queries enable the search for conditions and code fragments that match a given specification. Similarly, Solar-Lezama *et al.* [21] build a framework for writing programs with "holes" and letting a search algorithm find proper implementations for them. The approach of reactive synthesis [19] is similar to ours in the type of artefact that it produces. However, the techniques that we are using are more related to those explained above. Recently, Beyene *et al.* [1] have shown how constraint solving can be used also in the context of reactive synthesis.

Synthesis has recently been applied in the context of biology. Köksal *et al.* show how to synthesise state-machine-like models from gene mutation experiments using a novel counterexample-guided inductive synthesis (CEGIS) algorithm [12]. Their approach uses constraint solvers to search for program completions that match given specifications, as explained above. Both the data and the type of model are different to those dealt with here, which called for a new approach.

Recently, there have been several applications of synthesis to Boolean networks. Dunn *et al.* [6] and Xu *et al.* [25] show how to fit an existing static, topological regulatory network for embryonic stem cells to gene expression data in order to obtain an executable Boolean network, under the assumption that experimentally measured data represent stable states of the system. This assumption may be appropriate for cell lines maintained in culture, but it does not adapt well to developmental processes such as ours, where cells are transiting through intermediate states in order to develop into a particular lineage.

Recent work of Karp and Sharan [20] shows how to synthesise Boolean networks given a topological network and a set of perturbation experiments, by reduction to integer linear programming. In [17], Paoletti *et al.* synthesise a related class of models (which incorporate timing and spatial information) from perturbation data, via reducion to SMT. To the best of our knowledge, our approach is the first to synthesise gene regulatory network models directly from raw gene expression data, without the need of either genetic perturbation data or *a-priori* information about the topology of the network.

10   Conclusions and Future Work

We presented a technique for synthesising Boolean networks from single–cell resolution gene-expression data. This new and exciting type of data allows us to consider the state of each cell separately, giving rise to "state snapshots", which we treat as the states of an asynchronous Boolean network. Our key insight is that the update functions of each variable can be sought after separately, giving rise to reasonably sized satisfiability queries. We then combine the single gene update functions by considering the flow of time included in the data.

We are able to reconstruct rules from a manually curated Boolean network and produce a set of possible Boolean networks for the given experimental data, for which no similar curated Boolean network is available. The discussion with biologists about this Boolean network led to a set of predictions, which were then experimentally validated in the lab.

We are awaiting similar data from additional experiments to apply the same technique to. At the same time, we are considering the usage of advanced search techniques, as used in this paper, to the analysis of other types of high-throughput data. Future work in the experimental domain includes the validation of more of the links in our synthesised network, and the design of further gene perturbation experiments motivated by the results of computational perturbations. An interesting question for future research is whether techniques like ours, which achieve scalability by treating different aspects of a graph data structure seperately, are applicable to other domains where graph–like data is generated.

Acknowledgements. We thank B. Gottgens, V. Moignard, and A. Wilkinson for sharing with us the biological data, discussing with us its biological significance, and for discussions on the resulting Boolean network, and its meaningfulness. We thank R. Bodik, S. Srivastava and B. Hall for helpful discussions.

References

1. Beyene, T.A., Chaudhuri, S., Popeea, C., Rybalchenko, A.: A constraint-based approach to solving games on infinite graphs. In: 41st Symposium on Principles of Programming Languages, pp. 221–234. ACM (2014)
2. Bonzanni, N., Garg, A., Feenstra, K.A., Schtte, J., Kinston, S., Miranda-Saavedra, D., Heringa, J., Xenarios, I., Gottgens, B.: Hard-wired heterogeneity in blood stem cells revealed using a dynamic regulatory network model. Bioinformatics **29**(13), i80–i88 (2013)
3. Claessen, K., Fisher, J., Ishtiaq, S., Piterman, N., Wang, Q.: Model-checking signal transduction networks through decreasing reachability sets. In: Sharygina, N., Veith, H. (eds.) CAV 2013. LNCS, vol. 8044, pp. 85–100. Springer, Heidelberg (2013)
4. Cook, B., Fisher, J., Hall, B.A., Ishtiaq, S., Juniwal, G., Piterman, N.: Finding instability in biological models. In: Biere, A., Bloem, R. (eds.) CAV 2014. LNCS, vol. 8559, pp. 358–372. Springer, Heidelberg (2014)
5. Cook, B., Fisher, J., Krepska, E., Piterman, N.: Proving stabilization of biological systems. In: Jhala, R., Schmidt, D. (eds.) VMCAI 2011. LNCS, vol. 6538, pp. 134–149. Springer, Heidelberg (2011)
6. Dunn, S.-J., Martello, G., Yordanov, B., Emmott, S., Smith, A.G.: Defining an essential transcription factor program for nave pluripotency. Science **344**(6188), 1156–1160 (2014)
7. Garg, A., Di Cara, A., Xenarios, I., Mendoza, L., De Micheli, G.: Synchronous versus asynchronous modeling of gene regulatory networks. Bioinformatics **24**(17), 1917–1925 (2008)
8. Guo, G., Luc, S., Marco, E., Lin, T.-W., Peng, C., Kerenyi, M.A., Beyaz, S., Kim, W., Xu, J., Das, P.P., Neff, T., Zou, K., Yuan, G.-C., Orkin, S.H.: Mapping cellular hierarchy by single-cell analysis of the cell surface repertoire. Cell Stem Cell **13**(4), 492–505 (2013)
9. Peterson, H., Abu-Dawud, R., Garg, A., Wang, Y., Vilo, J., Xenarios, I., Adjaye, J.: Qualitative modeling identifies IL-11 as a novel regulator in maintaining self-renewal in human pluripotent stem cells. Front Physiol. **4**, 303 (2013)
10. Kauffman, S.A.: Metabolic stability and epigenesis in randomly constructed genetic nets. J. Theor. Biol. **22**, 437–467 (1969)
11. Kazemzadeh, L., Cvijovic, M., Petranovic, D.: Boolean model of yeast apoptosis as a tool to study yeast and human apoptotic regulations. Front Physiol. **3**, 446 (2012)
12. Koksal, A., Pu, Y., Srivastava, S., Bodik, R., Piterman, N., Fisher, J.: Synthesis of biological models from mutation experiments. In: POPL (2013)

13. Krumsiek, J., Marr, C., Schroeder, T., Theis, F.J.: Hierarchical differentiation of myeloid progenitors is encoded in the transcription factor network. PLoS One **6**(8), e22649 (2011)
14. Moignard, V., Gottgens, B.: Transcriptional mechanisms of cell fate decisions revealed by single cell expression profiling. Bioessays **36**, 419–426 (2014)
15. Moignard, V., Macaulay, I., Swiers, G., Buettner, F., Schutte, J., Calero-Nieto, F., Kinston, S., Joshi, A., Hannah, R., Theis, F., Jacobsen, S., de Bruijn, M., Gottgens, B.: Characterization of transcriptional networks in blood stem and progenitor cells using high-throughput single-cell gene expression analysis. Nat. Cell Biol. **15**(4), 363–372 (2013)
16. Moignard, V., Woodhouse, S., Haghverdi, L., Lilly, J., Tanaka, Y., Wilkinson, A., Buettner, F., Macaulay, I., Jawaid, W., Diamanti, E., Nishikawa, S., Piterman, N., Kouskoff, V., Theis, F., Fisher, J., Gottgens, B.: Decoding the regulatory network of early blood development from single-cell gene expression measurements. Nat. Biotechnol. **33**, 269–276 (2015)
17. Paoletti, N., Yordanov, B., Hamadi, Y., Wintersteiger, C.M., Kugler, H.: Analyzing and synthesizing genomic logic functions. In: Biere, A., Bloem, R. (eds.) CAV 2014. LNCS, vol. 8559, pp. 343–357. Springer, Heidelberg (2014)
18. Pina, C., Fugazza, C., Tipping, A.J., Brown, J., Soneji, S., Teles, J., Peterson, C., Enver, T.: Inferring rules of lineage commitment in haematopoiesis. Nat. Cell Biol. **14**, 287–294 (2012)
19. Pnueli, A., Rosner, R.: On the synthesis of a reactive module. In: 16th Symposium on Principles of Programming Languages, pp. 179–190. ACM Press (1989)
20. Sharan, R., Karp, R.M.: Reconstructing boolean models of signaling. J. Comput. Biol. **20**(3), 249–257 (2013)
21. Solar-Lezama, A., Rabbah, R.M., Bodík, R., Ebcioglu, K.: Programming by sketching for bit-streaming programs. In: Programming Language Design and Implementation, pp. 281–294. ACM (2005)
22. Srivastava, S., Gulwani, S., Foster, J.S.: From program verification to program synthesis. In: 37th Symposium on Principles of Programming Languages, pp. 313–326. ACM (2010)
23. Srivastava, S., Gulwani, S., Foster, J.S.: Template-based program verification and program synthesis. Int. J. Softw. Tools Technol. Transfer **15**(5–6), 497–518 (2013)
24. Wilkinson, D.: Stochastic Modelling for Systems Biology, 2nd edn. Chapman and Hall/CRC, Boca Raton, Florida (2012)
25. Xu, H., Ang, Y.-S., Sevilla, A., Lemischka, I.R., Ma'ayan, A.: Construction and validation of a regulatory network for pluripotency and self-renewal of mouse embryonic stem cells. PLoS Comput. Biol. **10**(8), e1003777 (2014)
26. Yen, J.Y.: Finding the k shortest loopless paths in a network. Manag. Sci. **17**(11), 712–716 (1971)
27. Zheng, D., Yang, G., Li, X., Wang, Z., Liu, F., He, L.: An efficient algorithm for computing attractors of synchronous and asynchronous boolean networks. PLOS ONE **8**, e60593 (2013)

Empirical Software Metrics for Benchmarking of Verification Tools

Yulia Demyanova, Thomas Pani[(✉)], Helmut Veith, and Florian Zuleger

Vienna University of Technology, Vienna, Austria
thomas.pani@tuwien.ac.at

Abstract. In this paper we study empirical metrics for software source code, which can predict the performance of verification tools on specific types of software. Our metrics comprise variable usage patterns, loop patterns, as well as indicators of control-flow complexity and are extracted by simple data-flow analyses. We demonstrate that our metrics are powerful enough to devise a machine-learning based portfolio solver for software verification. We show that this portfolio solver would be the (hypothetical) overall winner of both the 2014 and 2015 International Competition on Software Verification (SV-COMP). This gives strong empirical evidence for the predictive power of our metrics and demonstrates the viability of portfolio solvers for software verification.

1 Introduction

The success and gradual improvement of software verification tools in the last two decades is a multidisciplinary effort – modern software verifiers combine methods from a variety of overlapping fields of research including model checking, static analysis, shape analysis, SAT solving, SMT solving, abstract interpretation, termination analysis, pointer analysis etc.

The mentioned techniques all have their individual strengths, and a modern software verification tool needs to pick and choose how to combine them into a strong, stable and versatile tool. The trade-offs are based on both technical and pragmatic aspects: many tools are either optimized for specific application areas (e.g. device drivers), or towards the in-depth development of a technique for a restricted program model (e.g. termination for integer programs). Recent projects like CPA [10] and FrankenBit [20] have explicitly chosen an eclectic approach which enables them to combine different methods more easily.

There is growing awareness in the research community that the benchmarks in most research papers are only useful as proofs of concept for the individual contribution, but make comparison with other tools difficult: benchmarks are often manually selected, handcrafted, or chosen a posteriori to support a certain technical insight. Oftentimes, neither the tools nor the benchmarks are available to other researchers. The annual *International Competition on Software Verification* (SV-COMP, since 2012) [2,3,8,9] is the most ambitious attempt to remedy this situation. Now based on more than 5,500 C source files, SV-COMP

© Springer International Publishing Switzerland 2015
D. Kroening and C.S. Păsăreanu (Eds.): CAV 2015, Part I, LNCS 9206, pp. 561–579, 2015.
DOI: 10.1007/978-3-319-21690-4_39

has the most diverse and comprehensive collection of benchmarks available, and is a natural starting point for a more systematic study of tool performance.

In this paper, we demonstrate that the competition results can be explained by intuitive metrics on the source code. In fact, the metrics are strong enough to enable us to construct a portfolio solver which would (hypothetically) win SV-COMP 2014 [2] and 2015 [3]. Here, a portfolio solver is a SW verification tool which uses heuristic preprocessing to select one of the existing tools [19,24,32].

Table 1. Sources of complexity for 4 tools participating in SV-COMP'15, marked with $+/-/$N/A when supported/not supported/no information is available. Extracted from competition reports [7] and tool papers [14,17].

Source of complexity	CBMC	Predator	CPAchecker	SMACK	Corresp. feature
Unbounded loops	–	N/A	N/A	–	$\mathcal{L}^{SB}, \mathcal{L}^{ST}, \mathcal{L}^{simple}, \mathcal{L}^{hard}$
Pointers	+	+	+	+	PTR
Arrays	+	–	N/A	+	ARRAY_INDEX
Dynamic data structures	N/A	+	N/A	+	PTR_STRUCT_REC
Non-static pointer offsets	–	+	N/A	N/A	OFFSET
Non-static size of heap-allocated memory	+	+	N/A	N/A	ALLOC_SIZE
Pointers to functions	+	N/A	N/A	N/A	$m_{fpcalls}, m_{fpargs}$
Bit operations	+	–	+	–	BITVECTOR
Integer variables	+	+	+	+	SCALAR_INT
Recursion	–	–	–	+	$m_{reccalls}$
Multi-threading	+	–	–	–	THREAD_DESCR
External functions	+	–	N/A	N/A	INPUT
Structure fields	+	+	N/A	+	STRUCT_FIELD
Big CFG ($\geq$ 100 KLOC)	+	N/A	N/A	+	$m_{cfgblocks}, m_{maxindeg}$

Of course it is pointless to let a portfolio solver compete in the regular competition (except, maybe in a separate future track), but for anybody who just wants to verify software, it provides useful insights. Portfolio solvers have been successful (and controversial) in combinatorially cleaner domains such as SAT solving [25,33,37], quantified boolean satisfiability (QSAT) [30,31,34], answer set programming (ASP) [18,27], and various constraint satisfaction problems (CSP) [19,26,28]. In contrast to software verification, in these areas constituent tools are usually assumed to be correct.

As an approach to software verification, portfolio solving brings interesting advantages: (1) a portfolio solver optimally uses available resources, (2) it can avoid incorrect results of partially unsound tools, (3) machine learning in combination with portfolio solving allows us to select between multiple versions of the same tool with different runtime parameters, (4) the portfolio solver gives good insight into the state-of-the-art in software verification.

To choose the software metrics, we consider the zoo of techniques discussed above along with their target domains, our intuition as programmers, as well as the tool developer reports in their competition contributions. Table 1 summarizes these reports for tools CBMC, Predator, CPAchecker and SMACK: The first column gives obstacles the tools' authors identified, columns 2–5 show whether the feature is supported by respective tool, and the last column references the corresponding metrics, which we introduce in Sect. 2. The obtained metrics are naturally understood in three dimensions that we motivate informally first:

1. *Program Variables.* Does the program deal with machine or unbounded integers? Are the ints used as indices, bit-masks or in arithmetic? Dynamic data structures? Arrays? Interval analysis or predicate abstraction?
2. *Program Loops.* Reducible loops or goto programs? For-loops or ranking functions? Widening, loop acceleration, termination analysis, or loop unrolling?
3. *Control Flow.* Recursion? Function pointers? Multithreading? Simulink or complex branching?

Our hypothesis is that precise metrics along these dimensions allow us to predict tool performance. The challenge lies in identifying metrics which are predictive enough to understand the relationship between tools and benchmarks, but also simple enough to be used in a preprocessing and classification step. Sections 2.1, 2.2 and 2.3 describe metrics which correspond to the three dimensions sketched above, and are based on simple data-flow analyses.

Our algorithm for the portfolio is based on machine learning (ML) using *support vector machines* (SVMs) [12,15] over the metrics defined above. Figure 1 depicts our experimental results on SV-COMP'15: Our tool $\mathcal{TP}$ is the overall winner and outperforms all other tools – Sect. 4 contains a detailed discussion.

A machine-learning based method for selecting model checkers was previously introduced in [35]. Similar to our work, the authors use SVM classification with weights (cf. Sect. 3.1). Our approach is novel in the following ways:

- First, the results in [35] are not reproducible because (1) the benchmark is not publicly available, (2) the verification properties are not described, and (3) the weighting function – in our experience crucial for good predictions – is not documented.
- Second, we use a larger set of verification tools (22 tools vs. 3). Our benchmark is not restricted to device drivers and is 10 times larger (49 MLOC vs. 4 MLOC in [35]).
- Third, in contrast to structural metrics of [35] our metrics are computed using data-flow analysis. Based on tool designer reports (Table 1) we believe that they have superior predictive power. Precise comparison is difficult due to non-reproducibility of [35].

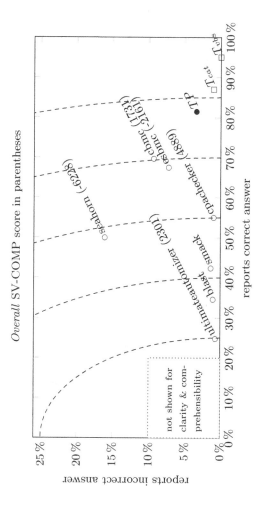

Fig. 1. Decisiveness-reliability plot for SV-COMP'15. The horizontal axis gives the percentage of correct answers c, the vertical axis the number of incorrect answers i. Dashed lines connect points of equal decisiveness $c + i$. The *Overall* SV-COMP score is given (if available) in parentheses.

While portfolio solvers are important, we also think that the software metrics we define in this work are interesting in their own right. Our results show that categories in SVCOMP have characteristic metrics. Thus, the metrics can be used to (1) characterize benchmarks not publicly available, (2) understand large benchmarks without manual inspection, (3) understand presence of language constructs in benchmarks.

Summarizing, in this paper we make the following contributions:

- We define software metrics along the three dimensions – program variables, program loops and control flow – in order to capture the difficulty of program analysis tasks (Sect. 2).
- We develop a machine-learning based portfolio solver for software verification that learns the best-performing tool from a training set (Sect. 3).
- We experimentally demonstrate the predictive power of our software metrics in conjunction with our portfolio solver on the software verification competitions SV-COMP'14 and SV-COMP'15 (Sect. 4).

2   Source Code Metrics for Software Verification

We introduce program features along the three dimensions – *program variables*, *program loops* and *control flow* – and describe how to derive corresponding metrics. Subsequent sections demonstrate their predictive power: In Sect. 3 we describe a portfolio solver for software verification based on our metrics. In Sect. 4 we experimentally demonstrate the portfolio's success, thus attesting the descriptive and predictive power of our metrics and the portfolio.

2.1   Variable Role Based Metrics

The first set of features that we introduce are *variable roles*. Intuitively, a variable role is a usage pattern of how a variable is used in a program.

```
int n = 0, y = x;                int fd = open(path, flags);
while (x) {                      int c, val=0;
  n++;                           while (read(fd, &c, 1) > 0 && isdigit(c)) {
  x = x & (x-1);                   val = 10*val + c-'0';
}                                }
  (a) bitvector, counter, linear          (b) character, file descriptor
```

Fig. 2. Different usage patterns of integer variables.

Example 1. Consider the C program in Fig. 2a, which computes the number of non-zero bits of the variable x. In every loop iteration, a non-zero bit of x is set to zero and the counter n is incremented. For a human reading the program, the statements n=0 and n++ in the loop body signal that n is a *counter*, and statement x = x & (x-1) indicates that x is a *bit vector*.

Example 2. Consider the program in Fig. 2b, which reads a decimal number from a text file and stores its numeric representation in variable val. Statement fd=open(path, flags) indicates that variable fd stores a *file descriptor* and statement isdigit(c) indicates that c is a *character*, because function isdigit() checks whether its parameter is a decimal digit character.

Criteria for Choosing Roles. We implemented 27 variable roles and give their informal definition in Table 2. Our choice of roles is inspired by standard concepts used by programmers. In order to create the list of roles we inspected the source code of the cBench benchmark [1] and came up with a minimum set of roles such that every variable is assigned at least one role.

Roles as Features for Selecting a Verification Tool. The developer reports in SV-COMP'15 [7] give evidence of the relevance of variable roles for selecting verification tools. Most often authors mention language constructs which – depending on whether they are fully, partially, or not modeled by a tool – constitute its strong or weak points. We give examples of such constructs in Table 1 and relate them to variable roles. A preliminary experiment in [16], where we have successfully used variable roles to predict categories in SV-COMP'13, gives further evidence for our claim.

Definition of Roles. We define roles using data-flow analysis, an efficient fixed-point algorithm popular in optimizing compilers [6]. Our current definition of roles is control-flow insensitive, and the result of analysis is a set of variables Res^R which are assigned role R. We give the definition of variable roles in [16].

Example 3. We describe the process of computing roles on the example of role LINEAR for the code in Fig. 2a. Initially, the algorithm assigns to Res^{LINEAR} the set of all variables $\{x, y, n\}$. Then it computes the greatest fixed point in three iterations. In iteration 1, variable x is removed, because it is assigned expression x & (x-1), resulting in $Res^{\text{LINEAR}} = \{y, n\}$. In iteration 2, variable y is removed, because it is assigned variable x, resulting in $Res^{\text{LINEAR}} = \{n\}$. In iteration 3, Res^{LINEAR} does not change, and the result of the analysis is $Res^{\text{LINEAR}} = \{n\}$.

Definition 1 (Variable Role Based Metrics). *For a given benchmark file f, we compute the mapping Res^R from variable roles to the program variables of f. We derive role metrics m_R that represent the relative occurrence of each variable role R: $m_R = |Res^R|/|Vars|$, where $R \in Roles$.*

2.2   Loop Pattern Based Metrics

The second set of program features we introduce is a classification of loops. The capability of Turing complete imperative languages to express unbounded

Table 2. List of variable roles with informal definitions. Type *struct_type* stands for a C structure, *any_type* for an arbitrary C type.

C type	Role name	Informal definition
int	ARRAY_INDEX	Occurs in an array subscript expression
	ALLOC_SIZE	Passed to a standard memory allocation function
	BITVECTOR	Used in a bitwise operation or assigned the result of a bitwise operation or a BITVECTOR variable
	BOOL	Assigned and compared only to 0,1, the result of a boolean operation or a BOOL variable
	BRANCH_COND	Used in the condition of an if statement
	CHAR	Used in a library function which manipulates characters, or assigned a character literal
	CONST_ASSIGN	Assigned only literals or CONST_ASSIGN variables
	COUNTER	Changed only in increment/decrement statements
	FILE_DESCR	Passed to a library function which manipulates files
	INPUT	Assigned the result of an external function or passed to it as a parameter by reference
	LINEAR	Assigned only linear combinations of LINEAR variables
	LOOP_BOUND	Used in a loop condition in a comparison operation, where it is compared to a LOOP_ITERATOR variable
	LOOP_ITERATOR	Occurs in loop condition, assigned in loop body
	MODE	Not used in comparison operations other than == and !=; assigned and compared to constant values only
	OFFSET	Added to or subtracted from a pointer
	SCALAR_INT	Scalar integer variable
	SYNT_CONST	Not assigned in the program (a global or an unused variable, or a formal parameter to a global function)
	THREAD_DESCR	Passed to a function of pthread library
	USED_IN_ARITHM	Used in addition/subtraction/multiplication/division
float	SCALAR_FLOAT	Scalar float variable
int*, float*	PTR_SCALAR	Pointer to a scalar value
*struct_type**	PTR_STRUCT	Pointer to a structure
	PTR_STRUCT_PTR	Pointer to a structure which has a pointer field
	PTR_STRUCT_REC	Pointer to a recursively defined structure
	PTR_COMPL_STRUCT	Pointer to a recursively defined structure with more than one pointer, e.g. doubly linked lists
*any_type**	HEAP_PTR	Assigned the result of a memory allocation
	PTR	Pointer to any value

iteration entails hard and in general undecidable problems for any non-trivial program analysis. On the other hand, in many cases iteration takes trivial forms, for example in loops enumerating a bounded range (counting). In [29] we introduce a family of *loop patterns* that capture such differences. Ability to reason about bounds or termination of loops allows a verification tool to discharge the (un)reachability of assertions after the loop, or to compute unrolling factors and soundness limits in the case of bounded model checking. Thus we expect our loop patterns to be useful program features for constructing our portfolio.

Criteria for Choosing Loop Patterns. We start with a termination procedure for a restricted set of bounded loops. This loop pattern is inspired by basic (bounded) FOR-loops, a frequently used programming pattern. It allows us to implement an efficient termination procedure using syntactic pattern matching and data-flow analysis. Additionally, this loop class lends itself to derive both a stronger notion of boundedness, and weaker notions (heuristics) of termination. We give an informal description of these patterns in Table 3; for details cf. [29]

Usefulness of Loop Patterns. In [29] we give evidence that these loop patterns are a common engineering pattern allowing us to describe loops in a variety of benchmarks, that they indeed capture classes of different empirical hardness, and that the hardness increases as informally described in Table 3.

Definition 2 (Loop Pattern Based Metrics). *For a given benchmark file f, we compute $\mathcal{L}^{SB}, \mathcal{L}^{ST}, \mathcal{L}^{simple}, \mathcal{L}^{hard}$, and the set of all loops Loops. We derive loop metrics m_P that represent the relative occurrence of each loop pattern P: $m_P = |\mathcal{L}^P|/|Loops|$ where $P \in \{ST, SB, simple, hard\}$.*

Table 3. List of loop patterns with informal descriptions.

Loop pattern	Empirical hardness	Informal definition
Syntactically bounded loops $\mathcal{L}^{SB}$	Easy	The number of executions of the loop body is bounded (considers outer control flow)
Syntactically terminating loops $\mathcal{L}^{ST}$	Intermediate	The loop terminates whenever control flow enters it (disregards outer control flow)
Simple loops $\mathcal{L}^{simple}$	Advanced	A heuristic derived from syntactically terminating loops by weakening the termination criteria. A good heuristic for termination
Hard loops $\mathcal{L}^{hard}$	Hard	Any loop that is not classified as simple

2.3 Control Flow Based Metrics

Complex control flow poses another challenge for program analysis. To measure its presence, we introduce five additional metrics: For *control flow complexity*, we count (a) the number of basic blocks in the control flow graph (CFG) $m_\text{cfgblocks}$, and (b) the maximum indegree of any basic block in the CFG m_maxindeg. To represent the use of *function pointers*, we measure (a) the ratio of call expressions taking a function pointer as argument m_fpcalls, and (b) the ratio of function call arguments that have a function pointer type m_fpargs. Finally, to describe the use of *recursion*, we measure the number of direct recursive function calls m_reccalls.

3 A Portfolio Solver for Software Verification

3.1 Preliminaries on Machine Learning

In this section we introduce standard terminology from the machine learning (ML) community as can for example be found in [11].

Data Representation. A *feature vector* is a vector of real numbers $\mathbf{x} \in \mathbb{R}^n$. A *labeling function* $L : X \to Y$ maps a set of feature vectors $X \subseteq \mathbb{R}^n$ to a set $Y \subseteq \mathbb{R}$, whose elements are called *labels*.

Supervised Machine Learning. In *supervised* ML problems, labeling function L is given as input. *Regression* is a supervised ML problem where labels are real numbers $Y \subseteq \mathbb{R}$. In *classification*, in contrast, labels belong to a finite set of integers $Y \subseteq \mathbb{Z}$. *Binary classification* considers two classes $Y = \{1, -1\}$, and a problem with more than two classes is called *multi-class classification*.

Given a set of feature vectors X, labeling function L and error measure function $Err : \mathbb{R}^s \times \mathbb{R}^s \to \mathbb{R}$, where $s = |X|$, a supervised ML algorithm searches for function $M : \mathbb{R}^n \to Y$ in some function space such that the value $Err(L(X), M(X))$ is minimal.

Support Vector Machine. A *support vector machine* (SVM) [12,15] is a supervised ML algorithm, parametrized by a *kernel function* $K(x_i, x_j) \equiv \phi(x_i)^T \phi(x_j)$, that finds a hyperplane $w\phi(x_i) - b = 0$ separating the data with different labels. In the case of binary classification,

$$M(x) = sign\left(\sum_{i=1}^{s} w_i L(x_i)\phi(x_i)^T \phi(x)\right) \text{ and } Err = \frac{1}{2}w^T w + C\sum_{i=1}^{s} \xi_i \quad (1)$$

where $sign(n) = \begin{cases} -1 & \text{if } n < 0 \\ 1 & \text{if } n \geq 0 \end{cases}$, $x_i \in X$ is a feature vector, $C > 0$ is the penalty parameter of the error term, function ϕ is implicitly given through kernel function

K, and w, b and ξ are existentially quantified parameters of the optimization problem

$$\min_{w,b,\xi} Err, \text{ subject to } L(x_i)(w^T\phi(x_i) + b) \geq 1 - \xi_i \text{ and } \xi_i \geq 0 \qquad (2)$$

with ξ_i measuring the degree of misclassification of point x_i.

The kernel function K and $C \in \mathbb{R}$ are parameters of SVM. An example of a non-linear kernel function is the *Radial Basis Function* (RBF): $K(x_i, x_j) = exp(-\gamma\|x_i - x_j\|^2)$, $\gamma > 0$.

Probabilistic Classification. *Probabilistic classification* is a generalization of the classification algorithm, which searches for a function $M^P : \mathbb{R}^n \to (Y \to [0,1])$ mapping a feature vector to a *class probability* distribution, which is a function $P : Y \to [0,1]$ from a set of classes Y to the unit interval. There is a standard algorithm for estimating class probabilities for SVM [36].

Creating and Evaluating a Model. Function M is called a *model*, the set X used for creating the model is called *training set*, and the set used for evaluating the model X' is called *test set*.

To avoid overly optimistic evaluation of the model, it is common to require that the training and test sets are disjoint: $X \cap X' = \emptyset$. A model which produces accurate results with respect to the error measure for the training set, but results in a high error for previously unseen feature vectors $x \notin X$, is said to *overfit*.

Data Imbalances. Labeling function L is said to be *imbalanced* when it exhibits an unequal distribution between its classes: $\exists y_i, y_j \in Y . Num(y_i)/Num(y_j) \sim 100$, where $Num(y) = |\{x \in X \mid L(x) = y\}|$, i.e. imbalances of the order 100:1 and higher. Data imbalances significantly compromise the performance of most standard learning algorithms [21].

A common solution for the imbalanced data problem is to use a *weighting function* $W : X \to \mathbb{R}$ [23]. *SVM with weights* is a generalization of SVM, where $Err = \frac{1}{2}w^T w + C \sum_{i=1}^{s} W(x_i)\xi_i$. W is usually chosen empirically.

An orthogonal solution of dealing with data imbalances is the reduction of a multi-class classification problem to multiple binary classification problems: *one-vs-all* classification creates one model per class i, with the labeling function $L_i(x) = \begin{cases} 1 & \text{if } L(x) = i \\ -1 & \text{otherwise} \end{cases}$, and the predicted value calculated as $M(x) = choose(\{i \mid M_i(x) = 1\})$, where a suitable operator *choose* is used to choose a single class from multiple predicted classes.

3.2   The Competition on Software Verification SV-COMP

Setup. A verification task in SV-COMP is given as a C source file f and a verification property p. The property is either a label reachability check or a memory safety check (comprising checks for freedom of unsafe deallocations, unsafe pointer dereferences, and memory leaks). The expected answer $ExpAns$ is provided for each task by the designers of the benchmark. The verification tasks are partitioned into *categories*, manually grouped by characteristic features such as usage of bitvectors, concurrent programs, linux device drivers, etc.

Scoring. The competition assigns a *score* to each tool's result on a verification task v. The *category score* of a tool is defined as the sum of scores for individual tasks in the category. In addition, medals are awarded to the three best tools in each category. The *Overall* SV-COMP score considers all verification tasks, with each constituent category score normalized by the number of tasks in it.

3.3   Tool Selection as a Machine Learning Problem

In this section, we first describe the setup of our portfolio solver $\mathcal{TP}$, and then define the notion of the *best-performing tool* t^{best} predicted by $\mathcal{TP}$.

Definitions. A *verification task* $v = \langle f, p, type \rangle$ is a triple of a source file f, the property p and property type $type$ (e.g. reachability or safety). Function $ExpAns : Tasks \rightarrow \{true, false\}$ maps verification task $v \in Tasks$ to $true$ if the property p holds for f and to $false$ otherwise. We identify each *verification tool* by a unique natural number $t \in \mathbb{N}$.

The result of a run of a tool t on a verification task v is a pair $\langle ans_{t,v}, runtime_{t,v} \rangle$, where $ans_{t,v} \in \{true, false, unknown\}$ is the tool's answer whether the property holds, and $runtime_{t,v} \in \mathbb{R}$ is the runtime of the tool in seconds. The *expected answer* for a task v is a boolean value $ExpAns(v)$.

Machine Learning Data. We compute feature vectors from the metrics and the results of the competition as follows: for verification task v we define feature vector $\mathbf{x}(v) = (m_{\text{ARRAY\_INDEX}}(v), \ldots, m_{\text{PTR}}(v), m_{\text{ST}}(v), \ldots, m_{\text{hard}}(v), m_{\text{cfgblocks}}(v), \ldots, m_{\text{reccalls}}(v), type(v))$, where the $m_i(v)$ are our metrics from Sect. 2 and $type(v) \in \{0, 1\}$ encodes if the property is reachability or memory safety.

The portfolio solver predicts a tool identifier $t \in \{1, \ldots, n\}$, which is a multi-class classification problem. We use a generalization of the one-vs-all classification to solve the problem. We define the labeling function $L_t(v)$ for tool t and task v as follows:

$$L_t(v) = \begin{cases} 1 & \text{if } ans_{t,v} = ExpAns(v) \\ 2 & \text{if } ans_{t,v} = unknown \\ 3 & \text{if } ans_{t,v} \neq unknown \wedge ans_{t,v} \neq ExpAns(v) \end{cases}$$

where we treat opted-out categories as if the tool answered *unknown* for all of the category's verification tasks.

Formulation of the Machine Learning Problem. Given $|Tools|$ classification problems for a task v, the portfolio algorithm chooses a tool t^{best} as follows:

$$t^{best} = \begin{cases} choose(TCorr(v)) & \text{if } TCorr(v) \neq \emptyset \\ choose(TUnk(v)) & \text{if } TCorr(v) = \emptyset \wedge TUnk(v) \neq \emptyset \\ t^{winner} & \text{if } TCorr(v) = \emptyset \wedge TUnk(v) = \emptyset \end{cases}$$

where $TCorr(v) = \{t \in Tools \mid M_t(v) = 1\}$, $TUnk(v) = \{t \in Tools \mid M_t(v) = 2\}$ and t^{winner} is the winner of the competition, e.g. CPAchecker in SV-COMP'15. We now describe two alternative ways of implementing the operator *choose*.

1. **"Success/Fail + Time":** $\mathcal{TP}^{SuccFailTime}$. We formulate $|Tools|$ additional regression problems, where the predicted value is the runtime of the tool $runtime_{t,v}$. We define $choose(T) = \arg\min_{t \in T} runtime_{t,v}$.

2. **"Success/Fail + Probability":** $\mathcal{TP}^{SuccFailProb}$. We define the operator $choose(T) = \arg\max_{t \in T} P_{t,v}$, where $P_{t,v}$ is class probability estimate.

In Table 4 we compare the two *choose* operators for category *Overall* in the setup of SV-COMP'14 according to 3 different criteria: the score, the percentage of correctly and incorrectly answered tasks and the place in the competition.

Configuration $\mathcal{TP}^{SuccFailProb}$ yields a higher score and number of correct answers with less runtime. We believe this is due to the tool runtimes varying in the range of 5 orders of magnitude (from tenth parts of a second to 15 min), which causes high error rates in the predicted runtime. We therefore use configuration $\mathcal{TP}^{SuccFailProb}$ and in the following refer to it as $\mathcal{TP}$.

Table 4. Comparison of 2 formulations of $\mathcal{TP}$.

Setting	Correct/Incorrect/ Unknown answers, %	Score	Runtime, s	Place
$\mathcal{TP}^{SuccFailTime}$	92/3/6	1384	279859	1
$\mathcal{TP}^{SuccFailProb}$	93/1/5	1494	132688	1

The Weighting Function. We analyzed the results of SV-COMP'14 and observed, that the labeling function in the formulation of $\mathcal{TP}^{SuccFailProb}$ is highly imbalanced: the label which corresponds to incorrect answers, $L_t(v) = 3$, occurs in less than 4 % for all tools.

We therefore use SVM with weights, in accordance with the standard practice in machine learning. We note that we use the same weighting function for our experiments in the setup of SV-COMP'15 without any changes. Given a task v and tool t, we calculate the weighting function W as follows:

$$W(v,t) = Potential(v) * Criticality(v) * Performance(t, Cat(v))$$
$$* Speed(t, Cat(v))$$

- where $Potential(v) = score_{max}(v) - score_{min}(v)$ is the difference of the maximal and minimal possible scores for task v. For example, in the setup of SV-COMP'14, if v is safe, then $score_{max}(v) = 2$ and $score_{min}(v) = -8$;
- $Criticality(v) = \dfrac{1}{|\{t \in Tools \mid ans_{t,v} = ExpAns(v)\}|}$ is inversely proportional (subject to a constant factor) to the probability of randomly choosing a tool which gives the expected answer;
- $Performance(t, c) = \dfrac{cat\_score(t, c)}{cat\_score(t^{cbest}, c)}$ is the ratio of the scores of tool t and the best in category c tool t^{cbest}, where given the score $score_{t,v}$ of tool t for task v, $t^{cbest} = \underset{t_i \in Tools}{\arg\max} \left(cat\_score(t_i, c) \right)$ and $cat\_score(t, c) = \sum_{\{v \in Tasks \mid Cat(v) = c\}} \left(score_{t,v} \right)$;
- $Speed(t, c) = \dfrac{ln(rel\_time(t, c))}{ln(rel\_time(t^{cfst}, c))}$ is the relative difference of the orders of magnitude of the fraction in total runtime of the time spent by tool t and the fastest in category c tool t^{cfst} respectively, where $rel\_time(t, c) = \left(cat\_time(t, c) \right) \Big/ \left(\sum_{t_i \in Tools} cat\_time(t_i, c) \right)$, $t^{cfst} = \underset{t_i \in Tools}{\arg\min} \left(cat\_time(t_i, c) \right)$ and $cat\_time(t, c) = \sum_{\{v \in Tasks \mid Cat(v) = c\}} runtime_{t,v}$.

Implementation of $\mathcal{TP}$. Finally, we discuss the details of the implementation of $\mathcal{TP}$. We use the SVM ML algorithm with the RBF kernel and weights implemented in the LIBSVM library [13]. To find optimal parameters for a ML algorithm with respect to the error measure function, we do exhaustive search on the grid, as described in [22].

4   Experimental Results

4.1   SV-COMP 2014 vs. 2015

As described in Sect. 3.2, SV-COMP provides two metrics for comparing tools: score and medal counts. As the scoring policy has recently changed (the penalties for incorrect answers were increased) after a close jury vote [4], we are interested in how stable the scores are under different scoring policies. The following table gives the three top-scoring tools in *Overall* and their scores in SV-COMP'14 and '15, as well as the top-scorers of SV-COMP'14 if the 2015 scoring policy had been applied, and vice versa:

Competition	Scoring	1st place (score)	2nd place (score)	3rd place (score)
SV-COMP'14	Original	CBMC (3,501)	CPAchecker (2,987)	LLBMC (1,843)
	Like '15	CPAchecker (3,035)	CBMC (2,515)	LLBMC (2,004)
SV-COMP'15	Original	CPAchecker (4,889)	Ult. Aut. (2,301)	CBMC (1,731)
	Like '14	CPAchecker (5,537)	SMACK (4,120)	CBMC (3,481)

Discussion. Clearly, the scoring policy has a major impact on the competition results: If the '15 policy is applied to SV-COMP'14, the first and second placed tools switch ranks. SV-COMP'15, applying the previous year's policy has an even stronger effect: Ultimate Automizer loses its silver medal to SMACK, a tool originally not among the top three, and CBMC almost doubles its points.

Given that SV-COMP score and thus also medal counts are rather volatile, we introduce *decisiveness-reliability plots* (DR-plots) in the next section to complement our interpretation of the competition results.

4.2 Decisiveness-Reliability Plots

To better understand the competition results, we create scatter plots where each data point $\mathbf{v} = (c, i)$ represents a tool that gives $c\%$ correct answers and $i\%$ incorrect answers. Figures 1 and 3 show such plots based on the verification tasks in SV-COMP'14 and '15. Each data point marked by an unfilled circle ○ represents one competing tool. The rectilinear distance $c + i$ from the origin gives a tool's *decisiveness*, i.e. the farther from the origin, the fewer times a tool reports "unknown". The angle enclosed by the horizontal axis and $\mathbf{v}$ gives a tool's *(un)reliability*, i.e. the wider the angle, the more often the tool gives incorrect answers. Thus, we call such plots *decisiveness-reliability plots* (DR-plots).

Discussion. Figures 1 and 3 show DR-plots for the verification tasks in SV-COMP'14 and'15. For 2014, all the tools are performing quite well on soundness: none of them gives more than 4% of incorrect answers. CPAchecker, ESBMC and CBMC are highly decisive tools, with more than 83% correct answers.

In 2015 (Fig. 1) the number of verification tasks more than doubled, and there is more variety in the results: We see that very reliable tools (BLAST, SMACK, and CPAchecker) are limited in decisiveness – they report "unknown" in more than 40% of cases. The bounded model checkers CBMC and ESBMC are more decisive at the cost of giving up to 10% incorrect answers. We also give *Overall* SV-COMP scores (where applicable) in parentheses. Clearly, tools close together in the DR-plot not necessarily have similar scores because of the different score weights prescribed by the SV-COMP scoring policy.

Referring back to Figs. 1 and 3, we also show the theoretic strategies T_{cat} and T_{vbs} marked by a square □: Given a verification task v, T_{cat} selects the tool winning the corresponding competition category $Cat(v)$. T_{vbs} is the *virtual best solver* (VBS) and selects the best performing tool per verification

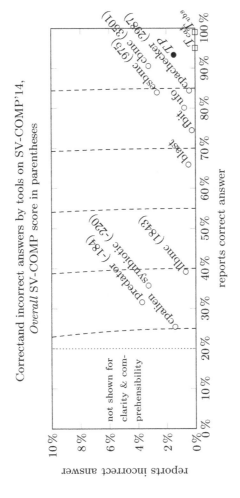

Correct and incorrect answers by tools on SV-COMP'14, *Overall* SV-COMP score in parentheses

Fig. 3. Decisiveness-reliability plot for SV-COMP'14.

(a) *Overall* SV-COMP score, runtime and medal counts for SV-COMP'14.

	blast	cbmc	cpa-che-cker	cpa-lien	esbmc	fbit	llbmc	ufo	$\mathcal{TP}$	T_{cat}	T_{vbs}
Overall	468	**1292**	1235	266	695	666	853	735	**1494**	1732	1840
	2066	**4991**	1865	776	4024	898	978	381	**2211**	1310	270
Medals	1/0/0	2/2/2	2/1/1	0/0/0	1/0/1	0/0/2	1/0/1	1/1/0	1/5/1	-	-

(b) *Overall* SV-COMP score, runtime and medal counts for SV-COMP'15.

	blast	cas-cade	cbmc	cpa-che-cker	pre-da-torhp	smack	ulti-mate-kojak	ulcseq	$\mathcal{TP}$	T_{cat}	T_{vbs}
Overall	737	806	684	**2228**	389	**1542**	1215	273	**2511**	3231	3768
	4546	5146	11936	**6288**	96	**8727**	7979	12563	**6260**	4360	1882
Medals	1/0/0	0/0/0	1/1/1	2/1/5	1/0/1	2/1/1	0/2/0	0/0/0	1/6/1	-	-

Fig. 4. Experimental results for the eight best competition participants in *Overall*, plus our portfolio $\mathcal{TP}$ and the idealized strategies T_{cat}, T_{vbs} on *random subsets* of SV-COMP, given as arithmetic mean of 10 experiments on the resp. test sets $test_{year}$. The first row shows the *Overall* SV-COMP score and beneath it the runtime in minutes. We highlight the gold, silver, and bronze medal in dark gray, light gray and white+bold font, respectively. The second row shows the number of gold/silver/bronze medals won in individual categories.

task. Both strategies illustrate that combining tools can yield an almost perfect solver, with $\geq 95\%$ correct and 0% incorrect answers. (Note that these figures may give an overly optimistic picture – after all the benchmarks are supplied by the competition participants.) The results for T_{vbs} compared to T_{cat} indicate that leveraging not just the category winner provides an advantage in both reliability and decisiveness. A useful portfolio would thus lie somewhere between CPAchecker, CBMC, T_{cat}, and T_{vbs}, i.e. improve upon the decisiveness of constituent tools while minimizing the number of incorrect answers.

4.3 Evaluation of Our Portfolio Solver

We implemented the ML-based portfolio $\mathcal{TP}$ for SV-COMP'14 in our tool *Verifolio* [5]. When competition results for SV-COMP'15 became available, we successfully evaluated the existing techniques on the new data. We present these results both in terms of the traditional metrics used by the competition (SV-COMP score and medals), and by its placement in DR-plots:

Setup. For our experiments we did not rebuild the infrastructure of SV-COMP, but use numeric results from the competition to compare our portfolio approach against other tools. Following a standard practice in ML [11], we randomly split the verification tasks of SV-COMP'*year* into a training set $train_{year}$ and a test set $test_{year}$ with a ratio of 60:40. We train our portfolio on $train_{year}$ and re-run the competition on $test_{year}$, with the portfolio participating as an additional tool. As the partitioning into training and test sets is randomized, we conduct the experiment 10 times and report the arithmetic mean of all figures. Figures 4a and b show the *Overall* SV-COMP scores, runtimes and medal counts. The DR-plots in Figs. 1 and 3 show the portfolio marked by a filled circle •.

Overhead of Feature Extraction. By construction, our portfolio incurs an overhead for feature extraction and prediction before actually executing the selected tool. We find this overhead to be negligible with a median time of $\tilde{x}_{\text{features}} = 0.5$ seconds for feature extraction and $\tilde{x}_{\text{prediction}} = 0.5$ seconds for prediction.

Discussion. First, we discuss our results in terms of *Overall* SV-COMP score and medals. The experimental results for SV-COMP'14 in Fig. 4a show that our portfolio overtakes the original *Overall* winner CBMC with 16 % more points. It wins a total of seven medals (1/5/1 gold/silver/bronze) compared to CBMC's six medals (2/2/2). For SV-COMP'15 (Fig. 4b), our portfolio $\mathcal{TP}$ is again the strongest tool, collecting 13 % more points than the original *Overall* winner CPAchecker. Both CPAchecker and $\mathcal{TP}$ collect 8 medals, with CPAchecker's 2/1/5 against $\mathcal{TP}$'s 1/6/1.

Second, we discuss the DR-plots in Figs. 1 and 3. Our portfolio $\mathcal{TP}$ positions itself between CPAchecker, CBMC and the theoretic strategies T_{cat} and T_{vbs}. Furthermore, $\mathcal{TP}$ falls halfway between the concrete tools and idealized strategies. We think this is a promising result, but also leaves room for future work. Here we invite the community to contribute further feature definitions, learning techniques, portfolio setups, etc. to enhance this approach.

Constituent Verifiers Employed by Our Portfolio. Our results could suggest that $\mathcal{TP}$ implements a trade-off between CPAchecker's conservative-and-sound and CBMC's decisive-but-sometimes-unsound approach. Contrarily, our experiments show that significantly more tools get selected by our portfolio solver. Additionally, we find that our approach is able to select domain-specific solvers: For example, in the *Concurrency* category, $\mathcal{TP}$ almost exclusively selects variants of CSeq, which translates concurrent programs into equivalent sequential ones.

Wrong Predictions. Finally, we investigate cases of wrong predictions made by the portolio solver, which are due to two reasons:

First, ML operates on the assumption that the behavior of a verification tool is the same for different verification tasks with the same or very similar metrics. However, sometimes this is not the case because tools are (1) unsound, e.g. SMACK in category Arrays, (2) buggy, e.g. BLAST in DeviceDrivers64, or (3) incomplete, e.g. CPAchecker in ECA.

Second, the data imbalances lead to the following bias in ML: For a verification tool that is correct most of the time, ML will prefer the error of predicting that the tool is correct (when in fact incorrect) over the error that a tool is incorrect (when in fact correct), i.e. "good" tools are predicted to be even "better".

References

1. Collective benchmark (cBench). http://ctuning.org/wiki/index.php/CTools: CBench. Accessed 6 Feb 2015
2. Competition on Software Verification 2014. http://sv-comp.sosy-lab.org/2014/. Accessed 6 Feb 2015
3. Competition on Software Verification 2015. http://sv-comp.sosy-lab.org/2015/. Accessed 6 Feb 2015
4. SV-COMP 2014 - Minutes. http://sv-comp.sosy-lab.org/2015/Minutes-2014.txt. Accessed 6 Feb 2015
5. Verifolio. http://forsyte.at/software/verifolio/. Accessed 11 May 2015
6. Aho, A.V., Sethi, R., Ullman, J.D.: Compilers: Princiles, Techniques, and Tools. Addison-Wesley, Reading (1986)
7. Baier, C., Tinelli, C. (eds.): TACAS 2015. LNCS, vol. 9035. Springer, Heidelberg (2015)
8. Beyer, D.: Status report on software verification. In: Ábrahám, E., Havelund, K. (eds.) TACAS 2014 (ETAPS). LNCS, vol. 8413, pp. 373–388. Springer, Heidelberg (2014)
9. Beyer, D.: Software verification and verifiable witnesses. In: Baier, C., Tinelli, C. (eds.) TACAS 2015. LNCS, vol. 9035, pp. 401–416. Springer, Heidelberg (2015)
10. Beyer, D., Henzinger, T.A., Théoduloz, G.: Configurable software verification: concretizing the convergence of model checking and program analysis. In: Damm, W., Hermanns, H. (eds.) CAV 2007. LNCS, vol. 4590, pp. 504–518. Springer, Heidelberg (2007)
11. Bishop, C.M.: Pattern Recognition and Machine Learning. Springer, New York (2006)
12. Boser, B.E., Guyon, I., Vapnik, V.: A training algorithm for optimal margin classifiers. In: Conference on Computational Learning Theory (COLT 1992), pp. 144–152 (1992)
13. Chang, C., Lin, C.: LIBSVM: a library for support vector machines. ACM TIST 2(3), 27 (2011)
14. Clarke, E., Kroning, D., Lerda, F.: A tool for checking ANSI-C programs. In: Jensen, K., Podelski, A. (eds.) TACAS 2004. LNCS, vol. 2988, pp. 168–176. Springer, Heidelberg (2004)
15. Cortes, C., Vapnik, V.: Support-vector networks. Mach. Learn. 20(3), 273–297 (1995)
16. Demyanova, Y., Veith, H., Zuleger, F.: On the concept of variable roles and its use in software analysis. In: Formal Methods in Computer-Aided Design (FMCAD 2013), pp. 226–230 (2013)
17. Dudka, K., Peringer, P., Vojnar, T.: Byte-precise verification of low-level list manipulation. In: Logozzo, F., Fähndrich, M. (eds.) Static Analysis. LNCS, vol. 7935, pp. 215–237. Springer, Heidelberg (2013)
18. Gebser, M., Kaminski, R., Kaufmann, B., Schaub, T., Schneider, M.T., Ziller, S.: A portfolio solver for answer set programming: preliminary report. In: Delgrande, J.P., Faber, W. (eds.) LPNMR 2011. LNCS, vol. 6645, pp. 352–357. Springer, Heidelberg (2011)
19. Gomes, C.P., Selman, B.: Algorithm portfolios. Artif. Intell. 126(1–2), 43–62 (2001)
20. Gurfinkel, A., Belov, A.: FRANKENBIT: bit-precise verification with many bits. In: Ábrahám, E., Havelund, K. (eds.) TACAS 2014 (ETAPS). LNCS, vol. 8413, pp. 408–411. Springer, Heidelberg (2014)

21. He, H., Garcia, E.A.: Learning from imbalanced data. Knowl. Data Eng. **21**(9), 1263–1284 (2009)
22. Hsu, C.W., Chang, C.C., Lin, C.J., et al.: A practical guide to support vector classification (2003)
23. Huang, Y.M., Du, S.X.: Weighted support vector machine for classification with uneven training class sizes. Mach. Learn. Cybern. **7**, 4365–4369 (2005)
24. Huberman, B.A., Lukose, R.M., Hogg, T.: An economics approach to hard computational problems. Science **275**(5296), 51–54 (1997)
25. Kadioglu, S., Malitsky, Y., Sabharwal, A., Samulowitz, H., Sellmann, M.: Algorithm selection and scheduling. In: Lee, J. (ed.) CP 2011. LNCS, vol. 6876, pp. 454–469. Springer, Heidelberg (2011)
26. Lobjois, L., Lemaître, M.: Branch and bound algorithm selection by performance prediction. In: Mostow, J., Rich, C. (eds.) National Conference on Artificial Intelligence and Innovative Applications of Artificial Intelligence Conference, pp. 353–358 (1998)
27. Maratea, M., Pulina, L., Ricca, F.: The multi-engine ASP solver ME-ASP. In: del Cerro, L.F., Herzig, A., Mengin, J. (eds.) JELIA 2012. LNCS, vol. 7519, pp. 484–487. Springer, Heidelberg (2012)
28. O'Mahony, E., Hebrard, E., Holland, A., Nugent, C., OSullivan, B.: Using case-based reasoning in an algorithm portfolio for constraint solving. In: Irish Conference on Artificial Intelligence and Cognitive Science (2008)
29. Pani, T.: Loop patterns in C programs. Diploma Thesis (2014). http://forsyte.at/static/people/pani/sloopy/thesis.pdf
30. Pulina, L., Tacchella, A.: A multi-engine solver for quantified boolean formulas. In: Bessière, C. (ed.) CP 2007. LNCS, vol. 4741, pp. 574–589. Springer, Heidelberg (2007)
31. Pulina, L., Tacchella, A.: A self-adaptive multi-engine solver for quantified boolean formulas. Constraints **14**(1), 80–116 (2009)
32. Rice, J.R.: The algorithm selection problem. Adv. Comput. **15**, 65–118 (1976)
33. Roussel, O.: Description of ppfolio. http://www.cril.univ-artois.fr/~roussel/ppfolio/solver1.pdf
34. Samulowitz, H., Memisevic, R.: Learning to solve QBF. In: Proceedings of the Conference on Artificial Intelligence (AAAI), pp. 255–260 (2007)
35. Tulsian, V., Kanade, A., Kumar, R., Lal, A., Nori, A.V.: MUX: algorithm selection for software model checkers. In: Working Conference on Mining Software Repositories, pp. 132–141 (2014)
36. Wu, T.F., Lin, C.J., Weng, R.C.: Probability estimates for multi-class classification by pairwise coupling. J. Mach. Learn. Res. **5**, 975–1005 (2004)
37. Xu, L., Hutter, F., Hoos, H.H., Leyton-Brown, K.: SATzilla: portfolio-based algorithm selection for SAT. J. Artif. Intell. Res. (JAIR) **32**, 565–606 (2008)

Interpolation, IC3/PDR, and Invariants

Property-Directed Inference of Universal Invariants or Proving Their Absence

A. Karbyshev[1]($\boxtimes$), N. Bjørner[2], S. Itzhaky[3], N. Rinetzky[1], and S. Shoham[4]

[1] Tel Aviv University, Tel Aviv, Israel
karbyshev@post.tau.ac.il
[2] Microsoft Research, Redmond, USA
[3] Massachusetts Institute of Technology, Cambridge, USA
[4] The Academic College of Tel Aviv Yaffo, Tel Aviv, Israel

Abstract. We present *Universal Property Directed Reachability* (PDR$^\forall$), a property-directed procedure for automatic inference of invariants in a universal fragment of first-order logic. PDR$^\forall$ is an extension of Bradley's PDR/IC3 algorithm for inference of propositional invariants. PDR$^\forall$ terminates when it either discovers a concrete counterexample, infers an inductive universal invariant strong enough to establish the desired safety property, or finds a *proof that such an invariant does not exist*. We implemented an analyzer based on PDR$^\forall$, and applied it to a collection of list-manipulating programs. Our analyzer was able to automatically infer universal invariants strong enough to establish memory safety and certain functional correctness properties, show the absence of such invariants for certain natural programs and specifications, and detect bugs. All this, without the need for user-supplied abstraction predicates.

1 Introduction

We present *Universal Property Directed Reachability* (PDR$^\forall$), a procedure for automatic inference of quantified inductive invariants, and its application for the analysis of programs that manipulate unbounded data structures such as singly-linked and doubly-linked list data structures. For a correct program, the inductive invariant generated ensures that the program satisfies its specification. For an erroneous program, PDR$^\forall$ produces a concrete counterexample. Historically, this has been addressed by abstract interpretation [17] algorithms, which automatically infer sound inductive invariants, and bounded model checking algorithms, which explore a limited number of loop iterations in order to systematically look for bugs [6,13]. We continue the line of recent works [2,32] which simultaneously search for invariants and counterexamples. We follow Bradley's PDR/IC3 algorithm [9] by repeatedly strengthening a candidate invariant until it either becomes inductive, or a counterexample is found.

In our experience, the correctness of many programs can be proven using universal invariants. Hence, we simplify matters by focusing on inferring universal first-order invariants. When PDR$^\forall$ terminates, it yields one of the following outcomes:

© Springer International Publishing Switzerland 2015
D. Kroening and C.S. Păsăreanu (Eds.): CAV 2015, Part I, LNCS 9206, pp. 583–602, 2015.
DOI: 10.1007/978-3-319-21690-4_40

```
void split(h, g){
  i:=h; j:=null; k:=null;
  while (i ≠ null){
    if ¬C(i) then {
      if i = h then h:=i.n
      else j.n:=i.n;
      if g = null then g:=i
      else k.n:=i;
      k:=i; i:=i.n;
      k.n:=null;}
    else {j:=i; i:=i.n}
}}
```

requires:
$g = null \wedge H = h \wedge (\forall x, y.\, n^*(x,y) \leftrightarrow L(x,y))$
ensures:
$(\forall z.\, h \neq null \wedge n^*(h,z) \to C(z)) \wedge$
$(\forall z.\, g \neq null \wedge n^*(g,z) \to \neg C(z)) \wedge$
$(\forall z.\, z \neq null \to (L(H,z) \leftrightarrow n^*(h,z) \vee n^*(g,z))) \wedge$
$(\forall x, y.$
$\quad L(H,x) \wedge L(x,y) \wedge C(x) \wedge C(y) \to n^*(x,y)) \wedge$
$(\forall x, y.$
$\quad L(H,x) \wedge L(x,y) \wedge \neg C(x) \wedge \neg C(y) \to n^*(x,y))$

(a) A procedure that moves all the elements not satisfying $C(\cdot)$ from list h to list g and its specification. h,g,i,j, and k are pointers to list nodes, and l.n denotes the "next" field of node l. The ghost variables H and L record the head of the original list and the reachability order between its elements.

```
void filter(h){
  i:=h; j:=null;
  while (i ≠ null){
    if ¬C(i) then
      if i = h then h:=i.n
      else j.n:=i.n;
    else j:=i;
    i:=i.n
}}
```

$I = L_1 \wedge L_2 \wedge L_3 \wedge L_4 \wedge L_5 \wedge L_6 \wedge L_7$, where
$L_1 = i \neq h \wedge i \neq null \to n^*(j,i)$
$L_2 = i \neq h \to C(h)$
$L_3 = n^*(h,j) \vee i \neq j$
$L_4 = \forall x_1.\, i \neq h \wedge n^*(j,x_1) \wedge x_1 \neq j \to n^*(i,x_1)$
$L_5 = i \neq h \to C(j)$
$L_6 = \forall x_2.\, z = h \vee j = null \vee$
$\qquad \neg n^*(h,x_2) \vee n^*(h,j) \vee \neg C(j)$
$L_7 = \forall x_3.\, j \neq null \wedge n^*(h,x_3) \wedge$
$\qquad x_3 \neq h \wedge \neg C(x_3) \to n^*(j,x_3)$

(b) A procedure that deletes all the nodes not satisfying $C(\cdot)$ from list h and its inferred loop invariant.

Fig. 1. Motivating examples. $n^*(x, y)$ means a (possibly empty) path of n-fields from x to y.

(i) a universal inductive invariant strong enough to show that the program respects the property, (ii) a concrete counterexample which shows that the program violates the desired safety property, or (iii) a *proof that the program cannot be proven correct using a universal invariant* in a given vocabulary.

Diagram Based Abstraction. Unlike previous work [2,32], we neither assume that the predicates which constitute the invariants are known, nor apriori bound the number of universal quantifiers. Instead, we rely on first-order theories with a *finite model property*: for such theories, SMT-based tools are able to either return UNSAT, indicating that the negation of a formula φ is valid, or construct a *finite model* σ of φ. We then translate σ into a *diagram* [10]—a formula describing the set of models that extend σ—and use the diagram to construct a *universal* clause to strengthen a candidate invariant.

Property-Directed Invariant Inference. Similarly to IC3, PDR$^\forall$ iteratively constructs an increasing sequence of candidate inductive invariants $F_0 \cdots F_N$. Every F_i over-approximates the set $\mathcal{R}_i$ of states that can be reached by up to i execution steps from a given set of *initial* states. In every iteration, PDR$^\forall$

uses SMT to check whether one of the candidate invariants became inductive. If so, then the program respects the desired property. If not, PDR$^\forall$ iteratively strengthens the candidate invariants and adds new ones, guided by the considered property. Specifically, it checks if there exists a *bad* state σ which satisfies F_N but not the property. If so, we use SMT again to check whether there is a state σ_a in F_{N-1} that can lead to a state in the *diagram* φ of σ in one execution step. If no such state exists, the candidate invariant F_N can be strengthened by conjoining it with the negation of φ. Otherwise, we recursively strengthen F_{i-1} to exclude σ_a from its over-approximation of $\mathcal{R}_{i-1}$. If the recursive process tries to strengthen F_0, we stop and use a bounded model checker to look for a counterexample of length N. If no counterexample is found, PDR$^\forall$ *determines that no universal invariant strong enough to prove the desired property exists* (see Lemma 1). We note that PDR$^\forall$ is not guaranteed to terminate, although in our experience it often does.

Example 1. Procedure split(), shown in Fig. 1(a), moves the elements not satisfying the condition C from the list pointed to by h to the list pointed by g. PDR$^\forall$ can infer tricky inductive invariants strong enough to prove several interesting properties: (i) memory safety, i.e., no null dereference and no memory leaks; (ii) all the elements satisfying C are kept in h; (iii) all the elements which do not satisfy C are moved to g; (iv) no new elements are introduced; and (v) stability, i.e., the reachability order between the elements satisfying C is not changed. Our implementation verified that split() satisfies all the above properties fully automatically by inferring an inductive loop invariant consisting of 36 clauses (among them 19 are universal formulae) in 206 sec.

Example 2. Procedure filter(), shown in Fig. 1(b), removes and deallocates the elements not satisfying the condition C from the list pointed to by h. The figure also shows the loop invariant inferred by PDR$^\forall$ when it was asked to verify a simplified version of property (iii): all the elements which do not satisfy C are removed from h. The invariant highlights certain interesting properties of filter(). For example, clause L_4 says that if the head element of the list was processed and kept in the list (this is the only way $i \neq h$ can hold), then j becomes an immediate predecessor of i. Clause L_7 says that all the elements x_3 reachable from h and not satisfying C must occur after j.

Experimental Evaluation. We implemented PDR$^\forall$ on top of the decision procedure of [32], and applied it to a collection of procedures that manipulate (possibly sorted) singly linked lists, doubly-linked lists, and multi-linked lists. Our analysis successfully verified interesting specifications, detected bugs in incorrect programs, and established the absence of universal invariants for certain correct programs.

Main Contributions. The main contributions of this work can be summarized as follows.

- We present PDR$^\forall$, a pleasantly simple, yet surprisingly powerful, combination of PDR [9] with a strengthening technique based on diagrams [10]. PDR$^\forall$

enjoys a high-degree of automation because it does *not* require pre-defined abstraction predicates.

- The diagram-based abstraction is particularly interesting as it is determined "on-the-fly" according to the structural properties of the bad states discovered in PDR's traversal of the state space.
- We prove that the diagram-based abstraction is precise in the sense that if $\mathsf{PDR}^\forall$ finds a spurious counterexample then the program cannot be proven correct using a universal invariant. We believe that this is a unique feature of our approach.
- We implemented $\mathsf{PDR}^\forall$ on top of a decision procedure for logic AE^R [31], and applied it successfully to verify a collection of list-manipulating programs, detect bug, and prove the absence of universal invariants. We show that our technique outperforms an existing state-of-the-art less-automatic PDR-based verification technique [32] which uses the same decision procedure.

2   Preliminaries

Programs. We handle single loop programs, i.e., we assume that a program has the form while *Cond* do *Cmd*, where *Cmd* is loop-free. We encode more complicated control structures, e.g., nested or multiple loops, by explicitly recording the program counter. For clarity, in our examples we allow for a sequence of instructions preceding the loop. Technically, we encode their effect in the loop's pre-condition.

From Programs to Transition Systems. The semantics of a program is described by a *transition system*, which consists of a set of states and transitions between states.

Program States. We consider the states of the program at the beginning of each iteration of the loop. A program state is represented by a first-order model $\sigma = (\mathcal{U}, \mathcal{I})$ over a vocabulary $\mathcal{V}$ which consists of constants and relation symbols, where $\mathcal{U}$ is the *universe* of the model, and $\mathcal{I}$ is the interpretation function of the symbols in $\mathcal{V}$. For example, to represent memory states of list manipulating programs, we use a vocabulary $\mathcal{V}$ which associates every program variable x with a constant x, every boolean field C with a unary predicate $C(\cdot)$, and every pointer field n with a binary predicate $n^*(\cdot, \cdot)$ which represents its reflexive transitive closure.[1] We use a special constant $null$ to denote the null value. We depict memory states $\sigma = (\mathcal{U}, \mathcal{I})$ as directed graphs (see Fig. 2). Individuals in $\mathcal{U}$, representing heap locations, are depicted as circles labeled by their name. We draw an edge from the name of constant x and of a unary predicate C to an individual v if $\sigma \models x = v$ or $\sigma \models C(v)$, respectively. We draw an n^*-annotated edge between v and u if $\sigma \models n^*(v, u)$. For clarity, we do not show edges that can be inferred from the reflexive and transitive nature of n^*.

---

[1] We reason about list-manipulating programs using logic EA^R [32]. Hence, values of pointer fields n are defined indirectly by a formula over n^*, but n is not included in the vocabulary.

Transition Relation. The set of transitions of a program is defined using a *transition relation*. A transition relation is a set of models of a *double vocabulary* $\hat{\mathcal{V}} = \mathcal{V} \uplus \mathcal{V}'$, where vocabulary $\mathcal{V}$ is used to describe the *source* state of the transition and vocabulary $\mathcal{V}' = \{v' \mid v \in \mathcal{V}\}$ is used to describe its *target* state: A model $\sigma' = (\mathcal{U}, \mathcal{I}')$ over $\mathcal{V}'$ describes a program state $\sigma = (\mathcal{U}, \mathcal{I})$, where $\mathcal{I}(v) = \mathcal{I}'(v')$ for every symbol $v \in \mathcal{V}$.

Definition 1 (Reduct). *Let* $\hat{\sigma} = (\mathcal{U}, \mathcal{I})$ *be a model of* $\hat{\mathcal{V}}$, *and let* $\Sigma \subseteq \hat{\mathcal{V}}$. *The reduct of* $\hat{\sigma}$ *to* Σ *is the model* $(\mathcal{U}, \mathcal{I}_i)$ *of* Σ *where for every symbol* $v \in \Sigma$, $\mathcal{I}_i(v) = \mathcal{I}(v)$.

We often write a transition $\hat{\sigma}$ as a pair of states (σ_1, σ_2), such that σ_1 is the *reduct* of $\hat{\sigma}$ to vocabulary $\mathcal{V}$, and σ_2 is the state described by the *reduct* to $\mathcal{V}'$. Each transition (σ_1, σ_2) describes one possible execution of the loop body, *Cmd*, i.e., it relates the state σ_1 at the beginning of an iteration of the loop to the state σ_2 at the end of the iteration. We say that σ_2 is a successor of σ_1, and σ_1 is a predecessor of σ_2.

Properties and Assertions. *Properties* are sets of states. We express properties using logical formulae over $\mathcal{V}$. For example, we express properties of list-manipulation programs, e.g., their pre- and post-conditions, *Pre* and *Post*, respectively, using assertions written in a fragment of first-order logic with transitive closure. In our analysis, these assertions are translated into equisatisfiable first-order logic formulae [31]. We use $(\varphi)'$ to denote the formula obtained by replacing every constant and relation symbol in formula φ with its primed version.

Verification Problem. The *transition system* of a program is represented by a pair $TS = (Init, \rho)$, where *Init* is a first-order formula over $\mathcal{V}$ used to denote the *initial states* of the program, and ρ is a formula over $\hat{\mathcal{V}}$ used to denote its *transition relation*. A state σ is initial if $\sigma \models Init$, and a pair of states (σ_1, σ_2) is a transition if $(\sigma_1, \sigma_2) \models \rho$. We say that a state is *reachable by at most i* steps of ρ (or *i-reachable* for short, when ρ is clear from the context) if it can be reached by at most i applications of ρ starting from some initial state. We denote the set of i-reachable states by $\mathcal{R}_i$. We say that a state is *reachable* if it is i-reachable for some i. We say that *TS satisfies* a *safety property* $\mathcal{P}$ if all reachable states satisfy $\mathcal{P}$. We often define $Bad \stackrel{\text{def}}{=} \neg \mathcal{P}$, and refer to states satisfying *Bad* as *bad states*. We define $\rho \stackrel{\text{def}}{=} Cond \wedge wlp(Cmd, Id)$, where $wlp(Cmd, Id)$ denotes the weakest liberal precondition of the loop body and *Id* is a conjunction of equalities between $\mathcal{V}$ and $\mathcal{V}'$ (see [31] for more details). We define *Init* and *Bad* using the programs pre- and post- conditions: $Init \stackrel{\text{def}}{=} Pre$ and $Bad \stackrel{\text{def}}{=} \neg Cond \wedge \neg Post$. That is, a state is initial if it satisfies the pre-condition, and it is bad if it satisfies the negation of the loop condition (which indicates termination of the loop) but does not satisfy the post-condition. This captures the requirement that when the loop terminates the post-condition needs to hold.

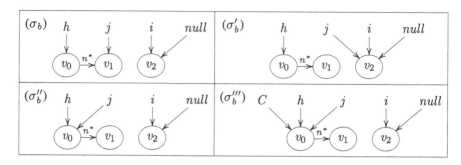

Fig. 2. Graphical depiction of models found during the analysis of the running example.

Example 3. In Example 2, $Init \stackrel{\text{def}}{=} (i = h) \land (j = null)$ and $Bad \stackrel{\text{def}}{=} (i = null) \land$
$\neg (h \neq null \to (\forall v.\, n^*(h, v) \to C(v)))$. Note that these refer to the pre- and
post-conditions that should hold right before the loop begins and right after it
terminates, respectively. Here, a state is bad if $i = null$ (i.e., it occurs when the
loop terminates) and h points to a non-empty list that contains an element not
having the property C.

Invariants. An *invariant* of a program is a property that should hold for all
reachable states. It is *inductive* if it is closed under application of ρ.

Definition 2 (Invariants). *Let $TS = (Init, \rho)$ be a transition system and $\mathcal{P}$ a
safety property over $\mathcal{V}$. A formula $\mathcal{I}$ is a* safety inductive invariant *(invariant,
in short) for TS and $\mathcal{P}$ if (i) $Init \Rightarrow \mathcal{I}$, and (ii) $\mathcal{I} \land \rho \Rightarrow (\mathcal{I})'$, and (iii) $\mathcal{I} \Rightarrow \mathcal{P}$.*

If there exists an invariant for TS and $\mathcal{P}$, then TS satisfies $\mathcal{P}$. An invariant is
universal if it is equivalent to a universal formula in prenex normal form. We
note that the invariants inferred by PDR$^\forall$ are conjunctions of *universal clauses*,
where a universal clause is a universally quantified disjunction of literals (positive
or negative atomic formulae).

3 Universal-Property-Directed Reachability

In this section, we present *Universal Property Directed Reachability* (PDR$^\forall$),
an algorithm for checking if a transition system TS satisfies a safety property $\mathcal{P}$. PDR$^\forall$ is an adaptation of Bradley's *property-directed reachability*
(IC3) algorithm [9] that uses universal formulae instead of propositional predicates [9,22,29] or predicate abstraction [32]. We use Example 2 as a running
example throughout this section.

Requirements. We require that the transition relation ρ, as well as the *Init* and
Bad conditions, are expressible in a first-order logic $\mathcal{L}$ (We can partly handle
transitive closure using the approach of [31]. See Sect. 5.) We require that every
satisfiable formula in $\mathcal{L}$ has a finite model, and assume to have a decision procedure $SAT(\psi)$, which checks if a formula ψ in $\mathcal{L}$ is satisfiable, and a function
$model(\psi)$, which returns a *finite* model σ of ψ if such a model exists and None
otherwise.

3.1 Diagrams as Structural Abstractions

$PDR^\forall$ iteratively strengthens a candidate invariant by retrieving program states that lead to bad states and checking whether the retrieved states are reachable. In that sense, $PDR^\forall$ is similar to IC3. The novel aspect of our approach is the use of *diagrams* [10] to generalize individual states into sets of states before checking for reachability. Diagrams provide a *structural abstraction* of states by existential formulae: The *diagram* of a *finite* model σ, denoted by $Diag(\sigma)$, is an existential cube which describes explicitly the relations between all the elements of the model.[2]

Definition 3 (Diagrams). *Given a finite model* $\sigma = (\mathcal{U}, \mathcal{I})$ *over alphabet* $\mathcal{V}$, *the* diagram *of* σ, *denoted by* $Diag(\sigma)$, *is a formula over alphabet* $\mathcal{V}$ *which denotes the set of models in which* σ *can be isomorphically embedded.* $Diag(\sigma)$ *is constructed as follows.*

- *For every element* $e_i \in \mathcal{U}$, *a fresh variable* x_{e_i} *is introduced.*
- $\varphi_{distinct}$ *is a conjunction of inequalities of the form* $x_{e_i} \neq x_{e_j}$ *for every pair of distinct elements* $e_i \neq e_j$ *in the model.*
- $\varphi_{constants}$ *is a conjunction of equalities of the form* $c = x_e$ *for every constant symbol* c *such that* $\sigma \models c = e$.
- φ_{atomic} *is a conjunction of atomic formulae which include for every predicate* $p \in \mathcal{V}$ *the atomic formula* $p(\bar{x}_e)$ *if* $\sigma \models p(\bar{e})$, *and* $\neg p(\bar{x}_e)$ *otherwise.*

Then: $Diag(\sigma) \overset{def}{=} \exists x_{e_1} \dots x_{e_{|\mathcal{U}|}} . \varphi_{distinct} \wedge \varphi_{constants} \wedge \varphi_{atomic}$.

Intuitively, one can think of $Diag(\sigma)$ as the formula produced by treating individuals in σ as existentially quantified variables and explicitly encoding the interpretation of every constant and every predicate using a conjunction of equalities, inequalities, and atomic formulae. For example, the diagram of σ_b, depicted in Fig. 2(σ_b), is

$$
\begin{aligned}
Diag(\sigma_b) \overset{def}{=} \ & \exists x_0, x_1, x_2. \, x_0 \neq x_1 \wedge x_0 \neq x_2 \wedge x_1 \neq x_2 \wedge \\
& h = x_0 \wedge j = x_1 \wedge i = x_2 \wedge null = x_2 \wedge \\
& \neg C(x_0) \wedge \neg C(x_1) \wedge \neg C(x_2) \wedge \\
& n^* x_0 x_0 \wedge n^* x_1 x_1 \wedge n^* x_2 x_2 \wedge n^* x_0 x_1 \wedge \\
& \neg n^* x_0 x_2 \wedge \neg n^* x_1 x_0 \wedge \neg n^* x_1 x_2 \wedge \neg n^* x_2 x_0 \wedge \neg n^* x_2 x_1 \ .
\end{aligned}
$$

The first line records the fact that the universe of σ_b consists of three elements. The second line characterizes the interpretations of all the constant symbols in σ_b. The other lines capture precisely the interpretation of predicates C and n^* in σ_b.

---

[2] Definition 3, as well as the property formulated by Lemma 1, are an adaptation of the standard model-theoretic notion of a diagram [10].

Lemma 1. *Let σ be a model over $\mathcal{V}$, and let ϕ be a closed existential first-order formula over $\mathcal{V}$. If $\sigma \models \phi$ then $Diag(\sigma) \Rightarrow \phi$.*

Semantically, Lemma 1 means that for any models σ and σ_i such that $\sigma_i \models Diag(\sigma)$ if $\sigma \models \phi$ then $\sigma_i \models \phi$. This implies that if a bad state is reachable from σ *and* the program can be proven correct using an inductive universal invariant $\mathcal{I}$ then *all* the states in σ's diagram are unreachable too: $\mathcal{I}$ is an inductive invariant, thus any state σ leading to a bad state must satisfy (closed existential) formula $\neg\mathcal{I}$. Hence, $Diag(\sigma) \Rightarrow \neg\mathcal{I}$, which means that all states satisfying $Diag(\sigma)$ are unreachable. In this sense, the abstraction based on diagrams is precise for programs with universal invariants.

3.2   Data Structures and Frames

$PDR^\forall$ is shown in Algorithm 1. It uses procedures *block()* and *analyzeCEX()*, shown in Algorithms 2 and 3, respectively, as subroutines. The algorithm uses an array F of *frames*, where a frame is a conjunction of universal clauses. For clarity, we refer to the ith entry of the array using subscript notation, i.e., F_i instead of $F[i]$. Intuitively, frame F_i over-approximates $\mathcal{R}_i$, the set of i-reachable states. The algorithm also maintains a *frame counter* N which records the number of frames it developed. We refer to F_0 as the *initial* frame, to F_N as the *frontier* frame, and to any F_i, where $0 \leq i < N$, as a *back* frame.

$PDR^\forall$ maintains several invariants which ensure that every frame F_i is an over-approximation of $\mathcal{R}_i$, and hence that the sequence of developed frames is an over-approximation of all the traces of the program of length $N + 1$ or less. Technically, this means that the algorithm constructs an *approximate reachability sequence*.

Definition 4. *Let $TS = (Init, \rho)$ be a transition system and $\mathcal{P}$ a safety property. A sequence $\langle F_0, F_1, \ldots, F_N \rangle$ is an* approximate reachability sequence *for TS and $\mathcal{P}$ if:*

(i) $Init \Rightarrow F_0$.
(ii) $F_i \Rightarrow F_{i+1}$, for all $0 \leq i < N$, i.e., for every state σ, if $\sigma \models F_i$ then $\sigma \models F_{i+1}$.
(iii) $F_i \wedge \rho \Rightarrow (F_{i+1})'$, for all $0 \leq i < N$, i.e., for every transition $(\sigma_1, \sigma_2) \models \rho$, if $\sigma_1 \models F_i$ then $\sigma_2 \models F_{i+1}$.
(iv) $F_i \Rightarrow \mathcal{P}$, for all $0 \leq i \leq N$.

Items (ii) and (iii) ensure that every frame includes the states of the previous frame and their successors, respectively. Together with item (i), it follows by induction that for every $0 < i \leq N$ the set of states (models) that satisfy F_i is a superset of the set $\mathcal{R}_i$. Furthermore, by item (iv) no frame includes a bad state.

Algorithm 1. PDR$^\forall$ ($Init, \rho, Bad$)

1 **if** $SAT(Init \wedge Bad)$ **then**
2   **exit** invalid: $model(Init \wedge Bad)$
3 $F_0 := Init$
4 $F_1 := true$
5 $N := 1$
6 **while** true **do**
7   **if** there exists $0 \leq j < N$
       such that $F_{j+1} \Rightarrow F_j$ **then**
8   **return** valid
9   **if** $\neg SAT(F_N \wedge Bad)$ **then**
10     $F_{N+1} := true$
11     $N := N + 1$
12   **else**
13     $\sigma_b := model(F_N \wedge Bad)$
14     $block(N, \sigma_b)$

Algorithm 2. $block(j, \sigma)$

21 $\varphi = Diag(\sigma)$
22 **if** $(j = 0) \vee (j = 1 \wedge SAT(\varphi \wedge Init))$ **then**
23     $analyzeCEX(j, N)$
24 **while** $SAT(F_{j-1} \wedge \rho \wedge (\varphi)')$ **do**
25     $\sigma_a = reduct(model(F_{j-1} \wedge \rho \wedge (\varphi)'))$
26     $block(j - 1, \sigma_a)$
27 **for** $i = 0 \dots j$ **do**
28     $F_i := F_i \wedge \neg\varphi$

Algorithm 3. $analyzeCEX(j, N)$

31 **if** $j = 0 \wedge$ there exists $\sigma_0, \dots, \sigma_N$ such that
32     $\sigma_0 \models Init$
33     $(\sigma_i, \sigma_{i+1}) \models \rho$ for every $0 \leq i < N$, and
34     $\sigma_N \models Bad$
35 **then exit** invalid: $\sigma_0, \dots, \sigma_N$
36 **else exit** No Universal Invariant Exists

3.3 Iterative Construction of an Approximate Reachability Sequence

PDR$^\forall$ is an iterative algorithm. At every iteration, the algorithm either strengthens the Nth frame, if it contains a bad state, or starts to develop the $N + 1$th frame, otherwise. In addition, in every iteration, it might also strengthen some of the back frames. Each strengthening of frame F_i is performed by determining a universal clause φ_i which holds for any i-reachable state, and then conjoining F_i with φ_i.

Initialization. The algorithm first checks that the initial states and the bad states do not intersect. If so, it exits and returns the state that satisfies both $Init$ and Bad as a counterexample (line 2). Otherwise, it sets F_0 to represent the set of initial states (line 3), F_1 to represent all possible states (line 4), and the frame counter to 1. Note that at this point, F_1 is a trivial over-approximation of the set of initial states and their successors, but it might contain bad states.

Iterative Construction. The algorithm then starts its iterative search for an inductive invariant (line 6). Recall that when the algorithm develops the Nth frame, it has already managed to determine an approximate reachability sequence $\langle F_0, \dots, F_{N-1} \rangle$. Hence, every iteration starts by checking whether a fixpoint has been reached (line 7). If true, then an inductive invariant proving unreachability of Bad has been found, and the algorithm returns **valid** (line 8). Otherwise, the algorithm keeps on strengthening the frontier frame F_N by searching for a *bad witness*, a bad state in the frontier frame (line 9). If no such state exists, it means that no bad state is N-reachable. Moreover, at this point $\langle F_0, \dots, F_N \rangle$ is an approximate reachability sequence. Thus, the iterative strengthening of F_N terminates and a new frontier frame is initialized to *true* (line 10 and 11).

If the frontier frame contains a bad witness, i.e. $F_N \wedge Bad$ is satisfiable, then there *might* be an N-reachable bad state. Due to our requirement for finite satisfiability of the logic, the bad witness is a *finite* model. Given a bad witness σ_b (line 13), the algorithm tries to determine whether it is indeed reachable, and thus the program does not satisfy its specification, or whether σ_b was discovered due to some over-approximation in one of the back frames. This check is done by invoking procedure *block*() with the index of the frontier frame and σ_b as parameters (line 14). The latter either returns a counterexample, determines that it is impossible to prove the specification using a universal invariant (in the given logic and vocabulary), or strengthens the frontier frame to exclude the *set of states in the diagram of* σ_b, and possibly strengthens some back frames too (see below). The iterative construction and strengthening of the frames continues until reaching a fixpoint, finding a counterexample, or determining the absence of a universal invariant.[3]

Example 4. When analyzing the running example, our algorithm discovers that state σ_b, shown in Fig. 2, is a bad witness when $F_1 = true$, and thus it invokes $block(1, \sigma_b)$. In this example, *block*() succeeds to block σ_b. Unfortunately, the strengthened frame F_1^1 (see below) still has bad models. Therefore, the iterative strengthening continues and the next iterations find σ_b', depicted in Fig. 2, as a bad witness model for F_1^1, σ_b'' as a bad witness model of F_1^2 and σ_b''' as a bad witness model of F_1^3. At that point, however, the algorithm determines that the strengthened frame F_1^4 does not have a bad witness. $\langle F_0, F_1^4 \rangle$ is now an approximate reachability sequence and $\mathsf{PDR}^\forall$ goes on and initializes a new frame, F_2, to *true*, and the search for an inductive invariant continues.

Diagram-Based Abstract Blocking. Procedure $block(j, \sigma)$, shown in Algorithm 2, gets an index of a frame $j = 0 \cdots N$ and a state σ which is included in the jth frame, i.e., $\sigma \models F_j$, and tries to determine whether σ is j-reachable. The unique aspect of our approach is the way in which it abstracts σ to a set of states in order to accelerate the strengthening routine. Namely, the use of diagrams. More specifically, $\mathsf{PDR}^\forall$ computes the diagram φ of σ (line 21) and then checks whether there is a j-reachable state satisfying φ. Importantly, due to Lemma 1, if a universal invariant exists then the generalization of σ to its diagram will not include any reachable state, hence the abstraction is precise in the sense that it maintains unreachability. In this case the strengthening of F_j is also guaranteed to succeed, excluding not only σ, but its entire diagram.

The check if the diagram φ of σ includes a j-reachable state is done *conservatively* by determining whether some state of φ is an initial state or has a predecessor in F_{j-1}. (Recall that F_{j-1} over-approximates $\mathcal{R}_{j-1}$.) The former is

---

[3] For efficiency, in our implementation we represent each frame as a set of clauses (with the meaning of conjunction) and check implication (line 7) by checking inclusion of these sets. To facilitate this fixpoint computation, any clause φ in F_i that is *inductive* in F_i, i.e., $F_i \wedge \rho \Rightarrow (\varphi)'$ is also propagated forward to F_{i+1}. In particular, this allows to initialize a new frontier frame F_N, for $1 < N$, to a tighter over-approximation of $\mathcal{R}_N$ than *true* (line 10) [22].

equivalent to checking if $\varphi \wedge Init$ is satisfiable. Note that if we reached the initial frame, i.e., if $j = 0$, then $\sigma \models Init$, hence the above formula is guaranteed to be satisfiable. Explicitly checking that $\varphi \wedge Init$ is satisfiable is required only at the second frame, i.e., if $j = 1$:

Lemma 2. *For every* $1 < j \leq N$, *when* $block(j, \sigma)$ *is called,* $F_i \Rightarrow \neg Diag(\sigma)$ *for every* $i \leq j - 1$. *In particular,* $Init \Rightarrow \neg Diag(\sigma)$.

If the algorithm finds an *adverse initial state*, i.e., an initial state satisfying φ, (line 22),[4] it invokes procedure $analyzeCEX()$ for further analysis (see below). Otherwise, the algorithm checks if the formula $\delta = F_{j-1} \wedge \rho \wedge (\varphi)'$ is satisfiable (line 24),[5] i.e., whether some state of φ has a predecessor in F_{j-1}. There can be two cases:

Case I. If δ is unsatisfiable then no state represented by φ is j-reachable. Hence, F_j remains an over-approximation of $\mathcal{R}_j$ even if any state of φ is excluded. The exclusion is done by conjoining the jth frame with the universal formula $\neg \varphi$ (line 28), and results in a strengthening of F_j. In fact, $\neg \varphi$ is conjoined to any back frame (line 27). We refer to the exclusion of the states of φ as the *blocking* of (the diagram of) σ from frame F_j.

Example 5. In our running example, in the first iteration $block(1, \sigma_b)$ updates F_1^0 to $F_1^1 = true \wedge \neg Diag(\sigma_b)$. This excludes σ_b, but also all states where $i = null$, C is empty, and j is n-reachable from h in *any* (nonzero) number of steps. In later iterations $block$ updates $F_1^2 = F_1^1 \wedge \neg Diag(\sigma_b')$, $F_1^3 = F_1^2 \wedge \neg Diag(\sigma_b'')$, and $F_1^4 = F_1^3 \wedge \neg Diag(\sigma_b''')$.

Case II. If δ is satisfiable, then there exists an *adverse* state σ_a in frame F_{j-1}, a state which is the predecessor of some state of the diagram of σ that we try to block at frame F_j. Note that σ_a is not necessarily a predecessor of σ itself. The adverse state σ_a is found by taking the reduct of a (finite) model of δ (line 25). If an adverse model σ_a exists then the algorithm *recursively* tries to block it from F_{j-1} (line 26). The recursive procedure continues until the adverse state is either blocked or the algorithm finds an adverse initial state (line 22). Note that blocking an adverse state during the development of the Nth frame leads to a strengthening of some back frame F_i, and thus tightens its over-approximation of $\mathcal{R}_i$.

Finding Concrete Counterexamples and Proving the Absence of Universal Invariants. Procedure $analyzeCEX()$, shown in Algorithm 3, is called when an adverse initial state is found. Such a state indicates that an abstract counterexample exists:

---

[4] If $Init$ is a universal formula, then Lemma 2 holds for $j = 1$ as well, hence $j = 1 \wedge SAT(\varphi \wedge Init)$ never holds, and its check can be omitted (line 22).

[5] As an optimization, one can consider $\delta' = F_{j-1} \wedge \neg \varphi \wedge \rho \wedge (\varphi)'$ instead of δ. The two formulae are equivalent since $F_{j-1} \Rightarrow \neg \varphi$ (by Lemma 2 for $j > 1$, and since it was checked for $j = 1$), but the strenthening of δ can make the satisfiability check cheaper.

594   A. Karbyshev et al.

Definition 5 (Abstract and Spurious Counterexamples). *A sequence of formulae* $\langle \phi_j, \phi_{j+1} \cdots \phi_N \rangle$ *is an* abstract counterexample *if the formulae* $\phi_j \wedge$ *Init,* $\phi_N \wedge Bad$, *and* $\varphi_i \wedge \rho \wedge (\phi_{i+1})'$, *for every* $i = j \cdots N - 1$, *are all satisfiable. The abstract counterexample is* spurious *if there exists no sequence of states* $\langle \sigma_j, \sigma_{j+1} \cdots \sigma_N \rangle$ *such that* $\sigma_j \models Init$, $\sigma_N \models Bad$, *and for every* $j \leq i < N$, $(\sigma_i, \sigma_{i+1}) \models \rho$.

An abstract counterexample does not necessarily describe a real counterexample. In fact, if $j \neq 0$, the counterexample is necessarily spurious (as, if a real counterexample shorter than N had existed, the algorithm would have already terminated during the development of the $N - 1$th frame). However, when $j = 0$, the algorithm determines if the abstract counterexample is real or spurious by checking whether a bad state can be reached by N applications of the transition relation (line 31). Technically, *analyzeCEX()* can be implemented using a symbolic bounded model checker [5]. If a real counterexample is found, the algorithm reports it (line 35). Otherwise, the obtained counterexample is *spurious*. Technically, this means that the property is neither verified nor falsified. In our case, the algorithm can determine that the verification effort is doomed: The spurious counterexample is in fact a proof for the absence of a universal invariant (see Proposition 1).

Generalization of Blocked Diagrams. Rather than blocking a diagram ϕ from frames $0 \cdots j$ by conjoining them with the clause $\neg\phi$ (line 28), our implementation uses a minimal unsat core of $\psi = ((Init)' \vee (F_{j-1} \wedge \rho)) \wedge (\varphi)'$ to define a clause L which implies $\neg\phi$ and is also disjoint from *Init* and unreachable from F_{j-1}. Blocking is done by conjoining L with F_i for every $i \leq j$.[6]

4   Correctness

In this section we formalize the correctness guarantees of $PDR^\forall$. We recall that if $PDR^\forall$ terminates it reports that either the program is safe, the program is not safe, providing a counterexample, or the program cannot be verified using a universal inductive invariant.

Lemma 3. *Let* $TS = (Init, \rho)$ *be a transition system and let* $\mathcal{P}$ *be a safety property. If* $PDR^\forall$ *returns* valid *then* TS *satisfies* $\mathcal{P}$. *Further, if* $PDR^\forall$ *returns a counterexample, then* TS *does not satisfy* $\mathcal{P}$.

Proof. $PDR^\forall$ returns valid if there exists i such that $F_{i+1} \Rightarrow F_i$. Therefore, $F_i \wedge \rho \Rightarrow (F_{i+1})' \Rightarrow (F_i)'$. Recall that, by the properties of an approximate reachability sequence, $Init \Rightarrow F_0 \Rightarrow F_i$ and $F_i \Rightarrow \mathcal{P}$. Therefore, F_i is an inductive invariant, which ensures that TS satisfies $\mathcal{P}$. The second part of the claim follows immediately from the definition of a counterexample. □

---

[6] We can also use inductive generalization, i.e., look for a minimal subclause L of $\neg\phi$ that is still inductive relative to F_{j-1}, meaning $((Init)' \vee (F_{j-1} \wedge L \wedge \rho)) \wedge (\neg L)'$ is unsatisfiable.

Proposition 1. *Let* $TS = (Init, \rho)$ *be a transition system and let* $\mathcal{P}$ *be a safety property. If* $PDR^\forall$ *obtains a spurious counterexample* $\langle \phi_j \cdots \phi_N \rangle$ *then there exists no universal safety inductive invariant* $\mathcal{I}$ *for* TS *and* $\mathcal{P}$.

Proof. Assume that there exists a universal safety inductive invariant $\mathcal{I}$ over $\mathcal{V}$. We show by induction on the distance $N - i = 0 \cdots N$, of F_i from F_N that every state σ_i generated by $PDR^\forall$ at frame F_i is such that $\sigma_i \models \neg\mathcal{I}$. This implies, by Lemma 1, that every diagram ϕ_i generated by $PDR^\forall$ at frame F_i is such that $\phi_i \Rightarrow \neg\mathcal{I}$, and hence $\phi_i \Rightarrow \neg Init$. (Recall that by definition $Init \Rightarrow \mathcal{I}$, i.e., $\neg\mathcal{I} \Rightarrow \neg Init$). This contradicts the existence of a spurious counterexample, where $\phi_j \wedge Init$ is satisfiable.

The base case of the induction pertains to F_N. It follows immediately from the property that a state σ_N generated at frame F_N is a model of the formula $F_N \wedge Bad$, and in particular is a model of $Bad = \neg\mathcal{P}$, i.e., $\sigma_N \models \neg\mathcal{P}$. Since $\mathcal{I} \Rightarrow \mathcal{P}$, or equivalently $\neg\mathcal{P} \Rightarrow \neg\mathcal{I}$, we conclude that $\sigma_N \models \neg\mathcal{I}$.

Consider a state generated at frame F_i. Then σ_i is the reduct of a model of the formula $F_i \wedge \rho \wedge (Diag(\sigma_{i+1}))'$ to $\mathcal{V}$. Moreover, by the induction hypothesis, $\sigma_{i+1} \models \neg\mathcal{I}$. Since $\neg\mathcal{I}$ is an existential formula, this means by Lemma 1 that $Diag(\sigma_{i+1}) \Rightarrow \neg\mathcal{I}$. We conclude that $F_i \wedge \rho \wedge (Diag(\sigma_{i+1}))' \Rightarrow F_i \wedge \rho \wedge (\neg\mathcal{I})'$. Therefore, σ_i is also (a reduct of) a model of the formula $F_i \wedge \rho \wedge (\neg\mathcal{I})'$. If we assume that $\sigma_i \models \mathcal{I}$, we would get that $\mathcal{I} \wedge \rho \wedge (\neg\mathcal{I})'$ is satisfiable, in contradiction $\mathcal{I}$ being inductive. Hence, $\sigma_i \models \neg\mathcal{I}$. $\square$

Example 6. Procedure `traverseTwo()`, presented in Figure 3 together with its pre- and post-condition, traverses two lists until it finds their last elements. If the lists have a shared tail then p and q should point to the same element when the traversal terminates. The program indeed satisfies this property. However, this cannot be proven correct using an inductive universal invariant: Take, as usual, $Init$ to be the procedure's precondition and $\mathcal{P}$ to be the safety property whose negation is $Bad = (i = null \wedge j = null) \wedge \neg post$, where $post$ is the procedure's postcondition. Consider the state σ_0 depicted in Figure 4. Clearly, this model satisfies $Init$. Therefore, if $\mathcal{I}$ exists, $\sigma_0 \models \mathcal{I}$. σ_0 is a predecessor of σ_1^t and hence it should be the case that $\sigma_1^t \models \mathcal{I}$. Now consider σ_1, which is a submodel of σ_1^t and interprets all constants as in σ_1. If $\mathcal{I}$ is universal, then $\sigma_1 \models \mathcal{I}$ as well. However, $\sigma_1 \not\models \mathcal{P}$, in contradiction to the property of a safety invariant. Indeed, when using $PDR^\forall$, the spurious counterexample $\langle \sigma_0, \sigma_1, \sigma_2 \rangle$ presented in Figure 4 is obtained. This indicates that no universal invariant for $\mathcal{P}$ exists. Note that state σ_1 is a predecessor of σ_2 and recall that σ_0 is a predecessor of σ_1^t. The spurious counterexample was obtained because σ_1^t satisfies the diagram of state σ_1.

5   Implementation and Empirical Evaluation

$PDR^\forall$ is parametric in the vocabulary, and can be implemented on top of any decision procedure for finite satisfiability of first-order logic formulae. The language of these formulae should be expressive enough to capture the assertions,

pre: $p = null \wedge q = null \wedge i = g \wedge g \neq null \wedge j = h \wedge h \neq null \wedge$
$\exists v. n^*(g, v) \wedge n^*(h, v) \wedge v \neq null$
post: $p = q \wedge p \neq null \wedge i = null \wedge j = null$
```
void traverseTwo(List g, List h) {
    while (i ≠ null ∨ j ≠ null){
        if i ≠ null then p := i; i := i.n;
        if j ≠ null then q := j; j := j.n}}
```

Fig. 3. A procedure that finds the last elements of two non-empty acyclic lists.

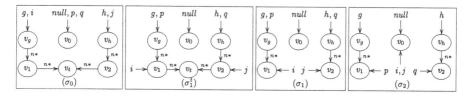

Fig. 4. A spurious counterexample found for procedure `traverseTwo()`, shown in Fig. 3.

transition system, and space of candidate invariants. Our algorithm is not guaranteed to terminate, thus the underlying logic does not have to be decidable. Our implementation, however, uses EA^R which is a decidable logic [31].

EA^R allows for relational first-order formulae with a quantifier prefix of the form $\exists^*\forall^*$ and a deterministic transitive-closure operator *, but forbids functional symbols. We use n^* to construct reachability constraints over the pointer field n, e.g., in Examples 1 and 2, and to define the "next" relation n [31] using a universal formula. We note that The latter can be done only when the prefix of the resulting formula is of the form $\exists^*\forall^*$.

EA^R satisfiability is reducible to effectively-propositional (EPR) satisfiability, also known as the Bernays-Schönfinkel-Ramsey class, and hence is decidable and enjoys the *small model property*, i.e., every satisfiable formula in EA^R is guaranteed to have a finite model. Technically, the reduction introduces axioms (EPR formulae) that capture the reflexivity, transitivity, acyclicity and linearity properties of the * operator [31].

Benchmarks. We implemented $PDR^\forall$ and applied it to a collection of procedures that manipulate singly-linked lists, doubly-linked lists, multi-linked lists, and implementations of an insertion-sort algorithm [16], and a union-find algorithm [16]. Our experiments were conducted using a 3.6GHz Intel Core i7 machine with 32GB of RAM, running Ubuntu 14.04. We used the 64bit version of Z3 4.4 [19] with the default settings to check satisfiability of EPR formulae. Table 1 summarizes our experimental results.

(a) Verification. Our analyzer successfully verified memory safety, i.e., the absence of null-dereferences and of memory leaks, preservation of data-structure integrity, meaning that the procedure never creates cycles in the list, and functional correctness of several singly- and doubly-linked list manipulating

Table 1. Experimental results. Running time is measured in seconds. N denotes the highest index for a developed frame F_i. "# Z3" denotes the number of calls to Z3. **AF** denotes "Abstraction Failure" of [32]. **TO** means timeout (> 1 hr). (a) Correct programs; "# Cl. (∀)" = number of (∀-)clauses in the inferred invariant. (b) Correct programs for which there is no universal inductive invariant. (c) Incorrect program; "C.e. size" is the maximal number of elements in a model that arises in the counterexample.

(a) Verification	Full				Memory safety				Memory safety [32]			
	Time	N	# Z3	# Cl. (∀)	Time	N	# Z3	# Cl. (∀)	Time	N	# Z3	# Cl. (∀)
— Singly-linked lists —												
concat	2.1	3	59	7 (4)	1.5	4	59	5 (2)	AF			
delete	15	5	279	23 (12)	1.5	3	59	7	9.7	4	108	11
delete-all	16	6	300	16 (9)	0.6	3	37	3 (1)	2.7	3	60	6
filter	26	5	336	19 (12)	2.6	4	98	9 (1)	6.6	5	144	9
insert-at	1.9	3	70	9 (2)	1.6	4	60	9 (1)	7.8	5	157	10
insert	3.2	3	71	9 (2)	1.4	3	59	7 (1)	2.1	3	48	7
merge	201	6	1251	34 (22)	12	5	255	13 (3)	AF			
reverse	13	5	218	12 (7)	6.0	7	183	5 (1)	8.4	6	266	5
split	206	8	1143	36 (19)	9.6	6	216	13	24	6	186	10
uf-find	37	7	531	21 (13)	4.9	9	201	7 (2)	8.3	11	309	10
uf-union	77	6	618	26 (12)	79	8	819	22 (4)	TO			
— Sorted singly-linked lists —												
sorted-insert	6.2	3	95	14 (6)	1.8	3	56	8 (1)	26	3	63	10
sorted-merge	655	8	1822	36 (22)	18	5	263	11 (3)	AF			
bubble-sort	112	11	931	24 (8)	2.0	5	53	4 (1)	3.5	6	54	2
insertion-sort	1934	14	4783	41 (18)	265	13	1878	37 (6)	TO			
— Doubly-linked lists —												
create	15	6	195	9 (5)	5.5	6	135	7 (2)	47	3	43	6
delete	4.2	3	68	11 (4)	1.5	3	36	5 (2)	403	6	98	8
insert-at	8.0	5	130	15 (6)	2.7	3	60	10 (3)	439	5	208	16
— Composite linked-list structures —												
nested-flatten	734	17	3018	34 (20)	262	14	1714	25 (10)	AF			
nested-split	278	9	930	25 (19)	7.3	4	152	9 (1)	AF			
overlaid-delete	163	6	918	26 (5)	60	5	518	23 (3)	TO			
ladder	117	7	723	30 (16)	9.2	6	152	13 (3)	12	4	70	7

(b) Absence of a universal invariant	Description	Time	N	Z3
shared-tail	See Example 6	3.6	2	42
comb	See Section 5(b)	2	3	52

(c) Bug finding	Bug description	Time	N	Z3	C.e. size
insert-at	Precondition is too weak (omitted $e \neq$ null)	0.4	1	11	4
filter	Forgot a corner case where $\neg C(h)$	3	1	21	4
insertion-sort	Typo: typed j instead of i	5	4	68	4
sorted-merge	Forgot to link the two segments	7.5	1	49	4

procedures. The precondition says that the expected input is a (possibly empty) acyclic list, and the post-condition is the one expected from the procedure's name. For example, the post-condition of `reverse()` is that it returns a list comprised of the same elements as in its input, but in reversed order. To verify the

598   A. Karbyshev et al.

absence of memory leaks, we used a unary predicate $alloc(\cdot)$ to record whether a node is allocated. To verify the other properties, we used auxiliary predicates to mark the elements of the input list and record the reachability order between them.

We also verified the correctness of several procedures that manipulate sorted lists: `sorted-insert()` inserts an element into its appropriate place in a sorted list, `sorted-merge()` creates a sorted list by merging two sorted ones, and `bubble-sort()` and `insertion-sort()` sort their input lists. We represented the order on data elements by a binary predicate together with the appropriate axioms.

In addition, we verified several procedures that manipulate multi-linked lists: `overlaid-delete()` takes an overlaid list and deletes a given element. (Overlaid lists use multiple pointer fields to index the same set of elements in different orders.) `nested-split()` moves all the elements not satisfying C into a sublist. `flatten()` takes a nested list and flattens it by concatenating its sublists. `ladder()` creates a copy t of a list h and places a pointer p from every element in h to its counterpart in list t. We then verify that the p field of every element in h points to a distinct element in list t. This property indicates, indirectly, that both lists have the same length. Finally, we verify the union-find algorithm. E.g., for compressing `find()` operation, we prove the it maintains the reachability between every node and its root and preserves the elements.

We compared our results to [32], where EA^R was used to verify properties of list-manipulating programs with PDR, using human-supplied (universally-quantified) abstraction predicates as templates. We note that [32] can also establish certain functional correctness properties, but theirs are strictly weaker than ours. For example, they do not verify that a reversed list does not contain more elements than in its input list.

(b) Verifying the Absence of Universal Invariants. Our tool was also able to show that certain properties cannot be verified with a universal invariant. It proved that procedure `shared-tail()`, described in Example 6, does not have a universal invariant. We applied our tool to procedure `comb()`, which is a simplified version of `ladder()` where the newly allocated elements are not linked together, hence resulting in a heap shaped like a comb. The tool discovered that it is not possible to use a universal invariant to prove that when `comb()` terminates there is no null-valued p-field in the input list.

(c) Bug Finding. We also ran our analysis on programs containing deliberate bugs. In all of the cases, the method was able to detect the bug and generate a concrete trace in which the safety or correctness properties are violated.

6   Related Work

Synthesizing quantified invariants has received significant attention. Several works have considered discovery of quantified predicates, e.g., based on counterexamples [18] or by extension of predicate abstraction to support free variables [24,33]. Our inferred invariants are comprised of universally quantified predicates, but unlike these approaches, our computation of the predicates is property directed and does *not* employ predicate abstraction. Additional works for generation of quantified invariants include using abstract domains of *quantified data automata* [25,26] or ones tailored to Presburger arithmetic with arrays [20], instantiating quantifier templates [8,38], applying symbolic proof techniques [30], or using abstractions based on separation logic [4,21].

Other works aim to identify loop invariants *given* a set of predicates as candidate ingredients. Houdini [23] is the first such algorithm of which we are aware. Santini [39,40] is a recent algorithm which is based on full predicate abstraction. In the context of IC3, predicate abstraction was used in [7,12,32], the last of which specifically targeting shape analysis. In contrast to previous work, our algorithm does not require a pre-defined set of predicates, and is therefore more automatic: The diagrams provide an "on-the-fly" abstraction mechanism.

PDR has been shown to work extremely well in other domains, such as hardware verification [9,22]. Subsequently, it was generalized to software model checking for program models that use linear real arithmetic [29] and linear rational arithmetic [11]. The latter employs a quantifier-elimination procedure for linear rational arithmetic to provide an approximate pre-image operation. In contrast, our use of diagrams allows us to obtain a natural approximation which is precise for programs that can be verified using universal invariants.

The reduction we use into EPR creates a parametrized array-based system (where the range of the arrays are Booleans). A number of tools have been developed for general array-based systems. The SAFARI [3] system is relevant. It is related to MCMT and Cubicle [14,15,27,28], SAFARI uses symbolic preconditions to propagate symbolic states in the form of cubes that are conjunctions of literals over array constraints, and uses interpolants to synthesize universal invariants. Our method for propagating and inductively generalizing diagrams differs by being based on PDR.

The logic used by our implementation has limited capabilities to express properties of list segments that that are not pointed to by variables [32]. This is similar to the self-imposed limitations on expressibility used in a number of shape analysis algorithms [4,21,34–37,41]. Past experience, as well as our own, has shown that despite these limitations it is still possible to successfully analyze a rich set of programs and properties.

7   Conclusions

$PDR^\forall$ is a combination of PDR/IC3 [9] with the model-theoretic notion of diagrams [10]. The latter provide PDR an aggressive strengthening scheme in which the structural properties of a bad state are abstracted "on-the-fly" by a formula describing all of its possible extensions, which are then blocked together within the same iteration of PDR's main refinement loop. This obviates the need for user-supplied abstraction predicates. This form of automation is particularly important when one tries to verify tricky programs, e.g., programs that manipulate unbounded data structures, against a variety (of possibly changing) specifications. Indeed, our implementation successfully analyzed multiple specifications of tricky list-manipulating programs, discovered counterexamples, and, uniquely to our approach, showed that certain programs cannot be proven correct using a universal invariant. Interestingly, we noticed that sometimes the tool had to work harder to verify simple properties than when it was asked to verify complicated ones. In particular, verifying partial correctness properties was done faster when verified together with memory safety than without. In hindsight, this might not be surprising due to the property guided nature of the analysis.

We are very pleased with the simplicity of our approach and believe that the notion of diagram-based abstractions is particularly useful for the verification of programs that manipulate unbounded state. In the future, we plan to apply it in other contexts too, e.g., for the verification of network programs [1].

Acknowledgments. We thank Mooly Sagiv and the reviewers for helpful comments. This work was supported by EU FP7 project ADVENT (308830), ERC grant agreement no. [321174-VSSC], by Broadcom Foundation and Tel Aviv University Authentication Initiative, and by BSF grant no. 2012259.

References

1. The Open Networking Foundation. http://opennetworking.org
2. Albarghouthi, A., Berdine, J., Cook, B., Kincaid, Z.: Spatial interpolants. CoRR, abs/1501.04100 (2015)
3. Alberti, F., Bruttomesso, R., Ghilardi, S., Ranise, S., Sharygina, N.: SAFARI: SMT-based abstraction for arrays with interpolants. In: Madhusudan, P., Seshia, S.A. (eds.) CAV 2012. LNCS, vol. 7358, pp. 679–685. Springer, Heidelberg (2012)
4. Berdine, J., Calcagno, C., Cook, B., Distefano, D., O'Hearn, P.W., Wies, T., Yang, H.: Shape analysis for composite data structures. In: Damm, W., Hermanns, H. (eds.) CAV 2007. LNCS, vol. 4590, pp. 178–192. Springer, Heidelberg (2007)
5. Biere, A., Cimatti, A., Clarke, E.M., Strichman, O., Zhu, Y.: Bounded model checking. Adv. Comput. **58**, 118–149 (2003)
6. Biere, A., Cimatti, A., Clarke, E., Zhu, Y.: Symbolic model checking without BDDs. In: Cleaveland, W.R. (ed.) TACAS 1999. LNCS, vol. 1579, pp. 193–207. Springer, Heidelberg (1999)
7. Birgmeier, J., Bradley, A.R., Weissenbacher, G.: Counterexample to induction-guided abstraction-refinement (CTIGAR). In: Biere, A., Bloem, R. (eds.) CAV 2014. LNCS, vol. 8559, pp. 831–848. Springer, Heidelberg (2014)
8. Bjørner, N., McMillan, K., Rybalchenko, A.: On solving universally quantified horn clauses. In: Logozzo, F., Fähndrich, M. (eds.) Static Analysis. LNCS, vol. 7935, pp. 105–125. Springer, Heidelberg (2013)
9. Bradley, A.R.: SAT-based model checking without unrolling. In: Jhala, R., Schmidt, D. (eds.) VMCAI 2011. LNCS, vol. 6538, pp. 70–87. Springer, Heidelberg (2011)
10. Chang, C., Keisler, H.: Model Theory. Studies in Logic and the Foundations of Mathematics. Elsevier Science, New York (1990)
11. Cimatti, A., Griggio, A.: Software model checking via IC3. In: Madhusudan, P., Seshia, S.A. (eds.) CAV 2012. LNCS, vol. 7358, pp. 277–293. Springer, Heidelberg (2012)

12. Cimatti, A., Griggio, A., Mover, S., Tonetta, S.: IC3 modulo theories via implicit predicate abstraction. In: Ábrahám, E., Havelund, K. (eds.) TACAS 2014 (ETAPS). LNCS, vol. 8413, pp. 46–61. Springer, Heidelberg (2014)

13. Clarke, E., Kroening, D., Yorav, K.: Behavioral consistency of C and Verilog programs using bounded model checking. In: Proceedings of the 40th Annual Design Automation Conference, DAC 2003, pp. 368–371. ACM, New York, NY, USA (2003)

14. Conchon, S., Goel, A., Krstić, S., Mebsout, A., Zaïdi, F.: Cubicle: a parallel SMT-based model checker for parameterized systems. In: Madhusudan, P., Seshia, S.A. (eds.) CAV 2012. LNCS, vol. 7358, pp. 718–724. Springer, Heidelberg (2012)

15. Conchon, S., Goel, A., Krstic, S., Mebsout, A., Zaïdi, F.: Invariants for finite instances and beyond. In: Formal Methods in Computer-Aided Design, FMCAD 2013, Portland, OR, USA, 20–23 October 2013, pp. 61–68. IEEE (2013)

16. Cormen, T., Leiserson, C., Rivest, R.: Introduction To Algorithms. MIT Press, Cambridge (1990)

17. Cousot, P., Cousot, R.: Abstract interpretation: a unified lattice model for static analysis of programs by construction or approximation of fixpoints. In: POPL, pp. 238–252 (1977)

18. Das, S., Dill, D.L.: Counter-example based predicate discovery in predicate abstraction. In: Aagaard, M.D., O'Leary, J.W. (eds.) FMCAD 2002. LNCS, vol. 2517, pp. 19–32. Springer, Heidelberg (2002)

19. de Moura, L., Bjørner, N.S.: Z3: an efficient SMT solver. In: Ramakrishnan, C.R., Rehof, J. (eds.) TACAS 2008. LNCS, vol. 4963, pp. 337–340. Springer, Heidelberg (2008)

20. Dillig, I., Dillig, T., Aiken, A.: Symbolic heap abstraction with demand-driven axiomatization of memory invariants. In: Cook, W.R., Clarke, S.. Rinard, M.C. (eds.) ACM SIGPLAN Conference on Object-Oriented Programming, Systems, Languages, and Applications, pp. 397–410. ACM (2010)

21. Distefano, D., O'Hearn, P.W., Yang, H.: A local shape analysis based on separation logic. In: Hermanns, H., Palsberg, J. (eds.) TACAS 2006. LNCS, vol. 3920, pp. 287–302. Springer, Heidelberg (2006)

22. Eén, N., Mishchenko, A., Brayton, R.: Efficient implementation of property directed reachability. In: FMCAD (2011)

23. Flanagan, C., M. Leino, K.R.: Houdini, an annotation assistant for ESC/Java. In: Oliveira, J.N., Zave, P. (eds.) FME 2001. LNCS, vol. 2021, pp. 500–517. Springer, Heidelberg (2001)

24. Flanagan, C., Qadeer, S.: Predicate abstraction for software verification. SIGPLAN Not. **37**(1), 191–202 (2002)

25. Garg, P., Löding, C., Madhusudan, P., Neider, D.: Learning universally quantified invariants of linear data structures. In: Sharygina, N., Veith, H. (eds.) CAV 2013. LNCS, vol. 8044, pp. 813–829. Springer, Heidelberg (2013)

26. Garg, P., Madhusudan, P., Parlato, G.: Quantified data automata on skinny trees: an abstract domain for lists. In: Logozzo, F., Fähndrich, M. (eds.) Static Analysis. LNCS, vol. 7935, pp. 172–193. Springer, Heidelberg (2013)

27. Ghilardi, S., Ranise, S.: Backward reachability of array-based systems by SMT solving: termination and invariant synthesis. Log. Methods Comput. Sci. **6**(4), 1–48 (2010)

28. Ghilardi, S., Ranise, S.: MCMT: a model checker modulo theories. In: Giesl, J., Hähnle, R. (eds.) IJCAR 2010. LNCS, vol. 6173, pp. 22–29. Springer, Heidelberg (2010)

29. Hoder, K., Bjørner, N.: Generalized property directed reachability. In: Cimatti, A., Sebastiani, R. (eds.) SAT 2012. LNCS, vol. 7317, pp. 157–171. Springer, Heidelberg (2012)
30. Hoder, K., Kovács, L., Voronkov, A.: Invariant generation in vampire. In: Abdulla, P.A., Leino, K.R.M. (eds.) TACAS 2011. LNCS, vol. 6605, pp. 60–64. Springer, Heidelberg (2011)
31. Itzhaky, S., Banerjee, A., Immerman, N., Nanevski, A., Sagiv, M.: Effectively-propositional reasoning about reachability in linked data structures. In: Sharygina, N., Veith, H. (eds.) CAV 2013. LNCS, vol. 8044, pp. 756–772. Springer, Heidelberg (2013)
32. Itzhaky, S., Bjørner, N., Reps, T., Sagiv, M., Thakur, A.: Property-directed shape analysis. In: Biere, A., Bloem, R. (eds.) CAV 2014. LNCS, vol. 8559, pp. 35–51. Springer, Heidelberg (2014)
33. Lahiri, S.K., Bryant, R.E.: Predicate abstraction with indexed predicates. ACM Trans. Comput. Logic 9(1), 4 (2007). doi:10.1145/1297658.1297662
34. Lev-Ami, T., Immerman, N., Sagiv, M.: Abstraction for shape analysis with fast and precise transformers. In: Ball, T., Jones, R.B. (eds.) CAV 2006. LNCS, vol. 4144, pp. 547–561. Springer, Heidelberg (2006)
35. Manevich, R., Yahav, E., Ramalingam, G., Sagiv, M.: Predicate abstraction and canonical abstraction for singly-linked lists. In: Cousot, R. (ed.) VMCAI 2005. LNCS, vol. 3385, pp. 181–198. Springer, Heidelberg (2005)
36. Podelski, A., Wies, T.: Counterexample-guided focus. In: POPL (2010)
37. Sagiv, M., Reps, T., Wilhelm, R.: Parametric shape analysis via 3-valued logic. TOPLAS 24(3), 217–298 (2002)
38. Srivastava, S., Gulwani, S.: Program verification using templates over predicate abstraction. In: PLDI, pp. 223–234 (2009)
39. Thakur, A., Lal, A., Lim, J., Reps, T.: PostHat and all that: attaining most-precise inductive invariants. TR-1790, Computer Science Department, University of Wisconsin, Madison, WI, April 2013
40. Thakur, A., Lal, A., Lim, J., Reps, T.: PostHat and all that: automating abstract interpretation. Electronic Notes in Theoretical Computer Science (2013)
41. Yorsh, G., Reps, T., Sagiv, M.: Symbolically computing most-precise abstract operations for shape analysis. In: Jensen, K., Podelski, A. (eds.) TACAS 2004. LNCS, vol. 2988, pp. 530–545. Springer, Heidelberg (2004)

Efficient Anytime Techniques for Model-Based Safety Analysis

Marco Bozzano, Alessandro Cimatti, Alberto Griggio,
and Cristian Mattarei$^{(\boxtimes)}$

Fondazione Bruno Kessler, Trento, Italy
mattarei@fbk.eu

Abstract. Safety analysis investigates system behavior under faulty conditions. It is a fundamental step in the design of complex systems, that is often mandated by certification procedures. Safety analysis includes two key steps: the construction of all minimal cut sets (MCSs) for a given property (i.e. the sets of basic faults that may cause a failure), and the computation of the corresponding probability (given probabilities for the basic faults).

Model-based Safety Analysis relies on formal verification to carry out these tasks. However, the available techniques suffer from scalability problems, and are unable to provide useful results if the computation does not complete.

In this paper, we investigate and evaluate a family of IC3-based algorithms for MCSs computation. We work under the monotonicity assumption of safety analysis (i.e. an additional fault can not prevent the violation of the property). We specialize IC3-based routines for parameter synthesis by optimizing the counterexample generalization, by ordering the exploration of MCSs based on increasing cardinality, and by exploiting the inductive invariants built by IC3 to accelerate convergence.

Other enhancements yield an "anytime" algorithm, able to produce an increasingly precise probability estimate as the discovery of MCSs proceeds, even when the computation does not terminate.

A thorough experimental evaluation clearly demonstrates the substantial advances resulting from the proposed methods.

Keywords: Formal methods · Safety analysis · Fault tree · IC3 · Parameter synthesis

1 Introduction

Safety analysis [1–3] is an essential step for the design of critical systems. Safety analysis activities aim at demonstrating that a given system meets the conditions that are required for its deployment and use in the presence of faults. In many application domains, such activities are mandatory to obtain system certification. Safety analysis includes two key steps: (i) the construction of all *minimal cut sets* (MCSs), i.e. (minimal) sets of faults that lead to a *top level*

© Springer International Publishing Switzerland 2015
D. Kroening and C.S. Păsăreanu (Eds.): CAV 2015, Part I, LNCS 9206, pp. 603–621, 2015.
DOI: 10.1007/978-3-319-21690-4_41

event (TLE), such as the loss of a desirable functionality; and (ii)the computation of the corresponding *fault probability* (i.e. the probability of reaching the TLE), given probabilities for the basic faults.

In recent years, there has been a growing interest in model-based safety analysis (MBSA) [3–9]. Its purpose is to automate the most tedious and error-prone activities that today are carried out manually. This is done by analyzing models where selected variables represent the occurrence of faults. Cut sets are assignments to such variables that lead to the violation of the property. Formal verification tools, notably those based on model checking [8,10] have been extended to automate traditional safety analysis activities, such as the generation of minimal cut sets, and to perform probabilistic evaluation.

The practical application of MBSA in an industrial setting poses two key problems. The first one is scalability. In addition to the sheer size of the models, a specific factor is the possibly huge number of relevant MCSs, corresponding to different fault combinations. The second problem is to support the state of the practice. In manual safety analysis, the exploration often proceeds according to the importance and likelihood of fault configurations: MCSs of lower cardinality, that are typically associated with higher probability, are explored before the ones with higher cardinality. When the analysis is considered to be sufficiently thorough, over-approximation techniques are used to assess the weight of the unexplored MCSs.

In this paper, we investigate and evaluate a family of efficient algorithms for safety analysis. We work under the *monotonicity assumption*, commonly adopted in safety analysis, that an additional fault can not prevent the violation of the property. We specialize IC3-based routines for parameter synthesis by optimizing the generalization of counterexamples, and by ordering the exploration of MCSs based on increasing cardinality. We also propose a way to accelerate convergence by exploiting the inductive invariants built by IC3.

The practical applicability of our approach is enhanced by proposing a method to precisely compute the under- and over-approximated probability of failure. This technique produces an increasingly precise estimation as the discovery of MCSs proceeds, with the advantage of providing an "anytime" algorithm.

The described approach was implemented within the xSAP platform for safety analysis [11,12], extending and integrating the model checking routines of the underlying NUXMV model checker [13]. We carried out a thorough experimental evaluation on a number of benchmarks from various sources. The results clearly demonstrate the substantial advances resulting from the proposed methods. First, we can complete the computation of all MCSs more efficiently, and for much larger problems than previously possible. Second, even when the computation fails to terminate due to the number of MCSs, the algorithms produce intermediate approximations of increasing precision at the growth of the available computation resources. Furthermore, although here we concentrate on invariant properties of finite-state systems, our techniques can be easily extended to consider also arbitrary LTL properties and infinite-state models (where faults are still expressed with propositional variables).

Related Work. The field of MBSA is receiving increasing attention [14]. Many works cover aspects of modeling (see for example [10,11,15,16]), and propose dedicated mechanisms for the description of faults, also in probabilistic settings. Here, we work within assumptions derived from practical industrial experience. In particular, we assume that the faults are specified as discrete variables in a qualitative transition system, and that probabilities are attached to the basic faults after MCSs have been computed.

The ESACS project [16] pioneered the idea of model-based safety assessment by means of model checking techniques. The work in [17] proposes an algorithmic approach to the automatic construction of fault trees. The approach relies on the structure of the system, and does not apply model checking techniques.

In this paper, we focus on the fully automated construction of MCSs for a given transition system. There are relatively few works addressing the problem [8,18,19]. They share two key differences with respect to the work presented here. First, they do not rely on recent IC3 [20] techniques; second, none of them tackles the problem of anytime techniques. Specifically, the approach in [18] proposes the idea of layering of the exploration in terms of cardinality of MCSs. The approach is SAT-based, using bounded model checking; it does not directly discuss the problem of reaching convergence, likely adopting an induction-based approach. [16] investigates the generation of orders between faulty events, using a BDD-based approach. Automated fault tree analysis in probabilistic settings is covered in [21]. In [8], an approach based on BDDs and dynamic cone of influence is proposed. The approach does not scale well for models containing many variables. In [19], techniques based on SAT-based bounded model checking are combined with BDD-based techniques in order to achieve completeness. The approach is shown to substantially outperform the engines used in a proprietary industrial tool.

The work on IC3-based parameter synthesis [22] can in principle address the problem tackled in this paper. Here we propose several enhancements based on the specific features of the problem, with dramatic improvements in terms of scalability.

Structure of the Paper. The rest of this paper is structured as follows. In Sect. 2 we overview SA, and in Sect. 3 we formally characterize the problem of MBSA. In Sect. 4 we discuss the available baseline, and in Sect. 5 we present our new algorithms for MCS computation. In Sect. 6 we discuss the anytime approximation. In Sect. 7 we experimentally evaluate the approach, and in Sect. 8 we draw some conclusions and present directions for future work.

2   Safety Analysis

Traditional techniques for safety analysis include Fault Tree Analysis (FTA) and Failure Mode and Effects Analysis (FMEA) [23,24]. FTA is a deductive technique, whereby an undesired state (the so called *top level event* – TLE) is specified, and the system is analyzed for the possible fault configurations (sets of faults, a.k.a. basic events) that may cause the top event to occur. Fault configurations are arranged in a tree, which makes use of logical gates to depict the logical interrelationships linking such events with the TLE, and which can be evaluated quantitatively, to determine the probability of the TLE. Of particular importance in safety analysis is the list of *minimal* fault configurations, i.e. the *Minimal Cut Sets (MCSs)*.

FMEA works in a bottom-up fashion, and aims at producing a tabular representation (called *FMEA table*) that represents the causality relationships between (sets of) faults and a list of properties (representing undesired states, as in the case of FTs). Although FMEA is different in spirit from FTA, generation of MCSs can also be used as a building block for computing FMEA tables, in particular under the assumption of monotonicity (i.e., any super-set of a MCS will still cause the TLE) [3,25].

More specifically, a cut set is a set of faults that represents a necessary, but not sufficient, condition that may cause a system to reach an unwanted state/behaviour. For instance, the cut set {battery1_failure, battery2_failure} may cause the safety hazard "fuel pump malfunctioning" in a 2-redundant electrical system. Moreover, minimality implies that every proper super-set of it cannot prevent the possibility to have the malfunction. When the safety hazard is reachable without triggering of any fault, the FT collapses to true, representing the empty cut set (which is evidently minimal).

An important aspect of safety assessment is the quantitative evaluation of FTs, i.e. the association of FT nodes with probabilities. In particular, the determination of the probability of the TLE is used to estimate the likelihood of the safety hazard it represents. Such computation can be carried out by evaluating the probability of the logical formula given by the disjunction of the MCSs (each MCS, in turn, being the conjunction of its constituent faults). It is standard practice, in particular for complex systems, to consider only cut sets up to a maximum cardinality – in order to simplify the computation. This approach is justified by the fact that, in practical cases, cut sets with high cardinality have low probabilities, and may be "safely" ignored. However, it is essential to have criteria to estimate the error which is inherent in such approximation, since under-approximating the probability of a hazard would not be acceptable.

3   Model-Based Safety Analysis

3.1   Minimal Cut Set Computation

We represent a plant using a transition system, as follows. A transition system is a tuple $S = \langle V, F, I, T \rangle$, where V is the set of state variables, $F \subseteq V$ is a set of parameters, the *failure mode variables*; I is the initial formula over V; T is the transition formula over V and V' (V' being the next version of the state variables). A state s (resp. s') is an assignment to the state variables V (V'). A trace of S is a sequence $\pi = s_0, s_1, \ldots, s_n$ of states such that s_0 satisfies I and for each k, $1 \leq k \leq n$, $\langle s_{k-1}, s_k \rangle$ satisfies T.

A cut set is formally defined as follows [8].

Definition 1 (Cut set). *Let $S = \langle V, F, I, T \rangle$ be a transition system, $FC \subseteq F$ a fault configuration, and TLE a formula over V (the top level event). We say that FC is a cut set of TLE, written $cs(FC, TLE)$ if there exists a trace $s_0, s_1, \ldots, s_k$ for S such that: i) $s_k \models TLE$; ii) $\forall f \in F \ f \in FC \iff \exists i \in \{0, \ldots, k\} \ (s_i \models f)$.*

Intuitively, a cut set is a fault configuration whose faults are active at some point along a trace witnessing the occurrence of the top level event. In safety analysis, it is important to identify the fault configurations that are minimal in terms of failure mode variables – as they represent simpler explanations for the top level event, and they have higher probability, under the assumption of independent faults. Minimal configurations, called *minimal cut sets*, are defined as follows.

Definition 2 (Minimal Cut Sets). *Let $S = \langle V, F, I, T \rangle$ be a transition system and $FConf = 2^F$ be the set of all fault configurations, and TLE a top level event. We define the set of cut sets and minimal cut sets of TLE as follows:*

$$CS(TLE) \quad = \{FC \in FConf \mid cs(FC, TLE)\}$$
$$MCS(TLE) = \{cs \in CS(TLE) \mid \forall cs' \in CS(TLE) \ (cs' \subseteq cs \Rightarrow cs' = cs)\}$$

The previous definition of MCS is based on the assumption that fault configurations are *monotonic*, i.e. activating additional faults cannot prevent triggering the top level event. This is an assumption that is commonly applied in practice, considering that it leads to a conservative over-approximation of the unreliability (probability of TLE). In cases where this is not desirable, the notion of MCS can be generalized to the more general one of *prime implicant* [26] i.e., with no monotonicity assumption. However, this is not considered here.

Algorithm 1. Probability computation.

Input: BDD (n), Probability map $(\mathcal{P})$, Hashtable $(cache)$
Result: Probability
1 **if** n in *cache* **then**
2   $\lfloor$ **return** $cache[n]$;
3 **if** $n = \top$ **then**
4   $\lfloor$ **return** *1.0*;
5 **if** $n = \bot$ **then**
6   $\lfloor$ **return** *0.0*;
7 pthen = Probability_computation(get_then_node(n), $\mathcal{P}$, *cache*);
8 pelse = Probability_computation(get_else_node(n), $\mathcal{P}$, *cache*);
9 pcur = $\mathcal{P}$(get_var(n));
10 $cache[n]$ = pcur $\cdot$ pthen + $(1.0 -$ pcur$) \cdot$ pelse;
11 **return** $cache[n]$;

3.2   Computing Faults Probability

Given a set of MCSs and a mapping $\mathcal{P}$ giving the probability for the basic faults, it is possible to compute the probability of the occurrence of the top-level event. Under the assumption that basic faults are independent[1], the probability of a single MCS σ is given by the product of the probabilities of its basic faults:

$$\mathcal{P}(\sigma) = \prod_{f_i \in \sigma} \mathcal{P}(f_i).$$

For a set of MCSs S, the probability can be computed using the above and the following recursive formula:

$$\mathcal{P}(S_1 \cup S_2) = \mathcal{P}(S_1) + \mathcal{P}(S_2) - \mathcal{P}(S_1 \cap S_2).$$

Interpreting the set of MCSs as a disjuction of partial assignments to the fault variables, then it is possible to represented such formula using a Binary Decision Diagram, a simple and efficient way of computing its probability is shown in Algorithm 1. The algorithm exploits the following facts:

(i) the probability of two disjoint sets is simply the sum of the two probabilities; and
(ii) the two children t and e of a BDD node with variable v correspond to the two disjoint sets of assignments for the formulae $v \wedge t$ and $\neg v \wedge e$ respectively;
(iii) if the variable v does not occur in the formula f, then f is independent from v, and so $\mathcal{P}(v \wedge f) = \mathcal{P}(v) \cdot \mathcal{P}(f)$;
(iv) $\mathcal{P}(\neg v) = 1 - \mathcal{P}(v)$ by definition.

4   Basic Algorithms for MCS Computation

BDD-Based Algorithms. The work in [8] presents a series of symbolic algorithms for the computation of MCSs using BDDs. The algorithms are based on a reachability analysis on the symbolic transition system extended with history variables for fault events. Intuitively, each state is decorated with the faults that have occurred in its history; at the end of the reachability, each state is thus associated with the set of cut sets that are required to reach it. MCSs are extracted by projecting the reachable states over the history variables and then minimizing the result, using standard routines provided by BDD packages.

Exploiting BMC. An improved version of the BDD-based routines is presented in [19], by exploiting Bounded Model Checking (BMC) as a preprocessing step. Essentially, the idea is to run BMC up to a maximum (user-defined) depth k to check the invariant property stating that the top level event can never be reached. Whenever a counterexample trace is found, a cut set cs (not necessarily minimal)

---

[1] Specific techniques for the case of common cause analysis are out of the scope of this paper.

is extracted from it, and the model is strengthened with constraints excluding all the supersets of cs. When no more counterexamples of length at most k are found, a BDD-based algorithm is invoked on the strengthened model, in order to discover the remaining cut sets not yet covered.

The approach can be generalized to completely avoid the use of BDDs. The idea is to use the BMC engine incrementally to enumerate cut sets, and combine it with a generic "black box" procedure for checking invariant properties, invoked periodically (e.g. before increasing the BMC bound k) to check whether all the MCSs have been enumerated.

MCS via Parameter Synthesis. The work in [22] presents an efficient extension of the IC3 algorithm (called ParamIC3) that allows to compute, given a model M depending on some parameters P, the set of all values of P such that the model satisfies a given invariant property. The algorithm works by complement, constructing the set of "good" parameters by incrementally blocking "bad" assignments extracted from counterexample traces generated by IC3.

The technique can be immediately exploited also for MCS computation as follows. First, the model is extended with history variables for fault events, as in [8]. The parameter synthesis algorithm is then invoked on the extended model, considering the history variables as parameters, and checking the property that the top level event is never triggered. Each "bad" assignment blocked by ParamIC3 (see [22]) corresponds to a fault configuration reaching the top level event. When the algorithm terminates, the MCS set can be extracted by simply dropping the subsumed bad assignments.

5   Efficient Algorithms for MCS Computation

In practice, the BDD-based routines of [8] show rather poor scalability, and are typically not applicable to problems of realistic size. Using BMC as a preprocessing step helps significantly [19], but ultimately also this technique is limited by the scalability problems of BDD-based approaches. The technique of [22], being based on the very-efficient IC3 algorithm, is much more promising. However, in the basic formulation given in the previous section, its performance is extremely poor when the number of possible fault configurations leading to the top level event is large. In this Section, we show how the situation can be dramatically improved by exploiting the monotonicity assumption on faults under which we are operating.

5.1   Monotonic Parameter Synthesis

The first (trivial) improvement exploits the definition of monotonicity to generalize the set of "bad" parameters to be blocked whenever IC3 generates a counterexample trace. This idea is similar to the *dynamic pruning* optimization of [8] for BDD-based computation. The monotonicity assumption ensures that if a set of faults F is sufficient to generate the top level event, so does any set

$S \supseteq F$. Therefore, any assignment to the (parameters corresponding to the) fault variables $\gamma = \{f_j, \ldots, f_k\} \cup \{\neg f_i, \ldots, \neg f_h\}$ extracted from an IC3 counterexample trace can be immediately generalized to $\gamma' = \{f_j, \ldots, f_k\}$, by dropping all the variables assigned to false.

The above optimization prevents the algorithm from explicitly considering all cut sets that are subsumed by the one just found, i.e. $F = \{f_j, \ldots, f_k\}$. However, F itself might not be minimal. In this case, IC3 would later have to find another configuration $G \subset F$, and the effort spent in blocking F would have been wasted.

We address this by modifying the branching heuristic of the SAT solver used by IC3. In the modified heuristic, (SAT variables corresponding to) faults are initially assigned to false, and they have higher priority than the other variables, so that no other variable is assigned by a SAT decision before all the fault variables are assigned. This ensures that fault variables are assigned to true only when necessary to satisfy the constraints.

The above idea is very simple to implement and integrate in the IC3-based algorithm (in total, it requires about 20 lines of code), and it provides a significant performance boost (as we will show in Sect. 7). However, it is still not sufficient to ensure that no redundant cut sets are generated. The reason is that, by the nature of IC3, ParamIC3 enumerates counterexample traces in an increasing order of length k, so that it only considers traces of length $k + 1$ when all the traces of length $\leq k$ have already been excluded.[2] This means that, if the shortest trace that leads to the top level event from a set F of faults is k, but there exists another set of faults $S \supset F$ that leads to the top level event in $h < k$ steps, then S will necessarily be blocked by ParamIC3 before F. In some extreme cases, this might make the heuristic completely ineffective.

5.2 Enumerating only MCS

We address the problem by incorporating in our algorithm a solution originally proposed in [18]. The idea is to force the algorithm to proceed by *layering*, by forcing the search to compute the cuts sets of increasing cardinality, instead of analyzing traces of increasing length. The pseudo-code for the basic version is shown in Algorithm 2. At each iteration of the main loop, the algorithm uses an "atmost" constraint c to limit the cardinality of the cut sets generated, by relaxing the invariant property to check from $\neg$TLE to $(\neg$TLE $\vee \neg c)$. The termination check is performed by invoking the "regular" version of IC3 on the model strengthened to exclude the already-computed cut sets, to check whether

---

[2] For readers familiar with IC3, strictly speaking this is not fully accurate: if the IC3 implementation uses a priority queue for managing counterexamples to induction [20], some counterexamples of length $h > k$ may be generated before all those of length $\leq k$ are blocked. However, the argument still holds in this case, so the issue can be ignored for simplicity.

Algorithm 2. Basic MCS enumeration with ParamIC3

Input: Model ($\mathcal{M} = \langle I, T \rangle$), Top level event (TLE), Faults ($\boldsymbol{F}$)
Result: MCS
1 bound = 1;
2 MCS = $\perp$;
3 **while** *True* **do**
4   c = make_atmost($\boldsymbol{F}$, bound);
5   region = ParamIC3($I \wedge \neg$ MCS, $T \wedge \neg$ MCS, ($\neg$TLE $\vee \neg$c), $\boldsymbol{F}$);
6   MCS = MCS $\vee \neg$ region;
7   done = IC3($I \wedge \neg$ MCS, $T \wedge \neg$ MCS, $\neg$TLE);
8   **if** *done* **then**
9   **return** *MCS*
10   **else**
11   bound = bound + 1;

---

there are other fault configurations that can reach the top level event. It is easy to see that Algorithm 2 enumerates only the MCSs, and thus it avoids the exponential blow-up suffered from ParamIC3 on the model of Example 1. However, it does so at a significant price, since it needs two IC3 calls per iteration. On less pathological examples, the overhead introduced might largely outweigh the potential benefits.

Algorithm 2 can be improved by exploiting the capability of IC3 (and so also of ParamIC3) of generating a proof for verified properties in the form of an *inductive invariant* entailing the property P. In our specific case, the inductive invariant ψ produced by ParamIC3 on line 5 of Algorithm 2 would satisfy the following: (i)$I \wedge \neg$MCS $\wedge$ region $\models \psi$; (ii)$\psi \wedge T \wedge \neg$MCS $\wedge$ region $\models \psi'$; and (iii)$\psi \wedge \neg$MCS $\wedge$ region $\models (\neg$TLE $\vee \neg$c). The first improvement is based on the observation that the inductive invariant can be fed back to ParamIC3 at the next iteration of the main loop, thus avoiding the need of restarting the search from scratch. The second improvement, instead, exploits the computed invariant to check whether all the MCSs have been enumerated, thus avoiding the second invocation of IC3 of line 7. This is done by checking with a SAT solver whether the current invariant ψ is strong enough to prove that the top level event cannot be reached by any fault configuration not covered by the already-computed cut sets. Note that this does not affect completeness, since in the worst case the atmost constraints simplifies to true after $|\boldsymbol{F}|$ iterations of the loop. However, the hope is that in practice the inductive invariant will allow to exit the loop much earlier. The enhanced algorithm is shown in Algorithm 3, where the improvements are displayed in red.

Algorithm 3. Enhanced MCS enumeration with ParamIC3

Input: Model ($\mathcal{M} = \langle I, T \rangle$), Top level event (TLE), Faults ($\boldsymbol{F}$)
Result: MCS

1 bound = 1;
2 MCS = $\bot$;
3 invar = $\top$;
4 **while** *True* **do**
5   c = make_atmost($\boldsymbol{F}$, bound);
6   region, invar = ParamIC3($I \wedge \neg$ MCS $\wedge$ invar, $T \wedge \neg$ MCS $\wedge$ invar,
                                           ($\neg$TLE $\vee \neg$c), $\boldsymbol{F}$);
7   MCS = MCS $\vee \neg$ region;
8   done = check_unsat($\neg$ MCS $\wedge$ invar $\wedge$ TLE);
9   **if** *done* **then**
10 | **return** *MCS*
11   **else**
12   ⌊ bound = bound + 1;

Example 1. Consider the following example, using the syntax of NUXMV [13]. There are N fault variables, and suppose the top level event occurs when the status variable becomes false, i.e., whenever at least one fault occurs. Therefore, the MCSs for this model are the N singleton sets containing one fault variable each. However, the TRANS constraint forces an inverse dependency between the number of steps to reach the top level event and the cardinality of the smallest cut sets needed: for k steps, the smallest cut sets have cardinality $N - k$, and there are $\binom{N}{k}$ of them. Therefore, even with the branching heuristic described above, ParamIC3 will generate an exponential number of counterexamples (since $\sum_{k=1}^{N} \binom{N}{k} = 2^N - 1$) before finding the MCSs. ◇

```
1  MODULE main
2  IVAR
3    fault_1 : boolean;
4    ...
5    fault_N : boolean;
6
7  DEFINE fault_count := fault_1 + ... + fault_N;
8
9  VAR counter : 1 .. N;
10     status : boolean;
11
12 ASSIGN
13   init(counter) := 1;
14   next(counter) := counter = 10 ? 1 : counter + 1;
15
16 TRANS (fault_count = 0) | (fault_count > (N - counter));
17
18 ASSIGN
19   init(status) := TRUE;
20   next(status) := (fault_count = 0);
```

6   Anytime Approximation

An additional benefit of Algorithm 3 compared to the other algorithms of Sects. 4 and 5 is that it provides an "anytime" approximation behaviour on the set of MCSs, in the sense that at any point during its execution, the candidate solution is a subset of all the MCSs. As pointed out in Sect. 2, however, such underapproximation is useful only if it is possible to estimate its error in terms of failure probability. Here, we show a simple but effective procedure for estimating the approximation error on the fly, during the execution of Algorithm 3. This allows to consider a bound on the error as an alternative stopping criterion for the algorithm, which might be useful in cases when the full computation of all the MCSs would be too expensive.

The idea is to keep two running bounds for the probability x of reaching the top-level event, such that at any point in the execution of the algorithm $P_L(\text{TLE}) \leq x \leq P_U(\text{TLE})$. Initially, we set $P_L(\text{TLE}) = 0$ and $P_U(\text{TLE}) = 1$. When a minimal cut set m_1 is found, $P_L(TLE)$ is incremented by computing the probability of the fault configurations represented by m_1 that are not covered by the already-computed MCSs. This can be done by constructing the BDD for the formula $m_1 \wedge \neg\text{MCS}$, and then computing its probability with Algorithm 1.[3]

For updating the upper bound $P_U(\text{TLE})$, instead, we exploit fact that Algorithm 3 proceeds by layers of increasing cardinality. More precisely, when ParamIC3 returns at line 7, we know that all the fault configurations of cardinality smaller or equal to the current bound that are not included in MCS will definitely not cause the top-level event. The probability P_{excluded} of these configurations can be computed with Algorithm 1 by constructing the BDD for the formula $\neg\text{make\_atmost}(F, \text{bound}) \wedge \neg\text{MCS}$. With this, the new value of $P_U(\text{TLE})$ is given by $1 - P_{\text{excluded}}$. An illustration of this idea is shown in Fig. 1. The red area represents the minimal cut sets found within a specific cardinality, and the blue one shows all the supersets of those cut sets. The white area denotes the configurations that cannot cause the TLE, whereas the gray one represents the unknown part. Figure 2 shows instead an example of the evolution of the error bounds during the execution of Algorithm 3 for one instance of our benchmark set: $P_L(\text{TLE})$ becomes non-zero after the first cut set found, and then grows continuously at every cut set, whereas $P_U(\text{TLE})$ decreases in steps, whenever an individual cardinality has been fully explored.

7   Experimental Evaluation

We have implemented the algorithms described in the previous sections in the xSAP [11,12] platform for model-based safety analysis. In this Section, we experimentally evaluate their performance and effectiveness. The benchmarks and executables for reproducing the results are available at https://es-static.fbk.eu/people/mattarei/dist/FTA2015/.

---

[3] For performance reasons, it might make sense to perform this computation for clusters of cut sets rather than for individual ones, trading granularity for efficiency.

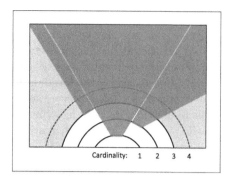

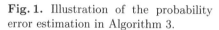

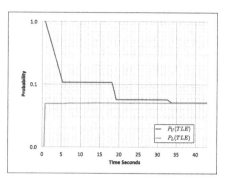

Fig. 1. Illustration of the probability error estimation in Algorithm 3.

Fig. 2. Example of evolution of probability error bounds.

7.1 Benchmarks

The benchmarks used for the evaluation come from a set of real-world test cases from the avionics domain, where safety assessment and Fault Tree Analysis are parts of the formal analysis of the models.

Aircraft Electrical System. The first set of benchmarks describes the architecture of an aircraft-oriented electrical system. These problems were developed as part of the MISSA project [27], and previously analyzed using OCAS, a proprietary model-based safety assessment platform, as well as the FSAP [28] toolset. This comparison is described in [19]. This family of benchmarks is composed of four different models, where each of them is a refinement of the previous one. The properties that are taken into account describe the situation when the system that manages the alternate/continuous current is malfunctioning. Each model has two properties, for a total of 8 benchmark instances. The size of the models varies from 35 to 297 state variables and from 437 to 14030 AND gates (in an And-Inverter-Graph representation [29] of the transition relation), whereas the number of faults is between 9 and 105.

Next-Gen Collision Avoidance. The second set of instances comes from the analysis of a novel, "next generation" air traffic control system that is being studied at NASA. Part of the activities involves the evaluation of different technological approaches in order to discover the safer and most efficient one. This process is supported by different analysis techniques, and one of those is based on formal model-based safety assessment. The formal model is composed of an on-ground Air Traffic Control System (ATC), a set of aircraft that rely on ground-based separation systems like the ATC (GSEP), and a set of aircraft that have self-separating capabilities (SSEP) as support of the standard ground-based approach.

The benchmark instances encode different architectural solutions for the Next-gen collision avoidance system. The system is composed of various numbers of GSEP and SSEP aircraft, and one ATC. The models contain 47 basic faults, and the objective is to compute the MCSs for the violation of the property "Two Aircraft shall not have a Loss of Separation", meaning that the distance between two aircraft is below a certain safety limit. The models are scaled by varying the number of aircraft of each kind (GSEP and SSEP, from 0 to 3 each) and the number communication rounds between each aircraft and the ATC (from 1 to 10). The size of the models varies from 162 to 330 state variables and from 1700 to 5110 AND gates.

Wheel Braking System. The third family of benchmarks models an aircraft-based wheel braking system (WBS), described in the Aerospace Information Report, version 6110 [30]. The model was developed in a joint project between FBK and The Boeing Company [31], and it is representative of an industrial system of significant size. The WBS describes a redundant architecture that takes as input the pedal information (the brake signal coming from the pilot), computes the braking force that has to be applied to the 8 wheels, and drives the hydraulic system in order to physically operate the right braking force. This system is characterized by three redundant sub units:

(i) normal brake system, receiving the pedal information and driving the hydraulic system. This unit is composed of two sub components that work in parallel in order to prevent that a single failure can cause the complete malfunctioning;

(ii) alternate brake system, receiving the pedal information and the output from the normal brake system: when the latter one is not operating as expected, it operates as backup by driving the hydraulic system;

(iii) emergency brake system, behaving similarly to the alternate one: it receives pedal information and both outputs from the normal and alternate sub systems, and operates as a backup of the alternate one.

The benchmark set consists of 4 different variants of the WBS architecture, expressing various kinds of faulty behaviour. The models contain 261 fault variables and 1482 state variables, whereas the number of AND gates varies between 35182 and 35975.

7.2   Performance Evaluation

In the first part of our analysis, we evaluate the performance of different techniques for the computation of the set of MCSs. We consider the following algorithms:

BDD is the procedure of [8];

BMC+BDD is the enhancement of [19] that uses BMC as a preprocessor. The BMC implementation uses the branching heuristic described in Sect. 5 for reducing the number of fault configurations to enumerate;

BMC+IC3 is the variant of the previous technique outlined in Sect. 4, using IC3 as a "black box" invariant checking procedure. (The branching heuristic of Sect. 5 for fault variables is used also in this case);

ParamIC3 is a basic version of ParamIC3, exploiting monotonicity for generalizing parameter regions to block;

ParamIC3+faultbranch is the enhanced version of ParamIC3 that uses the branching heuristic for fault variables of Sect. 5;

MCS-ParamIC3-simple is the basic MCS procedure described in of Algorithm 2. We use m-cardinality networks [32] for encoding the cardinality constraints;

MCS-ParamIC3 is the enhanced MCS procedure of Algorithm 3;

MCS-BMC+IC3 is an anytime variant of BMC+IC3, in which the BMC solver is forced to enumerate only MCSs, using cardinality constraints: whenever IC3 finds that a given cardinality has been fully enumerated, the bound of the atmost constraint is increased, and BMC is restarted;

MCS-BMC+IC3-swipe is a variant of the above, in which IC3 is invoked less frequently and BMC is limited to a maximum counterexample length k, instead of fully enumerating a given cardinality. This is expected to improve performance, at the price of losing the "anytime" feature.

We have run our experiments on a cluster of Linux machines with 2.5GHz Intel Xeon E5420 CPUs, using a timeout of 1 hour and a memory limit of 4Gb. The results are shown in Fig. 3. The plots show the number of solved instances (y-axis) in the given timeout (x-axis) for each of the algorithms considered. More information is provided in Table 1, where for each configuration we show the number of solved instances and the total execution time (excluding timeouts).

From the results, we can clearly see the benefits of the techniques discussed in Sect. 5. Using the specialized branching heuristic, ParamIC3+faultbranch performs very well in general, especially on the Elec.Sys and NextGen families. However, for the harder WBS instances, the heuristic is not enough. On the contrary, the cardinality-based enumeration introduces an overhead for easier problems, but it pays off for harder ones, making MCS-ParamIC3 the best performing overall. Moreover, even for simpler problems the integrated approach of Algorithm 3 is not very far from the performance of ParamIC3+faultbranch. More importantly, the anytime behaviour of MCS-ParamIC3 is extremely useful in all cases in which none of the algorithms terminates, i.e. in the majority of the WBS instances. Its usefulness is evaluated in Sect. 7.3.

7.3   Error Estimation

In order to assess the usefulness of the anytime behaviour, we evaluate the effectiveness of our technique for estimating error bounds on the probability of faults. For this, we consider the instances of the WBS benchmark set that could not be completed within the timeout, and for each of them we study the evolution of the probability bounds during the execution of MCS-ParamIC3. The results are summarized in Table 2, where we show the number of MCSs found

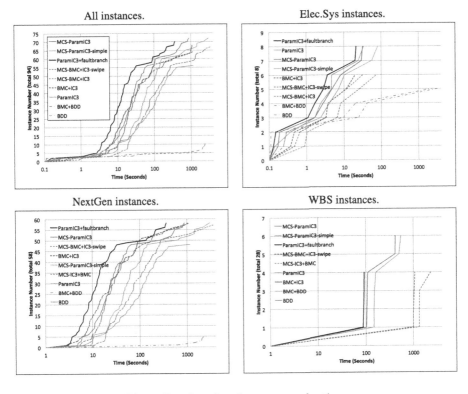

Fig. 3. Results of performance evaluation.

Table 1. Summary of scalability evaluation.

Algorithm	# solved				Total time (sec)
	All	Elec.Sys	NextGen	WBS	
MCS-ParamIC3	**72**	8	58	6	7837
MCS-ParamIC3-simple	**72**	8	58	6	19326
ParamIC3+faultbranch	**70**	8	58	4	3222
MCS-BMC+IC3-swipe	**68**	6	58	4	9896
MCS-BMC+IC3	**67**	6	57	4	23210
BMC+IC3	**64**	6	58	0	5477
ParamIC3	**56**	8	48	0	6787
BMC+BDD	**10**	5	5	0	10753
BDD	**5**	5	0	0	3377

Table 2. Evolution of probability error bounds on hard WBS instances.

Instance	card	# MCS	Time	P_L(TLE)	P_U(TLE)
M1-S18-WBS-R-0321	2	6	3.686	4.4999799997e-10	4.7856862743e-09
	3	627	27.937	4.5052040749e-10	4.5368234398e-10
	4	629	96.760	4.5052047798e-10	4.5052230781e-10
	5^a	38950	3549.163	4.5052047798e-10	4.5052230781e-10
M1-S18-WBS-R-0322-left	1	2	1.809	9.9999750001e-06	1.4392898712e-05
	2	2	3.827	1.0000324995e-05	1.0004616980e-05
	3	203	23.106	1.0000325102e-05	1.0000328223e-05
	4^a	46287	3271.215	1.0000325102e-05	1.0000328223e-05
M1-S18-WBS-R-0323	6	13689	480.034	1.0696143952e-28	3.5789505917e-22
	7^a	52035	3596.097	1.0701599223e-28	3.5789505917e-22
M1-S18-WBS-R-0324	2	1	3.603	2.5000000000e-11	4.3619410877e-09
	4	2	9.273	2.5000000001e-11	2.5001833724e-11
	5	8729	360.012	2.5000000003e-11	2.5000000881e-11
	6^a	23995	2905.057	2.5000000003e-11	2.5000000881e-11
M1-cmd_implies_braking_w1	1	13	4.508	1.1299483157e-04	1.1708790375e-04
	2	30	12.944	1.1299924596e-04	1.1300309322e-04
	3	7428	265.771	1.1299925205e-04	1.1299925473e-04
	4	3815	865.818	1.1299925205e-04	1.1299925205e-04
	5	1768	1956.225	1.1299925205e-04	1.1299925205e-04
	6	168	3465.792	1.1299925205e-04	1.1299925205e-04

[a]: cardinalities for which not all the MCSs could be computed within the timeout

of each cardinality, as well as the evolution of the probability bounds during the execution for a representative subset of the WBS instances (we could not include all instances for lack of space).

From the table, we can see how for most instances error bounds converge quickly towards the actual fault probability, and then continue improving very slowly, confirming the intuition of safety engineers that it is often enough to consider only MCSs of small cardinality in practice. There is only one case where the bounds are very loose, namely the M1-S18-WBS-R-323 instance. However, in this case the fault probability is several order of magnitudes smaller than for the other properties.

We remark that the probabilities for the basic faults are not artificially generated; on the contrary, they have been estimated by domain experts, and the error bounds that we have obtained matched their expectations. The table shows that, for these problems, the error estimation provided by our technique is precise enough to make our results useful in practice even when the computation of the set of MCSs does not terminate.

8 Conclusions and Future Work

In this paper we presented a family of algorithms for model-based safety analysis, based on IC3. The algorithms tightly integrate the generation and minimization of cut sets, and enable the computation of the hazard probability, both numerically and symbolically. Moreover, we introduced a method to provide an estimate for the remaining computation, when the generation does not terminate, and to safely approximate the final result. This makes the approach anytime, and makes it possible to deal with cases where the number of cut sets may explode.

There are several directions of ongoing and future work. First, we are extending our implementation to handle arbitrary LTL properties and infinite-state systems. Second, concerning the routines for MCS generation, we want to investigate the role of parallelization, based on partitioning/cofactoring the space of parameters. Another line of research which is orthogonal with respect to the generation of MCSs is their presentation in a more structured way, namely as a multi-level Fault Tree (rather than as DNF). Ongoing work includes generation of hierarchical FTs using contract-based design [25].

An important open challenge we wish to explore is the relaxation of the monotonicity assumption on faults. Traditionally, in the avionics and aerospace domain (from which our benchmarks are taken) non-monotonic analysis is rarely considered, as it does not provide significant benefits – most systems are indeed monotonic and, whenever they are not, monotonic analysis already provides an accurate over-approximation. However, in other domains this is known not to be the case: for example, in circuits two subsequent inversions may prevent the occurrence of a top level event. Given the hardness of the non-monotonic analysis, it may be also worth to compute a monotonic over-approximation and find other means to tighten the measure (or to compute the tightness of the approximation). Finally, we want to study strategies to detect non-monotonicity, as in some cases it may be unclear whether it holds or not.

References

1. Leveson, N.G.: Safeware: System Safety and Computers. Addison-Wesley, Boston (1995)
2. Storey, N.: Safety Critical Computer Systems. Addison-Wesley, Boston (1996)
3. Bozzano, M., Villafiorita, A.: Design and Safety Assessment of Critical Systems, an Auerbach Book. CRC Press (Taylor and Francis), Boca Raton (2010)
4. Bozzano, M., Villafiorita, A., et al.: ESACS: an integrated methodology for design and safety analysis of complex systems. In: Proceedings of ESREL 2003, pp. 237–245 (2003)
5. Bieber, P., Bougnol, C., Castel, C., Christophe Kehren, J.P., Metge, S., Seguin, C.: Safety assessment with AltaRica. In: Jacquart, R. (ed.) Building the Information Society. IFIP International Federation for Information Processing, vol. 156, pp. 505–510. Springer, Heidelberg (2004)
6. Bozzano, M., Cavallo, A., Cifaldi, M., Valacca, L., Villafiorita, A.: Improving safety assessment of complex systems: an industrial case study. In: Araki, K., Gnesi, S., Mandrioli, D. (eds.) FME 2003. LNCS, vol. 2805, pp. 208–222. Springer, Heidelberg (2003)
7. Joshi, A., Miller, S., Whalen, M., Heimdahl, M.: A proposal for model-based safety analysis. In: Proceedings of DASC. IEEE Computer Society (2005)

8. Bozzano, M., Cimatti, A., Tapparo, F.: Symbolic Fault Tree Analysis for Reactive Systems. In: Namjoshi, K.S., Yoneda, T., Higashino, T., Okamura, Y. (eds.) ATVA 2007. LNCS, vol. 4762, pp. 162–176. Springer, Heidelberg (2007)
9. Bozzano, M., Cimatti, A., Katoen, J.P., Nguyen, V., Noll, T., Roveri, M.: Safety, dependability and performance analysis of extended AADL models. Comput. J. **54**(5), 754–775 (2011)
10. Bozzano, M., Cimatti, A., Katoen, J.-P., Nguyen, V.Y., Noll, T., Roveri, M.: The COMPASS approach: correctness, modelling and performability of aerospace systems. In: Buth, B., Rabe, G., Seyfarth, T. (eds.) SAFECOMP 2009. LNCS, vol. 5775, pp. 173–186. Springer, Heidelberg (2009)
11. xSAP: The xSAP safety analysis platform. http://xsap.fbk.eu
12. Bittner, B., Bozzano, M., Cavada, R., Cimatti, A., Gario, M., Griggio, A., Mattarei, C., Micheli, A., Zampedri, G.: The xSAP safety analysis platform. In: 1504.07513
13. Cavada, R., Cimatti, A., Dorigatti, M., Griggio, A., Mariotti, A., Micheli, A., Mover, S., Roveri, M., Tonetta, S.: The NUXMV symbolic model checker. In: Biere, A., Bloem, R. (eds.) CAV 2014. LNCS, vol. 8559, pp. 334–342. Springer, Heidelberg (2014)
14. Morel, M.: Model-based safety approach for early validation of integrated and modular avionics architectures. In: Ortmeier, F., Rauzy, A. (eds.) IMBSA 2014. LNCS, vol. 8822, pp. 57–69. Springer, Heidelberg (2014)
15. Batteux, M., Prosvirnova, T., Rauzy, A., Kloul, L.: The altarica 3.0 project for model-based safety assessment. In: 11th IEEE International Conference on Industrial Informatics, INDIN 2013, Bochum, Germany, 29–31 July 2013, pp. 741–746. IEEE (2013)
16. Bozzano, M., Villafiorita, A.: Integrating fault tree analysis with event ordering information. In: Proceedings of ESREL 2003, pp. 247–254 (2003)
17. Majdara, A., Wakabayashi, T.: Component-based modeling of systems for automated fault tree generation. Reliab. Eng. Syst. Saf. **94**(6), 1076–1086 (2009)
18. Abdulla, P.A., Deneux, J., Stålmarck, G., Ågren, H., Åkerlund, O.: Designing safe, reliable systems using scade. In: Margaria, T., Steffen, B. (eds.) ISoLA 2004. LNCS, vol. 4313, pp. 115–129. Springer, Heidelberg (2006)
19. Bozzano, M., Cimatti, A., Lisagor, O., Mattarei, C., Mover, S., Roveri, M., Tonetta, S.: Safety assessment of AltaRica models via symbolic model checking. Sci. Comput. Program. **98**(4), 464–483 (2015)
20. Bradley, A.R.: SAT-based model checking without unrolling. In: Jhala, R., Schmidt, D. (eds.) VMCAI 2011. LNCS, vol. 6538, pp. 70–87. Springer, Heidelberg (2011)
21. Böde, E., Peikenkamp, T., Rakow, J., Wischmeyer, S.: Model based importance analysis for minimal cut sets. In: Cha, S.S., Choi, J.-Y., Kim, M., Lee, I., Viswanathan, M. (eds.) ATVA 2008. LNCS, vol. 5311, pp. 303–317. Springer, Heidelberg (2008)
22. Cimatti, A., Griggio, A., Mover, S., Tonetta, S.: Parameter synthesis with IC3. In: Proceedings of FMCAD, pp. 165–168. IEEE (2013)
23. SAE: ARP4761 Guidelines and Methods for Conducting the Safety Assessment Process on Civil Airborne Systems and Equipment, December 1996
24. Vesely, W., Stamatelatos, M., Dugan, J., Fragola, J., Minarick III, J., Railsback, J.: Fault Tree Handbook with Aerospace Applications. NASA Headquarters, Washington DC (2002)
25. Bozzano, M., Cimatti, A., Mattarei, C., Tonetta, S.: Formal safety assessment via contract-based design. In: Cassez, F., Raskin, J.-F. (eds.) ATVA 2014. LNCS, vol. 8837, pp. 81–97. Springer, Heidelberg (2014)

26. Coudert, O., Madre, J.: Fault tree analysis: 10^{20} prime implicants and beyond. In: Proceedings of RAMS (1993)
27. MISSA: The MISSA Project. http://www.missa-fp7.eu. Accessed 28 Jan 2015
28. Bozzano, M., Villafiorita, A.: The FSAP/NuSMV-SA safety analysis platform. STTT **9**(1), 5–24 (2007)
29. Biere, A., Heljanko, K., Wieringa, S.: AIGER (2011). http://fmv.jku.at/aiger/
30. SAE: AIR 6110. Contiguous Aircraft/ System Development Process Example, December 2011
31. Bozzano, M., Cimatti, A., Pires, A.F., Jones, D., Kimberly, G., Petri, T., Robinson, R., Tonetta, S.: A formal account of the AIR6110 wheel brake system. In: Proceedings of CAV, LNCS 9206 (2015)
32. Abío, I., Nieuwenhuis, R., Oliveras, A., Rodríguez-Carbonell, E.: A parametric approach for smaller and better encodings of cardinality constraints. In: Proceedings of CP (2013)

Boosting k-Induction with Continuously-Refined Invariants

Dirk Beyer, Matthias Dangl, and Philipp Wendler

University of Passau, Passau, Germany

Abstract. k-induction is a promising technique to extend bounded model checking from falsification to verification. In software verification, k-induction works only if auxiliary invariants are used to strengthen the induction hypothesis. The problem that we address is to generate such invariants (1) automatically without user-interaction, (2) efficiently such that little verification time is spent on the invariant generation, and (3) that are sufficiently strong for a k-induction proof. We boost the k-induction approach to significantly increase effectiveness and efficiency in the following way: We start in parallel to k-induction a data-flow-based invariant generator that supports dynamic precision adjustment and refine the precision of the invariant generator continuously during the analysis, such that the invariants become increasingly stronger. The k-induction engine is extended such that the invariants from the invariant generator are injected in each iteration to strengthen the hypothesis. The new method solves the above-mentioned problem because it (1) automatically chooses an invariant by step-wise refinement, (2) starts always with a lightweight invariant generation that is computationally inexpensive, and (3) refines the invariant precision more and more to inject stronger and stronger invariants into the induction system. We present and evaluate an implementation of our approach, as well as all other existing approaches, in the open-source verification-framework CPACHECKER. Our experiments show that combining k-induction with continuously-refined invariants significantly increases effectiveness and efficiency, and outperforms all existing implementations of k-induction-based verification of C programs in terms of successful results.

1 Introduction

Advances in software verification in recent years have lead to increased efforts towards applying formal verification methods to industrial software, in particular operating-systems code [3,4,34]. One model-checking technique that is implemented by half of the verifiers that participated in the 2015 Competition on Software Verification [7] is bounded model checking (BMC) [16,17,22]. For unbounded systems, BMC can be used only for falsification, not for verification [15]. This limitation to falsification can be overcome by combining BMC

A preliminary version of this article appeared as technical report [8].

© Springer International Publishing Switzerland 2015
D. Kroening and C.S. Păsăreanu (Eds.): CAV 2015, Part I, LNCS 9206, pp. 622–640, 2015.
DOI: 10.1007/978-3-319-21690-4_42

with mathematical induction and thus extending it to verification [26]. Unfortunately, inductive approaches are not always powerful enough to prove the required verification conditions, because not all program invariants are inductive [2]. Using the more general k-induction [38] instead of standard induction is more powerful [37] and has already been implemented in the DMA-race analysis tool SCRATCH [27] and in the software verifier ESBMC [35]. Nevertheless, additional supportive measures are often required to guide k-induction and take advantage of its full potential [25]. Our goal is to provide a powerful and competitive approach for reliable, general-purpose software verification based on BMC and k-induction, implemented in a state-of-the-art software-verification framework.

Our contribution is a new combination of k-induction-based model checking with automatically-generated continuously-refined invariants that are used to strengthen the induction hypothesis, which increases the effectiveness and efficiency of the approach. BMC and k-induction are combined in an algorithm that iteratively increments the induction parameter k (iterative deepening). The invariant generation runs in parallel to the k-induction proof construction, starting with relatively weak (but inexpensive to compute) invariants, and increasing the strength of the invariants over time as long as the analysis continues. The k-induction-based proof construction adopts the currently known set of invariants in every new proof attempt. This approach can verify easy problems quickly (with a small initial k and weak invariants), and is able to verify complex problems by increasing the effort (by incrementing k and searching for stronger invariants). Thus, it is both efficient and effective. In contrast to previous work [35], the new approach is sound. We implemented our approach as part of the open-source software-verification framework CPACHECKER [12], and we perform an extensive experimental comparison of our implementation against the two existing tools that use k-induction and against other common software-verification approaches.

Contributions. We make the following contributions:

- a novel approach for providing *continuously-refined invariants* from data-flow analysis with precision adjustment in order to repeatedly inject invariants to k-induction,
- an *effective and efficient tool* implementation of a framework for software verification with k-induction that allows to express all existing approaches to k-induction in a *uniform, module-based, configurable architecture*, and
- an extensive *experimental evaluation* of (a) all approaches and their implementations in the framework, (b) the two existing k-induction tools CBMC and ESBMC, and (c) the two different approaches predicate analysis and value analysis; the result being that the new technique outperforms all existing k-induction-based approaches to software verification.

Availability of Data and Tools. Our experiments are based on benchmark verification tasks from the 2015 Competition on Software Verification. All benchmarks, tools, and results of our evaluation are available on a supplementary web page[1].

---

[1] http://www.sosy-lab.org/~dbeyer/cpa-k-induction/
(successfully evaluated by the CAV 2015 Artifact Evaluation Committee)

```
1  int main() {
2    unsigned int x1 = 0, x2 = 0;
3    int s = 1;
4
5    while (nondet()) {
6      if (s == 1) x1++;
7      else if (s == 2) x2++;
8
9      s++;
10     if (s == 5) s = 1;
11
12     if ((s == 1) && (x1 != x2)) {
13       // Valid safety property
14       ERROR: return 1;
15     }
16   }
17 }
```

```
1  int main() {
2    unsigned int x1 = 0, x2 = 0;
3    int s = 1;
4
5    while (nondet()) {
6      if (s == 1) x1++;
7      else if (s == 2) x2++;
8
9      s++;
10     if (s == 5) s = 1;
11   }
12
13   if (s >= 4) {
14     // Violation: s may be 4
15     ERROR: return 1;
16   }
17 }
```

Fig. 1. Safe example program example-safe, which cannot be proven with existing k-induction-based approaches

Fig. 2. Unsafe example program example-unsafe, where some approaches may produce a wrong proof

Example. We illustrate the problem of k-induction that we address, and the strength of our approach, on two example programs. Both programs encode an automaton, which is typical, e.g., for software that implements a communication protocol. The automaton has a finite set of states, which is encoded by variable s, and two data variables x1 and x2. There are some state-dependent calculations (lines 6 and 7 in both programs) that alternatingly increment x1 and x2, and a calculation of the next state (lines 9 and 10 in both programs). The state variable cycles through the range from 1 to 4. These calculations are done in a loop with a non-deterministic number of iterations. Both programs also contain a safety property (the label ERROR should not be reachable). The program example-safe in Fig. 1 checks that in every fourth state, the values of x1 and x2 are equal; it satisfies the property. The program example-unsafe in Fig. 2 checks that when the loop exits, the value of state variable s is not greater or equal to 4; it violates the property.

First, note that the program example-safe is difficult or impossible to prove with many classical software-verification approaches other than k-induction: (1) BMC cannot prove safety for this program because the loop may run arbitrarily long. (2) Explicit-state model checking fails because of the huge state space (x1 and x2 can get arbitrarily large). (3) Predicate analysis with counterexample-guided abstraction refinement (CEGAR) and interpolation is able to prove safety, but only if the predicate $x1 = x2$ gets discovered. If the interpolants contain instead only predicates such as $x1 = 1$, $x2 = 1$, $x1 = 2$, etc., the predicate analysis will not terminate. Which predicates get discovered is hard to control and usually depends on internal interpolation heuristics of the satisfiability-modulo-theory (SMT) solver. (4) Traditional 1-induction is also not able to prove the program safe because the assertion is checked only in every fourth loop iteration (when s equals 1). Thus, the induction hypothesis is too weak (the program state s = 4, x1 = 0, x2 = 1 is a counterexample for the step case in the induction proof).

Intuitively, this program should be provable by k-induction with a k of at least 4. However, for every k, there is a counterexample to the inductive-step case that refutes the proof. For such a counterexample, set s = $-k$, x1 = 0, x2 = 1 at the beginning of the loop. Starting in this state, the program would increment s k times (induction hypothesis) and then reach s = 1 with property-violating values of x1 and x2 in iteration $k+1$ (inductive step). It is clear that s can never be negative, but this fact is not present in the induction hypothesis, and thus, the proof fails. This illustrates the general problem of k-induction-based verification: safety properties often do not hold in unreachable parts of the state space of a program, and k-induction alone does not distinguish between reachable and unreachable parts of the state space. Therefore, approaches based on k-induction without auxiliary invariants will fail to prove safety for program example-safe.

This program could of course be verified more easily if it were rewritten to contain a stronger safety property such as $s \geq 1 \wedge s \leq 4 \wedge (s = 2 \Rightarrow x1 = x2+1) \wedge$ $(s \neq 2 \Rightarrow x1 = x2)$ (which is a loop invariant and allows a proof by 1-induction without auxiliary invariants). However, our goal is to automatically verify real programs, and programmers usually neither write down trivial properties such as $s \geq 1$ nor more complex properties such as $s \neq 2 \Rightarrow x1 = x2$.

Our approach of combining k-induction with invariants proves the program safe with $k = 4$ and the invariant $s \geq 1$. This invariant is easy to find automatically using an inexpensive data-flow analysis, such as an interval analysis. For larger programs, a more complex invariant might be necessary, which might get generated at some point by our continuous strengthening of the invariant. Furthermore, stronger invariants can reduce the k that is necessary to prove a program. For example, the invariant $s \geq 1 \wedge s \leq 4 \wedge (s \neq 2 \Rightarrow x1 = x2)$ (which is still weaker than the full loop invariant above) allows to prove the program with $k = 2$. Thus, our strengthening of invariants can also shorten the inductive proof procedure and lead to better performance.

An existing approach tries to solve this problem of a too-weak induction hypothesis by initializing only the variables of the loop-termination condition to a non-deterministic value in the step case, and initializing all other variables to their initial value in the program [35]. However, this approach is not strong enough for the program example-safe and even produces a wrong proof (unsound result) for the program example-unsafe. This second example program contains a different safety property about s, which is violated. Because the variable s does not appear in the loop-termination condition, it is not set to an arbitrary value in the step case as it should be, and the inductive proof wrongly concludes that the program is safe because the induction hypothesis is too strong, leading to a missed bug and a wrong result. Our approach does not suffer from this unsoundness, because we add only invariants to the induction hypothesis that the invariant generation has proven to hold.

Related Work. The use of auxiliary invariants is a common technique in software verification [2, 9, 10, 18, 19, 20, 23, 30, 36], and techniques combining data-flow analysis and SMT solvers also exist [28, 31]. In most cases, the purpose is to speed up the analysis. For k-induction, however, the use of invariants is crucial in making the analysis terminate at all (cf. Fig. 1). There are several approaches to software verification using BMC in combination with k-induction.

Split-Case Induction. We use the *split-case k-induction* technique [26,27], where the base case and the step case are checked in separate steps. Earlier versions of SCRATCH [27] that use this technique transform programs with multiple loops into programs with only one single monolithic loop using a standard approach [1]. The alternative of recursively applying the technique to nested loops is discarded by the authors of SCRATCH [27], because the experiments suggested it was less efficient than checking the single loop that is obtained by the transformation. We also experimented with single-loop transformation, but our experimental results suggest that checking all loops at once in each case instead of checking the monolithic transformation result (which also encodes all loops in one) has no negative performance impact, so for simplicity, we omit the transformation. SCRATCH also supports *combined-case k-induction* [25], for which all loops are cut by replacing them with k copies each for the base and the step case, and setting all loop-modified variables to non-deterministic values before the step case. That way, both cases can be checked at once in the transformed program and no special handling for multiple loops is required. When using combined-case k-induction, SCRATCH requires loops to be manually annotated with the required k values, whereas its implementation of split-case k-induction supports iterative deepening of k as in our implementation. Contrary to SCRATCH, we do not focus on one specific problem domain [26,27], but want to provide a solution for solving a wide range of heterogeneous verification tasks.

Auxiliary Invariants. While both the split-case and the combined-case k-induction supposedly succeed with weaker auxiliary invariants than for example the inductive invariant approach [5], the approaches still do require auxiliary invariants in practice, and the tool SCRATCH requires these invariants to be annotated manually [25,27]. There are techniques for automatically generating invariants that may be used to help inductive approaches to succeed (e.g. [2,9,20]. These techniques, however, do not justify their additional effort because they are not guaranteed to provide the required invariants on time, especially if strong auxiliary invariants are required. Based on previous ideas of supporting k-induction with invariants generated by lightweight data-flow analysis [24], we therefore strive to leverage the power of the k-induction approach to succeed with auxiliary invariants generated by a data-flow analysis based on intervals. However, to handle cases where it is necessary to invest more effort into invariant generation, we increase the precision of these invariants over time.

Invariant Injection. A verification tool using a strategy similar to ours is PKIND [28,33], a model checker for Lustre programs based on k-induction. In PKIND, there is a parallel computation of auxiliary invariants, where candidate invariants derived by templates are iteratively checked via k-induction and, if successful, added to the set of known invariants [32]. While this allows for strengthening the induction hypothesis over time, the template-based approach lacks the flexibility that is available to an invariant generator using dynamic precision refinement [11], and the required additional induction proofs are potentially expensive. We implemented checking candidate invariants with k-induction as a possible strategy of our invariant generation component.

Unsound Strengthening of Induction Hypothesis. ESBMC does not require additional invariants for k-induction, because it assigns non-deterministic values only to the loop-termination condition variables before the inductive-step case [35] and thus retains more information than our as well as the SCRATCH implementation [25,27], but k-induction in ESBMC is therefore potentially unsound. Our goal is to perform a real proof of safety by removing all pre-loop information in the step case, thus treating the unrolled iterations in the step case truly as "any k consecutive iterations", as is required for the mathematical induction. Our approach counters this lack of information by employing incrementally-refined invariant generation.

Parallel Induction. PKIND checks the base case and the step case in parallel, and ESBMC supports parallel execution of the base case, the forward condition, and the inductive-step case. In contrast, our base case and inductive-step case are checked sequentially, while our invariant generation runs in parallel to the base- and step-case checks.

2 k-Induction with Continuously-Refined Invariants

Our verification approach consists of two algorithms that run concurrently. One algorithm is responsible for generating program invariants, starting with an imprecise invariant, continuously refining (strengthening) the invariant. The other algorithm is responsible for finding error paths with BMC, and for constructing safety proofs with k-induction, for which it periodically picks up the new invariant that the former algorithm has constructed so far. The k-induction algorithm uses information from the invariant generation, but not vice versa. In our presentation, we assume that each program contains at most one loop; in our implementation, we handle programs with multiple loops by checking all loops together.

Iterative-Deepening k-Induction. Algorithm 1 shows our extension of the k-induction algorithm to a combination with continuously-refined invariants. Starting with an initial value for the bound k, e.g., 1, we iteratively increase the value of k after each unsuccessful attempt at finding a specification violation or proving correctness of the program using k-induction. The following description of our approach to k-induction is based on split-case k-induction [25], where for the propositional state variables s and s' within a state-transition system that represents the program, the predicate $I(s)$ denotes that s is an initial state, $T(s, s')$ states that a transition from s to s' exists, and $P(s)$ asserts the safety property for the state s.

Base Case. Lines 3 to 5 implement the *base case*, which consists of running BMC with the current bound k. This means that starting from an initial program state, all paths of the program up to a maximum path length $k-1$ are explored. If an error path is found, the algorithm terminates.

Algorithm 1 Iterative-Deepening k-Induction

Input:

the initial value $k_{init} \geq 1$ for the bound k,

an upper limit k_{max} for the bound k,

a function $\text{inc} : \mathbb{N} \to \mathbb{N}$ with $\forall n \in \mathbb{N} : \text{inc}(n) > n$ for increasing the bound k,

the initial states defined by the predicate I,

the transfer relation defined by the predicate T, and

a safety property P

Output: true if P holds, **false** otherwise

1: $k := k_{init}$

2: **while** $k \leq k_{max}$ **do**

3:      $base\_case := I(s_0) \wedge \bigvee\limits_{n=0}^{k-1} \left(\bigwedge\limits_{i=0}^{n-1} T(s_i, s_{i+1}) \wedge \neg P(s_n) \right)$

4:      **if** $\text{sat}(base\_case)$ **then**

5:          **return false**

6:      $forward\_condition := I(s_0) \wedge \bigwedge\limits_{i=0}^{k-1} T(s_i, s_{i+1})$

7:      **if** $\neg \text{sat}(forward\_condition)$ **then**

8:          **return true**

9:      $step\_case_n := \bigwedge\limits_{i=n}^{n+k-1} (P(s_i) \wedge T(s_i, s_{i+1})) \wedge \neg P(s_{n+k})$

10:     **repeat**

11:         $Inv := \text{get\_currently\_known\_invariant}()$

12:         **if** $\neg \text{sat}(Inv(s_n) \wedge step\_case_n)$ **then**

13:             **return true**

14:     **until** $Inv = \text{get\_currently\_known\_invariant}()$

15:     $k := \text{inc}(k)$

16: **return unknown**

Algorithm 2 Continuous Invariant Generation using Configurable Program Analysis

Input:

a configurable program analysis with dynamic precision adjustment $\mathbb{D}$,

the initial states defined by predicate I,

a coarse initial precision π_0,

a safety property P

Output: true if P holds

1: $\pi := \pi_0$

2: $Inv := true$

3: **loop**

4:      $reached := \text{CPAAlgorithm}(\mathbb{D}, I, \pi)$

5:      **if** $\forall s \in reached : P(s)$ **then**

6:          **return true**

7:      $Inv := Inv \wedge \bigvee\limits_{s \in reached} s$

8:      $\pi := \text{RefinePrec}(\pi, reached)$

Forward Condition. Otherwise we check whether there exists a path with length $k' > k - 1$ in the program, or whether we have already fully explored the state space of the program (lines 6 to 8). In the latter case the program is safe and the algorithm terminates. This check is called the *forward condition* [29].

Inductive Step. Checking the forward condition can, however, only prove safety for programs with finite (and short) loops. Therefore, the algorithm also attempts an inductive proof (lines 9 to 14). The *inductive-step case* checks if, after every sequence of k loop iterations without a property violation, there is also no property violation before loop iteration $k+1$. For model checking of software, however, this check would often fail inconclusively without auxiliary invariants [8]. In our approach, we make use of the fact that the invariants that were generated so far by the concurrently-running invariant-generation algorithm hold, and conjunct these facts to the induction hypothesis. Thus, the inductive-step case proves a program safe if the following condition is unsatisfiable:

$$Inv(s_n) \wedge \bigwedge_{i=n}^{n+k-1} (P(s_i) \wedge T(s_i, s_{i+1})) \wedge \neg P(s_{n+k})$$

where Inv is the currently available program invariant, and $s_n, \ldots, s_{n+k}$ is any sequence of states. If this condition is satisfiable, then the induction check is inconclusive, and the program is not yet proved safe or unsafe with the current value of k and the current invariant. If during the time of the satisfiability check of the step case, a new (stronger) invariant has become available (condition in line 14 is false), we immediately re-check the step case with the new invariant. This can be done efficiently using an incremental SMT solver for the repeated satisfiability checks in line 12. Otherwise, we start over with an increased value of k.

Note that the inductive-step case is similar to a BMC check for the presence of error paths of length exactly $k + 1$. However, as the step case needs to consider any consecutive $k + 1$ loop iterations, and not only the first such iterations, it does not assume that the execution of the loop iterations begins in an initial state. Instead, it assumes that there is a sequence of k iterations without any property violation (induction hypothesis).

Continuous Invariant Generation. Our continuous invariant generation incrementally produces stronger and stronger program invariants. It is based on iterative refinement, each time using an increased precision. After each strengthening of the invariant, it can be used as injection invariant by the k-induction procedure. It may happen that this analysis proves safety of the program all by itself, but this is not its main purpose here.

Our k-induction module works with any kind of invariant-generation procedure, as long as its precision, i.e., its level of abstraction, is configurable. We implemented two different invariant-generation approaches: KI and DF, described below.

We use the design of Fig. 3 to explain our flexible and modular framework for k-induction: k-induction is a verification technique, i.e., an invariant generation. In this paper, the main algorithm is thus the k-induction, as defined in Algorithm 1.

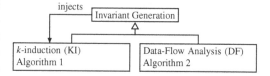

Fig. 3. Configurable design of a k-induction framework

We denote the algorithm by KI. If invariants are generated and injected into KI, we denote this injection by KI←. Thus, the use of generated invariants that are produced by a data-flow analysis (DF) are denoted by KI←DF. If the invariant generator continuously refines the invariants and repeatedly *injects* those invariants into KI, this is denoted by KI↺, more specifically, if data-flow analysis with dynamic precision adjustment (our new contribution) is used, we have KI↺DF, and if the PKIND approach is used, i.e., KI is used to construct invariants, we have KI↺KI. Now, since the second KI, which constructs invariants for injection into the first KI, can again get invariants injected, we can further build an approach KI↺KI↺DF that combines all approaches such that the invariant-generating KI benefits from the invariants generated with DF, and the main KI algorithm that tries to prove program safety benefits from both invariant generators.

KI. PKIND [33] introduced the idea to construct invariants for injection in parallel, using a template-based method that extracts candidate invariants from the program and verifies their validity using k-induction [32]. If the candidate invariants are found to be valid, they are injected to the main k-induction procedure. We re-implemented the PKIND approach in our framework (KI↺KI), using a separate instance of k-induction to prove candidate invariants. Being based on k-induction, the power of this technique is continuously increased by increasing k. We derive the candidate invariants by taking the negations of assumptions on the control-flow paths to error locations. Similar to our Algorithm 2, each time this k-induction algorithm succeeds in proving a candidate invariant, the previously-known invariant is strengthened with this newly generated invariant. In our tool, we used an instance of Algorithm 1 to implement this approach. We are thus able to further combine this technique with other auxiliary invariant-generation approaches.

DF. As a second invariant-generation approach (our contribution), we use the reachability algorithm CPAAlgorithm for configurable program analysis with dynamic precision adjustment [11]. Algorithm 2 shows our continuous invariant generation. The initial program invariant is represented by the formula *true*. We start with running the invariant-generating analysis once with a coarse initial precision (line 4). After each run of the program-invariant generation, we strengthen the previously-known program invariant with the newly-generated invariant (line 7, note that the program invariant *Inv* is not a safety invariant) and announce it globally (such that the k-induction algorithm can inject it).

If the analysis was able to prove safety of the program, the algorithm terminates (lines 5 to 6). Otherwise, the analysis is restarted with a higher precision. The CPAAlgorithm takes as input a configurable program analysis (CPA), a set of initial abstract states, and a precision. It returns a set of reachable abstract states that form an over-approximation of the reachable program states. Depending on the used CPA and the precision, the analysis by CPAAlgorithm can be efficient and abstract like data-flow analysis or expensive and precise like model checking.

For invariant generation, we choose an abstract domain based on expressions over intervals [8]. Note that this is not a requirement of our approach, which works with any kind of domain. Our choice is based on the high flexibility of this domain, which can be fast and efficient as well as precise. For this CPA, the precision is a triple (Y, n, w), where $Y \subseteq X$ is a specific selection of important program variables, n is the maximal nesting depth of expressions in the abstract state, and w is a boolean specifying whether widening should be used. Those variables that are considered important will not be over-approximated by joining abstract states. With a higher nesting depth, more precise relations between variables can be represented. The use of widening ensures timely termination (at the expense of a lower precision), even for programs with loops with many iterations, like those in the examples of Figs. 1 and 2. An in-depth description of this abstract domain is presented in a technical report [8].

3   Experimental Evaluation

We implemented all existing approaches to k-induction, compare all configurations with each other, and the best configuration with other k-induction-based software verifiers, as well as to two standard approaches to software verification: predicate and value analysis.

Benchmark Verification Tasks. As benchmark set we use verification tasks from the 2015 Competition on Software Verification (SV-COMP'15) [7]. We took all 3 964 verification tasks from the categories *ControlFlow*, *DeviceDrivers64*, *HeapManipulation*, *Sequentialized*, and *Simple*. The remaining categories were excluded because they use features (such as bit-vectors, concurrency, and recursion) that not all configurations of our evaluation support. A total of 1 148 verification tasks in the benchmark set contain a known specification violation. Although we cannot expect an improvement for these verification tasks when using auxiliary invariants, we did not exclude them because this would unfairly give advantage to the new approach (which spends some effort generating invariants, which are not helpful when proving existence of an error path).

Experimental Setup. All experiments were conducted on computers with two 2.6 GHz 8-Core CPUs (Intel Xeon E5-2560 v2) with 135 GB of RAM. The operating system was Ubuntu 14.04 (64 bit), using Linux 3.13 and OpenJDK 1.7. Each verification task was limited to two CPU cores, a CPU run time of 15 min, and a memory usage of 15 GB. The benchmarking framework BENCHEXEC[2] ensures precise and reproducible results.

Presentation. All benchmarks, tools, and the full results of our evaluation are available on a supplementary web page.[3] All reported times are rounded to two significant digits. We use the scoring scheme of SV-COMP'15 to calculate a score for each configuration. For every real bug found, 1 point is assigned, for every correct safety proof, 2 points are assigned. A score of 6 points is subtracted for every wrong alarm (false positive) reported by the tool, and 12 points are subtracted for every wrong proof of safety (false negative). This scoring scheme values proving safety higher than finding error paths, and significantly punishes wrong answers, which is in line with the community consensus [7] on difficulty of verification vs. falsification and importance of correct results. We consider this a good fit for evaluating an approach such as k-induction, which targets at producing safety proofs.

In Figs. 4 and 5, we present experimental results using a plot of quantile functions for accumulated scores as introduced by the Competition on Software Verification [6], which shows the score and CPU time for successful results and the score for wrong answers. A data point (x, y) of a graph means that for the respective configuration the sum of the scores of all wrong answers and the scores for all correct answers with a run time of less than or equal to y seconds is x. For the left-most point (x, y) of each graph, the x-value shows the sum of all negative scores for the respective configuration and the y-value shows the time for the fastest successful result. For the right-most point (x, y) of each graph, the x-value shows the total score for this configuration, and the y-value shows the maximal run time. A configuration can be considered better, the further to the right (the closer to 0) its graph begins (fewer wrong answers), the further to the right it ends (more correct answers), and the lower its graph is (less run time).

Comparison of k-Induction-Based Approaches. We implemented all approaches in the JAVA-based open-source software-verification framework CPACHECKER [12], which is available online[4] under the Apache 2.0 License. For the experiments, we used version 1.4.5-cav15 of CPACHECKER, with SMTINTERPOL [21] as SMT solver (using uninterpreted functions and linear arithmetic over integers and reals). The k-induction algorithm of CPACHECKER was configured to increment k by 1 after each try (in Algorithm 1, $\text{inc}(k) = k+1$). The precision refinement of the DF-based continuous invariant generation (Algorithm 2) was configured to increment the number of important program variables in the first, third, fifth, and any further precision refinements. The second precision refinement increments the expression-nesting depth, and the fourth disables the widening.

---

[2] https://github.com/dbeyer/benchexec
[3] http://www.sosy-lab.org/~dbeyer/cpa-k-induction/
[4] http://cpachecker.sosy-lab.org

Table 1. Results of k-induction-based configurations in CPACHECKER for all 3 964 verification tasks with different approaches for generating auxiliary invariants

Approach	KI	KI←DF (0,1,t)	(8,2,t)	(16,2,t)	(16,2,f)	KI↺-KI	KI↺-DF	KI↺-KI↺-DF
Score	2 246	3 944	4 117	4 062	3 992	3 535	4 249	**4 282**
Correct results	1 531	2 377	2 462	2 428	2 392	2 169	2 507	**2 519**
Wrong proofs	1	1	2	1	1	1	1	1
Wrong alarms	30	30	30	30	30	30	26	25
CPU time (h)	530	330	330	340	340	380	320	320
Wall time (h)	440	240	210	210	210	270	190	170
Times for correct results only:								
CPU time (h)	17	32	39	36	36	28	36	41
Wall time (h)	13	19	22	20	20	18	20	22
k-Values for correct safe results only:								
Max. final k	101	101	100	100	126	101	112	111
Avg. final k	1.7	1.4	1.7	1.8	1.8	1.8	1.8	1.9

We evaluated the following groups of k-induction approaches: (1) without any auxiliary invariants (KI), (2) with auxiliary invariants of different precisions generated by the DF approach (KI←DF), and (3) with continuously-refined invariants (KI↺-).

The k-induction-based configuration using no auxiliary invariants (KI) is an instance of Algorithm 1 where get_currently_known_invariant() always returns *true* as invariant and Algorithm 2 does not run at all.

The configurations using generated invariants (KI←DF) are also instances of Algorithm 1. Here, Algorithm 2 runs in parallel, however, it terminates after one loop iteration. We denote these configurations with triples (s, n, w) that represent the precision (Y, n, w) of the invariant generation with s being the size of the set of important program variables ($s = |Y|$). For example, the first of these configurations, $(0, 1, true)$, has no variables in the set Y of important program variables (i.e., all variables get over-approximated by the merge operator), the maximum nesting depth of expressions in the abstract state is 1, and the widening operator is used. The remaining configurations we use are $(8, 2, true)$, $(16, 2, true)$, and $(16, 2, false)$. These configurations were selected because they represent some of the extremes of the precisions that are used during dynamic invariant generation. It is impossible to cover every possible valid configuration within the scope of this paper.

There are three configurations using continuously-refined invariants: (1) using the k-induction approach similar to PKIND to generate invariants, refining by increasing k, denoted as KI↺-KI, (2) using the DF-based approach to generate invariants, refining by precision adjustment, denoted as KI↺-DF, and (3) using both approaches in parallel combination, denoted as KI↺-KI↺-DF. All configurations using invariant generation run the generation in parallel to the main k-induction algorithm, an instance of Algorithm 1.

Score and Reported Results. The configuration KI with no invariant generation receives the lowest score of 2 246, and (as expected) can verify only 1 531 programs successfully. This shows that it is indeed important in practice to enhance k-induction-based software verification with invariants. The configurations KI←DF using invariant generation produce similar numbers of correct results (around 2 400), improving upon the results of the plain k-induction without auxiliary invariants by a score of 1 700 to 1 800. Even though these configurations solve a similar number of programs, a closer inspection reveals that each of the configurations is able to correctly solve significant amounts of programs where the other configurations run into timeouts. This observation explains the high score of 4 249 points achieved by our approach of injecting the continuously-refined invariants generated with data-flow analysis into the k-induction engine (configuration KI↔DF). By combining the advantages of fast and coarse precisions with those of slow but fine precisions, it correctly solves 2 507 verification tasks, which is 45 more than the best of the chosen configurations without dynamic refinement. Using a k-induction-based invariant generation as done by PKIND (configuration KI↔KI) is also a successful technique for improving the amount of solvable verification tasks, and thus, combining both invariant-generation approaches with continuously refining their precision and injecting the generated invariants into the k-induction engine (configuration KI↔KI↔DF) is the most effective of all evaluated k-induction-based approaches, with a score of 4 282, and 2 519 correct results. The few wrong proofs produced by the configurations are not due to conceptual problems, but only due to incompleteness in the analyzer's handling of certain constructs such as unbounded arrays and pointer aliasing.

Performance. Table 1 shows that by far the largest amount of time is spent by the configuration KI (no auxiliary invariants), because for those programs that cannot be proved without auxiliary invariants, the k-induction procedure loops incrementing k until the time limit is reached. The wall times and CPU times for the correct results correlate roughly with the amount of correct results, i.e., on average about the same amount of time is spent on correct verifications, whether or not invariant generation is used. This shows that the overhead of generating auxiliary invariants is well-compensated.

The configurations with invariant generation have a relatively higher CPU time compared to their wall time because these configurations spend some time generating invariants in parallel to the k-induction algorithm. The results show, however, that the time spent for the continuously-refined invariant generation clearly pays off as the configuration using both data-flow analysis and k-induction for invariant generation is not only the one with the most correct results, but at the same time one of the two fastest configurations with only 320 h in total. Even though they produced much more correct results, the configurations KI↔KI↔DF and KI↔DF did not exceed the times of the chosen configurations using invariant generation without continuous refinement. The configuration KI↔KI using only k-induction to continuously generate invariants is slower, but produces results for some programs where the configuration

Table 2. Results of k-induction-based tools for all 3 964 verification tasks

Tool Configuration	CBMC	ESBMC sequential parallel		CPACHECKER KI←⊖ KI←⊖-DF	
Score	−4 372	1 674	1 716	**4 282**	
Correct results	1 949	2 050	2 059	**2 519**	
Wrong proofs	666	156	152	1	
Wrong alarms	5	9	13	25	
CPU time (h)	360	290	370	320	
Wall time (h)	360	290	200	170	
Times for correct results only:					
CPU time (h)	3.9	16	26	41	
Wall time (h)	3.9	16	13	22	
k-Values for correct safe results only:					
Max. final k	50	2 048	1 952	111	
Avg. final k	1.1	5.3	7.1	1.9	

KI←⊖-DF fails. The results show that the combination of the techniques reaps the benefits of both.

These results show that the additional effort invested in generating auxiliary invariants is well-spent, as it even decreases the overall time due to the fewer timeouts. As expected, the continuously-refined invariants solve many tasks quicker than the configurations using invariant generation with high precisions and without refinement.

Final value of k. The bottom of Table 1 shows some statistics about the final values of k for the correct safety proofs. There are only small differences between the maximum k values of most of the configurations. Interestingly, the configuration using non-dynamic invariant generation with high precision has a higher maximum final value of k than the others, because for the verification task afnp2014_true-unreach-call.c.i, a strong invariant generated only with this configuration allowed the proof to succeed. This effect is also observable in the continuously-refined configurations using invariants generated by data-flow analysis: They are also able to solve this verification task, and, by dynamically increasing the precision, find the required auxiliary invariant even earlier with loop bounds 112 and 111, respectively. There is also a verification task in the benchmark set, gj2007_true-unreach-call.c.i, where most configurations need to unroll a loop with bound 100 to prove safety, while the strong invariant generation technique allows the proof to succeed earlier, at a loop bound of 16. The continuously-refined configurations benefit from the same effect: KI←⊖-DF and KI←⊖-KI←⊖-DF solve this task at loop bounds 22 and 19, respectively.

Comparison with Other Tools. For comparison with other k-induction-based tools, we evaluated ESBMC and CBMC, two software model checkers with support for k-induction. For CBMC, we used version 5.1 in combination with a wrapper script for split-case k-induction provided by M. Tautschnig. For ESBMC we used version 1.25.2 in combination with a wrapper script that enables k-induction (based on the SV-COMP'13

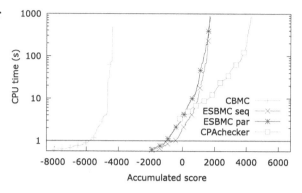

Fig. 4. Quantile functions of k-induction-based tools (CPACHECKER in configuration KI↶KI↶DF) for accumulated scores showing the CPU time for the successful results; linear scale between 0 s and 1 s, logarithmic scale beyond

submission [35]). We also provide results for the experimental parallel k-induction of ESBMC, but note that our benchmark setup is not focused on parallelization (using only two CPU cores and a CPU-time limit instead of wall time). The CPACHECKER configuration in this comparison is the one with continuously-refined invariants and both invariant generators (KI↶KI↶DF). Table 2 gives the results; Fig. 4 shows the quantile functions of the accumulated scores for each configuration. The results for CBMC are not competitive, which may be attributed to the experimental nature of its k-induction support.

Score. CPACHECKER in configuration KI↶KI↶DF successfully verifies almost 500 tasks (20 %) more than ESBMC. Furthermore, it has only 1 missed bug, which is related to unsoundness in the handling of some C features, whereas ESBMC has more than 150 wrong safety proofs. This large number of wrong results must be attributed to the unsound heuristic of ESBMC for strengthening the induction hypothesis, where it retains potentially incorrect information about loop-modified variables [35]. We have previously also implemented this approach in CPACHECKER and obtained similar results [8]. The large number of wrong proofs reduces the confidence in the soundness of the correct proofs. Consequently, the score achieved by CPACHECKER in configuration KI↶KI↶DF is much higher than the score of ESBMC (4 282 compared to 1 674 points). This clear advantage is also visible in Fig. 4. The parallel version of ESBMC performs somewhat better than its sequential version, and misses fewer bugs. This is due to the fact that the base case and the step case are performed in parallel, and the loop bound k is incremented independently for each of them. The base case is usually easier to solve for the SMT solver, and thus the base-case checks proceed faster than the step-case checks (reaching a higher value of k sooner). Therefore, the parallel version manages to find some bugs by reaching the relevant k in the base-case checks earlier than in the step-case checks, which would produce a wrong safety proof at reaching k. However, the number of wrong proofs is still much higher than with our approach, which is conceptually sound. Thus, the score of the new, sound approach is more than 2 500 points higher.

Performance. Table 2 shows that our approach needs only 10 % more CPU time than the sequential version of ESBMC for solving a much higher number of tasks, and even needs less CPU and wall time than the parallel version of ESBMC. This indicates that due to our invariants, we succeed more often with fewer loop unrollings, and thus in less time. It also shows that the effort invested for generating the invariants is well spent.

Final Value of k. The bottom of Table 2 contains some statistics on the final value of k that was needed to verify a program. The table shows that for safe programs, CPACHECKER needs a loop bound that is (on average) only about one third of the loop bound that ESBMC needs. This advantage is due to the use of generated invariants, which make the induction proofs easier and likely to succeed with a smaller number of k. The verification task array_true-unreach-call2.i is solved by ESBMC after completely unwinding the loop, therefore reaching the large k-value 2 048. In the parallel version, the (quicker) detached base case hits this bound while the inductive step case is still at $k = 1\,952$.

Comparison with Other Approaches. We also compare our combination of k-induction with continuously-refined invariants with other common approaches for software verification. We use for comparison two analyses based on CEGAR, a predicate analysis [13] and a value analysis [14]. Both are implemented in CPACHECKER, which allows us to compare the approaches inside the same tool, using the same run-time environment, SMT solver, etc., and focus only on the conceptual differences between the analyses.

Figure 5 shows a quantile plot to compare the configuration KI←⊖-KI←⊖-DF with CPACHECKER predicate analysis and value analysis. The predicate analysis solves 2 463 verification tasks in a total of 280 CPU hours, and achieves a score of 4 201. The value analysis solves 2 367 verification tasks in a total of 303 CPU hours, and achieves a score of 4 216 because it has a few wrong results less. The higher number of solved tasks (2 519) and the higher score (4 282)

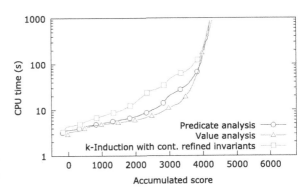

Fig. 5. Quantile functions of different approaches implemented in CPACHECKER (k-induction in configuration KI←⊖-KI←⊖-DF) for accumulated scores showing the CPU time for the successful results

of the k-induction-based configuration show that k-induction is clearly competitive with the state-of-the-art in software verification, if it is boosted by injecting continuously-refined invariants.

4 Conclusion

We have presented the novel idea of injecting invariants into k-induction that are generated using data-flow analysis with dynamic precision adjustment, and contribute a publicly available implementation of our idea within the software-verification framework CPACHECKER. Our extensive experiments show that the new approach outperforms all existing implementations of k-induction for software verification, and that it is competitive compared to other, more mature techniques for software verification. We showed that a sound, effective, and efficient k-induction approach to general-purpose software verification is possible, and that the additional resources required to achieve these combined benefits are negligible if invested judiciously. At the same time, there is still room for improvement of our technique. An interesting improvement would be to add an information flow between the two cooperating algorithms in the reverse direction. If the k-induction procedure could tell the invariant generation which facts it misses to prove safety, this could lead to a more efficient and effective approach to generate invariants that are specifically tailored to the needs of the k-induction proof. Already now, CPACHECKER is parsimonious in terms of unrollings, compared to other tools. The low k-values required to prove many programs show that even our current invariant generation is powerful enough to produce invariants that are strong enough to help cut down the necessary number of loop unrollings. k-induction-guided precision refinement might direct the invariant generation towards providing weaker but still useful invariants for k-induction more efficiently.

Acknowledgments. We thank M. Tautschnig and L. Cordeiro for explaining the optimal available parameters for k-induction, for the verifiers CBMC and ESBMC, respectively.

References

1. Aho, A.V., Sethi, R., Ullman, J.D.: Compilers: Principles, Techniques, and Tools. Addison-Wesley, Reading (1986)
2. Awedh, M., Somenzi, F.: Automatic invariant strengthening to prove properties in bounded model checking. In: Proceedings of DAC, pp. 1073–1076. ACM/IEEE (2006)
3. Ball, T., Cook, B., Levin, V., Rajamani, S.K.: SLAM and static driver verifier: technology transfer of formal methods inside microsoft. In: Proceedings of IFM, LNCS, vol. 2999, pp. 1–20. Springer (2004)
4. Ball, T., Levin, V., Rajamani, S.K.: A decade of software model checking with SLAM. Commun. ACM **54**(7), 68–76 (2011)
5. Barnett, M., Leino, K.R.M.: Weakest-precondition of unstructured programs. In: Proceedings of PASTE, pp. 82–87. ACM (2005)

6. Beyer, D.: Second competition on software verification. In: Proceedings of TACAS, LNCS, vol. 7795, pp. 594–609. Springer (2013)
7. Beyer, D.: Software verification and verifiable witnesses. In: Proceedings of TACAS, LNCS, vol. 9035, pp. 401–416. Springer (2015)
8. Beyer, D., Dangl, M., Wendler, P.: Combining k-induction with continuously-refined invariants. Technical Report MIP-1503, University of Passau, January 2015. arXiv:1502.00096
9. Beyer, D., Henzinger, T.A., Majumdar, R., Rybalchenko, A.: Invariant synthesis for combined theories. In: Proceedings of VMCAI, LNCS, vol. 4349, pp. 378–394. Springer (2007)
10. Beyer, D., Henzinger, T.A., Majumdar, R., Rybalchenko, A.: Path invariants. In: Procedings of PLDI, pp. 300–309. ACM (2007)
11. Beyer, D., Henzinger, T.A., Théoduloz, G.: Program analysis with dynamic precision adjustment. In: Proceedings of ASE, pp. 29–38. IEEE (2008)
12. Beyer, D., Keremoglu, M.:CPACHECKER: A tool for configurable software verification. In: Proceedings of CAV, LNCS, vol. 6806, pp. 184–190. Springer (2011)
13. Beyer, D., Keremoglu, M.E., Wendler, P.: Predicate abstraction with adjustable-block encoding. In: Proceedings of FMCAD, pp. 189–197. FMCAD (2010)
14. Beyer, D., Löwe, S.: Explicit-state software model checking based on CEGAR and interpolation. In: Proceedings of FASE, LNCS, vol. 7793, pp. 146–162. Springer (2013)
15. Biere, A.: Handbook of Satisfiability. IOS Press, Amsterdam (2009)
16. Biere, A., Cimatti, A., Clarke, E.M., Strichman, O., Zhu, Y.: Bounded model checking. Adv. Comput. **58**, 117–148 (2003)
17. Biere, A., Cimatti, A., Clarke, E., Zhu, Y.: Symbolic model checking without BDDs. In: Proceedings of TACAS, LNCS, vol. 1579, pp. 193–207. Springer (1999)
18. Bjørner, N., Browne, A., Manna, Z.: Automatic generation of invariants and intermediate assertions. Theor. Comput. Sci. **173**(1), 49–87 (1997)
19. Blanchet, B., Cousot, P., Cousot, R., Feret, J., Mauborgne, L., Miné, A., Monniaux, D., Rival, X.: A static analyzer for large safety-critical software. In: Proceedings of PLDI, pp. 196–207. ACM (2003)
20. Bradley, A.R., Manna, Z.: Property-directed incremental invariant generation. FAC **20**(4–5), 379–405 (2008)
21. Christ, J., Hoenicke, J., Nutz, A.: SMTInterpol: An interpolating SMT solver. In: Proceedings of SPIN, LNCS, vol. 7385, pp. 248–254. Springer (2012)
22. Cordeiro, L., Fischer, B., Silva, J.P.M.: SMT-based bounded model checking for embedded ANSI-C software. In: Proceedings of ASE, pp. 137–148. IEEE (2009)
23. Cousot, P., Halbwachs, N.: Automatic discovery of linear restraints among variables of a program. In: Procedings of POPL, pp. 84–96 (1978)
24. Donaldson, A.F., Haller, L., Kroening, D.: Strengthening induction-based race checking with lightweight static analysis. In: Proceedings of VMCAI, LNCS, vol. 6538, pp. 169–183. Springer, Heidelberg (2011)
25. Donaldson, A.F., Haller, L., Kroening, D., Rümmer, P.: Software verification using k-induction. In: Proceeding of Static Analysis. LNCS, vol. 6887, pp. 351–368. Springer (2011)
26. Donaldson, A.F., Kroening, D., Rümmer, P.: Automatic analysis of scratch-pad memory code for heterogeneous multicore processors. In: Proceedings of TACAS, LNCS, vol. 6015, pp. 280–295. Springer (2010)
27. Donaldson, A.F., Kröning, D., Rümmer, P.: Automatic analysis of DMA races using model checking and k-induction. FMSD **39**(1), 83–113 (2011)

28. Garoche, P.-L., Kahsai, T., Tinelli, C.: Incremental invariant generation using logic-based automatic abstract transformers. In: Proceedings of NFM, LNCS, vol. 7871, pp. 139–154. Springer (2013)

29. Große, D., Le, H.M., Drechsler, R.: Proving transaction and system-level properties of untimed SystemC TLM designs. In: Proceedings of MEMOCODE, pp. 113–122. IEEE (2010)

30. Gupta, A., Rybalchenko, A.: InvGen: an efficient invariant generator. In: Proceedings of CAV, LNCS, vol. 5643, pp. 634–640. Springer (2009)

31. Albarghouthi, A., Gurfinkel, A., Li, Y., Chaki, S., Chechik, M.: UFO: verification with interpolants and abstract interpretation. In: Proceedings of TACAS, LNCS, vol. 7795, pp. 637–640. Springer (2013)

32. Kahsai, T., Ge, Y., Tinelli, C.: Instantiation-based invariant discovery. In: Proceedings of NFM, LNCS, vol. 6617, pp. 192–206. Springer (2011)

33. Kahsai, T., Tinelli, C.: Pkind: a parallel k-induction based model checker. In: Proceedings of International Workshop on Parallel and Distributed Methods in Verification, EPTCS 72, pp. 55–62 (2011)

34. Khoroshilov, A., Mutilin, V., Petrenko, A., Zakharov, V.: Establishing linux driver verification process. In: Proceedings of PSI, LNCS, vol. 5947, pp. 165–176. Springer (2010)

35. Morse, J., Cordeiro, L., Nicole, D., Fischer, B.: Handling unbounded loops with ESBMC 1.20. In: Proceedings of TACAS, LNCS, vol. 7795, pp. 619–622. Springer (2013)

36. Sankaranarayanan, S., Sipma, H.B., Manna, Z.: Scalable analysis of linear systems using mathematical programming. In: Proceedings of VMCAI, LNCS, vol. 3385, pp. 25–41. Springer (2005)

37. Sheeran, M., Singh, S., Stålmarck, G.: Checking safety properties using induction and a SAT-solver. In: Proceedings of FMCAD, LNCS, vol. 1954, pp. 108–125. Springer (2000)

38. Wahl, T.: The k-induction principle (2013). http://www.ccs.neu.edu/home/wahl/Publications/k-induction.pdf

Fast Interpolating BMC

Yakir Vizel[1], Arie Gurfinkel[2][(✉)], and Sharad Malik[1]

[1] Electrical Engineering Department, Princeton University, Princeton, USA
[2] Carnegie Mellon Software Engineering Institute, Pittsburgh, USA
arie@sei.cmu.edu

Abstract. *Bounded Model Checking* (BMC) is well known for its simplicity and ability to find counterexamples. It is based on the idea of symbolically representing counterexamples in a transition system and then using a SAT solver to check for their existence or their absence. State-of-the-art BMC algorithms combine a direct translation to SAT with circuit-aware simplifications and work incrementally, sharing information between different bounds. While BMC is incomplete (it can only show existence of counterexamples), it is a major building block of several complete interpolation-based model checking algorithms. However, traditional interpolation is incompatible with optimized BMC. Hence, these algorithms rely on simple BMC engines that significantly hinder their performance. In this paper, we present a Fast Interpolating BMC (FIB) that combines state-of-the-art BMC techniques with interpolation. We show how to interpolate in the presence of circuit-aware simplifications and in the context of incremental solving. We evaluate our implementation of FIB in AVY, an interpolating property directed model checker, and show that it has a great positive effect on the overall performance. With the FIB, AVY outperforms ABC implementation of PDR on both HWMCC'13 and HWMCC'14 benchmarks.

1 Introduction

Bounded Model Checking (BMC) [4,5] has emerged as an efficient bug-finding model checking algorithm. It is based on an exploration of bounded paths in a transition system with respect to a property. The main idea behind it is to *unroll* the transition system up to a given bound k. Unrolling is done by duplicating the transition system k times, attaching the k copies together, and creating a formula, called the *BMC* or the *unrolling* formula, representing all paths of

This material is based upon work funded and supported by the Department of Defense under Contract No. FA8721-05-C-0003 with Carnegie Mellon University for the operation of the Software Engineering Institute, a federally funded research and development center. Any opinions, findings and conclusions or recommendations expressed in this material are those of the author(s) and do not necessarily reflect the views of the United States Department of Defense. This material has been approved for public release and unlimited distribution. DM-0002152.
.

length k. The formula is then constrained by the checked property and is passed to a SAT-solver. If the formula is found to be satisfiable, a counterexample of length k exists. Otherwise, the formula is unsatisfiable, thus no counterexample of length k exists.

State-of-the-art BMC engines are able to find a long counterexample or prove properties up to a large bound. We call such engines *fast*. Their efficiency lies in a variety of optimizations that use advances in SAT-solving, such as incrementality and assumptions [14,15] as well as circuit-aware simplifications [1]. Circuit-aware simplifications, such as SAT-sweeping [21], use high-level structure of the design to simplify the unrolling formula before sending it to the SAT-solver.

While BMC is incomplete, it is the basis of many complete SAT-based model checking algorithms, such as Interpolation-based Model Checking (IMC) [22,27,28], and k-induction, and others (e.g., [23,25]). We focus on the applications of BMC in IMC. IMC engines use a simple, non-optimized, BMC. This is largely due to the complexity of interpolation in the presence of circuit-aware simplifications and incremental SAT. For instance, simplifications destroy the structure of the unrolling formula, making interpolation difficult. Using simple BMC engines significantly hinders the performance of IMC.

In this paper, we present a *Fast Interpolating BMC* (FIB). FIB combines the state-of-the-art circuit-aware simplifications, incremental solving, and interpolation. The key insight is to apply simplifications in a way that enables to reconstruct the interpolants from the simplified formula to interpolants for the original formula. To deal with incremental SAT, we extend clausal proofs [18] and their interpolation [17] to the incremental setting.

To elaborate, let $F = A(X, Y) \wedge B(Y, Z)$ be an unsatisfiable formula. A *Craig interpolant* $I(Y)$ is a formula such that $A(X, Y) \rightarrow I(Y)$ and $I(Y) \wedge B(Y, Z) \rightarrow \perp$. An interpolant is dependent on the structure of F and its partitioning into A and B. A simplification procedure is not aware of the interpolation partitioning of F, and, thus, might destroy it, eliminating the ability to interpolate. For example, consider a case where a simplification procedures finds the variables $y_1, y_2 \in Y$ to be equivalent. The simplified formula is $F' = F[y_2 \leftarrow y_1]$, i.e., y_2 is substituted with y_1. An interpolant $I'(Y)$ with respect to F' it is not necessarily an interpolant with respect to F since I' does not have the information about y_1 being equal to y_2. This equality is a consequence of F, but after substitution, it is implicitly embedded in the simplified formula F', and thus lost.

In FIB, we simplify different partitions of the formula separately, explicitly propagating facts between partitions. This compactly logs the simplification steps. Since FIB takes control from the simplifier by managing the generated consequences, it can then use this information to reconstruct the interpolant $I'(Y)$ of the simplified formula F' to an interpolant that matches F.

Furthermore, since interpolation requires a proof-logging SAT-solver, we develop an incremental SAT-solver that logs proofs [18] incrementally. Unlike a regular incremental SAT-solver, a proof-logging solver must efficiently manage the proof and learned clauses. In the incremental setting, the proof grows with each call to the solver. This dramatically increases the memory requirements of the solver. We, therefore, introduce a heuristic to keep the proof as small as possible while maintaining the benefits of an incrementality.

We evaluate FIB on the benchmarks from the Hardware Model Checking Competitions (HWMCC'13 and '14). We show that the performance of FIB lies between that of a highly optimized (we use &bmc command of ABC [8]) and simple BMC engines. More importantly, to evaluate the impact of FIB in the context of IMC, we have integrated it in AVY [28], an advanced interpolation-based algorithm that was shown to be on-par with PDR. We compare AVY+FIB to AVY and to the implementation of PDR in ABC (pdr command). Our results show that AVY+FIB solves more instances on both HWMCC'13 and HWMCC'14 than either AVY or PDR. Additionally, when comparing run-time, AVY+FIB is the most efficient. Our experiments show the importance of a fast BMC engine in IMC.

We make the following contributions: (1) we show how to combine interpolation and an optimized BMC engine; (2) we implement our technique in a BMC engine called FIB and evaluate its performance and impact in the context of an advanced interpolation-based model checker AVY; and (3) our implementation is publicly available and can be used by others in future research.

Related Work. There is a large body of work on structure-aware formula simplification and the interaction between simplifications and SAT-solvers (e.g., [1,6,13,24]). However, these works do not deal with proofs or interpolation. The closest work that deals with proofs, simplifications, and logic synthesis is [9]. Their goal is to certify correctness of combinatorial equivalence checking (CEC). The key insight is that the proof of simplification steps naturally corresponds to extended resolution [26]. While this procedure can be used to construct an extended resolution proof that tracks both simplifications and SAT-solving, interpolation over extended resolution is difficult. For example, the interpolant is worst-case exponential in the size of the proof [7].

Alternatively, advanced SAT-preprocessing can be used to simulate circuit-aware simplifications directly on CNF [20]. For example, Blocked Clauses Elimination (BCE) [19] simulates Cone-Of-Influence (COI) reduction. Recently, a proof format, called DRAT, that can log such preprocessing efficiently, was introduced in [29]. However, since DRAT simulates extended resolution, interpolation is not trivial and the same problem as in [9] arises. In contrast, our approach uses existing simplification and interpolation procedures and guarantees that the interpolants are linear in the size of resolution proofs involved.

2   Preliminaries

In this section we describe the needed background for the reminder of the paper.

Propositional Satisfiability. Given a set U of Boolean variables, a *literal* ℓ is a variable $u \in U$ or its negation. A *clause* is a disjunction of literals. A propositional formula F in Conjunctive Normal Form (CNF) is a conjunction of clauses. It is often convenient to treat a clause as a set of literals, and a CNF as a set of clauses. For example, given a CNF formula F, a clause c and a literal ℓ, we write

$\ell \in c$ to mean that ℓ occurs in c, and $c \in F$ to mean that c occurs in F. A CNF is *satisfiable* if there exists a *satisfying assignment* such that every clause in it is evaluated to $\top$. Otherwise, it is *unsatisfiable*. A SAT-solver is a complete decision procedure that determines whether a given CNF is *satisfiable*. If the clause set is satisfiable then the SAT solver returns a satisfying assignment for it. Otherwise, if the solver is proof-logging, it produces a proof of unsatisfiability [16,17,23,30]. In this work we use DRUP-proofs [18]. A DRUP-proof π is a sequence of all clauses learned and deleted during the execution of the SAT-solver, in the order in which the learning and deletion happen.

We assume that the reader is familiar with the basic interface of an incremental SAT-solver [14]. We use the following API: (a) $\mathtt{Sat\_Add}(\varphi)$ adds clauses corresponding to the formula φ to the solver; (b) $\mathtt{Sat\_DB}$ is the set of all currently added clauses; (c) $\mathtt{Sat\_Reset}$ resets the solver to the initial state; (d) $\mathtt{To\_Cnf}(F)$ converts a formula F to CNF; (e) $\mathtt{Sat\_Solve}(A)$ returns true if $\mathtt{Sat\_DB}$ is satisfiable; Note that $\mathtt{Sat\_Solve}(A)$ optionally takes a set of literals A, called *assumptions*. If A is not empty, then $\mathtt{Sat\_Solve}(A)$ determines whether A and $\mathtt{Sat\_DB}$ are satisfiable together. We also use $\mathtt{Is\_Sat}(\varphi)$ for deciding whether φ is satisfiable, and $\mathtt{Sat\_Mus}(F)$ for a Minimal Unsatisfiable Subset (MUS) [11] of a CNF F. The MUS is computed relative to the clauses already added to the solver.

Modeling Hardware Circuits. A hardware circuit can be described by a propositional formula where state variables (registers), and primary inputs are represented by Boolean variables V and Z, respectively, and the logical operators correspond to the gates. Let V' be a set of primed Boolean variables representing a successor value of state variables V. For each variable $v \in V$, let $f_v(V, Z)$ be the *next-state function* (NSF) of v. The operation of the circuit is captured by a transition relation $Tr(V, Z, V') \equiv \bigwedge_{v' \in V'} v' = f_v(V, Z)$.

For example, a counter circuit shown in Fig. 1(a) can be modeled by a transition system $Tr(\{v_0, v_1, v_2\}, \emptyset, \{v_0', v_1', v_3'\})$ defined as a conjunction of the following NSFs:

$$v_0' = \neg v_0 \qquad\qquad v_1' = v_0 \neq v_1 \qquad\qquad v_2' = v_2$$

A state s is an assignment to the state variables V. It can be represented as a conjunction of literals that is satisfied in s. More generally, a formula over V represents the set of states that satisfy it. A transition system is a tuple $T = \langle V, Z, Init, Tr, P \rangle$, where the formulas $Init(V)$ and $P(V)$ over V represent the set of initial states and safe states of a circuit, respectively. We call $\neg P(V)$ the set of bad states. For simplicity, we assume that $Init(V) = \bigwedge_{v \in V} \neg v$ and $P(V)$ is a literal. $Tr(V, Z, V')$ is a transition relation associating a state s to its successor state s' under a given assignment of the inputs Z. For simplicity, we often omit the primary inputs Z from the transition relation, and omit V and Z from the signature of the transition system when they are clear from the context. We write V^i is to denote the variables in V after i steps of the transition relation. Thus, $V^0 \equiv V$ and $V^1 \equiv V'$.

Every propositional formula can be represented by a combinational circuit or a graph. One such representation is And Inverted Graph (AIG) [3]. A formula

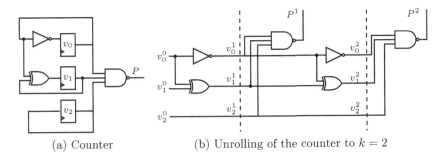

| (a) Counter | (b) Unrolling of the counter to $k = 2$ |

Fig. 1. A counter and its unrolling.

Input: A transition system $T = (Init, Tr, \neg P)$, and a number N
1 **if** Is_Sat($Init \wedge \neg P$) **then return** CEX
2 **for** $k \leftarrow 1$ **to** N **do**
3 | $G^k \leftarrow Init(V^0) \wedge (\bigwedge_{i=0}^{k-1} Tr(V^i, V^{i+1})) \wedge \neg P(V^k)$
4 | **if** Is_Sat(G^k) **then return** CEX
5 **end**
6 **return** No CEX of length $\leq N$

Fig. 2. A Simple BMC.

$\varphi(X)$ over a set of variables X corresponds to a circuit with a set of inputs X, internal nodes corresponding to logical operators, and an output O_φ that is set to 1 for all assignments to the input X that satisfy φ. Note that a circuit with multiple outputs represents multiple, independent, propositional formulas – one per output.

Bounded Model Checking. A transition system T is *unsafe* iff there exists a path from the initial state in $Init$ to a bad state in $\neg P$ that satisfies the transition relation. This path is called a *counterexample*. T is unsafe iff there exists a number k such that the following *k-unrolling* formula is satisfiable:

$$Init(V^0) \wedge \left(\bigwedge_{i=0}^{k-1} Tr(V^i, V^{i+1}) \right) \wedge \neg P(V^k) \qquad (1)$$

It is useful to view (1) as a combinatorial circuit with inputs V^0 and a single output representing the value of $\neg P(V^k)$. For example, a circuit corresponding to two unrollings of the counter in Fig. 1(a) is shown in Fig. 1(b). Each step of the unrolling (indicated by dashed lines in the figure) is called a *frame*.

SAT-based Bounded Model Checking (BMC) [5] determines whether a transition system is unsafe by deciding satisfiability of the unrolling formula (1) for increasing values of k. A simple BMC algorithm in shown in Fig. 2.

In practice, fast state-of-the-art BMC implementations combine the simple reduction of BMC to SAT with circuit-aware simplifications of the unrolling

Input: A transition system $T = (Init, Tr, \neg P)$, a number N

1 **if** Is_Sat$(Init \wedge \neg P)$ **then return** CEX

2 $G \leftarrow Init(V^0) \wedge \left(\bigwedge_{i=0}^{N} Tr(V^i, V^{i+1}) \right)$

3 $(G', E) \leftarrow$ Simplify$(G, \emptyset)$

4 **for** $k \leftarrow 1$ **to** N **do**

5   CONE $\leftarrow$ Get_Coi$(G', \neg P(V^k))$

6   Sat_Add(CONE)

7   **if** Sat_Solve$(\{\neg P(V^k)\})$ **then return** CEX

8 **end**

9 **return** *No CEX of length* $\leq N$

Fig. 3. Fast BMC.

formula. Furthermore, they use an incremental SAT interface to share learned clauses between checks for different values of k. To give a general account of circuit aware simplifications, we abstract them using a function

$$G'(X, Y), E'(Y) = \texttt{Simplify}(G(X, Y), E(X)) \tag{2}$$

that takes a formula $G(X, Y)$ and a set of input constraints E over X and returns a simplified formula $G'(X, Y)$ and a set of output constraints $E'(Y)$ such that:

$$E(X) \rightarrow (G'(X, Y) \equiv G(X, Y)) \qquad (E(X) \wedge G(X, Y)) \rightarrow E'(Y) \tag{3}$$

The form of admissible constraints in E depends on the simplification. For example, *constant propagation (CP)* or *ternary simulation* requires that $E(X)$ is of the form $\bigwedge_i x_i = c_i$, where $x_i \in X$ and $c_i \in \{0, 1\}$. The output constraints $E'(Y)$ for CP are also of the same form. Another, more general simplification, is *SAT-sweeping* [21] which, restricts the constraints to be equalities between inputs. For our purposes, the inner workings of the simplifications are not important, and we refer an interested reader to ample literature on this subject.

A pseudo-code of a fast BMC is shown in Fig. 3. Unlike simple BMC (Fig. 2), it first constructs a complete unrolling (line 2), then applies circuit-aware simplifications (line 3), and enters the main loop. In each iteration of the loop, it uses a function Get_Coi to find the *cone-of-influence* of the output at depth k (line 5), adds the clauses corresponding to the cone to the solver (line 6, and checks whether the current set of clauses is unsatisfiable together with assumption $\neg P(V^k)$ (line 7). For simplicity, we assume that conversion to CNF is deterministic and that Sat_Add silently ignores clauses that are already known to the solver. A fast BMC is significantly faster than simple BMC and can get much deeper into the circuit.

Craig interpolation. Given a pair of inconsistent formulas (A, B) (i.e., $A \wedge B \models \bot$), a *Craig interpolant* [10] for (A, B) is a formula I such that:

$$A \rightarrow I \qquad\qquad I \rightarrow \neg B \qquad\qquad \mathcal{L}(I) \subseteq \mathcal{L}(A) \cap \mathcal{L}(B) \tag{4}$$

where $\mathcal{L}(A)$ denotes the set of all variables in A. A *sequence (or path) interpolant* extends interpolation to a sequence of formulas. We write $\boldsymbol{F} = [F_1, \ldots, F_N]$ to denote a sequence with N elements, and F_i for the ith element of the sequence. Given an unsatisfiable sequence of formulas $\boldsymbol{A} = [A_1, \ldots, A_N]$, (i.e., $A_1 \wedge \cdots \wedge A_N \models \bot$) a *sequence interpolant* $\boldsymbol{I} = \text{SEQITP}(\boldsymbol{A})$ for $\boldsymbol{A}$ is a sequence of formulas $\boldsymbol{I} = [I_1, \ldots, I_{N-1}]$ such that:

$$A_1 \to I_1 \qquad \forall 1 < i < N \cdot I_{i-1} \wedge A_i \to I_i \qquad I_{N-1} \wedge A_N \to \bot \qquad (5)$$

and for all $1 \leq i \leq N$, $\mathcal{L}(I_i) \subseteq \mathcal{L}(A_1 \wedge \cdots \wedge A_i) \cap \mathcal{L}(A_{i+1} \wedge \cdots \wedge A_N)$.

3 Simplification-Aware Interpolation

We begin with an illustration of the difficulties of interpolation in the presence of circuit-aware simplifications. Consider the counter circuit and its unrolling G shown in Fig. 1. Recall, initially all registers are zero. Assume that we want an interpolant between the first and second frames G_0 and G_1, respectively, where $G = G_0 \wedge G_1$, under the assumption $\neg P^2 = \neg(v_0^2 \wedge v_1^2 \wedge v_2^2)$. Simplifying G using constant propagation, which replaces outputs of gates with constants based on the values of its inputs, reduces it to $v_0^2 = 0 \wedge v_1^2 = 1 \wedge v_2^2 = 0$ that is trivially unsatisfiable together with $\neg P^2$. However, the simplification destroys the partitioning structure of G, making interpolation meaningless. Alternatively, assume that the simplification does not eliminate intermediate values of the registers. Then, the simplification might reduce G to $G' = G_0' \wedge G_1'$, where

$$G_0' \equiv v_0^1 = 1 \wedge v_1^1 = 0 \wedge v_2^1 = 0 \qquad G_1' \equiv v_0^2 = 0 \wedge v_1^2 = 1 \wedge v_2^2 = 0$$

While the partitioning structure is preserved, not every interpolant of $(G_0', G_1' \wedge \neg P^2)$ is an interpolant of $(G_0, G_1 \wedge \neg P^2)$. For example, $\top$ is an interpolant in the first case, but not in the second. Such problems are even more severe for more complicated simplifications such as SAT-sweeping, in which case additionally variables that are local to a partition before the simplification might become shared between partitions after.

The source of the problems is that the reasoning done by the simplification is hidden from the interpolation procedure. One way to expose it is to use proof-logging simplifications. Let G be a circuit, and G' a simplified version of G such that $G \to G'$ and $G' \to \bot$. Then, there exists a resolution proof π_1 of $G \to G'$ and a resolution proof π_2 of $G' \to \bot$. If we require a simplification to produce π_1 while constructing G', and require a SAT-solver to produce π_2 while deciding satisfiability of G', then, we can construct a complete resolution proof $\pi = \pi_1 ; \pi_2$ of $G \to \bot$ and apply interpolation to π. In fact, this approach is used in [17] for interpolation in the presence of SAT pre-processing [12].

While there are suggestions in literature (e.g., [9]) on how to extract resolution proofs out of circuit-aware simplifications, this is non-trivial. It requires significant changes to existing simplifiers, and is particularly difficult for simplifications that are done as a by-product of using efficient data-structures such

Input: $G = G_0 \wedge G_1 \wedge \cdots \wedge G_k$
1 Initialize $\langle E_0 \leftarrow \emptyset, \ldots, E_{k+1} \leftarrow \emptyset \rangle$
2 **for** $i \leftarrow 0$ **to** k **do**
3 $\quad | \quad (G'_i, E_{i+1}) \leftarrow \texttt{Simplify}(G_i, E_i)$
4 **end**
5 **return** $(G'_0 \wedge \cdots \wedge G'_k, \langle E_1, \cdots, E_{k+1} \rangle)$

Fig. 4. Localized simplification ($\texttt{Loc\_Simp}(G)$).

as AIGs and BDDs. Furthermore, as shown in [9], circuit-aware simplifications correspond naturally to extended resolution proofs. However, interpolation over extended resolution is difficult, and the interpolants are worst-case exponential in the size of the proof. Furthermore, the proof logging is likely to incur a non-trivial overhead and is likely to be much more detailed than necessary for interpolation in our target applications.

In this section, we suggest an alternative light-weight approach. Instead of applying the simplifications to the complete unrolling, we apply them to each individual frame (or partition), and propagate constraints between frames. Instead of requiring simplifications to be proof-logging, we log the constraints that are exchanged. In our setting, simplifications preserve the partitioning of the original formula. We show how to use the logged constraints to reconstruct a sequence interpolant of the simplified formula to a sequence interpolant of the original formula. Finally, we propose a minimization algorithm to ensure that the final interpolant does not contain redundant constraints.

Constraint-Logging Simplifications. Let $G = G_0(V^0, V^1) \wedge \cdots \wedge G_k(V^k, V^{k+1})$ be a formula divided into k partitions. Note that variables are shared between two adjacent partitions only. Our constraint-logging simplification algorithm $\texttt{Loc\_Simp}$ is shown in Fig. 4. It processes the formula G left-to-right. In each step, it simplifies G_i using constraints E_i of the prefix, and generates new consequences E_{i+1} to be used by the next step. For example, if G is an unrolling formula, then E_i is a set of consequences that are implied by the states reachable in $(i+1)$ states from the initial state. Note that in this case, the initial state is embedded in G_0.

Let $G' = G'_0 \wedge \cdots \wedge G'_k$ be a formula obtained by $\texttt{Loc\_Simp}(G)$ and $E_1, \ldots, E_{k+1}$ be the corresponding trail of constraints. Assume that G' is unsatisfiable, and let $I = \langle I_1, \ldots, I_k \rangle$ be a sequence interpolant of G'. Recall that I is an interpolant w.r.t. the simplified formula G' and, therefore, may not be an interpolant w.r.t. the original formula G. The reason is that some of the consequences that were generated by the simplification are present implicitly in the simplified formula and, thus, are missing from the interpolant. This requires a post-processing step that adds the missing information to the sequence-interpolant.

Theorem 1. Let $G = G_0(V^0, V^1) \wedge \cdots \wedge G_k(V^k, V^{k+1})$ be a formula partitioned into k parts, and let $(G' = G'_0 \wedge \cdots \wedge G'_k, \langle E_1, \ldots, E_{k+1} \rangle)$ be the result of

Loc_Simp(G). *If G' is unsatisfiable and $\langle I'_1, \ldots, I'_k \rangle$ is a sequence-interpolant of G' then*

- *G is unsatisfiable, and*
- *$\langle I'_1 \wedge E_1, \ldots, I'_k \wedge E_k \rangle$ is a sequence-interpolant of G.*

Proof. Since $\langle I'_1, \ldots, I'_k \rangle$ is a sequence-interpolant of G' we know that:

$$G'_0 \rightarrow I'_1 \qquad \forall 1 \leq i < k \cdot (I'_i \wedge G'_i) \rightarrow I'_{i+1} \qquad I'_k \wedge G'_k \rightarrow \bot \qquad (6)$$

By construction, the trail $\langle E_0, \ldots, E_{k+1} \rangle$ satisfies:

$$G_0 \rightarrow E_1 \qquad \forall 1 \leq i \leq k \cdot (E_i \wedge G_i) \rightarrow E_{i+1} \qquad (7)$$

Finally, by the properties of Simplify, we have:

$$G_0 \rightarrow G'_0 \qquad \forall 1 \leq i < k \cdot (E_i \wedge G_i) \rightarrow G'_i \qquad (8)$$

Combining the above together, we get:

$$G_0 \rightarrow I'_1 \wedge E_1 \quad \forall 1 \leq i < k \cdot (I'_i \wedge E_i \wedge G_i) \rightarrow (I'_{i+1} \wedge E_{i+1}) \quad I'_k \wedge E_k \wedge G'_k \rightarrow \bot \qquad (9)$$

Theorem 1 gives a simple way to reconstruct a sequence-interpolant of the simplified formula to the original formula. However, the resulting interpolant is likely not to be minimal. Each E_i may contain many constraints that are not necessary for the validity of the sequence-interpolant. Thus, we propose an algorithm to minimize sequence interpolants. First, we formally define what we mean by *minimality*.

Definition 1. *Let $\bar{I} = \langle I_1, \ldots, I_k \rangle$ be a sequence-interpolant where each element I_i is a conjunction (or a set) of constraints. The sequence $\bar{I}$ is minimal if any other sequence obtained by removing at least one constraint from any of the I_i is not a sequence-interpolant.*

Our algorithm, Min_Itp, is shown in Fig. 5. It takes a partitioned formula G and a sequence interpolant $\boldsymbol{I}$ as input, and returns a minimal sequence interpolant $\boldsymbol{I}'$. It applies an iterative backward search for the necessary constraints from I_k to I_1. In each iteration, it computes the needed constraints $I'_i \subseteq I_i$ that ensures that $I'_i \wedge G_i \rightarrow I'_{i+1}$. This is accomplished by asserting $G_i \wedge \neg I'_{i+1}$ and computing an MUS of I_i relative to those background constraints. The soundness of Min_Itp follows from the loop invariant described above. The minimality follows from the minimality of the MUS computation.

Lemma 1. *Let $G = G_0(V^0, V^1) \wedge \cdots \wedge G_k(V^k, V^{k+1})$ be an unsatisfiable formula partitioned into k parts, and $\boldsymbol{I}$ be its sequence interpolant. Then, $\boldsymbol{I}' = $ Min_Itp$(G, \boldsymbol{I})$ is a minimal sequence interpolant for G.*

Input: $G = G_0 \wedge \cdots \wedge G_k$, $\boldsymbol{I} = \langle I_1, \ldots, I_k \rangle$
1   $I_{k+1} = \bot$
2   **for** $i \leftarrow k$ **to** 1 **do**
3 | Sat_Reset()
4 | Sat_Add($\neg I_{i+1}$)
5 | Sat_Add(G_i)
6 | $I_i' = $ Sat_Mus(I_i)
7   **end**
8   **return** $\langle I_1', \ldots, I_k' \rangle$

Fig. 5. Minimal sequence-interpolant Min_Itp($\mathsf{G}, \boldsymbol{I}$).

Recall that in the traditional interpolation techniques the size of the interpolant is linear in the size of the resolution proof. In the presence of the simplifications, the size of the interpolant is linear in the size of the resolution proof of the *simplified* formula and the number of constraints introduced by the simplification, whichever is greater. Let $F = A(X, Y) \wedge B(Y, Z)$ be an unsatisfiable formula and $F' = A'(X, Y) \wedge B'(Y, Z)$ be a simplified formula, where $(A', E) = \mathtt{Simplify}(A, \emptyset)$, and $B' = \mathtt{Simplify}(B, E)$. An interpolant I', computed with respect to F', is linear in the size of the resolution proof for F'. Let the size of E be bounded by $\psi(A)$ (i.e. $|E| \leq \psi(A)$), and let $I = I' \wedge E$ be the interpolant constructed by our method. Since I is generated by adding constraints from E to I', its size is bounded by $\max\{|I'|, \psi(A)\}$. Interestingly, for common simplifications like CP and SAT-sweeping, $\psi(A) = |Y|$, it can only generate as many consequences as the number of interface variables. Thus, in this case the size of interpolant is bounded by the number of shared variables or the size of the simplified proof, whichever is greater.

Fast Interpolating BMC. Using the machinery of simplification-aware interpolation, we now present our fast interpolating BMC (FIB) algorithm. The pseudocode of FIB is shown in Fig. 6. Structurally, it is similar to the fast BMC shown in Fig. 3. The first difference is that the unrolling formula G is partitioned into frames G_i. Second, instead of simplifying the unrolling, we use Loc_Simp to simplify each frame and collect the trail of side-constraints. Then, in each iteration of the main loop, the cone of influence of the current $\neg P(V^k)$ is computed and added to the SAT-solver. If the result is UNSAT, FIB computes an interpolant of the current simplified k-unrolling, extends it with the side-conditions, and minimizes using Min_Itp. The result is made available to the user using a call to yield. Thus, in addition to detecting counterexamples, FIB computes a trail of sequence interpolants. One sequence for each safe bound.

Note that we assume that it is possible to compute interpolants (see the call to $ttSat\_Itp$) in an incremental SAT-solver. That is, we expect interpolants to be available after the SAT-solver is called with assumptions, and during repeated calls to Sat_Solve with new clauses added in between. While in theory supporting interpolation in an incremental SAT-solver is straight-forward, it is difficult to do efficiently in practice. We address this issue in the next section.

Input: $T = (Init, Tr, P)$, a number $N \geq 0$
1 **if** Is_Sat($Init \wedge \neg P$) **then return** CEX
2 **else yield** $\langle P \rangle$
3 $G_0 \leftarrow Init(V^0) \wedge Tr(V^0, V^1)$
4 **for** $i \leftarrow 1$ **to** $N - 1$ **do** $G_i \leftarrow Tr(V^i, V^{i+1})$
5 $(G', \langle E_1, \ldots, E_N \rangle) = $ Loc_Simp($G_0 \wedge \cdots \wedge G_{N-1}$)
6 **for** $k \leftarrow 1$ **to** N **do**
7   CONE $\leftarrow$ Get_Coi($G', \neg P(V^k)$)
8   Sat_Add(CONE)
9   **if** Sat_Solve($\neg P(V^k)$) **then return** CEX
10      $\langle I'_1, \ldots, I'_k \rangle \leftarrow$ Sat_Itp(k)
11      $\langle I_1, \ldots, I_k \rangle \leftarrow \langle I'_1 \wedge E_1, \ldots, I'_k \wedge E_k \rangle$
12   **yield** Min_Itp($G, \langle I_1, \ldots, I_k \rangle$)
13 **end**
14 **return** *No CEX of length* $\leq N$

Fig. 6. Fast Interpolating BMC (FIB).

4 Interpolating Incremental SAT Solver

In this section, we describe our implementation of an interpolating incremental solver that supports both an incremental addition of clauses and solving with assumptions. The keys to our approach are DRUP [18] and DRUP-interpolation [17].

DRUP proofs were introduced in [18] in the context of SAT-solver certification. Since we use them for interpolation, we begin by reviewing DRUP-proofs and interpolation as they appear in [17]. Let F be an unsatisfiable propositional formula in CNF. A DRUP-proof π is a sequence of all clauses learned and deleted during the execution of the SAT-solver, in the order in which the learning and deletion happen. Meaning, the first clause in π is the first learned clause, and the last clause is the empty clause. Let $\pi = \langle c_0, \ldots, c_n \rangle$ be a DRUP-proof, then a non-deleted clause c_i is derivable by *trivial resolution* [2] from F and from all non-deleted clauses c_j for $0 \leq j < i$. The interpolation procedure in [17] labels each clause in $c_i \in \pi$ with a sequence of propositional formulæ $\bar{I}(c_i)$, where the label of the last clause, i.e. $\bar{I}(c_n)$, is the sequence-interpolant.

FIB uses the SAT-solver incrementally in two ways: (1) the solver is called with assumptions, and (2) new clauses are added. The two steps are iterated repeatedly. Because of multiple calls, the learned clauses that are currently part of the SAT-solver's database are being used in a consecutive calls to the solver.

We first address the problem of interpolation under assumptions. In the presence of assumptions, the final learned clause produced by the solver, provided that the instance is unsatisfiable, is not the empty clause, but a clause containing negated assumption literals. We claim that whenever the assumptions are local to each interpolation-partition the formula that marks the final clause is the sequence-interpolant.

Proposition 1. *Let* $F = F_1(X_1, Y_1, X_2) \wedge \cdots \wedge F_k(X_k, Y_k, X_{k+1})$ *be a propositional formula in CNF. Assume that* F *is unsatisfiable under assumptions* $\{a_1, \ldots, a_k\}$. *Let* $\pi = \{c_0, \ldots, c_n\}$ *be a corresponding DRUP-proof. If for all* $1 \leq i \leq k$, $a_i \in Y_i$, *then a* $\bar{I}(c_n)$ *is a sequence-interpolant of* $\bigwedge_{i=1}^{k}(F_i \wedge a_i)$.

Incremental addition of new clauses and multiple calls to Sat_Solve create new challenges to a proof-logging SAT solver. First, the solver must ensure that the DRUP-proof remains *consistent*. More precisely, every learned clause in a DRUP-proof must be derivable by *trivial resolution* [2] using original clauses and learned clauses that were part of Sat_DB when it was learned. This is tricky in an incremental setting because original clauses might be added after learned clauses. For example, assume that initially Sat_DB contained the set of original clauses F_1 and after some time the DRUP-proof is a sequence of two clauses (c_1, c_2). Then, by the DRUP property, c_2 follows from $F_1 \wedge c_1$ by trivial resolution. Next, assume that additional original clauses F_2 were added to the solver via Sat_Add. After some time, the DRUP-proof might be (c_1, c_2, c_3). At this point, the fact that c_2 is derivable only from F_1 and c_1 is lost. This makes it difficult to reconstruct (or even approximate) the original resolution proof produced by the SAT-solver to derive c_2. While this might be an issue if the goal is to validate the solver, it is not in our case. The database of clauses Sat_DB is growing monotonically. Thus, if a clause was derivable by a trivial resolution at one point, it remains derivable if new clauses are added to the database. Hence, in our implementation, we disregard the order in which the original clauses are added to the database. Thus, the proof that is found during interpolation might be significantly different from the original proof used implicitly by the SAT-solver.

Another challenge is memory requirement. In an incremental solver, learned clauses are re-used between the calls to Sat_Solve and the number of learned clauses grows monotonically. This is not an issue for non-interpolating solvers since they prune learned clauses even in a non-incremental mode. However, an interpolating solver that logs the DRUP-proof must keep all clauses ever learned in memory because even though a clause is deleted at one time, it might have participated in the proof at prior time. To address this, we use the following heuristic. Recall that DRUP-interpolation first finds the core clauses and then traverses them, rebuilding the proof and generating the interpolant. We change it to also mark as core the unit clauses that are on the trail during the last conflict. The intuition is that units are very strong consequences and are likely to be useful in other Sat_Solve calls. Finally, between every call to Sat_Solve, we prune the DRUP proof and the learned clauses from all non-core clauses. Thus, the only learned clauses that remain between Sat_Solve calls are clauses that appear in the last resolution proof, units on the trail, and clauses that are necessary to derive the units from Sat_DB.

5 Experiments

We have implemented FIB inside our model checking framework AVY[1]. We evaluate our implementation of FIB in two ways. First, we evaluate FIB as a

---

[1] Source code is available at: https://bitbucket.org/arieg/extavy.

BMC engine by comparing it with both a simple BMC and a fast BMC (&bmc) of ABC [8]. Second, we integrate FIB in AVY, an Interpolation-based Model Checker, and show the impact it has on performance, both in run-time and the number of solved instances. We use all of HWMCC'13 and '14 benchmarks, an Intel Xeon 2.4GHz processor with 128GB of memory, and a timeout of 900 s.

BMC Evaluation. We compare FIB to a simple BMC implementation, and then to a fast BMC of ABC. We expect FIB to perform in between the fast and simple BMCs. Figure 7 shows a comparison of runtime when running all the different BMC algorithms until depth 40 on the benchmarks in which at least one tool ran to completion. That is, at least one tool either finds a counterexample or proves no counterexamples of depth up to 40. As expected, FIB is more efficient than a simple BMC on most cases and ABC BMC is more efficient than FIB. Some of the difference are due to the way simplification is applied in FIB. We believe that with a more careful implementation this gap can be closed.

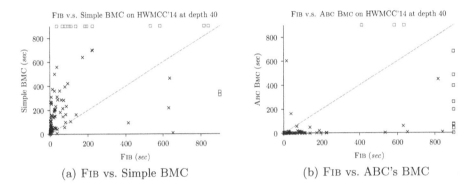

(a) FIB vs. Simple BMC   (b) FIB vs. ABC's BMC

Fig. 7. Runtime comparison between FIB, ABC's BMC (&bmc) and Simple BMC. Points above the line are in favor of FIB. Square represents a timeout.

Figure 8 shows a comparison of the depth reached during an execution of the algorithms for bound 40 in the presence of a predefined time limit. Clearly, FIB reaches deeper bounds compared to the simple BMC engine. Compared to ABC BMC, FIB is mostly on par with a few cases in favor of ABC. Note that the problem is exponential in the depth, so even a small increase is significant.

On a few test cases, we have noticed that FIB performs worse than a simple BMC engine. Analyzing those cases revealed that sometime the simplified formula, even though having less clauses and less variables, is harder for the SAT-solver. While this is not a common case, it may happen. Our intuition is that this is most likely due to the solver spending more time in a harder part of the search space.

Model Checking Evaluation. For these sets of experiments, we have integrated FIB in AVY and called it AVY+FIB. We compared AVY+FIB with the original

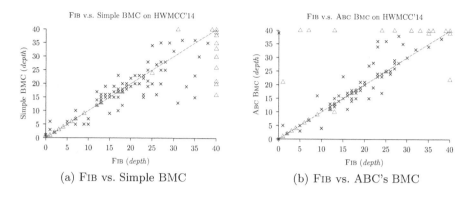

(a) FIB vs. Simple BMC   (b) FIB vs. ABC's BMC

Fig. 8. Depth comparison between FIB, ABC's BMC and Simple BMC. Triangles are cases solved to completion by at least one tool. Points below the line are in favor of FIB. Triangle represents timeout.

Table 1. Summary of solved instances on HWMCC'13 and HWMCC'14.

Benchmark	Status	AVY+FIB	AVY	PDR	VBS(AVY+FIB)	VBS(AVY)
HWMCC'13	SAFE	**67**	66	50	**76**	74
	UNSAFE	**19**	19	16	**22**	**22**
	Runtime (s)	**151,302**	156,806	167,302	–	–
HWMCC'14	SAFE	**60**	56	49	**64**	60
	UNSAFE	**28**	24	20	**31**	30
	Runtime (s)	**126,293**	139,336	150,586	–	–

AVY and with ABC implementation of PDR (pdr). Table 1 summarizes the number of solved instances by each algorithm and total runtime on the entire benchmark. AVY+FIB solves the most cases in both HWMCC'13 and HWMCC'14. On HWMCC'13 it solves 5 more cases than AVY and 32 more cases than PDR, and it cannot solve 4 cases solved by AVY and 12 cases solved by PDR. On HWMCC'14 it solves 8 more than AVY and 26 more than PDR, and it cannot solve 1 case solved by AVY and 7 cases solved by PDR.

Table 1 also shows two *Virtual Best* (VBS) results. The first corresponds to combining AVY+FIB and PDR, the second to combining AVY and PDR. As expected, the addition of AVY+FIB to PDR is the better option.

As we describe in Sect. 3, during the computation of an interpolant, the set of constraints generated by the simplifier is minimized. We measured the time minimization takes. The median value are 5.6 s and 4.78 s for HWMCC'13 and '14, respectively. This shows that in most cases this process is efficient.

Even though AVY+FIB uses a faster BMC engine than AVY, there are still cases solved by AVY and not by AVY+FIB. Analyzing those showed that sometimes simplification creates "noise" and forces a proof that is very dependent on the initial state. Since FIB propagates the initial values as far as it can, it might also increase the convergence bound of AVY. This behavior may hurt

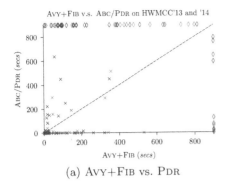

(a) AVY+FIB vs. PDR

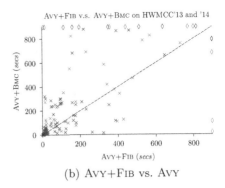

(b) AVY+FIB vs. AVY

Fig. 9. Runtime comparison of AVY+FIB, AVY+BMC and PDR on HWMCC'13 (green) and HWMCC'14 (blue) benchmarks. Rhombus represents a timeout.

performance, yet we rarely observe it in practice. Moreover, in some cases, even when the convergence bound is increased, AVY+FIB is still faster than AVY.

Considering total runtime, AVY+FIB is more efficient than both AVY and PDR. Figure 9 shows run-time comparison per test case for each HWMCC'13 and '14. Analyzing individual runtimes shows that AVY+FIB (just like AVY) is very different from PDR. Each of them performs better than the other on a different class of benchmarks. This is evident in Fig. 9(a) where most of the points are on the extremes (axis) of the plots. Figure 9(b) shows that AVY+FIB is more efficient than AVY on most of the benchmarks. We also analyzed the median value w.r.t. runtime on solved instances. AVY's median values on HWMCC'13 and '14 are 94.2 and 35.9, respectively. While for AVY+FIB, the values are 53.4 and 23.4 respectively.

6   Discussion and Conclusions

The paper presents a novel method for interpolation over BMC formulas when circuit-aware simplifications are applied. Our approach is based on the observation that for the purpose of interpolation, only the consequences generated by the simplifier need to be logged. These consequences can then be used to reconstruct an interpolant w.r.t. to the original formula from an interpolant computed w.r.t. the simplified formula. This approach is simpler than trying to reconstruct the proof itself.

We implemented our approach in an engine called FIB and evaluated its impact on model checking by incorporating it into AVY. The experimental results show that FIB improves the performance of AVY significantly.

FIB puts some restrictions on the way the simplifier operates. This can be seen in the gap between FIB and ABC's BMC engine. We believe that most of these restrictions can be removed and that interpolation is possible even when using an unrestricted simplifier. Enabling this may further close the gap between FIB and state-of-the-art BMC engines. We leave this challenge for future research.

References

1. Amla, N., Du, X., Kuehlmann, A., Kurshan, R.P., McMillan, K.L.: An analysis of SAT-Based model checking techniques in an industrial environment. In: Borrione, D., Paul, W. (eds.) CHARME 2005. LNCS, vol. 3725, pp. 254–268. Springer, Heidelberg (2005)
2. Beame, P., Kautz, H.A., Sabharwal, A.: Towards understanding and harnessing the potential of clause learning. J. Artif. Intell. Res. (JAIR) **22**, 319–351 (2004)
3. Biere, A.: Aiger: (AIGER is a format, library and set of utilities for And-Inverter Graphs (AIGs)). http://fmv.jku.at/aiger/
4. Biere, A., Cimatti, A., Clarke, E.M., Strichman, O., Zhu, Y.: Bounded model checking. Adv. Comput. **58**, 117–148 (2003)
5. Biere, A., Cimatti, A., Clarke, E., Zhu, Y.: Symbolic model checking without BDDs. In: Cleaveland, W.R. (ed.) TACAS 1999. LNCS, vol. 1579, pp. 193–207. Springer, Heidelberg (1999)
6. Bjesse, P., Borälv, A.: Dag-aware circuit compression for formal verification. In: 2004 International Conference on Computer-Aided Design (ICCAD 2004), 7–11 November 2004, San Jose, CA, USA, pp. 42–49 (2004)
7. Bonet, M.L., Pitassi, T., Raz, R.: No feasible interpolation for TC0-frege proofs. In: 38th Annual Symposium on Foundations of Computer Science, FOCS 1997, Miami Beach, Florida, USA, 19–22 October 1997, pp. 254–263. IEEE Computer Society (1997)
8. Brayton, R., Mishchenko, A.: ABC: an academic industrial-strength verification tool. In: Touili, T., Cook, B., Jackson, P. (eds.) CAV 2010. LNCS, vol. 6174, pp. 24–40. Springer, Heidelberg (2010)
9. Chatterjee, S., Mishchenko, A., Brayton, R.K., Kuehlmann, A.: On resolution proofs for combinational equivalence. In: Proceedings of the 44th Design Automation Conference, DAC 2007, San Diego, CA, USA, 4–8 June 2007, pp. 600–605 (2007)
10. Craig, W.: Linear reasoning. a new form of the Herbrand-Gentzen theorem. J. Symb. Log. **22**(3), 250–268 (1957)
11. Dershowitz, N., Hanna, Z., Nadel, A.: A scalable algorithm for minimal unsatisfiable core extraction. In: Biere, A., Gomes, C.P. (eds.) SAT 2006. LNCS, vol. 4121, pp. 36–41. Springer, Heidelberg (2006)
12. Eén, N., Biere, A.: Effective preprocessing in SAT through variable and clause elimination. In: Bacchus, F., Walsh, T. (eds.) SAT 2005. LNCS, vol. 3569, pp. 61–75. Springer, Heidelberg (2005)
13. Eén, N., Mishchenko, A., Sörensson, N.: Applying logic synthesis for speeding up SAT. In: Marques-Silva, J., Sakallah, K.A. (eds.) SAT 2007. LNCS, vol. 4501, pp. 272–286. Springer, Heidelberg (2007)
14. Eén, N., Sörensson, N.: An extensible SAT-solver. In: Giunchiglia, E., Tacchella, A. (eds.) SAT 2003. LNCS, vol. 2919, pp. 502–518. Springer, Heidelberg (2004)
15. Eén, N., Sörensson, N.: Temporal induction by incremental SAT solving. Electr. Notes Theor. Comput. Sci. **89**(4), 543–560 (2003)
16. Goldberg, E.I., Novikov, Y.: Verification of proofs of unsatisfiability for CNF formulas. In: DATE, pp. 10886–10891 (2003)
17. Gurfinkel, A., Vizel, Y.: Druping for interpolants. In: Formal Methods in Computer-Aided Design, FMCAD 2014, Lausanne, Switzerland, 21–24 October 2014, pp. 99–106 (2014)

18. Heule, M., Hunt Jr., W.A., Wetzler, N.: Trimming while checking clausal proofs. In: FMCAD, pp. 181–188 (2013)
19. Järvisalo, M., Biere, A., Heule, M.: Blocked clause elimination. In: Esparza, J., Majumdar, R. (eds.) TACAS 2010. LNCS, vol. 6015, pp. 129–144. Springer, Heidelberg (2010)
20. Järvisalo, M., Biere, A., Heule, M.: Simulating circuit-level simplifications on CNF. J. Autom. Reasoning **49**(4), 583–619 (2012)
21. Kuehlmann, A.: Dynamic transition relation simplification for bounded property checking. In: 2004 International Conference on Computer-Aided Design (ICCAD 2004), 7–11 November 2004, San Jose, CA, USA, pp. 50–57 (2004)
22. McMillan, K.L.: Interpolation and SAT-Based model checking. In: Hunt Jr., W.A., Somenzi, F. (eds.) CAV 2003. LNCS, vol. 2725, pp. 1–13. Springer, Heidelberg (2003)
23. McMillan, K.L., Amla, N.: Automatic abstraction without counterexamples. In: Tools and Algorithms for the Construction and Analysis of Systems, Proceedings of 9th International Conference, TACAS 2003, Held as Part of the Joint European Conferences on Theory and Practice of Software, ETAPS 2003, Warsaw, Poland, 7–11 April 2003, pp. 2–17 (2003)
24. Mishchenko, A., Chatterjee, S., Brayton,R.K.: Dag-aware AIG rewriting a fresh look at combinational logic synthesis. In: Proceedings of the 43rd Design Automation Conference, DAC 2006, San Francisco, CA, USA, 24–28 July 2006, pp. 532–535 (2006)
25. Sheeran, M., Singh, S., Stålmarck, G.: Checking safety properties using induction and a SAT-solver. In: Johnson, S.D., Hunt Jr., W.A. (eds.) FMCAD 2000. LNCS, vol. 1954, pp. 108–125. Springer, Heidelberg (2000)
26. Tseitin, G.S.: On the complexity of derivations in the propositional calculus. Stud. Math. Math. Logic **Part II**, 115–125 (1968)
27. Vizel, Y., Grumberg, O.: Interpolation-sequence based model checking. In: FMCAD, pp. 1–8 (2009)
28. Vizel, Y., Gurfinkel, A.: Interpolating property directed reachability. In: Biere, A., Bloem, R. (eds.) CAV 2014. LNCS, vol. 8559, pp. 260–276. Springer, Heidelberg (2014)
29. Wetzler, N., Heule, M.J.H., Hunt Jr., W.A.: DRAT-trim: efficient checking and trimming using expressive clausal proofs. In: Sinz, C., Egly, U. (eds.) SAT 2014. LNCS, vol. 8561, pp. 422–429. Springer, Heidelberg (2014)
30. Zhang, L., Malik, S.: Extracting small unsatisfiable cores from unsatisfiable Boolean formula. In: SAT (2003)

Counterexample-Guided Polynomial Loop Invariant Generation by Lagrange Interpolation

Yu-Fang Chen[1]([✉]), Chih-Duo Hong[1], Bow-Yaw Wang[1], and Lijun Zhang[2]

[1] Institute of Information Science, Academia Sinica, Taipei, Taiwan
yfc@iis.sinica.edu.tw
[2] State Key Laboratory of Computer Science, Institute of Software,
CAS, Beijing, China

Abstract. We apply multivariate Lagrange interpolation to synthesizing polynomial quantitative loop invariants for probabilistic programs. We reduce the computation of a quantitative loop invariant to solving constraints over program variables and unknown coefficients. Lagrange interpolation allows us to find constraints with less unknown coefficients. Counterexample-guided refinement furthermore generates linear constraints that pinpoint the desired quantitative invariants. We evaluate our technique by several case studies with polynomial quantitative loop invariants in the experiments.

1 Introduction

A probabilistic program may change its computation due to probabilistic choices. Consider, for instance, the Miller-Rabin algorithm for primality test [27]. Given a composite number, the algorithm reports incorrectly with probability at most 0.25. Since the outcome of the algorithm is not always correct, classical program correctness specifications [9,14,20] do not apply. For probabilistic programs, quantitative specifications are needed to reason about program correctness [8,23,24]. Instead of logic formulae, probabilistic programs are specified by numerical functions over program variables. Since a probabilistic program gives random outcomes, a numerical function may have different values on different executions. The expected value of a numerical function is then determined by the probability distribution induced by the executions of program.

Since probabilistic programs are specified by numerical functions, their correctness can be established by annotations with expectations. In particular, correctness of while loops can be proved by inferring special expectations called the *quantitative loop invariants* [24,25]. Similar to classical programs, finding general quantitative loop invariants is hard. Techniques for generating linear quantitative loop invariants however are available [1,15,22,25].

Interestingly, existing linear loop invariant generation techniques can be extended to synthesize polynomial invariants [1]. Observe that polynomial multivariate polynomials are linear combinations of monomials. For instance, any

© Springer International Publishing Switzerland 2015
D. Kroening and C.S. Păsăreanu (Eds.): CAV 2015, Part I, LNCS 9206, pp. 658–674, 2015.
DOI: 10.1007/978-3-319-21690-4_44

polynomial over x, y with degree 2 is a linear combination of the monomials $1, x, y, x^2, y^2$, and xy. It suffices to find coefficients of the monomials to represent any multivariate polynomial of a fixed degree. Linear loop invariant generation techniques can hence be applied to infer invariants of a fixed degree. The number of monomials however grows rapidly. Quadratic polynomials over 5 variables, for example, are linear combinations of 21 monomials. One then has to find as many coefficients. It is unclear whether the extended approach is still feasible.

In this paper, we develop a Lagrange interpolation-based technique to synthesize polynomial loop invariants for simple loops in probabilistic programs. Lagrange interpolation is a well-known method to construct explicit expressions for polynomials by sampling. For example, suppose that the values of $f(x)$ are known to be s_1, s_3, and s_4 at the sampling points 1, 3, and 4, respectively. By Lagrange interpolation, we immediately have an explicit expression of $f(x) = s_1 \cdot \frac{(x-3)(x-4)}{(1-3)(1-4)} + s_3 \cdot \frac{(x-1)(x-4)}{(3-1)(3-4)} + s_4 \cdot \frac{(x-1)(x-3)}{(4-1)(4-3)}$. Our new technique employs multivariate Lagrange interpolation. Similar to previous techniques [15,22], we use conditions of quantitative loop invariants as constraints. Lagrange interpolation moreover allows us to simplify the constraints and sometimes to determine several coefficients. In the example, suppose $f(3) = 1$ is known. Then it suffices to determine s_1 and s_4 to construct an explicit expression of $f(x)$. In contrast, if $f(x)$ is represented as $c_0 + c_1 x + c_2 x^2$, then $f(3) = 1$ only gives $c_0 + 3c_1 + 9c_2 = 1$ and determines none of the coefficients. Lagrange interpolation hence can reduce the number of unknown coefficients and make our technique more scalable.

Although there are less unknown coefficients, one still has to solve non-linear constraints. We give heuristics to determine coefficients efficiently. Our heuristics first perform random experiments and obtain linear constraints about coefficients. An SMT solver is then used to find candidate coefficients from the constraints. If there is no candidate, then the desired loop invariant does not exist. Otherwise, quantifier elimination verifies whether the candidate coefficients give a loop invariant. If so, our technique has found a quantitative loop invariant. Otherwise, we add more linear constraints to exclude infeasible coefficients.

We apply our technique to find quantitative loop invariants for ten annotated loops from non-trivial probabilistic programs. Our case studies range from gambler's ruin problem [13] to simulation of a fair coin with a biased coin [15]. Over 1000 random runs, our technique is able to synthesize polynomial quantitative loop invariants within 15 s on average. Besides, 97.5 % of the runs can finish within a 300 s timeout.

Related Work. Constraint-based techniques for automated loop invariants generation have been much progressed over the past years [4,5,17,18,21,22,29]. Gupta and Rybalchenko [18,19] proposed a GEGAR framework, so that static and dynamic information of a program can be exploited incrementally to restrict the search space of *qualitative* loop invariants. Sankaranarayanan *et al.* [29] used Gröbner bases to reduce the generation of algebraic polynomial loop invariants to solving non-linear constraints in the parametric linear form. These techniques however deal with classical programs and cannot be applied to probabilistic programs directly. McIver and Morgan [24] were among the first to consider *quantitative* loop invariants for probabilistic programs. Katoen *et al.* [22] studied the synthesis of quantitative loop invariants using a constraint-solving approach. The approach was further developed and implemented in the PRINSYS tool [15], which synthesizes quantitative invariants by solving constraints over unknown template coefficients. The performance of the tool however is sensitive to manually supplied templates. Recently, a technique based on abstract interpretation is proposed in [1]. It formulates linear loop invariants with the collecting semantics and synthesizes coefficients via fixed-point computation. Although the authors only report experiments on linear loop invariants, the technique can be extended to generate polynomial invariants by representing polynomials as linear combinations of monomials. The effectiveness of the extension however is unclear.

We have the following organization. After preliminaries, we review probabilistic programs in Sect. 3. Quantitative loop invariants are presented in Sect. 4. Section 5 introduces multivariate Lagrange interpolation. Our technical contribution is presented in Sect. 6. Applications are given in Sect. 7. We evaluate our technique in the following section. Section 9 concludes our presentation.

2   Preliminaries

Let $\mathbf{x}_m$ be a sequence of variables $x_1, x_2, \ldots, x_m$. We use $\mathbb{R}[\mathbf{x}_m^n]$ to denote the set of real coefficient polynomials over m variables of degree at most n. Observe that $\mathbb{R}[\mathbf{x}_m^n]$ can be seen as a vector space over $\mathbb{R}$ of dimension $d = \binom{m+n}{n}$. For instance, the set of d monomials $\{x_1^{d_1} x_2^{d_2} \cdots x_m^{d_m} : 0 \le d_1 + d_2 + \cdots + d_m \le n\}$ forms a basis of $\mathbb{R}[\mathbf{x}_m^n]$. Given $f \in \mathbb{R}[\mathbf{x}_m^n]$ and expressions $e_1, e_2, \ldots, e_m$, we use $f(e_1, e_2, \ldots, e_m)$ to denote the polynomial obtained by replacing x_i with e_i for $1 \le i \le m$ in f. Particularly, $f(v)$ is the value of f at $v \in \mathbb{R}^m$.

A *constraint* is a quantifier-free logic formula with equality, linear order, addition, division, and integer constants. A constraint is *linear* if it contains only linear expressions; otherwise, it is *non-linear*. A *quantified constraint* is a constraint with quantifiers over its variables. A *valuation* over $\mathbf{x}_m$ assigns a value to each variable in $\mathbf{x}_m$. A *model* of a constraint is a valuation which evaluates the constraint to true.

Given a quantified constraint, *quantifier elimination* removes quantifiers and returns a logically equivalent constraint. Given a linear constraint, a *Satisfiability Modulo Theory (SMT) solver* returns a model of the constraint if it exists.

3   Probabilistic Programs

A *probabilistic program* in the *probabilistic guarded command language* is of the following form:

$$P ::= \mathsf{skip} \mid \mathsf{abort} \mid x := E \mid P;P \mid P[p]P \mid \mathsf{if}\,(G)\,\mathsf{then}\,\{P\}\,\mathsf{else}\,\{P\} \mid \mathsf{while}\,(G)\,\{P\}$$

where E is an expression and G is a Boolean expression. For $p \in (0, 1)$, the *probabilistic choice command* $P_0[p]P_1$ executes P_0 with probability p and P_1 with probability $1 - p$. For instance, $x := 1 \, [0.75] \, x := 0$ sets x to 1 with probability 0.75 and to 0 with probability 0.25. A *program state* is a valuation over program variables. For simplicity, we assume program variables are in non-negative integers, and use 0 and 1 for the truth values false and true respectively.

Example 1. Consider the following probabilistic program:

$$z := 0; \; \mathsf{while} \, (0 < x < y) \, \{ \, x := x + 1 \, [0.5] \, x := x - 1; \; z := z + 1; \, \}$$

The program models a game where a player has x dollars at the beginning and keeps tossing a coin with head probability 0.5. The player wins one dollar for each head and loses one dollar for each tail. The game ends either when the player loses all his money, or when he wins $y - x$ dollars for a predetermined $y > x$. The variable z counts the number of tosses made by the player during the game.

3.1 Expectations

From an initial program state, a probabilistic program can have different final program states due to probabilistic choice commands. Particularly, a function over program variables gives different values on different final program states. Note that a probabilistic program induces a probability distribution on final program states. One therefore can discuss the expected value of any function over program variables with respect to that probability distribution. More precisely, one can take an expectation transformer [24] approach to characterize a probabilistic program by annotating the program with expectations.

Formally, an *expectation* is a function mapping program states to a non-negative real number. An expectation is called a *post-expectation* when it is to be evaluated on final program states. Similarly, an expectation is called a *pre-expectation* if it is to be evaluated on initial program states. Let $preE$ and $postE$ be expectations, and $prog$ a probabilistic program. We say a *quantitative* Hoare triple $\langle preE \rangle \, prog \, \langle postE \rangle$ *holds* if the expected value of $postE$ is no less than that of $preE$ before executing $prog$. Note that the expected values of $postE$ and $preE$ are functions over states and hence are compared pointwisely.

For any Boolean expression G, define the *indicator* function $[G] = 1$ if G is true and $[G] = 0$ otherwise. Consider an *qualitative* Hoare triple $\{P\} \, prog \, \{Q\}$ with a pre-condition P, a post-condition Q, and a classical program $prog$. Observe that $\{P\} \, prog \, \{Q\}$ holds if and only if $\langle [P] \rangle \, prog \, \langle [Q] \rangle$ holds. Expectations are therefore the quantitative analogue to predicates for classical programs.

3.2 Expectation Transformer for Probabilistic Programs

Let P and Q be probabilistic programs, g a post-expectation, x a program variable, E an expression, G a Boolean expression, and $p \in (0, 1)$. Define the *expectation transformer* $wp(\,\cdot\,, g)$ as follows [24].

$$wp(\mathsf{skip}, g) = g$$
$$wp(\mathsf{abort}, g) = 0$$
$$wp(x := E, g) = g[x/E]$$
$$wp(P;Q, g) = wp(P, wp(Q, g))$$
$$wp(\mathsf{if}\ (G)\ \mathsf{then}\ \{P\}\ \mathsf{else}\ \{Q\}, g) = [G] \cdot wp(P, g) + [\neg G] \cdot wp(Q, g)$$
$$wp(P[p]Q, g) = p \cdot wp(P, g) + (1 - p) \cdot wp(Q, g)$$
$$wp(\mathsf{while}\ (G)\ \{P\}, g) = \mu X.([G] \cdot wp(P, X) + [\neg G] \cdot g).$$

Here $g[x/E]$ denotes the formula obtained from g by replacing free occurrences of x by E. The least fixed point operator μ is defined over the domain of expectations [16]. It can be shown that $\langle f \rangle\ P\ \langle g \rangle$ if and only if $f \leq wp(P, g)$. That is, $wp(P, g)$ is the greatest lower bound of pre-expectation of P with respect to g. We say $wp(P, g)$ is the *weakest pre-expectation of P with respect to g*.

Example 2. The weakest pre-expectation of command $x := x + 1\,[p]\,x := x - 1$ with respect to x is computed below:

$$wp(x := x + 1\,[p]\,x := x - 1, x)$$
$$= p \cdot wp(x := x + 1, x) + (1 - p) \cdot wp(x := x - 1, x)$$
$$= p \cdot (x + 1) + (1 - p) \cdot (x - 1)$$
$$= x + 2p - 1$$

It follows that $\langle x + 2p - 1 \rangle\ x := x + 1\,[p]\,x := x - 1\ \langle x \rangle$ holds.

4   Quantitative Loop Invariants

Given a pre-expectation $preE$, a post-expectation $postE$, a Boolean expression G, and a loop-free probabilistic program $body$, we would like to verify whether

$$\langle preE \rangle\ \mathsf{while}\ (G)\ \{body\}\ \langle postE \rangle$$

holds or not. One way to solve this problem is to compute the weakest pre-expectation $wp(\mathsf{while}\ (G)\ \{body\}, postE)$ and check if it is not less than $preE$ pointwisely. However, the weakest pre-expectation of a while-command requires fixed point computation. To avoid the expensive computation, we can solve the problem by finding quantitative loop invariants.

Theorem 1 ([15,24]). *Let preE be a pre-expectation, postE a post-expectation, G a Boolean expression, and body a loop-free probabilistic program. To show*

$$\langle preE \rangle\ \mathsf{while}\ (G)\ \{body\}\ \langle postE \rangle,$$

it suffices to find a loop invariant I *which is an expectation such that*

1. *(boundary)* $preE \leq I$ *and* $I \cdot [\neg G] \leq postE$;
2. *(invariant)* $I \cdot [G] \leq wp(body, I)$;
3. *(soundness) the loop terminates from any state in G with probability 1, and*

(a) the number of iterations is finite;
(b) I is bounded above by some fixed constant; or
(c) the expected value of $I \cdot [G]$ tends to zero as the loop continues to iterate.

In this paper, we only focus on checking the boundary and invariant conditions in Theorem 1. One however can show that *any* polynomial expectation is sound for all examples we consider. In fact, one can establish the soundness of a large class of loop invariants before any specific invariant is found. For instance, it can be shown that any polynomial expectation satisfies the third soundness condition, as long as the probability of exiting the loop is bounded below by a non-zero constant in each iteration. We refer the reader to [24] for more details of sufficient conditions for soundness.

5 Multivariate Lagrange Interpolation

Fix a degree n of quantitative loop invariants and number of variables m. Let $d = \binom{m+n}{n}$. *Multivariate Lagrange interpolation* is a method to construct an explicit expression for any polynomial in $\mathbb{R}[\mathbf{x}_m^n]$ by sampling, see e.g., [6,26,30]. Given d *sampling points* $\mathbf{s}_1, \mathbf{s}_2, \ldots, \mathbf{s}_d \in \mathbb{R}^m$, we can compute a Lagrange basis as follows [28]. Let $\{b_1, b_2, \ldots, b_d\} = \{x_1^{d_1} x_2^{d_2} \cdots x_m^{d_m} : d_1 + d_2 + \cdots + d_m \leq n\}$ be the set of monomials in $\mathbb{R}[\mathbf{x}_m^n]$. For $1 \leq i \leq d$, define

$$M_i = \det \begin{bmatrix} b_1(\mathbf{s}_1) & \cdots & b_d(\mathbf{s}_1) \\ \vdots & & \vdots \\ b_1 & \cdots & b_d \\ \vdots & & \vdots \\ b_1(\mathbf{s}_d) & \cdots & b_d(\mathbf{s}_d) \end{bmatrix} \quad \leftarrow \text{the } i\text{th row}$$

Observe that $M_i \in \mathbb{R}[\mathbf{x}_m^n]$ for $1 \leq i \leq d$. Moreover, $M_i(\mathbf{s}_j) = 0$ for $i \neq j$ and $M_1(\mathbf{s}_1) = M_2(\mathbf{s}_2) = \cdots = M_d(\mathbf{s}_d) = r$ for some $r \in \mathbb{R}$. If $r = 0$, then there is a geometrical dependency among the sampling points $\mathbf{s}_1, \mathbf{s}_2, \ldots, \mathbf{s}_d$ [2], and thus no Lagrange basis could be determined from these points. If $r \neq 0$, define $B_i = M_i/r$ for $1 \leq i \leq d$. Then $\mathcal{B}(\mathbf{s}_1, \mathbf{s}_2, \ldots, \mathbf{s}_d) = \{B_i : 1 \leq i \leq d\} \subseteq \mathbb{R}[\mathbf{x}_m^n]$ is called a *Lagrange basis* of $\mathbb{R}[\mathbf{x}_m^n]$.

Observe that $B_i(\mathbf{s}_j) = [i = j]$ for $1 \leq i, j \leq d$. Thus $\sum_{i=1}^d f(\mathbf{s}_i) B_i(\mathbf{s}_j) = f(\mathbf{s}_j)$ for $1 \leq j \leq d$. Moreover, given any $f \in \mathbb{R}[\mathbf{x}_m^n]$, we can write $f = \sum_{i=1}^d f(\mathbf{s}_i) B_i$. Define the *Lagrange functional* $\mathcal{L}[\mathbf{s}_1, \mathbf{s}_2, \ldots, \mathbf{s}_d] : \mathbb{R}^d \to \mathbb{R}[\mathbf{x}_m^n]$ by

$$\mathcal{L}[\mathbf{s}_1, \mathbf{s}_2, \ldots, \mathbf{s}_d](c_1, c_2, \ldots, c_d) = \sum_{i=1}^d c_i B_i.$$

Then $f = \mathcal{L}[\mathbf{s}_1, \mathbf{s}_2, \ldots, \mathbf{s}_d](f(\mathbf{s}_1), f(\mathbf{s}_2), \ldots, f(\mathbf{s}_d))$ for any $f \in \mathbb{R}[\mathbf{x}_m^n]$. We shall call $f(\mathbf{s}_1), f(\mathbf{s}_2), \ldots, f(\mathbf{s}_d) \in \mathbb{R}$ the *coefficients* for f on basis $\mathcal{B}(\mathbf{s}_1, \mathbf{s}_2, \ldots, \mathbf{s}_d)$.

6   Interpolation of Loop Invariants

Suppose we would like to find a quantitative loop invariant $I \in \mathbb{R}[\mathbf{x}_m^n]$ for

$$\langle preE \rangle \text{ while } (G) \{ body \} \langle postE \rangle$$

where $preE$ is a pre-expectation, $postE$ is a post-expectation, G is a Boolean expression, and $body$ is a loop-free probabilistic program. Assume the soundness of I can be verified. We shall use Lagrange interpolation to find I.

Let $\mathbf{s}_1, \mathbf{s}_2, \ldots, \mathbf{s}_d \in \mathbb{R}^m$ be sampling points that determine a Lagrange basis. If the coefficients $I(\mathbf{s}_1), I(\mathbf{s}_2), \ldots, I(\mathbf{s}_d) \in \mathbb{R}$ are known, then

$$I = \mathcal{L}[\mathbf{s}_1, \mathbf{s}_2, \ldots, \mathbf{s}_d](I(\mathbf{s}_1), I(\mathbf{s}_2), \ldots, I(\mathbf{s}_d))$$

by Lagrange interpolation. Our idea therefore is to find the coefficients via constraint-solving. By the boundary and invariant conditions in Theorem 1, we have the following requirements about any loop invariant I:

$$
\begin{aligned}
preE &\leq I \\
I \cdot [\neg G] &\leq postE \\
I \cdot [G] &\leq wp(body, I).
\end{aligned}
\tag{1}
$$

Example 3. Consider

$$\langle xy - x^2 \rangle \ z := 0; \ \text{ while } (0 < x < y) \ \{ \ x := x + 1 \ [0.5] \ x := x - 1; \ z := z + 1; \ \} \ \langle z \rangle.$$

The following must hold for any loop invariant I

$$
\begin{aligned}
xy - x^2 &\leq I \\
I \cdot [x \leq 0 \vee y \leq x] &\leq z \\
I \cdot [0 < x < y] &\leq 0.5 \cdot I(x+1, y, z+1) + 0.5 \cdot I(x-1, y, z+1).
\end{aligned}
$$

Observe that $wp(x := x + 1 \ [0.5] \ x := x - 1; \quad z := z + 1, I(x, y, z)) = wp(x := x + 1 \ [0.5] \ x := x - 1, I(x, y, z + 1)) = 0.5 \cdot wp(x := x + 1, I(x, y, z + 1)) + 0.5 \cdot wp(x := x - 1, I(x, y, z + 1)) = 0.5 \cdot I(x + 1, y, z + 1) + 0.5 \cdot I(x - 1, y, z + 1)$.

Requirements (1) can have indicators on both sides of inequality, which is beyond the capability of the solvers we use. We would like to obtain a constraint by removing indicators in two steps. First, we rewrite the expectations to a normal form. An expectation is in *disjoint normal form (DNF)* if it is of the form $f = [P_1] \cdot f_1 + \cdots + [P_k] \cdot f_k$, where $P_1, P_2, \ldots, P_k$ are disjoint, that is, at most one of $P_1, P_2, \ldots, P_k$ evaluates to true on any valuation.

Theorem 2 ([22]). *Given an expectation of the form $f = [P_1] \cdot f_1 + \cdots + [P_k] \cdot f_k$, f is equivalent to the following expectation in DNF:*

$$\sum_{I \subseteq K} \left[\left(\bigwedge_{i \in I} P_i \right) \wedge \neg \left(\bigwedge_{j \in K \setminus I} P_j \right) \right] \cdot \sum_{i \in I} f_i$$

where $K = \{1, 2, \ldots, k\}$.

We then transform inequalities between expectations in DNF to constraints.

Theorem 3 ([15]). *Suppose* $f = [P_1] \cdot f_1 + \cdots + [P_k] \cdot f_k$ *and* $g = [Q_1] \cdot g_1 + \cdots + [Q_h] \cdot g_h$ *are expectations over* $\mathbf{x}_m$ *in DNF.* $f \leq g$ *iff for every* $\mathbf{x}_m$

$$\bigwedge_{j \in K} \bigwedge_{i \in H} ((P_j \wedge Q_i) \Rightarrow f_j \leq g_i) \quad \wedge$$

$$\bigwedge_{j \in K} \left(\left(\bigwedge_{i \in H} \neg Q_i \wedge P_j \right) \Rightarrow f_j \leq 0 \right) \wedge \bigwedge_{i \in H} \left(\left(\bigwedge_{j \in K} \neg P_j \wedge Q_i \right) \Rightarrow 0 \leq g_i \right)$$

where $K = \{1, 2, \ldots, k\}$ *and* $H = \{1, 2, \ldots, h\}$.

Example 4. By Theorems 2 and 3, requirements in Example 3 are equivalent to

$$xy - x^2 \leq I \quad \wedge$$
$$(x \leq 0 \vee y \leq x) \Rightarrow I \leq z \quad \wedge$$
$$(x \leq 0 \vee y \leq x) \Rightarrow 0 \leq z \quad \wedge$$
$$(0 < x < y) \Rightarrow I \leq 0.5 \cdot I(x+1, y, z+1) + 0.5 \cdot I(x-1, y, z+1) \quad \wedge$$
$$(0 < x < y) \Rightarrow 0 \leq 0.5 \cdot I(x+1, y, z+1) + 0.5 \cdot I(x-1, y, z+1)$$

for every x, y, z.

We define the *loop invariant constraint* $\phi[\mathbf{s}_1, \mathbf{s}_2, \ldots, \mathbf{s}_d](c_1, c_2, \ldots, c_d)$ as the constraint transformed from the requirements (1), where the quantitative loop invariant I is replaced by Lagrange functional $\mathcal{L}[\mathbf{s}_1, \mathbf{s}_2, \ldots, \mathbf{s}_d](c_1, c_2, \ldots, c_d)$.

Example 5. We have the following loop invariant constraint from Example 4.

$$\phi[\mathbf{s}_1, \mathbf{s}_2, \ldots, \mathbf{s}_{10}](c_1, c_2, \ldots, c_{10}) =$$
$$xy - x^2 \leq \mathcal{L}[\mathbf{s}_1, \mathbf{s}_2, \ldots, \mathbf{s}_{10}](c_1, c_2, \ldots, c_{10}) \quad \wedge$$
$$(x \leq 0 \vee y \leq x) \Rightarrow \mathcal{L}[\mathbf{s}_1, \mathbf{s}_2, \ldots, \mathbf{s}_{10}](c_1, c_2, \ldots, c_{10}) \leq z \quad \wedge$$
$$(0 < x < y) \Rightarrow 2 \cdot \mathcal{L}[\mathbf{s}_1, \mathbf{s}_2, \ldots, \mathbf{s}_{10}](c_1, c_2, \ldots, c_{10}) \leq$$
$$\mathcal{L}[\mathbf{s}_1, \mathbf{s}_2, \ldots, \mathbf{s}_{10}](c_1, c_2, \ldots, c_{10})(x+1, y, z+1) +$$
$$\mathcal{L}[\mathbf{s}_1, \mathbf{s}_2, \ldots, \mathbf{s}_{10}](c_1, c_2, \ldots, c_{10})(x-1, y, z+1).$$

With loop invariant constraints, it is easy to state our goal. Observe that $\exists \mathbf{s}_1, \mathbf{s}_2, \ldots, \mathbf{s}_d \exists c_1, c_2, \ldots, c_d \forall \mathbf{x}_m. \phi[\mathbf{s}_1, \mathbf{s}_2, \ldots, \mathbf{s}_d](c_1, c_2, \ldots, c_d)$ implies the existence of a quantitative loop invariant satisfying the boundary and invariant conditions in Theorem 1. Our strategy hence is to choose sampling points $\mathbf{s}_1, \mathbf{s}_2, \ldots, \mathbf{s}_d$ such that $\exists c_1, c_2, \ldots, c_d \forall \mathbf{x}_m. \phi[\mathbf{s}_1, \mathbf{s}_2, \ldots, \mathbf{s}_d](c_1, c_2, \ldots, c_d)$ holds.

We will choose sampling points to simplify the loop invariant constraint. Recall that sampling points are not unique in Lagrange interpolation. For a loop invariant constraint, we select sampling points so that several coefficients among $c_1, c_2, \ldots, c_d$ are determined. This helps us to evaluate the quantified loop invariant constraint $\exists c_1, c_2, \ldots, c_d \forall \mathbf{x}_m. \phi[\mathbf{s}_1, \mathbf{s}_2, \ldots, \mathbf{s}_d](c_1, c_2, \ldots, c_d)$.

To evaluate the quantified loop invariant constraint, observe that the Lagrange functional $\mathcal{L}[\mathbf{s}_1, \mathbf{s}_2, \ldots, \mathbf{s}_d](c_1, c_2, \ldots, c_d)$ is a multivariate polynomial over $c_1, c_2, \ldots, c_d$ and $\mathbf{x}_m$. A loop invariant constraint is hence non-linear. However, $\phi[\mathbf{s}_1, \mathbf{s}_2, \ldots, \mathbf{s}_d](c_1, c_2, \ldots, c_d)(\mathbf{e})$ is a linear constraint over coefficients for every *experiment* $\mathbf{e} \in \mathbb{Z}^m$, i.e., valuation over $\mathbf{x}_m$. We therefore use experiments to construct a series of linear constraints and find coefficients by an SMT solver.

Input: $\langle preE \rangle$ while (G) $\{body\}$ $\langle postE \rangle$: a loop over program variables $\mathbf{x}_m$; n : the degree of an loop invariant
Output: I : a loop invariant satisfying the boundary and invariant conditions in Theorem 1
$d \leftarrow \binom{m+n}{n}$;
$\mathbf{s}_1, \mathbf{s}_2, \ldots, \mathbf{s}_d \leftarrow$ SamplingPoints();
$C \leftarrow$ InitialConstraint($\mathbf{s}_1, \mathbf{s}_2, \ldots, \mathbf{s}_d$);
while C *has a model* **do**
    $\hat{c}_1, \hat{c}_2, \ldots, \hat{c}_d \leftarrow$ a model of C from an SMT solver;
    switch *RandomExperiments*(C) **do**
        case *Pass*:
            switch *UQElem*($\mathbf{x}_m, \phi[\mathbf{s}_1, \mathbf{s}_2, \ldots, \mathbf{s}_d](\hat{c}_1, \hat{c}_2, \ldots, \hat{c}_d)$) **do**
                case *True*: **return** $\mathcal{L}[\mathbf{s}_1, \mathbf{s}_2, \ldots, \mathbf{s}_d](\hat{c}_1, \hat{c}_2, \ldots, \hat{c}_d)$ **case** *CounterExample* ($\mathbf{e}$) : RefineConstraint($C, \mathbf{e}$)
            end
        case *CounterExample* ($\mathbf{e}$) : RefineConstraint($C, \mathbf{e}$)
    end
end
//No loop invariant

Algorithm 1: Quantitative loop invariant synthesis

Algorithm 1 shows our top-level algorithm. The algorithm starts by choosing sampling points (Sect. 6.1). The sampling points are then used to construct the initial linear constraint over coefficients (Sect. 6.2). The while loop evaluates the quantified loop invariant constraint $\exists c_1, c_2, \ldots, c_d \, \forall \mathbf{x}_m. \, \phi[\mathbf{s}_1, \mathbf{s}_2, \ldots, \mathbf{s}_d](c_1, c_2, \ldots, c_d)$. In each iteration, the algorithm selects coefficients $\hat{c}_1, \hat{c}_2, \ldots, \hat{c}_d$ by a model of the linear constraint obtained from an SMT solver. It then checks whether $\forall \mathbf{x}_m. \, \phi[\mathbf{s}_1, \mathbf{s}_2, \ldots, \mathbf{s}_d](\hat{c}_1, \hat{c}_2, \ldots, \hat{c}_d)$ is true. The algorithm does this by first trying a number of random experiments (Sect. 6.3). Only after the random experiments are passed, will the algorithm performs universal quantifier elimination to evaluate the quantified constraint (Sect. 6.4). If the random experiments fail, or quantifier elimination does not evaluate to true, our algorithm refines the linear constraint by a counterexample and reiterates (Sect. 6.5).

6.1   Choosing Sampling Points

In Lagrange interpolation, sampling points need be chosen in the first place. We would like to choose sampling points so that as many coefficients are determined as possible. To this end, observe that $\mathcal{L}[\mathbf{s}_1, \mathbf{s}_2, \ldots, \mathbf{s}_d](c_1, c_2, \ldots, c_d)(\mathbf{s}_i) = c_i$ for $1 \leq i \leq d$. In other words, $\phi[\mathbf{s}_1, \mathbf{s}_2, \ldots, \mathbf{s}_d](c_1, c_2, \ldots, c_d)(\mathbf{s}_i)$ can be significantly simplified if a sampling point s_i is used as an experiment. Consider, for instance, the boundary condition in our running example:

$$xy - x^2 \leq \mathcal{L}[s_1, s_2, \ldots, s_d](c_1, c_2, \ldots, c_d)(x, y, z); \text{ and}$$
$$(x \leq 0 \vee y \leq x) \Rightarrow \mathcal{L}[s_1, s_2, \ldots, s_d](c_1, c_2, \ldots, c_d)(x, y, z) \leq z$$

If $s_j = (0, 3, 0)$ is a sampling point, then the condition can be simplified to $0 \leq c_j$ and $c_j \leq 0$. Thus c_j is determined by choosing $(0, 3, 0)$ as both a sampling point and an experiment.

Ideally, one would choose sampling points so that all coefficients are determined. Unfortunately, such points tend to be geometrically dependent in practice. Thus we cannot expect to establish a Lagrange basis from these points exclusively. Instead, we try to find sampling points which yield a Lagrange basis and determine as many coefficients as possible. We adopt a weighted random search for this purpose. That is, we pick sampling points randomly according to their weights, so that points determining more coefficients are more likely to be picked. If the randomly selected sampling points fail to yield a Lagrange basis, we discard them and select other sampling points randomly again. In our experiments, this heuristic finds pretty good sampling points in reasonable time.

6.2 Initial Constraint

After sampling points are chosen, we compute the initial linear constraint over coefficients. Recall that $\mathcal{L}[s_1, s_2, \ldots, s_d](c_1, c_2, \ldots, c_d)(s_i) = c_i$ for $1 \leq i \leq d$. By taking sampling points as experiments, the loop invariant constraint $\phi[s_1, s_2, \ldots, s_d](c_1, c_2, \ldots, c_d)$ is simplified to a linear constraint over $c_1, c_2, \ldots, c_d$.

Example 6. Consider the loop invariant constraint in Example 5. We first choose 10 sampling points $s_1, \ldots, s_{10}$ (see table below) to establish a Lagrange basis. We then compute the initial constraints by simplifying the loop invariant constraint with the sampling points. For example, we obtain constraint $c_2 = 0$ from point $s_2 = (2, 2, 0)$ as follows:

$\phi[s_1, s_2, \ldots, s_{10}](c_1, c_2, \ldots, c_{10})(2, 2, 0)$

iff $(2 \cdot (2 - 2) \leq c_2) \wedge ((2 \leq 0 \vee 2 \leq 2) \Rightarrow c_2 \leq 0) \wedge$

$\quad (0 < 2 < 2 \Rightarrow 0 \leq -2c_1 - 42c_2 + 3c_3 + 27c_4 + 9c_5 + 6c_6 + 14c_7 - 12c_8 - 3c_{10})$

iff $0 \leq c_2 \wedge c_2 \leq 0$

iff $c_2 = 0$.

We list all initial constraints in the following table, where $\phi[s_1, s_2, \ldots, s_{10}](c_1, c_2, \ldots, c_{10})(s_i)$ is denoted by $\psi(s_i)$ for simplicity.

Note that our choice of sampling points helps the initial constraints determine 5 coefficients. If a standard monomial basis were used, none of the coefficients could be determined by the initial constraints.

i	$\mathbf{s}_i$	$\psi(\mathbf{s}_i)$	i	$\mathbf{s}_i$	$\psi(\mathbf{s}_i)$	i	$\mathbf{s}_i$	$\psi(\mathbf{s}_i)$
1	0,3,0	$c_1 = 0$	2	2,2,0	$c_2 = 0$	3	0,3,1	$0 \le c_3 \le 1$
4	1,1,0	$c_4 = 0$	5	1,1,2	$0 \le c_5 \le 2$	6	2,2,1	$0 \le c_6 \le 1$
7	3,3,0	$c_7 = 0$	8	0,0,1	$0 \le c_8 \le 1$	9	0,1,0	$c_9 = 0$
10	2,3,3	$6 \le 3c_{10} \le -4c_1 - 36c_2 + 5c_3 + 30c_4 + 12c_5 - 6c_6 + 16c_7 - 14c_8$						

6.3   Random Experiments

From a linear constraint of coefficients, we obtain a model $\hat{c}_1, \hat{c}_2, \ldots, \hat{c}_d$ of the linear constraint from an SMT solver. Recall that we would like to check if $\forall \mathbf{x}_m. \phi[\mathbf{s}_1, \mathbf{s}_2, \ldots, \mathbf{s}_d](\hat{c}_1, \hat{c}_2, \ldots, \hat{c}_d)$ is true. Before using expensive quantifier elimination immediately, we first perform a number of random tests. If $\phi[\mathbf{s}_1, \mathbf{s}_2, \ldots, \mathbf{s}_d]$ $(\hat{c}_1, \hat{c}_2, \ldots, \hat{c}_d)(\mathbf{e})$ evaluates to true for all random experiments $\mathbf{e} \in \mathbb{Z}^m$, the coefficients $\hat{c}_1, \hat{c}_2, \ldots, \hat{c}_d$ may induce a loop invariant. Otherwise, a witness experiment $\mathbf{e}$ is used to refine the linear constraint over coefficients.

When the coefficients do not induce a loop invariant, the random experiments make it possible to avoid expensive quantifier elimination and to obtain a witness experiment without resorting to an SMT solver. This possibility is important, because the solver we use does not always find a valid witness experiment.

6.4   Universal Quantifier Elimination

After random tests, we perform quantifier elimination check if $\forall \mathbf{x}_m. \phi[\mathbf{s}_1, \mathbf{s}_2, \ldots, \mathbf{s}_d](\hat{c}_1, \hat{c}_2, \ldots, \hat{c}_d)$ is true. If so, the polynomial $\mathcal{L}[\mathbf{s}_1, \mathbf{s}_2, \ldots, \mathbf{s}_d]$ $(\hat{c}_1, \hat{c}_2, \ldots, \hat{c}_d)$ is a quantitative loop invariant satisfying the boundary and invariant conditions. Otherwise, we obtain a witness experiment to refine our linear constraint.

Universal quantifier elimination is carried out in two steps. We first eliminate the quantifiers in the ordered field theory [3,11]. Intuitively, the ordered field theory formalizes real numbers $\mathbb{R}$. Since quantifier elimination tools such as REDLOG [10] employ algebra and real algebraic geometry, eliminating quantifiers over real numbers is more efficient than over integers. If $\forall \mathbf{x}_m. \phi[\mathbf{s}_1, \mathbf{s}_2, \ldots, \mathbf{s}_d]$ $(\hat{c}_1, \hat{c}_2, \ldots, \hat{c}_d)$ is true over $\mathbb{R}$, it is also true over $\mathbb{Z}$. Thus $\hat{c}_1, \hat{c}_2, \ldots, \hat{c}_d$ induces a quantitative loop invariant. Otherwise, we perform quantifier elimination over $\mathbb{Z}$.

If $\forall \mathbf{x}_m. \phi[\mathbf{s}_1, \mathbf{s}_2, \ldots, \mathbf{s}_d](\hat{c}_1, \hat{c}_2, \ldots, \hat{c}_d)$ evaluates to true over $\mathbb{Z}$, we are done. Otherwise, quantifier elimination gives a constraint equivalent to the quantified query. We then use an SMT solver to obtain a witness experiment. We abort the procedure if the solver times-out or fails to yield a valid witness experiment.

6.5   Constraint Refinement

Let $\mathbf{e} = (\hat{x}_1, \hat{x}_2, \ldots, \hat{x}_m) \in \mathbb{Z}^m$ be a witness experiment such that $\phi[\mathbf{s}_1, \mathbf{s}_2, \ldots, \mathbf{s}_d]$ $(\hat{c}_1, \hat{c}_2, \ldots, \hat{c}_d)(\mathbf{e})$ evaluates to false. Recall that we would like to find coefficients $c_1, c_2, \ldots, c_d$ such that $\phi[\mathbf{s}_1, \mathbf{s}_2, \ldots, \mathbf{s}_d](c_1, c_2, \ldots, c_d)$ is true for every valuations over $\mathbf{x}_m$. Particularly, $\phi[\mathbf{s}_1, \mathbf{s}_2, \ldots, \mathbf{s}_d](c_1, c_2, \ldots, c_d)(\hat{x}_1, \hat{x}_2, \ldots, \hat{x}_m)$ must also be true for such coefficients. Note that $\phi[\mathbf{s}_1, \mathbf{s}_2, \ldots, \mathbf{s}_d](c_1, c_2, \ldots, c_d)(\hat{x}_1, \hat{x}_2, \ldots, \hat{x}_m)$ is a linear constraint on coefficients $c_1, c_2, \ldots, c_d$ that excludes the incorrect coefficients $\hat{c}_1, \hat{c}_2, \ldots, \hat{c}_d$. By adding the linear constraint to the current set of constraints, our algorithm will find different coefficients in the next iteration.

Table 1. Summary of results. The name of each experiment is shown in column Name. The annotated pre- and post-expectations are shown in columns preE and postE, respectively. Column Time lists the mean execution times our prototype took to verify the annotations, and TO denotes the timeout ratios. Besides, columns L, T, and S show the average times our prototype spent in sampling a Lagrange basis, making random tests and synthesizing coefficients, respectively. Finally, columns #L, #T, and #S show the average numbers of iterations our prototype has taken to find sampling points, make random tests, and refine constraints, respectively. The last six columns are calculated based on the runs that finished within timeouts.

Name	preE	postE	Time	TO	L	T	S	#L	#T	#S
Ruin	$xy - x^2$	z	3.6 s	0 %	0.3 s	2.8 s	0.3 s	5.2	61.5	5.0
Geo1	$x + 3zy$	x	3.0 s	0 %	1.4 s	1.5 s	0.1 s	21.4	32.1	1.0
Geo2	$x + \frac{15}{2}z$	x	8.0 s	0 %	1.4 s	4.9 s	0.2 s	22.3	108	3.8
Bin1	$x + \frac{1}{4}ny$	x	4.5 s	0 %	1.4 s	2.9 s	0.1 s	22.7	64.0	1.0
Bin2	$\frac{1}{8}n^2 - \frac{1}{8}n + \frac{3}{4}ny$	x	77.5 s	19 %	0.4 s	9.0 s	15.8 s	5.9	185	10.3
Sum	$\frac{1}{4}n^2 + \frac{1}{4}n$	x	2.5 s	0 %	0.1 s	1.9 s	0.4 s	1.2	42.7	5.8
Prod	$\frac{1}{4}n^2 - \frac{1}{4}n$	xy	15.7 s	5 %	0.3 s	4.3 s	2.3 s	4.2	97.0	6.5
Coin1	$\frac{1}{2} - \frac{1}{2}x$	$1 - x + xy$	2.0 s	0 %	0.4 s	1.2 s	0.3 s	5.7	27.1	3.6
Coin2	$\frac{1}{2} - \frac{1}{2}y$	$x + xy$	3.9 s	0 %	0.6 s	1.4 s	1.8 s	9.8	32.0	4.2
Coin3	$\frac{8}{3} - \frac{8}{3}x - \frac{8}{3}y + \frac{1}{3}n$	n	18.5 s	1 %	12.6 s	2.6 s	1.4 s	202	57.9	7.2

7 Applications

We have implemented a prototype in JavaScript to test our techniques. For each simple loop, we manually perform the weakest pre-expectation computation and the DNF transformation to translate the requirements (1) into loop invariant constraints. We then use our prototype to find a quantitative loop invariant based on the constraints. Our prototype uses GNU OCTAVE [12] to compute Lagrange interpolation, Z3 [7] to solve linear constraints, and REDLOG [10] to perform quantifier elimination. The experiments are done on an Intel Xeon 3.07 GHz Linux workstation with 16 GB RAM.

We consider six types of applications: gambler's ruin problem, geometric distribution, binomial distribution, sum of random series, product of random variables, and simulation of a fair coin. We also consider variants of geometric and binomial distributions. For the fair-coin simulation, we find three quantitative loop invariants to prove the correctness and the expected execution time of the simulation. In each probabilistic program, we annotate the while loop with a pre-expectation and a post-expectation. Note that the annotated pre-expectation is by construction a precise estimate of the annotated post-expectation at the entrance of the loop.

Our results are summarized in Table 1. We use a fixed random seed for all experiments and compute the averages over 100 random runs with a 300 s time-out. The prototype may synthesize different loop invariants in different runs of the same experiment. We now discuss the applications in more details.

Gambler's Ruin Problem. In Example 1, we consider a game where a player has x dollars initially and plays until he loses all his money or wins up to $y - x$ dollars for some $y > x$. The expected number of rounds before the game ends is $E[z] = x \cdot (y - x)$. Our prototype proves this result within 3.6 s on average.

Geometric Distribution. The geometric distribution describes the number of tails before the first head in a sequence of coin-tossing. When the probability of head is 0.25, we expect to see $\frac{1-0.25}{0.25} = 3$ tails before the first head. The following program computes a geometrically distributed random variable x:

$$x := 0; \ z := 1; \ \mathsf{while} \, (z \neq 0) \, \{ \ z := 0 \, [0.25] \, x := x + y; \ \}$$

Our prototype finds a quantitative loop invariant for the pre-expectation $E[x] = 3y$ within 3 s on average.

We moreover consider the following variant of the game. A player keeps flipping a coin until the head turns up. He wins k dollars if the tail turns up at the kth flip. The variant is modeled as follows.

$$x := 0; \ y := 0; \ z := 1; \ \mathsf{while} \, (z \neq 0) \, \{ \ y := y + 1; \ z := 0 \, [0.25] \, x := x + y; \ \}$$

The expected amount of money a player can win is $E[x] = \frac{1}{2} \left(0.25^{-2} - 1 \right) = \frac{15}{2}$. Our prototype proves this result within 8 s on average.

Binomial Distribution. The binomials distribution describes the number of heads that appear in a fixed number of coin-tossing. If the probability of head is 0.25 and the number of tosses is n, then the expected number of heads is $0.25n$. The following program computes a binomially distributed random variable x:

$$x := 0; \ \mathsf{while} \, (0 < n) \, \{ \ x := x + y \, [0.25] \, \mathsf{skip}; \ n := n - 1; \ \}$$

Our prototype proves $E[x] = 0.25ny$ within 4.5 s on average. We moreover consider the following variant. A player flips a coin for n times. At the kth flip, he wins k dollars if the head turns up and wins y dollars otherwise. This game can be modeled as follows.

$$x := 0; \ \mathsf{while} \, (0 < n) \, \{ \ x := x + n \, [0.25] \, x := x + y; \ n := n - 1; \ \}$$

The expected amount of money a player can win is $E[x] = 0.25 \cdot \frac{1}{2} n(n+1) + (1 - 0.25) \cdot ny = \frac{1}{8} n^2 - \frac{1}{8} n + \frac{3}{4} ny$. Our prototype proves this result within 77.5 s on average.

Sum of Random Series. Consider a game where a player flips a coin for n times. The player wins k dollars if the head turns up at the kth flip. The following program models this game when the head probability of the coin is 0.5:

$$x := 0; \ \text{while} \ (0 < n) \ \{ \ x := x + n \ [0.5] \ \text{skip}; \ n := n - 1; \ \}$$

The expected amount of money the player can win from this game is $E[x] = 0.5 \cdot \sum_{i=1}^{n} i = 0.5 \cdot \frac{1}{2}n(n+1)$ dollars. Our prototype proves this result within 2.5 s on average.

Product of Dependent Random Variables. We consider a game where two players flip a coin for n times. The first player wins one dollar for each head and the second player wins one dollars for each tail. When the head probability of the coin is 0.5, this game can be modeled by the following program where variables x, y represent the amount of money won by the respective players:

$$\text{while} \ (0 < n) \ \{ \ x := x + 1 \ [0.5] \ y := y + 1; \ n := n - 1; \ \}$$

It can be shown that $E[xy] = \frac{1}{4}(n^2 - n)$. Our prototype proves this result within 15.7 s on average.

Simulation of a Fair Coin. We consider an algorithm that simulates a fair coin flip using biased coins [15]:

$$x := 0; \ y := 0; \ n := 0;$$
$$\text{while} \ (x = y) \ \{ \ x := 1 \ [0.25] \ x := 0; \ y := 1 \ [0.25] \ y := 0; \ n := n + 1; \ \}$$

The algorithm uses two biased coins x and y with head probability 0.25. The main loop flips the two coins at each iteration and terminates when the coins show different outcomes. The value of x is then taken as the final outcome, with 1 representing the head and 0 representing the tail.

To see that the algorithm indeed simulates a fair coin flip, we prove

$$0.5 - 0.5x \leq wp(loop, 1 - x + xy) \quad \text{and} \quad 0.5 - 0.5y \leq wp(loop, x + xy),$$

where $loop$ denotes the while-loop in the program. Since $x = y = 0$ before the loop starts and $xy = 0$ after the loop stops, we see that $0.5 \leq E[1 - x]$ and $0.5 \leq E[x]$ on termination. Since $x \in \{0, 1\}$, it follows that $\Pr\{x = 1\} = \Pr\{x = 0\} = 0.5$ on termination and thus the correctness of the algorithm is concluded.

Observe moreover that the number of iterations until the two coins show different outcomes is the geometric distribution with head probability $0.25 \cdot 2(1 - 0.25) = 0.375$. Hence, the expected number of iterations is $E[n] = \frac{1 - 0.375}{0.375} + 1 = \frac{8}{3}$. This result is verified by our prototype within 18.5 s on average.

8 Evaluation

Our technique is closely related to the PRINSYS tool [15], which implements the constraint-based quantitative invariant synthesis approach developed in [22].

PRINSYS receives a probabilistic program and a template with unknown coefficients. It derives loop invariant constraints from the template and exploits SMT-solvers to perform quantifier elimination and simplification for the constraints. The tool generates a formula, which is in effect a conjunction of nonlinear inequalities, describing all coefficients that make the supplied template an inductive loop invariant. A concrete quantitative invariant has to be derived manually by extracting solutions from the formula.

For our prototype, the input is a quantitative Hoare triple and there are three possible outputs: "unknown" (due to timeout or invalid counterexamples), "disproved" with a witness (a valuation of program variables), and "proved" with a proof (a quantitative loop invariant). For PRINSYS, it receives a program and a template, and outputs a constraint describing all inductive loop invariants in form of the template. To verify a specific Hoare triple with PRINSYS, one has to encode the interested pre- and post-expectations as well as the form of possible invariants into the same template. Designing a template for PRINSYS is a tricky task that needs to be done on a case-by-case basis. In contrast, our technique does not require manually supplied templates, though the degree of loop invariants has to be fixed a priori.

One could use templates to represent non-linear loop invariants. We nevertheless failed to verify any of our non-linear examples with PRINSYS. In particular, we could not generate formulae that subsume the quantitative loop invariants computed by our prototype. This however does not imply that our examples are beyond the capability of PRINSYS, since we could not arguably try all templates manually. The designers of PRINSYS also examined their tool on some non-linear examples, e.g., the gambler's ruin problem, and reported negative results in [15]. Generally, when the supplied template is non-linear, it becomes intractable to derive a loop invariant, or even to decide the existence of a loop invariant, from the formula yielded by PRINSYS. Maybe a counterexample-refinement approach is helpful here, but this requires further research and experiments.

9   Conclusion

We propose an automated technique to generate polynomial quantitative invariants for probabilistic programs by Lagrange interpolation. Fixing the degree of loop invariants, our technique can infer polynomial quantitative loop invariants for simple loops. By choosing sampling points carefully, constraints are simplified so that coefficients of loop invariants can be determined. We also develop a counterexample-guided refining heuristics to find coefficients of quantitative loop invariants. We report applications in several case studies.

Our technique does not yet support parameters such as probability in probabilistic choice commands. Such parameters would induce non-linear constraints over coefficients and parameters. SMT solvers however could not find candidate coefficients and parameters as easily. Also, non-determinism is not implemented in our prototype. We plan to address both issues in our future work.

Acknowledgments. This work was supported by the Ministry of Science and Technology of Taiwan (103-2221-E-001 -019 -MY3, 103-2221-E-001 -020 -MY3) and the Natural Science Foundation of China (NSFC) under grant No. 61472473, 61428208, 61361136002, the CAS/SAFEA International Partnership Program for Creative Research Teams.

References

1. Chakarov, A., Sankaranarayanan, S.: Expectation invariants for probabilistic program loops as fixed points. In: Müller-Olm, M., Seidl, H. (eds.) Static Analysis. LNCS, vol. 8723, pp. 85–100. Springer, Heidelberg (2014)
2. Charles, K., Hang-Chin, L.: Vandermonde determinant and Lagrange interpolation in $\mathbb{R}^s$. In: Nonlinear and Convex Analysis: Proceedings in Honor of Ky Fan, vol. 107, p. 23. CRC Press (1987)
3. Collins, G.E.: Quantifier elimination for real closed fields by cylindrical algebraic decompostion. In: Automata Theory and Formal Languages 2nd GI Conference Kaiserslautern, 20–23 May 1975, pp. 134–183. Springer (1975)
4. Colón, M.A., Sankaranarayanan, S., Sipma, H.B.: Linear invariant generation using non-linear constraint solving. In: Hunt Jr., W.A., Somenzi, F. (eds.) CAV 2003. LNCS, vol. 2725, pp. 420–432. Springer, Heidelberg (2003)
5. Cousot, P.: Proving program invariance and termination by parametric abstraction, lagrangian relaxation and semidefinite programming. In: Cousot, R. (ed.) VMCAI 2005. LNCS, vol. 3385, pp. 1–24. Springer, Heidelberg (2005)
6. De Boor, C., Ron, A.: On multivariate polynomial interpolation. Constructive Approximation **6**(3), 287–302 (1990)
7. de Moura, L., Bjørner, N.S.: Z3: an efficient SMT solver. In: Ramakrishnan, C.R., Rehof, J. (eds.) TACAS 2008. LNCS, vol. 4963, pp. 337–340. Springer, Heidelberg (2008)
8. Den Hartog, J., de Vink, E.P.: Verifying probabilistic programs using a hoare like logic. Int. J. Found. Comput. Sci. **13**(03), 315–340 (2002)
9. Dijkstra, E.W.: A Discipline of Programming. Prentice-hall, Englewood Cliffs (1976)
10. Dolzmann, A., Sturm, T.: Redlog: computer algebra meets computer logic. Acm Sigsam Bulletin **31**(2), 2–9 (1997)
11. Dolzmann, A., Sturm, T., Weispfenning, V.: Real quantifier elimination in practice. In: Matzat, B.H., Greuel, G.-M., Hiss, G. (eds.) Algorithmic Algebra and Number Theory, pp. 221–247. Springer, Heidelberg (1999)
12. Eaton, J.W., Bateman, D., Hauberg, S.: GNU Octave. Network thoery, London (1997)
13. Uslar, M., Specht, M., Rohjans, S., Trefke, J., Gonzalez, J.M.V.: Introduction. In: Uslar, M., Specht, M., Rohjans, S., Trefke, J., Gonzalez, J.M.V. (eds.) The Common Information Model CIM. POWSYS, vol. 2, pp. 3–48. Springer, Heidelberg (2012)
14. Floyd, R.W.: Assigning meanings to programs. Math. Aspects Comput. Sci. **19**(1), 19–32 (1967)
15. Gretz, F., Katoen, J.-P., McIver, A.: PRINSYS—on a quest for probabilistic loop invariants. In: Joshi, K., Siegle, M., Stoelinga, M., D'Argenio, P.R. (eds.) QEST 2013. LNCS, vol. 8054, pp. 193–208. Springer, Heidelberg (2013)

16. Gretz, F., Katoen, J.P., McIver, A.: Operational versus weakest pre-expectation semantics for the probabilistic guarded command language. Perform. Eval. **73**, 110–132 (2014)
17. Gulwani, S., Srivastava, S., Venkatesan, R.: Program analysis as constraint solving. In: ACM SIGPLAN Notices, vol. 43, pp. 281–292. ACM (2008)
18. Gupta, A., Majumdar, R., Rybalchenko, A.: From tests to proofs. In: Kowalewski, S., Philippou, A. (eds.) TACAS 2009. LNCS, vol. 5505, pp. 262–276. Springer, Heidelberg (2009)
19. Gupta, A., Rybalchenko, A.: InvGen: an efficient invariant generator. In: Bouajjani, A., Maler, O. (eds.) CAV 2009. LNCS, vol. 5643, pp. 634–640. Springer, Heidelberg (2009)
20. Hoare, C.A.R.: An axiomatic basis for computer programming. CACM **12**(10), 576–580 (1969)
21. Kapur, D.: Automatically generating loop invariants using quantifier elimination-preliminary report. In: IMACS International Conference on Applications of Computer Algebra. Citeseer (2004)
22. Katoen, J.-P., McIver, A.K., Meinicke, L.A., Morgan, C.C.: Linear-invariant generation for probabilistic programs: In: Cousot, R., Martel, M. (eds.) SAS 2010. LNCS, vol. 6337, pp. 390–406. Springer, Heidelberg (2010)
23. Kozen, D.: Semantics of probabilistic programs. JCSS **22**(3), 328–350 (1981)
24. McIver, A., Morgan, C.C.: Abstraction, Refinement and Proof for Probabilistic Systems. Springer, Heidelberg (2006)
25. Morgan, C.: Proof rules for probabilistic loops. In: Proceedings of the BCS-FACS 7th Refinement Workshop, Workshops in Computing. Springer Verlag. (1996)
26. Olver, P.J.: On multivariate interpolation. Stud. Appl. Math. **116**(2), 201–240 (2006)
27. Rabin, M.O.: Probabilistic algorithm for testing primality. J. Number Theory **12**(1), 128–138 (1980)
28. Saniee, K.: A simple expression for multivariate Lagrange interpolation. SIAM Undergraduate Research Online **1**(1) (2008)
29. Sankaranarayanan, S., Sipma, H.B., Manna, Z.: Non-linear loop invariant generation using Gröbner bases. ACM SIGPLAN Notices **39**(1), 318–329 (2004)
30. Sauer, T., Xu, Y.: On multivariate Lagrange interpolation. Math. Comput. **64**(211), 1147–1170 (1995)

Author Index

d in the United States
masters